2002
U.S. Master
Tax Guide.

CCH Editorial Staff Publication

CCH

CCH INCORPORATED
Chicago

This publication is designed to provide accurate and authoritative information in regard to the subject matter covered. It is sold with the understanding that the publisher is not engaged in rendering legal, accounting, or other professional service. If legal advice or other expert assistance is required, the services of a competent professional person should be sought.

ISBN 0-8080-0659-2 (paperback edition)
ISBN 0-8080-0658-4 (hardbound edition)

U.S. Master Tax Guide®
Quick Tax Facts

CCH

Key Figures for the 2001 Tax Year

STANDARD DEDUCTIONS

Married, Filing Joint Return	$	7,600
Surviving Spouse	$	7,600
Head of Household	$	6,650
Unmarried (not S.S. or H.H.)	$	4,550
Married, Filing Separate Return	$	3,800
Dependent Standard Deduction (Minimum)	$	750
Additional Amount for Blindness and/or Age	$	900
Additional Amount as Above if Unmarried and not S.S.	$	1,100

EXEMPTIONS

Personal and Dependent Amount	$	2,900
Estate Amount	$	600
Simple Trust Amount	$	300
Complex Trust Amount	$	100
Joint Returns or Surviving Spouse (Phaseout)	$	199,450
Head of Household (Phaseout)	$	166,200
Unmarried (not S.S. or H.H.) (Phaseout)	$	132,950
Married, Filing Separate Return (Phaseout)	$	99,725

ITEMIZED DEDUCTIONS

Married, Filing Separate Return (Phaseout)	$	66,475
Others (Phaseout)	$	132,950

TRANSPORTATION

Fringe Benefit: Employer-provided passes and vehicles	$	65/mo.
Fringe Benefit: Qualified parking limit	$	180/mo.
Luxury Auto Excise Tax Base Amount	$	38,000
Business Mileage Rate		34.5¢
Charitable Mileage Rate		14¢
Medical and Moving Mileage Rate		12¢
Depreciation Component of Standard Mileage Rate		15¢
High Cost Per Diem Travel Rate (10/1/01–9/30/02)	$	204
Low Cost Per Diem Travel Rate (10/1/01–9/30/02)	$	125

RETIREMENT/PENSION PLANS

Maximum Annual Benefit for Defined Benefit Plan	$	140,000
Maximum Annual Contribution Defined Contribution Plan	$	35,000
Highly Compensated Employee Definition (In general)	$	85,000
SEP De minimis Compensation Amount	$	450
SEP Nondiscrimination Compensation Amount	$	170,000
401(k) Maximum Compensation Amount	$	170,000
401(k) Maximum Exclusion	$	10,500
IRA Deduction Limit (In general)	$	2,000
SIMPLE Contribution Limit	$	6,500

As of November 26, 2001, there still remains the possibility that Congress may pass legislation that might affect these figures for the 2001 tax year. For details concerning the House and Senate proposals, see ¶1 of the *U.S. Master Tax Guide*. For late-breaking coverage of tax legislation, visit the Guide's website at http://tax.cchgroup.com/mtg.

CCH®

Key Figures for the 2001 Tax Year

CAPITAL GAIN RATES (MAXIMUM FOR NONCORPORATE TAXPAYERS)

Adjusted Net Capital Gain (Assets held more than 12 months)	20%
For those in 15% bracket	10%
For those in 15% bracket (Assets held more than 5 years)	8%
For Recaptured Gain on Real Estate	25%
For Most Collectibles	28%

HOME SALE GAIN EXCLUSION

Joint Filers	$ 500,000
Single Filers	$ 250,000

ESTATE AND GIFT TAXES

Unified Credit Shelter Amount	$ 675,000
Annual Gift Tax Exclusion Amount (Per donee)	$ 10,000
State Death Tax Threshold Amount	$ 60,000
Estate/Gift Tax Rate (Maximum rate before phaseout)	55%

PAYROLL TAXES

Soc. Sec. (Self-employed) Combined Rate (OASDI+Medicare)	15.3%
Soc. Sec. (Employer or Employee) Rate (OASDI+Medicare)	7.65%
OASDI Maximum Base	$ 80,400
FUTA Rate	6.2%
FUTA Wage Base	$ 7,000

ADJUSTED GROSS INCOME LIMITS

Casualty Loss Threshold	10%
Medical Deduction Threshold	7.5%
Miscellaneous Itemized Deduction Floor	2%

EDUCATION PROVISIONS

Hope Scholarship Credit	$ 1,500
Lifetime Learning Credit	$ 1,000
Student Loan Interest Deduction	$ 2,500
U.S. Savings Bond Interest Exclusion (Phaseout)	
Married, filing joint return	$ 83,650
Single, S.S. or H.H.	$ 55,750
Married, filing separate return	$ 0

KEY PENALTY RATES

Failure to File Return	5%/month (max. 25%)
Failure to Pay Tax	1/2 of 1% per month
Substantial Understatement	20%
Failure to Supply Social Security Number	$50 per occurrence

As of November 26, 2001, there still remains the possibility that Congress may pass legislation that might affect these figures for the 2001 tax year. For details concerning the House and Senate proposals, see ¶1 of the *U.S. Master Tax Guide*. For late-breaking coverage of tax legislation, visit the *Guide's* website at http://tax.cchgroup.com/mtg.

Preface

CCH is proud to serve the community of tax professionals by explaining the maze of tax rules, restrictions, and requirements with this edition of the *U.S. Master Tax Guide®*. The 85th Edition of this industry standard is designed to provide fast and reliable answers to tax questions affecting individuals and businesses. In all, 29 chapters contain comprehensive, timely, and precise explanation of the ever-changing federal income tax rules for individuals, businesses, and estates and trusts.

In 2001, the Tax Code became a vehicle for economic stimulus. The Economic Growth and Tax Relief Reconciliation Act of 2001 (P.L. 107-16) brought about changes that immediately affected taxpayers while also providing changes that will phase in and out throughout the next decade. This 2002 Edition reflects the changes from P.L. 107-16 that affect 2001 tax returns. Following the terrorist attacks in New York and Washington, DC, Congress went to work on a relief and economic stimulus package. After two months, the House of Representatives and the Senate arrived at two wide-ranging sets of legislative proposals. At this time, there still remains the possibility of a compromise package being passed before year-end that may affect the 2001 tax year.

In an effort to keep users of the *Guide* current on events taking place after we go to press, CCH has established a website at **http://tax.cchgroup.com/mtg** for any late-breaking 2001 year-end tax legislation or other significant developments that might affect the *Guide's* coverage.

As in previous editions, major legislative provisions are highlighted at ¶ 1 and reflected throughout the *Guide*, while important nonlegislative tax developments are conveniently highlighted at ¶ 2 and concisely explained for quick reference and understanding.

Also, the *Guide* comes complete with many time-saving features that help users quickly and easily determine how particular tax items and situations should be treated (see the following page for a listing and description of these "Key Features"). The *Guide* also contains a handy Quick Tax Facts card that can be detached for an at-a-glance reference to key tax figures and other often-referenced amounts.

Not only does the *U.S. Master Tax Guide®* assist in the preparation of 2001 tax returns, it also serves as a reference tool for more comprehensive tax research and tax planning via extensive footnotes and other references to the Internal Revenue Code, Income Tax Regulations, and CCH's STANDARD FEDERAL TAX REPORTS® and FEDERAL ESTATE AND GIFT TAX REPORTER.

For additional analysis of new and complex tax issues, we point you to a companion resource to the *Guide*. CCH's *Analysis of Top Tax Issues for 2002* identifies and examines the key tax controversies that have developed over the course of 2001. This publication addresses issues from the perspective of how ongoing transactions should be arranged as a result of each "hot issue." It provides insights into how these issues play out and how they should be handled when planning for 2002 and beyond. To order this vital resource, call 1-800-248-3248.

November 2001

Key Features

In addition to 29 chapters of concise tax law explanations, the *U.S. Master Tax Guide®* provides a wealth of information in the pages that lead up to Chapter 1. Some of these time-saving tools are described below, listed by paragraph location:

OVERVIEW (¶ 1-5): The Overview division contains a collection of informative features to facilitate research and dealing with clients. Included are:

- "New Legislation," a highlight of provisions from this year's enacted tax legislation.
- "What to Watch on 2001 Returns," a listing of important nonlegislative tax developments, including key inflation-adjusted amounts.
- "Where to File," a listing of income tax return mailing addresses.
- "Government Agency and Tax/Accounting Directories," a feature comprised of addresses and telephone numbers for numerous federal agencies and tax and accounting organizations.
- "Due Dates in 2002," a tax calendar showing filing dates for 2001 tax returns and tax payments throughout 2002.

TAX RATES (¶ 11-53): This section contains the 2001 and 2002 (unofficial) tax rate schedules for individuals and estates and trusts, the 2001 tax tables for individuals, the corporate tax rate schedule and related rates, and the estate and gift tax rate schedule, as well as a listing of excise and other taxes.

CHECKLISTS (¶ 55-59): A collection of checklists designed to provide tax return preparers with quick answers (and references) to common questions regarding the inclusion of items in income, the deductibility of certain expenses, and the treatment of various medical expenses.

COMPUTATION OF TAXABLE INCOME (¶ 61-64): Provides a summary overview of how taxable income is computed for an individual, a corporation, a partnership, and an estate or trust. References are provided to detailed explanations within the *Guide*.

SPECIAL TAX TABLES (¶ 83-88A): This is a collection of often-used interest rates and percentages including:

- applicable federal rates (AFRs)
- adjusted applicable federal rates
- federal long-term tax-exempt rates
- low-income housing credit percentages
- earned income credit amounts

Also presented are the average itemized deductions for 1999 (the latest year of available figures), broken down by AGI ranges, as well as the AGI thresholds for a number of tax items subject to phaseout restrictions in 2001.

CPE CREDIT: An extra benefit for tax professionals is that continuing education credit may be earned in conjunction with the *Guide*. The accompanying *Federal Taxation Refresher Course—Study Guide* is designed to help further readers' understanding and application of the concepts presented in the *Guide*. CPE credit may be earned by successfully completing and submitting the Course answer sheets to CCH for grading. See the *Course* introduction for more information.

ADDITIONAL FORMATS: To provide flexibility for users, the *Guide* is available in a loose-leaf edition with quarterly updates, a hardbound edition, and a CD-ROM edition that may be purchased with or without the softbound print edition. The *Guide* also anchors *U.S. Master Tax Guide Plus*, an electronic tax research library available on the Internet or monthly CDs that combines the quick-reference ease and reliability of the *Guide* with current primary sources including the Internal Revenue Code, Income Tax Regulations, cases, IRS rulings and more.

USER COMMUNITY: CCH has established a website at http://tax.cchgroup.com/mtg for users of the *Guide* to visit periodically in order to stay current with significant post-publication developments.

Washington News Staff

Jeff Carlson, M.A.
Paula L. Cruickshank
Kathryn Hough

Catherine Hubbard, M.G.
Rosalyn Johns

Joyce Mutcherson-Ridley
William Pegler

Electronic and Print Production

Lilian Bajor
Ce'on Barnes
Brian A. Berens
Miranda Blunt
Stella Brown
Barbara Brumleve
William E. Buonincontro
Gina Carbone
Julia Careau
Angela D. Cashmore
Elizabeth Dudek
Tara K. Fenske
Christopher Freeman
Mary Ellen Guth
Ann Hartmann
Kathleen M. Higgins
Jenny Holland

Kristine J. Jacobs
Judith Jones
Kenneth R. Kuehl
Andrea M. Lacko
Faina Lerin
Rebecca Little
Chantal M. Mahler
Andrejs Makwitz
Jennifer McCarthy
Diane L. McComb
Helen Miller
Loretta Miller
Molly Munson
Robyn Terrell
Holly J. Porter
Diana Roozeboom

Christine Roth
Jennifer Schencker
David Schuster
Jennifer Seay
Diane Shultz
Sandy Silverman
Eileen Slivka
Monika Stefan
Jennifer Swanson
Jason Switt
Emily Urban
Jim Waddick
Matthew Widmer
Jamie Wild
Lynn Wilson
Laura Zenner
Christopher Zwirek

7

CONTENTS Paragraph

Tax Tables—Features

Filing 2001 Returns

OVERVIEW

¶ 1   New Legislation

2001 Legislation. The key phrase surrounding tax legislation in 2001 was "economic stimulus." Congress and the President attempted to jump-start the economy with a massive, decade-long tax package that came together in late May. Then they attempted to follow up with additional provisions to spark the lagging economy, coupled with relief for the victims of the terrorist attacks in New York and Washington, DC.

Year-end efforts. Following the September 11, 2001, attacks in New York and Washington, DC, the House and Senate spent the next two months assembling competing relief and stimulus packages to assist the victims and to further aid the sluggish economy. While the proposals are far apart at press time, the President remains insistent on providing economic help for the 2001 tax year. Therefore, there is still a distinct possibility that tax practitioners will be faced with unanticipated compliance challenges as they enter the upcoming filing season. The following provisions from the House proposal would have the greatest potential to affect 2001 tax returns and 2001 year-end tax planning if enacted (Senate agreement and alternatives have been noted):

    (1) provide a supplemental tax rebate for those that did not receive the full rebate under P.L. 107-16 (also in Senate version);

    (2) accelerate depreciation on a wide range of property (variation in Senate version);

    (3) repeal corporate AMT;

    (4) increase the Code Sec. 179 expense limit from $24,000 to $35,000 (also in Senate version);

    (5) lengthen the carryback period for net operating losses from two years to five years (also in Senate version);

    (6) accelerate the reduction of the 28-percent marginal rate (as added by P.L. 107-16, discussed below);

    (7) reduce the 20% and 10% capital gain rates to 18% and 8%, respectively;

    (8) increase the dollar limit for offsetting net capital losses against ordinary income to $4,000 and then again to $5,000 ($5,000 limit in Senate version);

    (9) extend permanently the Subpart F exception for active financing income (one-year extension in Senate version);

(10) extend most of the expiring tax provisions (see below) by two years (one-year extension in Senate version);

(11) overturn the Supreme Court's *Gitlitz* decision with respect to discharge in indebtedness of an S corporation; and

(12) limit the use of the non-accrual experience method of accounting.

With some wide differences between the two proposals and the Administration's expectations, compromise efforts are expected to linger well into December and could result in a bill being presented to President Bush that is a mix of the two packages, plus possible new provisions. As we go to press, these issues remain unresolved. For information on late-breaking legislative developments that still may affect the 2001 tax year, visit the *U.S. Master Tax Guide's* website at http://tax.cchgroup.com/mtg.

A decade of change. On June 7, 2001, President Bush signed the Economic Growth and Tax Relief Reconciliation Act of 2001 (P.L. 107-16)—a bipartisan compromise putting various tax proposals within a budget framework that calls for $1.35 trillion in tax cuts over 11 years. The new law reflects compromises on tax rate reduction, estate tax repeal, marriage penalty relief, education incentives, child tax credit increase, pension reform, and alternative minimum tax relief. However, to meet budgetary constraints, provisions are phased in and out over the next 10 years, with an anticipated sunset in 2011 that would reinstate the Code as it was prior to this enactment.

The following highlights some of the new and more immediate changes:

(1) a new 10% bracket and reductions to other brackets for 2001 and beyond;

(2) the eventual repeal of the itemized deduction and personal exemption phaseouts;

(3) increases to the child tax credit for 2001 and beyond;

(4) changes to the dependent care credit and the adoption credit, as well as the creation of a new credit under the general business credit for employers providing child care;

(5) changes to the student loan interest deduction and education IRA rules, as well as a new 2002 "above-the-line" deduction for higher education expenses;

(6) numerous changes implementing the eventual repeal of the estate and generation-skipping transfer taxes;

(7) numerous changes regarding pension contributions, funding, distributions and rollovers;

(8) a short deferral period for all or a part of the required corporate quarterly estimated tax payments due in September 2001 and 2004; and

(9) increases to the AMT exemption amounts for 2001—2004.

The following table outlines additional changes that will take place over the next few years, subject to any 2001 year-end legislative changes.

	2001	*2002*	*2003*	*2004*
Tax rate brackets				
39.6%	39.1%	38.6%	38.6%	37.6%
36%	35.5%	35%	35%	34%
31%	30.5%	30%	30%	29%
28%	27.5%	27%	27%	26%
15%	15%	15%	15%	15%
Child tax credit .... $	600	$600	$600	$600
IRA contributions ...... $	2,000	$3,000	$3,000	$3,000
IRA catch-ups	N/A	$500	$500	$500
Elective deferrals ...... $	10,500	$11,000	$12,000	$13,000
Elective catch-ups				
—401(k) and				
SIMPLEs	N/A	$500	$1,000	$1,500
—other plans......	N/A	$1,000	$2,000	$3,000
AMT exemption				
—single .... $	35,750	$35,750	$35,750	$35,750
—married filing				
jointly .... $	49,000	$49,000	$49,000	$49,000
Estate tax				
—top rate	55%	50%	49%	48%
—exemption				
amount	$675,000	$1 million	$1 million	$1.5 million

Expiring provisions. It seems that every year-end finds some tax provisions set to expire. In the past, Congress has responded with late-season legislation or even retroactive extensions. The following are some of the tax items set to expire December 31, 2001:

(1) personal tax credits allowed against regular tax and AMT (¶ 1371);

(2) work opportunity credit (¶ 1342);

(3) welfare-to-work credit (¶ 1343);

(4) tax credit for electricity production from wind, closed-loop biomass and poultry waste (¶ 1339);

(5) limitation on percentage depletion for oil and gas from marginal wells (¶ 1294);

(6) zone academy bond limitations (¶ 1344A); and

(7) electric vehicle credit and deduction (phaseout begins in 2002) (¶ 1286, ¶ 1321).

As we go to press, legislation that would extend these provisions or make them permanent is being considered by both the House and the Senate as part of larger economic stimulus packages. Visit http://tax.cchgroup.com/mtg for late-breaking developments that may extend some or all of these items.

Looking ahead, Archer MSAs (¶ 860 and ¶ 1020) and the excise tax on luxury automobiles are two provisions set to expire on December 31, 2002.

¶ 2   What to Watch on 2001 Returns

The *Guide* reflects all of the important administrative and judicial developments of 2001 . . . final regulations, major court decisions, and important rulings of the Internal Revenue Service. Legislative highlights are at ¶ 1. Below are nonlegislative highlights of the changes in 2001 with the greatest impact on individuals and businesses.

Individuals

Income levels at which individuals must file income tax returns have increased for 2001 . . . . ¶ 109

Basic standard deduction amounts have increased for 2001 . . . . ¶ 126

The deduction for each personal exemption has increased to $2,900 for 2001 . . . . ¶ 133

Inflation-adjusted income amounts that trigger the reduction of allowable itemized deductions and personal exemptions for high-income taxpayers have increased for 2001 . . . . ¶ 88A, ¶ 133, ¶ 1014

"Kiddie" tax amount is $1,500 for 2001 . . . . ¶ 706

The standard mileage rate for all business use of a car in 2001 is 34.5 cents per mile . . . . ¶ 947

Per diem rates for 2001 under the high-low method of substantiating travel expenses are at $201 for high-cost localities and $124 for low-cost localities . . ¶ 954A

Student loan interest, up to $2,500 in 2001, may be deducted "above-the-line" by qualifying taxpayers. This is an increase from $2,000 in 2000 . . . . ¶ 1082

The deduction for health insurance premiums paid by self-employed individuals remains at 60% in 2001, the same amount as in 2000 . . . . ¶ 908

Depreciation, Amortization and Depletion

Inflation-adjusted limits on depreciation deductions for luxury cars has increased for cars placed in service during 2001 . . . . ¶ 1214

The maximum Code Sec. 179 deduction for 2001 is $24,000 . . . . ¶ 1208

Tax Credits

For 2001, the maximum earned income credit for eligible taxpayers with no qualifying children is $364, with one qualifying child is $2,428, and with two or more qualifying children is $4,008 . . . . ¶ 87, ¶ 1375

The child tax credit was set to be $500 in 2001, but has been increased to $600 . ¶ 1302

The education tax credits (Hope and lifetime learning) remain at $1,500 and $1,000, respectively . . . . ¶ 1303

Withholding

The 2001 OASDI wage base for FICA and self-employment tax purposes is $80,400 . . . . ¶ 47, ¶ 49, ¶ 2648, ¶ 2670

The 2001 wage threshold for "Nanny Tax" reporting is $1,300 . . . . ¶ 2650

¶ 3   Where to File Returns

Individuals. Listed below are the mailing addresses for filing individual income tax returns. See ¶ 122. See also ¶ 2701 for a discussion of service centers.

Note: The IRS has undertaken a two-year plan to reorganize its processing of tax returns. As a result of these efforts, some taxpayers *may* have different filing service centers than those used previously.

☐ Per the IRS, if an addressed envelope came with your return, please use it. If you do not have one, or if you moved during the year, mail your return to the Internal Revenue Service Center for the place where you live. No street address is needed. To facilitate processing, each form (1040, 1040A, 1040EZ) uses a different ZIP+4 ZIP Code extension. Also, different extensions are used if you are making a payment or not. Check your form's instructions for the proper extension.

If you are located in:	*Mail your return to:*
Florida, Georgia, North Carolina, South Carolina, West Virginia	Atlanta, GA 39901
New Jersey, New York (New York City and counties of Nassau, Rockland, Suffolk, and Westchester)	Holtsville, NY 00501
Massachusetts, Michigan, New York (all other counties), Rhode Island	Andover, MA 05501
Illinois, Iowa, Kansas, Minnesota, Missouri, Oklahoma, Utah, Wisconsin	Kansas City, MO 64999
Connecticut, Delaware, District of Columbia, Indiana, Maine, Maryland, New Hampshire, Pennsylvania, Vermont	Philadelphia, PA 19255
Ohio	Cincinnati, OH 45999
Arizona, Colorado, Idaho, Montana, New Mexico, Texas, Wyoming	Austin, TX 73301
Nebraska, North Dakota, South Dakota, Washington	Ogden, UT 84201
Alaska, California, Hawaii, Nevada, Oregon	Fresno, CA 93888
Alabama, Arkansas, Kentucky, Louisiana, Mississippi, Tennessee, Virginia	Memphis, TN 37501
All A.P.O. and F.P.O. addresses, American Samoa, nonpermanent residents of Guam or the Virgin Islands, Puerto Rico (or if excluding income under Code Sec. 933), a foreign country (U.S. citizens and those filing Form 2555, 2555-EZ, or 4563)	Philadelphia, PA 19255
Guam: permanent residents	Department of Revenue and Taxation, Government of Guam, P.O. Box 23607, GMF, GU 96921
Virgin Islands: permanent residents	V.I. Bureau of Internal Revenue, 9601 Estate Thomas, Charlotte Amalie, St. Thomas, VI 00802

¶ 3

Corporations and Partnerships. A corporation or partnership should file Form 1120 or Form 1065 in accordance with the "Where to File" addresses listed in the instructions to the forms. A corporation or partnership is "located in" the place where it has its principal place of business or principal office or agency. If a corporation or partnership is without a principal office or agency or principal place of business in the United States, returns are to be filed with the Philadelphia Service Center.

Estates and Trusts. Generally, a fiduciary of an estate or trust should file Form 1041 in accordance with the instructions to Form 1041. For locations in a U.S. possession or foreign country, file with the Philadelphia Service Center. (A fiduciary is "located in" the place where he (it) resides or has his (its) principal place of business.) However, the table does not apply to the fiduciary of a charitable or split interest trust (described in Code Sec. 4947(a)) or of a pooled income fund (described in Code Sec. 642(c)(5)). The fiduciary of such a trust must consult a special table contained in the instructions to Form 1041.

Private Delivery Services. Certain private delivery services designated by the IRS are available to meet the "timely mailed as timely filing/paying" rule for tax returns and payments. The IRS last published this list of the designated private delivery services in September 2001 (Notice 2001-62), adding UPS Worldwide services. This is the first change to the list since 1997 (Notice 97-26). The IRS commented in 1999 that a new list will only be published when there is a change to it. The allowable private delivery services are:

● Airborne Express (Airborne): Overnight Air Express Service, Next Afternoon Service, and Second Day Service.

● DHL Worldwide Express (DHL): DHL "Same Day" Service and DHL USA Overnight.

● Federal Express (FedEx): FedEx Priority Overnight, FedEx Standard Overnight, and FedEx 2Day.

● United Parcel Service (UPS): UPS Next Day Air, UPS Next Day Air Saver, UPS 2nd Day Air, UPS 2nd Day Air A.M., UPS Worldwide Express Plus, and UPS Worldwide Express.

The private delivery service will provide information for getting written proof of the mailing date.

¶ 4   Government Agency and Tax/Accounting Directories

Listed below are mailing addresses and telephone numbers for key federal government agencies as well as tax and accounting organizations.

FEDERAL GOVERNMENT OFFICES—GENERAL LISTING

Department of Commerce
> 1401 Constitution Ave NW Washington DC 20230 202-482-2000

Department of Justice
> 950 Pennsylvania Ave Washington DC 20530 202-514-2000

Department of The Treasury
> 1500 Pennsylvania Ave NW Washington DC 20220 202-622-2000

Executive Office of the President
> Office of Admin.
> Rm 5001 725 17th St NW Washington DC 20503 202-395-3000
> Office of the US Trade Representative
> 600 Seventeenth St NW Washington DC 20508 202-395-3230
> Office of the Vice President of the US
> Old Executive Office Bldg Washington DC 20501 202-456-2326
> The White House Office
> 1600 Pennsylvania Ave NW Washington DC 20500 202-456-1414

Export-Import Bank
> 811 Vermont Ave NW Washington DC 20571 800-565-3946

Federal Deposit Insurance Corporation
> 550 Seventeenth St NW Washington DC 20429 202-393-8400

Federal Reserve System Board of Governors
> 20th & C St NW Washington DC 20551 202-452-3000

Federal Reserve System Research & Statistics
> 20th & C St NW Washington DC 20551 202-452-3301

General Accounting Office
> 441 G Street NW Washington DC 20548 202-512-3000

General Services Administration
> 1800 F St NW Washington DC 20405 202-501-0800

Government Printing Office
> 732 N Capitol St NW Washington DC 20401 202-512-0000

Library of Congress
> 101 Independence Ave SE Washington DC 20540 202-707-5000

National Archives and Records Administration
> 700 Pennsylvania Ave NW Washington DC 20408 800-234-8861

Office of Management & Budget
> 725 17th St NW Washington DC 20503 202-395-3080

Railroad Retirement Board
> 844 N Rush St Chicago Il 60611 312-751-4776

Securities and Exchange Commission
> 450 Fifth St NW Washington DC 20549 202-942-8088

Small Business Administration
> 409 3rd St SW 5th Floor Washington DC 20416 800-827-5722

Social Security Administration
> 6401 Security Blvd Baltimore MD 21235 800-772-1213

United States Tax Court
> 400 2nd St. NW Washington DC 20217 202-606-8751

¶ 4

FEDERAL GOVERNMENT OFFICES—SPECIALIZED LISTINGS

MAJOR FEDERAL EXECUTIVE PROCUREMENT AGENCIES
General Services Administration
  Business Service Center
  100 Penn Sq E Philadelphia PA 19107 215-656-5525
  Federal Procurement Data Center
  7th & D St SW Rm 5652 Washington DC 20407 202-401-1529
Justice Department
  1331 Pennsylvania Ave NW Rm 1010 National Place Bldg Washington DC
  20530 202-616-0521
Treasury Department
  1500 Pennsylvania Ave Attn: 1310 G Street Ste 400 W Washington DC 20220
  202-622-0530

SMALL BUSINESS ADMINISTRATION
SBA Answer Desk
  409 3rd St SW Washington DC 20416 800-827-5722

AICPA, NAEA, NATP, NSA AND STATE ACCOUNTING SOCIETIES
AICPA Main Office
  1211 Avenue of Americas New York NY 10036-8775 888-777-7077
National Association of Enrolled Agents
  Ste 302 200 Orchard Ridge Dr Gaithersburg, MD 20878 301-212-9608
National Association of Tax Professionals
  720 Association Dr Appleton WI 54914-1483 800-558-3402
National Society of Accountants Main Office
  1010 N Fairfax St Ste 200 Alexandria VA 22314 703-549-6400
AL Society of CPAs
  1103 S Perry St Montgomery AL 36104 334-834-7650
AK Society of CPAs
  Ste 105 341 W Tudor Anchorage AK 99503 907-562-4334
AZ Society of CPAs
  Ste 100 2120 N Central Ave Phoenix AZ 85004 602-252-4144
AR Society of CPAs
  11300 Executive Center Dr Little Rock AR 72211 501-664-8739
CA Society of CPAs
  1235 Radio Rd Redwood City CA 94065 650-802-2600
CO Society of CPAs
  Ste 500 7979 E Tufts Denver CO 80237 303-773-2877
CT Society of CPAs
  845 Brook St Bldg 2 Rocky Hill CT 06067 860-525-1153
DE Society of CPAs
  3512 Silverside Rd 8th The Commons Wilmington DE 19810 . . 302-478-7442
DC Institute of CPAs
  1023 15th ST NW Washington DC 20005 202-789-1844
FL Institute of CPAs
  325 W College Ave Tallahassee FL 32301 850-224-2727
GA Society of CPAs
  Ste 2700 3340 Peachtree Rd Atlanta GA 30326 404-231-8676
Greater Washington Society
  8th Fl 1023 15th ST NW Washington DC 20005 202-789-1844

HI Society of CPAs
    PO Box 1754 Honolulu HI 96806 808-537-9475
ID Society of CPAs
    Ste 240 250 Bob White Ct Boise ID 83706 208-344-6261
IL CPA Society
    Ste 1600 222 S Riverside Plaza Chicago IL 60606 312-993-0393
IN Society of CPAs
    Ste 305 8250 Woodfield Crossing Blvd Indianapolis IN 46240 .. 317-726-5001
IA Society of CPAs
    Ste 300 950 Office Pk Rd West Des Moines IA 50265 515-223-8161
KS Society of CPAs
    1080 SW Wanamaker Rd Ste 200 Topeka KS 66604 785-272-4366
KY Society of CPAs
    1735 Alliant Ave Louisville KY 40299 502-266-5272
LA Society of LA CPAs
    Ste 500 2400 Veterans Blvd Kenner LA 70062 504-464-1040
ME Society of CPAs
    Ste 8 153 US Rte 1 Scarborough ME 04074 207-883-6090
MD Association of CPAs
    Ste 10 1300 York Rd Lutherville MD 21093 410-296-6250
MA Society of CPAs
    105 Chauncy St Boston MA 02111 617-556-4000
MI Society of CPAs
    5480 Corporate Dr PO Box 5068 Troy MI 48007-5068 248-267-3700
MN Society of CPAs
    Ste 1230 7900 Xerxes Ave S Bloomington MN 55431 952-831-2707
MS Society of CPAs
    Ste 246 4500 I55N Highland Village Jackson MS 39211 601-366-3473
MO Society of CPAs
    Ste 10 275 N Lindbergh Blvd St Louis MO 63141 314-997-7966
MT Society of CPAs
    33 S Last Chance Gulch Ste 2B Helena MT 59601 406-442-7301
NE Society of CPAs
    Ste 330 635 S 14th St Lincoln NB 68508 402-476-8482
NV Society of CPAs
    Ste 205 5250 Neil Rd Reno NV 89502 775-826-6800
NH Society of CPAs
    1750 Elm St Ste 403 Manchester NH 03104 603-622-1999
NJ Society of CPAs
    425 Eagle Rock Ave Roseland NJ 07068-1723 973-226-4494
NM Society of CPAs
    Ste 450 1650 University NE Albuquerque NM 87102 505-246-1699
NY Society of CPAs
    530 Fifth Ave NY NY 10036 212-719-8300
NC Society of CPAs
    PO Box 80188 Raleigh NC 27623 919-469-1040
ND Society of CPAs
    2701 South Colombia Rd Grand Forks ND 58201 701-775-7100
OH Society of CPAs
    535 Metro Place S Dublin OH 43017 614-764-2727
OK Society of CPAs
    Ste 910 1900 NW Expwy Oklahoma City OK 73118 405-841-3800

¶4

OR Society of CPAs
      PO Box 4555 Beaverton OR 97076-4555 503-641-7200
PA Institute of CPAs
      1650 Arch St 17th Floor Philadelphia PA 19103 215-496-9272
PR Society of CPAs
      Capitol Ctr Bldg South Tower 239 Ave Arterial Hostos Ste 1401 San Juan PR
      00918-1477 787-754-1950
RI Society of CPAs
      45 Royal Little Dr Providence RI 02904 401-331-5720
SC Association of CPAs
      570 Chris Dr West Columbia SC 29169 803-791-4181
SD Society of CPAs
      Ste 100 1000 W. Ave North Sioux Falls SD 57104 605-334-3848
TN Society of CPAs
      201 Powell Pl Brentwood TN 37027 615-377-3825
TX Society of CPAs
      Ste 150 14860 Montfort Dallas TX 75254 800-428-0272
UT Society of CPAs
      Ste 320 220 E Morris Ave Salt Lake City UT 84115 801-466-8022
VT Society of CPAs
      Ste 500 100 State St Montpelier VT 05602 802-229-4939
VA Society of CPAs
      4309 Cox Rd Glen Allen VA 23060 804-270-5344
WA Society of CPAs
      902-140th Ave NE Bellevue WA 98005 425-644-4800
WV Society of CPAs
      900 Lee St Ste 1201 Charleston WV 25301 304-342-5461
WI Institute of CPAs
      235 N Executive Dr Brookfield WI 53008 262-785-0445
WY Society of CPAs
      1603 Capitol Ave Ste 413 Cheyenne WY 82001 307-634-7039

¶4

¶ 5   Due Dates in 2002

Each date shown below is the prescribed last day for filing the return or making the payment of tax indicated. For income tax returns, the due dates apply to calendar-year taxpayers only. Employment tax due dates are determined on a calendar-year basis for all taxpayers. **If any due date falls on a Saturday, Sunday or legal holiday, the due date is the next succeeding day that is not a Saturday, Sunday, or legal holiday (national, District of Columbia, or state-wide in the state where the return is to be filed).**

Note: Following the terrorist attacks on New York and Washington, DC, the IRS extended the filing deadlines for affected taxpayers with original deadlines between September 11, 2001 and November 30, 2001. See Notice 2001-61 and Notice 2001-63 for specific details.

This day
2002   **Tax Return Due Dates**

Jan. 15th— **Estimated Taxes.** Final installment of 2001 estimated tax (Form 1040-ES) by individuals unless income tax return is filed with final payment by January 31, 2002. Payment in full of estimated tax by farmers and fishermen unless income tax returns are filed by March 1, 2002.

Final installment of 2001 estimated tax (Form 1041-ES) by trusts, and by calendar-year estates and certain residuary trusts in existence more than two years, unless Form 1041 is filed and taxes are paid in full by January 31, 2002.

Jan. 31st— **Employers' Taxes.** Employers of nonagricultural and nonhousehold employees file return on Form 941 for withheld income and FICA taxes in last quarter of 2001.[1]

Employers of agricultural workers must file the annual Form 943 to report income and FICA taxes withheld on 2001 wages.[1]

Employers must file Form 940, annual return of federal unemployment (FUTA) taxes for 2001.[1]

Withholding. Employees' statements (Form W-2 and Form 1099-R) for amounts withheld in 2001 to be furnished by employer to employees. Statements for amounts withheld on certain gambling winnings (Form W-2G) to be furnished by payer to recipients.

Individuals. Individuals (other than farmers and fishermen) who owed, but did not pay, estimated tax on January 15 must file final 2001 income tax return and pay tax in full to avoid late payment penalty.

Trusts and Estates. Trusts, as well as estates and certain residuary trusts in existence more than two years, that owed but did not pay estimated tax on January 15 must file final 2001 income tax return and pay tax in full to avoid late payment penalty.

Information Returns. Annual statements must be furnished to recipients of dividends and liquidating distributions (Form 1099-DIV); interest, including interest on bearer certificates of deposit (Form 1099-INT); patronage dividends (Form 1099-PATR); original issue discount (Form 1099-OID); proceeds from broker and barter exchange transactions (Form 1099-B); proceeds from real estate transactions (Form 1099-S); certain government payments, including unemployment compensation and state and local tax refunds of $10

---

[1] If timely deposits in full payment of tax due were made, the due date for Forms 940, 941, and 943 is February 10.

¶ 5

**This day
2002**   **Tax Return Due Dates**—continued
Jan. 31st—continued

or more (Form 1099-G); royalty payments of more than $10, rent or other business payments of more than $600, prizes and awards of more than $600, broker payments in lieu of dividends or tax-exempt interest of $10 or more, crop insurance proceeds of $600 or more, fishing boat proceeds, and medical and health care payments of $600 or more, (Form 1099-MISC); debt canceled by certain financial entities including financial institutions, credit unions, and Federal Government agencies of $600 or more (Form 1099-C); distributions from retirement or profit-sharing plans, IRAs, SEPs, or insurance contracts (Form 1099-R).

Business recipients of more than $600 of interest on any mortgage must furnish Form 1098 to payer.

Information called for on Form 8300 must be provided to each payer in a transaction of more than $10,000 in cash at any time during 2001. (Form 8300 must have been filed with the IRS by the 15th day after the date of the transaction.)

Partnerships must provide Form 8308 to the transferor and transferee in any exchange of a partnership interest that involved unrealized receivables or substantially appreciated inventory items.

Trustees or issuers of IRAs or SEPs must provide participants with a statement of the account's value.

Feb. 15th— **Individuals.** Last day for filing Form W-4 by employees who wish to claim exemption from withholding of income tax for 2002.

Feb. 28th— **Information Returns.** Annual 1099 series returns (together with transmittal Form 1096 for paper filings or Form 4804 for magnetic media filings) must be filed with the IRS to report payments to recipients who received Form 1099 on January 31, as indicated above.

Business recipients of more than $600 of interest from an individual on any mortgage must file Form 1098 with the IRS (together with transmittal Form 1096 for paper filings or Form 4804 for magnetic media filings).

Form 5452, report of nontaxable corporate distributions made to shareholders during calendar year 2001.

Withholding. Form W-2 "A" copies for 2001 (together with transmittal Form W-3) must be filed with the Social Security Administration.

Form W-2G and Form 1099-R for 2001 "A" copies (together with transmittal Form 1096 for paper filings or Form 4804 for magnetic media filings) must be filed with the IRS.

Mar. 1st— **Individuals.** Last day for farmers and fishermen who owed, but did not pay, estimated tax on January 15 to file 2001 calendar-year income tax return and pay tax in full to avoid late payment penalty.

Mar. 15th— **Corporations.** Due date of 2001 income tax returns (Form 1120 or Form 1120-A) for calendar-year U.S. corporations or calendar-year foreign corporations with offices in the U.S. Fiscal-year U.S. corporations and foreign corporations with a U.S. office must file by the 15th day of the 3rd month following the close of the tax year.

¶ 5

**This day
2002**   **Tax Return Due Dates**—continued
Mar. 15th—continued

Due date of 2001 income tax returns for calendar-year S corporations (Form 1120S).

Last date for filing application (Form 7004) by calendar-year corporations for automatic six-month extension to file 2001 income tax return.

Calendar-year corporations' 2001 information return (Form 5471) with respect to foreign corporations. (Fiscal-year corporations file form with income tax return.)

Last date for a calendar-year corporation to file an amended income tax return (Form 1120X) for the calendar year 1998.[2]

Withholding. File returns on Form 1042 and Form 1042S to report tax withheld at the source from nonresident aliens, foreign corporations, foreign partnerships and foreign fiduciaries of a trust or estate.

Apr. 15th— Individuals. Income tax and self-employment tax returns of individuals for calendar year 2001 and income tax returns of calendar-year decedents who died in 2001. (Form 1040, Form 1040A, or Form 1040EZ.) Fiscal-year individuals must file returns or requests for extension by the 15th day of the 4th month after the close of the tax year.

Last day for calendar-year individuals to file application (Form 4868) for automatic four-month extension to file 2001 income tax return.

Individuals' information returns (Form 5471) with respect to foreign corporations to be filed with Form 1040.

Last day for individuals to file amended income tax returns (Form 1040X) for the calendar year 1998.

Estimated Tax. Using Form 8109, calendar-year corporations pay 25% of estimated tax if requirements are met before April 1, 2002. Fiscal-year corporations are to make payments on the 15th day of the 4th, 6th, 9th and 12th months of the tax year.

Payment of first installment of 2002 estimated income taxes by calendar-year individuals (other than farmers and fishermen) (Form 1040ES). Estimated tax payments for fiscal-year individuals are due on the 15th day of the 4th, 6th and 9th months of the tax year and the 1st month of the following tax year.

Trusts (and calendar-year estates and certain residuary trusts in existence more than two years) must make first payment of estimated taxes for 2002 (Form 1041-ES). Fiscal-year estates must make payments on the 15th day of the 4th, 6th, and 9th months of the fiscal year and the 1st month of the following fiscal year.

Trusts and Estates. Fiduciary income tax return (Form 1041) for calendar year 2001. (Fiscal-year estates must file by the 15th day of the 4th month following close of the tax year.)

Estates seeking an extension of time to file return must have submitted an application on Form 2758 in time for it to be processed by the filing date.

Last day for trusts to file application (Form 8736) for automatic three-month extension of time to file 2001 income tax return.

---

[2] In general, fiscal-year corporations must file within three years of the date the original return was due.

¶5

This day
2002   **Tax Return Due Dates**—continued
Apr. 15th—continued
Last day for estates and trusts to file amended tax returns for calendar year 1998.

Partnerships. Last day for filing income tax return (Form 1065) for calendar-year 2001. Returns for fiscal-year partnerships are due on the 15th day of the 4th month after the close of the tax year.

Last day for calendar-year U.S. partnerships to file application (Form 8736) for automatic three-month extension to file 2001 income tax return.

Last day for calendar-year partnership to file an amended return for 1998.

Information Returns. Annual information return (Form 1041-A) for split-interest trusts and complex trusts claiming charitable deductions under Code Sec. 642(c) and annual information return (Form 5227) for Code Sec. 4947(a)(2) trusts must be filed.

Apr. 30th— **Employers' Taxes.** Employers of nonagricultural and nonhousehold employees must file return on Form 941 to report income tax withholding and FICA taxes for the first quarter of 2002.[3]

May 15th— **Exempt Organizations.** Annual information return (Form 990) for 2001 by calendar-year organizations exempt or claiming exemption from tax under Code Sec. 501 or Code Sec. 4947(a)(1). Fiscal-year organizations must file by 15th day of 5th month after close of the tax year.

Calendar-year private foundations (and Code Sec. 4947(a) trusts treated as private foundations) must file Form 990-PF and, for tax years beginning after August 5, 2001, private foundations must pay the first quarter installment of estimated excise tax on net investment or tax on unrelated business income. Fiscal-year organizations must file by 15th day of 5th month after close of tax year, for both Form 990-PF and estimated taxes referred to above.

Calendar-year Code Sec. 501(a) organizations with unrelated business income must file income tax return on Form 990-T. Fiscal-year organizations must file by 15th day of 5th month following close of tax year.

Corporations requesting an extension of time to file Form 990 may file Form 7004 for an automatic six-month extension. Other entities must file Form 2758 in time for it to be processed by the filing deadline to request a nonautomatic extension.

May 31st— **Information Returns.** Annual statement to IRS regarding 2001 account balances for an IRA or SEP (Form 5498). Participants and IRS must be provided with IRA plan contribution information.

June 15th— **Individuals.** Last day for nonresident alien individuals not subject to withholding to file income tax return for calendar year 2001.

Estimated Tax. Calendar-year corporations must pay second installment of 2002 estimated tax.

---

[3] If timely deposits in full payment of taxes due were made, the due date for Form 941 is May 10.

¶ **5**

This day
2002   **Tax Return Due Dates**—continued
June 15th—continued

> Payment of second installment of 2002 estimated tax by individuals (other than farmers and fishermen), by trusts and by estates and certain residuary trusts in existence more than 2 years. Nonresident aliens who have no wages subject to U.S. withholding must make first payment (Form 1040ES(NR)).

> **Corporations.** Last day for foreign corporations that do not maintain an office or place of business in U.S. to file income tax return (Form 1120F) for calendar year 2001.

July 15th— **Trusts.** Last day for filing 2001 Form 1041 for trusts that obtained an automatic three-month filing extension.

> **Partnerships.** Last day for filing 2001 Form 1065 for partnerships that obtained an automatic three-month filing extension.

July 31st— **Employers' Taxes.** Employers of nonagricultural and nonhousehold employees must file return on Form 941 to report income tax withholding and FICA taxes for the second quarter of 2002.[4]

Aug. 15th— **Individuals.** Last day for filing 2001 income tax return by calendar-year individuals who obtained automatic four-month filing extension.

Sept. 15th— **Estimated Tax.** Payment of third installment of 2002 estimated tax by calendar-year corporations.

> Payment of third installment of 2002 estimated tax by individuals (other than farmers and fishermen), by trusts and by estates and certain residuary trusts in existence more than 2 years.

> Last day for filing 2001 income tax return by calendar-year corporations that obtained automatic six-month filing extension.

> **Exempt Organizations.** Last day for exempt calendar-year farmers' cooperatives to file 2001 income tax returns (Form 990-C). Fiscal-year cooperatives must file by the 15th day of the 9th month following the close of the tax year. An automatic six-month extension of the filing date may be obtained by filing Form 7004.

Oct. 31st— **Employers' Taxes.** Employers of nonagricultural and nonhousehold employees must file return on Form 941 to report income tax withholding and FICA taxes for the third quarter of 2002.[5]

Dec. 15th— **Estimated Tax.** Payment of last installment of 2002 estimated tax by calendar-year corporations.

This day
2003

Jan. 15th— **Estimated Tax.** Final installment of 2002 estimated tax by individuals, trusts and estates and certain residuary trusts in existence more than two years. (Payment of estimated tax in full by individuals, trusts and estates that are first required to pay estimated tax for calendar year 2002.) Payment not necessary if returns filed and tax paid in

---

[4] If timely deposits in full payment of taxes due were made, the due date for Form 941 is August 10.

[5] If timely deposits in full payment of taxes due were made, the due date for Form 941 is November 10.

¶ 5

**This day
2003**   **Tax Return Due Dates**—continued
Jan. 15th—continued
full by January 31, 2003. Payment of estimated tax in full by farmers and fishermen who are not filing final returns by March 1, 2003.

Jan. 31st— Individuals. Final income tax return for 2002 by calendar-year individuals and by trusts and estates in existence more than two years who owed but did not pay 2002 estimated tax otherwise due January 15th.

Employment Tax Deposits

Income Tax Withholding, FICA Taxes, Backup Withholding. Employment taxes are withheld income tax, FICA contributions and backup withholding on reportable payments. Generally, an employer must make either MONTHLY or SEMI-WEEKLY deposits during a calendar year based upon the aggregate amount of employment taxes paid during the "lookback" period. The lookback period for each calendar year is the 12-month period that ended the preceding June 30. Thus, an employer's obligation to make deposits in 2002 will be based upon the aggregate employment taxes paid during the period July 1, 2000, through June 30, 2001. (New employers are considered to have an aggregate tax liability of zero for any calendar quarter in which the employer did not exist.) See ¶ 2650.

Monthly Deposits. Monthly deposits are required if the aggregate amount of employment taxes reported by the employer for the lookback period is $50,000 or less. Monthly deposits are due on the 15th day of the following month in which the payments were made.

Semi-Weekly Deposits. An employer is a semi-weekly depositor for the entire calendar year if the aggregate amount of employment taxes during the lookback period exceeds $50,000. Further, a monthly depositor will become a semi-weekly depositor on the first day after the employer becomes subject to the One-Day Rule, discussed below. Semi-weekly deposits are generally due on either Wednesday or Friday—depending upon the timing of the employer's pay period. Employers with payment dates (paydays) that fall on Wednesday, Thursday or Friday must deposit the employment taxes on or before the following Wednesday. Employers with payment dates that fall on Saturday, Sunday, Monday or Tuesday must make their deposit on or before the following Friday. However, an employer will always have three banking days in which to make the deposit. Thus, if any of the three weekdays following the close of a semi-weekly period is a holiday, then the employer will have an additional banking day in which to make the deposit.

One-Day Rule. If an employer has accumulated $100,000 or more of undeposited employment taxes, then the taxes must be deposited by the close of the next banking day.

Federal Unemployment Taxes. The calendar year is divided into four quarters for purposes of determining when deposits of federal unemployment tax are necessary. The periods end on March 31, June 30, September 30 and December 31. If the employer owes more than $100 in undeposited federal unemployment tax at the end of a quarter, then the tax owed must be deposited by the end of the next month.

¶ 5

2002

January

S	M	T	W	T	F	S
		1	2	3	4	5
6	7	8	9	10	11	12
13	14	15	16	17	18	19
20	21	22	23	24	25	26
27	28	29	30	31		

February

S	M	T	W	T	F	S
					1	2
3	4	5	6	7	8	9
10	11	12	13	14	15	16
17	18	19	20	21	22	23
24	25	26	27	28		

March

S	M	T	W	T	F	S
					1	2
3	4	5	6	7	8	9
10	11	12	13	14	15	16
17	18	19	20	21	22	23
24/31	25	26	27	28	29	30

April

S	M	T	W	T	F	S
	1	2	3	4	5	6
7	8	9	10	11	12	13
14	15	16	17	18	19	20
21	22	23	24	25	26	27
28	29	30				

May

S	M	T	W	T	F	S
			1	2	3	4
5	6	7	8	9	10	11
12	13	14	15	16	17	18
19	20	21	22	23	24	25
26	27	28	29	30	31	

June

S	M	T	W	T	F	S
						1
2	3	4	5	6	7	8
9	10	11	12	13	14	15
16	17	18	19	20	21	22
23/30	24	25	26	27	28	29

July

S	M	T	W	T	F	S
	1	2	3	4	5	6
7	8	9	10	11	12	13
14	15	16	17	18	19	20
21	22	23	24	25	26	27
28	29	30	31			

August

S	M	T	W	T	F	S
				1	2	3
4	5	6	7	8	9	10
11	12	13	14	15	16	17
18	19	20	21	22	23	24
25	26	27	28	29	30	31

September

S	M	T	W	T	F	S
1	2	3	4	5	6	7
8	9	10	11	12	13	14
15	16	17	18	19	20	21
22	23	24	25	26	27	28
29	30					

October

S	M	T	W	T	F	S
		1	2	3	4	5
6	7	8	9	10	11	12
13	14	15	16	17	18	19
20	21	22	23	24	25	26
27	28	29	30	31		

November

S	M	T	W	T	F	S
					1	2
3	4	5	6	7	8	9
10	11	12	13	14	15	16
17	18	19	20	21	22	23
24	25	26	27	28	29	30

December

S	M	T	W	T	F	S
1	2	3	4	5	6	7
8	9	10	11	12	13	14
15	16	17	18	19	20	21
22	23	24	25	26	27	28
29	30	31				

¶5

Schedules and Tables

TAX RATES

NOTE: The 2001 Tax Rate Schedules reproduced below are based on the 2001 Form 1040 instructions. The projected 2002 Tax Rate Schedules were prepared by CCH Editors based on the inflation-adjustment provisions of Section 1(f) of the Internal Revenue Code and the average of the Consumer Price Indexes (all urban consumers), published by the Department of Labor for each month in the 12-month period ended August 31, 2001. Please note that the official 2002 tax rate tables had not been released by the Internal Revenue Service at the date of publication.

The 2001 and 2002 tax rate schedules reflect the changes enacted by the Economic Growth and Tax Relief Reconciliation Act of 2001 (EGTRRA) (P.L. 107-16). The 2001 and 2002 tax rate schedules for single individuals are at ¶ 11; for married individuals filing jointly and surviving spouses, see ¶ 13; for married individuals filing separately, see ¶ 15; for heads of households, see ¶ 17; and for estates and nongrantor trusts, see ¶ 19.

Besides the immediate impact on 2001 and 2002 tax brackets of lower tax rates and the incorporation of a 10% rate bracket (for all rate schedules except estates and trusts), EGTRRA also phases in additional decreases to the tax rates over the next few years. For more details on how the brackets will be structured in future years, see ¶ 21.

TAX RATE SCHEDULES FOR 2001 AND 2002

¶ 11   SCHEDULE X: Single Individuals

2001

Taxable Income Over	But Not Over	Pay	% on + Excess	of the amount over—
$ 0—	$ 27,050	$ 0	15 %	$ 0
27,050—	65,550	4,057.50	27.5	27,050
65,550—	136,750	14,645.00	30.5	65,550
136,750—	297,350	36,361.00	35.5	136,750
297,350—	....	93,374.00	39.1	297,350

Example: Nancy Gary, a single individual, has gross income of $102,000 in 2001. She has no dependents and claims a standard deduction because she lacks sufficient itemized deductions. Her taxable income is $94,550 ($102,000 − $4,550 standard deduction − $2,900 personal exemption). Her tax is $23,490 ($14,645 + .305 ($94,550 − $65,550)).

2002 (Projected)

Taxable Income Over	But Not Over	Pay	% on + Excess	of the amount over—
$ 0—$	6,000	$ 0	10 %	$ 0
6,000—	27,950	600.00	15	6,000
27,950—	67,700	3,892.50	27	27,950
67,700—	141,250	14,625.00	30	67,700
141,250—	307,050	36,690.00	35	141,250
307,050—	....	94,720.00	38.6	307,050

¶ 13   SCHEDULE Y-1: Married Filing Jointly and Surviving Spouses

2001

Taxable Income Over	But Not Over	Pay	% on + Excess	of the amount over—
$ 0—$	45,200	$ 0	15 %	$ 0
45,200—	109,250	6,780.00	27.5	45,200
109,250—	166,500	24,393.75	30.5	109,250
166,500—	297,350	41,855.00	35.5	166,500
297,350—	....	88,306.75	39.1	297,350

Example: Barbara and Ken Doosee have a combined income of $150,000 in 2001. They have two dependent children and allowable itemized deductions (consisting solely of medical expense deductions) totaling $16,000. They file a joint return. Their taxable income is $122,400 ($150,000 − $16,000 itemized deductions − $11,600 (four personal exemptions)). Their tax is $28,404.50 ($24,393.75 + .305 ($122,400 − $109,250)).

2002 (Projected)

Taxable Income Over	But Not Over	Pay	% on + Excess	of the amount over—
$ 0—$	12,000	$ 0	10 %	$ 0
12,000—	46,700	1,200.00	15	12,000
46,700—	112,850	6,405.00	27	46,700
112,850—	171,950	24,265.50	30	112,850
171,950—	307,050	41,995.50	35	171,950
307,050—	....	89,280.50	38.6	307,050

¶ 15   SCHEDULE Y-2: Married Individuals Filing Separately

2001

Taxable Income Over	But Not Over	Pay	% on + Excess	of the amount over—
$ 0—$ 22,600		$ 0	15 %	$ 0
22,600— 54,625		3,390.00	27.5	22,600
54,625— 83,250		12,196.88	30.5	54,625
83,250— 148,675		20,927.50	35.5	83,250
148,675—.........		44,153.38	39.1	148,675

2002 (Projected)

Taxable Income Over	But Not Over	Pay	% on + Excess	of the amount over—
$ 0—$ 6,000		$ 0	10 %	$ 0
6,000— 23,350		600.00	15	6,000
23,350— 56,425		3,202.50	27	23,350
56,425— 85,975		12,132.75	30	56,425
85,975— 153,525		20,997.75	35	85,975
153,525—.........		44,640.25	38.6	153,525

¶ 17   SCHEDULE Z: Heads of Households

2001

Taxable Income Over	But Not Over	Pay	% on + Excess	of the amount over—
$ 0—$ 36,250		$ 0	15 %	$ 0
36,250— 93,650		5,437.50	27.5	36,250
93,650— 151,650		21,222.50	30.5	93,650
151,650— 297,350		38,912.50	35.5	151,650
297,350—.......		90,636.00	39.1	297,350

2002 (Projected)

Taxable Income Over	But Not Over	Pay	% on + Excess	of the amount over—
$ 0—$ 10,000		$ 0	10 %	$ 0
10,000— 37,450		1,000.00	15	10,000
37,450— 96,700		5,117.50	27	37,450
96,700— 156,600		21,115.00	30	96,700
156,600— 307,050		39,085.00	35	156,600
307,050—.......		91,742.50	38.6	307,050

¶ 19 INCOME TAX RATE SCHEDULES FOR USE BY ESTATES AND NONGRANTOR TRUSTS

2001

Taxable Income Over	But Not Over	Pay	% on + Excess	of the amount over—
$ 0—$	1,800	$ 0	15 %	$ 0
1,800—	4,250	270.00	27.5	1,800
4,250—	6,500	943.75	30.5	4,250
6,500—	8,900	1,630.00	35.5	6,500
8,900—......		2,482.00	39.1	8,900

2002 (Projected)

Taxable Income Over	But Not Over	Pay	% on + Excess	of the amount over—
$ 0—$	1,850	$ 0	15 %	$ 0
1,850—	4,400	277.50	27	1,850
4,400—	6,750	966.00	30	4,400
6,750—	9,200	1,671.00	35	6,750
9,200—......		2,528.50	38.6	9,200

¶ 21 Tax Rate Changes Beyond 2001

The Economic Growth and Tax Relief Reconciliation Act of 2001 (EGTRRA) (P.L. 107-16), implemented a staged decrease in the existing tax rates, while adding a 10% bracket for individuals. Notwithstanding future legislation, the tax rates in place by 2006 will be a far cry from what was in place for 2001. At the beginning of 2001, there were five brackets—15%, 28%, 31%, 36% and 39.6%. Here's how the tax rate brackets will evolve over the next few years.

10% bracket. For 2001, the new 10% bracket was administered through the tax rebate checks. For 2002 - 2007, the 10% bracket applies to singles (including those married filing separate) on the first $6,000 of taxable income, to heads of households on the first $10,000 of taxable income, and to joint filers on the first $12,000 of taxable income. It is important to note that the 10% bracket applies to individual rate schedules but not for the estate and trust rate schedule (¶ 19).

After 2007, the 10% bracket applies to singles (including those married filing separate) on the first $7,000 of taxable income, to heads of households on the first $10,000 of taxable income (no change), and to joint filers on the first $14,000 of taxable income.

Other brackets. EGTRRA phases in a rate reduction for all brackets except the 15% bracket in three stages, as follows:

Tax Years

2002—2003	27.5% rate reduced to	27%
	30.5% rate reduced to	30%
	35.5% rate reduced to	35%
	39.1% rate reduced to	38.6%
2004—2005	27% rate reduced to	26%
	30% rate reduced to	29%
	35% rate reduced to	34%
	38.6% rate reduced to	37.6%
2006 and after	26% rate reduced to	25%
	29% rate reduced to	28%
	34% rate reduced to	33%
	37.6% rate reduced to	35%

Planning for change. With the rates decreasing every two years, tax practitioners will need to keep aware of the effect on their clients' withholding (¶ 2601) and estimated taxes (¶ 2682). To review the rate schedules for 2001 and the projected schedules for 2002, see ¶ 11-¶ 17. Also, as ordinary tax rates move closer to the capital gains tax rates (¶ 1736), some investment decisions will need to be reconsidered as the gap narrows and lessens the potential tax impact on certain transactions. Finally, as the rates continue to decline, AMT may play a larger role as "regular" tax liability amounts decrease without a corresponding drop in AMT (¶ 1401 and ¶ 1405).

2001 TAX TABLE—INDIVIDUALS

¶ 25   2001 Tax Table for Use with Form 1040

□ The Tax Table on pages 30-41 is for use with Form 1040. A similar Tax Table applies to Forms 1040A and 1040EZ, except that the table for Form 1040A refers to taxable income on line 25, Form 1040A, and the table for Form 1040EZ refers to taxable income on line 6, Form 1040EZ.

□ **Note:** The Tax Table reproduced in the *Guide* is for use with Form 1040 by taxpayers with taxable income of less than $100,000. Because Forms 1040A and 1040EZ cannot be filed by taxpayers with taxable incomes of $50,000 or more, tax tables for use with those forms end at taxable income of $50,000.

2001 TAX TABLE   Based on Taxable Income. For persons with taxable incomes of less than $100,000.

Read down the income columns of the tax table until you find the line covering the taxable income shown on line 39 of Form 1040 (line 25 of Form 1040A or line 6 of Form 1040EZ). Then read across that income line until you find the column heading that describes your filing status. Enter the tax found there on line 40, Form 1040 (line 26, Form 1040A or line 10, Form 1040EZ).

2001 Tax Table

Caution. Dependents, see the worksheet on page 33.

Use if your taxable income is less than $100,000.
If $100,000 or more, use the Tax Rate Schedules.

Example. Mr. and Mrs. Brown are filing a joint return. Their taxable income on line 39 of Form 1040 is $25,300. First, they find the $25,300–25,350 income line. Next, they find the column for married filing jointly and read down the column. The amount shown where the income line and filing status column meet is $3,799. This is the tax amount they should enter on line 40 of their Form 1040.

Sample Table

At least	But less than	Single	Married filing jointly *	Married filing separately	Head of a household
			Your tax is—		
25,200	25,250	3,784	3,784	4,112	3,784
25,250	25,300	3,791	3,791	4,126	3,791
25,300	25,350	3,799	(3,799)	4,139	3,799
25,350	25,400	3,806	3,806	4,153	3,806

If line 39 (taxable income) is— / And you are—

At least	But less than	Single	Married filing jointly *	Married filing separately	Head of a household
			Your tax is—		
0	5	0	0	0	0
5	15	2	2	2	2
15	25	3	3	3	3
25	50	6	6	6	6
50	75	9	9	9	9
75	100	13	13	13	13
100	125	17	17	17	17
125	150	21	21	21	21
150	175	24	24	24	24
175	200	28	28	28	28
200	225	32	32	32	32
225	250	36	36	36	36
250	275	39	39	39	39
275	300	43	43	43	43
300	325	47	47	47	47
325	350	51	51	51	51
350	375	54	54	54	54
375	400	58	58	58	58
400	425	62	62	62	62
425	450	66	66	66	66
450	475	69	69	69	69
475	500	73	73	73	73
500	525	77	77	77	77
525	550	81	81	81	81
550	575	84	84	84	84
575	600	88	88	88	88
600	625	92	92	92	92
625	650	96	96	96	96
650	675	99	99	99	99
675	700	103	103	103	103
700	725	107	107	107	107
725	750	111	111	111	111
750	775	114	114	114	114
775	800	118	118	118	118
800	825	122	122	122	122
825	850	126	126	126	126
850	875	129	129	129	129
875	900	133	133	133	133
900	925	137	137	137	137
925	950	141	141	141	141
950	975	144	144	144	144
975	1,000	148	148	148	148
1,000					
1,000	1,025	152	152	152	152
1,025	1,050	156	156	156	156
1,050	1,075	159	159	159	159
1,075	1,100	163	163	163	163
1,100	1,125	167	167	167	167
1,125	1,150	171	171	171	171
1,150	1,175	174	174	174	174
1,175	1,200	178	178	178	178
1,200	1,225	182	182	182	182
1,225	1,250	186	186	186	186
1,250	1,275	189	189	189	189
1,275	1,300	193	193	193	193
1,300	1,325	197	197	197	197
1,325	1,350	201	201	201	201
1,350	1,375	204	204	204	204
1,375	1,400	208	208	208	208
1,400	1,425	212	212	212	212
1,425	1,450	216	216	216	216
1,450	1,475	219	219	219	219
1,475	1,500	223	223	223	223
1,500	1,525	227	227	227	227
1,525	1,550	231	231	231	231
1,550	1,575	234	234	234	234
1,575	1,600	238	238	238	238
1,600	1,625	242	242	242	242
1,625	1,650	246	246	246	246
1,650	1,675	249	249	249	249
1,675	1,700	253	253	253	253
1,700	1,725	257	257	257	257
1,725	1,750	261	261	261	261
1,750	1,775	264	264	264	264
1,775	1,800	268	268	268	268
1,800	1,825	272	272	272	272
1,825	1,850	276	276	276	276
1,850	1,875	279	279	279	279
1,875	1,900	283	283	283	283
1,900	1,925	287	287	287	287
1,925	1,950	291	291	291	291
1,950	1,975	294	294	294	294
1,975	2,000	298	298	298	298
2,000					
2,000	2,025	302	302	302	302
2,025	2,050	306	306	306	306
2,050	2,075	309	309	309	309
2,075	2,100	313	313	313	313
2,100	2,125	317	317	317	317
2,125	2,150	321	321	321	321
2,150	2,175	324	324	324	324
2,175	2,200	328	328	328	328
2,200	2,225	332	332	332	332
2,225	2,250	336	336	336	336
2,250	2,275	339	339	339	339
2,275	2,300	343	343	343	343
2,300	2,325	347	347	347	347
2,325	2,350	351	351	351	351
2,350	2,375	354	354	354	354
2,375	2,400	358	358	358	358
2,400	2,425	362	362	362	362
2,425	2,450	366	366	366	366
2,450	2,475	369	369	369	369
2,475	2,500	373	373	373	373
2,500	2,525	377	377	377	377
2,525	2,550	381	381	381	381
2,550	2,575	384	384	384	384
2,575	2,600	388	388	388	388
2,600	2,625	392	392	392	392
2,625	2,650	396	396	396	396
2,650	2,675	399	399	399	399
2,675	2,700	403	403	403	403
2,700	2,725	407	407	407	407
2,725	2,750	411	411	411	411
2,750	2,775	414	414	414	414
2,775	2,800	418	418	418	418
2,800	2,825	422	422	422	422
2,825	2,850	426	426	426	426
2,850	2,875	429	429	429	429
2,875	2,900	433	433	433	433
2,900	2,925	437	437	437	437
2,925	2,950	441	441	441	441
2,950	2,975	444	444	444	444
2,975	3,000	448	448	448	448
3,000					
3,000	3,050	454	454	454	454
3,050	3,100	461	461	461	461
3,100	3,150	469	469	469	469
3,150	3,200	476	476	476	476
3,200	3,250	484	484	484	484
3,250	3,300	491	491	491	491
3,300	3,350	499	499	499	499
3,350	3,400	506	506	506	506
3,400	3,450	514	514	514	514
3,450	3,500	521	521	521	521
3,500	3,550	529	529	529	529
3,550	3,600	536	536	536	536
3,600	3,650	544	544	544	544
3,650	3,700	551	551	551	551
3,700	3,750	559	559	559	559
3,750	3,800	566	566	566	566
3,800	3,850	574	574	574	574
3,850	3,900	581	581	581	581
3,900	3,950	589	589	589	589
3,950	4,000	596	596	596	596
4,000					
4,000	4,050	604	604	604	604
4,050	4,100	611	611	611	611
4,100	4,150	619	619	619	619
4,150	4,200	626	626	626	626
4,200	4,250	634	634	634	634
4,250	4,300	641	641	641	641
4,300	4,350	649	649	649	649
4,350	4,400	656	656	656	656
4,400	4,450	664	664	664	664
4,450	4,500	671	671	671	671
4,500	4,550	679	679	679	679
4,550	4,600	686	686	686	686
4,600	4,650	694	694	694	694
4,650	4,700	701	701	701	701
4,700	4,750	709	709	709	709
4,750	4,800	716	716	716	716
4,800	4,850	724	724	724	724
4,850	4,900	731	731	731	731
4,900	4,950	739	739	739	739
4,950	5,000	746	746	746	746

(Continued on page 60)

* This column must also be used by a qualifying widow(er).

-59-

¶ 25

2001 Tax Table—*Continued*　　Caution. Dependents, see the worksheet on page 33.

If line 39 (taxable income) is—		And you are—				If line 39 (taxable income) is—		And you are—				If line 39 (taxable income) is—		And you are—			
At least	But less than	Single	Married filing jointly *	Married filing separately	Head of a household	At least	But less than	Single	Married filing jointly *	Married filing separately	Head of a household	At least	But less than	Single	Married filing jointly *	Married filing separately	Head of a household
		Your tax is—						Your tax is—						Your tax is—			
5,000						**8,000**						**11,000**					
5,000	5,050	754	754	754	754	8,000	8,050	1,204	1,204	1,204	1,204	11,000	11,050	1,654	1,654	1,654	1,654
5,050	5,100	761	761	761	761	8,050	8,100	1,211	1,211	1,211	1,211	11,050	11,100	1,661	1,661	1,661	1,661
5,100	5,150	769	769	769	769	8,100	8,150	1,219	1,219	1,219	1,219	11,100	11,150	1,669	1,669	1,669	1,669
5,150	5,200	776	776	776	776	8,150	8,200	1,226	1,226	1,226	1,226	11,150	11,200	1,676	1,676	1,676	1,676
5,200	5,250	784	784	784	784	8,200	8,250	1,234	1,234	1,234	1,234	11,200	11,250	1,684	1,684	1,684	1,684
5,250	5,300	791	791	791	791	8,250	8,300	1,241	1,241	1,241	1,241	11,250	11,300	1,691	1,691	1,691	1,691
5,300	5,350	799	799	799	799	8,300	8,350	1,249	1,249	1,249	1,249	11,300	11,350	1,699	1,699	1,699	1,699
5,350	5,400	806	806	806	806	8,350	8,400	1,256	1,256	1,256	1,256	11,350	11,400	1,706	1,706	1,706	1,706
5,400	5,450	814	814	814	814	8,400	8,450	1,264	1,264	1,264	1,264	11,400	11,450	1,714	1,714	1,714	1,714
5,450	5,500	821	821	821	821	8,450	8,500	1,271	1,271	1,271	1,271	11,450	11,500	1,721	1,721	1,721	1,721
5,500	5,550	829	829	829	829	8,500	8,550	1,279	1,279	1,279	1,279	11,500	11,550	1,729	1,729	1,729	1,729
5,550	5,600	836	836	836	836	8,550	8,600	1,286	1,286	1,286	1,286	11,550	11,600	1,736	1,736	1,736	1,736
5,600	5,650	844	844	844	844	8,600	8,650	1,294	1,294	1,294	1,294	11,600	11,650	1,744	1,744	1,744	1,744
5,650	5,700	851	851	851	851	8,650	8,700	1,301	1,301	1,301	1,301	11,650	11,700	1,751	1,751	1,751	1,751
5,700	5,750	859	859	859	859	8,700	8,750	1,309	1,309	1,309	1,309	11,700	11,750	1,759	1,759	1,759	1,759
5,750	5,800	866	866	866	866	8,750	8,800	1,316	1,316	1,316	1,316	11,750	11,800	1,766	1,766	1,766	1,766
5,800	5,850	874	874	874	874	8,800	8,850	1,324	1,324	1,324	1,324	11,800	11,850	1,774	1,774	1,774	1,774
5,850	5,900	881	881	881	881	8,850	8,900	1,331	1,331	1,331	1,331	11,850	11,900	1,781	1,781	1,781	1,781
5,900	5,950	889	889	889	889	8,900	8,950	1,339	1,339	1,339	1,339	11,900	11,950	1,789	1,789	1,789	1,789
5,950	6,000	896	896	896	896	8,950	9,000	1,346	1,346	1,346	1,346	11,950	12,000	1,796	1,796	1,796	1,796
6,000						**9,000**						**12,000**					
6,000	6,050	904	904	904	904	9,000	9,050	1,354	1,354	1,354	1,354	12,000	12,050	1,804	1,804	1,804	1,804
6,050	6,100	911	911	911	911	9,050	9,100	1,361	1,361	1,361	1,361	12,050	12,100	1,811	1,811	1,811	1,811
6,100	6,150	919	919	919	919	9,100	9,150	1,369	1,369	1,369	1,369	12,100	12,150	1,819	1,819	1,819	1,819
6,150	6,200	926	926	926	926	9,150	9,200	1,376	1,376	1,376	1,376	12,150	12,200	1,826	1,826	1,826	1,826
6,200	6,250	934	934	934	934	9,200	9,250	1,384	1,384	1,384	1,384	12,200	12,250	1,834	1,834	1,834	1,834
6,250	6,300	941	941	941	941	9,250	9,300	1,391	1,391	1,391	1,391	12,250	12,300	1,841	1,841	1,841	1,841
6,300	6,350	949	949	949	949	9,300	9,350	1,399	1,399	1,399	1,399	12,300	12,350	1,849	1,849	1,849	1,849
6,350	6,400	956	956	956	956	9,350	9,400	1,406	1,406	1,406	1,406	12,350	12,400	1,856	1,856	1,856	1,856
6,400	6,450	964	964	964	964	9,400	9,450	1,414	1,414	1,414	1,414	12,400	12,450	1,864	1,864	1,864	1,864
6,450	6,500	971	971	971	971	9,450	9,500	1,421	1,421	1,421	1,421	12,450	12,500	1,871	1,871	1,871	1,871
6,500	6,550	979	979	979	979	9,500	9,550	1,429	1,429	1,429	1,429	12,500	12,550	1,879	1,879	1,879	1,879
6,550	6,600	986	986	986	986	9,550	9,600	1,436	1,436	1,436	1,436	12,550	12,600	1,886	1,886	1,886	1,886
6,600	6,650	994	994	994	994	9,600	9,650	1,444	1,444	1,444	1,444	12,600	12,650	1,894	1,894	1,894	1,894
6,650	6,700	1,001	1,001	1,001	1,001	9,650	9,700	1,451	1,451	1,451	1,451	12,650	12,700	1,901	1,901	1,901	1,901
6,700	6,750	1,009	1,009	1,009	1,009	9,700	9,750	1,459	1,459	1,459	1,459	12,700	12,750	1,909	1,909	1,909	1,909
6,750	6,800	1,016	1,016	1,016	1,016	9,750	9,800	1,466	1,466	1,466	1,466	12,750	12,800	1,916	1,916	1,916	1,916
6,800	6,850	1,024	1,024	1,024	1,024	9,800	9,850	1,474	1,474	1,474	1,474	12,800	12,850	1,924	1,924	1,924	1,924
6,850	6,900	1,031	1,031	1,031	1,031	9,850	9,900	1,481	1,481	1,481	1,481	12,850	12,900	1,931	1,931	1,931	1,931
6,900	6,950	1,039	1,039	1,039	1,039	9,900	9,950	1,489	1,489	1,489	1,489	12,900	12,950	1,939	1,939	1,939	1,939
6,950	7,000	1,046	1,046	1,046	1,046	9,950	10,000	1,496	1,496	1,496	1,496	12,950	13,000	1,946	1,946	1,946	1,946
7,000						**10,000**						**13,000**					
7,000	7,050	1,054	1,054	1,054	1,054	10,000	10,050	1,504	1,504	1,504	1,504	13,000	13,050	1,954	1,954	1,954	1,954
7,050	7,100	1,061	1,061	1,061	1,061	10,050	10,100	1,511	1,511	1,511	1,511	13,050	13,100	1,961	1,961	1,961	1,961
7,100	7,150	1,069	1,069	1,069	1,069	10,100	10,150	1,519	1,519	1,519	1,519	13,100	13,150	1,969	1,969	1,969	1,969
7,150	7,200	1,076	1,076	1,076	1,076	10,150	10,200	1,526	1,526	1,526	1,526	13,150	13,200	1,976	1,976	1,976	1,976
7,200	7,250	1,084	1,084	1,084	1,084	10,200	10,250	1,534	1,534	1,534	1,534	13,200	13,250	1,984	1,984	1,984	1,984
7,250	7,300	1,091	1,091	1,091	1,091	10,250	10,300	1,541	1,541	1,541	1,541	13,250	13,300	1,991	1,991	1,991	1,991
7,300	7,350	1,099	1,099	1,099	1,099	10,300	10,350	1,549	1,549	1,549	1,549	13,300	13,350	1,999	1,999	1,999	1,999
7,350	7,400	1,106	1,106	1,106	1,106	10,350	10,400	1,556	1,556	1,556	1,556	13,350	13,400	2,006	2,006	2,006	2,006
7,400	7,450	1,114	1,114	1,114	1,114	10,400	10,450	1,564	1,564	1,564	1,564	13,400	13,450	2,014	2,014	2,014	2,014
7,450	7,500	1,121	1,121	1,121	1,121	10,450	10,500	1,571	1,571	1,571	1,571	13,450	13,500	2,021	2,021	2,021	2,021
7,500	7,550	1,129	1,129	1,129	1,129	10,500	10,550	1,579	1,579	1,579	1,579	13,500	13,550	2,029	2,029	2,029	2,029
7,550	7,600	1,136	1,136	1,136	1,136	10,550	10,600	1,586	1,586	1,586	1,586	13,550	13,600	2,036	2,036	2,036	2,036
7,600	7,650	1,144	1,144	1,144	1,144	10,600	10,650	1,594	1,594	1,594	1,594	13,600	13,650	2,044	2,044	2,044	2,044
7,650	7,700	1,151	1,151	1,151	1,151	10,650	10,700	1,601	1,601	1,601	1,601	13,650	13,700	2,051	2,051	2,051	2,051
7,700	7,750	1,159	1,159	1,159	1,159	10,700	10,750	1,609	1,609	1,609	1,609	13,700	13,750	2,059	2,059	2,059	2,059
7,750	7,800	1,166	1,166	1,166	1,166	10,750	10,800	1,616	1,616	1,616	1,616	13,750	13,800	2,066	2,066	2,066	2,066
7,800	7,850	1,174	1,174	1,174	1,174	10,800	10,850	1,624	1,624	1,624	1,624	13,800	13,850	2,074	2,074	2,074	2,074
7,850	7,900	1,181	1,181	1,181	1,181	10,850	10,900	1,631	1,631	1,631	1,631	13,850	13,900	2,081	2,081	2,081	2,081
7,900	7,950	1,189	1,189	1,189	1,189	10,900	10,950	1,639	1,639	1,639	1,639	13,900	13,950	2,089	2,089	2,089	2,089
7,950	8,000	1,196	1,196	1,196	1,196	10,950	11,000	1,646	1,646	1,646	1,646	13,950	14,000	2,096	2,096	2,096	2,096

* This column must also be used by a qualifying widow(er).

(Continued on page 61)

-60-

¶ 25

Caution. Dependents, see the worksheet on page 33.   **2001 Tax Table**—*Continued*

If line 39 (taxable income) is—		And you are—			
At least	But less than	Single	Married filing jointly *	Married filing separately	Head of a household
		Your tax is—			

14,000

At least	But less than	Single	Married filing jointly	Married filing separately	Head of a household
14,000	14,050	2,104	2,104	2,104	2,104
14,050	14,100	2,111	2,111	2,111	2,111
14,100	14,150	2,119	2,119	2,119	2,119
14,150	14,200	2,126	2,126	2,126	2,126
14,200	14,250	2,134	2,134	2,134	2,134
14,250	14,300	2,141	2,141	2,141	2,141
14,300	14,350	2,149	2,149	2,149	2,149
14,350	14,400	2,156	2,156	2,156	2,156
14,400	14,450	2,164	2,164	2,164	2,164
14,450	14,500	2,171	2,171	2,171	2,171
14,500	14,550	2,179	2,179	2,179	2,179
14,550	14,600	2,186	2,186	2,186	2,186
14,600	14,650	2,194	2,194	2,194	2,194
14,650	14,700	2,201	2,201	2,201	2,201
14,700	14,750	2,209	2,209	2,209	2,209
14,750	14,800	2,216	2,216	2,216	2,216
14,800	14,850	2,224	2,224	2,224	2,224
14,850	14,900	2,231	2,231	2,231	2,231
14,900	14,950	2,239	2,239	2,239	2,239
14,950	15,000	2,246	2,246	2,246	2,246

15,000

At least	But less than	Single	Married filing jointly	Married filing separately	Head of a household
15,000	15,050	2,254	2,254	2,254	2,254
15,050	15,100	2,261	2,261	2,261	2,261
15,100	15,150	2,269	2,269	2,269	2,269
15,150	15,200	2,276	2,276	2,276	2,276
15,200	15,250	2,284	2,284	2,284	2,284
15,250	15,300	2,291	2,291	2,291	2,291
15,300	15,350	2,299	2,299	2,299	2,299
15,350	15,400	2,306	2,306	2,306	2,306
15,400	15,450	2,314	2,314	2,314	2,314
15,450	15,500	2,321	2,321	2,321	2,321
15,500	15,550	2,329	2,329	2,329	2,329
15,550	15,600	2,336	2,336	2,336	2,336
15,600	15,650	2,344	2,344	2,344	2,344
15,650	15,700	2,351	2,351	2,351	2,351
15,700	15,750	2,359	2,359	2,359	2,359
15,750	15,800	2,366	2,366	2,366	2,366
15,800	15,850	2,374	2,374	2,374	2,374
15,850	15,900	2,381	2,381	2,381	2,381
15,900	15,950	2,389	2,389	2,389	2,389
15,950	16,000	2,396	2,396	2,396	2,396

16,000

At least	But less than	Single	Married filing jointly	Married filing separately	Head of a household
16,000	16,050	2,404	2,404	2,404	2,404
16,050	16,100	2,411	2,411	2,411	2,411
16,100	16,150	2,419	2,419	2,419	2,419
16,150	16,200	2,426	2,426	2,426	2,426
16,200	16,250	2,434	2,434	2,434	2,434
16,250	16,300	2,441	2,441	2,441	2,441
16,300	16,350	2,449	2,449	2,449	2,449
16,350	16,400	2,456	2,456	2,456	2,456
16,400	16,450	2,464	2,464	2,464	2,464
16,450	16,500	2,471	2,471	2,471	2,471
16,500	16,550	2,479	2,479	2,479	2,479
16,550	16,600	2,486	2,486	2,486	2,486
16,600	16,650	2,494	2,494	2,494	2,494
16,650	16,700	2,501	2,501	2,501	2,501
16,700	16,750	2,509	2,509	2,509	2,509
16,750	16,800	2,516	2,516	2,516	2,516
16,800	16,850	2,524	2,524	2,524	2,524
16,850	16,900	2,531	2,531	2,531	2,531
16,900	16,950	2,539	2,539	2,539	2,539
16,950	17,000	2,546	2,546	2,546	2,546

17,000

At least	But less than	Single	Married filing jointly	Married filing separately	Head of a household
17,000	17,050	2,554	2,554	2,554	2,554
17,050	17,100	2,561	2,561	2,561	2,561
17,100	17,150	2,569	2,569	2,569	2,569
17,150	17,200	2,576	2,576	2,576	2,576
17,200	17,250	2,584	2,584	2,584	2,584
17,250	17,300	2,591	2,591	2,591	2,591
17,300	17,350	2,599	2,599	2,599	2,599
17,350	17,400	2,606	2,606	2,606	2,606
17,400	17,450	2,614	2,614	2,614	2,614
17,450	17,500	2,621	2,621	2,621	2,621
17,500	17,550	2,629	2,629	2,629	2,629
17,550	17,600	2,636	2,636	2,636	2,636
17,600	17,650	2,644	2,644	2,644	2,644
17,650	17,700	2,651	2,651	2,651	2,651
17,700	17,750	2,659	2,659	2,659	2,659
17,750	17,800	2,666	2,666	2,666	2,666
17,800	17,850	2,674	2,674	2,674	2,674
17,850	17,900	2,681	2,681	2,681	2,681
17,900	17,950	2,689	2,689	2,689	2,689
17,950	18,000	2,696	2,696	2,696	2,696

18,000

At least	But less than	Single	Married filing jointly	Married filing separately	Head of a household
18,000	18,050	2,704	2,704	2,704	2,704
18,050	18,100	2,711	2,711	2,711	2,711
18,100	18,150	2,719	2,719	2,719	2,719
18,150	18,200	2,726	2,726	2,726	2,726
18,200	18,250	2,734	2,734	2,734	2,734
18,250	18,300	2,741	2,741	2,741	2,741
18,300	18,350	2,749	2,749	2,749	2,749
18,350	18,400	2,756	2,756	2,756	2,756
18,400	18,450	2,764	2,764	2,764	2,764
18,450	18,500	2,771	2,771	2,771	2,771
18,500	18,550	2,779	2,779	2,779	2,779
18,550	18,600	2,786	2,786	2,786	2,786
18,600	18,650	2,794	2,794	2,794	2,794
18,650	18,700	2,801	2,801	2,801	2,801
18,700	18,750	2,809	2,809	2,809	2,809
18,750	18,800	2,816	2,816	2,816	2,816
18,800	18,850	2,824	2,824	2,824	2,824
18,850	18,900	2,831	2,831	2,831	2,831
18,900	18,950	2,839	2,839	2,839	2,839
18,950	19,000	2,846	2,846	2,846	2,846

19,000

At least	But less than	Single	Married filing jointly	Married filing separately	Head of a household
19,000	19,050	2,854	2,854	2,854	2,854
19,050	19,100	2,861	2,861	2,861	2,861
19,100	19,150	2,869	2,869	2,869	2,869
19,150	19,200	2,876	2,876	2,876	2,876
19,200	19,250	2,884	2,884	2,884	2,884
19,250	19,300	2,891	2,891	2,891	2,891
19,300	19,350	2,899	2,899	2,899	2,899
19,350	19,400	2,906	2,906	2,906	2,906
19,400	19,450	2,914	2,914	2,914	2,914
19,450	19,500	2,921	2,921	2,921	2,921
19,500	19,550	2,929	2,929	2,929	2,929
19,550	19,600	2,936	2,936	2,936	2,936
19,600	19,650	2,944	2,944	2,944	2,944
19,650	19,700	2,951	2,951	2,951	2,951
19,700	19,750	2,959	2,959	2,959	2,959
19,750	19,800	2,966	2,966	2,966	2,966
19,800	19,850	2,974	2,974	2,974	2,974
19,850	19,900	2,981	2,981	2,981	2,981
19,900	19,950	2,989	2,989	2,989	2,989
19,950	20,000	2,996	2,996	2,996	2,996

20,000

At least	But less than	Single	Married filing jointly	Married filing separately	Head of a household
20,000	20,050	3,004	3,004	3,004	3,004
20,050	20,100	3,011	3,011	3,011	3,011
20,100	20,150	3,019	3,019	3,019	3,019
20,150	20,200	3,026	3,026	3,026	3,026
20,200	20,250	3,034	3,034	3,034	3,034
20,250	20,300	3,041	3,041	3,041	3,041
20,300	20,350	3,049	3,049	3,049	3,049
20,350	20,400	3,056	3,056	3,056	3,056
20,400	20,450	3,064	3,064	3,064	3,064
20,450	20,500	3,071	3,071	3,071	3,071
20,500	20,550	3,079	3,079	3,079	3,079
20,550	20,600	3,086	3,086	3,086	3,086
20,600	20,650	3,094	3,094	3,094	3,094
20,650	20,700	3,101	3,101	3,101	3,101
20,700	20,750	3,109	3,109	3,109	3,109
20,750	20,800	3,116	3,116	3,116	3,116
20,800	20,850	3,124	3,124	3,124	3,124
20,850	20,900	3,131	3,131	3,131	3,131
20,900	20,950	3,139	3,139	3,139	3,139
20,950	21,000	3,146	3,146	3,146	3,146

21,000

At least	But less than	Single	Married filing jointly	Married filing separately	Head of a household
21,000	21,050	3,154	3,154	3,154	3,154
21,050	21,100	3,161	3,161	3,161	3,161
21,100	21,150	3,169	3,169	3,169	3,169
21,150	21,200	3,176	3,176	3,176	3,176
21,200	21,250	3,184	3,184	3,184	3,184
21,250	21,300	3,191	3,191	3,191	3,191
21,300	21,350	3,199	3,199	3,199	3,199
21,350	21,400	3,206	3,206	3,206	3,206
21,400	21,450	3,214	3,214	3,214	3,214
21,450	21,500	3,221	3,221	3,221	3,221
21,500	21,550	3,229	3,229	3,229	3,229
21,550	21,600	3,236	3,236	3,236	3,236
21,600	21,650	3,244	3,244	3,244	3,244
21,650	21,700	3,251	3,251	3,251	3,251
21,700	21,750	3,259	3,259	3,259	3,259
21,750	21,800	3,266	3,266	3,266	3,266
21,800	21,850	3,274	3,274	3,274	3,274
21,850	21,900	3,281	3,281	3,281	3,281
21,900	21,950	3,289	3,289	3,289	3,289
21,950	22,000	3,296	3,296	3,296	3,296

22,000

At least	But less than	Single	Married filing jointly	Married filing separately	Head of a household
22,000	22,050	3,304	3,304	3,304	3,304
22,050	22,100	3,311	3,311	3,311	3,311
22,100	22,150	3,319	3,319	3,319	3,319
22,150	22,200	3,326	3,326	3,326	3,326
22,200	22,250	3,334	3,334	3,334	3,334
22,250	22,300	3,341	3,341	3,341	3,341
22,300	22,350	3,349	3,349	3,349	3,349
22,350	22,400	3,356	3,356	3,356	3,356
22,400	22,450	3,364	3,364	3,364	3,364
22,450	22,500	3,371	3,371	3,371	3,371
22,500	22,550	3,379	3,379	3,379	3,379
22,550	22,600	3,386	3,386	3,386	3,386
22,600	22,650	3,394	3,394	3,394	3,394
22,650	22,700	3,401	3,401	3,411	3,401
22,700	22,750	3,409	3,409	3,424	3,409
22,750	22,800	3,416	3,416	3,438	3,416
22,800	22,850	3,424	3,424	3,452	3,424
22,850	22,900	3,431	3,431	3,466	3,431
22,900	22,950	3,439	3,439	3,479	3,439
22,950	23,000	3,446	3,446	3,493	3,446

* This column must also be used by a qualifying widow(er).

(Continued on page 62)

¶ 25

2001 Tax Table—Continued   **Caution.** Dependents, see the worksheet on page 33.

If line 39 (taxable income) is— At least	But less than	Single	Married filing jointly *	Married filing separately	Head of a household
23,000				Your tax is—	
23,000	23,050	3,454	3,454	3,507	3,454
23,050	23,100	3,461	3,461	3,521	3,461
23,100	23,150	3,469	3,469	3,534	3,469
23,150	23,200	3,476	3,476	3,548	3,476
23,200	23,250	3,484	3,484	3,562	3,484
23,250	23,300	3,491	3,491	3,576	3,491
23,300	23,350	3,499	3,499	3,589	3,499
23,350	23,400	3,506	3,506	3,603	3,506
23,400	23,450	3,514	3,514	3,617	3,514
23,450	23,500	3,521	3,521	3,631	3,521
23,500	23,550	3,529	3,529	3,644	3,529
23,550	23,600	3,536	3,536	3,658	3,536
23,600	23,650	3,544	3,544	3,672	3,544
23,650	23,700	3,551	3,551	3,686	3,551
23,700	23,750	3,559	3,559	3,699	3,559
23,750	23,800	3,566	3,566	3,713	3,566
23,800	23,850	3,574	3,574	3,727	3,574
23,850	23,900	3,581	3,581	3,741	3,581
23,900	23,950	3,589	3,589	3,754	3,589
23,950	24,000	3,596	3,596	3,768	3,596
24,000					
24,000	24,050	3,604	3,604	3,782	3,604
24,050	24,100	3,611	3,611	3,796	3,611
24,100	24,150	3,619	3,619	3,809	3,619
24,150	24,200	3,626	3,626	3,823	3,626
24,200	24,250	3,634	3,634	3,837	3,634
24,250	24,300	3,641	3,641	3,851	3,641
24,300	24,350	3,649	3,649	3,864	3,649
24,350	24,400	3,656	3,656	3,878	3,656
24,400	24,450	3,664	3,664	3,892	3,664
24,450	24,500	3,671	3,671	3,906	3,671
24,500	24,550	3,679	3,679	3,919	3,679
24,550	24,600	3,686	3,686	3,933	3,686
24,600	24,650	3,694	3,694	3,947	3,694
24,650	24,700	3,701	3,701	3,961	3,701
24,700	24,750	3,709	3,709	3,974	3,709
24,750	24,800	3,716	3,716	3,988	3,716
24,800	24,850	3,724	3,724	4,002	3,724
24,850	24,900	3,731	3,731	4,016	3,731
24,900	24,950	3,739	3,739	4,029	3,739
24,950	25,000	3,746	3,746	4,043	3,746
25,000					
25,000	25,050	3,754	3,754	4,057	3,754
25,050	25,100	3,761	3,761	4,071	3,761
25,100	25,150	3,769	3,769	4,084	3,769
25,150	25,200	3,776	3,776	4,098	3,776
25,200	25,250	3,784	3,784	4,112	3,784
25,250	25,300	3,791	3,791	4,126	3,791
25,300	25,350	3,799	3,799	4,139	3,799
25,350	25,400	3,806	3,806	4,153	3,806
25,400	25,450	3,814	3,814	4,167	3,814
25,450	25,500	3,821	3,821	4,181	3,821
25,500	25,550	3,829	3,829	4,194	3,829
25,550	25,600	3,836	3,836	4,208	3,836
25,600	25,650	3,844	3,844	4,222	3,844
25,650	25,700	3,851	3,851	4,236	3,851
25,700	25,750	3,859	3,859	4,249	3,859
25,750	25,800	3,866	3,866	4,263	3,866
25,800	25,850	3,874	3,874	4,277	3,874
25,850	25,900	3,881	3,881	4,291	3,881
25,900	25,950	3,889	3,889	4,304	3,889
25,950	26,000	3,896	3,896	4,318	3,896

If line 39 (taxable income) is— At least	But less than	Single	Married filing jointly *	Married filing separately	Head of a household
26,000				Your tax is—	
26,000	26,050	3,904	3,904	4,332	3,904
26,050	26,100	3,911	3,911	4,346	3,911
26,100	26,150	3,919	3,919	4,359	3,919
26,150	26,200	3,926	3,926	4,373	3,926
26,200	26,250	3,934	3,934	4,387	3,934
26,250	26,300	3,941	3,941	4,401	3,941
26,300	26,350	3,949	3,949	4,414	3,949
26,350	26,400	3,956	3,956	4,428	3,956
26,400	26,450	3,964	3,964	4,442	3,964
26,450	26,500	3,971	3,971	4,456	3,971
26,500	26,550	3,979	3,979	4,469	3,979
26,550	26,600	3,986	3,986	4,483	3,986
26,600	26,650	3,994	3,994	4,497	3,994
26,650	26,700	4,001	4,001	4,511	4,001
26,700	26,750	4,009	4,009	4,524	4,009
26,750	26,800	4,016	4,016	4,538	4,016
26,800	26,850	4,024	4,024	4,552	4,024
26,850	26,900	4,031	4,031	4,566	4,031
26,900	26,950	4,039	4,039	4,579	4,039
26,950	27,000	4,046	4,046	4,593	4,046
27,000					
27,000	27,050	4,054	4,054	4,607	4,054
27,050	27,100	4,064	4,061	4,621	4,061
27,100	27,150	4,078	4,069	4,634	4,069
27,150	27,200	4,092	4,076	4,648	4,076
27,200	27,250	4,106	4,084	4,662	4,084
27,250	27,300	4,119	4,091	4,676	4,091
27,300	27,350	4,133	4,099	4,689	4,099
27,350	27,400	4,147	4,106	4,703	4,106
27,400	27,450	4,161	4,114	4,717	4,114
27,450	27,500	4,174	4,121	4,731	4,121
27,500	27,550	4,188	4,129	4,744	4,129
27,550	27,600	4,202	4,136	4,758	4,136
27,600	27,650	4,216	4,144	4,772	4,144
27,650	27,700	4,229	4,151	4,786	4,151
27,700	27,750	4,243	4,159	4,799	4,159
27,750	27,800	4,257	4,166	4,813	4,166
27,800	27,850	4,271	4,174	4,827	4,174
27,850	27,900	4,284	4,181	4,841	4,181
27,900	27,950	4,298	4,189	4,854	4,189
27,950	28,000	4,312	4,196	4,868	4,196
28,000					
28,000	28,050	4,326	4,204	4,882	4,204
28,050	28,100	4,339	4,211	4,896	4,211
28,100	28,150	4,353	4,219	4,909	4,219
28,150	28,200	4,367	4,226	4,923	4,226
28,200	28,250	4,381	4,234	4,937	4,234
28,250	28,300	4,394	4,241	4,951	4,241
28,300	28,350	4,408	4,249	4,964	4,249
28,350	28,400	4,422	4,256	4,978	4,256
28,400	28,450	4,436	4,264	4,992	4,264
28,450	28,500	4,449	4,271	5,006	4,271
28,500	28,550	4,463	4,279	5,019	4,279
28,550	28,600	4,477	4,286	5,033	4,286
28,600	28,650	4,491	4,294	5,047	4,294
28,650	28,700	4,504	4,301	5,061	4,301
28,700	28,750	4,518	4,309	5,074	4,309
28,750	28,800	4,532	4,316	5,088	4,316
28,800	28,850	4,546	4,324	5,102	4,324
28,850	28,900	4,559	4,331	5,116	4,331
28,900	28,950	4,573	4,339	5,129	4,339
28,950	29,000	4,587	4,346	5,143	4,346

If line 39 (taxable income) is— At least	But less than	Single	Married filing jointly *	Married filing separately	Head of a household
29,000				Your tax is—	
29,000	29,050	4,601	4,354	5,157	4,354
29,050	29,100	4,614	4,361	5,171	4,361
29,100	29,150	4,628	4,369	5,184	4,369
29,150	29,200	4,642	4,376	5,198	4,376
29,200	29,250	4,656	4,384	5,212	4,384
29,250	29,300	4,669	4,391	5,226	4,391
29,300	29,350	4,683	4,399	5,239	4,399
29,350	29,400	4,697	4,406	5,253	4,406
29,400	29,450	4,711	4,414	5,267	4,414
29,450	29,500	4,724	4,421	5,281	4,421
29,500	29,550	4,738	4,429	5,294	4,429
29,550	29,600	4,752	4,436	5,308	4,436
29,600	29,650	4,766	4,444	5,322	4,444
29,650	29,700	4,779	4,451	5,336	4,451
29,700	29,750	4,793	4,459	5,349	4,459
29,750	29,800	4,807	4,466	5,363	4,466
29,800	29,850	4,821	4,474	5,377	4,474
29,850	29,900	4,834	4,481	5,391	4,481
29,900	29,950	4,848	4,489	5,404	4,489
29,950	30,000	4,862	4,496	5,418	4,496
30,000					
30,000	30,050	4,876	4,504	5,432	4,504
30,050	30,100	4,889	4,511	5,446	4,511
30,100	30,150	4,903	4,519	5,459	4,519
30,150	30,200	4,917	4,526	5,473	4,526
30,200	30,250	4,931	4,534	5,487	4,534
30,250	30,300	4,944	4,541	5,501	4,541
30,300	30,350	4,958	4,549	5,514	4,549
30,350	30,400	4,972	4,556	5,528	4,556
30,400	30,450	4,986	4,564	5,542	4,564
30,450	30,500	4,999	4,571	5,556	4,571
30,500	30,550	5,013	4,579	5,569	4,579
30,550	30,600	5,027	4,586	5,583	4,586
30,600	30,650	5,041	4,594	5,597	4,594
30,650	30,700	5,054	4,601	5,611	4,601
30,700	30,750	5,068	4,609	5,624	4,609
30,750	30,800	5,082	4,616	5,638	4,616
30,800	30,850	5,096	4,624	5,652	4,624
30,850	30,900	5,109	4,631	5,666	4,631
30,900	30,950	5,123	4,639	5,679	4,639
30,950	31,000	5,137	4,646	5,693	4,646
31,000					
31,000	31,050	5,151	4,654	5,707	4,654
31,050	31,100	5,164	4,661	5,721	4,661
31,100	31,150	5,178	4,669	5,734	4,669
31,150	31,200	5,192	4,676	5,748	4,676
31,200	31,250	5,206	4,684	5,762	4,684
31,250	31,300	5,219	4,691	5,776	4,691
31,300	31,350	5,233	4,699	5,789	4,699
31,350	31,400	5,247	4,706	5,803	4,706
31,400	31,450	5,261	4,714	5,817	4,714
31,450	31,500	5,274	4,721	5,831	4,721
31,500	31,550	5,288	4,729	5,844	4,729
31,550	31,600	5,302	4,736	5,858	4,736
31,600	31,650	5,316	4,744	5,872	4,744
31,650	31,700	5,329	4,751	5,886	4,751
31,700	31,750	5,343	4,759	5,899	4,759
31,750	31,800	5,357	4,766	5,913	4,766
31,800	31,850	5,371	4,774	5,927	4,774
31,850	31,900	5,384	4,781	5,941	4,781
31,900	31,950	5,398	4,789	5,954	4,789
31,950	32,000	5,412	4,796	5,968	4,796

* This column must also be used by a qualifying widow(er).

(Continued on page 63)

¶ 25

Caution. Dependents, see the worksheet on page 33. **2001 Tax Table—*Continued***

If line 39 (taxable income) is— At least	But less than	And you are— Single	Married filing jointly *	Married filing separately	Head of a household	If line 39 (taxable income) is— At least	But less than	And you are— Single	Married filing jointly *	Married filing separately	Head of a household	If line 39 (taxable income) is— At least	But less than	And you are— Single	Married filing jointly *	Married filing separately	Head of a household
		Your tax is—						Your tax is—						Your tax is—			
32,000						**35,000**						**38,000**					
32,000	32,050	5,426	4,804	5,982	4,804	35,000	35,050	6,251	5,254	6,807	5,254	38,000	38,050	7,076	5,704	7,632	5,926
32,050	32,100	5,439	4,811	5,996	4,811	35,050	35,100	6,264	5,261	6,821	5,261	38,050	38,100	7,089	5,711	7,646	5,939
32,100	32,150	5,453	4,819	6,009	4,819	35,100	35,150	6,278	5,269	6,834	5,269	38,100	38,150	7,103	5,719	7,659	5,953
32,150	32,200	5,467	4,826	6,023	4,826	35,150	35,200	6,292	5,276	6,848	5,276	38,150	38,200	7,117	5,726	7,673	5,967
32,200	32,250	5,481	4,834	6,037	4,834	35,200	35,250	6,306	5,284	6,862	5,284	38,200	38,250	7,131	5,734	7,687	5,981
32,250	32,300	5,494	4,841	6,051	4,841	35,250	35,300	6,319	5,291	6,876	5,291	38,250	38,300	7,144	5,741	7,701	5,994
32,300	32,350	5,508	4,849	6,064	4,849	35,300	35,350	6,333	5,299	6,889	5,299	38,300	38,350	7,158	5,749	7,714	6,008
32,350	32,400	5,522	4,856	6,078	4,856	35,350	35,400	6,347	5,306	6,903	5,306	38,350	38,400	7,172	5,756	7,728	6,022
32,400	32,450	5,536	4,864	6,092	4,864	35,400	35,450	6,361	5,314	6,917	5,314	38,400	38,450	7,186	5,764	7,742	6,036
32,450	32,500	5,549	4,871	6,106	4,871	35,450	35,500	6,374	5,321	6,931	5,321	38,450	38,500	7,199	5,771	7,756	6,049
32,500	32,550	5,563	4,879	6,119	4,879	35,500	35,550	6,388	5,329	6,944	5,329	38,500	38,550	7,213	5,779	7,769	6,063
32,550	32,600	5,577	4,886	6,133	4,886	35,550	35,600	6,402	5,336	6,958	5,336	38,550	38,600	7,227	5,786	7,783	6,077
32,600	32,650	5,591	4,894	6,147	4,894	35,600	35,650	6,416	5,344	6,972	5,344	38,600	38,650	7,241	5,794	7,797	6,091
32,650	32,700	5,604	4,901	6,161	4,901	35,650	35,700	6,429	5,351	6,986	5,351	38,650	38,700	7,254	5,801	7,811	6,104
32,700	32,750	5,618	4,909	6,174	4,909	35,700	35,750	6,443	5,359	6,999	5,359	38,700	38,750	7,268	5,809	7,824	6,118
32,750	32,800	5,632	4,916	6,188	4,916	35,750	35,800	6,457	5,366	7,013	5,366	38,750	38,800	7,282	5,816	7,838	6,132
32,800	32,850	5,646	4,924	6,202	4,924	35,800	35,850	6,471	5,374	7,027	5,374	38,800	38,850	7,296	5,824	7,852	6,146
32,850	32,900	5,659	4,931	6,216	4,931	35,850	35,900	6,484	5,381	7,041	5,381	38,850	38,900	7,309	5,831	7,866	6,159
32,900	32,950	5,673	4,939	6,229	4,939	35,900	35,950	6,498	5,389	7,054	5,389	38,900	38,950	7,323	5,839	7,879	6,173
32,950	33,000	5,687	4,946	6,243	4,946	35,950	36,000	6,512	5,396	7,068	5,396	38,950	39,000	7,337	5,846	7,893	6,187
33,000						**36,000**						**39,000**					
33,000	33,050	5,701	4,954	6,257	4,954	36,000	36,050	6,526	5,404	7,082	5,404	39,000	39,050	7,351	5,854	7,907	6,201
33,050	33,100	5,714	4,961	6,271	4,961	36,050	36,100	6,539	5,411	7,096	5,411	39,050	39,100	7,364	5,861	7,921	6,214
33,100	33,150	5,728	4,969	6,284	4,969	36,100	36,150	6,553	5,419	7,109	5,419	39,100	39,150	7,378	5,869	7,934	6,228
33,150	33,200	5,742	4,976	6,298	4,976	36,150	36,200	6,567	5,426	7,123	5,426	39,150	39,200	7,392	5,876	7,948	6,242
33,200	33,250	5,756	4,984	6,312	4,984	36,200	36,250	6,581	5,434	7,137	5,434	39,200	39,250	7,406	5,884	7,962	6,256
33,250	33,300	5,769	4,991	6,326	4,991	36,250	36,300	6,594	5,441	7,151	5,444	39,250	39,300	7,419	5,891	7,976	6,269
33,300	33,350	5,783	4,999	6,339	4,999	36,300	36,350	6,608	5,449	7,164	5,458	39,300	39,350	7,433	5,899	7,989	6,283
33,350	33,400	5,797	5,006	6,353	5,006	36,350	36,400	6,622	5,456	7,178	5,472	39,350	39,400	7,447	5,906	8,003	6,297
33,400	33,450	5,811	5,014	6,367	5,014	36,400	36,450	6,636	5,464	7,192	5,486	39,400	39,450	7,461	5,914	8,017	6,311
33,450	33,500	5,824	5,021	6,381	5,021	36,450	36,500	6,649	5,471	7,206	5,499	39,450	39,500	7,474	5,921	8,031	6,324
33,500	33,550	5,838	5,029	6,394	5,029	36,500	36,550	6,663	5,479	7,219	5,513	39,500	39,550	7,488	5,929	8,044	6,338
33,550	33,600	5,852	5,036	6,408	5,036	36,550	36,600	6,677	5,486	7,233	5,527	39,550	39,600	7,502	5,936	8,058	6,352
33,600	33,650	5,866	5,044	6,422	5,044	36,600	36,650	6,691	5,494	7,247	5,541	39,600	39,650	7,516	5,944	8,072	6,366
33,650	33,700	5,879	5,051	6,436	5,051	36,650	36,700	6,704	5,501	7,261	5,554	39,650	39,700	7,529	5,951	8,086	6,379
33,700	33,750	5,893	5,059	6,449	5,059	36,700	36,750	6,718	5,509	7,274	5,568	39,700	39,750	7,543	5,959	8,099	6,393
33,750	33,800	5,907	5,066	6,463	5,066	36,750	36,800	6,732	5,516	7,288	5,582	39,750	39,800	7,557	5,966	8,113	6,407
33,800	33,850	5,921	5,074	6,477	5,074	36,800	36,850	6,746	5,524	7,302	5,596	39,800	39,850	7,571	5,974	8,127	6,421
33,850	33,900	5,934	5,081	6,491	5,081	36,850	36,900	6,759	5,531	7,316	5,609	39,850	39,900	7,584	5,981	8,141	6,434
33,900	33,950	5,948	5,089	6,504	5,089	36,900	36,950	6,773	5,539	7,329	5,623	39,900	39,950	7,598	5,989	8,154	6,448
33,950	34,000	5,962	5,096	6,518	5,096	36,950	37,000	6,787	5,546	7,343	5,637	39,950	40,000	7,612	5,996	8,168	6,462
34,000						**37,000**						**40,000**					
34,000	34,050	5,976	5,104	6,532	5,104	37,000	37,050	6,801	5,554	7,357	5,651	40,000	40,050	7,626	6,004	8,182	6,476
34,050	34,100	5,989	5,111	6,546	5,111	37,050	37,100	6,814	5,561	7,371	5,664	40,050	40,100	7,639	6,011	8,196	6,489
34,100	34,150	6,003	5,119	6,559	5,119	37,100	37,150	6,828	5,569	7,384	5,678	40,100	40,150	7,653	6,019	8,209	6,503
34,150	34,200	6,017	5,126	6,573	5,126	37,150	37,200	6,842	5,576	7,398	5,692	40,150	40,200	7,667	6,026	8,223	6,517
34,200	34,250	6,031	5,134	6,587	5,134	37,200	37,250	6,856	5,584	7,412	5,706	40,200	40,250	7,681	6,034	8,237	6,531
34,250	34,300	6,044	5,141	6,601	5,141	37,250	37,300	6,869	5,591	7,426	5,719	40,250	40,300	7,694	6,041	8,251	6,544
34,300	34,350	6,058	5,149	6,614	5,149	37,300	37,350	6,883	5,599	7,439	5,733	40,300	40,350	7,708	6,049	8,264	6,558
34,350	34,400	6,072	5,156	6,628	5,156	37,350	37,400	6,897	5,606	7,453	5,747	40,350	40,400	7,722	6,056	8,278	6,572
34,400	34,450	6,086	5,164	6,642	5,164	37,400	37,450	6,911	5,614	7,467	5,761	40,400	40,450	7,736	6,064	8,292	6,586
34,450	34,500	6,099	5,171	6,656	5,171	37,450	37,500	6,924	5,621	7,481	5,774	40,450	40,500	7,749	6,071	8,306	6,599
34,500	34,550	6,113	5,179	6,669	5,179	37,500	37,550	6,938	5,629	7,494	5,788	40,500	40,550	7,763	6,079	8,319	6,613
34,550	34,600	6,127	5,186	6,683	5,186	37,550	37,600	6,952	5,636	7,508	5,802	40,550	40,600	7,777	6,086	8,333	6,627
34,600	34,650	6,141	5,194	6,697	5,194	37,600	37,650	6,966	5,644	7,522	5,816	40,600	40,650	7,791	6,094	8,347	6,641
34,650	34,700	6,154	5,201	6,711	5,201	37,650	37,700	6,979	5,651	7,536	5,829	40,650	40,700	7,804	6,101	8,361	6,654
34,700	34,750	6,168	5,209	6,724	5,209	37,700	37,750	6,993	5,659	7,549	5,843	40,700	40,750	7,818	6,109	8,374	6,668
34,750	34,800	6,182	5,216	6,738	5,216	37,750	37,800	7,007	5,666	7,563	5,857	40,750	40,800	7,832	6,116	8,388	6,682
34,800	34,850	6,196	5,224	6,752	5,224	37,800	37,850	7,021	5,674	7,577	5,871	40,800	40,850	7,846	6,124	8,402	6,696
34,850	34,900	6,209	5,231	6,766	5,231	37,850	37,900	7,034	5,681	7,591	5,884	40,850	40,900	7,859	6,131	8,416	6,709
34,900	34,950	6,223	5,239	6,779	5,239	37,900	37,950	7,048	5,689	7,604	5,898	40,900	40,950	7,873	6,139	8,429	6,723
34,950	35,000	6,237	5,246	6,793	5,246	37,950	38,000	7,062	5,696	7,618	5,912	40,950	41,000	7,887	6,146	8,443	6,737

* This column must also be used by a qualifying widow(er).

(Continued on page 64)

2001 Tax Table—*Continued*   Caution. Dependents, see the worksheet on page 33.

If line 39 (taxable income) is— At least	But less than	Single	Married filing jointly *	Married filing separately	Head of a household
41,000					
41,000	41,050	7,901	6,154	8,457	6,751
41,050	41,100	7,914	6,161	8,471	6,764
41,100	41,150	7,928	6,169	8,484	6,778
41,150	41,200	7,942	6,176	8,498	6,792
41,200	41,250	7,956	6,184	8,512	6,806
41,250	41,300	7,969	6,191	8,526	6,819
41,300	41,350	7,983	6,199	8,539	6,833
41,350	41,400	7,997	6,206	8,553	6,847
41,400	41,450	8,011	6,214	8,567	6,861
41,450	41,500	8,024	6,221	8,581	6,874
41,500	41,550	8,038	6,229	8,594	6,888
41,550	41,600	8,052	6,236	8,608	6,902
41,600	41,650	8,066	6,244	8,622	6,916
41,650	41,700	8,079	6,251	8,636	6,929
41,700	41,750	8,093	6,259	8,649	6,943
41,750	41,800	8,107	6,266	8,663	6,957
41,800	41,850	8,121	6,274	8,677	6,971
41,850	41,900	8,134	6,281	8,691	6,984
41,900	41,950	8,148	6,289	8,704	6,998
41,950	42,000	8,162	6,296	8,718	7,012
42,000					
42,000	42,050	8,176	6,304	8,732	7,026
42,050	42,100	8,189	6,311	8,746	7,039
42,100	42,150	8,203	6,319	8,759	7,053
42,150	42,200	8,217	6,326	8,773	7,067
42,200	42,250	8,231	6,334	8,787	7,081
42,250	42,300	8,244	6,341	8,801	7,094
42,300	42,350	8,258	6,349	8,814	7,108
42,350	42,400	8,272	6,356	8,828	7,122
42,400	42,450	8,286	6,364	8,842	7,136
42,450	42,500	8,299	6,371	8,856	7,149
42,500	42,550	8,313	6,379	8,869	7,163
42,550	42,600	8,327	6,386	8,883	7,177
42,600	42,650	8,341	6,394	8,897	7,191
42,650	42,700	8,354	6,401	8,911	7,204
42,700	42,750	8,368	6,409	8,924	7,218
42,750	42,800	8,382	6,416	8,938	7,232
42,800	42,850	8,396	6,424	8,952	7,246
42,850	42,900	8,409	6,431	8,966	7,259
42,900	42,950	8,423	6,439	8,979	7,273
42,950	43,000	8,437	6,446	8,993	7,287
43,000					
43,000	43,050	8,451	6,454	9,007	7,301
43,050	43,100	8,464	6,461	9,021	7,314
43,100	43,150	8,478	6,469	9,034	7,328
43,150	43,200	8,492	6,476	9,048	7,342
43,200	43,250	8,506	6,484	9,062	7,356
43,250	43,300	8,519	6,491	9,076	7,369
43,300	43,350	8,533	6,499	9,089	7,383
43,350	43,400	8,547	6,506	9,103	7,397
43,400	43,450	8,561	6,514	9,117	7,411
43,450	43,500	8,574	6,521	9,131	7,424
43,500	43,550	8,588	6,529	9,144	7,438
43,550	43,600	8,602	6,536	9,158	7,452
43,600	43,650	8,616	6,544	9,172	7,466
43,650	43,700	8,629	6,551	9,186	7,479
43,700	43,750	8,643	6,559	9,199	7,493
43,750	43,800	8,657	6,566	9,213	7,507
43,800	43,850	8,671	6,574	9,227	7,521
43,850	43,900	8,684	6,581	9,241	7,534
43,900	43,950	8,698	6,589	9,254	7,548
43,950	44,000	8,712	6,596	9,268	7,562

If line 39 (taxable income) is— At least	But less than	Single	Married filing jointly *	Married filing separately	Head of a household
44,000					
44,000	44,050	8,726	6,604	9,282	7,576
44,050	44,100	8,739	6,611	9,296	7,589
44,100	44,150	8,753	6,619	9,309	7,603
44,150	44,200	8,767	6,626	9,323	7,617
44,200	44,250	8,781	6,634	9,337	7,631
44,250	44,300	8,794	6,641	9,351	7,644
44,300	44,350	8,808	6,649	9,364	7,658
44,350	44,400	8,822	6,656	9,378	7,672
44,400	44,450	8,836	6,664	9,392	7,686
44,450	44,500	8,849	6,671	9,406	7,699
44,500	44,550	8,863	6,679	9,419	7,713
44,550	44,600	8,877	6,686	9,433	7,727
44,600	44,650	8,891	6,694	9,447	7,741
44,650	44,700	8,904	6,701	9,461	7,754
44,700	44,750	8,918	6,709	9,474	7,768
44,750	44,800	8,932	6,716	9,488	7,782
44,800	44,850	8,946	6,724	9,502	7,796
44,850	44,900	8,959	6,731	9,516	7,809
44,900	44,950	8,973	6,739	9,529	7,823
44,950	45,000	8,987	6,746	9,543	7,837
45,000					
45,000	45,050	9,001	6,754	9,557	7,851
45,050	45,100	9,014	6,761	9,571	7,864
45,100	45,150	9,028	6,769	9,584	7,878
45,150	45,200	9,042	6,776	9,598	7,892
45,200	45,250	9,056	6,787	9,612	7,906
45,250	45,300	9,069	6,801	9,626	7,919
45,300	45,350	9,083	6,814	9,639	7,933
45,350	45,400	9,097	6,828	9,653	7,947
45,400	45,450	9,111	6,842	9,667	7,961
45,450	45,500	9,124	6,856	9,681	7,974
45,500	45,550	9,138	6,869	9,694	7,988
45,550	45,600	9,152	6,883	9,708	8,002
45,600	45,650	9,166	6,897	9,722	8,016
45,650	45,700	9,179	6,911	9,736	8,029
45,700	45,750	9,193	6,924	9,749	8,043
45,750	45,800	9,207	6,938	9,763	8,057
45,800	45,850	9,221	6,952	9,777	8,071
45,850	45,900	9,234	6,966	9,791	8,084
45,900	45,950	9,248	6,979	9,804	8,098
45,950	46,000	9,262	6,993	9,818	8,112
46,000					
46,000	46,050	9,276	7,007	9,832	8,126
46,050	46,100	9,289	7,021	9,846	8,139
46,100	46,150	9,303	7,034	9,859	8,153
46,150	46,200	9,317	7,048	9,873	8,167
46,200	46,250	9,331	7,062	9,887	8,181
46,250	46,300	9,344	7,076	9,901	8,194
46,300	46,350	9,358	7,089	9,914	8,208
46,350	46,400	9,372	7,103	9,928	8,222
46,400	46,450	9,386	7,117	9,942	8,236
46,450	46,500	9,399	7,131	9,956	8,249
46,500	46,550	9,413	7,144	9,969	8,263
46,550	46,600	9,427	7,158	9,983	8,277
46,600	46,650	9,441	7,172	9,997	8,291
46,650	46,700	9,454	7,186	10,011	8,304
46,700	46,750	9,468	7,199	10,024	8,318
46,750	46,800	9,482	7,213	10,038	8,332
46,800	46,850	9,496	7,227	10,052	8,346
46,850	46,900	9,509	7,241	10,066	8,359
46,900	46,950	9,523	7,254	10,079	8,373
46,950	47,000	9,537	7,268	10,093	8,387

If line 39 (taxable income) is— At least	But less than	Single	Married filing jointly *	Married filing separately	Head of a household
47,000					
47,000	47,050	9,551	7,282	10,107	8,401
47,050	47,100	9,564	7,296	10,121	8,414
47,100	47,150	9,578	7,309	10,134	8,428
47,150	47,200	9,592	7,323	10,148	8,442
47,200	47,250	9,606	7,337	10,162	8,456
47,250	47,300	9,619	7,351	10,176	8,469
47,300	47,350	9,633	7,364	10,189	8,483
47,350	47,400	9,647	7,378	10,203	8,497
47,400	47,450	9,661	7,392	10,217	8,511
47,450	47,500	9,674	7,406	10,231	8,524
47,500	47,550	9,688	7,419	10,244	8,538
47,550	47,600	9,702	7,433	10,258	8,552
47,600	47,650	9,716	7,447	10,272	8,566
47,650	47,700	9,729	7,461	10,286	8,579
47,700	47,750	9,743	7,474	10,299	8,593
47,750	47,800	9,757	7,488	10,313	8,607
47,800	47,850	9,771	7,502	10,327	8,621
47,850	47,900	9,784	7,516	10,341	8,634
47,900	47,950	9,798	7,529	10,354	8,648
47,950	48,000	9,812	7,543	10,368	8,662
48,000					
48,000	48,050	9,826	7,557	10,382	8,676
48,050	48,100	9,839	7,571	10,396	8,689
48,100	48,150	9,853	7,584	10,409	8,703
48,150	48,200	9,867	7,598	10,423	8,717
48,200	48,250	9,881	7,612	10,437	8,731
48,250	48,300	9,894	7,626	10,451	8,744
48,300	48,350	9,908	7,639	10,464	8,758
48,350	48,400	9,922	7,653	10,478	8,772
48,400	48,450	9,936	7,667	10,492	8,786
48,450	48,500	9,949	7,681	10,506	8,799
48,500	48,550	9,963	7,694	10,519	8,813
48,550	48,600	9,977	7,708	10,533	8,827
48,600	48,650	9,991	7,722	10,547	8,841
48,650	48,700	10,004	7,736	10,561	8,854
48,700	48,750	10,018	7,749	10,574	8,868
48,750	48,800	10,032	7,763	10,588	8,882
48,800	48,850	10,046	7,777	10,602	8,896
48,850	48,900	10,059	7,791	10,616	8,909
48,900	48,950	10,073	7,804	10,629	8,923
48,950	49,000	10,087	7,818	10,643	8,937
49,000					
49,000	49,050	10,101	7,832	10,657	8,951
49,050	49,100	10,114	7,846	10,671	8,964
49,100	49,150	10,128	7,859	10,684	8,978
49,150	49,200	10,142	7,873	10,698	8,992
49,200	49,250	10,156	7,887	10,712	9,006
49,250	49,300	10,169	7,901	10,726	9,019
49,300	49,350	10,183	7,914	10,739	9,033
49,350	49,400	10,197	7,928	10,753	9,047
49,400	49,450	10,211	7,942	10,767	9,061
49,450	49,500	10,224	7,956	10,781	9,074
49,500	49,550	10,238	7,969	10,794	9,088
49,550	49,600	10,252	7,983	10,808	9,102
49,600	49,650	10,266	7,997	10,822	9,116
49,650	49,700	10,279	8,011	10,836	9,129
49,700	49,750	10,293	8,024	10,849	9,143
49,750	49,800	10,307	8,038	10,863	9,157
49,800	49,850	10,321	8,052	10,877	9,171
49,850	49,900	10,334	8,066	10,891	9,184
49,900	49,950	10,348	8,079	10,904	9,198
49,950	50,000	10,362	8,093	10,918	9,212

* This column must also be used by a qualifying widow(er).

(Continued on page 65)

¶25

Caution. Dependents, see the worksheet on page 33. **2001 Tax Table—Continued**

If line 39 (taxable income is)— At least	But less than	And you are— Single	Married filing jointly*	Married filing separately	Head of a household
50,000					
50,000	50,050	10,376	8,107	10,932	9,226
50,050	50,100	10,389	8,121	10,946	9,239
50,100	50,150	10,403	8,134	10,959	9,253
50,150	50,200	10,417	8,148	10,973	9,267
50,200	50,250	10,431	8,162	10,987	9,281
50,250	50,300	10,444	8,176	11,001	9,294
50,300	50,350	10,458	8,189	11,014	9,308
50,350	50,400	10,472	8,203	11,028	9,322
50,400	50,450	10,486	8,217	11,042	9,336
50,450	50,500	10,499	8,231	11,056	9,349
50,500	50,550	10,513	8,244	11,069	9,363
50,550	50,600	10,527	8,258	11,083	9,377
50,600	50,650	10,541	8,272	11,097	9,391
50,650	50,700	10,554	8,286	11,111	9,404
50,700	50,750	10,568	8,299	11,124	9,418
50,750	50,800	10,582	8,313	11,138	9,432
50,800	50,850	10,596	8,327	11,152	9,446
50,850	50,900	10,609	8,341	11,166	9,459
50,900	50,950	10,623	8,354	11,179	9,473
50,950	51,000	10,637	8,368	11,193	9,487
51,000					
51,000	51,050	10,651	8,382	11,207	9,501
51,050	51,100	10,664	8,396	11,221	9,514
51,100	51,150	10,678	8,409	11,234	9,528
51,150	51,200	10,692	8,423	11,248	9,542
51,200	51,250	10,706	8,437	11,262	9,556
51,250	51,300	10,719	8,451	11,276	9,569
51,300	51,350	10,733	8,464	11,289	9,583
51,350	51,400	10,747	8,478	11,303	9,597
51,400	51,450	10,761	8,492	11,317	9,611
51,450	51,500	10,774	8,506	11,331	9,624
51,500	51,550	10,788	8,519	11,344	9,638
51,550	51,600	10,802	8,533	11,358	9,652
51,600	51,650	10,816	8,547	11,372	9,666
51,650	51,700	10,829	8,561	11,386	9,679
51,700	51,750	10,843	8,574	11,399	9,693
51,750	51,800	10,857	8,588	11,413	9,707
51,800	51,850	10,871	8,602	11,427	9,721
51,850	51,900	10,884	8,616	11,441	9,734
51,900	51,950	10,898	8,629	11,454	9,748
51,950	52,000	10,912	8,643	11,468	9,762
52,000					
52,000	52,050	10,926	8,657	11,482	9,776
52,050	52,100	10,939	8,671	11,496	9,789
52,100	52,150	10,953	8,684	11,509	9,803
52,150	52,200	10,967	8,698	11,523	9,817
52,200	52,250	10,981	8,712	11,537	9,831
52,250	52,300	10,994	8,726	11,551	9,844
52,300	52,350	11,008	8,739	11,564	9,858
52,350	52,400	11,022	8,753	11,578	9,872
52,400	52,450	11,036	8,767	11,592	9,886
52,450	52,500	11,049	8,781	11,606	9,899
52,500	52,550	11,063	8,794	11,619	9,913
52,550	52,600	11,077	8,808	11,633	9,927
52,600	52,650	11,091	8,822	11,647	9,941
52,650	52,700	11,104	8,836	11,661	9,954
52,700	52,750	11,118	8,849	11,674	9,968
52,750	52,800	11,132	8,863	11,688	9,982
52,800	52,850	11,146	8,877	11,702	9,996
52,850	52,900	11,159	8,891	11,716	10,009
52,900	52,950	11,173	8,904	11,729	10,023
52,950	53,000	11,187	8,918	11,743	10,037

If line 39 (taxable income is)— At least	But less than	And you are— Single	Married filing jointly*	Married filing separately	Head of a household
53,000					
53,000	53,050	11,201	8,932	11,757	10,051
53,050	53,100	11,214	8,946	11,771	10,064
53,100	53,150	11,228	8,959	11,784	10,078
53,150	53,200	11,242	8,973	11,798	10,092
53,200	53,250	11,256	8,987	11,812	10,106
53,250	53,300	11,269	9,001	11,826	10,119
53,300	53,350	11,283	9,014	11,839	10,133
53,350	53,400	11,297	9,028	11,853	10,147
53,400	53,450	11,311	9,042	11,867	10,161
53,450	53,500	11,324	9,056	11,881	10,174
53,500	53,550	11,338	9,069	11,894	10,188
53,550	53,600	11,352	9,083	11,908	10,202
53,600	53,650	11,366	9,097	11,922	10,216
53,650	53,700	11,379	9,111	11,936	10,229
53,700	53,750	11,393	9,124	11,949	10,243
53,750	53,800	11,407	9,138	11,963	10,257
53,800	53,850	11,421	9,152	11,977	10,271
53,850	53,900	11,434	9,166	11,991	10,284
53,900	53,950	11,448	9,179	12,004	10,298
53,950	54,000	11,462	9,193	12,018	10,312
54,000					
54,000	54,050	11,476	9,207	12,032	10,326
54,050	54,100	11,489	9,221	12,046	10,339
54,100	54,150	11,503	9,234	12,059	10,353
54,150	54,200	11,517	9,248	12,073	10,367
54,200	54,250	11,531	9,262	12,087	10,381
54,250	54,300	11,544	9,276	12,101	10,394
54,300	54,350	11,558	9,289	12,114	10,408
54,350	54,400	11,572	9,303	12,128	10,422
54,400	54,450	11,586	9,317	12,142	10,436
54,450	54,500	11,599	9,331	12,156	10,449
54,500	54,550	11,613	9,344	12,169	10,463
54,550	54,600	11,627	9,358	12,183	10,477
54,600	54,650	11,641	9,372	12,197	10,491
54,650	54,700	11,654	9,386	12,212	10,504
54,700	54,750	11,668	9,399	12,227	10,518
54,750	54,800	11,682	9,413	12,243	10,532
54,800	54,850	11,696	9,427	12,258	10,546
54,850	54,900	11,709	9,441	12,273	10,559
54,900	54,950	11,723	9,454	12,289	10,573
54,950	55,000	11,737	9,468	12,304	10,587
55,000					
55,000	55,050	11,751	9,482	12,319	10,601
55,050	55,100	11,764	9,496	12,334	10,614
55,100	55,150	11,778	9,509	12,349	10,628
55,150	55,200	11,792	9,523	12,365	10,642
55,200	55,250	11,806	9,537	12,380	10,656
55,250	55,300	11,819	9,551	12,395	10,669
55,300	55,350	11,833	9,564	12,410	10,683
55,350	55,400	11,847	9,578	12,426	10,697
55,400	55,450	11,861	9,592	12,441	10,711
55,450	55,500	11,874	9,606	12,456	10,724
55,500	55,550	11,888	9,619	12,471	10,738
55,550	55,600	11,902	9,633	12,487	10,752
55,600	55,650	11,916	9,647	12,502	10,766
55,650	55,700	11,929	9,661	12,517	10,779
55,700	55,750	11,943	9,674	12,532	10,793
55,750	55,800	11,957	9,688	12,548	10,807
55,800	55,850	11,971	9,702	12,563	10,821
55,850	55,900	11,984	9,716	12,578	10,834
55,900	55,950	11,998	9,729	12,593	10,848
55,950	56,000	12,012	9,743	12,609	10,862

If line 39 (taxable income is)— At least	But less than	And you are— Single	Married filing jointly*	Married filing separately	Head of a household
56,000					
56,000	56,050	12,026	9,757	12,624	10,876
56,050	56,100	12,039	9,771	12,639	10,889
56,100	56,150	12,053	9,784	12,654	10,903
56,150	56,200	12,067	9,798	12,670	10,917
56,200	56,250	12,081	9,812	12,685	10,931
56,250	56,300	12,094	9,826	12,700	10,944
56,300	56,350	12,108	9,839	12,715	10,958
56,350	56,400	12,122	9,853	12,731	10,972
56,400	56,450	12,136	9,867	12,746	10,986
56,450	56,500	12,149	9,881	12,761	10,999
56,500	56,550	12,163	9,894	12,776	11,013
56,550	56,600	12,177	9,908	12,792	11,027
56,600	56,650	12,191	9,922	12,807	11,041
56,650	56,700	12,204	9,936	12,822	11,054
56,700	56,750	12,218	9,949	12,837	11,068
56,750	56,800	12,232	9,963	12,853	11,082
56,800	56,850	12,246	9,977	12,868	11,096
56,850	56,900	12,259	9,991	12,883	11,109
56,900	56,950	12,273	10,004	12,898	11,123
56,950	57,000	12,287	10,018	12,914	11,137
57,000					
57,000	57,050	12,301	10,032	12,929	11,151
57,050	57,100	12,314	10,046	12,944	11,164
57,100	57,150	12,328	10,059	12,959	11,178
57,150	57,200	12,342	10,073	12,975	11,192
57,200	57,250	12,356	10,087	12,990	11,206
57,250	57,300	12,369	10,101	13,005	11,219
57,300	57,350	12,383	10,114	13,020	11,233
57,350	57,400	12,397	10,128	13,036	11,247
57,400	57,450	12,411	10,142	13,051	11,261
57,450	57,500	12,424	10,156	13,066	11,274
57,500	57,550	12,438	10,169	13,081	11,288
57,550	57,600	12,452	10,183	13,097	11,302
57,600	57,650	12,466	10,197	13,112	11,316
57,650	57,700	12,479	10,211	13,127	11,329
57,700	57,750	12,493	10,224	13,142	11,343
57,750	57,800	12,507	10,238	13,158	11,357
57,800	57,850	12,521	10,252	13,173	11,371
57,850	57,900	12,534	10,266	13,188	11,384
57,900	57,950	12,548	10,279	13,203	11,398
57,950	58,000	12,562	10,293	13,219	11,412
58,000					
58,000	58,050	12,576	10,307	13,234	11,426
58,050	58,100	12,589	10,321	13,249	11,439
58,100	58,150	12,603	10,334	13,264	11,453
58,150	58,200	12,617	10,348	13,280	11,467
58,200	58,250	12,631	10,362	13,295	11,481
58,250	58,300	12,644	10,376	13,310	11,494
58,300	58,350	12,658	10,389	13,325	11,508
58,350	58,400	12,672	10,403	13,341	11,522
58,400	58,450	12,686	10,417	13,356	11,536
58,450	58,500	12,699	10,431	13,371	11,549
58,500	58,550	12,713	10,444	13,386	11,563
58,550	58,600	12,727	10,458	13,402	11,577
58,600	58,650	12,741	10,472	13,417	11,591
58,650	58,700	12,754	10,486	13,432	11,604
58,700	58,750	12,768	10,499	13,447	11,618
58,750	58,800	12,782	10,513	13,463	11,632
58,800	58,850	12,796	10,527	13,478	11,646
58,850	58,900	12,809	10,541	13,493	11,659
58,900	58,950	12,823	10,554	13,508	11,673
58,950	59,000	12,837	10,568	13,524	11,687

* This column must also be used by a qualifying widow(er).

(Continued on page 66)

¶25

2001 Tax Table—Continued   Caution. Dependents, see the worksheet on page 33.

Left column

If line 39 (taxable income) is—		And you are—			
At least	But less than	Single	Married filing jointly *	Married filing separately	Head of a household
		Your tax is—			
59,000					
59,000	59,050	12,851	10,582	13,539	11,701
59,050	59,100	12,864	10,596	13,554	11,714
59,100	59,150	12,878	10,609	13,569	11,728
59,150	59,200	12,892	10,623	13,585	11,742
59,200	59,250	12,906	10,637	13,600	11,756
59,250	59,300	12,919	10,651	13,615	11,769
59,300	59,350	12,933	10,664	13,630	11,783
59,350	59,400	12,947	10,678	13,646	11,797
59,400	59,450	12,961	10,692	13,661	11,811
59,450	59,500	12,974	10,706	13,676	11,824
59,500	59,550	12,988	10,719	13,691	11,838
59,550	59,600	13,002	10,733	13,707	11,852
59,600	59,650	13,016	10,747	13,722	11,866
59,650	59,700	13,029	10,761	13,737	11,879
59,700	59,750	13,043	10,774	13,752	11,893
59,750	59,800	13,057	10,788	13,768	11,907
59,800	59,850	13,071	10,802	13,783	11,921
59,850	59,900	13,084	10,816	13,798	11,934
59,900	59,950	13,098	10,829	13,813	11,948
59,950	60,000	13,112	10,843	13,829	11,962
60,000					
60,000	60,050	13,126	10,857	13,844	11,976
60,050	60,100	13,139	10,871	13,859	11,989
60,100	60,150	13,153	10,884	13,874	12,003
60,150	60,200	13,167	10,898	13,890	12,017
60,200	60,250	13,181	10,912	13,905	12,031
60,250	60,300	13,194	10,926	13,920	12,044
60,300	60,350	13,208	10,939	13,935	12,058
60,350	60,400	13,222	10,953	13,951	12,072
60,400	60,450	13,236	10,967	13,966	12,086
60,450	60,500	13,249	10,981	13,981	12,099
60,500	60,550	13,263	10,994	13,996	12,113
60,550	60,600	13,277	11,008	14,012	12,127
60,600	60,650	13,291	11,022	14,027	12,141
60,650	60,700	13,304	11,036	14,042	12,154
60,700	60,750	13,318	11,049	14,057	12,168
60,750	60,800	13,332	11,063	14,073	12,182
60,800	60,850	13,346	11,077	14,088	12,196
60,850	60,900	13,359	11,091	14,103	12,209
60,900	60,950	13,373	11,104	14,118	12,223
60,950	61,000	13,387	11,118	14,134	12,237
61,000					
61,000	61,050	13,401	11,132	14,149	12,251
61,050	61,100	13,414	11,146	14,164	12,264
61,100	61,150	13,428	11,159	14,179	12,278
61,150	61,200	13,442	11,173	14,195	12,292
61,200	61,250	13,456	11,187	14,210	12,306
61,250	61,300	13,469	11,201	14,225	12,319
61,300	61,350	13,483	11,214	14,240	12,333
61,350	61,400	13,497	11,228	14,256	12,347
61,400	61,450	13,511	11,242	14,271	12,361
61,450	61,500	13,524	11,256	14,286	12,374
61,500	61,550	13,538	11,269	14,301	12,388
61,550	61,600	13,552	11,283	14,317	12,402
61,600	61,650	13,566	11,297	14,332	12,416
61,650	61,700	13,579	11,311	14,347	12,429
61,700	61,750	13,593	11,324	14,362	12,443
61,750	61,800	13,607	11,338	14,378	12,457
61,800	61,850	13,621	11,352	14,393	12,471
61,850	61,900	13,634	11,366	14,408	12,484
61,900	61,950	13,648	11,379	14,423	12,498
61,950	62,000	13,662	11,393	14,439	12,512

Middle column

If line 39 (taxable income) is—		And you are—			
At least	But less than	Single	Married filing jointly *	Married filing separately	Head of a household
		Your tax is—			
62,000					
62,000	62,050	13,676	11,407	14,454	12,526
62,050	62,100	13,689	11,421	14,469	12,539
62,100	62,150	13,703	11,434	14,484	12,553
62,150	62,200	13,717	11,448	14,500	12,567
62,200	62,250	13,731	11,462	14,515	12,581
62,250	62,300	13,744	11,476	14,530	12,594
62,300	62,350	13,758	11,489	14,545	12,608
62,350	62,400	13,772	11,503	14,561	12,622
62,400	62,450	13,786	11,517	14,576	12,636
62,450	62,500	13,799	11,531	14,591	12,649
62,500	62,550	13,813	11,544	14,606	12,663
62,550	62,600	13,827	11,558	14,622	12,677
62,600	62,650	13,841	11,572	14,637	12,691
62,650	62,700	13,854	11,586	14,652	12,704
62,700	62,750	13,868	11,599	14,667	12,718
62,750	62,800	13,882	11,613	14,683	12,732
62,800	62,850	13,896	11,627	14,698	12,746
62,850	62,900	13,909	11,641	14,713	12,759
62,900	62,950	13,923	11,654	14,728	12,773
62,950	63,000	13,937	11,668	14,744	12,787
63,000					
63,000	63,050	13,951	11,682	14,759	12,801
63,050	63,100	13,964	11,696	14,774	12,814
63,100	63,150	13,978	11,709	14,789	12,828
63,150	63,200	13,992	11,723	14,805	12,842
63,200	63,250	14,006	11,737	14,820	12,856
63,250	63,300	14,019	11,751	14,835	12,869
63,300	63,350	14,033	11,764	14,850	12,883
63,350	63,400	14,047	11,778	14,866	12,897
63,400	63,450	14,061	11,792	14,881	12,911
63,450	63,500	14,074	11,806	14,896	12,924
63,500	63,550	14,088	11,819	14,911	12,938
63,550	63,600	14,102	11,833	14,927	12,952
63,600	63,650	14,116	11,847	14,942	12,966
63,650	63,700	14,129	11,861	14,957	12,979
63,700	63,750	14,143	11,874	14,972	12,993
63,750	63,800	14,157	11,888	14,988	13,007
63,800	63,850	14,171	11,902	15,003	13,021
63,850	63,900	14,184	11,916	15,018	13,034
63,900	63,950	14,198	11,929	15,033	13,048
63,950	64,000	14,212	11,943	15,049	13,062
64,000					
64,000	64,050	14,226	11,957	15,064	13,076
64,050	64,100	14,239	11,971	15,079	13,089
64,100	64,150	14,253	11,984	15,094	13,103
64,150	64,200	14,267	11,998	15,110	13,117
64,200	64,250	14,281	12,012	15,125	13,131
64,250	64,300	14,294	12,026	15,140	13,144
64,300	64,350	14,308	12,039	15,155	13,158
64,350	64,400	14,322	12,053	15,171	13,172
64,400	64,450	14,336	12,067	15,186	13,186
64,450	64,500	14,349	12,081	15,201	13,199
64,500	64,550	14,363	12,094	15,216	13,213
64,550	64,600	14,377	12,108	15,232	13,227
64,600	64,650	14,391	12,122	15,247	13,241
64,650	64,700	14,404	12,136	15,262	13,254
64,700	64,750	14,418	12,149	15,277	13,268
64,750	64,800	14,432	12,163	15,293	13,282
64,800	64,850	14,446	12,177	15,308	13,296
64,850	64,900	14,459	12,191	15,323	13,309
64,900	64,950	14,473	12,204	15,338	13,323
64,950	65,000	14,487	12,218	15,354	13,337

Right column

If line 39 (taxable income) is—		And you are—			
At least	But less than	Single	Married filing jointly *	Married filing separately	Head of a household
		Your tax is—			
65,000					
65,000	65,050	14,501	12,232	15,369	13,351
65,050	65,100	14,514	12,246	15,384	13,364
65,100	65,150	14,528	12,259	15,399	13,378
65,150	65,200	14,542	12,273	15,415	13,392
65,200	65,250	14,556	12,287	15,430	13,406
65,250	65,300	14,569	12,301	15,445	13,419
65,300	65,350	14,583	12,314	15,460	13,433
65,350	65,400	14,597	12,328	15,476	13,447
65,400	65,450	14,611	12,342	15,491	13,461
65,450	65,500	14,624	12,356	15,506	13,474
65,500	65,550	14,638	12,369	15,521	13,488
65,550	65,600	14,653	12,383	15,537	13,502
65,600	65,650	14,668	12,397	15,552	13,516
65,650	65,700	14,683	12,411	15,567	13,529
65,700	65,750	14,698	12,424	15,582	13,543
65,750	65,800	14,714	12,438	15,598	13,557
65,800	65,850	14,729	12,452	15,613	13,571
65,850	65,900	14,744	12,466	15,628	13,584
65,900	65,950	14,759	12,479	15,643	13,598
65,950	66,000	14,775	12,493	15,659	13,612
66,000					
66,000	66,050	14,790	12,507	15,674	13,626
66,050	66,100	14,805	12,521	15,689	13,639
66,100	66,150	14,820	12,534	15,704	13,653
66,150	66,200	14,836	12,548	15,720	13,667
66,200	66,250	14,851	12,562	15,735	13,681
66,250	66,300	14,866	12,576	15,750	13,694
66,300	66,350	14,881	12,589	15,765	13,708
66,350	66,400	14,897	12,603	15,781	13,722
66,400	66,450	14,912	12,617	15,796	13,736
66,450	66,500	14,927	12,631	15,811	13,749
66,500	66,550	14,942	12,644	15,826	13,763
66,550	66,600	14,958	12,658	15,842	13,777
66,600	66,650	14,973	12,672	15,857	13,791
66,650	66,700	14,988	12,686	15,872	13,804
66,700	66,750	15,003	12,699	15,887	13,818
66,750	66,800	15,019	12,713	15,903	13,832
66,800	66,850	15,034	12,727	15,918	13,846
66,850	66,900	15,049	12,741	15,933	13,859
66,900	66,950	15,064	12,754	15,948	13,873
66,950	67,000	15,080	12,768	15,964	13,887
67,000					
67,000	67,050	15,095	12,782	15,979	13,901
67,050	67,100	15,110	12,796	15,994	13,914
67,100	67,150	15,125	12,809	16,009	13,928
67,150	67,200	15,141	12,823	16,025	13,942
67,200	67,250	15,156	12,837	16,040	13,956
67,250	67,300	15,171	12,851	16,055	13,969
67,300	67,350	15,186	12,864	16,070	13,983
67,350	67,400	15,202	12,878	16,086	13,997
67,400	67,450	15,217	12,892	16,101	14,011
67,450	67,500	15,232	12,906	16,116	14,024
67,500	67,550	15,247	12,919	16,131	14,038
67,550	67,600	15,263	12,933	16,147	14,052
67,600	67,650	15,278	12,947	16,162	14,066
67,650	67,700	15,293	12,961	16,177	14,079
67,700	67,750	15,308	12,974	16,192	14,093
67,750	67,800	15,324	12,988	16,208	14,107
67,800	67,850	15,339	13,002	16,223	14,121
67,850	67,900	15,354	13,016	16,238	14,134
67,900	67,950	15,369	13,029	16,253	14,148
67,950	68,000	15,385	13,043	16,269	14,162

* This column must also be used by a qualifying widow(er).

(Continued on page 67)

¶ 25

Caution. Dependents, see the worksheet on page 33.　　2001 Tax Table—*Continued*

68,000

At least	But less than	Single	Married filing jointly*	Married filing separately	Head of a household
68,000	68,050	15,400	13,057	16,284	14,176
68,050	68,100	15,415	13,071	16,299	14,189
68,100	68,150	15,430	13,084	16,314	14,203
68,150	68,200	15,446	13,098	16,330	14,217
68,200	68,250	15,461	13,112	16,345	14,231
68,250	68,300	15,476	13,126	16,360	14,244
68,300	68,350	15,491	13,139	16,375	14,258
68,350	68,400	15,507	13,153	16,391	14,272
68,400	68,450	15,522	13,167	16,406	14,286
68,450	68,500	15,537	13,181	16,421	14,299
68,500	68,550	15,552	13,194	16,436	14,313
68,550	68,600	15,568	13,208	16,452	14,327
68,600	68,650	15,583	13,222	16,467	14,341
68,650	68,700	15,598	13,236	16,482	14,354
68,700	68,750	15,613	13,249	16,497	14,368
68,750	68,800	15,629	13,263	16,513	14,382
68,800	68,850	15,644	13,277	16,528	14,396
68,850	68,900	15,659	13,291	16,543	14,409
68,900	68,950	15,674	13,304	16,558	14,423
68,950	69,000	15,690	13,318	16,574	14,437

69,000

At least	But less than	Single	Married filing jointly*	Married filing separately	Head of a household
69,000	69,050	15,705	13,332	16,589	14,451
69,050	69,100	15,720	13,346	16,604	14,464
69,100	69,150	15,735	13,359	16,619	14,478
69,150	69,200	15,751	13,373	16,635	14,492
69,200	69,250	15,766	13,387	16,650	14,506
69,250	69,300	15,781	13,401	16,665	14,519
69,300	69,350	15,796	13,414	16,680	14,533
69,350	69,400	15,812	13,428	16,696	14,547
69,400	69,450	15,827	13,442	16,711	14,561
69,450	69,500	15,842	13,456	16,726	14,574
69,500	69,550	15,857	13,469	16,741	14,588
69,550	69,600	15,873	13,483	16,757	14,602
69,600	69,650	15,888	13,497	16,772	14,616
69,650	69,700	15,903	13,511	16,787	14,629
69,700	69,750	15,918	13,524	16,802	14,643
69,750	69,800	15,934	13,538	16,818	14,657
69,800	69,850	15,949	13,552	16,833	14,671
69,850	69,900	15,964	13,566	16,848	14,684
69,900	69,950	15,979	13,579	16,863	14,698
69,950	70,000	15,995	13,593	16,879	14,712

70,000

At least	But less than	Single	Married filing jointly*	Married filing separately	Head of a household
70,000	70,050	16,010	13,607	16,894	14,726
70,050	70,100	16,025	13,621	16,909	14,739
70,100	70,150	16,040	13,634	16,924	14,753
70,150	70,200	16,056	13,648	16,940	14,767
70,200	70,250	16,071	13,662	16,955	14,781
70,250	70,300	16,086	13,676	16,970	14,794
70,300	70,350	16,101	13,689	16,985	14,808
70,350	70,400	16,117	13,703	17,001	14,822
70,400	70,450	16,132	13,717	17,016	14,836
70,450	70,500	16,147	13,731	17,031	14,849
70,500	70,550	16,162	13,744	17,046	14,863
70,550	70,600	16,178	13,758	17,062	14,877
70,600	70,650	16,193	13,772	17,077	14,891
70,650	70,700	16,208	13,786	17,092	14,904
70,700	70,750	16,223	13,799	17,107	14,918
70,750	70,800	16,239	13,813	17,123	14,932
70,800	70,850	16,254	13,827	17,138	14,946
70,850	70,900	16,269	13,841	17,153	14,959
70,900	70,950	16,284	13,854	17,168	14,973
70,950	71,000	16,300	13,868	17,184	14,987

71,000

At least	But less than	Single	Married filing jointly*	Married filing separately	Head of a household
71,000	71,050	16,315	13,882	17,199	15,001
71,050	71,100	16,330	13,896	17,214	15,014
71,100	71,150	16,345	13,909	17,229	15,028
71,150	71,200	16,361	13,923	17,245	15,042
71,200	71,250	16,376	13,937	17,260	15,056
71,250	71,300	16,391	13,951	17,275	15,069
71,300	71,350	16,406	13,964	17,290	15,083
71,350	71,400	16,422	13,978	17,306	15,097
71,400	71,450	16,437	13,992	17,321	15,111
71,450	71,500	16,452	14,006	17,336	15,124
71,500	71,550	16,467	14,019	17,351	15,138
71,550	71,600	16,483	14,033	17,367	15,152
71,600	71,650	16,498	14,047	17,382	15,166
71,650	71,700	16,513	14,061	17,397	15,179
71,700	71,750	16,528	14,074	17,412	15,193
71,750	71,800	16,544	14,088	17,428	15,207
71,800	71,850	16,559	14,102	17,443	15,221
71,850	71,900	16,574	14,116	17,458	15,234
71,900	71,950	16,589	14,129	17,473	15,248
71,950	72,000	16,605	14,143	17,489	15,262

72,000

At least	But less than	Single	Married filing jointly*	Married filing separately	Head of a household
72,000	72,050	16,620	14,157	17,504	15,276
72,050	72,100	16,635	14,171	17,519	15,289
72,100	72,150	16,650	14,184	17,534	15,303
72,150	72,200	16,666	14,198	17,550	15,317
72,200	72,250	16,681	14,212	17,565	15,331
72,250	72,300	16,696	14,226	17,580	15,344
72,300	72,350	16,711	14,239	17,595	15,358
72,350	72,400	16,727	14,253	17,611	15,372
72,400	72,450	16,742	14,267	17,626	15,386
72,450	72,500	16,757	14,281	17,641	15,399
72,500	72,550	16,772	14,294	17,656	15,413
72,550	72,600	16,788	14,308	17,672	15,427
72,600	72,650	16,803	14,322	17,687	15,441
72,650	72,700	16,818	14,336	17,702	15,454
72,700	72,750	16,833	14,349	17,717	15,468
72,750	72,800	16,849	14,363	17,733	15,482
72,800	72,850	16,864	14,377	17,748	15,496
72,850	72,900	16,879	14,391	17,763	15,509
72,900	72,950	16,894	14,404	17,778	15,523
72,950	73,000	16,910	14,418	17,794	15,537

73,000

At least	But less than	Single	Married filing jointly*	Married filing separately	Head of a household
73,000	73,050	16,925	14,432	17,809	15,551
73,050	73,100	16,940	14,446	17,824	15,564
73,100	73,150	16,955	14,459	17,839	15,578
73,150	73,200	16,971	14,473	17,855	15,592
73,200	73,250	16,986	14,487	17,870	15,606
73,250	73,300	17,001	14,501	17,885	15,619
73,300	73,350	17,016	14,514	17,900	15,633
73,350	73,400	17,032	14,528	17,916	15,647
73,400	73,450	17,047	14,542	17,931	15,661
73,450	73,500	17,062	14,556	17,946	15,674
73,500	73,550	17,077	14,569	17,961	15,688
73,550	73,600	17,093	14,583	17,977	15,702
73,600	73,650	17,108	14,597	17,992	15,716
73,650	73,700	17,123	14,611	18,007	15,729
73,700	73,750	17,138	14,624	18,022	15,743
73,750	73,800	17,154	14,638	18,038	15,757
73,800	73,850	17,169	14,652	18,053	15,771
73,850	73,900	17,184	14,666	18,068	15,784
73,900	73,950	17,199	14,679	18,083	15,798
73,950	74,000	17,215	14,693	18,099	15,812

74,000

At least	But less than	Single	Married filing jointly*	Married filing separately	Head of a household
74,000	74,050	17,230	14,707	18,114	15,826
74,050	74,100	17,245	14,721	18,129	15,839
74,100	74,150	17,260	14,734	18,144	15,853
74,150	74,200	17,276	14,748	18,160	15,867
74,200	74,250	17,291	14,762	18,175	15,881
74,250	74,300	17,306	14,776	18,190	15,894
74,300	74,350	17,321	14,789	18,205	15,908
74,350	74,400	17,337	14,803	18,221	15,922
74,400	74,450	17,352	14,817	18,236	15,936
74,450	74,500	17,367	14,831	18,251	15,949
74,500	74,550	17,382	14,844	18,266	15,963
74,550	74,600	17,398	14,858	18,282	15,977
74,600	74,650	17,413	14,872	18,297	15,991
74,650	74,700	17,428	14,886	18,312	16,004
74,700	74,750	17,443	14,899	18,327	16,018
74,750	74,800	17,459	14,913	18,343	16,032
74,800	74,850	17,474	14,927	18,358	16,046
74,850	74,900	17,489	14,941	18,373	16,059
74,900	74,950	17,504	14,954	18,388	16,073
74,950	75,000	17,520	14,968	18,404	16,087

75,000

At least	But less than	Single	Married filing jointly*	Married filing separately	Head of a household
75,000	75,050	17,535	14,982	18,419	16,101
75,050	75,100	17,550	14,996	18,434	16,114
75,100	75,150	17,565	15,009	18,449	16,128
75,150	75,200	17,581	15,023	18,465	16,142
75,200	75,250	17,596	15,037	18,480	16,156
75,250	75,300	17,611	15,051	18,495	16,169
75,300	75,350	17,626	15,064	18,510	16,183
75,350	75,400	17,642	15,078	18,526	16,197
75,400	75,450	17,657	15,092	18,541	16,211
75,450	75,500	17,672	15,106	18,556	16,224
75,500	75,550	17,687	15,119	18,571	16,238
75,550	75,600	17,703	15,133	18,587	16,252
75,600	75,650	17,718	15,147	18,602	16,266
75,650	75,700	17,733	15,161	18,617	16,279
75,700	75,750	17,748	15,174	18,632	16,293
75,750	75,800	17,764	15,188	18,648	16,307
75,800	75,850	17,779	15,202	18,663	16,321
75,850	75,900	17,794	15,216	18,678	16,334
75,900	75,950	17,809	15,229	18,693	16,348
75,950	76,000	17,825	15,243	18,709	16,362

76,000

At least	But less than	Single	Married filing jointly*	Married filing separately	Head of a household
76,000	76,050	17,840	15,257	18,724	16,376
76,050	76,100	17,855	15,271	18,739	16,389
76,100	76,150	17,870	15,284	18,754	16,403
76,150	76,200	17,886	15,298	18,770	16,417
76,200	76,250	17,901	15,312	18,785	16,431
76,250	76,300	17,916	15,326	18,800	16,444
76,300	76,350	17,931	15,339	18,815	16,458
76,350	76,400	17,947	15,353	18,831	16,472
76,400	76,450	17,962	15,367	18,846	16,486
76,450	76,500	17,977	15,381	18,861	16,499
76,500	76,550	17,992	15,394	18,876	16,513
76,550	76,600	18,008	15,408	18,892	16,527
76,600	76,650	18,023	15,422	18,907	16,541
76,650	76,700	18,038	15,436	18,922	16,554
76,700	76,750	18,053	15,449	18,937	16,568
76,750	76,800	18,069	15,463	18,953	16,582
76,800	76,850	18,084	15,477	18,968	16,596
76,850	76,900	18,099	15,491	18,983	16,609
76,900	76,950	18,114	15,504	18,998	16,623
76,950	77,000	18,130	15,518	19,014	16,637

* This column must also be used by a qualifying widow(er).

(Continued on page 68)

¶25

2001 Tax Table—Continued   **Caution.** Dependents, see the worksheet on 33.

* This column must also be used by a qualifying widow(er).

77,000 – 79,000

At least	But less than	Single	Married filing jointly *	Married filing separately	Head of a household
77,000					
77,000	77,050	18,145	15,532	19,029	16,651
77,050	77,100	18,160	15,546	19,044	16,664
77,100	77,150	18,175	15,559	19,059	16,678
77,150	77,200	18,191	15,573	19,075	16,692
77,200	77,250	18,206	15,587	19,090	16,706
77,250	77,300	18,221	15,601	19,105	16,719
77,300	77,350	18,236	15,614	19,120	16,733
77,350	77,400	18,252	15,628	19,136	16,747
77,400	77,450	18,267	15,642	19,151	16,761
77,450	77,500	18,282	15,656	19,166	16,774
77,500	77,550	18,297	15,669	19,181	16,788
77,550	77,600	18,313	15,683	19,197	16,802
77,600	77,650	18,328	15,697	19,212	16,816
77,650	77,700	18,343	15,711	19,227	16,829
77,700	77,750	18,358	15,724	19,242	16,843
77,750	77,800	18,374	15,738	19,258	16,857
77,800	77,850	18,389	15,752	19,273	16,871
77,850	77,900	18,404	15,766	19,288	16,884
77,900	77,950	18,419	15,779	19,303	16,898
77,950	78,000	18,435	15,793	19,319	16,912
78,000					
78,000	78,050	18,450	15,807	19,334	16,926
78,050	78,100	18,465	15,821	19,349	16,939
78,100	78,150	18,480	15,834	19,364	16,953
78,150	78,200	18,496	15,848	19,380	16,967
78,200	78,250	18,511	15,862	19,395	16,981
78,250	78,300	18,526	15,876	19,410	16,994
78,300	78,350	18,541	15,889	19,425	17,008
78,350	78,400	18,557	15,903	19,441	17,022
78,400	78,450	18,572	15,917	19,456	17,036
78,450	78,500	18,587	15,931	19,471	17,049
78,500	78,550	18,602	15,944	19,486	17,063
78,550	78,600	18,618	15,958	19,502	17,077
78,600	78,650	18,633	15,972	19,517	17,091
78,650	78,700	18,648	15,986	19,532	17,104
78,700	78,750	18,663	15,999	19,547	17,118
78,750	78,800	18,679	16,013	19,563	17,132
78,800	78,850	18,694	16,027	19,578	17,146
78,850	78,900	18,709	16,041	19,593	17,159
78,900	78,950	18,724	16,054	19,608	17,173
78,950	79,000	18,740	16,068	19,624	17,187
79,000					
79,000	79,050	18,755	16,082	19,639	17,201
79,050	79,100	18,770	16,096	19,654	17,214
79,100	79,150	18,785	16,109	19,669	17,228
79,150	79,200	18,801	16,123	19,685	17,242
79,200	79,250	18,816	16,137	19,700	17,256
79,250	79,300	18,831	16,151	19,715	17,269
79,300	79,350	18,846	16,164	19,730	17,283
79,350	79,400	18,862	16,178	19,746	17,297
79,400	79,450	18,877	16,192	19,761	17,311
79,450	79,500	18,892	16,206	19,776	17,324
79,500	79,550	18,907	16,219	19,791	17,338
79,550	79,600	18,923	16,233	19,807	17,352
79,600	79,650	18,938	16,247	19,822	17,366
79,650	79,700	18,953	16,261	19,837	17,379
79,700	79,750	18,968	16,274	19,852	17,393
79,750	79,800	18,984	16,288	19,868	17,407
79,800	79,850	18,999	16,302	19,883	17,421
79,850	79,900	19,014	16,316	19,898	17,434
79,900	79,950	19,029	16,329	19,913	17,448
79,950	80,000	19,045	16,343	19,929	17,462

80,000 – 82,000

At least	But less than	Single	Married filing jointly *	Married filing separately	Head of a household
80,000					
80,000	80,050	19,060	16,357	19,944	17,476
80,050	80,100	19,075	16,371	19,959	17,489
80,100	80,150	19,090	16,384	19,974	17,503
80,150	80,200	19,106	16,398	19,990	17,517
80,200	80,250	19,121	16,412	20,005	17,531
80,250	80,300	19,136	16,426	20,020	17,544
80,300	80,350	19,151	16,439	20,035	17,558
80,350	80,400	19,167	16,453	20,051	17,572
80,400	80,450	19,182	16,467	20,066	17,586
80,450	80,500	19,197	16,481	20,081	17,599
80,500	80,550	19,212	16,494	20,096	17,613
80,550	80,600	19,228	16,508	20,112	17,627
80,600	80,650	19,243	16,522	20,127	17,641
80,650	80,700	19,258	16,536	20,142	17,654
80,700	80,750	19,273	16,549	20,157	17,668
80,750	80,800	19,289	16,563	20,173	17,682
80,800	80,850	19,304	16,577	20,188	17,696
80,850	80,900	19,319	16,591	20,203	17,709
80,900	80,950	19,334	16,604	20,218	17,723
80,950	81,000	19,350	16,618	20,234	17,737
81,000					
81,000	81,050	19,365	16,632	20,249	17,751
81,050	81,100	19,380	16,646	20,264	17,764
81,100	81,150	19,395	16,659	20,279	17,778
81,150	81,200	19,411	16,673	20,295	17,792
81,200	81,250	19,426	16,687	20,310	17,806
81,250	81,300	19,441	16,701	20,325	17,819
81,300	81,350	19,456	16,714	20,340	17,833
81,350	81,400	19,472	16,728	20,356	17,847
81,400	81,450	19,487	16,742	20,371	17,861
81,450	81,500	19,502	16,756	20,386	17,874
81,500	81,550	19,517	16,769	20,401	17,888
81,550	81,600	19,533	16,783	20,417	17,902
81,600	81,650	19,548	16,797	20,432	17,916
81,650	81,700	19,563	16,811	20,447	17,929
81,700	81,750	19,578	16,824	20,462	17,943
81,750	81,800	19,594	16,838	20,478	17,957
81,800	81,850	19,609	16,852	20,493	17,971
81,850	81,900	19,624	16,866	20,508	17,984
81,900	81,950	19,639	16,879	20,523	17,998
81,950	82,000	19,655	16,893	20,539	18,012
82,000					
82,000	82,050	19,670	16,907	20,554	18,026
82,050	82,100	19,685	16,921	20,569	18,039
82,100	82,150	19,700	16,934	20,584	18,053
82,150	82,200	19,716	16,948	20,600	18,067
82,200	82,250	19,731	16,962	20,615	18,081
82,250	82,300	19,746	16,976	20,630	18,094
82,300	82,350	19,761	16,989	20,645	18,108
82,350	82,400	19,777	17,003	20,661	18,122
82,400	82,450	19,792	17,017	20,676	18,136
82,450	82,500	19,807	17,031	20,691	18,149
82,500	82,550	19,822	17,044	20,706	18,163
82,550	82,600	19,838	17,058	20,722	18,177
82,600	82,650	19,853	17,072	20,737	18,191
82,650	82,700	19,868	17,086	20,752	18,204
82,700	82,750	19,883	17,099	20,767	18,218
82,750	82,800	19,899	17,113	20,783	18,232
82,800	82,850	19,914	17,127	20,798	18,246
82,850	82,900	19,929	17,141	20,813	18,259
82,900	82,950	19,944	17,154	20,828	18,273
82,950	83,000	19,960	17,168	20,844	18,287

83,000 – 85,000

At least	But less than	Single	Married filing jointly *	Married filing separately	Head of a household
83,000					
83,000	83,050	19,975	17,182	20,859	18,301
83,050	83,100	19,990	17,196	20,874	18,314
83,100	83,150	20,005	17,209	20,889	18,328
83,150	83,200	20,021	17,223	20,905	18,342
83,200	83,250	20,036	17,237	20,920	18,356
83,250	83,300	20,051	17,251	20,936	18,369
83,300	83,350	20,066	17,264	20,951	18,383
83,350	83,400	20,082	17,278	20,972	18,397
83,400	83,450	20,097	17,292	20,990	18,411
83,450	83,500	20,112	17,306	21,007	18,424
83,500	83,550	20,127	17,319	21,025	18,438
83,550	83,600	20,143	17,333	21,043	18,452
83,600	83,650	20,158	17,347	21,061	18,466
83,650	83,700	20,173	17,361	21,078	18,479
83,700	83,750	20,188	17,374	21,096	18,493
83,750	83,800	20,204	17,388	21,114	18,507
83,800	83,850	20,219	17,402	21,132	18,521
83,850	83,900	20,234	17,416	21,149	18,534
83,900	83,950	20,249	17,429	21,167	18,548
83,950	84,000	20,265	17,443	21,185	18,562
84,000					
84,000	84,050	20,280	17,457	21,203	18,576
84,050	84,100	20,295	17,471	21,220	18,589
84,100	84,150	20,310	17,484	21,238	18,603
84,150	84,200	20,326	17,498	21,256	18,617
84,200	84,250	20,341	17,512	21,274	18,631
84,250	84,300	20,356	17,526	21,291	18,644
84,300	84,350	20,371	17,539	21,309	18,658
84,350	84,400	20,387	17,553	21,327	18,672
84,400	84,450	20,402	17,567	21,345	18,686
84,450	84,500	20,417	17,581	21,362	18,699
84,500	84,550	20,432	17,594	21,380	18,713
84,550	84,600	20,448	17,608	21,398	18,727
84,600	84,650	20,463	17,622	21,416	18,741
84,650	84,700	20,478	17,636	21,433	18,754
84,700	84,750	20,493	17,649	21,451	18,768
84,750	84,800	20,509	17,663	21,469	18,782
84,800	84,850	20,524	17,677	21,487	18,796
84,850	84,900	20,539	17,691	21,504	18,809
84,900	84,950	20,554	17,704	21,522	18,823
84,950	85,000	20,570	17,718	21,540	18,837
85,000					
85,000	85,050	20,585	17,732	21,558	18,851
85,050	85,100	20,600	17,746	21,575	18,864
85,100	85,150	20,615	17,759	21,593	18,878
85,150	85,200	20,631	17,773	21,611	18,892
85,200	85,250	20,646	17,787	21,629	18,906
85,250	85,300	20,661	17,801	21,646	18,919
85,300	85,350	20,676	17,814	21,664	18,933
85,350	85,400	20,692	17,828	21,682	18,947
85,400	85,450	20,707	17,842	21,700	18,961
85,450	85,500	20,722	17,856	21,717	18,974
85,500	85,550	20,737	17,869	21,735	18,988
85,550	85,600	20,753	17,883	21,753	19,002
85,600	85,650	20,768	17,897	21,771	19,016
85,650	85,700	20,783	17,911	21,788	19,029
85,700	85,750	20,798	17,924	21,806	19,043
85,750	85,800	20,814	17,938	21,824	19,057
85,800	85,850	20,829	17,952	21,842	19,071
85,850	85,900	20,844	17,966	21,859	19,084
85,900	85,950	20,859	17,979	21,877	19,098
85,950	86,000	20,875	17,993	21,895	19,112

(Continued on page 69)

¶25

Caution. Dependents, see the worksheet on page 33.　　2001 Tax Table—*Continued*

If line 39 (taxable income) is—		And you are—			
At least	But less than	Single	Married filing jointly *	Married filing separately	Head of a household
		Your tax is—			
86,000					
86,000	86,050	20,890	18,007	21,913	19,126
86,050	86,100	20,905	18,021	21,930	19,139
86,100	86,150	20,920	18,034	21,948	19,153
86,150	86,200	20,936	18,048	21,966	19,167
86,200	86,250	20,951	18,062	21,984	19,181
86,250	86,300	20,966	18,076	22,001	19,194
86,300	86,350	20,981	18,089	22,019	19,208
86,350	86,400	20,997	18,103	22,037	19,222
86,400	86,450	21,012	18,117	22,055	19,236
86,450	86,500	21,027	18,131	22,072	19,249
86,500	86,550	21,042	18,144	22,090	19,263
86,550	86,600	21,058	18,158	22,108	19,277
86,600	86,650	21,073	18,172	22,126	19,291
86,650	86,700	21,088	18,186	22,143	19,304
86,700	86,750	21,103	18,199	22,161	19,318
86,750	86,800	21,119	18,213	22,179	19,332
86,800	86,850	21,134	18,227	22,197	19,346
86,850	86,900	21,149	18,241	22,214	19,359
86,900	86,950	21,164	18,254	22,232	19,373
86,950	87,000	21,180	18,268	22,250	19,387
87,000					
87,000	87,050	21,195	18,282	22,268	19,401
87,050	87,100	21,210	18,296	22,285	19,414
87,100	87,150	21,225	18,309	22,303	19,428
87,150	87,200	21,241	18,323	22,321	19,442
87,200	87,250	21,256	18,337	22,339	19,456
87,250	87,300	21,271	18,351	22,356	19,469
87,300	87,350	21,286	18,364	22,374	19,483
87,350	87,400	21,302	18,378	22,392	19,497
87,400	87,450	21,317	18,392	22,410	19,511
87,450	87,500	21,332	18,406	22,427	19,524
87,500	87,550	21,347	18,419	22,445	19,538
87,550	87,600	21,363	18,433	22,463	19,552
87,600	87,650	21,378	18,447	22,481	19,566
87,650	87,700	21,393	18,461	22,498	19,579
87,700	87,750	21,408	18,474	22,516	19,593
87,750	87,800	21,424	18,488	22,534	19,607
87,800	87,850	21,439	18,502	22,552	19,621
87,850	87,900	21,454	18,516	22,569	19,634
87,900	87,950	21,469	18,529	22,587	19,648
87,950	88,000	21,485	18,543	22,605	19,662
88,000					
88,000	88,050	21,500	18,557	22,623	19,676
88,050	88,100	21,515	18,571	22,640	19,689
88,100	88,150	21,530	18,584	22,658	19,703
88,150	88,200	21,546	18,598	22,676	19,717
88,200	88,250	21,561	18,612	22,694	19,731
88,250	88,300	21,576	18,626	22,711	19,744
88,300	88,350	21,591	18,639	22,729	19,758
88,350	88,400	21,607	18,653	22,747	19,772
88,400	88,450	21,622	18,667	22,765	19,786
88,450	88,500	21,637	18,681	22,782	19,799
88,500	88,550	21,652	18,694	22,800	19,813
88,550	88,600	21,668	18,708	22,818	19,827
88,600	88,650	21,683	18,722	22,836	19,841
88,650	88,700	21,698	18,736	22,853	19,854
88,700	88,750	21,713	18,749	22,871	19,868
88,750	88,800	21,729	18,763	22,889	19,882
88,800	88,850	21,744	18,777	22,907	19,896
88,850	88,900	21,759	18,791	22,924	19,909
88,900	88,950	21,774	18,804	22,942	19,923
88,950	89,000	21,790	18,818	22,960	19,937

If line 39 (taxable income) is—		And you are—			
At least	But less than	Single	Married filing jointly *	Married filing separately	Head of a household
		Your tax is—			
89,000					
89,000	89,050	21,805	18,832	22,978	19,951
89,050	89,100	21,820	18,846	22,995	19,964
89,100	89,150	21,835	18,859	23,013	19,978
89,150	89,200	21,851	18,873	23,031	19,992
89,200	89,250	21,866	18,887	23,049	20,006
89,250	89,300	21,881	18,901	23,066	20,019
89,300	89,350	21,896	18,914	23,084	20,033
89,350	89,400	21,912	18,928	23,102	20,047
89,400	89,450	21,927	18,942	23,120	20,061
89,450	89,500	21,942	18,956	23,137	20,074
89,500	89,550	21,957	18,969	23,155	20,088
89,550	89,600	21,973	18,983	23,173	20,102
89,600	89,650	21,988	18,997	23,191	20,116
89,650	89,700	22,003	19,011	23,208	20,129
89,700	89,750	22,018	19,024	23,226	20,143
89,750	89,800	22,034	19,038	23,244	20,157
89,800	89,850	22,049	19,052	23,262	20,171
89,850	89,900	22,064	19,066	23,279	20,184
89,900	89,950	22,079	19,079	23,297	20,198
89,950	90,000	22,095	19,093	23,315	20,212
90,000					
90,000	90,050	22,110	19,107	23,333	20,226
90,050	90,100	22,125	19,121	23,350	20,239
90,100	90,150	22,140	19,134	23,368	20,253
90,150	90,200	22,156	19,148	23,386	20,267
90,200	90,250	22,171	19,162	23,404	20,281
90,250	90,300	22,186	19,176	23,421	20,294
90,300	90,350	22,201	19,189	23,439	20,308
90,350	90,400	22,217	19,203	23,457	20,322
90,400	90,450	22,232	19,217	23,475	20,336
90,450	90,500	22,247	19,231	23,492	20,349
90,500	90,550	22,262	19,244	23,510	20,363
90,550	90,600	22,278	19,258	23,528	20,377
90,600	90,650	22,293	19,272	23,546	20,391
90,650	90,700	22,308	19,286	23,563	20,404
90,700	90,750	22,323	19,299	23,581	20,418
90,750	90,800	22,339	19,313	23,599	20,432
90,800	90,850	22,354	19,327	23,617	20,446
90,850	90,900	22,369	19,341	23,634	20,459
90,900	90,950	22,384	19,354	23,652	20,473
90,950	91,000	22,400	19,368	23,670	20,487
91,000					
91,000	91,050	22,415	19,382	23,688	20,501
91,050	91,100	22,430	19,396	23,705	20,514
91,100	91,150	22,445	19,409	23,723	20,528
91,150	91,200	22,461	19,423	23,741	20,542
91,200	91,250	22,476	19,437	23,759	20,556
91,250	91,300	22,491	19,451	23,776	20,569
91,300	91,350	22,506	19,464	23,794	20,583
91,350	91,400	22,522	19,478	23,812	20,597
91,400	91,450	22,537	19,492	23,830	20,611
91,450	91,500	22,552	19,506	23,847	20,624
91,500	91,550	22,567	19,519	23,865	20,638
91,550	91,600	22,583	19,533	23,883	20,652
91,600	91,650	22,598	19,547	23,901	20,666
91,650	91,700	22,613	19,561	23,918	20,679
91,700	91,750	22,628	19,574	23,936	20,693
91,750	91,800	22,644	19,588	23,954	20,707
91,800	91,850	22,659	19,602	23,972	20,721
91,850	91,900	22,674	19,616	23,989	20,734
91,900	91,950	22,689	19,629	24,007	20,748
91,950	92,000	22,705	19,643	24,025	20,762

If line 39 (taxable income) is—		And you are—			
At least	But less than	Single	Married filing jointly *	Married filing separately	Head of a household
		Your tax is—			
92,000					
92,000	92,050	22,720	19,657	24,043	20,776
92,050	92,100	22,735	19,671	24,060	20,789
92,100	92,150	22,750	19,684	24,078	20,803
92,150	92,200	22,766	19,698	24,096	20,817
92,200	92,250	22,781	19,712	24,114	20,831
92,250	92,300	22,796	19,726	24,131	20,844
92,300	92,350	22,811	19,739	24,149	20,858
92,350	92,400	22,827	19,753	24,167	20,872
92,400	92,450	22,842	19,767	24,185	20,886
92,450	92,500	22,857	19,781	24,202	20,899
92,500	92,550	22,872	19,794	24,220	20,913
92,550	92,600	22,888	19,808	24,238	20,927
92,600	92,650	22,903	19,822	24,256	20,941
92,650	92,700	22,918	19,836	24,273	20,954
92,700	92,750	22,933	19,849	24,291	20,968
92,750	92,800	22,949	19,863	24,309	20,982
92,800	92,850	22,964	19,877	24,327	20,996
92,850	92,900	22,979	19,891	24,344	21,009
92,900	92,950	22,994	19,904	24,362	21,023
92,950	93,000	23,010	19,918	24,380	21,037
93,000					
93,000	93,050	23,025	19,932	24,398	21,051
93,050	93,100	23,040	19,946	24,415	21,064
93,100	93,150	23,055	19,959	24,433	21,078
93,150	93,200	23,071	19,973	24,451	21,092
93,200	93,250	23,086	19,987	24,469	21,106
93,250	93,300	23,101	20,001	24,486	21,119
93,300	93,350	23,116	20,014	24,504	21,133
93,350	93,400	23,132	20,028	24,522	21,147
93,400	93,450	23,147	20,042	24,540	21,161
93,450	93,500	23,162	20,056	24,557	21,174
93,500	93,550	23,177	20,069	24,575	21,188
93,550	93,600	23,193	20,083	24,593	21,202
93,600	93,650	23,208	20,097	24,611	21,216
93,650	93,700	23,223	20,111	24,628	21,230
93,700	93,750	23,238	20,124	24,646	21,245
93,750	93,800	23,254	20,138	24,664	21,261
93,800	93,850	23,269	20,152	24,682	21,276
93,850	93,900	23,284	20,166	24,699	21,291
93,900	93,950	23,299	20,179	24,717	21,306
93,950	94,000	23,315	20,193	24,735	21,322
94,000					
94,000	94,050	23,330	20,207	24,753	21,337
94,050	94,100	23,345	20,221	24,770	21,352
94,100	94,150	23,360	20,234	24,788	21,367
94,150	94,200	23,376	20,248	24,806	21,383
94,200	94,250	23,391	20,262	24,824	21,398
94,250	94,300	23,406	20,276	24,841	21,413
94,300	94,350	23,421	20,289	24,859	21,428
94,350	94,400	23,437	20,303	24,877	21,444
94,400	94,450	23,452	20,317	24,895	21,459
94,450	94,500	23,467	20,331	24,912	21,474
94,500	94,550	23,482	20,344	24,930	21,489
94,550	94,600	23,498	20,358	24,948	21,505
94,600	94,650	23,513	20,372	24,966	21,520
94,650	94,700	23,528	20,386	24,983	21,535
94,700	94,750	23,543	20,399	25,001	21,550
94,750	94,800	23,559	20,413	25,019	21,566
94,800	94,850	23,574	20,427	25,037	21,581
94,850	94,900	23,589	20,441	25,054	21,596
94,900	94,950	23,604	20,454	25,072	21,611
94,950	95,000	23,620	20,468	25,090	21,627

* This column must also be used by a qualifying widow(er).

(Continued on page 70)

¶ 25

2001 Tax Table—*Continued*   Caution. Dependents, see the worksheet on page 33.

If line 39 (taxable income) is—		And you are—				If line 39 (taxable income) is—		And you are—			
At least	But less than	Single	Married filing jointly *	Married filing separately	Head of a household	At least	But less than	Single	Married filing jointly *	Married filing separately	Head of a household
		Your tax is—						Your tax is—			
95,000						**98,000**					
95,000	95,050	23,635	20,482	25,108	21,642	98,000	98,050	24,550	21,307	26,173	22,557
95,050	95,100	23,650	20,496	25,125	21,657	98,050	98,100	24,565	21,321	26,190	22,572
95,100	95,150	23,665	20,509	25,143	21,672	98,100	98,150	24,580	21,334	26,208	22,587
95,150	95,200	23,681	20,523	25,161	21,688	98,150	98,200	24,596	21,348	26,226	22,603
95,200	95,250	23,696	20,537	25,179	21,703	98,200	98,250	24,611	21,362	26,244	22,618
95,250	95,300	23,711	20,551	25,196	21,718	98,250	98,300	24,626	21,376	26,261	22,633
95,300	95,350	23,726	20,564	25,214	21,733	98,300	98,350	24,641	21,389	26,279	22,648
95,350	95,400	23,742	20,578	25,232	21,749	98,350	98,400	24,657	21,403	26,297	22,664
95,400	95,450	23,757	20,592	25,250	21,764	98,400	98,450	24,672	21,417	26,315	22,679
95,450	95,500	23,772	20,606	25,267	21,779	98,450	98,500	24,687	21,431	26,332	22,694
95,500	95,550	23,787	20,619	25,285	21,794	98,500	98,550	24,702	21,444	26,350	22,709
95,550	95,600	23,803	20,633	25,303	21,810	98,550	98,600	24,718	21,458	26,368	22,725
95,600	95,650	23,818	20,647	25,321	21,825	98,600	98,650	24,733	21,472	26,386	22,740
95,650	95,700	23,833	20,661	25,338	21,840	98,650	98,700	24,748	21,486	26,403	22,755
95,700	95,750	23,848	20,674	25,356	21,855	98,700	98,750	24,763	21,499	26,421	22,770
95,750	95,800	23,864	20,688	25,374	21,871	98,750	98,800	24,779	21,513	26,439	22,786
95,800	95,850	23,879	20,702	25,392	21,886	98,800	98,850	24,794	21,527	26,457	22,801
95,850	95,900	23,894	20,716	25,409	21,901	98,850	98,900	24,809	21,541	26,474	22,816
95,900	95,950	23,909	20,729	25,427	21,916	98,900	98,950	24,824	21,554	26,492	22,831
95,950	96,000	23,925	20,743	25,445	21,932	98,950	99,000	24,840	21,568	26,510	22,847
96,000						**99,000**					
96,000	96,050	23,940	20,757	25,463	21,947	99,000	99,050	24,855	21,582	26,528	22,862
96,050	96,100	23,955	20,771	25,480	21,962	99,050	99,100	24,870	21,596	26,545	22,877
96,100	96,150	23,970	20,784	25,498	21,977	99,100	99,150	24,885	21,609	26,563	22,892
96,150	96,200	23,986	20,798	25,516	21,993	99,150	99,200	24,901	21,623	26,581	22,908
96,200	96,250	24,001	20,812	25,534	22,008	99,200	99,250	24,916	21,637	26,599	22,923
96,250	96,300	24,016	20,826	25,551	22,023	99,250	99,300	24,931	21,651	26,616	22,938
96,300	96,350	24,031	20,839	25,569	22,038	99,300	99,350	24,946	21,664	26,634	22,953
96,350	96,400	24,047	20,853	25,587	22,054	99,350	99,400	24,962	21,678	26,652	22,969
96,400	96,450	24,062	20,867	25,605	22,069	99,400	99,450	24,977	21,692	26,670	22,984
96,450	96,500	24,077	20,881	25,622	22,084	99,450	99,500	24,992	21,706	26,687	22,999
96,500	96,550	24,092	20,894	25,640	22,099	99,500	99,550	25,007	21,719	26,705	23,014
96,550	96,600	24,108	20,908	25,658	22,115	99,550	99,600	25,023	21,733	26,723	23,030
96,600	96,650	24,123	20,922	25,676	22,130	99,600	99,650	25,038	21,747	26,741	23,045
96,650	96,700	24,138	20,936	25,693	22,145	99,650	99,700	25,053	21,761	26,758	23,060
96,700	96,750	24,153	20,949	25,711	22,160	99,700	99,750	25,068	21,774	26,776	23,075
96,750	96,800	24,169	20,963	25,729	22,176	99,750	99,800	25,084	21,788	26,794	23,091
96,800	96,850	24,184	20,977	25,747	22,191	99,800	99,850	25,099	21,802	26,812	23,106
96,850	96,900	24,199	20,991	25,764	22,206	99,850	99,900	25,114	21,816	26,829	23,121
96,900	96,950	24,214	21,004	25,782	22,221	99,900	99,950	25,129	21,829	26,847	23,136
96,950	97,000	24,230	21,018	25,800	22,237	99,950	100,000	25,145	21,843	26,865	23,152
97,000											
97,000	97,050	24,245	21,032	25,818	22,252						
97,050	97,100	24,260	21,046	25,835	22,267						
97,100	97,150	24,275	21,059	25,853	22,282						
97,150	97,200	24,291	21,073	25,871	22,298						
97,200	97,250	24,306	21,087	25,889	22,313						
97,250	97,300	24,321	21,101	25,906	22,328						
97,300	97,350	24,336	21,114	25,924	22,343						
97,350	97,400	24,352	21,128	25,942	22,359						
97,400	97,450	24,367	21,142	25,960	22,374						
97,450	97,500	24,382	21,156	25,977	22,389						
97,500	97,550	24,397	21,169	25,995	22,404						
97,550	97,600	24,413	21,183	26,013	22,420						
97,600	97,650	24,428	21,197	26,031	22,435						
97,650	97,700	24,443	21,211	26,048	22,450						
97,700	97,750	24,458	21,224	26,066	22,465						
97,750	97,800	24,474	21,238	26,084	22,481						
97,800	97,850	24,489	21,252	26,102	22,496						
97,850	97,900	24,504	21,266	26,119	22,511						
97,900	97,950	24,519	21,279	26,137	22,526						
97,950	98,000	24,535	21,293	26,155	22,542						

$100,000 or over — use the Tax Rate Schedules on page 71

* This column must also be used by a qualifying widow(er).

CORPORATION INCOME TAX RATES FOR 2001

¶ 33   Corporations

2001

| Taxable Income | | | | of the |
Over	But Not Over	Pay	% on + Excess	amount over—
$ 0—$ 50,000		$ 0	15 %	$ 0
50,000—	75,000	7,500	25	50,000
75,000—	100,000	13,750	34	75,000
100,000—	335,000	22,250	39	100,000
335,000—	10,000,000	113,900	34	335,000
10,000,000—	15,000,000	3,400,000	35	10,000,000
15,000,000—	18,333,333	5,150,000	38	15,000,000
18,333,333—	....	6,416,667	35	18,333,333

Taxable income of certain personal service corporations is taxed at a flat rate of 35%.

¶ 34   Controlled Group of Corporations

A controlled group of corporations is subject to the same rates as those listed above as though the group was one corporation. See ¶ 289.

¶ 35   Personal Holding Companies

In addition to the regular corporate income taxes, a special tax is imposed on any personal holding company. The additional tax is 39.1% (38.6% for tax years beginning in 2002) of undistributed personal holding company income. See ¶ 275.

¶ 36   Insurance Companies and Regulated Investment Companies

The regular corporate tax rates apply to a company's taxable income (see ¶ 2370). In the case of regulated investment companies, the corporate tax rates apply to investment company taxable income. See ¶ 2311.

¶ 37   Accumulated Earnings Tax

A tax (payable in addition to the regular tax payable by a corporation) is imposed at the rate of 39.1% (38.6% for tax years beginning in 2002) on accumulated taxable income exceeding the $250,000 ($150,000 for personal service corporations engaged in the field of health, law, engineering, architecture, accounting, actuarial science, performing arts, or consulting) minimum accumulated earnings credit. See ¶ 251.

¶ 38   Foreign Corporations

The income of a foreign corporation that is not effectively connected with a U.S. trade or business is taxed at a rate of 30%. Domestic corporate rates apply to the income of a foreign corporation that is effectively connected with a U.S. trade or business. See ¶ 2425.

¶ 33

¶ 39   Real Estate Investment Trusts

The regular corporate tax rates apply, but they apply to "real estate investment trust taxable income." See ¶ 2329.

ESTATE AND GIFT TAXES

¶ 40   Computation of Taxes

Estate Taxes. Estate taxes are computed by applying the unified rate schedule (¶ 42) to the aggregate of cumulative lifetime transfers and transfers at death and subtracting the gift taxes payable on the lifetime transfers. The unified rate schedule is effective for gifts made after December 31, 1976, and to estates of decedents dying after that date until the scheduled repeal of the estate tax in 2010 (Economic Growth and Relief Reconciliation Act of 2001 (P.L. 107-16)). See ¶ 2912 and following.

Gift Taxes. Gift taxes are computed by applying the unified rate schedule (¶ 42) to cumulative lifetime taxable transfers and subtracting the taxes payable for prior taxable periods. Although the estate tax is being repealed in 2010, the gift tax will remain in effect. There is an annual exclusion of $10,000 (projected to increase to $11,000 in 2002) per donee for gifts, with an annual maximum of $20,000 (projected to increase to $22,000 in 2002) per donee applicable to spouses who utilize gift-splitting. Additionally, there is an unlimited exclusion for payments of tuition and medical expenses. See ¶ 2906-¶ 2911.

Generation-Skipping Transfer Tax. The tax on generation-skipping transfers (GST) is computed with reference to a flat rate equal to the product of the maximum estate tax rate (55% in 2001, 50% in 2002) and the inclusion ratio with respect to the transfer. The GST tax is also scheduled to be repealed in 2010. See ¶ 2942.

¶ 41   Unified Credit

Amount of Credit. The applicable credit amount (formerly, the unified credit) for estates of decedents dying during 2001 is $220,550 ($345,800 in 2002 and 2003). The applicable credit amount exempts $675,000 (the applicable exclusion amount) from estate and gift tax liability in 2001 ($1 million in 2002 and 2003). The applicable exclusion amount for estate tax purposes will gradually increase to $3.5 million in 2009; however, for gift tax purposes, the applicable exclusion amount will remain at $1 million. It is subtracted from the taxpayer's estate or gift tax liability. Although the credit must be used to offset gift taxes on lifetime transfers, regardless of the amount so used, the full credit is allowed against the tentative estate tax at death.[1]

---

[1] This is so because, under Code Sec. 2001(b)(1), any gifts to which the unified credit was previously applied are added back to the taxable estate to compute the tentative estate tax. After reducing the tentative tax by the amount of gift taxes payable, the full unified credit amount is subtracted to arrive at estate tax payable. Thus, what may at first appear to be a double application of the unified credit is eliminated by way of a calculation that effectively increases the estate tax payable in the amount of the unified gift tax credit used to shelter lifetime gifts.

¶ 42   Unified Transfer Tax Rate Schedule

The unified rate schedule applying to estates of decedents dying and gifts made after 1983 and before 2002 appears below.

Table A—Unified Rate Schedule Through 2001

Column A	Column B	Column C	Column D
Taxable amount over	Taxable amount not over	Tax on amount in column A	Rate of tax on excess over amount in column A
			Percent
$ 0	$ 10,000	$ 0	18
10,000	20,000	1,800	20
20,000	40,000	3,800	22
40,000	60,000	8,200	24
60,000	80,000	13,000	26
80,000	100,000	18,200	28
100,000	150,000	23,800	30
150,000	250,000	38,800	32
250,000	500,000	70,800	34
500,000	750,000	155,800	37
750,000	1,000,000	248,300	39
1,000,000	1,250,000	345,800	41
1,250,000	1,500,000	448,300	43
1,500,000	2,000,000	555,800	45
2,000,000	2,500,000	780,800	49
2,500,000	3,000,000	1,025,800	53
3,000,000	. . . .	1,290,800	55

The top estate and gift tax rate will incrementally decrease to 45 percent between 2002 and 2009, the year prior to the scheduled repeal of the estate tax (Code Sec. 2001(c), as amended by P.L. 107-16). For estates of decedents dying, and gifts made, in 2002, the top estate and gift tax rate is as follows:

2002

Over (1)	But not over (2)	Tax on (1)	Rate on Excess (1)
$1,500,000	$2,000,000	$ 555,800	45
2,000,000	2,500,000	780,800	49
2,500,000	. . . .	1,025,800	50

The gift tax will continue after the repeal of the estate tax; however, the top tax rate will be 35 percent applicable to transfers over $500,000. Although the estate tax is scheduled to be repealed in 2010, because of budgetary constraints, it will be reestablished in 2011 under 2001 rules. The changes are discussed in Chapter 29.

Benefits phased out for transfers exceeding $10,000,000. The benefits of the graduated rates and the unified credit under the unified transfer tax system are phased out beginning with cumulative transfers rising above $10,000,000. This is accomplished by adding five percent of the excess of any transfer over $10,000,000 to the tentative tax computed in determining the ultimate transfer tax liability. For estates of decedents dying, and gifts made, after 1987 and before 1998, the tax is levied on amounts transferred in excess of $10,000,000 but not exceeding $21,040,000, in order to recapture the benefit of any transfer tax rate below 55 percent as well as the unified credit. For decedents dying after 1997 and before 2002

(the surcharge was repealed by P.L. 107-16), the tax is levied on amounts in excess of $10,000,000 but not exceeding $17,184,000.

¶ 43   Credit for State Death Taxes

The table below is to be used in calculating the amount of the credit available for state death taxes paid with respect to property included in a decedent's gross estate. However, for estates of decedents dying in 2002, the state death tax credit will be reduced by 25 percent beginning in 2002 (Code Sec. 2011(b), as amended by P.L. 107-16). Further reductions will occur as follows: 50 percent for the estates of decedents dying in 2003 and 75 percent for the estates of decedents dying in 2004. Looking ahead, the credit will be repealed completely for the estates of decedents dying after 2004, at which time it will become a deduction until the phaseout of the federal estate tax is complete in 2010.

State Death Tax Credit Table [1]

Adjusted Taxable Estate [2]		Credit =	+	%	Of Excess Over
At least	But less than				
$ 0	$ 40,000	$ 0	0	$ 0
40,000	90,000	0	.8	40,000
90,000	140,000	400	1.6	90,000
140,000	240,000	1,200	2.4	140,000
240,000	440,000	3,600	3.2	240,000
440,000	640,000	10,000	4	440,000
640,000	840,000	18,000	4.8	640,000
840,000	1,040,000	27,600	5.6	840,000
1,040,000	1,540,000	38,800	6.4	1,040,000
1,540,000	2,040,000	70,800	7.2	1,540,000
2,040,000	2,540,000	106,800	8	2,040,000
2,540,000	3,040,000	146,800	8.8	2,540,000
3,040,000	3,540,000	190,800	9.6	3,040,000
3,540,000	4,040,000	238,800	10.4	3,540,000
4,040,000	5,040,000	290,800	11.2	4,040,000
5,040,000	6,040,000	402,800	12	5,040,000
6,040,000	7,040,000	522,800	12.8	6,040,000
7,040,000	8,040,000	650,800	13.6	7,040,000
8,040,000	9,040,000	786,800	14.4	8,040,000
9,040,000	10,040,000	930,800	15.2	9,040,000
10,040,000	....	1,082,800	16	10,040,000

¶ 45   Nonresident Aliens

The gift and estate tax rates that are applicable to U.S. citizens are also applicable to the estate of a nonresident alien. Where permitted by treaty, the estate of a nonresident alien is allowed a credit equal to the unified credit available to a U.S. citizen multiplied by the proportion of the decedent's entire gross estate situated in the United States. In computing the credit, property is not treated as situated in the United States if such property is exempt from tax under any treaty. In other cases, a unified credit of $13,000 is allowed.

---

[1] There is a limitation on the credit in estates of nonresident aliens. See Code Sec. 2102.

[2] The adjusted taxable estate is the taxable estate reduced by $60,000.

The additional 5% rate applicable to transfers in excess of $10 million but not exceeding $17,184,000 is adjusted to reflect the fact that in some cases the estate of a nonresident noncitizen does not receive the same unified credit available to U.S. citizens. Accordingly, the additional 5% rate applies to the taxable transfers of nonresident noncitizens prior to 2002 in excess of $10 million only to the extent necessary to phase out the benefit of the graduated rates actually allowed by statute or treaty.

The estate of a resident of a U.S. possession is entitled to a unified credit equal to the greater of (1) $13,000 or (2) $46,800 multiplied by the proportion of the decedent's entire gross estate situated in the United States. See ¶ 2940 and ¶ 2941.

OTHER TAXES

¶ 47   Self-Employment Taxes

A tax of 15.3% is imposed on net earnings from self-employment. The rate consists of a 12.4% component for old-age, survivors, and disability insurance (OASDI) and a 2.9% component for medicare. The OASDI rate (12.4%) applies to net earnings within the OASDI earnings base, which is $80,400 for 2001 and $84,900 for 2002. The medicare rate (2.9%) applies to all net earnings since there is no limit on the amount of earnings subject to the medicare portion of the tax.

¶ 49   Social Security Taxes

Social Security, Hospital Insurance. A combined tax rate of 7.65% (6.2% for old-age, survivors, and disability insurance (OASDI) and 1.45% for hospital insurance (medicare)) is imposed on both employer and employee. The OASDI rate (6.2%) applies to wages within the OASDI wage base, which is $80,400 for 2001 and $84,900 for 2002. The medicare rate (1.45%) applies to all wages since there is no limit on the amount of earnings subject to the medicare portion of the tax.

Medicare Payments. Medicare Part B premiums ($50 per month for 2001 and $54 per month for 2002) qualify as deductible medical expenses. See ¶ 1019.

Unemployment Compensation. A tax rate of 6.2% is imposed on the first $7,000 of wages paid to a covered employee by an employer who employs one or more persons in covered employment in each of 20 days in a year, each day being in a different week, or who has a payroll for covered employment of at least $1,500 in a calendar quarter in the current or preceding calendar year. Because employers are allowed credits against the 6.2% FUTA rate through participation in state unemployment insurance laws, the net FUTA rate actually paid by most employers is 0.8% except when credit reductions are in effect in a state. (The tax also applies to any person who paid any one household employee cash wages of $1,300 or more in 2001 (and 2002) or who paid total cash wages of at least $1,000 for domestic service during any calendar quarter in the current or preceding calendar year.) For wages paid in 2001 and 2002, the FUTA rate remains at 6.2%.

Railroad Retirement Tax. For 2001, a tier I tax of 7.65% (consisting of a medicare portion (1.45%) and an OASDI portion (6.2%)) applies to employers and employees. The OASDI portion (6.2%) is imposed on annual compensation within a compensation base of $80,400 for 2001 and $84,900 for 2002. There is no limit on the amount of earnings subject to the medicare portion of the tax. A tier II tax of 4.9% for employees and 16.1% for employers is imposed on annual compensation within a compensation base of $59,700 in 2001 ($63,000 in 2002).

¶ 47

¶ 53   Excise Taxes

Identified below are various excise taxes.

Gasoline

Gasoline (per gallon) .... 18.4¢

Gasohol

Gasohol, 10% alcohol (per gallon) .... 13.1¢
Gasohol, 7.7% alcohol (per gallon) .... 14.242¢
Gasohol, 5.7% alcohol (per gallon) .... 15.322¢
Nongasoline/ethanol mixture (per gallon) .... 19.1¢
Nonethanol, 10% alcohol (per gallon) .... 12.4¢
Nonethanol, 7.7% alcohol (per gallon) .... 13.78¢
Nonethanol, 5.7% alcohol (per gallon) .... 14.98¢
Nongasoline/nonethanol mixture (per gallon) .... 18.4¢
Gasoline, if used to produce 10% ethanol-based gasohol (per gallon) .... 14.555¢
Gasoline, if used to produce 7.7% ethanol-based gasohol (per gallon) .... 15.513¢
Gasoline, if used to produce 5.7% ethanol-based gasohol (per gallon) .... 16.308¢
Gasoline, if used to produce 10% non-ethanol-based gasohol (per gallon) .... 13.777¢
Gasoline, if used to produce 7.7% non-ethanol-based gasohol (per gallon) ...... 14.929¢
Gasoline, if used to produce 5.7% non-ethanol-based gasohol (per gallon) ...... 15.885¢

Special Fuels

Diesel fuel (except if used on a farm for farming purposes) (per gallon) .... 24.4¢
Diesel fuel sold for diesel/alcohol mixture, ethanol-based (per gallon) .... 21.11¢
Diesel fuel sold for diesel/alcohol mixture, non-ethanol-based (per gallon) .... 20.44¢
Diesel/alcohol mixture, ethanol-based (per gallon) .... 19.1¢
Diesel/alcohol mixture, non-ethanol-based (per gallon) .... 18.4¢
Diesel fuel for use in trains (per gallon) .... 4.4¢
Diesel fuel for certain intercity buses (per gallon) .... 7.4¢
Special motor fuel (per gallon) .... 18.4¢
Special motor fuel/alcohol mixture, ethanol (per gallon) .... 13¢
Special motor fuel/alcohol mixture, non-ethanol (per gallon) .... 12.4¢
Inland waterways fuel use tax (per gallon) .... 24.4¢
Commercial aviation fuel (other than gasoline) (jet fuel) (per gallon) .... 4.4¢
Noncommercial aviation fuel (gasoline) (per gallon) .... 19.4¢
Noncommercial aviation fuel (other than gasoline) (jet fuel) (per gallon) .... 21.9¢
Noncommercial aviation fuel/alcohol mixture, ethanol (per gallon) .... 8.6¢
Noncommercial aviation fuel sold for aviation/alcohol mixture, ethanol (per gallon) .... 9.444¢
Noncommercial aviation fuel/alcohol mixture, non-ethanol (per gallon) .... 7.9¢
Noncommercial aviation fuel sold for aviation/alcohol mixture, non-ethanol (per gallon) .... 8.778¢
Compressed natural gas (per thousand cubic feet) .... 48.54¢
Liquefied petroleum gas (LPG) .... 13.6¢
Liquefied natural gas .... 11.9¢
Kerosene (per gallon) .... 24.4¢
Kerosene sold for kerosene/alcohol mixture, ethanol-based (per gallon) .... 21.11¢
Kerosene sold for kerosene/alcohol mixture, non-ethanol-based (per gallon) .... 20.44¢
Kerosene/alcohol mixture, ethanol-based (per gallon) .... 19¢
Kerosene/alcohol mixture, non-ethanol-based (per gallon) .... 18.4¢

LUXURY ITEMS
Passenger vehicles (2001) .... 4% of excess over $38,000

HEAVY TRUCKS, TRAILERS
Truck chassis or body (suitable for use with a vehicle in excess of 33,000 lbs. gross
    vehicle weight) .... 12% of retail price
Trailer and semitrailer chassis or body (suitable for use with a trailer or semitrailer
    in excess of 26,000 lbs. gross vehicle weight) .... 12% of retail price
Parts and accessories installed on taxable vehicles within 6 months after being
    placed in service (when cost of parts or accessories exceeds $200) . 12% of retail price

HIGHWAY-TYPE TIRES
Tires not more than 40 lbs. .... No tax
Tires 41 lbs. through 70 lbs. .... .15¢ per pound in excess of 40 pounds
Tires 71 lbs. through 90 lbs. .... $4.50 + 30¢ per pound in excess of 70 pounds
Tires over 90 lbs. .... $10.50 + 50¢ per pound in excess of 90 pounds

GAS GUZZLER TAX
Mileage ratings per gallon of at least 22.5 .... $ 0
Mileage ratings per gallon of at least 21.5 but less than 22.5 1,000
Mileage ratings per gallon of at least 20.5 but less than 21.5 1,300
Mileage ratings per gallon of at least 19.5 but less than 20.5 1,700
Mileage ratings per gallon of at least 18.5 but less than 19.5 2,100
Mileage ratings per gallon of at least 17.5 but less than 18.5 2,600
Mileage ratings per gallon of at least 16.5 but less than 17.5 3,000
Mileage ratings per gallon of at least 15.5 but less than 16.5 3,700
Mileage ratings per gallon of at least 14.5 but less than 15.5 4,500
Mileage ratings per gallon of at least 13.5 but less than 14.5 5,400
Mileage ratings per gallon of at least 12.5 but less than 13.5 6,400
Mileage ratings per gallon of less than 12.5 7,700

FACILITIES AND SERVICES
Communications
Telephone and teletypewriter service, prepaid telephone cards 3%
Transportation by air
Domestic passenger tickets .... .7.5% plus $2.75 (from 1/1/01-12/31/01) for each flight
                       segment (excepting segments to or from rural airports)
International passenger tickets (per person per departure) (from
    1/1/01-12/31/01) $6.40
International passenger tickets (per person for each arrival and departure) (from
    1/1/01-12/31/01) $12.80
Air freight waybill 6.25%

Transportation by water
Persons $3.00
Port use tax on imports (harbor maintenance tax) .... $0.125% of cargo value

ALCOHOL TAXES
Distilled spirits (per gallon)... $13.50
Beer (per barrel) .... $18.00 (31 gallons or less)

Wines
Not more than 14% alcohol (per gallon) $1.07
More than 14 to 21% alcohol (per gallon) $1.57
More than 21 to 24% alcohol (per gallon) $3.15

¶ 53

Artificially carbonated wines (per gallon)................................. $3.30

More than 24% alcohol (per gallon)..................................... $13.50

Champagne and other sparkling wines (per gallon) $3.40

TOBACCO TAXES

Cigarettes (per 1,000) ....$17 or $35.70 per 1,000

Cigarette papers (per 50 papers).. $1.06

Cigarette tubes (per 50 tubes) .... 2.13¢

Cigars (per 1,000)..................................$1.594 to $42.50 per 1,000

Snuff (per pound) .... 51¢

Chewing tobacco (per pound) .... 17¢

Pipe tobacco (per pound)........... .... 95.67¢

Roll-you-own tobacco (per pound) .... 95.67¢

WAGERING TAXES

State authorized wagers placed with bookmakers and lottery operators 0.25%

License fee on person accepting wagers (each year) $50

HIGHWAY MOTOR VEHICLE USE TAX

Vehicles of less than 55,000 lbs. ....No tax

Vehicles of 55,000 lbs.—75,000 lbs. (per year)...$100 per year + $22 for each 1,000 lbs. (or fraction thereof) over 55,000 lbs.

Vehicles over 75,000 lbs. (per year) $550

FIREARMS

Transfer taxes (per firearm) .... $5 (concealable weapons) or $200

Occupational taxes (per year) ... $1,000 (importers or manufacturers), or $500 (dealers, small importers or manufacturers)

Pistols and revolvers .... 10% of mfr. price

Firearms other than pistols and revolvers .... 11% of mfr. price

Ammunition (shells and cartridges)............................ 11% of mfr. price

OTHER TAXES

Electric outboard motors and sonar devices .... 3% of sales price, not to exceed $30

Sport fishing equipment .... 10% of mfr. price

Arrow component parts (point, nock, shaft or vane) .... 12.4% of mfr. price

Bows.. 11% of mfr. price

Coal—underground mines (per ton sold)................................. $1.10

Coal—surface mines (per ton sold) .... 55¢

Vaccines.................................... 75¢ per dose on taxable vaccines

Preparing Income Tax Returns

CHECKLISTS

¶ 55   Checklist for Items of Income

The determination of whether an item of income is includible in income and, thus, taxable, or whether it is excludable from income is crucial to the determination of tax liability. An item that is includible increases tax liability, depending on the amount, whereas an excludable item decreases tax liability. The following chart, which is arranged alphabetically by income item, indicates whether the item is includible or excludable from income. A reference to further details in the STANDARD FEDERAL TAX REPORTER is also provided.

Income Item	Includible in Income	Paragraph Reference
Accident and health insurance premiums, employer-paid (except for long-term care benefits provided through flexible spending accounts and subject to limitation as to medical savings accounts)	No	¶ 6803.01
Accident and health plans proceeds (under insurance purchased by taxpayer or under employee supported plans) where premiums did not give taxpayer a previous medical expense deduction	No	¶ 6662.035
Agreement not to compete, payments received for	Yes	¶ 30,422.033
Airline deregulation benefits, special rule, unemployment compensation	Yes	¶ 6412.15
Alimony, support and separate maintenance payments, receipt of	Yes	¶ 6094.01
Allowances received by dependents of members of the Armed Forces	No	¶ 7501.01
Annuities (amounts in excess of cost)	Yes	¶ 6114.022
Annuities, interest on advance premiums	Yes	¶ 5504.023
Antitrust action, punitive damages recovered	Yes	¶ 5900.03
Armed Forces pay (except "combat zone" or "missing" status pay)	Yes	¶ 5507.037; ¶ 7082.021
Athletic facilities on employer's premises, value of use	No	¶ 7438.057
Awards, generally	Yes	¶ 6204.01
Back pay	Yes	¶ 5507.129
Bad debts, prior taxes and interest on taxes, recovery of, provided no tax benefit in prior year	No	¶ 7062.043; ¶ 7062.047
Bargain purchases from employer to extent discount exceeds gross profit percentage	Yes	¶ 7438.026
Barter income	Yes	¶ 5508.028
Beauty contest winners, receipt of scholarships and amounts for personal appearances	Yes	¶ 7183.305

References in Checklists are to the 2002 Standard Federal Tax Reports.

¶ 55

Income Item	Includible in Income	Paragraph Reference
Bequests and devises, generally	No	¶ 6553.01
Bonds, state, city, etc., interest on, generally	No	¶ 6602.01
Bonuses	Yes	¶ 5507.024
Buried treasure	Yes	¶ 5504.6916
Business interruption insurance proceeds:		
. based on income experience	Yes	¶ 29,650.053
. based on per diem idleness	No	¶ 29,650.053
Business profits	Yes	¶ 5504.01
Business subsidies for construction or contributions by customer or potential customer	Yes	¶ 7202.021
Capital contributions to corporation	No	¶ 7202.01
Car pool receipts by car owner for transportation of other employees	No	¶ 5504.144
Car used for business purposes by full-time car salesperson, value of use	No	¶ 7438.038
Checks, uncashed by payee, for previously deducted items	Yes	¶ 5507.698
Child or dependent care plan benefits, employer-subsidized, limited	No	¶ 7381.01
Child support payments	No	¶ 6094.027
Christmas bonuses from employer, based on percentage of salary (aside from token gifts such as hams, turkeys, etc., given for goodwill)	Yes	¶ 5507.2942
Civil Rights Act violation, back pay recovery	Yes	¶ 5900.021
Clergy fees and contributions received unless earned as agent of religious order	Yes	¶ 5507.04
"Combat zone" pay, military	No	¶ 5507.037; ¶ 7082.021
Commissions	Yes	¶ 5507.022
Commodity credit loans, receipt of (optional)	Yes	¶ 6304.01
Compensation, property received, value of	Yes	¶ 5508.021
Contract cancellation, payments received for	Yes	¶ 21,005.126
Damages:		
. back pay	Yes	¶ 5507.129
. loss of anticipatory benefits (business)	Yes	¶ 5900.14
. personal physical injuries or sickness	No	¶ 5900.021; ¶ 6662.04
. slander or libel of personal reputation	Yes	¶ 5900.025
Death benefits, employer-paid	Yes	¶ 6507.01
Debts, nongratuitous cancellation of	Yes	¶ 5802.021
Defamation damage award, compensating injury to business and professional reputation	Yes	¶ 5900.025
Dependent care assistance program payments, limited	No	¶ 7381.01
Disability payments, other than for loss of wages, all taxpayers, including veterans	No	¶ 6662.01
Disability pensions, Veterans' Administration	No	¶ 6662.01; ¶ 6662.046
Disaster unemployment payments	Yes	¶ 6412.021
Discharge of indebtedness, nongratuitous	Yes	¶ 5802.021
Dividends, stock distributed in lieu of money	Yes	¶ 15,402.01
Drawing account, excess cancelled by employer	Yes	¶ 5507.154
Educational assistance, employer-provided under a nondiscriminatory plan, for courses beginning after December 31, 2001 (including graduate-level courses)	No	¶ 7353.01
Embezzlement proceeds	Yes	¶ 5901.021
Employee achievement awards, qualified	No	¶ 5507.024; ¶ 6204.03
Employee discount, qualified	No	¶ 7438.025

References in Checklists are to the 2002 Standard Federal Tax Reports.

¶ **55**

Income Item	Includible in Income	Paragraph Reference
Employment contract, amounts received by employee for cancellation	Yes	¶ 5507.297; ¶ 21,005.116
Endowment policies, generally as to non-annuity payments until cost is recovered...............	No	¶ 6114.01; ¶ 6114.0405
Farm income	Yes	¶ 5602.01
Farmers, government payments to offset operating losses or lack of profits........................	Yes	¶ 5602.03
Fellowships and scholarships, degree programs	No	¶ 7183.01
Financial counseling fees, employer-paid	Yes	¶ 5507.2927
Foreign earned income, limited election	No	¶ 28,049.01
Foster parents, reimbursements for care of a qualified foster child	No	¶ 7402.01
Fringe benefits, if no additional cost service, qualified employee discount, working condition fringe, *de minimis* fringe, qualified transportation fringe, qualified moving expense reimbursement	No	¶ 7438.01
Future services, prepayment for.................	Yes	¶ 21,005.027
Gain on sale of personal residence:		
. up to $250,000 ($500,000 for joint filers)	No	¶ 7266.024
Gains:		
. condemnation of nonresidential property unless award is used for replacement	Yes	¶ 29,650.01; ¶ 29,650.319
. discount on later sale or redemption of bonds purchased with excess number of interest coupons detached (stripped bonds)..................	Yes	¶ 31,481.023
. obligations purchased or satisfied for less than face value...................................	Yes	¶ 5804.51
. partner's sale of asset to partnership...........	Yes	¶ 25,182.01
. sales of depreciable property	Yes	¶ 30,909.01
. sales of goodwill	Yes	¶ 30,422.032
. sales of patents	Yes	¶ 30,653.01
. sales of property, generally	Yes	¶ 5700.01
. sales of stock in foreign corporations	Yes	¶ 30,968.01
. sales of stock of foreign investment company	Yes	¶ 30,921.01
. swap-fund transfers	Yes	¶ 16,405.03
Gambling winnings:		
. illegal	Yes	¶ 5901.40
. legal	Yes	¶ 5504.22
Gifts	No	¶ 6553.03
Government employees, additional compensation as inducement to accept foreign service employment ("post differentials")......................	Yes	¶ 28,063.01
Health insurance proceeds, not paid by the insured's employer or financed by the insured's employer through contributions that were not included in the employee's gross income	No	¶ 6662.035
Hedging transactions, commodity futures transactions	Yes	¶ 30,426.03
Hobby income (nonprofit activities, deductions limited)	Yes	¶ 12,177.01
Illegal transactions, gains from: gambling, betting, lotteries, illegal businesses, embezzlement, protection money, etc........................	Yes	¶ 5901.01
Illness, employee's compensation during, except to extent qualifying as insurance benefits	Yes	¶ 6662.0355
Incentive stock options	No	¶ 19,806.021

References in Checklists are to the 2002 Standard Federal Tax Reports.

¶ 55

Income Item	Includible in Income	Paragraph Reference
Income tax refunds:		
. state, to extent of tax benefit from prior deduction	Yes	¶ 5504.041
Inheritances	No	¶ 6553.01
Insider's profits	Yes	¶ 5504.2645
Insurance proceeds:		
. business interruption insurance, based on lost income	Yes	¶ 29,650.053
. use or occupancy, actual loss of net profits	Yes	¶ 29,650.053
Interest-free loans:		
. loans in excess of *de minimis* amount, deemed interest	Yes	¶ 43,960.01
. loans within *de minimis* amount	No	¶ 43,960.066
Interest on:		
. bank deposits or accounts	Yes	¶ 5704.023
. bonds, debentures, or notes	Yes	¶ 5704.044
. claim awarded by judgment	Yes	¶ 5704.279
. condemnation awards	Yes	¶ 30,575.166
. deferred legacies	Yes	¶ 5704.347
. federal obligations	Yes	¶ 6602.03
. insurance contracts	Yes	¶ 6504.045
. refund of federal taxes	Yes	¶ 21,005.922
Involuntary conversions, gain from, if reinvested	No	¶ 29,650.01
Juror's mileage allowance	No	¶ 5504.5006
Jury fees	Yes	¶ 5507.021
Layoff pay benefits:		
. supplemental unemployment benefit plan, company-financed	Yes	¶ 5507.032
Lease cancellation, payments received for	Yes	¶ 5706.031
Leased retail space, cash or rent reductions received for construction or improvements	No	¶ 5706.025
Legal services plan, employer contributions and value of benefits received	Yes	¶ 7244.01
Lessee's improvements, value of to lessor upon termination of lease	No	¶ 7022.01
Libel or slander of personal reputation, exemplary damages	Yes	¶ 5900.03
Life insurance dividends, veterans' converted, interest on	No	¶ 5504.74
Life insurance, group-term premiums paid by employer, to extent of employer's cost of $50,000 or less of insurance	No	¶ 6367.01
Life insurance proceeds, paid on death of the insured	No	¶ 6504.01
Living expenses paid by insurance while damaged home being repaired	No	¶ 7302.01
Lodging and meals, *unless* furnished on employer's premises for employer's convenience and the employee must accept lodging as a condition of employment	Yes	¶ 7222.01; ¶ 7222.021
Lodging, cost of, furnished on employer's premises for employer's convenience and employee must accept lodging as a condition of employment	No	¶ 7222.021
Losses, previously deducted, reimbursement for or expense items	Yes	¶ 7062.01
Meals, cost of, furnished on employer's premises for employer's convenience	No	¶ 7222.01
Medical care reimbursements, employer-financed accident and health plan	No	¶ 6702.01
Mileage allowance	Yes	¶ 5507.3267
Military personnel, basic pay	Yes	¶ 5507.037

References in Checklists are to the 2002 Standard Federal Tax Reports.

¶ 55

Income Item	Includible in Income	Paragraph Reference
Military service, employer-payments to employees...	Yes	¶ 5507.107
Mortgage indebtedness, prepayment at a discount to the extent of the discount	Yes	¶ 5802.295
Moving expenses, qualified, employer-reimbursement (under qualified fringe benefit rules)	No	¶ 12,623.035
Mustering-out pay, military personnel.............	Yes	¶ 5507.037
National Labor Relations Board, back-pay award ...	Yes	¶ 5507.129
National Service Life Insurance dividends	No	¶ 5504.74
Nobel prize and similar awards if donated by recipient to qualified entity	No	¶ 6204.025
Obligations, federal interest on	Yes	¶ 6602.03
Old age, disability, survivors' benefit payments, Social Security or Railroad Retirement Acts, below base amount..................................	No	¶ 6421.03
Parsonage, rental value of, furnished to a minister or rabbi as part of compensation; rental allowances if used to rent or provide a home	No	¶ 6852.01
Partnership, distributive share of taxable income	Yes	¶ 25,124.01
Patents, sale to controlled foreign corporation.......	Yes	¶ 30,982.01
Peace Corps volunteers, basic living and travel allowances	No	¶ 28,063.01
Pensions:		
. annuities, etc., for personal injuries or sickness resulting from active service in armed forces of any country, National Oceanic and Atmospheric Administration, or U.S. Public Health Service ..	No	¶ 6662.045
. distributions attributable to employer contributions	Yes	¶ 6140.0236; ¶ 6140.03
Personal physical injuries, damages	No	¶ 6662.01
Political campaign contributions, with exceptions ...	No	¶ 6553.42
Prizes	Yes	¶ 6204.01
Professional fees.............................	Yes	¶ 5507.022
Pulitzer prize and similar awards if donated by recipient to qualified entity	No	¶ 6204.025
Punitive damages	Yes	¶ 5900.03
Purchases, nondiscriminatory employee-discounts ...	No	¶ 7438.025
Railroad Retirement Act benefits, below base amount	No	¶ 6421.01
Rebates, credits, price reductions received by customers..................................	No	¶ 5504.492
Rent reductions received by retail tenants for construction or improvements	No	¶ 5706.025
Rents	Yes	¶ 5706.01
Retirement pay attributable to employer contributions other than veterans' disability retirement pay...........................	Yes	¶ 5507.033
Reward, informer's	Yes	¶ 5504.2642
Royalties	Yes	¶ 5706.01
Salaries, including those of state and federal employees and amounts employer withholds for income, Social Security, and Railroad Retirement taxes...................................	Yes	¶ 5507.021; ¶ 5507.043; ¶ 5507.044
Scholarships and fellowships, degree programs, qualified..................................	No	¶ 7183.01
Security deposits, when retained by lessor	Yes	¶ 21,005.027
Sickness and injury benefits:		
. employer's plan, subject to limitations	No	¶ 6662.035
. workers' compensation equivalent..............	No	¶ 6662.025

References in Checklists are to the 2002 Standard Federal Tax Reports.

¶ 55

Income Item	Includible in Income	Paragraph Reference
Social Security old age, disability and survivor's benefits, below base amount	No	¶ 6421.01
State contracts, profits on	Yes	¶ 5504.023; ¶ 5511
Stock distributions in general	No	¶ 15,402.01
. convertible preferred stock or debentures	Yes	¶ 15,402.01
. disproportionate distributions	Yes	¶ 15,402.01
. distributions of common and preferred stock	Yes	¶ 15,402.01
. dividends on preferred stock	Yes	¶ 15,402.01
. increasing shareholder's proportionate interest ...	Yes	¶ 15,402.01
. in lieu of money	Yes	¶ 15,402.01
Stock options incentive	No	¶ 19,806.021
Strike benefits, generally.......................	Yes	¶ 6553.03
Strike benefits, union and non-union employees in need, paid in form of food, clothes, etc.	No	¶ 6553.03
Supper money, employer-paid, occasional due to overtime work	No	¶ 7438.053
Supplemental security income (SSI) payments	No	¶ 5507.034; ¶ 6421.021
Support payment, received from former spouse......	Yes	¶ 6094.01
Surviving spouse, decedent's salary continued, limited depending on intent........................	No	¶ 5507.4741
Survivor annuities, paid to family of public safety officer	No	¶ 5507.045; ¶ 6507.05
Taxes:		
. employees', employer-paid	Yes	¶ 5508.046
. refunds of, not previously deducted or deducted without tax benefit	No	¶ 5504.041; ¶ 7062.043
Tenancy, payments for surrender of..............	Yes	¶ 30,575.206
Tips	Yes	¶ 5507.023
Treasure trove	Yes	¶ 5504.6916
Treaty-exempt income	No	¶ 26,805.001
Tuition, employer-paid under qualified plans for classes beginning after December 31, 2001 (including graduate-level courses)	No	¶ 7353.01
Unemployment benefit plans, supplemental payments	Yes	¶ 6412.021
Unemployment benefits	Yes	¶ 6412.021
U.S. Savings Bonds, earned increase during year, if cash-method taxpayer elects..................	Yes	¶ 6602.04
Use and occupancy insurance proceeds, income experience	Yes	¶ 29,650.053
Vacation fund allowance, union agreement	Yes	¶ 5507.47
Veterans Administration payments	No	¶ 5504.027
Veterans' benefits, generally....................	No	¶ 5504.027
Veterans' bonuses, state	No	¶ 5504.775
Wages.....................................	Yes	¶ 5507.021
Workers' Compensation Acts, payments under	No	¶ 6662.01; ¶ 6662.025
"Wrap-around" annuity contracts sold by life insurance companies, interest on	Yes	¶ 6114.48

References in Checklists are to the 2002 Standard Federal Tax Reports.

¶ 55

¶ 57 Checklist for Deductions

The Internal Revenue Code permits a number of wide-ranging deductions that may be taken into account in arriving at taxable income. However, the Code contains a number of rules and restrictions concerning the expenses that qualify as deductions and the taxpayers who may claim them. Although deductions generally reduce taxable income, deductions from gross income, available to all qualifying taxpayers, must be distinguished from deductions from adjusted gross income, available only to those taxpayers who itemize. Certain miscellaneous itemized deductions, including unreimbursed employee business expenses and investment expenses, are deductible by an individual only if the aggregate amount of such deductions exceeds two percent of adjusted gross income (see ¶ 6064.01 of the STANDARD FEDERAL TAX REPORTER). In addition, deductions that can be taken currently must be distinguished from those that can be taken over a number of tax years through depreciation or amortization.

The chart below lists a number of expenses that a taxpayer might incur. The chart indicates for each expense a symbol(s) representing the possible availability of a deduction, its timing, and whether it is deductible from gross income or adjusted gross income. Many deductions have special rules. The chart also provides the STANDARD FEDERAL TAX REPORTER paragraph number where further information on the deduction may be found.

The following symbols are used:

D/GI = Deductible from gross income

D/AGI = Deductible from adjusted gross income

D/Am = Deductible over a period of time

ND = Nondeductible

Abandonment of business real
property . . . . .D/GI, ¶ 9902.177
Accident and health plans
. employer contributions . . . . .D/GI,
¶ 8522.386
Accounting fees
. business . . . . .D/GI, ¶ 8520.315
. capital transactions . . . . . .D/Am,
¶ 13,709.01
. connected with trade or
business . . . . .D/GI, ¶ 8520.315
. investors . . . . . D/AGI, ¶ 12,523.03
. organization of business . . . .D/Am,
¶ 12,371.01, ¶ 13,352.01
. reorganization of business . . . .ND,
¶ 13,709.83
Accounting system, installation . . . .D/GI,
¶ 13,709.135
Administrative expenses of estate . D/AGI,
¶ 24,308.021
Admissions to political dinners,
programs, inaugural balls, etc. . . . ND,
¶ 14,552.025
Advertising expenses
. business cards . . .D/GI, ¶ 8851.133
. catalogs
. . long term . .D/Am, ¶ 21,817.2075

. generally . . . . . . .D/GI, ¶ 8851.01
. home demonstrations . . . . . .D/GI,
¶ 8851.1337
. political convention
programs and other political
publications . . . . .ND, ¶ 14,552.021
. prizes and contests . . . . . . .D/GI,
¶ 8851.1657
. promotional activities . . . . .D/GI,
¶ 8851.1659
Airline pilot, special clothing . . . . D/AGI,
¶ 8524.265
Airplane, heavy maintenance
expenses . . . . .D/GI, ¶ 8526.5175
Alcohol fuels credit, unused . . . . . .D/Am,
¶ 12,430.01
Alimony payments . . . . .D/GI, ¶ 12,573.01
Amortization of premium on
taxable bonds (optional) . . . . D/AGI,
¶ 11,855.01
Appraisal fees
. acquisition of capital asset . . . .ND,
¶ 13,709.121
. connection with trade or
business . . . . . D/AGI, ¶ 8520.3152
Architect's fees (capital
expenditure) . . . . . .D/Am, ¶ 13,709.149

References in Checklists are to the 2002 Standard Federal Tax Reports.

¶ 57

Attorney's and accountant's fees in contesting tax claims (nonbusiness) ...... D/AGI, ¶ 8526.462

Attorney's fees

. accounting suit by former partner, defense of .... D/GI, ¶ 13,603.243

. acquisition of corporate control .... ND, ¶ 8526.4213

. business debts, collection of .D/GI, ¶ 8526.429

. condemnation proceeding, defense of .... ND, ¶ 8526.4198

. disbarment proceedings .... D/GI, ¶ 8526.032

. divorce, ¶ 13,603.223

.. obtaining alimony ...... D/GI, ¶ 13,603.223

.. proceedings.... ND, ¶ 13,603.223

.. property settlement .... ND, ¶ 13,603.223

. personal affairs ... ND, ¶ 13,603.01

. slander prosecution (personal) ...... ND, ¶ 13,603.253

. tax advice on investments . D/AGI, ¶ 12,523.346

. title clearance

.. land .... ND, ¶ 8526.469

.. stock .... ND, ¶ 13,709.93

. will preparation .ND, ¶ 13,603.259

Automobile expenses

. business use by employee

.. unreimbursed . D/AGI, ¶ 8590.01

. business use by self-employed person

.. chauffeur's salary .... D/GI, ¶ 8590.1344

.. cost of car .... D/GI, D/Am, ¶ 8590.033

.. garage rentals .D/GI, ¶ 8590.024

.. gas .... D/GI, ¶ 8590.024

.. insurance .... D/GI, ¶ 8590.252

.. license fees ... D/GI, ¶ 8590.024

.. loss on sale .... D/GI, ¶ 8590.037

.. oil and lubrication ...... D/GI, ¶ 8590.024

.. parking...... D/GI, ¶ 8590.024

.. repairs ...... D/GI, ¶ 8590.024

.. tires .... D/GI, ¶ 8590.024

.. washing ..... D/GI, ¶ 8590.024

. nonbusiness casualty loss (limited) ..... D/AGI, ¶ 10,005.01

. pleasure use .... ND, ¶ 13,603.109

Bad debts, ¶ 10,650.01

. business ..... D/GI, ¶ 10,650.021

. nonbusiness ... D/GI, ¶ 10,650.021, ¶ 10,700.01, ¶ 10,700.03

Bar examination fees .... ND, ¶ 8634.1172

Baseball player's uniforms .... D/AGI, ¶ 8524.265

Baseball team equipment for business publicity .... D/GI, ¶ 8851.184

Black lung benefits trust, employer contributions .... D/GI, ¶ 12,291.01

Bookmakers, business expenses ..... D/GI, ¶ 8521.1260

Building replacements (capital expenditure) .... D/Am, ¶ 8630.51

Burglar alarm system, cost of installing (business capital expenditure) ..... D/Am, ¶ 13,709.119

Burial expenses .... ND, ¶ 12,543.047

Business bad debts .... D/GI, ¶ 10,650.021

Business conventions

. cruise ship (limited) ...... D/GI, ¶ 14,408A.059

. foreign conventions (limited) .... D/GI, ¶ 14,408A.0591

. political conventions (must be related to trade or business)...... D/GI, ¶ 8550.2835

. travel expenses .D/GI, ¶ 8550.025, ¶ 8550.275-¶ 8550.284

Business expenses ...... D/GI, ¶ 8520.01

Business meals .... 50% D/GI, ¶ 8523.024, ¶ 8570.021, ¶ 14,408A.027

Business startup expenses ... D/GI, D/Am, ¶ 12,371.01

Campaign contributions .... ND, ¶ 8952.53

Capital expenditures .... ND, D/Am, ¶ 13,709.01

Capital loss individual (limited) .... D/GI, ¶ 30,392.01

Car expenses (see "Automobile expenses")

Career counseling costs . D/AGI, ¶ 8524.25

Caribbean convention expenses (business) ...... D/GI, ¶ 14,408A.0591

Carrying charges deductible as interest where installment sales contract states carrying charge separately .... D/AGI, ¶ 9200.03

Casualty losses, personal, deduction limited to amount of each loss in excess of $100 and then only to the extent losses exceed 10% of adjusted gross income .... D/AGI, ¶ 10,005.041

Charitable contributions

. corporations (limited) ...... D/GI, ¶ 11,680.021

References in Checklists are to the 2002 Standard Federal Tax Reports.

.. computer technology
equipment to schools and
public libraries .D/GI, ¶ 11,680.037
. individuals (limited) . . . . . D/AGI,
¶ 11,670.01
.. appreciated property . . . D/AGI,
¶ 11,660.04—¶ 11,660.047
. where organization carries
on lobbying activities . . . . .ND,
¶ 11,620.052
Child support payments . . .ND, ¶ 6094.027
Circulation expenditures,
newspapers, magazine periodicals
. . . . .D/GI, ¶ 12,032.01
Clean fuel vehicle property
(limited) . . . . .D/GI, ¶ 12,133.01
Clinical testing deduction if credit is
elected . . . . .ND, ¶ 14,954.025
Club dues (limited) . . . D/AGI, ¶ 8853.025
Coal royalty contracts
. expenses related to . . . . ND,
¶ 14,311.01
. if there is no production, or
no income, under contracts . . . . D/
AGI, ¶ 14,311.01
Commissions
. paid as compensation . . . . . .D/GI,
¶ 5507.022
. sale of real estate or securities
.. dealers . . . . . . D/GI, ¶ 8521.046,
¶ 8521.049
.. other taxpayers .ND, ¶ 8521.1357
Commissions on sale of real estate
and securities, dealer only (other
than taxpayers deduct from
selling price) . . . . . . .D/GI, ¶ 8521.046,
¶ 8521.049
Commuting expenses . . . .ND, ¶ 8550.269
Compensation, reasonable .D/GI, ¶ 8636.01
Computer software (business use)
. development costs . .D/GI, D/Am,
¶ 12,047.057
. leased software .D/GI, ¶ 12,047.115
. purchased software . . . . . .D/Am,
¶ 12,047.115
Contributions by employer to
employer-financed accident and
health plans for benefit of
employees . . . . .D/GI, ¶ 8752.01
Contributions by employer to state
unemployment insurance and
state disability funds . .D/GI, ¶ 8752.025
Contributions by members to a
labor union (voluntary) . .ND, ¶ 8853.20
Contributions paid (within certain
limits) during year to charitable,

etc., organizations . D/AGI, ¶ 11,670.01,
¶ 11,620.04
Convention (political) programs,
cost of advertising in . .ND, ¶ 14,552.021
Conventions (see "Business conventions")
Cooperative housing corporation,
share of taxes or interest paid by . . . . D/
AGI, ¶ 12,603.01, ¶ 12,603.15
Copyright costs . . . . . .D/Am, ¶ 11,016.021
Cost recovery, business property or
property held for the production
of income . . . . .D/Am, ¶ 11,004.01
Cruise ship business conventions
(limited) . . . . .D/GI, ¶ 14,408A.059
Custodian fees . . . . . . D/AGI, ¶ 13,709.591
Defending title to property (capital
expenditure) . . . . .ND, ¶ 8526.469
Demolition of structure . . .ND, ¶ 14,901.01
Dependents. D/AGI, ¶ 8005.03, ¶ 8250.021
Depletion . . . . .D/Am, ¶ 23,924.01
Depreciation, business property or
property held for production of
income . . . . .D/Am, ¶ 11,004.01
. election to expense (limited)
. . . . .D/GI, ¶ 12,126.01
Diaper service . . . . .ND, ¶ 12,543.71
Disbarment proceedings, attorneys'
fees and expenses in defending . . . D/GI,
¶ 8526.032
Doctor's staff privilege fees at
hospital (capital expenditures) . .D/Am,
¶ 13,709.323
Dues
. chamber of commerce . . . . .D/GI,
¶ 8853.155
. charitable, religious,
educational organizations . D/AGI,
¶ 8853.15-¶ 8853.175
. clubs organized for business,
pleasure, recreation, or any
other social purpose . . . . .ND,
¶ 14,408A.035
. professional associations . . . D/GI,
¶ 8634.102-¶ 8634.1142
. union dues . . . . . D/AGI, ¶ 8853.20
Education expenses
. higher education expenses
(2002-2005) . . . . .D/GI, ¶ 12,772.01
Education expenses (employee)
. maintaining or improving
required skills . . . D/AGI, ¶ 8632.01
. minimum requirements for
job . . . . .ND, ¶ 8632.3865
. new trade or business . . . . .ND,
¶ 8632.3873

References in Checklists are to the 2002 Standard Federal Tax Reports.

Educational assistance plan
payments . . . . .D/GI, ¶ 7353.023
Efficiency engineers' fees . . . . .D/GI,
¶ 8520.317
Embezzlement loss . . . .D/GI, ¶ 10,101.024
Employee's expenses
. entertaining customers
. . reimbursed expenses . . . . .D/GI,
¶ 8524.025
. . unreimbursed expenses . .50% D/
AGI, ¶ 8523.021
. meals and lodging away from home
. . reimbursed . . . .D/GI, ¶ 8550.021
. . unreimbursed lodging . . . D/AGI,
¶ 8550.075
. . unreimbursed meals . . . . .50% D/
AGI, ¶ 14,408A.051
. move to a new work location
. . . . .D/GI, ¶ 12,623.021
. transportation expenses
. . unreimbursed (limited) . D/AGI,
¶ 8550.075
Employees' life insurance, paid by
employer
. employee beneficiary . . . . .D/GI,
¶ 8522.386
. employer beneficiary . . . . . . .ND,
¶ 14,008.035
Employees, payments for injuries
to, not compensated by insurance;
disability benefits . . .D/GI, ¶ 8752.2959
Employees, severance payments . . . .D/GI,
¶ 8752.676
Employees, training expenses . . . . .D/GI,
¶ 8752.676
Employment, fees for obtaining . . . D/AGI,
¶ 8524.03, ¶ 8524.25
Employment taxes
. employer's payment under Federal
Unemployment Tax Act
. . employer (but not
deductible if paid on wages
of domestics) . . . .D/GI, ¶ 9502.042,
¶ 9502.30
. employer's taxes under Federal
Insurance Contributions Act
. . employer (deductible only
as business expense) . . . . . . .D/GI,
¶ 9502.042
. employer's taxes under Railroad
Retirement Act
. . employer (deductible only
as business expense) . . . . . . .D/GI,
¶ 9502.28
. Federal Unemployment Tax
Act . . . . .D/GI, ¶ 9502.042

. Railroad Retirement Act . . .D/GI,
¶ 9502.28
. Social Security Act . . . . .D/GI,
¶ 9502.29
Entertainment expenses (business,
nonemployee)
. athletic club dues . . . . .ND,
¶ 14,408A.035
. facilities owned and used by
the taxpayer . . .ND, ¶ 14,408A.036
. food
. . furnished to employees on
premises . . . . . . .D/GI, ¶ 7438.052
. . meals directly related to
business . . . .50% D/GI, ¶ 8523.024
. . provided for customers . .50% D/
GI, ¶ 8523.024
Environmental cleanup costs
(brownsfield) . . . . . . .D/GI, ¶ 12,465.01
Environmental impact statement,
preparation of . . . . .D/Am, D/GI,
¶ 12,047.122
Estate tax . . . . .ND, ¶ 9502.035
Excess deductions on termination of
estate or trust . . . . D/AGI, ¶ 24,308.049
Excise taxes on personal goods . . . . . .ND,
¶ 9504.032
Expenditures violating public policy
. . . . .ND, ¶ 8858.01
Farmers, expenses for
. fertilizers, lime, etc. . . . . . . .D/GI,
¶ 12,143.01
. soil and water conservation .D/GI,
¶ 8756.026
Federal income tax . . . . .ND, ¶ 9504.01
Federal National Mortgage Association
. first buyers, excess of issue
price over market value on
date of issuance . . .D/GI, ¶ 8860.01
Fiduciaries' fees . . . . D/AGI, ¶ 24,267.463
Finance charges other than carrying
charges or loan fees (limited) . . . D/AGI,
¶ 9200.01
Fines and penalties
. child labor violations . . . . .ND,
¶ 8954.3265
. Fair Labor Standards Act
awards . . . . . . .D/GI, ¶ 8954.3265
. federal income tax penalties
. . . . .ND, ¶ 9502.0315
. generally . . . . .ND, ¶ 8954.01
. NLRB awards . .D/GI, ¶ 8954.3265
. overweight or over-length
trucks . . . . .ND, ¶ 8954.322
. violations of federal law . . . . . .ND,
¶ 8954.325

References in Checklists are to the 2002 Standard Federal Tax Reports.

¶ **57**

. Walsh-Healey Act awards .... ND,
¶ 8954.3265
Firefighter
. meals and lodging on
overnight duty at station ... ND,
D/AGI, ¶ 8570.1474, ¶ 13,603.265
. rubber coat, helmet, boots,
etc. .... D/AGI, ¶ 8524.265
Fishing boat crews (commercial),
members' protective clothing... D/AGI,
¶ 8524.265
Foreign conventions (with
limitations)...... D/GI, ¶ 14,408A.0591
Foreign taxes (unless taken as credit)
. by payor ..... D/AGI, ¶ 9502.032
Forfeitures
. business transactions
.. advance payments .... D/GI,
¶ 9805.103
.. lease deposits .. D/GI, ¶ 9805.163
.. purchase price .D/GI, ¶ 9805.172
. interest
.. premature withdrawal
from time savings account .. D/GI;
¶ 9805.165
Fringe benefits
. cost of providing non-cash
benefits......... D/GI, ¶ 9051.01
Funeral expenses ...... ND, ¶ 12,543.047
Furnishings and fixtures, business
cost .... D/Am ¶ 11,279.335
Gambling losses (limited)....... D/AGI,
¶ 10,105.01, ¶ 10,105.30
Gift tax .... ND, ¶ 9502.035
Gifts (business), but limited to $25
per donee per year .D/GI, ¶ 14,408A.038
Gifts to charity
. corporations (limited) ..... .D/GI,
¶ 11,680.021
.. computer technology
equipment to schools and
public libraries .D/GI, ¶ 11,680.037
. individuals (limited) ..... D/AGI,
¶ 11,670.01
.. appreciated property ... D/AGI,
¶ 11,660.04—¶ 11,660.047
. where organization carries
on lobbying activities .... ND,
¶ 11,620.052
Gifts to employees
. awards for length of service
(limited) ..... .D/GI, ¶ 14,408A.045
. gifts valued above $25 ...... ND,
¶ 8520.334, ¶ 14,408A.055
. gifts valued at $25 or less ... D/GI,
¶ 8520.334

Gifts to individuals ...... ND, ¶ 11,620.03
Golden parachutes
. excess parachute payments ... ND,
¶ 15,152.01, ¶ 34,941.01
. parachute payments ...... D/GI,
¶ 15,152.01-¶ 15,152.066
Golf course
. maintenance and operating
costs.......... D/GI, ¶ 8521.124,
¶ 8630.1292
. original construction........ ND,
¶ 8630.1292, ¶ 13,709.237
Hobby losses .... ND, ¶ 12,177.01
Home office (limited) .. D/GI, ¶ 14,854.021
. employee ... D/AGI, ¶ 14,854.021
. principal place of business .. D/GI,
¶ 14,854.027
. storage of product samples .. D/GI,
¶ 14,854.021
House rent .. ND, ¶ 13,603.01, ¶ 13,603.295
Husband to wife, allowance paid as
housewife's salary .... ND, ¶ 13,603.171
Illegal business, legitimate expenses
...D/GI, ND, ¶ 8521.1255-¶ 8521.1269,
¶ 15,051.01
Illegal drugs .... ND, ¶ 15,051.01
Impairment-related work expenses
. attendant care services at
work .... D/AGI, ¶ 6064.01
. necessary expenses at work
.... D/AGI, ¶ 6064.01
Import duties (unless as a business
expense)............. ND, ¶ 9502.032
Improvements made by lessee,
depreciation and amortization ... D/Am,
¶ 12,105.42
Income tax (state) .... D/AGI, ¶ 9502.031
Income tax liability, cost of
determining..... D/AGI, ¶ 12,523.3844
Income tax returns, cost of
preparing (non-business) ...... D/AGI,
¶ 8526.462, ¶ 12,523.3844, ¶ 12,523.44
Individual retirement account,
contributions (limited).......... D/GI,
¶ 18,922.01
Infringement litigation in course of
business .... D/GI, ¶ 8526.449
Inheritance tax .... ND, ¶ 9502.035
Injuries to employees, payments for,
not compensated by insurance ... D/GI,
¶ 8752.01
Insurance expenses
. business
.. casualty ..... D/GI, ¶ 8522.3815
.. malpractice ... D/GI, ¶ 8522.392

References in Checklists are to the 2002 Standard Federal Tax Reports.

. individual . . . . D/AGI, ¶ 12,543.01
(medical)
. insured employees
. . employee or other
beneficiary . . . . . .D/GI, ¶ 8522.386
. . employer beneficiary . . . . . .ND,
¶ 14,008.03
. . key employees .D/GI, ¶ 14,008.01
. personal residence .ND, ¶ 13,603.01
. required for credit
. . premiums paid by creditor
. . . . .D/GI, ¶ 14,008.035
. . premiums paid by debtor . . .ND,
¶ 14,008.035
Intangible assets (as defined in
Code Sec. 197) . . . . .D/Am, ¶ 12,455.01
Interest and carrying charges
related to a commodity straddle
position in excess of income
generated by straddle position . . . ND,
¶ 13,709.028
Interest (with exceptions and
limitations, see below) . . . . D/AGI,
¶ 9104.01
. education loans (limited) . . .D/GI,
¶ 12,695.01
. interest related to tax-
exempt income . . . . .ND, ¶ 9104.01,
¶ 14,054.01
. interest related to life
insurance contracts (limited)
. . D/AGI, ¶ 9104.048, ¶ 14,008.021
. personal obligations
(limited). .ND, ¶ 9104.01, ¶ 9402.01
. points, purchase of
residence. . . . . . . D/AGI, ¶ 9402.01
. prepaid . . .D/Am, D/GI, ¶ 9402.04
. property held for production
of rent or royalties .D/GI, ¶ 9104.01
. trade or business debts . . . . .D/GI,
¶ 9104.01
Interest forfeiture
. premature withdrawal from
time savings account . . . . . . .D/GI,
¶ 9805.165
Interest on tax deficiencies
. corporation . . . . .D/GI, ¶ 9400A.04
individual-generally . . . . .ND,
¶ 9400A.04, ¶ 9400A.50
. . related to trade or
business . . . .D/GI, ND, ¶ 9400A.04
Investigatory costs
. acquisition of specific
business . . . . .ND, ¶ 12,371.25
. . business search . . .D/GI, D/Am,
¶ 12,371.25

Investor's expenses (except incurred
in earning tax-exempt interest) . D/AGI,
¶ 12,523.03
ISO 9000 costs . . . . . . .D/GI, ¶ 8520.3175
Job hunting expenses
. new trade or business . . . . . . .ND,
¶ 8524.03, ¶ 8524.25
. resume preparation costs . D/AGI,
¶ 8524.03, ¶ 8524.25
. same trade or business . . . . D/AGI,
¶ 8524.03, ¶ 8524.25
. travel and transportation to
new area . . . . . . D/AGI, ¶ 8524.03,
¶ 8524.25
Jockey's riding apparel. . . . . D/AGI,
¶ 8524.265
Labor union dues . . . . . . D/AGI, ¶ 8853.20
Laundry, dry cleaning, pressing
charges (business travel) . . . . . . D/AGI,
¶ 8550.021
Legal expenses and fees
. business . . . . . .D/GI, ¶ 8526.021—
¶ 8526.05
. investors . . . . D/AGI, ¶ 8526.4394,
¶ 12,523.025
. production of income . . . . . D/AGI,
¶ 12,523.3375
. tax determination . . . . D/AGI,
¶ 12,523.346
Legislators
. congressional living expenses, away
from home
. . expenses of moving to
capital . . . . . . D/AGI, ¶ 8570.1218,
¶ 12,623.117
. state
. . local transportation . . . . D/AGI,
¶ 8570.1222
. . meals and lodging . . . . . . D/AGI,
¶ 8570.1222
. . travel expenses . . . . D/AGI,
¶ 8570.1222
License fees
. treated as personal property
tax. . . . . D/AGI, ¶ 9502.398
Life insurance premiums, debts incurred to
purchase, paid by employer, ¶ 8636.27
. employee or other
beneficiary . . . . .D/GI, ¶ 14,008.01
. employer beneficiary . . . . . . .ND,
¶ 5508.24, ¶ 14,008.03
Loan cost—stock reacquisition . . . . . . .ND,
¶ 9052.01
Lobbying expense
. appearances before
legislative bodies . . .ND, ¶ 8952.021

References in Checklists are to the 2002 Standard Federal Tax Reports.

. expenditures to influence
voters . . . . .ND, ¶ 8952.021
. professional lobbyist's
expenses . . . . . .D/GI, ¶ 8952.0664,
¶ 8952.468

Losses
. gambling (trade or business)
. . . . D/AGI, ¶ 6005.028
. net operating loss . . . . .D/GI,
¶ 12,014.01
. sale or exchange of property
. . business property . . . . . . .D/GI,
¶ 9804.03
. . related parties . .ND, ¶ 14,161.02
. . capital assets (business
motive). . . . . .D/GI, ¶ 9804.03
. theft or casualty
. . individual property . . . . D/AGI,
¶ 9804.02, ¶ 9807.01
. . rent- or royalty-generating
property . . . . .D/GI, ¶ 9808.01
. worthless stock and
securities . . . . . .D/GI, ¶ 10,001.01

Lump sum distribution-ordinary
income portion . . . .D/GI, ¶ 18,217A.026

Machinery
. incidental repairs . . . . .D/GI,
¶ 8630.025

Materials and supplies, business
(incidentals) . . . . .D/GI, ¶ 8610.01

Maternity clothes. . . . . . .ND, ¶ 12,543.71

Meals provided for employees
. employer's cost of providing
meals on premises. . . . . .D/GI,
¶ 7438.052
. meals directly related to
business . . . .50% D/GI, ¶ 8523.024

Medical, dental and hospital
expenses (to the extent exceeding
7.5% of adjusted gross income)
(for a detailed list of such
expenses, see ¶ 470) . D/AGI, ¶ 12,543.01

Medical, dental and hospital
expenses less than 7.5% of
adjusted gross income . .ND, ¶ 12,543.01

Medical insurance premiums (see ¶ 470)

Medical savings account . . . . .D/GI,
¶ 12,675.01

Mine development expenditures . . . .D/GI,
¶ 24,094.01

Mine exploration expenditures . . . . .D/GI,
¶ 24,115.01

Moving expenses
. meals . . . . .ND, ¶ 12,623.50
. other expenses

. . employee, reimbursed . . . .D/GI,
¶ 12,623.01
. . employee, unreimbursed . . .D/GI
¶ 12,623.021
. . self employed. . . . . .D/GI,
¶ 12,623.021

Moving machinery . . . . . .D/GI, ¶ 8520.50

Musician's clothing, used
exclusively in business . . . . .D/AGI,
¶ 8524.265

National Labor Relations Board
award to employees, payment by
employer . . . . .D/GI, ¶ 8954.3265

Net operating loss deduction . . . . . .D/GI,
¶ 12,014.01

New business, cost of starting up . . .D/GI,
D/Am, ¶ 12,371.01

Nonbusiness bad debts (limited) . . . .D/GI,
¶ 10,700.021

Nontrade or nonbusiness expenses
incurred in preserving income-
producing property . D/AGI, ¶ 12,523.01

Nurse's uniform . . . . . . D/AGI, ¶ 8524.265

Office in home (limited)
. employee . . . D/AGI, ¶ 14,854.021,
. principal place of business . .D/GI,
¶ 14,854.027

Office supplies . . . . .D/GI, ¶ 8610.01

Operating loss in prior or
subsequent year . . . .D/GI, ¶ 12,014.023

Organization expenses of
corporation (amortizable over not
less than 60 months) .D/Am, ¶ 13,352.01

Original construction of greens on a
golf course . . . . .ND, ¶ 13,709.237,
¶ 8630.1292

Outside salesperson
. meals—see Meals, employees'
business
. moving expenses—see Moving
expenses
. travel expenses. . . . . .D/AGI,
¶ 8550.021

Package design costs . . .D/Am, ¶ 13,709.03

Partners' fixed or guaranteed
payments for services or for use of
capital (allowed as business
deduction to partnership) . . . . . .D/GI,
¶ 25,183.01

Partnership organization expenses,
unless election to amortize . . . . .ND,
¶ 25,223.01

Passport fee, business trip .D/GI, ¶ 9502.41

Passport fee (except for business
purposes) . . . . .ND, ¶ 9502.41

Penalties. . . . . . . generally ND, ¶ 8954.01

References in Checklists are to the 2002 Standard Federal Tax Reports.

¶ **57**

. Environmental Protection Agency:
.. Clean Air Act violation . . . . .ND,
¶ 8954.021
.. nonconformance penalty . .D/GI,
¶ 8954.022
. penalty on early withdrawal
of time deposit . . . .D/GI, ¶ 9104.03
Performing artists (limitation on gross income)
. employee business expenses
. . . . .D/GI, ¶ 6005.025
Permanent improvements
. business property . . . . .D/Am,
¶ 13,709.325
. tenants . . . . . .D/Am, ¶ 13,854.035,
¶ 12,105.42
"Points" on home mortgage (if customarily required in geographic area in which indebtedness was incurred) . . . . D/AGI,
¶ 9402.04, ¶ 21,817.04
Police officer's uniform and cost of cleaning . . . . D/AGI, ¶ 8524.265
Political contributions
. corporations, businesses,
etc. . . . . .ND, ¶ 8952.53
. individuals. . . . . . . .ND, ¶ 8952.53,
¶ 14,552.01
Political publications, cost of advertising in . . . . .ND (generally),
¶ 14,552.021
Postage costs, business . . .D/GI, ¶ 8610.14,
¶ 8851.1652
Premiums paid on a business insurance "professional overhead expense disability policy" . . . . . . .D/GI,
¶ 8522.385
Prepaid interest or finance charges .D/Am,
¶ 9402.04
Prizes and contests—see "Promotional activities"
Professional associations, dues
. unreimbursed employee
expense . . . . . D/AGI, ¶ 8634.102—
¶ 8634.1142
Professional books and journals and information services
. unreimbursed employee
expense . . . . . . D/AGI, ¶ 8634.01,
¶ 8634.1201—¶ 8634.121
Promotional activities
. coupons . . . . . . .D/GI, ¶ 21,015.01
. prizes and contests . . . . . . .D/GI,
¶ 8851.1657
Protective clothing. . . . . D/AGI, ¶ 8524.05
Raffle tickets, cost of . . . .ND, ¶ 11,620.511

Railroad retirement tax paid by
employers . . . . .D/GI, ¶ 9502.28
Railway trainman's uniform . . . . . D/AGI,
¶ 8524.265
Reconditioning and health-restoring expenses of employees paid by employers . . . . .D/GI, ¶ 8520.246
Reforestation costs . . . . . . .D/GI, D/Am,
¶ 23,929.195
Reimbursed expenses (otherwise deductible) . . . . .D/GI, ¶ 8524.025
Removal of architectural and transportation barriers to the handicapped and elderly (limited) . . . . D/AGI, ¶ 12,264.01
Rent, business property . .D/GI, ¶ 8754.01
Reorganization expenditures, unless election to amortize (capital expenditure) . . . . .ND, ¶ 13,709.83
Repairs to business property . . . .D/GI, D/Am, ¶ 8630.01
Repairs to personal residence . . . . . . .ND,
¶ 8630.574
Research and experimental expenditures connected with a trade or business . . . . . . .D/GI, D/Am,
¶ 12,047.01
Retirement plans, contributions to
. employer . . . . .D/GI, ¶ 18,347.01
. individuals (limited) . . . . . .D/GI,
¶ 18,922.0226
. self-employed individuals . . .D/GI,
¶ 17,933.01
. simplified employee pension contributions . . . . . .D/GI, ¶ 18,922.0245
Return, federal or state income tax, gift tax, etc., cost of having prepared (including investor) . . D/AGI,
¶ 8520.73, ¶ 12,523.3844
Safe deposit boxes, rental for protection of income producing property
. investor . . . . . . D/AGI, ¶ 12,523.03
. trader . . . . ¶ 12,523.23
.. business use. . .D/GI, ¶ 12,523.23
Salaries
. bonuses . . . . .D/GI, ¶ 8642.01
. commissions . . . .D/GI, ¶ 5507.022
. related parties. . . .D/GI, ¶ 8638.01
Salespersons' expenses
. reimbursed . . . . . .D/GI, ¶ 8524.01,
. unreimbursed . . D/AGI ¶ 8524.01,
.. automobile expenses . . . . D/AGI,
¶ 7438.038, ¶ 8590.01
.. entertaining customers,
reimbursed . . . . . .D/GI, ¶ 8523.021

References in Checklists are to the 2002 Standard Federal Tax Reports.

¶ 57

.. entertaining customers, unreimbursed .... .50% D/AGI, ¶ 8523.277
.. gifts to customers (up to $25) .... D/AGI, ¶ 14,408A.038
.. membership dues in business or social clubs ...... .ND, ¶ 14,408A.035
.. subscriptions to business, professional or trade publications, if for business reasons ..... D/AGI, ¶ 8524.2509
.. transportation expenses, unreimbursed .. D/AGI, ¶ 8550.075
.. travel expenses .... D/AGI, ¶ 14,408A.05
Self-employment tax (limited to 50%) .... .D/GI, ¶ 9502.043
Servants, social security taxes paid for .... .ND, ¶ 9502.30
Severance payments .... .D/GI, ¶ 8752.676
Shareholder's proxy fight expenses .... D/ AGI, ¶ 12,523.3593
Social security taxes
. employees .... .ND, ¶ 9502.042
. employers .. D/GI (only as business expense), ¶ 9502.042
Soil and water conservation expenditures, farmers ... .D/GI, D/Am, ¶ 8756.026
Stamp taxes
. dealers/investors .... .D/GI, ¶ 9502.032
. trade or business .D/GI, ¶ 9502.032
. transfer of personal residence .... .ND, ¶ 9502.032
Start-up expenditures, business .. D/GI, D/ Am, ¶ 12,371.01
Stock redemption costs .... .ND, ¶ 9052.01
Subscriptions, professional journals (self-employed) ...... .D/GI, ¶ 8634.02
Supplemental unemployment compensation benefits, repayments by recipients .... .D/GI, ¶ 6005.04
Surgeon's uniform (employee) .... D/AGI, ¶ 8524.265
Tax penalty payments ..... .ND, ¶ 8954.33
Tax refresher course, lawyer's ..... .D/GI, ¶ 8632.645
Tax returns, cost of preparation
. business ..... .D/GI, ¶ 12,523.3844
. individual ... D/AGI, ¶ 12,523.132
Taxes (Deductible by Manufacturer, Producer, Importer or Corresponding

Person, but Not by Consumer) .... ¶ 9502.01
. automobile excise taxes ... .D/Am, ¶ 9502.35
Telephone service (as a business expense) .... .D/GI, ¶ 8520.74
Theft loss
. business ..... .D/GI, ¶ 10,101.136
. nonbusiness .. D/AGI, ¶ 10,101.01
Tires, truck used in business ...... .D/GI, ¶ 8590.1489, ¶ 8590.612
Title costs (perfecting or defending title to property, including costs of defending condemnation proceedings) (capital expenditure) ..... .D/Am, ¶ 8526.4682— ¶ 8526.471, ¶ 12,523.35
Tools, unreimbursed cost, useful life of one year or less .... D/AGI, ¶ 8524.04
Trade association dues, unreimbursed employee expenses .... D/AGI, ¶ 8853.50—¶ 8853.57
Trade or business expenses (securities dealers and traders) .. D/GI, ¶ 8521.04
Trademark and trade name expenditures ..... .D/Am, ¶ 31,044.055
Transfer taxes .... .ND, ¶ 9502.032
Travel expenses (employees)
. commuting expenses .... .ND, ¶ 8550.269
. reimbursed ..... .D/GI, ¶ 8550.29, ¶ 8550.48
. unreimbursed . D/AGI, ¶ 8550.022, ¶ 8550.075
.. baseball players (including meals and lodging) while away from "club town," also other business expenses at "club town" if tax "home" in a different city .. D/AGI, ¶ 8550.025
.. business and pleasure trips .... D/AGI, ¶ 8550.255
.. clergymen, church conventions travel, meals and lodging away from home .... D/AGI, ¶ 8550.28
.. commercial fishing boat crew members, for travel, meals, and lodging away from home port .... D/AGI, ¶ 8570.1165
.. congressmen, up to $3,000 of living expenses .... D/AGI, ¶ 8570.032, ¶ 8570.12

References in Checklists are to the 2002 Standard Federal Tax Reports.

¶ 57

. . expenses of traveling from
principal place to minor
place of business . . . . D/AGI,
¶ 8570.175
. . government employees,
expenses in excess of per
diem allowances . D/AGI, ¶ 8570.12
. . lawyers . . . . D/AGI, ¶ 8550.281,
¶ 8550.345
. . meals, reimbursed . . . . . . .D/GI,
¶ 8550.021, ¶ 14,417.421
. . meals, unreimbursed . . . .50% D/
AGI, ¶ 8550.075, ¶ 14,417.01
. . physician,   medical
conventions . . . D/AGI, ¶ 8550.283
. . railroad employees' meals
and lodging while away from
"home terminal" . . . . D/AGI,
¶ 8550.269, ¶ 8550.475
. . salespersons . . . . D/AGI,
¶ 8570.1505
. . teachers,   scientific
meetings and conventions . D/AGI,
¶ 8570.1254
. . truck drivers' (long line)
meals and lodging while
away from "home terminal"
. . . . D/AGI, ¶ 8570.154
Truck tires with life less than a year
. . . . . . .D/GI, ¶ 8590.1489, ¶ 8590.612

Truck use tax (unless as business
expense) . . . . .ND, ¶ 9502.039
Uncollectible notes (see Bad debts)
Uniform and special clothing costs
. baseball uniforms . . . . D/AGI,
¶ 8524.265
. clothing   required   for
business . . . . . D/AGI, ¶ 8524.2658
. employer-reimbursed costs . .D/GI,
¶ 8524.05
. jockey's riding apparel . . . D/AGI,
¶ 8524.265
. nurses' uniforms . . . . D/AGI,
¶ 8524.265
. protective clothing . . . . . . D/AGI,
¶ 8524.05
. work shoes, metal tipped . . D/AGI,
¶ 8524.2658
Union payments
. dues . . . . D/AGI, ¶ 8853.20
. fines . . . . D/AGI, ¶ 8853.205
Utilities, personal . . . . . .ND, ¶ 13,603.323
Wages and salaries . . . . . .D/GI, ¶ 8636.01
Waiters, waitresses
. special uniforms . . . . D/AGI,
¶ 8524.265
Work shoes, metal tipped for
protection of worker . . . . D/AGI,
¶ 8524.2658

References in Checklists are to the 2002 Standard Federal Tax Reports.

¶ 57

¶ 59   Checklist for Medical Expenses

Generally, a medical expense deduction is allowed for expenses incurred in the diagnosis, cure, mitigation, treatment or prevention of disease, or for the purpose of affecting any structure or function of the body for the individual or for the individual's spouse or dependents. The deduction covers expenses that have not been reimbursed by medical insurance or other sources.

Despite the broad scope of medical expenses, not every expense incurred for medical care is deductible. Also, there is a 7.5-percent floor on the medical expense deduction. The chart, below, lists specific types of expenses and whether or not a deduction for the expense is permitted. The user can easily check whether an official determination has been made as to the deductibility of a particular type of expense.

Medical Expense	Deductible	Authority
Abortion		
. legal	Yes	Rev. Rul. 73-201, 1973-1 CB 140, as clarified by Rev. Rul. 73-603, 1973-2 CB 76, and Rev. Rul. 97-9, 1997-1 CB 77
Accident and health insurance		
. medical care portion separately stated and reasonable in amount	Yes	Code Sec. 213(d)(1)(C) and (d)(6) and Reg. § 1.213-1(e)(4)
. medical care portion not separately stated or, if separately stated, not reasonable in amount	No	Code Sec. 213(d)(6) and Reg. § 1.213-1(e)(4)
Acupuncture	Yes	Rev. Rul. 72-593, 1972-2 CB 180
Adoption		
. medical costs of adopted child	Yes	Rev. Rul. 60-255, 1960-2 CB 105
. medical costs of natural mother	No	B.L. Kilpatrick, 68 TC 469, Dec. 34,493
Air conditioner		
. allergy relief	Yes	Rev. Rul. 55-261, 1955-1 CB 307
. cystic fibrosis relief	Yes	R. Gerard, 37 TC 826, Dec. 25,331 (Acq.)
. permanent improvement to property	No	G.W. Wade, 61-2 USTC ¶ 9709
Alcoholism, treatment of	Yes	Rev. Rul. 73-325, 1973-2 CB 75
Ambulance hire	Yes	Reg. § 1.213-1(e)(1)(ii)
Anticipated medical expenses	No	W.B. Andrews, 37 TCM 744, Dec. 35,144(M), TC Memo. 1978-174
Attendant to accompany blind or deaf student	Yes	Rev. Rul. 64-173, 1964-1 CB (Part 1) 121; R.A. Baer Est., 26 TCM 170, Dec. 28,352(M), TC Memo. 1967-34
Automobile (see Car)		
Baby sitting expenses to enable parent to see doctor	No	Rev. Rul. 78-266, 1978-2 CB 123
Birth control pills	Yes	Rev. Rul. 73-200, 1973-1 CB 140
Blind persons		
. attendant to accompany student	Yes	Rev. Rul. 64-173, 1964-1 (Part I) CB 121
. braille books and magazines, excess cost of regular editions	Yes	Rev. Rul. 75-318, 1975-2 CB 88
. seeing-eye dog	Yes	Rev. Rul. 55-261, 1955-1 CB 307
. special education (see Schools, special)		
. special educational aids to mitigate condition	Yes	Rev. Rul. 58-223, 1958-1 CB 156
Capital expenditures		
. home modifications for handicapped individual	Yes	Rev. Rul. 87-106, 1987-2 CB 67

References in Checklists are to the 2002 Standard Federal Tax Reports.

¶ 59

Medical Expense	Deductible	Authority
. permanent improvement to property	No	Reg. § 1.213-1(e)(1)(iii)
. primary purpose medical care	Yes	Reg. § 1.213-1(e)(1)(iii)
Car		
. depreciation on	No	M.S. Gordon, 37 TC 986, CCH Dec. 25,364; R.K. Weary, CA-10, 75-1 USTC ¶ 9173, 510 F.2d 435, cert. denied, 423 U.S. 838
. equipped to accommodate wheelchair passengers	Yes	Rev. Rul. 70-606, 1970-2 CB 66
. handicap controls	Yes	S.H. Weinzimer, 17 TCM 712, Dec. 23,100(M), TC Memo. 1958-137
. insurance, medical coverage for persons other than taxpayer, spouse and children	No	Rev. Rul. 73-483, 1973-2 CB 75
Chauffeur, salary of	No	W.E. Buck, 47 TC 113, CCH Dec. 28,175
Chemical dependency treatment (see Alcoholism, treatment of, and Drug addiction, recovery from)		
Childbirth preparation classes		
. "coach"	No	IRS Letter Ruling 8919009, 2-6-89, CCH IRS LETTER RULINGS REPORTS
. mother	Yes	IRS Letter Ruling 8919009, 2-6-89, CCH IRS LETTER RULINGS REPORTS
Chiropractors	Yes	Rev. Rul. 63-91, 1963-1 CB 54
Christian Science treatment	Yes	Rev. Rul. 55-261, 1955-1 CB 307
Clarinet and lessons, alleviation of severe teeth malocclusion	Yes	Rev. Rul. 62-210, 1962-2 CB 89
Clothing, suitable for use other than therapy	No	M.C. Montgomery, 51 TC 410, Dec. 29,270, aff'd on other issues, CA-6, 70-2 USTC ¶ 9466, 428 F2d 243
Computer data bank, storage and retrieval of medical records	Yes	Rev. Rul. 71-282, 1971-2 CB 166
Contact lenses	Yes	Reg. § 1.213-1(e)(1)(iii)
. replacement insurance	Yes	Rev. Rul. 74-429, 1974-2 CB 83
Contraceptives, prescription	Yes	Rev. Rul. 73-200, 1973-1 CB 140
Cosmetic surgery		
. necessary to ameliorate a deformity arising from a congenital abnormality, personal injury, or disfiguring disease	Yes	Code Sec. 213(d)(9); Senate Finance Committee Report to P.L. 101-508
. unnecessary	No	Code Sec. 213(d)(9); Senate Finance Committee Report to P.L. 101-508
Crime victims, compensated medical expenses of	No	Rev. Rul. 74-74, 1974-1 CB 18
Crutches	Yes	Reg. § 1.213-1(e)(1)(iii)
Dancing lessons	No	R.C. France, CA-6, 82-1 USTC ¶ 9225
Deaf persons		
. hearing aid	Yes	Rev. Rul. 55-261, 1955-1 CB 307
. hearing-aid animal	Yes	Rev. Rul. 68-295, 1968-1 CB 92
. lip reading expenses for the deaf	Yes	Rev. Rul. 55-261, 1955-1 CB 307
. notetaker, deaf student	Yes	R.A. Baer Est., 26 TCM 170, Dec. 28,352(M), TC Memo. 1967-34
. special education (see Schools, special)		
. telephone, specially equipped, including repairs	Yes	Rev. Rul. 71-48, 1971-1 CB 99, as amplified by Rev. Rul. 73-53, 1973-1 CB 139

References in Checklists are to the 2002 Standard Federal Tax Reports.

¶ 59

Medical Expense	*Deductible*	*Authority*
. television, closed-caption decoder	Yes	Rev. Rul. 80-340, 1980-2 CB 81
. visual alert system	Yes	IRS Letter Ruling 8250040, 9-13-82, CCH IRS LETTER RULINGS REPORTS
Dental fees	Yes	Reg. § 1.213-1(e)(1)(ii)
Dentures (artificial teeth)	Yes	Reg. § 1.213-1(e)(1)(ii)
Deprogramming services	No	IRS Letter Ruling 8021004, no date given, CCH IRS LETTER RULINGS REPORTS
Diagnostic fees	Yes	Reg. § 1.213-1(e)(1)(ii)
Diaper service	No	Rev. Rul. 55-261, 1955-1 CB 307
Diapers, disposable, used due to severe neurological disease	Yes	IRS Letter Ruling 8137085, 6-17-81, CCH IRS LETTER RULINGS REPORTS
Doctors' fees	Yes	Reg. § 1.213-1(e)(1)(i)
Domestic aid, type that would be rendered by nurse	Yes	Rev. Rul. 58-339, 1958-2 CB 106
Drug addiction, recovery from	Yes	Rev. Rul. 72-226, 1972-1 CB 96
Drugs, illegal/controlled substances, even when prescribed	No	Rev. Rul. 97-9, 1997-1 CB 77
Drugs, prescription	Yes	Code Sec. 213(b)
Dust elimination system	No	*F.S. Delp,* 30 TC 1230, Dec. 23,167
Dyslexia, language training	Yes	Rev. Rul. 69-607, 1969-2 CB 40
Ear piercing	No	Rev. Rul. 82-111, 1982-1 CB 48
Electrolysis	No	Code Sec. 213(d)(9); Senate Finance Committee Report to P.L. 101-508
Elevator, alleviation of cardiac condition	Yes	*J.E. Berry,* DC Okla., 58-2 USTC ¶ 9870, 174 FSupp 748; Rev. Rul. 59-411, 1959-2 CB 100, as modified by Rev. Rul. 83-33, 1983-1 CB 70
Eye examinations and glasses	Yes	Reg. § 1.213-1(e)(1)(ii), (iii)
Fallout shelter, prevention of disease	No	*F.H. Daniels,* 41 TC 324, Dec. 26,414
Fluoride device; on advice of dentist	Yes	Rev. Rul. 64-267, 1964-2 CB 69
Funeral expenses	No	*K.P. Carr,* 39 TCM 253, Dec. 36,352(M), TC Memo. 1979-400
Furnace	No	*J.L. Seymour,* 14 TC 1111, Dec. 17,675
Glasses	Yes	Reg. § 1.213-1(e)(1)(ii)
Gravestone	No	*C.W. Libby Est.,* 14 TCM 699, Dec. 21,110(M), TC Memo. 1955-180
Guide animals (see Service animals)		
Hair transplants, surgical	No	Code Sec. 213(d)(9); Senate Finance Committee Report to P.L. 101-508
Halfway house, adjustment to mental hospital	Yes	IRS Letter Ruling 7714016, no date given, CCH IRS LETTER RULINGS REPORTS
Handicapped persons (see, also, specific handicap or equipment)		
. home modification (see Capital expenses)		
. special training or education (see Schools, special)		
Health club dues		
. not related to a particular medical condition	No	Rev. Rul. 55-261, 1955-1 CB 307
. prescribed by physician for medical condition	Yes	Rev. Rul. 55-261, 1955-1 CB 307

References in Checklists are to the 2002 Standard Federal Tax Reports.

Medical Expense	Deductible	Authority
Health Maintenance Organization (HMO)	Yes	IRS Publication No. 502, "Medical and Dental Expenses" (for 2000 returns)
Hearing aids (see Deaf persons)		
Hospital care, in-patient	Yes	Reg. § 1.213-1(e)(1)(v)
Hospital services	Yes	Reg. § 1.213-1(e)(1)(ii)
Hygienic supplies	No	Reg. § 1.213-1(e)(2); O.G. Russell, 12 TCM 1276, Dec. 19,973(M)
Indian medicine man	Yes	R.H. Tso, 40 TCM 1277, Dec. 37,260(M), TC Memo. 1980-339
Insulin	Yes	Code Sec. 213(b)
Insurance		
. accident and health insurance (see Accident and health insurance)		
. long term care insurance (within limits)	Yes	Code Sec. 213(d)(1)(D); Code Sec. 7702B
. Medicare A coverage	Yes	Rev. Rul. 79-175, 1979-1 CB 117
. premiums for loss of income	No	Reg. § 1.213-1(e)(4)
. premiums for loss of life, limb or sight	No	Reg. § 1.213-1(e)(4)
. premiums for medical care	Yes	Reg. § 1.213-1(e)(4)
. self-employed	Yes	Code Sec. 162(l)
Iron lung	Yes	Rev. Rul. 55-261, 1955-1 CB 307
Laboratory fees	Yes	Reg. § 1.213-1(e)(1)(ii)
Laetrile, prescribed	No	Rev. Rul. 97-9, 1997-1 CB 77
Lamaze classes (see Childbirth preparation classes)		
Lead paint, removal	Yes	Rev. Rul. 79-66, 1979-1 CB 114
Legal expenses		
. authorization of treatment for mental illness	Yes	Rev. Rul. 71-281, 1971-2 CB 165
. divorce upon medical advice	No	J.H. Jacobs, 62 TC 813, Dec. 32,773
Lifetime medical care, prepaid; retirement home	Yes	Rev. Rul. 75-302, 1975-2 CB 86, as clarified by Rev. Rul. 93-72, 1993-2 CB 77; Rev. Rul. 75-303, 1975-2 CB 87
Limbs, artificial	Yes	Reg. § 1.213-1(e)(1)(ii)
Lodging		
. care not provided in hospital or equivalent outpatient facility	No	A.L. Polyak, 94 TC 337, CCH Dec. ¶ 46,443
. limited to $50 per night	Yes	Code Sec. 213(d)(2)
Long term care expenses	Yes	Code Sec. 213(d)(1)(C); Code Sec. 7702B
Marriage counseling	No	Rev. Rul. 75-319, 1975-2 CB 88
Maternity clothes	No	Rev. Rul. 55-261, 1955-1 CB 307
Mattress, prescribed for alleviation of arthritis	Yes	Rev. Rul. 55-261, 1955-1 CB 307
Nursing home, medical reasons	Yes	W.B. Counts, 42 TC 755, Dec. 26,893 (Acq.)
Nursing services (including board and social security tax if paid by taxpayer)	Yes	Rev. Rul. 57-489, 1957-2 CB 207
Obstetrical expenses	Yes	Reg. § 1.213-1(e)(1)(ii)
Operations		
. illegal	No	Reg. § 1.213-1(e)(1)(ii)
. legal	Yes	Reg. § 1.213-1(e)(1)(ii)
Optometrists	Yes	Rev. Rul. 55-261, 1955-1 CB 307
Orthodontia	Yes	Reg. § 1.213-1(e)(1)(ii)
Orthopedic shoes, excess cost	Yes	IRS Letter Ruling 8221118, 2-26-82, CCH IRS LETTER RULINGS REPORTS
Osteopaths	Yes	Rev. Rul. 63-91, 1963-1 CB 54

References in Checklists are to the 2002 Standard Federal Tax Reports.

Medical Expense	Deductible	Authority
Oxygen equipment, breathing difficulty	Yes	Rev. Rul. 55-261, 1955-1 CB 307
Patterning exercises, handicapped child	Yes	Rev. Rul. 70-170, 1970-1 CB 51
Plumbing, special fixtures for handicapped	Yes	Rev. Rul. 70-395, 1970-2 CB 65
Prosthesis	Yes	Reg. § 1.213-1(e)(1)(iii)
Psychiatric care	Yes	Rev. Rul. 55-261, 1955-1 CB 307
Psychologists	Yes	Rev. Rul. 63-91, 1963-1 CB 54
Psychotherapists	Yes	Rev. Rul. 63-91, 1963-1 CB 54
Reclining chair for cardiac patient	Yes	Rev. Rul. 58-155, 1958-1 CB 156
Remedial reading for dyslexic child	Yes	Rev. Rul. 69-607, 1969-2 CB 40
Residence, loss on sale, move medically recommended	No	Rev. Rul. 68-319, 1968-1 CB 92
Retirement home, cost of medical care	Yes	H.W. Smith Est., 79 TC 313, Dec. 39,273 (Acq.)
Sanitarium rest home, cost of, medical, educational, or rehabilitative reasons	Yes	Reg. § 1.213-1(e)(1)(v)
Schools, special, relief of handicap	Yes	Rev. Rul. 58-533, 1958-2 CB 108; Rev. Rul. 69-499, 1969-2 CB 39; Rev. Rul. 70-285, 1970-1 CB 52
Scientology "audits" and "processing"	No	D.H. Brown, CA-8, 75-2 USTC ¶ 9718, 523 F2d 365, aff'g 62 TC 551, Dec. 32,701; Rev. Rul. 78-190, 1978-1 CB 74
Self-help, medical	No	B. Doody, 32 TCM 547, Dec. 32,006(M), TC Memo. 1973-126
Service animals		
. hearing-aid animal	Yes	Rev. Rul. 68-295, 1968-1 CB 92
. other	Yes	Senate Finance Committee Report to P.L. 100-647
. seeing-eye dog	Yes	Rev. Rul. 55-261, 1955-1 CB 307
Sexual dysfunction, treatment for	Yes	Rev. Rul. 75-187, 1975-1 CB 92
Smoking, program to stop	Yes	Rev. Rul. 99-28, IRB 1999-25, 6
Spiritual guidance	No	M. Miller, 40 TCM 243, Dec. 36,911(M), TC Memo. 1980-136
Sterilization operation, legal	Yes	Rev. Rul. 73-603, 1973-2 CB 76, clarifying Rev. Rul. 73-201, 1973-1 CB 140
Swimming pool, treatment of polio or arthritis	Yes	C.B. Mason, DC Hawaii, 57-2 USTC ¶ 10,012; Rev. Rul. 83-33, 1983-1 CB 70
Tattoos	No	Rev. Rul. 82-111, 1982-1 CB 48
Taxicab to doctor's office	Yes	Rev. Rul. 55-261, 1955-1 CB 307
Teeth, artificial	Yes	Reg. § 1.213-1(e)(1)(ii)
Telephone, specially equipped		
. deaf persons	Yes	Rev. Rul. 71-48, 1971-1 CB 99, amplified by Rev. Rul. 73-53, 1973-1 CB 139
. modified for person in an iron lung	Yes	Rev. Rul. 55-261, 1955-1 CB 307
Television, closed caption decoder	Yes	Rev. Rul. 80-340, 1980-2 CB 81
Toilet articles	No	O.G. Russell, 12 TCM 1276, Dec. 19,973(M)
Transplant, donor's costs of	Yes	Rev. Rul. 68-452, 1968-2 CB 111; Rev. Rul. 73-189, 1973-1 CB 139
Transportation, cost incurred essentially and primarily for medical care	Yes	Code Sec. 213(d)(1)(B) and Reg. § 1.213-1(e)(1)(iv)
Trips, general health improvement	No	Reg. § 1.213-1(e)(1)(iv)
Vacations, health restorative	No	Reg. § 1.213-1(e)(1)(iv) and Rev. Rul. 57-130, 1957-1 CB 108

References in Checklists are to the 2002 Standard Federal Tax Reports.

¶ 59

Medical Expense	Deductible	Authority
Vacuum cleaner, alleviation of dust allergy	No	Rev. Rul. 76-80, 1976-1 CB 71
Vasectomy, legal	Yes	Rev. Rul. 73-201, 1973-1 CB 140, clarified by Rev. Rul. 73-603, 1973-2 CB 76, and Rev. Rul. 97-9, 1997-1 CB 77
Visual alert system for hearing impaired	Yes	IRS Letter Ruling 8250040, 9-13-82, CCH IRS Letter Rulings Reports
Weight loss program for treatment of specific disease	Yes	IRS Letter Ruling 8004111, 10-31-79, CCH IRS LETTER RULINGS REPORTS
Weight loss programs to improve appearance, prescribed	No	Rev. Rul. 79-151, 1979-1 CB 116; IRS Publication 502
Wheelchair	Yes	Reg. § 1.213-1(e)(1)(iii)
Wig, alleviation of mental discomfort resulting from disease	Yes	Rev. Rul. 62-189, 1962-2 CB 88
X-rays	Yes	Reg. § 1.213-1(e)(1)(ii)

References in Checklists are to the 2002 Standard Federal Tax Reports.

¶ 59

Return Flow Charts

COMPUTATION OF TAXABLE INCOME

	Par.

¶ 61   Individuals

The computation of an individual's taxable income involves several steps. Items that constitute income for tax purposes must be sifted from items that do not constitute income. Similarly, expenses that are deductible must be sifted from expenses that are not deductible. In addition, deductible expenses must be divided into expenses that are deductible from gross income and those that are deductible as itemized deductions.

The following outline summarizes the computation of taxable income by an individual and highlights those items that often enter into this computation.

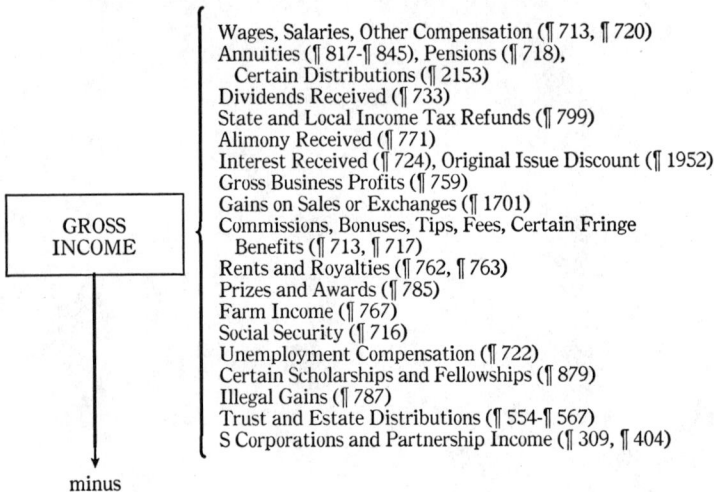

GROSS INCOME	Wages, Salaries, Other Compensation (¶ 713, ¶ 720) Annuities (¶ 817-¶ 845), Pensions (¶ 718), Certain Distributions (¶ 2153) Dividends Received (¶ 733) State and Local Income Tax Refunds (¶ 799) Alimony Received (¶ 771) Interest Received (¶ 724), Original Issue Discount (¶ 1952) Gross Business Profits (¶ 759) Gains on Sales or Exchanges (¶ 1701) Commissions, Bonuses, Tips, Fees, Certain Fringe Benefits (¶ 713, ¶ 717) Rents and Royalties (¶ 762, ¶ 763) Prizes and Awards (¶ 785) Farm Income (¶ 767) Social Security (¶ 716) Unemployment Compensation (¶ 722) Certain Scholarships and Fellowships (¶ 879) Illegal Gains (¶ 787) Trust and Estate Distributions (¶ 554-¶ 567) S Corporations and Partnership Income (¶ 309, ¶ 404)

minus

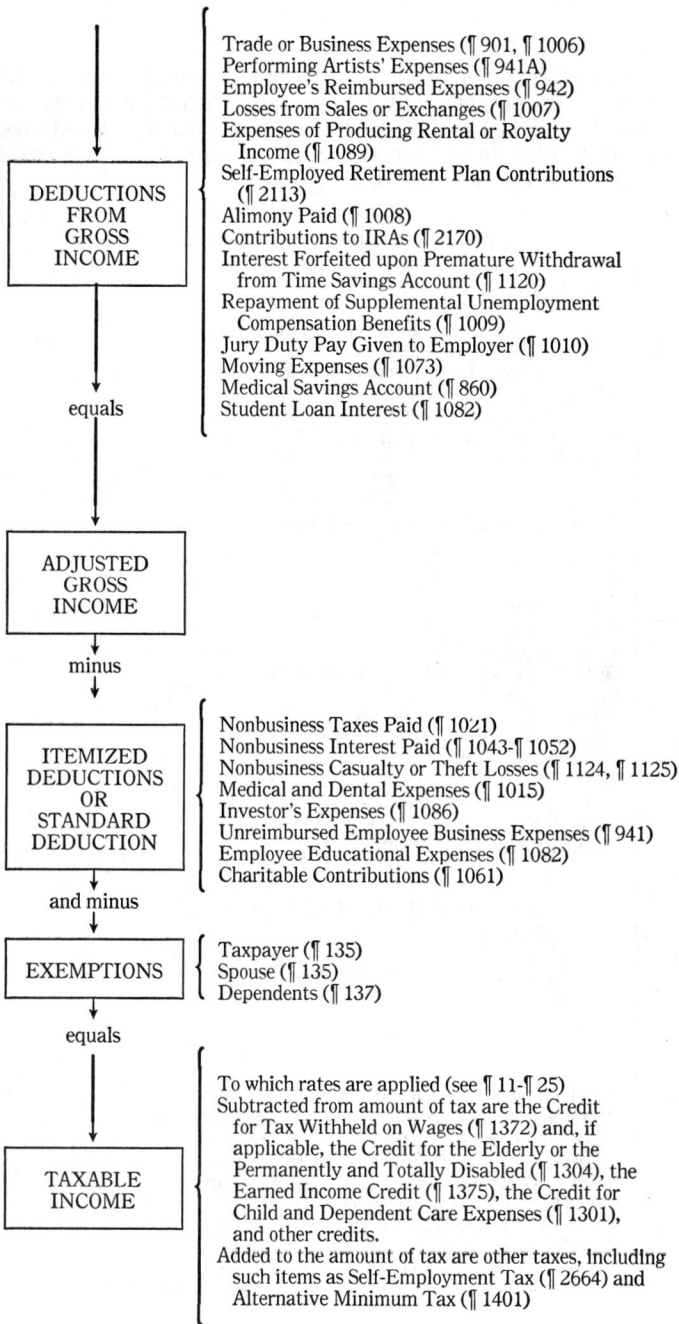

DEDUCTIONS FROM GROSS INCOME

- Trade or Business Expenses (¶ 901, ¶ 1006)
- Performing Artists' Expenses (¶ 941A)
- Employee's Reimbursed Expenses (¶ 942)
- Losses from Sales or Exchanges (¶ 1007)
- Expenses of Producing Rental or Royalty Income (¶ 1089)
- Self-Employed Retirement Plan Contributions (¶ 2113)
- Alimony Paid (¶ 1008)
- Contributions to IRAs (¶ 2170)
- Interest Forfeited upon Premature Withdrawal from Time Savings Account (¶ 1120)
- Repayment of Supplemental Unemployment Compensation Benefits (¶ 1009)
- Jury Duty Pay Given to Employer (¶ 1010)
- Moving Expenses (¶ 1073)
- Medical Savings Account (¶ 860)
- Student Loan Interest (¶ 1082)

equals

ADJUSTED GROSS INCOME

minus

ITEMIZED DEDUCTIONS OR STANDARD DEDUCTION

- Nonbusiness Taxes Paid (¶ 1021)
- Nonbusiness Interest Paid (¶ 1043-¶ 1052)
- Nonbusiness Casualty or Theft Losses (¶ 1124, ¶ 1125)
- Medical and Dental Expenses (¶ 1015)
- Investor's Expenses (¶ 1086)
- Unreimbursed Employee Business Expenses (¶ 941)
- Employee Educational Expenses (¶ 1082)
- Charitable Contributions (¶ 1061)

and minus

EXEMPTIONS

- Taxpayer (¶ 135)
- Spouse (¶ 135)
- Dependents (¶ 137)

equals

TAXABLE INCOME

- To which rates are applied (see ¶ 11-¶ 25)
- Subtracted from amount of tax are the Credit for Tax Withheld on Wages (¶ 1372) and, if applicable, the Credit for the Elderly or the Permanently and Totally Disabled (¶ 1304), the Earned Income Credit (¶ 1375), the Credit for Child and Dependent Care Expenses (¶ 1301), and other credits.
- Added to the amount of tax are other taxes, including such items as Self-Employment Tax (¶ 2664) and Alternative Minimum Tax (¶ 1401)

¶61

¶ 62   Corporations

The computation of a corporation's taxable income involves several steps. Items that constitute income for tax purposes must be segregated from items that do not constitute income. Similarly, expenses that are deductible must be segregated from expenses that are not deductible. In addition, deductible expenses must be classified as either ordinary expenses or special deductions.

The following outline summarizes the computation of taxable income by a corporation and highlights those items that often enter into this computation.

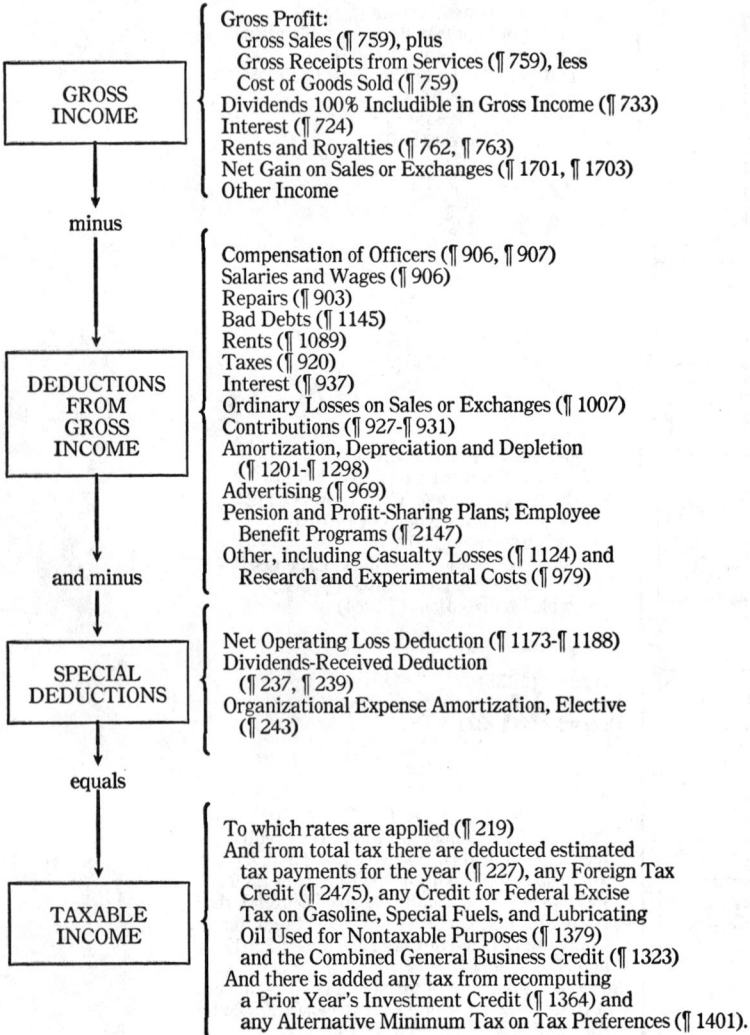

GROSS INCOME

Gross Profit:
Gross Sales (¶ 759), plus
Gross Receipts from Services (¶ 759), less
Cost of Goods Sold (¶ 759)
Dividends 100% Includible in Gross Income (¶ 733)
Interest (¶ 724)
Rents and Royalties (¶ 762, ¶ 763)
Net Gain on Sales or Exchanges (¶ 1701, ¶ 1703)
Other Income

minus

DEDUCTIONS FROM GROSS INCOME

Compensation of Officers (¶ 906, ¶ 907)
Salaries and Wages (¶ 906)
Repairs (¶ 903)
Bad Debts (¶ 1145)
Rents (¶ 1089)
Taxes (¶ 920)
Interest (¶ 937)
Ordinary Losses on Sales or Exchanges (¶ 1007)
Contributions (¶ 927-¶ 931)
Amortization, Depreciation and Depletion
    (¶ 1201-¶ 1298)
Advertising (¶ 969)
Pension and Profit-Sharing Plans; Employee
    Benefit Programs (¶ 2147)
Other, including Casualty Losses (¶ 1124) and
    Research and Experimental Costs (¶ 979)

and minus

SPECIAL DEDUCTIONS

Net Operating Loss Deduction (¶ 1173-¶ 1188)
Dividends-Received Deduction
    (¶ 237, ¶ 239)
Organizational Expense Amortization, Elective
    (¶ 243)

equals

TAXABLE INCOME

To which rates are applied (¶ 219)
And from total tax there are deducted estimated
    tax payments for the year (¶ 227), any Foreign Tax
    Credit (¶ 2475), any Credit for Federal Excise
    Tax on Gasoline, Special Fuels, and Lubricating
    Oil Used for Nontaxable Purposes (¶ 1379)
    and the Combined General Business Credit (¶ 1323)
And there is added any tax from recomputing
    a Prior Year's Investment Credit (¶ 1364) and
    any Alternative Minimum Tax on Tax Preferences (¶ 1401).

¶ 63   Partnerships

Although a partnership does not pay tax, it must nevertheless report its income and expenses so that its partners may account for partnership income and expenses on their income tax returns.

Many types of income and expenses are separately stated and flow through to the partners. Similarly, many types of deduction and some types of credit information are separately stated and flow through to the partners. See ¶ 431. The remaining income and deductions that are not separately reported are combined into the partnership's taxable income or loss.

The separately stated income and expense items, information regarding credits, and the partnership's ordinary income or loss are reported on Schedule K. These income, deduction and credit items are allocated to each partner on Schedule K-1, **a** copy of which is furnished to each partner.

The following outline summarizes the computation of the partnership's income or loss (i.e., its bottom-line income or loss as reflected on page 1, Form 1065) and highlights those items that often enter into this computation.

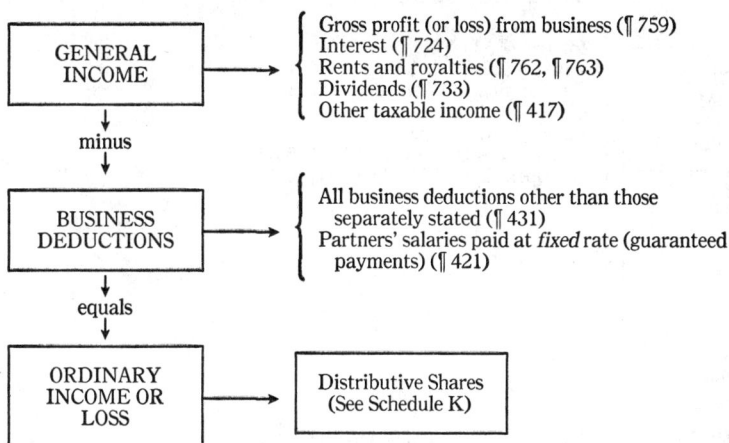

```
┌─────────────┐        ⎧ Gross profit (or loss) from business (¶ 759)
│  GENERAL    │        ⎪ Interest (¶ 724)
│  INCOME     │──────▶ ⎨ Rents and royalties (¶ 762, ¶ 763)
└─────────────┘        ⎪ Dividends (¶ 733)
      ↓                ⎩ Other taxable income (¶ 417)
    minus
      ↓
┌─────────────┐        ⎧ All business deductions other than those
│  BUSINESS   │        ⎪   separately stated (¶ 431)
│  DEDUCTIONS │──────▶ ⎨ Partners' salaries paid at *fixed* rate (guaranteed
└─────────────┘        ⎩   payments) (¶ 421)
      ↓
    equals
      ↓
┌─────────────┐        ┌──────────────────────┐
│  ORDINARY   │        │ Distributive Shares   │
│ INCOME OR   │──────▶ │ (See Schedule K)      │
│   LOSS      │        └──────────────────────┘
└─────────────┘
```

¶ 64   Estates and Trusts

Estates and trusts are distinct entities for income tax purposes. They are subject to the same income taxes as individuals and are taxed in much the same manner as individuals. However, estates and trusts are not subject to self-employment tax. Although an estate or trust is a taxable entity, it is nevertheless a conduit of income to be distributed. Income is taxed to the estate or trust unless distributed. A deduction is allowed for distributed income, which becomes taxable to the beneficiary distributees.

The following outline summarizes the computation of taxable income by a trust or estate and highlights those items that often enter into this computation.

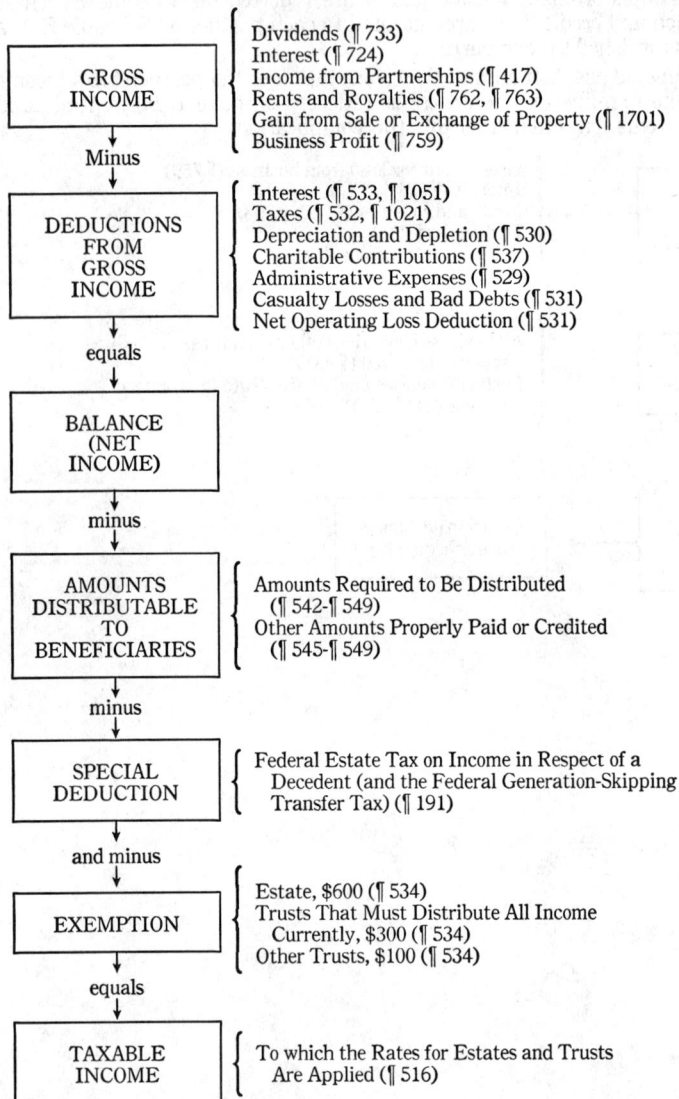

GROSS INCOME	Dividends (¶ 733) Interest (¶ 724) Income from Partnerships (¶ 417) Rents and Royalties (¶ 762, ¶ 763) Gain from Sale or Exchange of Property (¶ 1701) Business Profit (¶ 759)

Minus

DEDUCTIONS FROM GROSS INCOME	Interest (¶ 533, ¶ 1051) Taxes (¶ 532, ¶ 1021) Depreciation and Depletion (¶ 530) Charitable Contributions (¶ 537) Administrative Expenses (¶ 529) Casualty Losses and Bad Debts (¶ 531) Net Operating Loss Deduction (¶ 531)

equals

BALANCE (NET INCOME)

minus

AMOUNTS DISTRIBUTABLE TO BENEFICIARIES	Amounts Required to Be Distributed
	    (¶ 542-¶ 549)
	Other Amounts Properly Paid or Credited
	    (¶ 545-¶ 549)

minus

SPECIAL DEDUCTION	Federal Estate Tax on Income in Respect of a
	    Decedent (and the Federal Generation-Skipping
	    Transfer Tax) (¶ 191)

and minus

EXEMPTION	Estate, $600 (¶ 534) Trusts That Must Distribute All Income Currently, $300 (¶ 534) Other Trusts, $100 (¶ 534)

equals

TAXABLE INCOME	To which the Rates for Estates and Trusts Are Applied (¶ 516)

¶ 64

SPECIAL TAX TABLES

¶ 83 Applicable Federal Rates

Following are the monthly applicable federal interest rates for January through November 2001, published by the IRS for purposes of testing imputed interest in below-market interest loans (¶ 795) and debt-for-property transactions (¶ 1954). The rates are also relevant under the golden parachute rules (¶ 907) and for testing interest in connection with deferred payments for the use of property (¶ 1859).

In the case of below-market interest loans that are demand or gift loans, an amount deemed the "foregone" interest is treated as transferred from the lender to the borrower and retransferred by the borrower to the lender as interest. In order to simplify the computation of such foregone interest, the IRS prescribes a "blended annual rate," which is 4.98% on loans from January 1 through December 31, 2001.

	Period for Compounding			
	Annual	*Semiannual*	*Quarterly*	*Monthly*
January 2001				
Short-Term				
AFR	5.90	5.82	5.78	5.75
110% AFR	6.50	6.40	6.35	6.32
120% AFR	7.10	6.98	6.92	6.88
130% AFR	7.71	7.57	7.50	7.45
Mid-Term				
AFR	5.61	5.53	5.49	5.47
110% AFR	6.17	6.08	6.03	6.00
120% AFR	6.75	6.64	6.59	6.55
130% AFR	7.32	7.19	7.13	7.08
150% AFR	8.47	8.30	8.22	8.16
175% AFR	9.91	9.68	9.57	9.49
Long-Term				
AFR	5.78	5.70	5.66	5.63
110% AFR	6.37	6.27	6.22	6.19
120% AFR	6.96	6.84	6.78	6.74
130% AFR	7.55	7.41	7.34	7.30

Period for Compounding

		Annual	Semiannual	Quarterly	Monthly
February 2001					
	Short-Term				
AFR		5.18	5.11	5.08	5.06
110% AFR		5.70	5.62	5.58	5.56
120% AFR		6.22	6.13	6.08	6.05
130% AFR		6.75	6.64	6.59	6.55
	Mid-Term				
AFR		5.07	5.01	4.98	4.96
110% AFR		5.59	5.51	5.47	5.45
120% AFR		6.10	6.01	5.97	5.94
130% AFR		6.62	6.51	6.46	6.42
150% AFR		7.66	7.52	7.45	7.40
175% AFR		8.96	8.77	8.68	8.61
	Long-Term				
AFR		5.48	5.41	5.37	5.35
110% AFR		6.04	5.95	5.91	5.88
120% AFR		6.60	6.49	6.44	6.40
130% AFR		7.15	7.03	6.97	6.93
March 2001					
	Short-Term				
AFR		4.86	4.80	4.77	4.75
110% AFR		5.35	5.28	5.25	5.22
120% AFR		5.84	5.76	5.72	5.69
130% AFR		6.34	6.24	6.19	6.16
	Mid-Term				
AFR		5.07	5.01	4.98	4.96
110% AFR		5.59	5.51	5.47	5.45
120% AFR		6.10	6.01	5.97	5.94
130% AFR		6.62	6.51	6.46	6.42
150% AFR		7.66	7.52	7.45	7.40
175% AFR		8.96	8.77	8.68	8.61
	Long-Term				
AFR		5.58	5.50	5.46	5.44
110% AFR		6.14	6.05	6.00	5.98
120% AFR		6.71	6.60	6.55	6.51
130% AFR		7.28	7.15	7.09	7.05
April 2001					
	Short-Term				
AFR		4.63	4.58	4.55	4.54
110% AFR		5.10	5.04	5.01	4.99
120% AFR		5.58	5.50	5.46	5.44
130% AFR		6.04	5.95	5.91	5.88
	Mid-Term				
AFR		4.94	4.88	4.85	4.83
110% AFR		5.44	5.37	5.33	5.31
120% AFR		5.95	5.86	5.82	5.79
130% AFR		6.44	6.34	6.29	6.26
150% AFR		7.45	7.32	7.25	7.21
175% AFR		8.72	8.54	8.45	8.39
	Long-Term				
AFR		5.43	5.36	5.32	5.30
110% AFR		5.99	5.90	5.86	5.83
120% AFR		6.53	6.43	6.38	6.35
130% AFR		7.09	6.97	6.91	6.87

¶ 83

	Period for Compounding			
	Annual	Semiannual	Quarterly	Monthly

May 2001

Short-Term

	Annual	Semiannual	Quarterly	Monthly
AFR	4.25	4.21	4.19	4.17
110% AFR	4.68	4.63	4.60	4.59
120% AFR	5.11	5.05	5.02	5.00
130% AFR	5.54	5.47	5.43	5.41

Mid-Term

	Annual	Semiannual	Quarterly	Monthly
AFR	4.77	4.71	4.68	4.66
110% AFR	5.25	5.18	5.15	5.12
120% AFR	5.73	5.65	5.61	5.58
130% AFR	6.21	6.12	6.07	6.04
150% AFR	7.19	7.07	7.01	6.97
175% AFR	8.41	8.24	8.16	8.10

Long-Term

	Annual	Semiannual	Quarterly	Monthly
AFR	5.43	5.36	5.32	5.30
110% AFR	5.99	5.90	5.86	5.83
120% AFR	6.53	6.43	6.38	6.35
130% AFR	7.09	6.97	6.91	6.87

June 2001

Short-Term

	Annual	Semiannual	Quarterly	Monthly
AFR	4.15	4.11	4.09	4.08
110% AFR	4.57	4.52	4.49	4.48
120% AFR	4.99	4.93	4.90	4.88
130% AFR	5.41	5.34	5.30	5.28

Mid-Term

	Annual	Semiannual	Quarterly	Monthly
AFR	5.02	4.96	4.93	4.91
110% AFR	5.53	5.46	5.42	5.40
120% AFR	6.04	5.95	5.91	5.88
130% AFR	6.55	6.45	6.40	6.36
150% AFR	7.58	7.44	7.37	7.33
175% AFR	8.87	8.68	8.59	8.53

Long-Term

	Annual	Semiannual	Quarterly	Monthly
AFR	5.75	5.67	5.63	5.60
110% AFR	6.34	6.24	6.19	6.16
120% AFR	6.92	6.80	6.74	6.71
130% AFR	7.51	7.37	7.30	7.26

July 2001

Short-Term

	Annual	Semiannual	Quarterly	Monthly
AFR	4.07	4.03	4.01	4.00
110% AFR	4.48	4.43	4.41	4.39
120% AFR	4.90	4.84	4.81	4.79
130% AFR	5.31	5.24	5.21	5.18

Mid-Term

	Annual	Semiannual	Quarterly	Monthly
AFR	5.12	5.06	5.03	5.01
110% AFR	5.65	5.57	5.53	5.51
120% AFR	6.16	6.07	6.02	5.99
130% AFR	6.69	6.58	6.53	6.49
150% AFR	7.73	7.59	7.52	7.47
175% AFR	9.06	8.86	8.76	8.70

Long-Term

	Annual	Semiannual	Quarterly	Monthly
AFR	5.82	5.74	5.70	5.67
110% AFR	6.41	6.31	6.26	6.23
120% AFR	7.01	6.89	6.83	6.79
130% AFR	7.60	7.46	7.39	7.35

	Period for Compounding			
	Annual	*Semiannual*	*Quarterly*	*Monthly*

August 2001

Short-Term

	Annual	Semiannual	Quarterly	Monthly
AFR	3.94	3.90	3.88	3.87
110% AFR	4.34	4.29	4.27	4.25
120% AFR	4.73	4.68	4.65	4.64
130% AFR	5.13	5.07	5.04	5.02

Mid-Term

AFR	4.99	4.93	4.90	4.88
110% AFR	5.49	5.42	5.38	5.36
120% AFR	6.01	5.92	5.88	5.85
130% AFR	6.51	6.41	6.36	6.33
150% AFR	7.54	7.40	7.33	7.29
175% AFR	8.82	8.63	8.54	8.48

Long-Term

AFR	5.72	5.64	5.60	5.57
110% AFR	6.30	6.20	6.15	6.12
120% AFR	6.88	6.77	6.71	6.68
130% AFR	7.46	7.33	7.26	7.22

September 2001

Short-Term

AFR	3.82	3.78	3.76	3.75
110% AFR	4.20	4.16	4.14	4.12
120% AFR	4.59	4.54	4.51	4.50
130% AFR	4.97	4.91	4.88	4.86

Mid-Term

AFR	4.82	4.76	4.73	4.71
110% AFR	5.31	5.24	5.21	5.18
120% AFR	5.79	5.71	5.67	5.64
130% AFR	6.29	6.19	6.14	6.11
150% AFR	7.27	7.14	7.08	7.04
175% AFR	8.50	8.33	8.25	8.19

Long-Term

AFR	5.57	5.49	5.45	5.43
110% AFR	6.13	6.04	6.00	5.97
120% AFR	6.70	6.59	6.54	6.50
130% AFR	7.27	7.14	7.08	7.04

October 2001

Short-Term

AFR	3.58	3.55	3.53	3.52
110% AFR	3.95	3.91	3.89	3.88
120% AFR	4.31	4.26	4.24	4.22
130% AFR	4.67	4.62	4.59	4.58

Mid-Term

AFR	4.59	4.54	4.51	4.50
110% AFR	5.05	4.99	4.96	4.94
120% AFR	5.52	5.45	5.41	5.39
130% AFR	5.99	5.90	5.86	5.83
150% AFR	6.93	6.81	6.75	6.72
175% AFR	8.11	7.95	7.87	7.82

Long-Term

AFR	5.39	5.32	5.29	5.26
110% AFR	5.94	5.85	5.81	5.78
120% AFR	6.48	6.38	6.33	6.30
130% AFR	7.04	6.92	6.86	6.82

¶83

| | Period for Compounding | | | |
	Annual	Semiannual	Quarterly	Monthly
November 2001				
Short-Term				
AFR	2.73	2.71	2.70	2.69
110% AFR	3.00	2.98	2.97	2.96
120% AFR	3.28	3.25	3.24	3.23
130% AFR	3.55	3.52	3.50	3.49
Mid-Term				
AFR	4.13	4.09	4.07	4.06
110% AFR	4.55	4.50	4.47	4.46
120% AFR	4.97	4.91	4.88	4.86
130% AFR	5.39	5.32	5.29	5.26
150% AFR	6.23	6.14	6.09	6.06
175% AFR	7.29	7.16	7.10	7.06
Long-Term				
AFR	5.31	5.24	5.21	5.18
110% AFR	5.84	5.76	5.72	5.69
120% AFR	6.39	6.29	6.24	6.21
130% AFR	6.93	6.81	6.75	6.72

¶ 84   Adjusted Applicable Federal Rates

Code Sec. 1288 provides that, in determining original issue discount on tax-exempt obligations, an adjustment must be made to the applicable federal rates (¶ 83) to take into account the tax exemption for interest on the obligations.

Adjusted Applicable Federal Rates

January 2001

	Annual Compounding	Semiannual Compounding	Quarterly Compounding	Monthly Compounding
Short-term rate	4.18%	4.14%	4.12%	4.10%
Mid-term rate	4.52%	4.47%	4.45%	4.43%
Long-term rate	5.24%	5.17%	5.14%	5.12%

February 2001

	Annual Compounding	Semiannual Compounding	Quarterly Compounding	Monthly Compounding
Short-term rate	3.91%	3.87%	3.85%	3.84%
Mid-term rate	4.25%	4.21%	4.19%	4.17%
Long-term rate	4.92%	4.86%	4.83%	4.81%

March 2001

	Annual Compounding	Semiannual Compounding	Quarterly Compounding	Monthly Compounding
Short-term rate	3.44%	3.41%	3.40%	3.39%
Mid-term rate	3.98%	3.94%	3.92%	3.91%
Long-term rate	4.87%	4.81%	4.78%	4.76%

April 2001

	Annual Compounding	Semiannual Compounding	Quarterly Compounding	Monthly Compounding
Short-term rate	3.37%	3.34%	3.33%	3.32%
Mid-term rate	3.89%	3.85%	3.83%	3.82%
Long-term rate	4.87%	4.81%	4.78%	4.76%

¶ 84

May 2001

	Annual Compounding	Semiannual Compounding	Quarterly Compounding	Monthly Compounding
Short-term rate	3.37%	3.31%	3.30%	3.29%
Mid-term rate	3.89%	3.85%	3.83%	3.82%
Long-term rate	4.89%	4.83%	4.80%	4.78%

June 2001

	Annual Compounding	Semiannual Compounding	Quarterly Compounding	Monthly Compounding
Short-term rate	3.46%	3.43%	3.42%	3.41%
Mid-term rate	3.99%	3.95%	3.93%	3.92%
Long-term rate	5.01%	4.95%	4.92%	4.90%

July 2001

	Annual Compounding	Semiannual Compounding	Quarterly Compounding	Monthly Compounding
Short-term rate	3.16%	3.14%	3.13%	3.12%
Mid-term rate	3.87%	3.83%	3.81%	3.80%
Long-term rate	5.00%	4.94%	4.91%	4.89%

August 2001

	Annual Compounding	Semiannual Compounding	Quarterly Compounding	Monthly Compounding
Short-term rate	3.01%	2.99%	2.98%	2.97%
Mid-term rate	3.83%	3.79%	3.77%	3.76%
Long-term rate	4.94%	4.88%	4.85%	4.83%

September 2001

	Annual Compounding	Semiannual Compounding	Quarterly Compounding	Monthly Compounding
Short-term rate	2.90%	2.88%	2.87%	2.86%
Mid-term rate	3.73%	3.70%	3.68%	3.67%
Long-term rate	4.85%	4.79%	4.76%	4.74%

October 2001

	Annual Compounding	Semiannual Compounding	Quarterly Compounding	Monthly Compounding
Short-term rate	2.72%	2.70%	2.69%	2.68%
Mid-term rate	3.57%	3.54%	3.52%	3.51%
Long-term rate	4.71%	4.66%	4.63%	4.62%

November 2001

	Annual Compounding	Semiannual Compounding	Quarterly Compounding	Monthly Compounding
Short-term rate	2.39%	2.38%	2.37%	2.37%
Mid-term rate	3.41%	3.38%	3.37%	3.36%
Long-term rate	4.74%	4.69%	4.66%	4.64%

¶84

¶ 85 Federal Long-Term Tax-Exempt Rates

Code Sec. 382 provides that the long-term tax-exempt rate for purposes of net operating loss carryforwards is the highest of the adjusted federal long-term rates (¶ 84) for the three months ending with the month in which the particular ownership change occurs. Each rate below is the highest for the three-month period.

Long-Term Tax-Exempt Rates

Month	Rate
January 2001	5.39%
February 2001	5.31%
March 2001	5.24%
April 2001	4.92%
May 2001	4.89%
June 2001	5.01%
July 2001	5.01%
August 2001	5.01%
September 2001	5.00%
October 2001	4.94%
November 2001	4.85%

¶ 86 Applicable Credit Percentages for Low-Income Housing

Code Sec. 42 provides that applicable credit percentages for low-income housing are to be computed so that the present value of the 10 annual credit amounts at the beginning of the 10-year credit period equals either 70% or 30% of the qualified basis of the low-income units in a project. The discount rate for determining the present value in these computations is a rate equal to 72% of the average of the month's AFR for mid-term and long-term obligations. The applicable credit percentage for new construction or rehabilitation expenditures not federally subsidized is indicated under the 70% rate column. The applicable credit percentage for subsidized construction or rehabilitation expenditures and the acquisition of existing housing is indicated under the 30% rate column. See ¶ 1334.

Applicable Credit Percentages for Low-Income Housing

Month	70% Rate	30% Rate
January 2001	8.33%	3.57%
February 2001	8.23%	3.53%
March 2001	8.24%	3.53%
April 2001	8.21%	3.52%
May 2001	8.19%	3.51%
June 2001	8.26%	3.54%
July 2001	8.28%	3.55%
August 2001	8.25%	3.54%
September 2001	8.21%	3.52%
October 2001	8.16%	3.50%
November 2001	8.10%	3.47%

¶ 87 Earned Income Credit

The earned income credit tables are used in conjunction with the Form 1040 or Form 1040A, and Schedule EIC. The appropriate Schedule must be filed with the taxpayer's tax return in order to claim the earned income credit. The credit, as computed on the Schedules, is entered on line 61a, Form 1040, or on line 39a, Form 1040A. Form 1040EZ may be used to claim the earned income credit in limited circumstances.

□ The tables on the following pages refer to lines on Schedule EIC, which Form 1040 filers must attach to claim the earned income credit. Taxpayers filing Form 1040A should use similar tables appearing in the Form 1040A instructions.

2001 Earned Income Credit (EIC) Table

⚠ CAUTION — This is **not** a tax table.

1. To find your credit, read down the "At least - But less than" columns and find the line that includes the amount you were told to look up from your EIC Worksheet.

2. Then, read across to the column that includes the number of qualifying children you have. Enter the credit from that column on your EIC Worksheet.

Example. If you have one qualifying child and the amount you are looking up from your EIC Worksheet is $4,875, you would enter $1,658.

If the amount you are looking up from the worksheet is—		And you have— No children	One child	Two children
At least	But less than	*Your credit is—*		
4,800	4,850	364	1,641	1,930
4,850	4,900	364	1,658	1,950
4,900	4,950	364	1,675	1,970
4,950	5,000	364	1,692	1,990

At least	But less than	No children	One child	Two children
$1	$50	$2	$9	$10
50	100	6	26	30
100	150	10	43	50
150	200	13	60	70
200	250	17	77	90
250	300	21	94	110
300	350	25	111	130
350	400	29	128	150
400	450	33	145	170
450	500	36	162	190
500	550	40	179	210
550	600	44	196	230
600	650	48	213	250
650	700	52	230	270
700	750	55	247	290
750	800	59	264	310
800	850	63	281	330
850	900	67	298	350
900	950	71	315	370
950	1,000	75	332	390
1,000	1,050	78	349	410
1,050	1,100	82	366	430
1,100	1,150	86	383	450
1,150	1,200	90	400	470
1,200	1,250	94	417	490
1,250	1,300	98	434	510
1,300	1,350	101	451	530
1,350	1,400	105	468	550
1,400	1,450	109	485	570
1,450	1,500	113	502	590
1,500	1,550	117	519	610
1,550	1,600	120	536	630
1,600	1,650	124	553	650
1,650	1,700	128	570	670
1,700	1,750	132	587	690
1,750	1,800	136	604	710
1,800	1,850	140	621	730
1,850	1,900	143	638	750
1,900	1,950	147	655	770
1,950	2,000	151	672	790
2,000	2,050	155	689	810
2,050	2,100	159	706	830
2,100	2,150	163	723	850
2,150	2,200	166	740	870

At least	But less than	No children	One child	Two children
2,200	2,250	170	757	890
2,250	2,300	174	774	910
2,300	2,350	178	791	930
2,350	2,400	182	808	950
2,400	2,450	186	825	970
2,450	2,500	189	842	990
2,500	2,550	193	859	1,010
2,550	2,600	197	876	1,030
2,600	2,650	201	893	1,050
2,650	2,700	205	910	1,070
2,700	2,750	208	927	1,090
2,750	2,800	212	944	1,110
2,800	2,850	216	961	1,130
2,850	2,900	220	978	1,150
2,900	2,950	224	995	1,170
2,950	3,000	228	1,012	1,190
3,000	3,050	231	1,029	1,210
3,050	3,100	235	1,046	1,230
3,100	3,150	239	1,063	1,250
3,150	3,200	243	1,080	1,270
3,200	3,250	247	1,097	1,290
3,250	3,300	251	1,114	1,310
3,300	3,350	254	1,131	1,330
3,350	3,400	258	1,148	1,350
3,400	3,450	262	1,165	1,370
3,450	3,500	266	1,182	1,390
3,500	3,550	270	1,199	1,410
3,550	3,600	273	1,216	1,430
3,600	3,650	277	1,233	1,450
3,650	3,700	281	1,250	1,470
3,700	3,750	285	1,267	1,490
3,750	3,800	288	1,284	1,510
3,800	3,850	293	1,301	1,530
3,850	3,900	296	1,318	1,550
3,900	3,950	300	1,335	1,570
3,950	4,000	304	1,352	1,590
4,000	4,050	308	1,369	1,610
4,050	4,100	312	1,386	1,630
4,100	4,150	316	1,403	1,650
4,150	4,200	319	1,420	1,670
4,200	4,250	323	1,437	1,690
4,250	4,300	327	1,454	1,710
4,300	4,350	331	1,471	1,730
4,350	4,400	335	1,488	1,750

At least	But less than	No children	One child	Two children
4,400	4,450	339	1,505	1,770
4,450	4,500	342	1,522	1,790
4,500	4,550	346	1,539	1,810
4,550	4,600	350	1,556	1,830
4,600	4,650	354	1,573	1,850
4,650	4,700	358	1,590	1,870
4,700	4,750	361	1,607	1,890
4,750	4,800	364	1,624	1,910
4,800	4,850	364	1,641	1,930
4,850	4,900	364	1,658	1,950
4,900	4,950	364	1,675	1,970
4,950	5,000	364	1,692	1,990
5,000	5,050	364	1,709	2,010
5,050	5,100	364	1,726	2,030
5,100	5,150	364	1,743	2,050
5,150	5,200	364	1,760	2,070
5,200	5,250	364	1,777	2,090
5,250	5,300	364	1,794	2,110
5,300	5,350	364	1,811	2,130
5,350	5,400	364	1,828	2,150
5,400	5,450	364	1,845	2,170
5,450	5,500	364	1,862	2,190
5,500	5,550	364	1,879	2,210
5,550	5,600	364	1,896	2,230
5,600	5,650	364	1,913	2,250
5,650	5,700	364	1,930	2,270
5,700	5,750	364	1,947	2,290
5,750	5,800	364	1,964	2,310
5,800	5,850	364	1,981	2,330
5,850	5,900	364	1,998	2,350
5,900	5,950	364	2,015	2,370
5,950	6,000	364	2,032	2,390
6,000	6,050	358	2,049	2,410
6,050	6,100	355	2,066	2,430
6,100	6,150	351	2,083	2,450
6,150	6,200	347	2,100	2,470
6,200	6,250	343	2,117	2,490
6,250	6,300	339	2,134	2,510
6,300	6,350	335	2,151	2,530
6,350	6,400	332	2,168	2,550
6,400	6,450	328	2,185	2,570
6,450	6,500	324	2,202	2,590
6,500	6,550	320	2,219	2,610
6,550	6,600	316	2,236	2,630

At least	But less than	No children	One child	Two children
6,600	6,650	313	2,253	2,650
6,650	6,700	309	2,270	2,670
6,700	6,750	305	2,287	2,690
6,750	6,800	301	2,304	2,710
6,800	6,850	297	2,321	2,730
6,850	6,900	293	2,338	2,750
6,900	6,950	290	2,355	2,770
6,950	7,000	286	2,372	2,790
7,000	7,050	282	2,389	2,810
7,050	7,100	278	2,406	2,830
7,100	7,150	274	2,428	2,850
7,150	7,200	270	2,428	2,870
7,200	7,250	267	2,428	2,890
7,250	7,300	263	2,428	2,910
7,300	7,350	259	2,428	2,930
7,350	7,400	255	2,428	2,950
7,400	7,450	251	2,428	2,970
7,450	7,500	247	2,428	2,990
7,500	7,550	244	2,428	3,010
7,550	7,600	240	2,428	3,030
7,600	7,650	236	2,428	3,050
7,650	7,700	232	2,428	3,070
7,700	7,750	228	2,428	3,090
7,750	7,800	225	2,428	3,110
7,800	7,850	221	2,428	3,130
7,850	7,900	217	2,428	3,150
7,900	7,950	213	2,428	3,170
7,950	8,000	209	2,428	3,190
8,000	8,050	205	2,428	3,210
8,050	8,100	202	2,428	3,230
8,100	8,150	198	2,428	3,250
8,150	8,200	194	2,428	3,270
8,200	8,250	190	2,428	3,290
8,250	8,300	186	2,428	3,310
8,300	8,350	182	2,428	3,330
8,350	8,400	179	2,428	3,350
8,400	8,450	175	2,428	3,370
8,450	8,500	171	2,428	3,390
8,500	8,550	167	2,428	3,410
8,550	8,600	163	2,428	3,430
8,600	8,650	160	2,428	3,450
8,650	8,700	156	2,428	3,470
8,700	8,750	152	2,428	3,490
8,750	8,800	148	2,428	3,510

Need more information or forms? See page 7.

- 48 -　　(Continued on page 49)

SPECIAL TAX TABLES □ Earned Income Credit

85

2001 Earned Income Credit (EIC) Table Continued (Caution. This is not a tax table.)

At least	But less than	No children	One child	Two children
8,800	8,850	144	2,428	3,530
8,850	8,900	140	2,428	3,550
8,900	8,950	137	2,428	3,570
8,950	9,000	133	2,428	3,590
9,000	9,050	129	2,428	3,610
9,050	9,100	125	2,428	3,630
9,100	9,150	121	2,428	3,650
9,150	9,200	117	2,428	3,670
9,200	9,250	114	2,428	3,690
9,250	9,300	110	2,428	3,710
9,300	9,350	106	2,428	3,730
9,350	9,400	102	2,428	3,750
9,400	9,450	98	2,428	3,770
9,450	9,500	94	2,428	3,790
9,500	9,550	91	2,428	3,810
9,550	9,600	87	2,428	3,830
9,600	9,650	83	2,428	3,850
9,650	9,700	79	2,428	3,870
9,700	9,750	75	2,428	3,890
9,750	9,800	72	2,428	3,910
9,800	9,850	68	2,428	3,930
9,850	9,900	64	2,428	3,950
9,900	9,950	60	2,428	3,970
9,950	10,000	56	2,428	3,990
10,000	10,050	52	2,428	4,008
10,050	10,100	49	2,428	4,008
10,100	10,150	45	2,428	4,008
10,150	10,200	41	2,428	4,008
10,200	10,250	37	2,428	4,008
10,250	10,300	33	2,428	4,008
10,300	10,350	29	2,428	4,008
10,350	10,400	26	2,428	4,008
10,400	10,450	22	2,428	4,008
10,450	10,500	18	2,428	4,008
10,500	10,550	14	2,428	4,008
10,550	10,600	10	2,428	4,008
10,600	10,650	7	2,428	4,008
10,650	10,700	3	2,428	4,008
10,700	10,750	*	2,428	4,008
10,750	13,100	0	2,428	4,008
13,100	13,150	0	2,422	4,001
13,150	13,200	0	2,414	3,990
13,200	13,250	0	2,406	3,980
13,250	13,300	0	2,398	3,969
13,300	13,350	0	2,390	3,959
13,350	13,400	0	2,382	3,948
13,400	13,450	0	2,374	3,937
13,450	13,500	0	2,366	3,927
13,500	13,550	0	2,358	3,916
13,550	13,600	0	2,350	3,906
13,600	13,650	0	2,342	3,895
13,650	13,700	0	2,334	3,885
13,700	13,750	0	2,326	3,874
13,750	13,800	0	2,318	3,864
13,800	13,850	0	2,310	3,853
13,850	13,900	0	2,302	3,843
13,900	13,950	0	2,294	3,832
13,950	14,000	0	2,286	3,822
14,000	14,050	0	2,278	3,811
14,050	14,100	0	2,270	3,801
14,100	14,150	0	2,262	3,790
14,150	14,200	0	2,254	3,779
14,200	14,250	0	2,246	3,769
14,250	14,300	0	2,238	3,758
14,300	14,350	0	2,230	3,748
14,350	14,400	0	2,222	3,737
14,400	14,450	0	2,214	3,727
14,450	14,500	0	2,206	3,716
14,500	14,550	0	2,198	3,706
14,550	14,600	0	2,190	3,695
14,600	14,650	0	2,182	3,685
14,650	14,700	0	2,174	3,674
14,700	14,750	0	2,166	3,664
14,750	14,800	0	2,158	3,653
14,800	14,850	0	2,150	3,643
14,850	14,900	0	2,142	3,632
14,900	14,950	0	2,134	3,622
14,950	15,000	0	2,126	3,611
15,000	15,050	0	2,118	3,600
15,050	15,100	0	2,110	3,590
15,100	15,150	0	2,102	3,579
15,150	15,200	0	2,094	3,569
15,200	15,250	0	2,086	3,558
15,250	15,300	0	2,078	3,548
15,300	15,350	0	2,070	3,537
15,350	15,400	0	2,062	3,527
15,400	15,450	0	2,054	3,516
15,450	15,500	0	2,046	3,506
15,500	15,550	0	2,038	3,495
15,550	15,600	0	2,030	3,485
15,600	15,650	0	2,023	3,474
15,650	15,700	0	2,015	3,464
15,700	15,750	0	2,007	3,453
15,750	15,800	0	1,999	3,443
15,800	15,850	0	1,991	3,432
15,850	15,900	0	1,983	3,421
15,900	15,950	0	1,975	3,411
15,950	16,000	0	1,967	3,400
16,000	16,050	0	1,959	3,390
16,050	16,100	0	1,951	3,379
16,100	16,150	0	1,943	3,369
16,150	16,200	0	1,935	3,358
16,200	16,250	0	1,927	3,348
16,250	16,300	0	1,919	3,337
16,300	16,350	0	1,911	3,327
16,350	16,400	0	1,903	3,316
16,400	16,450	0	1,895	3,306
16,450	16,500	0	1,887	3,295
16,500	16,550	0	1,879	3,285
16,550	16,600	0	1,871	3,274
16,600	16,650	0	1,863	3,264
16,650	16,700	0	1,855	3,253
16,700	16,750	0	1,847	3,242
16,750	16,800	0	1,839	3,232
16,800	16,850	0	1,831	3,221
16,850	16,900	0	1,823	3,211
16,900	16,950	0	1,815	3,200
16,950	17,000	0	1,807	3,190
17,000	17,050	0	1,799	3,179
17,050	17,100	0	1,791	3,169
17,100	17,150	0	1,783	3,158
17,150	17,200	0	1,775	3,148
17,200	17,250	0	1,767	3,137
17,250	17,300	0	1,759	3,127
17,300	17,350	0	1,751	3,116
17,350	17,400	0	1,743	3,106
17,400	17,450	0	1,735	3,095
17,450	17,500	0	1,727	3,085
17,500	17,550	0	1,719	3,074
17,550	17,600	0	1,711	3,063
17,600	17,650	0	1,703	3,053
17,650	17,700	0	1,695	3,042
17,700	17,750	0	1,687	3,032
17,750	17,800	0	1,679	3,021
17,800	17,850	0	1,671	3,011
17,850	17,900	0	1,663	3,000
17,900	17,950	0	1,655	2,990
17,950	18,000	0	1,647	2,979
18,000	18,050	0	1,639	2,969
18,050	18,100	0	1,631	2,958
18,100	18,150	0	1,623	2,948
18,150	18,200	0	1,615	2,937
18,200	18,250	0	1,607	2,927
18,250	18,300	0	1,599	2,916
18,300	18,350	0	1,591	2,906
18,350	18,400	0	1,583	2,895
18,400	18,450	0	1,575	2,884
18,450	18,500	0	1,567	2,874
18,500	18,550	0	1,559	2,863
18,550	18,600	0	1,551	2,853
18,600	18,650	0	1,543	2,842
18,650	18,700	0	1,535	2,832
18,700	18,750	0	1,527	2,821
18,750	18,800	0	1,519	2,811
18,800	18,850	0	1,511	2,800
18,850	18,900	0	1,503	2,790
18,900	18,950	0	1,495	2,779
18,950	19,000	0	1,487	2,769
19,000	19,050	0	1,479	2,758
19,050	19,100	0	1,471	2,748
19,100	19,150	0	1,463	2,737
19,150	19,200	0	1,455	2,726
19,200	19,250	0	1,447	2,716
19,250	19,300	0	1,439	2,705
19,300	19,350	0	1,431	2,695
19,350	19,400	0	1,423	2,684
19,400	19,450	0	1,415	2,674
19,450	19,500	0	1,407	2,663
19,500	19,550	0	1,399	2,653
19,550	19,600	0	1,391	2,642
19,600	19,650	0	1,383	2,632
19,650	19,700	0	1,375	2,621
19,700	19,750	0	1,367	2,611
19,750	19,800	0	1,359	2,600
19,800	19,850	0	1,351	2,590
19,850	19,900	0	1,343	2,579
19,900	19,950	0	1,335	2,569
19,950	20,000	0	1,327	2,558
20,000	20,050	0	1,319	2,547
20,050	20,100	0	1,311	2,537
20,100	20,150	0	1,303	2,526
20,150	20,200	0	1,295	2,516
20,200	20,250	0	1,287	2,505
20,250	20,300	0	1,279	2,495
20,300	20,350	0	1,271	2,484
20,350	20,400	0	1,263	2,474
20,400	20,450	0	1,255	2,463
20,450	20,500	0	1,247	2,453
20,500	20,550	0	1,239	2,442
20,550	20,600	0	1,231	2,432
20,600	20,650	0	1,224	2,421
20,650	20,700	0	1,216	2,411
20,700	20,750	0	1,208	2,400
20,750	20,800	0	1,200	2,390
20,800	20,850	0	1,192	2,379
20,850	20,900	0	1,184	2,368
20,900	20,950	0	1,176	2,358
20,950	21,000	0	1,168	2,347
21,000	21,050	0	1,160	2,337
21,050	21,100	0	1,152	2,326
21,100	21,150	0	1,144	2,316
21,150	21,200	0	1,136	2,305
21,200	21,250	0	1,128	2,295
21,250	21,300	0	1,120	2,284
21,300	21,350	0	1,112	2,274
21,350	21,400	0	1,104	2,263
21,400	21,450	0	1,096	2,253
21,450	21,500	0	1,088	2,242
21,500	21,550	0	1,080	2,232
21,550	21,600	0	1,072	2,221
21,600	21,650	0	1,064	2,211
21,650	21,700	0	1,056	2,200
21,700	21,750	0	1,048	2,189
21,750	21,800	0	1,040	2,179
21,800	21,850	0	1,032	2,168
21,850	21,900	0	1,024	2,158
21,900	21,950	0	1,016	2,147
21,950	22,000	0	1,008	2,137
22,000	22,050	0	1,000	2,126
22,050	22,100	0	992	2,116
22,100	22,150	0	984	2,105
22,150	22,200	0	976	2,095
22,200	22,250	0	968	2,084
22,250	22,300	0	960	2,074

*If the amount you are looking up from the worksheet is at least $10,700 but less than $10,710, your credit is $1. Otherwise, you cannot take the credit.

(Continued on page 50)

- 49 -

Need more information or forms? See page 7.

¶ 87

86   U.S. Master Tax Guide

2001 Earned Income Credit (EIC) Table *Continued*   (Caution. This is **not** a tax table.)

If the amount you are looking up from the worksheet is— At least	But less than	And you have— No children	One child	Two children
22,300	22,350	0	952	2,063
22,350	22,400	0	944	2,053
22,400	22,450	0	936	2,042
22,450	22,500	0	928	2,032
22,500	22,550	0	920	2,021
22,550	22,600	0	912	2,010
22,600	22,650	0	904	2,000
22,650	22,700	0	896	1,989
22,700	22,750	0	888	1,979
22,750	22,800	0	880	1,968
22,800	22,850	0	872	1,958
22,850	22,900	0	864	1,947
22,900	22,950	0	856	1,937
22,950	23,000	0	848	1,926
23,000	23,050	0	840	1,916
23,050	23,100	0	832	1,905
23,100	23,150	0	824	1,895
23,150	23,200	0	816	1,884
23,200	23,250	0	808	1,874
23,250	23,300	0	800	1,863
23,300	23,350	0	792	1,853
23,350	23,400	0	784	1,842
23,400	23,450	0	776	1,831
23,450	23,500	0	768	1,821
23,500	23,550	0	760	1,810
23,550	23,600	0	752	1,800
23,600	23,650	0	744	1,789
23,650	23,700	0	736	1,779
23,700	23,750	0	728	1,768
23,750	23,800	0	720	1,758
23,800	23,850	0	712	1,747
23,850	23,900	0	704	1,737
23,900	23,950	0	696	1,726
23,950	24,000	0	688	1,716
24,000	24,050	0	680	1,705
24,050	24,100	0	672	1,695
24,100	24,150	0	664	1,684
24,150	24,200	0	656	1,673
24,200	24,250	0	648	1,663
24,250	24,300	0	640	1,652
24,300	24,350	0	632	1,642
24,350	24,400	0	624	1,631
24,400	24,450	0	616	1,621
24,450	24,500	0	608	1,610
24,500	24,550	0	600	1,600
24,550	24,600	0	592	1,589
24,600	24,650	0	584	1,579
24,650	24,700	0	576	1,568
24,700	24,750	0	568	1,558
24,750	24,800	0	560	1,547
24,800	24,850	0	552	1,537
24,850	24,900	0	544	1,526

If the amount you are looking up from the worksheet is— At least	But less than	And you have— No children	One child	Two children
24,900	24,950	0	536	1,516
24,950	25,000	0	528	1,505
25,000	25,050	0	520	1,494
25,050	25,100	0	512	1,484
25,100	25,150	0	504	1,473
25,150	25,200	0	496	1,463
25,200	25,250	0	488	1,452
25,250	25,300	0	480	1,442
25,300	25,350	0	472	1,431
25,350	25,400	0	464	1,421
25,400	25,450	0	456	1,410
25,450	25,500	0	448	1,400
25,500	25,550	0	440	1,389
25,550	25,600	0	432	1,379
25,600	25,650	0	425	1,368
25,650	25,700	0	417	1,358
25,700	25,750	0	409	1,347
25,750	25,800	0	401	1,337
25,800	25,850	0	393	1,326
25,850	25,900	0	385	1,315
25,900	25,950	0	377	1,305
25,950	26,000	0	369	1,294
26,000	26,050	0	361	1,284
26,050	26,100	0	353	1,273
26,100	26,150	0	345	1,263
26,150	26,200	0	337	1,252
26,200	26,250	0	329	1,242
26,250	26,300	0	321	1,231
26,300	26,350	0	313	1,221
26,350	26,400	0	305	1,210
26,400	26,450	0	297	1,200
26,450	26,500	0	289	1,189
26,500	26,550	0	281	1,179
26,550	26,600	0	273	1,168
26,600	26,650	0	265	1,158
26,650	26,700	0	257	1,147
26,700	26,750	0	249	1,136
26,750	26,800	0	241	1,126
26,800	26,850	0	233	1,115
26,850	26,900	0	225	1,105
26,900	26,950	0	217	1,094
26,950	27,000	0	209	1,084
27,000	27,050	0	201	1,073
27,050	27,100	0	193	1,063
27,100	27,150	0	185	1,052
27,150	27,200	0	177	1,042
27,200	27,250	0	169	1,031
27,250	27,300	0	161	1,021
27,300	27,350	0	153	1,010
27,350	27,400	0	145	1,000
27,400	27,450	0	137	989
27,450	27,500	0	129	979

If the amount you are looking up from the worksheet is— At least	But less than	And you have— No children	One child	Two children
27,500	27,550	0	121	968
27,550	27,600	0	113	957
27,600	27,650	0	105	947
27,650	27,700	0	97	936
27,700	27,750	0	89	926
27,750	27,800	0	81	915
27,800	27,850	0	73	905
27,850	27,900	0	65	894
27,900	27,950	0	57	884
27,950	28,000	0	49	873
28,000	28,050	0	41	863
28,050	28,100	0	33	852
28,100	28,150	0	25	842
28,150	28,200	0	17	831
28,200	28,250	0	9	821
28,250	28,300	0	**	810
28,300	28,350	0	0	800
28,350	28,400	0	0	789
28,400	28,450	0	0	778
28,450	28,500	0	0	768
28,500	28,550	0	0	757
28,550	28,600	0	0	747
28,600	28,650	0	0	736
28,650	28,700	0	0	726
28,700	28,750	0	0	715
28,750	28,800	0	0	705
28,800	28,850	0	0	694
28,850	28,900	0	0	684
28,900	28,950	0	0	673
28,950	29,000	0	0	663
29,000	29,050	0	0	652
29,050	29,100	0	0	642
29,100	29,150	0	0	631
29,150	29,200	0	0	620
29,200	29,250	0	0	610
29,250	29,300	0	0	599
29,300	29,350	0	0	589
29,350	29,400	0	0	578
29,400	29,450	0	0	568
29,450	29,500	0	0	557
29,500	29,550	0	0	547
29,550	29,600	0	0	536
29,600	29,650	0	0	526
29,650	29,700	0	0	515
29,700	29,750	0	0	505
29,750	29,800	0	0	494
29,800	29,850	0	0	484
29,850	29,900	0	0	473
29,900	29,950	0	0	463
29,950	30,000	0	0	452
30,000	30,050	0	0	441
30,050	30,100	0	0	431

If the amount you are looking up from the worksheet is— At least	But less than	And you have— No children	One child	Two children
30,100	30,150	0	0	420
30,150	30,200	0	0	410
30,200	30,250	0	0	399
30,250	30,300	0	0	389
30,300	30,350	0	0	378
30,350	30,400	0	0	368
30,400	30,450	0	0	357
30,450	30,500	0	0	347
30,500	30,550	0	0	336
30,550	30,600	0	0	326
30,600	30,650	0	0	315
30,650	30,700	0	0	305
30,700	30,750	0	0	294
30,750	30,800	0	0	284
30,800	30,850	0	0	273
30,850	30,900	0	0	262
30,900	30,950	0	0	252
30,950	31,000	0	0	241
31,000	31,050	0	0	231
31,050	31,100	0	0	220
31,100	31,150	0	0	210
31,150	31,200	0	0	199
31,200	31,250	0	0	189
31,250	31,300	0	0	178
31,300	31,350	0	0	168
31,350	31,400	0	0	157
31,400	31,450	0	0	147
31,450	31,500	0	0	136
31,500	31,550	0	0	126
31,550	31,600	0	0	115
31,600	31,650	0	0	105
31,650	31,700	0	0	94
31,700	31,750	0	0	83
31,750	31,800	0	0	73
31,800	31,850	0	0	62
31,850	31,900	0	0	52
31,900	31,950	0	0	41
31,950	32,000	0	0	31
32,000	32,050	0	0	20
32,050	32,100	0	0	10
32,100	32,121	0	0	2
32,121 or more		0	0	0

**If the amount you are looking up from the worksheet is at least $28,250 but less than $28,281, your credit is $3. Otherwise, you cannot take the credit.

Need more information or forms? See page 7.   - 50 -

¶ 87

¶ 88   Average Itemized Deductions

For those taxpayers who itemize their deductions on Schedule A of Form 1040, the following chart should be of special interest. This chart (which is based on *preliminary* statistics for *1999* returns) shows the average deductions of taxpayers for *1999* for interest (¶ 1043), taxes (¶ 1021), medical and dental expenses (¶ 1015), and charitable contributions (¶ 1058). While it may be interesting for those who itemize their deductions to compare them with these average figures, the chart should not be considered as indicating amounts that would be allowed by the Internal Revenue Service. In any case, taxpayers must be able to substantiate claimed itemized deductions.

Preliminary Average Itemized Deductions for 1999 by AGI Ranges. (Source: IRS Publication No. 1136, *Statistics of Income Bulletin—Spring 2001* (Rev. May 2001).)

PRELIMINARY AVERAGE ITEMIZED DEDUCTIONS FOR 1999 BY ADJUSTED GROSS INCOME RANGES

Adjusted Gross Income Ranges	Medical Expenses	Taxes	Interest	Contributions
$ 20,000 to $ 30,000	$ 5,241	$ 2,315	$ 6,034	$ 1,613
$ 30,000 to $ 50,000	4,863	3,058	6,292	1,686
$ 50,000 to $ 75,000	5,441	4,337	7,121	2,034
$ 75,000 to $ 100,000	6,945	5,916	8,298	2,527
$ 100,000 to $ 200,000	11,835	9,229	10,941	3,684
$ 200,000 or more	31,727	38,253	24,846	21,403

¶ 88A   AGI Phaseout Thresholds for 2001

Adjusted gross income (AGI) levels in excess of certain phaseout thresholds limit the following deductions, credits and other tax benefits. This chart provides the beginning point for the *2001* thresholds and the ending point of the phaseout (where applicable).

Tax Item	Taxpayers Affected	Phaseout—Begin	Phaseout—End
Itemized Deductions (Overall Limit)	single, head of household, joint filers	$132,950	phaseout varies by taxpayer
	married filing separate	$ 66,475	phaseout varies by taxpayer
7.5% Floor on Medical Deductions	those itemizing medical expenses	7.5% of AGI	N/A
2% Floor on Misc. Itemized Deductions	those itemizing misc. expenses	2% of AGI	N/A
10% Floor on Casualty Loss	those itemizing casualty loss	10% of AGI	N/A
Personal Exemption	single	$132,950	$255,450
	head of household	$166,200	$288,700
	joint filers	$199,450	$321,950
	married filing separate	$ 99,725	$160,975
Child Tax Credit*	single, head of household	$ 75,000	phaseout varies by taxpayer
	married filing separate	$ 55,000	phaseout varies by taxpayer
	joint filers	$110,000	phaseout varies by taxpayer

Tax Iten.	Taxpayers Affected	Phaseout—Begin	Phaseout—End
Dependent Care Credit*	joint filers, head of household, single	30% credit if AGI not over $10,000	20% credit if AGI over $28,000
Elderly and Disabled Credit	single, head of household	$ 7,500	phaseout varies by taxpayer
	joint filers	$ 10,000	phaseout varies by taxpayer
	married filing separate	$ 5,000	phaseout varies by taxpayer
Adoption Credit*	all filers	$ 75,000	$115,000
Earned Income Credit*	no child	$ 5,950	$ 10,710
	one child	$ 13,090	$ 28,281
	two or more children	$ 13,090	$ 32,121
HOPE Credit*	single, head of household	$ 40,000	$ 50,000
	joint filers	$ 80,000	$100,000
Lifetime Learning Credit*	single, head of household	$ 40,000	$ 50,000
	joint filers	$ 80,000	$100,000
Student Loan Interest Deduction*	single, head of household	$ 40,000	$ 55,000
	joint filers	$ 60,000	$ 75,000
Savings Bonds Interest Exclusion	single, head of household	$ 55,750	$ 70,750
	joint filers	$ 83,650	$113,650
Education Savings Accounts (formerly Education IRAs)	single, head of household, married filing separate	$ 95,000	$110,000
	joint filers	$150,000	$160,000
IRA Deduction	single, head of household	$ 33,000	$ 43,000
	joint filers	$ 53,000	$ 63,000
	married filing separate	$ 0	$ 10,000
Roth IRA Eligibility	single, head of household	$ 95,000	$110,000
	joint filers	$150,000	$160,000
	married filing separate	$ 0	$ 10,000
First-time DC Homebuyer*	single, head of household, married filing separate	$ 70,000	$ 90,000
	joint filers	$110,000	$130,000
	married filing separate	$ 50,000	$ 75,000
Rental Real Estate Passive Losses	single, head of household, joint filers	$100,000	$150,000
Mortgage Bond Subsidy Recapture	all filers	AGI relative to area median income	N/A

---

* Modified AGI, as defined by the relevant Code Sections, is used instead of AGI.

Chapter 1

INDIVIDUALS

January Payments of Estimated Tax

101. Final Adjustments to the 2001 Estimated Tax. As 2001 ends, the first responsibility of the calendar-year taxpayer is to review payments of estimated tax for 2001 to make sure that these tax payments and the income tax withheld from wages during the year are at least sufficient to avoid penalties (¶ 2875) on the last installment, which is due January 15, 2002.

The 2001 estimated tax payments (plus income tax withheld from wages) are credited against tax due for 2001 (¶ 124). Any underpayment of tax must be made up by a payment with the final return, and any overpayment is either refunded or credited against the estimated tax for the next year, whichever the taxpayer elects on the return. See ¶ 2679 and following.

105. Overpayment. An individual who has been making payments of estimated tax for 2001, and who finds that by paying the installment scheduled for January 15, 2002, he or she will overpay the 2001 tax, may:

(1) make the payment as scheduled on or before January 15, 2002, file the return on or before April 15, 2002, and direct whether the overpayment should be refunded or credited toward the 2002 estimated tax;

(2) reduce the payment due on or before January 15, 2002, so that the estimated tax payments plus withholding will meet the tax liability that will be shown on the return to be filed on or before April 15, 2002;

(3) pay enough estimated tax to cover the minimum requirement as described at ¶ 2875 in order to avoid a penalty on the January 15, 2002, payment and then pay any difference on the final return, filed on or before April 15, 2002; or

(4) file the final return on or before January 31, 2002, add up all payments of estimated tax plus any withholding, and use this return for a final accounting of 2001 tax liability.

¶ 105

107. Underpayment. The law provides a penalty for underpayment of estimated tax. However, a taxpayer can avoid this penalty by paying the minimum installment authorized under one of the exceptions described at ¶ 2682.[1]

The taxpayer may file the tax return for calendar year 2001 on or before January 31, 2002, and pay any balance of tax that may still be due for 2001. Under this method, no penalty will apply for failure to make the last quarterly installment and any penalty for underpayment of any of the three earlier installments will not be increased any further. See ¶ 2688. See also ¶ 2691 for special rules on 2001 payments of estimated tax for farmers and fishermen.

Who Must File a Return

109. Citizens and Residents. For each tax year, a return must be made by a U.S. citizen or a resident alien who has at least a specified minimum amount of gross income. The income levels at which individuals must file income tax returns for 2001 (even though no tax is owed) are generally as follows (Code Sec. 6012): [2]

Single individual (also individuals treated as unmarried for tax purposes; see ¶ 173)	$ 7,450
Single individual, 65 or older	8,550
Married individual, separate return	2,900
Married couple, joint return	13,400
Married couple, joint return, one spouse 65 or older	14,300
Married couple, joint return, both spouses 65 or older	15,200
Head of household	9,550
Head of household, 65 or older	10,650
Qualifying widow(er)	10,500
Qualifying widow(er), 65 or older	11,400

The above income levels for a married couple filing a joint return are not applicable if, at the close of their tax year, the couple does not share the same household or if some other taxpayer is entitled to a dependency exemption for either spouse (e.g., a married student who is supported by a parent). In such a case, a return for 2001 must be filed if gross income equals $2,900 or more (Code Sec. 6012(a)(1)(A)(iv)).[3]

With respect to a dependent child or other individual who is neither blind nor age 65 or older for whom a dependency exemption is allowed to another taxpayer, a return must be filed for the 2001 tax year if the individual (1) has over $750 of unearned income (projected by CCH to remain $750 in 2002), (2) has over $4,550 of earned income (projected by CCH to increase to $4,700 in 2002), or (3) has a total of unearned and earned income which exceeds the larger of (a) $750 or (b) earned income (up to $4,300) plus $250 (see ¶ 126). All married dependents under age 65 with gross income of at least $5 whose spouse files a separate return on Form 1040 and itemizes deductions on Schedule A must file a return.

If a child under age 14 had no earned income, received unearned income (interest and dividends, including Alaska Permanent Fund dividends) in an amount less than $7,500 as indexed for inflation (projected by CCH to remain $7,500 in 2002) that was not subject to backup withholding, and made no estimated tax payments, the parents may elect to report the income on their return. If this election is made, the child need not file a return. See ¶ 114.

Dependents who are blind and/or age 65 or older must file returns if (1) their earned income exceeds their maximum standard deduction amount, (2) they have unearned income in excess of the sum of $750 plus additional standard deduction amounts to which they are entitled, or (3) their gross income exceeds the total of earned income up to the regular standard deduction amount or $750, whichever is larger, plus the applicable additional standard deduction amounts. See ¶ 126.

Footnote references are to paragraphs of the 2002 Standard Federal Tax Reports.

¶ **107**

[1] ¶ 39,560.01, ¶ 39,560.021, ¶ 39,560.048   [2] ¶ 35,142, ¶ 35,150.21   [3] ¶ 35,142, ¶ 35,150.21

Even if the income levels noted above are not reached, an individual is required to file a return if (1) net earnings from self-employment in 2001 are at least $400, (2) advance earned income credit payments were received during 2001, (3) FICA and/or Medicare taxes are due on 2001 tip income not reported to the employer or if uncollected FICA, Medicare, and/or RRTA taxes are due on tips reported to the employer or on group-term life insurance, (4) liability for alternative minimum tax is incurred, (5) tax on an IRA or a qualified retirement plan is due, (6) tax is due from the recapture of an investment credit, a low-income housing credit, or recapture tax on the disposition of a home purchased with a federally subsidized mortgage, or (7) wages of $108.28 or more were earned from a church or qualified church-controlled organization that is exempt from employer FICA and Medicare taxes.

The income-level test applies to *gross* income and not to *adjusted* gross income. Also, the amount includes foreign earned income excludable under Code Sec. 911 (see ¶ 2401) (Reg. § 1.6012-1(a)(3)).[4]

Any person who is required to file an income tax return must report on that return the amount of tax-exempt interest received or accrued during the tax year (Code Sec. 6012(d)).[5] See ¶ 724 et seq.

If the applicable gross income test is met, a return must be filed even though the individual's exemptions and deductions are such that no tax will be due. And even when the gross income test is not met, a return should be filed whenever a refund of tax or the earned income credit is available.

Example. John, a 66-year-old retired single person, worked at a part-time job in 2001 and earned wages of $3,000 from which his employer withheld a total of $75 in income taxes for the year. Although John is not required to file a return because he did not meet the $8,550-or-more gross income test for a single person 65 or older, he should file a return to receive a refund of the $75 in withheld income tax. (Certain taxpayers may be exempt from withholding if they had no income tax liability for their preceding tax year and expect none for the current year. See ¶ 2634.)

112. Resident Alien. Generally, a resident alien is taxable on income from all sources, including sources outside the United States, at the same rates and in the same manner as is a United States citizen.[6]

An alien individual is treated as a U.S. resident for any calendar year in which the individual (1) is a lawful permanent resident of the U.S. at any time during such year, (2) elects to be treated as a U.S. resident (this election is revocable only with IRS consent), or (3) satisfies the substantial presence test requiring presence in the U.S. for at least 31 days during the current calendar year and at least 183 days during the three-year period that includes the current calendar year and the preceding two calendar years. In computing the 183-day test, the individual may include all the days present during the current calendar year, one-third of the days present during the preceding calendar year, and one-sixth of the days present during the second preceding calendar year. However, exceptions to this rule apply (Code Sec. 7701(b)).[7] See ¶ 2421.

114. Child or Dependent. A child or dependent is taxed on income, including wages, income from property, and trust income (see ¶ 554 et seq.). No exemption will be allowed to an individual eligible to be claimed as a dependent on another taxpayer's return. The basic standard deduction for dependents is limited to the greater of $750 (projected by CCH to remain $750 in 2002) or the sum of $250 plus earned income (up to the regular standard deduction) (see ¶ 126). Therefore, a dependent who has gross income of $750 or less will not be taxed on that amount and does not have to file an income tax return.[8]

Footnote references are to paragraphs of the 2002 Standard Federal Tax Reports.
[4] ¶ 35,143, ¶ 35,150.022   [7] ¶ 43,080, ¶ 43,116A—   [8] ¶ 3270.035
[5] ¶ 35,142   ¶ 43,125A
[6] ¶ 3290.01

Investment income of a child under age 14 is generally taxed at the parents' top marginal rate if such income exceeds the sum of the $750 standard deduction (projected by CCH to remain $750 in 2002) and the greater of $750 or the itemized deductions directly connected to the production of that investment income. This rule applies to a child's investment income regardless of its source and requires a calculation of the parents' "allocable parental tax" (Code Sec. 1(g)).[9] See ¶ 126 and ¶ 706.

Even though, under state law, compensation for a child's personal services may be treated as belonging to the parent, and even though the money is not retained by the child, for federal income tax purposes, it is considered gross income of the child (Reg. § 1.73-1).[10] If a child's income tax is not paid, an assessment made against the child will be treated as if it were also made against the child's parent, to the extent that the tax is attributable to amounts received for the child's services (Code Sec. 6201(c)).[11]

A parent may elect on Form 8814 to include on his or her return the unearned income of a child under the age of 14 on January 1, 2002, whose income is less than $7,500 (projected by CCH to remain $7,500 in 2002) and consists solely of interest, dividends, capital gain distributions, or Alaska Permanent Fund dividends. This election is not available if estimated tax payments were made for the tax year in the child's name and social security number or if the child is subject to backup withholding. Electing parents are taxed on their child's income in excess of $1,500 for the 2001 tax year (projected by CCH to remain $1,500 in 2002). Also, they must report an additional tax liability equal to the lesser of $75 in 2001 (projected by CCH to remain $75 in 2002) or 10% (projected by CCH to remain 10% in 2002) of the child's income exceeding $750 in 2001 (Code Sec. 1(g)(7)(A)(ii) and Code Sec. 1(g)(7)(B)(ii)).[12]

If a guardian or other person is charged with the care of a minor (or a person under a disability) or the minor's property, the return for the minor should be filed by the responsible person, unless already filed by the minor or some other person. See ¶ 504.

116. Identifying Number. Every taxpayer must record his taxpayer identification number (TIN) on his return. Generally, this is the taxpayer's social security number. If a taxpayer does not have a social security number, he should apply for one on Form SS-5. Taxpayers must provide TINs for dependents and qualifying children for EITC, child care credit and dependency exemption purposes (Code Sec. 21(e)(10), Code Sec. 32(c) and Code Sec. 151)).[13] For tax returns due after September 21, 1996, individuals claiming the earned income tax credit must include TINs for themselves, their spouses (if married) and any qualifying children on the return (Code Sec. 32(c)(1)(F)). Failure to include a correct TIN will be treated as a mathematical or clerical error under Code Sec. 6213(g)(2), as will instances when the information provided differs from the information on file with the IRS.

The parent of any child to whom the rules governing taxation of unearned income of minor children apply (see ¶ 114) must provide his or her "identifying number" to the child for inclusion on the child's tax return (Code Sec. 1(g)(6)).[14]

When and Where Return Is Filed

118. Due Date. The individual income tax return is due on or before the 15th day of the 4th month following the close of the tax year (April 15 in the case of a calendar-year taxpayer) (Reg. § 1.6072-1(a)).[15] If the due date falls on a Saturday, Sunday, or legal holiday, the return may be filed on the next succeeding day that is not a Saturday, Sunday, or legal holiday (Reg. § 301.7503-1).[16]

Footnote references are to paragraphs of the 2002 Standard Federal Tax Reports.

¶ **116**

[9] ¶ 3260	[12] ¶ 3260, ¶ 3280	[15] ¶ 36,721
[10] ¶ 6151	[13] ¶ 36,960, ¶ 36,964	[16] ¶ 42,631
[11] ¶ 37,502, ¶ 37,504.025	[14] ¶ 3260	

A nonresident alien who has wages *not* subject to withholding, generally may file a return as late as the 15th day of the 6th month after the close of the tax year (June 15 in the case of a calendar-year taxpayer). A nonresident alien who has wages subject to withholding must file a return by the 15th day of the 4th month following the close of the tax year (Reg. § 1.6072-1(c)).[17]

120. Extension for Filing. An individual may obtain an automatic extension of four months for filing Forms 1040, 1040A or 1040EZ if the individual files, on or before the due date of the return, an application (Form 4868) accompanied by a proper estimate of tax due for the year (see ¶ 2509).[18] A U.S. citizen or resident who, on April 15, 2002, lives and has a main place of business or post of duty outside the U.S. and Puerto Rico, or who is in military or naval service on duty outside the U.S. and Puerto Rico, is given an automatic two-month extension without the necessity of filing Form 4868. However, an explanatory statement must be attached to the taxpayer's return (Reg. § 1.6081-5).[19] Also, interest will be charged on any unpaid tax from the original due date of the return. For further details, see ¶ 2509.

122. Where to File Returns. The individual's return is filed with the Internal Revenue Service Center for the region in which the individual's residence or principal place of business is located (Reg. § 1.6091-2).[20] However, payment vouchers for electronically filed returns are to be sent to a different address (see IRS Publication 1045). In addition, nonresident aliens are to file Form 1040NR at the Philadelphia Service Center. For filing locations, see ¶ 3.

The Return Form

124. Forms in Use for 2001. Three principal forms are available for use by the majority of individuals for 2001. These forms include Form 1040 and a shorter return form, Form 1040A. In addition, certain taxpayers with no dependents may use Form 1040EZ, which is substantially shorter and easier to fill out than either of the other 1040 forms. If the applicable filing conditions are met, any of the forms in the 1040 series may serve as a separate return or as a joint return. However, if a married person files Form 1040 as a separate return and itemizes deductions, a spouse can either file Form 1040 and itemize deductions or file Form 1040A and claim a standard deduction of zero. These rules do not apply to a spouse who is eligible to file as unmarried or as head of household (see ¶ 173).

Form 1040EZ. For the 2001 tax year, the simplified income tax return, Form 1040EZ, may be used by taxpayers who: (1) have single or joint filing status (if you are a nonresident alien at any time in 2001, your filing status can only be married filing jointly); (2) claim no dependents; (3) do not claim a student loan interest deduction or an educational credit; (4) are under age 65 on January 1, 2002 and are not blind at the end of 2001; (5) have taxable income of less than $50,000; (6) have income from *only* wages, salaries, tips, unemployment compensation, taxable scholarships and fellowships, qualified state tuition program earnings, Alaska Permanent Fund dividends, and taxable interest income not exceeding $400; (7) have received no advance earned income credit payments; and (8) owe no household employment taxes on wages paid to a household employee. If you do not meet *all* eight requirements, you must use either Form 1040 or Form 1040A. If social security tax is owing on tip income, the taxpayer must use Forms 1040 and 4137 (Social Security and Medicare Tax on Unreported Tip Income). No tax credits (other than the earned income credit, and, in 2001 only, the rate reduction credit), itemized deductions, or adjustments to income may be taken on Form 1040EZ. The "Single" or "Married Filing Jointly" column of the Tax Table (¶ 25) must be used to find the amount of income tax, which is entered on the appropriate line of Form 1040EZ.

An individual who has no qualifying children and who received less than a total of $10,710 (projected by CCH to increase to $11,060 in 2002) in taxable and

---

Footnote references are to paragraphs of the 2002 Standard Federal Tax Reports.
[17] ¶ 36,721   [19] ¶ 36,795, ¶ 36,796.01   [20] ¶ 36,808
[18] ¶ 36,793

nontaxable earned income may be able to take the earned income credit on Form 1040EZ if the taxpayer or his spouse was at least age 25 at the end of 2001. The IRS will calculate the EIC for taxpayers who indicate that they desire such a computation on the appropriate line of the form.

Form 1040A. Form 1040A is a two-page form accompanied by four schedules. It is to be used by an individual, a married couple filing jointly or separately, a head of household, or a qualifying widow(er) with a dependent child (¶ 175) who does not itemize personal deductions, whose gross income consists only of wages, salaries, tips, taxable scholarship and fellowship grants, IRA distributions, pensions or annuities, taxable social security or railroad retirement benefits, unemployment compensation, dividends, interest, and Alaska Permanent Fund dividends, and whose taxable income is less than $50,000. If the taxpayer receives more than $400 of either taxable interest income or dividend income, claims the exclusion of interest from series EE U.S. savings bonds issued after 1989 (¶ 730), receives interest or dividends as a nominee, receives interest from a seller-financed mortgage where the buyer used the property as a personal residence (¶ 726), claims the credit for child and dependent care expenses (¶ 1301), receives employer-provided dependent care benefits (¶ 869), claims the credit for the elderly or the disabled (¶ 1304), or is eligible for the earned income credit (¶ 1375), the respective parts of Schedules 1 through 3 or Schedule EIC for Form 1040A must be completed. To claim the adoption credit (¶ 1306), Form 8839 must be attached. To claim the education credit (¶ 1303), Form 8863 must be attached. The child tax credit (¶ 1302) is figured on the child tax credit worksheet and is entered on the appropriate line of Form 1040A. To claim the additional child tax credit, Form 8812 must be attached. The rate reduction credit, available in 2001 only, is claimed by completing the worksheet found in the instructions (¶ 1310A). The IRA deduction (¶ 2170), nondeductible IRA contributions (¶ 2173), alternative minimum tax liability (¶ 1400 and following), and advance EIC payments may also be claimed on Form 1040A. A taxpayer who made estimated tax payments (¶ 2679 and following) and wishes to apply any part of the refund to 2002 estimated tax, or who is subject to an underpayment of estimated tax penalty determined on Form 2210, can reflect these items on Form 1040A.

However, Form 1040A may *not* be used by an individual who is required to file any of the schedules necessary to support Form 1040 (other than the information contained in the Schedules to Form 1040A), has taxable income of $50,000 or more, or if any of the following applies to the taxpayer:

(1) itemizes deductions;

(2) claims any credit against tax (see the discussion of Form 1040, below) other than (a) the credits allowable for child and dependent care (¶ 1301), earned income (¶ 1375), or the elderly or the disabled (¶ 1304), (b) the adoption credit (¶ 1306), (c) the education credit (¶ 1303), (d) the child tax credit (¶ 1302), or (e) the rate reduction credit for 2001 only (¶ 1310A);

(3) realizes taxable gain on the sale of a personal residence (¶ 1705 and following);

(4) claims any adjustments to income (other than the deduction for certain contributions made to an IRA (¶ 2168) or the deduction for student loan interest (¶ 1082));

(5) receives in any month tips of $20 or more that are not reported fully to the employer, has a Form W-2 that shows allocated tips that must be reported in income, owes social security and Medicare tax on tips not reported to the employer, or has a Form W-2 that shows any uncollected social security, Medicare, or RRTA tax on tips or on group-term life insurance;

(6) is a nonresident alien at any time during the year and does not file a joint return or is married at the end of the year to a nonresident alien or dual-status alien who has U.S.-source income and who has not elected to be treated

¶ 124

as a resident alien (however, such a married taxpayer may use Form 1040A if considered unmarried and eligible to use the head of household tax rate);

(7) owes or claims any of the items set out as "Other Taxes" in the discussion of Form 1040, below, with the exception of advance earned income credit payments and alternative minimum tax;

(8) receives income from (a) self-employment (net earnings of at least $400) (¶ 2667), (b) rents and royalties (¶ 762 and ¶ 763), (c) taxable state and local income tax refunds, (d) alimony received (¶ 771), (e) capital gains (¶ 1735), (f) business income (¶ 759), or (g) farm income (¶ 767);

(9) is the grantor of, or transferor to, a foreign trust;

(10) can exclude either foreign earned income received as a U.S. citizen (¶ 2402) or resident alien or certain income received from sources in a U.S. possession while a resident of American Samoa for all of 2001 (¶ 2410);

(11) receives or pays accrued interest on securities transferred between interest payment dates;

(12) earns wages of $108.28 or more from a church or church-controlled organization that is exempt from employer social security taxes;

(13) receives any nontaxable dividends or capital gain distributions;

(14) is reporting original issue discount in an amount more or less than that shown on Form 1099-OID;

(15) receives income as a partner (¶ 415, ¶ 431), an S corporation shareholder (¶ 309), or a beneficiary of an estate or trust (¶ 554-¶ 556); or

(16) has financial accounts in foreign countries (exceptions apply if the combined value of the accounts was $10,000 or less during all of 2001 or if the accounts were with a U.S. military banking facility operated by a U.S. financial institution).

An individual otherwise eligible to use Form 1040A should use Form 1040 if allowable itemized deductions exceed the appropriate standard deduction amount. See ¶ 126.

Form 1040. The basic Form 1040 is a single-sheet, two-page form. To it are added any necessary supporting schedules, depending upon the particular circumstances of the individual taxpayer. The chart that appears at ¶ 61 illustrates an individual's computation of taxable income on Form 1040. Items listed on the chart are explained at the paragraphs indicated.

The Tax Table (¶ 25) is used to determine the amount of tax if taxable income is less than $100,000 (see ¶ 128). If taxable income is $100,000 or more, the appropriate Tax Rate Schedule (¶ 11-¶ 17) must be used to compute the tax (see ¶ 130). Further, taxpayers who realized a net capital gain may owe less tax if they calculate their liability using Schedule D, Part IV (see ¶ 126).

Generally, Form 8615 (Tax for Children Under Age 14 Who Have Investment Income of More Than $1,500) must be used to calculate the tax for any child who was under age 14 on January 1, 2002, and who had more than $1,500 of investment income (see ¶ 126). However, taxpayers who elect to be taxed on the unearned income of their children who are under age 14 (see ¶ 114) must add to the amount of tax for Form 1040 the tax calculated on Form 8814 (Parent's Election to Report Child's Interest and Dividends). They do not file Form 8615. The Form 8814 amount must be entered in the space provided on Form 1040. Also included in the total is any tax from Form 4972 (Tax on Lump-Sum Distributions) (see ¶ 2153), Form 5329 (Additional Taxes on Qualified Plans (Including IRAs) and Other Tax-Favored Accounts) (see ¶ 2157), and Schedule J (Farm Income Averaging) (see ¶ 767).

Credits. A number of credits whose excess over tax liability is not refundable in the current year are subtracted from the resulting tax *in the following order:* (1) credit for child and dependent care expenses (¶ 1301); (2) credit for the elderly or for

¶ 124

the permanently and totally disabled (¶ 1304); (3) education credits (¶ 1301); (4) rate reduction credit for 2001 only (¶ 1310A); (5) child tax credit (¶ 1302); (6) adoption credit (¶ 1306); (7) mortgage interest credit (¶ 1308); (8) first-time homebuyer credit for District of Columbia (¶ 1310); (9) foreign tax credit (¶ 2475); (10) general business credit (¶ 1323), which consists of (a) investment tax credit, to the extent available (¶ 1345 and following), (b) work opportunity credit (¶ 1342), (c) welfare-to-work credit for individuals who begin work for the employer after December 31, 1997 (¶ 1343), (d) alcohol fuels credit (¶ 1326), (e) research credit (¶ 1330), (f) low-income housing credit (¶ 1334), (g) disabled access credit (¶ 1338), (h) enhanced oil recovery credit (¶ 1336), (i) renewable electricity production credit (¶ 1339), (j) Indian employment credit (¶ 1340), (k) credit for employer-paid FICA and Medicare taxes on employee cash tips (¶ 1341), (l) orphan drug credit (¶ 1344), (m) credit for contributions to selected community development corporations (¶ 1325), and (n) new markets credit (¶ 1335); (11) empowerment zone employment credit (¶ 1339A); (12) credit for prior year alternative minimum tax (¶ 1370); (13) qualified electric vehicle credit (¶ 1321); and (14) credit for fuel from a nonconventional source (¶ 1319).

Taxpayers who have qualifying children under age 17 are entitled to the child credit. The amount of the credit for 2001 is $600 per child (¶ 1302). Taxpayers may also claim the Hope scholarship credit for qualifying tuition and related expenses paid after December 31, 1997, for education furnished in academic periods beginning after that date and the lifetime learning credit for qualifying tuition and related expenses paid after June 30, 1998, for education furnished in academic periods after that date (¶ 1303).

Other Taxes. The following taxes are then added: (1) self-employment tax (¶ 2664); (2) alternative minimum tax (¶ 1401); (3) recapture of any investment tax credit (¶ 1364), low-income housing credit (¶ 1334), federal mortgage subsidy (¶ 1308), or qualified electric vehicle credit (¶ 1321); (4) FICA, Medicare, and/or RRTA tax owing on tip income not reported to the employer, and employee FICA, Medicare, and/or RRTA tax on tips where the employer did not withhold proper amounts (¶ 2639); (5) excess contribution, excess distribution, and premature distribution taxes for IRAs and qualified pension or annuity plans, excess accumulations in qualified pension plans (including IRAs) and Archer MSAs, or early distribution tax for a modified endowment contract entered into after June 20, 1988 (¶ 2157, ¶ 2174, ¶ 2179); (6) advance earned income credit payments received (¶ 1375); (7) household employment taxes (¶ 2650); (8) the "Section 72(m)(5) excess benefits tax" imposed on a 5% owner of a business who receives a distribution of excess benefits from a qualified pension or annuity plan; (9) uncollected FICA, Medicare, and/or RRTA tax on tips with respect to employees who received wages that were insufficient to cover the FICA, Medicare, and RRTA tax due on tips reported to their employers; (10) uncollected FICA, Medicare, and/or RRTA tax on group-term life insurance (¶ 721); (11) any excise tax due on "golden parachute" payments (¶ 2609); and (12) tax on accumulated distribution of trusts (¶ 907).

Payments. To arrive at final tax due or refund owed, the taxpayer subtracts from the above balance the following: (1) federal income tax withheld (¶ 2601 and following); (2) 2001 estimated tax payments and amounts applied from 2000 returns (¶ 2679 and following); (3) earned income credit (¶ 1375); (4) amounts paid with applications for automatic filing extensions (¶ 2509); (5) excess social security tax withheld from individuals paid more than a total of $80,400 in wages by two or more employers and/or excess RRTA tax withheld from individuals paid more than a total of $59,700 by two or more employers (¶ 2648); (6) credit for excise tax on gasoline and special fuels used in business and credit on certain diesel-powered vehicles (¶ 1379); and (7) a shareholder's share of capital gains tax paid by a regulated investment company (¶ 2309).

The following schedules and forms are added to the basic Form 1040 as needed:

¶ 124

(1) Schedule A for itemizing deductions; (2) Schedule B for reporting (a) more than $400 of dividend income and/or other stock distributions, (b) more than $400 of taxable interest income or claiming the exclusion of interest from series EE U.S. savings bonds issued after 1989 used for higher educational expenses, and (c) declaring any interests in foreign accounts and trusts; (3) Schedule C or Schedule C-EZ for claiming profit or loss from a sole proprietorship; (4) Schedule D for reporting capital gains and losses; (5) Schedule E for reporting income or loss from (a) rents and royalties, (b) partnerships and S corporations, (c) estates and trusts, and (d) real estate mortgage investment conduits (REMICs); (6) Schedule EIC for providing information regarding the earned income credit; (7) Schedule F for computing income and expenses from farming; (8) Schedule H for reporting employment taxes for domestic workers paid $1,300 or more during 2001; (9) Schedule J for reporting farm income averaging; (10) Schedule R for claiming the tax credit for the elderly or the disabled; (11) Schedule SE for computing the tax due on income from self-employment; (12) Form 4797 for reporting gains and losses from sales of business assets or from involuntary conversions other than casualty or theft losses (reported on Form 4684); (13) Form 6251 for computing the alternative minimum tax; (14) Form 4562 for reporting depreciation and amortization; (15) Form 2106 or 2106-EZ for computing employee business expenses; (16) Form 8582 for computing the amount of passive activity loss; (17) Form 3903 for calculating moving expenses; (18) Form 4835 for reporting farm rental income and expenses; (19) Form 8283 for claiming a deduction for a noncash charitable contribution where the total claimed value of the contributed property exceeds $500; (20) Form 8606 for reporting nondeductible IRA contributions, for figuring the basis of an IRA, and for calculating nontaxable distributions; (21) Form 8615 for computing the tax for children under age 14 who have investment income in excess of $1,500 in 2001; and (22) Form 8829 for figuring allowable expenses for business use of a home.

The following forms are for computing and claiming credits: (1) Form 4136 to claim the credit for federal tax on gasoline and special fuels; (2) Form 3468 to claim the investment credit, to the extent available; (3) Form 5884 to calculate the work opportunity credit; (4) Form 2441 to figure the child and dependent care credit; (5) Form 1116 to compute the foreign tax credit; (6) Form 2439, Copy B, to support the regulated investment company tax credit; (7) Form 6478 to compute the alcohol fuels credit; (8) Form 6765 to compute the credit for increasing research activities; (9) Form 3800 if more than one of the components of the general business credit are claimed; (10) Form 4255 to compute the recapture of investment credit for regular and energy property; (11) Form 8830 to claim the enhanced oil recovery credit; (12) Form 8396 to figure the mortgage interest credit and any carryforwards; (13) Forms 8586 and 8609 and Schedule A for Form 8609 to compute the low-income housing credit available for buildings placed in service during 2001; (14) Form 8611 to compute the recapture of the low-income housing credit; (15) Form 8801 to compute the credit for prior year alternative minimum tax; (16) Form 8812 to claim the additional child tax credit; (17) Form 8826 to claim the disabled access credit; (18) Form 8828 to compute the recapture of a federal mortgage subsidy; (19) Form 8835 to claim the renewable electricity production credit; (20) Form 8834 to determine eligibility for the qualified electric vehicle credit; (21) Form 8845 to claim the Indian employment credit; (22) Form 8846 to claim the credit for employer-paid FICA and Medicare taxes on employee cash tips; (23) Form 8847 to claim the credit for contributions to selected community development corporations; (24) Form 8844 to claim the empowerment zone employment credit; (25) Form 8839 to claim the adoption credit; (26) Form 8863 to claim the education credits; (27) Form 8820 to claim the orphan drug credit; and (28) Form 8874 to claim the new markets credit.

In addition, Form 4137 is used to compute social security (FICA) and Medicare tax on tip income that is not reported to an employer, and Form 5329 is used to compute the various penalty taxes applicable to retirement arrangements and plans.

¶124

Adjustments to Income. Adjustments to income (on page 1 of Form 1040) are principally those deductions that may be taken whether or not the standard deduction is employed. They include deductions for contributions to self-employed retirement plans or individual retirement arrangements (¶ 2113, ¶ 2168), student loan interest (¶ 1005, ¶ 1082), Archer medical savings accounts (MSAs) (¶ 860, ¶ 1020), moving expenses (¶ 1073), one-half of self-employment tax (¶ 2664), the forfeited interest penalty for premature withdrawals from a time savings account (¶ 1120), alimony paid (¶ 771), expenses of qualified performing artists (¶ 941A), jury duty pay given to an employer (¶ 941, ¶ 1010), forestation or reforestation amortization (¶ 1287), repayment of supplemental unemployment benefits (¶ 1009), contributions to Code Sec. 501(c)(18) pension plans (¶ 601), employee business expenses of fee-basis state or local government officials (Code Sec. 62(a)(2)(C)) (¶ 941), the deduction for a clean-fuel vehicle placed in service in 2001 (¶ 1286), and deductible expenses incurred with respect to the rental of personal property (¶ 1085).

The self-employed health insurance deduction is 60% for 2001. The deduction is claimed in the Adjusted Gross Income section of Form 1040. The self-employed health insurance deduction increases to 70% in 2002 and 100% in 2003 and later years (Code Sec. 162(l), see ¶ 908).

IRS Computation of Tax. Any taxpayer who files an individual tax return by the due date, April 15, 2002, can have the IRS compute the tax under certain conditions. These returns must have all applicable lines completed and be signed and dated. The inclusion of a daytime telephone number will speed processing should any questions arise. If you have overpaid your tax liability, a refund will be sent to you. You will be billed for any balance due on your tax liability. You must pay the amount due to avoid interest or the penalty for late payment by the later of 30 days from the billing date or the due date of your return.

Form 1040EZ. Lines 1 through 9 that are applicable to the taxpayer should be completed. If the filing status is married, filing jointly, then in the left margin next to Line 6 each spouse must separately list their total income. The IRS will also calculate the earned income credit. Write "EIC" in the space to the right of the words "See page 15" on Line 9a. Then enter the amount and type of nontaxable earned income on Line 9b.

Form 1040A. To enable the IRS to compute the tax using Form 1040A, complete Lines 1 through 25, 27 through 31, 35, and 37 through 40 including any schedules and forms asked for on those lines which are applicable to the taxpayer. If the taxpayer wishes the IRS to calculate the credit for the elderly and disabled and/ or earned income credit, Lines 28 and 39(a) should be left blank. For calculation of the credit for the elderly and disabled, write "CFE" in the space to the left of Line 28 and attached a completed Schedule 3 to the return. The box on Schedule 3 for filing status and age should be checked, and Part II and Part III, Lines 11 and 13 should be completed if necessary. To have the earned income credit calculated, write "EIC" directly to the right of Line 39(a) and enter the total of nontaxable earned income on Line 39(b). Schedule EIC must also be completed and attached to Form 1040A. When filing a joint return, the taxable income of each spouse must be separately listed in the margin to the left of Line 25. However, the IRS will not figure the tax for taxpayers who are claiming the credit for child and dependent care expenses, the adoption credit, or who are required to file Form 8615 (see ¶ 126).

Form 1040. The IRS will figure the tax for a taxpayer using Form 1040 who (1) files a signed and dated return by April 15, 2002 (inclusion of a daytime telephone number will speed up processing should any questions arise), (2) does not itemize deductions, (3) does not receive foreign earned income or claim a deduction or exclusion in connection with working abroad (Form 2555 or 2555-EZ), (4) does not request application of a refund to next year's tax, (5) has taxable income that (a) is less than $100,000 and (b) consists only of wages, salaries, tips, dividends, interest, taxable social security benefits, unemployment compensation, IRA distributions,

¶ 124

pensions and/or annuities, (6) does not elect to report a child's interest and dividends (Form 8814), (7) owes no social security or Medicare tax on unreported tip income (Form 4137), (8) did not receive an accumulation distribution made by a trust (Form 4970), (9) did not receive a lump-sum distribution from a qualified retirement plan (Form 4972), (10) did not realize profit or loss from an at-risk activity (Form 6198), (11) is not liable for alternative minimum tax (Form 6251), (12) is not required to file Form 8615 (see ¶ 126), (13) does not claim a credit for adoption expenses (Form 8839), and (14) does not claim a deduction for contributions to a Archer MSA or long-term care insurance contract (Form 8853). Lines 1-39 and 41-65 are to be completed if applicable (the "Total" lines should not be computed), along with any related forms or schedules. Line 59, indicating income tax withheld, must be filled in. If eligible for the earned income credit, the taxpayer should write "EIC" next to Line 61(a) and enter the amount of any nontaxable earned income on Line 61(b) and, if he has a qualifying child, should fill in Schedule EIC and attach it to the return. If eligible for the tax credit for the elderly or for the permanently and totally disabled, the taxpayer should write "CFE" on the dotted line next to Line 45 and attach Schedule R with the necessary information completed. The box on Schedule R for filing status and age must be checked, and Part II and Lines 11 and 13 of Part III, if applicable, must be filled in. If a joint return is being filed, the taxable income of each spouse must be separately listed under the words "Adjustments to Income" on the front of Form 1040. Finally, all necessary forms and schedules must be attached to the return.

Rounding Off Amounts. Dollar amounts on the return and accompanying schedules and forms may be rounded off to the nearest whole-dollar.

Computing the Tax

126. Taxable Income and Rates. Certain taxpayers must use the Tax Table (¶ 128) to compute their tax; other taxpayers must use the Tax Rate Schedules (¶ 130). Under either method, taxable income must first be computed. Taxable income is equal to adjusted gross income (¶ 1005) minus allowances for deductions and exemptions (¶ 133). See the chart at ¶ 61. Thus, taxable income for a taxpayer who does not itemize deductions is equal to adjusted gross income minus the applicable standard deduction and allowable exemptions. Taxable income for a taxpayer who itemizes is equal to adjusted gross income minus total itemized deductions and allowable exemptions.

Standard Deduction. Taxpayers who do not itemize their deductions are entitled to a standard deduction (Code Sec. 63(c)).[21] Taxpayers have the choice of itemizing deductions or taking the applicable standard deduction amount, whichever figure will result in a higher deduction. An individual whose AGI exceeds a specified threshold amount must reduce the amount of otherwise allowable itemized deductions (¶ 1014).

The amount of the standard deduction varies according to the taxpayer's filing status. This deduction, together with the taxpayer's personal and dependency exemptions, applies to reduce adjusted gross income in arriving at taxable income. Listed below are the standard deduction amounts available in 2001 to individuals other than those who are age 65 or older or who are blind:

Filing status	2001 standard deduction amount
Married filing jointly and surviving spouses	$7,600
Married filing separately	3,800
Head of household filers	6,650
Single filers	4,550

A special rule applies to an individual for whom a dependency exemption is allowable to another taxpayer. Such individual's basic standard deduction may not exceed the greater of $750 (projected by CCH to remain $750 in 2002) or the sum of

---

Footnote references are to paragraphs of the 2002 Standard Federal Tax Reports.
[21] ¶ 6020

$250 and the individual's earned income, up to the applicable standard deduction amount ($4,550 for single taxpayers) (projected by CCH to increase to $4,700 in 2002) (Code Sec. 63(c)(5)).[22] Thus, a child who may be claimed as a dependent by his parents and who has no earned income and $750 of interest or dividend income will have a $750 standard deduction. A scholarship or fellowship grant that is not excludable from the dependent's income (see ¶ 879) is considered earned income for standard deduction purposes.[23]

Note that the standard deduction for dependents other than those age 65 or older or blind cannot exceed the basic standard deduction amount shown above. If the taxpayer is age 65 or older or blind, the standard deduction is increased by the additional amount allowed to such taxpayers (see below).

Standard Deduction Marriage Penalty Relief. Beginning in 2005, the standard deduction for married filers and surviving spouses will increase over a five-year period until it is twice the size of the standard deduction for single filers (Code Sec. 63(c)(7), as added by the Economic Growth and Tax Relief Reconciliation Act of 2001 (P.L. 107-16)). The standard deduction for single filers is multiplied by the applicable percentage to determine the standard deduction for joint filers: 174% in 2005, 184% in 2006, 187% in 2007, 190% in 2008, and 200% (double) in 2009 and later. The standard deduction for married taxpayers filing separately will be increased in 2005 to equal the standard deduction claimed by single filers (Code Sec. 63(c)(2), as amended by P.L. 107-16).

Elderly and/or Blind Taxpayers. Taxpayers who are age 65 or older or who are blind receive an additional standard deduction amount that is added to the basic standard deduction shown in the above table. The additional amount for married individuals (whether filing jointly or separately) and surviving spouses is $900 (projected by CCH to remain $900 in 2002), while the additional amount for single individuals is $1,100 (projected by CCH to increase to $1,150 in 2002) (Code Sec. 63(f)).[24] Two additional amounts are allowed to an individual who is both over 65 and blind. Thus, married taxpayers filing jointly, both of whom are over 65 and blind, would claim four of the additional standard deduction amounts.

Generally, to qualify for the additional standard deduction amount, a taxpayer must be age 65 (or blind) before the close of the tax year. However, an individual who reaches age 65 on January 1st of any year is deemed to have reached that age on the preceding December 31st.[25] A taxpayer claiming the additional amount for blindness must obtain a certified statement from a doctor or registered optometrist. The statement, which should be kept with the taxpayer's records, must state that: (1) the individual cannot see better than 20/200 in the better eye with glasses or contact lenses or (2) the individual's field of vision is 20 degrees or less.

A married taxpayer filing separately may claim the additional amounts for a spouse who had no gross income and was not claimed as a dependent by another taxpayer. A taxpayer who claims a dependency exemption for an individual who is blind or age 65 or older may not claim the additional standard deduction amounts for that individual.

Taxpayers Ineligible for Standard Deduction. When married taxpayers file separate returns, both spouses should either itemize their deductions or claim the standard deduction. If one spouse itemizes and the other does not, the non-itemizing spouse's standard deduction amount will be zero, even if such spouse is age 65 or older or blind. However, the IRS has determined that this rule may not apply if one spouse qualifies to file as "head-of-household" (Service Center Advice 200030023). A zero standard deduction amount also applies to nonresident aliens, estates or trusts, common trust funds, or partnerships, and to individuals with short tax years due to a change in their annual accounting period (Code Sec. 63(c)(6)).[26] Taxpayers who

Footnote references are to paragraphs of the 2002 Standard Federal Tax Reports.

¶ 126

| [22] ¶ 6020 | [24] ¶ 6020, ¶ 6023.034 | [26] ¶ 6020 |
| [23] ¶ 7170.06 | [25] ¶ 6023.034 | |

itemize even though their itemized deductions are less than the standard deduction must enter "IE" (itemized elected) next to the appropriate line.

Example. A husband and a wife who are eligible to file a joint return elect to file separate returns. The husband itemizes. The wife, whose adjusted gross income is $12,100, has itemized deductions of $1,070, and her standard deduction is zero. Her taxable income is $8,130—adjusted gross income of $12,100 less $1,070 in itemized deductions less the $2,900 personal exemption.

Standard Deduction Amounts Projected by CCH for 2002. Standard deduction amounts for 2002 are projected as follows:

Filing status	2002 standard deduction amount
Married filing jointly and surviving spouses	$7,850
Married filing separately	3,925
Head of household filers	6,900
Single filers	4,700

Tax Rates in 2001. There are five tax rate brackets applicable to individual taxpayers for 2001: 15%, 27.5%, 30.5%, 35.5%, and 39.1%. The phaseout of personal exemptions is an additional adjustment apart from the tax rate structure (see ¶ 133) (Code Sec. 1(a)-Code Sec. 1(e)).[27] See ¶ 11-¶ 17 for the 2001 tax rate schedules.

Under the language of P.L. 107-16, the new 10-percent tax bracket will not be effective until after December 31, 2001. Most individuals will receive the benefit of a 10-percent bracket in the form of an advance rebate check which will be mailed by the IRS without any action on the part of taxpayers (Code Sec. 6428, as added by P.L. 107-16). To ensure all qualified taxpayers receive the full benefit of the tax rate reduction, a rate reduction credit may be claimed on the 2001 income tax return for those who, although qualified, failed to receive the advance rebate check.

The rate reduction credit is 5 percent (the difference between the 15-percent and 10-percent rates) of the amount of 2001 taxable income that would be eligible for the 10-percent rate if that rate were in effect in 2001. Generally, the credit is $300 for single taxpayers and married taxpayers filing separately ($6,000 × 5%), $600 for married taxpayers filing jointly and surviving spouses ($12,000 × 5%), and $500 for head of households ($10,000 × 5%). The credit may not exceed the sum of the taxpayer's regular and AMT tax liability reduced by all nonrefundable credits.

Individuals who were claimed as a dependent on another taxpayer's 2000 return, nonresident alien individuals, and estates and trusts are not eligible for the credit. At the time of publication, Congress is working towards the passage of a technical corrections act to clarify the language in the 2001 Act. This would allow individuals who were disqualified from receiving the rebate checks due to their filing status in 2000 to qualify for the rate reduction credit if they are no longer a disqualified individual in 2001.

The amount of the check is not included in a taxpayer's gross income. When taxpayers file their 2001 returns, they will reconcile the amount of the advance rebate check received with the credit actually due based on 2001 taxable income, filing status, and tax liability. If a taxpayer's advance rebate check was greater than the credit actually due, the difference does not need to be returned. If the taxpayer received less than the correct amount, the difference is claimed as a credit against 2001 tax liability.

Tax Rates in 2002 and Later. The Economic Growth and Tax Relief Reconciliation Act of 2001 reduces the rate brackets applicable to individual taxpayers as follows:

Tax years beginning during calendar year:		Rate brackets				
2002 and 2003	10%	15%	27%	30%	35%	38.6%
2003 and 2005	10%	15%	26%	29%	34%	37.6%
2006 and later	10%	15%	25%	28%	33%	35 %

Footnote references are to paragraphs of the 2002 Standard Federal Tax Reports.

[27] ¶ 3260

The 10-percent bracket will apply to the first $6,000 of taxable income for single filers and married taxpayers filing separately; the first $12,000 of taxable income for married taxpayers filing jointly and surviving spouses; and the first $10,000 of taxable income for head of household filers (Code Sec. 1(i)(1)(B), as added by P.L. 107-16). The $6,000 and $12,000 limits increase to $7,000 and $14,000, respectively, after 2008.

Marriage Penalty Relief. Beginning in 2005, the amount of taxable income that falls within the 15-percent rate bracket for married taxpayers filing jointly and surviving spouses will be increased over four years until it includes twice the amount of taxable income that falls within the 15-percent tax bracket for single filers (Code Sec. 1(f)(8), as added by P.L. 107-16). The phase-in is accomplished by measuring the taxable income that falls within the 15-percent bracket for joint filers as a percentage of the taxable income that falls within the 15-percent bracket for single filers. The applicable percentages are: 180 percent in 2005, 187 percent in 2006, 197 percent in 2007, and 200 percent (i.e., double) in 2008 and later.

The size of the 15-percent bracket amount for married taxpayer's filing separately will increase to the size of the 15-percent bracket for single filers during this same period. Stated as a percentage of the taxable income that falls within the 15-percent bracket for single individuals, the amount of taxable income falling within the 15-percent tax bracket for married filing separate filers will be: 90 percent in 2005, 93.5 percent in 2006, 96.5 percent in 2007, and 100 percent in 2008 and thereafter.

Another aspect of the marriage penalty relief is an increase in the standard deduction for joint filers to twice the size of the standard deduction for single filers over five years beginning in 2005. In 2005, the standard deduction for married taxpayer's filing separate also increases to equal the standard deduction for single filers. See *Standard Deduction Marriage Penalty Relief*, above.

Tax Calculation on Form 8615. Generally, Form 8615 must be used to calculate the tax for any child who was under age 14 on January 1, 2002, and who had more than $1,500 of investment income. However, if neither of the child's parents was alive on December 31, 2001, Form 8615 cannot be used to figure the tax (see ¶ 706). Taxpayers required to calculate their tax on Form 8615 may compute taxable income using Form 1040, 1040A, or 1040NR. Form 8615 is not filed if the child's parent elects to include the child's unearned income on the parent's return (see ¶ 114).

Tax Calculation on Schedule D, Part IV. Taxpayers who had a net capital gain use Schedule D, Part IV to compute their tax.

128. Tax Table Simplifies Computation. A table prepared by the IRS (reproduced at ¶ 25) simplifies determination of the tax. The table is based on taxable income and applies to taxpayers who file Form 1040 and have taxable income of less than $100,000. A similar tax table (ending at $50,000 rather than $100,000) must be used by filers of Forms 1040A and 1040EZ.

Taxpayers may *not* use the table if they have taxable income of $100,000 or more or if they file short-period returns because of a change in their annual accounting periods (¶ 1507 and ¶ 1509). Also, estates and nongrantor trusts may not use the table; instead, they must use the Tax Rate Schedule at ¶ 19.

> **Example.** An unmarried individual has adjusted gross income of $26,240. He has itemized deductions of $4,680. Since his itemized deductions exceed the allowable standard deduction ($4,550), he elects to itemize. His taxable income is $18,660—adjusted gross income of $26,240 less $4,680 in itemized deductions less the $2,900 personal exemption amount. His tax is $2,801 using the Tax Table.

130. Tax Rate Schedules. A taxpayer who may not use the Tax Table (¶ 25) must determine taxable income and apply the appropriate tax rate schedule (¶ 11-¶ 17) in order to compute his tax (unless he is required to compute his tax on

Form 8615, uses the Schedule D, Part IV (see ¶ 126), or the worksheet for capital gain distributions from mutual funds).

>   **Example.** Married taxpayers who file a joint return for 2001 have adjusted gross income of $145,950, four exemptions, and no itemized deductions. Their taxable income is $126,750 ($145,950 less $7,600 for the standard deduction less $11,600 for four exemptions). Their tax is $29,731 ($24,393.75 + 30.5% of $17,500 ($126,750 − $109,250)) and is computed by using the Tax Rate Schedule Y-1 at ¶ 13.

Exemption Amount

133. Exemption Amount. The amount of a personal exemption (for taxpayer and his spouse) and of a dependency exemption (for taxpayer's dependents) is $2,900 for 2001. This amount is adjusted annually to reflect the inflation rate (Code Sec. 151(d)).[28] For 2002, the exemption amount is projected by CCH to increase to $3,000. The exemption is denied to claimants who fail to provide the dependent's correct taxpayer identification number on the return claiming the exemption (Code Sec. 151(e)).

The deduction for exemptions may be reduced or eliminated for higher-income taxpayers (Code Sec. 151(d)).[29] The exemption for a taxpayer whose adjusted gross income exceeds the set threshold amount, based on filing status, is reduced by 2% for each $2,500 ($1,250 for a married person filing separately) or fraction thereof by which AGI exceeds the threshold amount. The 2001 threshold amounts are: (1) $199,450 for joint returns or a surviving spouse; (2) $166,200 for a head of household; (3) $132,950 for single taxpayers; and (4) $99,725 for married persons filing separately. Phaseout thresholds for 2002, as projected by CCH, increase to $206,000 (for joint returns or a surviving spouse), $171,650 (for a head of household), $137,300 (for single taxpayers), and $103,000 (for married persons filing separately).

Exemptions Phaseout Repealed. In tax years beginning in 2006 and 2007, the amount of the exemption phaseout reduction that would otherwise apply is reduced by one-third and for tax years beginning in 2008 and 2009 by two-thirds. For tax years beginning after 2009, the exemption phaseout is repealed (Code Sec. 151(d)(3)(E) and (F), as added by P.L. 107-16).

135. Exemptions. Generally, the exemptions allowed to a taxpayer are his "personal" exemption of $2,900 (projected by CCH to increase to $3,000 in 2002) and an exemption of $2,900 (projected by CCH to increase to $3,000 in 2002) for each dependent.

A husband and wife filing a joint return are allowed at least two "personal" exemptions of $2,900 in 2001 since each spouse is regarded as a taxpayer, plus any exemptions for dependents (¶ 137 et seq.). If a husband and wife file separate returns, each must take his or her own exemptions on the return. If, however, a husband or wife files a separate return and the other spouse has no gross income and is not the dependent of another taxpayer, the combined personal exemptions of the spouses may be claimed on the separate return (Reg. § 1.151-1(b)).[30] Additionally, a taxpayer who files a separate return may *not* claim two exemptions for his spouse— one as a spouse and one as a dependent (Code Sec. 152(a)(9)).[31]

If the husband and wife file a joint return, neither can be claimed as a "dependent" on the return of any other person (Reg. § 1.151-1(b)).[32] For an exception, see ¶ 145.

Also, no exemption will be allowed to an individual who is eligible to be claimed as a dependent on another taxpayer's return. Thus, students who work part-time during the year or for the summer may not claim personal exemptions on their own

---

Footnote references are to paragraphs of the 2002 Standard Federal Tax Reports.

[28] ¶ 8000, ¶ 8005.12   [30] ¶ 8001   [32] ¶ 8001
[29] ¶ 8000   [31] ¶ 8007

returns if their parents (or other taxpayers) are entitled to claim them on their returns. However, if dependents who are not allowed their own exemptions have gross income in an amount not exceeding $750 (projected by CCH to remain $750 in 2002), they will not be taxed on that amount and need not file income tax returns (see ¶ 109).

A resident alien may claim his own personal exemption and, if he files a joint return, may claim a similar exemption for his spouse. However, unless one of the elections noted at ¶ 152 applies, the filing of a joint return is not permissible if either he or his spouse was a nonresident alien during any part of the tax year (Code Sec. 6013(a)(1); Reg. § 1.6013-1(b)).[33] For nonresident aliens, see ¶ 2444.

137. Exemption for Dependent. Five tests must be met before an exemption for a dependent is allowed:

(1) The claimed dependent must have less than $2,900 (projected by CCH to increase to $3,000 in 2002) of gross income for the calendar year. This gross income test does not apply if the dependent is a child of the taxpayer and either is under age 19 at the close of the calendar year or is a full-time student under age 24 at the end of the calendar year (see ¶ 143 for rules regarding students);

(2) Over half of the dependent's total support for that calendar year must have been furnished by the taxpayer (with exceptions relating to multiple support agreements (¶ 147) and children of divorced parents (¶ 139));

(3) The dependent must fall within one of the following relationships:

(a) Son or daughter, grandchild, stepchild, or adopted child;

(b) Brother or sister;

(c) Brother or sister by the half blood;

(d) Stepbrother or stepsister;

(e) Mother or father, ancestor of either;

(f) Stepfather or stepmother;

(g) Son or daughter of taxpayer's brother or sister;

(h) Brother or sister of taxpayer's father or mother;

(i) Son-in-law, daughter-in-law, father-in-law, mother-in-law, brother-in-law, or sister-in-law (the widow of a taxpayer's deceased wife's brother is not considered a sister-in-law);[34] *or*

(j) A person (other than the taxpayer's spouse) who, during the taxpayer's entire tax year, lives in the taxpayer's home and is a member of the taxpayer's household (but not if the relationship between the person and the taxpayer is in violation of local law) (Code Sec. 152(a) and Code Sec. 152(b)); [35]

(4) The dependent must not have filed a joint return with his spouse (but see ¶ 145); and

(5) The dependent must be a citizen, national, or resident of the United States, a resident of Canada or Mexico at some time during the calendar year in which the tax year of the taxpayer begins, or an alien child adopted by and living with a U.S. citizen or national as a member of his household for the entire tax year (Code Sec. 152(b)(3); Reg. § 1.152-2(a)(2)).[36]

A legally adopted child or a child placed in the taxpayer's home for adoption by an authorized agency is considered to be a child by blood. The same status is given to a foster child who meets the conditions stated in category (3)(j), above, and is cared for by the foster parent as his own child. Thus, such an adopted or foster child fits into the (3)(a) category above (Code Sec. 152(b)(2)).[37]

The relationship of affinity, once existing, is not destroyed for income tax purposes by divorce or by the death of a spouse.

Footnote references are to paragraphs of the 2002 Standard Federal Tax Reports.

[33] ¶ 35,160, ¶ 35,161 [35] ¶ 8007, ¶ 8250.48 [37] ¶ 8007
[34] ¶ 8005.85 [36] ¶ 8007, ¶ 8050

Example. Mr. Golden contributes more than half the support of his wife's mother. Mrs. Golden divorces Mr. Golden, but he continues to contribute more than half the support of his former mother-in-law. Mr. Golden may continue to claim his former mother-in-law as a dependent on his separate return.

Assuming that the support test is met, a full exemption may be claimed for a child born at any time during the tax year, so long as the child lives momentarily and the birth is recognized under state or local law as a "live" birth.[38]

139. Exemptions for Children of Divorced Parents. Generally, the dependency exemption for children of divorced taxpayers will go to the parent who has custody of the child for the greater part of the calendar year. This rule applies only if the child receives over one-half of his or her support from parents who are divorced, legally separated, or have lived apart for the last six months of the calendar year. In addition, the child must have been in the custody of one or both parents for more than one-half of the calendar year (Code Sec. 152(e)).[39]

There are three exceptions to the rule that a custodial parent is entitled to the dependency exemption.[40] The first exception arises when there is a multiple support agreement that allows the child to be claimed as a dependent by a taxpayer other than the custodial parent (see ¶ 147). The second exception is when the custodial parent releases his or her right to the child's dependency exemption to the noncustodial parent. This release must be executed in writing (Form 8332 or similarly worded release) and attached to the noncustodial parent's tax return for each year the exemption is released. The final exception is when a pre-1985 divorce decree or separation agreement between the parents grants the exemption to the noncustodial parent and the noncustodial parent provides at least $600 for the support of the child for the year in question.

When a parent has remarried, support received from the parent's spouse is treated as received from the parent (Code Sec. 152(e)(5)).[41]

141. How the "Dependency" Exemption Is Claimed. On a joint return, the dependency exemption is allowed if the prescribed relationship (¶ 137) exists between one of the spouses and the claimed dependent (other conditions being satisfied) (Reg. § 1.152-2(d)).[42]

On a separate return, however, only a person who meets the requirements outlined at ¶ 137 can be claimed as a dependent by the taxpayer.

Example. Mr. and Mrs. Parker file a joint tax return. If Mr. Parker provides more than one-half of the support for Mrs. Parker's uncle, the exemption may be claimed on their joint return, even though the uncle does not live with them. If Mr. and Mrs. Parker file separate returns, Mr. Parker may claim the exemption for the uncle only if the uncle is a member of Mr. Parker's household and lives with him for the entire tax year.

In a community property state (¶ 710), if a child's support is derived from community income, some or all of the exemptions may, by agreement, be taken by either the husband or wife on a separate return. A single $2,900 (projected by CCH to increase to $3,000 in 2002) exemption amount may *not* be divided between them.[43]

143. Dependent's Income. Generally, in order to claim a person as a dependent, that person may *not* have gross income of $2,900 (projected by CCH to increase to $3,000 in 2002) or more for the year. But a taxpayer's child (¶ 137) who has not attained age 19 or who was under age 24 and was a full-time student at a regular educational institution or was pursuing a full-time, accredited, on-farm training course during each of five calendar months in 2001 may be claimed as a

---

Footnote references are to paragraphs of the 2002 Standard Federal Tax Reports.

| 38 ¶ 8250.36 | 40 ¶ 8007, ¶ 8200 | 42 ¶ 8050 |
| 39 ¶ 8007 | 41 ¶ 8007 | 43 ¶ 8005.23 |

¶ 143

dependent (if the taxpayer satisfies the support test), regardless of the amount of the child's income. The five calendar months need not be consecutive. In fixing the $2,900 income ceiling, any income excludable from the claimed dependent's gross income (such as exempt interest, disability, or social security) is disregarded. This income (except a student's scholarship), however, if used to any extent for support of the dependent, must be taken into account (to the extent that it was so used) to determine whether the taxpayer has furnished more than one-half of the claimed dependent's support (Reg. § 1.151-3(b), Reg. § 1.152-1).[44]

> **Example.** Paul's mother, who lived in his home, earned $450 in 2001 from baby-sitting. She was injured in an accident and received $2,650 in damages. Paul contributed $1,950 for her support in 2001. The damages award is not taxable income and is not counted for purposes of the $2,900 gross income test, but, if the mother spent at least $1,500 of this amount (plus the $450 she received for baby-sitting) in 2001 for her own support, Paul could not claim her as a dependent, because he would not have furnished more than one-half of her support. If less than $1,950 was spent by the mother for her own support, Paul would be entitled to the exemption for a dependent.

If the taxpayer is on a fiscal-year basis, the determinations as to whether the dependent had gross income, whether the taxpayer furnished the chief support, and whether a child is under age 19 or is a student under age 24 are all made on the basis of the calendar year in which the fiscal year begins (Reg. § 1.151-2(a), Reg. § 1.152-1(a)).[45]

If a parent is barred from claiming an exemption for a child who was a student age 24 or over during 2001 or whose gross income was $2,900 or more, the child may claim an exemption on his own return (Code Sec. 151(c)(1)(B)).[46]

A dependent who has earned wages in 2001 on which income tax has been withheld should file a return even though claimed as a dependent by another. The return will serve as a claim for refund of the tax withheld where the dependent incurs no tax liability. If a dependent child of the taxpayer has only earned income in excess of $4,550, $1 or more of unearned income and gross income in excess of $750, or self-employment income of $400 or more, a return must be filed whether or not the child is claimed as a dependent (see ¶ 109 and ¶ 2670).

Income received by a permanently and totally disabled individual at a sheltered workshop school is disregarded in determining that individual's status as a dependent.[47]

145. Exemption for Married Child. Generally, a parent may claim a married child as a dependent only if the child does not file a joint return and otherwise qualifies as a dependent. If the support test is met, a parent may claim a married child and their spouse as dependents, even though they file a joint return, if neither is *required* to file a return for the year (the filing being merely for the purpose of claiming a refund and neither has any independent tax liability if filing individually).[48]

147. Support of Dependent. A taxpayer must furnish more than one-half of the *total* support provided during the calendar year before claiming an exemption for a dependent (Reg. § 1.152-1).[49] (But see the special rule for children of divorced parents at ¶ 139.) If more than half of the support is provided by two or more people, the dependency exemption is not necessarily lost. A person can be treated, for purposes of the exemption, as having provided more than half of an individual's support if: (1) no one person provided over half of the support; (2) over half of the support was received from persons who each would have been entitled to claim the exemption had they contributed more than half of the support; (3) over 10 percent of the support was provided by the person claiming the exemption; and (4) each

Footnote references are to paragraphs of the 2002 Standard Federal Tax Reports.

¶ 145
44 ¶ 8000, ¶ 8003, ¶ 8008   46 ¶ 8000   48 ¶ 8005.56
45 ¶ 8002, ¶ 8008   47 ¶ 8000   49 ¶ 8008

person who contributed more than 10 percent of the support signs a written declaration (Form 2120) stating that they will not claim the exemption, which is attached to the return of the taxpayer claiming the exemption (Reg. § 1.152-3).[50]

"Total" support is determined on a yearly basis and is the sum of (1) the fair rental value of lodging furnished to a dependent, (2) the costs of all items of expense paid out directly by or for the benefit of the dependent, such as clothing, education, medical and dental care, gifts, transportation, church contributions, and entertainment and recreation, and (3) a proportionate share of the expenses incurred in supporting the whole household that cannot be directly attributed to each individual, such as food.[51] Item (3) does not include items that represent the cost of maintaining a house, such as heat, electricity, repairs, taxes, etc., because these costs are accounted for in the fair rental value of the lodging furnished the dependent. Medical care includes the premiums paid on a medical care policy, but not the benefits provided by the policy. Medicare benefits, both basic and supplementary, as well as Medicaid,[52] are also disregarded in determining support.[53]

Some capital expenditures qualify as items of support, such as the cost of an automobile purchased for a dependent and the cost of furniture and appliances provided to the dependent.[54] However, the following have been held or ruled not to be items of support: (1) income and social security taxes paid by a dependent child from his own income; (2) funeral expenses of a dependent; (3) costs incurred by a parent in exercising visitation rights; and (4) life insurance premium costs.[55]

In determining whether a taxpayer furnished more than one-half of a dependent's total support, the support provided by the taxpayer, by the dependent, and by third parties must be taken into account.[56] In addition, only the amount of the cash actually expended for items of support is taken into account. However, the source and tax status of money used to provide support is, generally, not controlling. It may come from taxable income, tax-exempt receipts, and loans. Furthermore, the year in which the support is received, and not the year of payment of the indebtedness incurred, is controlling in determining whether over one-half of the support is furnished by the taxpayer, regardless of his method of tax accounting.[57]

In the case of the taxpayer's child (as defined at ¶ 137) or stepchild who is a student, any amounts received as scholarships (including the value of accommodations furnished to a student nurse)[58] do not have to be taken into account (Reg. § 1.152-1(c)).[59] Educational benefits received under the United States Navy's educational assistance program are not considered to be scholarships.[60]

Survivor and old-age insurance benefits received under the Social Security Act and used for support are considered as having been contributed by the recipient to his own support.[61] Benefit payments made to an individual under state public assistance laws and measured solely by the needs of the recipient are considered as having been used entirely by that individual for his own support unless it is shown otherwise.[62] Amounts expended by a state for the training and education of handicapped children (including mentally retarded children who qualify as "students" and are in a state institution that qualifies as an "educational institution") are not considered to constitute support, except where the state assumes custody of the child involved.[63] AFDC (aid to families with dependent children) payments are considered support by the state and not by the parent.[64]

149. Effect of Death on Exemption. The $2,900 (projected by CCH to increase to $3,000 in 2002) exemption amount for 2001 is not reduced because of the death of a taxpayer, his spouse, or a dependent during the tax year.[65]

Footnote references are to paragraphs of the 2002 Standard Federal Tax Reports.

[50] ¶ 8100	[56] ¶ 8005.045	[61] ¶ 8005.71
[51] ¶ 8005.54, ¶ 8005.80	[57] ¶ 8005.81	[62] ¶ 8005.60
[52] ¶ 8005.80	[58] ¶ 8005.62	[63] ¶ 8005.72
[53] ¶ 8005.80	[59] ¶ 8008	[64] ¶ 8005.60
[54] ¶ 8005.80	[60] ¶ 8005.62	[65] ¶ 8005.055, ¶ 8008
[55] ¶ 8005.38, ¶ 8005.80		

¶ 149

Example 1. A child is born on December 31, 2001, and dies in January, 2002. A full exemption is allowed for the child in both years, assuming that the support test is met.

The death of one spouse will not deprive the survivor of the right to claim the exemptions of the deceased. The crucial date for determining marital status is the last day of the tax year; however, where a spouse dies during the tax year, such determination is made as of the date of death (Code Sec. 7703(a)).[66]

On the final separate return of a decedent, in addition to the deceased's own exemptions, the exemptions for the surviving spouse may be taken if the survivor had no gross income and was not a dependent of anyone else. Further, since the dependency exemption is based upon furnishing over half the support during the calendar year in which the tax year of the taxpayer begins, a decedent who furnished over half the support to a person otherwise qualifying as a dependent would be entitled to the full exemption for such dependent, without proration.

Example 2. Allen furnishes the full support for his aged father up to the date of his (Allen's) death on September 1, 2001, and over one-half of the total support for the year. A $2,900 exemption is allowed for the father on Allen's final return. But if Allen died on April 1 and his brother, Bob, supported the father for the balance of the year, incurring a larger expense than Allen did during the first part of the year, Bob alone would be entitled to the exemption. If the support in the latter case was furnished equally by Bob and another brother, Carl, from April 1 on, and if none of the three brothers furnished over half of the father's support for the calendar year, any one of them (including the executor of Allen's estate, on Allen's final return) could take the exemption if the other two renounced their right to the exemption for that year (¶ 147). Regardless of the amount of support, no exemption is allowed any of the three brothers for their father if the father has gross income of $2,900 or more during calendar year 2001.

Joint Return

152. Who May File? A husband and wife may file a joint return even though one spouse has no income or deductions (Reg. § 1.6013-1),[67] but only if (1) their tax years begin on the same date, (2) they are not legally separated under a decree of divorce or separate maintenance on the last day of the tax year, and (3) neither is a nonresident alien at any time during the year. However, a U.S. citizen or resident and his or her nonresident alien spouse can elect to file a joint return if they agree to be taxed on their worldwide income and supply all necessary books and records and other information pertinent to the determination of tax liability (Code Sec. 6013(g)).[68] Further, a one-time election to file a joint return is available in the year when a nonresident alien spouse becomes a resident (Code Sec. 6013(h)).[69]

If a husband and wife are on a calendar-year basis or have fiscal years that begin on the same date, they can file a joint return. If, however, they have different tax years, for some reason other than the intervention of death (see ¶ 164), then they cannot file a joint return. If newly married spouses with different tax years want to change the year of one spouse to coincide with that of the other so as to be able to file jointly, they may do so by following the rules described at ¶ 1513.

A husband and wife may file a joint return even though they have different accounting methods (e.g., where one is on the cash basis and the other is on the accrual basis) if such methods clearly reflect their income.

Even though a husband and wife are not living together on the last day of the tax year, they may still file a joint return if they are *not* legally separated under a decree of divorce or separate maintenance on that date (Reg. § 1.6013-4).[70] Spouses

Footnote references are to paragraphs of the 2002 Standard Federal Tax Reports.

¶ 152

66 ¶ 43,170   68 ¶ 35,160   70 ¶ 35,165
67 ¶ 35,161   69 ¶ 35,160

who are separated under an interlocutory decree of divorce are considered husband and wife and are entitled to file a joint return until the decree becomes final.[71] But certain married individuals living apart may file separate returns as heads of households (Code Sec. 2(c) and Code Sec. 7703(b)).[72] See ¶ 173.

Spouses of military personnel serving in a combat zone and missing in action may file a joint return for any tax year beginning before the date that is two years after the termination of combat activities in that zone (Code Sec. 6013(f)).

154. Election to File Joint Return. There can be a change of election from a separate return or returns to a joint return. Generally, this change of election is achieved by the filing of a Form 1040X within three years of the last date prescribed by law for the filing of the separate return or returns, without taking into account any extension of time granted to either spouse (Code Sec. 6013(b)(2)).[73] Additionally, the change to a joint return cannot be made (1) after either spouse timely files a petition with the Tax Court pursuant to a notice of deficiency which was mailed to either spouse for the tax year; (2) after either spouse commences a suit in any court for the recovery of any part of the tax for such tax year; (3) after either spouse enters into a closing agreement with respect to such tax year; or (4) after either spouse has compromised any civil or criminal case arising with respect to such tax year. Once a joint return has been filed for a tax year, the spouses may not thereafter file separate returns after the time for filing the return of either spouse has expired (Reg. § 1.6013-1(a)).[74] The exception being if either spouses dies during the tax year, then only the executor or administrator of the estate of the deceased spouse may elect to change from a separate to a joint return. See also ¶ 168.

However, the Tax Court has ruled that a couple could elect to file joint returns even though the IRS had previously prepared and filed returns for the husband with a status of married filing separately (*J.V. Millsap*).[75] The IRS's filing of substitute returns did not bar the taxpayer from contesting either the deficiency or the IRS's choice of his filing status. The former standard, i.e., that the IRS's choice precludes taxpayers from selecting a different filing status (*R.E. Smalldridge*),[76] will be applied only when the issue is appealable to the U.S. Court of Appeals for the Tenth Circuit.

156. Joint v. Separate Return. The gross income and deductions of a husband and wife are aggregated on a joint return. Deductions that are limited to a percentage of the adjusted gross income (e.g., medical expenses) are computed on combined adjusted gross income. Similarly, losses of a husband and wife from sales or exchanges of capital assets are combined. The "taxable income" (¶ 126) on a joint return, for this purpose, is the entire taxable income. Although there are two taxpayers on a joint return, there is only one taxable income and only one adjusted gross income amount (Reg. § 1.6013-4).[77] The total exemptions of a husband and wife are subtracted in determining taxable income.

The filing of a joint return will result in a savings of tax in those instances in which differences in the tax rate brackets for joint and separate returns result in higher tax rates for married individuals filing separately.

> **Example.** For 2001, Joe has taxable income in the amount of $14,500, and his wife, Trisha, has taxable income in the amount of $22,950. If they elect to file a joint return, they will not be subject to the 27.5% tax rate because their combined taxable income of $37,450 does not exceed $45,200 (see ¶ 13). However, if they opt to file separate returns, $350, which represents the portion of Trisha's income that exceeds $22,600, falls within the 27.5% tax bracket (see ¶ 15).

Similarly, it might be advantageous to file jointly if a couple's tax situation triggers alternative minimum tax liability. Both the greater exemption amount

Footnote references are to paragraphs of the 2002 Standard Federal Tax Reports.

[71] ¶ 35,165, ¶ 35,171.39 [74] ¶ 35,161   [76] ¶ 35,171.026,
[72] ¶ 3310, ¶ 43,170   [75] ¶ 35,171.026,   ¶ 35,171.687
[73] ¶ 35,160   ¶ 35,171.687   [77] ¶ 35,165

available to joint filers ($49,000 as opposed to $24,500) and the higher phaseout of exemption amount ($150,000 compared to $75,000) allow couples filing jointly to shelter a larger amount of preference income from the tax.[78] See ¶ 1405.

Also, if only one spouse has income, it would be impractical for the income earner to use married filing separately status, claiming two exemptions, because such status carries a basic standard deduction of only $3,800 (projected by CCH to increase to $3,925 in 2002). Joint filers have a basic standard deduction of $7,600 in 2001 (projected by CCH to increase to $7,850 in 2002). See ¶ 126. It should be noted that a married person generally may not claim the credit for the elderly or permanently disabled (¶ 1304), the child and dependent care credit (¶ 1301), the earned income credit (¶ 1375), or the educational credits (¶ 1303) unless he and his spouse file a joint return.

There are circumstances under which married taxpayers might reduce their tax liability by filing separate returns. For example, a spouse whose medical expenses are high, but not high enough to exceed 7.5% of the adjusted gross income reported on a joint return, may exceed the AGI threshold on a separate return (see ¶ 1015). In light of the 2%-of-AGI floor on miscellaneous itemized deductions (see ¶ 1011), a spouse who incurs substantial unreimbursed employee business or investment expenses might be better off filing separately. The same rationale holds true for casualty and disaster loss deductions, which are subject to a 10%-of-AGI floor (see ¶ 1137).

Actual tax comparisons should be made using both joint and separate returns if there is doubt as to which method produces more favorable results. Considerations other than tax savings might enter into the decision to file a separate, rather than a joint, return. For example, one spouse may wish to avoid a deficiency liability assessed against the other spouse (see ¶ 162).

Marriage Penalty Relief. Beginning in 2005, the amount of taxable income that falls within the 15-percent rate bracket for married taxpayers filing jointly and surviving spouses increases over a four-year period until it includes twice the amount of taxable income that falls within the 15-percent tax bracket for single filers. The size of the 15-percent bracket amount for married taxpayers filing separately is also increased to the size of the 15-percent bracket for single filers during this same period. See ¶ 126.

162. Liability on Joint Return. A husband and wife are generally liable jointly and individually for the entire tax on a joint return. For tax liabilities arising prior to July 22, 1998, an "innocent spouse" could be relieved of the tax liability, interest and penalties only if certain specific threshold requirements were met. Effective for any tax liability, interest and penalties arising on or after July 22, 1998, and for any tax liability that remains unpaid, is a less strict set of requirements to obtain "innocent spouse" relief. These standards make it easier to qualify for relief and to prevent abuse of the "innocent spouse." One must now elect the form of relief being sought on Form 8857 (Request for Innocent Spouse Relief (and Separation of Liability and Equitable Relief)) within two years of the IRS beginning collection of a tax deficiency or assessment. The types of relief available to the electing spouse are (1) innocent spouse, (2) separation of liability, or (3) equitable relief. Any determination by the IRS is reviewable in Tax Court.[79] Notice of the election for relief is required to be given to the non-electing spouse who may participate in any hearings on the relief requested.[80] The Tax Court has held that the non-electing spouse has the right to a "stand-alone" hearing regarding the appropriateness of granting relief to the electing spouse (*T. Corson,* 114 TC 354, CCH Dec. 53,882 and *K.A. King,* 115 TC 118, CCH Dec. 53,994). There are additional requirements for jurisdictions located in community property states.[81]

Footnote references are to paragraphs of the 2002 Standard Federal Tax Reports.

[78] ¶ 5100
[79] ¶ 35,192.028
[80] ¶ 35,192.027
[81] ¶ 35,192.021, ¶ 35,192.024

To qualify for the innocent spouse relief election, the taxpayer must meet *all* the following requirements: (1) filed a joint return which has an *understatement of tax* due to *erroneous items* of the spouse, (2) establish that at the time of signing the tax return the taxpayer did not know, or have reason to know, there was an understatement of tax, and (3) taking into account all the facts and circumstances, it would be unfair to hold the innocent spouse liable for the understatement of tax.[82] A key element for the IRS will be whether the electing spouse received any substantial benefits or later was divorced, separated from or deserted by the other spouse.

The "innocent spouse" may elect to obtain relief by separation of liabilities.[83] To qualify, an individual must have (1) filed a joint return and (2) either (a) be no longer married to, or be legally separated from, the spouse with whom the joint return was filed or (b) must *not* have been a member of the same household with the spouse for a 12-month period ending on the date of the filing of Form 8857 (Request for Innocent Spouse Relief). The burden of proof on income and deductions is on the taxpayer who elects relief under separation of liability.

Finally, should one fail to qualify for either of the first two types of relief, one may still obtain relief from the tax liabilities, interest and penalties by electing equitable relief.[84] The taxpayer must show that, under *all* facts and circumstances, it would be unfair to be held liable for the understatement or underpayment of taxes. One should note that under equitable relief, the "innocent spouse" can receive relief from tax liabilities caused by underpayment of taxes (Code Sec. 6015; IRS Publication 971; IRS Publication 555).

163. Injured Spouse Claim. In situations when married taxpayers file a joint return and one spouse has not paid child or spousal support or certain federal debts, such as student loans, all or part of the tax overpayment shown on the delinquent spouse's return may be used to satisfy the past-due debt. However, the nonobligated spouse may be entitled to a refund of his or her part of the overpayment if that individual (1) is not required to pay the past-due amount, (2) received and reported income, such as wages, taxable interest, etc., on the joint return, and (3) made and reported payments, such as withheld federal income taxes or estimated taxes, on the joint return.

To make this type of claim, the nonobligated spouse must write "Injured Spouse" in the upper left corner of Form 1040 and attach Form 8379 (Injured Spouse Claim and Allocation). If the joint return has already been filed for 2001 or prior years, the nonobligated spouse should file Form 8379 by itself to claim the refund.

164. Effect of Death on Joint Return. A joint return may be filed when one or both spouses died during the year, and the tax year of both began on the same day, whether such year is a fiscal or calendar year. When a joint return is filed, it is treated as if the tax years of both spouses ended on the closing date of the surviving spouse's tax year (Reg. § 1.6013-3).[85]

166. When Surviving Spouse May Not File Joint Return. A joint return may not be filed in the year a spouse dies if the surviving spouse has remarried before the close of the tax year. However, the survivor may file a joint return with the new spouse if all other requirements are met. Also, the survivor may not file a joint return with the deceased spouse if the tax year of either spouse is a fractional part of a year resulting from a change of accounting period (Reg. § 1.6013-1(d)).[86]

> **Example.** Stan and Tracy file joint returns on a calendar-year basis. Tracy dies on March 1, 2001. Thereafter, Stan receives permission to change his accounting period to a fiscal year beginning July 1, 2001. A joint return cannot be filed for the short tax year ending June 30, 2001.

Footnote references are to paragraphs of the 2002 Standard Federal Tax Reports.

[82] ¶ 35,192.073	[84] ¶ 35,192.023	[86] ¶ 35,161
[83] ¶ 35,192.35	[85] ¶ 35,164	

168. Who Files the Return? Generally, where one spouse dies, a joint return can be filed only by the executor/administrator and the survivor. The surviving spouse, alone, however, *may file a joint* return if: (1) no return was filed by the decedent for the tax year at issue; (2) no executor or administrator was appointed; and (3) no executor or administrator was appointed before the last day for filing the return of the surviving spouse, including any extensions of time for filing.

Even if all of the above tests are met, an administrator or executor, subsequently appointed, may disaffirm a joint return made by the surviving spouse by filing a separate return for the decedent. This disaffirmance must be made within one year after the last day allowed for filing the return of the surviving spouse (including extensions). If a disaffirmance is made, then the already filed joint return will be considered the survivor's separate return. The survivor's tax will be figured on the basis of this joint return, with all of the items properly includible in the return of the deceased spouse deleted from the joint return (Reg. § 1.6013-1(d)).[87]

Head of a Household

171. Special Tax Table. A portion of the benefits that the more favorable tax rates bestow upon a married couple filing a joint return are given to an unmarried individual who qualifies as the "head of a household." See Tax Rate Schedule Z (¶ 17) and the "Head of a Household" column in the Tax Table (¶ 25). See ¶ 128 and ¶ 130 for determining whether the schedule or the table is used.

173. Who Is a Head of Household? In order to qualify for head of household status, a taxpayer must not be married or a surviving spouse (¶ 175) at the close of the tax year. In addition, the taxpayer must maintain as his home a household which, for more than one-half of the tax year, is the principal place of abode of one or more of the following:

(1) A son or daughter, grandchild, or stepchild. If one of the above is married at the close of the taxpayer's tax year, the taxpayer must be able to claim the person as a dependent (but not merely by virtue of a multiple support agreement (¶ 147)). For purposes of this requirement, an adopted child or a foster child that has been a member of the taxpayer's household for the entire year shall be treated as the taxpayer's child by blood. A taxpayer qualified for "head of a household" status, even though his daughter filed a joint return with her deceased husband, because all parties had lived with the taxpayer during the entire tax year.[88]

(2) Any other person (see (3)(a)-(i) at ¶ 137) eligible to be claimed as a dependent, except for those eligible to be claimed under a multiple support agreement (¶ 147). A dependent satisfying the member of taxpayer's household test (see (3)(j) at ¶ 137) is not sufficient to qualify a taxpayer for head of household status.

An individual also qualifies for head of household status if a *separate* household is maintained, for the tax year, for a parent. The separate household must be the parent's principal place of abode, and the parent must qualify as the child's dependent (see ¶ 137). A parent's principal place of abode can include residence in a rest home or home for the aged. An institutionalized or hospitalized dependent, other than a parent, may also qualify a taxpayer as head of a household if the taxpayer can prove that the taxpayer's home was the "principal" place of abode of the dependent, even though the dependent may never return home because of the nature of the infirmity.[89]

The marital status of an individual for the purpose of applying the "head of household" rates is determined at the end of a tax year. A taxpayer is considered to be unmarried at the end of a tax year if his spouse was a nonresident alien at any time during the tax year or if he is legally separated from his spouse under a decree

---

Footnote references are to paragraphs of the 2002 Standard Federal Tax Reports.

¶ **168**   [87] ¶ 35,161   [88] ¶ 3340.12   [89] ¶ 3340.16

of divorce or separate maintenance at the close of the tax year. A taxpayer under an interlocutory decree of divorce is not legally separated.[90] A widow or widower may not use the "head of household" rates in those tax years in which he or she is eligible to use the joint tax rates under the "surviving spouse" rules discussed at ¶ 175.

A married taxpayer will be considered unmarried and eligible for head of household status if the taxpayer's spouse was not a member of the household for the last six months of the year and if the household is the principal place of abode of a child for whom the taxpayer is entitled to a dependency exemption.[91] However, the taxpayer will still be eligible for head-of-household status if no dependency exemption is available for a child because the taxpayer waived the exemption or because of the existence of a pre-1985 divorce decree or separation agreement (¶ 139).[92]

An individual "maintains a household" only if the individual furnishes (with funds the source of which are attributable to the taxpayer) more than one-half the cost of maintaining the home during the tax year and if at least one of the persons described in (1) and (2) above (with an exception for institutionalized or hospitalized dependents) lives there for more than one-half of the year (except for temporary absence, such as time spent at school). Birth or death of such a person during the year will not disqualify the taxpayer as the head of a household if the person lived in the household for the part of the year during which he was alive (Reg. § 1.2-2(c)).[93]

The cost of maintaining a household includes the expenses incurred for the mutual benefit of the occupants by reason of its use as the principal place of abode. These expenses include property taxes, mortgage interest, rent, utility charges, upkeep and repairs, property insurance, food consumed on the premises, and other household expenses. They do not include the cost of clothing, education, medical treatment, vacations, life insurance, transportation, food consumed off the premises, or the value of services rendered by the taxpayer or by any person who qualifies the taxpayer as head of a household (Reg. § 1.2-2(d)).[94]

Widow or Widower

175. Surviving Spouse. A surviving spouse may use the joint return tax rates for two tax years following the year of death of the husband or wife, but *only* if the survivor remains unmarried and maintains as a home a household (see ¶ 173) that, for the entire tax year, is the principal place of abode of a son or daughter, adopted child, foster child, or stepchild who is a member of the surviving spouse's household and for whom the taxpayer is entitled to the dependency exemption (¶ 137) (Code Sec. 2(a)).[95] As to joint returns for the year of death, see ¶ 164.

A widow or widower who qualifies as a "surviving spouse" uses the joint return rate schedule (Schedule Y-1) at ¶ 13 or Tax Table at ¶ 25 and must use Form 1040 or 1040A. This benefit is afforded a survivor only if he or she was entitled to file a joint return with the deceased spouse during the latter's lifetime.

It should be emphasized that the benefit entitles the survivor only to the joint return *tax rates;* it does not authorize him or her to file a joint return or claim any personal exemptions other than his or her own and those of the dependent or dependents for whom the household is maintained.

For 2001, a qualifying widow or widower with dependent children is generally entitled to joint return rate benefits if the spouse died at any time during 1999 or 2000.

In determining eligibility for filing as a surviving spouse, the date of death of a person serving in a combat zone and missing in action is considered to be two years after the termination of combat activities in that zone (Code Sec. 2(a)(3)), unless death has been established at an earlier time.

Footnote references are to paragraphs of the 2002 Standard Federal Tax Reports.

[90] ¶ 3340.03, ¶ 3340.17	[92] ¶ 3335.01, ¶ 8007	[94] ¶ 3325
[91] ¶ 3335.01, ¶ 8007	[93] ¶ 3325	[95] ¶ 3310

Tax Treatment of Decedent's Final Return

178. Who Must File. A taxpayer's tax year ends on the date of his death.[96] The final return of a decedent for the part of the year up to and including the date of his death [97] is filed on Form 1040, 1040A, or 1040EZ. A return is required if the decedent met the gross income filing test (¶ 109) for the short period. A return must also be made for the decedent if earnings from self-employment amounted to $400 or more or if the decedent is owed a refund. See ¶ 2664-¶ 2676.

The return for the decedent must be filed by his administrator, executor, or any other person charged with responsibility for the decedent's affairs. Whoever files the return for the decedent may file a separate return or a joint return (¶ 164-¶ 168). All personal exemptions to which the decedent was entitled while he was alive may be claimed. If a refund is due, Form 1310 (Statement of Person Claiming Refund Due a Deceased Taxpayer) is to be attached to the return.

180. Due Date. The final return of a decedent is due by the date on which the return would have been due had death not occurred. See ¶ 118. Thus, for a calendar-year taxpayer who died in 2001, the final return is due by April 15, 2002 (Reg. § 1.6072-1(a)).[98]

182. How Income Is Treated. When a cash-basis taxpayer dies, only income actually or constructively received up to the date of death is included in the final return. If the decedent was on the accrual basis, income accrued up to the date of death is included in the final return. However, income that accrues *only because of death* is not included (Code Sec. 451; Reg. § 1.451-1(b)).[99] These rules also apply to successive decedents as to rights to receive "income in respect of a prior decedent" (Reg. § 1.691(a)-1(c)).[100]

Any amount of gross income not reported on the return of the decedent is, when received, includible in the income of the person receiving such amounts by inheritance or survivorship. This may be the decedent's estate. Or, if the estate does not collect an item of income but distributes the right to receive it to a testamentary trust or to the heir, next of kin, legatee, or devisee, it is included in the income of such trust, heir, next of kin, legatee, or devisee (Code Sec. 691(a); Reg. § 1.691(a)-2).[101]

The depreciation recapture rules under Code Sec. 1245 and Code Sec. 1250 (see ¶ 1779-¶ 1795) apply to sales or other dispositions of property subject to those rules where the income therefrom is treated as income on the decedent's final return or as income in respect of a decedent under Code Sec. 691. But these rules do not apply to transfers of depreciable property at death (Code Sec. 1245(b)(2) and Code Sec. 1250(d)(2)).[102]

184. Installment Obligation. Collections on an installment obligation acquired from a decedent are treated as items of income in respect of a decedent if the decedent had been reporting the profit on the installment basis (Code Sec. 691(a)(4); Reg. § 1.691(a)-5).[103]

If, however, the obligor of the installment obligation acquires the uncollected obligation, then the decedent's estate is considered to have made a taxable disposition of the installment obligation. Thus, any previously unreported gain will be recognized by the estate. This rule also applies if the obligation is canceled because of the death of the payee or if the estate allows the obligation to become unenforceable because it is canceled by the executor.[104]

187. Deductions. Deductible expenses and other items are not accrued on the final return of a decedent (unless his accounting method requires it), but are deductible instead by the estate or person who pays them or is liable for their

---

Footnote references are to paragraphs of the 2002 Standard Federal Tax Reports.

[96] ¶ 21,817.03	[99] ¶ 21,002, ¶ 21,003	[102] ¶ 30,902, ¶ 31,000
[97] ¶ 20,501	[100] ¶ 24,901	[103] ¶ 24,900, ¶ 24,905
[98] ¶ 36,721	[101] ¶ 24,900, ¶ 24,902	[104] ¶ 24,900, ¶ 24,906.29

¶ 178

payment (Code Sec. 461; Reg. § 1.461-1(b)).[105] Similar treatment is given the foreign tax credit (Code Sec. 691(b); Reg. § 1.691(b)-1).[106]

Expenses for medical care of the decedent, paid out of his estate within one year from the date of his death, are deductible on the decedent's final return (Reg. § 1.213-1(d)). However, the estate must attach a statement (in duplicate) to the decedent's return waiving the right to claim the deduction on the estate tax return.[107]

Business expenses, income-producing expenses, interest, and taxes for which the decedent was liable but which were not properly allowable as a deduction on his last return will be allowed when paid (a) as a deduction by the estate or (b) if the estate was not liable, then as a deduction by the person who by reason of the decedent's death acquires—subject to such obligation—an interest in property of the decedent (Reg. § 1.691(b)-1(a)).[108]

The percentage depletion deduction is allowed only to the person who receives the income in respect of the decedent to which the deduction relates (Reg. § 1.691(b)-1(b)).[109]

189. How Recipient Treats Decedent's Income. A decedent's income that is to be accounted for by the recipient retains the same character it would have had in the hands of the decedent (Code Sec. 691(a)(3); Reg. § 1.691(a)-3).[110] Thus, if the income would have been earned income, exempt income, or interest to the decedent, it is the same kind of income to the recipient.

191. Deduction of Death Taxes. If a person includes in gross income an item of income that had accrued as of the date of death of a decedent or prior successive decedents, so that it was included in the valuation of the estate for estate tax purposes, that person may take a corresponding deduction based on the estate tax attributable to the net value of the income item (Code Sec. 691(c); Reg. § 1.691(c)-1).[111] This deduction is taken by individuals on Form 1040 and by estates and trusts on Form 1041. In the case of individuals, it may be taken only if deductions are itemized on Schedule A.[112] For individuals, as well as for estates and trusts, the deduction is not subject to the 2%-of-AGI floor on miscellaneous deductions (Code Sec. 67(b)(7)).[113]

In the case of any generation-skipping transfer tax imposed on a taxable termination or a direct skip as a result of the death of the transferor, a deduction is available for the portion of such tax attributable to items of gross income that were not properly includible in the gross income of the trust before the date of such termination (Code Sec. 691(c)(3)).[114]

Footnote references are to paragraphs of the 2002 Standard Federal Tax Reports.

[105] ¶ 21,802, ¶ 21,805	[109] ¶ 24,907	[112] ¶ 24,911.11
[106] ¶ 24,900, ¶ 24,907	[110] ¶ 24,900, ¶ 24,903	[113] ¶ 6060, ¶ 24,911.025
[107] ¶ 12,541	[111] ¶ 24,900, ¶ 24,909	[114] ¶ 24,900
[108] ¶ 24,907		

Chapter 2

CORPORATIONS

TAX ON CORPORATIONS

Organizations Taxed as Corporations

201. How Organizations Are Taxed. A corporation, like any business other than a sole proprietorship or a single-member limited liability corporation (in states where permitted), is formed by business associates to conduct a business venture and divide profits among investors (Reg. § 301.7701-2).[1] A corporation files a charter or articles of incorporation in a state, in a U.S. possession, or with the U.S. government. It prepares by-laws, has its business affairs overseen by a board of directors, and issues stock. Under the "check-the-box" regulations, entities formed under a corporation statute are automatically classified as corporations and may not elect to be treated as any other kind of entity (Reg. § 301.7701-2).[2] Further, other entities with more than one member are allowed to elect corporate status on Form 8832, "Entity Classification Election." Thus, an entity that is a partnership under the laws of the state in which it is formed may elect to be taxed as a C corporation or an S corporation under the Code (Reg. § 301.7701-3).[3] However, an entity organized under a state's corporation statute cannot elect to be taxed as a partnership.

Partnerships that are publicly traded are taxed as corporations unless 90 percent or more of the gross income consists of qualifying passive-type income (Code Sec. 7704(d); Reg. § 1.7704-1, Reg. § 1.7704-3).[4]

For tax purposes, the predominant forms of business enterprise are C corporations, S corporations, partnerships, limited liability companies (LLCs), and sole proprietorships. To choose among these is to choose among significant differences in federal income tax treatment. Although many of the Code's provisions apply to all of these entities, some areas of the law are specially tailored for each type. The

---

Footnote references are to paragraphs of the 2002 Standard Federal Tax Reports.

[1] ¶ 43,082
[2] ¶ 43,082
[3] ¶ 43,083

[4] ¶ 43,180, ¶ 43,181B, ¶ 43,181D

classification of an entity will have a lingering tax impact throughout the entity's existence.

Of the types of business organization, C corporations are subject to the toughest tax bite. Their earnings are taxed twice. First, a *corporate* income tax is imposed on its net earnings and then, after the earnings are distributed to shareholders as dividends, each shareholder must pay taxes separately on his or her share of the dividends (Code Sec. 11 and Code Sec. 301(c)).[5] Since no tax deduction may be claimed by a corporation for its distribution of dividends, there is no chance of lessening the overall tax drain. However, a corporation can reduce, or even eliminate, its federal income tax liability by distributing its income as salary to shareholder-employees who actually perform valuable services to the corporation. Although this can reduce taxation on the corporation level, nevertheless, those who receive distributions from a corporation in exchange for services must pay tax on the distributions, which are treated as salary (Reg. § 1.351-1(a)(1)(i)).[6]

This scheme of taxation differs radically from that applied to S corporations, partnerships, limited liability companies, and sole proprietorships. These entities do not pay an entity-level tax on their earnings. There is no partnership income tax (Code Sec. 701).[7] Nor (in most cases) is there an S corporation income tax, limited liability company income tax, or sole proprietorship income tax (Code Sec. 1363).[8] Only the owners or members of these entities are taxed on their share of the entity's earnings.

For more on S corporations, see ¶ 301. Partnerships are discussed at ¶ 401, while LLCs are discussed at ¶ 402B. Foreign corporations are discussed at ¶ 2425. Sole proprietorships, which are really no more than the alter egos of individuals, are discussed throughout this book as part of the material on individual income taxation.

For the tax treatment of corporate distributions to the shareholders, see ¶ 733–¶ 757.

203. Tax-Free Contributions in Exchange for Stock. A corporation is formed by the transfer of money or property from shareholders to the corporate entity in return for corporate stock.

If one or more shareholders transfer money or property to a corporation solely in exchange for stock of that corporation, and if the shareholders control the corporation immediately after the exchange, neither the shareholders nor the corporation recognizes any gain or loss (Code Sec. 351(a) and Code Sec. 1032).[9] To be considered in "control," the shareholders as a group must own immediately after the transaction (1) at least 80 percent of the total combined voting power of all classes of stock entitled to vote and (2) at least 80 percent of the total number of shares of all other classes of stock (Code Sec. 368(c)).[10]

Money or property transferred to a controlled corporation generally includes all property, tangible or intangible, with certain limitations. Stock issued for services, indebtedness of the corporation which is not evidenced by a security, or interest on indebtedness of the corporation which accrued on or after the beginning of the transferor's holding period for the debt are not considered as issued in return for property (Code Sec. 351(d)).[11]

Corporate shareholders can be individuals, estates, trusts, partnerships or other corporations (Code Sec. 351; Reg. § 1.351-1(a)(1)).[12] However, the rules permitting tax-free transfers to a corporation in exchange for corporate stock do not apply if the corporation is an investment company or "swap fund" (Code Sec. 351(e)(1)).[13]

Regulations address what constitutes "immediately after the transaction." The rules provide that no gain or loss is recognized in certain otherwise taxable transactions if one corporation transfers its own stock to another corporation (usually a

---

Footnote references are to paragraphs of the 2002 Standard Federal Tax Reports.

[5] ¶ 3365, ¶ 15,302	[8] ¶ 32,060	[11] ¶ 16,402
[6] ¶ 16,403	[9] ¶ 16,402, ¶ 29,622	[12] ¶ 16,402
[7] ¶ 25,060	[10] ¶ 16,750	[13] ¶ 16,402

subsidiary) pursuant to a plan by which the second corporation immediately transfers the stock of the first corporation in exchange for money or other property (Reg. § 1.1032-3).[14] The IRS notes that the immediacy requirement should not be construed to permit the acquiring corporation to hold issuing corporation stock for a period of time during which the value of the stock could fluctuate.

Generally, the tax-free organization of a business is not wholly negated if the transferor owners receive additional property along with the stock when they transfer property to the corporation. However, the owners are taxed on any additional property received ("boot"). Thus, gain is recognized, but only to the extent of the cash received, plus the fair market value of the other property received. No loss is recognized on the transfer (Code Sec. 351(b); Reg. § 1.351-2(a)).[15]

Assumption of Liabilities. If property transferred in what would otherwise be a Code Sec. 351[16] tax-free transaction is subject to liabilities, the acceptance of the transfer or the assumption of the liabilities does not prevent the transaction from being tax free. This rule does not apply if the principal purpose of the transfer is tax avoidance or if liabilities assumed by the transferee exceed the transferor's basis in the property (Code Sec. 357).[17]

Bankruptcy. A debtor must recognize gain or loss upon its transfer of assets to a controlled corporation pursuant to a plan approved by a bankruptcy court (other than a reorganization plan) in which the stock is exchanged (Code Sec. 351(e)(2)).[18] Essentially, the transaction is treated as if the property had first been transferred to the creditors and then transferred by them to the controlled corporation. If less than all the stock is transferred to creditors, only a proportionate share of the gain or loss must be recognized. Both the basis of the stock and of the assets are adjusted for the gain or loss recognized on the transfer to the corporation.

Reporting Requirements. If a person receives stock of a corporation in exchange for property and no gain or loss is recognized, the person and the corporation must each attach to their tax returns a complete statement of all the facts pertinent to the exchange, including (Reg. § 1.351-3):[19]

(1) a description of the property transferred or of the interest in such property, together with a statement of the cost or other basis, adjusted to the date of transfer;

(2) with respect to stock of the controlled corporation received in the exchange, a statement of (a) the kind of stock and preferences, if any, (b) the number of shares of each class received, and (c) the fair market value per share of each class at the date of the exchange;

(3) with respect to securities of the controlled corporation received in the exchange, a statement of (a) the principal amount and terms and (b) the fair market value at the date of exchange;

(4) the amount of money received, if any;

(5) with respect to other property received, (a) a complete description of each separate item, (b) the fair market value of each separate item at the date of exchange, and (c) in the case of a corporate shareholder, the adjusted basis of the other property in the hands of the controlled corporation immediately before the distribution of such other property to the corporate shareholder in connection with the exchange; and

(6) with respect to liabilities of the transferors assumed by the controlled corporation, a statement of (a) the nature of the liabilities, (b) when and under what circumstances created, (c) the corporate business reason for assumption by the controlled corporation, and (d) whether such assumption eliminates the transferor's primary liability.

Footnote references are to paragraphs of the 2002 Standard Federal Tax Reports.

¶ 203

[14] ¶ 29,624F	[16] ¶ 16,402	[18] ¶ 16,402
[15] 16,402, ¶ 16,404B	[17] ¶ 16,520	[19] ¶ 16,404C

Return of Corporation and Payment of Taxes

211. Annual and Short-Period Returns. A corporation must file an income tax return even if it has no income or if no tax is due (Code Sec. 6012(a)(2)).[20] Form 1120, "U.S. Corporation Income Tax Return," must be filed on or before the 15th day of the third month that follows the close of its tax year (Code Sec. 6012(a)(2) and Code Sec. 6072(b); Reg. § 1.6012-2 and Reg. § 1.6072-2).[21] If the last day of a corporation's tax year does not end on the last day of a month (as in the case of a dissolved corporation whose tax year ends on the date of dissolution), the return is due on or before the 15th day of the third full month following the date of dissolution. A shorter version of the form, Form 1120-A, "U.S. Corporation Short-Form Income Tax Return," may be filed by a corporation that has gross receipts of less than $500,000, if all the following amounts are under $500,000: (1) gross receipts, (2) total income (includes dividends received, interest, rent, royalties, capital gains and certain other income), and (3) total assets from Form 1120, Schedule L, line 15. Further, all dividend income must come from domestic corporations, and the dividends must qualify for the 70-percent deduction (see ¶ 737). Also, the corporation must not be a member of a controlled group, a personal holding company, filing a consolidated return, filing its final return, or dissolving or liquidating, among other restrictions.

If the due date for filing a return falls on a Saturday, Sunday, or legal holiday, the return must be filed by the first following business day (Code Sec. 7503; see ¶ 2549).[22] Timely mailing generally is regarded as timely filing (Code Sec. 7502; see ¶ 2553).[23]

A corporation's tax year may be a calendar year or a fiscal year (Code Sec. 441(b)(1), (d), and (e)).[24] Its return may not cover a period of more than a year. In a slight exception to this rule, a corporation may elect to use an annual filing period that fluctuates between 52 and 53 weeks (Code Sec. 441(f); see ¶ 1505).[25] A return may cover less than a year if a corporation was formed during the year or dissolved during the year (Code Sec. 443(a)(2) and Reg. § 1.443-1(a)(2)).[26] For example, if a corporation elects the calendar year method but starts operations on August 1, it must report income from August 1 to December 31. If it dissolves on June 30, it must file a short-period return covering the period from January 1 to June 30. In addition to filing its regular income tax return, a corporation that has adopted a resolution to dissolve itself or liquidate all or part of its stock must file Form 966, "Corporate Dissolution or Liquidation" (Code Sec. 6043 and Reg. § 1.6043-1).[27]

213. Accounting Methods. Generally, a corporation (other than a personal service corporation) must use the accrual method of accounting if its average annual gross receipts exceed an average of $5 million for the three tax years preceding the current tax year (Code Sec. 448(c)).[28] A corporation engaged in farming operations also must use the accrual method (Code Sec. 447) unless it has gross receipts of $1 million or less ($25 million for a family farming corporation).[29] Securities dealers must use the "mark-to-market" method of accounting (Code Sec. 475).[30]

214. Corporate Taxable Income. A corporation pays tax on its "taxable income" (Code Sec. 11).[31] Taxable income is the corporation's total income for the year (such as gross receipts, dividends received, interest, rents and royalties) minus a corporation's deductions for the year (such as compensation and salaries paid, repairs, maintenance, rents paid, interest paid, depreciation, advertising and deductible amounts paid into pension and profit-sharing plans and other employee

Footnote references are to paragraphs of the 2002 Standard Federal Tax Reports.

[20] ¶ 35,142	[24] ¶ 20,302	[28] ¶ 20,800
[21] ¶ 35,142, ¶ 35,145,	[25] ¶ 20,302	[29] ¶ 20,700
¶ 36,720, ¶ 36,724	[26] ¶ 20,500, ¶ 20,501	[30] ¶ 22,265
[22] ¶ 42,630	[27] ¶ 35,880, ¶ 35,881	[31] ¶ 3365
[23] ¶ 42,620		

¶214

benefit programs). See the flowchart at ¶ 63 that outlines the determination of a corporation's taxable income.

215. Due Date for Taxes. The due date for the payment of a corporation's taxes is the same as the due date for the filing of a return (Code Sec. 6151).[32] However, corporations that anticipate a tax liability of $500 or more must estimate their taxes and make quarterly estimated tax payments (including estimated payments of the minimum tax) using Form 8109 federal tax deposit forms (Code Sec. 6655(f) and (g)(1)(A)(ii); Reg. § 1.6302-1).[33] If the liability exceeds the total estimated payments, the corporation must pay the remaining amount by the due date of its return. Failure to pay estimated taxes may be penalized (see ¶ 225). For an extension of time to file returns or to pay taxes, see ¶ 2509 and ¶ 2537.

Rate of Taxation

219. Graduated Tax Rates. Corporations are subject to the following tax rates on their taxable income (Code Sec. 11 and Code Sec. 1201): [34]

If taxable income is:

Over—	But not over—	Tax is—	Of the amt. over—
$ 0	$ 50,000	15%	$ 0
50,000	75,000	$ 7,500 + 25%	50,000
75,000	100,000	13,750 + 34%	75,000
100,000	335,000	22,250 + 39%	100,000
335,000	10,000,000	113,900 + 34%	335,000
10,000,000	15,000,000	3,400,000 + 35%	10,000,000
15,000,000	18,333,333	5,150,000 + 38%	15,000,000
18,333,333	—	35%	0

The 38-percent rate is imposed to phase out the benefits of the lower brackets for high-income corporations.

Personal Service Corporations. The corporate graduated rates do not apply to personal service corporations. Such corporations are instead taxed at a flat rate of 35 percent of taxable income. Qualified personal service corporations perform services in the fields of health, law, engineering, architecture, accounting, actuarial science, the performing arts, or consulting. Substantially all of the stock of a personal service corporation is held by employees, retired employees, or their estates (Code Sec. 11(b)(2)).[35] See, also, ¶ 1575. For information on personal service corporations, see ¶ 273.

Foreign Corporations. Foreign corporations are taxed at regular U.S. corporate rates on most income that is effectively connected with a U.S. trade or business and at a flat 30-percent rate on U.S.-source fixed or determinable income that is not effectively connected (see ¶ 2425-¶ 2460). Tax treaties between the U.S. and foreign countries may provide for lower rates or exemptions from taxation.

220. Additional Taxes. In addition to the regular corporate income tax, the alternative minimum tax (AMT) may be imposed on a corporation having tax preference items. See Chapter 14. Also, certain corporations used by their shareholders for the purpose of avoiding taxes might be subject to the accumulated earnings tax (¶ 251-¶ 271) or the personal holding company tax (¶ 275-¶ 287). Also, the IRS has the right to reallocate income from personal service corporations (¶ 273).

A corporation is treated as a "small corporation" exempt from the AMT if it is the corporation's first year or (1) it was treated as a small corporation exempt from the AMT for all prior tax years beginning after 1997, and (2) its average annual gross receipts for the three-tax-year period (or portion thereof) ending before its current tax year did not exceed $7.5 million (see ¶ 1401). The $7.5 million amount is reduced to $5 million for the corporation's first three-tax-year period (Code Sec. 55(e).[36]

Footnote references are to paragraphs of the 2002 Standard Federal Tax Reports.

¶ 215

[32] ¶ 37,080	[34] ¶ 3365, ¶ 30,352	[36] ¶ 5100
[33] ¶ 38,061, ¶ 39,565	[35] ¶ 3365	

Estimated Tax

225. Penalty for Underpayment of Estimated Tax. A corporation that anticipates a tax bill of $500 or more must estimate its income tax liability for the
current tax year and pay four quarterly estimated tax installments (with Form
8109) during that year (Code Sec. 6655).[37] Any underpayment of a required
installment results in an addition to tax on the amount of the underpayment for the
period of underpayment (Code Sec. 6655). The addition to tax is based on current
interest rates (see ¶ 2838 and ¶ 2890).

The period of underpayment begins with the due date of the underpaid
installment and ends with the earlier of (1) the date that the underpayment is
satisfied or (2) the 15th day of the third month after the close of the tax year (Code
Sec. 6655(b)).[38] Each estimated tax payment is credited against unpaid installments
in the order in which they are required to be paid.

In determining the required amount of any installment (¶ 227), a corporation
must take into account its regular corporate (or insurance company) income tax, the
corporate alternative minimum tax (¶ 1401 and following), and the four-percent tax
on gross transportation income of a foreign corporation (Code Sec. 887).[39] No
addition to tax applies if the tax shown on the return (or the actual tax if no return
is filed) is less than $500 (Code Sec. 6655).[40]

If there is an underpayment, Form 2220 should be attached to the return to
show whether the addition to tax applies and, if so, the amount of the penalty.

What is the Tax? The tax liabilities to which corporate estimated tax applies
are the corporate income tax imposed by Code Sec. 11[41] or by the alternative
minimum tax (Code Sec. 55(b)),[42] the environmental tax (Code Sec. 59A),[43] and the
gross transportation income tax (Code Sec. 887).[44] For this purpose, the 30-percent
tax on foreign corporations not connected with a U.S. business is considered a Code
Sec. 11 tax (Code Sec. 6655(g)(1)).[45] The total expected tax liability is reduced by
the sum of the credits against tax. Special rules apply for estimating the book
income adjustment by corporations that use the annualization method to calculate
estimated tax liability.

227. Time and Amount of Installment Payments. For calendar-year corporations, estimated tax installments are due on April 15, June 15, September 15,
and December 15. Installments of fiscal-year corporations are due on the 15th day of
the fourth, sixth, ninth, and twelfth months of the tax year (Code Sec. 6655).[46] If
any due date falls on a Saturday, Sunday or legal holiday, the payment is due on the
first following business day. Thus, since June 15, 2002 is on a Saturday, and
September 15 and December 15 fall on a Sunday, the due dates for these installments are moved to June 17, September 16, and December 16, 2002.

There is a short deferral for all or a part of the required quarterly estimated tax
payment of corporations that have an estimated payment due in September in 2004.
Only 80 percent of the corporate estimated tax payments otherwise due on September 15, 2004 is due on that date. The remaining 20 percent is due on October 1, 2004
(Act Sec. 801 of the Economic Growth and Tax Relief Reconciliation Act of 2001,
which provided a similar deferral for September 2001 payments).

Corporations required to deposit taxes in excess of $200,000 must transfer their
tax deposits electronically from their accounts to the IRS's general account (Reg.
§ 31.6302-1(h)(2)(B)(ii)).[47]

To avoid a penalty, each installment must equal at least 25 percent of the
lesser of (1) 100 percent of the tax shown on the current year's tax return (or of the
actual tax if no return is filed) or (2) 100 percent of the tax shown on the
corporation's return for the preceding tax year, provided a positive tax liability was
shown and the preceding tax year consisted of 12 months (Code Sec. 6655(d))[48] (but

---

Footnote references are to paragraphs of the 2002 Standard Federal Tax Reports.

[37] ¶ 39,565
[38] ¶ 39,565
[39] ¶ 27,580
[40] ¶ 39,565
[41] ¶ 3365
[42] ¶ 5100
[43] ¶ 5450
[44] ¶ 27,850
[45] ¶ 39,565
[46] ¶ 39,565
[47] ¶ 38,055B
[48] ¶ 39,565

¶ 227

see special limitation on "large corporations" below). A lower installment amount may be paid if it is shown that use of an annualized income method or, for corporations with seasonal incomes, an adjusted seasonal method would result in a lower required installment (see ¶ 229).

A corporation that first meets the requirements for estimated tax payments before a particular installment due date must pay estimated tax as follows:

Determination dates	Percentages of the estimated tax to be paid by the 15th day of the—			
	4th month	6th month	9th month	12th month
Requirements met prior to 4th month of the tax year	25	25	25	25
Requirements met prior to 6th month of the tax year (but after 3rd month)	..	50	25	25
Requirements met prior to 9th month of the tax year (but after 5th month)	..	..	75	25
Requirements met prior to 12th month of the tax year (but after 8th month)	..	..	..	100

Example. The X Corporation, a calendar-year taxpayer, estimates at the end of March 2002 that its federal income tax for 2002 would be $800,000. Accordingly, it pays $200,000 [25% of ($800,000 × 100%)] of estimated tax by April 15, 2002, and another $200,000 by June 17, 2002 (June 15 falls on a Saturday). At the end of August 2002, a recalculation shows that its 2002 tax is expected to be $1,000,000. Assuming that there is no later change in the estimated tax, the estimated tax installments for September and December are computed as follows:

Estimated tax required to be paid by 9/17/2002 [75% of ($1,000,000 × 100%)]	$ 750,000
Less payments made in April and June	400,000
Payment due in September	$ 350,000
Payment due in December [25% of ($1,000,000 × 100%)]	$ 250,000
Total estimated tax payments	$1,000,000

Large Corporations. A "large corporation"—one with taxable income of at least $1 million in any one of the three immediately preceding tax years—is prohibited from using its prior year's tax liability (method (2), above) except in determining the first installment of its tax year (Code Sec. 6655(d)(2) and (g)(2)).[49] Any reduction in a large corporation's first installment as a result of using the prior year's tax must be recaptured in the corporation's second installment. In applying the $1 million test, taxable income is computed without regard to net operating loss carryovers or capital loss carrybacks. Also, a controlled group of corporations (¶ 291) must divide a single $1 million amount among its members.

229. Annualization and Seasonal Income Methods. A corporation may compute any annualized income installment by computing its taxable income (including alternative minimum taxable income and modified alternative minimum taxable income) for the corresponding portion of the tax year on an annualized basis, computing the tax, and paying the following percentages of the tax after deducting all prior required installments for the tax year (Code Sec. 6655(e)(1)).[50] A corporation can choose between using the standard monthly periods or either of two optional monthly periods.

Installment	Standard Monthly Periods	Optional Monthly Periods #1	Optional Monthly Periods #2
1st	first 3 months	first 2 months	first 3 months
2nd	first 3 months	first 4 months	first 5 months
3rd	first 6 months	first 7 months	first 8 months
4th	first 9 months	first 10 months	first 11 months

Footnote references are to paragraphs of the 2002 Standard Federal Tax Reports.

¶ 229   [49] ¶ 39,565   [50] ¶ 39,565

An election to use either of the two optional monthly periods is effective only for the year of election. The election must be made on or before the date required for the first installment payment (Code Sec. 6655(e)(2)(C)(iii)).[51]

To annualize income, multiply the income for the applicable period by 12 and divide by the number of months in the period (Reg. § 1.6655-3).[52] A corporation that uses the annualization method and switches to another method during the same tax year must, in its first installment under the new method, recapture 100 percent of any reduction achieved in the earlier installments (Code Sec. 6655(e)(1)).

Adjusted Seasonal Installments. Adjusted seasonal installments may be used only if, in each of the three preceding tax years, taxable income for the same six-month period averaged 70 percent or more of annual taxable income. An adjusted seasonal installment is the excess (if any) of (a) 100 percent of the amount determined by following the four steps set forth below over (b) the aggregate amount of all prior required installments for the tax year. The steps are as follows: (1) take the taxable income for the portion of the tax year up to the month in which the installment is due (filing month); (2) divide this amount by the "base period percentage" for such months; (3) determine the tax on the result; and (4) multiply the tax by the base period percentage for the filing month and all preceding months during the tax year. For any period of months, the "base period percentage" is the average percentage that the taxable income for the corresponding months in each of the three preceding tax years bears to the taxable income for those years (Code Sec. 6655(e)(3)).[53]

231. Quick Refund for Estimated Tax Overpayment. A corporation may apply for an adjustment (i.e., a refund of an overpayment of estimated tax) immediately after the close of its tax year if its overpayment is at least 10 percent of the expected tax liability and amounts to at least $500. "Overpayment," for this purpose, is the excess of the estimated tax paid over what the corporation expects its final income tax liability to be at the time the application is filed. The application must be filed by the 15th day of the 3rd month after the close of the tax year and before the day on which the corporation files its income tax return for the tax year for which a quick refund is requested (Code Sec. 6425 and Code Sec. 6655(h); Reg. § 1.6425-1—Reg. § 1.6425-3).[54] Application must be made on Form 4466, "Corporation Application for Quick Refund of Overpayment of Estimated Tax." An extension of time to file Form 1120 will not extend the time for filing Form 4466.

Special Deductions for Corporations

235. Base to Which Rates Apply. The tax rates described in ¶ 219, above, are applied to taxable income. The term "taxable income" means the gross income of the corporation, minus deductions allowed by Code Sec. 1 through Code Sec. 1400C (Reg. § 1.11-1).[55] The principal items of corporation income include gross sales receipts, dividends and interest received, rent and royalty income, and capital gains. The common deductions for a corporation in computing its taxable income include compensation paid to officers and workers, expenses for repairs and mainte-nance of corporation property, taxes, licenses, interest paid, depreciation and deple-tion, advertising, and deductible amounts paid to pension and profit-sharing plans and employee benefit programs. In addition, a corporation may be entitled to the special deductions described below. See the flowchart at ¶ 63 that outlines the determination of a corporation's taxable income.

Footnote references are to paragraphs of the 2002 Standard Federal Tax Reports.

[51] ¶ 39,565	[54] ¶ 38,840—¶ 38,843,	[55] ¶ 3370
[52] ¶ 39,570	¶ 39,565	
[53] ¶ 39,565		

¶ 235

237. Dividends Received from Other Corporations. A corporation is entitled to a special deduction from gross income for dividends received from a domestic corporation that is subject to income tax (Code Sec. 243).[56] This deduction is: (1) 70 percent of dividends received from corporations owned less than 20 percent (by stock vote and value) by the recipient corporation; (2) 80 percent of dividends received from a "20-percent-owned corporation," i.e., a corporation having at least 20 percent (but generally less than 80 percent) of its stock owned by the recipient corporation; (3) 100 percent of qualifying dividends received from members of the same affiliated group (generally, 80 percent or more common ownership) to which the recipient corporation belongs (¶ 239); and (4) 100 percent of dividends received by a small business investment company (¶ 2392). These rules also apply to dividends received from a foreign corporation that are paid out of the earnings and profits of a taxable domestic predecessor corporation (see ¶ 241).

The aggregate amount of dividends-received deductions that may be taken by a corporation is limited to 70 percent (80 percent in the case of 20-percent-owned corporations) of its taxable income, computed without regard to any net operating loss deduction, dividends-received deduction, dividends-paid deduction in the case of public utilities, the deduction for the U.S.-source portion of dividends from 10-percent-owned foreign corporations, the deduction for certain dividends received from wholly owned foreign subsidiaries, capital loss carryback, or adjustment for nontaxed portions of extraordinary dividends received. This limitation is applied first with respect to any 80 percent deductible dividends and then separately for 70 percent deductible dividends (after reducing taxable income by the 80 percent deductible dividends), but it does not apply for the year if the full deduction results in a net operating loss (Code Sec. 246(b)(2)).[57] Further, it does not apply in the case of small business investment companies.

The dividends-received deduction cannot be taken in computing the accumulated earnings tax (¶ 251) or the tax on personal holding companies (¶ 275). The deduction is allowed to a resident foreign corporation as well as to a domestic corporation. No deduction is allowed for dividends received from a corporation exempt from income tax (including an exempt farmers' cooperative) during the tax year or the preceding year (Code Sec. 246(a)).[58]

Holding Period. No dividends-received deduction is allowed for stock held by a corporation for 45 days or less during the 90-day period beginning on the date 45 days before the ex-dividend date of the stock. If the stock is cumulative preferred stock with an arrearage of dividends, it must be held at least 91 days during the 180-day period beginning on the date 90 days before the ex-dividend date.

The holding period is reduced for any period during which the taxpayer's risk of loss with respect to the stock is diminished because the taxpayer has (1) an option to sell, is under an obligation to sell, or has made (and not closed) a short sale of substantially identical stock or securities; (2) granted an option to purchase substantially identical stock or securities; or (3) reduced the risk by virtue of holding one or more other positions with respect to substantially similar or related property (Code Sec. 246(c)).[59]

Debt-Financed Portfolio Stock. The dividends-received deduction is reduced for dividends received from debt-financed portfolio stock by a percentage related to the amount of debt incurred to purchase such stock. The deduction is calculated by multiplying the difference between 100 percent and the average portfolio indebtedness by 70 percent (80 percent in the case of 20-percent-owned corporations) (Code Sec. 246A).[60] However, any required deduction is limited to the amount of the interest deduction allocable to the related dividend. This deduction does not apply to dividends that are eligible for 100-percent dividends-received deduction for (1) qualifying dividends received from a member of an affiliated group and (2) dividends received from a small business investment company.

Footnote references are to paragraphs of the 2002 Standard Federal Tax Reports.

¶ 237 [56] ¶ 13,051   [58] ¶ 13,200   [60] ¶ 13,250
[57] ¶ 13,200   [59] ¶ 13,200, ¶ 13,203

Other Limitations. Capital gain dividends from a regulated investment company (mutual fund) or a real estate investment trust, and distributions that are a return of capital, do not qualify for the dividends-received deduction.

Additionally, the dividends-received deduction is not allowed to the extent that the taxpayer is under an obligation (pursuant to a short sale or otherwise) to make related payments with respect to positions in substantially similar or related property (Code Sec. 246(c)(1)(B)).[61]

A corporation may take the dividends-received deduction for dividends on preferred stock of a public utility, unless the utility is entitled to a dividends-paid deduction under Code Sec. 247 (Reg. § 1.243-2(d)).[62] In the latter event, the deduction is limited under Code Sec. 244.[63]

No deduction is allowed with respect to a dividend received pursuant to distributions under Code Sec. 936(h)(4) (¶ 2463) made to qualify for the possessions tax credit or the Virgin Islands rebate (Code Sec. 246(e)).[64]

Extraordinary Dividends. If a dividend is deemed to be "extraordinary," a corporate taxpayer may be required to reduce its basis in the stock by the nontaxed portion of the dividend, i.e., the amount offset by the dividends-received deduction. This rule generally applies if the dividend exceeds 10 percent (5 percent in the case of preferred dividends) of (1) the taxpayer's adjusted basis in the stock or (2) the fair market value of the stock just before the ex-dividend date, and if the taxpayer has not held the stock for more than two years before the day the dividend is declared, agreed to, or announced. Generally, if the nontaxed portion of the dividend exceeds basis, gain must be recognized in the tax year in which the dividend is received instead of recognized upon the later sale or disposition of the stock. The Conference Committee Report to the IRS Restructuring and Reform Act of 1998 clarifies that, except as provided in regulations to be issued, Code Sec. 1059 does not cause current gain recognition to the extent that the consolidated return regulations require the creation or increase of an excess loss account with respect to a distribution. Thus, the current Reg. § 1.1059(e)-1(a)[65] does not result in gain recognition with respect to distributions within a consolidated group to the extent such distribution results in the creation or increase of an excess loss account under the consolidated return regulations.

239. 100-Percent Dividends-Received Deduction for Affiliates. Affiliated corporations that do not, or cannot, file consolidated returns (¶ 295) are allowed a 100-percent dividends-received deduction for "qualifying dividends" received from members of the affiliated group (Code Sec. 243(a)(3); Reg. § 1.1502-47(f)(5)).[66]

A qualifying dividend is any dividend received by a corporation that is a member of the same affiliated group as the corporation distributing it. The term also includes a dividend paid by an affiliated corporation that has made an election pertaining to the Puerto Rico and possessions tax credit.

If the affiliated group includes at least one life insurance company, no dividend by any member of the group will be treated as qualified unless a special election is in effect for the tax year in which the dividend is received (Code Sec. 243(b)).[67]

If any member of an affiliated group elects the foreign tax credit, then all members of the group that pay or accrue foreign taxes must elect the credit in order for any dividend paid by a member of the group to qualify for the 100 percent dividends-received deduction (Code Sec. 243(b)(2)).[68]

241. Dividends from Foreign Corporations. A domestic corporation is entitled to a 70-percent (80-percent in the case of 20-percent-owned corporations—see ¶ 237) deduction of the U.S.-source portion of dividends received from a foreign corporation that is at least 10-percent owned, by vote and value, by the domestic corporation. The U.S.-source portion of a dividend is the amount that bears the same

---

Footnote references are to paragraphs of the 2002 Standard Federal Tax Reports.

[61] ¶ 13,200	[64] ¶ 13,200	[67] ¶ 13,051
[62] ¶ 13,053	[65] ¶ 30,020B	[68] ¶ 13,051
[63] ¶ 13,100	[66] ¶ 13,051, ¶ 33,193	**¶241**

ratio to the dividend as undistributed U.S. earnings bear to total undistributed earnings (Code Sec. 245(a)).[69]

A 100-percent dividends-received deduction is allowed to a domestic corporation for dividends paid by a wholly owned foreign subsidiary out of its earnings and profits for the tax year. All of the foreign subsidiary's gross income must be effectively connected with a U.S. trade or business (Code Sec. 245(b)).[70]

A U.S. corporation is generally allowed a 100-percent deduction for any dividends received from a foreign sales corporation that are distributed out of earnings and profits attributable to foreign trade income (Code Sec. 245(c)).[71] In addition, a 70-percent (80-percent in the case of 20-percent-owned corporations) deduction is provided for dividends received from an FSC that made the distribution out of earnings and profits attributable to effectively connected income received or accrued by an FSC.

Debt-Financed Portfolio Stock. Any reduction in the dividends-received deduction resulting from the rules concerning debt-financed portfolio stock (¶ 237) must be computed before applying the above ratios.

243. Organizational and Start-Up Expenditures. A newly organized corporation may elect to treat its organizational expenditures as deferred expenses and deduct them ratably over a period of not less than 60 months, beginning with the first month in which the corporation is actively in business (Code Sec. 248; Reg. § 1.248-1).[72] The organizational expenditures must be incurred before the end of the first tax year in which the corporation is in business. A corporation using the cash method may amortize its organizational expenditures even though it may not have paid the expenses within the first tax year.

Organizational expenditures are deducted using IRS Form 4562, "Depreciation and Amortization." The deduction is entered at Part VI, line 40 of the form.

Organizational expenditures are those which are (1) connected directly with the creation of the corporation, (2) chargeable to capital account, and (3) of a character that would be amortizable over the life of the corporation if its life were limited by its charter. They include expenses of temporary directors and organizational meetings, state fees for incorporation privileges, accounting service costs incident to organization, and legal service expenditures, such as for drafting of documents, minutes of organizational meetings, and terms of the original stock certificates.

Expenditures connected with issuing or selling stock or with the transfer of assets to a corporation are not amortizable (Reg. § 1.248-1(b)(3)).[73] Preopening or start-up expenses, such as employee training, advertising, and expenses of lining up suppliers or potential customers, are not organizational expenses. However, a new business may be eligible to amortize start-up expenditures under Code Sec. 195.[74]

Corporate expenditures that are incurred in investigating the creation or acquisition of an active trade or business or in creating such a trade or business, but do not qualify for 60-month amortization as organizational expenses, may qualify for similar amortization under Code Sec. 195 (Rev. Rul. 99-23).[75] See ¶ 904.

SPECIAL TAXES AND EXEMPTIONS

Accumulated Earnings Tax

251. Rate and Nature of Tax. In addition to being liable for regular income taxes, every corporation (other than a domestic or foreign personal holding company (¶ 277), tax-exempt organization, or passive foreign investment company, as defined in Code Sec. 1297) may be liable for the accumulated earnings tax (Code Sec. 532). This is an extra tax, in the nature of a penalty, imposed if a corporation is formed

---

Footnote references are to paragraphs of the 2002 Standard Federal Tax Reports.

¶ 243

[69] ¶ 13,150	[72] ¶ 13,350, ¶ 13,351	[75] ¶ 12,370,
[70] ¶ 13,150	[73] ¶ 13,351	¶ 13,709.055,
[71] ¶ 13,150	[74] ¶ 12,370	

for the purpose of preventing the imposition of income tax upon its shareholders, or the shareholders of any other corporation, by permitting earnings or profits to accumulate instead of being distributed (Code Sec. 531-Code Sec. 537).[76]

The tax is imposed on "accumulated taxable income" at the highest rate applicable to individuals. These rates (as enacted by P.L. 107-16) are 39.1 percent for tax years beginning in 2001, 38.6 percent for 2002 and 2003, 37.6 percent for 2004 and 2005, and 35 percent for tax years beginning after 2005.

An underpayment of tax, such as that which would result from imposition of accumulated earnings tax, may be subject to the negligence penalties described at ¶ 2856 (Rev. Rul. 75-330).[77] Interest on underpayment of the tax is computed from the date the corporation's tax return is due without regard to extensions (Code Sec. 6601(b)(4)).[78]

253. Income on Which Tax Is Levied. The tax is imposed on "accumulated taxable income" of the tax year. "Accumulated taxable income" means taxable income, with the adjustments described below, minus the sum of the dividends-paid deduction (¶ 259) and the accumulated earnings credit (¶ 261). The following adjustments to taxable income must be made in determining accumulated taxable income (Code Sec. 535; Reg. § 1.535-2): [79]

(1) A deduction is allowed for federal income taxes, as well as for income, war, and excess profits taxes of foreign countries and U.S. possessions (to the extent not allowed as deductions in computing taxable income) accrued during the tax year, regardless of the accounting method used, but not including the accumulated earnings tax or the personal holding company tax.

(2) The deduction for charitable contributions is unlimited (even if in excess of the 10-percent-of-taxable-income limitation imposed on corporations).

(3) No deduction is allowed for dividends received or for dividends paid by public utilities on certain preferred stock.

(4) The net operating loss deduction is not allowed.

(5) A deduction is allowed for current net capital losses, but such deduction must be reduced by the lesser of (a) nonrecaptured capital gains deductions or (b) the amount of accumulated earnings and profits at the close of the preceding tax year. The term "nonrecaptured capital gains deductions" means the total amount of excluded net capital gains (less allowable capital gains tax).

(6) Deduction is allowed for current net capital gains (less allowable capital gains tax), but such deduction is to be reduced by any net capital losses (which are treated as short-term capital losses for the current year). In the case of a foreign corporation, only net capital gains that are effectively connected with the conduct of a trade or business within the United States that are not exempt under treaty are taken into account.

(7) No capital loss carryback or carryover is allowed.

Although exempt interest income is excludable from accumulated taxable income for purposes of determining the accumulated earnings tax base, it is considered for purposes of determining whether earnings and profits have been accumulated beyond the reasonable needs of the business (see ¶ 265).[80]

Holding or Investment Companies. If a corporation is a mere holding or investment company, special rules apply in determining its accumulated taxable income: (1) current capital losses may not be deducted, (2) current net short-term capital gains are deductible only to the extent of any capital loss carryovers, and (3) accumulated earnings and profits cannot be less than they would have been had the rules in (1) and (2) been applied in computing earnings and profits (Code Sec. 535(b)(8)).[81]

Footnote references are to paragraphs of the 2002 Standard Federal Tax Reports.

[76] ¶ 23,001—¶ 23,070   [78] ¶ 39,410   [80] ¶ 23,018.897
[77] ¶ 39,651G   [79] ¶ 23,040, ¶ 23,042   [81] ¶ 23,040

¶253

257. Re-sourcing Income of U.S.-Owned Foreign Corporations. For purposes of the accumulated earnings tax, if 10 percent or more of the earnings and profits of any foreign corporation is derived from sources within the United States or is effectively connected with the conduct of a trade or business in the United States, then any distribution out of such earnings and profits (and any interest payment) retains its character as U.S. source income upon receipt by a U.S.-owned foreign corporation (Code Sec. 535(d)(1)).[82] "United States-owned foreign corporation" means any foreign corporation in which 50 percent or more of voting power or total value is held directly or indirectly by U.S. persons (Code Sec. 535(d)(2)).[83]

259. Dividends-Paid Deduction. The "dividends paid deduction" (Code Sec. 561—Code Sec. 565)[84] does not enter into the computation of ordinary corporate income taxes. It is a consideration only in determining the taxation of a regulated investment company (Code Sec. 851),[85] a real estate investment trust (Code Sec. 856),[86] the personal holding company tax (Code Sec. 541),[87] the foreign personal holding company tax (Code Sec. 551),[88] and the accumulated earnings tax (Code Sec. 531).[89]

261. Accumulated Earnings Credit. For a corporation other than a mere holding or investment company, the accumulated earnings credit allowed in computing accumulated taxable income (¶ 253) is an amount equal to the part of the earnings and profits of the tax year retained for the reasonable needs of the business, reduced by the net capital gain (which is itself reduced by the amount of income tax attributable to it).

A minimum amount of $250,000 ($150,000 for personal service corporations (¶ 219)) may be accumulated from past and present earnings combined by all corporations, including holding or investment companies. This minimum amount is the only credit allowable to a holding or investment company (Code Sec. 535(c)).[90]

Only one $250,000 accumulated earnings credit is allowed to a controlled group of corporations (¶ 291) (Code Sec. 1561(a)(2)).[91] The single credit is to be divided equally among the corporations unless the IRS issues regulations permitting an unequal allocation.

263. Basis of Liability. Although the accumulated earnings tax is computed as a percentage of the corporation's accumulated taxable income (see ¶ 251, above), liability for the tax hinges on whether the corporation was formed or availed of to avoid the income tax on income otherwise receivable by its shareholders. A corporation can be subject to the accumulated earnings tax for a year in which it has accumulated taxable income on hand even though, because of a stock redemption, no earnings and profits were accumulated for the tax year.[92]

The courts have shifted the focus of attention from earnings and profits to liquidity.[93] The reason for this change in emphasis is that the earnings-and-profits figure often is no indication of the funds available to the corporation to meet its business needs and pay dividends to its shareholders. Whether a corporation can be subjected to the accumulated earnings tax is therefore determined by comparing the reasonable needs of its business (see ¶ 265) to its total liquid assets at the end of the year. Liquid assets include the corporation's cash and marketable securities.

265. Reasonable Needs of the Business. In order to justify an accumulation of income, there must be a reasonable business need for it and a definite plan for its use. Since a corporation is given a credit (¶ 261) for its reasonable business needs (including reasonably anticipated needs) in figuring the accumulated earnings tax, the resolution of most disputes hinges on this issue.

Footnote references are to paragraphs of the 2002 Standard Federal Tax Reports.

[82] ¶ 23,040	[87] ¶ 23,152	[91] ¶ 33,340
[83] ¶ 23,040	[88] ¶ 23,310	[92] ¶ 23,045.37
[84] ¶ 23,450—¶ 23,530	[89] ¶ 23,001	[93] ¶ 23,045.022,
[85] ¶ 26,400	[90] ¶ 23,040	¶ 23,045.65, ¶ 23,074.36
[86] ¶ 26,500		

The Code does not contain a comprehensive definition of reasonable business needs. However, a number of acceptable and unacceptable grounds for accumulating income are listed in the regulations (Reg. § 1.537-2).[94] Acceptable grounds are (1) business expansion and plant replacement, (2) acquisition of a business through purchase of stock or assets, (3) debt retirement, (4) working capital, and (5) investments or loans to suppliers or customers necessary to the maintenance of the corporation's business. The self-insurance of product liability risks is a business need for which earnings and profits may be accumulated to a reasonable extent without incurring liability for the accumulated earnings tax (Code Sec. 537(b)(4) and Reg. § 1.537-2(b)(6)).[95] Unacceptable grounds are (1) loans to shareholders and expenditures for their personal benefit, (2) loans to relatives or friends of shareholders or to others who have no reasonable connection with the business, (3) loans to a sister (commonly controlled) corporation, (4) investments that are not related to the business, and (5) accumulations to provide against unrealistic hazards (Reg. § 1.537-2(c)).[96]

Courts have used an operating-cycle approach to determine the amount of working capital a corporation needs. An operating cycle consists of (1) an inventory cycle (conversion of cash and raw materials into inventory), (2) a receivables cycle (conversion of inventory into accounts receivable and cash), and possibly (3) a credit cycle (accounts payable turnover).[97]

A stock redemption under Code Sec. 303 to pay death taxes and expenses (¶ 745) and a redemption of stock in order to bring a private foundation within the 20 percent excess business holdings limit (¶ 640) are good cause for an accumulation of income (Code Sec. 537(a)).[98] Although other types of stock redemptions are not accorded this certainty, accumulations to redeem a minority interest (or the interest of one of two 50 percent stockholders) have been approved where they would eliminate dissent, would prevent the minority interest from falling into hostile hands, or were an essential ingredient of an employee incentive plan. Court decisions in this area show that except in rare circumstances, the redemption of a majority interest is not good cause for accumulating income.[99]

267. Burden of Proof. On the issue of whether a corporation has accumulated income in excess of the reasonable needs of its business, the burden of proof in the Tax Court is on the government in two instances. First, the burden is on the government if, in advance of a formal deficiency notice, it does not notify the corporation by certified or registered mail of its intention to assess a deficiency based in whole or in part on the accumulated earnings tax or fails to state the tax years at issue. Second, in the event of such notification, the burden falls on the government if the corporation responds within 60 days with a statement of the grounds on which it relies to establish the reasonableness of all or any part of its accumulation of income (Code Sec. 534; Reg. § 1.534-2).[100] In other courts, the burden of proof is wholly on the corporation.

269. Tax Avoidance Intent. One of the conditions that must exist before a corporation can be subject to the accumulated earnings tax is an intent to avoid the income tax on its shareholders (Code Sec. 533).[101] If the corporation accumulates income beyond the reasonable needs of its business (or if it is a mere holding or investment company), a presumption of tax avoidance intent arises. This presumption can be overcome by showing that tax avoidance was not one of the purposes of the accumulation of income (*Donruss Co. and Shaw-Walker*).[102]

271. Publicly Held Corporations. The accumulated earnings tax may be imposed on a corporation without regard to the number of shareholders, meaning that widely held corporations are subject to the tax (Code Sec. 532(c)).[103]

Footnote references are to paragraphs of the 2002 Standard Federal Tax Reports.

[94] ¶ 23,072
[95] ¶ 23,070
[96] ¶ 23,070
[97] ¶ 23,074.625

[98] ¶ 23,070
[99] ¶ 23,018.895
[100] ¶ 23,020, ¶ 23,022, ¶ 23,025.40

[101] ¶ 23,015
[102] ¶ 23,018.26
[103] ¶ 23,010

Personal Service Corporations

273. Personal Service Corporations. A personal service corporation is one that furnishes personal services performed by employee-owners (Code Sec. 269A).[104] Employee-owners are those who own, directly or indirectly, more than 10 percent of the outstanding stock of the corporation on any day during the company's tax year. If a corporation meets these requirements and also has as its principal purpose the avoidance or evasion of federal income tax by reducing the income of any employee-owner or securing tax benefits for any employee-owner that would not otherwise be available, the IRS may reallocate income, deductions and other tax attributes between the personal service corporation and the employee-owner. The purpose of evading or avoiding income tax can be shown by a reduction in the tax liability of, or the increase of tax benefits to, an employee-owner or by any other increase in tax benefits.

Personal Holding Companies

275. Tax on Personal Holding Companies. In addition to the regular tax on corporate income, a special tax is imposed on the "*undistributed* personal holding company income" of a personal holding company (Code Sec. 541; Reg. § 1.541-1).[105] The personal holding company tax is aimed at so-called "incorporated pocketbooks" and "incorporated talent"—that is, at corporations established to receive and hold investment income or compensation of their shareholders.

The tax is imposed at the highest rate applicable to individuals. These rates (as enacted by P.L. 107-16) are 39.1 percent for tax years beginning in 2001, 38.6 percent for 2002 and 2003, 37.6 percent for 2004 and 2005, and 35 percent for later tax years. See ¶ 126.

The tax applies only to undistributed income, which, typically, is the corporation's taxable income less the amount of its federal income tax and the dividends paid by it. In computing the dividends-paid deduction under Code Sec. 562,[106] a distribution of property that has appreciated in the hands of the personal holding company is measured by its adjusted basis (Reg. § 1.562-1(a)).[107] The U.S. Supreme Court has upheld the regulation to this effect (*A. Fulman*).[108] There are, however, a number of adjustments that may apply depending on the circumstances (Code Sec. 545).[109]

277. Personal Holding Company Defined. A "personal holding company" (Code Sec. 542; Reg. § 1.542-1—Reg. § 1.542-3)[110] is any corporation (other than those mentioned in ¶ 279) if (1) at least 60 percent of adjusted ordinary gross income for the tax year is personal holding company income (¶ 281) and (2) at any time during the last half of the tax year more than 50 percent in value of its outstanding stock is owned, directly or indirectly, by or for not more than five individuals (¶ 285). For this purpose, the following are considered individuals: (1) a qualified pension, profit-sharing, and stock bonus plan (Code Sec. 401(a));[111] (2) a trust that provides for the payment of supplemental unemployment compensation under certain conditions (Code Sec. 501(c)(17));[112] (3) a private foundation (Code Sec. 509(a));[113] and (4) a part of a trust permanently set aside or used exclusively for the purposes described in Code Sec. 642(c).[114] For foreign personal holding companies, see ¶ 2472.

Personal holding company taxes are computed and reported on Schedule PH, "U.S. Personal Holding Company (PHC) Tax," which is attached to the corporation's Form 1120, "U.S. Corporation Income Tax Return."

Footnote references are to paragraphs of the 2002 Standard Federal Tax Reports.

[104] ¶ 14,300	[108] ¶ 23,453.30,	[112] ¶ 22,602
[105] ¶ 23,152, ¶ 23,153	¶ 23,474.12	[113] ¶ 22,800
[106] ¶ 23,470	[109] ¶ 23,250	[114] ¶ 24,280
[107] ¶ 23,471	[110] ¶ 23,190—¶ 23,193	
	[111] ¶ 17,502	

¶ 273

279. Exceptions. The term "personal holding company" does not include:

(1) a corporation exempt from tax under Code Sec. 501 et seq.;

(2) a bank as defined in Code Sec. 581 or a domestic building and loan association;

(3) a life insurance company;

(4) a surety company;

(5) a foreign personal holding company (as defined in Code Sec. 552);

(6) some lending and finance companies if they meet prescribed tests as to the source or amount of their interest income and the amount of loans to stockholders;

(7) a foreign corporation *all* of whose outstanding stock during the last half of the tax year is owned by nonresident alien individuals directly or indirectly through foreign estates, trusts, partnerships, or other foreign corporations;

(8) a small business investment company (unless a shareholder, directly or indirectly, owns 5 percent or more of a concern to which the company supplies funds);

(9) a corporation subject to the jurisdiction of a court in a bankruptcy or similar proceeding unless the case was started to avoid the tax; or

(10) a passive foreign investment company (as defined in Code Sec. 1297) (Code Sec. 542(c)).[115]

281. Personal Holding Company Income. The term "personal holding company income" (Code Sec. 543)[116] means the portion of the adjusted ordinary gross income that consists of:

(1) Dividends, interest, royalties (other than mineral, oil and gas, copyright, or computer software royalties), and annuities. However, such income does not include interest received by a broker or dealer in connection with any securities or money market instruments held as property under Code Sec. 1221(1),[117] margin accounts, or any financing for a customer secured by securities or money market instruments.

(2) Rents, unless they constitute 50 percent or more of the adjusted ordinary gross income and unless the sum of (a) dividends paid during the tax year, (b) dividends paid after the close of the tax year but, nevertheless, considered to be paid on the last day of the tax year under Code Sec. 563(d) as limited by Code Sec. 563(b), and (c) consent dividends for the tax year equals or exceeds the amount by which personal holding company income exceeds 10 percent of the ordinary gross income.[118]

(3) Mineral, oil, and gas royalties, unless (a) they constitute 50 percent or more of the adjusted ordinary gross income, (b) the other personal holding company income for the tax year is not more than 10 percent of the ordinary gross income, and (c) the ordinary and necessary business expense deductions, other than compensation for personal services rendered by shareholders, and apart from deductions otherwise specifically allowable under Code sections other than Code Sec. 162,[119] are 15 percent or more of adjusted ordinary gross income.

(4) Copyright royalties, unless (a) apart from royalties derived from the works of shareholders, they make up 50 percent or more of the ordinary gross income, (b) personal holding company income for the tax year (not taking into account copyright royalties and dividends in any corporation in which the taxpayer owns at least 50 percent of all classes of voting stock and at least 50 percent of the value of all classes of stock) is 10 percent or less of the ordinary gross income, and (c) business deductions (other than deductions for compensation for services rendered by shareholders, deductions for royalties, and deduc-

---

Footnote references are to paragraphs of the 2002 Standard Federal Tax Reports.

[115] ¶ 23,190, ¶ 31,620   [117] ¶ 30,420   [119] ¶ 8500
[116] ¶ 23,210   [118] ¶ 23,490

tions specifically allowable under sections other than Code Sec. 162)[120] equal or exceed 25 percent of the amount by which the ordinary gross income exceeds the sum of royalties paid or accrued and depreciation allowed.

(5) Rents from the distribution and exhibition of produced films (that is, rents from a film interest acquired before the film production was substantially complete) unless such rents are 50 percent or more of the ordinary gross income.

(6) Amounts received as compensation for the use of, or right to use, tangible property of the corporation where, at any time during the tax year, 25 percent or more in value of the outstanding stock of the corporation is owned, directly or indirectly, by or for an individual entitled to the use of the property, whether such right is obtained directly from the corporation or by means of a sublease or other arrangement. But this paragraph applies only if the corporation's other personal holding company income (computed with certain adjustments) for the tax year is more than 10 percent of its ordinary gross income.

(7) Amounts received by a corporation from contracts for personal services, including gain from the sale or other disposition thereof, if (a) some person other than the corporation has the right to designate (by name or by description) the individual who is to perform the services or if the individual who is to perform the services is designated (by name or by description) in the contract and (b) at some time during the tax year 25 percent or more in value of the outstanding stock of the corporation is owned, directly or indirectly, by or for the individual who has performed, is to perform, or may be designated (by name or by description) as the one to perform such services.

(8) Income required to be reported by a corporate beneficiary under the income tax provisions relating to estates and trusts.

(9) Instead of the net operating loss deduction of Code Sec. 172,[121] a deduction is allowed for the net operating loss for the preceding year without certain specialized deductions (Code Sec. 545(b)(4)).[122]

Special Dividend and Interest Exclusions. The personal holding company income of a securities broker-dealer excludes interest received with respect to (1) securities or money market instruments held as inventory, (2) margin accounts, or (3) any financing for a customer secured by securities or money market instruments (Code Sec. 543(a)(1)(D)).[123]

Active Computer Software Royalties. "Active computer software royalties" received in connection with the licensing of computer software are excluded from personal holding company income (and from foreign personal holding company income; see ¶ 2472) (Code Sec. 543(d)).[124] To qualify for the exclusion: (1) the royalties must be derived by a corporation actively engaged in the trade or business of developing, manufacturing or producing computer software; (2) the royalties must make up at least 50 percent of the corporation's gross income; (3) business and research expenses relating to the royalties must equal or exceed 25 percent of ordinary gross income; and (4) dividends must equal or exceed the excess of personal holding company income by 10 percent of ordinary gross income. If one member of an affiliated group receives software royalties, it will be treated as having met the above requirements if another member meets the requirements (Code Sec. 543(d)).[125]

283. Adjusted Ordinary Gross Income. In determining whether 60 percent or more of a corporation's "adjusted ordinary gross income" is personal holding company income, the following adjustments must be made (Code Sec. 543(b)(2)):[126]

(1) Rental income must be reduced by deductions for depreciation and amortization, property taxes, interest, and rents paid that are attributable to such income.

Footnote references are to paragraphs of the 2002 Standard Federal Tax Reports.

[120] ¶ 8500	[123] ¶ 23,210	[125] ¶ 23,210
[121] ¶ 12,002	[124] ¶ 23,210	[126] ¶ 23,210
[122] ¶ 23,250		

(2) Income from mineral, oil, and gas royalties and from working interests in oil and gas wells must be reduced by deductions for depreciation, amortization and depletion, property and severance taxes, interest, and rents paid which are attributable to such income.

(3) Interest on U.S. bonds held for sale by a dealer who is making a primary market for these obligations and interest on condemnation awards, judgments and tax refunds must be excluded.

(4) Rent received from the lease of tangible personal property manufactured by a taxpayer engaged in substantial manufacturing or production of property of the same type must be reduced by deductions for depreciation and amortization, taxes, rent and interest paid that are attributable to such income.

All capital gains are excluded in determining whether the 60-percent test has been met because it is based on *adjusted ordinary gross income* (Code Sec. 543(b)(2)).[127]

285. Stock Ownership. Constructive ownership rules apply in determining whether (1) a corporation is a personal holding company, so far as the determination is based on stock ownership (¶ 277), (2) amounts received under a personal service contract are personal holding company income (¶ 281), (3) copyright royalties are personal holding company income, or (4) compensation for the use of property is personal holding company income (¶ 281) (Code Sec. 544; Reg. § 1.544-1-Reg. § 1.544-7).[128] Under the constructive ownership rules:

(1) Stock owned, directly or indirectly, by or for a corporation, partnership, estate, or trust is considered as being owned proportionately by its shareholders, partners, or beneficiaries.

(2) An individual is considered as owning the stock owned, directly or indirectly, by or for his family (brothers and sisters (whole or half blood), spouse, ancestors, and lineal descendants), or by or for his partner.

(3) If any person has an option to acquire stock, such stock is considered as owned by such person. An option to acquire an option, and each one of a series of such options, is regarded as an option to acquire stock. This rule is applied in preference to rule (2), above, when both rules apply (Code Sec. 544(a)(6)).[129]

(4) Constructive ownership is treated as actual ownership, but not to the extent of chain application in item (2), above.

(5) Outstanding securities convertible into stock (whether or not during the tax year) are considered as outstanding stock, but only if the effect of the inclusion of all such securities is to make the corporation a personal holding company (Code Sec. 544(b)).[130]

287. Deficiency Dividend Deduction. If a deficiency is determined in the personal holding company tax, the corporation may then distribute dividends and, in redetermining the undistributed personal holding company income, reduce or eliminate the deficiency by means of a deduction for "deficiency dividends" in the amount of the dividends so paid. The distribution must be made within 90 days after the deficiency determination. Claim for the deduction must be filed within 120 days of the determination (Code Sec. 547; Reg. § 1.547-1—Reg. § 1.547-7).[131]

Controlled Corporate Group

289. Allocation of Tax Benefits. A controlled group of corporations is allowed only one set of graduated income tax brackets (¶ 219) and one $250,000 accumulated earnings credit (¶ 261). Controlled groups are also allowed one $40,000 exemption amount for alternative minimum tax purposes (¶ 1405). Each of these items is to be allocated equally among the members of the group unless they all consent to a different apportionment (Code Sec. 1561).[132]

Footnote references are to paragraphs of the 2002 Standard Federal Tax Reports.

[127] ¶ 23,210   [129] ¶ 23,230   [131] ¶ 23,290—¶ 23,297
[128] ¶ 23,230—¶ 23,237   [130] ¶ 23,230   [132] ¶ 33,340

Dividends-Received Deduction. Since a parent-subsidiary controlled group (see ¶ 291) is also an affiliated group, a 100-percent dividends-received deduction may be taken from dividends paid from one member to another (¶ 239). A 70-percent deduction is allowed for distributions between members of a brother-sister controlled group.

291. What Is a Controlled Group? There are two types of controlled corporate groups—parent-subsidiary and brother-sister.

A *parent-subsidiary controlled group* exists if (1) one or more chains of corporations are connected through stock ownership with a common parent corporation, (2) 80 percent or more of the voting power or value of the stock of each corporation in the group other than the parent is owned by one or more corporations in the group, and (3) the common parent owns at least 80 percent of the voting power or value of the stock of one of the other corporations in the group (not counting stock owned directly by other members) (Code Sec. 1563(a)(1)).[133]

A *brother-sister controlled group* exists if (1) five or fewer persons (individuals, estates, or trusts) own at least 80 percent of the voting stock or value of shares of each of two or more corporations *and* (2) these five or fewer persons own more than 50 percent of the voting power or value of shares of each corporation, considering a particular person's stock only to the extent that it is owned identically with regard to each corporation (Code Sec. 1563(a)(2)).[134]

293. Controlled Corporations—Expenses, Interest and Losses. Controlled groups of corporations are subject to the related parties' transaction rules of Code Sec. 267,[135] under which controlled members must use a matching rule that defers the deductibility of an expense or interest by a payor until the payment is included in the payee's income (Code Sec. 267(a)(2)).[136] Also, losses on sales between members of a controlled group must be deferred until the property is sold to an unrelated person (Code Sec. 267(f)(2)).[137] The loss deferral rule does not apply, however, to sales to a DISC, to sales of inventory in the ordinary course of business if one of the parties is a foreign corporation, or to loan repayment losses attributable to foreign currency value reductions (Code Sec. 267(f)(3)).[138]

Consolidated Return

295. Consolidated Return. The privilege of filing a consolidated return is extended to an affiliated group of corporations under Code Sec. 1501 and Code Sec. 1504(b).[139]

An "affiliated group" is defined as one or more chains of includible corporations connected through stock ownership with a common parent that is an includible corporation provided that (1) the common parent must directly own stock possessing at least 80 percent of the total voting power of at least one of the other includible corporations and having a value equal to at least 80 percent of the total value of the stock of the corporation, and (2) stock meeting the 80-percent test in each includible corporation other than the common parent must be owned directly by one or more of the other includible corporations (Code Sec. 1504(a)).[140]

A consolidated return may be filed only if all corporations that were members of the affiliated group *at any time* during the tax year consent to all the consolidated return regulations prior to the last day for filing the return. The making of a consolidated return is such consent. The common parent corporation, when filing a consolidated return, must attach Form 851, "Affiliations Schedule." In addition, for the first year a consolidated return is filed, each subsidiary must attach a Form 1122 (consent to be included in the consolidated return).

Footnote references are to paragraphs of the 2002 Standard Federal Tax Reports.

¶291

[133] ¶ 33,360
[134] ¶ 33,360, ¶ 33,382.85
[135] ¶ 14,150
[136] ¶ 14,150
[137] ¶ 14,150
[138] ¶ 14,150
[139] ¶ 33,121, ¶ 33,260
[140] ¶ 33,260

The following corporate organizations are denied the privilege (Code Sec. 1504(b)):[141]

(1) corporations that are exempt under Code Sec. 501 (except that such organizations may be affiliated with other such organizations at least one of which is organized only to hold title for exempt organizations and from which the others derive income);

(2) insurance companies subject to tax under Code Sec. 801 (see, however, Code Sec. 1504(c));[142]

(3) foreign corporations;

(4) corporations electing the Sec. 936 possessions tax credit (¶ 2463);

(5) regulated investment companies and real estate investment trusts (but see ¶ 2326 for circumstances in which a REIT may treat income and deductions of a qualified subsidiary as its own);

(6) DISCs (Code Sec. 992(a));[143] and

(7) S corporations.

297. Advantages and Disadvantages. The advantages in filing consolidated returns include: (1) offsetting operating losses of one company against the profits of another (but see the rule for dual resident companies below); (2) offsetting capital losses of one company against the capital gains of another (but see ¶ 2285 on newly acquired corporations); (3) avoidance of tax on intercompany distributions; (4) deferral of income on intercompany transactions; (5) use by the corporate group of the excess of one member's foreign tax credit over its limitation; and (6) designation of the parent company as agent of the group for all tax purposes.

The disadvantages include: (1) the effect on later years' returns; (2) deferral of losses on intercompany transactions; (3) additional bookkeeping required to keep track of deferred intercompany transactions; (4) intercompany profit in inventories still within group must be reflected in annual inventory adjustments; (5) possible elimination of foreign tax credits when the limiting fraction is diminished because of lack of foreign income on the part of some members; and (6) possible accumulated earnings tax liability when the consolidated accumulated earnings and profits of the group exceed the minimum credit amount.

Dual Resident Companies. If a U.S. corporation is subject to foreign tax on its worldwide income, or on a residence basis as opposed to a source basis, any net operating loss it incurs in a year cannot reduce the taxable income of any other member of a U.S. affiliated group for any tax year (Reg. § 1.1503-2(c)).[144]

Preferred Dividends. Income out of which a member of an affiliated group, other than a common parent, distributes preferred dividends to a nonmember may not be offset by the group's net operating losses or capital losses (Code Sec. 1503(f)[(e)]).[145] Taxes on that income may not be offset by most group tax credits.

Golden Parachutes. All members of an affiliated group are treated as a single corporation when determining excessive payments that are contingent on a change in corporate control (Code Sec. 280G(d)(5) and ¶ 907).[146]

Footnote references are to paragraphs of the 2002 Standard Federal Tax Reports.
[141] ¶ 33,260 [143] ¶ 28,960 [145] ¶ 33,240
[142] ¶ 33,260 [144] ¶ 33,242 [146] ¶ 15,150

Chapter 3

S CORPORATIONS

S Corporation Status

301. Corporate Income Taxed to Shareholders. An S corporation is a corporation that is eligible to choose S corporation status (¶ 305) and whose shareholders have all consented to the corporation's choice (¶ 306). In general, an S corporation does not pay any income tax. Instead, the corporation's income and deductions are passed through to its shareholders. The shareholders then must report the income and deductions on their own income tax returns.

An S corporation must file an annual return on Form 1120S, "U.S. Income Tax Return for an S Corporation," which is due on or before the 15th day of the 3rd month following the close of the corporation's tax year (Code Sec. 6072(b)).[1] The tax year of an S corporation generally must be a calendar year. However, a fiscal tax year can be used if the corporation establishes a business purpose to the satisfaction of the IRS or makes an election to use another tax year and makes "required payments" to the IRS (Code Sec. 1378).[2] To the extent the special S corporation rules do not apply, S corporations are governed by the "regular" or C corporation rules. Thus, the taxation of income earned by, and the allocation of losses incurred by, S corporations closely parallels the taxation of partnerships with respect to items of partnership income and loss. However, S corporations generally continue to be treated as regular corporations for purposes of the Code rules (subchapter C rules) relating to corporate distributions, redemptions, liquidations, reorganizations, and the like (Code Sec. 1371).[3]

305. Corporations Eligible to Elect S Corporation Status. To become an S corporation, an organization must be a "small business corporation" (Code Sec. 1361(a)).[4] Thus, all the following requirements must be met (Code Sec. 1361(b)); Reg. § 1.1361-1(b)):[5]

(1) The entity must be a domestic corporation that is organized under the laws of any state or U.S. territory. An unincorporated association that is taxed as a corporation for Code purposes (Code Sec. 7701)[6] may elect S corporation status (Reg. § 1.1361-1(c)).[7]

(2) The corporation may have as shareholders only individuals, estates or certain trusts. Partnerships and corporations cannot be shareholders.

(3) Only citizens or residents of the United States can be shareholders.

(4) The corporation can have only one class of stock.

Footnote references are to paragraphs of the 2002 Standard Federal Tax Reports.

¶ 301

[1] ¶ 36,720	[4] ¶ 32,021	[6] ¶ 43,080
[2] ¶ 32,260, ¶ 32,262.073	[5] ¶ 32,021, ¶ 32,024A	[7] ¶ 32,024A
[3] ¶ 32,140		

A few limited types of corporations are ineligible to be "small business corporations" (Code Sec. 1361(b)(2)).[8]

Shareholder Limitations. A qualifying S corporation can have no more than 75 shareholders. For purposes of this limitation, a husband and wife (and their estates) are counted as a single shareholder without regard to how they hold their shares. All "eligible" shareholders must be individuals, estates, certain defined trusts, or certain tax-exempt organizations.

The term "eligible shareholders" includes a grantor trust (where the grantor is regarded as the shareholder), a voting trust (where each beneficiary is treated as a shareholder), and any testamentary trust that receives S corporation stock. However, the trust is treated as an eligible shareholder only for two years after the deemed owners death (Code Sec. 1361(c)(2)(A); Reg. § 1.1361-1(h)).[9]

Stock Ownership Through LLCs. Shareholders' ownership of the stock of an S corporation through their respective limited liability company (LLC) does not terminate the corporation's S election (IRS Letter Ruling 200107025). In this situation, none of the LLCs or limited partnerships formed by the shareholders elected treatment as an association taxable as a corporation but, instead, existed according to their default classification under Reg. § 301.7701-3.[10] As a result, each shareholder was treated as the direct owner of the S corporation stock.

Electing Small Business Trusts. An "electing trust" can be an S corporation shareholder (Code Sec. 1361(e)).[11] An electing trust is one that does not have as a beneficiary any person other than (1) an individual, (2) an estate, or (3) an organization eligible to accept charitable contributions under Code Sec. 170 (other than political entities) and does not have "potential current beneficiaries." This kind of trust is different from a qualified subchapter S trust (see QSSTs, below).

Any portion of such a trust that consists of S corporation stock is treated as a separate trust and will be taxed at the highest rate of tax for estates and trusts with limited deductions and credits and no exemption amount for alternative minimum tax purposes.

Also, an electing small business trust cannot have any interest acquired by purchase, and a specific election to be treated as an electing trust must have been filed by the trustee. This election is irrevocable without the consent of the IRS. This type of trust does not include a qualified subchapter S trust (see below) or a trust that is exempt from income tax.

In the case of an electing small business trust, each potential current beneficiary of the trust is treated as a shareholder, except that for any period if there is no potential current beneficiary of the trust, the trust itself is treated as the shareholder during this period (Code Sec. 1361(c)(6)).[12]

Neither a charitable remainder trust nor a trust that qualifies as an individual retirement account is an eligible S corporation shareholder (Rev. Rul. 92-48, Rev. Rul. 92-73).[13]

Exempt Organizations as Shareholders. Certain tax-exempt organizations can be S corporation shareholders. These are qualified pension, profit-sharing and stock bonus plans, charitable organizations and any other organization exempt from taxation under Code Sec. 501.

QSSTs. A qualified subchapter S trust (QSST) whose beneficiary chooses to be treated as owner of the S corporation stock held by the trust also may hold stock in an S corporation (Code Sec. 1361(d)).[14] A QSST must own stock in at least one S corporation and must distribute all of its income to one individual who is a citizen or resident of the United States. In addition, under Code Sec. 1361(d)(3),[15] the terms of the trust must provide: (1) there may be only one income beneficiary at any time; (2) trust corpus may be distributed only to the income beneficiary; (3) each income

---

Footnote references are to paragraphs of the 2002 Standard Federal Tax Reports.

[8] ¶ 32,021	[11] ¶ 32,021	[14] ¶ 32,021
[9] ¶ 32,021, ¶ 32,024A	[12] ¶ 32,021	[15] ¶ 32,021
[10] ¶ 43,083	[13] ¶ 32,026.40	

¶ 305

interest must end no later than the death of the income beneficiary; and (4) if the trust terminates at any time during the life of the income beneficiary, it must distribute all of its assets to the beneficiary. However, successive income beneficiaries are permitted. The income beneficiary's election to treat the trust as a qualified subchapter S trust may be revoked only with the consent of the IRS. The election is effective for up to two months and 15 days before the election date. A separate election must be made for each subchapter S trust holding and must be made by each successive income beneficiary.[16]

C Corporation or S Corporation Subsidiaries. The Small Business Job Protection Act of 1996 (P.L. 104-188) included rules allowing an S corporation to have a C corporation or an S corporation subsidiary. An S corporation can hold qualifying wholly owned subsidiaries (Code Sec. 1361(b)(3))[17] and can own 80 percent or more of the stock of a C corporation. The C corporation subsidiary can elect to join in the filing of a consolidated return with its affiliated C corporations, but the S corporation cannot join in the election. Dividends received by an S corporation from a subsidiary C corporation of which the S corporation owns 80 percent or more of the stock are not treated as passive investment income from stock ownership. Instead, the classification of the income is determined by whether the subsidiary C corporation generated the income through the active conduct of a trade or business (Code Sec. 1362(d)(3)(E)).[18]

Single Class of Stock. A qualifying S corporation may have only one class of stock outstanding. These shares must confer identical rights to distribution and liquidation proceeds (Reg. § 1.1361-1(l)(1)).[19] Differences in voting rights, however, are permitted. A corporate obligation that qualifies as "straight debt" is not considered a second class of stock (Code Sec. 1361(c)(5); Reg. § 1.1361-1(l)(5)).[20] Buy-sell and redemption agreements restricting transferability of the stock are generally disregarded in determining whether the corporation has a single class of stock (Reg. § 1.1361-1(l)(2)(iii)).[21]

Qualified Subchapter S Subsidiary. An S corporation is permitted to own a qualified subchapter S subsidiary (QSSS or QSub). This includes any domestic corporation that qualifies as an S corporation and is 100 percent owned by an S corporation parent which elects to treat it as a QSSS. A QSSS is not taxed as a separate corporation, and all its tax items are treated as belonging to the parent (Code Sec. 1361(b)(3)).

Stock of an S corporation does not include stock received for the performance of services that is substantially nonvested, unless the holder has made a Reg. § 1.83-3(b)[22] election to include the value of the stock in income (Reg. § 1.1361-1(b)(3)).[23] However, stock warrants, call options, or other similar stock rights to purchase stock (collectively, "options") generally are treated as stock of the corporation if the options are substantially certain to be exercised at a strike price substantially below fair market value. This rule does not apply if the option was issued (1) to a commercial lender, (2) in connection with the performance of services, provided the option is nontransferable and does not have a readily ascertainable fair market value when issued, or (3) at a strike price that is at least 90 percent of the stock's fair market value (Reg. § 1.1361-1(l)(4)(iii)).[24] Form 8869, "Qualified Subchapter S Subsidiary Election," should be used by all S corporations to elect QSub treatment for wholly owned corporate subsidiaries.

306. How to Make S Election. The election of S corporation status must be made by a qualified corporation, with the unanimous consent of the shareholders, on or before the 15th day of the 3rd month of its tax year in order for the election to be effective beginning with the year when made. The election is made on Form 2553, "Election by a Small Business Corporation," and filed with the IRS Service Center where the corporation files its Form 1120S. The corporation must meet all of the

---

Footnote references are to paragraphs of the 2002 Standard Federal Tax Reports.

¶306

[16] ¶ 32,021	[19] ¶ 32,021, ¶ 32,024A	[22] ¶ 6383
[17] ¶ 32,021	[20] ¶ 32,021, ¶ 32,026.03	[23] ¶ 32,024A
[18] ¶ 32,040	[21] ¶ 32,024A	[24] ¶ 32,024A

eligibility requirements for the pre-election portion of the tax year, and all persons who were shareholders during the pre-election portion also must consent to the election. If these requirements are not met during the pre-election period, the election becomes effective the following year (Code Sec. 1362(a) and (b); Reg. § 1.1362-6).[25] However, the IRS can treat a late-filed election as timely made upon a showing of reasonable cause for the late filing. The S corporation must file an election within 12 months of the original due date of the election, but in no event later than the unextended due date of the tax return for the first year the corporation intends to be an S corporation. A statement that the filing is made pursuant to Rev. Proc. 98-55[26] must be at the top of the Form 2553, and the reasons why the election was not made on time must be attached to the election. This leeway period applies to shareholder elections, such as QSST elections and electing small business trust elections.

307. Termination of S Election. S corporation status is automatically terminated if any event occurs that would prohibit the corporation from making the election in the first place. The election is terminated as of the date on which the disqualifying event occurs. However, if a corporation, for three consecutive years, has both accumulated earnings and profits as well as passive investment income that exceeds 25 percent of its gross receipts, its election is terminated beginning with the following tax year (Code Sec. 1362(d)(3); Reg. § 1.1362-2(b)).[27]

An S corporation election may be revoked with the consent of shareholders holding more than 50 percent of the outstanding shares of stock (voting and nonvoting) on the day the revocation is made. A revocation may designate a prospective effective date (Code Sec. 1362(d)(1); Reg. § 1.1362-2(a)).[28] If no date is specified, a revocation made on or before the 15th day of the 3rd month of a corporation's tax year is retroactively effective on the first day of the tax year. A revocation made after this date is effective on the first day of the following tax year (Code Sec. 1362(d)(1)(C); Reg. § 1.1362-2(a)(2)).[29]

If an election is terminated or revoked, the corporation may not reelect S corporation status without IRS consent until the 5th year after the year in which the termination or revocation became effective (Code Sec. 1362(g); Reg. § 1.1362-5).[30] However, any termination of the subchapter S election in a tax year beginning before January 1, 1997, is not taken into account. Thus, any small business corporation that terminated its subchapter S election within the five-year period immediately preceding January 1, 1997, may reelect subchapter S status without the IRS's consent. An S corporation whose status as a qualified subchapter S subsidiary (QSub or QSSS) has terminated cannot elect to be treated as a qualified subchapter S subsidiary within five years (Code Sec. 1361(b)(3)(D)).[31]

Inadvertent Terminations. However, if a corporation's S election is inadvertently terminated or inadvertently invalid when made, and the corporation makes a timely correction, the IRS can waive the termination or can permit the election (Code Sec. 1362(f); Reg. § 1.1362-4(a)).[32] In such a case, the corporation must correct any condition that barred the corporation from qualifying as a small business corporation and must obtain any required shareholder consents. All shareholders must agree to make such adjustments as may be required by the IRS (Code Sec. 1362(f)).[33]

Election to End Tax Year. Further, if a shareholder terminates his interest in the S corporation and all "affected" shareholders consent to the termination, the tax year can be treated as two tax years, the first of which ends on the date of termination. For this purpose, affected shareholders include the shareholder whose interest is terminated and all shareholders to whom such shareholder has transferred shares during the tax year (Code Sec. 1377(a)(2)).[34]

Footnote references are to paragraphs of the 2002 Standard Federal Tax Reports.

[25] ¶ 32,040, ¶ 32,047	[29] ¶ 32,040, ¶ 32,043	[32] ¶ 32,045
[26] ¶ 32,053.41	[30] ¶ 32,040, ¶ 32,046	[33] ¶ 32,040
[27] ¶ 32,040, ¶ 32,043	[31] ¶ 32,021	[34] ¶ 32,240
[28] ¶ 32,040, ¶ 32,043		

Taxation of Shareholders

309. Tax Treatment of Shareholders—In General. Each shareholder of an S corporation separately accounts for his pro rata share of corporate items of income, deduction, loss, and credit in his tax year in which the corporation's tax year ends (Code Sec. 1366(a)).[35] Such items must be separately stated whenever they could affect the shareholder's individual tax liability (Reg. § 1.1366-1(a)).[36] A shareholder's share of each item generally is computed daily according to the number of shares held by him on each day of the corporation's tax year (Reg. § 1.1366-1, Reg. § 1.1377-1).[37] However, a shareholder's currently deductible share of the corporation's losses and deductions is limited to the total of his adjusted basis in the corporation's stock and any debt the corporation may owe him. Disallowed losses and deductions may be carried forward to any subsequent year in which he has a restored basis in the stock or debt (Code Sec. 1366(d)).[38] Following the termination of an S corporation election, any disallowed loss or deduction is allowed if the shareholder's basis in his stock is restored (1) within one year after the effective date of the termination or by the due date for the last subchapter S return, whichever is later, or (2) within 120 days after a determination that the corporation's S election had terminated for a previous year (Code Sec. 1366(d) and Code Sec. 1377(b)).[39]

At-Risk and Passive Activity Rules. The at-risk rules disallow losses that exceed an investor's amount at risk. Generally, at risk is the amount of investment that an investor could lose. The at-risk rules apply to all individuals, including S corporation shareholders, and are applied at the shareholder level (Code Sec. 465(a)(1)).[40] The at-risk amount is determined at the close of the S corporation's tax year. Thus, an S corporation shareholder who realizes that his or her at-risk amount is low, and wishes to deduct an anticipated S corporation net loss, can make additional contributions to the entity. See ¶ 2045.

Likewise, passive activity loss (PAL) rules generally are applied at the shareholder level (Code Sec. 469).[41] However, several determinations that affect the application of the PAL rules must be made at the corporate level. For example, the determination of whether an activity constitutes a trade or business as opposed to a rental activity is made at the corporate level. The distinction between portfolio and non-portfolio income is also made at the corporate level. This information is conveyed to the shareholder via Schedule K-1 which is generated by the corporation when preparing its tax return. The shareholder then uses the information to apply the PAL and at-risk limitations when preparing his individual tax return. See ¶ 2053.

315. Shareholder's Original Basis in Stock. An S corporation shareholder's basis in his stock is determined under the same rules as apply to C corporation shareholders. Thus, the original basis of the shareholder's stock is the purchase price for the stock (money or the fair market value of any property given in exchange for the stock) (Code Sec. 1012).[42] Stock acquired by gift normally carries over the donor's basis (Code Sec. 1015(a)).[43] The basis of stock acquired from a decedent is its fair market value on the date of the decedent's death or on the alternate valuation date, if elected (Code Sec. 1014(a)).[44]

317. Adjustments to Shareholder's Stock Basis. The stock basis of each S corporation shareholder is *increased* by the portion of (1) all income items of the corporation (including tax-exempt income) that are separately computed and passed through to shareholders, (2) the income of the corporation that is not separately computed, and (3) the excess of the corporation's deductions for depletion over the basis of the property subject to depletion (Code Sec. 1367(a)(1); Reg.

Footnote references are to paragraphs of the 2002 Standard Federal Tax Reports.

[35] ¶ 32,080	[39] ¶ 32,080, ¶ 32,240	[42] ¶ 29,330
[36] ¶ 32,081	[40] ¶ 21,850	[43] ¶ 29,390
[37] ¶ 32,081, ¶ 32,240C	[41] ¶ 21,960	[44] ¶ 29,370
[38] ¶ 32,080		

§ 1.1367-1(b)).[45] A shareholder's basis is *decreased* by the portion of (1) distributions that are not includible in the shareholder's income due to the provisions of Code Sec. 1368 (¶ 309), (2) all loss and deduction items of the corporation that are separately stated and passed through to shareholders, (3) the nonseparately computed loss of the corporation, (4) any expense of the corporation not deductible in computing its taxable income and not properly chargeable to the capital account, and (5) the amount of the shareholder's deduction for depletion with respect to oil and gas wells to the extent that it does not exceed his proportionate share of the adjusted basis of such property (Code Sec. 1367(a)(2); Reg. § 1.1367-2(e)).[46] If a shareholder's stock basis is reduced to zero, the remaining net decrease attributable to losses and deductions is applied to reduce any basis in debt owed to the shareholder by the corporation. Distributions may not be applied against basis in debt. Any net increase in basis in a subsequent year is applied to restore the basis of indebtedness before it may be applied to increase the shareholder's stock basis (Code Sec. 1367(b)(2); Reg. § 1.1367-2(e)).[47]

Adjustment to Basis in Indebtedness. Detailed rules on the adjustments in the basis of a shareholder's basis in corporate indebtedness are found at Reg. § 1.1367-2.[48]

Cancellation of Indebtedness. The U.S. Supreme Court held that discharge of indebtedness income (Code Sec. 108)[49] passes through to S corporation shareholders to increase the basis of their S corporation stock (*D.A. Gitlitz*).[50] The Court further reasoned that while discharge of indebtedness income usually is included in gross income, under the plain language of the Code this income is not included in gross income if an S corporation is insolvent. As a result, discharge of indebtedness income is passed through to S corporation shareholders before it is used to reduce the S corporation's tax attributes. Thus, the shareholders are able to deduct losses up to the amount of their stock basis, and any remaining suspended loss is treated as corporate net operating loss which is then reduced by the amount of the discharged debt (Code Sec. 1366).[51]

321. Taxable Income. Items of income and loss attributable to an S corporation are passed through to the shareholders. Computation of an S corporation's taxable income parallels the computation of the taxable income of an individual, except that organizational expenditures may be amortized under Code Sec. 248,[52] and the reduction in certain corporate tax benefits provided in Code Sec. 291[53] must be made if the S corporation was a C corporation for any of the three immediately preceding tax years. Furthermore, items that a shareholder must report separately must be computed separately, and certain deductions, such as those for personal exemptions, charitable contributions, medical expenses, alimony, and net operating losses, are not allowed the corporation (Code Sec. 1363(b)).[54]

322. Fringe Benefits. Only those benefits received by employee-shareholders owning two percent or less of the S corporation stock are deductible by the corporation as a business expense. Employee-shareholders owning more than two percent of the S corporation stock are treated in the same manner as partners in a partnership (Code Sec. 1372(a)). For purposes of this rule, a two-percent-plus shareholder is any person who owns, or is considered as owning by reason of the Code Sec. 318 attribution rules, more than two percent of the outstanding stock of the S corporation or stock having more than two percent of the total combined voting power of all of the stock of the S corporation (Code Sec. 1372(b)).[55]

Health Insurance Expenses. For tax years beginning in 2001, an employee-shareholder who owns more than two percent of the S corporation stock, and who is thus treated as a partner (Code Sec. 1372(a)),[56] is entitled to deduct an amount

---

Footnote references are to paragraphs of the 2002 Standard Federal Tax Reports.

[45] ¶ 32,100, ¶ 32,100B	[49] ¶ 7002	[53] ¶ 15,190
[46] ¶ 32,100, ¶ 32,100C	[50] ¶ 7010.73	[54] ¶ 32,060
[47] ¶ 32,100, ¶ 32,100C	[51] ¶ 32,080	[55] ¶ 32,160
[48] ¶ 32,100C	[52] ¶ 13,350	[56] ¶ 32,160

¶ 322

equal to 60 percent of the amount paid for medical insurance for himself, his spouse and dependents. The deduction increases to 70 percent in 2002, and a 100-percent deduction is available in 2003 and thereafter (Code Sec. 162(l)(1) and Code Sec. 162(l)(5)).[57] This amount is taken as an individual deduction from gross income in arriving at adjusted gross income.

For purposes of the deduction, a two-percent-plus shareholder's wages from the S corporation are treated as the shareholder's earned income. No deduction is allowed in excess of an individual's earned income (within the meaning of Code Sec. 401(c)) derived from the trade or business with respect to which the plan providing the health insurance coverage is established.

Tax Treatment of Distributions

323. S Corporation Distributions. Distributions of cash or property are taxed according to a priority system that depends upon whether the S corporation has earnings and profits. An S corporation has no earnings and profits unless these are attributable to tax years when the corporation was not an S corporation or to S corporation years beginning before 1983. An S corporation may also succeed to the earnings and profits of an acquired or merged corporation (IRS Letter Ruling 9046036).[58] For an S corporation without earnings and profits, distributions are treated first as a nontaxable return of capital to the extent of the shareholder's stock basis and then as a gain from the sale or exchange of property (Code Sec. 1368(b); Reg. § 1.1368-1(c)).[59] For a corporation with earnings and profits, unless an election is made (see ¶ 333), distributions are treated as follows: (1) a nontaxable return of capital to the extent of the corporation's "accumulated adjustments account" (AAA) (see ¶ 325), (2) dividends to the extent of the S corporation's accumulated earnings and profits, (3) a nontaxable return of capital to the extent of the shareholder's remaining stock basis, and (4) gain from the sale or exchange of property (Code Sec. 1368(c); Reg. § 1.1368-1(d)).[60] Before applying these rules, the shareholder's stock basis and the AAA are adjusted for the corporate items passed through from the corporate tax year during which the distribution is made.

The accumulated earnings and profits of an S corporation during its first tax year beginning after that date are reduced by the earnings and profits accumulated in any tax year beginning before January 1, 1983, for which the corporation was an S corporation (Act Sec. 1311(a), P.L. 104-188). This reduction ensures that an S corporation's accumulated earnings and profits are solely attributable to tax years for which its S election was not in effect and eliminates unnecessarily complicated corporate recordkeeping.

325. Accumulated Adjustments Account. The accumulated adjustments account is used to compute the tax effect of distributions made by an S corporation with accumulated earnings and profits. The AAA is zero on the first day of an S corporation's first tax year. It is *increased* by (1) all corporate income items (excluding tax-exempt income items) that are separately stated and passed through, (2) nonseparately computed corporate income, and (3) the excess of deductions for depletion over the basis of the property subject to depletion (Reg. § 1.1368-2). The regulations define tax-exempt income as income that is permanently excludable in all circumstances from the gross income of an S corporation and its shareholders (Reg. § 1.1366-1(a)(2)(viii)).[61]

The AAA is *decreased* by (1) certain nontaxable corporate distributions, (2) all loss and deduction items of the corporation that are separately stated and passed through (other than items that are not deductible in computing taxable income and not properly chargeable to the capital account), (3) the nonseparately computed loss of the corporation, (4) the nondeductible amounts that are unrelated to the production of tax-exempt income, and (5) the amount of the shareholder's deduction for oil

and gas depletion. No adjustment is made for federal taxes arising when the corporation was a C corporation. Because the AAA may become negative, the account becomes positive only after the negative balance is restored by later income (Code Sec. 1368(e)(1)(A); Reg. § 1.1368-2).[62] The amount in the accumulated adjustments account as of the close of a tax year is determined without regard to any net negative adjustment for the tax year. A negative adjustment occurs in any tax year in which negative adjustments to the account exceed increases to the account.

Distributions received by an S corporation shareholder in a stock redemption that is treated as a Code Sec. 301 distribution are treated as a distribution that reduces the S corporation's AAA (Rev. Rul. 95-14).[63] For a distribution in redemption of an S corporation's stock, if the redemption is treated as an exchange under Code Sec. 302 or Code Sec. 303, the AAA is decreased by an amount determined by multiplying the account balance by the number of shares redeemed and dividing the product by the total number of shares outstanding. This adjustment is made before the distribution rules are applied (Code Sec. 1368(e)(1)(B)).[64]

The AAA relates only to the most recent continuous period in which the corporation has been an S corporation. However, the period does not include tax years beginning before January 1, 1983 (Code Sec. 1368(e)(2); Reg. § 1.1368-2(a)).[65] If corporate distributions during a tax year exceed the amount in the AAA at the end of that year, the balance of the account is allocated among distributions in proportion to their respective sizes (Code Sec. 1368(c)).[66] (See, also, ¶ 329.)

329. Post-Termination Distributions. If an S corporation terminates its election, the corporation has the opportunity for a limited period of time to unfreeze the income that was previously taxed to shareholders under the passthrough rules but that was not actually distributed by the corporation. Specifically, any cash distribution by the corporation with respect to its stock during the post-termination transition period (Code Sec. 1377(b)(1))[67] is applied against and reduces stock basis to the extent that the amount of the distribution does not exceed the AAA (Code Sec. 1371(e)(1)).[68]

The term "post-termination transition period" means:

(1) the period beginning on the day after the last day of the corporation's last tax year as an S corporation and ending on the later of: (a) the day which is one year after such last day or (b) the due date for filing the return for the last tax year as an S corporation (including extensions);

(2) the 120-day period beginning on the date of any determination pursuant to an audit of the taxpayer which follows the termination of the corporation's election and which adjusts a subchapter S item of income, loss, or deduction of the corporation arising during the S period (Code Sec. 1368(e)(2));[69] or

(3) the 120-day period beginning on the date of a determination that the corporation's election had terminated for a previous tax year (Code Sec. 1362(a)).[70]

If the AAA is not exhausted by the end of the post-termination transition period, it disappears. Any distributions made thereafter are taxed under the usual subchapter C rules (that is to say, first, as a distribution of current earnings and profits; second, as a distribution of accumulated earnings and profits; third, as a return of capital to the extent of the shareholder's basis; and, finally, as a capital gain). Because the AAA is always reflected in the basis of the shareholder's stock, failure to exhaust it during the transition period moves it, in effect, below current and accumulated earnings and profits in the priority system for distributions. The grace period for post-termination distributions applies only to cash distributions. It

---

Footnote references are to paragraphs of the 2002 Standard Federal Tax Reports.

[62] ¶ 32,120, ¶ 32,120C   [65] ¶ 32,120, ¶ 32,120C   [68] ¶ 32,140
[63] ¶ 32,121.20   [66] ¶ 32,120   [69] ¶ 32,120
[64] ¶ 32,120   [67] ¶ 32,240   [70] ¶ 32,040

¶ 329

does not apply to noncash distributions. A noncash distribution is taxed under the usual subchapter C rules.[71]

333. Election to Distribute Earnings First. An S corporation can avoid the priority system (¶ 323) for treatment of distributions by electing to treat distributions as dividends. An S corporation might elect to treat a distribution as taxable dividends if it wants to avoid S-status termination for excess passive investment income.[72] However, all shareholders who receive a distribution during the tax year must consent to such treatment (Code Sec. 1368(e)(3)).[73] If such an election is made, the corporation is not required to distribute its entire AAA at the end of its tax year before it can pay a dividend.

Taxation of Corporation

335. Tax Treatment of the Corporation. Since an S corporation is a pass-through entity, it is generally not subject to federal income taxes. However, an S corporation may be liable for (1) the tax imposed on built-in gains or capital gains (Code Sec. 1374) (¶ 337), [74] (2) the tax on excess net passive income (Code Sec. 1375) (¶ 341), [75] (3) the tax from the recapture of a prior year's investment credit, [76] and (4) the LIFO recapture tax (Code Sec. 1363(d)) (¶ 339).[77] If the S corporation was incorporated after 1982, immediately became an S corporation and has no earnings or profits, only the capital gains tax applies. If the S corporation was incorporated and elected S corporation status before 1987, the tax on built-in gains does not apply. S corporations are required to make estimated tax payments (¶ 2679) attributable to the corporate-level tax liabilities listed above (Code Sec. 6655(g)(4)).[78]

337. Tax on Built-In Gains. The tax on built-in gains is a corporate-level tax on S corporations that dispose of assets that appreciated in value during years when the corporation was a C corporation. Current Code Sec. 1374[79] applies only to corporations that made S corporation elections after 1986. Former Code Sec. 1374 continues to apply to corporations that made S elections before 1987.

An S corporation may be liable for tax on its built-in gains if: (1) it was a C corporation prior to making its S corporation election; (2) the S corporation election was made after 1986; (3) it has a net recognized built-in gain within the recognition period; and (4) the net recognized built-in gain for the tax year does not exceed the net unrealized built-in gain minus the net recognized built-in gain for prior years in the recognition period, to the extent that such gains were subject to tax (Code Sec. 1374(c)).[80]

A recognized built-in loss is any loss recognized during the recognition period on the disposition of any asset to the extent that the S corporation establishes that: (1) the asset was held by the S corporation at the beginning of its first tax year as an S corporation and (2) the loss is not greater than the excess of (a) the adjusted basis of the asset at the beginning of the corporation's first tax year as an S corporation over (b) the fair market value of the asset at that time (Code Sec. 1374(d)(4)).[81]

Recognition Period. The recognition period is the ten-year period beginning on the first day on which the corporation is an S corporation or acquires C corporation assets in a carryover basis transaction (Code Sec. 1374(d)(7); Reg. § 1374-1(d)).[82] For example, if the first day of the recognition period is July 12, 2000, the last day of the recognition period will be July 11, 2010.

The tax is computed by applying the highest corporate income tax rate to the S corporation's net recognized built-in gain for the tax year. The amount of the net recognized built-in gain is taxable income. However, any net operating loss carryforward arising in a tax year in which the corporation was a C corporation is allowed as a deduction against the net recognized built-in gain of the S corporation. Capital loss

---

Footnote references are to paragraphs of the 2002 Standard Federal Tax Reports.

[71] ¶ 32,240E	[75] ¶ 32,201	[79] ¶ 32,201
[72] ¶ 32,120B	[76] ¶ 32,140.80	[80] ¶ 32,201
[73] ¶ 32,120	[77] ¶ 32,060	[81] ¶ 32,201
[74] ¶ 32,201	[78] ¶ 39,565	[82] ¶ 32,201; ¶ 32,201C

¶ 333

carryforwards may also be used to offset recognized built-in gains (Code Sec. 1374(b) and (d); Reg. § 1.1374-5).[83]

Furthermore, business tax credit carryovers of an S corporation, arising in a tax year in which the corporation was a C corporation, can offset the built-in gains tax of the S corporation (Code Sec. 1374(b)(3)(B); Reg. § 1.1374-6).[84]

The term "net recognized built-in gain" means the lesser of (1) the amount that would be the taxable income of the S corporation if only recognized built-in gains and recognized built-in losses were taken into account or (2) the corporation's taxable income. In the case of a corporation that made its S corporation election on or after March 31, 1988, any net recognized built-in gain that is not subject to the built-in gains tax due to the net income limitation is carried forward (Code Sec. 1374(d)(2); Reg. § 1.1374-2).[85]

The amount of recognized built-in gain passed through and taxed to shareholders is reduced by the tax imposed on the built-in gain and paid by the S corporation (Code Sec. 1366(f)(2)).[86]

339. LIFO Recapture. A C corporation that maintains its inventory using the last-in, first-out (LIFO) method for its last tax year before an S corporation election becomes effective must include in gross income a LIFO recapture amount when it converts to S corporation status. LIFO recapture is also required for transfers of inventory from a C corporation to an S corporation in a tax-free reorganization (Code Sec. 1363(d); Reg. § 1.1363-2).[87] The LIFO recapture amount is the amount, if any, by which the amount of the inventory assets using the first-in, first-out (FIFO) method exceeds the inventory amount of such assets under the LIFO method (¶ 1559).

The tax attributable to the inclusion in income of any LIFO recapture amount is payable by the corporation in four equal installments. The first payment is due on or before the due date of the corporate tax return for the electing corporation's last tax year as a C corporation. The three subsequent installments are due on or before the respective due dates of the S corporation's returns for the three succeeding tax years. No interest is payable on these installments if they are paid by the respective due dates.

341. Excess Net Passive Income. S corporations with subchapter C earnings and profits and with total net passive investment income totaling more than 25 percent of gross receipts are subject to an income tax computed by multiplying the corporation's excess net passive income by the highest corporate income tax rate (Code Sec. 1375(a); Reg. § 1.1375-1).[88] "Passive investment income" means gross receipts derived from royalties, rents, dividends, interest (excluding interest on installment sales of inventory to customers and income of certain lending and financing businesses), annuities, and sales or exchanges of stock or securities to the extent of any gains therefrom (Code Sec. 1362(d)(3)(D)).[89] However, such income derived by an S corporation in the ordinary course of its trade or business is generally excluded from the definition of passive investment income (Reg. § 1.1362-2(c)(5)).[90] "Net passive income" means passive investment income reduced by any allowable deduction directly connected with the production of such income except for the net operating loss deduction under Code Sec. 172[91] (¶ 1182) and the special deductions allowed to corporations by Code Sec. 241—Code Sec. 249[92] (¶ 235-¶ 243).

"Excess net passive income" is the amount that bears the same ratio to net passive income as the amount of passive investment income that exceeds 25 percent of gross receipts bears to passive investment income. "Excess net passive income" cannot exceed the corporation's taxable income for the year computed without

---

Footnote references are to paragraphs of the 2002 Standard Federal Tax Reports.

[83] ¶ 32,201; ¶ 32,202H	[87] ¶ 32,060, ¶ 32,061B	[90] ¶ 32,043
[84] ¶ 32,201; ¶ 32,202J	[88] ¶ 32,220, ¶ 32,221	[91] ¶ 12,002
[85] ¶ 39,201; ¶ 32,202B	[89] ¶ 32,040	[92] ¶ 13,002¶ 13,400
[86] ¶ 32,080		

regard to any net operating loss deduction (Code Sec. 172)[93] and without regard to the special deductions allowed by Code Sec. 241—Code Sec. 249,[94] other than the amortization deduction for organizational expenditures of Code Sec. 248[95] (Code Sec. 1375(b)(1)(B); Reg. § 1.1375-1(b)(1)(ii)).[96] Passive investment income is determined without taking into account any recognized built-in gain or loss during the recognition period (Code Sec. 1375(b)(4)).[97] This means that S corporations without earnings and profits cannot be taxed on excess net passive income if they have no taxable income. This can happen if the corporation has net operating losses and income from passive investments. The tax is not merely carried over; there is no tax due if during the year the corporation did not have taxable income.

The tax on excess net passive income reduces each item of passive income by the amount of tax attributable to it and thereby reduces the amount of passive investment income that each shareholder must take into account in computing gross income (Code Sec. 1366(f)(3)).[98]

The only credits allowable against the passive investment income tax are those for certain uses of gasoline and special fuels under Code Sec. 34 (Code Sec. 1375(c); Reg. § 1.1375-1(c)).[99]

The IRS may waive the tax on excess net passive income if the S corporation establishes that it made a good-faith determination at the close of the tax year that it had no C corporation earnings and profits and that it distributed such earnings and profits within a reasonable time after determining that they existed (Code Sec. 1375(d); Reg. § 1.1375-1(d)).[100]

345. Fringe Benefits. As noted at ¶ 322, for fringe benefit purposes, an S corporation is treated as a partnership, and a more-than-two-percent shareholder is treated as a partner. Amounts paid for fringe benefits of a partner, or benefits provided in kind, generally constitute guaranteed payments that are deductible by the partnership (¶ 421). Accordingly, the cost of fringe benefits provided by an S corporation to a more-than-two-percent shareholder, including the payment of accident and health insurance premiums, is deductible by the corporation (Code Sec. 1372; Rev. Rul. 91-26).[101]

349. Foreign Income. Foreign taxes paid by an S corporation pass through as such to the shareholders, who can elect to treat them as deductions or credits on their individual returns (Code Sec. 1373(a)).[102] Since an S corporation is not eligible for the foreign tax credit for taxes paid by a foreign corporation in which it is a shareholder, such taxes do not pass through to the S corporation's shareholders. The foreign loss recapture rules apply to an S corporation that previously passed foreign losses through to the shareholders and subsequently terminates its S corporation status. For the purpose of computing the amount of foreign losses that must be recaptured, the making or termination of an S corporation election is treated as the disposition of a business (Code Sec. 1373(b)).[103]

Audit Provisions

353. Administrative and Judicial Proceedings. The audit provisions applicable to S corporations that were enacted by the Tax Equity and Fiscal Responsibility Act of 1982 have been repealed, and new rules, requiring consistency between the returns of the S corporation and its shareholders, have been adopted (Code Sec. 6037(c)).[104]

Footnote references are to paragraphs of the 2002 Standard Federal Tax Reports.

¶ 345

[93] ¶ 12,002	[97] ¶ 32,220	[101] ¶ 32,160
[94] ¶ 13,002, ¶ 13,400	[98] ¶ 32,080	[102] ¶ 32,180, ¶ 32,181.01
[95] ¶ 13,350	[99] ¶ 32,220, ¶ 32,221	[103] ¶ 32,180
[96] ¶ 32,220, ¶ 32,221	[100] ¶ 32,220, ¶ 32,221	[104] ¶ 35,520

Chapter 4

PARTNERSHIPS

Association v. Partnership

401. Partnership Distinguished. A "partnership" includes a syndicate, group, pool, joint venture, or other unincorporated organization that carries on any business, financial operation, or venture, and that is not, within the meaning of the Code, a trust, estate, or corporation (Code Sec. 761).[1] A noncorporate entity with at least two members can be classified either as a partnership or as an association taxable as a corporation. A noncorporate entity with one member can be taxed either as a corporation or as a sole proprietorship (Reg. § 301.7701-3).[2]

401A. Limited Partnerships A limited partnership has one or more general partners and one or more limited partners. Limited partnerships are formed under the limited partnership laws of each state. Unlike general partnerships in which all the partners are responsible for partnership liabilities, limited partners are not responsible for partnership liabilities beyond the agreed amount of their investments. In addition, under state law, limited partners cannot participate in partnership management.

Limited Liability Limited Partnerships. A few states have passed legislation allowing limited liability limited partnerships (LLLPs). These entities operate like a traditional limited partnership, but the "general partner" also has limited liability.

401B. Limited Liability Partnerships. Limited liability partnerships (LLPs) generally are used by professionals such as accountants or attorneys. An LLP is a general partnership in which each individual partner remains liable for his or her own malpractice and the liabilities arising out of the wrongful acts or omissions of those over whom the partner has supervisory duties. The rising use of LLPs reflects changed perceptions as to the traditional concepts of joint and several liability for large professional partnerships with hundreds of partners scattered over the country or even on different continents.

Footnote references are to paragraphs of the 2002 Standard Federal Tax Reports.

[1] ¶ 25,600   [2] ¶ 43,082   **¶ 401B**

LLPs must be allowed under the law of the state in which it is doing business. All the states and the District of Columbia have LLP enabling legislation. Some states offer members of LLPs limited protection from partnership liabilities, such as limiting the protection to malpractice claims against other partners. Other states offer full protection from liabilities, including the partnership's contractual liabilities. These are called "full shield" states.

As a practical matter, LLPs are most likely to be used to give liability protection to partners in an existing partnership. The conversion of an existing partnership to an LLP does not create a new partnership. In such a case, the partnership is required to continue to use the same method of accounting used before its registration. Each partner's total percentage interest in the partnership's profits, losses and capital remains the same after the registration as an LLP.

The IRS has ruled that the registration of a general partnership as a registered limited liability partnership does not cause a termination of the partnership for purposes of Code Sec. 708(b) (Rev. Rul. 95-55).[3]

402. Exclusion from Partnership Provisions. Unincorporated organizations may elect not to be taxed as partnerships if they are used either for investment purposes only or for the joint production, extraction, or use—but not the sale—of property under an operating agreement. The exclusion also can be used by securities dealers for a short period for the purpose of underwriting, selling, or distributing a particular issue of securities. The exclusion can be elected only if the partners' incomes can be determined without computing the entity's income first (Code Sec. 761(a)).[4]

An unincorporated organization may elect to be completely or only partially excluded from the partnership provisions. However, the IRS will not allow an organization making the partial election to be excluded from the tax-year conformity rules of Code Sec. 706 or from the limitations on the allowance of losses (Rev. Rul. 57-215)[5] (see ¶ 416 and ¶ 425).[6] Unlike the check-the-box regulations (¶ 402A), this election removes the entity from all or a portion of the subchapter K partnership provisions. An election made under the check-the-box regulations, on the other hand, treats the entity as a nonpartnership for all Code purposes.

402A. Check-the-Box Regulations. Most entities that qualify for partnership treatment also qualify for electing out of partnership treatment under the "check-the-box" regulations (Reg. § 301.7701-3).[7] Under these rules, most entities that are not corporations may choose how they are to be taxed without specially qualifying as one form of entity or another under local law. An entity with two or more members can be classified either as a partnership or as an association taxed as a corporation. An entity with only one member can be classified as an association or can be disregarded as an entity separate from its owner. A single-member limited liability company cannot elect partnership status.

The default classification for entities existing before January 1, 1997, is the classification the entity claimed immediately prior to that date. For new entities that do not file an election, an entity with two or more members is classified as a partnership. An entity with one member is ignored and the taxpayer is treated as acting directly in business dealings.

An election not to be taxed as a partnership under the check-the-box regulations applies to all Code provisions. This is different from an election under Code Sec. 761 (see ¶ 402) which removes a partnership only from the provisions of Code Sec. 701—Code Sec. 777.

Footnote references are to paragraphs of the 2002 Standard Federal Tax Reports.

¶ 402

3 ¶ 25,200; ¶ 25,202.27	5 ¶ 25,602.11	7 ¶ 43,083
4 ¶ 25,600	6 ¶ 25,602.11	

Limited Liability Companies

402B. Limited Liability Companies. A state-registered limited liability company (LLC) can be taxed as a partnership for federal income tax purposes, but its members, like corporate shareholders, are not personally liable for the entity's debts and liabilities. Under the check-the-box rules, an LLC can elect partnership status to avoid taxation at the entity level as an "association taxed as a corporation."

Unlike limited partners, LLC members may participate in management without risking personal liability. No limitations are placed on the number of owners (there is a maximum of 75 shareholders for S corporations) and different types of shareholders. Additional advantages over S corporations include the ability to make disproportionate allocations and distributions (Code Sec. 704) and to distribute appreciated property to members without the recognition of gain (Code Sec. 731(b)). Members may also exchange appreciated property for membership interests without recognition of gain or loss (Code Sec. 721).

Conversion from Partnership to LLC. A conversion of a partnership into an LLC that is taxed as a partnership for federal income tax purposes is treated as a nontaxable partnership-to-partnership conversion. The conversion is treated as a contribution of assets to the new partnership under Code Sec. 721 and does not result in gain or loss to the partners. The tax results are the same whether the LLC is formed in the same state as the former partnership or in a different state. Upon such a conversion, the tax year of the converting partnership does not close with respect to any of the partners, and the resulting LLC does not need to obtain a new taxpayer identification number (Rev. Rul. 95-37).[8]

Publicly Traded Partnerships

403. Special Tax Rules. Publicly traded partnerships (PTPs) are taxed as corporations unless 90 percent or more of their gross income is derived from qualifying passive income sources (such as interest, dividends, real property rents, gain from the disposition of real property, mining and natural resource income, and gain from the disposition of capital assets or Code Sec. 1231(b) property held for the production of such income) (Code Sec. 7704).[9] A PTP is a partnership with interests traded on an established securities market or readily tradable on a secondary market (or its substantial equivalent), including master limited partnerships. A partnership that was publicly traded on December 17, 1987, is treated as a corporation in tax years beginning after December 31, 1997 (Reg. § 1.7704-2(a)(1)).[10]

However, after 1997, a publicly traded partnership (also called an "electing 1987 partnership") is not taxed as a corporation if it elects to be taxed on its gross income from the active conduct of a trade or business. The tax is 3.5 percent of the partnership's gross income from the active conduct of the enterprise. The partnership's gross income must include its share of gross trade or business income of any higher- or lower-tier partnership. The tax imposed under this provision cannot be offset by tax credits. Further, the election not to be taxed as a corporation must end as of the day on which there has been the addition of a substantial new line of business with respect to the partnership.

The election to be subject to the tax on gross trade or business income, once made, remains in effect until revoked by the partnership and cannot be reinstated (Code Sec. 7704(g)).[11]

The passive loss rules are applied separately to each PTP not treated as a corporation (Code Sec. 469(k)).[12] As a result, a passive activity loss from one PTP cannot be used to offset passive income from any other PTP.

Footnote references are to paragraphs of the 2002 Standard Federal Tax Reports.

[8] ¶ 25,243.13 [10] ¶ 43,181 [12] ¶ 21,960
[9] ¶ 43,180 [11] ¶ 43,180

¶403

Return and Payment of Tax

404. Partners, Not Partnership, Subject to Tax. A partnership does not pay federal income tax; rather, income or loss "flows through" to the partners who are taxable in their individual capacities on their distributive shares of partnership taxable income. However, the partnership is a tax-reporting entity that must file an annual partnership return (see ¶ 406). In determining federal income tax, a partner must take into account separately his distributive share of certain items (listed at ¶ 431) of partnership income, gain, loss, deduction or credit. A partner's distributive share of partnership items is includible on his individual income tax return (or corporate income tax return for corporate partners) for his tax year in which the partnership tax year ends (Code Sec. 706(a)).[13] See the flowchart at ¶ 63 that outlines the determination of a partner's distributive share.

A partner is generally not taxed on distributions of cash or property received from the partnership, except to the extent that any money distributed exceeds the partner's adjusted basis in his partnership interest immediately before the distribution (see ¶ 453). Taxable gain can also result from distributions of property that was contributed to a partnership with a "built-in gain" (where property has a fair market value in excess of its adjusted basis) and from property distributions that are characterized as sales and exchanges (see ¶ 432).

406. Return Used by Partnership. Annual information reporting on Form 1065 is required regardless of whether the partnership has taxable income for the tax year. Although Code Sec. 6063[14] states that the return may be signed by any one of the partners, Form 1065 instructions require the signature of a general partner. A U.S. partnership's return on Form 1065 is due on or before the 15th day of the fourth month following the close of the tax year. A foreign partnership that has U.S.-source income is not required to file a partnership return if the partnership has no effectively connected income and no U.S. partners at any time during the partnership's tax year (Reg. § 1.6031(a)-1(b)(3)(ii)).[15]

A partnership that fails to file Form 1065 or files an incomplete return is liable for a penalty of $50 per partner per month for a maximum of five months unless reasonable cause is shown. A partnership may not contest the penalty assessment in the Tax Court but must pay the entire penalty and sue for refund (Code Sec. 6698).[16] Certain domestic partnerships with 10 or fewer partners do not have to pay the penalty if all partners have fully reported their distributive shares on timely filed income tax returns (Rev. Proc. 84-35).[17]

A partnership may apply for an automatic three-month filing extension on Form 8736. An additional extension of no more than three months may be granted upon a showing of reasonable cause by filing Form 8800 (Code Sec. 6081).[18]

410. Reorganization, Dissolution, or Changes in Membership. The tax year of a partnership closes with respect to a partner whose entire interest in the partnership is terminated, whether by a sale of the entire interest or otherwise (Code Sec. 706(a)(2)(A)).[19] The sale of a portion of a partnership interest does not result in the closing of the partnership's tax year.

In the case of a sale, exchange or liquidation of a partner's entire interest in a partnership, the partner must include his share of partnership tax items in his income for the tax year in which his partnership interest terminates. This is often called the "closing the books" method. However, a partnership does not have to make an interim closing of the books to make this allocation to a retiring partner. Instead, a retiring partner's share of income may, by agreement among the partners, be estimated by taking a pro rata portion of the amount of such items the partner would have included in his income had he remained a partner until the end of the partnership tax year. The proration may be based on the portion of the tax year that

---

Footnote references are to paragraphs of the 2002 Standard Federal Tax Reports.

¶ 404

[13] ¶ 25,160	[16] ¶ 39,995	[18] ¶ 36,780
[14] ¶ 36,640	[17] ¶ 40,000.10	[19] ¶ 25,160
[15] ¶ 35,383		

has elapsed prior to the sale, exchange or liquidation, or may be determined under any other method that is reasonable (Reg. § 1.706-1(c)(2)(ii)).[20] The transfer of a partnership interest by gift does not close the partnership tax year with respect to the donor. However, the share of the partnership income up to the date of the gift is taxed to the donor (Reg. § 1.706-1(c)(5)).[21]

Changes in Partnership Interests During Tax Year. If there is a change in any partner's interest in the partnership (for instance, because of the retirement of a partner, entry of a new partner or simply a change in the partnership agreement), each remaining partner's distributive share must take into account the varying interests in the partnership tax year. Generally, this rule may be satisfied either by using an interim closing of the books or by prorating income, losses, etc., for the entire year on the basis of the number of days that the partner was a member of the partnership. However, special rules apply with respect to cash-method partnerships and tiered partnerships (Code Sec. 706(d)(2); Reg. § 1.706-1(c)(2)(ii)).[22]

If there is a change in any partner's interest in the partnership, the distributive shares of certain cash-method items are determined by assigning the appropriate portion of each item to each day to which it is attributable and then by allocating the daily portions among the partners in proportion to their interests in the partnership at the close of each day (Code Sec. 706(d); Reg. § 1.706-1(c)).[23] For this purpose, cash-method items are (1) interest, (2) taxes, (3) payments for services or for the use of property, and (4) any other item specified in the regulations. Cash-method items deductible or includible within the tax year but attributable to a time period before the beginning of the tax year (for example, payment during the tax year for services performed in the prior tax year) are assigned by Code Sec. 706(d)(2)(C) to the first day of the tax year. If persons to whom such items are allocable are no longer partners on the first day of the tax year, then their portion of the items must be capitalized by the partnership and allocated to the basis of partnership assets pursuant to Code Sec. 755.[24] Cash-method items attributable to periods following the close of the tax year (for example, properly deductible prepaid expenses) are assigned to the last day of the tax year.

In the case of changes in a partner's interest in an upper-tier partnership that has an ownership interest in a lower-tier partnership, each partner's distributive share of any items of the upper-tier partnership attributable to the lower-tier partnership is determined by (1) assigning the appropriate portion of each such item to the appropriate days of the upper-tier partnership's tax year on which the upper-tier partnership is a partner in the lower-tier partnership and (2) allocating the assigned portion among the partners in proportion to their interests in the upper-tier partnership as of the close of each day (Code Sec. 706(d)(3)).[25]

Partnership Audits

415. Administrative and Judicial Proceedings at Partnership Level. The determination of the tax treatment of partnership items is made at the partnership level in a single administrative partnership proceeding, rather than in separate proceedings with each partner. Special rules (the TEFRA rules) govern proceedings that must be conducted at the partnership level for the assessment and collection of tax deficiencies or for tax refunds arising out of the partners' distributive shares of income, deductions, credits, etc. (Code Secs. 6221-6233).[26] (Also see ¶ 482 and following for special rules applying to electing large partnerships.)

Notice of the beginning of administrative proceedings and the resulting final partnership administrative adjustment must be given to all partners (whose names and addresses are furnished to the IRS) except those with less than a one-percent interest in partnerships with more than 100 partners. However, a group of partners having an aggregate profits interest of five percent or more may request notice to be

---

Footnote references are to paragraphs of the 2002 Standard Federal Tax Reports.

[20] ¶ 25,161
[21] ¶ 25,161
[22] ¶ 25,160, ¶ 25,161
[23] ¶ 25,160
[24] ¶ 25,580
[25] ¶ 25,160
[26] ¶ 37,565—¶ 37,910

mailed to a designated partner (Code Sec. 6223).[27] Each partnership is supposed to name a "tax matters partner" who is to receive notice on behalf of small partners not entitled to notice and to keep all partners informed of all administrative and judicial proceedings at the partnership level (Code Sec. 6231).[28] Settlement agreements may be entered into between the tax matters partner and the IRS that bind the parties to the agreement and may extend to other partners who request to enter into consistent settlement agreements (Code Sec. 6224).[29] This rule has been applied even in cases where the designated tax matters partner had resigned from the partnership but had not formally resigned as tax matters partner (*Monetary II Ltd. Partnership*).[30]

Consistency Requirement. Each partner is required to treat partnership items on his return in a manner consistent with the treatment of such items on the partnership return. A partner may be penalized for intentional disregard of this requirement (Code Sec. 6222).[31] The consistency requirement may be waived if the partner files a statement (Form 8082) identifying the inconsistency or shows that it resulted from an incorrect schedule furnished by the partnership.

The IRS may apply the entity-level audit procedures when it appears from the return that such procedures should apply. The IRS's determination will stand even if it later proves to be erroneous (Code Sec. 6231(g)).[32]

Innocent Spouse Relief. Retroactive to partnership tax years beginning after September 3, 1982 (TEFRA), innocent spouse relief is available with respect to partnership-level proceedings (Code Sec. 6230).[33]

If the spouse of a partner in a TEFRA partnership asserts that the innocent spouse rules apply with respect to a liability attributable to any adjustment to a partnership item, then the spouse may file a request for an abatement of the assessment with the IRS. The spouse must file the request within 60 days after the notice of a computational adjustment has been mailed by the IRS. Upon receipt of the request, the IRS must abate the assessment. If the IRS chooses to reassess the abated tax, it then has 60 days after the date of the abatement in which to make any reassessment. In such a scenario, the regular deficiency procedures apply (Code Sec. 6230(a)(3)(A); Temporary Reg. § 301.6231(a)(12)-1T).[34]

If the taxpayer claiming innocent spouse relief files a Tax Court petition under Code Sec. 6213[35] with respect to the request for abatement, the Tax Court can determine only whether the innocent spouse requirements have in fact been satisfied. For purposes of this determination, the treatment of the TEFRA partnership items under the settlement, the final partnership administrative adjustment (FPAA) or the court decision that gave rise to the liability in question is conclusive (Code Sec. 6230(a)(3)(B)).[36]

Small Partnership Exception. The audit rules do not apply to partnerships with 10 or fewer partners if each partner is a natural person (other than a nonresident alien), a C corporation or an estate, and each partner's share of any partnership item is the same as his distributive share of every other partnership item. However, these small partnerships may elect to have the uniform audit rules apply (Code Sec. 6231(a)(1)(B)).[37] The partnership also can specially allocate items without jeopardizing its exception from the audit rules. Once a small partnership elects to have the audit rules apply, the election cannot be revoked without IRS consent (Code Sec. 6231(a)(1)(B)(ii)).[38]

Partnership Tax Year

416. Required Tax Year. Generally, a partnership cannot have a tax year other than its "majority-interest taxable year" (Code Sec. 706(b)).[39] This is the tax

---

Footnote references are to paragraphs of the 2002 Standard Federal Tax Reports.

[27] ¶ 37,590	[32] ¶ 37,770	[36] ¶ 37,750
[28] ¶ 37,770	[33] ¶ 37,750	[37] ¶ 37,770
[29] ¶ 37,640	[34] ¶ 37,750	[38] ¶ 37,770
[30] ¶ 37,749.10	[35] ¶ 37,545	[39] ¶ 25,160
[31] ¶ 37,570		

¶416

year that, on each "testing day," constitutes the tax year of one or more partners having an aggregate interest in partnership profits and capital of more than 50 percent. The testing day is the first day of the partnership's tax year (determined without regard to the majority interest rule). In general, a partnership that changes to a majority-interest tax year is not required to change to another tax year for the two tax years following the year of change.

If partners who own a majority interest have different tax years, then the tax year of the partnership must be the same as the tax year of all of the partnership's principal partners (partners who individually own five percent or more of the partnership's profits or capital). Partnerships that are unable to determine a tax year under either of the foregoing methods must adopt a tax year that results in the least aggregate deferral of income to the partners (Temporary Reg. § 1.706-1T).[40] A partnership may avoid the tax year rules set forth above if it can establish a business purpose for selecting a different tax year (Code Sec. 706(b)(1)(C); Temporary Reg. § 1.706-1T(b)).[41]

Code Sec. 444 Election. Certain partnerships are permitted to make an election under Code Sec. 444(a) to have a tax year other than the required tax year, which for most partnerships is a calendar year (Code Sec. 444).[42] For any tax year for which an election is made, a partnership generally must make a "required payment" that is intended to represent the tax on the income deferred through the use of a tax year other than a required year. The payment is due on May 15 of the calendar year following the calendar year in which the Code Sec. 444 election year begins (Code Sec. 7519; Temporary Reg. § 1.7519-2T(a)(4)(ii)).[43] See ¶ 1501.

Partnership Taxable Income

417. Partnership as Pass-Through Entity. While a partnership is not subject to tax, its "taxable income" is the key feature by which the partnership passes through its income or loss to partners (Code Sec. 701).[44] Each partner generally must account for his distributive share of partnership taxable income in computing his income tax. The partner's share of partnership tax items is reported to him by the partnership on Schedule K-1 of Form 1065. A partner's basis in his partnership interest is increased by his distributive share of partnership taxable income, while the partner's basis generally decreases by the amount distributed to him by the partnership. Thus, if a partnership distributes all its taxable income by the end of the partnership tax year, the basis of each partner's interest in the partnership will not change (Code Sec. 705 and Code Sec. 731(a)).[45]

The taxable income of a partnership is computed in the same manner as that of an individual except that the following are not allowed to a partnership: (1) the deduction for personal exemptions, (2) the deduction for foreign taxes, (3) the net operating loss deduction, (4) the deduction for charitable contributions, (5) individuals' itemized deductions (medical expenses, etc.) enumerated in Code Sec. 211— Code Sec. 219, (6) the capital loss carryover, and (7) the depletion deduction under Code Sec. 611 with respect to oil and gas wells (Code Sec. 703(a); Reg. § 1.703-1).[46] In addition, certain items of gain, loss, etc. (enumerated at ¶ 431) must be separately stated.

418. Anti-Abuse Regulations. Regulations give the IRS the power to recast transactions that attempt to use the partnership provisions for tax-avoidance purposes (Reg. § 1.701-2).[47] Under the rules, a partnership must be *bona fide* and each partnership transaction must be entered into for a substantial business purpose. The form of each transaction must be respected under substance-over-form rules. Finally, the tax consequences to each partner of partnership operations and transactions must accurately reflect the partners' economic agreement and clearly reflect each partner's income.

Footnote references are to paragraphs of the 2002 Standard Federal Tax Reports.
[40] ¶ 25,162
[41] ¶ 25,160, ¶ 25,162
[42] ¶ 20,600
[43] ¶ 42,770, ¶ 42,773
[44] ¶ 25,060
[45] ¶ 25,140, ¶ 25,320
[46] ¶ 25,100, ¶ 25,101
[47] ¶ 25,061B, ¶ 25,100, ¶ 25,101

¶418

Whether there is a "principal purpose" of "substantially" reducing the present value of the partners' aggregate tax liability is determined at the partnership level.

In abusive situations, the IRS can treat a partnership as the aggregate of its partners, in whole or in part, as appropriate to carry out the purpose of any Code or regulation provision. However, to the extent that a Code or regulation provision prescribes treatment of the partnership as an entity and the treatment and ultimate tax results are clearly contemplated by the provision, the IRS will not recast a transaction.

419. Elections by Partnerships. Most elections affecting the computation of income derived from a partnership must be made by the partnership. Thus, elections as to methods of accounting, methods of computing depreciation, the Code Sec. 179 expensing election, the election not to use the installment sales provision, the option to expense intangible drilling and development costs, etc., must be made by the partnership and must apply to all partners, insofar as the partnership transactions are concerned (Reg. § 1.703-1(b)).[48] In the case of an involuntary conversion of partnership property, the partnership also must purchase replacement property and elect nonrecognition of gain treatment (Rev. Rul. 66-191).[49]

Individual partners must make the elections to (1) use as a credit or as a deduction their distributive shares of foreign taxes of the partnership, (2) deduct or capitalize their shares of the partnership's mining exploration expenditures, and (3) reduce basis in connection with discharge of indebtedness under Code Sec. 108 (Code Sec. 703(b)).[50]

Regulations provide for an automatic six-month extension for making elections if the time for making the election also is the due date of the return for which the election is made (Reg. § 301.9100-1, Reg. § 301.9100-2, and Reg. § 301.9100-3).

421. Guaranteed Payments to Partners. Any fixed payments to partners for services or for the use of capital made without regard to partnership income are treated as though paid to a nonpartner for purposes of computing partnership gross income and business expense deductions (see ¶ 432). Thus, guaranteed payments are regarded as ordinary income to the recipient and are deductible by the partnership as ordinary and necessary business expenses (assuming they are, in fact, "ordinary and necessary" (see ¶ 902)) (Code Sec. 707(c); Reg. § 1.707-1(c)).[51] This rule applies only to the extent that the amounts paid are in fact "guaranteed payments" determined without regard to the income of the partnership (Code Sec. 707(c); Reg. § 1.707-4).[52] The partner must report the payments on his return for the tax year within or with which ends the partnership year in which the partnership deducted the payments as paid or accrued under its method of accounting.

> **Example 1.** In the AB partnership, Ann is the managing partner and is entitled to receive a fixed annual payment of $10,000 for her services, without regard to the income of the partnership. Her distributive share of partnership profit and loss is 10 percent. After deducting her guaranteed payment, the partnership has $30,000 ordinary income. Ann must include $13,000 ($10,000 guaranteed payment plus $3,000 distributive share) as ordinary income for her tax year within or with which the partnership tax year ends. If the partnership had shown a $10,000 loss after deduction of Ann's guaranteed payment, her guaranteed payment ($10,000) would be reported as income and her $1,000 distributive share of the loss, subject to the loss limitations of Code Sec. 704(d) (see ¶ 425), would be taken into account by her on her return.

If a partner is entitled to a minimum payment and the percentage of profits is less than the minimum payment, the guaranteed payment is the difference between the minimum payment and the distributive share of the profits determined before the deduction of the minimum payment (Reg. § 1.707-1(c)).[53] Only the amount of

Footnote references are to paragraphs of the 2002 Standard Federal Tax Reports.

¶419
48 ¶ 23,950.218, ¶ 25,101   50 ¶ 25,100   52 ¶ 25,180, ¶ 25,181C
49 ¶ 29,650.704   51 ¶ 25,180, ¶ 25,181 53 ¶ 25,181

the guaranteed payment may qualify as a deductible business expense of the partnership.

Example 2. The AB partnership agreement provides that Ann is to receive 30% of partnership income before taking into account any guaranteed payments, but not less than $10,000. The income of the partnership is $60,000, and Ann is entitled to $18,000 (30% of $60,000) as her distributive share. Because her distributive share exceeds the minimum amount that was guaranteed, no part of the $18,000 is a guaranteed payment. If the partnership had income of only $20,000, Ann's distributive share would have been $6,000 (30% of $20,000), and the remaining $4,000 payable to Ann would have been a guaranteed payment.

A partner who receives a guaranteed salary payment is not regarded as an employee of the partnership for the purpose of withholding of income or Social Security taxes or for pension plans. The guaranteed salary is includible in self-employment income for the purpose of the self-employment tax along with the partner's share of ordinary income or loss of the partnership (Reg. § 1.707-1(c); Rev. Rul. 56-675).[54]

Fringe Benefits. The value of fringe benefits provided to a partner for services rendered in the capacity as a partner is generally treated as a guaranteed payment (Rev. Rul. 91-26).[55] As such, the value of the benefit is generally deductible by the partnership as an ordinary and necessary business expense; the value of the benefit is included in the partner's gross income, unless a Code provision allowing exclusion of the benefit specifically provides that the exclusion applies to partners.

Thus, a payment of premiums by a partnership for a partner's health or accident insurance is generally deductible by the partnership and included in the partner's gross income. As an alternative, a partnership may choose to account for premiums paid for a partner's insurance by reducing that partner's distributions; in this case the premiums are not deductible by the partnership and all partners' distributive shares are unaffected by payment of the premiums. For tax years beginning in 1999 through 2001, a partner is permitted to deduct 60 percent of the cost of the health insurance premiums paid on his behalf. These limits increase to 70 percent for 2002. For 2003 and thereafter, the rate is 100 percent of the cost (Code Sec. 162(l)).[56]

423. Net Operating Loss Deduction of Partners. The benefit of the net operating loss deduction (¶ 1173) is not allowed to the partnership but only to the partners. For purposes of determining his individual net operating loss, each partner takes into account his distributive share of income, gain, loss, deduction, or credit of the partnership as if each item were realized directly from the source from which realized by the partnership or incurred in the same manner as incurred by the partnership (Reg. § 1.702-2).[57]

Limitations on Partnership Loss Deductions

425. Loss Limited to Partner's Basis. The amount of partnership loss (including capital loss) that may be recognized by a partner is limited to the amount of the adjusted basis (before reduction by the current year's loss) of his interest in the partnership at the end of the partnership tax year in which the loss occurred. Any disallowed loss is carried forward to and may be deducted by the partner in subsequent partnership tax years (to the extent that his basis exceeds zero before deducting the loss) (Reg. § 1.704-1(d)).[58] Techniques that have been used to increase a partner's basis so that he can deduct losses that otherwise would be unavailable are: (1) making additional contributions to the capital of the partnership (¶ 443), (2) refraining from drawing salary or other distributions from the partnership (¶ 453),

---

Footnote references are to paragraphs of the 2002 Standard Federal Tax Reports.

[54] ¶ 25,181, ¶ 25,183.30   [56] ¶ 8500, ¶ 25,183.16   [58] ¶ 25,121
[55] ¶ 25,183.16   [57] ¶ 25,084

and (3) increasing the partner's share of partnership liabilities if this is permitted under the "substantial economic effect" rules (¶ 428).

426. Partners and the At-Risk Rules. The rules limiting a partner's deduction for any tax year to the amount he is at risk in the partnership for that year (¶ 2045) apply at the partner level, not the partnership level. A partner is not at risk for any portion of a partnership liability for which he has no personal liability. The at-risk loss limitation rules are applied before taking into account the basis limitation for partners' losses or computing any passive activity loss for the year (Code Sec. 465).[59]

Special Real Estate Exception. The at-risk rules generally apply to the holding of real property in the same manner as they apply to other activities. However, a special exception to the general rule that a taxpayer is not at risk for the amount of nonrecourse liabilities applies to the holding of real estate. A taxpayer is at risk with respect to qualified nonrecourse financing that is secured by the real property used in the activity of holding real estate. Generally, qualified nonrecourse financing is nonconvertible financing provided by a person actively and regularly engaged in the business of lending money for which no one is personally liable and that is secured by real estate used in the activity. Thus, a loan provided by such entities as banks, credit unions and insurance companies is considered qualified nonrecourse financing if the real property secures the debt (Code Sec.465(b)(6)).[60]

427. Partnerships and the Passive Activity Loss Rules. The passive activity loss limitations (see ¶ 2053) apply at the partner level to each partner's share of any loss or credit attributable to a passive activity of the partnership (Code Sec. 469).[61] A partnership may engage in both passive and nonpassive activities. For example, a partnership may engage in business that is a passive activity of its limited partners (who normally do not participate in the management of a limited partnership), and it also may have investment assets that produce portfolio income (not a passive activity). Thus, a partner who disposes of his interest in a partnership must allocate any gain or loss among the various activities of the partnership in order to determine the amount that is passive gain or loss and the amount that is nonpassive gain or loss. In general, the allocation is made in accordance with the relative value of the partnership's assets.

To allow a partner to make these calculations, a partnership must report separately a partner's share of income or losses and credits from each (1) trade or business activity, (2) rental real estate activity, and (3) rental activity other than rental real estate. A partnership's portfolio income, which is excluded from passive income, must also be separately reported (Code Sec. 703).[62]

Generally, a passive activity of a partner is (1) a trade or business activity in which the partner does not materially participate or (2) any rental activity. Except as provided (Temporary Reg. § 1.469-5T(e)(2)),[63] an interest in an activity as a limited partner in a limited partnership is not one in which the partner materially participates. If a partnership reports amounts from more than one activity on a partner's Schedule K-1 and one or more of the activities is passive to the partner, the partnership must attach a statement detailing the income, losses, deductions, and credits from each passive activity and the line of Schedule K-1 on which that amount is included.

Partner's Distributive Share of Partnership Items

428. Allocations Under Partnership Agreement Must Have Substantial Economic Effect. A partner's distributive share of income, gain, loss, deduction or credit is generally determined by the partnership agreement. Allocations of any partnership item under the partnership agreement must have substantial economic effect if they are to be recognized for Code purposes. If a partnership agreement

---

Footnote references are to paragraphs of the 2002 Standard Federal Tax Reports.

¶ 426
[59] ¶ 21,850
[60] ¶ 21,850
[61] ¶ 21,960
[62] ¶ 25,100
[63] ¶ 21,965

does not provide for the allocation of partnership items or if partnership allocations lack substantial economic effect, the partner's distributive share is determined in accordance with his interest in the partnership (Code Sec. 704; Reg. § 1.704-1(b)).[64]

Economic Effect. Allocations have economic effect if they are consistent with the underlying economic arrangement of the partners. For instance, a limited partner who has no risk under the partnership agreement other than his initial capital contribution generally may not be allocated losses attributable to a partnership recourse liability to the extent such losses exceed his capital contribution. These "recourse" losses generally must be allocated to the partners (usually the general partners) who bear the ultimate burden of discharging the partnership's liability. A partnership's "nonrecourse deductions"—those attributable to those liabilities of the partnership for which no partner bears personal liability (for example, a mortgage secured only by a building and the land on which it is located)—are deemed to lack economic effect and, consequently, must be allocated according to the partners' interests in the partnership (Reg. § 1.704-2).[65] See ¶ 448 for a discussion of the allocation of tax basis with respect to recourse and nonrecourse liabilities.

Partnership allocations may be deemed to have substantial economic effect if a set of complicated *optional* safe harbor provisions are met. Generally, to satisfy the safe harbor, a partnership must maintain its "book" capital accounts as set forth by Reg. § 1.704-1 and make tax allocations consistent with the capital accounts. A second safe harbor set forth in Reg. § 1.704-2 applies to the allocation of nonrecourse deductions.

Substantiality. The economic effect of an allocation generally is substantial if there is a reasonable possibility that the allocation will substantially affect the dollar amounts to be received by the partners from the partnership, independent of tax consequences (Reg. § 1.704-1(b)(2)(iii)).[66]

Contributed Property. Income, gain, loss, and deductions attributable to property contributed to a partnership by a partner must be allocated among the partners to take into account the variation between the property's fair market value and its basis to the partnership at the time of contribution. (The partnership's basis in the contributed property at the time of contribution in exchange for a partnership interest is the basis of the property in the hands of the contributing partner.) The potential gain or loss ("built-in gain or loss") with respect to the contributed property must be allocated to the contributing partner. A similar rule applies to contributions by cash-method partners of accounts payable and other accrued but unpaid items (Code Sec. 704(c)).[67] The distribution of built-in gain or loss property within seven years of its contribution to the partnership may result in the recognition of gain or loss to the contributing partner if distributed to the other partners (see ¶ 453). For contributions of property made after June 8, 1997, the distribution period is seven years from the date of contribution. For contributions of property made before June 9, 1997, the distribution period is five years.

430. Disproportionate Distributions. The disproportionate distribution rules apply if an actual or constructive distribution to a partner changes his proportionate interest in the partnership's unrealized receivables or inventory. The purpose of these rules is to prevent conversion of ordinary income to capital gain on the distribution or a change in share of unrealized receivables or substantially appreciated inventory.

A disproportionate distribution is treated as a sale or exchange of the receivables or inventory items from the partnership to the partner (Code Sec. 751(b)).[68] This results in ordinary income rather than capital gain. Under Code Sec. 751(f), these rules cannot be avoided through the use of tiered partnerships. Sale or exchange treatment does not apply to a distribution of property that the distributee contributed to the partnership or to payments to a retiring partner or a successor in interest of a deceased partner.

Footnote references are to paragraphs of the 2002 Standard Federal Tax Reports.
[64] ¶ 25,120, ¶ 25,121   [66] ¶ 25,121   [68] ¶ 25,500
[65] ¶ 25,130   [67] ¶ 25,120

Although the "substantially appreciated inventory" test was changed to apply to all appreciated inventory in the case of a sale or exchange of a partnership interest (see ¶ 434), it remains in effect for disproportionate distributions from a partnership to its partners. Inventory is considered to be "substantially appreciated" if its fair market value exceeds the partnership's basis in the property by 120 percent or more. The inventory need not appreciate in value after the partnership acquired it to satisfy the 120-percent test.

431. Separate Reporting of Partnership Items. In determining tax, each partner must account separately for his distributive share of the following partnership items (Code Sec. 702):[69] (1) short-term capital gains and losses, (2) long-term capital gains and losses, (3) gains and losses from sales or exchanges of property used in a trade or business or subject to involuntary conversion (¶ 1747), (4) charitable contributions (¶ 1061), (5) dividends for which there is a dividends-received deduction (¶ 237), (6) taxes paid or accrued to foreign countries and to U.S. possessions (¶ 2475), (7) taxable income or loss, exclusive of items requiring separate computation, and (8) other items required to be stated separately either by Reg. § 1.702-1 [70] or because separate statement could affect the income tax liability of any partner. These include the following: recovery of bad debts, prior taxes, and delinquency amounts; gains and losses from wagering transactions (¶ 787); soil and water conservation expenditures (¶ 982); deductible investment expenses (¶ 1085); medical and dental expenses (¶ 1015); alimony payments (¶ 771); amounts paid to cooperative housing corporations (¶ 1040); intangible drilling and development costs (¶ 989); alternative minimum tax adjustments and tax preference items (¶ 1425, ¶ 1430); investment tax credit recapture (¶ 1364); recapture of mining exploration expenditures (¶ 987); information necessary for partners to compute oil and gas depletion allowances (¶ 1289); cost of recovery property being currently expensed (¶ 1208); the work opportunity tax credit (¶ 1342); alcohol fuels credit (¶ 1326); net earnings from self-employment (¶ 2670); investment interest (¶ 1094); income or loss to the partnership on certain distributions of unrealized receivables and inventory items to a partner (¶ 453); any items subject to a special allocation under the partnership agreement (¶ 428); and contributions (and the deductions for contributions) made on a partner's behalf to qualified retirement plans (¶ 2113).

In general, the need for a separate statement of various partnership items can be seen in the separate treatment of these items on Form 1065 and Schedules K and K-1.

Partnerships that regularly carry on a trade or business are required to furnish to tax-exempt partners a separate statement of items of unrelated business taxable income (Code Sec. 6031(d)).[71]

432. Members' Dealings with Own Partnership. A partner who engages in a transaction with the partnership, other than in his capacity as a partner, is generally treated as if he were a nonpartner (Code Sec. 707(a)).[72] Moreover, transactions may be deemed to be between the partnership and a nonpartner if direct or indirect allocations and distributions to a partner are related to the partner's performance of services for, or to the transfer of property to, the partnership and, when viewed together, are properly characterized as a payment to the partner acting other than in his capacity as a member of the partnership (Code Sec. 707(a)(2)(A)).[73] This rule prevents the use of disguised payments to circumvent the requirement that a partnership capitalize certain expenses (such as syndication and organization expenses).

Disguised Sales. Another rule is intended to prevent partners from disguising a sale or exchange of property as a contribution to the partnership. Under the "disguised sale" rule, if a partner directly or indirectly transfers money or other property to a partnership and there is a related direct or indirect transfer of money or property to that partner (or another partner) from the partnership, and the

---

Footnote references are to paragraphs of the 2002 Standard Federal Tax Reports.

[69] ¶ 25,080	[71] ¶ 35,381	[73] ¶ 25,180
[70] ¶ 25,081	[72] ¶ 25,180	

transfers, when viewed together, are properly characterized as a sale or exchange of the property, the selling partner is required to recognize gain or loss on the disguised sale (Code Sec. 707(a)(2)(B)).[74]

Whether a transfer constitutes a disguised sale is based on facts and circumstances. However, contributions and distributions made within a two-year period are presumed to be a sale, while such transactions occurring more than two years apart are presumed not to be a sale (Reg. § 1.707-3(c) and (d)).[75] Certain key exceptions to these presumptions are enumerated for guaranteed payments for capital, reasonable preferred returns, and operating cash flow distributions (Reg. § 1.707-4).[76]

Transactions Between Controlled Partnerships. Special rules also apply to controlled partnerships. Loss is not allowed from a sale or exchange of property (other than an interest in the partnership) between a partnership and a person whose interest in the partnership's capital *or* profits is more than 50 percent. Loss is also not allowed if the sale or exchange is between two partnerships in which the same persons own more than 50 percent of the capital or profits interests (Code Sec. 707(b)(1)).[77] In either case, if one of the purchasers or transferees realizes gain on a later sale, the gain is taxable only to the extent it exceeds the amount of the disallowed loss attributable to the property sold. Gain recognized on transactions involving controlled partnerships are treated as ordinary income if the property sold or exchanged is not a capital asset in the hands of the transferee (Code Sec. 707(b)(2)).[78]

Code Sec. 267(a)(1) disallows deductions for losses from the sale or exchange of property between persons who are in one of the twelve relationships ("related taxpayers") described in Code Sec. 267(b), including a partnership and a corporation controlled by the same persons. See ¶ 1717. Although this loss-denial rule does not apply to a transaction between a partnership and a partner, it does apply to a transaction between a partnership and a person who has a relationship with a partner that is otherwise specified in Code Sec. 267(b) (Reg. § 1.267(b)-1(b)).[79] Under Code Sec. 267(a)(2), accrued interest and expense deductions are not deductible until paid if the amount giving rise to the deduction is owed to a related cash-method taxpayer. For purposes of this rule, a partnership and persons holding interests in the partnership (actually or constructively) or persons related (under Code Sec. 267(b) or 707(b)(1)) to actual or constructive partners are treated as related persons (Code Sec. 267(e)(1)).[80] See ¶ 905 and ¶ 1527.

Sale and Liquidation of Partner's Interest

434. Purchase or Sale of a Partnership Interest. The sale or exchange of a partnership interest generally is treated as the sale of a single capital asset rather than a sale of each of the underlying partnership properties (Code Sec. 741).[81] The amount of gain or loss is based on the partner's basis in his partnership interest and the amount realized on the sale (Code Sec. 721).[82] (The sale of a partnership interest to a partner or to a nonpartner should be distinguished from the redemption of a partner's interest by the partnership. Redemptions are discussed at ¶ 435.)

Despite the general rule that the gain or loss on the sale of a partnership interest is a capital gain or loss, a partner may recognize ordinary income or loss under the constructive sale rules if he receives a disproportionate distribution of partnership unrealized receivables or inventory (see ¶ 430).

If a partner abandons or forfeits his partnership interest, he recognizes a loss in the amount of his basis in his partnership interest. If the partnership has liabilities, the abandoning partner is deemed to have received a distribution from the partnership when he is relieved of the liabilities. In such a case, the partner's loss is his basis in his interest less any liabilities of which he is relieved. An abandonment of a partnership interest, if there are no partnership liabilities from which the partner is

---

[74] ¶ 25,180	[77] ¶ 25,180	[80] ¶ 14,150
[75] ¶ 25,181B	[78] ¶ 25,180	[81] ¶ 25,440
[76] ¶ 25,181C	[79] ¶ 14,153	[82] ¶ 25,240

relieved, results in an ordinary loss because no sale or exchange has taken place (*P.B. Citron; G.G. Gannon; P. Hutchinson*).[83] If there are partnership liabilities of which the abandoning partner is relieved, the resulting gain or loss is a capital gain or loss (*A.O. Stilwell*).[84] Even a *de minimis* actual or deemed distribution generally results in a capital loss treatment to the partner. Capital loss is also mandated if the transaction is, in substance, a sale or exchange (Rev. Rul. 93-80).[85]

Unrealized Receivables and Inventory. A partner recognizes ordinary income or loss on any portion of a sale of a partnership interest that is attributable to his share of the partnership's unrealized receivables and inventory (Code Sec. 751(a)).[86] The gain is measured by the portion of the selling price attributable to unrealized receivables and inventory and the partner's basis in these assets. The partner's basis is the basis the partner's share of partnership unrealized receivables and inventory would have if these assets were distributed to him in a current distribution (Reg. § 1.751-1(a)(2)).[87] Capital gain or loss is determined by subtracting his remaining basis from the rest of the amount realized (Reg. § 1.741-1(a)).[88]

Note, the former rules that recognized income attributable to "substantially appreciated inventory" are no longer applicable with regard to the purchase and sale of a partnership interest. However, they do still apply if a partnership makes disproportionate distributions of partnership property. See ¶ 430.

435. Partnership Interest Redeemed by Partnership. If a partner's interest is liquidated solely through a distribution of partnership property other than money, no gain is recognized. The partner's basis in his partnership interest is transferred to the distributed assets, and any gain is recognized when the assets are disposed of (Code Sec. 731(a)).[89]

If a partner receives money as all or part of his liquidating distribution, he recognizes gain to the extent that the value of the cash or marketable securities exceeds his basis in the partnership interest (Code Sec. 732(b)).[90] A partner recognizes loss if no property other than money, unrealized receivables and inventory items are distributed to him, and his basis in his partnership interest exceeds the amount of money plus the basis of the distributed receivables and inventory (Code Sec. 731(a)).[91] However, if the partner is relieved of any or all of his share of partnership liabilities, the relief from liability is treated the same as a cash distribution (Reg. § 1.731-1(a)(1)).[92]

If a partner receives cash and unrealized receivables and inventory for his partnership interest, loss can be recognized in the amount by which the basis in the partnership interest exceeds the amount of money, plus the basis of the distributed receivables and inventory (Code Sec. 731(a)(2)).[93]

> **Example.** Martin has an adjusted basis in his partnership interest of $10,000. He retires from the partnership and receives as a distribution in liquidation of his interest his share of partnership property. This share is $5,000 cash and inventory with a basis to him of $3,000. Martin can recognize a loss of $2,000, his basis minus the money received and his basis in the inventory distributed to him ($10,000 − ($5,000 + $3,000) = $2,000).

If a partner receives money or property in exchange for any part of his partnership interest, the amount attributable to the partner's share of the partnership's unrealized receivables or inventory items results in ordinary income or loss. This treatment applies to the unrealized receivables portion of the payments to a retiring partner or successor in interest of a deceased partner only if that part is not treated as paid in exchange for partnership property. The rationale behind this rule is that the inventory or the accounts receivable would give rise to ordinary income

---

Footnote references are to paragraphs of the 2002 Standard Federal Tax Reports.

[83] ¶ 25,442.12,	[86] ¶ 25,500	[90] ¶ 25,340
¶ 25,422.545,	[87] ¶ 25,501	[91] ¶ 25,320
¶ 25,422.545	[88] ¶ 25,441	[92] ¶ 25,321
[84] ¶ 25,422.545	[89] ¶ 25,320	[93] ¶ 25,320
[85] ¶ 25,442.12		

¶ 435

had the partnership interest not been sold. However, if the partner does not sell the distributed inventory items within five years from the date of distribution, the gain can be recognized as a capital gain (Code Sec. 735(a)(2)).[94] For purposes of this rule, the term "inventory" does not include real estate or depreciable trade or business property (Code Sec. 735(c)(1)).[95] (Compare the general definition of "inventory" at ¶ 436, below.)

For exchanges of partnership interests involving unrealized receivables or inventory, the partnership must file an information return describing the exchange and furnish statements to each party (Reg. § 1.6050K-1).[96] (See also ¶ 453, "Distributions of Partnership Assets.")

436. "Unrealized Receivables" and "Inventory Items" Defined. The term "unrealized receivables" includes any rights to income that have not been included in gross income under the method of accounting employed by the partnership (Reg. § 1.751-1(c)).[97] For the most part, this classification relates to cash-method partnerships that have acquired a contractual or legal right to income for goods or services. In the usual case, the term does not apply to an accrual-method partnership because it has already included unrealized receivables in gross income.

The term "unrealized receivables" also includes certain property to the extent of the amount of gain that would have been realized and treated as ordinary income by the partnership if it had sold the property at its fair market value at the time of the sale or exchange of the partnership interest being considered (Reg. § 1.751-1(d)(2)).[98]

The term "inventory items" is broader than the term itself might suggest. It includes other assets that would not be treated as capital assets or Sec. 1231 assets (property used in a trade or business or involuntary conversion property) if they were sold by the partnership (or by the partner, if he had held them). Thus, the term might include a copyright, literary composition, etc.

Distributions of inventory made in exchange for all or a part of a partner's interest in other partnership property, including money, are governed by the "substantially appreciated" rule. Thus, gain from such distributions is taxed as ordinary income if the fair market value exceeds 120 percent of the partnership's adjusted basis of the inventory. The 120-percent test is applied to the total of *all* partnership inventory items, not to specific items or groups of items (Reg. § 1.751-1(d)).[99] Gains from such distributions are taxed as ordinary income if the fair market value exceeds 120 percent of the partnership's adjusted basis in the inventory.

438. Retiring Partner's or Successor's Shares. Payments made in liquidation of the interest of a retiring or deceased partner are considered distributions by the partnership to the extent that the payments are in exchange for the partner's interest in partnership property (Code Sec. 736(b) and Code Sec. 761(d)).[100] This provision does not apply if the estate or other successor in interest of a deceased partner continues as a partner in its own right under local law. In addition, it applies only to payments made by the partnership and not to transactions, such as the sale of a partnership interest, between the partners (Reg. § 1.736-1(a)(1)).[101]

Under Code Sec. 731, distributions are generally nontaxable except to the extent that money distributed exceeds the partner's adjusted basis for his partnership interest (see ¶ 453); the excess is treated as capital gain. However, all gain relating to inventory is treated as being from the sale of a noncapital asset (Code Sec. 751(b)).[102] The partners' valuation in an arm's-length agreement of a retiring or deceased partner's interest in partnership property is presumptively correct (Reg. § 1.736-1(b)(1)).[103]

Footnote references are to paragraphs of the 2002 Standard Federal Tax Reports.

[94] ¶ 25,400	[98] ¶ 25,501	[101] ¶ 25,421
[95] ¶ 25,400	[99] ¶ 25,501	[102] ¶ 25,500
[96] ¶ 36,241	[100] ¶ 25,420, ¶ 25,600	[103] ¶ 25,421
[97] ¶ 25,501		

Payments for unrealized receivables and goodwill are treated as distributive shares of partnership income or as guaranteed payments if capital is not a material income producing factor and the retiring or deceased partner was a general partner.[104] Such payments are deductible by the partnership. If these two requirements are not met, payments for goodwill are treated as payments for partnership property and do not create a deduction for the partnership. However, payments for goodwill can be treated as payments for property if:[105]

(1) goodwill was originally purchased by the partnership or otherwise acquired in a transaction resulting in a cash basis to the partnership, *or*

(2) the partnership agreement calls for a reasonable payment for goodwill.

Such payments result in capital gain or loss to the extent of the partnership's basis in the goodwill. In fixing the amount attributable to goodwill, an amount arrived at under an arm's-length agreement generally is accepted by the IRS. A formula approach involving the capitalization or earnings in excess of a fair market rate or return on the partnership's net tangible assets may be used, but only where there is no better basis for making such a determination (Rev. Rul. 68-609).[106]

These excluded amounts and other payments not considered made for an interest in the partnership property are treated as either distributive shares of partnership income or as guaranteed payments (Code Sec. 736(a)).[107] If the payments are determined by reference to partnership income, they are taxable as a distributive share to the recipient; if not, they are treated as "guaranteed payments" (¶ 421). Thus, if the payments consist of a percentage of partnership profits, they reduce the distributive shares of income of the remaining partners. If they are guaranteed payments, the effect is the same because they are deductible as business expenses in determining partnership taxable income. In either event, the payments are treated as ordinary income in the hands of the recipient partner.

Example 1. Partnership ABC is a personal service partnership and its balance sheet is as follows:

Assets			Liabilities and Capital		
	Adjusted basis	Market value		Adjusted basis	Market value
Cash	$13,000	$13,000	Liabilities.....	$ 3,000	$ 3,000
Accounts re-			Capital:		
ceivable	0	30,000	A	10,000	21,000
Capital and Sec.			B	10,000	21,000
1231 assets ..	20,000	23,000	C	10,000	21,000
Total.....	$33,000	$66,000	Total......	$ 33,000	$66,000

General Partner A retires from the partnership in accordance with an agreement whereby his share of liabilities (⅓ of $3,000) is assumed. In addition, he is to receive $9,000 in the year of retirement plus $10,000 in each of the two succeeding years, a total of $30,000 (including his $1,000 share of liabilities), for his partnership interest. The value of A's interest in the partnership's section 736(b) property is $12,000 (one-third of $36,000, the sum of $13,000 cash and $23,000, the fair market value of Sec. 1231 assets). The accounts receivable are not included in A's interest in partnership property because A is a general partner in a partnership in which capital is not a material income-producing factor. Assuming that the basis of A's interest is $11,000 ($10,000, the basis of his capital investment, plus $1,000, his share of partnership liabilities), he will realize a capital gain of $1,000 on the sale of his interest in partnership property. The $18,000 balance to be received by him will be treated as guaranteed payments taxable to A as ordinary income.

Footnote references are to paragraphs of the 2002 Standard Federal Tax Reports.

[104] ¶ 25,420   [106] ¶ 25,422.04   [107] ¶ 25,420
[105] ¶ 25,422.04

¶ 438

The $10,000 that A receives in each of the three years would ordinarily be allocated as follows: $4,000 as payments for A's interest in section 736(b) property ($12,000/$30,000 × $10,000) and the balance of $6,000 as guaranteed payments. While the $1,000 capital gain is normally recognized in the first year, A may elect to prorate the gain over the three-year period.

Example 2. Assume the same facts as in Example 1, above, except that the agreement provides for payments to A for three years of a percentage of annual income instead of a fixed amount. In such case, all payments received by A will be treated as payments for A's interest in partnership property, until he has received $12,000. Thereafter, the payments will be treated as a distributive share of partnership income to A (Reg. § 1.736-1(b)(7)).[108]

For income tax purposes, a retired partner or a deceased partner's successor is treated as a partner until his interest has been completely liquidated (Reg. § 1.736-1(a)(6)).[109]

440. Partner Receiving Income "In Respect of a Decedent." All payments to the successor of a deceased partner under Code Sec. 736(a), relating to payments made in liquidation of a deceased partner's interest and considered as a distributive share or guaranteed payment (see ¶ 438), are income "in respect of a decedent" (Code Sec. 753).[110] Under Code Sec. 691 the payments are taxed to the recipient when received to the extent that they are not properly includible in the short tax year ending with the decedent's death.

The estate or heir of a deceased partner is also treated as receiving income in respect of a decedent to the extent that amounts are received from an outsider in exchange for rights to future payments by the partnership representing distributive shares or guaranteed payments (Reg. § 1.753-1(a)).[111]

Partnership Contributions and Basis

443. Contribution to Partnership. No gain or loss is recognized, either by the partnership or by any of its partners, upon a contribution of property to the partnership in exchange for a partnership interest (Code Sec. 721(a)).[112] This is true whether the contribution is made to an existing partnership or to a newly formed partnership (Reg. § 1.721-1).[113] However, a partner must recognize any gain realized on the transfer of appreciated property to a partnership that would be treated as an investment company if the partnership were incorporated (Code Sec. 707(c) and Code Sec. 721(b)).[114] Further, the value of a capital interest in a partnership that is transferred to a partner in exchange for his services is taxable to him as ordinary income, provided that the interest is not subject to a substantial risk of forfeiture (see ¶ 1933) (Reg. § 1.721-1(b)).

The receipt of a profits interest (as opposed to a capital interest) in exchange for services rendered is not taxable as ordinary income (Rev. Proc. 93-27).[115]

The basis of a partner's interest acquired in exchange for his contribution to the partnership is the amount of the money contributed plus the adjusted basis to the contributing partner of any property contributed (Code Sec. 722).[116] If a partner receives a partnership interest as compensation for services rendered or to be rendered, resulting in taxable income to the incoming partner, that income is added to the basis of his interest (Reg. § 1.722-1).[117] If the contributed property is subject to debt or if liabilities of the partner are assumed by the partnership, the basis of the contributing partner's interest is reduced by the portion of the indebtedness assumed by the other partners. Such assumption of the partner's debt by others is

---

Footnote references are to paragraphs of the 2002 Standard Federal Tax Reports.

[108] ¶ 25,421	[112] ¶ 25,240	[115] ¶ 25,243.12
[109] ¶ 25,421	[113] ¶ 25,241	[116] ¶ 25,260
[110] ¶ 25,540	[114] ¶ 25,180, ¶ 25,240	[117] ¶ 25,261
[111] ¶ 25,541		

¶443

treated as a distribution of money to him and as a contribution of money by those assuming the debt (Code Sec. 752).[118] See ¶ 447.

The adjusted basis to the partnership of property contributed by a partner is the adjusted basis of such property in the hands of the contributing partner at the time of the contribution and any gain he recognized on the transfer to the partnership under Code Sec. 721(b) (Code Sec. 723).[119] However, it has been held that the basis of a nonbusiness asset (for example, a personal automobile) converted to a business asset upon contribution to a partnership was its fair market value at the time of contribution (*L.Y.S. Au*).[120] The holding period of a contributed asset includes the period during which it was held by the contributing partner (Reg. § 1.723-1).[121]

Under Code Sec. 724,[122] unrealized receivables and inventory items contributed by the partner to the partnership retain their ordinary income character in the hands of the partnership. That is to say, unrealized receivables remain ordinary income property up to the time of disposal by the partnership and inventory items remain ordinary income property for the five-year period beginning on the date of contribution (Code Sec. 735(a)).[123] In addition, a partner's contribution of property with a built-in capital loss (when the fair market value of the property is less than its adjusted basis) results in retention of the property's capital loss status in the hands of the partnership to the extent of built-in loss for the five-year period beginning on the date of contribution.

To prevent avoidance of these rules through the partnership's exchange of contributed unrealized receivables, inventory items, or capital loss property in a nonrecognition transaction (or series of transactions), the rule applies to any substituted basis property resulting from the exchange. It does not apply, however, to any stock in a C corporation received in a Code Sec. 351 exchange (Code Sec. 735).[124]

445. Increases and Decreases in Basis of Partner's Interest. The basis of a partner's interest is *increased* by his distributive share of partnership taxable income, the partnership's tax-exempt income, and the excess of the partnership deductions for depletion over the basis to the partnership of the depletable property. The basis of the partner's interest is *decreased* (but not below zero) by distributions to him from the partnership (applying the rules at ¶ 453) and by the sum of his share of partnership losses, his share of partnership expenditures not deductible in computing its taxable income and not chargeable to capital account, and his depletion deduction for oil and gas wells (Code Sec. 705(a)).[125] Distributions are to be taken into account before losses in adjusting the partner's interest basis (Rev. Rul. 66-94).[126]

> **Example.** Partner A of ABC partnership has an $8,000 basis for her partnership interest. During the tax year, she receives cash distributions of $5,000, and her share of the partnership's losses is $4,000. Her interest is adjusted as follows:
>
> | | | |
> |---|---:|---:|
> | Basis at beginning of year | . $8,000 | |
> | Less cash distributions | 5,000 | $3,000 |
> | Less share of losses ($4,000) but only to the extent that the basis is not reduced below zero | | 3,000 |
> | Adjusted basis for interest | | 0 |

Because basis is decreased by distributions received before reduction by A's share of partnership losses, no gain is recognized under Code Sec. 731 on the cash distribution. However, $1,000 of A's share of partnership loss is disallowed and carried forward to subsequent tax years (see ¶ 425).

Footnote references are to paragraphs of the 2002 Standard Federal Tax Reports.

¶ 445

[118] ¶ 25,520	[121] ¶ 25,281	[124] ¶ 25,400
[119] ¶ 25,280	[122] ¶ 25,300	[125] ¶ 25,140
[120] ¶ 25,282.02	[123] ¶ 25,400	[126] ¶ 25,144.12

Bases of partnership interests may also be determined by reference to proportionate shares of the adjusted basis of partnership property that would be distributable if the partnership were to be terminated. This alternative rule is available only in limited circumstances if a partner cannot practicably apply the general rule or when the IRS approves (Code Sec. 705(b); Reg. § 1.705-1(b)).[127]

For purposes of determining a partner's basis in his partnership interest or for determining gain or loss on a distribution, advances or drawings of money or property against a partner's distributive share of income are treated as current distributions made on the last day of the partnership's tax year (Reg. § 1.731-1(a)(1)(ii)).[128] Money received by a partner under an obligation to repay the partnership is not a distribution but is a loan that is treated as a transaction between the partnership and a nonpartner (Reg. § 1.707-1(a) and Reg. § 1.731-1(c)(2)).[129]

447. Liabilities Treated as Distributions or Contributions. Any increase in a partner's share of partnership liabilities, including a partner's assumption of partnership liabilities or receipt of partnership property subject to a liability (limited to the fair market value of the encumbered property), is treated as a contribution of money that increases a partner's basis in his interest (Code Sec. 722 and Code Sec. 752(a)).[130] A decrease in a partner's share of partnership liabilities is treated as a distribution of money by the partnership, which decreases the distributee partner's basis in his partnership interest (but not below zero) (Code Sec. 733 and Code Sec. 752(b)).[131] When a partner's basis has been reduced to zero, such "deemed distributions" can result in a taxable gain. See ¶ 453.

448. Allocation of Liabilities Among Partners. Partners' shares of partnership liabilities (and corresponding allocations of basis) depend upon whether the liability is "recourse" or "nonrecourse." In addition, separate rules apply in the case of nonrecourse debts of the partnership if a partner is the lender or has guaranteed repayment of the debt.

Recourse Liabilities. Liabilities are recourse to the extent that a partner bears the economic risk of loss if the liability is not satisfied by the partnership. Recourse liabilities are allocated in accordance with the partners' economic risk of loss (Reg. § 1.752-2(a)).[132] As a general matter, economic risk of loss is borne by a partner to the extent that he must make a contribution to the partnership (including the obligation to restore a deficit capital account) or pay a creditor if all partnership assets, including money, were deemed worthless and all partnership liabilities were due and payable (Reg. § 1.752-2(b)(1)).[133] Thus, a limited partner cannot be allocated recourse liabilities in excess of his capital contribution and future contribution obligations unless he has agreed to restore any deficit in his capital account or to indemnify other partners for their obligations with respect to a liability. A partner does not bear the economic risk of loss if he is entitled to reimbursement (for example, through an indemnification agreement or a state law right to subrogation) from other partners or the partnership (Reg. § 1.752-2(b)(5)).[134] Recourse liabilities must be allocated to a partner if a related person bears the risk of loss for the liability (Reg. § 1.752-4(b)).[135]

Nonrecourse Liabilities. Nonrecourse liabilities are those for which no partner bears the economic risk of loss—for example, a mortgage on an office building that is secured only by a lien on the building and on the rents, but with no personal obligation to repay the loan on the part of any of the owners. Such liabilities are generally shared by the partners in a manner that correlates with their allocations of deductions attributable to such liabilities under Code Sec. 704(b). See ¶ 428. A partner's share of nonrecourse liabilities of a partnership equals the sum of: (1) the partner's share of partnership minimum gain, (2) the amount of any taxable gain under Code Sec. 704(c) that would be allocated to the partner if the partnership

---

Footnote references are to paragraphs of the 2002 Standard Federal Tax Reports.

[127] ¶ 25,140, ¶ 25,141   [130] ¶ 25,260, ¶ 25,520   [133] ¶ 25,523
[128] ¶ 25,321   [131] ¶ 25,360, ¶ 25,520   [134] ¶ 25,523
[129] ¶ 25,181, ¶ 25,321 [132] ¶ 25,523   [135] ¶ 25,525

¶ 448

disposed of all partnership property subject to one or more nonrecourse liabilities of the partnership in full satisfaction of the liabilities and no other consideration, and (3) the partner's share of the excess nonrecourse liabilities as determined in accordance with the partner's share of partnership profits (Reg. § 1.752-3(a)).[136]

Although excess nonrecourse liabilities are allocated in accordance with the partners' respective profits interests, the partnership agreement may state their profits interests for purposes of sharing nonrecourse liabilities, provided that the stated sharing ratios are reasonably consistent with the allocation of some significant item of partnership income or gain among the partners (Reg. § 1.752-3(a)(3)).[137] Because no partner bears the economic risk of loss for nonrecourse liabilities, limited partners may be allocated shares of such liabilities (and the basis in such liabilities) in amounts exceeding their total capital contribution obligations.

Partner Nonrecourse Loans and Guarantees. A partner who lends money to the partnership on a nonrecourse basis bears the economic risk of loss for the liability. Likewise, a partner who guarantees an otherwise nonrecourse liability bears the risk of loss to the extent of his guarantee (Reg. § 1.752-2(d)(2)).[138]

A loss incurred on the abandonment or worthlessness of a partnership interest qualifies as an ordinary loss if there is neither an actual nor a deemed distribution to the partner upon the abandonment or determination of worthlessness. However, even a *de minimis* actual or deemed distribution will generally result in capital loss treatment to the partner. Capital loss treatment is also mandated if the transaction is, in substance, a sale or exchange (Rev. Rul. 93-80).[139]

Distributions of Partnership Assets

453. Gain or Loss on Distribution. The income of a partnership is taxable to the partners in accordance with their distributive shares (see ¶ 428). It does not matter when or if the income is distributed to the partners. However, distributions to partners decrease the partners' bases for their partnership interests. (See ¶ 445.)

> **Example 1.** A partner contributes $100,000 to the capital of a partnership. During the first year, his share of the partnership taxable income is $25,000, but only $10,000 of this amount is actually distributed to him. The $25,000 taxable income increases his basis to $125,000, and the $10,000 distribution decreases it to $115,000.

No gain or loss is recognized by a partnership on a distribution of property to a partner, including money (Code Sec. 731(b)).

If a distribution of money exceeds a partner's basis for his interest, gain is recognized by the partner as though he had sold or exchanged his partnership interest (Code Sec. 731(a)).[140] This applies both to current distributions (that is, those not in liquidation of an entire interest) and to distributions in liquidation of a partner's entire interest in a partnership (Reg. § 1.731-1(a)).[141]

> **Example 2.** A purchased a partnership interest for $10,000. During the first year, A receives a cash distribution of $10,000 and a distribution of property with a fair market value of $3,000. He recognizes no gain on the distributions since the amount of money distributed does not exceed A's basis for his partnership interest ($10,000). If he had received a cash distribution of $13,000, a $3,000 gain would have been recognized.

Distribution of marketable securities generally is treated the same as a distribution of money. The securities are valued at their fair market value on the date of the distribution (Code Sec. 731(c); Reg. § 1.731-2).[142]

Gain is determined only by reference to *money* distributed. Generally, a partner recognizes no gain on a distribution of property (other than money) until he

---

Footnote references are to paragraphs of the 2002 Standard Federal Tax Reports.

[136] ¶ 25,524	[139] ¶ 9804.33	[141] ¶ 25,321
[137] ¶ 25,524	[140] ¶ 25,320	[142] ¶ 25,320, ¶ 25,321B
[138] ¶ 25,523		

sells or otherwise disposes of the distributed property. Thus, if the taxpayer in Example 2 had received property in kind rather than cash, no gain would have been realized (Reg. § 1.731-1(a)).[143]

However, a distribution of property encumbered by a liability may cause a partner's share of partnership liabilities to decrease, resulting in a "deemed distribution" of money to that partner (see ¶ 447). For instance, if a partner receives a distribution of property subject to secured liability, the liability becomes a personal liability of the distributee partner, and there is a decrease in the liabilities of all other partners who had been allocated a share of the liability (Code Sec. 752(b)).[144] These partners must decrease the bases in their partnership interests in the amount of their "deemed distributions" (but not below zero), and any amounts deemed distributed in excess of their respective bases are taxable as capital gain.

The nonrecognition rules of Code Sec. 731 may not apply if, within "a short period" before or after property is contributed to a partnership, there is a distribution of either (1) other partnership property to the contributing partner or (2) the contributed property to another partner. If the distribution was made in order to effect an exchange of property between the partnership and a partner or between two or more partners, then the transaction will be treated as an exchange, and the "disguised sale" rules (¶ 432) may apply (Code Sec. 707(a)(2)(B); Reg. § 1.731-1(c)(3)).[145] Under Reg. § 1.707-3(c), there is a presumption that distributions made within two years of a contribution are made as part of a sale arrangement. However, the resumption can be rebutted if the facts and circumstances clearly establish that there is no sale (Reg. § 1.707-4).[146]

Loss is recognized only if the distribution terminates the partner's interest—and then only if the distribution is limited to money, unrealized receivables, or inventory items (¶ 436). The amount of the recognized loss is the excess of the adjusted basis of the partner's interest over the sum of any money distributed and the basis to him (which is ordinarily the same as the basis to the partnership (see ¶ 456)) of any unrealized receivables or inventory items (Code Sec. 731(a)(2)).[147]

> **Example 3.** A partner whose basis for his partnership interest is $10,000 retires from the partnership, receiving $5,000 in cash and inventory items having a basis to the partnership of $3,000. The taxpayer has a capital loss of $2,000.

These provisions do not apply to the extent that payments are made in liquidation to a retiring or deceased partner and are treated as a distributive share or guaranteed payment (¶ 438), to a distribution for unrealized receivables or appreciated inventory items (¶ 436) (Code Sec. 731(d)), or if the rules governing precontribution gain (¶ 454) are called into play.[148]

454. Property Distribution Within Certain Periods of Contribution. A partner who contributes property may have to recognize gain or loss if the contributed property is distributed to another partner within five years of the contribution (for property contributed before June 9, 1997) or within seven years (for property contributed after June 8, 1997) (Code Sec. 704(c)).[149] Property contributed pursuant to a written binding contract in effect on June 8, 1997, and in effect at all times until the contribution is made is treated under the old five-year rule. The gain or loss recognized under this rule is limited to the difference between the property's tax basis and its fair market value at the time of contribution. Upon distribution of the property within the five-year period, the "precontribution" gain or loss recognized is equal to the amount that would have been allocated to the contributing partner had the partnership sold, rather than distributed, the property. Appropriate adjustments must be made to the basis of the contributing partner's partnership interest and to the basis of the distributed property to reflect any gain or loss recognized (see ¶ 445 and ¶ 456).

Footnote references are to paragraphs of the 2002 Standard Federal Tax Reports.

143 ¶ 25,321	146 ¶ 25,181B	148 ¶ 25,320
144 ¶ 25,520	147 ¶ 25,320	149 ¶ 25,120
145 ¶ 25,180, ¶ 25,321		

The recognition rule does not apply if the property is distributed to the contributing partner (or its successor). Also, the rule does not apply with respect to certain distributions made as part of an exchange of like-kind property.

A similar rule may cause a partner contributing appreciated property to recognize precontribution gain if he receives a distribution of other partnership property (except money) within a seven-year period (Code Sec. 737(b)).[150] Precontribution gain must be recognized to the extent that it exceeds the partner's basis for his partnership interest at the time the distribution is received.

456. Basis of Property Distributed to Partner. The basis of property received in a distribution, other than in liquidation of a partner's interest, is ordinarily the same as the basis in the hands of the partnership immediately prior to distribution. In no case may the basis of property in the hands of the distributee exceed the basis of his partnership interest reduced by the amount of money distributed to him in the same transaction (Code Sec. 732(a)).[151]

> **Example 1.** Taxpayer has a basis of $10,000 for his partnership interest. He receives a nonliquidating distribution of $4,000 in cash and property with a basis to the partnership of $8,000. The basis to the partner of the distributed property is $6,000 ($10,000 minus $4,000). (The partnership can "recover" the $2,000 difference by making the election described at ¶ 459.)

The basis of property distributed *in liquidation* of a partner's interest is the basis of the distributee's partnership interest less any money received in the same transaction (Code Sec. 732(b)).[152]

A distributee partner's basis adjustment is allocated among distributed assets, first to unrealized receivables and inventory items in an amount equal to the partnership's basis in each such property, as under prior law (Code Sec. 732(c)).[153] Under these rules, the term "unrealized receivables" includes any property the sale of which would create ordinary income. This would include, for example, depreciation-recapture property. However, the amount of unrealized receivables is limited to that amount that would be treated as ordinary income if the property were sold at fair market value (Code Sec. 708).[154]

Basis is allocated first to the extent of each distributed property's adjusted basis to the partnership. Any remaining basis adjustment that is an increase is allocated among properties with unrealized appreciation in proportion to their respective amounts of unrealized appreciation (to the extent of each property's appreciation) and then in proportion to their respective fair market values.

> **Example 2.** A partnership has two assets, a tractor and a steam shovel. Both assets are distributed to a partner whose adjusted basis in his partnership interest is $55,000. The tractor has a basis to the partnership of $5,000 and a fair market value of $40,000. The steam shovel has a basis to the partnership of $10,000 and a fair market value of $10,000. Basis is first allocated to the tractor in the amount of $5,000 and to the steam shovel in the amount of $10,000 (their adjusted bases to the partnership). The remaining basis adjustment is an increase of $40,000 (the partner's $55,000 basis minus the partnership's total basis of $15,000 in the distributed assets). Basis is then allocated to the tractor in the amount of $35,000, its unrealized appreciation, with no allocation to the steam shovel attributable to unrealized appreciation because its fair market value equals the partnership's adjusted basis. The remaining basis adjustment of $5,000 is allocated in the ratio of the assets' fair market values, which is $4,000 to the tractor (for a total basis of $44,000) and $1,000 to the steam shovel (for a total basis of $11,000).

If the remaining basis adjustment is a decrease, it is allocated among properties with unrealized depreciation in proportion to their respective amounts of unrealized

Footnote references are to paragraphs of the 2002 Standard Federal Tax Reports.

¶ 456

150 ¶ 25,425
151 ¶ 25,340
152 ¶ 25,340
153 ¶ 25,340
154 ¶ 25,200

depreciation (to the extent of each property's depreciation), and then in proportion to their respective adjusted bases, taking into account the adjustments already made.

The result of these changes is that a partner's substituted basis in distributed partnership property is allocated among multiple properties based on the fair market value of the distributed properties. Under the prior rules, allocations were based on the partnership's proportionate basis in the distributed properties.

Optional Basis Adjustments. If a partner has acquired his partnership interest (1) by purchase from a former partner or another partner or (2) from a deceased partner, he can elect to have a special basis adjustment for property other than money received in a distribution from the partnership within two years after the partnership interest was acquired. This can be done if the partnership has not made an election to have the special basis adjustment apply to its assets. The partner's election will accomplish substantially the same result as if the partnership had made the election (Code Sec. 732(d)). This special basis adjustment is the difference between the amount paid for his interest, that is, his basis for his partnership interest and his share of the adjusted basis of the partnership assets.

The special basis adjustment applies to property received in current distributions as well as to distributions in complete liquidation of the partner's interest. Reg. § 1.732-1(d)(1)(iv) provides that if the partner makes the election when a distribution of depreciable or depletable property is received, the special basis adjustment is not diminished by any depletion or depreciation on that portion of the basis of partnership property which arises from the special basis adjustment. Depletion or depreciation on that portion for the period before distribution is allowed or allowable only if the partnership made the election.

If a transferee-partner wishes to make the election, it must be made on his tax return for the year of the distribution if the distribution includes any property subject to depreciation, depletion, or amortization. If it does not include any such property, the election may be made with the return for any tax year not later than the first tax year in which the basis of the distributed property is pertinent in determining income tax.

459. Optional Adjustment to Basis of Partnership Assets. If the basis of distributed assets in the hands of the distributee partner is less than the basis of the assets in the hands of the partnership, there may be an "unused" basis. The partnership may elect to adjust the basis of its remaining assets to take up this unused basis (Code Sec. 734; Code Sec. 754; Code Sec. 755).[155] See ¶ 470.

If gain is recognized by a partner because of a distribution of money, as described in ¶ 453, a similar increase in the partnership's basis of its remaining assets may be made. If an election is made, the partnership may have to decrease the basis of its remaining assets. The decrease would be required for the excess of the basis of distributed assets to the partner over the basis that the partnership had for those assets, in the event of a distribution in liquidation of a partner's interest. Decrease would also be required to the extent that any distribution to a partner resulted in loss to the partner (Code Sec. 734(b)(2)).[156] As explained at ¶ 453, loss results to the partner only if the distribution terminates the partner's interest and generally consists only of money, unrealized receivables, and inventories.

Example. An equal three-person partnership has the following assets:

	Partnership's Basis	Fair Market Value
Cash	$12,000	$12,000
Land	6,000	12,000
Securities	9,000	12,000
Total	$27,000	$36,000

If a partner retires and the partnership pays him $12,000 for the fair market value of his partnership interest, the partnership is really distributing $4,000 as his pro rata share of the partnership's cash and paying him $8,000 for his 1/3 interest in the land and in the securities. However, the retiring partner's share of the partnership's basis for these properties totals only $5,000. Therefore, the partnership, if it wishes to reflect the $3,000 excess cost, may elect to adjust the basis of the land and securities.

A partnership is barred from increasing the adjusted basis of remaining property following a distribution of an interest in another partnership if such other partnership has not made a consistent Code Sec. 754 election. In other words, tiered partnerships must make consistent elections (Code Sec. 734(b)).[157]

The allocation of any increase or decrease in basis is made among the various partnership assets or categories of assets. These rules contemplate generally that the allocation will be made first to "like-kind" assets and will reduce the difference between fair market value and basis of each asset adjusted (Code Sec. 755).[158]

462. Character of Gain or Loss on Disposition of Distributed Property. A partner recognizes ordinary gain or loss on the disposition of unrealized receivables or inventory items distributed by the partnership (¶ 436), regardless of whether the inventory has substantially appreciated in value (Code Sec. 735).[159] In the case of inventory items, this rule applies only if the sale takes place within five years of the date of distribution. If the sale takes place after this period, gain may be treated as capital gain if the assets are capital assets in the hands of the partner at that time (Reg. § 1.735-1).[160]

If a partner disposes of distributed unrealized receivables or inventory items in a nonrecognition transaction (or series of transactions), these rules apply to treat gain or loss on the substituted basis property as ordinary income or loss, except in the case of stock in a C corporation received in a Code Sec. 351 exchange (Code Sec. 735(c)).[161] The House Committee Report to the Deficit Reduction Act of 1984 (P.L. 98-369) states that it is intended that the basis tainting rules regarding distributed property apply only for the period during which the underlying rules as to character of gain or loss under Code Sec. 735 would apply if the property were not disposed of in a nonrecognition transaction. For example, if an inventory item was distributed by the partnership, and the partner subsequently disposed of it in a nonrecognition transaction, ordinary income treatment would apply to any substitute basis property only for the duration of the five-year period beginning on the date of the original distribution.

467. Adjustment of Basis on Sale of Partnership Interest. Generally, the transfer of a partnership interest does not affect the basis of partnership assets. However, the partnership may elect to adjust the basis of partnership assets to reflect the difference between the transferee's basis for his partnership interest (generally, the purchase price) and his proportionate share of the adjusted basis of all partnership property (his share of the partnership's adjusted basis in the partnership property). The election applies where there is a "transfer of an interest in a partnership by sale or exchange or upon the death of a partner" and not upon the contribution of property (including money) to the partnership (Code Sec. 743 and Reg. § 1.743-1(a)).[162]

The amount of the increase or decrease is an adjustment affecting the transferee partner only. In addition, a partner's proportionate share of the adjusted basis of partnership property is determined in accordance with his interest in partnership capital. Where, however, an agreement on contributed property is in effect, the agreement must be taken into account in determining a partner's proportionate share (Reg. § 1.743-1(b)).[163]

Footnote references are to paragraphs of the 2002 Standard Federal Tax Reports.

[157] ¶ 25,380	[160] ¶ 25,401	[162] ¶ 25,480, ¶ 25,481
[158] ¶ 25,580	[161] ¶ 25,400	[163] ¶ 25,481
[159] ¶ 25,400		

The basis adjustment must be allocated among the partnership assets in accordance with the rules set out in Code Sec. 755.[164] See ¶ 459.

470. Election for Basis Adjustment. An election to make the basis adjustments described at ¶ 459 and ¶ 467 is made in a written statement filed with the partnership return for the first year to be covered by the election. The election will apply to all property distributions and transfers of partnership interests taking place in the year of the election and in all subsequent partnership tax years until revoked (Reg. § 1.754-1(a)).[165]

Family Partnerships

474. Income-Splitting Device. The family partnership is a common device for splitting income among family members and having more income taxed in the lower tax brackets. A family member will be recognized as a partner for income tax purposes if he owns a capital interest in a partnership in which capital is a material income-producing factor, whether or not he purchased the interest. If capital is *not* a material income-producing factor, a partnership resulting from a gift of an interest might be disregarded as an invalid attempt to assign income. In any event, if all the income is attributable to the personal efforts of the donor, the donor would be taxed on the entire income. In addition, the donee's distributive share of income must be proportionate to his capital interest, and his control over the partnership must be consistent with his status as partner (Code Sec. 704(e); Reg. § 1.704-1(e)).[166]

Organization, Syndication, Start-Up Costs

477. Syndication and Organization Fees. No deduction is allowed a partnership or a partner for the costs of organizing a partnership (organization fees) or of selling partnership interests (syndication fees). Guaranteed payments (¶ 421) made to partners for their services in organizing a partnership are capital expenditures and are not deductible by the partnership. The partnership, however, may elect to amortize organization fees (but not syndication fees) over a period of not less than 60 months beginning with the month it begins business (Code Sec. 709).[167]

481. Start-Up Expenditures. Expenditures that do not qualify for 60-month amortization as organization fees but that are incurred in investigating the creation or acquisition of an active trade or business, in creating such a trade or business or in any activity engaged in for profit and for the production of income before, and in anticipation of, the start of the business may qualify for similar amortization under Code Sec. 195.[168] In the case of start-up expenses incurred by the partnership itself and for which an election is made, the amortization deduction is taken into account in computing partnership income. In the case of qualifying investigatory expenses incurred in connection with acquiring a partnership interest, the deduction is taken by the partner who has incurred the expenses. See ¶ 904.

Electing Large Partnerships

482. Simplified Reporting for Electing Large Partnerships. Large partnerships with 100 or more members in the preceding tax year may elect "large partnership" status. An electing large partnership combines most items of partnership income, deduction, credit and loss at the partnership level and passes through net amounts to the partners. Special rules apply to partnerships engaging in oil and gas activities and to partnerships with residual interests in real estate mortgage investment conduits (REMICs). Service partnerships and commodity pools generally are unable to elect large partnership treatment.

A partnership may lose its large partnership status if the number of partners falls below 100 during any partnership tax year. Rules for determining the treat-

---

Footnote references are to paragraphs of the 2002 Standard Federal Tax Reports.

[164] ¶ 25,580   [166] ¶ 25,120, ¶ 25,121   [168] ¶ 12,370
[165] ¶ 25,561   [167] ¶ 25,220

¶ 482

ment of a partnership whose membership falls below 100 will be provided by regulations.

An electing large partnership does not terminate for tax purposes solely because 50 percent or more if its interests are sold or exchanged within a 12-month period.

484. Deductions and Credits Generally Combined at Partnership Level. Miscellaneous itemized deductions are not separately reported to the partners. In place of applying the two-percent floor for itemized deductions, 70 percent of the itemized deductions are disallowed at the partnership level (Code Sec. 773(b)(3)).[169] The 70-percent cut is designed to approximate the amount of the deduction that would be lost to the individual partners under the two-percent floor. The remaining 30 percent is allowed at the partnership level in determining the large partnership's taxable income and is not subject to the two-percent floor at the partner level.

Tax credits other than the low-income housing credit, the rehabilitation credit and the credit for producing fuel from nonconventional sources are reported as a single item. Credit recapture also is recognized at the partnership level.

485. Gains and Losses of Electing Large Partnerships. For electing large partnerships, the netting of capital gains and losses occurs at the partnership level. Passive activity items are separated from capital gains stemming from partnership portfolio income. Each partner separately takes into account the partner's distributive shares of net capital gain or net capital loss for passive activity and portfolio items (Code Sec. 773).[170]

Any partnership gains and losses under Code Sec. 1231 (¶ 1747) are netted at the partnership level. Net gain is treated as long-term capital gain and is subject to the rules described above, and any net loss is treated as ordinary loss and consolidated with the partnership's other taxable income.

488. Audit Procedures for Electing Large Partnerships. The partnership audit rules normally applicable to partnerships do not apply to electing large partnerships. An electing large partnership, like other partnerships, appoints a representative to handle IRS matters. Unlike under the TEFRA rules, the representative does not have to be a partner (Code Sec. 6255(b)).[171] Only the partnership, and not the individual partners, will receive notice of partnership adjustments (Code Sec. 6245(b)).[172] Only the partnership has the right to appeal the adjustment (Code Sec. 6247(a)).[173] After a partnership-level adjustment, prior-year partners and prior tax years generally will not be affected. However, prior years can be affected if there has been a partnership dissolution or a finding that the shares of a distribution to partners was erroneous. Instead, the adjustments generally are passed through to current partners.

Chapter 5

TRUSTS □ ESTATES

ORDINARY TRUST RULES

Trust or Corporation

501. Trust, Estate and Fiduciary Defined. A trust is considered a separate taxable entity for federal income tax purposes. A "trust," for federal tax law purposes, usually involves an arrangement created by will or inter vivos instrument under which the trustees take title to the property for the purpose of protecting or conserving it for the beneficiaries under the ordinary rules applied in chancery and probate courts (see also ¶ 502). Usually, the beneficiaries of such a trust do no more than accept its benefits. However, even if the beneficiaries are the persons who planned or created it, the trust will still be recognized as a separate taxable entity if its purpose was to vest in trustees responsibility for protecting and preserving property for beneficiaries who cannot share in the discharge of this responsibility (Reg. § 301.7701-4)[1] and the grantors do not retain any impermissible powers. See ¶ 573 et seq. for rules governing special types of trusts, such as grantor trusts and charitable trusts.

Decedents' estates are also considered separate taxable entities for income tax purposes during the period of administration. See ¶ 504-¶ 506 for the tax treatment of other types of "estates."

The term "fiduciary" applies to a person who occupies a position of special confidence toward another, who holds in trust property in which another person has the beneficial title or interest, or who receives and controls income of another. Thus, trustees, executors and certain receivers are considered fiduciaries. However, the term "agent" does not denote a fiduciary for federal income tax purposes, even

---

though a "fiduciary relationship" may be said to exist for state law purposes. Where a person receives income as an agent, intermediary debtor or conduit, and the income is paid over to another, that person is not considered a fiduciary for tax purposes (Reg. § 301.7701-6; Reg. § 301.7701-7).[2]

Small Business Trusts. An electing small business trust is permitted to be a shareholder in an S corporation. An electing small business trust is a trust that does not have any beneficiaries other than individuals, or estates eligible to be S corporation shareholders, except that charitable organizations may hold contingent remainder interests. The portion of any electing small business trust that consists of stock in one or more S corporations is treated as a separate trust (Code Sec. 641(c)). See ¶ 301.

Qualified Domestic Trusts. A qualified domestic trust is a trust that meets certain requirements and that is subject to a special estate tax (Code Sec. 2056A). Property that is transferred from a citizen decedent to a nonresident alien spouse will not qualify for the usual marital deduction, for purposes of the gift and estate tax, unless it is transferred from the decedent to a qualified domestic trust. See ¶ 2926.

502. Business and Investment Trusts. A "business" or commercial trust is created as a means of carrying on a profit-making business, usually using capital or property supplied by the beneficiaries. The trustees or other designated persons are, in effect, managers of the undertaking, whether appointed or controlled by the beneficiaries. This arrangement more closely resembles an association, which may be taxed as a corporation or a partnership and is distinguishable from the type of trust discussed at ¶ 501. The fact that the trust property is not supplied by the beneficiaries is not sufficient to avoid the trust being classified and taxed as a corporation (Reg. § 301.7701-4(b)).[3]

An "investment" trust may also be taxed as an association, rather than a trust, if there is a power under the trust agreement to vary the investment of the certificate holders (Reg. § 301.7701-4(c)).[4] However, if this power is lacking, the arrangement is classified as a trust.

Unit investment trusts, as defined in the Investment Company Act of 1940, that are set up to hold mutual fund shares for investors are not taxed as trusts; their income is taxed directly to the investors (Reg. § 1.851-7).[5]

503. Liquidating Trust. A liquidating trust formed for the primary purpose of liquidating and distributing the assets transferred to it is taxed as a trust, and not as an association, despite the possibility of profit.[6] All the activities of the trust must be reasonably necessary to, and consistent with, the accomplishment of the primary purpose of liquidation and distribution. If the liquidation is unreasonably prolonged, or if the liquidation purpose becomes so obscured by business activities that the declared purpose of liquidation can be said to have been lost or abandoned, the arrangement is no longer a liquidating trust (Reg. § 301.7701-4(d)).[7]

504. Return for Persons Under a Disability. A guardian for a minor or a legally disabled person is required to file Form 1040 (U.S. Individual Income Tax Return), Form 1040A or Form 1040EZ as an agent for such person if the individual would be required to file a return. However, a minor can file a return or have someone else file it, relieving the minor's guardian of the obligation to file a return for the minor (Code Sec. 6012(b)(2); Reg. § 1.6012-3(b)(3)).[8] For the tax year during which an incompetent is declared competent and the fiduciary is discharged, the former incompetent must file the tax return. The estate of an incompetent is not a separate tax entity from the incompetent. Thus, no fiduciary return on Form 1041 (U.S. Fiduciary Income Tax Return) is required (Reg. § 1.641(b)-2(b)).[9] However, an agent making the return for another should file Form 2848 (Power of Attorney

---

Footnote references are to paragraphs of the 2002 Standard Federal Tax Reports.

¶ 502

[2] ¶ 24,267.025, ¶ 43,094	[5] ¶ 26,407	[8] ¶ 24,267.025, ¶ 35,142,
[3] ¶ 43,090, ¶ 43,091.01	[6] ¶ 43,090	¶ 35,146
[4] ¶ 43,090, ¶ 43,091.01	[7] ¶ 43,090	[9] ¶ 24,265

and Declaration of Representative) with the taxpayer's return. Both the agent and the taxpayer for whom the return is made may be liable for penalties.[10] One spouse may execute a valid return on behalf of his or her mentally incompetent or disabled spouse prior to appointment of a legal guardian, even without formal power of attorney.[11]

505. Trustees in Bankruptcy of Individual Debtors. The property held by a trustee in bankruptcy for an individual under Chapter 7 (liquidation) or Chapter 11 (business reorganization) of Title 11 of the U.S. Code is considered the estate of the debtor. Such an estate is treated as a separate taxable entity (Code Sec. 1398).[12]

A separate taxable entity is not created when the case is brought under Chapter 13 of Title 11 of the U.S. Code, which involves adjustment of debts of an individual with regular income. Further, no separate taxable entity is considered to have been created if a Chapter 7 or Chapter 11 case is dismissed (Code Sec. 1398(b)(1)). A separate taxable entity also is not created when an individual is in receivership.

The fiduciary of a Chapter 7 or Chapter 11 bankruptcy estate is obligated to file the estate's return, or if the bankruptcy plan creates a liquidating trust, the fiduciary must file the trust's return (Code Sec. 6012(b)(4)).[13] The bankruptcy trustee must file a Form 1041 for the bankruptcy estate for any tax year in which the estate in bankruptcy has gross income that equals or exceeds the sum of the personal exemption amount plus the basic standard deduction for married persons filing separately (Code Sec. 6012(a)(9)). For 2001, that sum is $6,700. For 2002, that sum is unofficially projected to be $6,925. The tax year for which the fiduciary files a return begins on the date of the filing of the petition in bankruptcy. The return may be for a calendar year or a fiscal year. A trustee in bankruptcy has no authority to file a return on Form 1040 for a bankrupt individual. The individual must file an individual return.

506. Receiver, Trustee in Bankruptcy of Corporate Debtors. The commencement of bankruptcy proceedings for a partnership or corporation does not create a separate taxable entity (Code Sec. 1399).[14] Thus, there is no obligation imposed upon the bankruptcy trustee to file a Form 1041 on behalf of the estate.

However, a receiver, trustee in dissolution, trustee in bankruptcy, or assignee who, by order of a court, has possession of or holds title to all or substantially all the property or business of a corporation must file the income tax return for such corporation on Form 1120 (U.S. Corporation Income Tax Return). The title holder or party in possession must file the return on behalf of the corporation whether or not that party is operating the property or business of the corporation. A receiver in charge of only *a small part* of the property of a corporation, such as a receiver in mortgage foreclosure proceedings involving merely a small portion of its property, need not make the return (Reg. § 1.6012-3(b)(4)).[15]

Bankrupt partnerships must file their returns on Form 1065 (U.S. Partnership Return of Income).

507. Termination of Estates and Trusts. An estate is recognized as a taxable entity only during the period of administration or settlement—i.e., the period actually required by the executor or administrator to perform the ordinary duties of administration, such as collection of assets, payment of debts and legacies, etc. This is so whether the period is longer or shorter than that specified under local law for the settlement of estates. However, the administration of an estate may not be unduly prolonged. For federal tax purposes, the estate will be considered terminated after the expiration of a reasonable period for the performance of the duties of administration or when all the assets of the estate have been distributed except for a

---

Footnote references are to paragraphs of the 2002 Standard Federal Tax Reports.

[10] ¶ 35,143	[12] ¶ 24,267.025	[14] ¶ 32,420
[11] ¶ 35,143, ¶ 35,150.734	[13] ¶ 35,142	[15] ¶ 35,146

reasonable amount set aside in good faith for the payment of contingent liabilities and expenses (Reg. § 1.641(b)-3(b)).[16]

A trust is recognized as a taxable entity until trust property has been distributed to successors, plus a reasonable time after this event necessary for the trustee to complete the administration of the trust. Further, like an estate, a trust is considered terminated when all the assets have been distributed except for a reasonable amount set aside in good faith to pay unascertained or contingent liabilities and expenses (other than a claim by a beneficiary in that capacity) (Reg. § 1.641(b)-3(b)).[17]

Once an estate or trust is considered terminated for tax purposes, the gross income, credits, and deductions of the estate or trust subsequent to termination are considered to be the gross income, credits, or deductions of the person or persons who succeed to the property (Reg. § 1.641(b)-3(d)).[18]

Fiduciary Return

510. Return of Estate or Trust by Fiduciary. A fiduciary must file a return on Form 1041 for the trust or estate if: (1) the trust (other than a trust exempt under Code Sec. 501(a)) for the tax year has any taxable income or has gross income of $600 or more, regardless of the amount of taxable income; (2) the estate has gross income of $600 or more for the tax year; (3) any beneficiary of the estate or trust is a nonresident alien (unless the trust is exempt under Code Sec. 501(a)) (Code Sec. 6012(a)(3); Reg. § 1.6012-3);[19] or (4) an individual's bankruptcy estate under Chapter 7 or Chapter 11 of the Bankruptcy Code has gross income equal to or in excess of the sum of the personal exemption amount plus the basic standard deduction applicable to married individuals filing separately (Code Sec. 6012(a)(9)).[20] The bankruptcy trustee must file a Form 1041 for the bankruptcy estate for any tax year in which the estate in bankruptcy has gross income that equals or exceeds the sum of the personal exemption amount plus the basic standard deduction for married persons filing separately (Code Sec. 6012(a)(9)). For 2001, that sum is $6,700. For 2002, that sum is unofficially projected to be $6,925.

When there is more than one fiduciary, the return can be filed by any one of them. However, when an estate has both domiciliary and ancillary representatives, each representative must file a return (Reg. § 1.6012-3(a)(1) and (3)).[21]

A trustee of two or more trusts must file a separate return for each trust, even though the trusts were created by the same grantor for the same beneficiaries (Reg. § 1.6012-3(a)(4)).[22] However, see ¶ 515.

The return must be filed on or before the 15th day of the 4th month following the close of the tax year (Reg. § 1.6072-1(a)).[23] In filing its first return, an estate may choose the same accounting period as the decedent, or it may choose a calendar tax year or any fiscal year it wishes. If it chooses the decedent's accounting period, its first return will be for a short period to cover the unexpired term of the decedent's regular tax year (Code Sec. 441 and Code Sec. 443).[24] An exemption of $600 (Code Sec. 642(b)) is allowed on a short-period return, without proration (see ¶ 534).[25]

With a few limited exceptions, trusts (other than those that are ignored for tax purposes under the rules discussed at ¶ 573 and following) must adopt a calendar tax year (Code Sec. 644).[26] An existing trust that is required to change its tax year must annualize any income earned in the short year. The Form 1041 for a trust must generally be filed on or before April 15 following the close of the tax year. Trusts may request an automatic three-month extension of the filing deadline by submit-

---

Footnote references are to paragraphs of the 2002 Standard Federal Tax Reports.

[16] ¶ 24,266	[20] ¶ 35,142	[24] ¶ 20,302, ¶ 20,500
[17] ¶ 24,266	[21] ¶ 35,146	[25] ¶ 24,280
[18] ¶ 24,266	[22] ¶ 35,146	[26] ¶ 24,350
[19] ¶ 35,142, ¶ 35,146, ¶ 35,150.55	[23] ¶ 36,721, ¶ 36,723.01	

¶ 510

ting Form 8736 (Application for Automatic Extension of Time To File U.S. Return for a Partnership, REMIC, or for Certain Trusts) on or before the return's due date.

The fiduciary of an estate or trust need not file a copy of the will or trust instrument with the estate or trust income tax return unless the IRS requests it. If the IRS does request a copy of the will or trust instrument, the fiduciary should file it (including any amendments), accompanied by a written declaration of truth and completeness and a statement indicating the provisions of the will or trust instrument that determine the extent to which the income of the estate or trust is taxable to the estate or trust, the beneficiaries, or the grantor (Reg. § 1.6012-3(a)(2)).[27]

An estate or trust that is obligated to file an income tax return must furnish a copy of Schedule K-1 (Form 1041) to each beneficiary (1) who receives a distribution from the trust or estate for the year or (2) to whom any item with respect to the tax year is allocated. This statement must contain the information required to be shown on the return and be furnished on or before the date on which the return is to be filed (Code Sec. 6034A).[28] In addition, a copy must be attached to the fiduciary's Form 1041. For each failure to file a correct payee statement, a $50 penalty may be assessed (Code Sec. 6722).[29]

Payment of Tax and Estimated Tax. The entire income tax liability of an estate or trust must be paid on or before the due date for its return (Reg. § 1.6151-1(a)).[30] In addition, estates that have been in existence more than two years and both new and existing trusts must pay estimated tax in the same manner as individuals. See ¶ 518.

512. Personal Liability of Fiduciary. Any fiduciary (other than a trustee acting under Chapter 11 of the Bankruptcy Code) who pays any debt due by the decedent or the estate, in whole or in part, before federal tax obligations are satisfied becomes personally liable for the tax of the estate to the extent of such payments. However, the fiduciary is not liable for amounts paid out for debts that have priority over the federal taxes due and owing on the estate, such as a decedent's funeral expenses or probate administration costs (31 U.S.C. § 3713).[31] Further, an executor or administrator who pays other debts is not personally liable unless the executor or administrator has either personal knowledge of a tax due the United States or knowledge that would put a reasonably prudent person on inquiry that such tax debts exist.[32] Discharge of the fiduciary does not terminate the fiduciary's personal liability for the payment of other debts of the estate without satisfying prior tax claims.

Method of Taxing Estate or Trust

514. Estate or Trust as Separate Entity. An estate or trust is a separate taxable entity.[33] In general, its entire income must be reported on Form 1041, which must be filed by the fiduciary (see ¶ 510). If income is required to be distributed currently or is properly distributed to a beneficiary, the estate or trust is regarded as a conduit with respect to that income. It is allowed a deduction for the portion of gross income that is currently distributable to the beneficiaries or is properly paid or credited to them (see ¶ 545). Generally, the beneficiaries are taxed on the part of the income currently distributed and the estate or trust on the portion that it has accumulated. The income allocated to a beneficiary retains the same character in the beneficiary's hands that it had in the hands of the estate or trust.[34]

515. Multiple Trusts. One grantor may create several trusts, and the income may be taxed separately for each trust. When there is an intention to create separate trusts for multiple beneficiaries, the fact that the corpus of each trust is kept in one fund will not necessarily defeat the grantor's intention. Although it is not necessary to divide the corpus physically in order to carry out the intentions of the

---

Footnote references are to paragraphs of the 2002 Standard Federal Tax Reports.

[27] ¶ 35,146	[30] ¶ 37,081	[33] ¶ 24,267.01
[28] ¶ 35,460, ¶ 35,461.01	[31] ¶ 40,730	[34] ¶ 24,383, ¶ 24,425
[29] ¶ 40,230	[32] ¶ 40,735.10	

parties, it is necessary to comply literally with the terms of the trust instrument in other respects.[35]

However, two or more trusts will be treated as one trust if (1) the trusts have substantially the same grantor or grantors and substantially the same primary beneficiary or beneficiaries and (2) a principal purpose of the trusts is the avoidance of income tax (Code Sec. 643(f)).[36] A special safe-harbor provision applies to any trust that was irrevocable on March 1, 1984, except to the extent that corpus is contributed to the trust after that date.

516. Tax Rates. An estate or trust computes its tax liability by using the separate estate and trust income rate schedule for 2001 at ¶ 19. As is the case with individual taxpayers, the tax is based on 15%, 27.5%, 30.5%, 35.5% and 39.1% tax rates for 2001. However, each rate becomes effective at a much lower taxable income level for estates and trusts than for individuals. The highest tax rate of 39.1% applies to a trust or estate with taxable income over $8,900 for 2001 (compared to $297,350 for individuals). The projected 2002 tax brackets are also provided at ¶ 19.

The taxable income of an estate or trust for purposes of the regular income tax is determined by subtracting from its gross income (¶ 520) allowable deductions (¶ 529 et seq.), amounts distributable to beneficiaries (to the extent of distributable net income) (¶ 543), and the proper exemption (¶ 534) (Code Sec. 641; Reg. § 1.641(a)-1 and Reg. § 1.641(b)-1).[37] The chart at ¶ 64 will help in understanding Form 1041.

The alternative minimum tax of an estate or trust is computed by determining distributable net income under the general rules contained in ¶ 543, subject to further adjustments under the minimum tax rules. The alternative minimum tax is computed on Schedule H, Form 1041. See, also, ¶ 1401 et seq.

Grantor and employees' trusts are subject to special tax treatment. See ¶ 573 et seq. and ¶ 2101 et seq.

A trustee of a revocable trust and the executor of a decedent's estate may join in an election to treat the revocable trust as part of the decedent's estate (Code Sec. 645). Such an election allows the revocable trust to enjoy certain income tax treatment that would previously have been accorded only to the decedent's estate.

Electing Small Business Trust. An electing small business trust, a trust that is an S corporation shareholder, is taxed in a different manner than other trusts. First, the portion of the trust that consists of stock in one or more S corporations is treated as a separate trust for purposes of computing the income tax attributable to the S corporation stock held by the trust, and this portion of the trust's income is taxed at the highest rate imposed on estates and trusts. The taxable income attributable to this portion includes (1) the items of income, loss or deduction allocated to the trust as an S corporation shareholder under the rules of subchapter S, (2) gain or loss from the sale of the S corporation stock, and (3) any state or local income taxes and administrative expenses of the trust properly allocable to the S corporation stock. Otherwise allowable capital losses are allowed only to the extent of capital gains. Moreover, no deduction is allowed for amounts distributed to beneficiaries, and, except as described above, no additional deductions or credits are allowed. Also, this income is not included in the distributable net income of the trust and, therefore, is not included in the beneficiaries' income. Furthermore, no item relating to the S corporation stock is apportioned to any beneficiary. Special rules apply upon termination of all or a part of the trust (Code Sec. 641(c)). See ¶ 301.

517. Establishing the Tax Year. Although estates may select or retain any tax year, all trusts (except for trusts exempt from tax under Code Sec. 501(a) and charitable trusts) must use the calendar year (Code Sec. 644).[38]

Footnote references are to paragraphs of the 2002 Standard Federal Tax Reports.

¶516

[35] ¶ 24,267.67	[37] ¶ 24,260, ¶ 24,262,	[38] ¶ 24,350
[36] ¶ 24,320, ¶ 24,334.034	¶ 24,264	

518. Estimated Tax. In general, trusts and estates are required to make quarterly estimated tax payments in the same manner as individuals. However, estates and grantor trusts that receive the residue of a probate estate under the grantor's will are only required to make estimated tax payments beginning with tax years ending two or more years after the decedent's death.

Trusts or estates with a short tax year must pay installments of tax on or before the 15th day of the fourth, sixth and ninth months of the tax year and the 15th day of the first month of the following tax year. The amount of each installment in a short tax year is determined by dividing the required annual payment (see ¶ 2679) by the number of payments required for that year.[39]

The general estimated tax rules for individuals set forth at ¶ 2679 et seq. apply to most trusts and estates that are required to make estimated tax payments. (The corporate estimated tax provisions apply to trusts taxed under Code Sec. 511 and private foundations. See ¶ 225 et seq.) However, trusts and estates generally have 45 days (rather than the 15 days allowed individuals) to compute the payments under the estimated tax annualization rules. The payment due dates are unchanged. An estate's fiduciary may elect, on Form 1041-T (Allocation of Estimated Tax Payments to Beneficiaries), to distribute excess estimated tax payments to the beneficiaries during the tax year that the fiduciary reasonably expects to be the estate's last tax year. If the payments of estimated tax made by a trust exceed the trust's tax liability as shown on the Form 1041, the trustee may elect to treat any or all of the overpayment as a payment made by the beneficiary and credited toward the beneficiary's tax liability. A trust's election is made on Form 1041-T and must be filed on or before the 65th day after the close of the tax year (March 6, 2002, for calendar tax year 2001).[40]

Gross Income of Estate or Trust

520. Gross Income of Estate or Trust. The gross income of an estate or trust is generally determined in the same manner as that of an individual (Reg. § 1.641(a)-2).[41] The gross income of an estate or trust includes all items of gross income received during the tax year, including (1) income accumulated in trust for the benefit of unborn or unascertained persons or persons with contingent interests; (2) income accumulated or held for future distribution under the terms of the will or trust; (3) income that is to be distributed currently by the fiduciary to the beneficiaries, and income collected by the guardian of an infant that is to be held or distributed as the court may direct; (4) income received by the estate of a deceased person during the period of administration or settlement of the estate; and (5) income that, at the discretion of the fiduciary, may be either distributed to the beneficiaries or accumulated (Code Sec. 641(a); Reg. § 1.641(a)-2).[42]

Although all the items above are includible in the gross income of the estate or trust, the liability for tax on the income may rest on either the beneficiary or the trust as a separate entity. See ¶ 542 for tax consequences of distributions to beneficiaries.

The allocation of income and deductions between a decedent's estate and the surviving spouse in community property states depends on state community property laws. In most states, the surviving spouse is taxable on one-half of the income flowing from the community property of the estate.[43]

522. Income from Real Estate. State law determines whether income from real estate during the period of administration is taxable to the decedent's estate or to the heirs or devisees. The IRS has ruled that, where state law provides that real property is subject to administration, income derived from the property is taxable to the estate, even though legal title may pass directly to the heirs or devisees.

Footnote references are to paragraphs of the 2002 Standard Federal Tax Reports.
[39] ¶ 39,560.82
[40] ¶ 24,334.036, ¶ 39,560.027
[41] ¶ 24,263, ¶ 24,267.01
[42] ¶ 24,260, ¶ 24,263
[43] ¶ 2350.2473

¶ 522

However, where the administrator is not entitled to possession or control of real property, income from the property is taxable to the heirs or devisees and not to the estate. Even if the property is not subject to the administrator's control, all or a part of the gain from a sale of property is taxable to the estate to the extent that the property was sold, under state law, to raise funds for its administration.[44]

523. Income from Personal Property. Income from personal property, including a gain from the sale or exchange of such property, is taxable to the estate. This is so because title to personal property vests in the administrator or executor immediately upon appointment and does not pass to the heirs or legatees until the estate is fully administered and distribution is ordered or approved by the courts, notwithstanding the fact that the basis of the property distributed relates back to the date of the decedent's death.[45]

524. Sale of Property by Estate or Trust. The computation of the gain or loss realized upon the sale of property acquired by an estate, trust or beneficiary is made under special basis rules, the applicability of which is dependent upon the method of acquisition and the nature of the property sold. See ¶ 1601 et seq.

526. Gain on Transfer to Beneficiary. Generally, no gain or loss results from a transfer of property from an estate or trust to a beneficiary under the terms of a will or trust instrument unless the distribution is in satisfaction of the beneficiary's right to receive a specific dollar amount or specific property other than that which is distributed (Reg. § 1.661(a)-2(f)(1)).[46]

A special rule limits gain on transfers to qualified heirs of property for which a special use valuation election under Code Sec. 2032A was made (Code Sec. 1040).[47]

A marital deduction trust (established for a spouse to take advantage of the estate tax marital deduction) comprising a portion of the residuary estate and measured by a percentage of the value of the adjusted gross estate is considered as being for a fixed dollar amount. Upon a distribution of property to such a trust, the estate realizes gain or loss measured by the difference between the fair market value at the date of distribution and the federal estate tax value of the property.[48]

Distribution of a stated percentage of trust corpus to the beneficiary before termination of the trust is not considered a satisfaction of an obligation of the trust for a definite amount of cash or equivalent value in property. Instead, it is treated as a partial distribution of a share of the trust principal. There is no sale or exchange, and the trustee does not realize taxable income.[49] However, a trustee or executor may elect to recognize gain or loss on the distribution of noncash property to a beneficiary as if the property had been sold to the beneficiary at its fair market value (Code Sec. 643(e)(3)).[50] This election is to be made on the return for the year of distribution and applies to all distributions made by the estate or trust during its entire tax year. Thus, an election to recognize gain or loss cannot be made separately for each distribution.

In the event this election is made, the beneficiary's basis in the distributed property is the estate's or trust's adjusted basis just prior to the distribution, adjusted by the gain or loss recognized by the estate or trust. If the election is not made, the beneficiary's basis will be the same as the trust's or estate's, and any gain or loss will be recognized by the beneficiary when the beneficiary disposes of the property.

527. Foreign Estates. A nonresident alien estate is taxed on its income received from U.S. sources, including capital gains and dividends received. However, the estate is allowed a deduction for distributions to both nonresident aliens and U.S. beneficiaries to the extent that these distributions are not in excess of its distributable net income. The portion of the distribution allocated to capital gains is not

includible in the gross income of nonresident alien beneficiaries if they have not resided in the United States for a period of at least 183 days. The portion of a distribution that represents dividends is, however, includible in the gross income of nonresident alien beneficiaries. The fiduciary must withhold U.S. taxes from these dividend distributions at the statutory rate or at the applicable treaty rate (Rev. Rul. 68-621, 1968-2 CB 286).[51]

Ordinary Deductions of Estate or Trust

528. Deductions and Credits Generally. In general, trusts and estates are allowed the same credits and deductions as individuals. However, special rules govern the computation of certain deductions and the allocation of certain credits and deductions between the beneficiaries and the estate or trust. See ¶ 529 et seq. Further, the estate or trust is permitted to claim a deduction for certain distributions to beneficiaries. See ¶ 544-545.

Two-Percent Floor on Itemized Deductions. In general, an estate or trust is subject to the two-percent-of-adjusted-gross-income floor on miscellaneous itemized deductions (¶ 1012). The AGI of an estate or trust is computed in the same manner as it is for an individual, except that the following deductions are allowed from gross income: (1) deductions for expenses paid or incurred in connection with the administration of the estate or trust that would not have been incurred had the property not been so held; (2) the Code Sec. 642(b) deduction, relating to the amount allowed to estates and trusts in lieu of the Code Sec. 151 personal exemption; and (3) the distribution deductions allowed under Code Sec. 651 and Code Sec. 661. Investment services fees that are not unique to the administration of a trust, however, are subject to the two-percent floor.[52] The IRS has the regulatory authority to apply the two-percent floor at the beneficiary level, rather than the entity level, with respect to simple trusts (Code Sec. 67(e)).[53]

For purposes of the income taxation of estates and trusts, excludable gain—50 percent of any gain from the sale or exchange of qualified small business stock held for more than five years (Code Sec. 1202(a))—cannot also be taken as a charitable deduction nor is it taken into account in computing the exclusion of capital gains in determining distributable net income (Code Sec. 642(c)(4) and Code Sec. 643(a)(3)).[54]

529. Expenses. In general, an estate or trust is allowed deductions for those ordinary and necessary expenses incurred in carrying on a trade or business,[55] those incurred in the production of income or the management or conservation of income-producing property, and those incurred in connection with the determination, collection, or refund of any tax.[56] Reasonable amounts paid or incurred by a fiduciary on account of administration, including fiduciaries' fees and expenses of litigation, are deductible, even though the estate or trust might not be engaged in a trade or business, unless the expenses were for the production or collection of tax-exempt income.

No deductions are allowable for (a) expenses that are allocable to one or more classes of income exempt from tax (other than interest income) or (b) any amount relating to expenses for the production of income that is allocable to tax-exempt interest income. See, also, ¶ 970. The IRS allows a deduction for an executor's or administrator's commissions, as paid or accrued, except the portion allocable to tax-exempt income. An estate can deduct the value of periodic alimony payments made by the estate under the rules regarding deductions for distributions to beneficiaries.[57]

Footnote references are to paragraphs of the 2002 Standard Federal Tax Reports.

[51] ¶ 24,267.4985
[52] ¶ 6064.75, ¶ 24,308.021
[53] ¶ 6060, ¶ 6060.704, ¶ 6064.03
[54] ¶ 24,280, ¶ 24,320, ¶ 30,372
[55] ¶ 8500
[56] ¶ 12,520
[57] ¶ 6094.31, ¶ 24,267.403, ¶ 24,400, ¶ 24,407.56

¶ 529

Double Deductions Prohibited. Amounts deductible as administration expenses or losses for estate tax (or generation-skipping transfer tax) purposes are not also deductible by the estate for income tax purposes. However, the estate can deduct such items for income tax purposes if it files a statement (in duplicate) that the items have not been allowed as deductions for estate tax purposes and that all rights to deduct them for such purposes are waived (Code Sec. 642(g); Reg. § 1.642(g)-1).[58]

The prohibition against double deductions by estates extends to trusts and other persons for expenses or losses incurred.[59] Expenses incurred by an estate in selling property to raise funds to pay administration expenses and taxes are also subject to the prohibition against double deductions. Such expenses cannot be claimed as a deduction (or offset against the selling price of the property) in computing the taxable income of the estate unless the estate waives the right to take such deduction for estate tax purposes (Code Sec. 642(g)). However, deductions for taxes, interest, business expenses, and other items accrued at the date of the decedent's death are allowed, for both estate and income tax purposes, as claims against the estate (Code Sec. 2053(a)) and deductions in respect of a decedent (Code Sec. 691(b)),[60] respectively (Reg. § 1.642(g)-2).[61]

530. Depreciation and Depletion. Depreciation and depletion deductions must be apportioned between trust and beneficiary and between estate and beneficiary (Code Sec. 167(d), Code Sec. 611(b), and Code Sec. 642(e)), except for certain term interests created or acquired after July 27, 1989, where the remainder interest is held by a related party (see ¶ 1201).[62] In the case of a trust, the allowable deduction for depreciation or depletion is apportioned between the income beneficiaries and the trustee on the basis of the trust income allocable to each. However, if the trust instrument or local law requires or permits the trustee to maintain a reserve for depreciation or depletion, the deduction is first allocated to the trustee to the extent that income is set aside for such a reserve.[63]

Any part of the deduction in excess of the income set aside for the reserve is then apportioned between the income beneficiaries and the trust on the basis of the trust income (in excess of the income set aside for the reserve) allocable to each. No effect is given to any allocation of the depreciation or depletion deduction that gives any beneficiary or the trustee a share of the deduction greater than a pro rata share of the trust income. The allocation is disregarded despite any provisions in the trust instrument, unless the trust instrument or local law requires or permits the trustee to maintain a reserve for depreciation or depletion.

In the case of an estate, the depreciation or depletion allowance is apportioned between the estate and the heirs, legatees and devisees on the basis of the income from the property allocable to each.[64] Although an estate or trust is entitled to take ACRS or MACRS depreciation on qualified assets, neither can make a Code Sec. 179 election to expense depreciable business assets described at ¶ 1208.

531. Losses and Bad Debts. An estate or trust can deduct losses from a trade or business or from transactions entered into for profit (Code Sec. 165(c) and Code Sec. 212). Similarly, the rules governing nonbusiness casualty and theft losses discussed at ¶ 1124 apply to an estate or trust. Thus, after the $100-per-occurrence floor has been satisfied, losses in excess of nonbusiness casualty and theft gains are deductible to the extent they exceed 10 percent of the adjusted gross income of the estate or trust. For this purpose, an estate's or trust's administration expenses are allowable as a deduction in computing its AGI (Code Sec. 165(h)(4)(C)).[65]

A nonbusiness casualty or theft loss sustained or discovered during the settlement of an estate is deductible on the estate's income tax return only if it has not been allowed for estate tax purposes. A statement to this effect should be filed with

Footnote references are to paragraphs of the 2002 Standard Federal Tax Reports.

[58] ¶ 24,280, ¶ 24,299	[62] ¶ 11,002, ¶ 23,920,	[64] ¶ 11,048, ¶ 11,049.01,
[59] ¶ 24,280	¶ 24,280	¶ 23,922
[60] ¶ 24,900	[63] ¶ 11,048, ¶ 23,922	[65] ¶ 9802
[61] ¶ 24,300		

¶ 530

the return for the year for which the deduction is claimed (Code Sec. 165(h)(4)(D); Reg. § 1.165-7(c); Reg. § 1.165-8(b)).[66]

An estate or trust is entitled to claim bad debt deductions under the rules governing individuals. The distinction is maintained between business debts, which may be deducted in the year in which they become partially or totally worthless, and nonbusiness debts, which may be deducted as short-term capital losses only if they become totally worthless.[67] An estate or trust is allowed a deduction for net operating loss carryovers and carrybacks (Reg. § 1.642(d)-1).[68] See ¶ 1173 and following; see, also, ¶ 543 and ¶ 556. However, an estate cannot deduct a capital loss or NOL sustained by a decedent during the decedent's last tax year. These losses must be deducted on the decedent's final return.[69]

532. Taxes. An estate or trust is entitled to the same deductions for taxes as individuals.[70] See ¶ 1021. Code Sec. 691(c) permits an offset of the allocable federal estate tax against income "in respect of a decedent." See ¶ 191. The portion of state income taxes allocable to exempt income, other than exempt interest income, is nondeductible. That portion of state income taxes attributable to exempt interest income and to income subject to federal income tax is deductible under Code Sec. 164.[71]

533. Interest. Paid or accrued interest is deductible by an estate or trust (Code Sec. 163).[72] However, there are a number of limitations on the deductibility of interest. Interest is not deductible on a debt incurred, or continued, to purchase or carry obligations the interest upon which is wholly exempt from federal income taxes. Personal interest of an estate or trust is nondeductible (see ¶ 1045). Further, the deduction for investment interest may not exceed net investment income for the tax year (Code Sec. 163(d)).[73] Net capital gain attributable to the disposition of property held for investment is generally excluded from investment income for purposes of computing this limitation. However, a special election is available to increase net capital gain includible in investment income by reducing the amount eligible for the maximum rate on capital gains (Code Sec. 1(h) and Code Sec. 163(d)(4)(iii)(B)). See ¶ 1094.

534. Exemption. An estate can claim a personal exemption of $600. A "simple" trust (¶ 542)—one that is required to distribute all of its income currently—is allowed an exemption of $300. All other trusts ("complex" trusts) are entitled to a $100 exemption (Code Sec. 642(b)).[74] If a final distribution of assets has been made during the year, all income of the estate or trust must be reported as distributed to the beneficiaries, without reduction for the amount claimed for the exemption.

535. Unused Loss Carryovers and Excess Deductions on Termination. A net operating loss, a capital loss carryover (see ¶ 562), and deductions in excess of gross income for the year in which an estate or trust terminates can be deducted by a beneficiary succeeding to the property of the trust or estate. Excess deductions on termination of an estate or trust are allowed only in computing taxable income and must be taken into account in computing the beneficiary's tax preference items. Such deductions may not be used in computing adjusted gross income. In computing excess deductions, the deductions for personal exemptions and for amounts set aside for charitable purposes are disregarded (Code Sec. 642(h); Reg. § 1.642(h)-1—Reg. § 1.642(h)-5).[75] The deduction is claimed as an itemized deduction or capital loss (depending on its nature) on the beneficiary's tax return filed for the year in which the trust or estate terminates.

Footnote references are to paragraphs of the 2002 Standard Federal Tax Reports.

[66] ¶ 9802, ¶ 10,004, ¶ 10,100
[67] ¶ 10,602, ¶ 10,691
[68] ¶ 24,296
[69] ¶ 24,267.451, ¶ 24,908.01

[70] ¶ 9500
[71] ¶ 14,054.03, ¶ 14,054.60, ¶ 24,267.4887
[72] ¶ 9102

[73] ¶ 9102
[74] ¶ 24,280, ¶ 24,286
[75] ¶ 24,280, ¶ 24,301, ¶ 24,305

The bankruptcy estate of an individual debtor in a liquidation (Chapter 7) or reorganization (Chapter 11) proceeding succeeds to certain tax attributes of the debtor, including any net operating loss (NOL) carryover (Code Sec. 1398(g)). The tax attributes that become part of the estate are determined as of the first day of the debtor's tax year in which the bankruptcy case commences. If any carryback year of the estate is a tax year before the estate's first tax year, the carryback is taken into account in the tax year of the debtor that corresponds to such carryback year and, accordingly, may offset the pre-bankruptcy income of the debtor (Code Sec. 1398(j)(2)(A)). When the estate closes upon the issuance of a final decree, any unused NOL carryover is returned to the debtor (Code Sec. 1398(i)). The debtor, however, cannot carry an unused NOL carryback from a tax year that ended after commencement of the bankruptcy case to a tax year that precedes the tax year in which the bankruptcy case was commenced (Code Sec. 1398(j)(2)(B)).

Charitable Contribution Deductions

537. Charitable Deduction Rules. Estates and complex trusts are allowed an unlimited charitable deduction for amounts that are *paid* to recognized charities out of gross income (other than unrelated business income) under the terms of the governing instrument during the tax year (Code Sec. 642(c)).[76] The trustee or administrator may elect to treat payments made during the year following the close of a tax year as having been paid in the earlier year for deduction purposes. This election must be made no later than the time, including extensions, prescribed by law for filing the income tax return for the tax year in which payment is made (Code Sec. 642(c)(1)).[77] The election for any tax year is binding for the year for which it is made and may not be revoked after the time for making the election has expired (Reg. § 1.642(c)-1(b)).[78]

Estates may also claim an unlimited deduction for amounts of gross income permanently set aside for charitable purposes. The income must be permanently set aside for a purpose specified in Code Sec. 170(c) or it must be used exclusively for religious, charitable, scientific, literary or educational purposes or for the establishment, acquisition, maintenance or operation of a nonprofit public cemetery.[79] For most complex trusts, the unlimited deduction does not apply for gross income that is permanently set aside for charitable purposes under the governing instrument (but not actually paid) (Reg. § 1.642(c)-2(b)).[80]

Pooled income funds (¶ 593) may claim a set-aside deduction only for gross income attributable to gain from the sale of a long-term capital asset that is permanently set aside for the benefit of the charity. No deduction is allowed with respect to gross income of the fund that is (1) attributable to income other than net long-term capital gains or (2) earned with respect to amounts transferred to the fund before August 1, 1969. The investment and accounting requirements applicable to trusts are also applicable to pooled income funds (Reg. § 1.642(c)-2).[81]

The unlimited charitable contribution deduction under Code Sec. 642(c) can be claimed only for contributions from income. Amounts bequeathed to charity that are paid out of corpus under state law are not deductible from income as charitable contributions or as distributions to beneficiaries.[82] Payments in compromise of bequests to charity are deductible.

The charitable deduction is normally computed on Form 1041, Schedule A. Where unrelated business income is involved, a separate schedule, rather than Schedule A, can be filed showing the computation of the deduction. Pooled income funds claiming the set-aside deduction for long-term capital gain are required to compute their deduction on a separate schedule, which is attached to the return.

Footnote references are to paragraphs of the 2002 Standard Federal Tax Reports.

¶ **537**

[76] ¶ 24,280,	[78] ¶ 24,288	[81] ¶ 24,290
¶ 24,308.058,	[79] ¶ 24,280, ¶ 24,290	[82] ¶ 24,308.115
¶ 24,308.1135	[80] ¶ 24,290	
[77] ¶ 24,280		

Every trust claiming a charitable deduction under Code Sec. 642(c) (and every Code Sec. 4947(a)(2) split-interest trust, including a pooled income fund) is required to file an information return (Code Sec. 6034). The information return is usually filed on Form 1041-A, due on or before April 15, 2002, for the 2001 calendar tax year. A nonexempt charitable trust, described in Code Sec. 4947(a)(1) and not treated as a private foundation, must also file a Form 990 if its gross receipts are normally more than $25,000. Such a trust may file a Form 990 to satisfy its Form 1041 filing requirement if the trust has zero taxable income (Code Sec. 6033). Both the trust and the trustee can be liable for a penalty of $20 per day up to a maximum of $10,000 for failure to timely file Form 1041-A. In the case of an organization having gross receipts exceeding $1,000,000 for any year, with respect to the return required under Code Sec. 6033 for such year, a $100 daily penalty applies instead of the $20 penalty and the maximum penalty will not exceed $50,000 rather than $10,000. Penalties also apply for filing a false or fraudulent return (Code Sec. 6652(c)).[83] When all trust net income must be distributed currently each year to the beneficiaries, the trust is relieved of filing Form 1041-A (Code Sec. 6034; Reg. § 1.6034-1).[84] For Code Sec. 664 charitable remainder trusts, see ¶ 590.

538. Disallowance of and Limitations on Deduction. A trust is not entitled to an unlimited charitable deduction under Code Sec. 642(c) for income that is allocable to its unrelated business income for the tax year (Code Sec. 681(a)).[85] The "unrelated business income" of a trust is computed in much the same manner as the unrelated business income of a tax-exempt organization (Code Sec. 501(a), Code Sec. 501(c)(3) and Code Sec. 512). See ¶ 655 and ¶ 687. However, in computing its unrelated business taxable income, a trust can claim deductions for *payments* to charities, subject to the percentage limitations applicable to individuals' charitable deductions (Code Sec. 170(b)). See ¶ 1058 et seq.

Charitable deductions are not allowed for otherwise deductible gifts to an organization upon which the private foundation termination tax has been imposed. General contributors will be denied deductions after the organization is notified of the loss of its private foundation status. Substantial contributors (see ¶ 635) will be denied deductions in the year in which the IRS takes action to terminate the private foundation status of an organization (Code Sec. 508(d)(1)).[86]

Deductions are also denied for contributions to any private foundation, charitable trust, or split-interest trust, as defined in Code Sec. 4947, that fails to meet the governing-instrument requirements of Code Sec. 508(e) (Code Sec. 508(d)(2)).[87] Deductions for gifts and bequests to any organization are disallowed during the period that the organization fails to notify the IRS that it is claiming exempt status as a charitable organization (a church, an organization with gross receipts of $5,000 or less, and certain other organizations designated by the IRS are exempt from the notification requirements) (Code Sec. 508(d)(2)).[88] Charitable deductions are also disallowed for bequests and gifts to a foreign private foundation after the IRS notifies it that it has engaged in a prohibited transaction or for a year in which such an organization loses its exempt status for engaging in such a transaction (Code Sec. 4948(c)(4)).[89]

Credits of Estate or Trust

540. Tax Credits. Generally, the credits allowed to individuals are allowed to estates and trusts. The credits typically must be apportioned between the estate or trust and the beneficiaries on the basis of the income allocable to each. These credits include the nonconventional source fuels credit (¶ 1319), the foreign tax credit (¶ 2475), the credit for prior year minimum tax (¶ 1370), and the component credits of the current year business credit (¶ 1323).[90]

Footnote references are to paragraphs of the 2002 Standard Federal Tax Reports.
[83] ¶ 39,480
[84] ¶ 35,440, ¶ 35,441
[85] ¶ 24,840, ¶ 24,844.01
[86] ¶ 22,790
[87] ¶ 22,790
[88] ¶ 22,790
[89] ¶ 34,160
[90] ¶ 24,264

The general business tax credit [91] is a limited nonrefundable credit against income tax that is claimed after all other nonrefundable credits are claimed (see ¶ 1323). The amount of the general business tax credit may not exceed the "net income tax" minus the greater of the tentative minimum tax or 25 percent of the net regular tax liability over $25,000. For estates and trusts, the $25,000 amount must be reduced to an amount that bears the same ratio to $25,000 as the portion of the income of the estate or trust that is not allocated to the beneficiaries bears to the total income of the estate or trust. Any unused credit can be carried back one year and forward 20 years for credits that arose in tax years beginning after 1997 and back three years and forward 15 years for credits that arose in tax years before 1998 (Code Sec. 39).[92]

Estates and trusts are also entitled to claim various refundable credits, including the credit for federal income tax withheld on wages (¶ 1372), the regulated investment company credit (¶ 1384), the credit for federal excise taxes paid on fuels (¶ 1379), and the credit for backup withholding (¶ 2645).

Deduction for Distribution to Beneficiary

542. "Simple" v. "Complex" Trust. A "simple" trust is one that is required to distribute all of its income currently whether or not distributions of current income are in fact made. The trust instrument for a simple trust does not provide for charitable contributions (Code Sec. 651; Reg. § 1.651(a)-1).[93] A trust may be a simple trust even though under local law or under the trust instrument capital gains must be allocated to corpus. The "income" required to be distributed in order to qualify for classification as a simple trust is the income under local law and the governing instrument (Code Sec. 643(b)).[94] Generally, this will include only ordinary income, because capital gains, under most trust instruments and state laws, are considered corpus. A trust will lose its classification as a simple trust (but not its $300 exemption) for any year during which it distributes corpus. Thus, a trust can never be a simple trust during the year of termination or in a year of partial liquidation (Reg. § 1.651(a)-3).[95] See ¶ 544. A foreign trust will not ordinarily be treated as a simple trust if it makes a loan of cash, cash equivalents or marketable securities to a grantor, or beneficiary who is a U.S. person, or a party related to such taxpayers (Code Sec. 643(i)(2)(D)).

The term "complex trust" applies to all trusts other than those described above. Generally, the same rules that apply to complex trusts also apply to estates. For simple and complex trusts and for estates, the deduction for distributions to beneficiaries is determined by reference to distributable net income (see ¶ 543).

543. Distributable Net Income. Distributable net income is an amount that sets the limit on the deduction of a domestic estate or trust for distributions to beneficiaries. It may also limit the amount of the distribution taxable to the beneficiary, and it is a factor in applying the conduit rule (see ¶ 559).

The distributable net income of a domestic estate or trust generally consists of the same items of gross income and deductions that make up the taxable income of the estate or trust. However, there are important modifications: (1) no deduction is allowed for distributions to beneficiaries; (2) the deduction for the personal exemption is disallowed; (3) tax-exempt interest on state and local bonds is included; (4) any tax-exempt interest and foreign income of a foreign trust that is determined without regard to Code Sec. 894 (income exempt under treaty) is included, reduced by any disbursements, expenses, losses, etc., allocable to such income; (5) capital gains allocable to corpus that are not paid, credited, or required to be distributed to any beneficiary during the tax year or paid, permanently set aside, or to be used for a charitable purpose as specified in Code Sec. 642(c) are excluded; (6) capital losses are excluded except to the extent of their use in determining the amount of capital

---

[91] ¶ 4250, ¶ 4251.01	[93] ¶ 24,360, ¶ 24,361	[95] ¶ 24,363
[92] ¶ 4300, ¶ 4301.01	[94] ¶ 24,320	

¶ **542**

gains paid, credited, or required to be distributed to any beneficiary during the tax year; and (7) in the case of a simple trust, extraordinary dividends or taxable stock dividends that the fiduciary, acting in good faith, allocates to corpus are excluded (Code Sec. 643(a); Reg. § 1.643(a)-0—Reg. § 1.643(a)-7).[96] The distributable net income of the estate or trust is determined by taking into account a net operating loss deduction.[97] See, also, ¶ 556.

For purposes of this chapter, the term "income" without specifying that "gross," "taxable," "distributable net," or another special concept is intended, it refers to income of the estate or trust for the tax year determined under the terms of its governing instrument and applicable local law—that is, income as it would be computed in an accounting to the court having jurisdiction over the estate or trust (Code Sec. 643(b); Reg. § 1.643(b)-1).[98] Trust provisions that depart fundamentally from concepts of local law on this point are not recognized for tax purposes.

544. Deduction for Distributions to Beneficiaries of a Simple Trust. A simple trust (¶ 542) may deduct the amount of income that the trustee is under a duty to distribute currently, even if the trustee makes the actual distribution after the close of the tax year. If other amounts are distributed—such as a payment from corpus to meet the terms of an annuity payable from income or corpus—the complex trust rules apply for that year, except that the $300 exemption (¶ 534) is still allowed (Reg. § 1.642(b)-1). If the income (in the accounting sense (¶ 543)) required to be distributed exceeds the distributable net income, the distribution deduction is limited to the distributable net income, computed without including exempt income (and related deductions) (Code Sec. 651; Reg. § 1.651(b)-1).[99]

545. Deduction for Distributions to Beneficiaries of Estate or Complex Trust. A complex trust (¶ 542) or estate may deduct any amount of income for the tax year that is required to be distributed currently. This includes any amount required to be distributed that may be paid out of income or corpus, to the extent that it is in fact paid out of income. A complex trust or estate may also deduct any other amounts properly paid or credited or required to be distributed in the tax year, including amounts distributable at the discretion of the fiduciary and a distribution in kind.[100] The amount to be taken into account in determining the deduction depends on whether the estate or trust elected to recognize gain on the distribution. See ¶ 526. In no case may the deduction exceed the distributable net income of the estate or trust (Code Sec. 661(a); Reg. § 1.661(a)-2).[101]

Where income is of varying types, the deduction for distributions is allocated in the same proportion as the total of each class of items bears to the total distributable net income. However, items will be allocated in accordance with a trust instrument or local law providing for a different method of allocation (Code Sec. 661(b); Reg. § 1.661(b)-1).[102] No deduction is allowed to the estate or trust for that part of a beneficiary's distribution that consists of income that is not included in the gross income of the estate or trust, such as tax-exempt interest income (Code Sec. 661(c); Reg. § 1.661(c)-1).[103]

In applying the above rule for determining the elements of a beneficiary's distribution (in the absence of specific allocation provisions in the trust instrument or state law providing otherwise), still another rule must be applied. All deductions entering into the computation of distributable net income (including charitable contributions) are allocated among the different types of income that make up such distributable net income according to the principles in Reg. § 1.652(b)-3.[104] These principles require that:

(1) There be allocated to items of gross income the deductions *directly* attributable to such gross income. (Thus, real estate taxes, repairs, the trustee's

---

Footnote references are to paragraphs of the 2002 Standard Federal Tax Reports.

[96] ¶ 24,320, ¶ 24,321—	[99] ¶ 24,360, ¶ 24,366	[102] ¶ 24,400, ¶ 24,403
¶ 24,327	[100] ¶ 24,400, ¶ 24,402	[103] ¶ 24,400, ¶ 24,405
[97] ¶ 24,296	[101] ¶ 24,400, ¶ 24,402	[104] ¶ 24,386
[98] ¶ 24,320, ¶ 24,329		

¶ 545

share of depreciation, fire insurance premiums, etc., would presumably be allocated to rental income.)

(2) All other deductions be allocated to any of the items of gross income included in computing distributable net income. (For example, allocate all other deductions to ordinary income.) However, a trust with nontaxable income must allocate a portion of these deductions to nontaxable income. The amount allocated to any one item of gross income may not exceed the amount of that item of gross income after its reduction for expenses directly attributable to it under step (1), above.

(3) The amounts determined under (1) and (2), above, be deducted from the separate items of gross income. Any excess of deductions may be assigned to any other class of income. However, excess deductions attributable to tax-exempt income may not be offset against any other class of income.

There is no prohibition against allocating the deduction under step (2) to every item of gross income distributed in the ratio that the amount of a particular type of income bears to the entire amount of income distributed. For an illustration of these allocations, see the examples at ¶ 559.

546. 65-Day Election. The fiduciary of an estate or a complex trust can elect annually to treat any distribution or any portion of any distribution to a beneficiary made within the first 65 days following the end of a tax year as having been distributed in the prior year. The election, which is to be made on Form 1041, is irrevocable for the year involved and is binding for that year only. The amount to which the election can apply is the greater of (1) the estate or trust's income or (2) distributable net income (¶ 543) for the tax year, reduced by any amounts paid, credited, or required to be distributed during the tax year other than those amounts that are subject to the 65-day election (Code Sec. 663(b); Reg. § 1.663(b)-1).[105] There is no 65-day election for accumulation distributions (¶ 567).

548. Annuities Distributable from Income or Corpus. In the case of recurring distributions, payments by a trust or estate (where the amounts to be distributed, paid, or credited are a charge upon the corpus or the income) are usually taxable to the beneficiary and deductible by the trust or estate, to the extent that they are made from income (Code Sec. 661(a)(1); Reg. § 1.661(a)-2(c)).[106]

549. Widow's Allowance. A widow's (or dependent's) statutory allowance or award for support during administration of the estate is deductible by an estate if it is paid pursuant to a court order or decree or under local law. The allowance can be paid from either income or principal, but the deduction is limited to the estate's distributable net income for the year (Reg. § 1.661(a)-2(e)).[107] Such payments are includible in the recipient's income to the extent of his or her share of the estate's distributable net income (Reg. § 1.662(a)-2(c) and Reg. § 1.662(a)-3(b)).[108] In addition, the IRS will treat such allowances as distributions to beneficiaries, even though the allowances are treated as debts of the estate under local law.[109]

How the Beneficiary Is Taxed

554. Taxation of Simple Trust Beneficiary. The income (as defined at ¶ 543) required to be distributed to a beneficiary of a simple trust is taxable to the beneficiary, whether or not distributed during the tax year, up to the amount of distributable net income. If the income required to be distributed exceeds distributable net income, only a proportionate part of each item is includible in the beneficiary's income. In making this apportionment, each item retains the same character (such as rent, dividends, etc.) that it had in the hands of the trust, unless the trust instrument specifically allocates a particular type of income to a particular benefici-

Footnote references are to paragraphs of the 2002 Standard Federal Tax Reports.

¶ **546**　[105] ¶ 24,440, ¶ 24,444　[107] ¶ 24,402　[109] ¶ 24,431.039
　　　[106] ¶ 24,400, ¶ 24,402　[108] ¶ 24,422, ¶ 24,423

ary, and deductions reflected in the computation of distributable net income are to be allocated among the various types of income in accordance with the rules explained at ¶ 545, above (Code Sec. 652; Reg. § 1.652(a)-1—Reg. § 1.652(b)-3).[110] The amounts reported on the beneficiary's return must be consistent with the amounts reported on the trust return (Code Sec. 6034A(c)).

556. Taxation of Beneficiary of Estate or Complex Trust. A beneficiary of a complex trust or of a decedent's estate must include in taxable income the income (as defined at ¶ 543) that is required to be distributed, whether or not it is actually distributed during the tax year, plus any other amounts that are properly paid, credited, or required to be distributed for that year (Code Sec. 662; Reg. § 1.662(a)-1).[111] (Special rules at ¶ 567-¶ 571 apply to distributions by trusts out of accumulated income.) If a fiduciary elects to treat a distribution to a beneficiary made in the year as an amount paid in a prior year (see the rules relating to the 65-day election at ¶ 546), the amount covered by the election is included in the beneficiary's income for the year for which the trust takes the deduction.

If the amount of income required to be distributed currently exceeds distributable net income (computed without the "unlimited" charitable deduction at ¶ 537), the beneficiary includes in income an amount that bears the same ratio to distributable net income as the amount of income required to be distributed currently to the beneficiary bears to the amount required to be distributed currently to all beneficiaries (Reg. § 1.662(a)-2).[112]

If the income required to be distributed, plus any other amounts properly paid, credited, or required to be distributed to a beneficiary for the tax year, exceeds the distributable net income for that year, then the beneficiary's share of such other amounts is a proportionate part of distributable net income (after subtracting the amounts required to be distributed) equal to the proportion that the beneficiary's share of these other amounts is of the total other amounts for all beneficiaries (Reg. § 1.662(a)-3).[113] The amount to be used in determining the beneficiary's share of estate or trust income depends on whether the estate or trust elected to recognize gain on the distribution. For the election rules, see ¶ 526.

If a net operating loss carryback of the estate or trust reduces the distributable net income of the estate or trust for the prior tax year to which the NOL is carried, the beneficiary's tax liability for such prior year may be recomputed based upon the revised distributable net income of the estate or trust (Rev. Rul. 61-20).[114]

In allocating the various types of income to the beneficiaries so as to give effect to all these rules, the amount reflected in the trust or estate's distributable net income is determined first. It is charged with directly related expenses and a proportionate part of other expenses, including the "unlimited" charitable deduction (¶ 537) to the extent it is chargeable to income of the current year. Then, each beneficiary's share of income paid, credited, or required to be distributed to the beneficiary is multiplied by fractions, for each class of income, in which the numerator is the amount of such income included in distributable net income (whether the aggregate is more or less than the distributable net income) and the denominator is the distributable net income. However, if the governing instrument specifies or local law requires a different allocation, such allocation is to be followed (Reg. § 1.662(b)-1; Reg. § 1.662(b)-2).[115] These computations are illustrated at ¶ 559.

Special provisions exclude from classification as income "required to be distributed currently" any "unlimited" charitable contribution (¶ 537) or a gift or bequest of a specific sum of money or specific property (other than an amount that can be paid or credited only from income of an estate or trust) if it is paid or distributed all at once or in not more than three installments. In determining the number of installments, gifts or bequests of personal and household effects, cars, and the like

---

Footnote references are to paragraphs of the 2002 Standard Federal Tax Reports.

[110] ¶ 24,380—¶ 24,386   [112] ¶ 24,422   [114] ¶ 24,431.493
[111] ¶ 24,420, ¶ 24,421   [113] ¶ 24,423   [115] ¶ 24,425, ¶ 24,426

¶ 556

are to be disregarded. Also disregarded are transfers of specific real estate, title to which passes directly from the decedent to the devisee under local law (Code Sec. 663(a); Reg. § 1.663(a)-1; Reg. § 1.663(a)-2).[116]

The amounts reported on the beneficiary's return must be consistent with the amounts reported on the trust or estate return (Code Sec. 6034A(c)).

557. Separate Shares as Separate Trusts. Where a trust or an estate has two or more beneficiaries and is to be administered in well-defined and separate shares, these shares are to be treated as separate trusts in determining the amount of distributable net income allocable to the beneficiaries. This rule limits the tax liability of a beneficiary on a corpus distribution where the income is being accumulated for the benefit of another beneficiary. The separate-share treatment is mandatory and not elective. A trustee or an executor may be required to apply it even though separate and independent accounts are not maintained for each share and even though there is no physical segregation of assets.

The separate-share rule does not affect situations in which a single trust instrument creates not one but several separate trusts, as opposed to separate shares in the same trust. The separate-share rule also does not apply to trusts that provide for successive interests (such as a trust that provides a life estate to A and a remainder to B).

The treatment of separate shares as separate trusts applies only for determining distributable net income in computing the distribution deduction allowable to the trust and the amount includible in the income of the beneficiary. It cannot be applied to obtain more than one deduction for the personal exemption or to split the income of the trust into several shares so as to be taxed at a lower-bracket rate (Code Sec. 663(c); Reg. § 1.663(c)-1—Reg. § 1.663(c)-4).[117]

ow the "Complex" Trust Rules Operate. The examples below illustrate, ɔr a uniform set of facts, computations of distributable net income, the ɔutive share of a beneficiary, and the taxable income of the trust. No "throw-' distributions (¶ 567-¶ 571) are involved.

Example 1. Trust income: A "complex" trust has the following items of income in 2001:

Dividends	$16,000
Taxable interest	10,000
Exempt interest	10,000
Rent	4,000
Long-term capital gain allocable to corpus	6,000

The trust has expenses as follows:

Expenses directly allocable to rent	$ 2,000
Commissions allocable to income	3,000
Commissions allocable to corpus	1,500

On these facts, the trust would have income of $40,000, as the term is interpreted by the regulations (see ¶ 543). The income items consist of dividends, taxable interest, exempt interest and rent (see Reg. § 1.643(d)-2(a)). No expenses or charges against income or corpus are subtracted; only "receipts" treated as income under local law and the governing instrument are counted (e.g., rent). Also, the long-term capital gain is excluded from this income in order to apply the conduit rule as illustrated below because it is not income under local law. It is, of course, included in the taxable income computation.

Example 2. Distributable net income: In computing distributable net income of the trust, an amount that will be an interim factor in later computations, the "net" amount of tax-exempt interest is added to the net income of the trust (after subtracting any charitable contribution). The "net" amount of tax-exempt interest is the full amount of such interest

---

Footnote references are to paragraphs of the 2002 Standard Federal Tax Reports.

¶ **557**

[116] ¶ 24,440, ¶ 24,441, ¶ 24,442   [117] ¶ 24,440, ¶ 24,446— ¶ 24,449

minus any expenses directly allocable to it and a proportionate part of all "general" expenses such as commissions. As noted in Example 1, there are $4,500 in general expenses (i.e., expenses not directly allocable to rental income), so $10,000/$40,000 of $4,500, or $1,125, is allocated to the exempt interest ($10,000), leaving a net of $8,875. This $1,125 must also be excluded from the deductions claimed by the trust as an expense "indirectly" related to the production of exempt interest income and therefore disallowed by Code Sec. 265. Accordingly, distributable net income is $33,500, computed as follows:

Dividends	$16,000
Taxable interest	10,000
Exempt interest ($10,000 less expenses allocable to exempt interest of $1,125)	8,875
Rent...	4,000
Total	$38,875

Deductions:

Rent expense	$2,000	
Commissions ($4,500 less $1,125 allocable to exempt interest)	3,375	5,375
Distributable net income		$33,500

Example 3. Taxable income of beneficiary: There is one beneficiary to whom the trustee must distribute $20,000 under the terms of the trust instrument. The first step in computing the amount taxable to the beneficiary is to determine the extent to which each income item is reflected in distributable net income, allocating expenses to the various items. Those allocable to exempt interest have already been reflected in the $8,875 figure carried into distributable net income in Example 2 so no further allocation of that item is needed. Allocation is needed for dividends, rent, and taxable interest income, but this allocation does not have to be proportionate. Expenses directly related to any source or type of income must, of course, be allocated directly to that income, but *general* expenses can be allocated to any taxable income the taxpayer wishes when computing distributable net income, as long as no deficit is created for any item. In this example, it is assumed the trustee allocates all general expenses to taxable interest. Accordingly, the trustee charges the entire $3,375 of expenses to the taxable interest ($10,000) so that the $33,500 distributable net income, for the purpose of applying the "conduit" rule, is deemed to have been derived from:

Rent...	$ 2,000
Taxable interest	6,625
Dividends	16,000
Tax-exempt interest	8,875
	$33,500

The total corresponds to the distributable net income and is only an intermediate or "identification" step. The next step, because the amounts actually distributable are less than the amount of distributable net income, is to multiply each of the above amounts by $20,000/$33,500 to determine what part of each is taxable to the beneficiary and deductible by the trust. Using these figures (the same result could be obtained by determining $2,000/$33,500 of $20,000, $6,625/$33,500 of $20,000, and so on), the apportionment is as follows:

Rent	$ 1,194.03
Taxable interest	3,955.22
Dividends..	9,552.24
Tax-exempt interest....................................	5,298.51
	$20,000.00

The beneficiary's share of income and deductions is reported on Schedule K-1 of Form 1041. The beneficiary will omit the $5,298.51 tax-exempt interest in reporting income from the trust. The $9,552.24 dividend and $3,955.22 taxable interest income should be reported on the beneficiary's Form 1040.

Example 4. Taxable income of the trust: The trust is allowed a deduction for the amount required to be distributed currently up to the amount of its distributable net income, but not for any portion that consists of tax-exempt income. The deduction for distributions, therefore, is $14,701.49 ($20,000 minus $5,298.51). Taxable income of the trust is then computed as follows:

Dividends	$16,000.00	
Interest	10,000.00	
Rent	4,000.00	
Long-term capital gain	6,000.00	$36,000.00
Less:		
Expenses allocable to rent	$ 2,000.00	
Commissions allocable to income ($3,000 minus the $750 [$10,000/$40,000] allocable to exempt interest)	2,250.00	
Commissions allocable to corpus ($1,500 minus the $375 [$10,000/$40,000] allocable to exempt interest)	1,125.00	
Distribution to beneficiary	14,701.49	
Exemption	100.00	20,176.49
Taxable income		$15,823.51

561. Income Paid or Credited to Heir, Legatee, or Beneficiary. An estate in the process of administration or a trust that accumulates or distributes income at the discretion of the fiduciary is allowed a deduction for income that is "properly paid, credited, or required to be distributed" during the tax year it is earned to a legatee, heir, or beneficiary, who is taxable accordingly (Code Sec. 662(a)(2)).[118] A testamentary trustee can be a legatee or beneficiary for the purpose of a taxable distribution.[119]

The IRS has ruled that where the will is silent, the law of the state controls for the purpose of determining whether income or gain during the period of administration is "properly paid or credited" to a legatee.[120] Income of a trust is taxable to the beneficiaries where there is no direction as to distribution or accumulation and state law requires distribution.[121]

562. Capital Gain or Loss of Estate or Trust. Capital gain is taxed to the estate or trust where the gain must be or is added to principal. However, where the gain is actually distributed to beneficiaries during the tax year, it is included in the computation of distributable net income and, therefore, is taxed to the beneficiary (Reg. § 1.643(a)-3(a)(2)).[122]

A net capital loss of an estate or trust will reduce the taxable income of the estate or trust, but no part of the loss is deductible by the beneficiaries. If the estate or trust distributes all of its income, the capital loss will not result in a tax benefit for the year of the loss. Losses from the sale or exchange of capital assets are generally excluded in computing distributable net income. However, they may be used to determine the net amount of capital gains that are paid, credited, or required to be distributed to any beneficiary during the tax year (Reg. § 1.643(a)-3).[123] On termination of an estate or trust, any unused capital loss carryover of the estate or trust is available to the beneficiaries (Code Sec. 642(h); Reg. § 1.642(h)-1).[124] See ¶ 535.

Footnote references are to paragraphs of the 2002 Standard Federal Tax Reports.

¶ 561

[118] ¶ 24,420	[121] ¶ 24,431.65	[123] ¶ 24,324
[119] ¶ 24,407.7951	[122] ¶ 24,324	[124] ¶ 24,280, ¶ 24,301
[120] ¶ 24,407.78		

564. Gift or Bequest. A trust or estate may not deduct as a distribution to a beneficiary and a beneficiary does not include in income a gift or bequest of a specific sum that is paid or credited in not more than three installments. However, an amount will not be treated as an excluded gift or bequest if the governing instrument provides that the specific sum is payable only from the income of the estate or trust (Code Sec. 663(a); Reg. § 1.663(a)-1).[125]

565. Different Tax Year. If the tax year of a beneficiary is different from that of the estate or trust, the amount to be included in the gross income of the beneficiary must be based on the distributable net income of the estate or trust and the amounts paid, credited, or required to be distributed to the beneficiary for any tax year or years of the estate or trust ending with or within his tax year (Code Sec. 652(c) and Code Sec. 662(c); Reg. § 1.652(c)-1 and Reg. § 1.662(c)-1).[126]

The Throwback Rules

567. What the Throwback Provision Accomplishes. Special "throwback rules" generally apply to trust distributions made in tax years beginning before August 6, 1997. Although the throwback rules have been repealed for most trusts, they continue to apply to trusts created before March 1, 1984 that would be treated as multiple trusts under Code Sec. 643(f) and to foreign trusts and domestic trusts that were once treated as foreign trusts.

The throwback rules are designed to prevent the accumulation of trust income by a complex or accumulation trust over a period of years with a distribution to a beneficiary only in low-income years. The rules have the effect of carrying back to preceding years any distributions in excess of distributable net income (ordinary income) for the distribution year and taxing them to the beneficiaries in the same manner as if distributed in the year the income was accumulated by the trust. This additional income is taxed to the beneficiary in the year that the beneficiary receives the accumulation distribution, but the beneficiary's tax liability is computed on Form 4970 (Tax on Accumulation Distribution of Trusts) under special rules. Schedule J of Form 1041 (Trust Allocation of an Accumulation Distribution) is used to determine the amount, the year, and the character of the additional distributions taxable to beneficiaries under the throwback rules. The beneficiary is allowed an offset or credit against the partial tax for the proportionate part of the trust's tax for the prior year, thus eliminating any double tax on the income. Beneficiaries of estates are not subject to the throwback rules (Code Sec. 665-Code Sec. 667).[127]

SPECIAL TRUST RULES

Grantor Trust

571. Overview of Grantor Trust Rules. Under the grantor trust rules, a person (the grantor) who transfers property to a trust and retains certain powers or interests is treated as the owner of the trust for income tax purposes. As a result, the income and deductions attributable to the trust for income are included in the grantor's income.[128]

573. Family Trust Generally. Income-producing property is often conveyed in trust for the benefit of a family member in an effort to split any income generated by the property or to otherwise lessen the original owner's tax liability. There must be an actual transfer of property to accomplish the desired tax savings; it is not enough to transfer income generated by the property.

Footnote references are to paragraphs of the 2002 Standard Federal Tax Reports.
125 ¶ 24,440, ¶ 24,441   127 ¶ 24,480, ¶ 24,500,   128 ¶ 24,680
126 ¶ 24,380, ¶ 24,387,   ¶ 24,520
¶ 24,420, ¶ 24,427

¶**573**

Limitations in the law (¶ 574-¶ 588) prevent a taxpayer from escaping tax on the income from property where the taxpayer in effect remains the owner of the property by retaining control over the trust. In addition, intrafamily transfers of income-producing property can no longer be used to reduce income tax liability by shifting income from the parents' high marginal rate to their child's generally lower tax bracket if the child is under age 14. Instead, if the net unearned income of the child exceeds the sum of the $750 standard deduction in 2001 (unofficially projected to be $750 in 2002) and the greater of $750 in 2001 (unofficially projected to be $750 in 2002) or the itemized deductions directly related to the production of that unearned income, it is taxed at the parents' top marginal rate (see ¶ 706).[129]

574. "Family Estate Trusts." A "family estate trust," i.e., a trust to which an individual transfers personal assets and the right to income in exchange for the beneficial enjoyment of such assets and compensation, will be taxed as a grantor trust. The grantor's assignment of lifetime services or salary to the trust is not recognized for income tax purposes. Such trusts are deemed a "nullity" for income tax purposes and their income is taxable to the persons who created them. Acceptance of this broad economic principle deprives a grantor of any possible refuge in the technicalities of the grantor trust provisions.[130] Expenses incurred in setting up these family estate trusts are not deductible under Code Sec. 212.[131]

575. "Pre-Need Funeral Trusts." A pre-need qualified funeral trust is not treated as a grantor trust and the tax on the annual earnings of the trust is payable by the trustee if a trustee elects this special tax treatment (Code Sec. 685). Generally, a qualified pre-need funeral trust is an arrangement that would otherwise be treated as a grantor trust, under which an individual purchases funeral services or merchandise for himself or for another individual from a funeral home prior to death and funds the purchase via contributions, not in excess of $7,500 for 2001 (Rev. Proc. 2001-13) (unofficially projected to be $7,700 in 2002), to a trust. The contributions are held, invested and reinvested by the trust solely to make payments for such services or property to the seller upon the individual's or the other trust beneficiaries' death. If the election is made, the income tax rate schedule generally applicable to estates and trusts is applied to the trust by treating each beneficiary's interest as a separate trust. However, the trust is not entitled to a personal exemption in calculating the tax. The trustee's election must be made separately for each such "separate" trust. No gain or loss is recognized to a purchaser of a pre-need funeral trust contract as a result of any payment from the trust to the purchaser due to the cancellation of the contract.

576. Reversionary Interest in Grantor. Trust income is generally taxed to the grantor if the trust corpus will revert to either the grantor or the grantor's spouse. A grantor is considered to be the owner of any portion of a trust in which the grantor has a reversionary interest in either the trust corpus or the income if the value of the reversionary interest exceeds five percent of the value of that portion of the trust. The value of the reversionary interest is measured as of the inception of the portion of the trust in which the grantor holds an interest. In determining whether the grantor's reversionary interest exceeds five percent of the value of that portion of the trust, it is assumed that any discretionary powers will be exercised to maximize the value of the reversionary interest. Any postponement of the reacquisition or enjoyment of the reversionary interest is considered to be a new transfer in trust; however, no income is to be included in the grantor's income that would not have been included in the absence of the postponement. A grantor is exempt from this rule if the grantor retains a reversionary interest that takes effect only upon the death of a minor lineal descendant (under age 21) and if the beneficiary has the entire present interest in the trust or a trust portion (Code Sec. 673).[132]

578. Powers Held by Grantor's Spouse. A grantor is treated as holding any power or interest in a trust that is held by a person who was the grantor's

spouse at the time the power or interest was created or who became the grantor's spouse subsequent to the creation of the power or interest, with respect to periods that the individual was the grantor's spouse. Thus, the grantor trust provisions cannot be avoided by having the spouse of the grantor possess prohibited powers or interests (e.g., spousal remainder trusts) (Code Sec. 672(e)).[133] However, individuals who are legally separated under a decree of divorce or separate maintenance are not considered to be married.

579. Power to Control Beneficial Enjoyment. A grantor is taxed on the trust income if the grantor or the grantor's spouse (as defined at ¶ 578, above) retains the power to control the beneficial enjoyment (Code Sec. 674; Reg. § 1.674(a)-1).[134] However, there are a number of exceptions listed in the regulations (Reg. § 1.674(b)-1—Reg. § 1.674(d)-2).[135]

581. Retention of Administrative Powers. The grantor is taxed on the trust income if the grantor or the grantor's spouse (as defined at ¶ 578, above) retains administrative powers enabling the grantor to obtain, by dealings with the trust, financial benefits that would not be available in an arm's-length transaction (Code Sec. 675; Reg. § 1.675-1).[136] The borrowing of trust corpus or income by the grantor or the grantor's spouse (as defined at ¶ 578, above) at any time during a tax year results in the grantor's being taxed on the trust income for that entire year, even if the grantor repays the loan with interest during the same year.[137]

582. Power to Revoke Trust. If a grantor creates a trust and reserves a right to revoke it, the income of the trust is treated as the grantor's income. However, the trust income will not be taxed to the grantor if the power can only affect the beneficial enjoyment of the income after the occurrence of an event such that the grantor would not be treated as the owner under Code Sec. 673 if the power were a reversionary interest. But the grantor may be treated as the owner after the occurrence of the event unless the power is then relinquished. [138]

584. Income for Grantor's Benefit. The grantor is taxable on income that is or may be accumulated or distributed to the grantor or to the grantor's spouse or used to pay life insurance premiums on either's life, except for policies irrevocably payable to charities (Code Sec. 677(a)).[139] If trust income may be used to any extent in satisfaction of the grantor's legal obligation to support a beneficiary (such as a child, but not a spouse), to that extent it is regarded as distributable to the grantor. But if the discretion to so use the income is not in the grantor, acting as such, but in another person, in the trustee, or in the grantor acting as trustee or co-trustee, then that income is includible in the grantor's gross income to the extent that it is used for the beneficiary's support or maintenance (Code Sec. 677(b); Reg. § 1.677(b)-1).[140]

In addition, any capital gain that, under state law, is added to trust corpus is taxable to the grantor if the corpus reverts to the grantor upon termination of the trust (Reg. § 1.671-3(b)(2) and Reg. § 1.677(a)-1(f)).[141]

585. Income Taxable to Person Other Than Grantor. A person other than the grantor of a trust may be taxed on the trust's income if that person has a power, exercisable alone, to vest the corpus or income of the trust in that person (Code Sec. 678(a); Reg. § 1.678(a)-1).[142] These rules apply, for example, in the case of a trust that is established by a father for the benefit of his children, but under which the grantor's brother may at any time take the trust property. The brother is then treated as the owner and the income is taxed to him. These rules do not apply if the power is renounced or disclaimed within a reasonable period of time (Reg. § 1.678(d)-1).[143]

Footnote references are to paragraphs of the 2002 Standard Federal Tax Reports.

[133] ¶ 24,700,	[137] ¶ 24,686.6135,	[141] ¶ 24,684, ¶ 24,781
¶ 24,705.021	¶ 24,742.01	[142] ¶ 24,800, ¶ 24,801,
[134] ¶ 24,720, ¶ 24,721	[138] ¶ 24,710	¶ 24,805.01
[135] ¶ 24,722—¶ 24,725	[139] ¶ 24,780, ¶ 24,783.01	[143] ¶ 24,804
[136] ¶ 24,740, ¶ 24,741	[140] ¶ 24,780, ¶ 24,782	

A U.S. person who is a beneficiary of a trust is treated as the grantor to the extent that the beneficiary transferred property, directly or indirectly, to a foreign person who otherwise would have been treated as the owner under the grantor trust rules.[144]

586. Return for Grantor Trust. Generally, items of income, deduction, or credit that are treated as belonging to a trust grantor or another person are not reported by the trust on Form 1041. Instead, these items are reflected on the income tax return of the grantor (or other person who is taxable on the trust income). A separate statement should be attached to Form 1041 stating the name, taxpayer identification number and address of the person to whom the income is taxable and setting forth the income deductions and credits (Reg. § 1.671-4).[145] Alternative reporting methods may be available for certain grantor trusts (Reg. § 1.671-4(b)).[146]

588. Foreign Grantor Trust Rules. Any U.S. person transferring property to a foreign trust (other than an employee's trust) that has a U.S. beneficiary will be treated as the owner of that portion of the trust attributable to the property transferred (Code Sec. 678(b) and Code Sec. 679).[147] The transferor is required to file an annual information return (Code Sec. 6048(c) and Code Sec. 6677(a)).[148] Also, the U.S. grantor trust rules generally will not apply to any portion of a trust that would otherwise be deemed to be owned by a foreign person (Code Sec. 672(f)).

Charitable Trust

590. Charitable Remainder Trusts. Whenever there is a noncharitable income beneficiary, gifts of remainder interests in trusts will qualify for a charitable contribution deduction only if the trust is a charitable remainder *annuity trust* or a charitable remainder *unitrust* (Code Sec. 664).[149] Charitable contribution deductions are denied for gifts of remainder interests in all other types of trusts. (However, if the grantor gives *all* the interests in a trust to charity, the above rules are not applicable, and a deduction is allowable.)

(1) An *annuity trust* is a trust from which a sum certain or a specified amount is to be paid to the income beneficiary or beneficiaries. The specified amount may not be less than five percent, and cannot be more than 50 percent, of the initial net fair market value of all property placed in trust, and it must be paid at least annually to the income beneficiary. Furthermore, the value of the remainder interest must usually be at least 10 percent of the initial net fair market value of all property placed in trust. There are several provisions designed to provide relief to trusts that do not meet the "10-percent" test. No contributions can be made to a charitable remainder annuity trust after the initial contribution, and the governing instrument must contain a prohibition against future contributions.

(2) A *unitrust* is a trust that specifies that the income beneficiary or beneficiaries are to receive annual payments based on a fixed percentage of the net fair market value of the trust's assets as determined each year. The fixed percentage cannot be less than five percent, and cannot be more than 50 percent, of the net fair market value. In the alternative, however, a qualified charitable remainder unitrust can provide for the distribution each year of five percent of the net fair market value of its assets or the amount of the trust income, whichever is lower. For this purpose, trust income excludes capital gains and trust assets must be valued annually. This payment requirement may not be discretionary with the trustee. Unitrusts may have additional contributions made to them. For most transfers in trust, the value of the remainder interest with respect to each contribution to the unitrust must be at least 10 percent of the net fair market value of such contributed property as of the date the property is contributed to the trust. If an additional contribution would cause the trust to fail the "10-percent" remainder test, then the contribution will be treated as a transfer to a separate trust under regulations to be

---

Footnote references are to paragraphs of the 2002 Standard Federal Tax Reports.

¶ 586

[144] ¶ 24,705.04	[146] ¶ 24,685	[148] ¶ 36,000, ¶ 39,815
[145] ¶ 24,685	[147] ¶ 24,800, ¶ 24,820	[149] ¶ 24,460

prescribed by the IRS. Other provisions may provide relief to trusts that fail to meet the "10-percent" test.

Charitable remainder annuity trusts and unitrusts cannot have noncharitable remainder interests. Generally, the remainder interests must pass to a charity upon the termination of the last income interest and the trust instrument must contain a provision that determines how the final payment of a specified distribution is to be made.[150] However, a charitable trust may make certain limited "qualified gratuitous" transfers of qualified employer securities to an ESOP without adversely affecting the status of the charitable remainder trust.

There may be more than one noncharitable income beneficiary, either concurrently or successively, and the income interest may be a life estate or for a term of years not in excess of 20 years. However, a contingency clause may be placed in the trust instrument providing that the noncharitable interest is to terminate and the charitable interest is to be accelerated upon the happening of an event such as the remarriage of the noncharitable beneficiary (Code Sec. 664(f)).[151] The income beneficiary can receive only a specified or fixed amount from the trust, and the trustee cannot have additional power to invade corpus or to alter, amend, or revoke the trust for the benefit of the noncharitable income beneficiary. The trustee cannot be restricted from investing in income-producing assets.[152]

Taxation of Trust and Beneficiary. A charitable remainder annuity trust or a unitrust is exempt from tax unless it has unrelated business income, in which case it is taxed as a complex trust. However, an exempt charitable remainder trust is subject to the income and excise taxes imposed on private exempt foundations. Under either an annuity trust or a unitrust, the amount paid to the income beneficiary is considered as having the following characteristics in the beneficiary's hands: it will be ordinary income to the extent of the trust's ordinary income for the tax year and its undistributed ordinary income from prior years; it will be capital gain to the extent of the trust's capital gains for the tax year and its undistributed capital gains, determined on a cumulative net basis, for prior years; it will be considered other income to the extent of the trust's other income for the tax year and its undistributed other income from prior years; any remaining amount will be considered a distribution of principal (Code Sec. 664; Reg. § § 1.664-1—1.664-4).[153]

The fiduciary of a charitable remainder annuity trust or unitrust must file Form 5227 (Split-Interest Trust Information Return). The fiduciary must also file Form 1041-A unless all net income is required to be distributed currently to the beneficiaries. Such returns must be filed on or before the 15th day of the fourth month following the close of the tax year of the trust.[154]

591. Private Foundation Rules Applicable to Trusts. The income and excise taxes imposed on private exempt foundations extend to certain nonexempt charitable trusts. First, the investment income tax and the excise taxes on prohibited transactions apply to any nonexempt trust that devotes *all* of its "unexpired interests" to charitable, religious, educational, and other purposes that enable contributors to obtain a charitable deduction. "Unexpired interests" include life or term income interests, interests in trust corpus and remainder interests. Such charitable trusts are subject to all of the other private foundation rules (except for the Code Sec. 508(a)-(c) notification requirements). See ¶ 616 and ¶ 631 (Code Sec. 4947).[155]

Second, a nonexempt, split-interest trust is subject to excise taxes on the following four prohibited transactions: self-dealing, excess business holdings, investments that jeopardize charitable purposes, and taxable expenditures (lobbying, electioneering, etc.). A split-interest trust has both charitable and noncharitable beneficiaries, so it does not devote *all* of its unexpired interests to charitable purposes. The investment income tax and failure to distribute sanction do not apply to a split-interest trust. Further, the four excise taxes apply to income to be paid to

---

Footnote references are to paragraphs of the 2002 Standard Federal Tax Reports.

[150] ¶ 24,468	[152] ¶ 24,468.03	[154] ¶ 24,468.20
[151] ¶ 24,460	[153] ¶ 24,460—¶ 24,466	[155] ¶ 34,140

trust beneficiaries under the terms of the trust instrument only if the trust was a "charitable remainder annuity trust" or a "charitable remainder unitrust" (¶ 590 and ¶ 631). The taxes do not, in any event, apply to amounts in trust for which a deduction is not allowable if segregated from deductible amounts.

The taxes on excess business holdings and on jeopardizing investments do not apply to a split-interest trust if the charity is only an income beneficiary and its beneficial interest is no more than 60 percent of the value of the trust property or if the charity's only interest in the trust is as a remainderman. Split-interest trusts are treated like private foundations with regard to the rules on governing instruments and the tax on involuntary termination of status for repeated or willful violations (¶ 631).

593. Pooled Fund Arrangements. Income, estate, and gift tax charitable contribution deductions are allowed for the value of remainder interests in property transferred to a pooled income fund (Code Sec. 642(c)(3)).[156] Generally, a pooled income fund is a trust to which a person transfers an irrevocable remainder interest in property for the benefit of a public charity while retaining an income interest in the property for the life of one or more beneficiaries living at the time of the transfer (Reg. § 1.642(c)-5). To protect the value of depreciable property that will pass to the charitable remainderman, the governing instrument of the pooled income fund must provide for the creation of a depreciation reserve.[157] In addition, the fund (1) must commingle all property contributed to it, (2) cannot invest in tax-exempt securities and (3) must be maintained by the recipient charity with no donor or income beneficiary acting as a trustee. However, the charity does not have to act as trustee of the fund.

Each person who has an income interest resulting from a transfer of property to the fund must be paid an annual income based on the fund's yearly rate of return; the trust cannot accumulate income for any beneficiary. A pooled income fund's method of calculating its yearly rate of return must be supported by a full statement attached to the fund's annual income tax return. A pooled income fund cannot include contributions of property from sources other than pooled income funds and general endowment funds (Code Sec. 642(c)(5)).[158] Such a fund and its beneficiaries are taxable under the rules applicable to trusts, except that the substantial owner rules do not apply.

595. Common Trust Fund. Each participant in a common trust fund—maintained by a bank—must report its share of the taxable income of the fund, whether or not distributed or distributable. The taxable income of a common trust fund is computed in much the same manner as an individual's taxable income, except for the exclusion of capital gains and losses and the deduction for charitable contributions (Code Sec. 584).[159]

Chapter 6

EXEMPT ORGANIZATIONS

Qualification and Application

601. Who May Be Tax Exempt? Under Code Sec. 501, a variety of organizations, e.g., nonprofit groups organized for charitable or mutual benefit purposes, may qualify for exemption from income taxation. However, they may be subject to income tax (see ¶ 655) if they have income from the operation of a business enterprise not related to the purpose for which they received their exemption (Code Sec. 511; Reg. § 1.511-1—§ 1.511-3).[1] Rental income arising from debt-financed sale and leaseback is also taxable (Code Sec. 514).[2] See ¶ 687. Exempt private foundations may be subject to sanctions, primarily in the form of excise taxes, for engaging in prohibited activities (see ¶ 635-¶ 644) or for accumulating income (Code Sec. 4940—Code Sec. 4948).[3]

Private foundations that are subject to the 2-percent excise tax on net investment income under Code Sec. 4940[4] and tax-exempt organizations that are subject to the tax on unrelated business income under Code Sec. 511 will be treated as corporations and be required to make estimated payments on such taxes. The quarterly estimated payments of the excise tax or the tax on unrelated business income must be made under rules similar (but see ¶ 650) to those that apply to corporate income taxes (Code Sec. 6655(g)(3)).[5] See ¶ 631 and following.

The general exemptions from income tax, under Code Sec. 501(c) and Reg. § 1.501(c)(2)-1—§ 1.501(e)-1, along with the proper forms for application for recognition of exempt status, are:[6]

(1) *Corporation organized under an Act of Congress as a U.S. instrumentality* if declared exempt under the Internal Revenue Code or organizing legislation enacted before July 18, 1984 (Code Sec. 501(c)(1)). (No application form.)

(2) *Corporation organized for the exclusive purpose of holding title to property,* collecting income from such property, and turning over the entire amount of such income, less expenses, to an exempt organization (Code Sec. 501(c)(2)). However, there are limits on the amount of unrelated business income that a corporation organized solely to hold title to property may receive and still retain its exempt status. See the discussion of a *title holding corporation or trust* below. (Form 1024 (Application for Recognition of Exemption Under Section 501(a) or for Determination Under Section 120).)

(3) *Corporation and any community chest, fund, or foundation, organized and operated exclusively for religious, charitable, scientific, testing for public safety, literary or educational purposes, or to foster national or international amateur sports*

Footnote references are to paragraphs of the 2002 Standard Federal Tax Reports.

[1] ¶ 22,820—¶ 22,825	[3] ¶ 34,000,¶ 34,160	[5] ¶ 39,565
[2] ¶ 22,850	[4] ¶ 34,000	[6] ¶ 22,602, ¶ 22,606

competition (so long as none of its activities involve the providing of athletic facilities or equipment) or for the prevention of cruelty to children or animals, no part of the net earnings of which inures to the benefit of any private shareholder or individual, no substantial part of the activities of which is carrying on propaganda, or otherwise attempting to influence legislation, and which does not attempt to participate or intervene in any political campaign (Code Sec. 501(c)(3)). (Form 1023 (Application for Recognition of Exemption Under Section 501(c)(3) of the Internal Revenue Code).)

Because of the need for the IRS to combat efforts on the part of some individuals and organizations to utilize a church form of organization to avoid taxes, and the equally important need to protect legitimate churches from undue IRS interference in their activities, the Code contains detailed rules governing the circumstances under which the IRS may inquire into or examine churches (Code Sec. 7611; Reg. § 301.7611-1).[7]

An educational organization includes a child-care center whose services are available to the general public and whose purpose is to enable individuals to be gainfully employed (Code Sec. 501(k)).[8] Educational institutions that practice racial discrimination cannot qualify for exemption.[9]

(4) *Civic league, an organization not organized for profit but operated exclusively for the promotion of social welfare, or a local association of employees,* the membership of which is limited to the employees of a designated employer in a particular municipality, and the net earnings of which are devoted exclusively to charitable, educational, or recreational purposes (Code Sec. 501(c)(4)). (Form 1024.) In addition, no part of the net earnings may inure to the benefit of any private shareholder or individual (Code Sec. 501(c)(4)(B)).

Except in the case of a charitable risk pool available to certain tax-exempt 501(c)(3) organizations, any organization described in (3) or (4), above, is entitled to tax-exempt status only if no substantial part of its activities consists of providing commercial-type insurance. If the organization provides insurance that is not substantial, that activity must be treated as an unrelated trade or business of the tax-exempt organization but will be taxed under the rules that pertain to insurance companies (Code Sec. 501(m)).[10]

A qualified charitable risk pool means any organization that is organized and operated solely to pool insurable risks of its members (other than risks related to medical malpractice), provides information to its members on loss control and risk management, and meets certain other requirements (Code Sec. 501(n)).[11]

(5) *Labor, agricultural, or horticultural organization* (Code Sec. 501(c)(5)). The term "agricultural" includes the harvesting of aquatic animal and vegetable resources (Code Sec. 501(g)). Also, an employer-funded pension plan for union employees that was jointly managed by labor and management was held to be a tax-exempt labor organization.[12] (Form 1024.)

(6) *Business league, chamber of commerce, real estate board, board of trade, or professional football league,* not organized for profit and no part of the net earnings of which inures to the benefit of any private shareholder or individual (Code Sec. 501(c)(6)). (Form 1024.)

(7) *Club organized for pleasure, recreation, and other nonprofit purposes* (social and recreation clubs), substantially all of the activities of which are for such purposes and no part of the net earnings of which inures to the benefit of any private shareholder (Code Sec. 501(c)(7)). (Form 1024.) No exemption is available for a club with a governing instrument or other written policy that discriminates against a person on the basis of race, religion, or color (Code Sec. 501(i)).

(8) *Fraternal beneficiary society, order, or association* (a) operating under the lodge system or for the exclusive benefit of the members of a fraternity that is itself operating under the lodge system and (b) providing for the payment of life, sickness,

Footnote references are to paragraphs of the 2002 Standard Federal Tax Reports.

¶601
7 ¶ 42,910, ¶ 42,912　　9 ¶ 22,604.1154　　11 ¶ 22,602
8 ¶ 22,602　　　　　　10 ¶ 22,602　　　　12 ¶ 22,613.51

accident, or other benefits to its members or their dependents (Code Sec. 501(c)(8)). (Form 1024.)

(9) *Voluntary employees' beneficiary association* (VEBA) providing for the payment of life, sickness, accident or other benefits to members, their dependents, or beneficiaries, if no part of its net earnings inures (other than through such payment) to the benefit of any private shareholder or individual (Code Sec. 501(c)(9)). (Form 1024.) A VEBA will not qualify for exemption unless it meets certain participation and anti-discrimination requirements that are similar to those applying to qualified pension, profit-sharing and stock bonus plans (see ¶ 2117) (Code Sec. 505).[13]

(10) *Domestic fraternal society, or association,* operating under the lodge system the net earnings of which are devoted exclusively to religious, charitable, scientific, literary, educational, or fraternal purposes and which does *not* provide for payment of life, sickness, accident or other benefits (Code Sec. 501(c)(10)). (Form 1024.)

(11) *Teachers' retirement fund association* of a purely local character if (a) no part of its net earnings inures (other than through payment of retirement benefits) to the benefit of any private shareholder or individual and (b) the income consists solely of amounts from public taxation, from assessments upon the teaching salaries of members, or from investments (Code Sec. 501(c)(11)). (No application form.)

(12) *Benevolent life insurance association* of a purely local character, *mutual ditch or irrigation company, mutual or cooperative telephone company,* or like organization, but only if 85 percent or more of the income (disregarding certain income) consists of amounts collected from members for the sole purpose of meeting losses and expenses (Code Sec. 501(c)(12)). (Form 1024.)

(13) *Cemetery company* that is owned and operated exclusively for the benefit of its members or that is not operated for profit, and any corporation chartered solely for the purpose of disposal of bodies by burial or cremation and is not permitted by its charter to engage in any business not necessarily incident to that purpose, no part of the net earnings of which inures to the benefit of any private shareholder or individual (Code Sec. 501(c)(13)). (Form 1024.)

(14) *Credit union without capital stock,* organized and operated for mutual purposes and without profit; mutual nonprofit corporation or association without capital stock, organized before September 1, 1957, and operated for the purpose of providing reserve funds for, and insurance of, shares or deposits in various financial institutions; and mutual nonprofit corporations or associations organized before September 1, 1957 and operated to provide reserve funds for certain financial institutions, as long as 85 percent or more of the income is attributable to providing such reserve funds and to investments. Mutual savings banks that have capital stock represented by shares and that are subject to, and operate under, federal or state laws relating to mutual savings banks (Code Sec. 591)[14] are tax exempt (Code Sec. 501(c)(14)). (No application form.)

(15) *Insurance companies or associations other than life* (including interinsurers and reciprocal underwriters) if the net written premiums (or, if greater, direct written premiums) for the tax year do not exceed $350,000 (Code Sec. 501(c)(15)). (Form 1024.)

(16) *Corporation—farmers' and fruit growers' cooperative—*organized by an association exempt under the provisions described at ¶ 696, or by the members of such an association, for the purpose of financing the crop operations of the members or other producers, and operated in conjunction with the association (Code Sec. 501(c)(16)). (There are certain capital stock restrictions.) (No application form.)

(17) *A trust or trusts forming part of a nondiscriminatory plan providing for the payment of supplemental unemployment compensation benefits* if certain requirements, similar to Code Sec. 414, are met (Code Sec. 501(c)(17)). (Form 1024.)

(18) *Nondiscriminatory employee pension trust or trusts created before June 25, 1959,* forming part of a plan providing for payment of benefits under a pension

---

plan funded only by employee contributions (Code Sec. 501(c)(18)). Employees who participate in this type of a pension plan may elect to make deductible contributions if the plan satisfies a special nondiscrimination test similar to the one applicable to a 401(k) plan. If the test is not satisfied, rules similar to the rules applicable to excess contributions under a 401(k) plan apply. (See ¶ 2111.) (No application form.)

(19) *A post or organization of past or present members of the U.S. Armed Forces,* or an auxiliary unit or related society, trust, or foundation, where at least 75 percent of the members are past or present Armed Forces Members and no part of the net earnings inure to the benefit of any private shareholder or individual (Code Sec. 501(c)(19)). (Form 1024.)

(20) *Organization or trust forming part of a qualified group legal services plan under Code Sec. 120.* It will not be prevented from so qualifying merely because it provides legal services or indemnification against the cost of legal services unassociated with a qualified group legal services plan (Code Sec. 501(c)(20)). (Form 1024.) This exemption applies for tax years beginning before July 1, 1992, and the organization must meet nondiscrimination requirements (Code Secs. 120(e) and 505).[15]

(21) *A trust established by coal operators* in the U.S. and maintained for the purpose of satisfying liability for claims of compensation pursuant to the Black Lung Acts (Code Sec. 501(c)(21)). Such trusts may be subject to excise taxes on self-dealing acts, improper expenditures, and excess contributions made to the trusts (Code Secs. 4951-4953).[16] (No application form.)

(22) *Condominium and residential real estate management associations* (which are taxed at a special 30-percent rate) may elect to be treated as tax-exempt organizations with respect to exempt function income. In addition, if certain qualifications are met, qualifying timeshare associations may elect to be taxed at a rate of 32 percent on their "timeshare association income" (Code Sec. 528).[17] (Form 1120-H (U.S. Income Tax Return for Homeowners Associations).)

(23) *Political organization,* to the extent of exempt function income. Income from investments (less direct expenses incurred in earning that income) is subject to tax at a 35-percent rate (Code Sec. 527).[18] (Form 1120-POL (U.S. Income Tax Return for Certain Political Organizations).)

(24) *A trust set up by a corporation* in connection with the termination of its pension, profit sharing, or stock bonus plan (Code Sec. 501(c)(24)).

(25) *A title-holding corporation or trust* that has no more than 35 shareholders, has only one class of stock or beneficial interest, is operated for the exclusive purpose of holding title to real property and distributing income to eligible shareholders and is able to dismiss investment advisors. An eligible shareholder includes a qualified pension, profit sharing or stock bonus plan, a governmental pension plan, a federal or state political subdivision, or a Code Sec. 501(c)(3) organization (Code Sec. 501(c)(25)). Also, a qualified subsidiary of a Code Sec. 501(c)(25) title-holding company is not to be treated as a separate corporation. "Real property" does not include any interest as a tenant in common (or similar interest) or any indirect interest, but it includes certain leased personal property. The receipt of otherwise disqualifying unrelated business taxable income (UBTI) that is incidentally derived from the holding of real property by a title holding company is not treated as a disqualifying event. However, if the amount of disqualifying income received exceeds 10 percent of the company's gross income for the tax year, the company must establish that the receipt of the excess income was inadvertent and must take reasonable steps to change the circumstances that gave rise to the income (Code Sec. 501(c)(25)(G)).

(26) *State-sponsored membership organizations* that provide high-risk individuals with health coverage. In addition to other requirements, the organization must provide such medical coverage on a not-for-profit basis through either insurance

Footnote references are to paragraphs of the 2002 Standard Federal Tax Reports.

¶601   [15] ¶ 22,652.01   [17] ¶ 22,920   [18] ¶ 22,900
[16] ¶ 34,180—¶ 34,221

issued by the organization or an HMO under an arrangement with the organization (Code Sec. 501(c)(26)).

(27) *State-sponsored worker's compensation reinsurance organizations.* In addition to other requirements, the organization must have been established by a state before June 1, 1996, exclusively for the purpose of reimbursing its members for losses arising under worker's compensation acts (Code Sec. 501(c)(27)).

See ¶ 603, ¶ 604, ¶ 607, ¶ 610 and ¶ 696 for other exempt organization classifications.

603. Qualified Tuition Programs. Qualified tuition programs (QTPs), also called Section 529 plans, were expanded by the Economic Growth and Tax Relief Reconciliation Act of 2001. The new law extends Code Sec. 529 qualified tuition programs to private institutions of higher learning, in addition to continuing to cover state (public) programs. An eligible educational institution generally includes colleges, universities, vocational schools or other post-secondary educational institutions. In addition, distributions from public programs, even to the extent of earnings, will be entirely tax free to the extent used for qualified higher education expenses for tax years beginning after December 31, 2001. (Investment gains arising prior to this date are taxed to the student.) For private college and university programs, however, distributed earnings will not be tax free with respect to distributions made in tax years until 2004.[19]

Except as provided in regulations, tuition programs maintained by eligible institutions may not be treated as qualified unless the program provides that amounts are held in a "qualified trust" and the entity has received a ruling from the IRS that the program satisfies the applicable requirements under Code Sec. 529(b)(1)(A).

A "qualified trust" is a trust created or organized in the United States for the exclusive benefit of designated beneficiaries and meets the Code Sec. 408(a)(2) and Code Sec. 408(a)(5) IRA requirements. Thus, the trustee must be a bank or other person who (1) demonstrates to the satisfaction of the IRS that the person who administers the trust will meet applicable IRA requirements and (2) demonstrates that the trust's assets will not be commingled with other property except in a common trust fund or common investment fund (Code Sec. 529(b)(1)).

Distributions that are not used by the designated beneficiary to pay for qualified higher education expenses are included as gross income by the recipient.

Rollovers. The transfer of amounts from one QTP to another for the benefit of a designated beneficiary is not considered to be a distribution. This treatment does not apply for more than one transfer within any 12-month period with respect to the same beneficiary (Code Sec. 529(c)(3)(C)).

The transfer of amounts to the credit of another designated beneficiary is not considered to be a distribution as long as the beneficiary receiving the credit is a family member of the original beneficiary. In addition, the designated beneficiary of a QTP may be changed as long as the new beneficiary is a member of the family of the old beneficiary (Code Sec. 529(c)(3)(C)).

604. Religious or Apostolic Association. A religious or apostolic association, if it has a common or community treasury, is also exempt from income taxation. The exemption applies even if the association engages in business, provided that the members, at the time of filing their returns, include in their gross income their entire pro rata shares of the taxable income, whether distributed or not. Any amount so included in gross income is treated as a dividend received (Code Sec. 501(d); Reg. § 1.501(d)-1).[20] There is no official exemption application form. Such an organization must file a return on Form 1065 (U.S. Partnership Return of Income) for each tax year for information purposes (Reg. § 1.6033-2).[21]

607. Cooperative Hospital Service Organization. Exempt charitable status is available to a cooperative hospital service organization that performs one or

---

Footnote references are to paragraphs of the 2002 Standard Federal Tax Reports.
[19] ¶ 22,940   [20] ¶ 22,602, ¶ 22,659   [21] ¶ 35,422   **¶607**

more special services. Some special services are data processing, purchasing (which includes purchasing insurance on a group basis, such as malpractice and general liability insurance), laboratory, billing and collection (including the purchase of patron accounts receivable on a recourse basis), food, personnel, and clinical services. Special services must be provided for two or more tax-exempt hospitals, including hospitals owned and operated by the federal, state, or local government (Code Sec. 501(e)).[22] (Form 1023.) A cooperative laundry serving tax-exempt hospitals is not a tax-exempt organization.[23]

610. Cooperative Service Organizations of Operating Educational Organizations. A cooperative arrangement formed and controlled by a group of exempt educational organizations for the collective investment of their funds may qualify for tax-exempt status (Code Sec. 501(f)).[24] Such an organization qualifies for exemption under Code Sec. 501(c)(3) only if the other relevant requirements of that provision are also met. (Form 1023.)

613. Lobbying by Certain Public Charities—An Elective Alternative. As noted at ¶ 601, item (3), a charitable, educational, etc., organization jeopardizes its exempt status if a substantial part of its activities is propagandizing or otherwise attempting to influence legislation. For example, an exempt organization that educates voters is prohibited from endorsing candidates, fund-raising, or distributing statements.[25] There is an alternative to this "substantial part of activities" standard; this alternative standard is available for determining the permissible level of lobbying activities of a public charity (other than a church or convention of churches). Eligible public charities may elect (on Form 5768 (Election/Revocation of Election by an Eligible Section 501(c)(3) Organization to Make Expenditures to Influence Legislation)) a sliding scale limitation on expenditures made to influence legislation (Code Sec. 501(h); Reg. § 1.501(h)-2).[26]

The basic permitted level for lobbying expenditures (but not grass roots lobbying) is 20% of the first $500,000 of the organization's exempt-purpose expenditures for the year, plus 15% of the second $500,000, plus 10% of the third $500,000, plus 5% of any additional expenditures. This, however, is subject to an overall maximum limit of $1 million for any one year. In addition, in the case of so-called grass roots lobbying—i.e., attempts to influence the general public on legislative matters, the basic permitted level is limited to 25% of the general lobbying level described above (Code Sec. 4911(b) and (c); Reg. § § 56.4911-1(c) and 56.4911-2(b)).[27] If both lobbying expenditures and grass roots expenditures exceed the permitted levels, then the 25% tax is imposed on the greater of the two.

An excise tax of 25% is imposed on the amount above these limits (Code Sec. 4911(a); Reg. § 56.4911-1(a)).[28] However, if an organization's lobbying expenditures normally—on an average over a four-year period—exceed 150% of these limits (computed on Part VI, Schedule A of Form 990), the organization will lose its tax-exempt status.

614. Political Expenditures. A 10-percent tax is imposed on each political expenditure of an entity that, but for such expenditure, would be exempt from tax as a Code Sec. 501(c)(3) organization. If the political expenditure is not corrected within the taxable period, an additional tax equal to 100 percent of the expenditure is imposed on the organization (Code Sec. 4955(a)(1)).[29]

A 2½ percent tax is also imposed on any exempt organization manager who agrees to any expenditure by the organization that the manager knows to be a political expenditure, unless the manager did not agree willfully. There is an additional 50% tax imposed on a manager if he does not agree to correct the expenditure. If more than one manager agreed to the expenditures, the liability for the tax is joint and several. For any single political expenditure, the first tax cannot

---

Footnote references are to paragraphs of the 2002 Standard Federal Tax Reports.

22 ¶ 22,602, ¶ 22,662	26 ¶ 22,602, ¶ 22,664,	28 ¶ 33,960, ¶ 33,962
23 ¶ 22,662.30	¶ 22,666	29 ¶ 34,240
24 ¶ 22,602	27 ¶ 22,602, ¶ 22,666,	
25 ¶ 22,666.20	¶ 33,960, ¶ 33,962,	
	¶ 33,963	

¶610

exceed $5,000 and the second cannot exceed $10,000. A manager is any director, officer, or trustee or any other individual with comparable responsibilities.

Corrections. The correction of an expenditure is defined as (1) recovery of the expenditure to the extent possible, (2) establishment of safeguards to prevent future political expenditures, and (3) where full recovery is impossible, such additional action as may be prescribed in regulations (Code Sec. 4955(f)(3)).

Political Expenditures. A political expenditure is generally defined as any amount paid or incurred by an organization in connection with any participation or intervention in any political campaign on behalf of, or in opposition to, any candidate for public office (Code Sec. 4955(d)).

Reporting. The organization must include on Form 990 any amounts paid under this provision by the organization or managers. Also, any reimbursement paid by the organization to a manager must be reported (Code Sec. 6033(b)(10)(C)).[30]

615. Feeder Organizations. An organization whose main purpose is to run a trade or business, the profits of which are paid to one or more tax-exempt entities, is known as a feeder organization (Code Sec. 502).[31] The feeder organization is taxable unless its activities are an integral part of the exempt parent organization's activities. The following activities are excluded from the definition of trade or business:

(1) the deriving of rents if the rents received would not be subject to the unrelated business income tax (Code Sec. 512(b)(3));

(2) any trade or business in which substantially all the work of carrying on such trade or business is performed by unpaid individuals or volunteers; and

(3) any trade or business that sells merchandise which has been donated or contributed.

616. Notification Requirements for Code Sec. 501(c)(3) Organizations. Organizations, including private foundations, claiming exempt status as a charitable, religious, educational, etc., organization under Code Sec. 501(c)(3) (see ¶ 601) must notify the IRS that they are applying for recognition of exempt status on Form 1023 within 15 months from the end of the month in which organized (Code Sec. 508(a)(1)).[32] Unless excepted as noted below, an organization that fails to file a timely notice may not qualify for exempt status for any period prior to the date of actual notice (Code Sec. 508(a)(2)).[33]

Any organization (other than a private foundation (¶ 631)) whose annual gross receipts normally do not exceed $25,000 (Code Sec. 508(c)(1); Reg. § 1.508-1(a)(3); Rev. Proc. 83-23) [34] is excepted from the above exempt-status notification requirements. Churches and their affiliates are also exempt. However, these organizations should establish exemption with the IRS by obtaining a ruling or determination letter (Reg. § 1.508-1(a)(4)).[35] See ¶ 619. Also excepted are subordinate organizations protected by the group exemption and notice of the parent (Reg. § 1.508-1(a)(3)).[36]

Notice That Organization Is Not a Private Foundation. A second notification is required of a Code Sec. 501(c)(3) organization claiming public charity status (nonprivate foundation status). The organization is required to notify the IRS on Form 1023 that it is not a private foundation and must do so within 15 months from the end of the month in which it was organized (Code Sec. 508(b) and (c)).[37] Exempt organizations that fail to file a timely notice of nonprivate foundation status will be presumed to be private foundations subject to the various restrictions and taxes on such groups (¶ 631). Those organizations excepted from the new-organization-notification requirement, above, are also excepted from filing the nonprivate foundation notice (Reg. § 1.508-1(a)(2)).[38] The filing requirement is also the same.

Footnote references are to paragraphs of the 2002 Standard Federal Tax Reports.

[30] ¶ 35,420	[34] ¶ 22,790, ¶ 22,791,	[37] ¶ 22,790
[31] ¶ 22,670	¶ 35,425,013	[38] ¶ 22,791
[32] ¶ 22,790	[35] ¶ 22,791	
[33] ¶ 22,790	[36] ¶ 22,791	

¶616

617. Disclosure of Nondeductibility. Tax-exempt organizations that have annual gross receipts in excess of $100,000 and that are ineligible to receive tax-deductible charitable contributions must expressly disclose the nondeductibility of fundraising solicitations. An express statement that makes the disclosure in a conspicuous and easily recognizable format must be present if the solicitation is in a print medium or over the telephone, television, or radio (Code Sec. 6113).[39]

A penalty of $1,000, with a maximum of $10,000 a year, is imposed for each day there is a failure to comply, unless the failure is due to reasonable cause. The daily penalty for intentional disregard is the greater of $1,000 a day or 50 percent of the aggregate cost of the solicitations, with no maximum limitation (Code Sec. 6710).[40]

619. Proof of Exemption. Although an organization is theoretically exempt from tax if it meets the requirements of the statute (Reg. § 1.508-1(a)(4)),[41] it must file an income tax return as well as an annual information return[42] until a ruling or determination letter is obtained from the IRS establishing such exemption. At such time, a claim for refund should be filed because an exemption is usually effective as of the date of formation if the statutory requirements were met at that time, unless the organization has failed to file timely notice of application for recognition of exempt status (usually through inadequate information on Form 1023).[43] Every organization claiming exemption must file the proper application form. See, also, ¶ 616.

620. Excess Benefit Transactions. An excise tax penalty may be imposed as an intermediate sanction when a Code Sec. 501(c)(3) or Code Sec. 501(c)(4) organization engages in an "excess benefit transaction."[44] The excise tax is imposed on the "disqualified person" who improperly benefits from the transaction and on organization managers who knowingly participate in the transaction (Code Sec. 4958). Private foundations are subject to different sanctions (see ¶ 635). An excess benefit transaction is one in which a disqualified person engages in a non-fair-market-value transaction with an organization or receives unreasonable compensation (Code Sec. 4958(c)). A disqualified person is a person who is in a position to exercise substantial influence over the affairs of the organization as well as family members and entities in which a disqualified person holds at least a 35-percent ownership interest (Code Sec. 4958(f)).

Penalty Imposed. A disqualified person is subject to a tax of 25 percent of the excess benefit (Code Sec. 4958(a)(1)). A manager who knowingly participates in the excess benefit transaction is subject to a penalty of 10 percent of the excess benefit (to a maximum of $10,000) (Code Sec. 4958(a)(2)). An additional penalty of 200 percent of the excess benefit may be imposed on the disqualified person if the transaction is not corrected by the earlier of (1) the date the notice of deficiency is mailed and (2) the date on which the tax is imposed. For IRS authority to abate these penalties, see ¶ 647.

622. Retroactive Revocation of Exemption. Although a change of IRS position as to exempt status of an organization is usually effective prospectively, retroactive revocation can result (Code Sec. 7805(b)).[45] Generally, retroactive revocation is appropriate where the IRS has not been fully or correctly informed as to the material facts on which the exemption ruling was based or there have been material changes in law or fact subsequent to the time the original ruling was issued.[46]

625. Information Return. An annual return stating gross income, receipts, contributions, disbursements, etc. is required of most organizations exempt from income tax under Code Sec. 501, including private foundations (Code Sec. 6033(a)(1)).[47] Churches, the exclusively religious activities of a religious order, and church-, denomination- or interdenomination-sponsored foreign mission societies are

---

Footnote references are to paragraphs of the 2002 Standard Federal Tax Reports.

¶617

[39] ¶ 37,040	[42] ¶ 22,604.075	[45] ¶ 43,270
[40] ¶ 40,115	[43] ¶ 22,604.10	[46] ¶ 22,609.4825
[41] ¶ 22,791	[44] ¶ 34,250	[47] ¶ 35,420

exempt from this requirement, along with certain foreign organizations, and organizations that normally have annual gross receipts of $25,000 or less (a religious, educational, or charitable organization, an organization for prevention of cruelty to children or animals, a fraternal lodge system beneficiary society providing life insurance, etc., benefits, an exempt federal instrumentality or its subsidiary, and controlled groups of religious organizations) (Code Sec. 6033(a)(2); Rev. Proc. 83-23). A tax-exempt organization (other than a charitable organization described in Code Sec. 501(c)(3)) must include on its annual return the total nondeductible lobbying expenditures for the tax year and the total amount of the dues or similar payments that are allocable to such expenditures. In addition, members must generally be given notification of the nondeductible portion of their dues (Code Sec. 6033(e)).[48]

The annual return of exempt organizations not excluded as noted above must be filed on Form 990 (Return of Organization Exempt from Income Tax). Schedule A must accompany Form 990 filed by Code Sec. 501(c)(3) organizations. Exempt private foundations must file their returns on Form 990-PF. See ¶ 631.

Both exempt and nonexempt farmers' cooperatives generally must file Form 990-C. Requirements for exempt status are set forth at ¶ 696. Cooperatives formed to purchase food for members or for purposes other than those listed in Code Sec. 521(b)(1) should file Form 1120. Religious and apostolic organizations exempt under Code Sec. 501(d) must file a return on Form 1065. Black lung benefit trusts exempt under Code Sec. 501(c)(21) must file a return on Form 990-BL. Political organizations (Code Sec. 527) must file Form 1120-POL, and condominium or residential management associations (Code Sec. 528) must file Form 1120-H. For returns by a stock bonus, pension or profit-sharing trust that qualifies for exemption under Code Sec. 401, see ¶ 2145. In addition, Code Sec. 501(c)(3) organizations are required to report annually on Form 990 any amounts paid under Code Sec. 4911, Code Sec. 4912 and Code Sec. 4955 by the organization or by organization managers. In addition, a Code Sec. 501(c)(3) organization must also report any amount of excise tax on excess benefit transactions paid by the organization, organization manager or any disqualified person during the tax year (Code Sec. 6033(b)(10)).

Forms 990 and 990-PF and related returns must be filed on or before the 15th day of the fifth month following the close of the accounting period. Form 1065, to be filed by a religious or apostolic association, must be filed on or before the 15th day of the fourth month following the close of the tax year for which the return is required to be filed (Reg. § 1.6033-2(e)).[49]

A copy of Form 990-PF with attachments (and, in some cases, additional information) will satisfy some state and local filing requirements. If the copy of Form 990-PF (and Form 4720 (Return of Excise Taxes on Charities and Other Persons Under Chapters 41 and 42 of the Internal Revenue Code), if any) must be filed with some state official other than the attorney general, a copy must still be furnished to the attorney general of that state. Form 4720 is required where there is an initial excise tax on prohibited activity or accumulation of income (Reg. § 1.6033-2(a)(2)(ii)(j)).[50]

A penalty of $20 per day (to a maximum of $10,000 or five percent of the organization's gross receipts, whichever is less) is imposed on each exempt organization whose gross receipts are $1,000,000 or less and that fails to file an annual information return, files a late return without reasonable cause (Code Sec. 6652(c)(1))[51] or fails to file the special information return on dissolution or substantial contraction (¶ 628). Organizations with gross receipts in excess of $1,000,000 for any year are subject to penalty of $100 per day (maximum of $50,000). An additional penalty of $10 a day (maximum $5,000) is imposed on any officer, trustee, employee, etc., who fails to file the return without reasonable cause after reasonable demand by the IRS (Code Sec. 6652(c)(1)(B)).[52]

Footnote references are to paragraphs of the 2002 Standard Federal Tax Reports.

[48] ¶ 35,420,	[49] ¶ 35,422	[51] ¶ 39,480
¶ 35,425.066,	[50] ¶ 35,422	[52] ¶ 39,480
¶ 35,425.33		

¶ 625

Tax-exempt organizations, including private foundations, must make available for public inspection, at the organization's principal regional and district offices (having three or more employees) during regular business hours, a copy of its application for exemption and its three most recent annual information returns (Code Sec. 6104(e)).[53] Organizations do not have to honor requests if they reasonably believe that the request is part of a harassment campaign (Reg. § 301.6104(d)-3).[54]

New regulations have changed the requirements for public inspection by expanding them to provide for easier access by the public. The regulations that affect private foundations were effective as of March 13, 2000, while the regulations affecting other exempt organizations were effective as of June 8, 1999 (Reg. § 301.6104(d)-1 and Reg. § 301.6104(d)-2, respectively).

The regulations allow requests to be made either in person or in writing. Copies of an organization's Form 990 must be furnished immediately for requests made in person and within 30 days for written requests. Organizations are permitted to charge only a reasonable fee for reproduction and mailing costs. The regulations also deal with how an exempt organization can comply with these disclosure requirements by posting information on the Internet. Failure to comply with the public inspection requirements results in a penalty of $20 per day, with a maximum of $10,000 for any annual return (Code Sec. 6652(c)(1)(C)).[55] There is no maximum penalty for failure to provide the exemption application. The penalty for willful failure to file is increased to $5,000, as required by Code Sec. 6104(e)(3).

628. Information on Dissolution. Each organization exempt from tax during any of its last five tax years (except churches, organizations other than private foundations with $25,000 (Rev. Proc. 83-23) or less in annual gross receipts, and other organizations specified in Reg. § 1.6043-3(b))[56] must provide information on its annual information return (Form 990) regarding its liquidation, dissolution, termination, or substantial contraction (Code Sec. 6043(b)).[57] Penalties for failure to comply may be imposed.

629. Disclosure of Quid Pro Quo Contributions. Most charitable organizations are required to inform donors through written statements that quid pro quo contributions in excess of $75 are deductible only to the extent that the contributions exceed the value of goods or services provided by the organization. Also, they must provide the donor with a good faith estimate of the value of those goods and services (Code Sec. 6115).[58] Penalties of $10 per contribution (with a maximum penalty of $5,000) will be imposed upon charities that do not make proper disclosures, absent reasonable cause (Code Sec. 6714).[59] Quid pro quo contributions do not include contributions to an organization organized exclusively for religious purposes in return for which the donor receives solely an intangible religious benefit that generally is not sold in a commercial transaction outside a religious context (Code Sec. 6115).[60]

Private Foundations

631. Private Foundation Defined. The term "private foundation" is defined in a negative way (Code Sec. 509).[61] It includes all Code Sec. 501(c)(3) organizations other than those in four distinct categories: (1) maximum (50%) charitable deduction donees, (2) broadly publicly supported organizations receiving more than 1/3 of their annual support from members and the public and not more than 1/3 from investment income and unrelated business income, (3) supporting organizations, and (4) public safety testing organizations.

A private foundation is denied tax-exempt status unless its governing instrument specifically prohibits it from engaging in the prohibited activities or the accumulation of income discussed at ¶ 635-¶ 644 (Code Sec. 508(e)).[62] See ¶ 1068.

Footnote references are to paragraphs of the 2002 Standard Federal Tax Reports.

[53] ¶ 36,900	[57] ¶ 35,880	[60] ¶ 37,065
[54] ¶ 36,910E	[58] ¶ 37,065	[61] ¶ 22,800
[55] ¶ 39,480	[59] ¶ 40,180	[62] ¶ 22,790
[56] ¶ 35,885		

¶ 628

The initial tax on undistributed income (¶ 637), acts of self-dealing (¶ 635), excess business holdings (¶ 640), investments which jeopardize charitable purpose (¶ 642), or taxable expenditures (¶ 644) is reportable on Form 4720, filed in conjunction with Form 990-PF (see ¶ 625).

If, at any time of the year, a private foundation has had assets of at least $5,000, supplementary information must be furnished on Form 990-PF regarding foundation managers; grants, scholarships and similar benefits; other significant program activity; and securities and other assets held.

633. Investment Income Taxed. An annual 2-percent excise tax is imposed on the net investment income of a private foundation (Code Sec. 4940) [63] and is reported on the foundation's annual return, Form 990-PF. This tax is reduced to 1 percent if the corporation satisfies certain requirements as to the level of distributions to charities and was not liable during any base-period year for the tax imposed by Code Sec. 4942 on undistributed income. Also, an exemption from the tax is provided for an "operating" foundation that expends at least 85 percent of the lesser of its adjusted net income or its minimum investment return in carrying on its exempt activities and that is broadly supported by, and governed by representatives of, the general public (Code Sec. 4940(d) and (e)).[64] A private foundation that constituted an operating foundation (as defined in Code Sec. 4942(j)(3)) for its last tax year ending before January 1, 1983, is treated as an operating foundation as of January 1, 1983. It would thus meet the requirements of Code Sec. 4940(d)(2)(B).

635. Prohibitions on Self-Dealing. Foundation financial transactions with disqualified persons (acts of self-dealing) are substantially restricted (Code Sec. 4941).[65] The prohibited acts of self-dealing are comprehensively defined in the law.

A "disqualified person" includes: a substantial contributor (one who contributes more than $5,000 if it is more than 2 percent of the total contributions received before the end of the foundation's tax year (Code Sec. 507(d)(2)(A)));[66] a foundation manager; the owner of more than 20 percent of a business or trust which is a substantial contributor; a member of the family (spouse, ancestor, child, grandchild, great grandchild, or spouse of any such descendants) of any of the preceding; or a corporation, trust, estate, or partnership more than 35 percent of which is owned or held by any of the preceding; or a government official (Code Sec. 4946).[67] The disqualified person is subject to a tax of 5 percent of the amount involved in the self-dealing, and the foundation manager who knowingly participates is subject to a tax of 2½ percent of the amount involved. A second-level tax of 200 percent (50 percent on the manager) applies if the prohibited act is not corrected within what is called the "taxable period." This is a period that begins on the date on which the self-dealing act occurs and ends on the earliest of (1) the date on which the deficiency notice for the first-level tax is mailed, (2) the date on which the first-level tax is assessed, or (3) the date on which the act of self-dealing is completely corrected. However, the second-level tax is not assessed if the taxpayer files a Tax Court petition to redetermine that tax and if the prohibited act is corrected by the end of the taxable period. A third-level tax, equal to the sum of the first- and second-level liabilities, may be added for repeated or flagrant violations of the self-dealing provisions (Code Secs. 4941 and 6684; Reg. § 53.4941(b)-1).[68] If more then one person is liable for these taxes with respect to any one act of self-dealing, then all such persons are jointly and severally liable for these taxes.

637. Failure to Distribute Income. A private foundation, other than a private operating foundation, must make annual expenditures or distributions for exempt purposes generally equal to its minimum investment return, which is 5 percent of a foundation's net investment assets (Code Sec. 4942).[69] Failure to do so will result in an excise tax on a percentage of its accumulated income. The tax is initially 15 percent of undistributed income—100 percent if the failure to distribute

---

Footnote references are to paragraphs of the 2002 Standard Federal Tax Reports.

63 ¶ 34,000	67 ¶ 34,120	69 ¶ 34,040
64 ¶ 34,000	68 ¶ 34,020, ¶ 34,022,	
65 ¶ 34,020	¶ 39,865	
66 ¶ 22,771		

is not corrected within a specified period. In order to avoid the first-level tax, a private foundation must distribute an amount equal to its minimum investment return, including interest from tax-exempt government bonds in excess of expenses of earning it (except net long-term capital gains), before the first day of the second (or succeeding) tax year following the year earned. The second-level tax of 100 percent applies if the foundation fails to make the necessary charitable distributions within a "taxable period" that begins on the first day of the tax year and that ends on the earlier of (1) the date on which the deficiency notice for the initial tax is mailed or (2) the date on which the initial tax is assessed (Code Sec. 4942(b)).[70] A third level of tax comes into play if there have been repeated or flagrant acts.

640. Involvement in Unrelated Business. Statutory restrictions on unrelated business ownership limit to 20 percent the combined ownership of a business enterprise by a private foundation and all disqualified persons (see ¶ 635) and tax any excess holdings which are not divested (Code Sec. 4943).[71] If third parties who are not disqualified persons have effective control of the business enterprise, the foundation, together with disqualified persons, may own up to 35 percent. There are more liberal divestiture rules for private foundations in existence at the time of the original enactment of private foundation rules (May 26, 1969). As with the self-dealing and payout provisions, two levels of taxes apply—5 percent of the value of excess business holdings; 200 percent if not corrected.

642. Investments Jeopardizing Exempt Purpose. An initial tax of 5 percent is imposed on a private foundation's investment made in such a manner as to jeopardize the carrying out of the foundation's exempt purpose (Code Sec. 4944).[72] "Jeopardizing" investments are generally those that show a lack of reasonable business care and prudence in providing for the foundation's short- and long-term financial needs. A 5-percent tax (not to exceed $5,000) may be imposed on a foundation's manager who knowingly participates in such an investment. A second-level tax of 25 percent (5 percent on the manager, up to a maximum of $10,000) may be imposed if the jeopardy situation is not corrected within the "taxable period" as defined at ¶ 637.

644. Lobbying and Other Prohibited Expenditures. A private foundation that makes a prohibited "taxable expenditure" is subject to an initial tax of 10 percent of the amount improperly expended (Code Sec. 4945).[73] There is also a 2½ percent tax (to a maximum of $5,000) on a manager who knowingly participates. Taxable expenditures include amounts paid by a private foundation for lobbying, electioneering, grants to individuals (unless awarded on a nondiscriminatory basis), and, in certain circumstances, grants to nonpublic charity organizations. Second-level sanctions of 100 percent are imposed on the foundation and 50 percent (up to $10,000) on the manager if the taxable expenditure is not corrected within the "taxable period" as described at ¶ 637.

647. Abatement of Taxes. The IRS has discretionary authority to withhold or abate assessment of the taxes referred to at ¶ 620, ¶ 637, ¶ 640, ¶ 642 and ¶ 644 that are imposed in the first instance ("first-tier" taxes as distinguished from the increased taxes that are imposed upon failure to correct the violation within specified periods of time), provided that the violation was due to reasonable cause and not to willful neglect and, provided further, that the violation was corrected within the applicable period of time (Code Sec. 4962).[74]

Second-Tier Taxes. The IRS also can abate the second-tier taxes that have been assessed against a private foundation if the foundation voluntarily corrects the act. The foundation must do so within a correction period that begins on the date of the taxable event and ends 90 days after the deficiency notice for the second-tier tax is mailed by the IRS (Code Sec. 4961).[75]

Footnote references are to paragraphs of the 2002 Standard Federal Tax Reports.

¶ 640

[70] ¶ 34,040	[72] ¶ 34,080	[74] ¶ 34,280
[71] ¶ 34,060	[73] ¶ 34,100	[75] ¶ 34,260

649. Termination of Private Foundation Status. Private foundation status need not be permanent (Code Sec. 507).[76]

Voluntary termination may be achieved by an organization that was a private foundation on October 9, 1969, or thereafter, by notifying the IRS of the plan to terminate and by paying back (1) any income, estate, and gift tax benefits (with interest) that it and all of its substantial contributors (¶ 635) have received since 1913 or (2) the value of its net assets, whichever is lower. Alternatively, without a tax payback, a foundation may elect to distribute all of its assets to an organization, contributions to which qualify for the maximum 50-percent deduction, or it may operate as a public charity itself for at least 5 years.

Involuntary termination of private foundation status by the IRS may result if the foundation commits repeated violations or a willful and flagrant violation of any of the private foundation provisions. The foundation is subject to a termination tax-payback of the value of its aggregate tax benefits (since 1913) or its net assets, whichever is lower.

Recently, the Tax Court held that a joint venture agreement between an exempt and non-exempt entity resulted in the involuntary termination of the exempt entity's status.[77] The case dealt with a health care organization that entered into a partnership with a for-profit health care facility (medical group) to expand the number of services it could provide to its patients. The court determined that the agreement allowed the for-profit entity to effectively control the tax-exempt entity and that this control compromised the exempt's charitable purpose.

650. Estimated Tax Payments. For purposes of determining underpayments of estimated tax, the due date for a calendar-year private foundation's first-quarter estimated tax payment for excise tax liability on net investment income or UBTI is May 15. Similarly, fiscal-year foundations are required to make their first-quarter estimated tax payments no later than the 15th day of the fifth month of their tax year (Code Sec. 6655(g)(3)).[78]

Declaratory Judgments

652. Status Determinations in Court. The U.S. Court of Federal Claims, the U.S. Tax Court, and the U.S. District Court for the District of Columbia have jurisdiction to issue declaratory judgments in cases involving a controversy as to a determination or failure to make a determination by the IRS with respect to the initial or continuing qualification of: (1) a charitable, educational, etc., organization under Code Sec. 501(c)(3);[79] (2) a qualified charitable donee under Code Sec. 170(c)(2);[80] (3) a private foundation under Code Sec. 509(a);[81] or (4) a private operating foundation under Code Sec. 4942(j)(3)[82] (see ¶ 637) (Code Sec. 7428). [83]

Unrelated Business Taxable Income

655. Organizations Subject to Tax. Although, under Code Sec. 501, a variety of nonprofit philanthropic or mutually beneficial organizations may be granted tax-exempt status, they may become subject to tax on income from a business enterprise not related to their exempt purpose (Code Sec. 511(a); Reg. § § 1.511-1—1.511-3).[84]

Unrelated business taxable income (UBTI) must be derived from an activity that constitutes a trade or business that is regularly carried on and is not substantially related to the organization's tax-exempt purposes.

Almost all types of exempt organizations are subject to the tax on unrelated business income. The only organizations exempt from the tax are government instrumentalities (except colleges or universities that are agencies or instrumentalities of any government or any political subdivision thereof) and, under certain

---

Footnote references are to paragraphs of the 2002 Standard Federal Tax Reports.

[76] ¶ 22,771	[80] ¶ 11,600	[83] ¶ 41,720
[77] ¶ 22,609.405	[81] ¶ 22,800	[84] ¶ 22,820—¶ 22,823,
[78] ¶ 39,565	[82] ¶ 34,040	¶ 22,825
[79] ¶ 22,602		

circumstances, federally licensed businesses carried on before May 27, 1959, by a religious institution or an educational institution maintained by it.

The proceeds from bingo games conducted by most exempt organizations and political organizations are not unrelated business income if the games are conducted in accordance with local law and do not compete with profit-making businesses (Code Sec. 513(f)).[85] Tax-exempt organizations that derive income from other games of chance are subject to tax on unrelated business income.

658. Rates and Payment. Unless the organization is taxable as a trust, its UBTI is subject to regular corporate taxes. Trusts are taxed at the rates applicable to estates and trusts (see ¶ 13) (Code Sec. 511; Reg. § 1.511-1).[86] Returns are made on Form 990-T (Reg. § 1.6012-2(e)),[87] to be filed at the same time as the organization's annual information return. All Form 990-T filers are required to make quarterly payments of estimated taxes as if they were corporations. Form 990-W should be used by tax-exempt organizations to compute estimated tax.

661. Specific Deduction. The first $1,000 of unrelated business income is not subject to tax (Code Sec. 512(b)(12)).[88]

664. Necessity That Business Be "Regularly" Carried On. UBTI is the gross income from any unrelated trade or business "regularly" carried on, minus business deductions directly connected with it (Code Sec. 512(a); Reg. § 1.512(a)-1).[89] In the case of a social club, voluntary employees' beneficiary association, group legal services plan or an organization for the payment of supplemental unemployment benefits, unrelated business income is subject to tax only to the extent that it is not set aside for the purposes that constitute the basis for the organization's exemption (Code Sec. 512(a)(3)).[90]

667. Necessity That Business Be "Unrelated" to Other Functions. To be taxable, income must be from a business *not substantially related* to the exercise of the charitable, educational, or other purpose on which the exemption of the organization is based (Code Sec. 513; Reg. § 1.513-1).[91]

670. Exempt Types of "Unrelated" Income. In addition to the specific $1,000 exemption (¶ 661), Code Sec. 512(b) [92] specifically excludes (with some limitations) from tax these income items and related deductions (¶ 682):

(1) royalties, dividends, interest and annuities, except certain annuities and interest derived from controlled corporations (¶ 673);

(2) rents from real property, except rents from some types of personalty-realty combinations and rents from personal property leased with real property that are an incidental amount of the total rents under the lease (¶ 676) or debt-financed income (¶ 687);

(3) gains or losses on sale or exchange of certain property (¶ 679);

(4) income of a college, university or hospital, from research performed for any person and income from research for the United States or any of its agencies or instrumentalities, or for a state or political subdivision;

(5) in the case of an organization operated primarily to carry on research, the results of which are freely available to the public, all income from research performed for any person;

(6) income of labor unions and agricultural or horticultural organizations used to establish or operate a retirement home, hospital or similar facility for the exclusive use of aged or infirm members, if such income qualified for exclusion for pre-1976 tax years (P.L. 94-455);

(7) income realized by Code Sec. 501(c)(3)-(5) [93] organizations (see ¶ 601, above) from qualified public entertainment activities conducted in connection

---

Footnote references are to paragraphs of the 2002 Standard Federal Tax Reports.

85 ¶ 22,846.029	88 ¶ 22,830	91 ¶ 22,840, ¶ 22,841
86 ¶ 22,820, ¶ 22,821	89 ¶ 22,830, ¶ 22,831	92 ¶ 22,830
87 ¶ 35,145	90 ¶ 22,830, ¶ 22,837.01	93 ¶ 22,602

with an international, national, state or local fair or exposition (Code Sec. 513(d));[94]

(8) income derived by labor, agricultural, and horticultural organizations and business trade associations (Code Sec. 501(c)(5) and (6) organizations—see ¶ 601) from qualified convention or trade show activities conducted to promote the products and services of the industry in general (Code Sec. 513(d));[95]

(9) securities loaned to a broker followed by the return of identical securities to the lender, including any payments received by the lender for use of the securities;

(10) income from the rental or exchange of membership lists by tax-exempt charitable organizations;

(11) annual dues not exceeding $116 in 2001 (Rev. Proc. 2001-13) (this amount is unofficially projected to increase to $119 for 2002) that are paid to tax-exempt agricultural or horticultural organizations (Code Sec. 512(d)); and

(12) the activity of soliciting and receiving qualified sponsorship payments (Code Sec. 513(i)).

A hospital that performs services noted at ¶ 607 (services that a tax-exempt cooperative hospital service organization may perform) is not subject to the unrelated business tax on the income from such services, provided (1) the services are performed at cost, (2) the services are furnished solely to one or more tax-exempt hospitals, each having facilities serving not more than 100 inpatients, and (3) the services, had they been performed by the recipient hospital, would fall within such hospital's tax-exempt activities (Code Sec. 513(e)).[96]

An unrelated trade or business does not include the exchanging or renting of member or donor lists between tax-exempt organizations to which deductible contributions can be made or activities relating to the distribution of low-cost articles ($7.60 or less in 2001 under Rev. Proc. 2001-13 and unofficially projected to be $7.80 or less for 2002) incidental to the solicitation of charitable contributions for tax-exempt charitable organizations (Code Sec. 513(h)).

673. Dividends, Interest, Annuities and Royalties (Investment Income). Generally, dividends, interest, payments with respect to securities loans, amounts received or accrued as consideration for entering into agreements to make loans, annuities, royalties and income derived from notional principal contracts, as well as income from an exempt organization's ordinary and routine investments that is substantially similar to these forms of income, are not "unrelated business income" unless derived from debt-financed property (¶ 687) (Code Sec. 512(b); Reg. § 1.512(b)-1(a)).[97] See, however, "Controlled Corporation," below.

The Tax Court and an appellate court have held that amounts paid to an exempt organization, as part of an affinity credit card program, in exchange for the use of its name and logo, which were intangible assets, constituted royalties that were not taxable unrelated business income.[98]

Investment Income of Certain Membership Organizations. An exempt social and recreational club, voluntary employees' beneficiary association, a trust forming part of a nondiscriminatory plan providing for the payment of supplemental unemployment compensation benefits, or an organization or trust forming part of a qualified group legal services plan is taxable on its investment income. Generally, the organizations are taxable on gross income, less deductions relating to production of income, except "exempt function income"—that is, (1) dues, fees, and charges for providing facilities and services for members, dependents, and guests and (2) income set aside for charitable purposes or by a voluntary employees' beneficiary association to provide insurance benefits (Code Sec. 512(a)(3)).[99] Also, a tax-exempt organization will not be subject to unrelated business income tax on the gain it realizes from a land sale if the gain is related to its exempt function.[100] However, an

---

[94] ¶ 22,840
[95] ¶ 22,840
[96] ¶ 22,840
[97] ¶ 22,830, ¶ 22,835
[98] ¶ 22,837.83
[99] ¶ 22,830
[100] ¶ 22,837.85

exempt social club may not offset against its investment income losses from the sale of food and beverages to nonmembers unless a profit motive for such sales exists.[101] A title-holding corporation whose income is payable to one of the above membership organizations is treated as the taxpayer.

To eliminate a possible bypass for the club or other membership organization through termination of tax-exempt status, Code Sec. 277 provides that a *nonexempt* social club or other membership organization operated primarily to furnish goods or services to members may deduct the cost of furnishing these goods, services, insurance, etc., *only to the extent of membership-related income.* A nonexempt social club is not allowed to claim the corporate dividends-received deduction.[102]

Controlled Corporation. Also subject to the unrelated business income tax is investment income in the form of interest, royalties, and rents received or accrued by an exempt organization from a subsidiary (exempt or nonexempt) in which it owns more than a 50-percent interest (80-percent interest for tax years beginning prior to August 6, 1997). An exception exists for any payment received or accrued during the first two tax years beginning on or after August 5, 1997, if the payment is received or accrued pursuant to a written binding contract in effect on June 8, 1997, and at all times thereafter before the payment; the constructive ownership rules of Code Sec. 318 are extended to apply to the control test (Code Sec. 512(b)(13)).[103]

676. Rents. Excludable from unrelated business income are amounts received from a rental of real property, including those rents from personal property leased with the realty that are an incidental amount of the total rents under the lease of the real property. Such rents will be considered "incidental" only if they do not exceed 10 percent of the total rents from all property leased (Reg. § 1.512(b)-1(c)).[104] However, taxable as unrelated business income are: (1) rents from real property leased with personal property if more than 50 percent of the rent is attributable to the personal property; (2) rents from both the realty and the personalty if the rentals are based on a percentage of the net income from the property (Code Sec. 512(b)(3));[105] and (3) unrelated income from debt-financed property (see ¶ 687).

679. Gains and Losses from Sales or Exchanges. Excluded from unrelated business income are all gains or losses from the sale, exchange or other disposition of property other than (1) stock in trade or other property of a kind properly includible in inventory or (2) property held primarily for sale to customers in the ordinary course of the trade or business. The exclusion applies to all gains or losses recognized, in connection with the organization's investment activities, from the lapse or termination of options to buy and sell securities whether or not written by the organization. Gain on options to buy or sell real property is also excluded (Code Sec. 512(b)(5); Reg. § 1.512(b)-1(d)).[106] The exclusion does not apply to gains derived from the sale or other disposition of debt-financed property (Code Sec. 512(b)(4))[107] (see ¶ 687). Gains from certain pension plan investments in the property of troubled financial institutions acquired after 1993 are excludable (Code Sec. 512(b)(16)).[108] Gross income from investments in publicly traded partnerships is treated the same as gross income from investments in other partnerships for purposes of computing UBTI (Code Sec. 512(c)).[109]

682. Deductions. In computing the unrelated business income of an exempt organization, those expenses that are deductible by commercial organizations are deductible by the exempt organization. Where facilities or personnel are used for both exempt functions and the conduct of an unrelated business, it is necessary to allocate expenses and income between the two uses on a reasonable basis. The portion of any such items allocated to the unrelated business is allowable as a deduction in computing UBTI.

Footnote references are to paragraphs of the 2002 Standard Federal Tax Reports.

¶676

101 ¶ 22,837.01	104 ¶ 22,835	107 ¶ 22,830
102 ¶ 14,600	105 ¶ 22,830	108 ¶ 22,830
103 ¶ 22,830, ¶ 22,835	106 ¶ 22,830, ¶ 22,835	109 ¶ 22,830

An organization is also allowed a charitable contributions deduction of up to 10 percent of its UBTI, computed without regard to the contributions deduction. A net operating loss deduction is also allowed. In computing this deduction for any year, the carrybacks and the carryovers and items attributable to exempt income and expenses are disregarded.

685. Advertising v. Sponsorship, Conventions, and Trade Shows Activities.
The profits of an exempt organization from advertising and other activity carried on for the production of income through the sale of goods or services, e.g., the sale of advertising in a periodical, journal, or magazine it publishes, may be taxable unrelated business income. (See ¶ 655, ¶ 664 and ¶ 667.) An activity does not lose its identity as a trade or business merely because it is carried on within a larger aggregate of similar activities or within a larger complex of other activities which may, or may not, be related to the exempt purpose (such as a tour group that promotes itself in the guise of education) (Code Sec. 513(c); Reg. § 1.513-1; Reg. § 1.513-7).[110]

However, certain qualified sponsorship payments solicited or received by tax-exempt organizations will not be subject to the tax. A qualified payment is any payment by a payor engaged in a trade or business that does not expect any substantial return benefit other than the use or acknowledgment of the payor's name, logo or product lines in connection with the activities of the tax-exempt organization. Such payments do not include advertising, including messages that contain qualitative or comparative language, price information, an endorsement, or an inducement to purchase, sell or use the payor's products and services (Code Sec. 513(i)).[111]

Organizations qualifying for tax exemptions under Code Sec. 501(c)(5) and (6) (e.g., labor and agricultural groups and business leagues) are not regarded as carrying on an unrelated trade or business when, as one of their major exempt activities, they present conventions and trade shows in an effort to generate interest in, and demand for, an industry's products[112] (see ¶ 670). Charges to exhibitors and public admission fees for entry to shows are not taxable. However, if a show is held primarily for selling exhibitors' products, income from the event is taxable (Reg. § 1.513-3).[113]

Taxable Income from Debt-Financed Property

687. Unrelated Debt-Financed Income. Code Sec. 514 provides that unrelated debt-financed income of an exempt organization is taxed as unrelated business income—in proportion to the debt existing on the income-producing property. This Code section was enacted to prevent a "bootstrap" sale and leaseback transaction, resulting in the conversion of ordinary income into capital gain, and to achieve acquisition of a business by a tax-exempt organization entirely from the earnings of the business. In a typical "bootstrap" sale and leaseback (1) shareholders of a closely held corporation sell their stock to an exempt organization with little or no down payment and a promissory note for the balance of the purchase price, (2) the corporation is immediately liquidated and its assets leased by the exempt organization to a new company, (3) the new company pays the exempt organization a percentage of its operating profit as rent, and (4) the exempt organization pays a percentage of the rents received to the selling shareholders to be applied on the promissory note.

Debt-financed property in general means any property that is held to produce income (e.g., rental real estate, corporate stock, etc.) and with respect to which there is an "acquisition indebtedness" (e.g., mortgage) at any time during the tax year or during the preceding 12 months if the property is disposed of during the tax year (Code Sec. 514(b); Reg. § 1.514(b)-1(a)).[114] See ¶ 691 for a list of exempt properties.

Footnote references are to paragraphs of the 2002 Standard Federal Tax Reports.

110 ¶ 22,840, ¶ 22,841   113 ¶ 22,843   114 ¶ 22,850, ¶ 22,853
111 ¶ 22,837.101
112 ¶ 22,840, ¶ 22,841,
¶ 22,843

The unrelated debt-financed income with respect to each debt-financed property is an amount that is the same percentage (not exceeding 100 percent) of total gross income derived during the tax year from such property as the "average acquisition indebtedness" is of the "average adjusted basis" (Reg. § 1.514(a)-1(a)(1)).[115] See ¶ 694.

689. Acquisition Indebtedness. The "acquisition indebtedness" with respect to the debt-financed property is the outstanding amount of principal indebtedness (1) incurred to acquire or improve the property, (2) incurred before acquisition or improvement if it would not have been incurred but for the acquisition or improvement, and (3) incurred after acquisition or improvement if it would not have been incurred but for the acquisition or improvement and was reasonably foreseeable at the time (Code Sec. 514(c); Reg. § 1.514(c)-1(a)).[116]

If the property is acquired *subject to* a mortgage, the amount of the mortgage is considered an "acquisition indebtedness" incurred in acquiring the property, even though the organization did not assume or agree to pay the indebtedness. However, when mortgaged property is received by devise, bequest or gift, there is a 10-year transition with regard to the debt secured by the mortgage (Code Sec. 514(c)(2)(B)).

"Acquisition indebtedness" does not include any amount of liability for taxes or special assessments by a state or local government that is secured by a lien until, and to the extent that, the amount becomes due and payable and the organization has had an opportunity to pay it (Code Sec. 514(c)(2)(C)).[117] Nor does it include certain liabilities incurred by a pension, profit-sharing or stock bonus trust to acquire or improve real property (excluding any interest in a mortgage) or liabilities incurred for such purposes by an educational institution qualified to receive deductible charitable contributions or a private foundation organized to support such an institution (Code Sec. 514(c)(9)).[118]

691. Exempt Properties. The following types of property are excluded from the definition of debt-financed property under Code Sec. 514(b):

(1) property all the use of which is substantially related to exercise or performance of the organization's exempt function (special rules apply to real property used as a medical clinic); (2) property to the extent that its income is subject to tax as income from the carrying on of an unrelated trade or business; (3) property to the extent that its income is derived from research activities and is excluded from gross income of an unrelated trade or business; and (4) property to the extent it is used in a business where (a) substantially all of the work of carrying on the business is performed without compensation, (b) the Code Sec. 501(c)(3) organization carrying on the business does so primarily for the convenience of members, students, patients, etc., or (c) the business consists of selling merchandise substantially all of which has been received as contributions.

For purposes of (1), (3), and (4), use of property by a related exempt organization is taken into account in determining use to which property is put (Reg. § 1.514(b)-1(c)).[119] Special rules apply to property put to related exempt uses, to life income contracts, and to real property located in the neighborhood of other property owned and used for exempt purposes by the exempt organization (Code Sec. 514(b); Reg. § 1.514(b)-1(c)-(e)).[120]

694. Computing the Tax. Unrelated business taxable income includes with respect to each debt-financed property (¶ 687) the percentage of total gross income derived for the year from the property. The percentage is "average acquisition indebtedness" divided by "average amount of the adjusted basis of debt financed property during that portion of the taxable year it is held by the organization." The percentage, however, may not exceed 100 percent (Reg. § 1.514(a)-1(a)).[121] Deductions with respect to each debt-financed property are

---

115 ¶ 22,851
116 ¶ 22,850, ¶ 22,854
117 ¶ 22,850

118 ¶ 22,850
119 ¶ 22,853

120 ¶ 22,850, ¶ 22,853
121 ¶ 22,851

¶ 689

allowed by applying the above fraction, except for deduction of capital loss resulting from the carryback or carryover of net capital losses (Code Sec. 514(a)).[122]

Cooperatives and Patrons

696. Return and Payment of Tax. A farmers', fruit growers' or like association, organized and operated on a cooperative basis for the purpose of marketing the products of members and returning to them the net proceeds, less marketing expenses, or for the purpose of purchasing supplies and equipment for members or other persons at cost plus expenses, may qualify for tax exemption (Code Sec. 521; Reg. § 1.521-1; Rev. Rul. 73-568).[123] Changing the form of the products (such as processing them into alcohol) does not jeopardize the exemption.[124] The official form for application for recognition of exempt status is Form 1028 (Application for Recognition of Exemption Under Section 521 of the Internal Revenue Code).

Form 990-C is the income tax return that must be filed by an "exempt" farmers' cooperative by September 15 (for a calendar-year corporation) or the 15th day of the ninth month following the close of a fiscal-year corporation's tax year (Code Sec. 6072(d); Reg. § 1.6072-2(d)).[125] Payment of the tax (on profits not distributed) is subject to the general rules described at ¶ 2529.

698. How Cooperatives and Patrons Are Taxed. Exempt cooperatives and corporations operating on a cooperative basis, with certain exceptions, are allowed a deduction (exclusion from income) for patronage dividends paid in money, qualified written notices of allocation, and property. The patron is taxed on such amounts. In addition, an exempt cooperative is allowed deductions for payments on a patronage basis arising from certain nonpatronage earnings. These payments are taxable to the patron. The patron is not taxed, however, on dividends that are directly attributable to the purchase of capital items or personal use items. Cooperatives and patrons may treat per-unit retain certificates and per-unit retain allocations paid in cash or other property similarly to patronage dividends. There are special rules, also, for deductions by an exempt or other cooperative upon the redemption of nonqualified written notices of allocation arising out of patronage and nonpatronage earnings (Code Secs. 1381-1388; Reg. §§ 1.1381-1—1.1388-1).[126] A federated cooperative (an association whose membership includes farmers' cooperatives) may also be exempt.[127] A cooperative is not denied tax-exempt treatment because it computes its net earnings by offsetting certain earnings and losses in determining any amount available for distribution to patrons (Code Secs. 521(b)(6) and 1388(j)(1)).[128] Cooperatives engaging in the practice of offsetting earnings and losses are required to notify their members that the amount of the member's distribution or allocation may have been affected by the cooperative's netting policy (Code Sec. 1388(j)(3)).[129]

A patronage dividend is an amount (1) paid to a patron on the basis of quantity or value of business done with or for such patron by the cooperative, (2) paid under an obligation to pay such amount that existed before the organization received the amount so paid, and (3) that is determined by reference to the net earnings of the organization from business done with or for its patrons (Code Sec. 1388(a)).

Footnote references are to paragraphs of the 2002 Standard Federal Tax Reports.

[122] ¶ 22,850
[123] ¶ 22,880, ¶ 22,881, ¶ 22,882.225
[124] ¶ 22,881, ¶ 22,882

[125] ¶ 36,720, ¶ 36,724
[126] ¶ 32,300—¶ 32,381
[127] ¶ 22,882.01, ¶ 22,882.225

[128] ¶ 22,880, ¶ 32,380
[129] ¶ 32,380

Chapter 7

INCOME

What Is "Income"

701. Gross Income Defined. For federal income tax purposes, "gross income" means all income from whatever source, except for those items specifically excluded by the Code (Code Sec. 61).[1]

Fifteen of the more common types of "gross income" are enumerated by Code Sec. 61. They are: (1) compensation for services, including fees, commissions, fringe benefits, and similar items; (2) gross income from business; (3) gains from dealings in property; (4) interest; (5) rents; (6) royalties; (7) dividends; (8) alimony and separate maintenance payments; (9) annuities; (10) income from life insurance and endowment contracts; (11) pensions; (12) income from discharge of debt; (13) partner's share of partnership income; (14) income "in respect of a decedent"; and (15) income from an interest in an estate or trust.

Although nearly every type of accession to wealth (except gifts and inheritances) appears to fall within this comprehensive definition, income items should be checked against the specific exclusions in Code Sec. 101–Code Sec. 139 (see ¶ 801 et seq.). For special rules relating to foreign income, see ¶ 2401 et seq. For a detailed list of income items and exclusions, see Checklist for Items of Income at ¶ 55.

702. Income from Capital or Labor. Court decisions have developed a concept of the term "income" that is quite different from the layman's concept. The Supreme Court has approved this definition: "Income may be defined as the gain derived from capital, from labor, or from both combined, provided it be understood to include profit gained through a sale or conversion of capital assets." In addition,

---

Footnote references are to paragraphs of the 2002 Standard Federal Tax Reports.

¶701   [1] ¶ 5502

the Supreme Court has repeatedly held that Congress's broad definition of what constitutes gross income was intended to tax all gain unless specifically exempted.[2]

In addition to those items specifically excluded from gross income by law (see ¶ 801 et seq.), certain other items are not considered income.

Return of Capital. A return of capital, such as repayment of a loan, is not income unless the loan had been previously deducted as a bad debt, resulting in a tax benefit.[3] Similarly, car pool reimbursements are not income even if only one person provides the car and does the driving.[4]

Damages. Damages (other than punitive damages) that compensate an injured person for personal physical injuries or physical sickness are excludable from gross income (Code Sec. 104(a)(2)). Damages received for personal nonphysical injuries, such as employment discrimination or injury to reputation, are generally taxable. See ¶ 852.

Interest on a judgment, including mandatory prejudgment interest, is generally includible in income.[5]

See ¶ 759 for treatment of damages awarded for business claims.

Housing Assistance. Rental assistance payments made by the Department of Housing and Urban Development under the National Housing Act and relocation payments made under the Housing and Community Development Act of 1974 are nontaxable. However, payments made by individuals or other nongovernmental entities are not considered payments for the general welfare and are taxable.[6]

Gift v. Income. The characterization of a payment or transfer as either a gift or as taxable income must be made on a case-by-case basis.[7] The Supreme Court has held that the value of a "gift" transferred to a business friend for furnishing the names of potential customers is taxable compensation.[8] See, also, ¶ 849.

Strike and Lockout Benefits. Strike benefits received from a labor union may be treated as nontaxable gifts when the benefits paid in the form of food, clothing, and rent are (1) given to both member and nonmember strikers, (2) dependent upon individual need, (3) dependent on the unavailability of unemployment compensation or local public assistance, and (4) given without condition. The fact that benefits are paid only to union members will not, of itself, be determinative as to taxability.[9]

Unrealized Appreciation. Unrealized appreciation in the value of property is not income.[10]

Ownership of Income

704. Tax Liability. In the vast majority of cases, the identity of the taxpayer is clear. The taxpayer is simply the person who is legally entitled to receive income. Thus, an individual who receives wages for services is obviously the person who must pay income tax on the wages. However, under some circumstances (see ¶ 705), a person may be taxed on income even though, at the time of payment, another receives it because of an anticipatory assignment of income.

705. Assignment of Income. The Supreme Court has held (in *Lucas v. Earl*) that an individual who gave his wife the legally enforceable right to receive the future income generated by his law practice was still taxable on that income.[11] In another case (*Helvering v. Horst*), the Supreme Court ruled that an individual who gave his son interest coupons, which were detached from bonds that he owned, was liable for the tax on the interest accrued before the gift and later paid to his son.[12] Generally, an individual can escape tax on income from property only if the individual makes a valid gift or assignment of the income-producing property itself as distinguished from an assignment of the income (however, see ¶ 706 for the taxation of the unearned income of children under the age of 14, below).

Footnote references are to paragraphs of the 2002 Standard Federal Tax Reports.

2 ¶ 5504.021
3 ¶ 5504.035, ¶ 5504.103
4 ¶ 5504.144
5 ¶ 6662.043
6 ¶ 5504.184
7 ¶ 6553.03
8 ¶ 5507.036, ¶ 5507.294
9 ¶ 6553.46
10 ¶ 5504.119
11 ¶ 2200.01, ¶ 5504.031, ¶ 6553.74
12 ¶ 2150.64

706. Unearned Income of Minor Child. The use of intra-family transfers of income-producing property to reduce income tax liability by shifting income from the parent's high marginal tax rate to a child's generally lower tax bracket is greatly limited before the child reaches age 14 (Code Sec. 1(g)).[13] During those years, a child's net unearned income in excess of the child's Code Sec. 63(c)(5)(A)[14] standard deduction ($750 for 2001 (Rev. Proc. 2001-13) and also $750 for 2002 (CCH projection)), reduced by the greater of the standard deduction or itemized deductions allocated to such income, is subject to tax at the top marginal tax rate of his or her parents. Since the applicable standard deduction is $750 for 2001, unearned income in excess of $1,500 is taxed at the parents' rates. This applies to children who have not reached age 14 before the close of the tax year and have either parent living at year end. The tax is computed on Form 8615.

> **Example.** A six-year-old child has $1,600 of unearned income and no earned income in 2001. His standard deduction of $750 is allocated against his unearned income, so that his net unearned income equals $850. The first $750 of that amount is taxed at the child's tax rate, while the remaining $100 of unearned income is taxed at the top rate of his parents.

The marginal tax rate of the parent with the greater amount of taxable income will apply in the case of married individuals filing separately. In the case of divorced parents, the custodial parent's taxable income is taken into account in determining the child's tax liability. The tax applies to a child's unearned income regardless of source and requires a calculation of the parents' allocable tax (Code Sec. 1(g)).[15]

The parent of a child under the age of 14 may elect to include the gross income of the child in excess of $1,500 in his or her income for the 2001 tax year by filing Form 8814.[16] See ¶ 114.

709. Joint Tenancy and Tenancy in Common. When property is held in joint tenancy with a right of survivorship, income from the property (and gain or loss upon its sale) is divided between the owners insofar as each is entitled, under state law, to share in the income.[17] There must be evidence that the joint ownership was bona fide and not used merely as a tax-avoidance scheme. These rules also apply to tenants in common.[18]

710. Community Property Income. In community property states (Arizona, California, Idaho, Louisiana, Nevada, New Mexico, Texas, Washington and Wisconsin),[19] property acquired by a husband and wife after their marriage is generally regarded as owned by them in community, and income from the property is divided equally between them. Although each state has exceptions in classifying income as separate or community property, the general rule is that salaries, wages, and other compensation for the services of either or both the husband and wife are community income. But it does not follow in every state that income from separate property is separate income. The states also differ in their treatment of property acquired by inheritance or intestate succession. However, the IRS can disallow the benefits of any community property law to a spouse for any income that the spouse treats as his or hers alone if that spouse fails to notify the other spouse of the nature and amount of income (Code Sec. 66(b)).[20]

711. Joint v. Separate Return in Community Property States. If separate returns are filed by a married couple residing in a community property state, one-half of the community income must be reported by each spouse. In Idaho, Louisiana, Texas and Wisconsin, income from the separate property of a spouse is community income, with one-half being allocable to each spouse. In the other community property states, income from separate property is separate income.[21]

Regardless of which rule is applied, it is usually more beneficial to file a joint return. For those taxpayers living in states where income from separate property

---

Footnote references are to paragraphs of the 2002 Standard Federal Tax Reports.

¶706

13 ¶ 3260, ¶ 3280.01	16 ¶ 3260	19 ¶ 2350.01
14 ¶ 6020	17 ¶ 2250.021	20 ¶ 6050, ¶ 6051.04
15 ¶ 3260	18 ¶ 2250.021	21 ¶ 2350.023

remains separate income, separate returns may be beneficial if one spouse has: (1) a nonbusiness casualty loss attributable to separate property that is not deductible on a joint return because it must be reduced by the $100 floor plus 10 percent of the taxpayer's adjusted gross income or (2) medical expenses that are not deductible on a joint return because of the 7.5 percent of adjusted gross income floor on medical expense deductions.

A U.S. citizen or resident who is married to a nonresident alien may elect to file a joint return if both agree to be taxed on their worldwide income (Code Sec. 6013(g)).[22] If the couple does not make this election and has community property income, certain community property laws will be inapplicable for income tax purposes (Code Sec. 879).[23] Further, there is a special one-time election that permits a nonresident alien spouse to file a joint return with his or her resident spouse for the year in which the former becomes a U.S. resident (Code Sec. 6013(g) and Code Sec. 6013(h)).[24] Moreover, if both spouses are nonresident aliens and one spouse's income is connected with a U.S. trade or business, such income is treated as income of that spouse only, regardless of foreign community property law (Code Sec. 879(a)).[25]

Separated Spouses and Innocent Spouse Relief in Community Property States. Community income is taxed to the party earning it if persons in a community property state are married at any time during the tax year, are separated for the entire year, file separate returns, and do not transfer to each other more than a *de minimis* amount of earned income (Code Sec. 66(a)).[26] Also, a spouse who files a separate return may be relieved of liability for tax on his or her share of community income earned by the other spouse if he or she did not know (or have reason to know) of community income items attributable to the other spouse. Further, the IRS may provide relief from a tax liability or deficiency where failure to do so would be inequitable (Code Secs. 66(c) and Rev. Proc. 2000-15).[27]

Salaries, Wages and Benefits

713. Compensation Is Income. All compensation for personal services, no matter what the form of payment, must be included in gross income.[28] Wages, salaries, commissions, bonuses, fringe benefits that do not qualify for statutory exclusions, tips, payments based on a percentage of profits, directors' fees, jury fees, election officials' fees, retirement pay and pensions, and other forms of compensation are income in the year received, and not in the year earned, unless the taxpayer reports income on the accrual basis.

> **Example.** A cash-basis salesperson who receives commissions in January 2001 for sales made in 2000 must include them in a 2001 return.

Under the claim-of-right doctrine, a taxpayer receiving income under a claim of right and without restrictions on its use or disposition is taxed on that income in the year received even though the right to retain the income is not yet fixed or the taxpayer may later be required to return it (see ¶ 1543).[29]

Compensation is income even though the amount is not fixed in advance, as in the case of marriage fees, baptismal offerings, and similar sums received by a member of the clergy.[30] A year-end bonus is usually taxable, particularly if based on salary or length of service. The value of a turkey, ham, or other nominally valued item distributed to an employee on holidays need not be reported as income even though the employer is entitled to deduct the cost as a business expense. However, a distribution of cash, a gift certificate, or a similar item of value readily convertible to cash must be included in the employee's income.[31] Severance pay and vacation pay are taxable as compensation.

The amount of compensation to be reported on the return is the gross amount before any reductions for withheld income tax or social security taxes, union dues,

---

Footnote references are to paragraphs of the 2002 Standard Federal Tax Reports.

[22] ¶ 35,160, ¶ 35,171.031	[26] ¶ 6050, ¶ 6051.021	[29] ¶ 21,005.122
[23] ¶ 27,460, ¶ 27,462.021	[27] ¶ 6050, ¶ 6051.035	[30] ¶ 5507.04
[24] ¶ 35,160, ¶ 27,462.01	[28] ¶ 5507.01	[31] ¶ 5507.036
[25] ¶ 27,460, ¶ 27,462.021		

¶713

insurance, or other deductions by the employer. One or more of these reductions might be allowable under some conditions, but they do not reduce the amount of gross income reported.

Restricted Property Transfers. The value of stock or other property provided to employees subject to certain restrictions is includible in income when the restrictions are removed, unless the recipient elects to recognize income upon receipt (Code Sec. 83). See ¶ 1681.

Fringe Benefits. Certain fringe benefits may be excluded from an employee's gross income. See ¶ 863. Benefits such as air flights, cars, computers, educational benefits, entertainment (see ¶ 910), or travel (see ¶ 949) may be excludable as working condition fringe benefits. However, these benefits may be includible in income to the extent the employee uses them for personal purposes. In general, an employee is required to include in income the amount by which the fair market value of a fringe benefit exceeds the sum of (1) the amount, if any, paid for the benefit and (2) the amount, if any, specifically excluded by some other provision of the law (Reg. § 1.61-21(b)(1)).

Employer-provided vehicle. The value of the personal use of an employer-provided car may be computed under annual lease value tables. The annual lease value of an automobile is computed by first determining the fair market value (FMV) of the automobile on the first date it was made available to any employee for personal use. Under a safe-harbor provision, the employer's cost can be substituted for FMV, provided certain conditions are met. Once the FMV is established, the Annual Lease Value Table, prepared by the IRS, is consulted to determine the annual lease value that corresponds to the FMV. The table is reproduced in Reg. § 1.61-21(d)(2)(iii).[32] The annual lease values include the FMV of maintenance and insurance for the automobile but do not include the cost of gasoline provided by the employer. The fuel provided can be valued either at its FMV or at 5.5 cents per mile for all miles driven within the United States, Canada, or Mexico by the employee (Reg. § 1.61-21(d)(3)).

Cents-per-mile valuation. The value of the personal use of an employer-provided vehicle may be determined by multiplying personal use mileage by the standard mileage rate (34.5 cents per mile in 2001) if certain requirements are satisfied (Reg. § 1.61-21(e)). For a car first made available to an employee in calendar-year 2001, the fair market value of the vehicle cannot exceed $15,400 (Rev. Proc. 2001-19). The standard mileage rate may be reduced by no more than 5.5 cents per mile if the employer does not pay for the cost of the fuel.

Employer-provided commuting vehicle. If certain requirements are met, the use of an employer-provided commuting vehicle is valued at $1.50 each way (to and from work) per employee (Reg. § 1.61-21(f)).[33] Even if two or more employees commute in the vehicle (e.g., car pool), each employee includes $1.50 each way in income. To qualify, personal use of the vehicle must be *de minimis* and the employer must require the employee or employees to commute to and/or from work in the vehicle for bona-fide noncompensatory business reasons.

Employer-provided transportation due to unsafe conditions. If it is unsafe for an employee, who would normally do so, to walk or use public transportation to get to work and certain other requirements are met, the employee includes only $1.50 per one-way commute in income with respect to cab fare or an employer-provided vehicle (Reg. § 1.61-21(k)).[34]

Noncommercial aircraft flights. The value of personal flights (domestic or international) on employer-provided noncommercial aircraft is determined under an IRS formula (Reg. § 1.61-21(g)) that is based on Standard Industry Fare Level (SIFL) flight mileage rates, a terminal charge and the weight of the aircraft.[35] If a trip made primarily for business purposes includes business and personal flights, the excess of the value of all the actual flights over the value of the flights that would

---

Footnote references are to paragraphs of the 2002 Standard Federal Tax Reports.

[32] ¶ 5906, ¶ 5907.03   [34] ¶ 5907.035   [35] ¶ 5906, ¶ 5907.042
            [33] ¶ 5906, ¶ 5907.032

have been taken if there had been no personal flights is included in income. If the trip is primarily personal, the value of the personal flights that would have been taken if there had been no business flights is included in income (Reg. § 1.61-21(g)(4)).

No amount is included in income if the employee takes a personal trip on a noncommercial aircraft and at least one-half of the aircraft's seating capacity is occupied by employees whose flights are primarily business related and excludable from income (Reg. § 1.61-21(g)(12)).

Golden parachute payments. Golden parachute payments are includible benefits (see ¶ 907).

Moving expense reimbursement. Moving expense reimbursements for expenses incurred are excludable as a qualified fringe benefit (see ¶ 1076).

Vacation and club expenses. That portion of an employee's vacation, athletic club, or health resort expenses that is paid by the employer is also taxable to the employee.[36]

Cafeteria Plans. Employer contributions under written "cafeteria" plans are excludable from the income of participants to the extent that they choose qualified benefits. See ¶ 861.

714. Compensation of Federal or State Employee. The salaries of all employees or officials of the United States government are taxed the same as those of other individuals. This is also true for state and local government employees.[37]

715. Treatment of Excessive Salaries. Although an employer is denied a deduction for compensation paid to the extent that the payment is unreasonable, the full amount of the payment is included in the recipient's income. In the case of an employee-shareholder, excessive compensation may be treated as dividend income. Excessive salaries are taxed only to the extent of the gain if the excess amounts are determined to be payments to the recipient for property rather than compensation (Reg. § 1.162-8).[38]

716. Social Security and Equivalent Railroad Retirement Benefits. A portion of a taxpayer's social security benefits or an equivalent portion of tier 1 railroad retirement benefits may be taxable (Code Sec. 86). The includible amount is the lesser of one-half of the annual benefits received or one-half of the excess of the taxpayer's provisional income over a specified base amount, at lower provisional income levels. However, at higher provisional income levels, up to 85% of the social security benefits may be included (see "85-Percent Inclusion," below). The Form 1040 instructions contain a worksheet for computing the taxable amount.

Provisional income is the taxpayer's modified adjusted gross income plus one-half of the social security or tier 1 railroad retirement benefits. Modified adjusted gross income is the taxpayer's adjusted gross income plus (a) any tax-exempt interest, including interest earned on savings bonds used to finance higher education, and (b) amounts excluded under an employer's adoption assistance program (¶ 1306), deducted for interest on education loans (¶ 1082) or as a qualified tuition expense (¶ 1082), or earned in a foreign country, a U.S. possession, or Puerto Rico and excluded from gross income (¶ 2401–¶ 2415). The base amount is: (a) $32,000 if married individual filing jointly, (b) $0 if married filing separately and the taxpayer lived with his or her spouse at any time during the year, and (c) $25,000 for any other filing status (Code Sec. 86(c)).[39]

> **Example 1.** John and Jane Mapes have an adjusted gross income of $24,000 for 2001. John, who is retired, receives social security benefits of $7,200 per year. The couple also receives $6,000 a year from a mutual fund that invests solely in tax-exempt municipal bonds. On their joint return for 2001, the Mapes would make the following computation to

---

Footnote references are to paragraphs of the 2002 Standard Federal Tax Reports.

[36] ¶ 5507.47
[37] ¶ 5507.043, ¶ 5507.044
[38] ¶ 8639, ¶ 8640.01
[39] ¶ 6420, ¶ 6421.03

determine how much (if any) of John's social security benefits must be included in their gross income:

(1)	Adjusted gross income.................................	$24,000
(2)	Plus: All tax-exempt interest	6,000
(3)	Modified adjusted gross income	$30,000
(4)	Plus: One-half of social security benefits	3,600
(5)	"Provisional income"	$33,600
(6)	Less: Base amount.................................	32,000
(7)	Excess above base amount	$ 1,600
(8)	One-half of excess above base amount	$ 800
(9)	One-half of social security benefits...................	3,600
(10)	Amount includible in gross income (lesser of (8) or (9))	$ 800

Although tier 2 railroad retirement benefits are not taken into account under the above rules, such benefits are taxed in the same manner as benefits paid under private employer retirement plans (Code Sec. 72(r)).[40]

85-Percent Inclusion. Up to 85 percent of an individual's social security benefits may be included in gross income. The rules affect married taxpayers filing jointly with provisional income in excess of $44,000, married taxpayers filing separately and not living apart the entire year with provisional income in excess of $0, and all other taxpayers with provisional income in excess of $34,000 (Code Sec. 86).[41]

Those who exceed the higher threshold "adjusted base" amounts must include in income the lesser of: (a) 85 percent of social security benefits or (b) 85 percent of the excess of provisional income over the threshold amount, plus the sum of the smaller of (i) the amount that would otherwise be includible if the second threshold did not apply or (ii) $4,500 ($6,000 for married persons filing a joint return).

> **Example 2.** Assume the same facts as above, except that the Mapes' provisional income is increased from $33,600 to $53,600. The includible amount is determined as follows:
>
> | | | |
> |---|---|--:|
> | (1) | Provisional income .... | $53,600 |
> | (2) | Adjusted base amount............................... | 44,000 |
> | (3) | Excess of (1) over (2)............................... | $ 9,600 |
> | (4) | 85% of amount in (3) .... | $ 8,160 |
> | (5) | Amount otherwise includible (½ of benefits in the Mapes' case)... | $ 3,600 |
> | (6) | Base amount for joint filers .... | $ 6,000 |
> | (7) | Lesser of (5) or (6)................................ | $ 3,600 |
> | (8) | Sum of amounts in (4) and (7) .... | $11,760 |
> | (9) | 85% of social security benefits .... | 6,120 |
> | (10) | Amount includible in gross income (lesser of (8) or (9)) ..... | $ 6,120 |

Supplemental security income (SSI) payments are not treated as social security benefits that may be partially includible in gross income.[42]

IRA Contributions. Employed individuals who are covered by a retirement plan and who are receiving social security benefits must make a special computation to determine the amount of an allowable IRA deduction. See ¶ 2170.

717. Tips. Tips received by cab drivers, waiters, barbers, hotel, railroad and cruise ship employees, etc., are taxable.[43] In the absence of proof of the actual amount of tips received, tip income may be reconstructed on the basis of average tips in a given locality for a given type of service.[44]

Tipped employees may use Form 4070A (not filed) to maintain a daily record of their tips. Cash, check, and credit card tips in excess of $20 per month are reported

---

Footnote references are to paragraphs of the 2002 Standard Federal Tax Reports.

¶717

[40] ¶ 6102, ¶ 6140.046	[42] ¶ 5507.034	[44] ¶ 5507.023,
[41] ¶ 6420, ¶ 6421.03	[43] ¶ 5507.023	¶ 5507.4651 et seq.

to the employer on Form 4070 or a similar statement by the 10th day of the following month (see ¶ 2601). An employer may also allow tips to be reported electronically. Form 4137 is used to compute an employee's liability for social security and medicare taxes on monthly tips in excess of $20 that were not reported to the employer or on tips allocated by a large food and beverage establishment (see ¶ 2601). If an employer was unable to withhold social security and medicare taxes on reported tip income, the uncollected taxes will be shown on Form W-2 and are reported as an additional tax on the tipped employee's income tax return. Noncash tips and tips of less than $20 per month are not subject to social security and medicare tax. These amounts, however, are subject to income tax and must be reported on the employee's return.

See ¶ 2601 regarding duty to report tips monthly to employer on Form 4070, ¶ 2639 regarding employer's withholding requirements, and ¶ 1341 regarding an employer credit for social security taxes on employee cash tips.

718. Pension. A pension paid to a retired employee is usually taxable compensation (Reg. § 1.61-11).[45] See ¶ 2101 et seq.

719. Salary Payments to Employee's Survivor. The IRS and the Tax Court have generally taken the position that salary payments made to the surviving spouse of a deceased employee are taxable income, while several U.S. Courts of Appeal have viewed the payments as tax-free gifts.[46]

720. Compensation Other Than in Cash. When services are paid for in property, the fair market value at the time of receipt must be included in gross income (Reg. § 1.61-2(d)).[47] A note received in payment for services, and not merely as security for such payment, comes within this rule and its fair market value must be included in income. A portion of each payment received under the note will be excludable from income as a recovery of capital.[48]

721. Group-Term and Split-Dollar Life Insurance. An employee must include in income the cost (based on the IRS uniform premium cost tables, reproduced below) of more than $50,000 of group-term life insurance provided by his employer (Code Sec. 79; Reg. § 1.79-1—Reg. § 1.79-3).[49] An employee's age is determined as of the last day of the employee's tax year.

> **Example 1.** X Corp. pays the premiums on a $70,000 group-term insurance policy on the life of its president, Dan Fox, with Fox's wife as beneficiary. Fox is 51 years old at the end of 2001. The IRS-established uniform cost for $1,000 of group-term coverage for twelve months in 2001 is $2.76 ($0.23 × 12) (Reg. § 1.79-3(d)(2)).[50] The cost of the policy includible in Fox's gross income is computed as follows:

Total insurance coverage	$70,000.00
"Tax-free" insurance	50,000.00
Insurance coverage subject to tax	$20,000.00
Taxable cost of policy includible in Fox's gross income ($2.76 × 20)	$55.20

The $50,000 limit relates to the group-term life insurance coverage which the employee receives during any part of the tax year.

> **Example 2.** An employee's group-term life insurance noncontributory coverage for the first six months of the tax year is $50,000 and for the remainder of the tax year is $95,000. The cost of $45,000 of such insurance for the second six months of the tax year is includible in her gross income.

Any amount paid by the employee toward the purchase of group-term life insurance coverage on the employee's life during the tax year reduces the amount includible in gross income. If a discriminatory group-term insurance plan exists, the

Footnote references are to paragraphs of the 2002 Standard Federal Tax Reports.

[45] ¶ 5710
[46] ¶ 5507.030
[47] ¶ 5506, ¶ 5508
[48] ¶ 5508.026
[49] ¶ 6360, ¶ 6362, ¶ 6364, ¶ 6367
[50] ¶ 6364

cost of the life insurance paid by the employer for the tax year is includible in the gross income of key employees and certain former key employees (Code Sec. 79(d)).[51]

Table 1—For Post-June 30, 1999 Coverage

Cost Per $1,000 of Protection for One-Month Period

Age	Cost
Under 25	5 cents
25 through 29	6 cents
30 through 34	8 cents
35 through 39	9 cents
40 through 44	10 cents
45 through 49	15 cents
50 through 54	23 cents
55 through 59	43 cents
60 through 64	66 cents
65 through 69	$1.27
70 and above	$2.06

"Split-Dollar" Life Insurance Policy. Under a "split-dollar" life insurance plan, the employer pays that part of each premium equal to the increase in the cash surrender value of the policy and the employee pays the rest of the premium. If the employee dies, the employer is paid an amount out of the proceeds about equal to the cash surrender value of the policy (or at least equal to its premium payments), with the remainder of the proceeds going to the employee's beneficiary.[52] The employee must include in gross income each year as wages an amount equal to the one-year term cost of the declining life insurance protection to which he is entitled, minus any part of the premium that he paid. Notice 2001-10 indicates that the IRS may issue future guidance (to apply prospectively) which characterizes an employer's premium payments as a series of below-market loans. This would result in an imputation of interest income to the employee. If a split-dollar arrangement is not considered a loan, the IRS indicates that it may issue prospective guidance which treats an employee's substantially vested interest in the policy's cash surrender value (i.e., the value in excess of the amount that the employer is entitled to) as taxable compensation under Code Sec. 83.

The PS-58 table which has been used to determine the value of current life insurance protection under a split-dollar arrangement is replaced by Table 2001, effective for tax years ending after December 31, 2001 (Notice 2001-10, revoking Rev. Rul. 55-747). Table 2001, however, may be used effective for tax years ending after January 9, 2001 (the date Notice 2001-10 was issued). Both tables are reproduced below. The use of Table 2001 will result in significant tax savings for employees. For example, the PS-58 rate for a worker age 45 is $6.30 for each $1,000 of insurance protection. The Table 2001 rate is $1.53.

An employer may also use the insurer's lower published premium rates that are available to all standard risks for initial one-year term insurance subject to specified conditions (Rev. Rul. 66-110, as modified by Notice 2001-10).

Table 2001

Interim Table of One-Year Term Premiums for $1,000
Life Insurance Protection

Age	Premium	Age	Premium
0	$ 0.70	9	0.16
1	0.41	10	0.16
2	0.27	11	0.19
3	0.19	12	0.24
4	0.13	13	0.28
5	0.13	14	0.33
6	0.14	15	0.38
7	0.15	16	0.52
8	0.16	17	0.57

Footnote references are to paragraphs of the 2002 Standard Federal Tax Reports.

¶**721**   [51] ¶ 6360   [52] ¶ 5508.032

Age	Premium	Age	Premium
18	0.59	59	6.06
19	0.61	60	6.51
20	0.62	61	7.11
21	0.62	62	7.96
22	0.64	63	9.08
23	0.66	64	10.41
24	0.68	65	11.90
25	0.71	66	13.51
26	0.73	67	15.20
27	0.76	68	16.92
28	0.80	69	18.70
29	0.83	70	20.62
30	0.87	71	22.72
31	0.90	72	25.07
32	0.93	73	27.57
33	0.96	74	30.18
34	0.98	75	33.05
35	0.99	76	36.33
36	1.01	77	40.17
37	1.04	78	44.33
38	1.06	79	49.23
39	1.07	80	54.56
40	1.10	81	60.51
41	1.13	82	66.74
42	1.20	83	73.07
43	1.29	84	80.35
44	1.40	85	88.76
45	1.53	86	99.16
46	1.67	87	110.40
47	1.83	88	121.85
48	1.98	89	133.40
49	2.13	90	144.30
50	2.30	91	155.80
51	2.52	92	168.75
52	2.81	93	186.44
53	3.20	94	206.70
54	3.65	95	228.35
55	4.15	96	250.01
56	4.68	97	265.09
57	5.20	98	270.11
58	5.66	99	281.05

PS-58

Uniform One-Year Term Premiums for $1,000
Life Insurance Protection

Age	Premium	Age	Premium
15	$ 1.27	34	3.02
16	1.38	35	3.21
17	1.48	36	3.41
18	1.52	37	3.63
19	1.56	38	3.87
20	1.61	39	4.14
21	1.67	40	4.42
22	1.73	41	4.73
23	1.79	42	5.07
24	1.86	43	5.44
25	1.93	44	5.85
26	2.02	45	6.30
27	2.11	46	6.78
28	2.20	47	7.32
29	2.31	48	7.89
30	2.43	49	8.53
31	2.57	50	9.22
32	2.70	51	9.97
33	2.86	52	10.79

Age	Premium	Age	Premium
53	11.69	68	40.59
54	12.67	69	44.17
55	13.74	70	48.06
56	14.91	71	52.29
57	16.18	72	56.89
58	17.56	73	61.89
59	19.08	74	67.33
60	20.73	75	73.23
61	22.53	76	79.63
62	24.50	77	86.57
63	26.63	78	94.09
64	28.98	79	102.23
65	31.51	80	111.04
66	34.28	81	120.57
67	37.31		

722. Unemployment Compensation. Recipients of unemployment compensation benefits must include in income the entire annual amount of benefits received (Code Sec. 85).[53] Payments to laid-off employees from company-financed supplemental unemployment benefit plans (also referred to as "guaranteed annual wage" plans) constitute taxable income to the employees in the year received.[54] Payors report unemployment compensation on Form 1099-G.

723. Deferred Compensation. Not all compensation is paid in the year when services are rendered. Some may be deferred to a later year. There are two types of deferred compensation arrangements—funded and unfunded.

Funded Arrangements. If deferred compensation is contributed to a trust or is used to purchase an annuity or other insurance contract, the arrangement is funded and is governed by the rules discussed in Chapter 21 ("Retirement Plans").

Unfunded Arrangements. If the deferral takes the form of an employer's unsecured promise (not represented by a note) to pay compensation for current services at some time in the future, and if the employee uses the cash method of accounting (as is virtually always the case), the amount promised is not includible in the employee's gross income until it is received or made available (Rev. Rul. 60-31).[55] This rule is not altered merely because the employee agrees with the employer in advance to receive compensation on a deferred basis, so long as the agreement is made before the taxpayer obtains an unqualified and unconditional right to the compensation (*J.F. Oates,*[56] Section 132 of the Revenue Act of 1978).[57]

Unfunded Plans of State and Local Governments and Other Tax-Exempt Organizations. The above-described treatment of unfunded deferred compensation plans is modified for participants in plans maintained by state and local governments and other tax-exempt organizations, except for churches and qualified church-controlled organizations (Code Sec. 457).[58] If the rules discussed below are satisfied by such plans or arrangements, the deferred compensation is includible in income only when received by, or unconditionally made available to, a participant. For distributions from a government plan after 2001, the deferred compensation is included in income only when actually paid. This change does not apply to plans of a tax-exempt organization (Code Sec. 457(a), as amended by the Economic Growth and Tax Relief Reconciliation Act of 2001 (P.L. 107-16)). If the rules are not satisfied, the present value of the deferred compensation is includible in gross income for the first tax year in which there is no substantial risk of forfeiture. Any interest or other earnings credited to the deferred compensation are taxable (under the annuity rules) only when made available.

In 2001, the plan or arrangement must limit the amount that may be deferred for any tax year to the lesser of $8,500 or 33⅓% of the participant's compensation that is currently includible in gross income (Code Sec. 457(b)(2), prior to amend-

---

Footnote references are to paragraphs of the 2002 Standard Federal Tax Reports.

¶722

[53] ¶6410, ¶6412	[55] ¶18,352.029	[57] ¶5905.01
[54] ¶5507.032, ¶5507.60	[56] ¶21,009.135	[58] ¶21,531

ment by P.L. 107-16). This limitation may be increased for the participant's last three tax years preceding normal retirement age under a special deferral provision that permits the participant to defer an additional amount equal to the aggregate of the deferral limitations not utilized in earlier tax years in which the employee was eligible to participate in the plan. The maximum amount that may be deferred under both the normal and special deferral provisions in any year is $15,000 (Code Sec. 457(b)(3), prior to amendment by P.L. 107-16). If an employee participates in more than one section 457 plan of a governmental or tax-exempt employer, the aggregate deferral cannot exceed $8,500 (as increased by the special deferral provision), allocated between the various plans as the employee determines.

The Economic Growth and Tax Relief Reconciliation Act of 2001 increases these limitations. For tax years beginning in 2002, the deferral limit is the lesser of $11,000 or 100% of the participant's compensation (Code Sec. 457(b)(2), as amended by P.L. 107-16). The maximum amount that can be deferred under the normal and special deferral provision is increased from $15,000 to $22,000 (Code Sec. 457(b)(3), as amended by P.L. 107-16). Effective for years beginning after 2001, P.L. 107-16 also repeals a coordination rule which required a dollar-for-dollar reduction of the Code Sec. 457 deferral limit by contributions to a section 403(b) tax sheltered annuity, elective deferrals under a section 401(k) plan, salary reduction contributions under a SEP, and contributions under a SIMPLE plan (Code Sec. 457(c)(2), prior to repeal by P.L. 107-16).[59] After 2001, individuals who are age 50 or older by the end of the plan year may make additional "catch-up" contributions, as explained at ¶ 2197A

Code Sec. 457 does not apply to a bona fide vacation leave, sick leave, compensatory time, severance pay, disability pay, or death benefit plan (Code Sec. 457(e)(11)). Also, Code Sec. 457 does not apply to nonelective deferred compensation attributable to services not performed as an employee (Code Sec. 457(e)(12)).

A Code Sec. 457 plan must also provide: (1) that compensation may be deferred for any month only if an agreement for such deferral has been entered into before the first day of that month; (2) that, except as may be required by (3), deferrals may not be distributed earlier than the calendar year in which the participant attains age 70½ or the date of the participant's separation from service ("severance from employment" for distributions after 2001) except in the case of unforeseeable emergency; and (3) minimum distribution rules as described in Code Sec. 401(a)(9) and discussed at ¶ 2133 and ¶ 2135 (Code Sec. 457(b)(4) and (5)).

Code Sec. 457 plans are also discussed at ¶ 2197A.

Unfunded Plans of Taxable Employers. An unfunded plan of a taxable employer is not subject to limitations similar to those that apply to a governmental or other tax-exempt employer. As a practical matter, however, such a plan is limited to providing benefits in excess of those permitted under qualified plans or benefits for highly compensated and managerial employees. This is because any other unfunded deferred compensation plan of a taxable employer would be subject to ERISA participation, vesting, funding, and fiduciary standards (ERISA Sec. 4(b)(5), ERISA Sec. 201(2), ERISA Sec. 301(a)(3), and ERISA Sec. 401(a)(1)).

Interest

724. Interest. All interest received or accrued is fully taxable (Reg. § 1.61-7)[60] except interest on (1) tax-exempt state or municipal bonds and (2) certain ESOP loans (¶ 725). A cash-basis taxpayer is taxed on interest when received. Interest on bank deposits, coupons payable on bonds, etc., is considered available and taxed to a cash-basis taxpayer under the doctrine of constructive receipt and is taxed when credited or due.

Footnote references are to paragraphs of the 2002 Standard Federal Tax Reports.
[59] ¶ 21,536.038,   [60] ¶ 5704
¶ 21,536.039

Interest earned on corporate obligations is generally taxed when actually received by, or credited to, a cash-basis taxpayer (Reg. § 1.61-7(a)). The same rule applies to interest on certificates of deposit, time obligations, and similar deposit arrangements on which interest is credited periodically and can be withdrawn without penalty even though the principal cannot be withdrawn without penalty prior to maturity. However, interest on a six-month certificate that is not credited or made available to the holder without penalty before maturity is not includible in the holder's income until the certificate is redeemed or matures (Rev. Rul. 80-157).[61]

Increments in value on growth savings certificates are taxable in the year that the increase occurs.[62] Any increment in the value of life insurance or annuity prepaid premiums or premium deposits is income when made available to the policyholder for withdrawal or when credited against premiums payable.[63] Interest on a judgment is taxable, even if the underlying award is nontaxable.[64]

When a bond with defaulted interest coupons is bought "flat" (that is, the price covers both principal and unpaid interest), any interest received that was in default on the date of purchase is not taxable but is a return of capital. If the bond is sold, this amount must be applied to reduce the basis, in turn increasing the gain or reducing the loss. If interest is received for a period which *follows* the date of purchase, it is taxable in full.[65]

Under the accrual method, interest is taxable as it accrues even though it is payable later. An exception to this rule is where it is discovered before the close of the tax year that the interest owed to the taxpayer will not be collected.[66]

725. Interest Earned on ESOP Loans. Banks, insurance companies, regulated investment companies (such as mutual funds), and corporations actively engaged in the business of lending money *may no longer* exclude from gross income 50 percent of the interest received on loans to an employee stock ownership plan (ESOP) or to an employer corporation, the proceeds of which are used by the plan to acquire employer securities (former Code Sec. 133).[67] The repeal is generally effective for loans made after August 20, 1996; however, it does not apply to loans made pursuant to written binding contracts in effect prior to June 10, 1996 and to certain refinanced loans.

726. Mortgage Interest. The Supreme Court *(Midland Mutual Life Ins. Co.)* has held that when a taxpayer forecloses on a mortgage and purchases the property at a foreclosure sale by bidding the full amount of the mortgage plus accrued unpaid interest, taxable income is realized in the amount of the accrued interest, even though the fair market value was less than the bid price. Other courts have applied the same rule to *voluntary* conveyances by the mortgagor in consideration for the cancellation of the principal and interest of the mortgage. But there is no interest income in the case of such a conveyance if the property is worth less than the principal of the loan.[68] Nor is any income realized if only the principal of the mortgage is bid.[69] For repossessions of real property, see ¶ 1841.

If a creditor bids in property for a debt, a loss may be deductible if the property when so bid in is worth less than the debt.[70] The First Circuit has held that the *Midland Mutual* decision as to interest income does not prevent deduction of a loss in such a case, even though the creditor bid in the property for more than the debt.[71] The Tax Court has ruled that the Reg. § 1.166-6 presumption that the fair market value is presumed to be the bid price applies in the absence of clear and convincing proof to the contrary.[72] See ¶ 1145 for a discussion of the bad debt deduction.

Seller-Provided Financing. A taxpayer who receives or accrues interest from seller-provided financing must include on his or her income tax return the name,

[61] ¶ 21,009.3247
[62] ¶ 5704.023
[63] ¶ 5504.023
[64] ¶ 6662.043
[65] ¶ 5704.046, ¶ 5704.3062
[66] ¶ 5704.033
[67] ¶ 7450
[68] ¶ 5704.043, ¶ 5704.338
[69] ¶ 5704.338
[70] ¶ 10,670.01
[71] ¶ 10,670.123
[72] ¶ 10,750.10

¶725

address and taxpayer identification number of the person from whom the interest was received or accrued (Code Sec. 6109(h)).[73] Failure to provide this required information will expose the taxpayer to information reporting penalties (¶ 2833).

727. Imputed Interest. Holders of bonds or other obligations issued at a discount may be required to include in income a portion of the discount as "imputed interest" in each year the obligation is held even though no interest corresponding to this amount is paid or accrued during the period. See ¶ 1952. Holders of notes or other debt instruments that were issued in exchange for property or services may be required to include in income "imputed interest" where no interest is provided in the debt instrument or the rate of interest is less than the applicable federal rate. See ¶ 1954. Other loans bearing interest at less than the applicable federal rate may also result in "imputed interest" income to the lender. See ¶ 795.

728. Bond Transaction Between Interest Dates. When a bond is sold between interest dates and an amount representing the interest earned up to the date of sale is added to the selling price, the buyer, upon later receiving the full interest payment, reports as income only the portion representing interest that accrued from the date of sale.[74] The seller must include in income in the year of the sale the portion of the selling price representing interest accrued to the date of sale. This interest adjustment has no effect on the cost of the bond and apparently has no connection with the adjustment for amortizable bond premium (¶ 1967). It is a purchase of accrued interest.

729. Private Activity Bonds. Although interest on obligations of a state or local government is generally excludable from gross income (Code Sec. 103(a)),[75] bond interest is not tax free when it is derived from nonexempt private activity bonds, state or local bonds that have not been issued in registered form, or arbitrage bonds (Code Sec. 103(b)).[76] Private activity bonds that qualify for tax exemption include exempt-facility bonds (enterprise zone facility bonds are included in this category (Code Sec. 1394)), qualified veterans' mortgage bonds, qualified student loan bonds, qualified redevelopment bonds, qualified Code Sec. 501(c)(3) bonds, and qualified mortgage and small-issue bonds.[77] Qualified private activity bonds must meet the applicable volume cap requirements of Code Sec. 146 [78] and the applicable requirements of Code Sec. 147 [79] (Code Sec. 141(e)).[80] Capital expenditures of public schools, except schools owned or operated by private, for-profit businesses, may be financed with private activity bonds. However, bonds issued after 2001 that are used to provide qualified public educational facilities can be treated as exempt facility bonds (Code Sec. 142(a)(13), as added by the Economic Growth and Tax Relief Reconciliation Act of 2001 (P.L. 107-16)). A qualified public educational facility is defined as a public school facility owned by a private, for-profit corporation pursuant to a public-private partnership agreement with a state or local educational agency (Code Sec. 142(k)(1), as added by P.L. 107-16).

A special exception allows qualified scholarship funding bonds to be treated as state and local bonds (Code Sec. 150(d)).[81] Such bonds must be issued by a not-for-profit corporation that is established and operated exclusively for the purpose of acquiring student loan notes incurred under the Higher Education Act of 1965 and is organized at the request of a state or political subdivision. Also, a qualified volunteer fire department may issue bonds that will be treated as issued by a political subdivision if it is operated under a written agreement with a political subdivision to provide fire-fighting or emergency medical services (Code Sec. 150(e)).[82]

Bonds issued by a governmental unit to fund the acquisition of existing electric and gas generating and transmission systems are generally treated as private

---

Footnote references are to paragraphs of the 2002 Standard Federal Tax Reports.

[73] ¶ 36,960, ¶ 36,965.034	[77] ¶ 7702, ¶ 7740, ¶ 7780,	[80] ¶ 7702
[74] ¶ 5704.047	¶ 7810, ¶ 7830.01	[81] ¶ 7930, ¶ 7935.021
[75] ¶ 6600, ¶ 6602	[78] ¶ 7850, ¶ 7854	[82] ¶ 7930, ¶ 7935.03
[76] ¶ 6600, ¶ 6602	[79] ¶ 7860, ¶ 7861	

activity bonds subject to the state-volume limitations in order to limit their issuance for this purpose (Code Sec. 141(d)).[83]

Generally, income of state and local governments that is derived from the exercise of an essential governmental function is tax exempt. However, arbitrage restrictions limit the ability of governmental units to profit from the investment of tax-exempt bond proceeds (Code Sec. 148). Subject to limited exceptions, investment profits earned before the funds are needed must be rebated to the government. A small issuer exception applies to bonds issued by small governmental units with general taxing powers provided that the aggregate amount of all tax-exempt bonds (other than private activity bonds) issued during a calendar year is not more than $5 million. However, the $5 million cap is increased an additional $5 million for bonds that are used to finance public school capital expenditures. For bonds issued after 2001, the additional $5 million cap is increased to $10 million (Code Sec. 148(f)(4)(D), as amended by P.L. 107-16). Thus, up to $15 million of bonds may be issued to finance public school capital expenditures without regard to the arbitrage restrictions.

730. United States Savings Bond. A taxpayer on the *accrual* basis must include the increase in value of a United States savings bond (issued at a discount and payable at par on maturity) each year in an amount equal to the increase in redemption value as indicated in the table of redemption values shown on the bond even if the interest will not be received until the bond is surrendered.[84]

On the *cash* basis, none of the increase in value of the bonds issued at a discount (Series E and EE) or interest on Series I bonds is taxable until the earlier of the year the bonds are cashed in or disposed of or the year in which they mature.[85] A taxpayer on the cash basis *may,* however, elect to treat the annual increase in value of Series EE (former Series E) and Series I bonds as income in each year.

Taxable income is not recognized when Series EE or E bonds on which interest reporting was postponed are traded for Series HH or H bonds unless cash is received in the trade. Any cash received is taxed to the extent of interest earned on the Series EE or E bonds. When the Series HH or H bonds mature (or, if earlier, when they are disposed of) the difference between their redemption value and cost is reported as interest income. Cost is the amount paid for the Series EE or E bonds plus any additional amount paid for the Series HH or H bonds. A taxpayer may elect to treat all previously unreported accrued interest on Series EE or E bonds traded for Series HH bonds as income in the year of the trade.

730A. Exclusion for U.S. Savings Bond Income Used for Higher Education. An individual who redeems any qualified U.S. savings bond in a year in which qualified higher education expenses are paid may exclude from income amounts received under such redemption, provided certain requirements are met (Code Sec. 135).[86] A qualified U.S. savings bond is any such bond issued after 1989 to an individual who has reached age 24 before the date of issuance and which was issued at a discount under 31 U.S.C. § 3105 (such as Series EE bonds). Qualified higher education expenses include tuition and fees required for enrollment or attendance at an eligible educational institution of either a taxpayer, the taxpayer's spouse, or any dependent of the taxpayer for whom the taxpayer is allowed a deduction under Code Sec. 151 (Code Sec. 135(c)(2)). Also, taxpayers are entitled to the exclusion if the redemption proceeds are contributed to a qualified tuition program.

The amount that may be excluded is limited when the aggregate proceeds of qualified U.S. savings bonds redeemed by a taxpayer during a tax year exceed the qualified higher education expenses paid during that year (Code Sec. 135(b)(1)). Qualified higher education expenses must be reduced by the sum of the amounts received with respect to an individual for a tax year as a qualified scholarship that is not includible in gross income under Code Sec. 117, as an educational assistance

allowance under certain chapters of title 38 of the United States Code, as a payment (other than a gift or inheritance) that is exempt from tax (such as employer-provided educational assistance), or as a payment, waiver, or reimbursement under a qualified tuition program (Code Sec. 135(d)(1)). The amount must be further reduced by expenses taken into account for the Hope Scholarship or Lifetime Learning credits and, in tax years beginning after 2001, amounts taken into account in determining the exclusion for distributions from a qualified tuition program or the exclusion for distributions from an education savings account (Code Sec. 135(d)(2), as amended by the Economic Growth and Tax Relief Reconciliation Act of 2001 (P.L. 107-16)).

The exclusion is subject to a phaseout in the years in which the bonds are cashed and the tuition is paid (Code Sec. 135(b)(2)(B)).[87] The phaseout for 2001 begins at $83,650 for joint returns and $55,750 for other returns and is complete at modified adjusted gross income of $113,650 or more for joint returns and $70,750 or more for other returns (Rev. Proc. 2001-13). In 2002, the joint return phaseout is projected to begin at $86,400 and end at $116,400; for other returns the phaseout is projected to begin at $57,600 and end at $72,600 (CCH projection).

Below the phaseout ranges, taxpayers may exclude bond interest up to the amount of qualified higher education expenses. Above these ranges, no exclusion is allowed. For those falling within the ranges, the amount of interest excludable from income is reduced, depending on the taxpayer's modified AGI. Modified AGI is adjusted gross income after applying (1) the partial exclusion for social security and tier 1 railroad retirement benefits (Code Sec. 86), (2) amounts deducted for contributions to individual retirement arrangements (Code Sec. 219), and (3) adjustments for limitations on passive activity losses and credits (Code Sec. 469), and before taking into account (4) the interest exclusion under discussion, (5) the foreign income exclusion (Code Sec. 911), and (6) the exclusion for income from sources within Guam, American Samoa, the Northern Mariana Islands, and Puerto Rico (Code Sec. 931 and Code Sec. 933) (Code Sec. 135(c)(4)).

Form. This exclusion is not available to married individuals who file separate returns. The amount of excludable savings bond interest is determined using Form 8815, which is then filed with the taxpayer's Form 1040 or Form 1040A.

731. Issues of U.S. Obligations. Except for a minor exception, interest on all obligations of the United States and its agencies and instrumentalities issued after February 28, 1941, is subject to federal taxes to the same extent as private obligations (Reg. § 1.103-4).[88]

732. Sale of Federal or State Obligations. The taxing of gain derived from the sale of tax-exempt county or municipal bonds is not in violation of the Constitution.[89] Losses so sustained are deductible, subject to capital loss limitations.

Dividends

733. Dividends. Dividends are fully includible in gross income. For income tax purposes, the term "dividend" means any distribution made by a corporation to its shareholders, whether in money or other property, out of its earnings and profits accumulated after February 28, 1913, or out of earnings and profits of the tax year (Code Sec. 316(a); Reg. § 1.316-1).[90] See ¶ 747.

If a dividend is in cash, the amount of the dividend is the amount of the cash. If the dividend is in both cash and noncash property, the amount of the dividend is the amount of the cash plus the fair market value of the property distributed. (See ¶ 735.) Special rules apply to distributions received by 20% corporate shareholders (Code Sec. 301(e)).[91]

733A. Corporate Debt v. Equity. The determination of whether an instrument issued by a corporation is to be treated as stock or as evidence of indebted-

---

Footnote references are to paragraphs of the 2002 Standard Federal Tax Reports.

[87] ¶ 7551.021   [89] ¶ 6602.36   [91] ¶ 15,302, ¶ 15,305.031
[88] ¶ 6606   [90] ¶ 15,702, ¶ 15,703   **¶733A**

ness for federal income tax purposes is resolved by weighing various factors, such as the source of the payments made to the holder and whether there is an unconditional promise to pay a sum certain together with a fixed rate of interest. For instruments issued after October 24, 1992, the corporate issuer's characterization of the nature of the instrument, made at the time of issuance, is binding upon the corporation and all the holders, but not the IRS. However, interest holders are not bound by the issuer's characterization if they disclose any inconsistent treatment on their tax returns (Code Sec. 385(c)).[92]

The IRS closely scrutinizes instruments containing a combination of debt and equity characteristics which are designed to be treated as debt for federal income tax purposes (Notice 94-47). Of particular interest are instruments that contain such equity features as an unreasonably long maturity or an ability to repay principal with the issuer's stock. No deduction is allowed for any interest paid or accrued on a "disqualified debt instrument" issued after June 8, 1997 (Code Sec. 163(l)). The term means any debt that is payable in equity of the issuer or a related party, specifically if: (1) a substantial portion of the principal or interest is required to be paid or converted, or at the issuer's or related party's option is payable in, or convertible into, equity of the issuer or a related party; (2) a substantial portion of the principal or interest is required to be determined, or may be determined at the option of the issuer or related party, by reference to the value of equity of the issuer or related party; or (3) the debt is part of an arrangement designed to result in payment of the instrument with or by reference to the equity.

In addition, the IRS examines corporate transactions designed to produce interest deductions with respect to a related issuance of stock and to provide companies with significant tax advantages in satisfying their equity capital requirements (Notice 94-48). The overall substance of an arrangement whereby a corporation creates a partnership that issues notes to investors and uses most of its capital to buy stock of the corporation is viewed by the IRS as merely an issuance of preferred stock by the corporation. Thus, such a corporation could not deduct an allocable portion of interest expense on the note without an offsetting inclusion of dividend income.

734. When Is a Dividend Received? A dividend on corporate stock is taxable when, in an unqualified manner, it is made subject to the demand of the shareholder (Reg. § 1.301-1).[93] Accordingly, an accrual-basis stockholder need not include the dividend in income until it is made subject to demand. Time of payment, rather than time of declaration, governs taxability. A dividend is taxable when the check is actually received, even though it may be dated and mailed in an earlier tax year, unless the recipient requested delivery by mail in order to delay recognition of income.[94]

Voluntary repayment of a dividend legally declared and distributed does not negate the receipt of dividend income by a shareholder.[95]

Dividends paid by regulated investment companies are not always taxable when received. See ¶ 2323.

735. Dividend Paid in Property. If any part of a dividend is paid in a form other than cash, the property received must be included in gross income at its fair market value at the date of distribution (regardless of whether this date is the same as that on which the distribution is includible in gross income) (Code Sec. 301(b)(1) and (3)).[96] When property is distributed to a corporate shareholder, the adjusted basis of the property in the hands of the distributing corporation at the time of the distribution (plus any gain recognized by the distributing corporation) is substituted for the fair market value of the property if the adjusted basis is less than the fair market value. See, also, ¶ 733, above.

Footnote references are to paragraphs of the 2002 Standard Federal Tax Reports.

¶ **734**

[92] ¶ 17,340, ¶ 17,351.01
[93] ¶ 15,303, ¶ 15,305.304
[94] ¶ 21,009.1235
[95] ¶ 15,704.46, ¶ 15,704.473
[96] ¶ 15,302, ¶ 15,305.024

The amount of income realized on a distribution is reduced (but not below zero) by the amount of any liability to which property is subject or which is assumed (Code Sec. 301(b)(2); Reg. § 1.301-1).[97] The basis of property received in a distribution is the fair market value of such property (Code Sec. 301(d)).

If a distribution is paid in property having a fair market value in excess of the corporation's earnings and profits (¶ 747), the dividend is limited to earnings and profits (accumulated and current). The portion of the distribution that is not a dividend is applied to reduce the basis of the stock. If the amount of the nondividend distribution exceeds the basis of the stock, the excess is treated as a gain from the sale or exchange of the stock (Code Sec. 301(c)).

736. Gain or Loss to Corporation on Nonliquidating Distributions. No gain or loss is recognized by a corporation on the distribution of its stock, or rights to its stock, to shareholders. Similarly, a corporation generally does not recognize gain or loss on the distribution to its shareholders of corporate property (Code Sec. 311(a)).[98] A corporation generally must recognize gain, however, when it distributes appreciated property to its shareholders in any ordinary, nonliquidating distribution to the extent that the fair market value of the property exceeds its adjusted basis (Code Sec. 311(b)).[99] If property is distributed subject to a liability, or if the distributee assumes a liability upon distribution, the fair market value of the property cannot be less, for purposes of determining gain, than the amount of the liability (Code Secs. 311(b)(2) and Code Sec. 336(b)). Gain or loss rules applicable to corporations on liquidating distributions are discussed at ¶ 2257.

738. Stock Dividends and Stock Rights. As a general rule, a stockholder need not include in gross income the value of stock received as a stock dividend (Code Sec. 305(a); Reg. § 1.305-1—Reg. § 1.305-8).[100] Cash that is paid in lieu of fractional shares may be taxable even though fractional shares themselves would not be taxable (Reg. § 1.305-3(c)).[101] But, contrary to the general rule, the following distributions by a corporation of its stock (or stock rights) are taxed as a dividend under the rules discussed at ¶ 733.

Distribution in Lieu of Money. If a corporate distribution is, at the election of any of the shareholders (whether exercised before or after the declaration), payable in either the distributing corporation's stock or other property, the distribution is treated as a taxable dividend (Reg. § 1.305-2).

Disproportionate Distribution. If a distribution (or series of distributions) results in the receipt of cash or other property by some shareholders, and in an increase in the proportionate interest of other shareholders in the corporation's assets or earnings and profits, then stock or stock rights distributed to a shareholder on the common stock of the corporation must be treated as a taxable distribution (Reg. § 1.305-3).

Convertible Preferred Stock. A shareholder receiving a distribution from a corporation of convertible preferred stock on common stock must pay tax on the value of the stock received, unless it is proven that the distribution will not result in a disproportionate distribution (Reg. § 1.305-6).

Distribution of Common and Preferred Stock. If, in a distribution or series of distributions, some common stockholders receive preferred stock while other common stockholders receive common stock, all of the stockholders involved in the distribution must pay a dividend tax on the stock they receive. An increase in the stockholders' proportionate interest in the corporation results (Reg. § 1.305-4).[102]

Transaction Increasing Shareholder's Proportionate Interest. Under Code Sec. 305(c) various transactions may be treated as a distribution with respect to any shareholder whose proportionate interest in the earnings and profits or assets of the

---

Footnote references are to paragraphs of the 2002 Standard Federal Tax Reports.

[97] ¶ 15,302, ¶ 15,303, ¶ 15,305.028
[98] ¶ 15,550
[99] ¶ 15,550, ¶ 15,554.03
[100] ¶ 15,400, ¶ 15,401— ¶ 15,401H, ¶ 15,402
[101] ¶ 15,401C
[102] ¶ 15,401H, ¶ 15,402

¶738

corporation is increased by such transactions (Reg. § 1.305-7).[103] A taxable distribution may result in these cases.

Dividend on Preferred Stock. Any distribution of stock or stock rights made on preferred stock is taxed as a dividend, with one limited exception (Reg. § 1.305-5). An increase in the conversion ratio of convertible preferred stock made solely to take account of stock dividends or stock splits on the stock into which the convertible stock can be converted is tax free.

The basis of the stock, stock rights, or fractional shares acquired in a nontaxable distribution is an allocable portion of the basis of the stock on which the distribution was made. The basis is allocated in proportion to the fair market value of each on the date of the distribution (not the record date) (Reg. § 1.307-1).[104] An exception is provided in the case of the issuance of rights having a fair market value of less than 15% of the fair market value of the stock on which they are issued. The basis of such rights is zero unless the taxpayer elects to allocate a portion of the basis of the old stock in a timely filed return for the year in which the rights were received. An election, once made, is irrevocable (Reg. § 1.307-2).[105]

Extraordinary Dividends. Any corporation that receives an extraordinary dividend with respect to any share of stock that it has not held for more than two years before the dividend announcement date must reduce its basis in such stock (but not below zero) by the nontaxed portion of the extraordinary dividend received. A dividend is extraordinary under the two-year rule if it equals or exceeds 10% (5% in the case of stock preferred as to dividends) of the shareholder's adjusted basis in the stock (Code Sec. 1059).[106]

Subscription Rights. Rights on common stock to subscribe to stock of another corporation may be taxable (Reg. § 1.1081-5).[107] Excepted by Code Sec. 1081(c) [108] is a distribution of the stock (or rights thereto—Code Sec. 1083(f)) [109] of another corporation made in compliance with an order of the Securities and Exchange Commission.[110]

739. Disposition of Section 306 Stock. A special provision (Code Sec. 306) is designed to prevent a stockholder from receiving a nontaxable stock dividend (other than common on common) or from receiving a stock distribution (other than common stock) in connection with a reorganization and disposing of it to avoid reporting dividend income (Code Sec. 306).[111]

If Sec. 306 stock is redeemed by a corporation, the amount realized is treated as a distribution of property to which Code Sec. 301 applies and, therefore, will be treated as ordinary income or as a taxable distribution to the extent that it is made out of earnings and profits (see ¶ 733, ¶ 742, and ¶ 747). If the stock is disposed of otherwise than by a redemption, the amount realized is treated as ordinary income to the extent that the amount realized is not more than the amount that would have been realized as a dividend if, instead of the stock, the corporation had distributed cash in an amount equal to the fair market value of the stock. Therefore, it would be ordinary income up to the stockholder's share of the amount of earnings and profits of the corporation available for distribution.

A shareholder who received a preferred stock dividend on common stock and who donated the dividend to a tax-exempt charitable foundation realized no income on the stock transfer. In addition, the donor would not realize any income from the later sale of the Sec. 306 stock by the foundation.[112]

740. Special Rules and Exceptions for Section 306 Stock. The rules governing gain realized on Sec. 306 stock do not apply to a disposition: [113] (1) if it is not a redemption, is not made, directly or indirectly, to a related person under the constructive ownership rules, and terminates the entire stock interest of the shareholder in the corporation (including stock constructively owned); (2) if it is a

Footnote references are to paragraphs of the 2002 Standard Federal Tax Reports.

103 ¶ 15,401G, ¶ 15,402	107 ¶ 30,125, ¶ 30,182	111 ¶ 15,450, ¶ 15,452
104 ¶ 15,501	108 ¶ 30,120	112 ¶ 15,452.19
105 ¶ 15,501B	109 ¶ 30,160	113 ¶ 15,450, ¶ 15,452.03
106 ¶ 30,020, ¶ 30,021	110 ¶ 30,132.01	

¶739

complete redemption of all the stock held in the corporation by the shareholder or in redemption of stock held by a shareholder who is not a corporation and in partial liquidation of the distributing corporation; (3) if it is redeemed in a complete liquidation of the corporation; (4) to the extent that gain or loss is not recognized with respect to the disposition; or (5) if the IRS is satisfied that the distribution of the stock and the disposition or redemption (simultaneously or previously) of the stock on which the distribution was made were not in pursuance of a plan having as one of its principal purposes the avoidance of income tax. The sale of Sec. 306 stock to an employees' trust was held not to be part of a tax-avoidance plan.[114]

Distribution in Redemption

742. Redemption of Stock as a Dividend. If a corporation cancels or redeems its stock in such a manner as to make the distribution "equivalent" to a dividend distribution, the amount received by the shareholder, to the extent that it is paid out of earnings and profits, is a taxable dividend (Reg. § 1.302-1).[115]

Whether a distribution in connection with a cancellation or redemption of stock is equivalent to a taxable dividend depends on the facts in each case. A cancellation or redemption of a part of the stock, pro rata among all the shareholders, will generally be considered as resulting in a dividend distribution (Reg. § 1.302-2).[116] A redemption can be treated as an exchange of stock, rather than as a dividend, if one of the following four tests is met (Code Sec. 302(b)): [117] (1) the redemption is substantially disproportionate with respect to the shareholder; (2) the redemption terminates the shareholder's entire interest in the corporation; (3) the redemption is not substantially equivalent to a dividend; or (4) the redemption is of stock held by a noncorporate shareholder and is made in partial liquidation of the redeeming corporation. Amounts received by a shareholder in a distribution in complete liquidation of a corporation are not equivalent to the distribution of a taxable dividend (Code Sec. 331).[118]

A distribution is substantially disproportionate as to a shareholder if, after the redemption, the shareholder owns less than 50% of the combined voting power of all classes of voting stock and there is an exchange of stock but not of a dividend. Further, the ratio of the shareholder's holdings of voting stock after the redemption to all the voting stock must be less than 80% of the ratio of the voting stock the shareholder owned immediately before the redemption to the entire voting stock in the corporation. In addition, a distribution is not substantially disproportionate unless the stockholder's ownership of common stock (whether voting or nonvoting) after and before redemption also meets the 80% test (Reg. § 1.302-3).[119]

If a shareholder is entirely bought out, the transaction is treated as an exchange of the stock, and no part of the distribution is taxed as a dividend (Reg. § 1.302-4).[120]

A distribution that is in redemption of stock held by a noncorporate shareholder in partial liquidation of the distributing corporation is a distribution in exchange for the stock and is not taxed as a dividend (Code Sec. 302(b)(4)).[121]

Stock Redemption Expenses. A corporation is not allowed a deduction for any amount paid or incurred in connection with any redemption of its stock or the stock of any related person. This restriction does not apply to deductions for interest paid or accrued within the tax year on indebtedness, deductions for dividends paid in connection with the redemption of stock in a regulated investment company, or deductions for amounts properly allocable to indebtedness and amortized over the term of the debt (Code Sec. 162(k)).[122]

Footnote references are to paragraphs of the 2002 Standard Federal Tax Reports.

[114] ¶ 15,452.21	[117] ¶ 15,325,	[120] ¶ 15,329
[115] ¶ 15,326, ¶ 15,330	¶ 15,330.023	[121] ¶ 15,325,
[116] ¶ 15,327	[118] ¶ 16,002, ¶ 16,004.01	¶ 15,330.027
	[119] ¶ 15,328	[122] ¶ 8500, ¶ 9052.01

743. Constructive Ownership of Stock. Whenever the law requires a constructive ownership rule to be applied in provisions relating to corporate distributions (such as distributions in redemption of stock noted at ¶ 742) and adjustments, the rule is that an individual shall be considered as owning the stock owned, directly or indirectly, by or for that individual, a spouse (if not legally separated under a decree of divorce or separate maintenance) and children (including adopted children), grandchildren, and parents (Code Sec. 318(a)(1)).

Stock constructively owned by an individual under the family attribution rule is not to be treated as owned by that individual for the purpose of again applying the constructive stock ownership rule to make another the owner of such stock (Reg. § 1.318-4).[123]

Stock owned, directly or indirectly, by or for a partnership, S corporation, or estate is considered as being owned proportionately by the partners, S corporation shareholders, or beneficiaries. Stock owned, directly or indirectly, by or for a partner, S corporation shareholder, or beneficiary is treated as being owned by the partnership, S corporation, or estate.

Stock owned, directly or indirectly, by or for a trust is considered as being owned by its beneficiaries in proportion to their actuarial interests in the trust. Stock owned, directly or indirectly, by or for a beneficiary of a trust is considered as being owned by the trust. However, a contingent beneficial interest of not more than 5% of the value of the trust property is not to be taken into account (Code Sec. 318(a)(2) and (3); Reg. § 1.318-2).[124]

If 50% or more in value of the stock in a corporation is owned, directly or indirectly, by or for any person, that person is considered as owning the stock owned, directly or indirectly, by or for the corporation in the proportion that the value of the stock the person owns bears to the value of all the stock in the corporation. The corporation, on the other hand, is considered as owning the stock owned, directly or indirectly, by or for any person holding 50% or more in value of its stock, directly or indirectly (Code Secs. 318(a)(2)(C) and (a)(3)(C)).[125]

744. Redemption of Stock Through Use of Related Corporations. If stock of an issuing corporation is acquired by a corporation that is controlled by the issuing corporation, the amount paid for the stock will be a dividend by the issuing corporation, provided that, under the rules outlined at ¶ 742, this amount would be considered a taxable dividend. Also, when the stock of one corporation is sold to a related corporation ("brother-sister" corporations), the sale proceeds are considered as distributed in redemption of the stock of the corporation which bought it, governed by the rules at ¶ 742. If the sales are related, it is immaterial whether they are made simultaneously (Reg. § 1.304-2).[126] Whether the sales are related is determined upon the facts and circumstances surrounding all the sales. To the extent that a redemption involving related corporations is treated as a distribution under Code Sec. 301, the transferor and the acquiring corporation are treated as if the transferor had transferred the stock involved to the acquiring corporation in exchange for stock of the acquiring corporation, in a Code Sec. 351(a) nontaxable contribution of capital, and then the acquiring corporation had redeemed the stock it was deemed to have issued (Code Sec. 304(a)(1)). In general, this treatment is effective for distributions or acquisitions after June 8, 1997.

745. Redemption of Stock to Pay Death Taxes and Expenses. A distribution of property by a corporation in redemption of its stock that has been included in the gross estate of a decedent for estate tax purposes can qualify as an exchange to the extent that the amount of the distribution does not exceed the sum of the estate, generation-skipping transfer, inheritance, legacy, and succession taxes (including interest) on the estate, plus the funeral and administration expenses allowable as

---

[123] ¶ 15,905, ¶ 15,906.052	[125] ¶ 15,900, ¶ 15,906.046	[126] ¶ 15,377, ¶ 15,378.01
[124] ¶ 15,900, ¶ 15,902, ¶ 15,906.05		

¶ 743

deductions from the gross estate for federal estate tax purposes (Code Sec. 303(a)).[127]

To qualify for this treatment, the redemption must have been made not later than 90 days after the period of limitations on assessment of the federal estate tax (three years after the return is filed) (Code Sec. 302(b)(1)). When a petition for redetermination of an estate tax deficiency has been filed with the Tax Court, the redemption period is extended to any time before the expiration of 60 days after the decision of the Tax Court becomes final. A distribution made more than 60 days after the decision of the Tax Court becomes final can be timely, providing it is made within 90 days after expiration of the three-year period.[128]

The value of the decedent's stock in a closely held company must exceed 35% of the gross estate, after the deductions for allowable funeral and administration expenses and losses, in order for such redemption not to be treated as a taxable dividend (Code Sec. 302(b)(2)). The shares must be redeemed from a person whose interest in the estate is reduced by payment of estate, generation-skipping transfer, inheritance, and succession taxes or funeral and administration expenses. The value of these redeemed shares is limited to the sum of such deductible expenses.[129]

If stock in a corporation is the subject of a generation-skipping transfer occurring at the same time and as a result of the death of an individual, the tax imposed is treated as an estate tax for purposes of the redemption rules. The period of distribution is measured from the date of the generation-skipping transfer, and the relationship of stock to the decedent's estate is measured with reference solely to the amount of the generation-skipping transfer (Code Sec. 303(d)).[130]

Earnings and Profits

747. Sources of Distributions. To be subject to income tax as a dividend, a distribution received by a shareholder must be paid out of *earnings and profits* of the distributing corporation. A "dividend" is any distribution made by a corporation to its shareholders (1) out of its earnings and profits accumulated after February 28, 1913, or (2) out of the earnings and profits of the tax year (computed as of the close of the tax year without diminution by reason of any distributions made during the tax year), without regard to the amount of the earnings and profits at the time the distribution was made (Code Sec. 316; Reg. § 1.316-1). [131]

In order to determine the source of a distribution, consideration should be given: first, to the earnings and profits of the tax year; second, to the earnings and profits accumulated since February 28, 1913, but only in the case when, and to the extent that, the distributions made during the tax year are not regarded as out of the earnings and profits of that year; third, to the earnings and profits accumulated before March 1, 1913, only after all of the earnings and profits of the tax year and all the earnings and profits accumulated since February 28, 1913, have been distributed; and fourth, to sources other than earnings and profits only after the earnings and profits have been distributed (Reg. § 1.316-2).[132]

If the current year's earnings and profits are sufficient to cover all distributions made during the year, each distribution is a taxable dividend. However, if the year's cash distributions exceed current earnings and profits, a part of the earnings and profits must be allocated proportionately to each distribution, on the basis of the following formula: distribution × (current earnings and profits ÷ total distributions). The remaining portion of each distribution not covered by current earnings and profits is then treated as a taxable dividend to the extent of accumulated earnings and profits. If these are not sufficient to cover the remaining portion of any distribution, they are to be applied against each distribution in chronological order until exhausted.

Footnote references are to paragraphs of the 2002 Standard Federal Tax Reports.

[127] ¶ 15,350, ¶ 15,353	[130] ¶ 15,350	[132] ¶ 15,703B,
[128] ¶ 15,353.022	[131] ¶ 15,702, ¶ 15,703,	¶ 15,704.021
[129] ¶ 15,353.01	¶ 15,704.021	

748. How to Compute "Earnings and Profits." In computing earnings and profits, all income that is exempt from tax or that is not taxable under the Constitution must be included, as well as all items includible in gross income under Code Sec. 61 (Reg. § 1.312-6).[133] Thus, exempt income such as life insurance proceeds and fully tax-exempt interest on state or municipal obligations is included. Gain or loss from a sale or other disposition must be included in earnings and profits at the time and to the extent that it is recognized for tax purposes (Reg. § 1.312-6).[134]

The general rule on the distribution of property (including cash) by a corporation is that the earnings and profits for future distributions are reduced by the amount of money distributed, the principal amount of any obligations of the corporation distributed, and the adjusted basis of any other property distributed (Reg. § 1.312-1).[135] If appreciated property is distributed with respect to stock, earnings and profits must be increased by the amount of the gain realized upon the distribution even if the gain is not recognized for purposes of computing taxable income. There are special rules for distributions to 20% corporate shareholders.

749. Effect of Deficit on Earnings and Profits. Even if there is an operating deficit at the beginning of the year, total dividends paid are taxable to the extent of profits for the *entire* year (Reg. § 1.316-1(e)).[136] See ¶ 747.

750. Effect of Loss on Earnings. A loss for a preceding year cannot be used to decrease the earnings and profits of the tax year (Reg. § 1.312-6(d)).[137]

751. Redemptions. A corporation that distributes amounts in redemption of its stock can reduce its post-February 28, 1913, accumulated earnings and profits only by the ratable share of those earnings and profits attributable to the redeemed stock (Code Sec. 312(n)(7)).[138]

752. Effect of Reorganization on Earnings. When a corporate reorganization results in no recognized gain or loss, the company's life as a continuing venture does not stop, so that what were "earnings and profits" of the original company remain, for purposes of distribution, "earnings and profits" of the continuing corporation.[139]

753. Effect of Nontaxable Distribution on Earnings. Nontaxable stock dividends or stock rights are not a distribution of earnings and profits. The same rule applies to distributions of the stock or securities (or rights to acquire stock or securities) of other corporations and distributions of property or money when they were nontaxable to the recipient when made (Code Sec. 312(d)).[140]

754. Distribution Other Than a Dividend. Any distribution that is a dividend is included in gross income. That part of a distribution which is not a dividend reduces the basis of the stock. Any excess of distributions over such basis is treated as a gain from the sale or exchange of property (Code Sec. 301(c)).[141]

755. Effect of Depreciation on Earnings and Profits. Depreciation claimed on the corporation's income tax return that is in excess of the straight-line method increases the corporation's current earnings and profits (Code Sec. 312(k)).[142] For tangible property placed in service in tax years beginning after 1986, the alternative MACRS method is used to compute depreciation in order to determine the corporation's earnings and profits (see ¶ 1247). For depreciable assets first placed in service after 1980, but before 1987, the adjustment to earnings and profits for depreciation is determined under the straight-line ACRS, using extended recovery periods (see ¶ 1252).[143] For assets placed in service before 1981, the amount of the depreciation

---

Footnote references are to paragraphs of the 2002 Standard Federal Tax Reports.

[133] ¶ 15,611	[138] ¶ 15,600,	[142] ¶ 15,600,
[134] ¶ 15,611	¶ 15,612.0364	¶ 15,612.032,
[135] ¶ 15,601,	[139] ¶ 15,612.0327	¶ 15,612.05
¶ 15,612.031	[140] ¶ 15,600,	[143] ¶ 15,612.51
[136] ¶ 15,703	¶ 23,045.053	
[137] ¶ 15,611, ¶ 15,612.45	[141] ¶ 15,302,	
	¶ 15,305.021	

deduction for the purpose of computing earnings and profits is generally the amount allowable under the traditional straight-line method, although a corporation that uses the permissible nonaccelerated depreciation method (such as the machine-hour method) can use that method for earnings and profits purposes.

Also, in computing the earnings and profits of a corporation, any amount that can be deducted currently under Code Sec. 179 or Code Sec. 179A [144] can be deducted ratably over a period of five years (beginning with the year such amount is deductible under Code Sec. 179) (Code Sec. 312(k)(3)(B)).[145]

756. Effect of Installment Sales. A corporation that sells property on the installment basis is treated for earnings and profits purposes as if it had not used the installment method (Code Sec. 312(n)(5)).[146]

757. Effect of LIFO Reserve Changes. A corporation's earnings and profits generally must be increased or decreased by the amount of any change in the corporation's LIFO recapture amount at the end of each tax year (Code Sec. 312(n)(4)).[147] The term "LIFO recapture amount" means the amount (if any) by which the inventory amount of the inventory assets under the first-in, first-out (FIFO) method exceeds the inventory amount of such assets under the last-in, first-out (LIFO) method.

Business Income

759. Business Profit. The definition of gross income in Code Sec. 61 [148] includes "gross income derived from business." As to a business, however, gross *income* is usually the same as gross *profit,* not gross *receipts.* Gross profit is the total receipts from sales minus the cost of the goods sold. In the case of most mercantile businesses, cost of goods sold includes the purchase price of the article sold plus delivery costs, warehousing, etc. In a manufacturing firm it includes the entire factory cost—materials, direct labor, and factory overhead, including depreciation attributable to manufacturing processes—applicable to goods manufactured and sold. Again, "cost of goods sold" should be distinguished from deductions allowed by law. Thus, salaries, rent, etc., are deductions and not "cost of goods sold." [149]

Damages for Lost Profit or Capital. Damage awards and amounts received in settlement of claims for business injury that represent compensation for lost profits are taxable as ordinary income. Included under this rule are proceeds from business interruption insurance, liquidated damages, and awards for breach of contract. Damages for injury to goodwill are a nontaxable return of capital to the extent that the amounts received do not exceed the taxpayer's basis in goodwill. Similarly, injury to or loss of capital is treated as a nontaxable return of capital to the extent of basis; any excess is treated as a capital gain if received for damage to a capital asset.[150] Punitive damages, such as treble damages under antitrust laws, constitute taxable ordinary income (Reg. § 1.61-14(a)).[151]

See ¶ 852 for damages arising out of employment discrimination claims.

760. Credits Included in Income. If the taxpayer claims a credit for gasoline and special fuels on Form 4136 (see ¶ 1379), the amount of the credit must be included in gross income to the extent that a business deduction for the products was taken.[152] A cash-basis taxpayer must claim the credit and include the amount in gross income in the same tax year. An accrual-basis taxpayer should include the credit in the gross income for the tax year in which the fuel was actually used.

A taxpayer who is eligible for the alcohol fuels credit (see ¶ 1326) must include the allowable credit in gross income for the tax year in which the credit is earned.[153]

Footnote references are to paragraphs of the 2002 Standard Federal Tax Reports.

[144] ¶ 12,120, ¶ 12,130
[145] ¶ 15,600, ¶ 15,612.05
[146] ¶ 15,600, ¶ 15,612.036
[147] ¶ 15,600, ¶ 15,612.0358

[148] ¶ 5502
[149] ¶ 5511, ¶ 5600.01, ¶ 5600.03
[150] ¶ 5900.14, ¶ 5900.15, ¶ 5900.26

[151] ¶ 5815
[152] ¶ 4150, ¶ 4151, ¶ 5602.35
[153] ¶ 6431.01

¶ 760

The total credit "allowable" is to be included even though the taxpayer cannot use the credit currently because of the credit limitation based on tax liability.

Rents and Royalties

762. Rents. Amounts received or accrued as rents in payment for the use of property must be included in gross income. As a general rule, the payment by a lessee of any expenses of a lessor is additional rental income of the lessor (Reg. § 1.61-8(c)).[154] Consideration received by the lessor for cancellation of a lease is in substitution for rental payments and, thus, not a return of capital. Any reduction in the value of property due to cancellation of a lease is a deductible loss only when fixed by a closed transaction.[155]

Expenses attributable to property held for the production of rents or royalties are deductible in computing "adjusted gross income." See ¶ 1089.

763. Royalties. Royalties from copyrights on literary, musical, or artistic works and similar property or from a patent on an invention are includible in gross income (Code Sec. 61).[156] Royalties received from oil, gas, or other mineral properties are also includible in gross income.[157] For the treatment of timber, coal and iron ore royalties, see ¶ 1772. For the depletion allowance for royalties, see ¶ 1289.

Forms. Royalties are generally reported on Part I of Schedule E of Form 1040. However, Schedule C or Schedule C-EZ (Form 1040) is used to report royalties received by the holder of an operating oil, gas, or mineral interest and self-employed writers, inventors, artists, etc.

764. Improvements by Lessee. No income is ordinarily derived by a lessor by reason of acquisition, upon termination of a lease, of improvements made by the lessee (Reg. § 1.109-1).[158] This exclusion applies to improvements that revert to the lessor upon expiration of a lease as well as to those acquired by the lessor upon forfeiture of a lease prior to the end of the full term. But when improvements are made in lieu of rent, the lessor has gross income to the extent of the fair market value of the improvements in the year they were made.[159]

Construction Allowances. A retail tenant that receives cash or rent reductions from the retail lessor with respect to a short-term (i.e., 15 years or less) lease entered into after August 5, 1997, does not include that amount in gross income if the amounts are used for qualified construction or improvement to the retail space (Code Sec. 110).

765. Lessor's Obligations Paid by Lessee. Property taxes paid by a tenant on behalf of a landlord are additional rent.[160] When the taxes paid are income to the lessor, they may be treated as if paid by the lessor in determining their deductibility. If a lessee agrees to pay, in lieu of rental, a dividend on the lessor's stock, or interest on its mortgages, the payments will result in rental income to the lessor.[161]

Farming Income

767. Farming Is a Business. Income from farming is treated in the same way as income from any other business. Every individual, partnership or corporation which cultivates, operates, or manages a farm for gain or profit, either as owner or tenant, is designated as a farmer. A person who cultivates or operates a farm for recreation or pleasure, and who experiences a continual net loss from year to year, generally lacks a profit motive and may not deduct the losses. See ¶ 1195.

In addition to filing Form 1040, an individual engaged in farming must file a Schedule F (Form 1040), "Farm Income and Expenses." Partnerships engaged in farming must file Form 1065, and corporations engaged in farming must file the

---

Footnote references are to paragraphs of the 2002 Standard Federal Tax Reports.

¶762

[154] ¶ 5705, ¶ 5706.021	[157] ¶ 5502, ¶ 5706.04	[160] ¶ 5706.021
[155] ¶ 5706.031	[158] ¶ 7021, ¶ 7022.01	[161] ¶ 5706.021
[156] ¶ 5502	[159] ¶ 7020, ¶ 7022.01	

appropriate Form 1120. The general rules for all cash-basis taxpayers also apply to a farmer on the cash basis. See ¶ 1515. A farmer must also file Schedule SE (Form 1040) for computing earnings from self-employment. See ¶ 2676.

Cash Basis. A farmer on the *cash basis* does not use inventories and must include in gross income all cash or the value of merchandise or other property *received* from the sale of livestock and produce which have been raised, profits from the sale of livestock or other items which have been bought, and gross income received from all other sources.[162] A cash-basis farmer may defer recognition of gain from the sale of a crop delivered in one year until the following year if a valid contract with the purchaser or the purchaser's agent prohibits payment until the following year, but not if the payment is deferred merely at the seller's request.[163]

Profit from the sale of livestock or other items bought by a farmer is computed by deducting the cost from the sales price. In the situation when animals are sold which originally were bought as draft or work animals, or for breeding or dairy purposes and not for resale, the profit is the difference between the sale price and the *depreciated* basis of the animal sold.

A cash-basis farmer who receives insurance proceeds as a result of destruction or damage to crops may elect to include the proceeds in income in the year after the year of damage if the farmer can show that the income from the crops would normally have been reported in the following year. This includes payments received under the Agricultural Act of 1949, Title II of the Disaster Assistance Act or Title I of the Disaster Assistance Act of 1989 as a result of damage to crops caused by drought, flood, or other natural disaster, or the inability to plant crops because of such a natural disaster (Code Sec. 451(d); Reg. § 1.451-6; Rev. Rul. 91-55).[164]

A cash-basis farmer who is forced to sell livestock due to drought, flood or other weather-related conditions in an area designated as eligible for assistance by the federal government may elect to be taxed on the forced sale income (gain that normally would not have been realized in the year of the forced sale) in the following year if the farmer can show that the income from the sale of livestock would normally have been reported in such following year (Code Sec. 451(e)).[165]

Accrual Basis. A farmer on the *accrual basis* must use inventories taken at the start and the end of the tax year (Reg. § 1.61-4(b)).[166]

Although most farmers are probably not required to use the accrual method of accounting, that method is required for certain farming corporations and partnerships and for all farming tax shelters (including farming syndicates) by virtue of Code Sec. 447.[167] See ¶ 2028 and ¶ 2032.

Gross profit of a farmer on the accrual basis is calculated by (1) adding the inventory value of livestock and products on hand at the end of the year with the amount received from the sale of livestock and products during the year (including miscellaneous receipts such as for the hire of machinery) and (2) deducting from that total the sum of the inventory value of livestock and products on hand at the beginning of the year and the cost of livestock and products bought during the year (Reg. § 1.61-4(b)).

Livestock raised or bought for sale must be inventoried. See ¶ 1569. Livestock bought for draft, breeding or dairy purposes and not for sale may be inventoried or, instead, be treated as capital assets subject to depreciation, if the method used is consistently followed from year to year. If inventoried livestock is sold, its cost must not be taken as an additional deduction in the return of income since the inventory will reflect such cost.

Aside from ordinary methods, two other inventory methods are available to the farmer—the "farm-price" method or the "unit-livestock-price" method. See ¶ 1569.

Footnote references are to paragraphs of the 2002 Standard Federal Tax Reports.

[162] ¶ 5601, ¶ 5602.041	[165] ¶ 21,002, ¶ 21,021.03	[167] ¶ 20,700
[163] ¶ 21,009.453	[166] ¶ 5601, ¶ 5602.042	
[164] ¶ 21,002, ¶ 21,018, ¶ 21,021.28		

Income Averaging. An individual engaged in a farming business may elect to average farm income over three years (Code Sec. 1301). The tax imposed in any tax year will equal the sum of the tax computed on taxable income reduced by the amount of farm income elected for averaging plus the increase in tax that would result if taxable income for each of the three prior tax years were increased by an amount equal to one-third of the elected farm income. Schedule J of Form 1040 is to be used to report the income averaging.

For income from the sale of farm property other than inventory, see Chapter 17. As to "tax shelter" farming operations, see ¶ 2028 and ¶ 2032.

For expenses of a farmer, see ¶ 982–¶ 985. For the application of the uniform capitalization rules, see ¶ 999.

768. Patronage Dividend. A cooperative and its patrons are taxed in such a way that the business earnings of the cooperative are taxable currently either to the cooperative or to the patrons. See ¶ 698.

769. Commodity Credit Corporation Loan. Normally, income from the sale of a crop is reported in the year of the sale. However, if the farmer has pledged all or part of the crop production to secure a Commodity Credit Corporation (CCC) loan, the farmer may elect to report the loan proceeds as income in the year received rather than reporting the income in the year of the sale. IRS permission is not required to begin reporting CCC loans in this manner, but once a loan has been reported in income in the year received, all succeeding loans must be reported in the same way unless the IRS grants permission to change the method of reporting. The election is made on Schedule F. The amount reported as income becomes the farmer's basis in the commodity and is used to determine gain or loss upon the ultimate disposition of the commodity (Code Sec. 77; Reg. § 1.77-1 and Reg. § 1.77-2).[168]

Alimony Payments

771. Classification. Alimony and separate maintenance payments are income to the recipient and are deductible by the payor if certain requirements are met (Code Sec. 62(a)(10); Code Sec. 71; Code Sec. 215).[169] However, different rules apply to payments made under post-1984 divorce or separation instruments (see ¶ 772–¶ 776) and to payments made under pre-1985 instruments (¶ 777). However, if a pre-1985 instrument is expressly modified to so provide, the rules for post-1984 instruments will apply to subsequent payments under that instrument.

Alimony payments are taken as a deduction from gross income in arriving at adjusted gross income and thus may be claimed by taxpayers who do not itemize.

772. Post-1984 Instruments. Payments made under a post-1984 divorce or separation instrument are includible in the gross income of the recipient and deductible by the payor if the following requirements are met: (1) the payment is in cash or its equivalent, (2) the payment is received by or on behalf of a spouse under a divorce or separation instrument, (3) such instrument does not designate the payment as one which is not includible in gross income and not allowable as a deduction under Code Sec. 215, (4) in the case of an individual who is legally separated from his or her spouse under a divorce decree or a separate maintenance decree, the payee spouse and the payor spouse must not be members of the same household at the time such payment is made, (5) there is no liability to make any payment for any period after the death of the payee spouse or to make any payment (either in cash or property) as a substitute for such payments after the death of the payee spouse, and (6) the spouses must not file joint returns with each other (Code Sec. 71(a); Code Sec. 71(b); Code Sec. 71(e)).[170]

A divorce or separation instrument is defined as (1) a divorce or separate maintenance decree or a written instrument incident to such a decree, (2) a written

Footnote references are to paragraphs of the 2002 Standard Federal Tax Reports.

¶ **768**

[168] ¶ 6300, ¶ 6301, ¶ 6302, ¶ 6304 [169] ¶ 6002, ¶ 6090, ¶ 12,570, ¶ 6094 [170] ¶ 6090, ¶ 6094

separation agreement, or (3) a decree that is not a divorce decree or separate maintenance decree but that requires a spouse to make payments for the support or maintenance of the other spouse (Code Sec. 71(b)(2)).[171]

773. Year of Taxability or Deductibility. Alimony payments are generally includible in income in the year received (Code Sec. 71(a); Reg. § 1.71-1)[172] and are deductible in the year paid (Code Sec. 215; Reg. § 1.215-1),[173] regardless of whether the taxpayer employs the cash or the accrual method of accounting. A recapture rule prevents "front-loading" of alimony payments; see below.

774. Three-Year Recapture of Excess Alimony Payments. A special recapture rule applies to "excess" alimony payments (Code Sec. 71(f)).[174] Its purpose is to prevent property settlement payments from qualifying for alimony treatment. The rule requires the recapture of excess amounts that have been treated as alimony either during the calendar year in which payments began (the "first post-separation year") or in the next succeeding calendar year (the "second post-separation year"). Excess alimony is to be recaptured in the payor spouse's tax year beginning in the second calendar year following the calendar year in which payments began (the "third post-separation year") by requiring that individual to include the excess in income. The payee, who previously included the payments in income as alimony, is entitled to deduct the amount recaptured from gross income in his or her tax year beginning in the third post-separation year.

Excess alimony, the amount that must be recaptured in the third post-separation year, is defined as the sum of the excess payments made in the first post-separation year plus the excess payments made in the second post-separation year.

The amount of excess payments in the first and second post-separation years is determined under a statutory formula. For the first recapture year, the excess payment amount is the excess (if any) of the total alimony paid in the first post-separation year over the sum of $15,000 and the average of the amount of alimony paid in the second post-separation year (minus excess payments for that year) and the amount of alimony paid in the third post-separation year. Thus, for the first post-separation year, the following formula would be used:

$$\begin{array}{l}\text{excess}\\\text{payments}\end{array} = \begin{array}{l}\text{alimony}\\\text{paid in}\\\text{1st year}\end{array} - \left(\$15{,}000 + \cfrac{\left[\left(\begin{array}{l}\text{alimony}\\\text{paid in}\\\text{2nd year}\end{array} - \begin{array}{l}\text{excess}\\\text{payments}\\\text{in 2nd year}\end{array}\right) + \begin{array}{l}\text{alimony}\\\text{paid in}\\\text{3rd year}\end{array}\right]}{2} \right)$$

To determine the excess payments in the first year it is necessary to determine the excess payments in the second year. The amount of excess payments in the second year is the excess (if any) of the amount of alimony paid during the second year over the sum of the amount of alimony paid in the third year plus $15,000.

$$\text{excess payments} = \begin{array}{l}\text{alimony paid}\\\text{in 2nd year}\end{array} - \left(\begin{array}{l}\text{alimony paid}\\\text{in 3rd year}\end{array} + \$15{,}000 \right)$$

Once the excess payments for both the first and second post-separation years have been determined, the results are added together to determine the amount that must be recaptured in the third post-separation year.

> **Example 1.** In 2001, Mr. Black makes payments totalling $50,000 to his ex-wife. He makes no payments in either 2002 or 2003. Assuming none of the exceptions (set forth below) apply, $35,000 will be recaptured in 2003. Mr. Black will have to report an additional $35,000 in income, while his ex-wife will be entitled to a $35,000 reduction in income.

Footnote references are to paragraphs of the 2002 Standard Federal Tax Reports.

[171] ¶ 6090, ¶ 6094.023   [173] ¶ 12,570, ¶ 12,571   [174] ¶ 6090, ¶ 6094.03
[172] ¶ 6090, ¶ 6091

¶774

Example 2. In 2001, Ms. Gold makes payments totalling $50,000 to her ex-husband. In 2002, she makes $20,000 in payments, but in 2003 she makes no payments. Assuming that none of the exceptions apply, the total amount that must be recaptured in the third year is $32,500. This represents $5,000 from the second year ($20,000 minus $15,000) and $27,500 from the first year. The amount recaptured from the first year equals the excess of $50,000 (the payments made) over the sum of $15,000 plus $7,500. The $7,500 is the average of the payments for years two and three after reducing the payments by the $5,000 recaptured for year two ($15,000 ($20,000 payment in year two plus $0 payment in year three minus the $5,000 that was required to be recaptured) divided by two equals $7,500).

IRS Publication 504 (Divorced or Separated Individuals) contains a worksheet for computing alimony recapture.

Exceptions to Recapture Rule. The recapture of excess payments is not required if the alimony payments terminate because either party dies or the payee-spouse remarries before the end of the third post-separation year. The rules also do not apply to temporary support payments received under an instrument described in Code Sec. 71(b)(2)(C). In addition, they do not apply where the payments fluctuate because of a continuing liability to pay—for at least three years—a fixed portion of income from the earnings of a business or property or from compensation from employment or self-employment (Code Sec. 71(f)(5)(C)).[175]

775. Indirect Alimony Payments. Unlike the rules for pre-1985 instruments, only one type of trust, the Code Sec. 682 trust, is contemplated in connection with divorce or separate maintenance under instruments executed after 1984 (or modified after 1984). When a beneficial interest in a trust is transferred or created incident to a divorce or separation, the beneficiary-spouse is entitled to the same treatment as the beneficiary of a regular trust, notwithstanding that the payments by the trust qualify as alimony or otherwise discharge a support obligation (Code Sec. 682).[176]

776. Child Support. Payments made under post-1984 instruments that fix an amount of money or part of the payment as child support are treated as child support for tax purposes and are not deductible (Code Sec. 71(c)).[177] If any amount specified in the instrument is to be reduced based on a contingency set out in the instrument relating to a child—such as attaining a specified age, dying, leaving school, or marrying—the amount of the specified reduction is treated as child support from the outset. The same rule applies if the reduction called for by the instrument is to occur at a time that can clearly be associated with such contingency. Thus, unlike the situation under pre-1985 law, payments that vary with the status of a child are not deductible.

Example. A 2001 divorce instrument provides that alimony payments will be reduced by $100 per month when a child reaches age 18. Under these circumstances, $100 of each payment is treated as child support.

777. Pre-1985 Instruments. Rules that are different from those discussed at ¶772-¶776 apply to payments under pre-1985 instruments that have not been modified (see ¶771) to have current law apply. The differences of current importance are these:

(1) The payments need not be in cash.

(2) The termination-at-death requirement does not apply.

(3) The parties have no power to opt out of alimony treatment for payments that otherwise meet the definition of alimony.

(4) The requirement that divorced or legally separated persons may not be members of the same household does not apply.

Footnote references are to paragraphs of the 2002 Standard Federal Tax Reports.

¶775   175 ¶6090   176 ¶24,860, ¶24,864   177 ¶6090

(5) To qualify as alimony, payments under pre-1985 instruments must be "periodic" (something of a misnomer for the concept involved). Payments are periodic to the extent that they are subject to modification in the case of one or more of the following contingencies: (a) death of either spouse, (b) remarriage of the payee, or (c) change in the economic status of either spouse. In addition, payments are treated as being periodic even if they are installments in discharge of a principal sum (stated or inferable) provided that they are payable over a period of more than 10 years, subject to the limitation that not more than 10% of the sum can be deductible/includible in any year. Even if the periodic payment requirement is satisfied, however, payments under pre-1985 instruments cannot qualify as alimony unless they are intended to be for the support of the payee.

(6) Undifferentiated "family support" payments under pre-1985 instruments are deductible as alimony (if all requirements are met), even if a determinable portion of each payment is for the support of children. Nothing comparable to the rule for post-1984 instruments (¶ 776) applies.

778. Property Transfers Between Spouses or Former Spouses Incident to Divorce. No gain or loss is recognized to the transferor on a transfer of property (outright or in trust) between spouses or between former spouses incident to divorce (Code Sec. 1041(a)),[178] nor is the value of the property included in the gross income of the transferee (Code Sec. 1041(b)(1)).[179] The transferee's basis is equal to the transferor's basis immediately before the transfer (Code Sec. 1041(b)(2)).[180] A transfer between former spouses is incident to divorce if it occurs within one year after the marriage ceases or is related to the cessation of the marriage (Code Sec. 1041(c)).[181]

Nonrecognition is not available to the transferor if the transferee is a nonresident alien (Code Sec. 1041(d))[182] or if there is a transfer in trust to the extent that liabilities assumed by the transferee (including liabilities to which the property is subject) exceed the transferor's adjusted basis in the property (Code Sec. 1041(e)).[183] The transferee's basis is increased for any such gain recognized by the transferor.

Prizes and Awards

785. Taxation of Prizes and Awards. Prizes and awards, other than certain types of fellowship grants and scholarships (see ¶ 879) and limited employee achievement awards, are includible in gross income (Code Sec. 74(a)). Awards for religious, charitable, scientific, educational, artistic, literary, or civic achievement are excluded from the recipient's income only if the award is transferred unused by the payor to a governmental unit or a tax-exempt charitable, religious, or educational organization designated by the recipient. In addition, the recipient must be selected without any action on his or her part to enter the contest or proceeding and is not required to render substantial future services as a condition to receiving the prize or award (Code Sec. 74).[184] Thus, Nobel and Pulitzer prize recipients may not exclude from income the value of such awards unless these conditions are met.

Employee achievement awards (items of tangible personal property) are excludable from gross income only to the extent that the cost of the award is deductible by the employer. The awards cannot represent disguised compensation, and the excludable amount can total no more than $400 for nonqualified awards or $1,600 for qualified awards (Code Sec. 74(c) and Code Sec. 274(j)(2)).[185] See ¶ 919.

Footnote references are to paragraphs of the 2002 Standard Federal Tax Reports.

[178] ¶ 29,802.01
[179] ¶ 29,802.01
[180] ¶ 29,802.01
[181] ¶ 29,802.031
[182] ¶ 29,802.01
[183] ¶ 29,802.021
[184] ¶ 6200, ¶ 6204
[185] ¶ 6200, ¶ 14,402

¶785

Gambling Income

787. Gambling and Other Gains. Gain arising from gambling, betting and lotteries is includible in gross income. A gain from an illegal transaction, such as bootlegging, extortion, embezzlement or fraud, is also includible.[186]

788. Gambling Losses. The law permits the deduction of wagering losses only to the extent of the taxpayer's gains from similar transactions (Code Sec. 165(d); Reg. § 1.165-10).[187] Nonbusiness gambling losses are deductible only as deductions itemized on Schedule A of Form 1040. If gambling is conducted as a business, the losses are deductible as business losses, but only to the extent of gains.[188]

Shareholder's or Employee's Bargain Purchase

789. Bargain Purchase. If a corporation transfers property to a shareholder, or an employer transfers property to an employee, at less than its fair market value, whether or not the transfer is in the form of a sale or exchange, the difference may be income to the purchaser—as dividends in the case of the shareholder and as compensation for personal services in the case of the employee (Reg. § 1.61-2).[189] However, qualified employee discounts are excluded from income. See ¶ 863.

In the case of a purchase at less than fair market value by a stockholder, the shareholder will be treated as having received a distribution from the transferor-corporation and will be subject to the general tax rules for including it in income (Reg. § 1.301-1).[190] If there is a later sale of the property, the gain or loss is measured by starting with a basis which is the amount paid for the property, increased by the amount previously included in income.

Discharge of Debt

791. Debt Canceled. Income from the discharge of indebtedness is includible in gross income unless it is excludable under Code Sec. 108. Four types of exclusions are provided in the following priority order: [191] (1) a debt discharge in a bankruptcy action under Title 11 of the U.S. Code in which the taxpayer is under the jurisdiction of the court and the discharge is either granted by or is under a plan approved by the court; (2) a discharge when the taxpayer is insolvent outside bankruptcy; (3) a discharge of qualified farm indebtedness; and (4) a discharge of qualified real property business indebtedness.

Form 982 is filed with a debtor's income tax return to report excluded income from the discharge of indebtedness.

The term "insolvent" refers to an excess of liabilities over the fair market value of assets immediately prior to discharge. This exclusion is limited to the insolvent amount. The taxpayer's insolvent amount includes the amount by which a nonrecourse debt exceeds the fair market value of the property securing the debt, but only to the extent that the excess nonrecourse debt is discharged.[192]

When an amount is excluded from gross income as the result of a discharge of indebtedness in a Title 11 case, a discharge of indebtedness during insolvency, or a discharge of qualified farm indebtedness, a taxpayer is required to reduce its tax attributes. The reduction in the foreign tax credit, minimum tax credit, passive activity credit, and general business credit carryovers is to be made at a rate of 33⅓ cents per dollar of excluded income (Code Sec. 108(b)(3)(B)).[193]

A corporation that satisfies a debt by transferring corporate stock to its creditor is treated as if it has paid the creditor with money equal to the fair market value of the stock. The corporation will thus have income from discharge of indebtedness to the extent that the principal of the debt exceeds the value of the stock (and any

---

Footnote references are to paragraphs of the 2002 Standard Federal Tax Reports.

[186] ¶ 5815, ¶ 5901.01, ¶ 5901.021	[189] ¶ 5506, ¶ 15,704.4803	[192] ¶ 7010.38
[187] ¶ 9802, ¶ 10,104	[190] ¶ 15,303	[193] ¶ 7002, ¶ 7010.03
[188] ¶ 10,105.01	[191] ¶ 7002, ¶ 7010.021	

other property transferred) (Code Sec. 108(e)(8)).[194] A similar rule applies to debtors (corporate or noncorporate) issuing debt instruments in satisfaction of indebtedness (Code Sec. 108(e)(10)).

Nonrecourse Debt. Discharge of indebtedness can result even if the canceled debt is nonrecourse (i.e., no person is personally liable for repayment of the debt). Thus, where property securing a nonrecourse debt is transferred in exchange for cancellation of the debt (such as a foreclosure sale), the amount realized from the sale or exchange includes the principal amount of the debt discharged.[195] The IRS has ruled that the "writedown" of the principal amount of a nonrecourse note by a holder who was not the seller of the property results in the realization of discharge of indebtedness income, even if there is no disposition of the property (Rev. Rul. 91-31).[196]

Farmers. Income arising from the discharge of qualified farm indebtedness owed to an unrelated lender, including a federal, state, or local government or agency, or instrumentality thereof, may be excluded from a taxpayer's income if certain requirements are met. The debt must be incurred directly in connection with the operation by the taxpayer of the trade or business of farming. Also, this relief applies only if at least 50% of the taxpayer's aggregate gross receipts for the three tax years preceding the tax year in which the discharge of indebtedness occurs is attributable to the trade or business of farming. The discharge of indebtedness income is excluded only to the extent absorbed by tax attributes (credits are reduced at a rate of 33⅓ cents per dollar of excluded income) and the adjusted bases of qualified property (any property held or used in a trade or business or for the production of income) (Code Sec. 108(g)).[197]

Basis reduction occurs first with respect to depreciable property, then with respect to land used in the business of farming, and finally with respect to other qualified property (Code Sec. 1017(b)(4)).

Qualified Real Property Business Indebtedness. A taxpayer other than a C corporation may elect to exclude from gross income amounts realized from the discharge of debt incurred or assumed in connection with real property used in a trade or business and secured by that property (Code Secs. 108(a)(1)(D) and 108(c)).[198] The debt must be incurred or assumed before 1993, or, if incurred or assumed after 1992, it must be incurred or assumed to acquire, construct, reconstruct, or substantially improve the real property. The excludable amount is limited to the excess of the outstanding principal amount of the debt over the fair market value of the business real property (reduced by the outstanding principal amount of any other qualified business indebtedness secured by the property). Also, the exclusion may not exceed the aggregate adjusted bases of depreciable real property held by the taxpayer immediately before discharge. The excluded amount reduces the basis of depreciable real property.

The election to treat debt as qualified real property business indebtedness must be filed with the taxpayer's timely income tax return (including extensions) for the tax year in which the discharge occurs (Reg. § 1.108(c)-5). The election, which is revocable with the consent of the IRS Commissioner, is made on Form 982. A taxpayer who fails to make a timely election must request consent to file a late election under Reg. § 301.9100-3.

Student Loans. A special income exclusion applies to the discharge of all or part of a student loan if, pursuant to the loan agreement, the discharge is made because the individual works for a specified period of time in certain professions for any of a broad class of employers (e.g., as a doctor or nurse in a rural area) (Code Sec. 108(f)).[199] The loan must be made by (1) a federal, state, or local government (or instrumentality, agency, or subdivision, thereof); (2) a tax-exempt public benefit corporation that has assumed control of a public hospital with public employees; or (3) an educational institution if (a) it received funds to loan from an entity described

---

Footnote references are to paragraphs of the 2002 Standard Federal Tax Reports.

[194] ¶ 7002, ¶ 7010.051   [196] ¶ 5802.34   [198] ¶ 7002, ¶ 7010.045
[195] ¶ 5802.34   [197] ¶ 7002, ¶ 7010.04 [199] ¶ 7002, ¶ 7010.049

in (1) or (2), above, or (b) the student serves, pursuant to a program of the institution, in an occupation or area with unmet needs under the direction of a governmental unit or a tax-exempt section 501(c)(3) organization (e.g., charitable, religious, educational, scientific organization). Loans refinanced through such a program by the institution (or certain tax-exempt organizations) also qualify for the exclusion.

793. Creditor's Financial Income. An accrual-basis creditor reports interest on loans or obligations as the interest is earned (over the term of the loan, as installment payments are due, etc.) or when it is received if payment is received earlier than when due. A cash-basis creditor reports such interest as it is received.

Rule of 78's. The IRS will not give any tax effect to a provision in a loan agreement that interest shall be allocated in accordance with the Rule of 78's because that method of allocating interest does not accurately reflect the true cost of borrowing.[200] A limited exception permits the Rule of 78's method for purposes of determining a lender's interest income where (1) the loan is a consumer loan, (2) the terms of the loan require the use of the Rule of 78's for allocating interest to the different periods over the term of the loan, and (3) the loan is self-amortizing, requires level payments at regular intervals at least annually over a period of no more than five years, and has no balloon payment at the end of the loan term.[201]

Loan Commission. A loan commission is taxed to an accrual-basis lender in the year the loan is made (earned at that time). A commission deducted from the face amount of the loan is taxed to a cash-basis lender only when received upon payment of the loan or sale of the obligation.[202]

"Points." When "points" (an adjustment of the stated interest rate earned at the commencement of the loan) are paid by the borrower out of funds not originating with the lender, they are taxed to a cash-basis lender in the year received and to an accrual-basis creditor when the right to receive arises, or when received, if earlier.[203]

Below-Market Interest Loans

795. Imputed Interest on Below-Market Interest Loans. Under Code Sec. 7872,[204] loans that carry little or no interest are generally recharacterized as arm's-length transactions in which the lender is treated as having made a loan to the borrower bearing the statutory federal rate of interest. Concurrently, there is deemed to be a transfer in the form of gift, dividend, contribution to capital, compensation, or other manner of payment (depending upon the nature of the loan) from the lender to the borrower which, in turn, is retransferred by the borrower to the lender to satisfy the accruing interest (Code Sec. 7872(a)(1)). This rule applies to (1) gift loans, (2) corporation-shareholder loans, (3) compensation loans between employer and employee or between independent contractor and client, (4) tax-avoidance loans, (5) any below-market interest loans in which the interest arrangement has a significant effect on either the lender's or borrower's tax liability, and (6) loans to any qualified continuing care facility not exempt under Code Sec. 7872(g).

In the case of a demand loan or a gift loan, the imputed interest amount is deemed to be transferred from the lender to the borrower on the last day of the calendar year of the loan. As for a term loan (other than a gift loan), there is an imputed transfer from the lender to the borrower, in an amount equal to the excess of the amount loaned over the present value of all payments required under the loan, which is deemed to have taken place on the date the loan was made.

Exceptions. A $10,000 *de minimis* exception applies to gift loans between individuals if the loan is not directly attributable to the purchase or carrying of income-producing assets (Code Sec. 7872(c)). There is also a $10,000 *de minimis* exception for compensation-related or corporation-shareholder loans that do not have tax avoidance as a principal purpose. Further, in the case of gift loans between

---

Footnote references are to paragraphs of the 2002 Standard Federal Tax Reports.

[200] ¶ 9104.0442	[202] ¶ 20,620.03	[204] ¶ 43,956, ¶ 49,960
[201] ¶ 9104.0442	[203] ¶ 20,620.0314	

individuals where the total amount outstanding does not exceed $100,000, the amount deemed transferred from the borrower to the lender at the end of the year will be imputed to the lender only to the extent of the borrower's annual net investment income (Code Sec. 7872(d)). If such income is less than $1,000, no imputed interest is deemed transferred to the lender.

Rules exempt certain below-market interest loans by individuals to continuing care facilities made pursuant to a continuing care contract (Code Sec. 7872(g)).[205] Also, in the case of an employer loan to an employee made in connection with the purchase of a principal residence at a new place of work, the applicable statutory federal rate for testing the loan is the rate as of the date the written contract to purchase the residence was entered into (Code Sec. 7872(f)(11)).[206]

Bartered Services

797. Value of Bartered Services. The value of bartered services must be included in gross income, usually on Schedule C or C-EZ (Form 1040). For example, in one "bartered services" transaction, the owner of an apartment building who permitted an artist to use an apartment rent free was required to include in gross income the value of a work of art received in return for the rent-free use of the apartment, and the artist was required to include in gross income the fair rental value of the apartment.[207]

If two individuals are members of a "barter club" and each agrees to exchange services, the value of the services received by each must be included in gross income. Barter clubs must report exchanges on Form 1099-B in accordance with the rules under Code Sec. 6045.[208] Trade or credit units equal to one dollar each, used by a barter club to account for transactions, are also includible in gross income.[209]

Recoveries

799. Tax Treatment of Recoveries. The receipt of an amount that was part of an earlier deduction or credit is considered a recovery and generally must be included, partially or totally, in income in the year of receipt (Code Sec. 111).[210] Common types of recoveries are refunds, reimbursements or rebates. Interest on amounts recovered is income in the year of the recovery.

When the refund or other recovery is for amounts that were paid in separate years, the recovery must be allocated between these years.

> **Example 1.** Marcia VanNauker paid her 2000 estimated state income tax liability of $4,000 in four equal installments in April, June, and September of 2000 and in January of 2001. In May of 2001, she received a $400 refund based upon her 2000 state income tax return. (Refunds of federal income taxes are never included in income because they are never allowed as a deduction from income.) Because the tax liability was paid in two years, the amount recovered must be allocated pro rata between the years in which the liability was paid. Because 75% of the liability was paid in 2000, 75% of the $400 refund (or $300) is for amounts paid in 2000 and is a recovery item in 2001 when received. The remaining $100 is offset against the otherwise deductible state tax payments made in 2001.

Itemized Deduction Recoveries. Recoveries of amounts claimed only as itemized deductions are not includible if the taxpayer did not itemize in the year for which the recovery was received. If a deduction is taken, the includible amount is limited to the amount of the deduction. Thus, the amount included is the lesser of the amount deducted or the amount recovered.

> **Example 2.** Brent Martin receives a $1,500 medical expense reimbursement in 2001 for expenses incurred in 2000. However, due to the

---

Footnote references are to paragraphs of the 2002 Standard Federal Tax Reports.

[205] ¶ 43,956, ¶ 43,960.04
[206] ¶ 43,956, ¶ 43,960.038
[207] ¶ 5508.028, ¶ 5508.15
[208] ¶ 35,920, ¶ 35,920.022
[209] ¶ 5508.028, ¶ 5508.15
[210] ¶ 7060, ¶ 7061, ¶ 7062.01

threshold on medical expenses, he was able to claim only a $450 deduction in 2000. The amount that he must include in income in 2001 is $450.

For situations in which a high-income individual's itemized deductions are reduced by 3 percent of AGI in excess of the threshold phaseout amount (in 2001, $132,950 ($66,475 for married filing separately)) or, if less, 80 percent of allowable deductions (see ¶ 1014), and, later, all or a portion of the previously deducted amount is recovered, the amount includible in income in the year of receipt is the difference between (1) the amount of the prior year's itemized deductions (after reduction) and (2) the deductions that would have been claimed (the greater of (a) itemized deductions (after reduction) or (b) the standard deduction) had the individual paid the proper amount in the prior year and not received a recovery or refund in a subsequent year (Rev. Rul. 93-75).

> **Example 3.** In 2000, Brian Cummings, a single individual, claimed $9,000 in itemized deductions that were reduced from $12,000 (a $3,000 reduction) because of the 3% itemized deduction phaseout. If $2,000 of state income tax is refunded in 2001, his itemized deductions for 2000, prior to reduction, would have been $10,000 ($12,000 minus $2,000). His itemized deductions after reduction would have been limited to $7,000 (a $3,000 reduction) as a result of the 3% phaseout. He derives a tax benefit to the extent of the difference between his total allowable itemized deductions for 2000 ($9,000) and the total itemized deductions he would have claimed had he paid the exact amount of his state tax liability ($7,000). Thus, the $2,000 refund is all includible in his gross income in 2001.

The total amount of all recoveries in a tax year must be included in the taxpayer's income if certain situations exist. Recoveries are includible if they are equal to or less than the amount by which the taxpayer's itemized deductions exceeded the standard deduction for his or her filing status in the prior year and the taxpayer had any taxable income in the prior year. Recoveries of state or local income taxes are reported on a different line of Form 1040 than other recoveries and, therefore, after the total amount that must be included has been determined a further allocation may be necessary for reporting purposes.

IRS Publication 525 contains a worksheet for computing the amount of a taxable itemized deduction recovery.

Nonitemized Deductions and Amounts Recovered for Credits. Recoveries of amounts for which a nonitemized deduction or a tax credit (other than the foreign tax credit or investment tax credit) was claimed in prior tax years must be included in income to the extent that the deduction or credit reduced the taxpayer's tax liability in the year of the deduction (Code Sec. 111(b)). Special rules apply when a deduction reduced taxable income but the taxpayer's actual tax liability was not reduced because of the application of the AMT rules or because tax credits were claimed that reduced the tax liability to zero. If the taxpayer has both itemized and nonitemized recoveries, the amount includible in income is determined by first figuring the nonitemized recoveries, then adding the nonitemized recoveries to taxable income, and, finally, figuring the itemized recoveries.

Chapter 8

EXCLUSIONS FROM INCOME

Nontaxable Income

801. What the Law Excludes. In addition to the items listed in Code Secs. 101-139 and some other special types of income specifically excluded by the law, the following are exempt from gross income: (1) items of income that, under the Constitution, are not taxable by the federal government; (2) items of income that are exempt from tax under the provisions of any act of Congress not inconsistent with, or repealed by, the revenue acts; and (3) items that are nontaxable under the provisions of foreign tax treaties designed to prevent double taxation.

These exclusions (and exemptions) should not be confused with *deductions* from gross income (losses, expenses, bad debts, etc.), which must be shown on a tax return. An exclusion generally does not have to be shown on a return.

Special Nonstatutory Exclusion

802. Special Nonstatutory Exclusion. Restitution or reparation payments received by persons who suffered Nazi persecution and survived the Holocaust are excludable from gross income (Act Sec. 803, Economic Growth and Tax Relief Reconciliation Act of 2001 (P.L. 107-16)). The exclusion of these payments extends to any interest earned thereon. These excludable payments are also *not* to be included in any tax provision that takes into account excluded income in computing modified adjusted gross income, such as the taxation of Social Security benefits. This special nonstatutory exclusion applies to any payments received on or after January 1, 2000. However, nothing in P.L. 107-16 is to be construed to create an inference to the proper tax treatment of any amounts received prior to January 1, 2000.

¶ **802**

Life Insurance

803. General Rule. Amounts received under a life insurance contract paid by
reason of the death of the insured are generally excluded from gross income.
Generally, all amounts payable on the death of the insured are excluded, whether
these amounts represent the return of premiums paid, the increased value of the
policy due to investment, or the death benefit feature (that is, the policy proceeds
exceeding the value of the contract immediately prior to the death of the insured).

It is immaterial whether the proceeds are received in a single sum or otherwise.
However, if the proceeds are left with the insurer under an agreement to pay
interest, any interest earned and paid is income to the recipient (Code Sec. 101; Reg.
§§ 1.101-1(a) and 1.101-3).[1]

A contract must qualify as a life insurance contract under applicable state or
foreign law and meet either a cash value accumulation test or a guideline premium/
cash value corridor test (Code Sec. 7702).[2] If a contract does not satisfy at least one
of these tests, it will be treated as a combination of term insurance and a currently
taxable deposit fund, and the policyholder must treat income on the contract as
ordinary income in any year paid or accrued (Code Sec. 7702(g)).[3]

Amounts received after December 31, 1996, under a life insurance contract on
the life of an insured, terminally or chronically ill individual may be excluded from
gross income. Similarly, if a portion of a life insurance contract is assigned or sold to
a viatical settlement provider, amounts received are excludable (Code Sec. 101(g)).

805. Installment Options. If the beneficiary of a life insurance policy receives the
proceeds in installments, any interest element in the life insurance proceeds
accruing after the date of the insured's death is included in the income of the
beneficiary (Code Sec. 101(d); Reg. § 1.101-4).[4] However, if the beneficiary is the
spouse of the decedent-insured who died before October 23, 1986, he or she is entitled
to exclude annually up to $1,000 of the amount otherwise taxable as interest
(Conference Committee Report on P.L. 99-514, Tax Reform Act of 1986).

807. Transfer for Value. If a life insurance policy is transferred for valuable
consideration, payments on account of the death of the insured are income to
the assignee to the extent that they exceed the premiums and other consideration
paid by that assignee. This rule, however, does not apply if the contract's basis in
the hands of the transferee is determined with reference to the transferor's basis,
such as a tax-free exchange or a gift. In such a case the proceeds are exempt. Nor
does the rule apply if the transfer of the contract was to the insured, a partner of the
insured, a partnership including the insured, or a corporation of which the insured
was a shareholder or officer (Code Sec. 101(a)(2); Reg. § 1.101-1(b)).[5] (See, also,
¶ 845.)

809. Dividends. Annuity policies that pay dividends in the nature of returns of
premiums are not taxable (1) until they exceed the premiums or other consideration paid for the insurance or (2) if they are paid for any reason other than the
death of the insured. However, dividends received on and after the "annuity
starting date" may be fully taxable (see ¶ 823) (Code Sec. 72(e); Reg. § 1.72-11(b)).[6]

Employee's Death Benefit

813. The $5,000 Exclusion—Repealed. The exclusion from income of up to
$5,000 of death benefits paid by or for an employer to the beneficiaries or the
estate of a deceased employee was repealed effective August 21, 1996.

Annuity

817. Exclusion Ratio. Under special rules for the taxation of amounts received as
an annuity under any annuity, endowment, or life insurance contract and paid

Footnote references are to paragraphs of the 2002 Standard Federal Tax Reports.

¶ 803
[1] ¶ 6502, ¶ 6503, ¶ 6508   [3] ¶ 43,150   [5] ¶ 6502, ¶ 6503
[2] ¶ 43,150   [4] ¶ 6502, ¶ 6510 [6] ¶ 6102, ¶ 6113

out for reasons other than death of the insured, the tax-free portion of annuity income is spread evenly over the annuitant's life expectancy. However, for pre-1987 contracts, the exclusion remains the same no matter how long the annuitant lives. These annuity rules also apply to contracts whose payments are made over a prescribed number of years (Code Sec. 72; Reg. § 1.72-1—Reg. § 1.72-11).[7] For Armed Forces personnel annuities, see ¶ 891.

Contracts, with some exceptions, will not be treated as annuity contracts unless they provide that (1) if the contract holder dies on or after the annuity starting date, but before the entire interest in the contract is distributed, the remainder must be distributed at least as rapidly as under the method used as of the day the holder died, and (2) the entire interest in the contract must be distributed within five years of the holder's death if death occurs before the annuity starting date (Code Sec. 72(s)).[8]

For post-1986 annuities, the exclusion of a portion of each annuity payment cannot be continued indefinitely. The annuitant is still required to compute the exclusion ratio as before, but, once the total of all exclusions taken for payments under the annuity contract equals the investment in the contract, all subsequent payments are fully taxed (Code Sec. 72(b)(2)).[9] On the other hand, if the annuitant dies before the investment in the contract is fully recovered tax free through the annuity exclusion, a deduction is provided for the annuitant's last year in an amount equal to the unrecovered portion of the investment (Code Sec. 72(b)(3)).[10]

819. The "Exclusion Ratio" Formula. The excludable portion of an annuity payment is the annuity payment multiplied by the exclusion ratio. The remainder is taxable to the recipient, whether it be the primary annuitant or a secondary annuitant under a joint or joint and survivor annuity. The exclusion ratio is the "investment in the contract" (¶ 821) divided by the "expected return" (¶ 825) under the contract as of the "annuity starting date" (¶ 823). For example, if, as of the annuity starting date, a taxpayer's investment in an annuity contract is $6,000 and his expected return is $10,000, his exclusion ratio is $6,000/$10,000, or 60%. If the taxpayer receives a monthly annuity payment of $200, the monthly exclusion is $120 ($200 × 60%).

821. "Investment in the Contract" Defined. The "investment in the contract" generally is the total amount of premiums or other consideration paid for the contract (other than contributions on behalf of self-employed individuals) less amounts, if any, received before the "annuity starting date" and not included in gross income (Code Sec. 72(c)(1); Reg. § 1.72-6).[11] A special adjustment is provided for a refund annuity. See ¶ 837.

Special rules for computing an employee's investment in an annuity received through an employer are explained at ¶ 2155.

823. "Annuity Starting Date" Defined. The "annuity starting date" is the first day of the first period for which an amount is received as an annuity under the contract. The first day of the first period for which an amount is received as an annuity is the later of (1) the date upon which the obligations of the contract become fixed or (2) the first day of the period (year, half-year, quarter, or month, depending on whether the payments are made annually, semi-annually, quarterly, or monthly) that ends on the date of the first annuity payment (Code Sec. 72(c)(4); Reg. § 1.72-4(b)).[12]

825. Computation of "Expected Return." The "expected return" under the contract is limited to amounts receivable as an annuity or as annuities. If no life expectancy is involved (as in the case of installment payments for a fixed number of years), the expected return is found by totaling the amounts to be received (Code Sec. 72(c)(3); Reg. § 1.72-5(c)).[13]

Footnote references are to paragraphs of the 2002 Standard Federal Tax Reports.

[7] ¶ 6102—¶ 6113	[10] ¶ 6102	[12] ¶ 6102, ¶ 6104
[8] ¶ 6102	[11] ¶ 6102, ¶ 6107	[13] ¶ 6102, ¶ 6106
[9] ¶ 6102		

To determine the expected return under contracts involving life expectancy, actuarial tables prescribed by the IRS must be used (Code Sec. 72(c)(3); Reg. § 1.72-5(a)).[14] The tables provide a multiplier (based on life expectancy) that is applied to the annual payment to obtain the expected return under the contract. The annuity tables are reproduced at ¶ 165 of CCH STANDARD FEDERAL TAX REPORTS and at ¶ 72-¶ 73 of the 2002 U.S. MASTER TAX GUIDE—Loose-Leaf Edition.

The expected return will vary, depending on when contributions were made and when amounts were received as an annuity. Gender-neutral tables must be used if the total investment in the contract is made after June 30, 1986. If there was an investment in the contract as of June 30, 1986, and there has been a further investment in the contract after that date, an individual may, instead of using the gender-neutral tables, elect to calculate the exclusion under a special rule. Under this rule, an exclusion amount is calculated using the gender-based tables—as if the investment in the contract as of June 30, 1986, were the only investment in the contract. Then a second exclusion is calculated, using the gender-neutral tables, as if the post-June 30, 1986, investment were the only investment. The two exclusion amounts are then added together to produce the final exclusion. Although, generally, the gender-based annuity tables formerly in effect must still be used if all contributions were made prior to June 30, 1986, an election may be made to use the updated tables if the annuity payments are received after June 30, 1986 (Reg. § 1.72-5 and Reg. § 1.72-6).[15]

For purposes of the examples, below, following is a portion of Table V (gender-neutral for post-June 30, 1986, investment in the contract (Reg. § 1.72-9))[16] for ordinary life annuities for one life:

TABLE V.—ORDINARY LIFE ANNUITIES—ONE LIFE—EXPECTED RETURN MULTIPLES

Age	Multiple	Age	Multiple
55	28.6	64	20.8
56	27.7	65	20.0
57	26.8	66	19.2
58	25.9	67	18.4
59	25.0	68	17.6
60	24.2	69	16.8
61	23.3	70	16.0
62	22.5	71	15.3
63	21.6	72	14.6

Example 1. In 2001, X purchases for $8,000 an annuity that provides for payments to him of $50 per month for life. At the annuity starting date, his age at his nearest birthday is 64 years. Table V (gender-neutral) must be used since all investment in the contract is post-June 1986 and it shows that for an individual of X's age, the multiple to be used in computing the expected return is 20.8. X's expected return and annual exclusion, therefore, are computed as follows:

Annual payment ($50 per month × 12 months)	$ 600
Table V multiple	20.8
Expected return ($600 × 20.8)	$12,480
Exclusion ratio	$\frac{8,000}{12,480}$, or 64.1%
Annual exclusion (64.1% of $600)	$ 385

If payments under the contract are made quarterly, semiannually or annually, or if the interval between the annuity starting date and the date of the first payment is less than the interval between future payments, an adjustment of the multiple found in the actuarial tables may be required (Reg. § 1.72-5). The amount of the adjustment is found in the following table.

Footnote references are to paragraphs of the 2002 Standard Federal Tax Reports.

¶ 825   [14] ¶ 6102, ¶ 6106   [15] ¶ 6106, ¶ 6107   [16] ¶ 165

If the number of whole months from the annuity starting date to the first payment date is	0-1	2	3	4	5	6	7	8	9	10	11	12
And payments under the contract are to be made:												
Annually	+.5	+.4	+.3	+.2	+.1	0	0	−.1	−.2	−.3	−.4	−.5
Semiannually ...	+.2	+.1	0	0	−.1	−.2	...	...	...	...	...	...
Quarterly.......	+.1	0	−.1	...	...	...	...	...	...	...	...	...

Example 2. Assume the same facts as in Example 1 except that the payments under the contract are to be made semiannually in the amount of $300, the first payment being made six full months from the annuity starting date. The table shows the adjustment to be "− .2". Therefore, X's multiple from Table V, 20.8, is adjusted by subtracting .2. His adjusted multiple then is 20.6, and his expected return and semiannual exclusion are computed as follows:

Annual payment ($300 × 2)	$ 600
Table V adjusted multiple	20.6
Expected return ($600 × 20.6)	$12,360
Exclusion ratio.......................... $\frac{8,000}{12,360}$, or 64.7%	
Semiannual exclusion (64.7% of $300)......................	$194.10

There is a simpler computation, illustrated in Example 3, below. But it may be used only if the annuity amount does not vary from year to year. The simple computation determines the annual exclusion by dividing the taxpayer's investment in the contract (cost) by the appropriate multiple from the actuarial tables.

Example 3. Assume the same facts as in Example 1. X's annual exclusion is computed as follows:

Cost of annuity	$8,000
Annual payment ($50 per month × 12 months)	$ 600
Table V multiple...	20.8
Annual exclusion $\dfrac{\$8,000}{20.8}$	$ 385
Annual taxable income ($600 less $385)	$ 215

827. Joint and Survivor Annuities and Joint Annuities. In the case of a joint and survivor annuity contract that provides the first annuitant with a fixed monthly income for life and, after his death, provides an identical monthly income for life to the second annuitant, the multiple used in computing expected return is found in Table II (gender-based) or Table VI (gender-neutral) under the ages of the living annuitants as of the annuity starting date (Reg. § 1.72-5(b)(1)).[17]

For purposes of the example, below, following is a portion of Table VI (gender-neutral for post-June 30, 1986, investment in the contract) providing expected return multiples for ordinary joint life and last survivor annuities for two lives.

TABLE VI.—ORDINARY JOINT LIFE AND LAST SURVIVOR ANNUITIES—TWO LIVES—EXPECTED RETURN Multiples

Ages	65	66	67	68	69	70	71	72
65......................	25.0	24.6	24.2	23.8	23.4	23.1	22.8	22.5
66......................	24.6	24.1	23.7	23.3	22.9	22.5	22.2	21.9
67......................	24.2	23.7	23.2	22.8	22.4	22.0	21.7	21.3
68......................	23.8	23.3	22.8	22.3	21.9	21.5	21.2	20.8
69......................	23.4	22.9	22.4	21.9	21.5	21.1	20.7	20.3
70......................	23.1	22.5	22.0	21.5	21.1	20.6	20.2	19.8
71......................	22.8	22.2	21.7	21.2	20.7	20.2	19.8	19.4
72......................	22.5	21.9	21.3	20.8	20.3	19.8	19.4	18.9

Footnote references are to paragraphs of the 2002 Standard Federal Tax Reports.

[17] ¶ 6106   ¶ **827**

Example. In 2001, Y purchased a joint and survivor annuity providing for payments of $200 a month to be made to Y for life and, upon his death, to his wife, Z, during her lifetime. At the annuity starting date Y's age at his nearest birthday is 68 and Z's is 66. The annuity cost $44,710. The expected return is as follows:

Annual payment ($200 × 12)	$ 2,400
Table VI multiple (age 68; age 66)	23.3
Expected return ($2,400 × 23.3)	$55,920

The annual exclusion for both Y and Z is computed as follows:

Exclusion ratio.............................	$\frac{44,710}{55,920}$, or 80%
Annual exclusion (80% of $2,400)	$1,920.00

If a joint and survivor annuity provides for a different monthly income, rather than an identical monthly income, payable to the second annuitant, the regulations call for a special computation of expected return that involves the use of both Table I and Table II or Table V and Table VI, whichever are applicable.[18]

If a contract involving two annuitants provides for fixed monthly payments to be made as a joint life annuity until the death of the first annuitant (in other words, only as long as both remain alive), the expected return for such a contract is determined under Table IIA or VIA (Reg. § 1.72-5(b)(4)).[19]

Adjustment of the multiple obtained from the annuity tables, as explained at ¶ 825 for single life annuities, may also be necessary for joint and survivor annuities and joint annuities.

829. Special Types of Annuities. The regulations contain detailed provisions on the computation of the exclusion ratio to be used for a contract that is acquired for a single consideration and that provides for the payment of two or more annuity obligations or elements (Reg. § 1.72-4(e), Reg. § 1.72-5(e), and Reg. § 1.72-6(b)).[20] In the case of variable annuities, the regulations set up a special rule for determining the portion of each payment to be "an amount received as an annuity" and excludable from gross income each year (Reg. § 1.72-2(b)(3)).[21] The regulations also set forth the computation of expected return for temporary life annuities (Reg. § 1.72-5(a)(3)-(5)).[22]

833. Annuity Tables. Actuarial tables are used in computing the expected return under commercial annuity contracts involving life expectancy. Tables I, II, IIA, III, and IV of Reg. § 1.72-9 are used if the investment in the contract does not include a post-June 1986 investment in the contract (as defined in Reg. § 1.72-6(d)(5)).[23] Tables V, VI, VIA, VII, and VIII of Reg. § 1.72-9 are used if the investment in the contract includes a post-June 1986 investment in the contract (as defined in Reg. § 1.72-6(d)(5)). These tables are reproduced at ¶ 165 of the CCH STANDARD FEDERAL TAX REPORTS and at ¶¶ 72-¶ 73 of the 2002 U.S. MASTER TAX GUIDE—Loose-Leaf Edition.

In the case of a contract under which amounts are received as an annuity after June 30, 1986, a taxpayer receiving such amounts may elect to treat the entire investment in the contract as a post-June 1986 investment in the contract and thus apply Tables V through VIII (Reg. § 1.72-9). A taxpayer may make the election in any tax year in which such amounts are received by attaching to the return for such tax year a statement of election to treat the entire investment in the contract as post-June 1986 investment in the contract. The statement must contain the taxpayer's name, address, and taxpayer identification number. The election is irrevocable and applies to all amounts that the taxpayer receives as an annuity under the contract in the tax year for which the election is made and in any subsequent tax year. Reg. § 1.72-6(d)(6) contains rules for treating the entire investment in the contract as post-June 1986 investment in the contract if the annuity starting date of

---

Footnote references are to paragraphs of the 2002 Standard Federal Tax Reports.

¶ 829

[18] ¶ 6106	[20] ¶ 6104, ¶ 6106, ¶ 6107	[22] ¶ 6106
[19] ¶ 6106	[21] ¶ 6102D	[23] ¶ 6107

the contract is after June 30, 1986, and the contract provides for a disqualifying form of payment or settlement, such as an option to receive a lump sum in full discharge of the obligation under the contract. Reg. § 1.72-6(d) contains special rules concerning the tables to be used and the separate computations required if the investment in the contract includes both a pre-July 1986 investment in the contract and a post-June 1986 investment in the contract.

835. Exclusion for Year Annuity Begins. If the first payment an annuitant receives is for a fractional part of a year, the annuitant need only determine the exclusion ratio, as a percentage, and apply it to the payment received for the fractional part of the payment period, resulting in the amount of the annuitant's exclusion for the tax year (Reg. § 1.72-4(a)).

> **Example.** John purchased an annuity that provides for semiannual payments of $3,000. The annuity starting date is November 1, and on December 31, John received $1,000 as his first payment under the contract. John's exclusion percentage is 70%. He may exclude 70% of $1,000, or $700, from his calendar-year income.

837. Refund Annuity. Generally, a contract contains a refund feature if (1) the annuity payments depend, in whole or in part, upon the continuing life of one or more persons; (2) there are payments on or after the death of the annuitant if a specified amount or a stated number of payments has not been made prior to death; and (3) the payments are in the nature of a refund of the consideration paid (Code Sec. 72(c)(2); Reg. § 1.72-7).[24] If a refund annuity contract is involved, including a contract for a life annuity with a minimum period of payments certain, an adjustment must be made to the original investment in the contract when determining the exclusion. The original investment in the contract must be reduced by the value of the refund payment or payments certain as of the annuity starting date (Code Sec. 72(b)(4) and (c); Reg. § 1.72-7).[25] The computation of the adjustment, which is explained in the Regulations, is detailed and involves the use of Table III (gender-based) or Table VII (gender-neutral) of Reg. § 1.72-9.[26] If an annuity has a refund feature, the investment in the contract must be reduced by the present value of the refund feature (Code Sec. 72(b)(4)).

839. Employee's Annuity. Subject to the exception noted below, a distribution from a qualified retirement plan (see Chapter 21) that takes the form of a periodic pension is taxable under the annuity rules described at ¶ 817 and following (Code Sec. 402(a) and Code Sec. 403(a)(1)). For purposes of those rules, the participant's investment in the contract (see ¶ 821) is the total amount of the participant's nondeductible contributions to the plan less any amounts withdrawn by the employee before commencement of the annuity that were not included in income (Reg. § 1.72-6; Reg. § 1.72-8; Reg. § 1.72-13; Reg. § 1.402(a)-1(a)(5)).[27]

Pre-November 19, 1996, Annuities. The IRS provides an alternative to application of the usual annuity rules for distributions from qualified plans when the annuity starting date is before November 19, 1996. This is a simplified safe-harbor method for determining the tax-free and taxable portions of certain annuity payments made from qualified employee plans, employee annuities, and annuity contracts (Notice 88-118).[28] Distributees who elect to use this method are considered to have complied with Code Sec. 72(b). Payors may also use this method to report the taxable portion of the annuity payments on Form 1099-R. This safe-harbor method may be used *only* if the following three conditions are met: (1) the annuity payments depend upon the life of the distributee or the joint lives of the distributee and beneficiary; (2) the annuity payments are made from an employee plan qualified under Code Sec. 401(a), an employee annuity under Code Sec. 403(a), or an annuity contract under Code Sec. 403(b); and (3) the distributee is less than age 75 when

---

Footnote references are to paragraphs of the 2002 Standard Federal Tax Reports.

[24] ¶ 6102, ¶ 6108   [27] ¶ 6107, ¶ 6109, ¶ 6119,   [28] ¶ 6140.0306
[25] ¶ 6102, ¶ 6108   ¶ 18,203
[26] ¶ 165

annuity payments commence or, if the distributee is age 75 or older, there are fewer than five years of guaranteed payments.

Under the safe-harbor method, the total number of monthly annuity payments expected to be received is based on the distributee's age at the annuity starting date rather than on the life expectancy tables in Reg. § 1.72-9. The same expected number of payments applies to a distributee whether the individual is receiving a single life annuity or a joint and survivor annuity. These payments are set forth in the following table:

Age of Distributee	Number of Payments
55 and under	300
56-60	260
61-65	240
66-70	170
71 and over	120

The investment in the contract is the aggregate amount of premiums and other consideration paid by the employee (generally the after-tax contributions to the plan) minus the aggregate amount received before the annuity starting date that was excluded from gross income. No refund feature adjustment (see ¶ 837) is required in computing the employee's investment in the contract.

Under the safe-harbor method, the distributee recovers the investment in the contract in level amounts over the number of monthly payments determined from the above table. The portion of each monthly annuity payment that is excluded from gross income by a distributee who uses the safe-harbor method for income tax purposes is a level dollar amount determined by dividing the investment in the contract, including any applicable death benefit exclusion, by the set number of annuity payments from the above table as follows:

$$\frac{\text{Investment}}{\text{Number of monthly payments}} = \text{Tax-free portion of monthly annuity}$$

For distributees with annuity starting dates after 1986, annuity payments received after the investment is recovered (generally, after the set number of payments has been received) are fully includible in gross income.

Example 1. At retirement, Jeff Anderson, age 65, begins receiving retirement benefits in the form of a joint and 50% survivor annuity to be paid for the joint lives of Jeff and his wife, Jan, age 59. Jeff's annuity starting date is January 1, 1996. Jeff contributed $24,000 to the plan and has received no distributions prior to the annuity starting date. He will receive a monthly retirement benefit of $1,000, and his wife Jan will receive a monthly survivor benefit of $500 upon his death. Under the safe-harbor method, Jeff's investment in the contract is $24,000 (the after-tax contributions to the plan). The set number of monthly payments for a distributee who is age 65 is 240. The tax-free portion of each $1,000 monthly annuity payment to Jeff is $100, determined by dividing Jeff's investment ($24,000) by the number of monthly payments (240). If Jeff has not recovered the full $24,000 investment at his death, Jan will also exclude $100 from each $500 monthly annuity payment. Any annuity payments received after 240 payments have been made will be fully includible in gross income. If Jeff and his wife die before 240 payments have been made, a deduction is allowed on the survivor's last income tax return in the amount of the unrecovered investment.

The dollar amount is excluded from each monthly payment even if the annuity payment amount changes. If the amount excluded is greater than the amount of the monthly annuity, because of decreased survivor payments, each monthly annuity payment is excluded completely until the entire investment is recovered. If annuity payments cease before the set number of payments has been made, a deduction for the unrecovered investment is allowed on the distributee's last tax return. Where

¶ 839

payments are made to multiple beneficiaries, the excludable amount is based on the oldest beneficiary's age. A pro rata portion is excluded by each beneficiary.

Tier 2 benefits received by retired railroad workers and their survivors under the Railroad Retirement Act are subject to federal income tax in the same manner as pension plan benefits paid by private employers (Code Sec. 72(r)).[29]

Post-November 18, 1996, Annuities.—The Small Business Job Protection Act of 1996 provided a simplified method similar to the above IRS method for determining the portion of an annuity distribution from a qualified retirement plan, qualified annuity, or tax-sheltered annuity that represents nontaxable return of basis (Code Sec. 72(d)). This rule applies in cases when the annuity starting date is after November 18, 1996.

Under the simplified method, the portion of each annuity payment that represents nontaxable return of basis is generally equal to the employee's total investment in the contract as of the annuity starting date, divided by the number of anticipated payments, which are determined by reference to the age of the participant as listed in the table below (Code Sec. 72(d)(1)(B)):

Age of Primary Annuitant on the Annuity Starting Date	Number of Anticipated Payments
55 and under	360
56-60	310
61-65	260
66-70	210
71 and over	160

For annuity starting dates after December 31, 1997, annuities paid over the life of a single individual have anticipated payments as listed in the table above. If, however, the annuity is payable over the lives of more than one individual, the number of anticipated payments is listed in the table below:

Combined Age of Annuitants	Number of Anticipated Payments
110 and under	410
More than 110 but not more than 120	360
More than 120 but not more than 130	310
More than 130 but not more than 140	260
More than 140	210

The investment in the contract is the amount of premiums and other consideration paid (generally, the after-tax contributions to the plan) minus the amount received before the annuity starting date that was excluded from gross income. The number of anticipated payments listed in the table above is based on the employee's age on the annuity starting date. If the number of payments is fixed under the terms of the annuity, that number is to be used rather than the number of anticipated payments listed in the table.

> **Example 2.** Assume the same facts as Example 1, except Jeff's annuity starting date is January 1, 1998. The set number of monthly payments per the chart above will be 310 (Jeff's age, 65, plus Jan's age, 59, at the starting date of the annuity equals 124). The tax-free portion of each $1,000 monthly annuity payment to Jeff is now $77.42, determined by dividing Jeff's investment ($24,000) by the number of monthly payments (310). The remaining facts of Example 1 are applicable here also.

The simplified method does not apply if the primary annuitant has attained age 75 on the annuity starting date unless there are fewer than five years of guaranteed payments under the annuity (Code Sec. 72(d)(1)(E)).

If, in connection with commencement of annuity payments, the recipient receives a lump-sum payment that is not part of the annuity stream, the payment is taxed under the annuity rules of Code Sec. 72(e) as if received before the annuity starting date and the investment in the contract used to calculate the simplified exclusion ratio for the annuity payments is reduced by the amount of the payment (Code Sec. 72(d)(1)(D)).

Footnote references are to paragraphs of the 2002 Standard Federal Tax Reports.

[29] ¶ 6102

For purposes of these rules, the investment in the contract is determined without regard to the adjustment made for a refund feature (Code Sec. 72(d)(1)(C)).

In any case where the annuity payments are not made on a monthly basis, appropriate adjustments will be made to take into account the period on which the payments are actually made (Code Sec. 72(d)(1)(F)).

Employee contributions under a defined contribution plan may be treated as a separate contract for purposes of these rules (Code Sec. 72(d)(2)).

841. Discharge of Annuity Obligation. Any amount received, whether in a single sum or otherwise, under an annuity, endowment or life insurance contract in full discharge of the obligation under the contract as a refund of the consideration paid for the contract or any amount received under such contract on its complete surrender, redemption or maturity is includible in gross income to the extent the amounts exceed the investment in the contract (Code Sec. 72(e); Reg. § 1.72-11).[30] The remainder is taxable to the recipient, whether the recipient is the primary annuitant or a secondary annuitant under a joint or joint and survivor annuity.

A penalty is imposed on a policyholder who receives a premature distribution (e.g., before age 59½) unless one of a number of exceptions (e.g., death, disability) applies (Code Sec. 72(q)).[31]

843. Installment Option. If an insured elects under an option in an insurance contract to receive the proceeds as an annuity, instead of a lump sum, and the election is made within 60 days after the day on which the lump sum first became payable, no part of it is taxable under the doctrine of constructive receipt (Code Sec. 72(h); Reg. § 1.72-12).[32] The installment payments are taxed in accordance with the annuity rules.

845. Transfer for Value. If a life insurance, endowment, or annuity contract is transferred for a valuable consideration, and the proceeds of the contract are paid to the transferee for reasons other than the death of the insured (for example, on surrender, redemption or maturity of the contract), the transferee (including a beneficiary of, or the estate of, a transferee) is taxed as follows: (1) if the proceeds are received as an annuity or in installments for a fixed period, the transferee computes the tax under the exclusion ratio formula or (2) if the proceeds are received in a lump sum, the transferee includes in income only that portion of the proceeds in excess of the consideration paid. Regardless of how the proceeds are received and taxed, the transferee's consideration paid consists of the actual value of the consideration paid for the transfer, plus the amount of premiums or other consideration paid after the transfer. This transferee rule, however, does not apply if the transferred contract has a basis for gain or loss in the hands of the transferee determined by reference to the transferor's basis, as in the case of a gift or tax-free exchange (Code Sec. 72(g); Reg. § 1.72-10).[33]

Bequest or Gift

847. Bequest. The value of property acquired by bequest, devise, or inheritance is excluded from gross income (Code Sec. 102; Reg. § 1.102-1).[34] But the *income* flowing from the property is not exempt, as, for example, that received as investment income from the property or as profit from a sale of the property. For the basis of inherited property, see ¶ 1633-¶ 1639.

The exclusion also does not apply if the bequest consists not of property but of income from property. Thus, a bequest of annual rent from the testator's property for 10 years is taxable income to the beneficiary.

A bequest of a specific sum or of specific property from an estate or trust may be exempt from tax if it is paid or credited all at once or in not more than three installments (Code Sec. 663(a)(1); Reg. § 1.663(a)-1).[35] An amount which is paid

---

Footnote references are to paragraphs of the 2002 Standard Federal Tax Reports.

¶ **841**

[30] ¶ 6102, ¶ 6113	[32] ¶ 6102, ¶ 6117	[34] ¶ 6550, ¶ 6551
[31] ¶ 6102	[33] ¶ 6102, ¶ 6112	[35] ¶ 24,440, ¶ 24,441

from the estate or trust income may qualify as a bequest for this purpose if the amount could have been paid from either income or principal; however, an amount that can only be paid from the estate or trust income will not be treated as bequest and, thus, will not be exempt even when paid in less than four installments.

849. Gift. The value of a gift is excludable from gross income, but *any income* from the gift, including profit upon sale, is taxable (Code Sec. 102(b)). A gift of income from the property of an estate or trust is not exempt except in the case of a gift of a specific sum or of specific property paid or credited all at once or in not more than three installments. See ¶ 847. For a donee's basis for gift property, see ¶ 1630.

Tips are not gifts and they are taxable (see, further, ¶ 717).[36] Food, clothing and rent payments furnished as strike benefits by a labor union to a needy worker participating in a strike may be considered gifts;[37] in determining whether a gift was made, the fact that benefits are paid only to union members is not controlling.[38]

The exclusion from gross income applicable to the value of property acquired by gift does not apply to any amount transferred by or for an employer to, or for the benefit of, an employee (Code Sec. 102(c)).[39] Certain employee achievement awards are excludable, however (see ¶ 785), and certain fringe benefits provided by employers are also excludable (see ¶ 863).

Employee Benefits

851. Occupational Disability or Insurance Benefit. Compensation received under a workers' compensation act for personal injuries or sickness and amounts received by a taxpayer under a policy of accident and health insurance are exempt from tax (Code Sec. 104(a)(1); Reg. § 1.104-1).[40] Code Sec. 104(a)(1) also applies to benefits having the characteristics of life insurance proceeds paid under a workers' compensation act to the survivor or survivors of a deceased employee (Reg. § 1.101-1(a)).[41]

Amounts received as a pension, annuity, or similar allowance for personal injuries or sickness resulting from active service in the armed forces of any country or in the Coast and Geodetic Survey or the Public Health Service, or as a disability annuity payable under section 808 of the Foreign Service Act of 1980, are also exempt (Code Sec. 104(a)(4); Reg. § 1.104-1).[42] The exclusion generally is limited to amounts received for combat-related injury or illness. However, the exclusion will not be less than the maximum amount of disability compensation from the Veterans Administration to which the individual is, or would be, entitled upon application (Code Sec. 104(b)).[43] See ¶ 702.

Benefits that are payable under state law for occupational injury or illness arising out of employment are nontaxable if the benefits are in the nature of workers' compensation payments (Reg. § 1.104-1(b)).[44]

Benefits received under an insurance contract indemnifying an individual against income lost by reason of loss of the use of his body or a portion of his body are tax exempt, as are payments under an income replacement policy in the event of illness.[45] However, amounts received under a policy designed to pay business overhead costs in the case of prolonged disability are taxable.[46] A lump-sum payment received under an employer-employee contributory disability insurance policy and paid with reference to a permanently disabling illness is excludable to the extent that it is attributable to the employee's contributions.[47] As to excludability of amounts attributable to employer's contributions, see ¶ 853. "No fault" insurance disability benefits received by a passenger injured in an automobile accident under

---

Footnote references are to paragraphs of the 2002 Standard Federal Tax Reports.

[36] ¶ 5507.4651	[40] ¶ 6660, ¶ 6661	[44] ¶ 6661
[37] ¶ 6553.46	[41] ¶ 6503	[45] ¶ 6662.0355
[38] ¶ 6553.46	[42] ¶ 6660, ¶ 6661	[46] ¶ 6662.295
[39] ¶ 6550	[43] ¶ 6660	[47] ¶ 6662.26

¶ **851**

the automobile owner's policy as compensation for loss of income or earning capacity are also excludable from gross income.[48]

If an otherwise excludable amount is for reimbursement of medical expenses previously deducted for tax purposes, the portion must be included in gross income to the extent of the prior deduction. If a portion of an award is specifically allocated to future injury-related medical expenses, the future expenses must be offset by the awarded portion and are not deductible to that extent.[49]

852. Personal Injuries. Amounts received as damages (other than punitive damages) on account of *personal physical injuries* or *physical sickness* are excludable from income (Code Sec. 104(a)(2)). Damages for emotional distress (including the physical symptoms of emotional distress) may not be treated as damages on account of a personal physical injury or sickness, except to the extent of an amount paid for medical care attributable to emotional distress. Accordingly, under Rev. Rul. 96-65, back pay received in satisfaction of a claim for denial of a promotion due to employment discrimination is not excludable because it is "completely independent of," and thus is not "damages received on account of," personal physical injuries or sickness. Damages of emotional distress in satisfaction of such a claim are also not excludable except to the extent paid for medical care attributable to emotional distress.

Damages received before August 21, 1996, from actions based on age, race, or sex discrimination violations were excluded from income, even when they were partially or wholly intended to compensate for lost wages. However, damage awards or settlement procedures that are more in the nature of severance pay than compensation for personal injuries are not excludable.[50] For example, the Supreme Court ruled that a woman who was the subject of sex discrimination could not exclude her award from income because the remedies provided in Title VII of the Civil Rights Act of 1964, the federal law under which she received the award, were not tort-type remedies (*T.A. Burke,* SCt, 92-1 USTC ¶ 50,254). Similarly, under the Age Discrimination in Employment Act, the Court in *Schleier* (SCt, 95-1 USTC ¶ 50,309) held that a settlement for back pay and liquidated damages under the ADEA was includible in gross income.[51]

Interest included in an award of damages for personal injury is includible in gross income.[52] Also, for damages received after August 20, 1996, punitive damages arising out of personal physical injury action cannot be excluded from gross income (Code Sec. 104(a)).[53] However, punitive damages may be excluded from income *if* received in a civil action for wrongful death and the applicable state law, in effect on September 13, 1995, provides that only punitive damages may be awarded (Code Sec. 104(c)).

853. Accident and Health Plans. Amounts received by employees under employer-financed accident and health plans may qualify for exclusion from income (Code Sec. 105; Reg. § 1.105-1).[54] A self-employed person is not an employee for purposes of this exclusion. The exclusion applies to a state government plan (including the District of Columbia) (Code Sec. 105(e)(2); Reg. § 1.105-5),[55] as well as to one of a private employer. Amounts received by employees as reimbursement for medical care and payments (computed without regard to the period of absence from work) for permanent injury or loss of bodily function under an employer-financed accident or health plan are excludable. Money, other than reimbursements for medical expenses, received by an employee from accident or health insurance because of personal injuries or sickness generally is includible in income if the amounts (1) are attributable to contributions from the employer to an insurance plan and were not included in the employee's income or (2) are paid directly by the employer (Code Sec. 105(a)).[56] Payments from an accident and health plan are also

Footnote references are to paragraphs of the 2002 Standard Federal Tax Reports.

¶ 852

[48] ¶ 6662.0355	[51] ¶ 6662.041	[54] ¶ 6700, ¶ 6701
[49] ¶ 6662.41	[52] ¶ 6662.513	[55] ¶ 6700, ¶ 6708
[50] ¶ 6662.04	[53] ¶ 6660	[56] ¶ 6700

excludable from an employee's income to the extent that the plan providing the benefits is funded by the employee (Reg. § 1.105-1(c)).[57]

The exclusion also applies to medical care payments that are made to reimburse the taxpayer, not only for the taxpayer's own medical expenses, but also for the medical expenses of a spouse or any dependents. The reimbursement is excludable in full in the year of receipt without limitation as to amount, even though the taxpayer does not actually pay the medical expenses until a later year. The exclusion does not apply to amounts deductible as medical expenses in any prior tax year (Reg. § 1.105-2).[58] Reimbursement of nondeductible expenses for cosmetic surgery is not excludable from gross income (see ¶ 1016).

Payments for permanent injury include payments for permanent loss of use of a member or function of the body, or the permanent disfigurement of the employee, a spouse, or a dependent. The payments must be based on the nature of the injury rather than on the length of time that the employee is absent from work (Code Sec. 105(c); Reg. § 1.105-3).[59]

Excess reimbursements paid to a highly compensated individual under an employer's self-insured medical reimbursement plan that fails to meet certain nondiscrimination requirements are includible in the individual's gross income (Code Sec. 105(h); Reg. § 1.105-11).[60] A highly compensated employee is an employee who is one of the five highest paid officers, who is among the highest paid 25% of all employees, or who is a shareholder owning more than 10% of the company's stock. The plan must not discriminate in terms of eligibility for coverage or in terms of benefits offered under the plan.

The entire amount of a reimbursement with respect to a benefit that is available only to highly compensated individuals is treated as an excess reimbursement includible in income. In the case of a plan that discriminates in terms of eligibility, the includible excess reimbursement is equal to all the medical expenses for which the highly compensated individual was reimbursed times a fraction, the numerator of which is the total amount reimbursed to all participants who are highly compensated individuals and the denominator of which is the total amount reimbursed to all employees under the plan for such plan year. If the plan discriminates in terms of eligibility *and* benefits, any amount which is included in income by reason of the benefits not being available to all other participants is not to be taken into account in determining the excess reimbursements that results from the plan being discriminatory in terms of eligibility.

There is no eligibility discrimination if the plan benefits (1) at least 70% of all employees or 80% of all eligible employees if at least 70% of all employees are eligible or (2) a class of employees found by the IRS not to be discriminatory in favor of highly compensated individuals. Certain employees, such as part-time workers, employees with less than three years of service, employees under age 25, and employees excluded as a result of a collective bargaining agreement, may be excluded from coverage. There is no benefits discrimination if the self-insured medical expense plan provides the same benefits for non-highly compensated employees as it does for highly compensated employees.

Railroad Unemployment Insurance. Benefits paid to an employee under the Railroad Unemployment Insurance Act for sick days are included in the employee's gross income unless an illness is due to an on-the-job injury (Code Sec. 105(i)).[61]

857. Application of Annuity Rules to Accident or Health Benefits. Amounts received as accident or health benefits are not taxable under the annuity rules at ¶ 817 (Reg. § 1.72-15(b)).[62] However, some employer-established plans pay participants both amounts taxable under the annuity rules (¶ 817-¶ 845, ¶ 2153) and amounts excludable from gross income as payments under an accident or health plan. Reg. § 1.72-15 provides specific rules for determining which amounts are

---

[57] ¶ 6701   [59] ¶ 6700, ¶ 6705   [61] ¶ 6700
[58] ¶ 6703   [60] ¶ 6700, ¶ 6711   [62] ¶ 6124

excludable.[63] Benefits attributable to the employee's contributions are excludable from gross income under the rules at ¶ 851. Benefits attributable to the employer's contributions are taxable except to the extent that they are excludable under the rules at ¶ 853.

859. Employer Contribution to Accident or Health Plans. Contributions by an employer to provide (through insurance or otherwise) the accident and health benefits described in ¶ 853 are not taxable to the employees (Code Sec. 106; Reg. § 1.106-1).[64] This rule also covers contributions made by a church to purchase health and accident insurance for its minister.[65] The employer's contributions are deductible expenses (Reg. § 1.162-10; Temp. Reg. § 1.162-10T).[66] A group health plan that fails to satisfy continuation coverage requirements or pediatric vaccine health care coverage requirements may be subject to an excise tax (Code Sec. 4980B).[67]

See ¶ 322 and ¶ 421 for treatment of an S corporation shareholder or partner whose accident or health insurance premiums are paid by the S corporation or partnership.

860. Medical Savings Accounts. Employers of small businesses and self-employed individuals can take advantage of Archer medical savings accounts (MSAs) to pay health care expenses, provided that accounts are used in conjunction with "high deductible" health insurance (Code Sec. 220). The MSA concept is being tested during a six-year (expanded from four years) pilot period running from 1997 through 2002. The number of taxpayers benefiting annually from an Archer MSA contribution is limited to a threshold level (generally 750,000 returns) (Code Sec. 220). Archer MSAs are like IRAs created for the purpose of defraying unreimbursed health care expenses on a tax-favored basis. For tax years beginning after December 31, 1998, another four-year pilot program permits eligible seniors to establish MSAs called "MedicarePlus Choice MSAs" (Code Sec. 138). See also ¶ 1020.

861. Cafeteria Plans. Cafeteria plans are employer-sponsored benefit packages that offer employees a choice between taking cash and receiving qualified benefits, such as accident and health coverage, group-term life insurance coverage, or coverage under a dependent care program (Code Sec. 125; Proposed Reg. § 1.125-1).[68] No amount is included in the income of a cafeteria plan participant who chooses among the benefits of the plan; however, if a participant chooses cash, it is includible in gross income as compensation. If qualified benefits are chosen, they are excludable to the extent allowed by law.

A cafeteria plan must limit its offering of benefits only between cash or qualified benefits, which, with the application of Code Sec. 125(a), are specifically excluded from gross income under a statutory provision. The term "qualified benefits" does not include benefits under Code Sec. 106(b) (Archer medical savings accounts), Code Sec. 117 (scholarships and fellowship grants), Code Sec. 127 (educational assistance benefits provided by an employer), and Code Sec. 132 (excludable fringe benefits). Also, "qualified benefits" do not include products that are advertised, marketed, or offered as long-term care insurance. A qualified benefit does include any group-term life insurance includible in gross income only because it exceeds the dollar limitations of Code Sec. 79.

The above rules do not apply to highly compensated employees for any benefit attributable to a plan year in which the plan discriminates in favor of the employees with respect to participation, contributions, and benefits. Nor do they apply to any benefit attributable to a plan year in which the statutory qualified benefits provided to key employees exceed 25% of the total of such benefits provided to all employees under the plan. The benefits must be included in the gross income of the highly compensated employee or key employee for the tax year in which the plan year ends. Reports on cafeteria plans are required (Code Sec. 6039D).[69]

Footnote references are to paragraphs of the 2002 Standard Federal Tax Reports.

[63] ¶ 6124	[66] ¶ 8750, ¶ 8751	[68] ¶ 7320, ¶ 7321
[64] ¶ 6800, ¶ 6801	[67] ¶ 34,600	[69] ¶ 35,660
[65] ¶ 6803.20		

¶ 859

Generally, a plan that provides deferred compensation is not included in the definition of a cafeteria plan. However, a profit-sharing or stock bonus plan or rural cooperative plan (within the meaning of Code Sec. 401(k)(7)) that includes a qualified cash or deferred arrangement (as defined in Code Sec. 401(k)(2) to the extent of amounts that a covered employee may elect to have the employer pay as contributions to a trust under such plan on behalf of the employee) or a plan of an educational institution (to the extent of amounts that a covered employee may elect to have the employer pay as contributions for post-retirement group life insurance if all contributions for such insurance have to be made before retirement and such life insurance does not have a cash surrender value at any time) may be classified as a cafeteria plan.

Flexible Spending Arrangements. A flexible spending arrangement (FSA) is a benefit that provides employees with coverage under which specified, incurred expenses may be reimbursed (subject to reimbursement maximums and other reasonable conditions). Flexible spending arrangements are sometimes referred to as "flexible spending accounts." These arrangements allow employees to make pre-tax contributions to FSA accounts for reimbursement of health and/or dependent care expenses. However, the employee does run the risk of forfeiture of any unused contribution by the end of the plan year.

863. Fringe Benefits. The following noncash benefits qualify for exclusion from an employee's gross income: (1) no-additional-cost services (e.g., free stand-by flights by airlines to their employees); (2) qualified employee discounts (e.g., reduced sales prices of products and services sold by the employer); (3) working condition fringe benefits (e.g., use of company car for business purposes); (4) *de minimis* fringe benefits (e.g., use of copying machine for personal purposes); (5) qualified transportation fringe benefits (e.g., transportation in a "commuter highway vehicle," transit passes, and qualified parking); and (6) qualified moving expense reimbursements (Code Sec. 132(a); Reg. § 1.132-1). Also, the value of any on-premises athletic facilities provided and operated by the employer is a nontaxable fringe benefit (Code Sec. 132(j)(4)).[70]

The above benefits may be extended to retired and disabled former employees, to widows and widowers of deceased employees, and to spouses and dependent children of employees. Applicable nondiscrimination conditions must be met (Code Sec. 132(h)).[71]

Denial of a deduction to an employer for its payment of travel expenses of a spouse, dependent, or other individual accompanying an employee on business travel does not preclude those items from qualifying as working condition fringe benefits (Reg. § 1.132-5).

The above benefits that are excluded from an employee's gross income also are excludable from the wage base for purposes of income tax, FICA, FUTA, and RRTA withholding purposes. In the case of taxable noncash fringe benefits in the form of the personal use of an employer-provided vehicle, income tax withholding may be avoided if the employer elects not to withhold and notifies the employee of such election (social security and railroad retirement taxes must be withheld). However, the value of the benefit must be included on the employee's Form W-2 (Code Sec. 3402(s)).[72] The IRS has issued detailed regulations governing the exclusion of fringe benefits from an employee's income.[73]

Qualified Moving Expense Reimbursement. A qualified moving expense reimbursement is an excludable fringe benefit. This is an amount received (directly or indirectly) by an individual from an employer as a payment for (or a reimbursement of) expenses that would be deductible as moving expenses under Code Sec. 217 if directly paid or incurred by the individual. The term does not include a payment for (or a reimbursement of) an expense actually deducted by an individual in a prior tax year (Code Sec. 132(g)). See ¶ 1073.

Footnote references are to paragraphs of the 2002 Standard Federal Tax Reports.

[70] ¶ 7420
[71] ¶ 7420
[72] ¶ 33,542, ¶ 33,591
[73] ¶ 5510, ¶ 7430, ¶ 7421

Transportation Fringe Benefits. In 2001, employees may exclude a maximum of $65 per month from gross income for the value of employer-provided transit passes or vanpooling in an employer-provided "commuter highway vehicle" (Code Sec. 132(f)).[74] For tax years beginning in 2002 and thereafter, the base amount for the exclusion (subject to inflation adjustment) will be increased from $65 to $100 (Code Sec. 132(f)(2)(A)). A qualifying vehicle must seat at least six adults (excluding the driver), and at least 80% of its mileage use must be reasonably expected to be for employees' commuting purposes and for trips when the vehicle is at least one-half full (excluding the driver).

Employees may exclude up to $180 per month from gross income for the value of employer-provided qualified parking in 2001 (projected by CCH to increase to $185 for 2002). The parking must be provided on or near the business premises of the employer or on or near a location from which the employee commutes to work by mass transit, in a commuter highway vehicle, or by carpool. The exclusion does not apply to parking on or near property used by the employee for residential purposes.

The exclusion for these types of transportation fringes also applies if an employer reimburses an employee's expenses for mass transit passes, vanpooling, or qualified parking. Effective for tax years beginning after December 31, 1997, employers may offer the employee a choice of one or more qualified transportation benefits or the cash equivalent without loss of the exclusion (Code Sec. 132(f)(4)). The amount is includible if the cash option is chosen. With respect to mass transit passes, employers must provide vouchers and not make cash reimbursements unless vouchers are not readily available for direct distribution by the employer to its employees.(Code Sec. 132(f)(4); Reg. § 1.132-9(b)).

869. Employer-Provided Child or Dependent Care Services. The value of child or dependent care services provided by an employer pursuant to a written plan generally is not includible in the employee's gross income (Code Sec. 129).[75] To qualify for dependent care assistance, the dependent must be (1) under 13 years old, (2) physically or mentally incapable of caring for himself, or (3) a spouse who is physically or mentally incapable of self-care (Code Sec. 21(b)(1)). The plan generally must not discriminate in favor of employees who are highly compensated. However, if a plan would qualify as a dependent care assistance program except for the fact that it fails to meet discrimination, eligibility, or other requirements of Code Sec. 129(d), then despite the failure the plan may still be treated as a dependent care assistance program in the case of employees who are not highly compensated. The amount excludable from gross income cannot exceed $5,000 ($2,500 in the case of a separate return by a married individual). The amount of any payment exceeding these limits is includible in gross income for the tax year in which the dependent care services were provided, even if payment for the services is received in a subsequent tax year (Code Sec. 129(a)(2)(B)).[76] The exclusion cannot exceed the earned income of an unmarried employee or the earned income of the lower-earning spouse of married employees. The exclusion does not apply unless the name, address, and taxpayer identification number of the person performing the child or dependent care services are included on the return of the employee benefiting from the exclusion (Code Sec. 129(e)(9)). However, the exclusion may be claimed even though the information is not provided if it can be shown that the taxpayer exercised due diligence in attempting to provide this information. See ¶ 1301 for child and dependent care credits.

871. Employer Payment of Employee's Educational Expenses. Up to $5,250 of payments received by an employee for tuition, fees, books, supplies, etc., under an employer's educational assistance program may be excluded from gross income (Code Sec. 127; Reg. § 1.127-1).[77] Excludable assistance payments may not cover tools or supplies that the employee retains after completion of the course or the cost of meals, lodging, or transportation. Although the courses covered by the plan need not be job related, an exception applies to courses involving sports, games,

or hobbies. These courses may only be covered if they involve the employer's business or are required as part of a degree program (Reg. § 1.127-2(c)).[78] The exclusion, which was scheduled to expire for expenses paid for courses beginning after 2001, has been permanently extended (Economic Growth and Tax Relief Reconciliation Act of 2001 (P.L. 107-16)). For expenses relating to courses beginning after December 31, 2001, the exclusion will now also apply to graduate-level courses.

Reports and Records. An employer who maintains an educational assistance plan must maintain records and file an information return (Form 5500, "Annual Return/Report of Employee Benefit Plan," with Schedule F, "Fringe Benefit Plan Annual Information Return" attached) for the plan (Code Sec. 6039D).[79]

873. Food and Lodging Provided by Employer. Meals that are excluded from an employee's income under Code Sec. 119 are considered a *de minimis* fringe benefit under Code Sec. 132.[80] If more than one-half of the employees are furnished meals for the convenience of the employer, all meals provided on the premises are treated as furnished for the convenience of the employer (Code Sec. 119(b)(4)). This provision became effective for tax years beginning before, on, or after July 22, 1998. Therefore, the meals are fully deductible by the employer, instead of possibly being subject to the 50-percent limit on business meal deductions, and excludable by the employees.

The value of meals and lodging furnished by an employer to an employee, a spouse, or dependents for the employer's convenience is not includible in the employee's gross income if, in the case of meals, they are furnished on the employer's business premises and if, in the case of lodging, the employee is required to accept the lodging on the employer's business premises as a condition of employment (Code Sec. 119; Reg. § 1.119-1).[81] The fact that the employer imposes a partial charge for meals or that the employee may accept or decline meals does not affect the exclusion if all other conditions are met, but cash reimbursements of the employee's meal expenses are included in gross income (Code Sec. 119(b)).[82] If meals are furnished for the convenience of the employer, they must be furnished for substantial noncompensatory business reasons (such as having the employee on call) rather than as additional compensation (Reg. § 1.119-1(a)(2)).[83] See also *Boyd Gaming Inc.,* 99-1 USTC ¶ 50,530.[84]

The term "business premises of the employer" generally means the place of employment of the employee. It can include a camp located in a foreign country if an employee is furnished lodging.

Faculty Housing. The value of campus lodging furnished to employees by educational or medical research institutions is excludable from the employee's gross income if an adequate rental is charged. A rental is considered inadequate and thus the exclusion will not apply to the extent of the excess of (a) the lesser of (1) 5% of the appraised value of the lodging or (2) an amount equal to the average of the rentals paid by nonemployees or nonstudents during the year for comparable lodging provided by the institution over (b) the rent paid by the employee for the calendar year (Code Sec. 119(d)).[85] The appraised value under (1), above, will be determined as of the close of the calendar year in which the tax year begins or, in the case of a rental period not greater than one year, at any time during the calendar year in which such period begins.

875. Minister's Home or Rental Allowance. The rental value of a dwelling furnished to a minister of the gospel is exempt from tax (Code Sec. 107; Reg. § 1.107-1),[86] as is a rental allowance to the extent that the allowance is used to rent or provide a home. This includes the portion of a retired minister's pension designated as a rental allowance by the national governing body of a religious denomination having complete control over the retirement fund.[87] The exemption also applies to the rental value of a residence furnished to a retired minister (but not a widow).[88]

Footnote references are to paragraphs of the 2002 Standard Federal Tax Reports.

[78] ¶ 7352	[82] ¶ 7220, ¶ 7222.59	[86] ¶ 6850, ¶ 6851
[79] ¶ 35,660	[83] ¶ 7221	[87] ¶ 6852.12
[80] ¶ 7420	[84] ¶ 7222.29	[88] ¶ 6852.27
[81] ¶ 7220, ¶ 7221	[85] ¶ 7220	

A minister is entitled to deduct mortgage interest and real property taxes paid on a personal residence even if the amounts expended are derived from a rental allowance that is excludable from the minister's gross income (Code Sec. 265(a)(6)).[89]

Reimbursed Living Expenses

877. Exclusion for Reimbursement. A taxpayer whose residence is damaged or destroyed by fire, storm, or other casualty and who must temporarily occupy another residence during the repair can exclude from gross income any insurance payments received as reimbursement for living expenses during such period. This also applies to a person who is denied access to his principal residence by governmental authorities because of the occurrence or threat of occurrence of a casualty (Code Sec. 123; Reg. § 1.123-1).[90]

This exclusion is limited to the excess of actual living expenses incurred by the taxpayer and members of the household over the normal living expenses they would have incurred during the period. The exclusion covers additional costs incurred in renting suitable housing and any extraordinary expenses for transportation, food, utilities, and miscellaneous items.

Scholarship or Fellowship Grant

879. Scholarship or Fellowship Grant Is Not Income. Any amount received as a qualified scholarship by an individual who is a candidate for a degree at a qualified educational organization, which normally maintains a regular faculty and curriculum and normally has a regularly enrolled body of students in attendance where its educational activities are regularly carried on, is excluded from that individual's gross income (Code Sec. 117; Reg. § 1.117-1).[91] A qualified scholarship includes any amount received by an individual as a scholarship or fellowship grant so long as the amount was used for qualified tuition and related expenses such as fees, books, supplies, and equipment required for courses of instruction at a qualified educational organization.

Tuition Reduction. The amount of any qualified tuition reduction to employees of educational institutions is, similarly, excluded from gross income (Code Sec. 117(d)).[92] The tuition reduction must be provided to an employee of a qualified educational organization (described above). The reduction can be for education provided by the employer or by another qualified educational organization. Moreover, it can be for education provided to the employee, the employee's spouse, dependent child, or other person treated as an employee under Code Sec. 132(h). However, it can only be used for education below the graduate level unless it is for the education of an employee who is a graduate student and who is engaged in teaching or research activities for the employer (Code Sec. 117(d)(5)[4]).[93] Any qualified tuition reduction may be excluded only if it does not discriminate in favor of highly compensated employees (Code Sec. 117(d)(3)).[94]

The exclusions for qualified scholarships and qualified tuition reductions will not apply to amounts representing payments for teaching, research, or other services performed by the student that are required as a condition for receiving the qualified scholarship or qualified tuition reduction (Code Sec. 117(c)).[95] Presumably, athletic scholarships awarded to students who are expected, but not required, to participate in sports would, as they have in the past, qualify for exclusion.[96] Effective for amounts received in tax years beginning after December 31, 2001, amounts received by degree candidates from the NHSC Scholarship Program or the Armed Forces Scholarship Program for tuition, fees, books, supplies and required equipment are

Footnote references are to paragraphs of the 2002 Standard Federal Tax Reports.

[89] ¶ 14,050	[92] ¶ 7170	[95] ¶ 7170
[90] ¶ 7300, ¶ 7301	[93] ¶ 7170	[96] ¶ 7183.22
¶ **877** [91] ¶ 7170, ¶ 7172	[94] ¶ 7170	

excluded from the recipient's gross income, even though there is a future service obligation connected to these qualified scholarships (Code Sec. 117(c)(2), as added by P.L. 107-16).

Government Cost-Sharing Payments

881. Certain Agricultural Cost-Sharing Payments Are Excludable. Recipients of agricultural and forestry cost-sharing payments made by state or federal governments may exclude the payments from gross income if (1) the Secretary of Agriculture determines that the payments were made primarily for soil and water conservation, environmental protection or restoration, wildlife habitat development, or forest improvement, and (2) the Treasury Department determines that the payments do not result in a substantial increase in the annual income derived from the property with respect to which the payments were made. No adjustment to the basis of the property involved is made for the payments and, therefore, no income tax deduction or credit may be taken with respect to them (Code Sec. 126).[97] Further, if the property (or improvement) purchased with the payments is disposed of within 20 years, the payment amounts are recaptured as ordinary income. A 100% recapture rate applies if disposition occurs within the first 10 years, with an annual decrease of 10% thereafter (Code Sec. 1255).[98]

Small Business Stock

882. Exclusion for Gain from Small Business Stock. Noncorporate taxpayers may exclude 50% of any gain from the sale or exchange of qualified small business stock issued after August 10, 1993, and held for more than five years. See ¶ 2396.

Foster Care Payments

883. Income Received for Foster Care. Payments made by a state or tax-exempt placement agency as "difficulty of care payments" or to reimburse a foster home provider for the expenses of caring for individuals placed in the home by a state agency or tax-exempt placement agency are excludable from gross income (Code Sec. 131).[99] Foster care payments are excludable only for foster care individuals who live in the foster care provider's home. Regular foster care payments are not excludable to the extent made for more than five individuals over age 18. In the case of "difficulty of care payments" (i.e., payments for additional care required by a physically, mentally, or emotionally handicapped person), payments are not excludable to the extent made for more than 10 individuals under age 19 and more than five individuals over 18 years of age.

Energy Conservation Subsidies

884. Subsidies for Energy Conservation Measures. The value of any subsidy provided (directly or indirectly) by a public utility to a customer for the purchase or installation of energy conservation measures for a dwelling unit is excluded from the customer's gross income (Code Sec. 136).[100] Energy conservation measures are any installations or modifications designed to reduce the consumption of electricity or natural gas or to improve management of energy demand.

Footnote references are to paragraphs of the 2002 Standard Federal Tax Reports.

[97] ¶ 7330   [99] ¶ 7400   [100] ¶ 7560
[98] ¶ 31,080, ¶ 31,081,
¶ 31,082

¶ 884

Cancellation of Debt

885. Income from Discharge of Debt. Generally, a taxpayer realizes income to the extent his debts are forgiven (Code Sec. 61(a)(12)). However, a taxpayer need not recognize income from the discharge of debts in bankruptcy proceedings under title 11 of the U.S. Code or when the taxpayer is insolvent outside bankruptcy (Code Sec. 108(a)(1)(A) and (B)). See ¶ 791. Certain taxpayers may also exclude from gross income amounts realized from the discharge of qualified real property business indebtedness and qualified farm indebtedness (Code Sec. 108(c) and Code Sec. 108(g)). See ¶ 791. For the cancellation of certain student loans, also see ¶ 791.

Military Exemptions

889. Income Generally. Except as noted in the following paragraphs, members of the U.S. Armed Forces include the same items in income as do civilians.

891. Armed Forces Benefits. A pension, annuity, or similar payment for *personal injuries* or *sickness* that resulted from combat-related service in the armed forces of *any* country or in the Coast and Geodetic Survey or the Public Health Service of the U.S., or a disability annuity under the provisions of section 808 of the Foreign Service Act of 1980, is exempt (Code Sec. 104(a)(4); Reg. § 1.104-1(e)).[101] See ¶ 851.

Retirement pay received from the government by Armed Service members is not exempt (Code Sec. 61(a)(11)).[102] Disability retirement pay that is computed on the basis of the percentage of disability is fully excludable from gross income, but disability retirement pay that is computed by reference to years of service is excludable only to the extent allowed under the percentage-of-disability method (Code Sec. 104).[103]

Dividends and proceeds from maturing government endowment insurance contracts under the National Service Life Insurance Act of 1940 and all other acts relating to veterans are exempt.[104] Interest on dividends left on deposit with the Veterans Administration is exempt. If an individual uses accumulated dividends to buy additional paid-up National Service Life Insurance, neither the dividends nor the paid-up insurance is taxable (Rev. Rul. 91-14).

Veterans' benefits under any law administered by the Veterans Administration are not includible in income.[105] This includes amounts paid to veterans or their families in the form of educational, training, or subsistence allowances, disability compensation and pension payments for disabilities, grants for homes designed for wheelchair living, grants for motor vehicles for veterans who lost their sight or the use of their limbs, and veterans' pensions (38 USC § 5301 et seq.).

893. Armed Forces Allowances. Allowances for subsistence, quarters, travel, and moving furnished to a commissioned officer, chief warrant officer, warrant officer, or enlisted personnel of the Armed Forces, Coast and Geodetic Survey, or Public Health Service are not taxable income.[106]

Housing and cost-of-living allowances received by Armed Forces members to cover the excess cost of quarters and subsistence while on permanent duty at a post outside the U.S. are excludable from gross income.[107] The same rule applies to family separation allowances received on account of overseas assignment.[108] The fact that a member of the military service, Coast and Geodetic Survey, or Public Health Service receives a tax-free housing allowance will not bar a deduction for mortgage interest or real property taxes on the member's home (Code Sec. 265(a)(6)).[109]

Footnote references are to paragraphs of the 2002 Standard Federal Tax Reports.

[101] ¶ 6660, ¶ 6661
[102] ¶ 5502, ¶ 5507.121
[103] ¶ 6660, ¶ 6662.79
[104] ¶ 5504.74
[105] ¶ 5504.785
[106] ¶ 5506, ¶ 7222.79
[107] ¶ 5507.111
[108] ¶ 5507.110
[109] ¶ 14,050, ¶ 14,054.0662

¶ 885

895. Combat Zone Compensation. Enlisted members of the Armed Forces and warrant officers (both commissioned and noncommissioned) may exclude from gross income all pay received for any month during any part of which they served in a combat zone or were hospitalized as a result of wounds, disease, or injury incurred while serving in a combat zone. The exclusion for months of hospitalization does not apply for any month beginning more than two years after the termination of combatant activities in the zone. The same exclusion applies to commissioned officers, but it is limited to $500 per month before November 21, 1995. After November 20, 1995, the limit is "the maximum enlisted amount." This amount is the highest rate of basic pay at the highest pay grade that enlisted personnel may receive plus the amount of hostile fire/imminent danger pay that the officer receives (Code Sec. 112; Reg. § 1.112-1).[110]

As of November 21, 1995, the special tax benefits are available to American military personnel serving in Bosnia, Herzegovina, Croatia and Macedonia. Effective March 24, 1999, the special tax benefits were extended to American military personnel serving in the Kosovo region (Notice 99-30, and see also Notice 96-34).

Disability income received by an individual for injuries received in a terrorist attack while the individual was performing services as a U.S. employee outside the United States is excludable from gross income (Code Sec. 104(a)(5)).[111]

896. Qualified Military Benefits. Before enactment of the Tax Reform Act of 1986, a variety of benefits for military personnel were excludable from gross income under a variety of statutes, regulations, and long-standing administrative practices. In the 1986 Act it was determined that, in the future, no such exclusions would be permitted except under some provision of the Internal Revenue Code. However, the Act added to the Code a provision that, in effect, "grandfathered" all of the previous non-Code exclusions (Code Sec. 134).[112] Under this provision, all such exclusions that were in effect on September 9, 1986, continue to be in effect. If a benefit in effect on September 9, 1986, is thereafter modified or adjusted for increases in the cost of living or the like under authority existing on that date, the adjustments are also excludable.

Benefits not otherwise categorized as qualified military benefits but provided in connection with an individual's status or service as a member of the uniformed services may be excluded from income under other Code sections if their requirements for exclusion are met.

Coverdell Education Savings Accounts

898. Coverdell Education Savings Accounts. For tax years beginning before 2002, joint filers with modified AGI below $150,000 ($95,000 for single filers) may contribute up to $500 per designated beneficiary (i.e., an individual under age 18) per year to a Coverdell Education Savings Account (CESA) (prior to July 26, 2001, CESAs were called Education Individual Retirement Accounts). The contribution is not deductible. Earnings on contributions will be distributed tax free provided that they are used to pay the beneficiary's postsecondary education expenses (Code Sec. 530(b)).[113] However, this income exclusion is not available for any year in which the Hope credit or the lifetime learning credit is claimed (see ¶ 1303). Amounts remaining in the account must be distributed within (1) 30 days after the beneficiary reaches age 30 or (2) 30 days after the death of the beneficiary (Code Sec. 530(b)(1)(E)).[114] See "Rollover" below.

The Economic Growth and Tax Relief Reconciliation Act of 2001 (P.L. 107-16) enacted a number of far-reaching changes. For tax years beginning after December 31, 2001, the maximum annual contribution increases to $2,000. In addition, the phaseout range for married individuals will begin at $190,000 and qualified ex-

---

Footnote references are to paragraphs of the 2002 Standard Federal Tax Reports.
[110] ¶ 7080, ¶ 7081   [112] ¶ 7500   [114] ¶ 22,950
[111] ¶ 6660   [113] ¶ 22,950

penses will include public, private and religious elementary and secondary school expenses. The age limit will not apply to beneficiaries with special needs. Further, coordination rules are provided that will allow a student to take advantage of the CESA provisions as well as the Hope and lifetime learning credits (Code Sec. 25A) and a qualified tuition program (Code Sec. 529) in the same tax year.

Under the coordination rules, qualified expenses will first be reduced for tax-exempt scholarships or fellowship grants (see ¶ 879) and any other tax-free educational benefits, as required by Code Sec. 25A(g). Expenses will then be reduced for amounts taken into account in determining the Hope and lifetime learning credits. Where a student receives distributions from both a CESA and a qualified tuition program that together exceed these remaining expenses, the expenses must be allocated between the distributions (Code Sec. 530(d)(2)(C)).

AGI Phaseout Ranges. The amount that a taxpayer is permitted to contribute to a CESA is limited if modified AGI exceeds certain threshold amounts (Code Sec. 530(c)(1)).[115] For 2001, the annual contribution limit is phased out for joint filers with modified AGI at or greater than $150,000 and less than $160,000, and for single filers with modified AGI at or greater than $95,000 and less than $110,000. Individuals with modified AGI at or above the $160,000/$110,000 phaseout limits are not allowed to make contributions to a CESA. After 2001, the phaseout range for joint filers will be between $190,000 and $220,000.

No contribution can be made by any person to a CESA established for a beneficiary during any tax year in which contributions are made by anyone to a qualified state tuition program on behalf of the same beneficiary (¶ 601).

Distributions. Generally, contributions to CESAs are treated as gifts to the beneficiaries. Distributions from CESAs are excludable from gross income to the extent that the distribution does not exceed the qualified higher education expenses incurred by the beneficiary during the year in which the distribution is made (Code Sec. 530(d)(2)(A)).[116] Qualified distributions, with the exception of room and board, are tax exempt regardless of whether the beneficiary attends an eligible educational institution on a full-time, half-time, or less than half-time basis. Room and board expenses constitute qualified higher education expenses only if the student is enrolled at an eligible institution on at least a half-time basis. (See the discussion of eligible education expenses, below.)

Distributions are deemed paid from both contributions (which are always tax free) and earnings (which may be excludable). The amount of contributions distributed is determined by multiplying the distribution by the ratio that the aggregate amount of contributions bears to the total balance of the account at the time the distribution is made (Code Sec. 530(d)(1)).[117]

If aggregate distributions exceed expenses during the tax year, qualified education expenses are deemed to be paid from a pro rata share of both principal and interest. Thus, the portion of earnings excludable from income is based on the ratio that the qualified higher education expenses bear to the total amount of the distribution. The remaining portion of earnings are included in the income of the distributee.

Distributions Not Used for Education. The tax imposed on any taxpayer who receives a payment or distribution from a CESA that is includible in gross income will be increased by an additional 10% (Code Sec. 530(d)(4)(A)).[118] The additional 10% penalty does not apply to distributions: (1) made to a beneficiary or the estate of a designated beneficiary after the beneficiary's death, (2) attributable to the designated beneficiary being disabled (as defined under Code Sec. 72(m)(7)), (3) made on account of a scholarship or allowance (as defined under Code Sec. 25A(g)(2))[119] received by the account holder to the extent the amount of the distribution does not exceed the amount of the scholarship or allowance, or (4) that

---

Footnote references are to paragraphs of the 2002 Standard Federal Tax Reports.

¶ 898

115 ¶ 22,950
116 ¶ 22,950
117 ¶ 22,950
118 ¶ 22,950
119 ¶ 3820

constitute the return of excess contributions and earnings thereon (although earnings are includible in income) (Code Sec. 530(d)(2)(A)).[120]

Rollovers. Amounts held in a CESA may be distributed and put into a CESA for a member of the beneficiary's family. These distributions will not be included in the distributee's gross income provided the rollover occurs within 60 days of the distribution. Similarly, any change in the beneficiary of a CESA does not constitute a distribution for gross income purposes if the new beneficiary is a member of the family of the original beneficiary. A person's family members are determined under Code Sec. 529(e)(2) (Code Sec. 530(d)(2)(A)).[121] Amounts held in a CESA may also be rolled over into another CESA for the benefit of the same beneficiary (e.g., to change the investment vehicle).

Qualified Higher Education Expenses. Tuition, fees, books, supplies and equipment required for the enrollment or attendance of a designated beneficiary at an eligible educational institution fall under the definition of qualified higher education expenses (Code Sec. 530(b)(2)).[122] The term also includes the room and board to the extent of the minimum room and board allowance applicable to the student as determined by the institution in calculating costs of attendance for federal financial aid programs. In tax years beginning after December 31, 2001, for students residing in housing owned or operated by an eligible educational institution, the term will be expanded to cover, if greater, the actual room and board expenses charged by the institution. Room and board expenses are considered qualified higher education costs only if (1) the designated beneficiary is enrolled in a degree, certificate, or other program leading to a recognized educational credential at an eligible educational institution and (2) the student carries at least one-half the normal full-time workload for the course of study pursued. In tax years beginning after December 31, 2001, funds from a CESA may be used to pay for elementary and secondary education expenses, including tutoring, computer equipment, room and board, uniforms and extended day program costs.

Eligible Educational Institution. An eligible educational institution is generally an accredited postsecondary educational institution offering credit toward a bachelor's degree, an associate's degree, a graduate-level or professional degree, or other recognized postsecondary credential. Generally, proprietary and postsecondary vocational institutions are eligible educational institutions (Code Sec. 530(b)(3)).[123] After 2001, educational expenses at elementary and secondary schools (i.e., kindergarten through grade 12) will be included. Schools may be public, private or religious.

Account Requirements. A CESA is a tax-exempt trust created in the United States exclusively for purposes of paying the qualified higher education expenses of the trust's designated beneficiary. The trust must be designated as a CESA at the time it is created or organized (Code Sec. 530(b)(1)).[124]

Prohibited Uses of Accounts. A CESA will lose its tax-exempt status if it engages in a prohibited transaction or is pledged as security for a loan. Prohibited transactions include loans and use of account assets by the beneficiary or a fiduciary (see Code Sec. 4975(c)).[125]

Transfers Upon Death or Divorce. Death or divorce of the designated beneficiary need not cause a taxable distribution to the spouse or ex-spouse. The transfer of a beneficiary's interest in a CESA to a spouse or ex-spouse under a divorce or separation agreement is not a taxable transfer, and after the transfer the interest in the account is treated as belonging to the spouse/ex-spouse (Code Sec. 530(d)(7)).[126]

Estate and Gift Tax Treatment. Any contribution to a CESA is treated as a completed gift of a present interest from the contributor to the beneficiary at the time of the contribution. Annual contributions are eligible for the gift tax exclusion under Code Sec. 2503(b) and are excludable for purposes of the generation-skipping transfer tax (Code Sec. 530(d)(3)).[127]

Footnote references are to paragraphs of the 2002 Standard Federal Tax Reports.

[120] ¶ 22,950
[121] ¶ 22,940
[122] ¶ 22,950

[123] ¶ 22,950
[124] ¶ 22,950
[125] ¶ 34,400

[126] ¶ 22,950
[127] ¶ 22,950

¶ 898

Chapter 9

DEDUCTIONS

Business Expenses

Trade or Business Expenses

901. Deductibility, Generally. A taxpayer, whether a corporation, an individual, a partnership, or a trust or estate, generally may deduct from gross income the ordinary and necessary expenses of carrying on a trade or business that are paid or incurred in the tax year (Reg. § 1.162-1).[1] However, a deduction is not permitted for any expenditure that is a capital expense. See ¶ 903. Expenses for property used for both business and personal activities must be allocated between the activities.

The Supreme Court has held that the origin and character of a claim control whether an expense is a deductible business expense or a nondeductible personal expense (*D. Gilmore*, SCt, 63-1 USTC ¶ 9285).[2] Business expenses incurred by a cash basis taxpayer while conducting a business but paid in a year after terminating the business are deductible as business expenses in the year paid (Rev. Rul. 67-12).[3]

A number of special tax incentives (e.g., tax credits and larger Section 179 deductions) may be available for taxpayers who operate businesses in areas designated as empowerment zones, enterprise communities, or renewal communities (Code Sec. 1400E).

902. Ordinary and Necessary. Whether an expense is ordinary and necessary is based upon the facts surrounding the expense. An expense is necessary if it is

---

Footnote references are to paragraphs of the 2002 Standard Federal Tax Reports.

¶901   [1] ¶ 8501   [2] ¶ 8526.4460   [3] ¶ 8520.1546

appropriate and helpful to the taxpayer's business. An expense is ordinary if it is one that is common and accepted in the particular business activity.[4]

903. Capital Expenditures. An expense that adds to the value or useful life of property is considered a capital expense (Reg. § 1.263(a)-1).[5] Generally, capital expenses must be deducted by means of depreciation, amortization or depletion. If the expense is not subject to depreciation, amortization or depletion, it is added to the cost basis of the property. Capital expenses include those for buildings, improvements or betterments of a long-term nature, machinery, architect's fees, and costs of defending or perfecting title to property (Reg. § 1.263(a)-2).[6] See Checklist at ¶ 57.

Expenses that keep property in an ordinarily efficient operating condition and do not add to its value or appreciably prolong its useful life are generally deductible as repairs (Reg. § 1.162-4).[7] Repairs include repainting, tuck-pointing,[8] mending leaks, plastering, and conditioning gutters on buildings.[9] However, the costs of installing a new roof [10] and bricking up windows to strengthen a wall [11] are capital expenditures.

Taxpayers may elect to currently deduct certain environmental cleanup costs (Code Sec. 198).[12] This deduction only pertains to the cleanup of hazardous substances located on sites within areas that meet specific requirements (Code Sec. 198(c)(2)(A)).[13] The expenses must have been paid or incurred after August 5, 1997 and before January 1, 2004 (Code Sec. 198(h)). The IRS has provided guidance for taxpayers who want to make this election (Rev. Proc. 98-47).[14] Individuals must include the total amount of the expenses on the line for "other expenses" on Schedule C, E, or F (as appropriate) for Form 1040.

In a situation that did not meet the requirements of Code Sec. 198, the IRS ruled that a corporation that discharged hazardous waste as part of its manufacturing process could claim a current business expense deduction for ongoing soil remediation and groundwater treatment costs because the costs did not produce permanent improvements or otherwise provide significant future benefits. Those expenses did not increase the value of the property after they were made in comparison to its value before it was contaminated and thus were not capital expenditures. However, the cost of constructing groundwater treatment facilities had a useful life substantially beyond the tax year and was required to be capitalized. In addition, because the construction of these facilities constituted production within the uniform capitalization rules, direct costs and a portion of indirect costs were required to be capitalized (Rev. Rul. 94-38).[15]

Legal fees, investment banker fees, and other expenses incurred by the target and acquiring corporations in a *friendly* takeover are capital expenses if they result in a long-term benefit. Expenses incurred in resisting a *hostile* takeover have been held to be currently deductible if the merger never took place.[16] Although the realization of future benefits is important to consider in determining whether an expense must be capitalized, the mere presence of some future benefit does not necessarily warrant capitalization. *Severance payments* made by a taxpayer to its employees in connection with a business down-sizing or an acquisition principally relate to previously rendered service and are therefore currently deductible (Rev. Rul. 94-77).[17]

904. Amortization of Business Start-Up Costs. Taxpayers who pay or incur business start-up costs and who subsequently enter the trade or business can elect to amortize these expenses over a period of not less than 60 months, starting with the month in which the business begins (Code Sec. 195(b)).[18] The election must be made no later than the date (including extensions) for filing the return for the tax year in which the business begins or is acquired (Code Sec. 195(c) and (d)). The

Footnote references are to paragraphs of the 2002 Standard Federal Tax Reports.

4 ¶ 8520.013	9 ¶ 8620	14 ¶ 12,465.30
5 ¶ 13,701	10 ¶ 13,701	15 ¶ 8630.1242
6 ¶ 13,703	11 ¶ 13,701	16 ¶ 8526.4234
7 ¶ 8620	12 ¶ 12,460	17 ¶ 8752.676
8 ¶ 8620	13 ¶ 12,460	18 ¶ 12,370

election is made by completing Part VI of Form 4562 (Depreciation and Amortization) and attaching a separate statement that provides such information as total start-up costs, date each cost was incurred, and a description of what each cost was for.[19] A taxpayer who does not make the election must capitalize the expenses (Code Sec. 195(a)).[20]

To qualify for amortization, the expense must be paid or incurred in connection with (1) investigating the creation or acquisition of an active trade or business, (2) creating an active trade or business, or (3) any activity engaged in for profit and for the production of income before the day on which the active trade or business begins, in anticipation of such activity becoming an active trade or business. In addition, the start-up expense must be a cost that would be allowable as a deduction if it were paid or incurred in connection with an existing active business in the same field as that entered into by the taxpayer (Code Sec. 195(c)).[21]

The term "start-up costs" does not include any amount with respect to which a deduction is allowable under Code Sec. 163(a) (interest on indebtedness), Code Sec. 164 (taxes), or Code Sec. 174 (research and experimental expenditures) (Code Sec. 195(c)).[22]

If the trade or business is disposed of completely by the taxpayer before the end of the 60-month (or longer) period, any remaining deferred expenses may be deductible as a loss under Code Sec. 165 (Code Sec. 195(b)(2)).[23]

Corporate organization fees are discussed at ¶ 243. Costs of organizing a partnership are discussed at ¶ 477 and ¶ 481.

905. Expenses, Interest Deductions and Losses—Related Taxpayers. When the payor and payee are related taxpayers (see ¶ 1717), and the payor is on the accrual method of accounting and the payee is on the cash method, no deduction will be allowed for any expense or interest payable to the payee until the payee includes the payment in income (Code Sec. 267(a)(2)).[24]

A similar rule denies a deduction for a loss (except for a loss from a distribution in corporate liquidation) for property sold or exchanged between related taxpayers. However, upon later sale or exchange of the property by the transferee at a gain, the gain is recognized only to the extent it exceeds the previously disallowed loss (Code Sec. 267(a) and Code Sec. 267(d)).[25]

Compensation Paid

906. Compensation for Personal Service. A taxpayer carrying on a trade or business is entitled to deduct a *reasonable* allowance for salaries or other compensation for personal services. The deduction is allowable for the year in which the salary is paid or incurred (Reg. § 1.162-7).[26] However, publicly held corporations are generally not able to deduct compensation paid to certain covered employees to the extent that such compensation exceeds $1 million per tax year (Code Sec. 162(m); Reg. § 1.162-27).[27] The $1 million limit does not apply to certain "performance based compensation" (Code Sec. 162(m)(4)(C)).[28]

A bonus is deductible if paid for services performed and if, when added to other salaries, it does not exceed reasonable compensation (Reg. § 1.162-9).[29]

Compensation paid to a relative is deductible if the relative performs needed services that would otherwise be performed by an unrelated party. The deduction is limited to the amount that would have been paid to a third party.[30]

Court decisions dealing with the question of excessive salaries, arising almost exclusively with closely held companies, show that each case is decided upon its particular facts. The IRS test is that *reasonable* compensation is the amount that would ordinarily be paid for like services by like enterprises in like circumstances.

Footnote references are to paragraphs of the 2002 Standard Federal Tax Reports.

¶ 905
19 ¶ 12,371.06   23 ¶ 12,370   27 ¶ 8500, ¶ 9051B
20 ¶ 12,370   24 ¶ 14,150   28 ¶ 8500
21 ¶ 12,370   25 ¶ 14,150   29 ¶ 8641
22 ¶ 12,370   26 ¶ 8635   30 ¶ 8637.752, 8638.01

Additional factors are personal ability, responsibility of the position, and economic conditions in the locality.[31] The U.S. Court of Appeals for the Seventh Circuit has used an "independent-investor" test. This test presumes that compensation is reasonable if the company's investors earn their expected rate of return (*Exacto Spring Corporation*, 99-2 USTC ¶ 50,964).[32]

Officer-stockholders of closely held corporations may deduct repayments of salary to their corporation that are made pursuant to an agreement requiring such repayments in the event that the IRS determines the salaries to be excessive. However, the officer-stockholders may claim the deduction only if the agreement is legally enforceable and was in existence *before* the payment of the amounts.[33]

Deferred Compensation. For unfunded deferred compensation plans, the employer's deduction for compensation is claimed when the compensation (or amount attributable to it) is included in the gross income of the recipient (Code Sec. 404(a)(5) and (b)(1)).[34] For the time of inclusion, see ¶ 723. Other benefits that are excluded from the recipient's gross income are deductible when they otherwise would have been includible in the recipient's gross income but for the exclusion (Code Sec. 404(b)(2)).[35] This rule also applies to compensation paid to independent contractors (Code Sec. 404(d)).[36]

A plan is unfunded if it consists of an unsecured promise to pay compensation at some time in the future. If the employer sets aside a reserve for the future obligation, the plan is unfunded if the employee has no rights in the reserve or its earnings and if the reserve remains solely the property of the employer or other payor, subject to the claims of creditors.[37]

A plan is presumed to defer compensation if the compensation is received after the 15th day of the third calendar month after the end of the employer's tax year in which the related services are rendered. This presumption may be overcome if the employer establishes that it was administratively or economically impractical to avoid the deferral of compensation beyond the 2½-month period. Payments within the 2½-month period are not treated as deferred compensation and may be accrued by an accrual-method employer in the year earned by the employee (Temporary Reg. § 1.404(b)-1T, Q&A-2).[38]

For a discussion of rules governing the employer's deduction for compensation for funded deferred compensation plans, see ¶ 2147-¶ 2151 and ¶ 2197.

907. Golden Parachute Contracts. A corporation that enters into a contract whereby it agrees to pay an employee amounts in excess of the employee's usual compensation in the event that control or ownership of the corporation changes is barred from taking a deduction for an "excess parachute payment" made to a "disqualified individual." The disqualified individual is subject to an excise tax of 20% of the excess parachute payment in addition to the income tax due (Code Sec. 4999).[39] The tax is reported on Line 58 of the 2001 Form 1040. A disqualified individual is an employee or independent contractor who performs personal services for any corporation and is an officer, shareholder, highly compensated person, or personal service corporation (Code Sec. 280G(c)).[40]

Parachute Payment Defined. A parachute payment is any payment in the nature of compensation to a disqualified individual if: (1) the payment is contingent on a change in the ownership or effective control of the corporation or a substantial portion of the corporation's assets and (2) the aggregate present value of such contingent payments equals or exceeds three times an individual's base amount. Any payment in the nature of compensation to a disqualified individual who violates any securities law or regulations is also considered a parachute payment. Reasonable compensation for personal services to be rendered on or after the date of change or for personal services actually rendered before the date of change are not treated as

---

Footnote references are to paragraphs of the 2002 Standard Federal Tax Reports.

[31] ¶ 8637.744, 8637.021   [35] ¶ 18,330   [38] ¶ 18,354
[32] ¶ 8637.227, 8367.021   [36] ¶ 18,330   [39] ¶ 34,940
[33] ¶ 8637.022, 8640.021   [37] ¶ 18,352.027   [40] ¶ 15,150
[34] ¶ 18,330

parachute payments. Additionally, parachute payments do not include payments to or from certain qualified plans (Code Sec. 280G(b)).[41]

Base Amount. The base amount is the individual's annualized includible compensation for a period, consisting of the most recent five tax years ending before the date on which the ownership or control of the corporation changed or the portion of this period during which the individual was an employee of the corporation (Code Sec. 280G(b)).[42]

"Excess Parachute Payment." An "excess parachute payment" is an amount equal to the excess of any parachute payment over the portion of the base amount allocated to the payment. The allocable base amount is subtracted from the parachute payment, and the remainder is the excess parachute payment (Code Sec. 280G(b)).[43]

Exceptions. Generally, a parachute payment does not include any payment made to a disqualified individual by (1) a small business corporation or (2) other corporations, if, immediately before the change, none of their stock was readily tradeable on an established securities market and shareholder approval requirements are met (Code Sec. 280G(b)(5)).[44]

908. Disability Payments; Contributions for Employee Benefits. An employer's deduction for contributions to a funded welfare benefit plan for sickness, accident, hospitalization or medical benefits is governed by Code Sec. 419 (Temporary Reg. § 1.162-10T).[45] See ¶ 2198 and ¶ 2199. Although amounts that are added to a self-insurance reserve account are not currently deductible, actual losses charged to the account are deductible.[46]

Group health plans that fail to provide continuing coverage to qualified beneficiaries may subject employers to an excise tax (Code Sec. 4980B).[47]

Self-Employed Persons. For 2001, self-employed persons may deduct from gross income 60% of amounts paid during the year for health insurance for themselves, spouses, and dependents from gross income (Code Sec. 162(l)(1)(B)).[48] The deduction is limited to the taxpayer's net earned income derived from the trade or business for which the insurance plan was established, minus the deductions for 50% of the self-employment tax and/or the deduction for contributions to Keogh, self-employed SEP or SIMPLE plans. The self-employed health insurance deduction increases to 70% in 2002, and 100% in 2003 and thereafter (Code Sec. 162(l)(1)). Amounts eligible for the deduction do not include amounts paid during any month, or part of a month, that the self-employed individuals were able to participate in a subsidized health plan maintained by their employers or their spouses' employers (Code Sec. 162(l)(2)(A)).

909. Life Insurance Premiums. Premiums paid by an employer for insurance on the life of an officer or employee are deductible only if it can be shown that: (1) premium payments are in the nature of additional compensation; (2) total compensation, including premiums, is not unreasonable; and (3) the employer is not directly or indirectly a beneficiary under the policy.[49] However, no deduction is allowed an employer for premiums paid under a split dollar (see ¶ 721) arrangement on the life of an employee.[50]

Premiums on group-term life insurance covering the lives of employees are deductible by the employer if the employer is not a direct or indirect beneficiary.[51] The payment of such premiums generally represents income to the employee to the extent that the coverage provided exceeds $50,000. See ¶ 721.

Generally, no deduction is allowed for interest paid or accrued on a debt incurred or continued to purchase or carry any single premium life insurance, endowment or annuity contract. If substantially all the premiums on a life insurance

---

Footnote references are to paragraphs of the 2002 Standard Federal Tax Reports.

¶908

[41] ¶ 15,150	[45] ¶ 8751	[49] ¶ 14,002, ¶ 14,004.01
[42] ¶ 15,150	[46] ¶ 8522.3947	[50] ¶ 5508.057,
[43] ¶ 15,150	[47] ¶ 34,600	¶ 14,004.165
[44] ¶ 15,150	[48] ¶ 8500	[51] ¶ 6360, ¶ 14,003

or endowment contract are paid within four years from date of purchase, or if an amount is deposited with the insurer for payment of a substantial number of future premiums on the contract, it is regarded as a single premium contract (Code Secs. 264(a)(2) and 264(c)).[52]

Interest on a debt incurred to purchase or continue a life insurance, endowment, or annuity contract pursuant to a plan of purchase contemplating the systematic borrowing of part or all of the increases in cash value is not deductible (Code Sec. 264(a)(3)).[53] However, Code Sec. 264(d) allows an interest deduction in limited situations.[54] Special rules may permit the deduction of interest incurred for key person policies owned by corporations (Code Sec. 264(e)).[55]

Entertainment, Meal and Gift Expenses

910. Entertainment Expense. Special limits are imposed by Code Sec. 274 on the deduction of business-related entertainment, meal and gift expenses. These limits are in addition to those imposed by other Code sections. For example, no deduction is allowed for the cost of entertainment, amusement, or recreation unless that cost is either (1) *directly related* to the active conduct of a trade or business or (2) *associated with* such business if the expense is for entertainment directly before or after a substantial and bona fide business discussion. (Specific exceptions to these general requirements are discussed at ¶ 915.) Entertainment includes entertaining guests at night clubs, sporting events, theaters, etc. A taxpayer's trade or business is considered in applying an objective test as to what constitutes entertainment. For example, if an appliance distributor conducts a fashion show for the spouses of retailers, the show would generally be considered entertainment (Code Sec. 274(a)(1)(A); Reg. § 1.274-2(b)(1)(ii)).[56]

The deduction for entertainment expenses may not exceed the portion that is related to the business. If there are both business and nonbusiness expenses at the same event, an allocation must be made, and only the business portion may be deducted.

Generally, only 50% of otherwise allowable meal and entertainment expenses are deductible (Code Sec. 274(n)).[57] See ¶ 916. There are numerous exceptions to the 50% limitation rule. See ¶ 917.

Transportation Workers. The deduction percentage of the cost of meals consumed while away from home by individuals subject to Department of Transportation hours of service rules (e.g., interstate truck drivers) is 60% for tax years beginning in 2001. The deduction will increase to 65% for tax years 2002 and 2003; 70% for tax years 2004 and 2005; 75% for tax years 2006 and 2007; and 80% for tax years 2008 and thereafter (Code Sec. 274(n)(3)).

Two-Percent Floor. In most situations, an employee's unreimbursed business expenses must be claimed as a miscellaneous itemized deduction, subject to the 2% floor. See ¶ 1011. The percentage limit (e.g., 50%) on meal and entertainment expenses must be taken into account prior to application of the 2% floor (see ¶ 916) (Code Sec. 67; Temporary Reg. § 1.67-1T(a)).[58] Some employees may deduct their unreimbursed expenses directly from gross income (see ¶ 941).

911. Directly Related Test. For an entertainment expense to meet the directly related test, the taxpayer must have had more than a general expectation of deriving income, or some other specific business benefit, at some indefinite future time. The taxpayer must engage in the active conduct of business with the person being entertained. In addition, the active conduct of business must be the principal aspect of the combined business and entertainment (Reg. § 1.274-2(c)).[59]

912. Associated Entertainment. Entertainment expenses associated with the active conduct of the taxpayer's business are deductible if they directly precede

---

Footnote references are to paragraphs of the 2002 Standard Federal Tax Reports.

[52] ¶ 14,002	[55] ¶ 14,002	[58] ¶ 6060, ¶ 6061
[53] ¶ 14,002	[56] ¶ 14,402, ¶ 14,405	[59] ¶ 14,405
[54] ¶ 14,002	[57] ¶ 14,402	

or follow a bona fide and substantial business discussion. This includes goodwill expenditures to obtain new business or encourage continuation of existing business relationships. The business discussion must be the principal aspect of the combined entertainment and business and must represent an active effort by the taxpayer to obtain income or other specific business benefit (Reg. § 1.274-2(d)).[60]

913. Entertainment Facility. No deduction is generally allowed for any expense for entertainment facilities, such as yachts, hunting lodges, swimming pools, tennis courts, or bowling alleys (Code Sec. 274(a)(1)(B)).[61] However, expenses for recreational facilities primarily for the benefit of employees generally are deductible (Reg. § 1.274-2(f)(2)(v)).[62]

913A. Club Dues. As a general rule, no business deduction is permitted for club dues. This rule extends to business, social, athletic, luncheon, sporting, airline and hotel clubs (Code Sec. 274(a)(3)). However, dues paid to professional or public service organizations (e.g., accounting associations, or Kiwanis and Rotary clubs) are deductible if paid for business reasons and the organization's principal purpose is *not* to conduct entertainment activities for members or their guests or to provide such parties with access to entertainment facilities (Reg. § 1.274-2(a)(2)(iii) and Reg. § 1.274-2(b)).[63]

914. Entertainment-Related Meals. Generally, an entertainment-related meal expense is *not* deductible unless the taxpayer establishes that the expense is directly related to the active conduct of a trade or business. However, if a meal expense directly precedes or follows a substantial and bona fide business discussion (including a business meeting at a convention), then it is deductible if it is established that the expense was associated with the active conduct of a trade or business. The taxpayer must be able to substantiate the expense (see ¶ 953) (Code Sec. 274(d); Temporary Reg. § 1.274-5T(c), (f)).[64]

There are two additional restrictions placed on the deduction of meal expenses: (1) meal expenses generally are not deductible if neither the taxpayer nor the taxpayer's employee is present at the meal, and (2) a deduction will not be allowed for food and beverages to the extent that such expense is lavish or extravagant under the circumstances. These restrictions do not apply to the expenses described in exceptions (2), (3), (4), (7), (8), and (9) at ¶ 915 (Code Sec. 274(k)).[65]

915. Exceptions to Entertainment Rules. The following entertainment expenses are deductible provided that they meet the ordinary and necessary requirements and are properly substantiated (Code Sec. 274(e); Reg. § 1.274-2(f)(2)).[66] However, they may be subject to the 50% limit rule. See ¶ 916 and ¶ 917.

(1) Food and beverages for employees furnished on the business premises.

(2) Expenses for services, goods, and facilities that are treated as compensation and as wages for withholding tax purposes.

(3) Reimbursed expenses, but only (a) where the services for which reimbursement is made are performed for an employer and the employer has not treated the expenses as wages subject to withholding or (b) where the services are performed for a person other than an employer and the taxpayer receiving the reimbursed expenses accounts to such person.

(4) Recreational expenses primarily for employees who, for this purpose, are not highly compensated (within the meaning of Code Sec. 414(q)). An example of such an expense is a company picnic.

(5) Expenses of employees', stockholders', agents' or directors' *business* meetings.

(6) Expenses directly related and necessary to attendance at a *business* meeting of a tax-exempt business league, including a real estate board, chamber of commerce or board of trade.

Footnote references are to paragraphs of the 2002 Standard Federal Tax Reports.

¶913

[60] ¶ 14,405	[63] ¶ 14,402, ¶ 14,405	[65] ¶ 14,402
[61] ¶ 14,402	[64] ¶ 14,402, ¶ 14,410	[66] ¶ 14,402, ¶ 14,405
[62] ¶ 14,405		

(7) Cost of goods, services and facilities made available to the public.

(8) Entertainment sold to customers in a bona fide transaction for adequate consideration.

(9) Goods, services, and facilities that are furnished to nonemployees as entertainment, amusement or recreation expenses and that are includible in the recipients' incomes.

916. 50% Limitation Rule. The amount allowable as a deduction for meal and entertainment expenses is generally limited to 50% of such expenses. Food and beverage costs incurred in the course of travel away from home fall within the scope of this rule. The 50% rule is applied only after determining the amount of the otherwise allowable deductions. For instance, the portion of a travel meal that is lavish and extravagant must first be subtracted from the meal cost before the 50% reduction is applied. Related expenses, such as taxes and tips in the case of meals and other charges, and room rental and parking fees in the case of entertainment expenses, must be included in the total expense before applying the 50% reduction. Allowable deductions for transportation costs to and from a business meal are not reduced (Code Sec. 274(n)).[67]

917. Exceptions to 50% Limitation Rule. The following expenses are *not* subject to the 50% limit on meal and entertainment expense deductions:

(1) Expenses described in categories (2), (3), (4), (7), (8), and (9) at ¶ 915.

(2) Food and beverage expenses associated with benefits that are excludable from the recipient's gross income as a *de minimis* fringe benefit (Code Sec. 274(n)(2)(B)).[68]

(3) The cost of a ticket package to a sporting event and related expenses if the event is organized to benefit a tax-exempt organization, all net proceeds of the event are contributed to such organization, and volunteers perform substantially all of the work in carrying out the event (Code Sec. 274(n)(2)(C)).[69] In other situations, a deduction for a ticket may not exceed the ticket's face value (Code Sec. 274(l)(1)).[70]

(4) An employee's meal expenses incurred while moving that are reimbursed by the employer and includible in the employee's gross income (see ¶ 1073).

(5) Expenses for food and beverages provided to employees on certain (a) vessels and (b) oil or gas platforms and drilling rigs and their support camps (Code Sec. 274(n)(2)(E)).[71]

See ¶ 910 for the rules that apply to certain transportation workers.

Skyboxes. When a skybox is rented for more than one event, the deduction may not exceed the price of non-luxury box seats (subject to the usual 50% limit) (Code Sec. 274(l)(2)).[72]

918. Business Gifts. Deductions for business gifts, whether made directly or indirectly, are limited to $25 per recipient per year. Items clearly of an advertising nature that cost $4 or less and signs, display racks, or other promotional materials given for use on business premises are not gifts (Code Sec. 274(b)(1) and Reg. § 1.274-3).[73]

919. Employee Achievement Awards. An employer may deduct the cost of an employee achievement award up to $400 for all *nonqualified plan awards*. The employer's deduction for the cost of *qualified plan awards* made to a particular employee is limited to $1,600 per year, taking into account all other qualified and nonqualified awards made to that employee during the tax year (Code Sec. 274(j)(2)).[74]

An employee achievement award is an item of tangible personal property awarded to an employee as part of a meaningful presentation for length of service or

Footnote references are to paragraphs of the 2002 Standard Federal Tax Reports.

[67] ¶ 14,402 [70] ¶ 14,402 [73] ¶ 14,402, ¶ 14,406
[68] ¶ 14,402 [71] ¶ 14,402 [74] ¶ 14,402
[69] ¶ 14,402 [72] ¶ 14,402

¶919

safety achievement under circumstances that do not create a significant likelihood of disguised compensation (Code Sec. 274(j)(3)(A)).[75]

A qualified plan award is an employee achievement award provided under an established written plan or program that does not discriminate in favor of highly compensated employees (within the meaning of Code Sec. 414(q)) as to eligibility or benefits. An employee achievement award is not a qualified plan award if the average cost of all employee achievement awards exceeds $400. Average cost calculation includes the entire cost of all qualified plan awards, ignoring employee achievement awards of nominal value (Code Sec. 274(j)(3)(B)).[76]

A length of service award will not qualify if it is received during the employee's first five years of service or if the employee has received a length of service award (other than an award excludable under Code Sec. 132(e), relating to *de minimis* fringe benefits) during the year or within the last four years. An award will not be considered a safety achievement award if made to a manager, administrator, clerical employee, or other professional employee or if, during the tax year, awards for safety achievement previously have been made to more than 10% of the employees, excluding managers, administrators, clerical employees, or other professional employees (Code Sec. 274(j)(4)).[77]

Taxes

920. Taxes Directly Attributable to Business. Business taxpayers can deduct the taxes listed at ¶ 1021 and any other state, local, and foreign taxes paid or accrued within the tax year to the extent that they are directly attributable to a trade or business or to property held for the production of rents or royalties. Any tax not listed at ¶ 1021 that is paid or accrued by the taxpayer in connection with the acquisition of property is treated as part of the cost of the acquired property or, if in connection with the disposition of property, as a reduction in the amount realized (Code Sec. 164(a)).[78]

The uniform capitalization rules require some taxpayers to capitalize certain taxes that would otherwise be deductible. See ¶ 990 et seq.

921. Unemployment Insurance Tax. The federal unemployment insurance tax is deductible as a business expense by the employer after application of state credits. On the accrual basis, the deduction may be accrued for the calendar year in which the wages were paid even though payment of the tax is not due until the following year. On the cash basis, the tax is deductible when paid.[79]

922. State Unemployment Insurance and Disability Fund Contributions. An employer covered by state unemployment insurance laws is entitled to deduct as taxes only those contributions that are classified as taxes under state law and are incurred in carrying on a trade or business or in the production of income.[80] In states that require employees to contribute to state unemployment compensation funds, such contributions may be claimed as *itemized* deductions (as state income taxes). Also, compulsory employee contributions to *state* disability funds (e.g., California, New Jersey, New York, Rhode Island, Washington and West Virginia) are deductible as itemized deductions (as state income taxes). However, employee contributions to *private* disability benefit plans (e.g., California, New Jersey and New York) are not deductible by employees.[81] See, also, the checklist at ¶ 57.

923. Social Security Tax. The federal social security tax on an employer is deductible by the employer as a business expense. The contribution of an employer on wages paid to a domestic worker is not deductible unless it is classified as a business expense.[82]

The tax imposed on employees by the Social Security Act is not deductible by the employee. If the employer pays the tax without deduction from the employee's

---

Footnote references are to paragraphs of the 2002 Standard Federal Tax Reports.

¶ 920

[75] ¶ 14,402	[78] ¶ 9500	[81] ¶ 9502.023,
[76] ¶ 14,402	[79] ¶ 9502.06	¶ 9502.063
[77] ¶ 14,402	[80] ¶ 9502.063	[82] ¶ 9502.30

wages under an agreement with the employee, the amount is deductible by the employer and is income to the employee (Rev. Rul. 86-14).[83]

A self-employed individual may deduct from gross income 50% of the self-employment tax imposed for the same tax year (Code Sec. 164(f)).[84] See, also, ¶ 2670.

924. Federal and State Income Taxes. Federal income taxes are not deductible in determining taxable income (Code Sec. 275).[85] However, they are deductible in determining the amount of a corporation's income subject to the accumulated earnings tax (¶ 251) (Reg. § 1.535-2) and the personal holding company tax (¶ 275) (Reg. § 1.545-2).[86] Corporations and partnerships may deduct their state income taxes as business expenses. State income taxes that are based on net business income may only be deducted by self-employed individuals on Schedule A of Form 1040 as an itemized deduction. However, if the state income tax is based on gross business income, the tax may be deducted as a business expense (Temporary Reg. § 1.62-1T(d)).[87]

Charitable Contributions

927. Corporate Limits. The deduction of a corporation, for a contribution or gift to an organization described at ¶ 1061, is limited to 10% of its taxable income for the year in which the deduction was made computed without regard to (1) the deduction for charitable contributions, (2) the deductions for dividends received and for dividends paid on certain preferred stock of public utilities, (3) any net operating loss carryback to the tax year, and (4) any capital loss carryback to the tax year (Code Sec. 170(b)(2); Reg. § 1.170A-11(a)).[88]

928. Five-Year Carryover for Corporations. A corporation is permitted to carry over to the five succeeding tax years contributions that exceed the 10% limitation, but deductions in those years are also subject to the maximum limitation (Code Sec. 170(d)(2); Reg. § 1.170A-11(c)).[89]

929. Accrual-Basis Corporations. Except for the carryover rule (¶ 928), a deduction is allowed only for a contribution paid during the tax year. An accrual-basis corporation may elect to treat as paid during the tax year all or a portion of a contribution that is actually paid within two and one-half months after the close of the tax year if it was authorized by the board of directors during the year (Code Sec. 170(a)(2); Reg. § 1.170A-11(b)).[90]

930. Contributions of Inventory or Scientific Property. Generally, the deduction for a charitable contribution of ordinary income property is the fair market value of that property less the amount that would have been ordinary income if the property had been sold at its fair market value on the date of the contribution (see ¶ 1062). There are, however, three exceptions to this rule in the case of contributions by corporations.

Inventory-Type Property. If a corporation (other than an S corporation) makes a gift of inventory, property held for sale to customers in the ordinary course of business, or depreciable or real property used in the trade or business, it may—if certain conditions are met—deduct its basis for the property plus one-half of the property's unrealized appreciation. However, the claimed deduction may not exceed twice the basis of the property (Code Sec. 170(e)(3)).[91] Moreover, no deduction is allowed for any part of the appreciation that would be ordinary income resulting from recapture. To qualify, the gift must be made to a qualified public charity or a private operating foundation and the donee's use of the property must be for the care of infants, the ill or needy.

Scientific Research Property. A corporation (other than an S corporation, a personal holding company, or a service organization) is entitled to the same deduc-

[83] ¶ 5508.0146	[86] ¶ 23,042, ¶ 23,252	[89] ¶ 11,600, ¶ 11,672
[84] ¶ 9500	[87] ¶ 6003	[90] ¶ 11,600, ¶ 11,672
[85] ¶ 14,500	[88] ¶ 11,600, ¶ 11,672	[91] ¶ 11,600, ¶ 11,672

tion for a qualified research contribution of certain ordinary income property to an institution of higher education or to an exempt scientific research organization for research purposes as that described above for inventory-type property (Code Sec. 170(e)(4)).[92]

To qualify as a research contribution: (1) the contributed property must have been constructed by the donor, (2) the contribution must be made within two years of construction, and (3) the original use of the property must be by the donee. Additional requirements must also be met (Code Sec. 170(e)(4)(B)).[93]

Computer Equipment. Effective for tax years beginning after December 31, 1997 and before January 1, 2004, a corporation is entitled to an increased deduction for a charitable contribution of computer technology or equipment to an elementary or secondary school (and public libraries after December 31, 2000). The amount of the deduction is equal to the taxpayer's basis in the donated property plus one-half of the amount of ordinary income that would have been realized if the property had been sold. The deduction may not exceed twice the taxpayer's basis in the donated property (Code Sec. 170(e)(6)).

931. Contribution Rules. The rules concerning a deduction for the following charitable contributions are the same regardless of whether the contribution is made by a corporate or a noncorporate taxpayer: (1) gifts of appreciated property, see ¶ 1062; (2) use of property—partial interests, see ¶ 1063; (3) reduction for interest, see ¶ 1065; (4) gift of future interest in tangible personal property, see ¶ 1069; (5) transfers in trust, see ¶ 1070; (6) appraisals, see ¶ 1071; and (7) denial of deduction, see ¶ 1068.

Interest

937. Business Expense. Interest expense incurred in a trade or business or in the production of rental or royalty income is deductible from gross income. See ¶ 1055 and ¶ 1056 for the rules on prepaid interest and ¶ 1094 for the rules on investment interest paid by noncorporate taxpayers.

937A. Interest on Income Tax Liability. Interest paid or accrued on income tax assessed on an individual's federal, state or local income tax liability is not a business deduction even though the tax due is related to income from a trade or business (Temporary Reg. § 1.163-9T(b)(2)(i)(A)).[94] This rule also applies to an individual's partnership and S corporation activities. See ¶ 2723 and ¶ 2724 for interest allocations pursuant to compromise and partial payments. Penalties on deficiencies and underestimated tax cannot be deducted.

938. Bank. A bank or trust company may deduct from gross income interest paid within the year on deposits and certificates of indebtedness (Reg. § 1.163-1(c)).[95]

939. Margin Account. Interest on a margin account is deductible by a cash basis investor when it is paid to the broker or when the interest becomes available to the broker through the investor's account.[96] See ¶ 1094 for investment interest.

940. Exceptions and Limitations. There are a number of Code sections which limit or preclude a taxpayer from claiming an interest deduction on certain types of indebtedness. See also ¶ 1045 for limits on personal interest.

Original Issue Discount Bonds. The interest deduction is generally limited (Code Sec. 163(e)).[97] See ¶ 1952.

Bonds Not in Registered Form. Failure to meet the registration requirement generally results in a denial of an interest deduction (Code Sec. 163(f)).[98] See ¶ 1963.

Commodity Straddles. Interest on debt incurred to purchase or carry commodity investments that are part of a straddle is not currently deductible. The interest

Footnote references are to paragraphs of the 2002 Standard Federal Tax Reports.

[92] ¶ 11,600	[95] ¶ 9103	[97] ¶ 9102
[93] ¶ 11,600	[96] ¶ 9104.048	[98] ¶ 9102
[94] ¶ 9400		

¶ 931

must be added to the basis of the commodity. Hedging transactions, however, are exempted from this capitalization rule (Code Sec. 263(g)).[99]

Mortgage Credit Certificates. The deduction for interest paid or accrued on indebtedness with respect to which an MCC has been issued is reduced by the amount of credit allowable (Code Sec. 163(g)).[100]

Corporate Indebtedness Incurred to Acquire Another Corporation's Stock. Generally, there is a $5 million annual limit on the interest deductible by a corporation on a debt incurred to acquire stock or two-thirds of the operating assets of another corporation (Code Sec. 279).[101]

Uniform Capitalization Rules. Interest paid or incurred during the production period and allocable to real property or tangible personal property may be required to be capitalized (Code Sec. 263A(f)).[102] See ¶ 993.

Employee's Expenses

941. Deductions from Gross Income. The performance of services as an employee is considered to be a trade or business. Thus, employee business expenses are generally deductible. *Reimbursed* employee business expenses are deductible from gross income (Code Sec. 62(a)(2)(A)).[103] However, in actual practice, employees do not claim the deductions on their returns because employers are instructed not to report the reimbursed amount in the employee's gross income (see ¶ 942). Generally, *unreimbursed* employee business expenses are deductible only as miscellaneous itemized deductions and the deduction is subject to a 2% floor (see ¶ 1011) and the 50% limit for meal and entertainment expenses (60% limit in 2001 for certain employees in the transportation industry) (see ¶ 910).[104] However, special rules apply to qualified performing artists (see ¶ 941A), statutory employees (see ¶ 941B), and impairment-related work expenses (see ¶ 1013). An employee is also allowed a deduction from gross income for jury duty pay surrendered to an employer in exchange for regular salary (Code Sec. 62(a)(13)) (see ¶ 1010).[105]

Expenses paid or incurred with respect to services performed by an official as an employee of a State or local government are deductible in computing adjusted gross income (Code Sec. 62(a)(2)(C)). The employee must be compensated in whole or in part on a fee basis.

941A. Performing Artist. A qualified performing artist may deduct business expenses in arriving at adjusted gross income on Form 2106 or 2106-EZ. Generally, to qualify for this deduction an individual must (1) render services in the performing arts during the tax year for at least two employers, (2) have total business deductions attributable to the performance of such services that exceed 10% of the income received from such services, and (3) have adjusted gross income of $16,000 or less (determined prior to the application of this provision) (Code Sec. 62(b)(1) and (2)).[106]

941B. Statutory Employees. Individuals who are considered to be "statutory employees" may deduct their allowable business expenses from gross income.[107] The term "statutory employees" includes:

(1) A full-time traveling or city salesperson who solicits orders from wholesalers, restaurants, or similar establishments on behalf of a principal. The merchandise sold must be for resale (e.g., food sold to a restaurant) or for supplies used in the buyer's business.

(2) A full-time life insurance agent whose principal business activity is selling life insurance and/or annuity contracts for one life insurance company.

(3) An agent-driver or commission-driver engaged in distributing meat, vegetables, bakery goods, beverages (other than milk), or laundry or dry cleaning services.

Footnote references are to paragraphs of the 2002 Standard Federal Tax Reports.

[99] ¶ 13,700　　[102] ¶ 13,800　　[105] ¶ 6002
[100] ¶ 9102　　[103] ¶ 6002　　[106] ¶ 6002
[101] ¶ 14,700, ¶ 14,708.30　　[104] ¶ 6004　　[107] ¶ 8524.2547

¶941B

(4) A home worker performing work on material or goods furnished by the employer.

An employer should indicate on the worker's Form W-2 whether the worker is classified as a statutory employee. Statutory employees report their wages, income and allowable expenses on Schedule C (or Schedule C-EZ). Statutory employees are not liable for self-employment tax because their employers are obligated to treat such individuals as employees for social security tax purposes.

942. Reimbursed Expenses of Employee. The tax treatment of an employee's business expenses depends upon whether the reimbursement or expense allowance arrangement is an accountable or nonaccountable plan.[108] Expenses that are reimbursed under an *accountable* plan (¶ 943) are not reported as income on an employee's Form W-2. As a result, employees should not account for them on their tax returns (Reg. § 1.62-2(c)(4)).[109] In this situation, the percentage limit on deductions for meals and entertainment applies to the employer (¶ 910). Any amounts considered paid under a *nonaccountable* plan must be included in the employee's income (Reg. § 1.62-2(c)(5)). If deductible business expenses exceed charges and reimbursements considered paid by an accountable plan, and these expenses are substantiated (¶ 953), then the excess expenses are deductible as miscellaneous itemized deductions, subject to the 2% floor (¶ 1011) and the 50% limit for meals and entertainment (¶ 910) (Code Sec. 62; Reg. § 1.62-1(e)).[110]

Withholding rules relating to employee expense reimbursements are explained at ¶ 2662 and ¶ 2663.

943. Accountable v. Nonaccountable Plans. A plan under which an employee is reimbursed for expenses or receives an allowance to cover expenses is an *accountable* plan only if the following three conditions are satisfied: (1) there must be a business connection for the expenses; (2) the employee must either substantiate or be deemed to have substantiated the expenses; and (3) the employee must return to the employer amounts in excess of the substantiated (or deemed substantiated) expenses (Reg. § 1.62-2(c)).[111] An expense allowance or reimbursement arrangement that would be partly an accountable plan and partly a nonaccountable plan if the two parts were separately considered will be treated as two separate arrangements, one an accountable plan and the other a nonaccountable plan (Reg. § 1.62-2(d)(2)).

Business Connection. The business connection requirement generally is satisfied if the expenses are incurred in connection with the performance of services as an employee. Advance payments must be made within a reasonable time of the date on which it is anticipated that the expense will occur or the advance will not be treated as meeting the business connection requirement (Reg.§ 1.62-2(f)(1)).[112]

Substantiation. The verification necessary to meet the accountable plan substantiation requirement depends upon whether the expense falls within one of the following categories of expenses: meals, lodging, entertainment, gifts and expenses attributable to the use of "listed property" (¶ 953). For these expenses, the accountable plan substantiation requirement is satisfied if enough information is submitted to the employer to satisfy the substantiation requirements of Code Sec. 274, including travel and automobile expenses deemed substantiated. (See ¶ 947 for deemed substantiation of car expenses and ¶ 954 for per diem rules for travel away from home.) If the expense is not in one of the categories stated above, such as expenses for printing a report, then the expense is considered substantiated if enough information is submitted to the employer to enable the employer to identify the specific nature of each expense and to conclude that the expense was attributable to the employee's business activities (Reg. § 1.62-2(e)(3)).[113]

Return of Excess Amounts. An employee must return amounts received in excess of those substantiated or deemed substantiated within a reasonable period of time.[114] If the employee fails to return the excess within a reasonable period of time,

---

Footnote references are to paragraphs of the 2002 Standard Federal Tax Reports.

¶ 942

[108] ¶ 6004
[109] ¶ 6004
[110] ¶ 6004
[111] ¶ 6004
[112] ¶ 6004
[113] ¶ 6004
[114] ¶ 6004

only amounts paid that are not in excess of the amounts substantiated will be treated as paid under an accountable plan. Excess amounts retained will be treated as paid under a nonaccountable plan and must be included in income by the employee. An accountable plan that reimburses expenses pursuant to an IRS-approved allowance (see ¶ 947 and ¶ 954 et seq.) must require the return of the portion that relates to days or miles of travel not substantiated. Further, the allowance must be reasonably calculated not to exceed anticipated expenses.

Reasonable Period of Time. The substantiation or return of excess amounts must take place within a reasonable period of time. A reasonable period depends on facts and circumstances, but the IRS has provided two safe harbor methods: the fixed date method and the periodic statement method (Reg. § 1.62-2(g)).[115] Under the fixed date method, the following are treated as occurring within a reasonable period of time: (1) advance payments—30 days before reasonably anticipated expenses are paid or incurred; (2) substantiation—60 days after expenses are paid or incurred; and (3) return of excess amounts—120 days after expenses are paid or incurred.

The periodic statement method is a safe harbor for determining reasonable time for the return of excess amounts. Under this method, the employer must (1) give each employee periodic statements (no less than quarterly) that set forth the amounts paid under the reimbursement arrangement in excess of the substantiated amount and (2) request that the employee either substantiate or return the excess amounts within 120 days of the statement date.

Transportation and Car Expenses

945. Local Transportation Expenses. Local transportation expenses are generally those incurred for the business use of a car. However, they also include the cost of travel by rail, bus, or taxi. Businesses (including self-employed persons and statutory employees) may deduct ordinary and necessary local transportation expenses from gross income (Reg. § 1.162-1(a)).[116] The manner of an employee's deduction for transportation expenses generally depends on whether the employee is reimbursed under an accountable plan. See ¶ 943.

Commuting Expenses. Commuting expenses between a taxpayer's residence and a business location within the area of the taxpayer's tax home generally are not deductible.[117] However, a deduction is allowed for expenses incurred in excess of ordinary commuting expenses for transporting job-related tools and materials.[118] An individual who works at two or more different places in a day may deduct the costs of getting from one place to the other.[119]

There is an exception to the general rule that commuting expenses are not deductible. If a taxpayer has at least one regular place of business away from home, then daily transportation expenses for commuting between the taxpayer's residence and a *temporary* work location in the same trade or business can be deducted (Rev. Rul. 99-7).[120] For this purpose, a temporary work location is defined using a one-year standard. If employment at a work location is realistically expected to last (and does in fact last) for one year or less, the employment is temporary, absent facts and circumstances to the contrary. Employment at a work location is not temporary, regardless of whether or not it lasts for more than one year, if it is realistically expected to last more than one year or there is no realistic expectation that employment will last for one year or less. A taxpayer may at first realistically expect that employment at a work location will last one year or less, but at a later date, realistically expect that the work will last for more than one year. In this situation, the employment will be treated as temporary until the date that the taxpayer's realistic expectation changes and will be treated as not temporary after that date (unless facts and circumstances indicate otherwise).

Footnote references are to paragraphs of the 2002 Standard Federal Tax Reports.

[115] ¶ 6004   [117] ¶ 8550.269   [119] ¶ 8570.175
[116] ¶ 8501   [118] ¶ 8590.25   [120] ¶ 8570.146

¶945

Prior to Rev. Rul. 99-7, the term "temporary work location" was defined as a work location where the taxpayer performed services on an irregular or short-term basis (Rev. Rul. 90-23).

For the rules concerning deductions while on a temporary assignment "away from home," see ¶951.

Travel from a Home Office. Individuals who use their homes as their principal place of business (¶961) are permitted to deduct transportation expenses between their homes and another work location in the same trade or business (Rev. Rul. 99-7).[121] This rule applies regardless of whether the work location is temporary or regular and regardless of the distance. A Tax Court decision permitted an individual to deduct daily transportation costs incurred in traveling between his home and numerous temporary work sites because the home was the individual's "regular place of business."[122] However, the IRS has ruled that it will not follow the Tax Court's decision in such a situation unless the residence is also the taxpayer's principal place of business (Rev. Rul. 94-47).[123] See ¶961 for a discussion of home office expenses.

946. Car Expense. Expenses for gasoline, oil, tires, repairs, insurance, depreciation, parking fees and tolls, licenses, and garage rent incurred for cars used in a trade or business are deductible. The deduction is allowed only for that part of the expenses that is attributable to business.[124] Generally, an employee's unreimbursed expenses can be deducted only as a miscellaneous itemized deduction subject to the 2% floor (Code Sec. 67).[125] See ¶941. See ¶1214 concerning depreciation of a car.

947. Substantiation of Car Expenses. A taxpayer can substantiate car expenses by keeping an exact record of the amount paid for gasoline, insurance, and other costs. However, the standard mileage rate method is a simplified method available to both employees and self-employed persons in computing deductions for car expenses in lieu of calculating the operating and fixed costs allocable to business purposes (Rev. Proc. 2000-48).[126]

Standard Mileage Rate. Under the standard mileage method, the taxpayer determines the amount of the allowable deduction by multiplying all the business miles driven during the year by the standard mileage rate. The standard mileage rate is 34.5 cents a mile for *all* miles driven in 2001 (Rev. Proc. 2000-48) (36.5 cents per mile in 2002 (Rev. Proc. 2001-54)). The business portion of parking fees and tolls may be deducted in addition to the standard mileage rate (Rev. Proc. 2000-48).

Rural mail carriers who receive a qualified reimbursement for expenses incurred for the use of their vehicles for performing the collection and delivery of mail in a rural route are allowed a deduction for an amount equal to the qualified reimbursements received (Code Sec. 162(o)).[127]

The standard mileage rate method may be utilized by self-employed individuals or employees who own or lease a car and operate only one car at a time for business purposes (Rev. Proc. 2000-48; Temporary Reg. § 1.274(d)-1T). The standard mileage rate is not available for cars used for hire (taxicabs) or two or more cars used simultaneously (fleet). Use of the standard mileage rate in the first year of business use is considered an election to exclude the car from MACRS depreciation (Rev. Proc. 2000-48) (¶1236).

Fixed and Variable Rate (FAVR) Method. An employee's car expenses will be deemed substantiated if the payor (usually the employer) reimburses the employee's expenses with a mileage allowance using a flat rate or a stated schedule that combines periodic fixed and variable payments. At least five employees must be covered by such an arrangement at all times during the calendar year, but at no time can the majority of covered employees be management employees. There are additional requirements that must be met (Rev. Proc. 2000-48).

Footnote references are to paragraphs of the 2002 Standard Federal Tax Reports.

[121] ¶8570.012	[124] ¶8501	[126] ¶8590.55
[122] ¶8570.146	[125] ¶6060	[127] ¶8500
[123] ¶8590.0414		

948. Interest on Car Loans. Interest paid by an employee on a car loan is nondeductible personal interest. See ¶ 1045. A self-employed taxpayer may claim the interest paid on the business portion of a car as a business expense. The remaining nonbusiness portion is nondeductible personal interest (Code Sec. 163(a)).[128]

Traveling Expenses Away from Home

949. Traveling Expenses Generally. A deduction is allowed for ordinary and necessary traveling expenses incurred by a taxpayer while *away from home* in the conduct of a trade or business (Code Sec. 162(a)(2); Reg. § 1.162-2).[129] Individuals are not "away from home" unless their duties require them to be away from the general area of their tax homes for a period substantially longer than an ordinary workday and it is reasonable for them to need to sleep or rest. In some cases, then, travel expenses may be deductible even though the taxpayer is away from home for a period of less than 24 hours.[130]

950. "Home" Defined. A taxpayer's "home" is considered to be (1) the taxpayer's regular or principal (if there is more than one regular) place of business or (2) if the taxpayer has no regular or principal place of business because of the nature of the work, the taxpayer's regular place of abode in a real and substantial sense.[131]

If a taxpayer fails to fall within either category, the taxpayer is an itinerant (i.e., one who has a home wherever one happens to be working) and, thus, is never "away from home" for purposes of the traveling expense deduction.[132]

When there are multiple areas of business activity or places of regular employment, the principal place of business is treated as the tax home. In determining the principal place, the following factors are considered: (1) the time spent on business activity in each area, (2) the amount of business activity in each area, and (3) the amount of the resulting financial return in each area. Business travel expenses incurred while away from the principal place of business are deductible.[133]

The tax home of a member of the U.S. Congress is the member's residence in the state or Congressional District that the member represents. However, deductions for meals and lodging while in Washington are limited to $3,000 per year, after applying the 2% floor (Code Sec. 162(a)).[134]

The Supreme Court has held that a member of the Armed Forces is not "away from home" while at the individual's permanent duty station.[135]

951. Temporary v. Indefinite Test. In determining when an individual is "away from home," the nature of the stay and the length of time away from the individual's principal place of business are of prime importance. If the assignment is *temporary* in nature, the taxpayer is considered "away from home" and a traveling expense deduction is allowed. If the assignment is for an *indefinite* period of time, the location of the assignment becomes the individual's new "tax home," and the individual may not deduct traveling expenses while there. When an individual works away from home, at a single location, for one year or more, the employment will be treated as indefinite and related travel expenses will not be deductible (Code Sec. 162(a)).[136] Employment expected to last more than one year is classified as indefinite, regardless of whether the work actually exceeds a year (Rev. Rul. 93-86).

The one-year rule does not apply to travel expenses of federal employees certified by the Attorney General while traveling on behalf of the United States in temporary duty status to investigate or prosecute, or to provide support services for the investigation or prosecution of, a federal crime (Code Sec. 162(a)).

952. Deductible Travel Expenses. The following expenses paid or incurred while traveling away from home ordinarily are deductible: travel, meals, and lodg-

---

Footnote references are to paragraphs of the 2002 Standard Federal Tax Reports.

[128] ¶ 9102	[131] ¶ 8570.1327	[134] ¶ 8500
[129] ¶ 8500, ¶ 8527	[132] ¶ 8570.1327	[135] ¶ 8570.0652
[130] ¶ 8550.269,	[133] ¶ 8570.1327	[136] ¶ 8500
¶ 8550.4661, ¶ 8570.154		

ing; transportation, plus a reasonable amount for baggage, necessary samples and display materials; hotel rooms, sample rooms, telephone and fax services, and public stenographers; and the costs (including depreciation—see ¶ 1211) of maintaining and operating a car for business purposes.[137]

Travel expenses are not allowed for a spouse, dependent, or other individual who accompanies the taxpayer on a business trip unless such person is an employee of the person who is paying or reimbursing the expenses, the travel of such person serves a bona fide business purpose, and the expenses of such person are otherwise deductible (Code Sec. 274(m)(3)).[138]

A taxpayer may deduct traveling expenses between the principal place of business and place of business at a temporary or minor post of duty. When the taxpayer's family lives at the temporary or minor post of duty, the taxpayer may still claim travel expenses. However, the deduction for meal and lodging is limited to the portion of the taxpayer's expenses that are allocable to the taxpayer's presence there in the actual performance of the taxpayer's duties (Rev. Rul. 55-604).[139]

The deduction for the cost of meals and lodging while away from home on business is limited to amounts that are not lavish or extravagant under the circumstances (Code Sec. 162(a)(2)).[140]

953. Code Sec. 274 Substantiation Requirements. In order to claim any deduction, a taxpayer must be able to prove that the expenses were in fact paid or incurred. The following expenses, which are deemed particularly susceptible to abuse, must generally be substantiated by adequate records or sufficient evidence corroborating the taxpayer's own statement: expenses with respect to travel away from home (including meals and lodging), entertainment expenses, business gifts, and expenses in connection with the use of "listed property" (such as cars and computers—see ¶ 1211). The expenses must be substantiated as to (1) amount, (2) time and place, and (3) business purpose. For entertainment and gift expenses, the business relationship of the person being entertained or receiving the gift must also be substantiated (Temporary Reg. § 1.274-5T(a)-(c)).[141]

Employee's Substantiation of Reimbursed Expenses. An employee's expenses are substantiated, for purposes of the accountable plan requirements (¶ 943), if the employee provides an adequate accounting of the expenses to the employer in the form of adequate records (Temporary Reg. § 1.274-5T(f)(4)).[142] The adequate accounting requirement can be satisfied as to the *amount* of lodging and/or meals and incidental expenses by using the per diem allowances discussed at ¶ 954—¶ 954B.

Substantiation by Adequate Records. A contemporaneous log is not required, but a record of the elements of the expense or use of the listed property made at or near the time of the expenditure or use, supported by sufficient documentary evidence, has a high degree of credibility. Adequate accounting generally requires the submission of an account book, expense diary or log, or similar record maintained by the employee and recorded at or near the time of incurrence of the expense. Documentary evidence, such as receipts or paid bills, is not generally required for expenses that are less than $75. Documentary evidence for lodging expenses is required (Temporary Reg. § 1.274-5T(c)(2)(iii)).[143] The employee should also maintain a record of any amounts charged to the employer.

The *Cohan* rule, which may be used by the courts to estimate the amount of a taxpayer's expenses when adequate records do not exist, may not be used to estimate the expenses covered by Code Sec. 274 (Temporary Reg. § 1.274-5T(a)(1)).[144] However, if a taxpayer has established that the records have been lost due to circumstances beyond the taxpayer's control, such as destruction by fire or flood, then the taxpayer has a right to substantiate claimed deductions by a reasonable construction of the expenditures or use (Temporary Reg. § 1.274-5T(c)(5)).[145]

Footnote references are to paragraphs of the 2002 Standard Federal Tax Reports.

[137] ¶ 8527	[140] ¶ 8500	[143] ¶ 14,410
[138] ¶ 14,402	[141] ¶ 14,410	[144] ¶ 14,410
[139] ¶ 8570.175	[142] ¶ 14,410	[145] ¶ 14,410

¶ 953

Employees of the executive and judicial branches and certain employees of the legislative branch of the federal government may substantiate their requests for reimbursement of ordinary and necessary business expenses with an account book or expense log instead of submitting documentary evidence (e.g., receipts or bills) (Rev. Proc. 97-45).

954. Per Diem Methods of Substantiating Meals and Lodging Expenses. A taxpayer must substantiate the amount, time, place, and business purpose of expenses paid or incurred in traveling away from home. Although the taxpayer has the option of keeping the actual records of travel expenses, the IRS has provided per diem allowances under which the *amount* of away-from-home meals and lodging expenses may be deemed to be substantiated. These per diem allowances eliminate the need for substantiating actual costs (Rev. Proc. 2001-47).[146] Per diem allowances may be used only if the time, place and business purpose of the travel are substantiated by adequate records or other evidence.

Although most frequently used in the employer-employee relationship, per diem allowances may be used in connection with arrangements between any payor and payee, such as between independent contractors and those contracting with them. However, employees related to the payor within the related party rules of Code Sec. 267(b) (using a 10% common ownership standard) cannot use per diem substantiation methods.

Employees. The per diem method can be used to substantiate an employee's *reimbursed* expenses only if the arrangement is considered an accountable plan and the allowance (1) is paid with respect to ordinary and necessary expenses incurred or which the employer reasonably expects to be incurred by an employee for lodging, meal and/or incidental expenses while traveling away from home in connection with the performance of services as an employee, (2) is reasonably calculated not to exceed the amount of the expense or the anticipated expenses, and (3) is paid at the applicable federal per diem rate, a flat rate or stated schedule.

Types of Per Diem Allowances. There are two types of per diem allowances: (1) M&IE only, which provides a per diem allowance for meals and incidental expenses only, and (2) lodging plus M&IE, which provides a per diem allowance to cover lodging as well as meals and incidental expenses. Incidental expenses include expenses for laundry, dry cleaning, and tips. However, telephone calls and taxicab fares are not considered incidental expenses and must be accounted for separately.

Allowances Exceeding Federal Rates. If expenses are substantiated using a per diem amount, regardless of whether it covers lodging plus M&IE or only M&IE, and reimbursement exceeds the relevant federal rates for that type of allowance, then the employee (or independent contractor) is required to include the excess in gross income. The excess portion is treated as paid under a nonaccountable plan; thus, it must be reported on the employee's W-2 and is subject to withholding.

954A. Lodging Plus Meals and Incidental Expenses Per Diem. Under the lodging plus M&IE per diem method, the amount of an employee's (or other payee's) *reimbursed* expenses that is deemed substantiated is equal to the lesser of the per diem allowance or the amount computed at the federal per diem rate for the locality of travel for the period in which the employee is away from home (Rev. Proc. 2001-47). Lodging receipts are not required if per diem allowances are used to substantiate such expenses. The locality of travel is the locality where the employee who is traveling on business away from home stops for sleep or rest. Employees and self-employed individuals may determine their allowable deductions for *un-reimbursed* meals and incidental expenses while away from home by using the applicable federal M&IE rate (see ¶ 954B). Under this method, lodging costs must be substantiated by required records (e.g., hotel receipts).

Per Diem Rates. The federal per diem rate for lodging plus M&IE depends upon the locality of travel. For various geographic areas within the continental

United States (the 48 contiguous states plus the District of Columbia) (CONUS), the federal per diem rate for a given locality is equal to the sum of a maximum lodging amount and the M&IE rate for that locality.

Federal per diem rates have also been established for nonforeign localities outside of the continental United States (OCONUS). These areas include Alaska, Hawaii, Puerto Rico, and possessions of the United States. Rates are also established for foreign travel (foreign OCONUS).

Rates for CONUS, OCONUS and foreign travel are published under the Federal Travel Regulations for government travel and are updated periodically. Per diem tables appear at ¶ 180.25 and following of the 2002 STANDARD FEDERAL TAX REPORTER or the tables may be found at ¶ 77—¶ 80 of the loose-leaf edition of the 2002 U.S. MASTER TAX GUIDE. For the last three months of 2001, taxpayers have the option of continuing to use the CONUS rates that were in effect from January 1, 2001 through September 30, 2001, or switching to the rates that went into effect on October 1, 2001 (Rev. Proc. 2001-47).

High-Low Method. In lieu of using the maximum per diem rate from the CONUS table, the high-low method, which is a simplified method for determining a lodging plus M&IE per diem, can be used to compute per diem allowances for travel within the continental United States. This method divides all CONUS localities into two categories: low-cost or high-cost localities.

For October 1, 2000, through September 30, 2001, the following per diem rates for lodging expenses and M&IE were set by the IRS for high-cost and low-cost localities (Rev. Proc. 2000-39):[147]

	Lodging expense rate	M&IE rate	Maximum per diem rate
High-cost locality....................	$159	$42	$201
Low-cost locality	90	34	124

For October 1, 2001 through September 31, 2002, the following per diem rates for lodging expenses and M&IE were set by the IRS for high-cost and low-cost localities (Rev. Proc. 2001-47):

	Lodging expense rate	M&IE rate	Maximum per diem rate
High-cost locality....................	$162	$42	$204
Low-cost locality	91	34	125

Certain areas are treated as high-cost only during designated periods of the year (e.g., a peak tourist season) and low-cost during other periods of time. Thus, employers who use the high-low method must determine whether the employee traveled in a high-cost area and if the area was classified as high-cost during the actual period of travel.

If the high-low method is used for an employee, then the payor may not use the actual federal maximum per diem rates for that employee during the calendar year for travel within the continental United States. However, the applicable federal rates for travel outside the continental United States (OCONUS rates) may be used, and the M&IE-only rate may be used or the reimbursement of actual expenses may be made.

Proration of M&IE Allowance. If an individual is traveling away from home for only a portion of the day, there are two alternative methods that may be used to prorate the per diem rate or the M&IE rate. Under the first method, 75% of the M&IE rate (or the M&IE portion of the per diem rate) is allowed for each partial day during which an employee or self-employed individual is traveling on business. Under the second method ("the reasonable business practice method"), the M&IE rate is prorated using any method that is consistently applied and in accordance with reasonable business practice. For example, if an employee travels from 9 a.m. one day until 5 p.m. the next day, a proration method that gives an amount equal to

Footnote references are to paragraphs of the 2002 Standard Federal Tax Reports.

¶**954A** [147] ¶ 14,417.421

2 times the M&IE rate will be treated as in accordance with reasonable business practice (Rev. Proc. 2001-47).

Transition Rules. Taxpayers who used the standard federal per diem substantiation method for reimbursement of an individual's travel expenses during the first nine months of calendar-year 2001 may not use the high-low substantiation method for reimbursement until January 1, 2002. Likewise, taxpayers who used the high-low substantiation method for reimbursement of an individual's travel expenses during the first nine months of calendar-year 2001 must continue to use that method for the remainder of calendar-year 2001. However, taxpayers who use the high-low method of substantiation during the first nine months of calendar-year 2001 to reimburse an individual's travel expense have the option of either continuing to use the rates and localities in effect for travel before October 1, 2002, or to use the rates and localities in effect for travel on or after October 1, 2001, and before January 1, 2002. The rates and localities that the taxpayer elects to use for reimbursement of an individual's travel expense must be used consistently during this October - December period (Rev. Proc. 2001-47).

954B. Meals-and-Incidental-Expense-Only Per Diem Allowances. An M&IE-only per diem allowance may be used to substantiate an employee's (or other payee's) meal and incidental expenses only if the payor (1) pays the actual expenses for lodging, either to the employee or to the one who furnishes the lodging, (2) provides the lodging in kind or (3) does not have a reasonable belief that lodging expenses were or will be incurred. The amount that is deemed substantiated is equal to the lesser of the per diem allowance or the amount computed at the federal M&IE rate for the locality of travel for the period that the employee is away from home.

Detailed per diem tables appear at ¶ 180.25 and following of the 2002 STANDARD FEDERAL TAX REPORTER or the tables may be found ¶ 77—¶ 80 of the loose-leaf edition of the 2002 U.S. MASTER TAX GUIDE.

If meal and incidental expenses are substantiated using a per diem allowance, the entire amount is treated as a food and beverage expense subject to the 50% limitation on meal and entertainment expenses.

The M&IE rate must be prorated for partial days of travel away from home. (See the discussion on proration at ¶ 954A.)

Self-Employed Persons and Employees. Self-employed individuals and employees whose expenses are not reimbursed may also use the M&IE-only rate to substantiate meal and incidental expenses while traveling away from home. The taxpayer must actually prove (through adequate records or sufficient corroborative evidence (see ¶ 953)) the time, place and business purpose of the travel (Rev. Proc. 2001-47). While the M&IE rate may be used, the amount of lodging costs must be proven by documentary evidence (e.g., a receipt).

Transportation Workers. An individual is in the transportation industry only if the individual's work (1) directly involves moving people or goods by airplane, barge, bus, ship, train, or truck and (2) regularly requires travel away from home that involves travel to localities with differing federal M&IE rates during a single trip.

The MI&E rates for travel from October 1, 2001, through September 30, 2002, for self-employed persons or employees in the transportation industry are $38 for CONUS travel and $42 for OCONUS travel (Rev. Proc. 2001-47). These are the same rates (i.e., $38 and $42, respectively) that were in effect for travel from January 1, 2000, through September 30, 2000, (Rev. Proc. 2000-9) [148] and for travel from October 1, 2000, through September 30, 2001 (Rev. Proc. 2000-39).

Transition Rules. Taxpayers under the calendar-year convention for the transportation industry, who used the federal M&IE rates during the first nine months of calendar year 2001 to substantiate the amount of an individual's travel expense, may not use the special transportation industry rates until January 1, 2002.

Likewise, taxpayers who used the special transportation industry rates for the first nine months of calendar year 2001 to substantiate the amount of an individual's travel expenses may not use the federal M&IE rates until January 1, 2002 (Rev. Proc. 2001-47).

955. Foreign Travel. Generally, traveling expenses (including meals and lodging) of a taxpayer who travels outside of the United States away from home must be allocated between time spent on the trip for business and time spent for pleasure. However, when the trip is for not more than one week or when the time spent on personal activities on the trip is less than 25% of the total time away from home, no allocation is required (Code Sec. 274(c)(2)).[149] Also, no allocation is required when the traveling expenses are incurred for a trip within the United States and the trip is entirely for business reasons (Reg. § 1.162-2(b)).[150] If, however, expenses were incurred on a purely personal side trip, they would be nondeductible even though all the travel was within the U.S.

When the foreign trip is longer than a week (seven consecutive days counting the day of return but not the day of departure) or 25% or more of the time away from home is spent for personal reasons, a deduction for travel expenses will be denied to the extent that they are not allocable to the taxpayer's business (or the taxpayer's management of income-producing property) (Code Sec. 274(c)(2)).[151]

No allocation is required on a foreign trip when (1) the individual traveling had no substantial control over the arranging of the business trip or (2) a personal vacation was not a major consideration in making the trip. An employee traveling under a reimbursement or expense account allowance arrangement is not considered as having substantial control over the arranging of a business trip unless the employee is a managing executive (an employee who can, without being vetoed, decide on whether and when to make the trip) or is a 10%-or-more owner of the employer (Reg. § 1.274-4(f)(5)).[152]

If the trip is primarily personal in nature, travel expenses are not deductible even though the taxpayer engages in some business activities while at the destination. However, business expenses incurred while at the destination are deductible even though the travel expenses are not (Reg. § 1.162-2(b)).[153]

For special rules governing expenses of attending foreign conventions, seminars, and other similar meetings, see ¶ 959 and ¶ 960.

956. State Legislators. A state legislator whose residence is further than 50 miles from the state capitol building may elect to be deemed to be away from home in the pursuit of a trade or business on any day that the legislature is in session (including periods of up to four consecutive days when the legislature is not in session) or on any day when the legislature is not in session but the legislator's presence is formally recorded at a committee meeting (Code Sec. 162(h)).[154]

957. Luxury Water Travel. A deduction for transportation by ocean liner, cruise ship, or other form of water transportation is limited to a daily amount equal to twice the highest per diem travel amount allowable to employees of the federal government while on official business away from home, but within the U.S. However, the limitation does not apply to any expense allocable to a convention, seminar, or other meeting that is held on a cruise ship (¶ 959). Separately stated meal and entertainment expenses are subject to the 50% limitation rule (¶ 916), prior to the application of the per diem limitation. Statutory exceptions to the percentage limitation rule (¶ 917) are applicable (Code Sec. 274(m)).[155]

958. Travel as a Form of Education. A deduction for travel expenses is not allowed if such expense would be deductible only on the basis that the travel itself constitutes a form of education (Code Sec. 274(m)).[156] See, also, ¶ 1082.

Footnote references are to paragraphs of the 2002 Standard Federal Tax Reports.

¶ 955

[149] ¶ 14,402
[150] ¶ 8527
[151] ¶ 14,402
[152] ¶ 14,408
[153] ¶ 8527
[154] ¶ 8500
[155] ¶ 14,402
[156] ¶ 14,402

959. Convention Expenses. Deductible travel expenses include those incurred in attending a convention related to the taxpayer's business, even though the taxpayer is an employee (Code Sec. 274(h)).[157] The fact that an employee uses vacation or leave time or that attendance at the convention is voluntary will not necessarily negate the deduction (Reg. § 1.162-2(d)).[158] See, also, ¶ 960.

Production-of-Income Expenses. Expenses for a convention or meeting in connection with investments, financial planning, or other income-producing property are not deductible (Code Sec. 274(h)(7)).[159]

Cruise Ships. A limited deduction is available for expenses incurred for conventions on U.S. cruise ships. This deduction (limited to $2,000 with respect to all cruises beginning in any calendar year) applies only if (1) all ports of such cruise ship are located in the U.S. or in U.S. possessions, (2) the taxpayer establishes that the convention is directly related to the active conduct of his trade or business, and (3) the taxpayer includes certain specified information in the return on which the deduction is claimed (Code Sec. 274(h)(2)).[160]

960. Foreign Conventions. No deduction is allowed for expenses allocable to a "foreign convention" unless the taxpayer establishes that the meeting is directly related to the active conduct of his trade or business and that, after taking certain factors into account, it is "as reasonable" for the meeting to be held outside the North American area as within it. The factors to be taken into account are: (1) the purpose of the meeting and the activities taking place at such meeting, (2) the purposes and activities of the sponsoring organization or group, (3) the places of residence of the active members of the sponsoring organization or group and the places at which other meetings of the organization or group have been held or will be held, and (4) such other relevant factors as the taxpayer may present.

The term "foreign convention" means any convention, seminar, or similar meeting held outside the United States, its possessions, the Trust Territory of the Pacific Islands, Canada, or Mexico. Costs incurred in attending Caribbean conventions may be deductible if the country is a designated beneficiary country and there is in effect a bilateral or multilateral agreement providing for the exchange of tax information with the United States. No deduction is allowed, however, in a country found to discriminate in its tax laws against conventions held in the U.S. (Code Sec. 274(h)).[161] Expenses for foreign conventions on cruise ships are not deductible.

Home Office and Vacation Home Expenses

961. Business Use of Home. Taxpayers are not entitled to deduct any expenses for using their homes for business purposes unless the expenses are attributable to a portion of the home (or separate structure) *used exclusively on a regular basis* (1) as the *principal place* of any business carried on by the taxpayer, (2) as a place of business that is used by patients, clients, or customers in meeting or dealing with the taxpayer in the normal course of business, or (3) in connection with the taxpayer's business if the taxpayer is using a separate structure that is appurtenant to, but not attached to, the home (Code Sec. 280A(c)).[162] If the taxpayer is an employee, the business use of the home must also be for the convenience of the employer. The allowable deduction is computed on Form 8829 (Expenses for Business Use of Your Home).

Generally, a specific portion of the taxpayer's home must be used solely for the purpose of carrying on a trade or business in order to satisfy the exclusive use test. This requirement is not met if the portion is used for both business and personal purposes. However, an exception is provided for a wholesale or retail seller whose dwelling unit is the sole fixed location of the trade or business. In this situation, the ordinary and necessary expenses allocable to space within the dwelling unit that is used as a storage unit for inventory or product samples are deductible provided that

---

Footnote references are to paragraphs of the 2002 Standard Federal Tax Reports.

[157] ¶ 14,402
[158] ¶ 8527
[159] ¶ 14,402
[160] ¶ 14,402
[161] ¶ 14,402
[162] ¶ 14,850

¶**961**

the space is used on a regular basis and is a separately identifiable space suitable for storage (Code Sec. 280A(c)(2)).[163] Another special exception applies to licensed day care operators (Code Sec. 280A(c)(4)).[164] See ¶ 964.

Tax Years Beginning After 1998. The phrase "principal place of business" includes a place of business that is used by the taxpayer for the administrative or management activities of any trade or business of the taxpayer if there is no other fixed location of such trade or business where the taxpayer conducts substantial administrative or management activities of the trade or business (Code Sec. 280A(c)(1)).

Taxpayers who perform administrative or management activities for their trade or business at places other than the home office are not automatically prohibited from taking the deduction based on failure to meet the principal place of business requirement. According to the House Committee Report to P.L. 105-34, the following taxpayers are *not* prevented from taking a home office deduction under the new definition:[165]

(1) taxpayers who do not conduct substantial administrative or management activities at a fixed location other than the home office, even if administrative or management activities (e.g., billing activities) are performed by other people at other locations;

(2) taxpayers who carry out administrative and management activities at sites that are not fixed locations of the business (e.g., cars or hotel rooms) in addition to performing the activities at the home office;

(3) taxpayers who conduct an insubstantial amount of administrative and management activities at a fixed location other than the home office (e.g., occasionally doing minimal paperwork at another fixed location); and

(4) taxpayers who conduct substantial nonadministrative and nonmanagement business activities at a fixed location other than the home office (e.g., meeting with, or providing services to customers, clients or patients at a fixed location other than the home office).

Tax Years Beginning Before 1999. The Supreme Court's decision in *Soliman* (93-1 USTC ¶ 50,014) [166] established the test that was previously used to determine whether a particular location was the taxpayer's *principal* business location. Under this test only the most important, consequential, or influential location could be the principal location. The Court said that while the ultimate determination depends upon the facts of each situation, two primary steps were to be followed in making the determination: (1) the relative importance of the functions performed at each business location must be analyzed, and (2) if (1) did not result in a definitive answer, the amount of time spent in the home business location was compared to the time spent in each of the other places where business was conducted. In some situations, after applying the two steps, the conclusion may be reached that the individual had no principal place of business. As mentioned above, after 1998, the definition of a "principal place of business" has been expanded to cover home offices used to conduct administrative or management activities (Code Sec. 280A(c)(1)).

Residential Telephone. An individual is denied a business deduction for basic local telephone service charges on the first line in the residence. Additional charges for long-distance calls, equipment, optional services (e.g., call waiting), or additional telephone lines may be deductible (Code Sec. 262(b)).[167]

963. Limitation on Deduction. The home office deduction is limited to the gross income from the activity, reduced by expenses that are deductible without regard to business use (such as home mortgage interest) and all other deductible expenses attributable to the activity but not allocable to the use of the unit itself. Thus, a deduction is not allowed to the extent that it creates or increases a net loss

---

Footnote references are to paragraphs of the 2002 Standard Federal Tax Reports.

¶ **963**

[163] ¶ 14,850	[165] ¶ 14,850.017	[167] ¶ 13,600
[164] ¶ 14,850	[166] ¶ 14,854.50	

from the business activity to which it relates. Any disallowed deduction may be carried over, subject to the same limit in carryover years (Code Sec. 280A(c)(5)).[168]

Example. A teacher operates a retail sales business, in which she makes a qualified business use of a home office. Assume that 25% of the general expenses for the dwelling unit are allocable to the home office. The taxpayer's gross income and expenses from the retail sales business are:

	Total	Allocable to Office
Gross income		$25,000
Home Office Expenses		
Interest and property taxes	$8,000	$2,000
Insurance, maintenance, utilities	2,000	500
Depreciation	6,000	1,500
Total home office expenses		$ 4,000
Expenses allocable to retail sales business, but not allocable to home office use (e.g., supplies, wages paid)		$24,000
Total expenses		$28,000

The teacher must apply both the deductions allocable to her retail sales business and the deductions for taxes and interest allocable to the business use of the home ($26,000) against the gross income from the activity ($25,000) in order to determine the limitation on her deduction. Because the limitation amount (negative $1,000) is zero or less, the teacher cannot deduct expenses for depreciation, insurance, maintenance, and utilities, which would otherwise qualify. For the tax year, the teacher has a business loss of $1,000, and may carry forward the unused $2,000 of expenses to a succeeding year, again subject to the limitation.

964. Day Care Services. Taxpayers who use their personal residences on a regular basis in the trade or business of providing qualifying day care services (for the care of children, handicapped persons, or the elderly) do not have to meet the "exclusive use" test (¶ 961) in order to deduct business-related expenses. However, the deduction is available only if the taxpayer has applied for, has been granted, or is exempt from having a license, certification, or approval as a day care center or as a family or group day care home under the provisions of applicable state law (Code Sec. 280A(c)(4)).[169]

The actual deduction of expenses allocable to day care use is limited as described at ¶ 963. Form 8829 (Expenses for Business Use of Your Home) must be filed.

965. Home Office Deduction by Employees. In order for employees to qualify for the home office deduction, they must meet the requirements cited at ¶ 961. In addition, the exclusive use of the home office must be for the convenience of their employers (Code Sec. 280A(c)(1)).[170] However, regardless of whether or not an employee meets the requirements, an employee is denied a home office deduction for any portion of the home rented to the employer (except for expenses such as home mortgage interest and real property taxes that are deductible absent business use) (Code Sec. 280A(c)(6)).[171] Generally, an employee's home office expenses must be taken as a miscellaneous itemized deduction subject to the 2% of adjusted gross income floor on Schedule A of Form 1040 (¶ 941). However, statutory employees claim their allowable home office deductions on Schedule C (Schedule C-EZ may not be used). See ¶ 941B.

966. Deductions on Rental Residence or Vacation Home. Special rules limit the amount of deductions that may be taken by an individual or an S corporation in connection with the rental of a residence or vacation home, or a portion thereof, that is also used as the taxpayer's residence (Code Sec. 280A).[172]

Minimum Rental Use. If the property is rented for less than 15 days during the year, no deductions attributable to such rental are allowable and no rental income is

---

Footnote references are to paragraphs of the 2002 Standard Federal Tax Reports.

168 ¶ 14,850	170 ¶ 14,850	172 ¶ 14,850
169 ¶ 14,850	171 ¶ 14,850	

¶966

includible in gross income. Deductions allowed without regard to whether or not the home is used for business or the production of income (e.g., mortgage interest, property taxes, or a casualty loss) may still be deducted.

Minimum Personal Use. If the home is not used by the taxpayer for personal purposes for the greater of (a) more than 14 days during the tax year or (b) more than 10% of the number of days during the year for which the home is rented at a fair market rental, the limitations in Code Sec. 280A do not apply. However, the deductibility of expenses still may be subject to the hobby loss rules of Code Sec. 183 if the rental of the residence is not engaged in for profit. See ¶ 1195.

Deduction Limitations. If the property is rented for 15 or more days during the tax year and it is used by the taxpayer for personal purposes for the greater of (a) more than 14 days or (b) more than 10% of the number of days during the year for which the home is rented, the rental deductions are limited. Under this limitation the amount of the rental activity deductions may not exceed the amount by which the gross income derived from such activity exceeds the deductions otherwise allowable for the property, such as interest and taxes. According to the IRS, expenses attributable to the use of the rental unit are limited in the same manner as that prescribed under the hobby loss rules at ¶ 1195 (i.e., the total deductions may not exceed the gross rental income and the expenses are further limited to a percentage that represents the total days rented divided by the total days used). However, the Tax Court has rejected this formula (the decision has been affirmed on appeal by both the Ninth and Tenth Circuit Courts of Appeals).[173] It is the Tax Court's position that mortgage interest and real estate taxes are not subject to the same percentage limitations as are other expenses because they are assessed on an annual basis without regard to the number of days that the property is used. As a result, the formula employed by the Tax Court computes the percentage limitation for interest and taxes by dividing the total days rented by the total days in the year. The following example illustrates the operation of the two methods for allocating rental unit expenses.

Example. During the year an individual rents out his vacation home for 91 days and uses the home for personal purposes for 30 days. The gross rental income from the unit is $2,700 for the year. He pays $621 of real property taxes and $2,854 of mortgage interest on the property for the year. The additional expenses for maintenance, repair and utilities total $2,693.

The IRS allocation of all expenses would be based on 75% (91 days rented ÷ 121 days used). In contrast, the Tax Court would allocate taxes and interest based on 25% (91 days rented ÷ 365 days) and use the 75% limitation for the additional expenses for maintenance, repair, etc.

	IRS	Tax Court
1. Gross rental income	$ 2,700	$ 2,700
2. Less: Interest ($2,854)	− 2,141	− 714
Property tax ($621)	− 466	− 155
3. Remaining available income	$ 93	$ 1,831
4. Utilities, maintenance, etc.	− 93	− 1,831
5. Net income	0	0
6. Unused expense allowable as itemized deductions:		
Interest	$ 713	$ 2,140
Property tax	155	466
7. Total allowable deductions	$ 3,568	$ 5,306

A vacation home is deemed to have been used by the taxpayer for personal purposes if for any part of the day the home is used (Code Sec. 280A(d)(2)):

Footnote references are to paragraphs of the 2002 Standard Federal Tax Reports.

[173] ¶ 14,854.30,
¶ 14,854.58

(1) for personal purposes by the taxpayer, any other person who owns an interest in the home, or the relatives (spouses, brothers, sisters, ancestors, lineal descendants, and spouses of lineal descendants) of either;

(2) by any individual who uses the home under a reciprocal arrangement, whether or not a rental is charged; and

(3) by any other individual who uses the home unless a fair rental is charged.

If the taxpayer rents the home at a fair rental value to any person (including a relative listed above), for use as that person's principal residence, the use by that person is not considered personal use by the taxpayer. This exception applies to a person who owns an interest in the home only if the rental is under a shared equity financing agreement.

The term "vacation home" means a dwelling unit, including a house, apartment, condominium, house trailer, boat, or similar property (Code Sec. 280A(f)(1)).

Bed and Breakfast Inns. The special restrictions on deductions related to a residence used for business and personal purposes do not apply to the portion of the residence used as a bed and breakfast inn (IRS Letter Ruling 8732002).[174]

967. Conversion of Property. Individuals who convert their principal residences into rental units (or vice versa) will not be considered to have used the unit for personal purposes for any day during the tax year which occurs before (or after) a qualified rental period for purposes of applying the deduction limitation (¶ 966) allocable to the qualified rental period. However, the expenses must be allocated between the periods of rental and personal use. A qualified rental period is a consecutive period of 12 or more months, beginning (or ending) during the tax year, during which the unit is rented or held for rental at its fair market value. The 12-month rental requirement does not apply if the residence is sold or exchanged before it has been rented or held for rental for the full 12 months (Code Sec. 280A(d)(4)).[175]

> **Example:** A taxpayer moved out of his principal residence on February 28, 2000, to accept employment in another town. The house was rented at its fair market value from March 15, 2000, through May 14, 2001. The use of the house as a principal residence from January 1 through February 28, 2000 is not counted as personal use. If, on June 1, 2001, the taxpayer moved back and reoccupied the home, the use of the house as a principal residence from June 1 through December 31, 2001, is not counted as personal use.

Other Business Expenses

968. Fire and Casualty Insurance Premiums. A premium paid for insurance against losses from fire, accident, storm, theft, or other casualty is deductible if it is an ordinary and necessary expense of a business (Reg. § 1.162-1).[176] However, the uniform capitalization rules may require that insurance costs on real or tangible personal property produced or acquired for resale be included in inventory or capitalized, rather than being deducted (see ¶ 990 et seq.).

A premium on a personal disability insurance policy is not deductible. A business or professional person may deduct premiums on a policy that pays overhead expenses during a period of disability, but the proceeds under such a policy are includible in gross income.[177] When an insurance premium is paid in advance for more than one year, only a pro rata portion of the premium is deductible for each year, regardless of the taxpayer's method of accounting.[178]

969. Advertising Expenses. Advertising expenses are deductible if they are reasonable in amount and bear a reasonable relation to the business. The expense may be for the purpose of developing goodwill as well as gaining immediate sales. The cost of advertising is deductible when paid or incurred, even though the

---

Footnote references are to paragraphs of the 2002 Standard Federal Tax Reports.

[174] ¶ 14,854.585   [176] ¶ 8501   [178] ¶ 21,805, ¶ 21,817.21
[175] ¶ 14,850   [177] ¶ 8522.385

¶969

advertising program extends over several years or is expected to result in benefits extending over a period of years (Rev. Rul. 92-80).[179] The Tax Court and the IRS require that the cost of printing a catalog that is not replaced annually be amortized over the expected life of the catalog. However, some courts have held to the contrary, taking the view that catalog costs are in the nature of an advertising expense.[180] The cost of public service or other impartial advertising, such as advertising designed to encourage the public to register and to vote, are deductible.[181]

Design Costs. The Tax Court has held that packaging design costs were a deductible advertising expense even though the design provided the company with significant future benefits (*RJR Nabisco*, 76 TCM 71, CCH Dec. 52,786(M) (Nonacq.)).[182]

No deduction may be claimed for expenses of advertising in political programs or for admission to political fund-raising functions and similar events (Code Sec. 276).[183] This includes admission to any dinner or program if any part of the proceeds of the event directly or indirectly inures to or for the use of a political party or a political candidate.

970. Expense of Earning Tax-Exempt Income. No deduction is allowed for any expense allocable to the earning of tax-exempt income.[184] No deduction is allowed for interest paid on a debt incurred or continued in order to purchase or carry tax-exempt bonds or other obligations, regardless of whether the interest expense was incurred in business, in a profit-inspired transaction, or in any other connection (Code Sec. 265(a)(2)).[185]

Generally, banks, thrift institutions, and all other financial institutions may not deduct any portion of their interest expenses allocable to tax-exempt interest on obligations acquired after August 7, 1986.[186] This includes amounts paid in respect of deposits, investment certificates, or withdrawable or repurchasable shares.

971. Circulation Expenses. Any expenditure to establish, maintain, or increase the circulation of a newspaper, magazine, or other periodical may be deducted in the year paid or incurred (Code Sec. 173; Reg. § 1.173-1),[187] even though the taxpayer reports only an allocable portion of the subscription income for each year of the subscription period (see ¶ 1537).[188] See ¶ 1435 for adjustments that may be required in computing alternative minimum taxable income.

972. Fines, Penalties, Kickbacks, Drug Trafficking. A fine or a penalty paid to a government for the violation of any law is not a deductible business expense (Code Sec. 162(f)).[189] Also, any illegal bribe or kickback paid directly or indirectly to a domestic government official or employee is nondeductible.[190] Bribes and kickbacks paid directly or indirectly to an employee or official of a foreign government are nondeductible if they are unlawful under the federal Foreign Corrupt Practices Act of 1977. No deduction is allowed for any payment made directly or indirectly to any person if the payment is a bribe, kickback, or other illegal payment under any U.S. law or under any generally enforced state law that subjects the payor to a criminal penalty or to the loss of license or privilege to engage in a trade or business (Code Sec. 162(c)(2); Reg. § 1.162-18).[191] A deduction is also denied for any kickback, rebate or bribe made by any provider of services, supplier, physician, or other person who furnished items or services for which payment is or may be made under the Social Security Act, or in whole or in part out of federal funds under a state plan approved under the Act, if the kickback, rebate or bribe is made in connection with the furnishing of such items or services or the making or receiving of such payments. For all the above purposes, a kickback includes a payment in consideration of the referral of a client, patient or customer (Code Sec. 162(c)(3); Reg. § 1.162-18).[192]

Footnote references are to paragraphs of the 2002 Standard Federal Tax Reports.

179 ¶ 8851.152	184 ¶ 14,050, ¶ 14,051	189 ¶ 8500
180 ¶ 21,817.206	185 ¶ 14,050	190 ¶ 8500
181 ¶ 8952.40	186 ¶ 14,050	191 ¶ 8500, ¶ 8857
182 ¶ 8851.028	187 ¶ 12,030, ¶ 12,031	192 ¶ 8500, ¶ 8857
183 ¶ 14,550	188 ¶ 12,032.01	

If a taxpayer is convicted of a criminal violation of the antitrust laws, which contain a treble damage provision, or enters a plea of guilty or "no contest" to a charged violation, no deduction is allowed for two-thirds of the amount paid to satisfy the judgment or in settlement of a suit brought under section 4 of the Clayton Act (Code Sec. 162(g); Reg. § 1.162-22).[193]

No deduction is allowed for a federal tax penalty.[194] No deduction or credit is allowed for amounts paid or incurred in the illegal trafficking in drugs listed in the federal Controlled Substances Act. However, a deduction for the cost of goods sold is permitted (Code Sec. 280E).[195] Damage awards paid in connection with the violation of a federal civil statute and similar penalties may be deductible if they are compensatory, rather than punitive, in nature.[196]

973. Legal Expenses. Legal expenses paid or incurred in connection with a business transaction or primarily for the purpose of preserving existing business reputation and goodwill are ordinarily deductible. The deductibility tests are substantially the same as those for other business expenses and preclude a current deduction for a legal expense incurred in the acquisition of capital assets.[197] It is not necessary that litigation be involved for legal fees to be deductible. In addition to attorney fees, legal expenses include fees or expenses of accountants and expert witnesses, as well as court stenographic and printing charges.[198]

A taxpayer may deduct, as a business expense, that part of the cost of tax return preparation that is properly allocable to the business, as well as expenses incurred in resolving asserted tax deficiencies relating to the business.[199]

For the deductibility of legal expenses arising from income-producing property or the determination of nonbusiness taxes, see ¶ 1092 and ¶ 1093.

974. Lobbying Expense. Business deductions for lobbying expenses directed towards influencing federal or state legislation are generally prohibited (Code Sec. 162(e)(1) and (2); Reg. § 1.162-20(c)).[200] However, the prohibition does not generally apply to in-house expenses that do not exceed $2,000 for a tax year (Code Sec. 162(e)(5)(B)).[201] Also, an exception exists for lobbying expenses that pertain to local legislation.[202]

975. Federal National Mortgage Association Stock. Initial holders of stock issued by the Federal National Mortgage Association may deduct, as a business expense, the excess of the price paid over the market price of the stock on the date of issuance (Code Sec. 162(d)).[203] The basis in the stock is reduced to reflect the deduction.

976. Political Contributions. Contributions made to a political candidate or party are not deductible as a business expense (Code Sec. 162(e)(2)(A)).[204]

977. Environmental Clean-Up Costs. A taxpayer may elect to currently deduct expenses for the clean up of certain hazardous substances (see ¶ 903).

Merchant's and Manufacturer's Expenses

978. Expenses of Mercantile and Manufacturing Businesses. Merchants and manufacturers generally are subject to the uniform capitalization rules. See the discussion at ¶ 990 et seq. However, ordinary and necessary business expenses not covered by such rules may be currently deducted (Reg. § 1.162-1).[205]

979. Research Expenditures. A taxpayer may elect to currently deduct certain research and experimental costs by claiming the deduction on the income tax return for the first tax year in which the costs are paid or incurred in connection with its business. Only costs of research in the laboratory or for experimental

---

Footnote references are to paragraphs of the 2002 Standard Federal Tax Reports.

[193] ¶ 8500, ¶ 8955	[198] ¶ 8526.4035	[202] ¶ 8500
[194] ¶ 8500 et seq.	[199] ¶ 8520.73	[203] ¶ 8500, ¶ 8859
[195] ¶ 15,050	[200] ¶ 8500, ¶ 8951,	[204] ¶ 8500
[196] ¶ 8953	¶ 8952	[205] ¶ 8501
[197] ¶ 12,521	[201] ¶ 8500	

purposes, whether carried on by the taxpayer or on behalf of the taxpayer by a third party, are deductible. Market research and normal product testing costs are not research expenditures. Once made, the election is applicable to all R&E costs incurred in the project for the current and all subsequent years. As an alternative, a taxpayer can elect to capitalize such costs and later amortize them ratably over a period of at least 60 months beginning with the month in which benefits are first realized from the expenditures, assuming that the property created does not have a determinable useful life at that time. Costs associated with property that has a determinable useful life must be amortized or depreciated over its useful life. The election to amortize must be made no later than the due date for the return for the tax year for which the election is made by attaching a statement to such return. The elections are not available for expenditures for land, oil or gas exploration, or for depreciable and depletable property used in experimental work (Code Sec. 174).[206] Amortization is claimed on Form 4562 (Depreciation and Amortization). Both elections are available for research expenditures incurred before a trade or business begins.[207]

The costs of obtaining a patent, including attorneys' fees paid or incurred in making and perfecting a patent application, qualify as research or experimental expenditures, but the costs of acquiring another's patent, model, production or process do not qualify (Reg. § 1.174-2(a)(1)).[208] When the election to defer expenses has been made, the right to amortize ceases when the patent issues. Unrecovered expenditures are recovered through depreciation over the life of the patent (Reg. § 1.174-4(a)(4)).[209] For a discussion of the special credit for increased research and experimental expenses, see ¶ 1330. A purchased patent may qualify as a Section 197 intangible and be amortized over 15 years (see ¶ 1288).

980. Computer Software Costs. The costs of developing software (for taxpayer's own use or for sale or lease to others) may be deducted currently or amortized over a five-year period (or shorter if established as appropriate), so long as such costs are treated consistently (Rev. Proc. 2000-50).[210]

For purchases after August 10, 1993, computer software which is not amortizable over 15 years as a Section 197 intangible (as defined at ¶ 1288) is depreciated using the straight-line method over three years beginning in the month it is placed in service (Code Sec. 167(f)). The cost of computer software that is included as part of the cost of computer hardware, and is not separately stated, is treated as part of the cost of the hardware (Reg. § 1.167(a)-(14)(b)).[211]

Computer software with a useful life of less than one year is currently deductible. A deduction is allowed for rental payments made for software leased for use in a trade or business.[212]

Web Site Development Costs. The IRS has yet to issue formal guidance on the treatment of web site development costs. See also ¶ 1201 and the 2002 U.S. MASTER DEPRECIATION GUIDE, ¶ 125.

Expenses of Professional Person

981. Professional Person. Expenses incurred for operating a car used in making professional calls, dues to professional organizations, rent paid for office space, and other ordinary and necessary business expenses are deductible by a professional person. Amounts for books and equipment may be deducted if the useful life of the item is not more than one year (Reg. § 1.162-6).[213]

No deduction is allowed for dues paid to any club organized for business, pleasure, recreation, or other social purposes (Code Sec. 274(a)(3)).[214] However, this disallowance does not extend to professional organizations (e.g., bar and accounting

---

Footnote references are to paragraphs of the 2002 Standard Federal Tax Reports.

[206] ¶ 12,040, ¶ 12,047	[209] ¶ 12,046	[212] ¶ 8754.1695
[207] ¶ 12,047.1805	[210] ¶ 8754.1695	[213] ¶ 8633
[208] ¶ 12,043	[211] ¶ 11,030D	[214] ¶ 14,402

associations) or public service organizations (e.g., Kiwanis and Rotary clubs) (Reg.§ 1.274-2(a)(2)(iii)(b)).[215] See, also, ¶ 913.

A professional who performs services as an employee and who incurs unreimbursed related expenses may deduct such expenses only as itemized deductions subject to the 2% of adjusted gross income floor. See ¶ 941 and ¶ 1011.

Information Services. Amounts paid for subscriptions to professional journals, and the cost of information services such as Federal or State Tax Reporters, Unemployment Reporters, Labor Law or Trade Regulation Reporters, Estate Tax Reporters, and other law reporters that have a useful life of one year or less are deductible by a lawyer, accountant or an employee who buys a service in connection with the performance of his duties.[216] The cost of a professional library having a more permanent value should be capitalized.

Other Expenses. A deduction is allowed to members of the clergy, lawyers, merchants, professors, and physicians for expenses incurred in attending business conventions (¶ 959).[217] (For foreign conventions, see ¶ 960.) A member of the medical profession is allowed a deduction for business entertainment, subject to the rules discussed at ¶ 910, so long as there is a direct relationship between the expense and the development or expansion of a medical practice.[218] A doctor's staff privilege fee paid to a hospital is a capital expenditure.[219] For other deductions, see the Checklist at ¶ 57.

Farmer's Expenses

982. Expenses. Deductions are permitted for expenses incurred in carrying on the business of farming, including a horticultural nursery business (Reg. § 1.162-12).[220] Special rules, however, apply to certain property produced in a farming business (see ¶ 999) and to farm tax shelters (see ¶ 2028). See ¶ 767 for income averaging rules.

Among allowable deductions are the following: tools, cost of feeding and raising livestock (excluding produce grown upon the farm and labor of the taxpayer), and cost of gasoline, repairs, and upkeep of a car or truck used wholly in the business of farming or a portion thereof if used for both farming and personal use.

For the accounting methods available to farmers, see ¶ 767. Special rules apply to deductions for prepaid feed and other supply costs of cash-basis farmers (see ¶ 1539). Farming syndicates are discussed at ¶ 2032.

Expenses for the purchase of farm machinery or equipment, breeding, dairy or work animals, a car, and drilling water wells for irrigation purposes are capital items usually subject to depreciation (Reg. § 1.162-12).[221]

Conservation Expenses. A farmer may generally deduct soil and water conservation expenditures that do not give rise to a deduction for depreciation, that are not otherwise deductible and that would increase the basis of the property absent the election to deduct them. However, current deductions for soil and water conservation expenses are limited to those that are consistent with a conservation plan approved by the Soil Conservation Service of the U.S.D.A. or, in the absence of a federally approved plan, a soil conservation plan of a comparable state agency. Expenses related to the draining or filling of wetlands or to land preparation for the installation or operation of center pivot irrigation systems may not be deducted under this provision (Code Sec. 175(c)(3)).[222] The deduction is limited annually to 25% of the taxpayer's *gross* income from farming. Excess expenses can be carried over to succeeding tax years, without time limitation, but in each year the total deduction is limited to 25% of that year's gross income from farming (Code Sec. 175; Reg. § 1.175-1—Reg. § 1.175-6).[223]

Footnote references are to paragraphs of the 2002 Standard Federal Tax Reports.

[215] ¶ 14,405	[218] ¶ 8523.2717	[221] ¶ 8755
[216] ¶ 8634.02	[219] ¶ 8634.043	[222] ¶ 12,060
[217] ¶ 8527	[220] ¶ 8755	[223] ¶ 12,060—¶ 12,066

Deductible soil and water conservation expenses include such costs as leveling, grading, construction, control and protection of diversion channels, drainage ditches, outlets and ponds, planting of windbreaks, and other treatment or moving of earth. No current deduction is allowed for the purchase, construction, installation or improvement of depreciable masonry, tile, metal or wood structures, appliances and facilities such as tanks, reservoirs, pipes, canals and pumps (Reg. § 1.175-2).[224] Assessments levied by a soil or water conservation or drainage district in order to defray expenses made by the district may also be deductible.

983. Land Clearing Expense. Land clearing expenditures must be capitalized and added to the farmer's basis in the land. However, business expenses for ordinary maintenance activities related to property already used in farming (e.g., brush clearing) are currently deductible.[225]

984. Development Costs. Generally, a farmer has the option of either deducting developmental expenses that are ordinary and necessary business expenses or capitalizing them (Reg. § 1.162-12).[226] However, plants produced by farms that have a preproductive period of more than two years must be capitalized. In the case of certain farms (corporations, partnerships, and tax shelters) that are required to use the accrual method, the expenses must be capitalized regardless of the length of the preproductive period (see ¶ 999). Special rules apply to farming syndicates; see ¶ 2032.

985. Expensing Fertilizer Cost. A farmer, other than a farm syndicate, may elect to deduct current expenses otherwise chargeable to capital account made for fertilizer, lime, ground limestone, marl, or other materials for enriching, neutralizing, or conditioning land used in farming. If no election is made, expenditures producing benefits extending over more than one year are capitalized and recovered by amortization (Reg. § 1.180-1).[227] The election, which is effective only for the tax year claimed, is made by claiming the deduction on the return (Reg. § 1.180-2).[228] For farm syndicates and prepayments by cash-basis farmers, see ¶ 1539, ¶ 2028 and ¶ 2032.

Landlord or Tenant Expenses

986. Landlord or Tenant. A tenant may deduct rent paid for business property as well as any amounts, such as property taxes and interest, which the lease requires the tenant to pay on behalf of the landlord (Reg. § 1.162-11).[229]

An amount paid by a *lessee* for cancellation of a lease on business property is generally deductible.[230] However, payments by the *lessor* for the cancellation of a lease have generally been regarded as capital expenditures.[231] If rent is prepaid, the taxpayer may only deduct that portion of the rent that pertains to the current tax year.[232] Some rental payments are subject to the uniform capitalization rules (see ¶ 990). For an improvement made by the lessee on leased premises, see ¶ 1234.

If an owner of property occupies part of the property as a personal residence and rents part of it, expenses and depreciation allocable to the rented space may be deductible. See also ¶ 966.

Mining Company's Expenses

987. Mine Exploration. Mining companies may elect to deduct domestic exploration expenses (except for oil or gas), provided that the amount deducted is recaptured once the mine reaches production stage or is sold (Code Sec. 617).[233] Recapture is accomplished by a company's electing either to (1) include in income for that year the previously deducted exploration expenditures chargeable to the mine, increase the basis of the property by the amount included in income, and

---

Footnote references are to paragraphs of the 2002 Standard Federal Tax Reports.

¶983

[224] ¶ 12,062
[225] ¶ 12,160.01
[226] ¶ 8755
[227] ¶ 12,141

[228] ¶ 12,142
[229] ¶ 8753
[230] ¶ 8754.06
[231] ¶ 13,709.307

[232] ¶ 8754.01, ¶ 21,817.635
[233] ¶ 24,110

subsequently recover this amount through depletion or (2) forgo depletion from the property (which includes or comprises the mine) until deductions forgone equal exploration expenditures previously deducted. Expenses not recaptured by one of these methods are recaptured on the sale or other disposition of the mining property with the amount recaptured treated as ordinary income. Certain transfers are not subject to these recapture rules (Code Sec. 617(b) and (d)(3)).[234]

Deductions allowed a corporation (other than an S corporation) for mineral exploration and development costs under Code Sec. 616(a) and Code Sec. 617(a) must be reduced by 30% (Code Sec. 291(b)).[235] The 30% of expenses that cannot be deducted must be capitalized and amortized over a 60-month period on Form 4562 (Depreciation and Amortization). Taxpayers may also elect to capitalize mine exploration expenses and amortize them over a 10-year period (Code Sec. 59(e)).[236] If the election is made, the expenses will not be tax preference items (see ¶ 1430).

988. Mine Development. Expenses paid or incurred with respect to a domestic mine or other natural deposit (other than oil or gas) after the existence of ores or minerals in commercially marketable quantities has been discovered can be deducted currently unless the taxpayer elects to treat them as deferred expenses and deduct them ratably as the ore or mineral is sold. Such expenses do not include those made for the acquisition or improvement of depreciable property. However, depreciation allowances are considered as development costs (Code Sec. 616; Reg. § 1.616-1).[237]

The 30% reduction in the allowable deduction and the election to amortize over a 10-year period (discussed at ¶ 987 in the case of exploration expenses) applies also to mine development expenses (Code Sec. 291(b)).[238]

988A. Foreign Mine Exploration and Development. Foreign mining exploration and development expenses (other than oil, gas, or geothermal wells) are to be recovered over a 10-year, straight-line amortization schedule beginning with the tax year in which the costs were paid or incurred. However, the taxpayer may elect to add such expenses to the adjusted basis of the property for purposes of computing cost depletion (Code Sec. 616(d) and Code Sec. 617(h)).[239]

989. Oil, Gas, or Geothermal Well Drilling Expense. Operators of a domestic oil, gas, or geothermal well may elect to currently deduct intangible drilling and development costs (IDCs) rather than charge such costs to capital, recoverable through depletion or depreciation. The election is binding upon future years. IDCs generally include all expenses made by the operator incident to and necessary for the drilling of wells and the preparation of wells for the production of oil, gas, or geothermal energy that are neither for the purchase of tangible property nor part of the acquisition price of an interest in the property. IDCs include labor, fuel, materials and supplies, truck rent, repairs to drilling equipment, and depreciation for drilling equipment (Code Sec. 263(c); Reg. § 1.612-4).[240]

An integrated oil company (generally, a producer that is not an independent producer) must reduce the deduction for IDCs otherwise allowable by 30%. The amount disallowed as a current expense deduction must be amortized over a 60-month period (Code Sec. 291(b)).[241] Taxpayers may elect to capitalize, rather than currently deduct, IDCs and amortize these expenditures over a 60-month period. If amortization is elected, the expenses will not constitute tax preference items (Code Sec. 59(e)(1), (6)).[242] See ¶ 1430.

If the operator has elected to capitalize intangible drilling and development costs, and the well later proves to be nonproductive (a dry hole), the operator may elect to deduct such costs as an ordinary loss. The election, once made, is binding for all years (Reg. § 1.612-4(b)(4)).[243] As to the recapture of intangible drilling expenses upon sale of oil, gas, or geothermal property, see ¶ 2025.

Footnote references are to paragraphs of the 2002 Standard Federal Tax Reports.

[234] ¶ 24,110
[235] ¶ 15,190
[236] ¶ 5400
[237] ¶ 24,090, ¶ 24,091
[238] ¶ 15,190
[239] ¶ 24,090, ¶ 24,110
[240] ¶ 13,700, ¶ 23,949
[241] ¶ 15,190
[242] ¶ 5400
[243] ¶ 23,949

¶989

Foreign Wells. Operators may not opt to currently deduct IDCs for wells located outside the U.S. Such costs must be recovered over a 10-year straight-line amortization schedule or, at the operator's election, added to the adjusted basis of the property for cost depletion. Dry hole expenses incurred outside the U.S. are currently deductible (Code Sec. 263(i)).[244]

Uniform Capitalization Rules

990. Uniform Capitalization Rules, Generally. Taxpayers subject to the uniform capitalization rules are required to capitalize direct costs and an allocable portion of most indirect costs that are associated with production or resale activities. The uniform capitalization rules apply to the following (Code Sec. 263A(a), Code Sec. 263A(b), Code Sec. 263A(c) and Code Sec. 263A(g)):[245]

(1) real or tangible personal property *produced* by the taxpayer for *use* in a trade or business or in an activity engaged in for profit;

(2) real or tangible personal property *produced* by the taxpayer for *sale* to customers; or

(3) real or personal property (both tangible and intangible) *acquired* by the taxpayer for *resale.* However, the uniform capitalization rules do not apply to *tangible* or *intangible* personal property acquired for resale if the taxpayer's annual gross receipts for the preceding three tax years do not exceed $10 million. Costs attributable to producing or acquiring property generally must be capitalized by charging such costs to capital accounts or basis, and costs attributable to property that is inventory in the hands of the taxpayer generally must be capitalized by including such costs in inventory.

Property Excepted from Rules. Among the classes of property excepted from the rules are: (1) property produced by the taxpayer for its own use other than in a trade or business or in an activity conducted for profit; (2) research and experimental expenditures (see ¶ 979); (3) intangible drilling and development costs under Code Sec. 263(c), Code Sec. 263(i) and Code Sec. 291(b)(2), and mine development and exploration costs pursuant to Code Sec. 616 and Code Sec. 617; (4) any property produced by the taxpayer pursuant to a long-term contract; (5) any costs incurred in raising, growing or harvesting trees (including the costs associated with the real property underlying such trees) other than trees bearing fruit, nuts or other crops and ornamental trees (those which are six years old or less when severed from the roots); and (6) costs (other than circulation expenditures) subject to amortization pursuant to Code Sec. 59(e) (Code Sec. 263A(c)).[246]

990A. Writers, Photographers, and Artists. Expenses paid or incurred by a self-employed individual (including expenses of a corporation owned by a free-lancer and directly related to the activities of a qualified employee-owner) in the business of being a writer, photographer, or artist whose personal efforts create or may reasonably be expected to create the product are exempt from uniform capitalization (Code Sec. 263A(h)).[247] Generally, expenses for producing jewelry, silverware, pottery, furniture and similar household items are not exempt.[248]

991. Costs Required to Be Capitalized. Generally, direct material and labor costs and indirect costs must be capitalized with respect to property that is produced or acquired for resale. Direct material costs include the costs of those materials that become an integral part of the subject matter and of those materials that are consumed in the ordinary course of the activity. Direct labor costs include the cost of labor that can be identified or associated with a particular activity such as basic compensation, overtime pay, vacation pay, and payroll taxes.

Indirect costs include all costs other than direct material and labor costs. Indirect costs require a reasonable allocation to determine the portion of such costs that are attributable to each activity of the taxpayer. Indirect costs include: repair

Footnote references are to paragraphs of the 2002 Standard Federal Tax Reports.

¶990
| 244 ¶ 13,700 | 246 ¶ 13,800 | 248 ¶ 13,800.072 |
| 245 ¶ 13,800 | 247 ¶ 13,800 | |

and maintenance of equipment or facilities; utilities; rental of equipment, facilities, or land; indirect labor and contract supervisory wages; indirect materials and supplies; depreciation, amortization and cost recovery allowance on equipment and facilities (to the extent allowable as deductions under Chapter 1 of the Code); certain administrative costs; insurance; contributions paid to or under a stock bonus, pension, profit-sharing or annuity plan, or other plan deferring the receipt of compensation; rework labor, scrap and spoilage; and certain engineering and design expenses (Code Sec. 263A(a)(2); Reg. § 1.263A-1(e)).[249]

992. Costs Not Required to Be Capitalized. Costs that are not required to be capitalized with respect to property produced or acquired for resale include marketing, selling, advertising and distribution expenses. The IRS has established procedures that allow for the capitalization or amortization of package design costs (Rev. Proc. 98-39).[250] Other costs that need not be capitalized include bidding expenses incurred in the solicitation of contracts not awarded the taxpayer; certain general and administrative expenses; and compensation paid to officers attributable to the performance of services that do not directly benefit or are not incurred by reason of a particular production activity (Reg. § 1.263A-1(e)(4)(iv)).[251]

993. Interest Capitalization Rules. Interest costs paid or incurred during the production period and allocable to real property or tangible personal property produced by the taxpayer which has a class life of at least 20 years, an estimated production period exceeding two years, or an estimated production period exceeding one year and a cost exceeding $1 million must be capitalized (Code Sec. 263A(f)).[252]

994. Property Acquired for Resale. Unless an election is made to use the simplified resale method at ¶ 995, the rules applicable to the production of property apply to costs incurred with respect to property acquired for resale in a trade or business or in an activity conducted for profit. Property held for resale may include literary, musical or artistic compositions, stocks, certificates, notes, bonds, debentures or other evidence of indebtedness or an interest in, right to subscribe to or purchase of any of the foregoing, and other intangible properties. However, in the case of personal property acquired for resale, a taxpayer is not subject to the uniform capitalization rules if its average annual gross receipts for the three preceding tax years (or, if less, the number of preceding tax years the taxpayer (and any predecessor) has been in existence) do not exceed $10 million. The uniform capitalization rules apply in the case of real property acquired for resale, regardless of the taxpayer's gross receipts (Code Sec. 263A(b)).[253]

995. Simplified Methods of Accounting for Resale Costs. Generally, taxpayers may elect to use one of the simplified resale methods for allocating costs to property acquired for resale. However, in the case of a single trade or business that consists of both production and resale activities, only the simplified production method (¶ 996) is available. Under the simplified resale methods, preliminary inventory balances are calculated without the inclusion of the additional costs (listed below) required to be capitalized. The amount of additional costs attributable to prior periods and the amount of additional costs determined to be capitalized for the current period are then taken into account with the inventory balances as initially calculated in order to arrive at an ending inventory balance.

The following categories of costs are required to be capitalized with respect to property acquired for resale, regardless of whether a taxpayer elects one of the simplified resale methods: (1) off-site storage or warehousing; (2) purchasing; (3) handling, processing, assembly, and repackaging; and (4) certain general and administrative expenses (Reg. § 1.263A-3(c)).[254]

996. Simplified Method of Accounting for Production Costs. An election to use the simplified production method may be made to account for the additional costs required to be capitalized with respect to property produced by the taxpayer

---

that is (1) stock in trade or other property properly includible in inventory or (2) property held primarily for sale to customers in the ordinary course of business.

Additional Categories. Categories of property eligible for the simplified production method also include properties constructed by a taxpayer for use in its trade or business if the taxpayer (1) is also producing inventory property and the constructed property is substantially identical in nature and is produced in the same manner as the inventory property or (2) produces such property on a routine and repetitive basis (Reg. § 1.263A-2(a)(5)).[255]

997. Simplified Service Cost Method. A simplified method is available for determining capitalizable mixed service costs for eligible property (Reg. § 1.263A-1).[256]

The election to use the simplified method must be made independently from other allowable simplified methods (Reg. § 1.263A-1(h)).[257]

999. Farming Business. The uniform capitalization rules apply to plants and animals produced by certain farming businesses (corporations, partnerships, and tax shelters) that are required to use the accrual method. For other farming businesses, the uniform capitalization rules apply only to plants produced in the farming business that have a preproductive period of more than two years (Code Sec. 263A(d)(1)).[258]

Generally, the rules do not apply to costs that are attributable to the replanting, cultivation, maintenance, and development of any plants (of the same type of crop) bearing an edible crop for human consumption (normally eaten or drunk by humans) that were lost or damaged as the result of freezing temperatures, disease, drought, pests, or casualty. Replanting or maintenance costs may be incurred on property other than the damaged property if the acreage is not in excess of the acreage of the damaged property (Code Sec. 263A(d)(2)).[259]

A farming business is a trade or business involving the cultivation of land or the raising or harvesting of any agricultural or horticultural commodity. Examples include a nursery or sod farm, the raising of ornamental trees (evergreen trees six years old or less when severed from their roots), the raising or harvesting of trees bearing fruit, nuts, or other crops, and the raising, shearing, feeding, caring for, training, and managing of animals (Code Sec. 263A(e)(4)).[260]

Any farmer (other than a corporation, partnership, or tax shelter required to use the accrual method) may elect *not* to have the uniform capitalization rules made applicable to any plant produced in his business. However, such election may *not* be made for any costs incurred within the first four years in which any almond or citrus trees were planted (Code Sec. 263A(d)(3) and (e); Reg. § 1.263A-1(b)(3)).[261]

Unless IRS consent is obtained, farmers may only make the election not to have the uniform capitalization rules apply for the first tax year during which the farmer produces property to which the uniform capitalization rules apply. Once the election is made, it is revocable only with the consent of the IRS (Code Sec. 263A(d)(3)).[262]

Footnote references are to paragraphs of the 2002 Standard Federal Tax Reports.

¶ 997

[255] ¶ 13,817	[258] ¶ 13,800	[261] ¶ 13,800, ¶ 13,811
[256] ¶ 13,811, ¶ 13,815.09	[259] ¶ 13,800	[262] ¶ 13,800
[257] ¶ 13,811, ¶ 13,815.09	[260] ¶ 13,800	

Chapter 10

DEDUCTIONS

Nonbusiness Expenses

Deductions, Generally

1001. Major Classifications. Deductions for individuals fall into two basic categories: (1) those taken from adjusted gross income if the taxpayer is eligible, and elects, to itemize deductions and (2) those taken from gross income regardless of whether the taxpayer itemizes. Itemized deductions should be claimed only if they exceed the taxpayer's standard deduction.[1]

1002. Standard Deduction. Individuals who do not itemize their deductions are entitled to a standard deduction amount which varies according to filing status. This amount, along with the taxpayer's personal and dependency exemptions, reduces adjusted gross income to arrive at taxable income.[2] See ¶ 126.

1003. Personal Expense. A personal, living or family expense is not deductible unless the Code specifically provides otherwise (Reg. § 1.262-1).[3] Nondeductible expenses include insurance premiums paid on taxpayer's own dwelling, life insurance premiums paid by the insured, and payments for house rent, food, clothing, domestic help, most education, and upkeep of an automobile.

Adjusted Gross Income

1005. Deductions Allowed. Adjusted gross income (AGI),[4] an intermediate figure between gross income and taxable income, is the starting point for computing the applicability of deductions, tax credits, and other tax benefits that are based on,

---

Footnote references are to paragraphs of the 2002 Standard Federal Tax Reports.

[1] ¶ 6020
[2] ¶ 6020
[3] ¶ 13,601
[4] ¶ 6002

or limited by, percentage of income (Reg. § 1.62-1T).[5] See the chart at ¶ 88A for a listing of the 2001 AGI phaseout thresholds.

"Adjusted gross income" means gross income minus deductions (Code Sec. 62):[6]

(1) on account of a trade or business carried on by the taxpayer (except for services as an employee) (¶ 1006),

(2) for trade or business expenses paid or incurred by a qualified performing artist for services in the performing arts as an employee (¶ 941A),

(3) allowed as losses from the sale or exchange of property (see ¶ 1007, ¶ 1701 et seq.),

(4) for expenses paid or incurred in connection with the performance of services as an employee under a reimbursement or other expense allowance arrangement with the employer or third party (¶ 942),

(5) attributable to rental or royalty property (¶ 1089),

(6) for depreciation or depletion allowed to a life tenant of property or to an income beneficiary of property held in trust, or to an heir, legatee, or devisee of an estate (¶ 1090),

(7) for contributions by self-employed persons to pension, profit-sharing, and annuity plans (¶ 2113),

(8) allowed for cash payments to individual retirement accounts (IRAs) and deductions allowed for cash payments to retirement savings plans of certain married individuals to cover a nonworking spouse (¶ 2170, ¶ 2172),

(9) for the ordinary income portion of a lump-sum distribution to the extent included in gross income (repealed effective for tax years beginning after December 31, 1999) (¶ 2153),

(10) for interest forfeited to a bank, savings association, etc., on premature withdrawals from time savings accounts or deposits (¶ 1120),

(11) for alimony payments (¶ 1008),

(12) for the amortization of reforestation expenses (¶ 1287),

(13) for certain repayments of supplemental unemployment compensation benefits to a trust described in Code Sec. 501(c)(9) or (17), required because of receipt of trade readjustment allowances (¶ 1009),

(14) for jury duty pay remitted to employer (¶ 1010),

(15) for moving expenses (¶ 1073),

(16) for the purchase of clean-fuel vehicle and refueling property (¶ 1286),

(17) for interest on education loans incurred on, before, or after August 5, 1997, with respect to loan interest payment due and paid after December 31, 1997 (Code Sec. 62(a)(17)) (¶ 1082),

(18) for contributions to an Archer medical savings account allowed by Code Sec. 220 (Code Sec. 62(a)(16)) (¶ 1020), and

(19) for expenses paid or incurred by a fee-basis state or local government official for services performed (¶ 941).

Employee expenses at (4), above, that are not reimbursed under an accountable plan are not deductible from gross income. See ¶ 942, ¶ 943.

1006. Trade or Business Deductions. Deductions directly attributable to a trade or business carried on by a taxpayer are used in computing the taxpayer's adjusted gross income. For this purpose, the performance of services as an employee is not considered to be a trade or business. However, the practice of a profession, not as an employee, is considered the conduct of a trade or business (Reg. § 1.62-1T(d)).[7] See ¶ 941 and following for the business deductions that are available to employees.

1007. Losses from Sales or Exchanges. Any allowable loss from the sale or exchange of property may be claimed as a deduction in arriving at adjusted

---

Footnote references are to paragraphs of the 2002 Standard Federal Tax Reports.

¶ 1006   [5] ¶ 6003   [6] ¶ 6002   [7] ¶ 6003

gross income (Reg. § 1.62-1T(c)(4)).[8] This includes allowable losses from sales or exchanges of capital assets and losses that are *treated* as losses from sales or exchanges of capital assets, such as losses on worthless stocks and bonds and on nonbusiness bad debts, as well as any allowable losses from sales or exchanges of noncapital assets. See ¶ 1735 and following. These deductions are allowed in addition to any losses attributable to a trade or business or to losses incurred in connection with property held for the production of rents or royalties. An individual's losses from sales of capital assets are generally limited to the individual's capital gains plus $3,000. See ¶ 1752.

A loss on an involuntary conversion *as such* is deductible in computing adjusted gross income only if it is attributable to property used in a trade or business or to property held for the production of rents or royalties. However, a taxpayer may be entitled to an itemized deduction for the involuntary conversion of property used for personal purposes if such loss arises from a casualty.[9] See ¶ 1713.

1008. Deduction for Alimony Paid. Alimony payments[10] are deductible from gross income in the year paid whether the taxpayer uses the cash or accrual method of accounting. Back alimony is deductible in the year paid if it would have been deductible if paid on schedule.[11] See ¶ 771 et seq. for details.

1009. Repayment of Supplemental Unemployment Compensation Benefits. Repayments of supplemental unemployment compensation benefits to trusts or voluntary employees' beneficiary associations required because of subsequent receipt of trade readjustment allowances under the Trade Act of 1974 are deductible from gross income.[12] Repayment of most other unemployment compensation benefits in a year after the year of receipt are deductible as an itemized deduction on Schedule A of Form 1040 (IRS Pub. 525). If the repayment of either type of unemployment compensation exceeds $3,000, the taxpayer may compute tax for the tax year of the repayment by using the claim-of-right method provided by Code Sec. 1341 (¶ 1543; IRS Pub. 525).[13]

1010. Jury Pay. Jury pay surrendered to an employer in return for continuing the employee's normal salary while on jury service is deductible from gross income.[14]

Floor on Miscellaneous Itemized Deductions

1011. Two-Percent Floor on Itemized Deductions. An individual is allowed certain itemized deductions only to the extent that the aggregate of such deductions exceeds two percent of the individual's adjusted gross income for the tax year (Code Sec. 67(a)).[15] These deductions are reported on Schedule A of Form 1040. An individual can elect to itemize such deductions if their total exceeds the applicable standard deduction (Code Sec. 63(d)).[16] Indirect deductions from pass-through entities (including nonpublicly offered mutual funds) that would not be allowed if paid or incurred directly by an individual are denied. However, such pass-through entities do not include estates, certain trusts, cooperatives, certain publicly offered mutual funds (RICs), and real estate investment trusts (REITs) (Code Sec. 67(c)).[17] Estates and trusts are generally treated as individuals. See ¶ 528.

Any limitation or restriction placed upon an itemized deduction, such as the 50 percent reduction for meals, generally applies prior to the two-percent floor (Reg. § 1.67-1T(a)(2)).[18]

A statutory employee, such as a full-time life insurance salesperson, is not treated as an employee for purposes of deducting expenses incurred in his business. Thus, such expenses may be claimed as trade or business expenses on Form 1040, Schedule C, and are not treated as miscellaneous itemized deductions (see ¶ 941B).[19]

Footnote references are to paragraphs of the 2002 Standard Federal Tax Reports.

[8] ¶ 6003	[12] ¶ 6002	[16] ¶ 6020
[9] ¶ 29,650.052	[13] ¶ 31,880	[17] ¶ 6060
[10] ¶ 6090, ¶ 12,570	[14] ¶ 6002	[18] ¶ 6061
[11] ¶ 6094.055	[15] ¶ 6060	[19] ¶ 6006.107

¶ 1011

1012. Itemized Deductions Not Subject to the Two-Percent Floor. The following itemized deductions (reported on Schedule A of Form 1040) are not subject to the two-percent floor discussed at ¶ 1011 (Code Sec. 67(b)):[20]

(1) Interest (see ¶ 1043 et seq.),

(2) Taxes (see ¶ 1021 and ¶ 1028 et seq.),

(3) Casualty, theft, and wagering losses (see ¶ 1101 et seq.),

(4) Charitable deductions (see ¶ 1058 et seq.),

(5) Medical and dental expenses (see ¶ 1015 et seq.),

(6) Deductions for impairment-related work expenses (see ¶ 1013),

(7) Deductions for estate tax in the case of income in respect of a decedent (see ¶ 191),

(8) Deductions allowable in connection with personal property used in a short sale (¶ 1944),

(9) Deductions relating to computation of tax when the taxpayer restores an amount in excess of $3,000 held under claim of right (see ¶ 1543),

(10) Deductions where annuity payments cease before an investment is recovered pursuant to Code Sec. 72(b)(3),

(11) Amortizable bond premiums (see ¶ 1967),

(12) Deductions of taxes, interest, and business depreciation by cooperative housing corporation tenant-stockholder (¶ 1040), and

(13) Deduction for gambling losses (¶ 788).

For a chart listing the average itemized deductions by AGI ranges, see ¶ 88.

1013. Impairment-Related Work Expenses. Expenses of a handicapped individual for attendant care services at his place of employment, other expenses in connection with his place of employment that are necessary for the individual to be able to work, and all ordinary and necessary expenses paid or incurred during the tax year in carrying on any business are not subject to the two-percent floor. Handicapped persons include any individuals who have a physical or mental disability (including blindness or deafness) which limits employment or who have any physical or mental impairment (including sight or hearing impairment) which substantially limits one or more major life activities (Code Sec. 67(d)).[21]

Phaseout of Itemized Deductions

1014. When AGI Exceeds Inflation-Adjusted Dollar Amount. An individual whose adjusted gross income exceeds a threshold amount is required to reduce the amount of allowable itemized deductions by three percent of the excess over the threshold amount (Code Sec. 68).[22] No reduction is required, however, in the case of deductions for medical expenses, investment interest, and casualty, theft or wagering losses. The 2001 threshold amount is $132,950 ($66,475 for married filing separately) (Rev. Proc. 2001-13). For 2002, the threshold amounts are $137,300 and $68,650, respectively, as projected by CCH. However, the reduction may never be more than 80 percent of allowable deductions, excluding deductions for medical expenses, investment interest, and casualty, theft or wagering losses. Thus, for example, if otherwise allowable itemized deductions are $10,000, the reduction amount cannot exceed $8,000.

This limitation is applied after any disallowance of miscellaneous itemized deductions subject to the two-percent floor (¶ 1011) has been taken into account (Code Sec. 68(d)) and the reduced amount is reported on Schedule A of Form 1040.[23]

Limit on itemized deductions phased out beginning in 2006. In tax years beginning after December 31, 2005, the limit on itemized deductions for high-income taxpayers will be phased out until it is fully repealed effective for tax years

Footnote references are to paragraphs of the 2002 Standard Federal Tax Reports.

¶ **1012**
[20] ¶ 6060
[21] ¶ 6060
[22] ¶ 6080
[23] ¶ 6080

beginning after 2009 (Code Sec. 68(f) and (g), as added by the Economic Growth and Tax Relief Reconciliation Act of 2001 (P.L. 107-16)).

Medical Expenses

1015. Medical and Dental Expenses. An individual is entitled to an itemized deduction for expenses paid during the tax year for the medical care of the individual, the individual's spouse, or a dependent to the extent that such expenses exceed 7.5 percent of adjusted gross income (Code Sec. 213(a)).[24] These expenses are reported on Schedule A of Form 1040. On a joint return, the percentage limitation is based on the total adjusted gross income of both husband and wife. The deduction may be taken for any person who was a dependent or spouse either at the time the services were rendered or at the time the expenses were paid (Reg. § 1.213-1(e)(3)).[25] For purposes of this deduction, "dependent" is defined at Code Sec. 152 (see ¶ 137), except (1) the amount of the dependent's gross income is not considered (Reg. § 1.213-1(a)(3))[26] and (2) a child of divorced parents is treated as the dependent of both parents for purposes of the medical expense deduction (Code Sec. 213(d)(5)).[27] The deduction, however, is limited to unreimbursed medical expenses (Code Sec. 213(a)).[28] Reimbursement received for expenses deducted in a previous tax year is includible in gross income in the year received to the extent previously deducted. Reimbursement for an earlier tax year in which no deduction was claimed is excludable when received (Reg. § 1.213-1(g)).[29]

Although medical expenses are generally deductible in the year paid (Reg. § 1.213-1(a)),[30] advance payments generally are not deductible until services are rendered. However, when expenses are prepaid for the future care of a retiree to a retirement home that is obligated to provide medical care or where expenses are prepaid and nonrefundable for an institution's future acceptance of a handicapped child, such medical expenses are deductible in the year paid.[31] Charges to credit cards qualify as payment of medical expenses in the year that such expenses are charged, regardless of when the credit card company is paid (Rev. Rul. 78-39).[32]

1016. What Are Medical Expenses? Medical expenses include amounts paid for the diagnosis, cure, mitigation, treatment, or prevention of disease or for the purpose of affecting any structure or function of the body; transportation cost of a trip primarily for and essential to medical care; qualified long-term care service; and for medical insurance (including premiums paid under the Social Security Act, relating to supplementary medical insurance for the aged or for any qualified long-term care insurance contracts that do not exceed certain limits) (Code Sec. 213(d)).[33] A medical expense deduction is allowed for lodging, but not meals, while away from home primarily for and essential to medical care. This lodging deduction is limited to amounts that are not lavish or extravagant and cannot exceed $50 per night for each individual (Code Sec. 213(d)(2)).[34] The deduction may also be claimed for a person who must accompany the individual seeking medical care.[35]

The costs of birth control pills prescribed by a physician, a legal abortion or a vasectomy are deductible.[36] Amounts for psychiatric treatment of sexual inadequacy are a medical expenditure, but marriage counseling fees are not.[37]

Expenses for elective cosmetic surgery are not deductible. Cosmetic surgery includes any procedure directed at improving the patient's appearance that does not meaningfully promote the proper function of the body or prevent or treat illness or disease (Code Sec. 213(d)(9)).[38]

The cost of weight-reduction or similar programs to improve general health or to alleviate physical or mental discomfort that is unrelated to a particular disease or

---

Footnote references are to paragraphs of the 2002 Standard Federal Tax Reports.

[24] ¶ 12,540	[30] ¶ 12,541	[35] ¶ 12,543.82
[25] ¶ 12,541	[31] ¶ 12,543.794	[36] ¶ 12,543.115
[26] ¶ 12,541	[32] ¶ 12,543.175	[37] ¶ 12,543.775,
[27] ¶ 12,540	[33] ¶ 12,540	¶ 12,543.7055
[28] ¶ 12,540	[34] ¶ 12,540	[38] ¶ 12,540
[29] ¶ 12,541		

defect is not deductible. However, a program prescribed by a doctor for treatment of a specific disease is deductible. This now includes smoking-cessation programs (whether or not prescribed) and prescription drugs to alleviate symptoms of nicotine withdrawal but not over-the-counter gums or patches (Rev. Rul. 99-28, revoking Rev. Rul. 76-162).

The Supreme Court denied a medical expense deduction for rent paid on an apartment for a patient who spent the winter months in Florida on the advice of his doctor. But the Court of Appeals for the Seventh Circuit allowed a medical expense deduction for a hotel bill incurred by a patient who was too weak to travel to his home town after being discharged from a hospital due to overcrowding.[39] (See the $50-per-night limit for lodging, above.) Medical expenses do not include amounts allowable as a "child care" credit (¶ 1301) (Code Sec. 213(e))[40] or funeral expenses.[41]

In lieu of a deduction for actual expenses incurred, for 2001, a standard mileage rate of 12 cents a mile (plus parking fees and tolls) is allowed in computing the cost of operating a car where transportation expenses are deductible as a medical expense (Rev. Proc. 2000-48) (13 cents a mile in 2002 (Rev. Proc. 2001-54)).[42]

Special schooling for a physically or mentally handicapped child or one needing psychiatric treatment is deductible.[43] Amounts paid for inpatient treatment of alcoholism or drug addiction at a therapeutic center and for meals and lodging furnished as a necessary incident to the treatment are deductible.[44] Amounts paid to acquire, train, and maintain a dog or other service animal for assisting a blind, deaf or physically disabled individual are deductible.[45]

If an individual is in a nursing home or a home for the aged because of his physical condition and the availability of medical care is a principal reason for his presence there, the entire cost of maintenance, including meals and lodging, is deductible. If an individual is in such an institution primarily for personal or family reasons, then only that portion of the cost attributable to medical or nursing care (excluding meals and lodging) is deductible. Payments to perform both nursing care and housework may be deducted only to the extent of the nursing cost.[46]

Capital expenditures for home improvements and additions that are added primarily for medical care qualify for the medical expense deduction only to the extent that the cost of the improvement exceeds any increase in the value of the affected property (Reg. § 1.213-1(e)(1)).[47] The entire cost of any improvement that does not increase the value of the property is deductible. Deductions have been allowed for the installation of an elevator, a swimming pool, and a central air-conditioning system. Furthermore, capital expenditures incurred to remove structural barriers to accommodate the condition of a physically handicapped person generally do not improve the value of the residence and, therefore, are fully deductible.[48] The entire cost of special equipment used to mitigate the effects of a physical impairment is also deductible.

See ¶ 59 for a checklist of medical expenses.

1017. Medicines and Drugs. In computing the deduction for medicine and drugs, only amounts paid for insulin and prescription drugs and medicines may be taken into account (Code Sec. 213(b)).[49]

> **Example.** A taxpayer with an adjusted gross income of $38,000 in 2001 paid $1,750 to a doctor for medical services, $1,325 to a hospital, $340 for prescription drugs, and $250 for over-the-counter (OTC) cold remedies and vitamins during 2001. His 2001 medical expense deduction is computed as follows:

Footnote references are to paragraphs of the 2002 Standard Federal Tax Reports.

39 ¶ 12,543.67	43 ¶ 12,543.786	47 ¶ 12,541
40 ¶ 12,540	44 ¶ 12,543.355	48 ¶ 12,543.48
41 ¶ 12,543.452	45 ¶ 12,543.138	49 ¶ 12,540
42 ¶ 12,543.035,	46 ¶ 12,543.726,	
¶ 12,543.82	¶ 12,543.727	

¶1017

Doctor	$1,750
Hospital...	1,325
Medicine and drugs	340
OTC remedies and vitamins.........................	0
2001 medical expenses	$3,415
Less: 7.5% of $38,000 (adjusted gross income)	2,850
Allowable deduction for 2001	$ 565

1018. Medical Expenses Paid After Death. A decedent's own medical expenses that are paid by the decedent's estate *within one year beginning on the day after the decedent's death* are treated as paid when incurred and may be deducted on the decedent's return for the year incurred if the estate waives an estate tax deduction for such expenses (Reg. § 1.213-1(d)).[50] Alternatively, the estate may deduct the medical expenses as a claim against the estate for federal estate tax purposes without fulfilling the above requirement (Code Sec. 2053; Reg. § 20.2053-4). Medical expenses disallowed for income tax purposes because of the 7.5% limitation (¶ 1015) may not be claimed on the estate tax return when the estate allocates medical expenses between a decedent's final income tax and estate tax return.[51]

1019. Health and Accident Insurance Premiums. A medical expense deduction is allowed for premiums paid for medical care insurance (including contact lens insurance),[52] subject to the 7.5% limitation (¶ 1015). If an amount is payable under an insurance contract for other than medical care (such as indemnity for loss of income or life, limb, or sight), no amount paid for the insurance is deductible unless the medical care charge is stated separately in the contract or furnished in a separate statement. Premiums paid by a taxpayer before age 65 for medical care insurance for the taxpayer, the taxpayer's spouse, or a dependent, effective after age 65, are considered to be medical expenses in the year paid if the premiums are payable (on a level payment basis) under the contract (1) for a period of 10 years or more or (2) until the year the taxpayer reaches age 65 (but in no case for a period of less than five years) (Reg. § 1.213-1(e)).[53]

The premiums for long-term care insurance contracts was added to the definition of "medical care" for tax years beginning after December 31, 1996. The premiums eligible for the medical deduction are those paid during the year for a qualified long-term care insurance contract. The amount of the premium that is deductible is limited by the age of the individual at the close of the tax year. The inflation-adjusted maximum deductible amount for 2001 is: age 40 or less, $230; age 41 through 50, $430; age 51 through 60, $860; age 61 through 70, $2,290; and age 71 or older, $2,860 (Code Sec. 213(d)(10); Rev. Proc. 2001-13).

Amounts paid as self-employment tax (¶ 2664) or as employee tax (¶ 2648) for hospital insurance under the Medicare program are not medical expenses. Similarly, the basic cost of Medicare insurance (Medicare A) is not deductible, unless voluntarily paid by the taxpayer for coverage. However, the cost of extra Medicare (Medicare B) is deductible.[54] Self-employed persons can deduct from gross income 60% of amounts paid for health insurance coverage in 2001, 70% in 2002, and 100% in 2003 and thereafter. For details, see ¶ 908.

Archer Medical Savings Accounts

1020. Archer Medical Savings Accounts. Employees of small employers and self-employed individuals may be permitted to maintain Archer medical savings accounts (Archer MSAs) to pay medical expenses, provided that the accounts are used in conjunction with high-deductible health insurance. This program is a test of the Archer MSA concept and is generally limited to the first 750,000 participants each year beginning in 1997. For 2001, a high-deductible health

---

Footnote references are to paragraphs of the 2002 Standard Federal Tax Reports.

[50] ¶ 12,541   [52] ¶ 12,543.77   [54] ¶ 12,543.49
[51] ¶ 12,543.185   [53] ¶ 12,541

¶ 1020

insurance plan is a plan that has the following deductibles and limitations: (1) for individual coverage: the minimum deductible is $1,600, maximum deductible is $2,400 and maximum out-of-pocket limitation is $3,200, and (2) for family coverage: the minimum deductible is $3,200, maximum deductible is $4,800 and maximum out-of-pocket limitation is $5,850 (Code Sec. 220(c)(2); Rev. Proc. 2001-13).

An Archer MSA is a tax-exempt trust or custodial account with a financial institution that is used solely to pay the unreimbursed health care expenses of the account holder, the account holder's spouse or dependents (IRS Pub. 969). Within the limits, contributions to an Archer MSA will be deductible if made by an eligible individual and excludable from income if made by an employer on behalf of an eligible individual. Such contributions made by an employer must be reported on the employee's W-2. Contributions to an Archer MSA are subject to an annual limitation which is a percentage of the deductible of the required health insurance plan. Contributions are further limited by the income earned from the business (in the case of a self-employed individual) or by compensation earned from an employer (in the case of an employee).

Distributions from an Archer MSA are tax free when used to pay for qualified medical expenses. Distributions from an Archer MSA that are not used for payment of qualified medical expenses are included in income and subject to an additional 15-percent tax unless made after the participant reaches age 65, dies or becomes disabled (Code Sec. 220).[55] The 15-percent additional tax is not treated as a tax liability for purposes of the alternative minimum tax (Code Sec. 26(b)(2)(Q) and Code Sec. 55(c)(1)). Individuals use Form 8853 to calculate their Archer MSA deductions and any taxable distributions. The Archer MSA program expiration date was extended through December 31, 2002 by the Community Renewal Tax Relief Act of 2000 (P.L. 106-554) (Code Sec. 220(i)(1)).

For tax years beginning after December 31, 1998, eligible seniors may establish medical savings accounts called MedicarePlus Choice MSAs. Eligible individuals will be able to use MedicarePlus Choice MSA contributions to pay health care expenses. MedicarePlus Choice MSAs must be used in conjunction with a high deductible MedicarePlus Choice MSA health plan. The program is a test and will be available on a first-come, first-serve basis to the first 390,000 eligible seniors. The MedicarePlus Choice pilot program ends December 31, 2002 (Code Sec. 138).[56]

Taxes, Generally

1021. Deductible Taxes. Taxes not directly connected with a trade or business or with property held for production of rents or royalties may be deducted only as an itemized deduction on Schedule A of Form 1040. The following is a list of such taxes (Code Sec. 164(a)):[57]

(1) State, local or foreign real property tax. (However, see ¶ 1026.)

(2) State or local personal property tax. Payment for registration and licensing of a car may be deductible as a personal property tax if it is imposed annually and assessed in proportion to the value of the car (Reg. § 1.164-3(c))[58] (¶ 1022).

(3) State, local or foreign income, war profits, or excess profits tax (¶ 1023 and ¶ 2475).

(4) Generation-skipping transfer tax imposed on income distributions (¶ 2942).

State and local taxes imposed on personal property are deductible if three conditions are met: (1) the tax is ad valorem (substantially in proportion to the value of the property); (2) the tax is imposed on an annual basis; and (3) the tax is imposed with respect to personal property (Reg. § 1.164-3(c)).[59]

Footnote references are to paragraphs of the 2002 Standard Federal Tax Reports.

¶ 1021

[55] ¶ 12,670
[56] ¶ 7630
[57] ¶ 9500
[58] ¶ 9506
[59] ¶ 9502.421

1022. Taxes Deductible When Paid or Accrued. The deduction for taxes is allowed only for the year in which the taxes are paid or accrued (Code Sec. 164(a)).[60] Cash-basis taxpayers deduct taxes in the year paid, regardless of when they were due. Accrual-basis taxpayers may generally deduct taxes in the year they accrue.[61] See ¶ 1515.

The date when a tax becomes due and payable is not necessarily its accrual date.[62] State income taxes accrue during the year in which the income is earned.[63] Uncontested additional assessments accrue at the same time they would have accrued upon a correct original assessment.[64] For accrual of real estate taxes, see ¶ 1031 and ¶ 1036.

A taxpayer who contests a tax and transfers cash or property to satisfy the tax may deduct the contested tax in the year of payment if (1) the contest exists after the transfer and (2) a deduction would have otherwise been allowed for the year of transfer. This rule does not apply to taxes imposed by a foreign country or U.S. possession (Code Sec. 461(f)).[65]

1023. Deduction of Foreign Income and Profits Taxes. Foreign income and profits taxes are deductible only if the taxpayer does not elect to claim a credit for them on his U.S. income tax return. The taxpayer must choose either the credit or the deduction; he may not elect to take a credit for part, and deduct part, of the taxes. Foreign taxes accrue in the period for which they are imposed.[66] See ¶ 2475-¶ 2485.

1024. Deduction of Advance Payments of State Income Taxes. Advance payments of estimated state income taxes made by a cash-basis taxpayer pursuant to state law are deductible in the year paid. However, if, on the date of payment, the taxpayer cannot reasonably determine that there was an additional amount owing, such payment is not deductible.[67]

1025. Nondeductible Taxes. The taxes that cannot be deducted either as taxes or as business expenses are (Code Sec. 275):[68]

(1) federal income taxes, including social security and railroad retirement taxes paid by employees and one-half of the self-employment tax imposed by Code Sec. 1401 [69] (¶ 2664);

(2) federal war profits and excess profits taxes;[70]

(3) estate, inheritance, legacy, succession, and gift taxes (¶ 2901);

(4) income, war profits, and excess profits taxes imposed by a foreign country or a U.S. possession, if the taxpayer chooses to take a foreign tax credit for these taxes or such taxes are paid or accrued with respect to foreign trade income of a foreign sales corporation (¶ 2470);[71]

(5) taxes on real property that must be treated as imposed on another taxpayer because of apportionment between buyer and seller (see ¶ 1032); and

(6) certain penalty taxes imposed under Chapters 41, 42, 43, 44, 46 and 54 of the Internal Revenue Code on public charities, private foundations, qualified pension plans, real estate investment trusts, and greenmail.

1026. Improvement Tax. Any tax that is in reality an assessment for local benefits such as street, sidewalk, and other like improvements is not deductible by a property owner, except where it is levied for the purpose of maintenance and repair or of meeting interest charges on local benefits. It is the taxpayer's burden to show the allocation of amounts assessed to the different purposes (Code Sec. 164(c)(1); Reg. § 1.164-4).[72]

Footnote references are to paragraphs of the 2002 Standard Federal Tax Reports.

[60] ¶ 9500
[61] ¶ 9502.04
[62] ¶ 9502.04
[63] ¶ 9502.445
[64] ¶ 9502.10
[65] ¶ 9502.0415
[66] ¶ 9502.01
[67] ¶ 9502.22
[68] ¶ 14,500
[69] ¶ 32,541
[70] ¶ 14,500
[71] ¶ 28,080
[72] ¶ 9500, ¶ 9508

1027. Self-Employment Tax. See ¶ 2664.

Real Property Taxes

1028. Deductibility. Local, state, and foreign real property taxes are generally deductible only by the person upon whom they are imposed in the year in which they were paid or accrued (Code Sec. 164(a); Reg. § 1.164-1(a)).[73] Real property taxes are taxes imposed on interests in real property and levied for the general public welfare. Such taxes do not include taxes assessed against local benefits (Reg. § 1.164-3(b)).[74] See ¶ 1026. State or local tax includes only taxes imposed by a state, including the District of Columbia, possessions of the U.S., or a political subdivision thereof. Foreign tax includes taxes imposed by the authority of a foreign country or its political subdivision (Reg. § 1.164-3(a) and Reg. § 1.164-3(d)).[75]

Stockholder-owners in a cooperative housing corporation may deduct amounts paid by the corporation to the extent of the stockholder-owner's proportionate share of the taxes paid (Code Sec. 216). See ¶ 1040. Condominium apartment owners may also deduct real property taxes paid on their personal interests in the property (Rev. Rul. 64-31). However, their homeowner association assessments are not deductible as real property taxes since the assessments are not paid to the state or a political subdivision (Rev. Rul. 76-495).[76]

Ministers and military personnel (see ¶ 1050) are allowed to deduct taxes paid on their homes even though they receive a parsonage or military allowance excludable from gross income (Code Sec. 265(a)(6)).[77] The New York renters' tax is not deductible as a property tax (Rev. Rul. 79-180).[78] Cash-basis mortgagors that pay taxes directly to the mortgagee are entitled to deduct the taxes when the mortgagee pays the taxing authority.[79]

1029. Real Property Construction Period Interest and Taxes. Interest and taxes on real property paid or incurred during the construction period generally must be capitalized (Code Sec. 263A).[80] See ¶ 991 and ¶ 993.

1030. Carrying Charges on Real Property. Taxpayers may elect to capitalize taxes on unimproved and unproductive real property (Code Sec. 266).[81] See ¶ 1614.

1031. Election to Accrue Real Property Tax. An accrual-basis taxpayer may elect to accrue real property taxes that are related to a definite period of time ratably over that period. Such an election may be made without IRS consent for the first tax year in which a taxpayer incurs real property taxes or at any other time with IRS consent (Code Sec. 461(c); Reg. § 1.461-1(c)).[82]

Should Election Be Made? Generally, the economic performance rule delays an accrual-method taxpayer's deduction for real property taxes until they are paid. However, if such taxes are a "recurring item," taxpayers may accrue the deduction on the lien or assessment date if certain requirements are met (Reg. § 1.461-4(g)(6) and Reg. § 1.461-5).[83]

Whether it is beneficial to make a Code Sec. 461(c) election or to adopt the recurring item exception for real property taxes depends on the taxpayer's tax year and the tax year and lien date of the jurisdiction in which the real property is located. Except where taxes are prepaid, either option is more favorable than the payment rule.

> **Example 1.** X is a calendar-year, accrual-method taxpayer who owns Blackacre in Cook County, Illinois, where the real property tax year is the calendar year and 2001 real property taxes were assessed and became a lien on the property on January 1, 2001. Taxes are due as follows: 1/2 on March 1, 2002, and 1/2 on August 1, 2002.

Footnote references are to paragraphs of the 2002 Standard Federal Tax Reports.

[73] ¶ 9500, ¶ 9501	[77] ¶ 14,050	[81] ¶ 14,100
[74] ¶ 9506	[78] ¶ 9507.82	[82] ¶ 21,802, ¶ 21,805
[75] ¶ 9506	[79] ¶ 9502.225	[83] ¶ 21,810, ¶ 21,811
[76] ¶ 9502.422	[80] ¶ 13,800	

Under its three options for accruing real property taxes, X would allocate its deduction between 2001 and 2002 as follows:

(1) *Payment rule.* 2001: none. 2002: $12/12$.

(2) *Ratable accrual.* 2001: $12/12$. 2002: none.

(3) *Recurring item exception.* 2001: $12/12$ (provided that X adopted the recurring item exception on either a timely filed original return or on an amended return filed after paying the second installment but before September 15, 2002). 2002: none.

Example 2. Assume X owns Greenacre in Alabama where taxes for the fiscal year from October 1, 2001, to September 30, 2002, were assessed and became a lien on the property on October 1, 2001. Taxes are due on October 1, 2002.

Under its three options for accruing real property taxes, X would allocate its deduction between 2001 and 2002 as follows:

(1) *Payment rule.* 2001: none. 2002: $12/12$.

(2) *Ratable accrual.* 2001: $3/12$. 2002: $9/12$.

(3) *Recurring item exception.* 2001: none (since taxes are not due until more than 8 ½ months after end of 2001). 2002: $12/12$. However, X could advance its entire deduction into 2001 by prepaying its real property taxes on or before September 15, 2002.

1032. Apportionment of Real Property Tax Upon Sale. The real property tax deduction must be apportioned between the seller and the buyer according to the number of days in the real property tax year (¶ 1033) that each holds the property. Where property is sold *during* any real property tax year, the taxes are considered as imposed upon the seller up to, but not including, the date of sale. The taxes are treated as imposed on the buyer beginning with the date of sale. Proration is required whether or not the seller and purchaser actually apportion the tax (Reg. § 1.164-6(a) and Reg. § 1.164-6(b)(1)).[84] However, when property is sold subsequent or prior to the real property tax year, see ¶ 1038.

Example 1. A sells his farm to B on August 1, 2001. Both use the cash- and calendar-year basis of accounting. Taxes for the real property tax year, April 1, 2001, to March 31, 2002, become due and payable on May 15, 2002. B pays the real estate taxes when they fall due. Regardless of any agreement between the parties, for federal income tax purposes $122/365$ of the real estate taxes are treated as imposed upon A and are deductible by him.

Example 2. Assume the same facts as in Example 1, except that A uses the accrual basis of accounting. If he has not elected to accrue the real property taxes ratably, he will be treated as having accrued $122/365$ of the taxes on the date of sale. The balance is deductible by B when he pays the taxes, if he is on the cash basis, unless the rule at ¶ 1035 applies because the seller (A) is personally liable for payment of the taxes. If he is on the accrual basis, he follows the rules explained at ¶ 1031.

1033. Real Property Tax Year Defined. The "real property tax year" is the period determined under state or local law that is regarded as the period to which the imposed tax relates. If a state and one or more local governmental units each imposes a tax, the real property tax year for each tax must be determined (Reg. § 1.164-6(c)).[85]

1034. Cash-Basis Sellers. The real estate tax apportioned to a cash-basis seller under the rules described at ¶ 1032 may be deducted in the tax year of the sale (whether or not actually paid in that tax year) if (1) the buyer is liable for the real estate tax for the real property tax year or (2) the seller is liable for the real estate tax for the real property tax year and the tax is not payable until after the

---

date of sale. Where the tax is not a liability of any person, the person who holds the property at the time the tax becomes a lien on the property is considered liable for the tax (Reg. § 1.164-6(d)(1) and Reg. § 1.164-6(d)(3)).[86]

1035. Cash-Basis Buyers. The real estate tax apportioned to a cash-basis buyer under the rules described at ¶ 1032 may be deducted by the buyer in the tax year of the sale, whether or not the tax is actually paid by the buyer in the tax year of the sale, if the seller is liable for the real estate tax. Where the tax is not a liability of any person, the person who holds the property at the time the tax becomes a lien on the property is considered liable for the tax (Reg. § 1.164-6(d)(2) and § 1.164-6(d)(3)).[87]

1036. Accrual-Basis Buyers and Sellers. If an accrual-basis buyer or seller has not made the election at ¶ 1031, the portion of tax imposed upon him (see ¶ 1032) that may not be deducted for any tax year by reason of his accounting method is treated as if accrued on the date of sale (Reg. § 1.164-6(d)(6)).[88]

1037. Excess Deduction. If a taxpayer deducted taxes in excess of the portion of such tax treated as imposed upon the taxpayer under ¶ 1032 for a tax year prior to the year of sale, the excess amount is included in the taxpayer's gross income in the year of sale, subject to the tax benefit rule (¶ 799) (Reg. § 1.164-6(d)(5)).[89]

> **Example.** In the county in which a cash-basis taxpayer owns property, the real property tax is due and payable on November 30 for the succeeding calendar year, which is also the real property tax year. The taxpayer paid his real property taxes on the due date for the 2001 real property tax year and deducted such taxes on his 2000 income tax return. On June 30, 2001, the taxpayer sold the real property. The taxes from January 1 through June 29, 2001, i.e., the $181/365$ portion, are treated as imposed on the taxpayer. The excess amount deducted by the taxpayer on his 2000 return is includible in his gross income in 2001.

1038. Property Sold Prior or Subsequent to Real Property Tax Year. If the tax becomes a personal liability or a lien before the beginning of the real property tax year to which it relates and the property is sold subsequent to the time the tax becomes a personal liability or a lien but prior to the beginning of the related real property tax year, the seller may not deduct any amount for real property taxes for the related real property tax year. The buyer, to the extent that the buyer holds the property for such real property tax year, may deduct the amount of the taxes for the tax year in which they are paid or accrued. Conversely, where the tax becomes a personal liability or a lien after the end of the real property tax year to which it relates and the property is sold prior to the time the tax becomes a personal liability or a lien but after the end of the related real property tax year, the buyer cannot deduct any amount for taxes for the related real property tax year. The seller, to the extent that he holds the property for such real property tax year, may deduct the amount of such taxes for the tax year they are paid or accrued (Reg. § 1.164-6(b)(1)(ii) and Reg. § 1.164-6(b)(1)(iii)).[90]

1040. Cooperative Housing Corporation. A tenant-stockholder may deduct amounts paid or accrued to the corporation to the extent that they represent his proportionate share of real estate taxes on the apartment building or houses and land on which situated and of interest on debt contracted in the acquisition, construction, alteration, rehabilitation, or maintenance of such building or houses or of the land on which situated (Code Sec. 216; Reg. § 1.216-1).[91] However, for the limitation on the interest deduction for residential property, see ¶ 1043 et seq.

Eighty percent or more of Cooperative Housing Corporation (CHC) gross income must come from its tenants before a tenant may deduct his share of the taxes and interest. For purposes of this 80% test, amounts received by such corporations from tenant-stockholders to defray expenses such as the costs of maid and secretarial

---

Footnote references are to paragraphs of the 2002 Standard Federal Tax Reports.

¶ **1035**

[86] ¶ 9603	[88] ¶ 9603	[90] ¶ 9603
[87] ¶ 9603	[89] ¶ 9603	[91] ¶ 12,600, ¶ 12,601

services, parking, utilities, recreation facilities, and cleaning and related services are included as gross income derived from tenants while amounts received from commercial leases and the operation of a business other than housing are excluded.[92] Stock owned or apartments leased by government entities empowered to acquire CHC shares in order to provide housing facilities are not taken into account (Code Sec. 216(b)(4)).[93]

Interest

1043. Interest Paid or Accrued. A taxpayer may generally deduct interest paid or accrued within the tax year on indebtedness (Code Sec. 163(a)).[94] The interest is reported on Schedule A of Form 1040. However, such interest must pertain to the debt of the taxpayer and must result from a debtor-creditor relationship based upon a valid and enforceable obligation to pay a fixed or determinable sum of money.[95] For example, interest paid by children on their parent's mortgage was not deductible.[96] There are numerous exceptions to and limitations on the deductibility of interest. See ¶ 940 and ¶ 1044-¶ 1056.

1044. Exceptions and Limitations. There are a number of Code sections that limit or preclude a taxpayer from claiming an interest deduction on certain types of indebtedness. See ¶ 940.

Investment Indebtedness Interest. The deduction by noncorporate taxpayers is limited to net investment income (Code Sec. 163(d)).[97] See ¶ 1094.

Life Insurance. Interest on loans incurred or continued to pay premiums on certain insurance contracts is nondeductible (Code Sec. 264(a)).[98] See ¶ 909.

Personal Interest. Personal interest is not deductible (Code Sec. 163(h)).[99] See ¶ 1045.

Prepaid Interest. Cash-basis taxpayers generally must capitalize prepaid interest and deduct it as if on the accrual basis (Code Sec. 461(g)).[100] See ¶ 1055.

Loan to Purchase and Carry Tax-Exempt Securities. A deduction for interest paid on a debt incurred or continued to purchase or carry tax-exempt bonds or other tax-exempt obligations is generally denied (Code Sec. 265(a)).[101] See ¶ 970.

Related Taxpayers. Accrual-basis taxpayers are placed on the cash basis for interest deductions owed to related cash-basis taxpayers (Code Sec. 267(a)).[102] Furthermore, a corporation will be disallowed a deduction for excessive interest paid to a tax-exempt related person, or on a loan guaranteed by certain tax-exempt or foreign related persons, for interest paid or accrued in tax years beginning after December 31, 1993 (Code Sec. 163(j)).[103]

Judicial Exceptions. The courts have denied a deduction for the interest charged upon conversion of a life insurance policy to a higher-premium policy[104] and for interest paid on loans to buy U.S. Treasury notes where there was nothing to be realized from the transaction beyond a tax deduction.[105]

1045. Personal Interest. Personal interest is not deductible. Personal interest is any interest incurred *by an individual* other than:

(1) interest paid or accrued on indebtedness properly allocable to a trade or business (other than services as an employee) (see ¶ 937);

(2) investment interest (see ¶ 1094);

(3) interest taken into account in computing income or loss from a passive activity of the taxpayer (see ¶ 2053);

(4) qualified residence interest (see ¶ 1047);

Footnote references are to paragraphs of the 2002 Standard Federal Tax Reports.

[92] ¶ 12,603.13
[93] ¶ 12,600
[94] ¶ 9102
[95] ¶ 9104.021, ¶ 9104.344
[96] ¶ 9104.728
[97] ¶ 9102
[98] ¶ 14,002
[99] ¶ 9102
[100] ¶ 21,802
[101] ¶ 14,050
[102] ¶ 14,150
[103] ¶ 9102
[104] ¶ 9104.0486
[105] ¶ 9104.364

(5) interest on the unpaid portion of the estate tax for the period during which there is an extension of time for payment of the tax on the value of a reversionary or remainder interest in property or when an estate consists largely of an interest in a closely held business; and

(6) interest on qualified education loans (see ¶ 1082) (Code Sec. 163(h)(2)).[106]

1047. "Qualified Residence Interest" Defined. Qualified residence interest is interest that is paid or accrued during the tax year on acquisition or home equity indebtedness with respect to any qualified residence. A qualified residence includes the principal residence of the taxpayer and one other residence (i.e., vacation home) that is used by the taxpayer for a number of days exceeding the greater of 14 days or 10 percent of the number of days during the tax year that it is rented out at a fair rental value. However, if a dwelling unit is not rented at any time during the tax year, such unit may be treated as a qualified residence regardless of personal use. Interest on a loan secured by a qualified residence in a state where the security instrument is otherwise restricted by a debtor protection law is qualified residence interest if it otherwise qualifies. Interest paid or accrued by a trust or estate on indebtedness secured by a beneficiary's qualified residence is qualified residence interest if the residence would be a qualified residence if owned by the beneficiary. Married taxpayers who file separate returns are treated as one taxpayer, with each entitled to take into account one residence unless both consent in writing to having only one taxpayer take into account both residences (Code Sec. 163(h)(3)).[107]

The receipt of mortgage interest is generally reported by the lender on Form 1098 (¶ 2565). In the case of seller-provided financing, taxpayers claiming a deduction for qualified residence interest must include on their returns the name, address and TIN of the person to whom interest is paid or accrued (Code Sec. 6109(h)).[108]

1048. Acquisition and Home Equity Indebtedness. Acquisition indebtedness is debt incurred in acquiring, constructing, or substantially improving a qualified residence and secured by such residence. Any such debt that is refinanced is treated as acquisition debt to the extent that it does not exceed the principal amount of acquisition debt immediately before refinancing.

Home equity indebtedness is all debt (other than acquisition debt) that is secured by a qualified residence to the extent it does not exceed the fair market value of the residence reduced by any acquisition indebtedness. Interest on such debt is deductible even if the proceeds are used for personal expenditures (IRS Pub. 936).[109]

1048A. Limits on Acquisition and Home Equity Indebtedness. Only a limited amount of interest paid or accrued is deductible as qualified residence interest. The aggregate amount of acquisition indebtedness may not exceed $1 million and the aggregate amount of home equity indebtedness may not exceed $100,000. These amounts are halved for a married individual filing a separate return. Interest attributable to the amount of debt equal to or under the above limits is fully deductible, while interest attributable to debt over such limits is nondeductible personal interest (¶ 1045). See ¶ 1048B for rules applicable to debt incurred on or before October 13, 1987.

> **Example 1.** In 2001, an individual buys a home to be used as his principal residence for $175,000 that is secured by a mortgage in the amount of $150,000. The mortgage qualifies as home acquisition debt since the loan amount does not exceed the home's cost.

> **Example 2.** An individual owns a home that has a fair market value in 2001 of $110,000. The balance of the mortgage (home acquisition debt) in 2001 is $95,000. The individual takes out a home equity loan in the

---

Footnote references are to paragraphs of the 2002 Standard Federal Tax Reports.

¶ 1047 106 ¶ 9102   108 ¶ 36,960   109 ¶ 9102
      107 ¶ 9102

amount of $42,500. His home equity debt is limited to $15,000—the smaller of (1) the $100,000 maximum limit or (2) the amount that the home's fair market value ($110,000) exceeds the home acquisition debt ($95,000).

1048B. Special Rules for Pre-October 13, 1987, Indebtedness. Indebtedness incurred on or before October 13, 1987, is treated as acquisition indebtedness on which the $1 million limitation at ¶ 1048A is inapplicable. However, the amount of such debt reduces the amount of the $1 million limitation available for new acquisition debt (e.g., for improvements).

Pre-October 13, 1987, debt is any debt incurred on or before October 13, 1987, that is secured by a qualified residence on October 13, 1987, and at all times thereafter before the interest is paid or accrued. Such debt also includes debt secured by a qualified residence to refinance existing pre-October 13 debt, to the extent that the principal amount of the refinancing does not exceed the principal amount of the refinanced debt immediately before the refinancing. Such refinancing may not extend the term of the debt beyond the term of the acquisition debt immediately before the refinancing. If acquisition debt is not amortized over its term, as in the case of a balloon note, interest on any otherwise qualified refinancing will be deductible for the term of the first refinancing of such acquisition debt, but not for more than 30 years after that first refinancing (Code Sec. 163(h)).[110]

1049. Redeemable Ground Rents. Annual or periodic payments of redeemable ground rent (except amounts paid in redemption of this rent) are treated as interest paid on mortgage indebtedness (Code Sec. 163(c)).[111] Therefore, it seems that such ground rents are subject to the rules pertaining to qualified residences. See ¶ 1047. A "redeemable ground rent" is defined as a ground rent payable under a freely assignable lease that (including possible renewal periods) is for a term in excess of 15 years (Code Sec. 1055(c)(1); Reg. § 1.1055-1).[112]

1050. Ministers and Military Personnel. Ministers and military personnel are allowed to deduct mortgage interest on their homes even though they receive a parsonage or military allowance that is excludable from gross income (Code Sec. 265(a)(6)).[113] However, it seems that such interest is subject to the qualified residence rules at ¶ 1047. Military personnel includes members of the Army, Navy, Air Force, Marine Corps, Coast Guard, National Oceanic and Atmospheric Administration, and Public Health Service.[114]

1051. Interest Paid on Delinquent Taxes. Nonbusiness interest imposed on delinquent federal taxes, state taxes and real estate taxes is generally nondeductible personal interest. See ¶ 1045. However, any interest expense accrued for federal estate taxes during an extension for payment of tax under Code Sec. 6163 or Code Sec. 6166 may be claimed as either a deduction from federal estate tax as an administrative expense or as an income tax deduction under Code Sec. 163(h)(2)(E),[115] provided that the right to an estate tax deduction for the interest expense has been waived (Code Sec. 642(g)).[116] Further, interest on federal and state income tax deficiencies accruing after death is generally deductible by the estate as an administration expense.[117]

The IRS maintains that interest paid on underpayments of an individual's federal, state, or local income tax liability is nondeductible personal interest regardless of the source of the income generating the tax liability (Temp. Reg. § 1.163-9T(b)(2)(i)(A)).[118] This regulation has been declared invalid by the Tax Court to the extent it denies a deduction for tax deficiency interest on income derived from the conduct of a trade or business. However, the appellate courts for the Fourth, Sixth, Eighth and Ninth Circuits have found Temp. Reg.

Footnote references are to paragraphs of the 2002 Standard Federal Tax Reports.

[110] ¶ 9102
[111] ¶ 9102
[112] ¶ 29,940, ¶ 29,941

[113] ¶ 14,050
[114] ¶ 14,050.024
[115] ¶ 9102

[116] ¶ 24,280
[117] ¶ 24,308.044
[118] ¶ 9400

§ 1.163-9T(b)(2)(i)(A) is valid with respect to the disallowance of interest paid on a tax liability whose source is a trade or business.[119]

Interest paid on sales and excise taxes incurred in connection with a trade or business or investment activity is not personal interest; interest paid by a transferee for a C corporation's delinquent taxes is not personal interest (Temp. Reg. § 1.163-9T(b)(2)(iii)).[120]

1052. Consumer Debt. Interest on consumer debt is nondeductible personal interest. See ¶ 1045.

Prepaid Interest

1055. Deductibility of Prepaid Interest by Cash-Basis Taxpayers. All cash-basis taxpayers are required to deduct prepaid interest over the period of the loan to the extent that the interest represents the cost of using the borrowed funds during each tax year in the period. Points paid on loans (other than certain home mortgage loans) are to be deducted ratably over the term of the loan (Code Sec. 461(g)).[121] Penalty payments made for the privilege of prepaying mortgage indebtedness are currently deductible as interest.[122]

The prepaid interest rule does not contemplate that interest will be treated as paid in equal payments over the term of the loan. Thus, interest paid on an amortizing loan as part of an equal constant payment (including principal and interest) is not subject to the prepaid interest rule merely because the payments consist of a larger interest portion in the earlier years of the loan than in later years.[123]

Points on a home mortgage loan for the purchase or improvement of, and secured by, a principal residence are deductible in the year paid to the extent that, under regulations, the payment of points is an established practice in the area involved and the amount of the payment does not exceed that generally charged in the area for a home loan (Code Sec. 461(g)(2)).[124]

As a matter of administrative practice, the IRS treats as deductible in the year paid any points paid by a cash-basis taxpayer with respect to a home mortgage that meets the following requirements (Rev. Proc. 94-27):[125]

(1) they must be designated as points on the RESPA settlement statement (Form HUD-1), for example, as "loan origination fees" (including amounts so designated on VA and FHA loans), "loan discount," "discount points," or "points";

(2) they must be calculated as a percentage of the principal loan amount;

(3) they must be paid to *acquire* the taxpayer's principal residence, and the loan must be secured by that residence;

(4) they must be paid directly by the taxpayer (which may include earnest money, an escrow deposit, or down payment applied at closing) and may not be derived from loan proceeds; points paid by a seller (including points charged to the seller) are considered directly paid by the taxpayer from funds not derived from loan proceeds if they are subtracted by the taxpayer from the purchase price of the residence in computing its basis; and

(5) they must conform to an established business practice of charging points for loans for the acquisition of personal residences in the area in which the residence is located, and the amount of points may not exceed the amount generally charged in that area. In this connection, the IRS emphasizes that no part of the amounts paid may be in lieu of appraisal, inspection, title, and attorney fees, property taxes, or other amounts that are ordinarily stated separately on the settlement statement.

The above safe harbor does not apply to the extent that the points exceed the limit on acquisition indebtedness discussed at ¶ 1048A. Nor does it apply to points

---

[119] ¶ 9400A.50	[122] ¶ 9402.023	[124] ¶ 21,802
[120] ¶ 9400	[123] ¶ 21,802.051	[125] ¶ 9402.65
¶ 1052 [121] ¶ 21,802		

paid on home improvement loans, second or vacation home loans, refinancing or home equity loans, or lines of credit. The fact that a taxpayer cannot satisfy the requirements of the safe harbor does not necessarily mean that points are not currently deductible; it does mean that the IRS will not automatically consider them to be currently deductible. In a recent letter ruling, the IRS allowed a couple to amortize home-purchase loan points over the life of the loan in a situation where the applicable standard deduction in the year the points were paid was greater than the couple's itemized deductions (including the total points paid) (IRS Letter Ruling 199905033).[126]

Points paid to refinance a home mortgage are not deductible in full in the year paid but must be deducted ratably over the period of the loan because such points are for repaying the taxpayer's existing indebtedness and are not paid in connection with the purchase or improvement of the home. However, the U.S. Court of Appeals for the Eighth Circuit, reversing the Tax Court, has allowed full deduction in the year paid for points on a long-term home mortgage loan refinancing a short-term balloon loan used to acquire the home.[127] Also, if part of the refinancing proceeds is used for improvements, the portion of the points allocable to the improvements may be deducted in the year paid. However, the portion allocable to the repayment of existing indebtedness or other purposes is deducted ratably over the period of the loan (Rev. Rul. 87-22).[128]

A loan discount (where a lender delivers to an individual borrower an amount smaller than the face amount of the loan and the difference is the agreed charge for the use of borrowed money) is interest.[129]

1056. Deductibility of Prepaid Interest by Accrual-Basis Taxpayers. Taxpayers who use the accrual method accrue interest ratably over the loan period and must deduct it ratably over such period, regardless of whether the interest is prepaid.[130]

Charitable Contributions

1058. Contributions by Individuals, Generally. The charitable deduction allowed to an individual for any one tax year is limited to a percentage of the individual's "contribution base." This percentage is determined by two factors: the type of organization to which the donation is made and the type of property donated (Code Sec. 170(b)(1)).[131] Any amount in excess of the percentage limitation for the tax year may be carried forward for a period of five years (Code Sec. 170(d)).[132] See ¶ 1060. An individual's contribution base is adjusted gross income, computed without regard to any net operating loss carryback (Code Sec. 170(b)(1)(F)).[133] When a husband and wife file a joint return, the percentage limitation depends on their aggregate contribution base (Reg. § 1.170A-8(a)).[134] Individuals also have a limit as to the amount of a charitable deduction allowed for gifts of appreciated property. See ¶ 1062. Such limitation is imposed before applying the percentage limitation (Code Sec. 170(e); Reg. § 1.170A-4).[135] Contributions are reported on Schedule A of Form 1040.

1059. Limits on Individuals' Contributions. Contributions to (but not for the use of) the following types of tax-exempt organizations qualify for the maximum deduction of 50 percent of a taxpayer's contribution base (see ¶ 1058) for the tax year: (1) churches or conventions or associations of churches; (2) educational institutions; (3) hospital or medical research organizations (not including a home health care organization,[136] convalescent home, homes for children or aged, or vocational institutions that train handicapped individuals); (4) endowment foundations in connection with a state college or university; (5) a government unit, state, federal or local, if the contribution is made for exclusively public purposes; (6) an

---

[126] ¶ 9402.04
[127] ¶ 9402.62
[128] ¶ 9402.60
[129] ¶ 9104.586

[130] ¶ 21,817.3253
[131] ¶ 11,600
[132] ¶ 11,600
[133] ¶ 11,600

[134] ¶ 11,661
[135] ¶ 11,600, ¶ 11,632
[136] ¶ 11,670.026, ¶ 11,670.562

¶ 1059

organization normally receiving a substantial part of its support from the public or a governmental unit; (7) a private operating foundation; (8) a private nonoperating foundation which distributes all contributions it receives to public charities and private operating foundations (or makes certain other qualifying distributions) within 2½ months after the end of its tax year; (9) organizations normally receiving (a) more than ⅓ of their support in each tax year from the public and other organizations ((1)-(7), above) in the form of grants, gifts, contributions, or membership fees, and gross receipts from an activity which is not an unrelated trade or business (less certain receipts), and (b) not more than ⅓ of their support from gross investment income and unrelated business taxable income (less taxes); and (10) private foundations that pool all contributions into a common fund and allow a substantial contributor to designate a recipient charity, income from the pool being distributed within 2½ months after the tax year in which it was realized and corpus attributable to any donor's contribution being distributed to a charity not later than one year after the death of the donor (or his surviving spouse if she has the right to designate the recipients of the corpus) (Code Sec. 170(b)(1)(A); Reg. § 1.170A-9).[137]

There is a special 30-percent limitation on certain capital gain property contributed by an individual to the ten types of organizations listed above (Code Sec. 170(b)(1)(C)).[138] See ¶ 1062.

The deduction limitation on contributions of ordinary income property to nonoperating foundations and organizations, such as war veterans' and fraternal organizations, public cemeteries, and gifts for the use of 50-percent organization donees is the lesser of (1) 30 percent of the taxpayer's contribution base or (2) the excess of 50 percent of the taxpayer's contribution base for the tax year over the amount of charitable contributions qualifying for the 50-percent deduction ceiling, including carryovers (Code Sec. 170(b)(1)(B)).[139] Gifts of capital gain property to these organizations are subject to a 20-percent AGI limitation (Code Sec. 170(b)(1)(D)).[140] See ¶ 1062.

For deduction limitations on charitable contributions by corporations, see ¶ 927.

1060. Five-Year Carryover by Individual. Individuals who make contributions to charitable organizations in excess of the deductible ceiling for the tax year may carry this excess deduction forward for a period of five years (Code Sec. 170(d); Reg. § 1.170A-10).[141] The amount of the excess that may be deducted in any carryover year is limited to the lesser of: (1) the remaining portion of any excess contribution not already deducted or (2) an amount equal to 50 percent (or 30 percent for capital gain carryover) of the taxpayer's adjusted gross income after first deducting the sum of the charitable contributions (to which the 50- or 30-percent limitation applies) paid in the carryover year and any excess contributions that have precedence in order of time over the present carryover.

1061. Contributions That Are Deductible. A contribution is deductible only if made to, or for the use of, the following qualified organization:

(1) The United States, a state, a local government, the District of Columbia, or a U.S. possession for exclusively public purposes.

(2) A corporation, trust, or community chest, fund, or foundation, created or organized in the United States or in any possession or under the law of the United States, any state, the District of Columbia, or any possession of the United States, organized and operated exclusively for religious, charitable, scientific, literary or educational purposes, or to foster national or international amateur sports competition, or for the prevention of cruelty to children or animals, no part of the net earnings of which inures to the benefit of any private shareholder or individual (e.g., nonprofit hospitals and churches and synagogues). Also, the organization must not be disqualified for tax exemption under Code Sec. 501(c)(3) by attempting to influence legislation.

Footnote references are to paragraphs of the 2002 Standard Federal Tax Reports.

¶ **1060**

[137] ¶ 11,600, ¶ 11,662	[139] ¶ 11,600	[141] ¶ 11,600, ¶ 11,663
[138] ¶ 11,600	[140] ¶ 11,600	

(3) A cemetery company owned and operated exclusively for the benefit of its members or any corporation chartered solely for burial purposes as a cemetery corporation and not operated for profit or for the benefit of any private shareholder or individual.

(4) A post or organization of war veterans, or its auxiliary society or unit, organized in the United States or its possessions, if no part of the net earnings inures to the benefit of any private shareholder or individual.

(5) For individuals only, a domestic fraternal society, order, or association, operating under the lodge system, but only if such contributions are to be used exclusively for religious, charitable, scientific, literary, or educational purposes, or for the prevention of cruelty to children or animals (Code Sec. 170(c)).[142]

Services. The value of service rendered to a charitable institution is not deductible as a contribution,[143] nor is the value of a blood donation, which is in the nature of service rendered.[144] But an out-of-pocket, unreimbursed expense, such as for uniforms, telephone or equipment, incurred in rendering such service is deductible as a contribution.[145] No deduction is allowed for an out-of-pocket expenditure made by any person on behalf of a charitable organization other than an organization described in Code Sec. 501(h)(5) (churches, etc.) if the expenditure is made for the purpose of influencing legislation (Code Sec. 170(f)(6)). A charitable or business deduction is also denied for contributions made to organizations that conduct lobbying activities relating to matters of direct financial interest to the donor, unless the donor could have claimed a business expense deduction if the donor had directly conducted the lobbying activities (Code Sec. 170(f)(9)).[146] See ¶ 974.

Travel Expenses. Deductions are allowed for transportation or other travel expenses (including meals and lodging) incurred in the performance of services away from home on behalf of a charitable organization if there is no significant element of personal pleasure, recreation, or vacation. If there is such an element, deductions will be denied even though the expenses are paid directly by the individual, indirectly through a contribution to the organization, or by reimbursement by the organization. This rule does not apply to the extent that an individual pays for travel for third parties who are participants in the charitable activity. However, deductions will be disallowed where two unrelated taxpayers pay each other's travel expenses or members of a group contribute to a fund that pays for all travel expenses (Code Sec. 170(j)).[147] Individuals who qualify for a deduction for the use of an automobile may use the statutory standard mileage rate of 14 cents per mile in lieu of a deduction based on the actual expenses incurred (Rev. Proc. 2000-48) (remains 14 cents per mile in 2002 (Rev. Proc. 2001-54)). Under the standard mileage rate method, additional deductions may be taken for parking fees and tolls. Depreciation and insurance are not deductible as part of the contribution (Code Sec. 170(i)).[148]

Fundraising Activities. The payment of money for a ticket to a charity event— e.g., a ball, bazaar, show, or athletic event—creates a presumption that the payment represents the purchase price for an item of value. The burden is on the taxpayer to show that the amount paid is not the purchase price or that the payment exceeds the fair market value of the admission or other privileges associated with the event. The purchase price of a raffle ticket is not deductible.[149]

> **Example.** An individual pays $12 to see a special showing of a motion picture, the net proceeds of which go to a qualified charitable organization. Printed on the ticket is "Contribution—$12." If the regular price for the movie is $5, the individual made a contribution of $7 to a qualified charitable organization.

Fundraising organizations that provide token benefits to contributors may advise those contributors that their donations are fully deductible only if the token benefits have an insubstantial value. In the case of potential donors who receive

---

Footnote references are to paragraphs of the 2002 Standard Federal Tax Reports.

[142] ¶ 11,600
[143] ¶ 11,620.655
[144] ¶ 11,620.65
[145] ¶ 11,620.67
[146] ¶ 11,600
[147] ¶ 11,600
[148] ¶ 11,600
[149] ¶ 11,620.511

items in the mail, the organization may advise that a contribution is fully deductible only if the item is low cost, provided for free, and not distributed at the donor's request or consent (See Rev. Proc. 90-12 and Rev. Proc. 97-57).[150] Disclosure by a charitable organization of *quid pro quo contributions* in excess of $75 is required for contributions made on or after January 1, 1994 (Code Sec. 6115).[151] See ¶ 629.

Eighty percent of an otherwise deductible payment made to a college or university for the right to purchase tickets to an athletic event is treated as a charitable contribution regardless of whether the tickets would have been available even if the payment had not been made (Code Sec. 170(l)).[152] The National Office of the IRS in an unpublished Technical Advice Memorandum extended this rule to include the offering of stadium skyboxes for football games. The memorandum held that the skybox limitation under Code Sec. 274(l) did not apply to this situation.

Transfers of property to a charitable organization directly related to the donor's business and made with a reasonable expectation of financial return commensurate with the value of the transfer will not qualify for a charitable deduction but may qualify as a trade or business expense (Reg. § 1.170A-1(c)(5)).[153]

For cash contributions, the taxpayer need only enter the total amount contributed on Form 1040, Schedule A, but written records are required to substantiate the deductions. For noncash contributions over $500 (over $5,000 in the case of C corporations other than closely held or personal service corporations), the taxpayer must complete Section A, Form 8283, giving details of the donation, and attach it to the taxpayer's return. If the noncash contribution exceeds $5,000, the taxpayer must obtain an appraisal for the contribution, complete Section B, Form 8283, giving details of the donation, and attach Section B to the taxpayer's tax return (Reg. § 1.170A-13).[154] See ¶ 1071.

Substantiation. Charitable contributions of $250 or more, made on or after January 1, 1994, must be substantiated by a contemporaneous written acknowledgment from the donee organization. However, substantiation is not required if the donee organization files a return with the IRS reporting the information that is required to be included in the written acknowledgment. Generally, the acknowledgment must include the amount of cash and a description of non-cash contributions, together with a description and good-faith estimate of the value of any goods or services (other than goods or services with insubstantial value) received for the contributions (Code Sec. 170(f)(8); Reg. § 1.170-13(f)).[155] Contributions made by payroll deduction may be substantiated with an employer-provided document, such as a pay-stub or Form W-2, showing the amount deducted and a donee-prepared document stating that the donee does not provide goods or services as whole or partial consideration for contributions made by payroll deduction. Substantiation is required only if $250 or more is deducted from a single paycheck (Reg. § 1.170A-13(f)(11)(i)(A)).[156]

Appraisal fees incurred by an individual in determining the fair market value of donated property are not to be treated as part of the charitable contribution, but they may be claimed as a miscellaneous deduction on Schedule A of Form 1040 (Rev. Rul. 67-461).[157]

Except for the carryover rule at ¶ 1060, a contribution is generally deductible only in the year of payment. However, contributions charged to a bank credit card are deductible in the year charged even though paid in a later year (Rev. Rul. 78-38).[158]

1062. Gifts of Appreciated Property. The amount deductible for a charitable contribution of appreciated property depends on whether it is ordinary income property or capital gain property, or a combination of both (Code Sec. 170(b) and (e); Reg. § 1.170A-4).[159]

Footnote references are to paragraphs of the 2002 Standard Federal Tax Reports.

[150] ¶ 11,620.512	[154] ¶ 11,685	[157] ¶ 11,700.10
[151] ¶ 37,065	[155] ¶ 11,600, ¶ 11,685	[158] ¶ 11,620.023
[152] ¶ 11,600	[156] ¶ 11,685	[159] ¶ 11,600, ¶ 11,632
¶ 1062 [153] ¶ 11,615		

Ordinary Income Property. Ordinary income property is property that, if sold at its fair market value on the date of contribution, would give rise to ordinary income or short-term capital gain. The deduction for such property is limited to the fair market value of the property less the amount that would be ordinary income. Such property includes inventory and stock in trade, artworks and manuscripts created by the donor, letters and memoranda, capital assets held for less than the required holding period for long-term capital gain treatment, and Code Sec. 306 stock (see ¶ 739 and ¶ 740) (Code Sec. 170(e)(1)(A); Reg. § 1.170A-4).[160]

Capital Gain Property. Capital gain property includes any asset on which a long-term capital gain would have been realized if the taxpayer had sold the asset for its fair market value on the date of contribution. As a general rule, gifts of capital gain property are deductible at their fair market value on the date of contribution. However, the individual's contribution must be reduced by the potential long-term gain (appreciation) if:

(1) the property is contributed to certain private nonoperating (grant-making) foundations (see, however, "Qualified Appreciated Stock," below) (Code Sec. 170(e)(1)(B)(ii));

(2) the gift is tangible personal property put to a use that is unrelated to the purpose or function upon which the organization's exemption is based; or

(3) the taxpayer elects to disregard the special 30% capital gains limitation in favor of the 50% limitation.[161]

Qualified Appreciated Stock. A deduction equal to the fair market value of qualified appreciated stock contributed to private nonoperating foundations is allowed (Code Sec. 170(e)(5)). Qualified appreciated stock is publicly traded stock that is capital gain property.

Combination Property. The amount of a deduction for a gift of property on which part of the gain that would result if it were sold at fair market value would be treated as ordinary income and part as capital gain is specially computed (Code Sec. 170(e)). First, the fair market value is reduced by the ordinary income that would have resulted from a sale at fair market value. The remainder of the fair market value is treated as capital gain property, subject to the above rules. The types of property to which this special computation would apply include those subject to depreciation recapture (¶ 1779-¶ 1788) and to recapture of farmland expenditures (¶ 1797), as well as interests in oil, gas, or geothermal property (¶ 2025).

1063. Use of Property—Partial Interests. Generally, a taxpayer is denied a charitable deduction for gifts to charity of the rent-free use of property and other nontrust gifts where less than the taxpayer's entire interest in the property is contributed, except in the following cases: (1) a contribution of an undivided portion of a taxpayer's entire interest in property—for example, a one-fourth interest in property; (2) a contribution of a remainder interest in a personal residence or farm; (3) a qualified conservation contribution; and (4) a charitable deduction would have been allowed had the interest been transferred in trust (Code Sec. 170(f)(3); Reg. § 1.170A-7).[162] See ¶ 538 and ¶ 1070.

1064. Care of Unrelated Student in the Home. A taxpayer may deduct as a charitable contribution unreimbursed amounts spent to maintain an elementary or high school student (other than a dependent or relative) in his home under a program sponsored by a charitable organization providing educational opportunities for students. The deduction is limited to the amount contributed but not more than $50 per month while the student is a member of the taxpayer's household and the student must be present in the home under a written agreement with the organization (Code Sec. 170(g); Reg. § 1.170A-2).[163]

1065. Reduction for Interest. If a liability is assumed by the recipient or by any other person, or if the contribution is of property that is subject to a liability,

---

Footnote references are to paragraphs of the 2002 Standard Federal Tax Reports.
[160] ¶ 11,600, ¶ 11,632   [162] ¶ 11,600, ¶ 11,651   [163] ¶ 11,600, ¶ 11,621
[161] ¶ 11,600

the charitable contribution must be reduced by the interest paid by the taxpayer-donor (whether prepaid or to be paid in the future by the taxpayer-donor) attributable to any period after the making of the contribution. If the gift is of a bond or other evidence of debt, the amount of the contribution is further reduced by the interest that is paid (or to be paid) by the taxpayer on indebtedness incurred or continued to purchase or carry such bond that is attributable to any period prior to the contribution (Code Sec. 170(f)(5); Reg. § 1.170A-3).[164]

1066. Contribution by Partnership. Although a partnership is not allowed to claim a charitable deduction in figuring its taxable income, each partner is allowed a deduction for the partner's distributive share of the partnership's charitable contribution (Code Sec. 702(a) and Code Sec. 703(a); Reg. § 1.702-1(a)).[165]

1068. Denial of Deduction. A contribution is not deductible unless it is made to, or for the use of, an organization that qualifies as one of the types described at ¶ 1061. Contributions made directly to an individual or to groups of individuals are not deductible,[166] including those made directly to individuals in the military.[167] Gifts to private schools and organizations, including churches, that practice racial discrimination in their admissions policies are not deductible.[168]

If a taxpayer makes a gift to a private foundation or a nonexempt trust (an annuity trust or unitrust), a deduction will be allowed only if the governing instrument specifically prohibits income accumulations and certain conflict-of-interest activities (¶ 635-¶ 644) (Code Sec. 508(d)).[169] The IRS has issued sample acceptable governing instrument clauses.[170] Many states have enacted statutes that accomplish the required governing instrument adjustments, and the IRS has published a list of those that satisfy the Code requirements.[171] See also ¶ 538 and ¶ 631.

An organization formed after October 9, 1969, and claiming exemption under Code Sec. 501(c)(3) (see ¶ 1061, item (2)) must file notice of intent to be exempt (¶ 616), exemption being retroactive to date of organization only if the notice was timely. Contributions to such an organization are deductible only if the notice is filed. Contributions made to a late-filing organization are not deductible if made before the date of filing (Code Sec. 170(f)(1)).[172] The IRS publishes a cumulative list of eligible organizations (IRS Pub 78), which is updated periodically.[173] For an updated list, one may consult the IRS Internet website, www.irs.gov.

Deductions are disallowed for contributions by a "substantial contributor" (¶ 635) to a foundation in a tax year in which there is an action resulting in a Code Sec. 507(c) (termination) tax (¶ 649) (Code Sec. 170(f)(1)).[174] Deductions are also denied for contributions made in connection with a church-related tax avoidance scheme. One common scheme involves the organization of a chapter of a "personal" church to which all the individual's assets are allegedly transferred, generating deductions for charitable contributions. Such deductions are routinely disallowed, and penalties and damages are usually assessed.[175]

1069. Gift of Future Interest in Tangible Personal Property. A charitable contribution deduction is not allowed where a taxpayer transfers to a charitable organization a future interest in tangible personal property, such as a painting, manuscript, sculpture, or other art objects, until all intervening interests in, and rights to, the actual possession or enjoyment of the property have expired or are held by persons other than related taxpayers and controlled partnerships (Code Sec. 170(a)(3); Reg. § 1.170A-5).[176]

1070. Transfer in Trust. No deduction is allowed for the value of a contribution of a remainder interest that the donor transfers in trust unless the trust is a

---

Footnote references are to paragraphs of the 2002 Standard Federal Tax Reports.

[164] ¶ 11,600, ¶ 11,631
[165] ¶ 25,080, ¶ 25,081, ¶ 25,100
[166] ¶ 11,620.111
[167] ¶ 11,620.111
[168] ¶ 11,620.051, ¶ 11,620.32
[169] ¶ 22,790
[170] ¶ 22,795.75
[171] ¶ 22,795.79
[172] ¶ 11,600
[173] ¶ 11,620.103
[174] ¶ 11,600
[175] ¶ 39,651G.225
[176] ¶ 11,600, ¶ 11,634

¶ **1066**

pooled income fund (¶ 593), a charitable remainder annuity trust, or a charitable remainder unitrust (¶ 590) (Code Sec. 170(f)(2); Reg. § 1.170A-6).[177]

1071. Appraisals for Noncash Contributions. Individuals, closely held corporations, personal service corporations, partnerships or S corporations that make a contribution of property (other than money or publicly traded securities) valued in excess of $5,000 must substantiate each contribution with a qualified appraisal of the value of the property. An appraisal summary, made on Section B, Form 8283, must be attached to the tax return on which the deduction is first claimed. The appraisal requirement is also triggered if a taxpayer donates a number of similar items (whether or not to the same donee), such as stamps or coins, with a total value in excess of $5,000. There is no appraisal requirement for publicly traded securities for which market quotations are readily available on an established securities market. For other publicly traded securities, a partially completed appraisal summary is required if the claimed value exceeds $5,000. The appraisal summary need only be partially completed for nonpublicly traded stock if the claimed value is greater than $5,000 but does not exceed $10,000 (Reg. § 1.170A-13(c)).[178] The qualified appraisal requirement is waived for closely held and personal service corporations that make contributions of inventory, stock in trade, or other property normally held for sale in its business after November 9, 1988 for the ill, needy, or infants.[179]

Moving Expense

1073. Moving Expense Deduction. An employee or self-employed individual may deduct as an adjustment to gross income the expenses of moving himself and his family from one location to another if the move is related to starting work in a new location and the amount is reasonable (Code Sec. 217).[180] The deduction is computed on Form 3903 and reported on Form 1040.

Deductible moving expenses are limited to the cost of (1) transportation of household goods and personal effects and (2) travel (including lodging but not meals) to the new residence (Code Sec. 217(b)).[181]

Where an automobile is used in making the move, a taxpayer may deduct either (1) the actual out-of-pocket expenses incurred (gasoline and oil, but not repairs, depreciation, etc.) or (2) a standard mileage allowance of 12 cents per mile in 2001 (Rev. Proc. 2000-48) (13 cents per mile in 2002 (Rev. Proc. 2001-54)).[182]

1075. Eligibility for Deduction. A taxpayer must meet a distance test, a length-of-employment test and a commencement-of-work test.

The new principal place of work must be at least 50 miles farther from the taxpayer's old residence than the old residence was from the taxpayer's old place of work. If there was no old place of work, the new place of work must be at least 50 miles from the old residence (Code Sec. 217(c)).[183]

During the 12-month period immediately following the move, the taxpayer must be employed full time for at least 39 weeks. A self-employed taxpayer must be employed or performing services full time for at least 78 weeks of the 24-month period immediately following the move and at least 39 weeks during the first 12 months. The full-time work requirement is waived, however, if death, disability, involuntary separation from work (other than for willful misconduct), or transfer to another location for the benefit of the employer occurs (Code Sec. 217(c) and (d)).[184]

In general, the move must have been in connection with the commencement of work at the new location and the moving expenses must be incurred within one year from the time the taxpayer first reports to the new job or business. If the move is not made within one year, the expenses ordinarily will not be deductible unless it can be

---

Footnote references are to paragraphs of the 2002 Standard Federal Tax Reports.

[177] ¶ 11,600, ¶ 11,635   [180] ¶ 12,620   [183] ¶ 12,620
[178] ¶ 11,685, ¶ 11,700   [181] ¶ 12,620   [184] ¶ 12,620
[179] ¶ 11,700.45   [182] ¶ 12,623.11

¶ 1075

shown that circumstances existed to prevent incurring the expenses within that period (Reg. § 1.217-2(a)(3)).[185]

An eligible taxpayer is permitted to deduct moving expenses even though the 39- or 78-week residence requirement has not been satisfied by the time prescribed for filing the return (including extensions) for the tax year in which the moving expenses were incurred and paid. However, a taxpayer who fails to meet the requirements must either file an amended return or include as gross income on the next year's return the amount previously claimed as expenses (Code Sec. 217(d); Reg. § 1.217-2(d)(3)).[186]

An individual who retires from an overseas job and returns to the U.S. or a survivor (spouse or dependent) of any decedent who worked outside the U.S. at the time of death is also eligible to deduct moving expenses if, within six months of the decedent's death, the survivor moves to the U.S. from a foreign residence that had been shared with the decedent (Code Sec. 217(i)).[187]

1076. Reimbursement by Employer. Gross income does not include qualified moving expense reimbursements. These are amounts received from an employer as a payment for or reimbursement of expenses that would be deductible as a moving expense if directly paid or incurred by the employee (Code Sec. 132(a)(6) and (g)).[188] See ¶ 863.

Any amount other than a qualified reimbursement received or accrued, directly or indirectly, by a taxpayer from the taxpayer's employer as a payment for or reimbursement of moving expenses must be included in the taxpayer's gross income as compensation for services (Code Sec. 82).[189] Such reimbursement or payment to or on behalf of a taxpayer by his employer is considered wages subject to the withholding (Code Sec. 3401(a)(15); Reg. § 31.3401(a)(15)-1).[190]

1077. Foreign Moves. A moving expense deduction is permitted in connection with the commencement of work at a new principal place of work located outside the U.S. and its possessions. The rules are similar to those discussed above except that a deduction is also allowed for reasonable expenses of moving household goods and personal effects to and from storage, and of storing them for part or all of the time during which the new place of work abroad continues to be a taxpayer's principal place of work (Code Sec. 217(h)).[191]

1078. Moves of Armed Forces Members. Moving and storage expenses that are furnished in kind by the military, or cash reimbursements or allowances to the extent of expenses actually paid or incurred incident to a permanent change of station for a member of the U.S. Armed Forces on active duty, are not includible in income. Such expenses need not be reported and such moves are exempt from the time and mileage requirements. See ¶ 1075. An income exclusion is also provided in those cases where the spouse and dependents of the member of the Armed Forces move to or from separate locations; any unreimbursed expenses are considered as incurred in a single move to a new principal place of work (Code Sec. 217(g)).[192]

Dues, Education, and Other Expenses

1080. Union Dues. Union dues, initiation fees and out-of-work-benefit assessments are deductible as an itemized deduction on Schedule A of Form 1040, subject to the 2% floor (¶ 1011).[193] The self-employed may deduct union dues as a business expense. See ¶ 1005.

1081. Job-Hunting Expenses. Individuals may deduct all expenses incurred in seeking employment in the *same* trade or business regardless of whether or not the search is successful. Such expenses include the typing, printing, and mailing of a resume, and travel and transportation expenses. If a person travels to an area seeking new employment in his present trade or business and also engages in

---

[185] ¶ 12,622	[188] ¶ 7420	[191] ¶ 12,620
[186] ¶ 12,620, ¶ 12,622	[189] ¶ 6374	[192] ¶ 12,620
[187] ¶ 12,620	[190] ¶ 33,502, ¶ 33,528	[193] ¶ 6006.16

personal activities, traveling expenses to and from the area are deductible only if the trip relates primarily to seeking the new employment. If the travel is primarily personal in nature, only the actual expenses of the search at the destination are deductible.[194]

Expenses are not deductible if an individual is seeking employment in a *new* trade or business even where employment is secured. An individual seeking his first job or switching his trade or business or a person with a long period of unemployment will be denied a deduction.[195]

To the extent that job-hunting expenses are deductible, they are only deductible as an itemized deduction on Schedule A of Form 1040, subject to the 2% floor (see ¶ 1011). An individual generally must complete Form 2106, "Employee Business Expenses," in order to claim such expenses if any expenses were reimbursed by an employer or a third party or if the individual is claiming any meal, entertainment, travel or transportation expenses.

1082. Education and Related Expenses. Education expenses are generally deductible (even if they lead to a degree) if the education that is undertaken (1) maintains or improves a skill *required* by the individual in the individual's employment or other trade or business or (2) meets the express *requirements* of the individual's employer, or the requirements of law or regulations, *imposed* as a condition to the retention by the individual of an established employment relationship, status, or rate of compensation (Reg. § 1.162-5).[196]

However, educational expenses that are personal or constitute an inseparable aggregate of personal and capital expenditures are not deductible, even though they may maintain or improve a skill or may meet the express requirements of the taxpayer's employer. Nondeductible capital or personal education expenses are those that (1) are required of the taxpayer in order to meet the minimum educational requirements for qualification in the taxpayer's present employment, trade, or business or (2) qualify the taxpayer for a new trade or business.

Taxpayers can claim an "above-the-line" deduction for qualified education expenses paid in tax years beginning after 2001 (Code Sec. 222, as added by P.L. 107-16). The maximum deduction is $3,000 for 2002 and 2003, and $4,000 for 2004 and 2005. Generally, taxpayers with an adjusted gross income below $65,000 ($130,000 for married filing jointly) can claim the deduction.[197]

The minimum education necessary to qualify for a position or other trade or business is determined from a consideration of such factors as requirements of the employer, laws or regulations, and the standards of the profession, trade, or business involved. The fact that the taxpayer is already employed does not mean that the taxpayer has met the minimum requirements for qualification in that employment so as to be entitled to a deduction under the improving-of-skills test. However, if new education requirements are established after the taxpayer has met the minimum requirements for qualification in his work, the taxpayer is treated as continuing to meet those qualification requirements, and expenses incurred in meeting the new requirements are deductible.

A change of duties is not a new trade or business if the new duties involve the same general work as is involved in the taxpayer's present employment. Thus, changing from an elementary to a secondary school teacher or from teaching one subject to another does not result in a new trade or business. Also, a change in duties from classroom teacher to principal is not a change in trade or business.

Unreimbursed expenditures for such items as tuition, books, laboratory fees, dues paid to professional societies, fees paid for professional journals, etc., are deducted by an employee as an itemized deduction, subject to the 2% floor (¶ 1011) (Reg. § 1.162-6).[198] The cost of technical books of relatively permanent value used in connection with professional work is a capital expenditure and must be depreciated (¶ 1201-¶ 1284).[199]

336

Travel as a Form of Education. Generally, no deduction is allowed for travel as a form of education (Code Sec. 274(m)).[200] This rule applies when a travel deduction would otherwise be allowable only on the ground that the travel itself served educational purposes. However, it does not apply when a deduction is claimed with respect to travel that is a necessary adjunct to engaging in an activity that gives rise to a business deduction relating to education: for example, a scholar of French literature travels to Paris in order to do specific library research that cannot be done elsewhere under circumstances that are otherwise deductible.[201]

Interest on Education Loans. Individuals are allowed to deduct interest paid during the tax year on any qualified education loan from gross income in arriving at adjusted gross income on Form 1040. The debt must be incurred by the taxpayer solely to pay qualified higher education expenses (Code Sec. 221(e)(1)). The deduction is limited to interest paid during the first 60 months in which such payments are required. However, the sixty-month limitation is repealed for tax years beginning after 2001. The original loan and all refinancings of the loan are treated as one loan for this purpose (Code Sec. 221(d)). The maximum deductible amount of interest is $2,500 for tax years beginning in 2001 and thereafter (Code Sec. 221(b)(1)).[202] In computing the deductible amount, the deduction that would otherwise be allowed (taking into account the above dollar limitation) is reduced by an amount that equals the otherwise allowable deduction times a fraction, the numerator being the excess of AGI over $40,000 ($60,000 if married filing jointly) and the denominator being $15,000. For tax years beginning after 2001, the AGI limits are increased to $50,000 ($100,000 if married filing jointly). The deductible amount cannot be reduced below zero (Code Sec. 221(b)(1)(B)).

1083. Uniforms and Special Clothing. The cost and upkeep of a uniform, including laundering and cleaning, are deductible only if the uniform is required as a condition of employment and is not adaptable to general wear. If the employee is reimbursed for uniform expenses under an accountable plan (¶ 943), reimbursement is not reported on the employee's Form W-2; therefore, it need not be accounted for on the employee's tax return (Reg. § 1.62-2(c)(4)).[203] If the cost exceeds the reimbursement, any excess is deductible as an itemized deduction, subject to the 2% floor (¶ 1011). Reimbursement made under a nonaccountable plan (¶ 943) must be included in income but may be deducted as an itemized deduction on Schedule A of Form 1040, subject to the 2% floor and limitations (Reg. § 1.62-2(c)(5)).[204] Armed Forces reservists may deduct the unreimbursed cost (less nontaxable uniform allowance) of a uniform required when in attendance at drills or other functions if prohibited from wearing it for regular use.[205]

A deduction is allowed for special items required in the employee's work that do not replace items of ordinary clothing, such as work shoes and special gloves for a railroad fireman, shop caps, high-top shoes, and leather-palm gloves used by a railroad car repairman, gloves used by a railroad brakeman, and boots required of a telephone company lineman.[206]

Production of Income

1085. Nontrade or Nonbusiness Expenses. An individual may deduct as an itemized deduction on Schedule A of Form 1040, subject to the 2% floor (¶ 1011), ordinary and necessary expenses paid or incurred during the tax year for the production or collection of income or for the management, conservation, or maintenance of property held for the production of income (Code Sec. 212; Reg. § 1.212-1(a)).[207] Expenses attributable to property held for rents or royalties are deductible from gross income and are not subject to the 2% floor (¶ 1089). Such

---

Footnote references are to paragraphs of the 2002 Standard Federal Tax Reports.

[200] ¶ 14,402	[204] ¶ 6004, ¶ 6006.0334	[207] ¶ 12,520, ¶ 12,521
[201] ¶ 14,402.0182	[205] ¶ 8524.265	
[202] ¶ 12,692	[206] ¶ 8524.2652,	
[203] ¶ 6004, ¶ 6006,	¶ 8524.2658	

¶ 1083   ¶ 6006.15

expenses must be reasonable in amount and bear a reasonable and proximate relation to the production or collection of taxable income or to the management, conservation, or maintenance of property held for the production of income (Reg. § 1.212-1(d)).[208] A deduction is not allowed for interest on indebtedness incurred or continued to purchase or carry obligations earning fully tax-exempt interest or other exempt income (Code Sec. 265(a)).[209] See, also, ¶ 1970.

1086. Investor's Expenses. Investment counsel fees, custodian fees, fees for clerical help, office rent, state and local transfer taxes, and similar expenses paid or incurred by an individual in connection with investments held by the individual are deductible as an itemized deduction on Schedule A of Form 1040, subject to the 2% floor (¶ 1011) (Reg. § 1.212-1(g)),[210] except where they relate to rents and royalties (¶ 1089). A dealer or trader in securities is not an investor and may deduct these items as business expenses (subject to the uniform capitalization rules; see ¶ 990 et seq.).[211]

1089. Deductions Attributable to Rental or Royalty Property. Ordinary and necessary expenses attributable to property held for the production of rents or royalties may be deducted in determining adjusted gross income (Reg. § 1.62-1T(c)).[212] These deductions include interest, taxes, depreciation, depletion, losses, etc. (Reg. § 1.212-1).[213] The property does not have to be actually producing income if it is held for the production of rents or royalties.[214]

Property held for the production of royalties includes intangible as well as tangible property. Therefore, depreciation on a patent or copyright may be deducted. Similarly, an operating owner, lessee, sublessor or sublessee, or purchaser of royalty interests can deduct his share of a depletion allowance on natural resources. See ¶ 1201 and ¶ 1289, respectively.

Where a property is devoted to rental purposes for part of a year and to personal use for the other part, a proration of expenses is required. See the example on proration at ¶ 963. See, also, ¶ 966 for special rules governing the deduction of expenses of rental vacation homes. For the applicability of the at-risk and passive activity rules, see ¶ 2045 and ¶ 2053.

1090. Deductions of Life Tenant or Income Beneficiary. When property is held by one person for life, with the remainder to another person, the deduction for depreciation or depletion is allowed to the life tenant and is computed as if the life tenant were the absolute owner of the property (Reg. § 1.167(h)-1 and Reg. § 1.611-1(c)).[215] After the life tenant's death, the deduction, if any, is allowed to the remainderman. For property held in trust or by an estate, the deduction is apportioned as explained at ¶ 530.

1091. Guardianship Expenses. A deduction is permitted for a reasonable amount paid or incurred for the services of a guardian or committee for a ward or minor, and for other ordinary and necessary expenses incurred in connection with the production or collection of income inuring to the ward or minor, or in connection with the management, conservation, or maintenance of income-producing property belonging to the ward or minor (Reg. § 1.212-1(j)).[216] Expenses of a competency proceeding are deductible if the purpose of the proceeding is the management and conservation of income-producing property owned by the taxpayer.[217]

1092. Expenses Connected with the Determination of Tax. Any ordinary and necessary expense incurred in connection with the determination, collection, or refund of *any tax* is deductible as an itemized deduction on Schedule A of Form 1040, subject to the 2% floor (¶ 1011) (Code Sec. 212(3)).[218] This includes tax return preparation fees allocable to an individual's Form 1040 and Schedules A and B.

Footnote references are to paragraphs of the 2002 Standard Federal Tax Reports.

[208] ¶ 12,521
[209] ¶ 14,050
[210] ¶ 12,521
[211] ¶ 8521.04, ¶ 8521.1475

[212] ¶ 6003
[213] ¶ 12,521
[214] ¶ 6005.03, ¶ 12,523.035
[215] ¶ 11,048, ¶ 23,922

[216] ¶ 12,521
[217] ¶ 12,523.13, ¶ 12,523.33
[218] ¶ 12,520

¶ 1092

However, Form 1040 expenses attributable to a trade or business, Schedule C and C-EZ, and those incurred for Schedules E and F are deductible from gross income and are not itemized deductions.[219] See ¶ 973.

This provision applies to estate and gift tax contests as well as to income tax contests. It also applies to state and local taxes as well as federal taxes and includes property taxes and state or city income taxes. Legal expenses incurred in determining tax liability include legal fees paid for obtaining a ruling on a tax question[220] and defending against a criminal indictment for tax evasion.[221] An allocation between tax and nontax matters should be made.

Appraisal fees may be deductible as an expense paid in connection with the determination of income tax liability. For example, appraisal fees incurred in determining the fair market value of property donated to a charity or to establish the amount of loss are deductible expenses.[222]

1093. Legal Expenses. Legal expenses are deductible, as miscellaneous itemized deductions on Schedule A of Form 1040, subject to the 2% floor (¶ 1011), if they are paid or incurred for the production of income or for the management, conservation, or maintenance of income-producing property.[223] Generally, legal expenses paid or incurred in recovering investment property and amounts of income includible in gross income are deductible (Reg. § 1.212-1(k)).[224] However, the U.S. Court of Appeals for the Sixth Circuit (*Nickell*) has ruled that legal expenses incurred in recovering stock were deductible only to the extent that they were allocable to the recovery of interest and dividends.[225] Legal expenses incurred in defending or perfecting title to property, in the acquisition or disposition of property, or in developing or improving property are not deductible and must be capitalized.

Generally, legal expenses paid by one spouse in resisting the other's monetary demands in divorce are nondeductible personal expenses. However, legal expenses for collecting alimony under a divorce decree are deductible, as a miscellaneous itemized deduction, subject to the 2% floor (¶ 1011).[226]

1094. Limitation on Deduction of Investment Interest. The deduction by a noncorporate taxpayer for interest on investment indebtedness that is reported on Form 4952 is limited to the taxpayer's net investment income (Code Sec. 163(d)).[227] Net investment income is the excess of investment income over investment expenses. The disallowed investment interest can be carried over to a succeeding tax year (Rev. Rul. 95-16).[228]

Interest subject to the investment interest limitation is interest on debt properly allocable to property held for investment. Property held for investment is generally defined as (1) property that produces interest, dividends, annuities, or royalties that are not derived in the ordinary course of a trade or business; (2) property that produces gain or loss not derived in the ordinary course of a trade or business from the sale or exchange of property that either produces item (1) types of income or that is held for investment (but which is not an interest in a passive activity); and (3) an interest in a trade or business activity that is not a passive activity and in which the taxpayer did not materially participate (Code Sec. 163(d)(5)(A); IRS Pub. 550). It does not include qualified residence interest (¶ 1047), interest properly allocable to a rental real estate activity in which the taxpayer actively participates (within the meaning of the passive loss rule (¶ 2062)), or interest that is taken into account in computing income or loss from a passive activity (¶ 2053).

Net capital gain from the disposition of investment property is not considered investment income. However, individuals may elect to treat all or any portion of such net capital gain as investment income by paying tax on the elected amounts at their ordinary income rates (Code Sec. 163(d)(4)(B)).[229] Thus, the taxpayer loses the benefit of the otherwise applicable maximum capital gains tax rate with respect to the elected amount (Code Sec. 1(h)).[230]

Footnote references are to paragraphs of the 2002 Standard Federal Tax Reports.

¶ **1093**

[219] ¶ 6005.109
[220] ¶ 12,523.421
[221] ¶ 12,523.3264
[222] ¶ 12,523.3848
[223] ¶ 12,521
[224] ¶ 12,521
[225] ¶ 12,523.35
[226] ¶ 12,523.3273
[227] ¶ 9102
[228] ¶ 9403.10
[229] ¶ 9102
[230] ¶ 3260

Chapter 11

DEUCTIONS

Losses □ Bad Debts

Losses

1101. Losses, Generally. Tax treatment of a loss depends upon the nature of the activity in which the loss was incurred. Losses are deductible in computing adjusted gross income only if they (1) are incurred in a trade or business, (2) result from a sale or exchange of property (¶ 1007), (3) are attributable to property held for the production of rents or royalties, or (4) are penalties for premature withdrawals of funds (¶ 1120). In addition, certain types of losses are deductible only if the property was used in a trade or business or for the production of income. An individual's deduction is limited to: (1) loss incurred in a trade or business, (2) loss incurred in a transaction entered into for profit, though not connected with a trade or business, and (3) loss of property not connected with a trade or business or a transaction entered into for profit arising from fire, storm, shipwreck, or other casualty, or from theft (Code Sec. 165(c)).[1] An individual cannot claim a casualty loss deduction for damage to insured property unless a timely insurance claim is filed (Code Sec. 165(h)(4)(E)).[2] The deduction for a loss cannot exceed the taxpayer's adjusted basis in the property (Reg. § 1.165-1(c)(1)).[3] In addition, any deduction must be reduced by the amount recovered from insurance or any other source (Reg. § 1.165-1(c)(4)).[4]

For the treatment of a loss on stock in a small business company, see ¶ 2395. For losses on wash sales of securities, see ¶ 1935. For the disallowance of losses on the sale, exchange, or worthlessness of bonds not issued in registered form, see ¶ 1963. For losses limited by the "at-risk" rules, see ¶ 2045. For losses from passive activities, see ¶ 2053.

1104. When Is a Loss Sustained? Generally, a loss is deductible only for the tax year in which it is sustained, i.e., the tax year in which its occurrence is evidenced by closed and completed transactions and is fixed by identifiable events occurring in such tax year (Reg. § 1.165-1(d)(1)).[5] No deduction may be claimed in the year of loss for any portion of the loss for which there remains a reasonable prospect of recovery. A deduction may be taken in the year in which it becomes reasonably certain that there will be no recovery (Reg. § 1.165-1(d)(2)).[6]

Footnote references are to paragraphs of the 2002 Standard Federal Tax Reports.

[1] ¶ 9802, ¶ 9802   [3] ¶ 9803, ¶ 10,005.039   [5] ¶ 9803, ¶ 10,005.05
[2] ¶ 9802, ¶ 10,005.051   [4] ¶ 9803   [6] ¶ 9803, ¶ 10,005.051   **¶ 1104**

No deduction is available for a *partial* loss resulting from the shrinkage in value of property, except as reflected in an inventory.[7] An exception to this rule is the chargeoff of the worthless part of a business debt (see ¶ 1145). See ¶ 1157 regarding changes in the deduction of an addition to a reserve for bad debts.

1107. Loss on Sale of Residence. A loss from a sale of residential property not purchased for investment purposes is not deductible by an individual. But loss on the sale of such property at the time it is being rented or otherwise used for income-producing purposes is deductible (Reg. § 1.165-9(a), (b)).[8] As to the basis for such a loss, see ¶ 1626. If the property is used as the taxpayer's personal residence after having been acquired as income-producing property, loss on its sale at the time it is being used as a residence is not deductible.[9]

1112. Capitalization of Demolition Costs and Losses. Any amount expended or loss sustained by an owner or lessee on account of the demolition of any structure (including a certified historic structure) must be capitalized as part of the basis of the land on which the structure was located (Code Sec. 280B).[10]

1115. Foreclosure Loss or Tax Sale. Where the owner of an equity interest receives less than his basis in real estate when it is sold upon foreclosure of the mortgage, his investment may represent a deductible loss only if the property foreclosed upon is business or investment property.[11] The nature of the loss—capital loss or ordinary loss—depends in each case upon the nature of the property foreclosed upon, i.e., whether it is a capital asset or required to be treated as a capital asset under Code Sec. 1231 (¶ 1747). The loss occurs when the redemption period expires or in the year the property became worthless where such property became worthless in an earlier year.[12] However, if there is no equity of redemption, the loss is fixed by the foreclosure sale and not by the decree of foreclosure that ordered the sale and preceded it.[13] These principles also apply to a sale for delinquent taxes.[14]

If real property is disposed of by reason of foreclosure or similar proceedings, the monthly percentage reduction of the amount of accelerated depreciation subject to recapture (see ¶ 1779) is determined as if the taxpayer ceased to hold the property on the date on which such proceedings were begun.[15]

1118. Abandonment and Obsolescence Losses. A loss may be allowed for the abandonment of a depreciable asset in the amount of its adjusted basis if the owner manifests an irrevocable intent to abandon (discard) the asset so that it will neither be used again by the taxpayer nor retrieved for sale, exchange, or other disposition (Reg. § 1.167(a)-8(a)).[16] An abandonment loss is an ordinary loss (whether or not the abandoned asset is a capital asset) and is reported on Form 4797, Part II, line 10 (IRS Publication 225).

If a nondepreciable asset is abandoned following a sudden termination of its usefulness, an obsolescence loss is allowed in an amount equal to its adjusted basis. An obsolescence loss, in the case of nondepreciable property, is deductible in the tax year in which it is sustained, even though the overt act of abandonment or the loss of title to the property may not occur in that year (Reg. § 1.165-2).[17]

1120. Interest Forfeited on Premature Withdrawals. Interest that was previously earned on a time savings account or deposit with a savings institution and that is later forfeited because of premature withdrawals is deductible from gross income in the year when the interest is forfeited (Code Sec. 62(a)(9)).[18]

> **Example.** John Cash opened a four-year time savings account in January 2000. He was credited with $400 in interest earned for 2000 and reported this income on his 2000 return. He withdrew the funds in October

---

Footnote references are to paragraphs of the 2002 Standard Federal Tax Reports.

[7] ¶ 9805.01	[11] ¶ 9805.155,	[15] ¶ 31,000, ¶ 31,006.028
[8] ¶ 10,102, ¶ 10,103.01	¶ 10,103.54	[16] ¶ 11,020, ¶ 11,021.021
[9] ¶ 10,102	[12] ¶ 21,817.45	[17] ¶ 9901, ¶ 9902.01
[10] ¶ 14,900, ¶ 14,901	[13] ¶ 21,817.451	[18] ¶ 6002, ¶ 6005.036,
	[14] ¶ 9808.453	¶ 9900.11

2001. This premature withdrawal triggered a penalty provision so that he received only $230 of interest for 2000, plus $195 in interest earned on the account for 2001. Thus, he has incurred a loss of $170 ($400 of interest reported for 2000 less $230 actually received with respect to that year). This loss should be claimed on his 2001 return. He should also report the $195 in interest earned for 2001 on his 2001 return.

The necessary information is provided on Form 1099-INT. In addition, the deduction must be claimed on Form 1040; no deduction is available on Form 1040A or 1040EZ.

1121. Wagering Loss. Losses from wagering are deductible to the extent of the gains from wagering, regardless of the legality of the activity under local law (Code Sec. 165(d)).[19] A professional gambler may deduct his losses directly from his gambling income. The nonprofessional must include all gambling income in his gross income but can claim the losses only as an itemized deduction.[20]

Casualty Losses

1124. Casualty Loss. Code Sec. 165(c)(3) limits any loss, in the case of nonbusiness property of individuals, to that arising from fire, storm, shipwreck, or other casualty, or from theft. Each loss is subject to a $100 floor (see ¶ 1134), and total losses are deductible only to the extent that the total loss amount for the year exceeds 10% of adjusted gross income (see ¶ 1137). Casualty and theft losses are reported on Form 4684.

A loss from a casualty arises from an event due to some sudden, unexpected, or unusual cause.[21] Damage to nonbusiness property caused by hurricane,[22] flood,[23] quarry blast,[24] vandalism,[25] sonic boom,[26] earthquake,[27] or earthslide[28] is deductible. Loss to shoreline buildings and structures from battering by waves and winds or flooding of buildings, but not damage from gradual erosion or inundation, is a casualty loss.[29] Damage or loss to property caused by an unusual and unprecedented drought can be treated as a casualty loss.[30] Although cash or property received as compensation for, or to repair or replace, damaged property reduces the amount of the loss,[31] the deduction will not be reduced by excludable gifts received by a disaster victim, even if such gifts are used to rehabilitate the property.[32]

A casualty includes damage to an automobile resulting from a collision, whether due to the faulty driving of another or the taxpayer, unless caused by the taxpayer's willful act (Reg. § 1.165-7(a)(13)).[33] The IRS takes the position that a casualty loss deduction for termite damage is not permitted because the "suddenness" test is not met, but some courts have allowed the deduction.[34] Storm damage to ornamental trees, as well as to orchards, is deductible as a casualty loss; however, loss of ornamental trees from Dutch elm or other diseases or insects lacks the "sudden force" requirement for classification as a casualty.[35]

A loss sustained as a result of negligent workmanship in repairing a leaky roof was a casualty loss.[36]

A casualty loss of nonbusiness property, as well as of business property, can result in a net operating loss (see ¶ 1176). The $100 floor and the 10%-of-AGI limitation are applied in the nonbusiness situation in determining an NOL.

If, as the result of insurance or other reimbursement, a taxpayer realizes a gain from a casualty or theft loss, recognition of the gain can be deferred under the

Footnote references are to paragraphs of the 2002 Standard Federal Tax Reports.

19 ¶ 9802, ¶ 10,105.01
20 ¶ 10,105.01
21 ¶ 10,005.023
22 ¶ 10,005.42
23 ¶ 10,005.33
24 ¶ 10,005.56
25 ¶ 10,005.85
26 ¶ 10,005.4645
27 ¶ 10,005.18
28 ¶ 10,005.63
29 ¶ 10,005.466
30 ¶ 10,005.17
31 ¶ 10,005.039
32 ¶ 10,005.117
33 ¶ 10,004
34 ¶ 10,005.671
35 ¶ 10,005.68, ¶ 10,005.80— ¶ 10,005.817
36 ¶ 10,005.904

involuntary conversion rules by making an election and purchasing qualifying replacement property within the applicable replacement period. See ¶ 1713.

1125. Embezzlement or Theft Loss. A loss from theft or embezzlement is generally deductible for the tax year in which the taxpayer discovers the loss (Code Sec. 165(e); Reg. § 1.165-8(a)(2)).[37] However, no deduction may be claimed in the year of discovery if there exists a claim for reimbursement with respect to which there is a reasonable prospect of recovery (Reg. § 1. 165-1(d)(3)). No deduction is available for lost or mislaid articles.[38] The deduction of theft losses is determined in the same way as other casualty losses as explained at ¶ 1131.

1128. Loss on Bank Deposits. Individuals may choose to treat the loss of a nonbusiness account in an insolvent or bankrupt financial institution as a personal casualty loss in the year in which the loss can reasonably be estimated (Code Sec. 165(l)).[39] If elected, the casualty loss is subject to the deduction limitations at ¶ 1134 and ¶ 1137. The election is made on Form 4684.

In lieu of the above election, an individual can elect to treat a loss with respect to funds deposited in a financial institution as an ordinary loss arising from a transaction entered into for profit in the year the loss can be reasonably estimated, provided that no portion of the deposit is federally insured. The aggregate amount of such losses for any tax year with respect to which an election may be made is limited to $20,000 ($10,000 in the case of a married individual filing separately) for each financial institution and must be reduced by the amount of insurance proceeds that the taxpayer can reasonably expect to receive under state law (Code Sec. 165(l)(5)). The loss is deducted on Schedule A (Form 1040) as a miscellaneous itemized deduction. The name of the financial institution and "Insolvent Financial Institution" should be written on line 22. A calculation of the deducted loss should be included with the return (IRS Publication 529).

Once made, these elections apply to all losses on deposits in the financial institution during the tax year and are revocable only with IRS consent. Taxpayers making the elections are foreclosed from deducting such losses as bad debts under Code Sec. 166 (Code Sec. 165(l)(7)).[40] The elections cannot be made by an individual who is an owner of 1% or more of the institution's stock, an officer of the institution, or certain relatives of these owners and officers (Code Sec. 165(l)(2)).

If these elections are not made, the loss is treated as a nonbusiness bad debt in the year of final determination of the actual loss and is deducted on Schedule D (Form 1040) as a short-term capital loss subject to the $3,000 annual limit (¶ 1145).

1131. Amount of Casualty or Theft Loss. The amount of a casualty loss (business/income-producing property or nonbusiness) is the *lesser* of (1) the difference between the fair market value (FMV) of the property immediately before the casualty and its FMV immediately after or (2) the adjusted basis of the property immediately before the casualty (Reg. § 1.165-7(b)).[41] However, if business property or income producing property is totally destroyed, the casualty loss is the adjusted basis of the property regardless of its fair market value (Reg. § 1.165-7(b)).

When money is stolen, the theft loss is the amount stolen. The amount of a theft loss in the case of nonbusiness property other than money is the lesser of the value of the property or its adjusted basis.[42] In the case of stolen business or income-producing property, the theft loss is the adjusted basis of the property stolen (Reg. § 1.165-7(b)).

A casualty loss is reduced by any salvage received. A casualty or theft loss is also reduced by any insurance or other compensation received (Code Sec. 165(a)). An individual cannot claim a personal casualty or theft loss to the extent the loss is covered by insurance unless a timely insurance claim is filed with respect to the loss (Code Sec. 165(h)(e)).

Footnote references are to paragraphs of the 2002 Standard Federal Tax Reports.

¶ 1125

[37] ¶ 9802, ¶ 10,100, ¶ 10,101.023	[39] ¶ 9802, ¶ 10,005.037	[41] ¶ 10,004
[38] ¶ 10,101.023	[40] ¶ 9802, ¶ 10,005.037	[42] ¶ 10,100, ¶ 10,101.113

A personal casualty loss is subject to a $100 floor and to a 10%-of-AGI limitation in determining the allowable deduction (see ¶ 1134 and ¶ 1137). The $100 floor and AGI limitations do not apply to a business or income-producing property casualty or theft loss.

When there is damage to different kinds of *business* property, loss must be computed separately for each single, identifiable property damaged or destroyed. This rule does not apply to *nonbusiness* property. Thus, if a tree is blown down in the front yard of a taxpayer's residence, the loss is the difference in the FMV of the taxpayer's whole property before and after damage to the tree (Reg. § 1.165-7(b)).[43]

1134. $100 Floor for Personal Casualty Loss. The deduction for a personal casualty loss is limited to the amount of each loss in excess of $100 (Code Sec. 165(h)(1); Reg. § 1.165-7).[44] The $100 floor applies separately to the loss from each single casualty or theft. If several items of nonbusiness property are damaged or stolen in the course of a single casualty or theft, the $100 floor is applied only once against the sum of the allowable losses established for each item (Reg. § 1.165-7(b)(4)(ii)).[45] In the case of married taxpayers filing a joint return, *only one* $100 floor applies to each casualty loss; if married taxpayers file separate returns, each spouse is subject to the $100 limitation for each casualty or theft loss (Reg. § 1.165-7(b)(4)(iii)).[46] When property is used for both business and personal purposes, the $100 floor applies only to the net loss attributable to that portion of the property used for personal purposes (Reg. § 1.165-7(b)(4)(iv)).[47]

1137. Ten-Percent-of-Adjusted-Gross-Income Limitation. Gains and losses from personal casualties and thefts are separately netted without regard to holding periods for the initial determination of whether there was a gain or loss (Code Sec. 165(h)).[48] The $100 floor is applied before the above netting occurs. If the recognized gains exceed the recognized losses, all such gains and losses are treated as capital gains and losses; the gains must be recalculated by combining short-term gains with short-term losses and long-term gains with long-term losses, and the results are then entered on Schedule D of Form 1040. If the recognized losses exceed the recognized gains after netting, all gains and losses will be treated as ordinary gains and losses; this allows losses to the extent of gains to be claimed in full as an itemized deduction on Schedule A, subject to the 10%-of-AGI floor. Form 4684 must be used to report gain or loss from a casualty or theft of nonbusiness property.

> **Example 1.** A taxpayer who has AGI of $50,000 (without regard to casualty gains or losses), a $25,000 casualty gain, and a $15,000 casualty loss (after the $100 floor) will report a $10,000 capital gain on Schedule D. The 10% floor does not apply in this computation.

> **Example 2.** A taxpayer who has AGI of $40,000, a $25,000 casualty loss (after the $100 floor), and a $15,000 casualty gain is allowed a $6,000 itemized deduction. The $10,000 loss resulting from netting the casualty gains against the casualty losses is deductible only to the extent that it exceeds 10% of AGI—$10,000 minus $4,000 equals $6,000.

Limitation for Estates and Trusts. The 10%-of-AGI limitation on personal casualty and theft losses applies to estates and trusts. AGI is computed in the same manner as it is for individuals, except that estates and trusts are allowed to deduct their administration expenses in arriving at AGI (Code Sec. 165(h)(4)(C)).[49] No deduction for a personal casualty loss may be taken if, at the time of filing a decedent's return, the loss has been claimed for estate tax purposes (Code Sec. 165(h)(4)(D)).[50]

1139. Basis of Damaged Property. The basis of damaged property is decreased by (1) the amount of any insurance or other reimbursement and (2) the

---

Footnote references are to paragraphs of the 2002 Standard Federal Tax Reports.

[43] ¶ 10,004
[44] ¶ 9802, ¶ 10,004, ¶ 10,005.041
[45] ¶ 10,004
[46] ¶ 10,004
[47] ¶ 10,004
[48] ¶ 9802
[49] ¶ 9802, ¶ 10,005.041
[50] ¶ 9802, ¶ 24,267.037

amount of the *deductible* loss. Any amount spent restoring the property or any gain recognized because insurance or other reimbursement exceeds the basis of the property prior to the casualty is added back to basis (Reg. § 1.165-1(c)).[51]

1141. Disaster Loss. If a taxpayer sustains a loss from a disaster in an area subsequently determined by the President of the United States to warrant federal assistance, a special rule may help the taxpayer to cushion his loss (Code Sec. 165(i)).[52] Disaster loss treatment is available with respect to a personal residence rendered unsafe by a disaster in a designated area and ordered to be demolished or relocated by the state or local government (Code Sec. 165(k)).[53]

The taxpayer has the option of (1) deducting the loss on his return for the year in which the loss occurred or (2) electing to deduct the loss on his return for the preceding tax year. The election to deduct a 2001 disaster loss in 2000 must be made on or before the due date (without extensions) of the taxpayer's 2001 return (April 15, 2002, for calendar-year individuals; March 15, 2002, for calendar-year corporations). The loss may be claimed by filing an amended 2000 return (see ¶ 2759). Revocation of such an election may be made before expiration of the time for filing the return for the year of the loss (even though Reg. § 1.165-11(e) states that revocation must be made within 90 days after election).[54] The calculation of the deduction for a disaster loss follows the same rules as those for any other personal casualty loss. However, if the taxpayer elects to claim a disaster loss on his return for the year immediately preceding the loss year, the AGI limitation is determined with respect to the preceding year's AGI.

The IRS is not prohibited from issuing guidance or other rules allowing an appraisal used to secure a loan or loan guarantee from the federal government to be used to establish the amount of a disaster loss for tax purposes. Should the IRS authorize a new valuation method, it would apply in a presidentially declared disaster area (Code Sec. 165(i)(4)).

Bad Debts

1145. Business Bad Debts. Business bad debts, which arise from the taxpayer's trade or business, differ from nonbusiness bad debts (see ¶ 1169) in that they can be deducted to the extent of their worthlessness at any time when they become partly or totally worthless and they can, generally, be deducted from gross income. A "business debt" is a debt (1) created or acquired in connection with the trade or business of the taxpayer who is claiming the deduction or (2) the worthlessness of which has been incurred in the taxpayer's trade or business (Reg. § 1.166-5(b)).[55] A business bad debt deduction, however, is not available to shareholders who have advanced money to a corporation as a contribution to capital[56] or to creditors who hold a debt that is evidenced by a bond, debenture, note, or other evidence of indebtedness that is issued by a corporation or by a governmental unit, with interest coupons or in registered form (Code Sec. 165(g)(2)(C)).[57] Nonbusiness bad debts are treated as short-term capital losses, subject to a $3,000 ($1,500 for married individuals filing separate returns) (see ¶ 1752 and ¶ 1757) per year deduction limitation, and are deductible only when totally worthless.

Guarantors. A noncorporate taxpayer who incurs a loss arising from his guaranty of a loan is entitled to deduct the loss only if the guaranty arose out of his trade or business or in a transaction entered into for profit. If the guaranty was connected with a trade or business, the resulting loss is an ordinary loss (business bad debt). If the guaranty was not connected with a true trade or business but was profit-inspired, the resulting loss is a short-term capital loss (nonbusiness bad debt) (Reg. § 1.166-9). No deduction is available if the guaranty payment does not fall within the above categories, if there is no legal obligation on the taxpayer to make the

---

Footnote references are to paragraphs of the 2002 Standard Federal Tax Reports.

[51] ¶ 9803, ¶ 10,005.039	[54] ¶ 10,200,	[56] ¶ 10,650.7301
[52] ¶ 9802, ¶ 10,201.01	¶ 10,201.073	[57] ¶ 9802
[53] ¶ 9802, ¶ 10,005.0755	[55] ¶ 10,691	

¶ 1141

guaranty payment, or if the guaranty was entered into after the debt became worthless.[58]

Employee Loans. An employee's rendering of services for pay is a trade or business for purposes of the bad debt provisions. Therefore, a loan to an employer to protect a job can give rise to a business bad debt deduction if the employer defaults. If a loan by a shareholder-employee is intended to protect the shareholder's job rather than to protect the shareholder's investment in the company, the failure to repay the loan results in a business bad debt deduction. The larger the shareholder's investment, the smaller his salary, and the larger his other sources of income, the more likely that a dominant nonbusiness motive existed for making the loan.[59]

Dominant Motivation Test. Since the tax treatment accorded business bad debts and nonbusiness bad debts differs, the taxpayer must show that his dominant motivation in making the payment was business-related in order to obtain the more favorable tax treatment.[60]

1148. Time of Deduction. A cash-basis taxpayer can deduct a bad debt only if an actual cash loss has been sustained or if the amount deducted was included in income. Nearly all accrual-basis taxpayers must use the specific chargeoff method to deduct business bad debts; the reserve method for computing and deducting bad debts on receivables may be used only by small banks and thrift institutions. Specific chargeoff is based on actual worthlessness and is not applicable merely because the taxpayer gives up attempts to collect (see ¶ 1157). A worthless debt arising from unpaid rent, interest, or a similar item is not deductible unless the income that such item represents has been reported for income tax purposes by a taxpayer on the accrual basis.[61]

1151. Secured Bad Debt. Where secured or mortgaged property is sold either to the secured party or to a third party for less than the amount of the debt, the creditor is entitled to a bad debt deduction in an amount equal to the difference between the sale price and the amount of the debt, to the extent that he can show that such difference is wholly or partially uncollectible. No bad debt deduction is allowable if a mortgage is foreclosed and the creditor buys the mortgaged property at a price equal to the unpaid indebtedness. However, loss or gain is realized on such a transaction and is measured by the difference between the amount of the obligations of the debtor that are applied to the purchase or bid price of the property and the fair market value of the property, to the extent that the obligations are capital or represent items the income from which has been returned by the creditor (Reg. § 1.166-6).[62] As to repossession of property sold on the installment plan, see ¶ 1838 and ¶ 1841.

1157. Reserve for Bad Debts. The reserve method for computing and deducting bad debts on receivables may be used only by small banks.[63] Consequently, nearly all accrual-basis taxpayers must use the specific charge-off method for receivables that become uncollectible in whole or in part. Thrift institutions that qualify as small banks can use the experience method of accounting. Thrift institutions that are treated as large banks are required to use the specific charge-off method (Code Sec. 593(f) and Code Sec. 593(g)).

1160. Guarantor's Reserve for Bad Debts. The reserve method is not available to dealers who guarantee, endorse, or provide indemnity agreements with respect to debts owed to others. Their losses are not deductible until sustained. If the dealer is subrogated to the rights of the original creditor, the loss will be deductible at the time the subrogation rights become wholly or partially worthless.[64]

1163. Reserve Method—Bank. Large banks (those with gross assets in excess of $500 million) cannot use the reserve method of computing deductions for bad

---

Footnote references are to paragraphs of the 2002 Standard Federal Tax Reports.

[58] ¶ 10,800.01	[61] ¶ 10,650.023	[63] ¶ 10,690.01, ¶ 23,650
[59] ¶ 10,800.01	[62] ¶ 10,701, ¶ 10,670.01,	[64] ¶ 10,800.01
[60] ¶ 10,700.03	¶ 10,750.01	

debts. Instead, they must use the specific charge-off method for accounts and loans that "go bad." The reserve method is available for small banks (those whose assets are $500 million or less) (Code Sec. 585).[65]

1166. Debts Owed by Political Parties. Generally, no deduction is allowable for a worthless debt owed by a political party. However, banks and accrual-basis taxpayers who are in the business of providing goods and services (such as polling, media, or organizational services) to political campaigns and candidates may be allowed to deduct such bad debts (Code Sec. 271(c)).[66]

1169. Nonbusiness Bad Debts. Nonbusiness bad debts do not include debts created or acquired in connection with a trade or business of the taxpayer or debts incurred in the taxpayer's trade or business (see ¶ 1145 for a discussion of business bad debts).[67] If a nonbusiness bad debt becomes *entirely* worthless within the tax year, the loss is treated as a short-term capital loss, regardless of how old the debt is.[68] For limitations on deduction of a capital loss, see ¶ 1752. No deduction is permitted unless and until the debt becomes totally worthless. For worthlessness of a debt evidenced by a bond or other security of a corporation or a government, see ¶ 1917.

Net Operating Losses

1173. Application of Net Business Loss. Nearly every taxpayer is allowed to carry back a net operating loss (NOL) from a trade or business to apply as a deduction against prior income and to deduct from succeeding years' income any unabsorbed loss (Code Sec. 172(b)).[69] Taxpayers entitled to the carryback and carryover privilege are: (1) corporations, other than the exceptions noted below, (2) individuals, (3) estates and trusts, (4) common trust fund participants, and (5) partners, who may deduct allocable partnership loss. Among those entities excepted from this privilege are regulated investment companies (Code Sec. 852(b)) and life insurance companies (Code Sec. 805(b)(4)).[70] Generally, no NOL deductions are available to partnerships and S corporations, but their investors may use their distributive shares to calculate individual NOLs (see ¶ 321 and ¶ 417).

Forms. Individuals, estates, and trusts compute the NOL for the loss year and the carrybacks and any carryforward on Form 1045 (Application for Tentative Refund) (Code Sec. 6411). Form 1045 is filed to claim a quick refund for the excess taxes paid in the carryback years that are attributable to the NOL.[71] Form 1045, however, may be used only if filed within one year after the close of the NOL year (but not before Form 1040 or Form 1041 for the NOL year is filed). Form 1045 is processed within the later of 90 days after being filed or 90 days after the last day of the month that includes the due date (including extensions) for filing Form 1040 or Form 1041 for the loss year (Code Sec. 6411(b)). As an alternative to Form 1045, an individual may file Form 1040X for each carryback year to claim a refund. Form 1040X must generally be filed within three years after the due date of the return for the NOL year. Estates and trusts file an amended Form 1041. (There is no Form 1041X; use Form 1041 as issued for the carryback year and check the "amended return" box). If an amended return is filed the taxpayer must still attach the NOL computations using the Form 1045 computation schedules. The IRS generally processes an amended return within six months after filing.

Corporations may file for a quick refund using Form 1139 (Corporation Application for a Quick Refund).[72] Form 1139 also needs to be filed within one year after the close of the NOL year (but not before the return for the NOL year is filed). A separate Form 1120X may be filed in place of Form 1139 for each carryback year, generally, within three years after the due date of the return for the NOL year.

A corporation that expects a NOL in the current tax year may file Form 1138 (Extension of Time for Payment of Taxes by a Corporation Expecting a Net Operating Loss Carryback) to extend the time for payment of the tax for the immediately preceding tax year (Code Sec. 6164; Reg. § 1.6164-1). The extension applies only to payments of tax that are required to be paid after Form 1138 is filed.[73] The extension expires at the end of the month in which the return for the tax year of the expected NOL is required to be filed (including extensions). However, if the corporation files Form 1139 before the extension period ends, the time for payments is further extended until the date that the IRS mails notice that it has allowed or disallowed the application.

Forms 1045 and 1139 may also be used to claim a quick refund of taxes from the carryback of a net capital loss (corporations only), unused general business credit, or claim of right adjustment under Code Sec. 1341(b)(1).

For additional information on Forms 1045 and 1139, see ¶ 2773.

1176. Net Operating Loss Defined. Simply stated, an NOL is the excess of allowable deductions over gross income, computed under the law in effect for the loss year, with the required adjustments (Code Sec. 172(c) and (d); Reg. § 1.172-2; Reg § 1.172-3).[74]

The following adjustments are made with respect to individuals:

(1) No deduction for NOL carryovers or carrybacks from other years is allowed.

(2) An individual may not take any personal or dependency exemptions into account and an estate or a trust cannot take the deduction available to it in lieu of the deduction for personal exemptions.

(3) Nonbusiness capital losses are deductible only to the extent of nonbusiness capital gains. Business capital losses are deductible only to the extent of the sum of (1) business capital gains and (2) any nonbusiness capital gains that remain after deducting nonbusiness capital losses and other nonbusiness deductions (item (4), below) (Reg. § 1.172-3(a)(2)).[75] The 50% exclusion for gain from qualified small business stock under Code Sec. 1202 is not allowed.

(4) Nonbusiness deductions are allowed only to the extent of nonbusiness income (including net nonbusiness capital gains). Further, any such excess may not be allowed against business capital gains (and thereby increase the NOL). Generally, nonbusiness income includes income from passive investments, such as interest, dividends, annuities, endowment income, etc. Salary is considered business income. A loss on a rental property is considered a business loss.[76] The nonbusiness deduction for a taxpayer who itemizes is the total of his itemized deductions other than the personal or business related casualty loss deduction. For one who does not itemize, the standard deduction is a nonbusiness deduction. Deductible contributions to a retirement plan by a self-employed individual on his own behalf are considered nonbusiness deductions (Code Sec. 172(d)(4); Reg. § 1.172-3(a)(3)(iv)).[77]

The following adjustments are made with respect to corporations:

(1) No deduction for NOL carryovers or carrybacks from other years is allowed.

(2) A corporation is entitled to deductions for dividends received from a domestic corporation, those received on certain preferred stock of public utilities, those received from certain foreign corporations, and those paid on certain preferred stock of public utilities, without regard to the limitations (based on taxable income) imposed on such deductions in computing taxable income (see ¶ 237 and ¶ 241) (Code Sec. 172(d)(5)).

1179. Carryover and Carryback. The NOL carryback or carryover is generally that part of the NOL that has not previously been applied against income for

---

Footnote references are to paragraphs of the 2002 Standard Federal Tax Reports.

[73] ¶ 12,014.0751
[74] ¶ 12,002, ¶ 12,004, ¶ 12,005, ¶ 12,014
[75] ¶ 12,005, ¶ 12,014.031
[76] ¶ 12,014.5085
[77] ¶ 12,002, ¶ 12,005, ¶ 12,014.033

other carryback or carryover years (Code Sec. 172(b)(2); Reg. § 1.172-4).[78] In computing the income of an intervening year that must be subtracted from an NOL to determine the portion still available to carry to a subsequent year, the following adjustments must be made (Reg. § 1.172-5):[79]

(1) The NOL deduction for the intervening year is computed by taking into account only carrybacks and carryovers from tax years preceding the loss year.

(2) For taxpayers other than corporations, capital losses are deductible only to the extent of capital gains.

(3) Personal and dependency exemptions are not allowed.

Generally, net operating losses can be carried back to the two years preceding the loss year and then forward to the 20 years following the loss year. For net operating losses in tax years beginning before August 6, 1997, taxpayers can carry back an NOL to the three years preceding the loss year and then forward to 15 years following the loss year. No deduction is allowed in the year the loss is incurred (Code Sec. 172(b); Reg. § 1.172-4).[80] The three-year carryback period is retained for the portion of the NOL that relates to casualty and theft losses of individual taxpayers and to NOLs that are attributable to presidentially declared disasters in the case of a small business or a farming business that elects to forgo the five-year carryback period for a farming loss (Code Sec. 172(b)(1)(F)). See "Farming Loss," below.

Election to Forgo Carryback. A taxpayer entitled to a carryback period for an NOL may elect to forgo the entire carryback period (Code Sec. 172(b)(3)).[81] If the election is made, the loss may be carried forward only. The election must be made by the return due date (including extensions) for the tax year of the NOL for which the election is to be in effect. The election is irrevocable for the year made. The election may also be made on an amended return filed within six months of the due date of an original timely return (excluding extensions).

Special Carrying Periods. Special carryback and carryforward periods apply in the case of specified liability losses and bad debt losses of commercial banks. A specified liability loss (product liability loss) is a separate net operating loss that can be carried back 10 years from the tax year of the loss (Code Sec. 172(b)(1)(C)).[82] The portion of a commercial bank's NOL incurred for any tax year after 1986 and before 1994 that is attributable to a bad debt deduction may be carried back 10 years and forward five years (Code Sec. 172(b)(1)(D)).[83] A real estate investment trust (REIT) generally cannot carry back an NOL to a tax year in which the entity operated as a REIT (Code Sec. 172(b)(1)(B)).[84]

Corporate Equity Reduction Transactions (CERTs). A C corporation may not carry back a portion of its NOL if $1 million or more of interest expense is incurred in a "major stock acquisition" of another corporation or in an "excess distribution" by the corporation. These transactions have been dubbed as CERTs (Code Sec. 172(h)).[85] The amount subject to the limitation is the lesser of (1) the corporation's deductible interest expense allocable to the CERT or (2) the amount by which the corporation's interest expense for the current tax year exceeds the average interest expense for the three tax years preceding the tax year in which the CERT occurs. The portion of the NOL that cannot be carried back may be carried forward.

Farming Loss. Effective for NOLs for tax years beginning after 1997, a farming loss may be carried back for five years (Code Sec. 172(b)(1)(G) and Code Sec. 172(i)). This loss is the amount of *any* NOL attributable to the income and deductions of a farming business. A taxpayer may elect to treat a farming loss as if it were not a farming loss. In this case, the two-year carryback period generally applies (Code Sec. 172(i)(3)).

Footnote references are to paragraphs of the 2002 Standard Federal Tax Reports.

[78] ¶ 12,002, ¶ 12,006, ¶ 12,014.037
[79] ¶ 12,007, ¶ 12,014.041
[80] ¶ 12,002, ¶ 12,006
[81] ¶ 12,002, ¶ 12,014.025
[82] ¶ 12,002, ¶ 12,014.054, ¶ 12,014.056
[83] ¶ 12,002, ¶ 12,014.05
[84] ¶ 12,002, ¶ 12,014.05
[85] ¶ 12,002, ¶ 12,014.059

¶1179

1182. Net Operating Loss Deduction. The NOL deduction that is subtracted from gross income is simply the sum of the carrybacks and carryovers to the tax year (Reg. § 1.172-1).[86] No adjustments need be made. As explained at ¶ 1179, however, certain adjustments must be made in determining the income for any year that must be offset against carryovers or carrybacks to find the portion of the loss that will still be available to carry to a later year.

1185. Carryovers and Carrybacks Between Predecessors and Successors. As a general rule, an NOL may be carried back or carried over only by the taxpayer who sustained the loss. A beneficiary of an estate or trust, however, is entitled to any carryover amount remaining unused after the last tax year of the estate or trust (Code Sec. 642(h); Reg. § 1.642(h)-1).[87] A successor corporation is allowed to carry over the NOL and certain other items of its predecessor under specified conditions (see ¶ 2277).

A divorced taxpayer who suffered an NOL in a year when he was single can carry it back to his portion of income in previous years when a joint return was filed. Only his signature is necessary for a valid refund claim.[88]

1188. Recomputation After Carryback. In a year in which an NOL is carried back, any income, deductions, or credits that are based on or limited to a percentage of adjusted gross income must be recomputed based on AGI after applying the NOL deduction for the carryback year. The charitable contribution deduction, however, is not recomputed. Taxable income is recomputed taking into account the NOL and the preceding adjustments. Income tax, alternative minimum tax, and any credits that are based on or limited to the amount of tax are then recomputed (Reg. § 1.172-5).[89]

Hobby Losses

1195. Hobby Expenses and Losses. Losses incurred by individuals, S corporations, partnerships, and estates and trusts that are attributable to an activity not engaged in for profit—so-called hobby losses—are generally deductible only to the extent of income produced by the activity (Code Sec. 183; Reg. § 1.183-1—Reg. § 1.183-4).[90] Some expenses that are deductible whether or not they are incurred in connection with a hobby, such as taxes, interest, and casualty losses, are deductible even if they exceed hobby income. These expenses, however, reduce the amount of hobby income against which hobby expenses can be offset (Code Sec. 183(b)(1)).[91] The hobby expenses then offset the reduced income, in the following order: (1) operating expenses other than amounts resulting in a basis adjustment and (2) depreciation and other basis adjustment items.[92] The itemized deduction for hobby expenses to the extent of income derived from the activity is subject to the 2% floor on miscellaneous itemized deductions (see ¶ 1011).

An activity is presumed not to be a hobby if profits result in any three of five consecutive tax years ending with the tax year in question, unless the IRS proves otherwise (Code Sec. 183(d)).[93] An activity involving the breeding, training, showing, or racing of horses is presumed not to be a hobby if profits result in two out of seven consecutive years. A special election on Form 5213 permits suspension of the presumption until there are five (or seven) years in existence from the time the taxpayer first engages in the activity. A taxpayer need not waive the statute of limitations for unrelated items on his return in order to take advantage of the presumption (Code Sec. 183(e)(4)).[94]

Footnote references are to paragraphs of the 2002 Standard Federal Tax Reports.

[86] ¶ 12,003
[87] ¶ 24,280, ¶ 24,301
[88] ¶ 12,014.443
[89] ¶ 12,007, ¶ 12,014.041

[90] ¶ 12,170, ¶ 12,171—
[91] ¶ 12,176, ¶ 12,177.025
[91] ¶ 12,170, ¶ 12,177.01
[92] ¶ 12,177.035

[93] ¶ 12,170, ¶ 12,177.01
[94] ¶ 12,170, ¶ 12,177.045

Chapter 12

DEDUCTIONS

Depreciation☐Amortization Depletion

DEPRECIATION AND AMORTIZATION

Allowance of Depreciation

1201. Property Subject to Depreciation. Taxpayers may deduct a reasonable allowance for the exhaustion, wear and tear of property used in a trade or business, or of property held for the production of income (Reg. § 1.167(a)-1).[1] Depreciation is not allowable for property used for personal purposes, such as a residence or a car used solely for pleasure.

Converted Residence. When an individual vacates a principal residence and offers it for sale, the Tax Court will consider it to be held for the production of income and depreciable for the period before the sale only if the individual is seeking a profit based on the post-conversion appreciation in value.[2] For allocation of depreciation in other situations when a home is used partly for business or rental purposes, see ¶ 961 et seq. When property held for personal use, such as a residence,

---

Footnote references are to paragraphs of the 2002 Standard Federal Tax Reports.

¶ 1201   [1] ¶ 11,003   [2] ¶ 11,007.512

is converted to business or income-producing use, the basis for depreciation is the lesser of the property's fair market value or adjusted basis on the date of conversion (Reg. § 1.167(g)-1).

Estates and Trusts. For depreciation by an estate or trust, see ¶ 530.

Inventory. Depreciation is allowed for tangible property, but not for inventories, stock in trade, land apart from its improvements, or a depletable natural resource (Reg. § 1.167(a)-2).[3]

Farmers. Farm buildings and other physical farm property (except land) are depreciable. Livestock acquired for work, breeding, or dairy purposes may be depreciated unless included in inventory (Reg. § 1.167(a)-6(b)).[4]

Intangibles. An intangible that is not amortizable under Code Sec. 197 (see ¶ 1288) may be depreciated under Code Sec. 167 using the straight-line method, provided that it has an ascertainable value and useful life that can be measured with reasonable accuracy.[5]

Software. Certain depreciable computer software generally acquired after August 10, 1993, that is not an amortizable Code Sec. 197 intangible may be depreciated using the straight-line method over 36 months (Code Sec. 167(f)(1)).[6] See ¶ 980.

Web Site Development Costs. The IRS has not issued formal guidance on the treatment of web site development costs. However, informal internal IRS guidance suggests that one appropriate approach is to treat these costs like an item of software and depreciate them over three years. See ¶ 125 of the CCH U.S. MASTER DEPRECIATION GUIDE for full text of this guidance. It is clear, however, that taxpayers who pay large amounts to develop sophisticated sites have been allocating their costs to items such as software development (currently deductible like research and development costs under Code Sec. 174) and currently deductible advertising expense.[7]

Residential Mortgage Servicing Rights. Depreciable residential mortgage servicing rights that are not Code Sec. 197 intangibles may be depreciated under the straight-line method over 108 months (Code Sec. 167(f)(3)).[8]

Term Interests. No depreciation or amortization deduction is allowed for certain term interests in property for any period during which the remainder interest is held directly (or indirectly) by a related person (Code Sec. 167(e)).[9]

Methods. The methods of depreciation are dependent on when the property was placed in service. The Modified Accelerated Cost Recovery System (MACRS) (¶ 1236) applies to tangible property generally placed in service after 1986 and the Accelerated Cost Recovery System (ACRS) applies to property placed in service after 1980 and before 1987 (¶ 1252). Under MACRS and ACRS, the cost or other basis of an asset is generally recovered over a specific recovery period. For assets placed in service before 1981 and assets that are excluded from MACRS and ACRS, the depreciation allowance for any tax year is limited to such ratable amount as is necessary to recover the remaining cost or other basis, less salvage value, during the remaining useful life of the property (class life ADR (¶ 1282) is to be used when it was elected). In no event may an asset that is not subject to MACRS or ACRS be depreciated below a reasonable salvage value (Reg. § 1.167(a)-1(a)).[10]

Depreciation based on a useful life is to be calculated over the estimated useful life of the asset while actually used by the taxpayer and not over the longer period of the asset's physical life (Reg. § 1.167(a)-1(b)).[11] For rules governing the depreciation of self-constructed assets, see the uniform capitalization rules at ¶ 990-¶ 999.

Post-1980 depreciation on tangible assets first placed in service before 1981 is to be computed under the method elected for the years they were placed in service. For assets placed in service after 1970 and before 1981, the taxpayer had a choice of the Asset Depreciation Range (ADR) System[12] (¶ 1282) or the general depreciation

---

Footnote references are to paragraphs of the 2002 Standard Federal Tax Reports.

[3] ¶ 11,006	[7] ¶ 13,709	[10] ¶ 11,003, ¶ 11,009.04
[4] ¶ 11,015	[8] ¶ 11,002, ¶ 11,009.03	[11] ¶ 11,003, ¶ 11,005.021
[5] ¶ 11,009.015	[9] ¶ 11,002, ¶ 11,049.035	[12] ¶ 11,029.021
[6] ¶ 11,002, ¶ 11,009.027		

rules (¶ 1216). For tangible assets first placed in service before 1971, the taxpayer could have elected the Class Life System (CLS) [13] for pre-1971 assets or the general depreciation rules.

Forms. Form 4562 is generally used to claim the depreciation or amortization deduction and is attached to the taxpayer's tax return. However, individuals and other noncorporate taxpayers (including S corporations) need not complete Form 4562 if their only depreciation (or amortization) deduction is for property (other than listed property (¶ 1211)) placed in service before the current tax year.

Basis for Depreciation

1203. Capital Sum Recoverable Through Depreciation Allowance. The capital sum recovered by depreciation is the adjusted basis of the property, which is the same adjusted basis used for determining gain upon its sale or other disposition (see ¶ 1604). For the effect of the investment credit on basis, see ¶ 1360. When property held for personal use, such as a residence, is converted to business or income-producing use, the basis for depreciation is the lesser of the property's fair market value or adjusted basis on the date of conversion (Reg. § 1.167(g)-1).[14]

When a building and land have been acquired for a lump sum, only the building is depreciated. The basis for depreciation cannot exceed the same proportion of the lump sum as the value of the building bore to the value of the entire property at the time of acquisition.

If property is subject to both depreciation and amortization, depreciation is allowable only for the portion that is not subject to the allowance for amortization and may be taken concurrently with amortization (Reg. § 1.167(a)-5).[15]

Proration of Depreciation Allowance

1206. Sale or Purchase During Tax Year. Depreciation begins in the tax year that an asset is placed in service and ends in the tax year that it is retired from service or is fully depreciated (Reg. § 1.167(a)-10).[16] Generally, an asset is considered placed in service when it is in a condition or state of readiness and availability for a specifically assigned function.

MACRS Depreciable Property. For tangible depreciable personal property placed in service after 1986, one-half year's depreciation is generally allowed, regardless of how long the property is held in the year it is placed in service or disposed of, unless the mid-quarter convention applies (¶ 1245). Special prorations by month (using a mid-month convention) are provided for depreciable real property (¶ 1243).

ACRS Recovery Property. For personal recovery property placed in service after 1980 and before 1987, one-half year's depreciation is allowed, regardless of how long it is held in the year that it is placed in service (see ¶ 1252). No deduction is allowed in the year of disposition of personal recovery property. Special prorations by month (using a mid-month convention) are provided for real recovery property (¶ 1261).

Pre-1981 Assets. For an asset purchased before 1981, only a part of a full year's depreciation was allowed in the year it was placed in service. The allowable deduction was computed by multiplying the first full year's depreciation allowance by the months the property was owned and dividing by 12. The same rule applies in the year of sale.[17]

Section 179 Expense Election

1208. Election to Expense Certain Depreciable Business Assets. An expense deduction is provided for taxpayers (other than estates, trusts or certain noncorporate lessors) who elect to treat the cost of qualifying property, called Sec.

Footnote references are to paragraphs of the 2002 Standard Federal Tax Reports.

¶ 1203   [13] ¶ 11,031.021   [15] ¶ 11,012, ¶ 11,014.021   [17] ¶ 11,025.03
          [14] ¶ 11,046, ¶ 11,007.045   [16] ¶ 11,024

179 property, as an expense rather than a capital expenditure (Code Sec. 179)[18]. The election, which is made on Form 4562, is attached to the taxpayer's original return (including a late-filed original return) or on an amended return filed by the due date of the original return (including extensions) for the year the property is placed in service and may not be revoked without IRS consent.[19].

Dollar Limitation. The maximum Code Sec. 179 deduction is $24,000 for tax years beginning in 2001 and 2002. Thereafter, the maximum deduction is $25,000 per year.

Investment Limitation. The dollar limitation is reduced by a dollar for each dollar of the cost of qualified property placed in service during the tax year over $200,000. Amounts disallowed under this rule may not be carried forward.

Taxable Income Limitation. The total cost of property that may be expensed for any tax year cannot exceed the total amount of taxable income derived from the active conduct of any trade or business during the tax year, including salaries and wages.

An amount disallowed as the result of the taxable income limitation is carried forward. The deduction for carryforwards and the amounts expensed for qualifying property placed in service in a carryforward year, however, may not exceed the maximum annual dollar cost ceiling, investment limitation, or, if lesser, the taxable income limitation.

Qualifying Property. To qualify as Code Sec. 179 property, the property must be tangible Code Sec. 1245 property, depreciable under Code Sec. 168, and acquired by purchase for use in the active conduct of a trade or business (Code Sec. 179(d)).[20] Code Sec. 50(b) property and air conditioning or heating units do not qualify as Code Sec. 179 property. Code Sec. 50(b) property includes property used predominantly outside of the U.S., property used with respect to lodging such as apartment buildings but not hotels and motels, and property used by tax-exempt organizations (unless the property is used predominantly in connection with an unrelated business income activity).

Recapture. The Code Sec. 179 expense deduction is treated as depreciation for recapture purposes. Thus, gain on a disposition of Sec. 179 property is generally treated as ordinary income to the extent of the Code Sec. 179 expense allowance claimed plus any depreciation claimed.

If business use of Sec. 179 property fails to exceed 50 percent during any year of the property's depreciation recovery period, a portion of the amount expensed is recaptured as ordinary income (Code Sec. 179(d)(10); Reg. § 1.179-1(e)). The recapture amount is the difference between the expense claimed and the depreciation that would have been allowed on the expensed amount for prior tax years and the tax year of recapture. Recapture is computed on Form 4797.

In the case of a listed property, such as a passenger automobile, the recapture rules described at ¶ 1211 for property used 50 percent or less for business apply in place of the above rule.

Enterprise Zones. Special rules apply to an enterprise zone business (Code Sec. 1397A).[21]

Limitations on Automobiles and Listed Property

1211. Business Usage Requirement for Listed Property. The availability of depreciation deductions for "listed property" is restricted (Code Sec. 280F).[22] This term embraces automobiles and other forms of transportation if the property's nature lends itself to personal use (airplanes, trucks, boats, etc.), entertainment, recreational and amusement property, computers and peripheral equipment, cellular telephones and similar telecommunications equipment, and any other property specified by regulation. Unless used more than 50% for business, MACRS deductions

---

Footnote references are to paragraphs of the 2002 Standard Federal Tax Reports.

[18] ¶ 12,120, ¶ 12,126   [21] ¶ 32,397, ¶ 32,398.01,   [22] ¶ 15,100, ¶ 15,108
[19] ¶ 12,120, ¶ 12,126.073   ¶ 32,399
[20] ¶ 12,120, ¶ 12,126.021

¶ 1211

for such property must be determined under the MACRS alternative depreciation system (ADS) (see ¶ 1247).

If the property satisfies the business use test in the year in which it is placed in service but fails to meet that test in a later tax year, depreciation deductions previously taken are subject to recapture in such later year. MACRS depreciation for years preceding the year in which the business use fell to 50% or less is recaptured to the extent that the MACRS depreciation for such years exceeds the depreciation that would have been allowed under the MACRS alternative depreciation system (ADS). Depreciation thereafter must be computed using ADS.

The above rules also apply to any portion of the cost of purchased "listed property" that a taxpayer elects to expense under Code Sec. 179 (¶ 1208). Thus, if the more-than-50%-business-use test is not satisfied in the year the property is placed in service, the property will not qualify for the expensing election. If the more-than-50%-business-use test is initially satisfied but is not met in a later tax year, the deduction taken under the Code Sec. 179 election will be treated as if it were a depreciation deduction for purposes of depreciation recapture.

Form 4797 is used to calculate any recapture amount.

See ¶ 1214 for additional limits on luxury cars.

1214. Limitations on Passenger Automobiles. Even though a passenger automobile is used more than 50% for business purposes, there are further limits on the annual depreciation that may be claimed (Code Sec. 280F(a)).[23] The maximum MACRS deduction (including the Code Sec. 179 expensing deduction (¶ 1208)) that may be claimed for a passenger automobile is shown in the following chart:

For Cars Placed in Service After	Before	Depreciation Allowable in—				
		Year 1	Year 2	Year 3	Year 4, etc.	Authority
6/18/84	1/1/85	$4,000	$6,000	$6,000	$6,000	Former 280F(a)(2)
12/31/84	4/3/85	4,100	6,200	6,200	6,200	Rev. Rul. 86-107
4/2/85	1/1/87	3,200	4,800	4,800	4,800	Former 280F(a)(2)
12/31/86	1/1/89	2,560	4,100	2,450	1,475	Current 280F(a)(2)
12/31/88	1/1/91	2,660	4,200	2,550	1,475	Rev. Proc. 89-64 Rev. Proc. 90-22
12/31/90	1/1/92	2,660	4,300	2,550	1,575	Rev. Proc. 91-30
12/31/91	1/1/93	2,760	4,400	2,650	1,575	Rev. Proc. 92-43
12/31/92	1/1/94	2,860	4,600	2,750	1,675	Rev. Proc. 93-35
12/31/93	1/1/95	2,960	4,700	2,850	1,675	Rev. Proc. 94-53
12/31/94	1/1/97	3,060	4,900	2,950	1,775	Rev. Proc. 95-9 Rev. Proc. 96-25
12/31/96	1/1/98	3,160	5,000	3,050	1,775	Rev. Proc. 97-20
12/31/97	1/1/99	3,160	5,000	2,950	1,775	Rev. Proc. 98-30
12/31/98	1/1/00	3,060	5,000	2,950	1,775	Rev. Proc. 99-14
12/31/99	1/1/02	3,060	4,900	2,950	1,775	Rev. Proc. 2000-18 Rev. Proc. 2001-19

The above maximum annual limits (often referred to as the luxury car limits) are based on 100% business use. If business use is less than 100%, the limits must be reduced to reflect the actual business use percentage.

Special rules apply to "clean fuel" and electric vehicles (¶ 1286).

If, after the normal recovery period for automobiles, the taxpayer continues to use the car in its trade or business, the unrecovered basis (referred to as "Sec. 280F unrecovered basis") may be deducted at the maximum annual rate provided in the chart for the fourth and succeeding years. This rule permits depreciation deductions beyond the normal recovery period. Unrecovered basis is determined as if business use had been 100 percent during each year of the recovery period.

> **Example.** On April 5, 2001, a calendar-year taxpayer purchased a car for $20,000. Business use of the car each year is 80%. Depreciation is computed under the general MACRS 200% declining-balance method over a five-year recovery period using a half-year convention subject to the

---

Footnote references are to paragraphs of the 2002 Standard Federal Tax Reports.

¶ 1214   [23] ¶ 15,100, ¶ 15,108

luxury car limitations. The regular recovery period depreciation for 2001 through 2006 is computed as follows:

Year	100% Business-Use MACRS Depreciation	Luxury Car Limit	Deduction: 80% of Lesser	Sec. 280F Unrecovered Basis
2001	$4,000	$3,060	$2,448	$16,940
2002	6,400	4,900	3,920	12,040
2003	3,840	2,950	2,360	9,090
2004	2,304	1,775	1,420	7,315
2005	2,304	1,775	1,420	5,540
2006	1,152	1,775	922	4,388

Note that the unrecovered basis is computed by subtracting the depreciation that would have been allowed (taking the applicable cap into consideration) if business use was 100%. Thus, for example, the unrecovered basis at the close of 2001 is $16,940 ($20,000 − $3,060). The $4,388 unrecovered basis at the close of the regular recovery period is deducted in the post recovery period years as follows:

Year	Unrecovered basis at beginning of year	Luxury Car Limit	Deduction: 80% of Lesser	Unrecovered basis at end of year
2007	$4,388	$1,775	$1,420	$2,613
2008	2,613	1,775	1,420	838
2009	838	1,775	670	0

Passenger Automobile Defined. For purposes of the depreciation caps, a passenger automobile includes any four-wheeled vehicle manufactured primarily for use on public streets, roads, and highways that has an *unloaded* gross vehicle weight (i.e., curb weight fully equipped for service but without passengers or cargo) of 6,000 pounds or less (Code Sec. 280F(d)(5)(A)). A truck or van (including a sport utility vehicle or minivan) is treated as a passenger automobile if it has a *gross* vehicle weight (i.e., maximum total weight of a loaded vehicle as specified by the manufacturer) of 6,000 pounds or less. Consequently, some large SUVs are not subject to the depreciation caps. Ambulances or hearses and vehicles used directly in the trade or business of transporting persons or property for hire (e.g., taxis and limousines) are not considered passenger automobiles.

Reporting. The allowable depreciation deduction is reported on Form 4562 (Part V).

1215. Leased Property Restrictions. The lessee of a passenger car (as defined for depreciation cap purposes at ¶ 1214) leased for business is required to include an additional amount in income to offset rental deductions for each tax year during which the car is leased (Code Sec. 280F(c)(2); Reg. § 1.280F-7).[24] The inclusion amount is based on the cost of the car and generally applies to cars with a fair market value exceeding an inflation-adjusted dollar amount (for example, $15,500 for a car with a lease term beginning in 2000 or 2001, $15,500 for a car with a lease term beginning in 1999, $15,800 for a lease term beginning in 1998 or 1997, and $15,500 for a lease term beginning in 1996 or 1995). An inclusion amount table is issued annually by the IRS in the same Revenue Procedure in which the annual depreciation caps are issued (see list of these Revenue Procedures at ¶ 1214). The same table is used for each year of the lease.

A lessee's inclusion amount for each tax year that the car is leased is computed as follows: (1) use the fair market value of the car on the first day of the lease term to find the appropriate dollar (inclusion) amounts on the IRS table (reproduced at ¶ 15,108.048 of the 2002 STANDARD FEDERAL TAX REPORTER and at ¶ 82 of the looseleaf edition of the U.S. MASTER TAX GUIDE); (2) prorate the dollar amount from the table for the number of days of the lease term included in the tax year; and (3) multiply the prorated amount by the percentage of business and investment use for the tax year. For the last tax year during any lease that does not begin and end in the same tax year, the dollar amount for the preceding tax year should be used.

Footnote references are to paragraphs of the 2002 Standard Federal Tax Reports.
[24] ¶ 15,100, ¶ 15,107

Example. A car costing $25,000 is leased for four years by a calendar-year taxpayer beginning on April 1, 2001 and is used 100% for business. The annual dollar amounts from the table (Rev. Proc. 2001-19) for leases beginning in 2001 are: $75 for the first tax year during the lease, $165 for the second tax year, $243 for the third tax year, $292 for the fourth tax year, and $337 for the fifth and following tax years. In 2001, the inclusion amount is $57 (275/365 × $75). The inclusion amounts for 2002, 2003, and 2004 are $165, $243, and $292 respectively since the vehicle is leased for the entire year during these tax years. In 2005, the inclusion amount is $72 (90/365 × $292 (the dollar amount for 2004, the preceding tax year, is used in the last year of the lease)).

Reporting. The inclusion amount is reported on Form 2106 by employees, Schedule C (Form 1040) by the self-employed, and Schedule F by farmers.

Listed Property Other Than Passenger Automobiles. Lessees of listed property (other than passenger automobiles) are required to include in income a usage-based inclusion amount in the first tax year that the business use percentage of such property is 50% or less (Code Sec. 280F(b); Reg. § 1.280F-7(b); Temp. Reg. § 1.280F-5T(g)).[25]

Depreciation Methods

1216. Methods of Computing Depreciation. Most tangible property placed in service after 1986 must be depreciated using methods prescribed under MACRS (¶ 1243). Depreciation for recovery property placed in service after 1980 and before 1987 is computed under ACRS (¶ 1252).

For property placed in service before 1981, post-1980 depreciation may be computed under the straight-line method (¶ 1224), the double declining-balance method (¶ 1226), the sum-of-the-years-digits method (¶ 1228), and other "consistent methods" (¶ 1231) (former Code Sec. 167(b)), depending on the taxpayer's election in the year the property was placed in service.[26] However, accelerated depreciation for pre-1981 realty is limited (former Code Sec. 167(j)).[27] One method of depreciation may have been used for a particular asset, and a different method may have been used for another asset of the same class whether held at the beginning of the year or acquired during the year. For item accounts, any method that resulted in a reasonable allowance may have been selected for each item of property, but such method must thereafter be applied consistently to that particular item. For group, classified or composite accounts, any method may have been selected for each account. Such method must be applied to that particular account consistently thereafter but need not necessarily have been applied to acquisitions of similar property in the same or later years, provided the acquisitions were set up in separate accounts (Reg. § 1.167(b)-0).[28]

1218. Methods for Depreciating Real Estate. Real property placed in service after 1986 is depreciated under MACRS (¶ 1236). Real property placed in service after 1980 and generally before 1987 is depreciated under ACRS (¶ 1252). Structural components placed in service after 1986 are depreciated under MACRS (see ¶ 1240). Post-1986 rehabilitation expenditures are subject to MACRS allowances (¶ 1236).

1221. Change in Depreciation Method. A change in depreciation method is a change in accounting method that generally requires the consent of the IRS (Reg. § 1.167(e)-1).[29] Procedures for obtaining automatic consent to change depreciation methods in specified situations (e.g., where incorrect depreciation has been claimed) are provided in Rev. Proc. 99-49 (Appendix 2.01).[30]

1224. "Straight-Line" or "Fixed-Percentage" Method of Depreciation. The "straight-line" method of computing the depreciation deduction assumes that the depreciation sustained is uniform during the useful life of the property. The cost

---

Footnote references are to paragraphs of the 2002 Standard Federal Tax Reports.

¶ 1216

[25] ¶ 15,108.054	[27] ¶ 11,059.01	[29] ¶ 11,042
[26] ¶ 11,037.021	[28] ¶ 11,032	[30] ¶ 11,043.021

or other basis, less estimated salvage value, is deductible in equal annual amounts over the estimated useful life (Reg. § 1.167(b)-1).[31] An asset may not be depreciated below its salvage value. Straight-line depreciation under MACRS and ACRS is generally computed in this manner, except that a recovery period is used instead of the useful life and salvage value is not considered (Code Sec. 168(b)(4)) [32] (¶ 1243 and ¶ 1252).

1226. Double Declining-Balance Method of Depreciation. Under this method, depreciation is greatest in the first year and smaller in each succeeding year (Reg. § 1.167(b)-2).[33] The depreciation basis is reduced each year by the amount of the depreciation deduction, and a uniform rate of up to 200% of the straight-line rate is applied to the resulting balances. Salvage is not taken into account in determining the annual allowances under the declining-balance method. However, an asset may not be depreciated below a reasonable salvage value (Reg. § 1.167(b)-2).[34] Under the MACRS rules, the double declining-balance method is used to depreciate 3-, 5-, 7-, and 10-year property (see ¶ 1243).

1228. Sum-of-the-Years-Digits Method. Under the sum-of-the-years-digits method, changing fractions are applied each year to the original cost or other basis, less salvage. The numerator of the fraction each year represents the remaining useful life of the asset and the denominator, which remains constant, is the sum of the numerals representing each of the years of the estimated useful life (the sum-of-the-years digits). This method, if elected, may be used for group, classified or composite accounts (Reg. § 1.167(b)-3).[35]

1229. Income Forecast Method. For property placed in service after August 5, 1997, the use of the income forecast method only applies to film, videotape, sound recordings, copyrights, books, patents, and other property that may be specified by IRS regulations. The income forecast method is not available to intangible property that is amortizable under Code Sec. 197 (see ¶ 1288) or to consumer durables subject to rent-to-own contracts (see ¶ 1240) (Code Sec. 167(g)(6); Rev. Rul. 60-358).[36]

Under the income forecast method, the cost of an asset (less any salvage value) placed in service after September 13, 1995, is multiplied by a fraction, the numerator of which is the net income from the asset for the tax year and the denominator of which is the total net income forecast to be derived from the asset before the close of the 10th tax year following the tax year in which the asset is placed in service. The unrecovered adjusted basis of the property as of the beginning of the 10th tax year is claimed as a depreciation deduction in the 10th tax year following the tax year in which the asset was placed in service.

If the income forecast changes during the 10-year period, the formula is as follows: the unrecovered depreciable cost of the asset at the beginning of the tax year of revision multiplied by a fraction, the numerator of which is the net income from the asset for the tax year of revision and the denominator of which is the revised forecasted total net income from the asset for the year of revision and the remaining years before the close of the 10th tax year following the tax year in which the asset was placed in service.

Generally, during the 3rd and 10th tax years after the asset is placed in service, a taxpayer is required to pay or may receive interest based on the recalculation of depreciation using actual income figures. This look-back rule does not apply to property that has a cost basis of $100,000 or less or if the taxpayer's income projections were within 10 percent of the income actually earned. Form 8866 is used to compute the interest due or owed.

1231. Other Consistent Methods. In addition to the depreciation methods explained at ¶ 1224-¶ 1228, a taxpayer may use any other consistent method, such as the sinking fund method, if the total deductions during the first two-thirds of

---

the useful life are not more than the total allowable under the declining-balance method (Reg. § 1.167(b)-4).[37]

Leased Property

1234. Lessee/Lessor Improvements, Lease Acquisition Costs. The cost of an addition or improvement made by the lessee to real property is depreciated under MACRS in the same manner as the MACRS deduction for the property would be calculated if the property had been placed in service at the same time as the addition or improvement (Code Sec. 168(i)(8)).[38] For example, the cost of replacing a roof on a residential rental building would be separately depreciated over 27.5 years using the straight-line method. If, upon termination of the lease, a lessee does not retain the improvement, loss is computed by reference to the improvement's adjusted basis at the time of the lease termination. A lessor that disposes of or abandons a leasehold improvement (made by the lessor) upon termination of the lease may use the adjusted basis of the improvement at such time to determine gain or loss (Code Sec. 168(i)(8)).

Lease Acquisition Costs. In amortizing the cost of acquiring a lease over the lease term, a renewal period is counted as part of the lease term if less than 75% of the acquisition cost is attributable to the unexpired lease period (not counting the renewal period) (Code Sec. 178).[39]

Modified Accelerated Cost Recovery System (MACRS)

1236. MACRS in General. MACRS is mandatory for most tangible depreciable property placed in service after December 31, 1986, unless transitional rules apply (Code Sec. 168).[40] However, post-1986 depreciation on property placed in service before 1987 will continue to be computed under the method used when the property was placed in service. Under MACRS, the cost of eligible property is recovered over a 3-, 5-, 7-, 10-, 15-, 20-, 27.5-, 31.5- or 39-year period, depending upon the type of property (see ¶ 1240) by using statutory recovery methods (see ¶ 1243) and conventions (see ¶ 1245). Special transferee rules under MACRS (Code Sec. 168(i)(7))[41] are similar to the ACRS transferee rules (see ¶ 1248). The recovery periods for all MACRS assets can be found in a table that appears in IRS Publication 946. This table is an updated version of the table that appears in Rev. Proc. 87-56.

MACRS Alternative Depreciation System (ADS). ADS must be used for tangible property used outside the United States, tax-exempt use property, tax-exempt bond-financed property, property imported from a foreign country for which an Executive Order is in effect because the country maintains trade restrictions or engages in other discriminatory acts, and property for which an ADS election has been made (Code Sec. 168(g))[42] (see ¶ 1247).

1238. Depreciable Property. Generally, most tangible depreciable property placed in service after 1986 that is not otherwise excluded is depreciated under MACRS. MACRS property is depreciable if it wears out, has a useful life that exceeds one year, and is used in a trade or business or for the production of income. Such property does not include property for which an election was made to use a depreciation method not expressed in terms of years, such as the unit of production or income forecast method; public utility property, unless a normalization method of accounting is used; motion picture films and videotapes; sound recordings; intangible property; and property placed in service before 1987 that is excluded from MACRS under the anti-churning rules (Code Sec. 168(f)).[43] Public utility property that does not qualify under MACRS (Code Sec. 168(f)(2) and Code Sec. 168(i)(9))[44] is depreciated under Code Sec. 167(a)[45] using the same depreciation method and

---

[37] ¶ 11,036, ¶ 11,037.031	[40] ¶ 11,250, ¶ 11,279	[43] ¶ 11,250, ¶ 11,279.021
[38] ¶ 11,250, ¶ 11,011.021	[41] ¶ 11,250, ¶ 11,279.054	[44] ¶ 11,250
[39] ¶ 12,100, ¶ 12,105.021	[42] ¶ 11,250, ¶ 11,279.04	[45] ¶ 11,002

¶ 1234

useful life as is used to compute the ratemaking depreciation allowance for the property.[46]

1240. Classes of Depreciable Property. The classes of depreciable property are defined in terms of Code Secs. 1245 and 1250 property and the class life as of January 1, 1986.[47] For purposes of the post-1986 rules, Code Sec. 1245 and Code Sec. 1250 property are defined under Code Sec. 1245(a)(3) and Code Sec. 1250(c), respectively (see ¶ 1785 and ¶ 1786), for purposes of determining gain. The class life (or assigned class life) of an asset affects its recovery period, the method of depreciation used, and the applicable convention. Under MACRS, assets are classified according to their present class life as follows:

Three-Year Property. Three-year property includes property with a class life of four years or less. Any race horse over two years old or any other horse over 12 years old at the time it is placed in service is also classified as three-year property (Code Sec. 168(e)(1) and (3)).[48] For property placed in service after August 5, 1997, certain "rent-to-own" consumer durable property (e.g., televisions and furniture) is three-year property (Code Sec. 168(e)(3)(iii)).[49] Breeding hogs (Rev. Proc. 87-56 Asset Class 01.236) and tractor units for use over the road (Rev. Proc. 87-56 Asset Class 00.26) are three-year property. A tractor unit is a highway truck designed to tow a trailer or semitrailer and which does not carry cargo on the same chassis as the engine (Reg. § 145.4051-1(e)(1)).

Five-Year Property. Five-year property generally includes property with a class life of more than four years and less than 10 years. This property includes: (1) cars, (2) light and heavy general-purpose trucks, (3) qualified technological equipment, (4) computer-based telephone central office switching equipment, (5) research and experimentation property that is Sec. 1245 property, (6) semi-conductor manufacturing equipment, (7) geothermal, solar and wind energy properties, (8) certain biomass properties that are small power production facilities, (9) computers and peripheral equipment, and (10) office machinery (typewriters, calculators, etc.) (Code Sec. 168(e)(1) and (3)).[50]

Furniture, appliances, window treatments, and carpeting used in residential rental property is five-year property (Announcement 99-82). Personal property used in wholesale or retail trade or in the provision of personal and professional services for which a specific recovery period is not otherwise provided is five-year property (Asset Class 57.0 of Rev. Proc. 87-56). For example, a professional library used by an accountant or attorney is five-year property. Examples of *personal* service businesses include hotels and motels, laundry and dry cleaning establishments, beauty and barber shops, photographic studios and mortuaries (Rev. Proc. 77-10). Examples of *professional* service businesses include services offered by doctors, dentists, lawyers, accountants, architects, engineers, and veterinarians (Rev. Proc. 77-10).

Five-year property also includes taxis (Rev. Proc. 87-56 Asset Class 00.22), buses (Rev. Proc. 87-56 Asset Class 00.23), airplanes not used in commercial or contract carrying of passengers or freight and all helicopters (Rev. Proc. 87-56 Asset Class 00.21), trailers and trailer-mounted containers (Rev. Proc. 87-56 Asset Class 00.27), breeding cattle and dairy cattle (Rev. Proc. 87-56 Asset Class 01.21), breeding sheep and breeding goats (Rev. Proc. 87-56 Asset Class 01.21), and assets used in construction by certain contractors, builders, and real estate subdividers and developers (Rev. Proc. 87-56 Asset Class 15.0).

Seven-Year Property. Seven-year property includes property with a class life of 10 years or more but less than 16 years (Code Sec. 168(e)(1)). This property includes office furniture, equipment and fixtures that are not structural components (Rev. Proc. 87-56 Asset Class 00.11). Desks, files, safes, overhead projectors, cell phones, fax machines and other communication equipment not included in any other class fall within this category. Seven-year property also includes: assets (except helicopters) used in commercial and contract carrying of passengers and freight by air (Rev. Proc. 87-56 Asset Class 45.0); certain livestock (Rev. Proc. 87-56 Asset Class

---

Footnote references are to paragraphs of the 2002 Standard Federal Tax Reports.

[46] ¶ 11,070.01
[47] ¶ 163.01, ¶ 11,279.021
[48] ¶ 11,250, ¶ 11,279.023
[49] ¶ 11,250, ¶ 11,279.023
[50] ¶ 11,250, ¶ 11,279.023

01.1); breeding or work horses 12 years old or less when placed in service (Rev. Proc. 87-56 Asset Class 01.221); other horses that are not three-year property (Rev. Proc. 87-56 Asset Class 01.225); machinery and equipment, grain bins, and fences used in agricultural activities (Rev. Proc. 87-56 Asset Class 01.1); assets used in recreation businesses (Rev. Proc. 87-56 Asset Class 80.0); and assets used in theme and amusement parks (Rev. Proc. 87-56 Asset Class 80.0). Railroad track and property (such as a fishing vessel) that does not have a class life and is not otherwise classified is seven-year property (Code Sec. 168(e)(3)(C)).[51]

10-Year Property. Ten-year property is property with a class life of 16 years or more and less than 20 years (Code Sec. 168(e)(1)).[52] Ten-year property includes vessels, barges, tugs, and similar means of water transportation not used in marine construction or as a fishing vessel (Rev. Proc. 87-56 Asset Class 00.28). MACRS deductions for trees or vines bearing fruit or nuts that are placed in service after 1988 are determined under the straight-line method over a 10-year recovery period (Code Sec. 168(b)(1)).[53] Single purpose agricultural or horticultural structures placed in service after 1988 are ten-year property (Code Sec. 168(e)(3)(D)(i)).

15-Year Property. Property with a class life of 20 years or more but less than 25 years is generally considered 15-year property (Code Sec. 168(e)(1)). It includes municipal wastewater treatment plants and telephone distribution plants and other comparable equipment used for the two-way exchange of voice, data communications, and retail motor fuels outlets (Code Sec. 168(e)(3)(E)).[54] A property qualifies as a retail motor fuels outlet (as opposed, for example, to a convenience store which is 39-year real property) if (1) 50 percent or more of gross revenues are derived from petroleum sales, or (2) 50 percent or more of the floor space is devoted to petroleum marketing sales, or (3) the property is 1,400 square feet or less (Rev. Proc. 97-10).[55]

Car wash buildings and related land improvements, section 1250 assets, including service station buildings and depreciable land improvements (whether personal or real property) used in marketing petroleum and petroleum products, and billboards are 15-year property (Rev. Proc. 87-56 Asset Class 57.1). Water transportation assets (other than vessels) used in the commercial and contract carrying of freight and passengers by water are 15-year property (Rev. Proc. 87-56 Asset Class 44.0).

Land improvements not specifically included in any other asset class and otherwise depreciable are 15-year property (Rev. Proc. 87-56 Asset Class 00.3). Examples of land improvements include sidewalks, driveways, curbs, roads, parking lots, canals, waterways, drainage facilities, sewers (but not municipal sewers), wharves and docks, bridges, and nonagricultural fences. Landscaping and shrubbery is a depreciable land improvement if it is located near a building and would be destroyed if the building were replaced (Rev. Rul. 74-265; IRS Publication 946). Playground equipment is a land improvement (IRS Letter Ruling 8848039).

20-Year Property. Twenty-year property includes property with a class life of 25 years and more, other than Code Sec. 1250 real property with a class life of 27.5 years or more. Water utility property and municipal sewers placed in service before June 13, 1996, and farm buildings (e.g., barns and machine sheds) are included within this class (Code Sec. 168(e)(1) and (3)).[56]

25-Year Property. Water utility property and municipal sewers placed in service after June 12, 1996 are included in this class (Code Sec. 168(c) and (e)(5)). The straight-line depreciation method is mandatory for 25-year property (Code Sec. 168(b)(3)(F)).

27.5-Year Residential Rental Property. Residential rental property (Code Sec. 168(e)(2)(A)) [57] includes buildings or structures with respect to which 80% or more of the gross rental income is from dwelling units. It also includes manufactured homes that are residential rental property and elevators and escalators.

Footnote references are to paragraphs of the 2002 Standard Federal Tax Reports.

¶ 1240

[51] ¶ 11,250, ¶ 11,279.023   [54] ¶ 11,250, ¶ 11,279.023   [56] ¶ 11,250, ¶ 11,279.023
[52] ¶ 11,250, ¶ 11,279.023   [55] ¶ 11,279.023   [57] ¶ 11,250, ¶ 11,279.023
[53] ¶ 11,250, ¶ 11,279.023

Nonresidential Real Property. Nonresidential real property is Code Sec. 1250 real property (see ¶ 1786) that is not (1) residential rental property or (2) property with a class life of less than 27.5 years. It includes property that either has no class life or whose class life is 27.5 years or more, including elevators and escalators (Code Sec. 168(e)(2)(B)).[58] The cost of nonresidential real property generally placed in service after May 12, 1993, is recovered over 39 years. For property placed in service after 1986 and before May 13, 1993, cost is recovered over 31.5 years.

Indian Reservation Property. For qualified Indian reservation property that is placed in service after 1993 and before 2004, special MACRS recovery periods are provided for both regular tax and alternative minimum tax purposes that permit faster writeoffs (Code Sec. 168(j)).[59]

Additions and Improvements. Additions and improvements to a property are depreciated under MACRS in the same way that the property would be depreciated if it were placed in service at the same time as the addition or improvement (Code Sec. 168(i)(6)). For example, a roof replaced on a commercial building in 2001 is treated as 39-year MACRS nonresidential real property even if the building is depreciated under ACRS or a pre-ACRS method.[60]

Structural Components of Buildings. Component depreciation is not allowed under-MACRS or ACRS. However, the Tax Court has ruled that elements of a building that are treated as personal property under the former investment tax credit rules (Reg. § 1.48-1(c)) may be separately depreciated under MACRS and ACRS (*Hospital Corp. of America*, 109 TC 21, Dec. 52,163).[61] The IRS has acquiesced to the court's holding that the former investment tax credit rules apply in determining whether an item is a structural component or personal property but nonacquiesced to its finding that various items were personal property under these rules (Notice of Acquiescence, 1999-35 I.R.B. 314).

The determination of whether an item is personal property or a structural component will often depend upon the specific facts. Case law on the issue is often contradictory. However, the following items, if related to the operation and maintenance of a building, are examples of structural components: bathtubs, boilers, ceilings (including acoustical ceilings), central air conditioning and heating systems, chimneys, doors, electrical and wiring, fire escapes, floors, hot water heaters, HVAC units, lighting fixtures, paneling, partitions (if not readily removable), plumbing, roofs, sinks, sprinkler systems, stairs, tiling, walls, and windows (Reg. § 1.48-1(e)(2)).

1243. Recovery Methods. Under MACRS, the cost of depreciable property is recovered using (1) the applicable depreciation method, (2) the applicable recovery period, and (3) the applicable convention (Code Sec. 168(a)). Instead of the applicable depreciation method, taxpayers may irrevocably elect to claim straight-line MACRS deductions over the regular recovery period. The election applies to all property in the MACRS class for which the election is made that is placed in service during the tax year and is made on the return for the year such property is first placed in service (Code Sec. 168(b)(5)). For example, if the election is made for 3-year property, it applies to all 3-year property placed in service in the tax year of the election.[62]

The cost of property in the 3-, 5-, 7-, and 10-year classes is recovered using the 200% declining-balance method over three, five, seven, and ten years, respectively, and the half-year convention, with a switch to the straight-line method in the year that maximizes the deduction (Code Sec. 168(b)(1)).[63] The cost of 15- and 20-year property is recovered using the 150% declining-balance method over 15 and 20 years, respectively, and the half-year convention, with a switch to the straight-line method to maximize the deduction (Code Sec. 168(b)(2)).[64] The cost of residential rental and nonresidential real property is recovered using the straight-line method and the mid-month convention (Code Sec. 168(b)(3)).[65]

Footnote references are to paragraphs of the 2002 Standard Federal Tax Reports.

[58] ¶ 11,250, ¶ 11,279.023
[59] ¶ 11,250, ¶ 11,279.031
[60] ¶ 11,279.05
[61] ¶ 11,279.051
[62] ¶ 11,279.033
[63] ¶ 11,250, ¶ 11,279.03
[64] ¶ 11,250, ¶ 11,279.03
[65] ¶ 11,250, ¶ 11,279.03

An election may be made to recover the cost of 3-, 5-, 7-, and 10-year property using the 150% declining-balance method over the regular recovery periods (the ADS recovery period for property placed in service before 1999) (see ¶ 1247) (Code Sec. 168(b)(2)(C)). This election, like the straight-line election described above, is made separately for each property class placed in service during the tax year of the election.[66] Generally, 3-, 5-, 7-, and 10-year property used in the trade or business of farming must be depreciated under the 150% declining balance method unless an election was made to deduct preproductive period expenditures, in which case the MACRS alternative depreciation system (ADS) must be used (Code Sec. 168(b)(2)(B)). Consequently, Tables 1-8, below, may not be used for such property.

Computation of Deduction Without Tables. The MACRS deduction on personal property is computed by first determining the rate of depreciation (dividing the number one by the recovery period).[67] This basic rate is multiplied by 1.5 or 2 for the 150% or 200% declining-balance method, as applicable, to determine the declining balance rate. The adjusted basis of the property is multiplied by the declining-balance rate and the half-year or mid-quarter convention (whichever is applicable) is applied in computing depreciation for the first year. The depreciation claimed in the first year is subtracted from the adjusted basis before applying the declining-balance rate in determining the depreciation deduction for the second year.

Under the MACRS straight-line method (used, for example, on real property or if ADS applies), a new applicable depreciation rate is determined for each tax year in the applicable recovery period. For any tax year, the applicable depreciation rate (in percentage terms) is determined by dividing one by the length of the applicable recovery period remaining as of the beginning of such tax year. The rate is applied to the unrecovered basis of such property in conjunction with the appropriate convention. If as of the beginning of any tax year the remaining recovery period is less than one year, the applicable depreciation rate under the straight-line method for that year is 100%.

> **Example 1.** An item of 5-year property is purchased by a calendar-year taxpayer in January of the current tax year at a cost of $10,000. The 200% declining-balance method and half-year convention apply. Depreciation computed without the use of the IRS tables is determined as follows: the declining-balance depreciation rate is determined and compared with the straight-line rate. A switch is made to the straight-line rate in the year depreciation equals or exceeds that determined under the declining-balance method. The applicable rate is applied to the unrecovered basis. The 200% declining-balance depreciation rate is 40% (1 divided by 5 (recovery period) times 2). The straight-line rate (which changes each year) is 1 divided by the length of the applicable recovery period remaining as of the beginning of each tax year (after considering the applicable convention for purposes of determining how much of the applicable recovery period remains as of the beginning of the year). For year four, the straight-line rate is .40 (1 divided by 2.5). For year five, the straight-line rate is .6667 (1 divided by 1.5). For year six, the straight-line rate is 100% because the remaining recovery period is less than one year.

Yr.	Method	Rate	Unrecovered Basis		Depreciation
1	DB	.40	× $10,000 × .5 (half-yr. conv.)	=	$ 2,000
2	DB	.40	× (10,000 − 2,000) = $8,000	=	3,200
3	DB	.40	× (8,000 − 3,200) = 4,800	=	1,920
4	SL	.40	× (4,800 − 1,920) = 2,880	=	1,152
5	SL	.6667	× (2,880 − 1,152) = 1,728	=	1,152
6	SL	1.000	× (1,728 − 1,152) = 576	=	576
				0	

Total . . . $10,000

The computation of MACRS without tables is discussed in detail by the IRS in Rev. Proc. 87-57.

Footnote references are to paragraphs of the 2002 Standard Federal Tax Reports.

¶ 1243   [66] ¶ 11,279.035   [67] ¶ 11,279.027

Computation of Deduction Using Tables. MACRS depreciation tables, which contain the annual percentage depreciation rates to be applied to the unadjusted basis of property in each tax year, may be used to compute depreciation instead of the above rules.[68] The tables incorporate the appropriate convention and a switch from the declining-balance method to the straight-line method in the year that the latter provides a depreciation allowance equal to, or larger than, the former. The tables may be used for any item of property (that otherwise qualifies for MACRS) placed in service in a tax year.

If a table is used to compute the annual depreciation allowance for any item of property, it must be used throughout the entire recovery period of such property. However, a taxpayer may not continue to use a table if there are any adjustments to the basis of the property for reasons other than (1) depreciation allowances or (2) an addition or improvement to such property that is subject to depreciation as a separate item of property.

Tables for the general depreciation system (GDS) and alternative depreciation system (ADS) under the straight-line method over the 2.5- through 50-year recovery periods that incorporate the mid-quarter convention and a table for the alternative depreciation system under the straight-line method over a 40-year recovery period that incorporates the mid-month convention are at ¶ 164.01 of the 2002 STANDARD FEDERAL TAX REPORTER and at ¶ 75 of the U.S. MASTER TAX GUIDE—Loose-Leaf Edition. Special tables are provided at those paragraphs for alternative minimum tax purposes.

The IRS MACRS tables discussed above may not be used in situations involving short tax years (see ¶ 1244).

Example (2). Depreciation on 5-year property purchased by a calendar-year taxpayer in January of the current tax year at a cost of $10,000 is computed under the general MACRS 200% declining-balance method over a five-year recovery period using the half-year convention.

If the depreciation tables provided by the IRS are used, depreciation is computed as follows: the applicable depreciation rate in Table 1 under the column for a 5-year recovery period for the applicable recovery year is applied to the unadjusted basis of the property.

Yr.	Rate	Unadj. Basis	Depreciation	Basis			
1	.20 ×	$10,000 =	$ 2,000	($10,000 −	$2,000) =	$8,000
2	.32 ×	10,000 =	3,200	(8,000 −	3,200) =	4,800
3	.192 ×	10,000 =	1,920	(4,800 −	1,920) =	2,880
4	.1152 ×	10,000 =	1,152	(2,880 −	1,152) =	1,728
5	.1152 ×	10,000 =	1,152	(1,728 −	1,152) =	576
6	.0576 ×	10,000 =	576	(576 −	576) =	0
		Total	$10,000			

An interactive calculator for computing MACRS deductions and creating depreciation schedules is available to subscribers of the following CCH internet tax products: Tax Research Network; CCH Essentials; and Omnitax. To access the calculator, click on "CCH Depreciation Toolkit" in the "Practice Aids" section of the product.

Footnote references are to paragraphs of the 2002 Standard Federal Tax Reports.
[68] ¶ 164.01

Table 1. General Depreciation System
Applicable Depreciation Method: 200 or 150 Percent
Declining Balance Switching to Straight Line
Applicable Recovery Periods: 3, 5, 7, 10, 15, 20 years
Applicable Convention: Half-year

If the Recovery Year is:	and the Recovery Period is:					
	3-year	5-year	7-year	10-year	15-year	20-year
	the Depreciation Rate is:					
1	33.33	20.00	14.29	10.00	5.00	3.750
2	44.45	32.00	24.49	18.00	9.50	7.219
3	14.81	19.20	17.49	14.40	8.55	6.677
4	7.41	11.52	12.49	11.52	7.70	6.177
5		11.52	8.93	9.22	6.93	5.713
6		5.76	8.92	7.37	6.23	5.285
7			8.93	6.55	5.90	4.888
8			4.46	6.55	5.90	4.522
9				6.56	5.91	4.462
10				6.55	5.90	4.462
11				3.28	5.91	4.462
12					5.90	4.461
13					5.91	4.462
14					5.90	4.461
15					5.91	4.462
16					2.95	4.461
17						4.462
18						4.461
19						4.462
20						4.461
21						2.231

Table 2. General Depreciation System
Applicable Depreciation Method: 200 or 150 Percent
Declining Balance Switching to Straight Line
Applicable Recovery Periods: 3, 5, 7, 10, 15, 20 years
Applicable Convention: Mid-quarter (property placed in service in first quarter)

If the Recovery Year is:	and the Recovery Period is:					
	3-year	5-year	7-year	10-year	15-year	20-year
	the Depreciation Rate is:					
1	58.33	35.00	25.00	17.50	8.75	6.563
2	27.78	26.00	21.43	16.50	9.13	7.000
3	12.35	15.60	15.31	13.20	8.21	6.482
4	1.54	11.01	10.93	10.56	7.39	5.996
5		11.01	8.75	8.45	6.65	5.546
6		1.38	8.74	6.76	5.99	5.130
7			8.75	6.55	5.90	4.746
8			1.09	6.55	5.91	4.459
9				6.56	5.90	4.459
10				6.55	5.91	4.459
11				0.82	5.90	4.459
12					5.91	4.460
13					5.90	4.459
14					5.91	4.460
15					5.90	4.459
16					0.74	4.460
17						4.459
18						4.460
19						4.459
20						4.460
21						0.557

Table 3. General Depreciation System
Applicable Depreciation Method: 200 or 150 Percent
Declining Balance Switching to Straight Line
Applicable Recovery Periods: 3, 5, 7, 10, 15, 20 years
Applicable Convention: Mid-quarter (property placed in
service in second quarter)

If the Recovery Year is:	and the Recovery Period is:					
	3-year	5-year	7-year	10-year	15-year	20-year
	the Depreciation Rate is:					
1	41.67	25.00	17.85	12.50	6.25	4.688
2	38.89	30.00	23.47	17.50	9.38	7.148
3	14.14	18.00	16.76	14.00	8.44	6.612
4	5.30	11.37	11.97	11.20	7.59	6.116
5		11.37	8.87	8.96	6.83	5.658
6		4.26	8.87	7.17	6.15	5.233
7			8.87	6.55	5.91	4.841
8			3.33	6.55	5.90	4.478
9				6.56	5.91	4.463
10				6.55	5.90	4.463
11				2.46	5.91	4.463
12					5.90	4.463
13					5.91	4.463
14					5.90	4.463
15					5.91	4.462
16					2.21	4.463
17						4.462
18						4.463
19						4.462
20						4.463
21						1.573

Table 4. General Depreciation System
Applicable Depreciation Method: 200 or 150 Percent
Declining Balance Switching to Straight Line
Applicable Recovery Periods: 3, 5, 7, 10, 15, 20 years
Applicable Convention: Mid-quarter (property placed in
service in third quarter)

If the Recovery Year is:	and the Recovery Period is:					
	3-year	5-year	7-year	10-year	15-year	20-year
	the Depreciation Rate is:					
1	25.00	15.00	10.71	7.50	3.75	2.813
2	50.00	34.00	25.51	18.50	9.63	7.289
3	16.67	20.40	18.22	14.80	8.66	6.742
4	8.33	12.24	13.02	11.84	7.80	6.237
5		11.30	9.30	9.47	7.02	5.769
6		7.06	8.85	7.58	6.31	5.336
7			8.86	6.55	5.90	4.936
8			5.53	6.55	5.90	4.566
9				6.56	5.91	4.460
10				6.55	5.90	4.460
11				4.10	5.91	4.460
12					5.90	4.460
13					5.91	4.461
14					5.90	4.460
15					5.91	4.461
16					3.69	4.460
17						4.461
18						4.460
19						4.461
20						4.460
21						2.788

Table 5.   General Depreciation System
Applicable Depreciation Method: 200 or 150 Percent
Declining Balance Switching to Straight Line
Applicable Recovery Periods: 3, 5, 7, 10, 15, 20 years
Applicable Convention: Mid-quarter (property placed in
service in fourth quarter)

If the Recovery Year is:	and the Recovery Period is:					
	3-year	5-year	7-year	10-year	15-year	20-year
	the Depreciation Rate is:					
1	8.33	5.00	3.57	2.50	1.25	0.938
2	61.11	38.00	27.55	19.50	9.88	7.430
3	20.37	22.80	19.68	15.60	8.89	6.872
4	10.19	13.68	14.06	12.48	8.00	6.357
5		10.94	10.04	9.98	7.20	5.880
6		9.58	8.73	7.99	6.48	5.439
7			8.73	6.55	5.90	5.031
8			7.64	6.55	5.90	4.654
9				6.56	5.90	4.458
10				6.55	5.91	4.458
11				5.74	5.90	4.458
12					5.91	4.458
13					5.90	4.458
14					5.91	4.458
15					5.90	4.458
16					5.17	4.458
17						4.458
18						4.459
19						4.458
20						4.459
21						3.901

¶ 1243

Table 6.

General Depreciation System
Applicable Depreciation Method: Straight Line
Applicable Recovery Period: 27.5 years
Applicable Convention: Mid-month

If the Recovery Year is:	And the Month in the First Recovery Year the Property is Placed in Service is: the Depreciation Rate is:											
	1	2	3	4	5	6	7	8	9	10	11	12
1	3.485	3.182	2.879	2.576	2.273	1.970	1.667	1.364	1.061	0.758	0.455	0.152
2	3.636	3.636	3.636	3.636	3.636	3.636	3.636	3.636	3.636	3.636	3.636	3.636
3	3.636	3.636	3.636	3.636	3.636	3.636	3.636	3.636	3.636	3.636	3.636	3.636
4	3.636	3.636	3.636	3.636	3.636	3.636	3.636	3.636	3.636	3.636	3.636	3.636
5	3.636	3.636	3.636	3.636	3.636	3.636	3.636	3.636	3.636	3.636	3.636	3.636
6	3.636	3.636	3.636	3.636	3.636	3.636	3.636	3.636	3.636	3.636	3.636	3.636
7	3.636	3.636	3.636	3.636	3.636	3.636	3.636	3.636	3.636	3.636	3.636	3.636
8	3.636	3.636	3.636	3.636	3.636	3.636	3.636	3.636	3.636	3.636	3.636	3.636
9	3.636	3.636	3.636	3.636	3.636	3.636	3.636	3.636	3.636	3.636	3.636	3.636
10	3.637	3.637	3.637	3.637	3.637	3.637	3.636	3.636	3.636	3.636	3.636	3.636
11	3.636	3.636	3.636	3.636	3.636	3.636	3.637	3.637	3.637	3.637	3.637	3.637
12	3.637	3.637	3.637	3.637	3.637	3.637	3.636	3.636	3.636	3.636	3.636	3.636
13	3.636	3.636	3.636	3.636	3.636	3.636	3.637	3.637	3.637	3.637	3.637	3.637
14	3.637	3.637	3.637	3.637	3.637	3.637	3.636	3.636	3.636	3.636	3.636	3.636
15	3.636	3.636	3.636	3.636	3.636	3.636	3.637	3.637	3.637	3.637	3.637	3.637
16	3.637	3.637	3.637	3.637	3.637	3.637	3.636	3.636	3.636	3.636	3.636	3.636
17	3.636	3.636	3.636	3.636	3.636	3.636	3.637	3.637	3.637	3.637	3.637	3.637
18	3.637	3.637	3.637	3.637	3.637	3.637	3.636	3.636	3.636	3.636	3.636	3.636
19	3.636	3.636	3.636	3.636	3.636	3.636	3.637	3.637	3.637	3.637	3.637	3.637
20	3.637	3.637	3.637	3.637	3.637	3.637	3.636	3.636	3.636	3.636	3.636	3.636
21	3.636	3.636	3.636	3.636	3.636	3.636	3.637	3.637	3.637	3.637	3.637	3.637
22	3.637	3.637	3.637	3.637	3.637	3.637	3.636	3.636	3.636	3.636	3.636	3.636
23	3.636	3.636	3.636	3.636	3.636	3.636	3.637	3.637	3.637	3.637	3.637	3.637
24	3.637	3.637	3.637	3.637	3.637	3.637	3.636	3.636	3.636	3.636	3.636	3.636
25	3.636	3.636	3.636	3.636	3.636	3.636	3.637	3.637	3.637	3.637	3.637	3.637
26	3.637	3.637	3.637	3.637	3.637	3.637	3.636	3.636	3.636	3.636	3.636	3.636
27	3.636	3.636	3.636	3.636	3.636	3.636	3.637	3.637	3.637	3.637	3.637	3.637
28	1.970	2.273	2.576	2.879	3.182	3.485	3.636	3.636	3.636	3.636	3.636	3.636
29	0.000	0.000	0.000	0.000	0.000	0.000	0.152	0.455	0.758	1.061	1.364	1.667

¶ 1243

Table 7.

General Depreciation System
Applicable Depreciation Method: Straight Line
Applicable Recovery Period: 31.5 years
Applicable Convention: Mid-month

If the Recovery Year is:	And the Month in the First Recovery Year the Property is Placed in Service is: the Depreciation Rate is:											
	1	2	3	4	5	6	7	8	9	10	11	12
1	3.042	2.778	2.513	2.249	1.984	1.720	1.455	1.190	0.926	0.661	0.397	0.132
2	3.175	3.175	3.175	3.175	3.175	3.175	3.175	3.175	3.175	3.175	3.175	3.175
3	3.175	3.175	3.175	3.175	3.175	3.175	3.175	3.175	3.175	3.175	3.175	3.175
4	3.175	3.175	3.175	3.175	3.175	3.175	3.175	3.175	3.175	3.175	3.175	3.175
5	3.175	3.175	3.175	3.175	3.175	3.175	3.175	3.175	3.175	3.175	3.175	3.175
6	3.175	3.175	3.175	3.175	3.175	3.175	3.175	3.175	3.175	3.175	3.175	3.175
7	3.175	3.175	3.175	3.175	3.175	3.175	3.175	3.175	3.175	3.175	3.175	3.175
8	3.175	3.175	3.175	3.175	3.175	3.175	3.175	3.175	3.175	3.175	3.175	3.175
9	3.174	3.174	3.174	3.174	3.174	3.174	3.174	3.174	3.174	3.174	3.174	3.174
10	3.175	3.175	3.175	3.175	3.175	3.175	3.175	3.175	3.175	3.175	3.175	3.175
11	3.174	3.174	3.174	3.174	3.174	3.174	3.174	3.174	3.174	3.174	3.174	3.174
12	3.175	3.175	3.175	3.175	3.175	3.175	3.175	3.175	3.175	3.175	3.175	3.175
13	3.174	3.174	3.174	3.174	3.174	3.174	3.174	3.174	3.174	3.174	3.174	3.174
14	3.175	3.175	3.175	3.175	3.175	3.175	3.175	3.175	3.175	3.175	3.175	3.175
15	3.174	3.174	3.174	3.174	3.174	3.174	3.174	3.174	3.174	3.174	3.174	3.174
16	3.175	3.175	3.175	3.175	3.175	3.175	3.175	3.174	3.174	3.174	3.175	3.175
17	3.174	3.174	3.174	3.174	3.174	3.174	3.174	3.175	3.175	3.175	3.174	3.174
18	3.175	3.175	3.175	3.175	3.175	3.175	3.175	3.174	3.174	3.174	3.175	3.175
19	3.174	3.174	3.174	3.174	3.174	3.174	3.174	3.175	3.175	3.175	3.174	3.174
20	3.175	3.175	3.175	3.175	3.175	3.175	3.175	3.174	3.174	3.174	3.175	3.175
21	3.174	3.174	3.174	3.174	3.174	3.174	3.174	3.175	3.175	3.175	3.174	3.174
22	3.175	3.175	3.175	3.175	3.175	3.175	3.175	3.174	3.174	3.174	3.175	3.175
23	3.174	3.174	3.174	3.174	3.174	3.174	3.174	3.175	3.175	3.175	3.174	3.174
24	3.175	3.175	3.175	3.175	3.175	3.175	3.175	3.174	3.174	3.174	3.175	3.175
25	3.174	3.174	3.174	3.174	3.174	3.174	3.174	3.175	3.175	3.175	3.174	3.174
26	3.175	3.175	3.175	3.175	3.175	3.175	3.175	3.174	3.174	3.174	3.175	3.175
27	3.174	3.174	3.174	3.174	3.174	3.174	3.174	3.175	3.175	3.175	3.174	3.174
28	3.175	3.175	3.175	3.175	3.175	3.175	3.175	3.174	3.174	3.174	3.175	3.175
29	3.174	3.174	3.174	3.174	3.174	3.174	3.174	3.175	3.175	3.175	3.174	3.174
30	3.175	3.175	3.175	3.175	3.175	3.175	3.175	3.174	3.174	3.174	3.175	3.175
31	3.174	3.174	3.174	3.174	3.174	3.174	3.174	3.175	3.175	3.175	3.174	3.174
32	1.720	1.984	2.249	2.513	2.778	3.042	3.175	3.174	3.175	3.174	3.175	3.174
33	0.000	0.000	0.000	0.000	0.000	0.000	0.132	0.397	0.661	0.926	1.190	1.455

¶ 1243

Table 7A.

General Depreciation System
Applicable Depreciation Method: Straight-Line
Applicable Recovery Period: 39 years
Applicable Convention: Mid-month—taken from the
IRS Pub. 946—CCH.

If the Recovery Year is:	And the Month in the First Recovery Year the Property is Placed in Service is: the Depreciation Rate is:											
	1	2	3	4	5	6	7	8	9	10	11	12
1	2.461	2.247	2.033	1.819	1.605	1.391	1.177	0.963	0.749	0.535	0.321	0.107
2–39	2.564	2.564	2.564	2.564	2.564	2.564	2.564	2.564	2.564	2.564	2.564	2.564
40	0.107	0.321	0.535	0.749	0.963	1.177	1.391	1.605	1.819	2.033	2.247	2.461

Table 8.
General and Alternative Depreciation Systems
Applicable Depreciation Method: Straight Line
Applicable Recovery Periods: 2.5 — 50 years
Applicable Convention: Half-year

If the Recovery Year is:	and the Recovery Period is:														
	2.5	**3.0**	**3.5**	**4.0**	**4.5**	**5.0**	**5.5**	**6.0**	**6.5**	**7.0**	**7.5**	**8.0**	**8.5**	**9.0**	**9.5**
	the Depreciation Rate is:														
1	20.00	16.67	14.29	12.50	11.11	10.00	9.09	8.33	7.69	7.14	6.67	6.25	5.88	5.56	5.26
2	40.00	33.33	28.57	25.00	22.22	20.00	18.18	16.67	15.39	14.29	13.33	12.50	11.77	11.11	10.53
3	40.00	33.33	28.57	25.00	22.22	20.00	18.18	16.67	15.38	14.29	13.33	12.50	11.76	11.11	10.53
4		16.67	28.57	25.00	22.22	20.00	18.18	16.67	15.39	14.28	13.33	12.50	11.77	11.11	10.53
5				12.50	22.23	20.00	18.18	16.66	15.38	14.29	13.33	12.50	11.76	11.11	10.52
6						10.00	18.19	16.67	15.39	14.28	13.34	12.50	11.77	11.11	10.53
7								8.33	15.38	14.29	13.33	12.50	11.76	11.11	10.52
8										7.14	13.34	12.50	11.77	11.11	10.53
9												6.25	11.76	11.11	10.52
10														5.56	10.53

If the Recovery Year is:	and the Recovery Period is:														
	10.0	**10.5**	**11.0**	**11.5**	**12.0**	**12.5**	**13.0**	**13.5**	**14.0**	**14.5**	**15.0**	**15.5**	**16.0**	**16.5**	**17.0**
	the Depreciation Rate is:														
1	5.00	4.76	4.55	4.35	4.17	4.00	3.85	3.70	3.57	3.45	3.33	3.23	3.13	3.03	2.94
2	10.00	9.52	9.09	8.70	8.33	8.00	7.69	7.41	7.14	6.90	6.67	6.45	6.25	6.06	5.88
3	10.00	9.52	9.09	8.70	8.33	8.00	7.69	7.41	7.14	6.90	6.67	6.45	6.25	6.06	5.88
4	10.00	9.53	9.09	8.69	8.33	8.00	7.69	7.41	7.14	6.90	6.67	6.45	6.25	6.06	5.88
5	10.00	9.52	9.09	8.70	8.33	8.00	7.69	7.41	7.14	6.89	6.67	6.45	6.25	6.06	5.88
6	10.00	9.53	9.09	8.69	8.33	8.00	7.69	7.41	7.14	6.90	6.66	6.45	6.25	6.06	5.88
7	10.00	9.52	9.09	8.70	8.34	8.00	7.69	7.41	7.15	6.89	6.67	6.45	6.25	6.06	5.88
8	10.00	9.53	9.09	8.69	8.33	8.00	7.69	7.41	7.14	6.90	6.66	6.45	6.25	6.06	5.88
9	10.00	9.52	9.09	8.70	8.34	8.00	7.70	7.41	7.15	6.89	6.67	6.45	6.25	6.06	5.88
10	10.00	9.53	9.09	8.69	8.33	8.00	7.69	7.41	7.14	6.90	6.66	6.45	6.25	6.06	5.89
11	5.00	9.52	9.09	8.70	8.34	8.00	7.70	7.41	7.15	6.89	6.67	6.45	6.25	6.06	5.88
12			4.55	8.69	8.33	8.00	7.69	7.41	7.14	6.90	6.66	6.45	6.25	6.06	5.89
13					4.17	8.00	7.70	7.40	7.15	6.89	6.67	6.45	6.25	6.06	5.88
14							3.85	7.41	7.14	6.90	6.66	6.45	6.25	6.06	5.89
15									3.57	6.89	6.67	6.45	6.25	6.06	5.88
16											3.33	6.46	6.25	6.06	5.89
17													3.12	6.07	5.88
18															2.94

¶1243

and the Recovery Period is:

the Depreciation Rate is:

If the Recovery Year is:	17.5	18.0	18.5	19.0	19.5	20.0	20.5	21.0	21.5	22.0	22.5	23.0	23.5	24.0	24.5
1	2.86	2.78	2.70	2.63	2.56	2.500	2.439	2.381	2.326	2.273	2.222	2.174	2.128	2.083	2.041
2	5.71	5.56	5.41	5.26	5.13	5.000	4.878	4.762	4.651	4.545	4.444	4.348	4.255	4.167	4.082
3	5.71	5.56	5.41	5.26	5.13	5.000	4.878	4.762	4.651	4.545	4.444	4.348	4.255	4.167	4.082
4	5.72	5.55	5.40	5.26	5.13	5.000	4.878	4.762	4.651	4.546	4.445	4.348	4.255	4.167	4.082
5	5.71	5.56	5.41	5.26	5.13	5.000	4.878	4.762	4.651	4.546	4.444	4.348	4.255	4.167	4.082
6	5.71	5.56	5.40	5.26	5.13	5.000	4.878	4.762	4.651	4.546	4.444	4.348	4.255	4.167	4.082
7	5.72	5.56	5.41	5.26	5.13	5.000	4.878	4.762	4.651	4.546	4.444	4.348	4.255	4.167	4.082
8	5.71	5.56	5.40	5.26	5.13	5.000	4.878	4.762	4.651	4.546	4.444	4.318	4.255	4.167	4.082
9	5.72	5.56	5.40	5.27	5.13	5.000	4.878	4.762	4.651	4.545	4.444	4.348	4.255	4.167	4.082
10	5.71	5.56	5.40	5.27	5.13	5.000	4.878	4.762	4.651	4.546	4.444	4.348	4.256	4.167	4.081
11	5.72	5.56	5.40	5.27	5.13	5.000	4.878	4.762	4.651	4.546	4.445	4.348	4.256	4.167	4.082
12	5.71	5.56	5.40	5.26	5.13	5.000	4.878	4.762	4.651	4.546	4.444	4.348	4.256	4.167	4.082
13	5.72	5.56	5.40	5.27	5.13	5.000	4.878	4.762	4.651	4.545	4.445	4.348	4.256	4.167	4.081
14	5.71	5.55	5.41	5.26	5.13	5.000	4.878	4.762	4.651	4.545	4.445	4.348	4.256	4.167	4.082
15	5.72	5.56	5.40	5.27	5.12	5.000	4.878	4.762	4.651	4.546	4.444	4.348	4.256	4.167	4.081
16	5.71	5.55	5.41	5.26	5.13	5.000	4.878	4.762	4.651	4.546	4.444	4.348	4.256	4.167	4.082
17	5.72	5.55	5.41	5.26	5.12	5.000	4.878	4.762	4.652	4.545	4.444	4.347	4.256	4.166	4.082
18	5.71	5.55	5.41	5.27	5.13	5.000	4.878	4.762	4.651	4.545	4.445	4.348	4.255	4.167	4.082
19		2.78	5.40	5.26	5.12	5.000	4.878	4.761	4.652	4.546	4.444	4.347	4.255	4.166	4.081
20				2.63	5.13	5.000	4.878	4.762	4.651	4.545	4.445	4.348	4.255	4.166	4.082
21						2.500	4.879	4.761	4.652	4.546	4.444	4.348	4.256	4.166	4.081
22								2.381	4.651	4.545	4.444	4.347	4.256	4.167	4.082
23										2.273	4.444	4.348	4.255	4.166	4.081
24												2.174	4.255	4.167	4.082
25														2.083	4.081

| | | | | | and the Recovery Period is: | | | | | | | | | | |
If the Recovery Year is:	25.0	25.5	26.0	26.5	27.0	27.5	28.0	28.5	29.0	29.5	30.0	30.5	31.0	31.5	32.0
					the Depreciation Rate is:										
1	2.000	1.961	1.923	1.887	1.852	1.818	1.786	1.754	1.724	1.695	1.667	1.639	1.613	1.587	1.563
2	4.000	3.922	3.846	3.774	3.704	3.636	3.571	3.509	3.448	3.390	3.333	3.279	3.226	3.175	3.125
3	4.000	3.922	3.846	3.774	3.704	3.636	3.571	3.509	3.448	3.390	3.333	3.279	3.226	3.175	3.125
4	4.000	3.922	3.846	3.774	3.704	3.636	3.571	3.509	3.448	3.390	3.333	3.279	3.226	3.175	3.125
5	4.000	3.922	3.846	3.774	3.704	3.636	3.571	3.509	3.448	3.390	3.333	3.279	3.226	3.175	3.125
6	4.000	3.922	3.846	3.774	3.704	3.636	3.572	3.509	3.448	3.390	3.333	3.279	3.226	3.175	3.125
7	4.000	3.922	3.846	3.773	3.704	3.637	3.571	3.509	3.448	3.390	3.333	3.279	3.226	3.175	3.125
8	4.000	3.922	3.846	3.773	3.704	3.637	3.572	3.509	3.448	3.390	3.333	3.279	3.226	3.175	3.125
9	4.000	3.922	3.846	3.773	3.704	3.637	3.572	3.509	3.448	3.390	3.333	3.279	3.226	3.175	3.125
10	4.000	3.922	3.846	3.773	3.703	3.636	3.571	3.509	3.448	3.390	3.333	3.279	3.226	3.175	3.125
11	4.000	3.921	3.846	3.773	3.703	3.636	3.572	3.509	3.448	3.390	3.333	3.279	3.226	3.175	3.125
12	4.000	3.922	3.846	3.773	3.704	3.636	3.572	3.509	3.448	3.390	3.334	3.279	3.226	3.175	3.125
13	4.000	3.921	3.846	3.773	3.703	3.637	3.571	3.509	3.448	3.390	3.333	3.279	3.226	3.174	3.125
14	4.000	3.922	3.846	3.773	3.703	3.636	3.572	3.509	3.449	3.390	3.334	3.279	3.226	3.174	3.125
15	4.000	3.921	3.846	3.773	3.704	3.637	3.572	3.509	3.448	3.390	3.333	3.278	3.226	3.174	3.125
16	4.000	3.921	3.846	3.773	3.703	3.636	3.572	3.509	3.449	3.390	3.334	3.279	3.226	3.174	3.125
17	4.000	3.922	3.846	3.773	3.703	3.637	3.572	3.509	3.448	3.390	3.333	3.278	3.226	3.174	3.125
18	4.000	3.921	3.846	3.773	3.704	3.636	3.571	3.508	3.449	3.390	3.334	3.279	3.226	3.174	3.125
19	4.000	3.922	3.847	3.773	3.703	3.637	3.572	3.509	3.448	3.390	3.333	3.279	3.226	3.174	3.125
20	4.000	3.921	3.846	3.773	3.704	3.636	3.571	3.508	3.449	3.390	3.334	3.279	3.226	3.174	3.125
21	4.000	3.922	3.847	3.773	3.703	3.637	3.572	3.509	3.448	3.389	3.333	3.279	3.226	3.174	3.125
22	4.000	3.921	3.846	3.773	3.704	3.636	3.571	3.508	3.449	3.389	3.334	3.279	3.225	3.174	3.125
23	4.000	3.922	3.847	3.773	3.703	3.637	3.572	3.509	3.448	3.389	3.333	3.279	3.225	3.174	3.125
24	4.000	3.921	3.847	3.773	3.704	3.636	3.571	3.508	3.449	3.389	3.334	3.279	3.225	3.174	3.125
25	4.000	3.922	3.846	3.773	3.703	3.637	3.572	3.509	3.448	3.389	3.333	3.278	3.225	3.174	3.125
26	4.000	3.921	3.847	3.774	3.704	3.636	3.571	3.508	3.449	3.389	3.334	3.279	3.225	3.174	3.125
27	2.000	3.921	3.846	3.773	3.703	3.637	3.572	3.509	3.448	3.389	3.333	3.278	3.225	3.175	3.125
28			1.923	3.774	1.852	3.636	3.571	3.508	3.449	3.389	3.334	3.279	3.225	3.175	3.125
29						3.636	1.786	3.509	3.448	3.389	3.334	3.279	3.226	3.174	3.125
30								3.509	1.724	3.389	3.333	3.278	3.225	3.175	3.125
31										3.390	1.667	3.279	3.226	3.174	3.125
32												3.278	1.613	3.175	3.125
33														3.174	1.562

If the Recovery Year is:	and the Recovery Period is: — the Depreciation Rate is:														
	32.5	33.0	33.5	34.0	34.5	35.0	35.5	36.0	36.5	37.0	37.5	38.0	38.5	39.0	39.5
1	1.538	1.515	1.493	1.471	1.449	1.429	1.408	1.389	1.370	1.351	1.333	1.316	1.299	1.282	1.266
2	3.077	3.030	2.985	2.941	2.899	2.857	2.817	2.778	2.740	2.703	2.667	2.632	2.597	2.564	2.532
3	3.077	3.030	2.985	2.941	2.899	2.857	2.817	2.778	2.740	2.703	2.667	2.632	2.597	2.564	2.532
4	3.077	3.030	2.985	2.941	2.899	2.857	2.817	2.778	2.740	2.703	2.667	2.632	2.597	2.564	2.532
5	3.077	3.030	2.985	2.941	2.899	2.857	2.817	2.778	2.740	2.703	2.667	2.632	2.597	2.564	2.532
6	3.077	3.030	2.985	2.941	2.899	2.857	2.817	2.778	2.740	2.703	2.667	2.632	2.597	2.564	2.532
7	3.077	3.030	2.985	2.941	2.899	2.857	2.817	2.778	2.740	2.703	2.667	2.632	2.597	2.564	2.532
8	3.077	3.030	2.985	2.941	2.899	2.857	2.817	2.778	2.740	2.703	2.667	2.632	2.597	2.564	2.532
9	3.077	3.030	2.985	2.941	2.899	2.857	2.817	2.778	2.740	2.703	2.667	2.632	2.597	2.564	2.532
10	3.077	3.030	2.985	2.941	2.899	2.857	2.817	2.778	2.740	2.703	2.667	2.632	2.597	2.564	2.532
11	3.077	3.030	2.985	2.941	2.899	2.857	2.817	2.778	2.740	2.703	2.667	2.632	2.598	2.564	2.532
12	3.077	3.030	2.985	2.941	2.899	2.857	2.817	2.778	2.740	2.703	2.667	2.632	2.597	2.564	2.532
13	3.077	3.030	2.985	2.941	2.899	2.857	2.817	2.778	2.740	2.703	2.667	2.632	2.598	2.564	2.531
14	3.077	3.030	2.985	2.941	2.899	2.857	2.817	2.778	2.740	2.703	2.667	2.631	2.597	2.564	2.532
15	3.077	3.030	2.985	2.941	2.899	2.857	2.817	2.778	2.740	2.703	2.666	2.632	2.598	2.564	2.532
16	3.077	3.031	2.985	2.941	2.899	2.857	2.817	2.778	2.740	2.703	2.666	2.632	2.597	2.564	2.532
17	3.077	3.030	2.985	2.941	2.899	2.857	2.817	2.778	2.740	2.702	2.667	2.631	2.598	2.564	2.532
18	3.077	3.031	2.985	2.941	2.899	2.857	2.817	2.778	2.739	2.703	2.666	2.632	2.597	2.564	2.532
19	3.077	3.031	2.985	2.941	2.899	2.857	2.817	2.778	2.740	2.702	2.667	2.631	2.598	2.564	2.531
20	3.077	3.030	2.985	2.941	2.899	2.857	2.817	2.778	2.740	2.703	2.666	2.632	2.597	2.564	2.532
21	3.077	3.031	2.985	2.941	2.899	2.857	2.817	2.778	2.740	2.702	2.667	2.631	2.598	2.564	2.532
22	3.077	3.030	2.985	2.941	2.899	2.857	2.817	2.778	2.740	2.703	2.666	2.632	2.597	2.564	2.532
23	3.077	3.031	2.985	2.941	2.899	2.857	2.817	2.778	2.739	2.702	2.667	2.631	2.598	2.564	2.532
24	3.077	3.030	2.985	2.941	2.899	2.857	2.817	2.778	2.740	2.703	2.666	2.632	2.597	2.564	2.532
25	3.077	3.031	2.985	2.942	2.899	2.857	2.817	2.778	2.740	2.702	2.667	2.631	2.598	2.564	2.531
26	3.077	3.030	2.985	2.941	2.899	2.857	2.817	2.778	2.739	2.703	2.666	2.632	2.597	2.564	2.532
27	3.077	3.031	2.985	2.942	2.899	2.857	2.817	2.778	2.740	2.702	2.667	2.631	2.598	2.564	2.532
28	3.077	3.030	2.985	2.941	2.899	2.858	2.817	2.778	2.739	2.703	2.666	2.632	2.597	2.564	2.531
29	3.077	3.031	2.985	2.942	2.899	2.857	2.817	2.778	2.740	2.702	2.667	2.631	2.598	2.564	2.532
30	3.077	3.030	2.985	2.941	2.899	2.858	2.817	2.778	2.739	2.703	2.666	2.632	2.597	2.564	2.531
31	3.076	3.031	2.986	2.942	2.899	2.857	2.817	2.778	2.740	2.702	2.667	2.631	2.598	2.564	2.532
32	3.077	3.030	2.985	2.941	2.899	2.858	2.816	2.778	2.739	2.703	2.666	2.632	2.597	2.564	2.531
33	3.076	3.031	2.986	2.942	2.899	2.857	2.817	2.778	2.740	2.702	2.667	2.631	2.598	2.564	2.532
34		1.515	2.985	2.941	2.899	2.857	2.017	2.778	2.740	2.703	2.666	2.632	2.597	2.565	2.531
35				1.471	2.899	2.857	2.816	2.778	2.740	2.702	2.667	2.631	2.598	2.565	2.532
36						1.429	2.816	2.777	2.739	2.703	2.666	2.632	2.597	2.564	2.331
37								1.389	2.739	2.703	2.667	2.631	2.598	2.565	2.532
38										2.703	2.667	2.631	2.597	2.565	2.532
39												1.316	2.597	2.565	2.531
40														1.282	2.531

and the Recovery Period is:
the Depreciation Rate is:

If the Recovery Year is:	40.0	40.5	41.0	41.5	42.0	42.5	43.0	43.5	44.0	44.5	45.0	45.5	46.0	46.5	47.0
1	1.250	1.235	1.220	1.205	1.190	1.176	1.163	1.149	1.136	1.124	1.111	1.099	1.087	1.075	1.064
2	2.500	2.469	2.439	2.410	2.381	2.353	2.326	2.299	2.273	2.247	2.222	2.198	2.174	2.151	2.128
3	2.500	2.469	2.439	2.410	2.381	2.353	2.326	2.299	2.273	2.247	2.222	2.198	2.174	2.151	2.128
4	2.500	2.469	2.439	2.410	2.381	2.353	2.326	2.299	2.273	2.247	2.222	2.198	2.174	2.151	2.128
5	2.500	2.469	2.439	2.410	2.381	2.353	2.326	2.299	2.273	2.247	2.222	2.198	2.174	2.151	2.128
6	2.500	2.469	2.439	2.410	2.381	2.353	2.326	2.299	2.273	2.247	2.222	2.198	2.174	2.150	2.128
7	2.500	2.469	2.439	2.410	2.381	2.353	2.326	2.299	2.273	2.247	2.222	2.198	2.174	2.150	2.128
8	2.500	2.469	2.439	2.410	2.381	2.353	2.326	2.299	2.273	2.247	2.222	2.198	2.174	2.151	2.128
9	2.500	2.469	2.439	2.410	2.381	2.353	2.326	2.299	2.273	2.247	2.222	2.198	2.174	2.150	2.128
10	2.500	2.469	2.439	2.410	2.381	2.353	2.326	2.299	2.273	2.247	2.222	2.198	2.174	2.151	2.128
11	2.500	2.469	2.439	2.410	2.381	2.353	2.326	2.299	2.273	2.247	2.222	2.198	2.174	2.150	2.128
12	2.500	2.469	2.439	2.410	2.381	2.353	2.326	2.299	2.273	2.247	2.222	2.198	2.174	2.151	2.128
13	2.500	2.469	2.439	2.410	2.381	2.353	2.326	2.299	2.273	2.247	2.222	2.198	2.174	2.150	2.128
14	2.500	2.469	2.439	2.410	2.381	2.353	2.326	2.299	2.273	2.247	2.222	2.198	2.174	2.151	2.128
15	2.500	2.469	2.439	2.410	2.381	2.353	2.326	2.299	2.273	2.247	2.222	2.198	2.174	2.150	2.128
16	2.500	2.469	2.439	2.410	2.381	2.353	2.326	2.299	2.273	2.247	2.222	2.198	2.174	2.151	2.128
17	2.500	2.469	2.439	2.409	2.381	2.353	2.326	2.299	2.273	2.247	2.222	2.198	2.174	2.150	2.127
18	2.500	2.469	2.439	2.410	2.381	2.353	2.325	2.299	2.273	2.247	2.222	2.198	2.174	2.151	2.128
19	2.500	2.469	2.439	2.409	2.381	2.353	2.326	2.299	2.273	2.247	2.222	2.198	2.174	2.150	2.127
20	2.500	2.469	2.439	2.410	2.381	2.353	2.325	2.299	2.273	2.247	2.222	2.198	2.174	2.151	2.128
21	2.500	2.469	2.439	2.409	2.381	2.353	2.326	2.299	2.273	2.247	2.222	2.198	2.174	2.150	2.128
22	2.500	2.469	2.439	2.410	2.381	2.353	2.325	2.299	2.273	2.247	2.222	2.198	2.174	2.151	2.128
23	2.500	2.469	2.439	2.409	2.381	2.353	2.326	2.299	2.272	2.247	2.222	2.198	2.174	2.150	2.128
24	2.500	2.469	2.439	2.410	2.381	2.353	2.325	2.299	2.273	2.247	2.222	2.198	2.174	2.151	2.127
25	2.500	2.469	2.439	2.409	2.381	2.353	2.326	2.299	2.272	2.247	2.222	2.198	2.174	2.150	2.128
26	2.500	2.469	2.439	2.410	2.381	2.353	2.325	2.299	2.273	2.247	2.222	2.198	2.174	2.151	2.127
27	2.500	2.469	2.439	2.409	2.381	2.353	2.326	2.299	2.272	2.247	2.222	2.198	2.174	2.150	2.128
28	2.500	2.469	2.439	2.410	2.381	2.353	2.325	2.299	2.272	2.247	2.222	2.197	2.174	2.151	2.127
29	2.500	2.469	2.439	2.409	2.381	2.353	2.326	2.299	2.272	2.247	2.222	2.198	2.174	2.150	2.128
30	2.500	2.469	2.439	2.410	2.381	2.353	2.326	2.299	2.273	2.247	2.223	2.198	2.174	2.151	2.128
31	2.500	2.469	2.439	2.410	2.381	2.353	2.325	2.299	2.272	2.248	2.223	2.197	2.174	2.150	2.127
32	2.500	2.470	2.439	2.409	2.381	2.353	2.326	2.299	2.273	2.248	2.223	2.198	2.174	2.151	2.128
33	2.500	2.469	2.439	2.410	2.381	2.353	2.326	2.298	2.272	2.248	2.223	2.197	2.173	2.150	2.127
34	2.500	2.470	2.439	2.409	2.381	2.353	2.326	2.299	2.273	2.248	2.223	2.198	2.174	2.151	2.128
35	2.500	2.469	2.139	2.410	2.381	2.353	2.325	2.298	2.272	2.248	2.222	2.197	2.173	2.150	2.127
36	2.500	2.470	2.439	2.409	2.381	2.353	2.326	2.299	2.272	2.247	2.222	2.198	2.174	2.151	2.128
37	2.500	2.469	2.439	2.410	2.381	2.353	2.326	2.298	2.272	2.247	2.222	2.197	2.174	2.150	2.128
38	2.500	2.470	2.439	2.409	2.381	2.353	2.325	2.299	2.272	2.247	2.222	2.198	2.173	2.151	2.127
39	2.500	2.469	2.439	2.410	2.381	2.353	2.326	2.298	2.273	2.247	2.222	2.198	2.174	2.150	2.128
40	2.500	2.469	2.439	2.410	2.380	2.353	2.326	2.298	2.273	2.247	2.222	2.197	2.173	2.151	2.128
41	1.250	2.469	2.439	2.409	2.381	2.352	2.325	2.299	2.273	2.248	2.222	2.198	2.174	2.150	2.127
42		1.220	1.220	2.409	2.381	2.353	2.326	2.298	2.273	2.248	2.223	2.198	2.174	2.151	2.127
43				2.409	1.190	2.352	2.325	2.299	2.272	2.247	2.223	2.198	2.174	2.150	2.128
44						2.352	1.163	2.298	2.273	2.247	2.222	2.198	2.173	2.151	2.128
45								2.299	1.136	2.248	2.223	2.197	2.174	2.150	2.127
46										2.247	1.111	2.198	2.173	2.151	2.128
47												2.197	1.087	2.150	2.127
48														2.150	1.064

If the Recovery Year is:	and the Recovery Period is:					
	47.5	48.0	48.5	49.0	49.5	50.0
			the Depreciation Rate is:			
1	1.053	1.042	1.031	1.020	1.010	1.000
2	2.105	2.083	2.062	2.041	2.020	2.000
3	2.105	2.083	2.062	2.041	2.020	2.000
4	2.105	2.083	2.062	2.041	2.020	2.000
5	2.105	2.083	2.062	2.041	2.020	2.000
6	2.105	2.083	2.062	2.041	2.020	2.000
7	2.105	2.083	2.062	2.041	2.020	2.000
8	2.105	2.083	2.062	2.041	2.020	2.000
9	2.105	2.083	2.062	2.041	2.020	2.000
10	2.105	2.083	2.062	2.041	2.020	2.000
11	2.105	2.083	2.062	2.041	2.020	2.000
12	2.105	2.083	2.062	2.041	2.020	2.000
13	2.105	2.083	2.062	2.041	2.020	2.000
14	2.105	2.083	2.062	2.041	2.020	2.000
15	2.105	2.083	2.062	2.041	2.020	2.000
16	2.105	2.083	2.062	2.041	2.020	2.000
17	2.105	2.083	2.062	2.041	2.020	2.000
18	2.105	2.083	2.062	2.041	2.020	2.000
19	2.105	2.084	2.062	2.041	2.020	2.000
20	2.105	2.083	2.062	2.041	2.020	2.000
21	2.105	2.084	2.062	2.041	2.020	2.000
22	2.105	2.083	2.062	2.041	2.020	2.000
23	2.105	2.084	2.062	2.041	2.020	2.000
24	2.105	2.083	2.062	2.041	2.020	2.000
25	2.105	2.084	2.062	2.041	2.020	2.000
26	2.106	2.083	2.062	2.041	2.020	2.000
27	2.105	2.084	2.062	2.041	2.020	2.000
28	2.106	2.083	2.062	2.041	2.020	2.000
29	2.105	2.084	2.062	2.041	2.020	2.000
30	2.106	2.083	2.062	2.041	2.020	2.000
31	2.105	2.084	2.062	2.041	2.021	2.000
32	2.106	2.083	2.062	2.041	2.020	2.000
33	2.105	2.084	2.062	2.041	2.021	2.000
34	2.106	2.083	2.062	2.040	2.020	2.000
35	2.105	2.084	2.062	2.041	2.021	2.000
36	2.106	2.083	2.062	2.040	2.020	2.000
37	2.105	2.084	2.061	2.041	2.021	2.000
38	2.106	2.083	2.062	2.040	2.020	2.000
39	2.105	2.084	2.061	2.041	2.021	2.000
40	2.106	2.083	2.062	2.040	2.020	2.000
41	2.105	2.084	2.061	2.041	2.021	2.000
42	2.106	2.083	2.062	2.040	2.020	2.000
43	2.105	2.084	2.061	2.041	2.021	2.000
44	2.106	2.083	2.062	2.040	2.020	2.000
45	2.105	2.084	2.061	2.041	2.021	2.000
46	2.106	2.083	2.062	2.040	2.020	2.000
47	2.105	2.084	2.061	2.041	2.021	2.000
48	2.106	2.083	2.062	2.040	2.020	2.000
49		1.042	2.061	2.041	2.021	2.000
50			1.020	2.020	2.000
51						1.000

1244. MACRS Short Tax Years. A short tax year is any tax year with less than 12 months. Special rules are provided for determining MACRS deductions that apply in the following situations: (1) property is placed in service in a short tax year, (2) a short tax year occurs during the recovery period of property, or (3) a disposition of property occurs before the end of the recovery period (Rev. Proc. 89-15). If any of the above situations exist, refinements are made to the use of the applicable conventions and the IRS MACRS depreciation tables at ¶ 1243 may *not* be used.[69]

The mid-month convention is applied without regard to the tax year unlike the half-year and mid-quarter conventions that are applied to the tax year. Accordingly, consideration of the tax year is necessary in establishing the deemed-placed-in-service and disposition dates under the latter two conventions.

Under the half-year convention, property placed in service or disposed of in a short tax year is deemed placed in service or disposed of on the midpoint of the short tax year, which always falls on either the first day or the midpoint of the month.

Under the mid-quarter convention, property is deemed placed in service or disposed of on the midpoint of the quarter, which always falls on either the first day or the midpoint of a month, in the short tax year that it is placed in service or disposed of.

Depreciation for the first recovery year in the recovery period is computed by multiplying the basis in the property by the applicable depreciation rate. The depreciation allowance allocable to the first tax year that includes a portion of the first recovery year is derived by multiplying the depreciation for the first recovery year by a fraction, the numerator of which is the number of months (including fractions of months) the property is deemed to be in service during the tax year under the applicable convention and the denominator of which is 12.

The correlation of a depreciation allowance between recovery years and tax years after the first tax year in the recovery period may be made under either an allocation or a simplified method.

1245. Applicable Convention. Specified averaging conventions apply to depreciation computations made under MACRS (Code Sec. 168(d)).[70] The recovery period begins on the date on which the property is placed in service under the applicable convention. The depreciation table percentages take into account the applicable convention in the first and last year of the regular recovery period. However, if property is disposed of prior to the end of the regular recovery period, the result obtained by using the table percentage for the year of disposition must be adjusted to take into account the applicable convention.

Half-Year Convention. Under the half-year convention, which can apply to property other than residential rental property and nonresidential real property, property is treated as placed in service or disposed of in the middle of the tax year. Thus, one-half of the depreciation for the first year of the recovery period is allowed in the tax year in which the property is placed in service, regardless of when the property is placed in service during the year.

A half-year of depreciation is allowed in the tax year of disposition if there is a disposition of property before the end of the recovery period.[71] The table percentage for the year of disposition does not take this into account; therefore, only one-half of the depreciation as computed using the applicable table percentage is allowed.

> **Example 1.** Five-year property costing $1,000 and subject to the half-year convention is placed in service in 1999 and sold in 2001. Using Table 1 at ¶ 1243, 1999 depreciation is $200 ($1,000 × 20%); 2000 depreciation is $320 ($1,000 × 32%); and 2001 depreciation is $96 ($1,000 × 19.20% × 50% to reflect half-year convention in year of disposition).

Mid-Month Convention. A mid-month convention applies to residential rental property, including low-income housing, and nonresidential real property. Property is deemed placed in service or disposed of during the middle of the month. The deduction is based on the number of months the property was in service. Thus, one-half month's depreciation is allowed for the month the property is placed in service and for the month of disposition if there is a disposition of property before the end of the recovery period.

> **Example 2.** A commercial building costing $100,000 is purchased by a calendar-year taxpayer in February 2000 and sold in August 2001. Using Table 7A at ¶ 1243, 2000 depreciation is $2,247 ($100,000 × 2.247% (first-year percentage for property placed in service in second month of tax year)) and 2001 depreciation is $1,603 ($100,000 × 2.564% (second-year percentage for property placed in service in second month) × 7.5/12 to reflect 7.5 months in service in 2001 (January through mid-August) under the mid-month convention).

Mid-Quarter Convention. Under the mid-quarter convention, all property placed in service, or disposed of, during any quarter of a tax year is treated as placed in service at the midpoint of the quarter (Code Sec. 168(d)(3)).[72] Depreciation under the mid-quarter convention may be determined using Tables 2-5, above.

The mid-quarter convention applies to all property, other than nonresidential real property and residential rental property, if more than 40% of the aggregate bases of such property is placed in service during the last three months of the tax year. Property placed in service and disposed of within the same tax year is disregarded for purposes of the 40% test.

Relief from the mid-quarter convention has been provided on account of the terrorist attacks of September 11, 2001. If the 3rd or 4th quarter of a taxpayer's tax year includes September 11, 2001, then the taxpayer may elect on Form 4562 to apply the half-year convention to all property placed in service during the tax year that would otherwise be subject to the mid-quarter convention (Notice 2001-70; Notice 2001-74).

In determining whether the mid-quarter convention is applicable, the aggregate basis of property placed in service in the last three months of the tax year must be computed regardless of the length of the tax year. Thus, if a short tax year consists of three months or less, the mid-quarter convention applies regardless of when the depreciable property is placed in service during the tax year.

The cost of Sec. 179 property purchased during the last three months of the year that is properly expensed is excluded from the aggregate basis of property placed in service in determining whether the mid-quarter convention applies. Thus, a taxpayer may be able to avoid the mid-quarter convention (if this is desirable) by allocating the Code Sec. 179 deduction to property placed in service in the last quarter.

For purposes of the 40% test, depreciable basis does not include adjustments resulting from transfers of property between members of the same affiliated group filing a consolidated return.

If the MACRS deduction for property subject to the mid-quarter convention is computed without tables, depreciation for the first year is determined by computing the depreciation for the full tax year and then multiplying it by the following percentages for the quarter of the tax year the property is placed in service: first quarter, 87.5%; second quarter, 62.5%; third quarter, 37.5%; and fourth quarter, 12.5%.

1247. MACRS Alternative Depreciation System (ADS). ADS must be used for (1) tangible property used outside the U.S., (2) tax-exempt use property,

---

(3) tax-exempt bond-financed property, (4) property imported from a foreign country for which an Executive Order is in effect because the country maintains trade restrictions or engages in other discriminatory acts, and (5) property for which an ADS election has been made (Code Sec. 168(g)).[73]

Under ADS, the deduction is computed by applying the straight-line method, the applicable convention and the applicable longer recovery period (12 years for personal property with no class life, 40 years for real property, 50 years for railroad grading and tunnel bores, and the class life for all other property) for the respective class of property (Code Sec. 168(g)(2)(C)).[74] ADS is also used to compute the earnings and profits of a foreign or domestic corporation. The allowable depreciation deductions for luxury cars and listed property used 50% or less in business are also determined under this method (see ¶ 1211 and ¶ 1214).

Electing ADS. In lieu of the regular MACRS deduction, taxpayers may irrevocably elect to apply the MACRS alternative depreciation system to any class of property for any tax year (Code Sec. 168(g)(7)).[75] If elected, ADS applies to all property in the MACRS class placed in service during the tax year. For example, if the election is made for five-year property, it applies to all five-year property placed in service in the year of the election. For residential rental property and nonresidential real property, the election may be made on a property-by-property basis.

1248. Special Transferee Rules. A transferee in certain corporate and partnership transactions is treated as the transferor and must use the latter's recovery period and method in computing the MACRS deduction for the portion of the transferee's basis that does not exceed the transferor's adjusted basis in the property (Code Sec. 168(i)(7)).[76] This rule applies to nonrecognition transfers under Code Sec. 332 (subsidiary liquidations) (¶ 2261); transfers to a controlled corporation (¶ 1731); transfers related to certain reorganizations (¶ 2209); contributions to a partnership (¶ 443); certain partnership distributions (¶ 453); and transactions between members of the same affiliated group during any tax year for which a consolidated return is made by such group. It does not apply to transactions relating to the sale or exchange of 50% or more of the total interest in a partnership's capital and profits within a 12-month period (Code Sec. 708(b)(1)(B)).

1249. Disposition of Depreciable Property. See ¶ 1779.

Accelerated Cost Recovery System (ACRS)

1252. Pre-1987 ACRS in General. The Accelerated Cost Recovery System (ACRS) must be used to compute the depreciation deduction for most tangible depreciable property placed in service after 1980 and before 1987.[77] Cost recovery methods and periods are the same for both new and used property, and salvage value is disregarded in computing ACRS allowances. Post-1980 depreciation on tangible assets first placed in service before 1981 is computed using the method elected by the taxpayer when the property was placed in service (including the Class Life ADR depreciation system (¶ 1284) and other methods of depreciation discussed at ¶ 1216 and following).

Under ACRS, the cost of eligible property is recovered over a 3-year, 5-year, 10-year, 15-year, 18-year, or 19-year period, depending on the type of property. ACRS applies to recovery property, as defined at ¶ 1255. The deduction is determined by applying the statutory table percentage for the appropriate class of property to its unadjusted basis. The unadjusted basis of property under ACRS is the basis of the property (as determined for purposes of computing gain or loss), unadjusted for depreciation, amortization or depletion. It does not include that

---

Footnote references are to paragraphs of the 2002 Standard Federal Tax Reports.

¶ 1248

[73] ¶ 11,250, ¶ 11,279.04   [75] ¶ 11,250, ¶ 11,279.04   [77] ¶ 11,258.01
[74] ¶ 11,250, ¶ 11,279.04   [76] ¶ 11,279.054

portion of the basis for which there is an election to amortize (¶ 1287) or to expense the cost of Code Sec. 179 property (¶ 1208) (pre-1987 Code Sec. 168(d)(1)).[78]

Straight-Line Election. An election to recover costs by using a straight-line method over the regular recovery period or a longer recovery period was also available under ACRS and was made on the taxpayer's return for the year in which the property was placed in service (pre-1987 Code Sec. 168(f)(4)).[79]

1255. Recovery Property. For ACRS purposes, recovery property is tangible depreciable property that is placed in service after 1980. It does not include property for which an election is made to compute depreciation on a method not based on a depreciation period (unit-of-production method, income forecast method, etc.), public utility property for which the normalization method of accounting is not used, intangible assets such as patents and copyrights (¶ 1201), property for which an election to amortize was made, or motion picture films and videotapes (pre-1987 Code Sec. 168(c), (e)).[80] For purposes of determining the class of recovery property into which an asset falls, recovery property is defined as either Code Sec. 1245 class property or Code Sec. 1250 class property.

Code Sec. 1245 class property includes tangible Code Sec. 1245 property, as defined at ¶ 1785, other than (1) elevators and escalators and (2) certain rapidly amortized realty. *Code Sec. 1250 class property* includes tangible Code Sec. 1250 property, as defined at ¶ 1786, and elevators and escalators.

1258. Personal Property. The ACRS statutory percentage for personal property placed in service after 1980 and before 1987 is determined under the table below, taking into account the type of property (3-year, 5-year, 10-year or 15-year) and the year in which the property is placed in service. The percentages for 3-, 5-, and 10-year property (which should be fully depreciated by now) are not reproduced.

Property	ACRS Percentages
15-year public utility:	
Year 1	5
Year 2	10
Year 3	9
Year 4	8
Year 5-6	7
Year 7-15	6

In determining the annual deduction, the applicable percentage to be applied to the unadjusted basis of the property depends on the number of years the property has been in service (the recovery year) (pre-1987 Code Sec. 168(b)(1)).[81] Generally, no recovery deduction is allowed in the year of disposition of personal property.

1261. Real Property. Under ACRS, the unadjusted basis of real property is recovered over a period of 19 years for real property placed in service after May 8, 1985, and before 1987. For real property placed in service after March 15, 1984, and before May 9, 1985, unadjusted basis is recovered over a period of 18 years. A 15-year recovery period applies to real property placed in service after 1980 and before March 16, 1984, and to low-income housing.[82]

In computing the ACRS deduction, a full-month convention is used for real recovery property placed in service before March 16, 1984, and for low-income housing, and a mid-month convention is used for real recovery property (other than low-income housing) placed in service after March 15, 1984. Under the full-month convention, real property placed in service at any time during a particular month is treated as placed in service on the first day of such month, thereby permitting a full

---

Footnote references are to paragraphs of the 2002 Standard Federal Tax Reports.

[78] ¶ 11,258.041
[79] ¶ 11,258.031
[80] ¶ 11,258.01, ¶ 11,258.045
[81] ¶ 11,258.023
[82] ¶ 11,258.025

month's cost recovery for the month the property is placed in service. For a disposition at any time during a particular month before the end of a recovery period, no cost recovery is permitted for such month of disposition. Under the mid-month convention, real property placed in service at any time during a particular month is treated as placed in service in the middle of such month, thereby permitting one-half month's cost recovery for the month the property is placed in service. For a disposition of real property during a month before the end of a recovery period, one-half month's cost recovery is allowed for the month of disposition.

In using the following tables, there are separate rate schedules depending upon the month in the first tax year that the property is placed in service. Further, where real property is sold before the end of the recovery period, the ACRS deduction for the year of disposition is to reflect only the months of the year during which the property was in service. For a short tax year, appropriate adjustments must also be made to the table amounts. A special rule applies where there is a disposition of real recovery property in the first recovery year.

Table I — 15-Year Real Property (other than low-income housing)

Year	1	2	3	4	5	6	7	8	9	10	11	12
1st	12%	11%	10%	9%	8%	7%	6%	5%	4%	3%	2%	1%
2nd	10%	10%	11%	11%	11%	11%	11%	11%	11%	11%	11%	12%
3rd	9%	9%	9%	9%	10%	10%	10%	10%	10%	10%	10%	10%
4th	8%	8%	8%	8%	8%	8%	9%	9%	9%	9%	9%	9%
5th	7%	7%	7%	7%	7%	7%	8%	8%	8%	8%	8%	8%
6th	6%	6%	6%	6%	7%	7%	7%	7%	7%	7%	7%	7%
7th	6%	6%	6%	6%	6%	6%	6%	6%	6%	6%	6%	6%
8th	6%	6%	6%	6%	6%	6%	5%	6%	6%	6%	6%	6%
9th	6%	6%	6%	6%	5%	6%	5%	5%	5%	6%	6%	6%
10th	5%	6%	5%	6%	5%	5%	5%	5%	5%	5%	6%	5%
11th	5%	5%	5%	5%	5%	5%	5%	5%	5%	5%	5%	5%
12th	5%	5%	5%	5%	5%	5%	5%	5%	5%	5%	5%	5%
13th	5%	5%	5%	5%	5%	5%	5%	5%	5%	5%	5%	5%
14th	5%	5%	5%	5%	5%	5%	5%	5%	5%	5%	5%	5%
15th	5%	5%	5%	5%	5%	5%	5%	5%	5%	5%	5%	5%
16th	—	—	1%	1%	2%	2%	3%	3%	4%	4%	4%	5%

Table II — Low-Income Housing (placed in service before May 9, 1985)

Year	1	2	3	4	5	6	7	8	9	10	11	12
1st	13%	12%	11%	10%	9%	8%	7%	6%	4%	3%	2%	1%
2nd	12%	12%	12%	12%	12%	12%	12%	13%	13%	13%	13%	13%
3rd	10%	10%	10%	10%	11%	11%	11%	11%	11%	11%	11%	11%
4th	9%	9%	9%	9%	9%	9%	9%	9%	10%	10%	10%	10%
5th	8%	8%	8%	8%	8%	8%	8%	8%	8%	8%	8%	9%
6th	7%	7%	7%	7%	7%	7%	7%	7%	7%	7%	7%	7%
7th	6%	6%	6%	6%	6%	6%	6%	6%	6%	6%	6%	6%
8th	5%	5%	5%	5%	5%	5%	5%	5%	5%	5%	6%	6%
9th	5%	5%	5%	5%	5%	5%	5%	5%	5%	5%	5%	5%
10th	5%	5%	5%	5%	5%	5%	5%	5%	5%	5%	5%	5%
11th	4%	5%	5%	5%	5%	5%	5%	5%	5%	5%	5%	5%
12th	4%	4%	4%	5%	4%	5%	5%	5%	5%	5%	5%	5%
13th	4%	4%	4%	4%	4%	4%	5%	4%	5%	5%	5%	5%
14th	4%	4%	4%	4%	4%	4%	4%	4%	4%	5%	4%	4%
15th	4%	4%	4%	4%	4%	4%	4%	4%	4%	4%	4%	4%
16th	—	—	1%	1%	2%	2%	2%	3%	3%	3%	4%	4%

Table III — Low-Income Housing (placed in service after May 8, 1985)

Year	1	2	3	4	5	6	7	8	9	10	11	12
1st	13.3%	12.2%	11.1%	10%	8.9%	7.8%	6.6%	5.6%	4.4%	3.3%	2.2%	1.1%
2nd	11.6%	11.7%	11.9%	12%	12.1%	12.3%	12.5%	12.6%	12.7%	12.9%	13%	13.2%
3rd	10%	10.1%	10.2%	10.4%	10.5%	10.7%	10.8%	10.9%	11.1%	11.2%	11.3%	11.4%
4th	8.7%	8.8%	8.9%	9%	9.1%	9.2%	9.3%	9.5%	9.6%	9.7%	9.8%	9.9%
5th	7.5%	7.6%	7.7%	7.8%	7.9%	8%	8.1%	8.2%	8.3%	8.4%	8.5%	8.6%
6th	6.5%	6.6%	6.7%	6.8%	6.9%	6.9%	7%	7.1%	7.2%	7.3%	7.4%	7.4%
7th	5.7%	5.7%	5.8%	5.9%	5.9%	6%	6.1%	6.1%	6.2%	6.3%	6.4%	6.5%
8th	4.9%	5%	5%	5.1%	5.2%	5.2%	5.3%	5.3%	5.4%	5.5%	5.5%	5.6%
9th	4.6%	4.6%	4.6%	4.6%	4.6%	4.6%	4.6%	4.6%	4.6%	4.7%	4.8%	4.8%
10th	4.6%	4.6%	4.6%	4.6%	4.6%	4.6%	4.6%	4.6%	4.6%	4.5%	4.6%	4.6%
11th	4.6%	4.6%	4.6%	4.6%	4.6%	4.6%	4.6%	4.6%	4.6%	4.6%	4.6%	4.6%
12th	4.5%	4.6%	4.6%	4.6%	4.6%	4.6%	4.6%	4.6%	4.6%	4.6%	4.6%	4.6%
13th	4.5%	4.5%	4.6%	4.5%	4.6%	4.6%	4.6%	4.6%	4.6%	4.5%	4.6%	4.6%
14th	4.5%	4.5%	4.5%	4.5%	4.5%	4.5%	4.5%	4.6%	4.6%	4.5%	4.5%	4.5%
15th	4.5%	4.5%	4.5%	4.5%	4.5%	4.5%	4.5%	4.5%	4.5%	4.5%	4.5%	4.5%
16th	—	0.4%	0.7%	1.1%	1.5%	1.9%	2.3%	2.6%	3%	3 4%	3.7%	4.1%

Table IV

18-Year Real Property
(placed in service after June 22, 1984)

Year	Month Placed in Service											
	1	2	3	4	5	6	7	8	9	10	11	12
1st	9%	9%	8%	7%	6%	5%	4%	4%	3%	2%	1%	0.4%
2nd	9%	9%	9%	9%	9%	9%	9%	9%	9%	10%	10%	10%
3rd	8%	8%	8%	8%	8%	8%	8%	8%	9%	9%	9%	9%
4th	7%	7%	7%	7%	7%	8%	8%	8%	8%	8%	8%	8%
5th	7%	7%	7%	7%	7%	7%	7%	7%	7%	7%	7%	7%
6th	6%	6%	6%	6%	6%	6%	6%	6%	6%	6%	6%	6%
7th	5%	5%	5%	5%	6%	6%	6%	6%	6%	6%	6%	6%
8-12th	5%	5%	5%	5%	5%	5%	5%	5%	5%	5%	5%	5%
13th	4%	4%	4%	5%	4%	4%	5%	4%	4%	4%	5%	5%
14-17th	4%	4%	4%	4%	4%	4%	4%	4%	4%	4%	4%	4%
18th	4%	3%	4%	4%	4%	4%	4%	4%	4%	4%	4%	4%
19th		1%	1%	1%	2%	2%	2%	3%	3%	3%	3%	3.6%

Table V

18-Year Real Property
(placed in service after March 15 and before June 23, 1984)

Year	Month Placed in Service										
	1	2	3	4	5	6	7	8	9	10-11	12
1st	10%	9%	8%	7%	6%	6%	5%	4%	3%	2%	1%
2nd	9%	9%	9%	9%	9%	9%	9%	9%	9%	10%	10%
3rd	8%	8%	8%	8%	8%	8%	8%	8%	9%	9%	9%
4th	7%	7%	7%	7%	7%	7%	8%	8%	8%	8%	8%
5th	6%	7%	7%	7%	7%	7%	7%	7%	7%	7%	7%
6th	6%	6%	6%	6%	6%	6%	6%	6%	6%	6%	6%
7th	5%	5%	5%	5%	6%	6%	6%	6%	6%	6%	6%
8-12th	5%	5%	5%	5%	5%	5%	5%	5%	5%	5%	5%
13th	4%	4%	4%	5%	5%	4%	4%	5%	4%	4%	4%
14-18th	4%	4%	4%	4%	4%	4%	4%	4%	4%	4%	4%
19th			1%	1%	1%	2%	2%	2%	3%	3%	4%

Table VI

19-Year Real Property

Year	Month Placed in Service											
	1	2	3	4	5	6	7	8	9	10	11	12
1st	8.8%	8.1%	7.3%	6.5%	5.8%	5.0%	4.2%	3.5%	2.7%	1.9%	1.1%	0.4%
2nd	8.4%	8.5%	8.5%	8.6%	8.7%	8.8%	8.8%	8.9%	9.0%	9.0%	9.1%	9.2%
3rd	7.6%	7.7%	7.7%	7.8%	7.9%	7.9%	8.0%	8.1%	8.1%	8.2%	8.3%	8.3%
4th	6.9%	7.0%	7.0%	7.1%	7.1%	7.2%	7.3%	7.3%	7.4%	7.4%	7.5%	7.6%
5th	6.3%	6.3%	6.4%	6.4%	6.5%	6.5%	6.6%	6.6%	6.7%	6.8%	6.8%	6.9%
6th	5.7%	5.7%	5.8%	5.9%	5.9%	5.9%	6.0%	6.0%	6.1%	6.1%	6.2%	6.2%
7th	5.2%	5.2%	5.3%	5.3%	5.3%	5.4%	5.4%	5.5%	5.5%	5.6%	5.6%	5.6%
8th	4.7%	4.7%	4.8%	4.8%	4.8%	4.9%	4.9%	5.0%	5.0%	5.1%	5.1%	5.1%
9th	4.2%	4.3%	4.3%	4.4%	4.4%	4.5%	4.5%	4.5%	4.5%	4.6%	4.6%	4.7%
10-19th	4.2%	4.2%	4.2%	4.2%	4.2%	4.2%	4.2%	4.2%	4.2%	4.2%	4.2%	4.2%
20th	0.2%	0.5%	0.9%	1.2%	1.6%	1.9%	2.3%	2.6%	3.0%	3.3%	3.7%	4.0%

¶ **1261**

Table VII

18-Year Real Property
(placed in service after June 22, 1984)
for Which Alternate ACRS Method Over an
18-Year Period Is Elected

Year	Month Placed in Service					
	1-2	3-4	5-7	8-9	10-11	12
1st	5%	4%	3%	2%	1%	0.2%
2-10th	6%	6%	6%	6%	6%	6%
11th	5%	5%	5%	5%	5%	5.8%
12-18th	5%	5%	5%	5%	5%	5%
19th	1%	2%	3%	4%	5%	5%

Table VIII

18-Year Real Property
(placed in service after March 15 and before June 23, 1984)
for Which Alternate ACRS Method Over an
18-Year Period Is Elected

Year	Month Placed in Service						
	1	2-3	4-5	6-7	8-9	10-11	12
1st	6%	5%	4%	3%	2%	1%	0.5%
2-10th	6%	6%	6%	6%	6%	6%	6%
11th	5%	5%	5%	5%	5%	5%	5.5%
12-18th	5%	5%	5%	5%	5%	5%	5%
19th		1%	2%	3%	4%	5%	5%

Table IX

19-Year Real Property
for Which Alternate ACRS Method Over a
19-Year Period Is Elected

Year	Month Placed in Service											
	1	2	3	4	5	6	7	8	9	10	11	12
1st	5.0%	4.6%	4.2%	3.7%	3.3%	2.9%	2.4%	2.0%	1.5%	1.1%	0.7%	0.2%
2-13th	5.3%	5.3%	5.3%	5.3%	5.3%	5.3%	5.3%	5.3%	5.3%	5.3%	5.3%	5.3%
14-19th	5.2%	5.2%	5.2%	5.2%	5.2%	5.2%	5.2%	5.2%	5.2%	5.2%	5.2%	5.2%
20th	0.2%	0.6%	1.0%	1.5%	1.9%	2.3%	2.8%	3.2%	3.7%	4.1%	4.5%	5.0%

Table X

18-Year Real Property
(placed in service after June 22, 1984) for Which Alternate ACRS Method
Over a 35-Year Period Is Elected

Year	Month Placed in Service				
	1-2	3-6	7-10	11	12
1st	3%	2%	1%	0.4%	0.1%
2-30th	3%	3%	3%	3%	3%
31st	2%	2%	2%	2.6%	2.9%
32-35th	2%	2%	2%	2%	2%
36th		1%	2%	2%	2%

Table XI *18-Year Real Property*
(placed in service after March 15 and before June 23, 1984)
15-Year Real Property and Low-Income housing
(placed in service before May 9, 1985) for Which Alternate
ACRS Method Over a 35-Year Period Is Elected

Year	Month Placed in Service		
	1-2	3-6	7-12
1st	3%	2%	1%
2-30th	3%	3%	3%
31-35th	2%	2%	2%
36th		1%	2%

Table XII *Low-Income Housing (placed in service after May 8, 1985)*
for Which Alternate ACRS Method Over a 35-Year Period Is Elected

Year	Month Placed in Service											
	1	2	3	4	5	6	7	8	9	10	11	12
1st	2.9%	2.6%	2.4%	2.1%	1.9%	1.7%	1.4%	1.2%	1.0%	0.7%	0.5%	0.2%
2-20th	2.9%	2.9%	2.9%	2.9%	2.9%	2.9%	2.9%	2.9%	2.9%	2.9%	2.9%	2.9%
21-35th	2.8%	2.8%	2.8%	2.8%	2.8%	2.8%	2.8%	2.8%	2.8%	2.8%	2.8%	2.8%
36th		0.3%	0.5%	0.8%	1.0%	1.2%	1.5%	1.7%	1.9%	2.2%	2.4%	2.7%

Table XIII *19-Year Real Property*
for Which Alternate ACRS Method Over a 35-Year Period Is Elected

Year	Month Placed in Service											
	1	2	3	4	5	6	7	8	9	10	11	12
1st	2.7%	2.5%	2.3%	2.0%	1.8%	1.5%	1.3%	1.1%	0.8%	0.6%	0.4%	0.1%
2-20th	2.9%	2.9%	2.9%	2.9%	2.9%	2.9%	2.9%	2.9%	2.9%	2.9%	2.9%	2.9%
21-35th	2.8%	2.8%	2.8%	2.8%	2.8%	2.8%	2.8%	2.8%	2.8%	2.8%	2.8%	2.8%
36th	0.2%	0.4%	0.6%	0.9%	1.1%	1.4%	1.6%	1.8%	2.1%	2.3%	2.5%	2.8%

Table XIV *18-Year Real Property*
(placed in service after June 22, 1984) 19-Year Real Property for Which
Alternate ACRS Method Over a 45-Year Period Is Elected

Year	Month Placed in Service											
	1	2	3	4	5	6	7	8	9	10	11	12
1st	2.1%	1.9%	1.8%	1.6%	1.4%	1.2%	1%	0.8%	0.6%	0.5%	0.3%	0.1%
2-11th	2.3%	2.3%	2.3%	2.3%	2.3%	2.3%	2.3%	2.3%	2.3%	2.3%	2.3%	2.3%
12-45th	2.2%	2.2%	2.2%	2.2%	2.2%	2.2%	2.2%	2.2%	2.2%	2.2%	2.2%	2.2%
46th	0.1%	0.3%	0.4%	0.6%	0.8%	1%	1.2%	1.4%	1.6%	1.7%	1.9%	2.1%

Table XV *18-Year Real Property*
(placed in service after March 15 and before June 23, 1984) 15-Year Real Property
and Low-Income housing (placed in service after December 31, 1980) for Which
Alternate ACRS Method Over a 45-Year Period Is Elected

Year	Month Placed in Service											
	1	2	3	4	5	6	7	8	9	10	11	12
1st	2.3%	2%	1.9%	1.7%	1.5%	1.3%	1.2%	0.9%	0.7%	0.6%	0.4%	0.2%
2-10th	2.3%	2.3%	2.3%	2.3%	2.3%	2.3%	2.3%	2.3%	2.3%	2.3%	2.3%	2.3%
11-45th	2.2%	2.2%	2.2%	2.2%	2.2%	2.2%	2.2%	2.2%	2.2%	2.2%	2.2%	2.2%
46th		0.3%	0.4%	0.6%	0.8%	1%	1.1%	1.4%	1.6%	1.7%	1.9%	2.1%

¶ 1261

1264. Predominant Use Outside the U.S. Under ACRS, the unadjusted basis of personal property used outside the U.S. is to be recovered over a period equal to the ADR class life for that property as of January 1, 1981.[83] Generally, no recovery deduction is allowed in the year of disposition of personal recovery property used predominantly outside the U.S. The unadjusted basis of real property and low-income housing used predominantly outside the U.S. is to be recovered over a period of 35 years. For real recovery property (other than low-income housing) placed in service after March 15, 1984, a mid-month convention is used. There are separate rate schedules depending on the month in the first tax year that the property is placed in service.

1267. Components of Sec. 1250 Class Property. Under ACRS, components of Sec. 1250 class property may not be depreciated separately. Composite depreciation is required on the entire building, unless the components qualify for amortization elections (pre-1987 Code Sec. 168(f)(1)).[84] The recovery period for any component part begins on the first day of the month in which the component is placed in service or, if later, when the building is placed in service.

Substantial Improvements. If a taxpayer makes a substantial improvement to a building, it is treated as a separate building rather than as one or more components. The taxpayer may use the regular ACRS deduction or may elect the straight-line ACRS deduction for the improvement over the regular or a longer recovery period regardless of the ACRS method that is used for the rest of the building.

1270. Short Tax Years. For a tax year of less than 12 months, the amount of the ACRS deduction is the amount that bears the same relationship to the amount of the deduction as the number of months and partial months in the short year bears to 12 (pre-1987 Code Sec. 168(f)(5)).[85] Generally, for real property and low-income housing placed in service or disposed of in a short tax year, the above rule does not apply and the deduction is based on the number of months the property is in service during the year, regardless of the length of the tax year and regardless of the recovery period and method used.

Any unrecovered allowance (the difference between the recovery allowance properly allowable for the short tax year and the recovery allowance that would have been allowable if such year were not a short tax year) is claimed in the tax year following the last year in the recovery period (Prop. Reg. § 1.168-2(f)(3)).[86] However, there is a maximum limitation on the amount of an unrecovered allowance that may be claimed as a recovery allowance in a tax year. The unrecovered allowance claimed as a recovery allowance in the tax year following the last year of the recovery period may not exceed the amount of the recovery allowance permitted for the last year of the recovery period, assuming that such year consists of 12 months. Any remainder is carried forward until exhausted.

1273. Sale v. Lease of Property. Whether a transaction is treated as a lease or as a purchase for tax purposes is important in determining who is entitled to claim depreciation and other deductions for related business expenses.[87] In most situations, the rules for determining whether a transaction is a lease or a purchase evolved from a series of court decisions and IRS rulings. Basically, the rules look to the economic substance of a transaction, not its form, to determine who is the owner of the property for tax purposes when the parties characterize it as a lease (Rev. Proc. 2001-28, Rev. Proc. 2001-29).

Motor Vehicle Leases. A qualified motor vehicle lease agreement that contains a terminal rental adjustment clause (a provision permitting or requiring the rental price to be adjusted upward or downward by reference to the amount realized by the lessor upon the sale of the vehicle) is treated as a lease if, but for the clause, it would

---

Footnote references are to paragraphs of the 2002 Standard Federal Tax Reports.
[83] ¶ 162.01   [85] ¶ 11,258.055   [87] ¶ 8754.022
[84] ¶ 11,258.05   [86] ¶ 11,252, ¶ 11,258.055

¶ 1273

be treated as a lease for tax purposes (Code Sec. 7701(h)). This provision applies only to qualified agreements with respect to a motor vehicle (including a trailer).[88]

1279. Dispositions of Depreciable Property. See ¶ 1779.

Class Life ADR System

1282. Post-1980 Depreciation Under ADR. If the Asset Depreciation Range (ADR) System was elected for tangible assets first placed in service after 1970 and before 1981, post-1980 depreciation on such assets must be computed under the ADR System.[89]

1284. ADR in General. Under ADR, all tangible assets were placed in specific classes. A class life (called "asset guideline period" in the regulations[90]) was given for each class of assets. In addition, each class of assets other than land improvements and buildings was given a range of years (called "asset depreciation range") that was about 20 percent above and below the class life. For details on the ADR system, see ¶ 11,029.01 and following of the 2002 STANDARD FEDERAL TAX REPORTER.

Deduction for Clean Fuel Vehicles and Refueling Property

1286. Clean Fuel Vehicle Property Deduction. A deduction from gross income is allowed for up to $2,000 of the cost of a clean fuel motor vehicle (up to $5,000 of the cost of a truck or van with a gross vehicle weight above 10,000 pounds and not exceeding 26,000 pounds; up to $50,000 of the cost of a truck or van with a gross vehicle weight above 26,000 pounds, or a bus with a seating capacity exceeding 20 adult passengers) in the year that the vehicle is placed in service (Code Sec. 62(a)(14) and Code Sec. 179A(a)).[91] The deduction applies to property placed in service after June 30, 1993, and before 2005. The deduction will be phased out by 25 percent for vehicles placed in service in calendar year 2002, by 50 percent in 2003, and by 75 percent in 2004 (Code Sec. 179A(b)(1)). Legislation is proposed that would defer the deduction phaseout.

A qualified clean fuel vehicle need not be depreciable property, but it must be acquired for use by the taxpayer, the original use must commence with the taxpayer, and it must meet certain environmental standards. The deduction pertains to that portion of the basis of a vehicle attributable to an engine which uses clean fuel, property installed (including installation costs) to convert a vehicle to the use of clean fuel, or in connection with the exhaust from such vehicles.

A clean-fuel vehicle is one that uses natural gas, liquefied natural gas, liquefied petroleum gas, hydrogen, electricity, or any other fuel that is at least 85% methanol, ethanol, any other alcohol, or ether.

No deduction is allowed for qualified electric vehicles, vehicles operated on rails, vehicles with less than four wheels, property used outside the U.S., or for costs that are expensed under Code Sec. 179. This deduction is not subject to the Code Sec. 280F limitation imposed on luxury cars (¶ 1214).

For property placed in service after August 5, 1997, and before January 1, 2005, the Code Sec. 280F limits on depreciation for "luxury" cars (¶ 1214) have been modified for electric vehicles and cars that have been equipped to qualify as clean-burning fuel vehicles. For electric passenger cars built by an original equipment manufacturer, the yearly statutory limits that apply to depreciation for luxury cars (¶ 1214) have been tripled and then adjusted for inflation (Code Sec. 280F(a)(1)(C)(ii)).[92]

Footnote references are to paragraphs of the 2002 Standard Federal Tax Reports.

88 ¶ 11,274.023	91 ¶ 6002, ¶ 12,130,	92 ¶ 15,100, ¶ 15,108.025
89 ¶ 11,029.01	¶ 12,133	
90 ¶ 11,026, ¶ 11,029.01		

¶ **1279**

The following chart provides the applicable depreciation caps for electric passenger cars:

Depreciation Caps for Electric Cars

For Electric Cars Placed in Service After	Before	Year 1	Year 2	Year 3	Year 4, etc.	Authority
8/5/97	1/1/98	$9,480	$15,100	$9,050	$5,425	Rev. Proc. 98-24
12/31/97	1/1/99	$9,380	$15,000	$8,950	$5,425	Rev. Proc. 98-30
12/31/98	1/1/00	$9,280	$14,900	$8,950	$5,325	Rev. Proc. 99-14
12/31/99	1/1/01	$9,280	$14,800	$8,850	$5,325	Rev. Proc. 2000-18
12/31/00	1/1/02	$9,280	$14,800	$8,850	$5,325	Rev. Proc. 2001-19

For passenger vehicles that initially used nonclean-burning fuel, but were modified to allow them to be propelled by clean-burning fuel, the Code Sec. 280F limits do not apply to the cost of the installed device that equips the car to use clean-burning fuel. The balance of the car's cost remains subject to the Code Sec. 280F limits (Code Sec. 280F(a)(1)(C)).[93]

A deduction from gross income is also allowed for the aggregate cost of qualified clean fuel vehicle refueling property up to $100,000 per location minus the aggregate amount of such property at such location previously deducted by the taxpayer or a related person (Code Sec. 179A(b)(2)).[94]

Qualified clean fuel vehicle refueling property is depreciable property (other than a building and its structural components) the original use of which begins with the taxpayer that either (a) stores or dispenses clean-burning fuel into the fuel tank of a clean fuel vehicle at a refueling location or (b) recharges electric vehicles at a recharging location (Code Sec. 179A(d)).[95]

These deductions are recaptured when property ceases to be eligible for them (Code Sec. 179A(e)(4); Reg. § 1.179A-1).[96] If the recapture event occurs within one, two, or three years after the property is placed in service, the portion of the deduction for clean-fuel vehicles recaptured is 100, 67, and 33 percent, respectively. The deduction for refueling property is recaptured ratably if such property ceases to be eligible during the recovery period for such property. For depreciable property, these deductions would be treated as depreciation deductions, and they would be recaptured upon the sale or disposition of property.

Amortization

1287. Amortization. Amortization is the recovery of certain capital expenditures, that are not ordinarily deductible, in a manner that is similar to straight-line depreciation. That portion of the basis of property that is recovered through amortization deductions may not also be depreciated.

Taxpayers may elect to amortize over a 60-month period the cost of certified pollution control facilities added to or used in connection with a plant in operation before 1976. When the property to be amortized is placed in service before 1981, the amortization deduction is available only for the portion of the property's basis attributable to the first 15 years of its useful life (Code Sec. 169).[97] Business taxpayers can elect to deduct up to $15,000 of the costs of removing certain architectural and transportation barriers for handicapped or elderly persons in the year paid or incurred instead of capitalizing and depreciating such costs (Code Sec. 190).[98] Rapid amortization is also allowed over an 84-month period for up to $10,000 annually of qualified reforestation expenditures (Code Sec. 194).[99]

Footnote references are to paragraphs of the 2002 Standard Federal Tax Reports.

[93] ¶ 15,100, ¶ 12,133.029 [96] ¶ 12,133.03 [98] ¶ 12,260, ¶ 12,264
[94] ¶ 12,130, ¶ 12,133 [97] ¶ 11,502, ¶ 11,517 [99] ¶ 12,330, ¶ 12,335
[95] ¶ 12,130, ¶ 12,133.022

1288. Amortization of Section 197 Intangibles. The capitalized cost of goodwill and most other intangibles acquired after August 10, 1993, and used in a trade or business or for the production of income are ratably amortized over a 15-year period generally beginning in the month of acquisition (Code Sec. 197).[100] Intangibles amortizable under this provision are referred to as "section 197 intangibles."

The following intangibles are section 197 intangibles: (1) goodwill, going concern value, and covenants not to compete entered into in connection with the acquisition of a trade or business (¶ 1743); (2) workforce in place; (3) information base; (4) a patent, copyright, formula, design, or similar item; (5) any customer-based intangible; (6) any supplier-based intangible; (7) any license, permit, or other right granted by a governmental unit or agency; and (8) any franchise, trademark, or trade name (Code Sec. 197(d)).[101]

Generally, self-created intangibles are not amortized under Code Sec. 197 unless created in connection with the acquisition of a trade or business. Exceptions are provided for government-granted licenses, permits, and rights, covenants not to compete entered into in connection with the purchase of a business, and franchises, trademarks, and trade names (Code Sec. 197(c)(2)).[102]

The following intangibles are specifically excluded from the definition of a section 197 intangible: (1) interests in a corporation, partnership, trust, or estate; (2) interests under certain financial contracts; (3) interests in land; (4) computer software not acquired in connection with the purchase of a business or which is readily available for purchase by the general public, is subject to a nonexclusive license, and has not been substantially modified (¶ 980); (5) certain separately acquired rights and interests, including an interest in a patent or copyright or an interest in a film, sound recording, videotape, book, or similar property; (6) interests under existing leases of tangible property; (7) interests under existing indebtedness; (8) sports franchises; (9) residential mortgage servicing rights; and (10) professional fees and transaction costs incurred in a corporate organization or reorganization (Code Sec. 197(e)).[103]

No loss may be claimed when an amortizable section 197 intangible is disposed of if any other section 197 intangibles acquired in the same transaction are retained. The bases of the retained section 197 intangibles are increased by the amount of the unrecognized loss (Code Sec. 197(f)).[104]

Generally, Code Sec. 197 applies to acquisitions made after August 10, 1993, or, on an elective basis, to all property acquired after July 25, 1991.[105] However, anti-churning rules prevent the provision from applying to section 197 intangibles that were not amortizable under prior law, if held or used by a taxpayer or a related person before the effective date and in certain other circumstances.[106]

DEPLETION

What Is Depletion?

1289. Deduction for Depletion. A deduction for depletion is allowed in determining the taxable income from natural resources. The deduction is similar to depreciation in that it allows the taxpayer to recover the cost of an asset over the resources' productive life. "Depletion" is the exhaustion of natural resources, such as mines, wells, and timberlands, as a result of production. The right to a depletion allowance is based upon the taxpayer's economic interest in the property (Reg.

Footnote references are to paragraphs of the 2002 Standard Federal Tax Reports.

[100] ¶ 12,450, ¶ 12,455	[103] ¶ 12,450, ¶ 12,455.034	[105] ¶ 12,455.06
[101] ¶ 12,450, ¶ 12,455.023	[104] ¶ 12,450, ¶ 12,455.035	[106] ¶ 12,455.044
[102] ¶ 12,450, ¶ 12,455.033		

¶ 1288

§ 1.611-1(b)(i)).[107] An economic interest exists if the taxpayer (1) has acquired by investment any interest in minerals in place or in standing timber and (2) looks to the income from the extraction of the minerals or severance of the timber for a return on investment.[108]

The basic method of computing depletion is "cost depletion" (Code Sec. 612).[109] The basis upon which the deduction is allowed is the adjusted basis of the property (Reg. § 1.612-1).[110] Determination of cost depletion first requires an estimate of the number of units (tons, barrels, etc.) that make up the deposit. Then that part of the cost or other adjusted basis of the property that is allocable to the depletable reserves is divided by the number of units. The quotient is the cost depletion per unit. This amount, multiplied by the number of units extracted and sold during the year, determines the cost depletion deductible for the year. Each year the "cost basis" of the property is reduced, but not below zero, by the amount of depletion deducted for that year, whether cost or percentage depletion was used. The remaining basis is used in computing cost depletion for the next year.

An alternative method of computing depletion, known as percentage depletion, may be used for almost all depletable property. However, timber is excluded from this method (Reg. § 1.611-1(a)(1)).[111] Under this method a flat percentage of *gross income* from the property is taken as the depletion deduction. The percentage depletion deduction may not exceed 50% (100% in the case of oil or gas properties) of the *taxable income* from the property (see ¶ 1294 for special rules concerning independent producers and royalty owners) computed without regard to the depletion allowance. In computing taxable income, the deductible mining expenses must be decreased by the amount of Sec. 1245 gains allocable to the property (Code Sec. 613(a)).[112] If cost depletion results in a greater deduction, cost depletion must be used (Reg. § 1.613-1).[113]

Ordinarily, the lease of a mineral property requires the lessee to make an advance payment, known as a bonus or advance royalty. In such a case, the lessor's cost depletion allowance must be allocated between the advance lump-sum payment and the royalties received during the period of extraction (Reg. § 1.612-3).[114] Unlike bonuses or advance royalties, "shut-in" oil payments and delay rentals are not depletable.[115]

Coal and iron ore royalties retained upon the disposition of coal and iron ore generally held for more than one year before mining are eligible for percentage depletion for any tax year in which the maximum rate of tax imposed on net capital gain equals or exceeds the maximum rate for ordinary income (Code Sec. 631(c)).[116]

Depletion is subject to recapture as ordinary income upon the sale or other disposition of an oil, gas, geothermal, or other mineral property at a gain (Code Sec. 1254).[117] Recapture is limited to the amount by which the depletion deduction reduced the adjusted basis of the disposed property.

Mineral Production Payments

1291. Mineral Production Payments. A mineral production payment is treated as a loan by the owner of the production payment to the owner of the mineral property (Code Sec. 636).[118] Thus, a carved-out mineral production payment—created when the owner of a mineral property sells or carves out a portion of the future production with payment secured by an interest in the minerals—is treated as a mortgage loan on the mineral property rather than as an economic interest in the property. All the income from the property is taxed to the seller (owner of the

Footnote references are to paragraphs of the 2002 Standard Federal Tax Reports.

[107] ¶ 23,922
[108] ¶ 23,924.027
[109] ¶ 23,940, ¶ 23,942
[110] ¶ 23,941, ¶ 23,942.021

[111] ¶ 23,922, ¶ 29,960, ¶ 23,963
[112] ¶ 23,960, ¶ 23,963
[113] ¶ 23,961, ¶ 23,963.01
[114] ¶ 23,946, ¶ 23,948.01

[115] ¶ 23,963.60
[116] ¶ 24,150, ¶ 24,156.021
[117] ¶ 31,060, ¶ 31,066
[118] ¶ 24,170, ¶ 24,176

working interest) and is subject to depletion by him. The owner of the production payment does not get depletion.

When the owner of a mineral interest sells the working interest, a retained production payment is treated as a purchase money mortgage loan and not as an economic interest in the mineral property. Accordingly, all the income from the property is taxed to the purchaser and is subject to depletion by him. The seller who retains the production payment is not entitled to depletion.

Percentage Depletion

1294. Oil and Gas Production. A 22% depletion rate is allowed for oil and gas production in the case of regulated natural gas and natural gas sold under a fixed contract (but not certain casinghead gas contracts[119]); a 10% rate applies to geopressurized methane gas wells (Code Sec. 613A(b)).[120]

A 15% depletion rate applies to independent producers and royalty owners with limitations based on average daily production (Code Sec. 613A(c)).[121] The rate applies to an average daily production of 1,000 barrels of oil and six million cubic feet of gas. The percentage depletion deduction is generally limited to the lesser of 65% of the *taxable income* before the depletion allowance (Code Sec. 613A(d)(1))[122] or 100% of the *taxable income from the property* before the depletion allowance (see ¶ 1289). For purposes of the 65% limit, taxable income is computed without regard to any net operating loss carryback or capital loss carryback. Any portion of a depletion allowance disallowed under the 65% limit may be carried over. Percentage depletion is also denied for lease bonuses, advance royalty payments, or other amounts payable without regard to actual production from an oil, gas or geothermal property (see ¶ 1296) (Code Sec. 613(e)(3) and Code Sec. 613A(d)(5)).[123]

For tax years beginning after December 31, 1997, and before January 1, 2002, the 100% taxable income limit on percentage depletion deductions for oil and gas properties has been suspended for marginal properties (Code Sec. 613A(c)(6)(H), as amended by P.L. 106-170).[124] Legislation is proposed that would extend this provision or make it permanent.

The 15% depletion rate for marginal oil or gas production properties held by independent producers or royalty owners increases by one percent (up to a maximum 25% rate) for each whole dollar that the reference price for crude oil for the preceding calendar year is less than $20 per barrel (Code Sec. 613A(c)(6)).[125] The allowance for depletion is computed using the increased rate with respect to the portion of the taxpayer's average daily marginal production of domestic crude oil and natural gas that does not exceed the taxpayer's depletable quantities of those products. An election may be made to have this rule apply to the pro rata portion of marginal production. The applicable percentage for marginal production for tax years beginning in 2001 is 15% (19% in 2000) (Notice 2001-53).

1296. Geothermal Deposits. Geothermal deposits (geothermal reservoirs consisting of natural heat that is stored in rocks or in an aqueous liquid or vapor (whether or not under pressure)) are eligible for a 15% depletion allowance (Code Sec. 613(e)).[126]

Footnote references are to paragraphs of the 2002 Standard Federal Tax Reports.

[119] ¶ 23,924.039, ¶ 23,988.01
[120] ¶ 23,980, ¶ 23,988.021
[121] ¶ 23,980, ¶ 23,988.024
[122] ¶ 23,980, ¶ 23,988.024
[123] ¶ 23,960, ¶ 23,980, ¶ 23,988.036
[124] ¶ 23,980, ¶ 23,988.044
[125] ¶ 23,980, ¶ 23,988.04
[126] ¶ 23,960, ¶ 23,965.03

1298. Coal or Other Minerals. Percentage depletion is allowed, under Code Sec. 613(b),[127] at the following percentages of "gross income from the property":

(a) 22%—sulphur and uranium; and, if from deposits in the United States, anorthosite, clay, laterite, and nephelite syenite (to the extent that alumina and aluminum compounds are extracted therefrom), asbestos, bauxite, celestite, chromite, corundum, fluorspar, graphite, ilmenite, kyanite, mica, olivine, quartz crystals (radio grade), rutile, block steatite talc, and zircon, and ores of the following metals: antimony, beryllium, bismuth, cadmium, cobalt, columbium, lead lithium, manganese, mercury, molybdenum, nickel, platinum and platinum group metals, tantalum, thorium, tin, titanium, tungsten, vanadium and zinc.

(b) 15%—if from deposits in the United States, gold, silver, copper, iron ore, and oil shale (except shale described in (e) below).

(c) 14%—metal mines (other than metals from deposits in the United States to which the 22% rate in (a) applies), rock asphalt, and vermiculite; if (a) above and (e) and (f) below do not apply, ball clay, bentonite, china clay, sagger clay, and clay used or sold for use for purposes dependent on its refractory properties.

(d) 10%—asbestos from deposits outside the United States, brucite, coal, lignite, perlite, sodium chloride, and wollastonite.

(e) 7½%—clay and shale used or sold for use in the manufacture of sewer pipe or brick, and clay, shale, and slate used or sold for use as sintered or burned lightweight aggregates.

(f) 5%—gravel, peat, pumice, sand, scoria, shale (except shale described in (b) and (e) above) and stone (except stone falling within the general 14% group described in (g)); clay used, or sold for use, in the manufacture of drainage and roofing tile, flower pots, and kindred products; also, if from brine wells, bromite, calcium chloride, and magnesium chloride.

(g) 14%—all other minerals not included in any of the categories listed above. For purposes of this paragraph, the term "all other minerals" does not include (A) soil, sod, dirt, turf, water, or mosses; (B) minerals from sea water, the air, or similar inexhaustible sources; or (C) oil and gas wells.

"Gross income from the property," on which percentage depletion is based, is that amount of income which comes from the extraction of the ores or minerals from the ground and the application of mining processes, including mining transportation (Code Sec. 613(c)).[128] Mining processes include certain specified treatment processes. In general, it can be said that the percentage depletion allowance is based on the mined product after application of those treatment processes applied by "ordinary" miners. Hence, an integrated miner-manufacturer computes gross income from mining at the point when the non-integrated miner disposes of the product. Gross income is computed by use of the representative market or field price. However, when it is impossible to determine such a field price, and where the IRS does not determine that a more appropriate method should be used, the proportionate profits method must be used (Reg. § 1.613-4(d)).[129]

Chapter 13

TAX CREDITS

NONREFUNDABLE CREDITS

Personal Credits

1301. Child and Dependent Care Credit. A nonrefundable credit is allowed for a portion of qualifying child or dependent care expenses paid for the purpose of allowing the taxpayer to be gainfully employed (Code Sec. 21).[1] The credit is computed on Form 2441,"Child and Dependent Care Expenses," or Schedule 2 of Form 1040A, whichever is applicable. To be eligible for the credit, the taxpayer must maintain a household for one of the following individuals:

(1) A dependent under age 13 for whom a dependency exemption may be claimed.

(2) Any other person who is physically or mentally incapable of caring for himself. In this case, the taxpayer must either (a) be able to claim the person as a dependent or (b) be able to claim the person as a dependent except for the fact that the person had income exceeding the exemption amount.

(3) The taxpayer's spouse who is physically or mentally incapable of self-care.

(4) Certain dependent children of divorced parents (see below).

Qualifying expenses include expenses paid for household services and for the care of a qualifying individual. Services outside the home qualify if they involve the care of a qualified child or a disabled spouse or dependent who regularly spends at least eight hours a day in the taxpayer's home. Payments to a relative also qualify for the credit unless the taxpayer claims a dependency exemption for the relative or if the relative is the taxpayer's child and is under age 19. However, no credit is

---

Footnote references are to paragraphs of the 2002 Standard Federal Tax Reports.

¶ **1301**   [1] ¶ 3502

allowed for expenses incurred to send a child or other dependent to an overnight camp.

Amount of Credit. The maximum amount of employment-related expenses to which the credit may be applied is $2,400 if one qualifying child or dependent is involved or $4,800 if two or more are involved less excludable employer dependent care assistance program payments. The credit is equal to 30% of employment-related expenses for taxpayers with adjusted gross income of $10,000 or less. For taxpayers with adjusted gross income over $10,000, the credit is reduced by one percentage point for each $2,000 of adjusted gross income (or fraction thereof) over $10,000. For taxpayers with AGIs of over $28,000, the credit is 20%.

Qualifying employment-related expenses are considered in determining the credit only to the extent of earned income—wages, salary, remuneration for personal services, net self-employment income, etc. For married taxpayers, expenses are limited to the earned income of the lower-earning spouse. Generally, if one spouse is not working, no credit is allowed. However, if the nonworking spouse is physically or mentally incapable of caring for himself or is a full-time student at an educational organization for at least five calendar months during the year, the law assumes an earned income—for each month of disability or school attendance—of $200 if there is one qualifying child or dependent or of $400 if there are two or more.

> **Example.** A widower pays a housekeeper $5,000 to take care of his home and 10-year-old daughter while he is working. For 2001, his adjusted gross income was $25,000. Since there is only one qualifying child, the maximum credit he can claim is $528 (22% of $2,400).

Generally, a married taxpayer must file a joint return to claim the credit. However, a married person living apart from his spouse under the circumstances described at ¶ 173 is considered unmarried for this purpose, except that the spouse must not have been a member of the household during the last six months of the tax year. Also, a divorced or legally separated taxpayer having custody of a disabled or under-age-13 child is entitled to the credit even though he or she has released the right to a dependency exemption for the child or is not entitled to the exemption under the terms of a pre-1985 divorce decree or settlement agreement (Code Sec. 21(e)).[2] Taxpayers must provide each dependent's taxpayer identification number in order to claim the credit, as well as the identifying number of the service provider (Code Sec. 21(e)(9); Code Sec. 21(e)(10); Notice 89-71).

Future Change. The applicable percentage and allowable employment-related expenses increase beginning in 2003. The maximum applicable percentage will be increased to 35 percent and the allowable employment-related expenses will be increased to $3,000 for one qualifying child and $6,000 for two or more qualifying children (Code Sec. 21, as amended by the Economic Growth and Tax Relief Reconciliation Act of 2001). Thus, the maximum credit will rise to $1,050 for one qualifying child and $2,100 for two or more qualifying children.

1302. Child Tax Credit. Taxpayers who have qualifying children, i.e., a child, descendant, stepchild, or eligible foster child who is a U.S. citizen and for whom the taxpayer may claim a dependency exemption and who is less than 17 years old as of the close of the tax year, are entitled to the child tax credit (Code Sec. 24).[3] The credit is allowed only for tax years consisting of 12 months. Beginning in 2001, the amount of the child tax credit will increase gradually over ten years to $1,000. For 2001 through 2004, the credit will be $600; for 2005 through 2008; the credit will be $700; for 2009, the credit will be $800; and for 2010 and thereafter, the credit will be $1,000 (Code Sec. 24(a), as amended by the Economic Growth and Tax Relief Reconciliation Act of 2001 (P.L. 107-16)).

Limitation of Child Tax Credit Based on AGI. The child tax credit begins to phase out when modified adjusted gross income (AGI) reaches $110,000 for joint filers, $55,000 for married taxpayers filing separately, and $75,000 for single

---

Footnote references are to paragraphs of the 2002 Standard Federal Tax Reports.

[2] ¶ 3502   [3] ¶ 3760   **¶ 1302**

U.S. Master Tax Guide

taxpayers. The credit is reduced by $50 for each $1,000, or fraction thereof, of modified AGI above the threshold (Code Sec. 24(b)).

Refundable Amount of Child Tax Credit. Effective after December 31, 2000, at least a portion of the child credit is refundable for all taxpayers, regardless of the amount of the taxpayer's regular tax or alternative minimum tax liability (see *Tax Liability Limitation* below). Beginning in 2001 and running through 2004, the child tax credit is refundable to the extent of 10 percent of the taxpayer's earned income in excess of $10,000 up to the per child credit amount. The percentage is increased to 15 percent in 2005 and thereafter. The $10,000 amount is to be inflation adjusted for years after 2001 (projected by CCH to increase to $10,300 in 2002). The amount of the nonrefundable credit is reduced by the amount of the refundable credit (Code Sec. 24(d), as amended by P.L. 107-16).

Supplemental Child Tax Credit. The supplemental credit has been repealed for 2001 and thereafter (Code Sec. 32(n), as repealed by P.L. 107-16).

Amount of Child Tax Credit for Three or More Children. For 2001, taxpayers with three or more children have two alternative methods to calculate their refundable child tax credit. One method is the percentage method explained above in *Refundable Amount of Child Tax Credit.* The other method to determine the refundable portion of the child tax credit is to calculate the excess of the taxpayer's share of social security taxes plus one-half of any self-employment taxes over his or her earned income credit. The taxpayer may then use whichever amount produces the greater child tax credit (Code Sec. 24(d), as amended by P.L. 107-16).

Tax Liability Limitation. Starting in 2002, the limitation on the nonrefundable portion of the child tax credit will be equal to the excess of the regular tax liability plus alternative minimum tax liability over the sum of the taxpayer's other nonrefundable tax credits (other than the child tax credit and the adoption credit) and the foreign tax credit. However, for 2001, the limitation remains equal to the regular and alternative minimum liability less the foreign tax credit (Code Sec. 24(d), as amended by P.L. 107-16).

1303. Credits for Higher Education Tuition. There are two education-related credits: the Hope scholarship credit and the lifetime learning credit. These credits may be claimed by individuals for tuition expenses incurred by students pursuing college or graduate degrees or vocational training (Code Sec. 25A).[4] The Hope scholarship credit provides a maximum allowable credit of $1,500 per student for each of the first two years of post-secondary education. The lifetime learning credit allows a credit of 20 percent of qualified tuition expenses paid by the taxpayer for any year the Hope credit is not claimed.

Specifically, the Hope scholarship credit initially allows taxpayers a 100-percent credit per eligible student for the first $1,000 of tuition expenses (but not room, board or books) and a 50-percent credit for the second $1,000 of tuition paid. The lifetime learning credit is equal to 20 percent of the amount of tuition paid by the taxpayer and is available for the first $5,000 of tuition for tax years beginning before 2003 and for the first $10,000 thereafter.

Eligibility. Both credits are available for qualified tuition and related expenses incurred for the taxpayer, the taxpayer's spouse, or the taxpayer's dependent at an eligible educational institution (Code Sec. 25A(b)(3) and (f)). The $1,500 maximum Hope credit is allowed per student. In contrast, the lifetime learning credit maximum is calculated per taxpayer and does not vary based on the number of students in the taxpayer's family. The credits are elective and nonrefundable (Code Sec. 25A(e)(1)). No double benefit is permitted; the credits are *not* permitted to more than one taxpayer in the same year (i.e., either parent or dependent child, if the parents choose not to claim the dependency exemption for the child (Proposed Reg. § 1.125A-1(g)), may take the credit) and cannot be claimed for the same expenses for which another tax benefit is also received.

Footnote references are to paragraphs of the 2002 Standard Federal Tax Reports.

¶ **1303**   [4] ¶ 3820

The $1,000 amount of tuition expenses eligible for the Hope scholarship credit and the amount used to compute the credit under the formula in Code Sec. 25A(b)(1) are adjusted for inflation beginning in the year 2002 (as are the income limitations below) (projected by CCH to remain $1,000 in 2002). No inflation adjustment is provided for the $5,000 and $10,000 tuition amounts used to determine the amount of the lifetime learning credit.

Income Limitations. The allowable amount of the credits is reduced for taxpayers who have modified adjusted gross income above certain amounts. Modified adjusted gross income is adjusted gross income increased by income earned outside the United States (amounts otherwise excluded from income under Code Secs. 911, 931, and 933). Income earned in Puerto Rico and U.S. possessions is considered to be earned abroad. The phaseout of the credits begins for most taxpayers when modified AGI reaches $40,000 (projected by CCH to increase to $41,000 in 2002); the credits are completely phased out when modified AGI reaches $50,000 (projected to increase to $51,000 in 2002). For joint filers the phaseout range is $80,000 to $100,000 (projected to increase to $82,000 to $102,000 in 2002) (Code Sec. 25A(d)). The Hope credit and the lifetime learning credit are not available to married taxpayers who file separate returns (Code Sec. 25A(g)).

Coordination with Other Provisions. For any tax year, a taxpayer is permitted to elect only one of the following with respect to one student: (1) the Hope credit, (2) the lifetime learning credit, or (3) the exclusion for distributions from a Coverdell education savings account (formerly known as an education IRA) used to pay higher education costs under Code Sec. 530.[5] This election is separate for each student. In addition, the amount of qualified higher education expenses, otherwise taken into account in determining the Series EE U.S. savings bond exclusion, is reduced by the amount taken into account in computing the credit (Code Sec. 25A(c)(2), (e)(2) and (g)(2)(C); Code Sec. 135(d)(2)(A)).

Qualified Tuition Programs. The Economic Growth and Tax Relief Reconciliation Act of 2001 expanded the availability of qualified tuition programs (QTPs) under Code Sec. 529 to private institutions and made distributions from these QTPs excludable for gross income after December 31, 2003 (see ¶ 603). Also, distributions from currently established state QTPs are excludable from income beginning after December 31, 2001. This exclusion must be coordinated with the education credit under the provisions of Code Sec. 25A(g) (Code Sec. 529(c), as amended by P.L. 107-16).

1304. Credit for the Elderly or the Permanently and Totally Disabled. A 15-percent tax credit for the elderly or the permanently and totally disabled applies to citizens or residents who are (1) 65 years of age before the close of the tax year or (2) under age 65, are retired on disability, and were permanently and totally disabled when they retired (Code Sec. 22).[6] Married taxpayers must file a joint return to claim the credit, unless the spouses live apart throughout the tax year. The credit is computed on Schedule R.

For individuals age 65 or older, the initial amount of allowable credit varies with filing status, as follows: [7]

Single individual	$5,000
Married individuals, joint return, one spouse is a qualified individual	5,000
Married individuals, joint return, both spouses are qualified individuals	7,500
Married individual, separate return	3,750

This initial amount is then reduced by amounts received as pension, annuity or disability benefits that are excludable from gross income and are payable under the Social Security Act (Title II), the Railroad Retirement Act of 1974, or a Veterans Administration program or that are excludable under a non-Code provision. No reduction is made for pension, annuity or disability benefits for personal injuries or sickness described in Code Sec. 104(a)(4) and Code Sec. 22(c)(3).

Footnote references are to paragraphs of the 2002 Standard Federal Tax Reports.

[5] ¶ 22,950   [6] ¶ 3550   [7] ¶ 3550   **¶ 1304**

The maximum amount determined above is further reduced by one-half of the excess of the adjusted gross income (AGI) over the following levels, based on filing status (Code Sec. 22(d)):

Single taxpayer	$ 7,500
Married taxpayers, combined AGI on joint return	10,000
Married individual filing separately	5,000

For permanently and totally disabled individuals under age 65, the applicable initial amount noted above may not exceed the amount of disability income. In determining their initial amounts, special rules apply to a married couple filing a joint return where both spouses qualify for the credit and at least one of them is under age 65 (Code Sec. 22(c)(2)(B)).[8]

Disability income for credit purposes means the total amount that is includible in an individual's gross income for the tax year under Code Sec. 72 or Code Sec. 105(a) to the extent the amount constitutes wages (or payments in lieu of wages) for periods during which the individual is absent from work due to permanent and total disability (Code Sec. 22(c)(2)(B)(iii)).

An individual is considered permanently and totally disabled for credit purposes if he is unable to engage in any substantial gainful activity by reason of any medically determinable physical or mental impairment that can be expected to result in death or to last for a continuous period of not less than 12 months. This impairment should be substantiated by a letter from a certified physician kept in the taxpayer's records (Code Sec. 22(a)(3)).

> **Example.** Alex, age 66 and single, has AGI of $8,700 for 2001 and receives $4,000 of nontaxable social security benefits for the year. To determine his credit for the elderly, he would make the following computation:
>
> | | |
> |---|---:|
> | Initial amount | $5,000 |
> | Less: Social security benefits | 4,000 |
> | Reduced initial amount | $1,000 |
> | Less: One-half of AGI above $7,500 | 600 |
> | Amount eligible for credit | $ 400 |
> | Credit: $400 × 15% | $ 60 |

1306. Adoption Credit. Taxpayers may claim a nonrefundable credit on Form 8839, "Qualified Adoption Expenses," of up to $5,000 ($6,000 in the case of a child with special needs) for qualified adoption expenses for each eligible child. The credit is phased out ratably for taxpayers with a modified adjusted gross over $75,000 and no credit is allowed to taxpayers with a modified adjusted gross income of $115,000 or more (Code Sec. 23).[9] A five-year carryforward is provided for the unused portion of such credit that exceeds the limitation imposed by Code Sec. 26.[10]

Qualified adoption expenses include reasonable and necessary adoption fees, court costs, attorney fees and other expenses which are directly related to the legal adoption of an eligible child. Expenses incurred in violation of state or federal law or in connection with the adoption of a child of the taxpayer's spouse are not eligible for the credit. Costs associated with a surrogate parenting arrangement are also ineligible for the credit (Code Sec. 23(d)(1)).

An eligible child is an individual who has not attained the age of 18 as of the time of the adoption or who is physically or mentally incapable of caring for himself. A child with special needs is any child who cannot or should not be returned to the home of his or her parents and a specific factor or condition makes it reasonable to conclude that the child cannot be placed with adoptive parents unless assistance is provided as determined by a state. Also, to qualify as a child with special needs, the child must be a citizen or resident of the United States (Code Sec. 23(d)(2)).

Footnote references are to paragraphs of the 2002 Standard Federal Tax Reports.

¶ 1306   [8] ¶ 3550   [9] ¶ 3700   [10] ¶ 3850

If adoption expenses are paid during a tax year prior to the tax year in which the adoption is finalized, the credit is allowed during the year the adoption is finalized. If adoption expenses are paid during or after the tax year in which the adoption is finalized, the credit is allowed for the tax year in which the expense is paid or incurred.

Taxpayers may not claim the credit for any expense for which another deduction or credit is allowed. This includes amounts excluded from gross income under Code Sec. 137[11] that are paid or incurred by an employer for the employee's qualified adoption expenses pursuant to an adoption assistance program. The dollar limits for the exclusion conform to the dollar limits for the credit (Code Sec. 137). However, any adoption expenses incurred in excess of the amount provided under an employer's adoption assistance program may be used to claim the adoption credit.

Amounts paid or expenses incurred by an employer for qualified adoption expenses under this program are not subject to income tax withholding but are subject to withholding for social security, Medicare, and FUTA taxes. Amounts paid directly to a third party or reimbursed to the taxpayer under an employer's adoption assistance program are to be report on Form W-2 in Box 13 under code T. Employees receiving such payments must make the appropriate adjustments on Form 1040 to include any taxable portion of adoption assistance program payments in gross income in accordance with Form 1040 instructions (Notice 97-9).

2001 Legislation. Starting in 2002, the adoption credit becomes permanent and the amount of eligible expenses increases to $10,000 per eligible child, including special needs children. The beginning point for the income phaseout rule will increase to $150,000 of modified adjusted gross income (Code Sec. 23(b), as amended by the Economic Growth and Tax Relief Reconciliation Act of 2001 (P.L. 107-16)). Both the dollar limitation and the income limitation amounts will be inflation-adjusted after 2002 (Code Sec. 23(h), as amended by P.L. 107-16).

P.L. 107-16 also made significant changes to the exclusion available for employer-sponsored adoption assistance programs. The amount which may be excluded increases to $10,000. Also, the exclusion becomes permanent for years after 2002 (Code Sec. 137, as amended by P.L. 107-16).

1307. Credit for Elective Deferrals and IRA Contributions. Starting in 2002, eligible taxpayers will be able to claim a nonrefundable credit for their contributions to elective deferral plans or individual retirement accounts (IRAs) (Code Sec. 25B, as added by the Economic Growth and Tax Relief Reconciliation Act of 2001 (P.L. 107-16)).[12] The credit amount will equal the eligible taxpayer's applicable percentage, determined by filing status and adjusted gross income, multiplied by the total qualified retirement savings contributions (not to exceed $2,000) in the tax year to certain specified retirement plans. The maximum credit amount is $1,000. The credit is in addition to the exclusion or deduction from gross income for making elective deferrals and IRA contributions that are otherwise allowed. The credit is set to terminate for tax years after 2006.

To be eligible, an individual making a contribution to a qualified retirement savings plan must be at least 18 years of age at the close of the tax year, must *not* be claimed as a dependent by someone else, and must *not* be a student as defined at Code Sec. 151(c)(4). A qualified retirement savings plan contribution is defined as the sum of:

(1) the amount of the qualified retirement contribution as defined in Code Sec. 219(e) (relating to retirement savings),

(2) any elective deferrals as defined in Code Sec. 402(g)(3) (relating to deferrals of certain specified employer contributions),

(3) any elective deferrals of compensation under an eligible Code Sec. 457(b) plan of a state or local government or tax-exempt organization, and

---

Footnote references are to paragraphs of the 2002 Standard Federal Tax Reports.

[11] ¶ 7600   [12] ¶ 3838   **¶ 1307**

(4) any voluntary employee contributions to any qualified retirement plan as defined at Code Sec. 4974(c).

This definition includes any contributions to Roth IRAs, but the amount must be reduced by any distributions from certain qualified retirement plans (Code Sec. 25B(d)(2), as added by P.L. 107-16). The amount of distributions is measured during a testing period defined as the current tax year, the two preceding tax years, and the following tax year up to the due date of the return including extensions. The applicable percentage is a maximum of 50 percent which phases out at $50,000 for joint return filers, at $37,500 for head of household filers, and at $25,000 for single and married filing separately filers. The applicable percentage is the percentage as determined in accordance with the following table:

Adjusted Gross Income						
Joint return		Head of a household		All other cases		Applicable percentage
Over	Not over	Over	Not over	Over	Not over	
$ 0	$30,000	$ 0	$22,500	$ 0	$15,000	50
30,000	32,500	22,500	24,375	15,000	16,250	20
32,500	50,000	24,375	37,500	16,250	25,000	10
50,000	—	37,500	—	25,000	—	0

1308. Credit for Interest on Certain Home Mortgages. Low-income homeowners who obtain qualified mortgage credit certificates (MCCs) from state or local governments may claim a tax credit on Form 8396, "Mortgage Interest Credit (For Holders of Qualified Credit Certificates Issued by State or Local Governmental Units or Agencies)," during any tax year for which the certificate is in effect for a portion of the interest paid or incurred. An MCC is in effect for interest attributable to the period beginning on the date the certificate is issued and ending when either (1) it is revoked by the issuing authority or (2) the taxpayer sells the residence or ceases to use it as a personal residence (Code Sec. 25). Any mortgage interest deduction under Code Sec. 163 must be reduced by any credit allowed under this provision (Code Sec. 163(g)).

The credit is an amount equal to the product of (1) the certificate credit rate (which may not be less than 10% or more than 50%) and (2) the interest paid or accrued by the taxpayer for the year on the remaining principal of the certified indebtedness (plus, a limited carryforward, if any). If the credit rate exceeds 20%, the tax credit for any year may not exceed $2,000 (Code Sec. 25(a)(2)(A)).[13]

A three-year carryforward is provided for the unused portion of such credit caused by the limitation imposed by Code Sec. 26. The amount of any unused credit which may be applied in any tax year is also limited by Code Sec. 25(e)(1)(B).

1310. Credit for First-Time Homebuyers for District of Columbia. First-time homebuyers who purchase a principal residence in the District of Columbia may claim a nonrefundable personal credit of up to $5,000 on Form 8859, "District of Columbia First-Time Homebuyer Credit." The credit is reduced for adjusted gross income in excess of $70,000 ($110,000 in the case of a joint return). The purchase must be after August 4, 1997, but before January 1, 2004 to qualify. Any unused credit may be carried forward indefinitely. Finally, a taxpayer must adjust the basis in the principal residence by the amount of credit taken (Code Sec. 1400C).

1310A. Rate Reduction Credit. The Economic Growth and Tax Relief Reconciliation Act of 2001 (P.L. 107-16) created a new 10-percent tax bracket. Most taxpayers received the benefit of this new tax bracket in the form of a tax rebate check issued by the IRS. To ensure that all taxpayers received the full benefit of the new tax bracket in 2001, a one-time credit was created for those who either did not

Footnote references are to paragraphs of the 2002 Standard Federal Tax Reports.

¶ **1308**   [13] ¶ 3800

receive or failed to qualify for a rebate check. The credit will be calculated on a worksheet in the form instructions, taking into account any advanced rebate check received, and recorded on the appropriate line of the form. The maximum amount of the credit is $300 for singles, $500 for head of households and $600 for joint return filers. However, P.L. 107-16 disqualified certain taxpayers based on their 2000 filing status from receiving advanced rebate checks. At the time of publication, legislation is proposed to clarify if these disqualified taxpayers, based on their change of filing status in 2001, may now claim the rate reduction credit. See ¶ 126.

Foreign Tax Credit

1311. Foreign Tax Credit. A taxpayer may deduct foreign income taxes paid or accrued or may apply them as a credit against U.S. income tax (Code Sec. 27).[14] See ¶ 2475. The credit is claimed on Form 1116, "Foreign Tax Credit," unless the total foreign taxes paid are less than $300 for single filers ($600 for married filing jointly). In such case, the credit may be claimed directly on Form 1040 if all filing requirements are satisfied. See ¶ 2477.

Alternative Fuels Credit

1319. Fuel Production from Nonconventional Source. A tax credit is allowed for the domestic production of oil, gas, and synthetic fuels derived from nonconventional sources (such as shale, tar sands, coal seams, and geopressured brine) that are sold to unrelated persons.[15] The credit is claimed by attaching a separate schedule to the tax return showing how the credit was computed. For 2000, the credit is $6.14 ($3.00 in case of a credit derived from gas from a tight formation) per 5.8 million BTUs (energy equivalent of one barrel of oil) produced and sold from facilities placed in service after 1979 and before 1993 or from wells drilled after 1979 and before 1993. Such fuels must be sold before 2003. The time period is extended for certain facilities placed in service before July 1, 1998, subject to a written binding contract in effect before 1997. The credit is reduced by an amount which bears the same ratio to the amount of the credit as (1) the amount by which the reference price for the calendar year in which the sale occurs ($26.73 for 2000) exceeds $23.50 bears to (2) $6. The base credit amount (except in the case of gas from a tight formation) and phaseout range amounts are adjusted for inflation. The inflation adjustment factor for 2000 is 2.0454 (Notice 2001-31). Producers of certain natural gases from nonconventional sources may not claim a credit for such fuels if they elect an incentive price for the gas under the Natural Gas Policy Act of 1978 (Code Sec. 29(e)). The Code makes no provision for carryover of any unused credit to future tax years.

Credit for Qualified Electric Vehicles

1321. Credit for Qualified Electric Vehicles. A nonrefundable credit calculated on Form 8834, "Qualified Electric Vehicle Credit," is allowed for 10 percent of the cost of a qualified electric vehicle in the year that it is placed in service for vehicles placed in service after June 30, 1993 and before 2005 (Code Sec. 30; Reg. § 1.30-1).[16] The maximum credit is $4,000 per qualified electric vehicle. The portion of the cost of a qualified electric vehicle that is expensed under Code Sec. 179 is ineligible for the credit.

The credit applies to a motor vehicle powered primarily by an electric motor drawing current from rechargeable batteries, fuel cells, or other portable sources of electric current. The original use of the vehicle must commence with the taxpayer. For vehicles placed in service in 2002 through 2004, the credit is reduced 25 percent each year (legislation proposed that would defer the credit phaseout). The basis of a qualified electric vehicle is reduced by the amount of the credit allowed. The credit

---

400 U.S. Master Tax Guide

is recaptured as an increase in tax in the year in which the vehicle ceases to be a qualified electric vehicle.

Business-Related Credits

1323. General Business Credit. The general business credit is a limited nonrefundable credit against income tax that is claimed after all other nonrefundable credits (Code Secs. 21, 22, 23, 25, 27, 29 and 30), except the credit for prior year minimum tax (Code Sec. 53).

The general business credit for a tax year is the sum of (1) the business credit carryforwards to the year, (2) the amount of the current year business credit, and (3) the business credit carrybacks to the year.

The current year general business credit is the sum of (1) the investment credit (¶ 1345), which is composed of (a) the rehabilitation credit, (b) the energy credit, and (c) the reforestation credit; (2) the work opportunity credit (for employees who begin work after September 30, 1996, and before December 31, 2001) (¶ 1342); (3) the welfare-to-work credit (for employees who begin work after December 31, 1997, and before December 31, 2001) (¶ 1343); (4) the alcohol fuels credit (¶ 1326); (5) the increased research expenditures credit (¶ 1330); (6) the low-income housing credit (¶ 1334); (7) the enhanced oil recovery credit (¶ 1336); (8) the disabled access credit (¶ 1338); (9) the renewable resources electricity production credit (¶ 1339); (10) the empowerment zone employment credit (for wages paid after 1993) (¶ 1339A); (11) the Indian employment credit (for wages paid after 1993) (¶ 1340); (12) the employer social security credit (for FICA taxes paid after 1993) (¶ 1341); (13) the orphan drug credit (¶ 1344); and (14) the new markets credit (¶ 1335).

The Economic Growth and Tax Relief Reconciliation Act of 2001 added two new credits to the general business credit which will be effective for tax years starting in 2002. These credits, which will follow the new markets credit in this order, are the small employer pension plan start-up costs credit (¶ 1344B) and the employer-provided child care credit (1344C). The current year business credit also includes the credit for contributions to certain community development corporations (applies to contributions on or after August 10, 1993) (¶ 1325) and the credit for unused payments into the trans-Alaska pipeline liability fund. Each of the credits of the general business credit is computed separately. If more than one of these components is claimed, or if there is a general business credit carryback or carryforward, Form 3800, "General Business Credit," along with the appropriate form must be filed with the return.

The components of the general business credit arising in a single year are deemed used in the same order in which they are listed above, with the following modifications. The empowerment zone employment credit is figured separately and, while a part of the general business credit, is not claimed on Form 3800. To accommodate unused carryovers of repealed credits, the former employee stock ownership credit (the so-called ESOP credit) is inserted into the above list between the credit for contributions to certain community development corporations and the credit for unused payments to the trans-Alaska pipeline liability fund. Also, the former regular investment credit is inserted in the list preceding the rehabilitation credit and the former additional investment credit for contributions to employee stock ownership plans (the so-called TRASOP credit) is inserted in the above list following the rehabilitation credit.

Limitations. The general business credit may not exceed a limitation based on the amount of tax liability. This limitation is determined separately for the general business credit attributable to (1) components other than the empowerment zone employment credit and (2) the empowerment zone employment credit component. For purposes of (1), the general business credit may not exceed net income tax less the greater of (a) the tentative minimum tax or (b) 25% of net regular tax liability above $25,000. For purposes of (2), the general business credit may not exceed net

¶ 1323

income tax less the greater of (a) 75% of the tentative minimum tax or (b) 25% of net regular tax liability above $25,000. The result under (2) is reduced by the general business credit allowed for the tax year that is attributable to the components other than the empowerment zone employment credit to arrive at the limitation on the general business credit attributable to the empowerment zone employment credit component. Net income tax is the sum of the regular tax (as defined in Code Sec. 26) and the alternative minimum tax imposed under Code Sec. 55, less all other nonrefundable credits (Code Secs. 21, 22, 23, 25, 27, 29 and 30, except the credit for prior year minimum tax (Code Sec. 53)). Net regular tax liability is the regular tax liability reduced by these credits.

For a married couple filing separate returns, the $25,000 figure above is limited to $12,500 for each spouse. If, however, one spouse has no current credit or unused credit, the spouse having current credit or unused credit may use the full $25,000 figure in determining his or her credit for the year. For a controlled group of corporations, the group may divide the $25,000 figure among its members in any way the members choose. For an estate or trust, the $25,000 figure is reduced to an amount that bears the same ratio to $25,000 as the portion of the estate's or trust's income that is not allocated to the beneficiaries bears to the total income of the estate or trust (Code Sec. 38(c)(3)(D)).

Carrybacks and Carryforwards of Unused Credits. When the general business credit exceeds the above limitation in any year, the excess or unused credit may be carried back one year and forward 20 years (3-year carryback and 15-year carryforward for credits that arise in tax years beginning before 1998) (Code Sec. 39).[17] The order in which these credits are claimed in any carryback or carryforward year is as follows: (1) carryforwards to that year on a first-in, first-out (FIFO) basis; (2) the business credit earned in that year; and (3) the carrybacks to that year on a FIFO basis.

Separate carryback and carryforward records must be maintained for the amount of the general business credit attributable to (1) the empowerment zone employment credit and (2) each of the other components of the general business credit (Code Sec. 38(c)(2)(A)). Separate recordkeeping is necessary because the empowerment zone employment credit may offset up to 25% of the taxpayer's alternative minimum tax (Code Sec. 38(c)(2)(A)). In addition, there are restrictions on the carryback/carryforward of certain credits such as the empowerment zone employment credit which may not be carried back to a tax year ending before 1994. For carryback/carryforward restrictions on other credits, see the respective credits.

1325. Credit for Contributions to CDCs. A nonrefundable credit may be claimed on Form 8847, "Credit for Contributions to Certain Community Development Corporations," for qualified cash contributions (including loans or investments) made to qualified community development corporations (CDCs).[18] Five percent of the amount contributed may be claimed as a credit for each tax year during a 10-year credit period beginning with the tax year in which the contribution is made. This credit is claimed as one of the components of the general business credit.

1326. Alcohol Fuels Credit. The alcohol fuels credit is the sum of the alcohol mixture credit, the alcohol credit, and the small ethanol producer credit (Code Sec. 40).[19]

The alcohol mixture credit is 60 cents per gallon for alcohol of at least 190 proof (45 cents per gallon for alcohol of at least 150 proof but less than 190 proof) utilized in the production of a qualified mixture fuel that is used by the producer or that is sold in the producer's trade or business.

The alcohol credit is 60 cents per gallon on alcohol of at least 190 proof (45 cents per gallon for alcohol of at least 150 proof but less than 190 proof) that is *not* a mixture with gas or a special fuel (other than any denaturant) and that is used by a

---

person as a fuel in a trade or business or that is sold at retail and placed in the fuel tank of the purchaser's vehicle.

An eligible small ethanol producer (a producer with a production capacity of up to 30 million gallons of alcohol per year) may claim the small ethanol producer credit of 10 cents per gallon on production of up to 15 million gallons per year of ethanol. The small ethanol producer credit is recaptured through a tax of 10 cents per gallon that is imposed if a producer fails to use the ethanol or ethanol mixture as fuel.

For alcohol blenders, the alcohol mixture credit and the alcohol credit are reduced as follows: for 190-or-greater proof ethanol, the credit rate is reduced from 60 to 54 cents per gallon, and for ethanol of at least 150 proof and less than 190 proof, the credit rate is reduced from 45 to 40 cents per gallon.

Any excise tax exemption for alcohol fuels reduces the amount of the income tax credit.

The alcohol fuels credit is computed on Form 6478, "Credit for Alcohol Used as Fuel," and is claimed as one of the components of the general business credit. Thus, it is subject to the limitation and the carryback and carryforward rules discussed at ¶ 1323. Taxpayers also have the option of electing to not claim the alcohol fuels credit.

The carryforward period for the alcohol fuels credit is limited. Generally, the credit may not be carried forward to tax years beginning after 2007. Thus, an alcohol fuels credit carryforward that is unused at the end of the 2007 tax year would be deductible in the following tax year under Code Sec. 196. However, an earlier termination of the carryforward period may occur if the tax rates under Code Sec. 4081(a)(2)(A) are 4.3 cents per gallon (Code Sec. 40(e)(1)(B)).

1330. Credit for Increased Research Expenditures. A credit for incremental research expenses (computed on Form 6765, "Credit for Increasing Research Activities") is claimed as one of the components of the general business credit (Code Sec. 41). The credit is available for amounts paid or incurred through June 30, 2004.

The credit is subject to the limitation and the carryback and carryforward rules discussed at ¶ 1323. The research credit that remains unused at the end of the carryforward period is allowed as a deduction in the year following the expiration of such period (Code Sec. 196). The deduction does not apply to unused amounts claimed under the reduced research credit election.

Temporary Credit Suspension. The credit attributable to the period beginning July 1, 1999 and ending September 30, 2000 cannot be claimed before October 1, 2000. The credit attributable to the period beginning October 1, 2000 and ending September 30, 2001 cannot be claimed before October 1, 2001. The amount of a credit suspended under these rules is determined by completing Form 6765. After a suspension period expires, the credit may be claimed by filing an amended return (Form 1040X or Form 1120X) or an application for a tentative refund (Form 1045 or Form 1139) or by claiming an adjustment to estimated taxes as explained in the Form 6765 instructions and Notice 2001-2. Additional guidance for corporations that file Form 7004 to obtain a six-month filing extension is provided in Notice 2001-29.

Amount of Credit. Unless an election is made to use the alternative incremental method, the research credit is the sum of (1) 20% of the excess of qualified research expenses for the current tax year over a base period amount and (2) 20% of the basic research payments made to a qualified organization. Special base period adjustments are required where there is an acquisition or disposition of the major portion of a business that paid or incurred research expenses.[20]

Base Amount. For purposes of calculating the credit under Code Sec. 41(a), the base period amount is the product of the taxpayer's (1) fixed-base percentage and

Footnote references are to paragraphs of the 2002 Standard Federal Tax Reports.

¶ 1330   [20] ¶ 4350

(2) average annual gross receipts for the four tax years preceding the credit period (Code Sec. 41(c)). The base amount may not be less than 50% of the qualified research expenses for the credit year. The fixed-base percentage (aggregate qualified research expenses compared to aggregate gross receipts for 1984 through 1988 tax years) may not exceed 16%.

Alternative Incremental Computation. A taxpayer may elect to compute the research credit using the alternative incremental credit (Code Sec. 41(c)(4)). The election must be made in the first tax year that begins after June 30, 1996, and applies to all future tax years unless the election is revoked with the consent of the IRS. The credit is equal to the sum of an increasing percentage of the amount of qualified research expenses in excess of a percentage of the base amount, divided into three tiers. For purposes of the alternative incremental computation, the base amount is the average gross receipts for the last four tax years. The tier one amount after June 30, 1999 is equal to 2.65% (1.65% for pre-July 1, 1999) of qualified research expenditures in excess of 1% of the base amount but not more than 1.5% of the base amount. The tier two amount after June 30, 1999 is equal to 3.2% (2.2% for pre-July 1, 1999) of qualified research expenditures in excess of 1.5% of the base amount but not in excess of 2% of the base amount. The amount of tier three after June 30, 1999 is equal to 3.75% (2.75% for pre-July 1, 1999) of qualified research expenditures in excess of 2% of the base amount (Code Sec. 41(c)(4)(A)).

Start-Up Company. A start-up company's fixed-base percentage is three percent for each of the first five tax years for which it has qualified research expenses. However, the fixed-base percentage for the sixth through tenth tax years in which qualified research expenses are incurred is a portion of the percentage which qualified research expenses bear to gross receipts for specified preceding years. For subsequent tax years, the fixed-base percentage is the whole percentage that qualified research expenses bear to gross receipts for any five years selected by the taxpayer from the fifth through tenth tax years. The definition of a start-up company includes a taxpayer who has both gross receipts and qualified research expenses for the first time in a tax year that begins after 1983 (Code Sec. 41(c)(3)(B)).

Deduction for Research and Experimental Expenditures. The business deduction for research and experimental expenditures under Code Sec. 174 must be reduced by the amount of the research credit (Code Sec. 280C(c)). Capitalized expenses must also be reduced by the amount of the research credit that exceeds the amount otherwise allowable as a deduction for such expenses.

An annual irrevocable election is available to claim a reduced research credit and thereby avoid reducing the research expense deduction (or capital expenditures) (Code Sec. 280C(c)). Under the election, the research credit must be reduced by the product of (1) the research credit computed in the regular manner and (2) the maximum corporate tax rate.

Qualified Research Expenses. Qualified research expenses are the same as those defined in Code Sec. 174 (see ¶ 979) other than expenses for foreign research; research in the social sciences, arts or humanities; or subsidized research. Credit-eligible research is limited to research undertaken to discover information that is (1) technological in nature and (2) intended to be useful in the development of a new or improved business component. Further, the research must relate to elements of a process of experimentation for a functional purpose, i.e., it must relate to a new or improved function, performance, reliability, or quality. Qualified research expenses cover in-house expenses for the taxpayer's own research (wages, including income from employees' exercise of stock options, for substantially engaging in or directly supervising or supporting research activities, supplies, and computer use charges) and 65 percent of amounts paid or incurred for qualified research done by a person other than an employee of the taxpayer. The percentage is increased to 75 percent of amounts paid or incurred for qualified research performed by a qualified research consortium. A qualified research consortium is a tax-exempt organization under

¶ 1330

either Code Secs. 501(c)(3) or 501(c)(6) that is not a private foundation and whose primary function is to conduct scientific research.

Special Rule for Pass-Thru Entities. For individuals with interests in unincorporated businesses, partners, trust or estate beneficiaries, or S corporation shareholders, any allowable pass-through of the credit cannot exceed the amount of tax attributable to the individual's taxable income allocable to that individual's interest in the entity (Code Sec. 41(g)).

1334. Low-Income Housing Credit. A nonrefundable income tax credit is available on a per unit basis for low-income units in qualified low-income buildings in qualified low-income housing projects (Code Sec. 42).[21] The owner of a qualified low-income housing project that is constructed, rehabilitated, or acquired may claim the credit in each of 10 tax years in an amount equal to (1) the applicable credit percentage appropriate to the type of project multiplied by (2) the qualified basis allocable to the low-income units in each qualified low-income building.

The credit is claimed over a 10-year period that begins with the tax year in which the project is placed in service or, at the taxpayer's election, the next tax year (but only if the building is a qualified low-income building as of the close of the first year of such period). The first-year credit is reduced to reflect the time during the year that any low-income units are unoccupied. If the reduction is made, a credit is allowed in the eleventh year in an amount equal to the reduction.

The credit is calculated on Form 8586, "Low-Income Housing Credit," and is claimed as a component of the general business credit.[22] As such, it is subject to the limitation and the carryback and carryforward rules discussed at ¶ 1323.

Usually, the applicable credit rates are the appropriate percentages issued by the IRS for the month in which the building is placed in service. Different percentages are provided for (1) new construction or rehabilitation and (2) subsidized construction or rehabilitation and the acquisition of existing housing. See ¶ 86. An irrevocable election is available to determine the credit percentage applicable to a building in advance of the date that it is placed in service.

Generally, rehabilitation expenditures are treated as expenditures for a separate new building provided that (1) the expenditures are allocable to, or substantially benefit, low-income units and (2) the expenditures incurred during any 24-month period are the greater of $3,000 per low-income unit or 10% of the adjusted basis of the building.

A credit is denied to otherwise qualified buildings unless the owner of the building is subject to an enforceable 30-year low-income use agreement with the housing agency (Code Sec. 42(h)(6)).

A qualified low-income housing project is any project for residential rental property that meets requirements for low-income tenant occupancy, gross rent restrictions, state credit authority, and IRS certification. The project must continue to meet these requirements for 15 years or recapture of a portion of the credit may occur. A qualified low-income building must be subject to MACRS depreciation.

Credits attributable to the operation of a qualified low-income housing project are not limited or disallowed by the rules applicable to activities not entered into for profit (see ¶ 1195) (Reg. § 1.42-4).[23]

1335. New Markets Tax Credit. The new markets tax credit has been created to increase investments in low-income communities. The credit is equal to five percent of the investment in a qualified community development entity (CDE) for the first three allowance dates and six percent of the investment for the next four allowance dates. The total credit available is equal to 39 percent of the investment over seven years. Active involvement of the low-income communities is required with strict penalties if the investment is terminated before seven years. There are national limitations on the amount of investments which can be used to claim the

Footnote references are to paragraphs of the 2002 Standard Federal Tax Reports.

¶ **1334**   [21] ¶ 4380   [22] ¶ 4380   [23] ¶ 4384A

new market tax credit for investments made after December 31, 2000. The Secretary of Treasury is authorized to allocate up to $1 billion in 2001 to qualified CDEs giving preference to those CDEs that demonstrate a history of successful investing in low-income areas. The limitation amount will increase to $3.5 billion for calendar years 2006 and 2007. In the event that the CDE does not use it yearly allocation within five years of the issue date, the CDE loses the unused balance and the Secretary of Treasury is authorized to reissue the unused allocation. In the event the Secretary of Treasury is unable to allocate the full amount of the yearly investment limitation, the unused allocation will be carried over and added to the following year's allocation amount. However, the carryover of the unused allocation amounts may not be carried forward beyond 2014.

The new markets tax credit is a part of and subject to the limitations and carryover rules of the general business credit (¶ 1323). The credit is calculated on Form 8874. The credit may not be carried back to tax years ending before January 1, 2001. Any unused credit at the end of the carryforward period will be allowed as a deduction in the following tax year (Code Sec. 196). Any termination event will require recapture of the credit amount claimed which will be treated as an increase to tax in the termination year. Any amounts of credit carried forward or carried back will need to be adjusted accordingly. Finally, the claiming of the new markets tax credit will necessitate an adjustment in the basis of the investment in the CDE (Code Sec. 45D).[24]

1336. Enhanced Oil Recovery Credit. Unless an election is made to have the enhanced oil recovery (EOR) credit not apply, this credit is available for up to 15% of qualified costs attributable to qualified domestic EOR projects (Code Sec. 43).[25] To the extent that a credit is allowed for these costs, the amount otherwise deductible or required to be capitalized and recovered through depreciation, depletion, or amortization must be reduced.

This credit is computed on Form 8830, "Enhanced Oil Recovery Credit," and is claimed as one of the components of the general business credit. Accordingly, it is subject to the limitation and the carryback and carryforward rules discussed at ¶ 1323. Any unused credit remaining after the expiration of the carryforward period is deductible (Code Sec. 196).

The amount of the credit allowable is phased out as the average wellhead price of uncontrolled domestic oil rises from $28 to $34 per barrel. The amount allowable as a credit is reduced by an amount that bears the same ratio to the amount of the credit as (1) the amount by which the reference price for the calendar year before the calendar year in which the tax year begins exceeds $28 bears to (2) $6. The credit is adjusted for inflation. Since the reference price for the 2000 calendar year ($26.73) does not exceed $28 multiplied by the inflation adjustment factor for the 2001 calendar year of 1.2353, the enhanced oil recovery credit for qualified costs paid or incurred in 2001 is determined without regard to the phaseout for crude oil price increases (Notice 2001-54).

A qualified EOR project is a domestic project involving one or more tertiary recovery methods defined in Code Sec. 193(b)(3) that can reasonably be expected to result in more than an insignificant increase in the amount of crude oil that will ultimately be recovered where the first injection of liquids, gases or other matter began after 1990 (Code Sec. 43(c)(2)).

1338. Disabled Access Credit. An eligible small business is entitled to a nonrefundable disabled access income tax credit for expenditures incurred to make a business accessible to disabled individuals (Code Sec. 44).[26] The amount of the credit is 50% of the amount of eligible access expenditures for a year that exceed $250 but that do not exceed $10,250.

The disabled access credit is computed on Form 8826, "Disabled Access Credit," and is claimed as one of the components of the general business credit.

Footnote references are to paragraphs of the 2002 Standard Federal Tax Reports.

[24] ¶ 4480   [25] ¶ 4386   [26] ¶ 4400   **¶ 1338**

Thus, this credit is subject to the limitation and the carryback and carryforward rules discussed at ¶ 1323. Any unused credit remaining at the end of the carryforward period is lost (Code Sec. 196(c)). No other deduction or credit is permitted for any amount for which a disabled access credit is allowed.

An eligible small business is any person that elects to claim the disabled access credit and that either (1) had gross receipts (less returns and allowances) for the preceding tax year that did not exceed $1 million or (2) had no more than 30 full-time employees during the preceding tax year.

Eligible access expenditures include reasonable and necessary amounts paid or incurred by an eligible small business for the purpose of enabling the business to comply with the requirements of the Americans with Disabilities Act of 1990. Eligible access expenditures also include the following expenditures: (1) for the purpose of removing architectural, communication, physical, or transportation barriers that prevent a business from being accessible to, or usable by, disabled individuals (other than amounts for new construction first placed in service after November 5, 1990); (2) to provide qualified interpreters or other effective methods of making aurally delivered materials available to hearing-impaired individuals; (3) to provide qualified readers, taped texts, and other effective methods of making visually delivered materials available to visually impaired individuals; (4) to acquire or modify equipment or devices for disabled individuals; or (5) to provide other similar services, modifications, materials, or equipment.

1339. Credit for Electricity Produced from Renewable Sources. A nonrefundable credit is available for the domestic production of electricity from qualified energy resources (closed-loop biomass facilities placed in service after 1992 and before January 1, 2002, wind facilities placed in service after 1993 and before January 1, 2002, or poultry waste facilities placed in service after December 31, 1999 and before January 1, 2002) (extension legislation proposed) (Code Sec. 45).[27] The credit is 1.5 cents (adjusted for inflation to 1.7 cents for 2001) per kilowatt hour of electricity produced from a qualified energy resource at a qualified facility during the 10-year period after the facility is placed in service that is sold during the tax year by the taxpayer to an unrelated person. The credit is reduced by an amount that bears the same ratio to the amount of the credit as (1) the amount by which the reference price for the calendar year in which the sale occurs (2.57 cents for 2001 for wind energy resources and 0 cents for closed-looped biomass and poultry waste energy resources) exceeds 8 cents (adjusted for inflation to 9.3 cents for 2001) bears to (2) 3 cents. The credit amount and reference price are adjusted annually for inflation. The inflation adjustment factor for 2001 is 1.1641 (Notice 2001-33).

The credit is claimed on Form 8835, "Renewable Electricity Credit," and is one of the components of the general business credit. Thus, it is subject to the limitation and the carryback and carryforward rules discussed at ¶ 1323. This credit may not be carried back to a tax year ending before 1993 for electricity produced from closed-loop biomass facilities or to a tax year ending before 1994 for electricity produced from wind energy facilities.

1339A. Empowerment Zone Employment Credit. Employers are entitled to a credit on the first $15,000 of wages paid to each full- or part-time employee who is a resident of an empowerment zone designated by the Secretary of Housing and Urban Development and the Secretary of Agriculture. To qualify, an employee must perform substantially all employment services within the zone and in the employer's trade or business. The credit percentage varies depending upon the empowerment zone and the year that wages are paid or incurred. Effective beginning in tax years in 2001, the credit percentage will be 20 percent for all designated empowerment zones for the duration of the designation (Code Sec. 1396, as amended by the Community Renewal Tax Relief Act of 2000).[28]

Footnote references are to paragraphs of the 2002 Standard Federal Tax Reports.

¶ **1339**   [27] ¶ 4410   [28] ¶ 32,393

Wages do not qualify for the credit if paid to certain individuals related to the employer, five-percent owners, individuals employed for fewer than 90 days, employees of golf courses, massage parlors, hot tub or suntan facilities, gambling facilities and liquor stores, and employees of farming businesses with owned or leased assets having a fair market value or basis exceeding $500,000. Additionally, wages used to claim the work opportunity credit (¶ 1342) may not be used to claim the empowerment zone credit (Code Sec. 1396(c)).

This credit is claimed on Form 8844, "Empowerment Zone Employment Credit," and is a component of the general business credit. Thus, it is subject to the limitation and the carryback and carryforward rules discussed at ¶ 1323. No unused portion of the credit may be carried back to a tax year ending before 1994. The amount of the credit claimed may not be deducted as wages.

1340. Indian Employment Credit. A nonrefundable credit is available to employers for the first $20,000 of certain wages and health insurance costs paid or incurred after 1993 in a tax year that begins before 2004 for qualified full- or part-time employees who are enrolled members of an Indian tribe or their spouses (Code Sec. 45A).[29] The credit is equal to 20% of the excess of eligible employee qualified wages and health insurance costs paid or incurred during a tax year over the amount of these costs paid or incurred during 1993. No deduction for wages is allowed for the portion of wages equal to the amount of the credit.

The credit is calculated on Form 8845, "Indian Employment Credit," and is claimed as one of the components of the general business credit. Thus, it is subject to the limitation and carryback and carryforward rules discussed at ¶ 1323. This credit may not be carried back to a tax year ending before August 10, 1993. Any unused credit at the end of the carryforward period is allowed as a deduction in the year following the expiration of the period (Code Sec. 196(c)).

Qualified wages are wages paid or incurred by an employer for services performed by a qualified employee excluding wages for which a work opportunity credit is allowed. Qualified health insurance costs are costs paid or incurred by an employer for a qualified employee, except for costs paid under a salary reduction agreement.

An individual who receives more than 50 percent of wages from services performed in the trade or business of the employer is a qualified employee for any period only if (1) the individual is an enrolled member of an Indian tribe or the spouse thereof; (2) substantially all of the services performed during the period by the employee for the employer are performed within an Indian reservation; and (3) the principal place of abode of the employee while performing the services is on or near the reservation on which the services are performed. Ineligible employees include employees who receive wages exceeding $30,000 (adjusted for inflation for years beginning after 1994).

1341. Credit for Employer-Paid Social Security Taxes on Employee Cash Tips. An employer in the food and beverage business may claim a nonrefundable income tax credit for a portion of employer social security taxes paid or incurred on employee cash tips (Code Sec. 45B).[30] The credit is equal to the employer's FICA obligation attributable to tips received exceeding those tips treated as wages for purposes of satisfying the minimum wage provisions of the Fair Labor Standards Act. For taxes paid after December 31, 1993, the credit is available whether or not the employee reported the tips and regardless of when the services were performed.

The credit is allowed for tips received from customers in connection with the providing, delivering, or serving of food or beverages for consumption if the tipping of employees delivering or serving food or beverages by customers is customary. The employer may not deduct any amount considered in determining this credit. An election may be made to have this credit not apply.

The credit is claimed on Form 8846, "Credit for Employer Social Security and Medicare Taxes Paid on Certain Employee Tips," and is one of the components of the general business credit. Thus, it is subject to the limitation and carryback and carryover rules discussed at ¶ 1323. This credit may not be carried back to a tax year ending before August 10, 1993. Any credit that remains unused at the end of the carryover period is lost.

1342. Work Opportunity Tax Credit. Unless an election is made to have the work opportunity credit not apply, a credit is available for wages paid by employers who hire individuals from certain target groups. The credit is taken for first-year wages paid to eligible individuals who begin work after September 30, 1996, and before January 1, 2002 (extension legislation proposed) (Code Sec. 51(c)(4)). The deduction for such wages must be reduced by the amount of the credit. It is computed on Form 5884, "Jobs Credit." It is a component of the general business credit and subject to the limitation rules and the carryback and carryforward rules discussed at ¶ 1323. No credit is allowed for wages paid to an individual for services rendered at the employer's plant or facility that are substantially similar to services performed by employees who are participants in a strike or who are affected by a lockout.

The work opportunity tax credit applies to eligible individuals who begin work after September 30, 1996, and before January 1, 2002 (Code Sec. 51).[31] The credit is 40 percent of the first $6,000 of wages ($3,000 for qualified summer youth employees) paid to each targeted group member during the first year of employment and 25 percent in the case of wages attributable to individuals meeting only minimum employment levels.

Target Groups. Individuals who fit into one of the following groups qualify for the work opportunity credit: (1) qualified IV-A (Aid to Families with Dependent Children (AFDC)) recipient, (2) qualified veteran, (3) qualified ex-felon, (4) high-risk youth, (5) vocational rehabilitation referral, (6) qualified summer youth employee, (7) qualified food stamp recipient, or (8) a qualified SSI recipient (Code Sec. 51(d)).

Minimum Employment Period. An employee must have completed a minimum of 120 hours of service for the wages to be taken into account for calculation of the work opportunity credit. The hours of service test is the only way the minimum employment period is measured for work opportunity credit purposes. If the 120-hour test is met, the employer is entitled to a credit of 25 percent if the employee performs less than 400 hours of service for the employer. For 400 or more hours of service, the percentage is 40 percent of the employee's wages.

1343. Credit for Employing Long-Term Family Assistance Recipients (Welfare-to-Work Credit). Commonly called the welfare-to-work credit, a credit is available for employers for wages paid to long-term family assistance recipients who begin work after December 31, 1997 (Code Sec. 51A).[32] The amount of the credit for a tax year is 35 percent of the qualified first-year wages for such year plus 50 percent of the qualified second-year wages for such year. The credit applies only to the first $10,000 of wages in each year with respect to any individual. Thus, the maximum total credit per qualified employee is $8,500 for the two years. The term "wages" is given a broad meaning for purposes of the welfare-to-work credit.

Qualified First-Year and Second-Year Wages. "Qualified" wages are wages paid or incurred by the employer during the tax year to individuals who are long-term family assistance recipients. "Qualified first-year wages" are qualified wages attributable to service rendered by the individual during the one-year period beginning with the day such individual began work for the employer. "Qualified second-year wages" are qualified wages attributable to service rendered during the one-year period beginning on the day after the last day of the period for determining first-year wages.

Footnote references are to paragraphs of the 2002 Standard Federal Tax Reports.

¶ **1342** [31] ¶ 4800 [32] ¶ 4820

Coordination with Other Code Provisions. Rules similar to the special rules of Code Sec. 52 and the provisions in Code Sec. 51 on the election to have the work opportunity credit not apply (Code Sec. 51(j)) and the treatment of successor employers and employees working for another employer (Code Sec. 51(k)) apply to the welfare-to-work credit. In addition, the Code Sec. 51 provisions on certifications (Code Sec. 51(d)(11)) (Form 8850, "Pre-Screening Notice and Certification Request for the Work Opportunity and Welfare-to-Work Credits"), notification to employers by the U.S. Employment Service (Code Sec. 51(g)), and ineligible individuals (Code Sec. 51(i)) are applicable as in effect on August 4, 1997 (the day before the enactment of the Taxpayer Relief Act of 1997).

The welfare-to-work credit, calculated on Form 8861, "Welfare-to-Work Credit," is deemed to be part of the general business credit subject to the limitation, carryback and carryforward rules discussed at ¶ 1323, and references to Code Sec. 51 in Code Sec. 38(b) (current year business credit), Code Sec. 280C (certain expenses for which credits are allowable), and Code Sec. 1396(c)(3) (empowerment zone employment credit) are treated as including references to the welfare-to-work credit. If a welfare-to-work credit is allowed to an employer with respect to an individual for any tax year, the individual is not treated as a member of a targeted group for such tax year for purposes of the Code Sec. 51 work opportunity credit (Notice 97-54). The credit is available through December 31, 2001 (extension legislation proposed).

1344. Orphan Drug Credit. Effective for qualified clinical testing expenses paid or incurred after May 31, 1997, the orphan drug credit has been made permanent. The credit is claimed on Form 8820, "Orphan Drug Credit," and is a component of the general business credit. Thus, it is subject to the limitation rules and the carryback and carryforward rules discussed at ¶ 1323. However, the orphan drug credit may not be carried back to a tax year ending before July 1, 1996. Subject to certain limitations, the credit is equal to 50 percent of the qualified clinical testing expenses incurred during the year (Code Sec. 45C).[33]

1344A. Academy Bond Credit. For bonds issued after December 31, 1997, an eligible taxpayer (certain financial institutions, including banks, insurance companies and corporations actively engaged in the business of lending money), who is holding a qualified zone academy bond on the credit allowance date, is entitled to a nonrefundable tax credit for each year in which the bond is held (Code Sec. 1397E).[34] The credit rate is the percentage that the Treasury estimates will permit qualified academy zone bonds to be issued without discount and without interest cost to the issuer of the bonds. The credit amount is included in the gross income of the taxpayer. Code Sec. 1397E(e) places a national limitation on the total amount of bonds that may be issued each year. For calendar years 1998, 1999, 2000 and 2001, the amount is $400,000,000. There is no amount authorized for calendar year 2002 and later (extension legislation proposed). The Secretary of Treasury is authorized to allocate the limitation amount among the states based on the proportion of the state population below the poverty line. The states are to allocate their share of the amount to the qualified academy zones. The states are authorized to allocate any unused calendar year allocation for up to three years after 1998 and 1999 and for up to two years after 2000 and 2001.

1344B. Small Employer Pension Plan Startup Costs Credit. Starting in 2002, a new tax credit may be claimed by eligible small businesses—the small employer pension plan startup costs credit (Code Sec. 45E, as added by the Economic Growth and Tax Relief Reconciliation Act of 2001).[35] The purpose of the credit is to encourage small businesses to establish and maintain retirement savings accounts for their employees. The credit amount equals 50 percent of the start-up costs incurred to create or maintain a new employee retirement plan. The credit is limited to $500 in any tax year and it may be claimed for qualified costs incurred in

---

each of the three years beginning with the tax year in which the plan becomes effective. The credit is part of and subject to the limitations and carryover rules of the general business credit (¶ 1323), except that no portion of the credit may be carried back to a tax year beginning before January 1, 2002.

An eligible small business is one that has not employed more than 100 employees who received at least $5,000 of compensation from that employer in the preceding year. An eligible plan includes a new qualified defined benefit plan, defined contribution plan (including a 401(k) plan), savings incentive match plan for employees (SIMPLE), or simplified employee pension (SEP) plan. Additionally, the plan must be a new plan established after December 31, 2001. Qualified costs are any ordinary and necessary expenses incurred to establish or administer an eligible plan or to educate employees about retirement planning. Qualified costs are not deductible to the extent that they are effectively offset by the tax credit. The credit is limited to the first $1,000 of qualified costs incurred in the first year the new plan is effective and in each of the following two years. The employer may elect to take the credit in the year immediately preceding the first year the new plan is effective, or elect not to claim the credit for a tax year.

1344C. Employer-Provided Child Care Credit. Starting in 2002, a new tax credit has been created for small and mid-sized businesses—the employer-provided child care credit (Code Sec. 45F, as added by the Economic Growth and Tax Relief Reconciliation Act of 2001).[36] The purpose of this credit is to encourage small and mid-sized businesses to provide child care services for their employees. The amount of the credit for a given tax year is the sum of 25 percent of the qualified child care expenditures and 10 percent of the qualified resource and referral expenditures. The maximum amount of credit allowed in any given year is $150,000. The credit is part of and subject to the limitations and carryover rules of the general business credit (¶ 1323). No double benefit is allowed for expenditures used to claim the employer-provided child care credit and the basis of the child care facility must be reduced by the amount of the credit taken. There is no deduction allowed in the year following the final year of any carryforward of unused employer-provided child care credit. In the event of an occurrence of a recapture event, the tax liability of that tax year must be increased by an amount equal to the applicable percentage (see Code Sec. 45F(d)(2)(A)) times the aggregate decrease in the general business credit as if all previously allowed employer-provided child care credits with respect to the employer's child care facility had been zero. Any carryforward or carryback amounts of the employer-provided child care credit must also be adjusted.

A qualified child care facility is a facility whose "principal use" is to provide child care assistance and that meets the requirements of all applicable laws and regulations of the state and local government in which it is located, including the licensing requirements applicable to a child care facility. The principal use requirement is waived for facilities located in the principal residence of the operator of the facility. Additional requirements for a facility to qualify to claim the credit are:

(1) enrollment must be open to the employees of the taxpayer during the tax year;

(2) at least 30 percent of the enrollees at the facility are the dependents of the taxpayer's employees, in the event the facility is the principal trade or business of the taxpayer; and

(3) the use of the child care facility cannot discriminate in favor of highly-compensated employees within the meaning of Code Sec. 414(q).

Qualified child care expenditures are any amounts paid or incurred:

(1) to acquire, construct, rehabilitate or expand property which is to used as a qualified child care facility of the taxpayer;

Footnote references are to paragraphs of the 2002 Standard Federal Tax Reports.

(2) for the operating costs of a qualified child care facility, including the costs related to the training of employees, scholarship programs, and providing increased compensation for employees with high levels of child care training; or

(3) under a contract with a qualified child care facility to provide child care services to the taxpayer's employees.

Costs associated with item (1) must qualify for a depreciation or amortization deduction and must not be the principal residence of the taxpayer. Expenses for items (2) and (3) shall not exceed the fair market value of such care. Further, qualified child care resources and referral expenditures are expenses paid or incurred by the taxpayer under a contract to provide child care services to the taxpayer's employees. These expenditures cannot discriminate in favor of highly-compensated employees within the meaning of Code Sec. 414(q). Finally, special rules will be set forth by the IRS for allocation of the credits to pass-thru entities and estates and trusts.

Investment Credit

1345. Investment Credit Components. The investment credit is the sum of three components: (1) the rehabilitation credit, (2) the energy credit, and (3) the reforestation credit (Code Sec. 46).[37] The investment credit is claimed on Form 3468, "Investment Credit," and is one of the components of the general business credit, subject to the limitation and the carryback and carryforward rules discussed at ¶ 1323.

Investment credit property of a partnership for a tax year is generally apportioned among partners according to the ratio in which the partners divide the general profits of the partnership. An S corporation's investment credit property for a tax year is apportioned among the shareholders on a daily basis according to each shareholder's proportion of ownership. Investment credit property of an estate or trust is apportioned between the estate or trust and the beneficiaries on the basis of the income allocable to each.

1347. Rehabilitation Investment Credit. The rehabilitation investment credit is 20 percent of qualified rehabilitation expenses (QRE) for certified historic structures and 10 percent of QRE for qualified rehabilitated buildings first placed in service before 1936 (other than certified historic structures) (Code Sec. 47).[38] No energy credit (¶ 1351) is allowed on that portion of the basis of property that is attributable to QRE (Code Sec. 48(a)(2)(B)). Certain restrictions apply to property which is used as lodging (Code Sec. 50(b)).

A building and its structural components constitute a qualified rehabilitated building (QRB) if they are (1) substantially rehabilitated for the tax year and (2) placed in service by any person before the beginning of the rehabilitation. Property other than a certified historic structure must also satisfy: (3) the applicable wall retention test, (4) an age requirement, and (5) a location-of-rehabilitation requirement (Code Sec. 47(c)(1); Reg. § 1.48-12(b)).[39] Property is considered substantially rehabilitated only if the expenditures during an elected 24-month measurement period (60-month period for phased rehabilitations) ending with or within the tax year are more than the greater of the adjusted basis of the property or $5,000.

QRE does not include an enlargement or new construction; the cost of acquisition; noncertified rehabilitation of a certified historic structure; rehabilitation of tax-exempt use property; expenditures, generally, that are not depreciated under the MACRS straight-line method over specified recovery periods; and a lessee-incurred expenditure if, on the date the rehabilitation of the building is completed, the remaining term of the lease (determined without regard to renewal periods) is less than the applicable recovery period (Reg. § 1.48-12(c)).[40]

Footnote references are to paragraphs of the 2002 Standard Federal Tax Reports.

[37] ¶ 4502   [39] ¶ 4600, ¶ 4609   [40] ¶ 4609
[38] ¶ 4600

Generally, the rehabilitation investment credit for QRE must be claimed in the tax year in which the property attributable to the expenditures is placed in service, provided that the building is a QRB for such tax year (Code Sec. 47(b)).[41] However, the credit may be claimed before the date the property is placed in service under the rules for qualified progress expenditures (Code Sec. 47(d)).[42]

1349. Advance Credits for Progress Expenditures. An election may be made to claim an advance rehabilitation investment credit for progress expenditures on certain rehabilitated buildings before such property is placed in service (Code Sec. 47(d)).[43] Property qualifying for an advance rehabilitation investment credit on progress expenditures includes a building that is being rehabilitated by or for the taxpayer if (1) the normal rehabilitation period for the building is two or more years, and (2) it is reasonable to expect that the building will be a QRB when it is placed in service.

The amount of QRE that is considered progress expenditures for which an advance rehabilitation investment credit may be claimed is the amount of QRE properly chargeable to the capital account for self-rehabilitated buildings. For non-self-rehabilitated buildings, the amount is the lesser of (a) the QRE paid to another person for the rehabilitation of the building during the tax year or (b) the portion of the overall cost of the rehabilitation completed during the tax year.

1351. Energy Investment Credit. The business energy investment credit is equal to 10% of the basis of energy property placed in service during the year (subject to reduction if the property is financed by tax-exempt private activity bonds or by subsidized energy financing) (Code Sec. 48).[44] No energy credit is allowed for that portion of the basis of property for which a rehabilitation investment credit (¶ 1347) is claimed. An advance energy investment credit may be claimed under special rules for progress expenditures.

Energy property includes equipment that uses solar energy to generate electricity, to heat or cool a structure, or to provide solar process heat. It also includes equipment that produces, distributes, or uses energy derived from geothermal deposits (but only, in the case of electricity generated by geothermal power, up to the electrical transmission stage). To qualify for the credit, the equipment must be depreciable (or amortizable) and must meet performance and quality standards prescribed by the regulations. In addition, the taxpayer must complete the construction, reconstruction or erection of the property or, if the property is acquired, the taxpayer must be the first person to use it.

1353. Reforestation Investment Credit. The reforestation credit is 10% of the amortizable basis of qualified timber property acquired during the tax year that is taken into account under Code Sec. 194 (Code Sec. 48).[45] Amortizable basis is the portion of the basis of qualified timber property attributable to reforestation expenditures that does not exceed $10,000 ($5,000 for a married individual who files a separate return). A trust is not entitled to the reforestation investment credit (Code Sec. 48 and Code Sec. 194).[46] Qualifying reforestation expenditures include all direct costs incurred in connection with the forestation or reforestation of commercial woodlands in the United States, including the costs of site preparation, seeds and seedlings, labor and tool costs, and depreciation on machinery and equipment.

1356. Investment Credit At-Risk Limitation. No investment credit is allowed for investment credit property to the extent that the property is financed with nonqualified nonrecourse borrowing (Code Sec. 49).[47] Thus, the credit base of investment credit property is reduced by the amount of nonqualified nonrecourse financing regarding the property as determined at the close of the tax year in which the property is placed in service. Decreases in nonqualified recourse financing on the

---

Footnote references are to paragraphs of the 2002 Standard Federal Tax Reports.

¶ 1349

[41] ¶ 4600	[44] ¶ 4651	[46] ¶ 4651, ¶ 12,330
[42] ¶ 4600	[45] ¶ 4651	[47] ¶ 4750
[43] ¶ 4600		

property in tax years following the year in which the property was placed in service increase the credit base of the property. This rule does not apply if the decrease occurs through the surrender or other use of property financed by nonqualified nonrecourse financing. Similarly, increases in nonqualified nonrecourse financing on the property in tax years following the year in which the property was placed in service decrease the credit base of the property and trigger recapture.

The limitation applies to investment credit property placed in service by individuals and by certain closely held corporations engaged in business activities that are subject to the loss limitation rules of Code Sec. 465. For a partnership or S corporation, the investment credit at-risk limitation applies at the partner or shareholder level.

The investment credit at-risk limitation does not apply to certain energy property. To come within this exception, nonqualified nonrecourse financing may not exceed 75 percent of the basis of energy property at the close of the tax year in which the property is placed in service. In addition, any nonqualified nonrecourse financing for such property must be a level payment loan (a loan repaid in substantially equal installments, including both principal and interest).

An increase in the amount at risk is treated as if it occurred in the year that the property was first placed in service for purposes of computing the investment credit and for computing any recapture of such credit. However, the investment credit attributable to the increase in the amount at risk is claimed by the taxpayer during the tax year in which the decrease in the amount of nonqualified nonrecourse financing occurs.

If at the close of a tax year there is a net increase in the amount of nonqualified nonrecourse financing regarding such property, thereby causing a decrease in the taxpayer's amount at risk, the investment credit must be recomputed and the decrease in investment credits for previous tax years is recaptured as additional tax in the year that the net increase in nonqualified nonrecourse financing occurs.

1358. Ineligible Property. No investment credit is allowed for the following types of property (Code Sec. 50(b)).[48]

Property used predominantly outside the United States is subject to limited exceptions.

Property used predominantly to furnish lodging (or in connection with the furnishing of lodging) is ineligible except in the case of nonlodging commercial facilities, a hotel or motel furnishing accommodations predominantly to transients, certified historic structures to the extent of that portion of the basis attributable to qualified rehabilitation expenditures, and energy property.

Property used by a tax-exempt organization (other than a farmers' cooperative) is ineligible for the investment credit unless it is used predominantly in an unrelated trade or business. Generally, property used by or leased to or by a governmental unit, foreign person, or foreign entity is not eligible for the investment credit. However, the portion of the property attributable to qualified rehabilitation expenditures or held under a short-term lease (generally under six months) does qualify for the investment credit.

1360. Basis Reduction. The basis of property for which an investment credit is claimed is reduced by the full amount of the rehabilitation credit and by 50% of the energy credit or the reforestation credit (Code Sec. 50).[49] The reduced basis is used to compute depreciation and any gain or loss on the disposition of property.

If the investment credit is recaptured on property for which an investment credit downward basis adjustment was made, the basis of the property immediately before the event resulting in recapture must be increased by the recapture amount for a rehabilitation credit and by 50 percent of the recapture amount for an energy or reforestation credit.

Footnote references are to paragraphs of the 2002 Standard Federal Tax Reports.
[48] ¶ 4752   [49] ¶ 4752   **¶ 1360**

In determining the amount of gain that is recaptured as ordinary income on a sale or disposition of depreciable personal property (Code Sec. 1245) or depreciable realty (Code Sec. 1250), the amount of the investment credit downward basis adjustment is treated as a deduction allowed for depreciation. Thus, the basis adjustment is treated as depreciation subject to ordinary income recapture.

For Code Sec. 1250 property, the recapture applies only to the excess of depreciation claimed over depreciation computed under the straight-line method, with the latter computed on the basis without reduction for the applicable investment credit downward basis adjustment.

If an investment credit for which a downward basis adjustment was made does not result in a tax benefit because it remains unused at the end of the 15-year general business credit carryover period for tax years prior to January 1, 1998 (20-year credit carryover period for tax years after December 31, 1997), a deduction is allowed under Code Sec. 196 to the taxpayer for 50 percent of the unused energy or reforestation credit (100 percent of the unused rehabilitation credit) attributable to the basis reduction.

1362. Special Investment Credit Rules. Special limitations apply to the amount of investment credit that may be claimed by thrift institutions, regulated investment companies, real estate investment trusts, noncorporate lessors, and certain other regulated companies (Code Sec. 50).[50]

1364. Early Disposition. When investment credit property (any property eligible for the rehabilitation, energy, or reforestation credit) is disposed of (including dispositions due to casualties or thefts) or ceases to be investment credit property before the end of its recapture period, the tax for the year of disposal or cessation is increased by the amount of the credit that is recaptured (Code Sec. 50).[51]

The amount of the recapture is a percentage of the original credit claimed, depending on how long the property is held before recapture is required. The recapture percentages are 100% within the first full year after placement in service, 80% within the second full year, 60% within the third full year, 40% within the fourth full year, 20% within the fifth full year, and zero thereafter.

Advance rehabilitation or energy credits on progress expenditures are also subject to recapture. For investment credit at-risk recapture, see ¶ 1356. Special recapture rules apply to certain energy property.

The recapture rules do not apply to the following transfers: (1) a transfer between spouses or incident to divorce as described in Code Sec. 1041, but a later disposition by the transferee will result in recapture to the same extent as if the disposition had been made by the transferor at that later date; (2) a transfer because of death; and (3) a transfer to which Code Sec. 381(a) (relating carryovers in corporate acquisitions) applies. Similarly, the recapture rules do not apply where there is a mere change in the form of operating a business, provided that the property is retained in the business and the taxpayer retains a substantial interest in the business.

Credit for Prior Year Minimum Tax

1370. Credit Against Regular Tax for Prior Year Minimum Tax Liability. A credit is allowed for the amount of adjusted net minimum tax for all tax years reduced by the minimum tax credit for all prior tax years (Code Sec. 53).[52] The credit may be carried forward indefinitely as a credit against regular tax liability. The credit is limited to the extent that the regular tax liability reduced by other nonrefundable credits exceeds the tentative minimum tax for the tax year. The credit may not be used to offset any future minimum tax liability. The credit is claimed on Form 8801, "Credit for Prior Year Minimum Tax—Individuals and Fiduciaries," by individuals and fiduciaries.

Footnote references are to paragraphs of the 2002 Standard Federal Tax Reports.

¶ **1362**   [50] ¶ 4752   [51] ¶ 4752   [52] ¶ 5002

The adjusted net minimum tax is the net minimum tax reduced by the amount that would have been the net minimum tax if only certain specified preferences and adjustments had been taken into account and had the 90% limit on the alternative minimum tax foreign tax credit not applied (Code Sec. 53(d)(1)(B)(ii)).[53] The adjustments are those described in Code Sec. 56(b)(1), including the standard deduction, personal exemptions, medical and dental expenses, miscellaneous itemized deductions, taxes, and interest expenses.

The exclusion-type preference items are certain depletion deductions exceeding adjusted basis, tax-exempt interest on specified private activity bonds, and one-half of the exclusion for gains on the sale of certain small business stock issued after August 10, 1993.

Adjusted net minimum tax is increased by the amount of the credit for producing fuels from nonconventional sources (¶ 1319) and the credit for qualified electric vehicles (¶ 1321) that are not allowed for a tax year because of the limitation based on a taxpayer's tentative minimum tax (Code Sec. 53(d)).[54]

In determining corporate credits for prior year minimum tax liability, adjusted net minimum tax is the sum of (a) the corporate net minimum tax liability (including such tax attributable to corporate exclusion preferences) and (b) the credit for producing fuels from nonconventional sources that are not allowed because of the limitation based on a taxpayer's tentative minimum tax (Code Sec. 53(d)(1)(B)(iv)).[55]

Limitations on Nonrefundable Credits

1371. Credit Limits. In addition to the limitations imposed on each credit, the aggregate amount of the nonrefundable credits cannot exceed the excess, if any, of the regular tax liability over the tentative minimum tax. Because of this limitation, it is important to note the order in which the nonrefundable credits are claimed since certain credits may be carried forward to future years while other credits are lost if not used in the current year. The nonrefundable credits are claimed in the following order: (1) the sum of the personal credits are claimed first: (a) Child and Dependent Care Credit (¶ 1301), (b) Credit for the Elderly or the Permanently and Totally Disabled (¶ 1304), (c) Educational Credits (¶ 1303), (d) Rate Reduction Credit (for 2001 only) (¶ 1310A), (e) Child Tax Credit (¶ 1302), (f) Adoption Credit (¶ 1306), (g) Credit for Interest on Certain Home Mortgages (¶ 1308), and (h) Credit for First-Time Homebuyers in the District of Columbia (¶ 1310) (note: the sum of the personal credits may be claimed only to the extent that they do not exceed the excess of the regular tax liability over the tentative minimum tax, as determined without regard to the alternative minimum tax foreign tax credit; however, in 2000 and 2001 the credits may be taken against both the regular tax liability and the alternative minimum tax liability (legislation proposed extending to 2002 and 2003) (Code Sec. 26(a)); (2) Foreign Tax Credit (¶ 1311); (3) Alternative Fuels Credit (¶ 1319); (4) Qualified Electric Vehicles Credit (Code Sec. 30) (¶ 1321); and (5) General Business Credit (¶ 1323) (note: the general business credit is claimed not only after the above listed credits but also after the refundable credits discussed at ¶ 1372 et seq.).

REFUNDABLE CREDITS

Credit for Taxes Withheld

1372. Credit for Taxes Withheld on Wages. A credit against the employee's income tax liability is granted for income taxes withheld from his salary or wages and for social security taxes overwithheld on the wages of a taxpayer with

more than one employer (Code Sec. 31).[56] For 2001, if a single employer withheld more than the maximum $4,984.80 of social security tax (6.2% tax rate on wage base of $80,400), the employee should request a refund from the employer. Overwithholding for this tax cannot be claimed as a refund on the employee's return. All wages are subject to the 1.45% Medicare tax. See ¶ 2648.

However, if a person has more than one employer and the employers' combined amounts withheld exceed the maximum, a credit for the excess social security tax may be claimed on Form 1040. If the employee is not required to file an income tax return, he may file a special refund claim (Reg. § 31.6413(c)-1).[57] See ¶ 2449 as to credits for tax withheld from nonresident aliens.

Earned Income Credit

1375. Earned Income Credit.

A refundable earned income credit is available to certain low-income individuals who have earned income, meet modified adjusted gross income thresholds, and do not have more than a certain amount of disqualified income for purposes of individuals having excess investment income (Code Sec. 32(a) and Code Sec. 32(i)).[58] The disqualified income limit for 2001 is $2,450 (projected to be $2,550 in 2002). Taxpayers claiming the credit must provide their social security number as well as the social security numbers of their spouse and dependents, if any. Failure to provide all required social security numbers is treated as a mathematical error (Code Sec. 6213(g)(2)).

Modified AGI. Modified adjusted gross income (MAGI) is defined as an individual's adjusted gross income calculated without regard to amounts for (1) capital losses, subject to certain limitations, (2) losses from trusts and estates, (3) losses from nonbusiness rents and royalties, and (4) 75 percent of the net losses from a trade or business. However, an individual's AGI is increased by any tax-exempt interest and nontaxable distributions from pensions, annuities, and IRAs unless they are rolled over into similar tax-favored vehicles (Code Sec. 32(c)(5)).

Disqualified Income. Disqualified income includes an individual's capital gain net income and net passive income in addition to interest, dividends, tax-exempt interest, and non-business rents or royalties. Credit percentages and phaseout percentages are provided for low-income individuals who have no qualifying children, one qualifying child, and more than one qualifying child. An individual who is a qualifying child of another taxpayer may not also claim such credit in the same tax year (Code Sec. 32(i)(2)).

Qualifying Child. A qualifying child is an individual who satisfies a relationship test, a residency test, and an age test, and for whom the taxpayer satisfies an identification requirement (Code Sec. 32(c)(3)).[59] The individual must be the taxpayer's child, a descendant thereof, adopted child, stepchild, or eligible foster child. A married child must also qualify as a dependent for whom the taxpayer is entitled to a dependency exemption. The child must share the same domestic principal place of abode with the taxpayer for more than one-half of the tax year (the entire tax year for eligible foster children). A child must be under the age of 19 (or a full-time student who is under the age of 24) at the close of the tax year or permanently and totally disabled at any time during the tax year. The taxpayer must specify the name and age of each qualifying child as well as the taxpayer identification number of a qualifying child on the return (Code Sec. 32(c)(3)).

No Qualifying Child. An individual who does not have a qualifying child may be eligible for this credit if (1) the principal residence of such individual is in the United States for more than one-half of the tax year, (2) the individual (or the spouse of the individual) is at least age 25 and under age 65 before the close of the

Footnote references are to paragraphs of the 2002 Standard Federal Tax Reports.

¶ 1375   [56] ¶ 4060   [58] ¶ 4080   [59] ¶ 4080
             [57] ¶ 38,754

tax year, and (3) the individual is not claimed as a dependent by another (Code Sec. 32(c)(1)(A)(ii)).

Restrictions on Claiming the Credit. The credit is denied to taxpayers who are not eligible to work in the United States. A nonresident alien usually cannot claim an earned income credit (Code Sec. 32(c)(1)(E)). Also, a person who claims a foreign earned income exclusion cannot claim an earned income credit (Code Sec. 32(c)(1)(D)).

Filing Requirements. Married persons must file a joint return in order to claim this credit. However, a married person living apart from a spouse under circumstances described at ¶ 173 need not file a joint return to claim the credit. Also, the credit may be claimed only for a full 12-month tax year, except in the case of death.

Earned Income. The credit is based on earned income, which includes all wages, salaries, tips, and other employee compensation (including union strike benefits), plus the amount of the taxpayer's net earnings from self-employment (determined with regard to the deduction for one-half of self-employment taxes (see ¶ 923)). For purposes of the earned income credit, earned income also includes nontaxable compensation such as the basic quarters and subsistence allowances for the military, parsonage allowances, the value of meals and lodging furnished for the convenience of the employer, and excludable employer-provided dependent care benefits. Earned income is determined without regard to community property laws (Code Sec. 32(c)(2)).

Earned income does not include interest and dividends, welfare benefits (including AFDC payments), veterans' benefits, pensions or annuities, alimony, social security benefits, workers' compensation, unemployment compensation, taxable scholarships or fellowships that are not reported on Form W-2, amounts that are subject to Code Sec. 871(a) (relating to income of nonresident alien individuals not connected with U.S. business), amounts received for services performed by prison inmates while in prison, or payments received from work activities (including work associated with the refurbishing of public housing) if sufficient private sector employment is not available and from community service programs (sections 407(d)(4) and 407(d)(7) of the Social Security Act). The amount of the earned income credit must also be reduced by the amount of the alternative minimum tax liability (Code Sec. 32(h)).[60]

Amount of Credit. The credit is determined by multiplying an individual's earned income that does not exceed a maximum amount (called the earned income amount) by the applicable credit percentage. The credit is reduced by a limitation amount determined by multiplying the applicable phaseout percentage by the excess of the amount of the individual's adjusted gross income (or earned income, if greater) over the phaseout amount. The earned income amount and the phaseout amount are adjusted yearly for inflation. The amount of allowable credit may be determined through the use of the tables that appear at ¶ 87.

For 2001, the maximum credit for one child is $2,428, two or more children is $4,008, and no qualifying children is $364 (Rev. Proc. 2001-13). For 2002, as projected by CCH, the maximum credits will be $2,506, $4,140 and $376, respectively (Code Sec. 32(b) and (j)).

Advance Payments. The earned income credit is refundable to the extent that it reduces the tax below zero. An eligible taxpayer may elect to receive advance payment of the credit through his or her paychecks. Form W-5 is to be used by eligible employees in order to notify their employers that they choose to receive advance payments instead of waiting until they file their annual tax returns.

The amount of the earned income credit that may be received as an advance payment for individuals who have one or more qualifying children is limited to 60% of the maximum credit available to an individual with one qualifying child. The

---

Footnote references are to paragraphs of the 2002 Standard Federal Tax Reports.
[60] ¶ 4080

advance payment of the earned income credit is not available to an individual who does not have a qualifying child (Code Sec. 3507(b)).

The advance payment is included on the taxpayer's Form W-2 and is shown on the return as part of the tax liability on Form 1040A and as an "other" tax due on Form 1040. The actual credit to which the taxpayer is entitled is treated as a payment. Any difference will be refunded to the taxpayer or has to be paid to the IRS by the taxpayer.

How to Claim the Credit. Taxpayers should use Form 1040, Schedule EIC, or Form 1040A, Schedule EIC, or Form 1040EZ to determine whether they are eligible for the credit. Credit amounts, which are determined by using the tables at ¶ 87, are also computed on these schedules. Taxpayers claiming the earned income tax credit *must* include a taxpayer identification number for themselves, their spouses (if married) and any qualifying children on their income tax return.

Earned income credit payments due a taxpayer are subject to interception by the Treasury Department to reimburse a state for any unpaid child-support obligations that have been assigned to the state, the U.S. Supreme Court has ruled.[61]

2001 Legislation. The Economic Growth and Tax Relief Reconciliation Act of 2001 (P.L. 107-16) made several important changes to the earned income credit which will apply beginning in 2002. To alleviate the marriage penalty, the phaseout amount will be increased by $1,000 for 2002 through 2004; by $2,000 for 2004 through 2006; and by $3,000 for 2007 and thereafter (Code Sec. 32(j), as amended by P.L. 107-16). The earned income definition is revised to exclude all forms of nontaxable employee compensation (Code Sec. 32(c), as amended by P.L. 107-16). The modified adjusted gross income calculation has been eliminated (Code Sec. 32(a), as amended by P.L. 107-16). Thus, the earned income credit will be based on the taxpayer's adjusted gross income. The relationship test will be broadened to include descendants of stepchildren (Code Sec. 32(c), as amended by P.L. 107-16). Additionally, the one-year residency requirement for foster children is eliminated (Code Sec. 32(c), as amended by P.L. 107-16). The rule which gave the qualifying child for two taxpayers to the one with the higher adjusted gross income has been modified. Now, there is a set of rules giving priority to the parent of the child (Code Sec. 32(c), as amended by P.L. 107-16). Finally, the earned income credit is no longer to be reduced by the amount of an individual's alternative minimum tax liability (Code Sec. 32(h), as repealed by P.L. 107-16).

Gasoline Tax Credit

1379. Credit for Federal Tax on Gasoline, Special Fuels. A credit for federal excise taxes on gasoline and special fuels may be taken where the fuel item is used for (1) farming purposes, (2) nonhighway purposes of a trade or business, (3) operation of intercity, local, or school buses, and (4) certain nontaxable purposes (Code Sec. 34).[62] The above credits are computed on Form 4136, "Credit for Federal Tax Paid on Fuels," which is attached to Form 1040 or Form 843, "Claim for Refund."

Regulated Investment Company Credit

1384. Credit for Capital Gain Tax. Undistributed capital gain of a regulated investment company must be included proportionately in the gross income of its shareholders. The capital gain tax that the company pays on this gain is treated as having been paid by the shareholders and is allowed as a credit against the tax (Code Sec. 852(b)(3)(D)(ii)).[63] In order to claim the credit, Copy B of Form 2439, "Notice to Shareholders of Undistributed Long-Term Capital Gains," must be attached to the taxpayer's return. See ¶ 2309.

Footnote references are to paragraphs of the 2002 Standard Federal Tax Reports.

¶ **1379**   [61] ¶ 4082.38   [62] ¶ 4150   [63] ¶ 26,433.022

Chapter 14

MINIMUM TAX

Calculating Alternative Minimum Tax

1401. The Minimum Tax Equation. Alternative minimum tax (AMT) rules have been devised to ensure that at least a minimum amount of income tax is paid by high-income corporate and noncorporate taxpayers (including estates and trusts) who reap large tax savings by making generous use of certain tax deductions and exemptions. Without the alternative minimum tax, some of these taxpayers might be able to escape income taxation entirely. In essence, the AMT functions as a recapture mechanism, reclaiming some of the tax breaks primarily available to high-income taxpayers, and represents an attempt to maintain tax equity.

A noncorporate taxpayer's AMT for a tax year is the excess of his tentative minimum tax over his regular tax (Code Sec. 55(a)) [1] (regular tax is discussed at ¶ 1420) and must be paid in addition to his regular tax. Thus, if a taxpayer's tentative minimum tax for a tax year is $75,000 while his regular tax is $50,000, he must pay an AMT of $25,000 in addition to the $50,000 regular tax for a total tax of $75,000. Form 6251, "Alternative Minimum Tax—Individuals," must be used by individuals to compute the AMT, while corporations must use Form 4626 "Alternative Minimum Tax—Corporations." Estates and trusts must use Schedule I of Form 1041 "U.S. Income Tax Return for Estates and Trusts."

The tentative minimum tax, in the case of a noncorporate taxpayer, is initially determined as the sum of 26 percent of the first $175,000 (or $87,500, in the case of married taxpayers filing separately) of alternative minimum taxable income (AMTI) in excess of the applicable exemption amount (¶ 1405) and 28 percent of any additional AMTI. Generally, the maximum rate of tax, including alternative minimum tax, on the net capital gain of an individual is 20 percent, any net capital gain which otherwise would be taxed at a 15-percent rate is taxed at a rate of 10 percent, and a special 25-percent rate is applied to the portion of the gain which represents unrecaptured depreciation on the sale of depreciable real estate (Code Sec. 55(b)(3)). A lower rate of 18 percent (8 percent for individuals in a 15-percent tax bracket) applies in tax years beginning after December 31, 2000 if the asset sold was held for more than five years (see ¶ 1736).

The tentative minimum tax of the noncorporate taxpayer is then reduced by the alternative minimum tax foreign tax credit (¶ 1410).

For tax years beginning in 1998, a corporation that meets certain gross receipts tests is considered to be a small corporation and, as a result, will not be subject to the alternative minimum tax (its tentative minimum tax is treated as zero) as long as it remains a small corporation (Code Sec. 55(e)). A small corporation is a corporation that has had average annual gross receipts of $5,000,000 or less over its 1994, 1995 and 1996 tax years and $7,500,000 or less over its 1995, 1996 and 1997 tax years. Once a corporation is recognized as a small corporation, it will continue to be exempt from the AMT for so long as its average annual gross receipts for the prior three-year period does not exceed $7,500,000. Also, a new corporation is treated as having a tentative minimum tax of zero, and, thus, is not subject to the AMT for the first tax year that the corporation is in existence. The allowable credit against the regular tax for prior year minimum tax liability (¶ 1370) of a small corporation is limited to the amount by which the corporation's regular tax liability (reduced by other credits) exceeds 25 percent of the excess (if any) of the corporation's regular tax (reduced by other credits) over $25,000. If a corporation ceases to be a small corporation, the AMT will apply only prospectively.

In the case of other corporations, the tentative minimum tax for the tax year is 20 percent of the excess of the alternative minimum taxable income over the AMTI exemption amount, reduced by the alternative minimum tax foreign tax credit.

Alternative Minimum Taxable Income. AMTI is the heart of minimum taxation. It is through this figure that excessive tax savings are recaptured. The base for computing AMTI is regular taxable income (including unrelated business taxable income, real estate investment trust taxable income, life insurance company taxable income, or any other income base, other than the alcohol fuels credit gross income of Code Sec. 87, used to calculate regular tax liability). This amount is then increased by a body of tax items, known as tax preference items (TPIs), which are the ultimate target of the minimum tax recapture apparatus. These items make up only a portion of the Code's available tax benefits but have been identified as a potential source of inordinate tax savings.

There are two ways in which TPIs are used to compute AMTI. In the first approach, all or a portion of the deductions or exclusions that have been claimed in computing regular taxation are directly added back to the regular taxable income base that makes up AMTI (Code Sec. 57).[2] For example, the excess of a depletion deduction for an interest in a mineral deposit over the adjusted basis of the interest must be added to the regular taxable income base (Code Sec. 57(a)(1)).[3] In the second form of recapture, the method used to compute a deduction for regular taxation is changed for minimum taxation (Code Sec. 56 and Code Sec. 58).[4] A change in methods will often, but not always, reduce the amount of a deduction originally claimed in regular taxation (or increase the amount of income originally subject to regular taxation) and thereby increase the taxable income base used in AMTI. For example, a corporation that uses the MACRS 200-percent declining balance method to compute a property's depreciation deduction for regular tax purposes may have to use the 150-percent declining balance method to compute AMTI (Code Sec. 56(a)(1)).[5] In the early years of that property's life, the regular tax MACRS deduction will exceed the deduction allowed for purposes of AMTI. For a given tax year, the excess of MACRS deductions over AMT deductions, if any, must be added back to the AMTI base. Tax preference items are discussed at ¶ 1425 and adjustments are covered at ¶ 1430-¶ 1440.

> **Example.** Jennifer, a single individual, has regular taxable income of $80,000 in 2001 and TPIs totaling $125,000. Her regular tax on the regular taxable income using tax rate schedules is $19,052. To compute her AMT, she must first establish her AMTI by adding the TPIs to regular taxable income ($205,000). Next, her tentative minimum tax must be

---

Footnote references are to paragraphs of the 2002 Standard Federal Tax Reports.

¶ 1401
[2] ¶ 5300
[3] ¶ 5300
[4] ¶ 5200, ¶ 5350
[5] ¶ 5200

computed by first subtracting her exemption amount of $12,625 (see ¶ 1405) from AMTI of $205,000 to arrive at the amount of $192,375. Since $192,375 exceeds $175,000, 28 percent of the $17,375 excess ($192,375 − $175,000) or $4,865 is added to 26 percent of $175,000, or $45,500, to arrive at a $50,365 tentative minimum tax from which any available alternative minimum tax foreign tax credit (AMT-FTC) is then subtracted. Assuming that there is no AMT-FTC, the $31,313 excess of the $50,365 tentative minimum tax over the $19,052 regular tax is the individual's AMT and must be paid in addition to her regular tax.

Minimum Tax on Children with Unearned Income. The alternative minimum tax of a child age 13 or younger who has net unearned income and who is subject to the regular tax "kiddie tax" rules (¶ 114 and ¶ 706) is limited (Code Sec. 59(j)).[6] AMT is limited to the child's share of the increase in the parents' alternative minimum tax that would result from increasing the parents' tentative minimum tax and regular tax by the sum of the tentative minimum taxes and regular taxes, respectively, of the child and all other siblings subject to the "kiddie tax." The child's share of the increase is determined under the "kiddie tax" rules (Code Sec. 1(g)(3)(B) and Code Sec. 59(j)(2)).

Exemption Amount

1405. Amount Excluded from Minimum Taxation. A specified amount of AMTI is exempt from alternative minimum taxation (Code Sec. 55(d)).[7] The amount varies according to the taxpayer's filing status and, following the Economic Growth and Tax Relief Reconciliation Act of 2001 (P.L. 107-16), the tax year at hand. For tax years before 2001 and after 2004, the AMT exemption amounts are (1) $45,000 for married individuals filing a joint return and surviving spouses, (2) $33,750 for unmarried individuals other than surviving spouses, and (3) $22,500 for married individuals filing a separate return and estates or trusts (other than electing small business trusts). The AMTI exemption amount is zero in the case of the portion of an electing small business trust is taxed as a separate trust. The portion of an electing small business trust that is used to hold the stock of an S corporation is taxed as a separate trust.

Following P.L. 107-16, the AMT exemption amounts for individuals increase for tax years beginning in 2001 through 2004. The new exemption amounts are (1) $49,000 for married individuals filing a joint return and surviving spouses, (2) $35,750 for unmarried individuals other than surviving spouses, and (3) $24,500 for married individuals filing a separate return (Code Sec. 55(d), as amended by P.L. 107-16). There is no increase in the alternative minimum tax exemption amount for estates and trusts. The figure remains unchanged at $22,500.

The exemption amounts are phased out for taxpayers with high AMTI. The exemption amounts are reduced by 25 cents for each $1 of AMTI in excess of (1) $150,000, in the case of married individuals filing a joint return and surviving spouses (the $49,000 exemption amount is completely phased out when AMTI is $346,000 or more ($45,000 amount phases out at $330,000)); (2) $112,500, in the case of unmarried individuals other than surviving spouses (the $35,750 exemption amount is completely phased out when AMTI is $255,500 or more ($33,750 amount phases out at $247,500)); and (3) $75,000, in the case of married individuals filing a separate return and estates or trusts (the $24,500 exemption amount is completely phased out when AMTI is $173,000 or more ($22,500 amount phases out at $165,000)). For married individuals filing a separate return, the maximum exemption phaseout is, in effect, the same as for married individuals filing jointly. This is accomplished by increasing the AMTI of the married individual filing a separate return by the lesser of (1) $24,500 (for 2001) or (2) 25 percent of the excess of AMTI

(as determined before this adjustment) over $165,000. None of the above exemption or phaseout amounts are adjusted for inflation.

> **Example 1.** For tax year 2001, an unmarried individual with AMTI of $150,000 may claim an exemption amount of only $26,375, rather than the full $35,750 available to individuals with AMTI of $112,500 or less. The exemption amount is determined by finding the excess of the individual's AMTI ($150,000) over $112,500, which is $37,500, multiplying the difference by 25% ($37,500 × .25 = $9,375), and subtracting the product from $35,750 ($35,750 − $9,375 = $26,375).

> **Example 2.** For tax year 2001, married individuals have a regular taxable income of $100,000 and tax preferences and adjustments totaling $40,000. Assume that the regular tax on $100,000 is $23,000. Their AMTI (regular taxable income plus tax preferences and adjustments) is $140,000 ($100,000+ $40,000). The AMTI is reduced by the applicable exemption amount of $49,000 and their tentative minimum tax is $23,660 ($91,000 × 26%). Thus, their AMT liability is $660 ($23,660 − $23,000).

Special Exemption Amounts for Certain Minor Children. The AMTI exemption amount of a minor child under age fourteen is equal to the lesser of $35,750 or the sum of the child's earned income plus $5,350 for tax years beginning in 2001 (Code Sec. 59(j)).

Small Business Trusts. Electing small business trusts have no exemption amount (Code Sec. 641(d)(2)(B)).

Credits Against Minimum Tax

1410. Alternative Minimum Tax Foreign Tax Credit. The only tax credit fully allowed to compute the AMT is the alternative minimum tax foreign tax credit (AMT-FTC), which may be no higher than 90 percent of the tentative minimum tax (¶ 1401 and Code Sec. 59(a)(2)). For purposes of this tentative minimum tax computation, AMTI is determined without including the alternative tax net operating loss deduction or intangible drilling cost preference exception for independent producers (see ¶ 1425 and ¶ 1430) and is determined after subtracting the AMTI exemption amount (Code Sec. 55(b)(1) and Code Sec. 59(a)).[8] An excess AMT-FTC for a tax year may be carried back or forward under the same ordering scheme allowed for carrybacks or carryforwards of regular tax FTCs, namely, to the second preceding tax year, the first preceding tax year, and then to the first through fifth succeeding tax years (Code Sec. 59(a)(2)(B)). The AMT-FTC for a tax year is determined by calculating the amount of foreign taxes on foreign source AMTI and then finding the limit on the size of an FTC that may be claimed during a tax year, which is accomplished by multiplying the tentative minimum tax by the ratio of a taxpayer's foreign source AMTI to worldwide AMTI. Alternatively, the taxpayer may elect to compute the AMT-FTC limit by multiplying the tentative minimum tax by the ratio of the taxpayer's foreign source regular taxable income to worldwide AMTI. A taxpayer may be subject to AMT even though any regular tax liability is eliminated by the foreign tax credit. The AMT liability can arise because the alternative minimum tax FTC is limited to 90 percent of the tentative minimum tax (Code Sec. 59(a)).[9]

Tax Liability Limitations. For taxpayers subject to AMT, the full benefit of other tax credits may be denied. In general, the sum of the nonrefundable child tax credit and all other nonrefundable personal tax credits is limited to the excess of the taxpayer's regular tax liability over the taxpayer's tentative minimum tax liability (determined without regard to the foreign tax credit) (Code Sec. 24(a)). For tax years beginning in 1998 and 1999, a taxpayer's nonrefundable personal tax credits

Footnote references are to paragraphs of the 2002 Standard Federal Tax Reports.

¶ **1410**　　　[8] ¶ 5100, ¶ 5400　　　[9] ¶ 5400

may be offset against the entire regular tax liability. However, for tax years beginning in 2000, the nonrefundable portion of the child tax credit may be offset against both the regular tax and alternative minimum tax liability. In addition, the general tax liability limitation (referred to as the alternative minimum tax offset) does not apply to the refundable child tax credit for families with three or more children beginning after 2001 (Code Sec. 24(d)).

Regular Tax

1420. Regular Tax Compared with Tentative Minimum Tax. The regular tax figure to which the tentative minimum tax is compared is a taxpayer's Chapter 1 tax reduced by his foreign and possessions tax credits (Code Sec. 55(c)).[10] Although the following taxes are imposed under Chapter 1, they are not included in the regular tax: (1) accumulated earnings taxes (Code Sec. 531); (2) personal holding company taxes (Code Sec. 541); (3) alternative minimum tax (Code Sec. 55); (4) 30 percent withholding taxes against the investment income of nonresident aliens and foreign corporations (Code Sec. 871(a) and Code Sec. 881); (5) foreign corporations' branch profits taxes (Code Sec. 884); (6) taxes on built-in gains of S corporations (Code Sec. 1374); (7) taxes on an S corporation's passive investment income (Code Sec. 1375); (8) taxes on early distributions from retirement plans (Code Sec. 72(m)(5)(B), Code Sec. 72(q), Code Sec. 72(t), and Code Sec. 72(v)); (9) excise taxes on the transfer of residual interests in REMICs to "disqualified organizations" (Code Sec. 860E(e)); (10) taxes on foreign expropriation loss recoveries (Code Sec. 1351(d)); (11) taxes on nonqualified withdrawals from certain Merchant Marine capital construction funds (Code Sec. 7518(g)(6)); (12) taxes that arise out of the recapture of investment tax credits (Code Sec. 49(b) or Code Sec. 50(a)) or low-income housing credits (Code Sec. 42(j) and Code Sec. 42(k)); (13) taxes that arise out of the recapture of mortgage bond federal subsidies (Code Sec. 143(m)); and (14) interest on tax liabilities deferred under the installment method (Code Sec. 453(l)(3) and Code Sec. 453A(c)). Also excluded from the regular tax are: (1) the additional tax on medical savings account distributions not used for qualified medical savings accounts (Code Sec. 220(f)(4)); (2) the additional tax on certain distributions from educational individual retirement accounts (Code Sec. 530(d)(3)); and (3) the "tax" on certain transfers of high-yield interests to disqualified holders (Code Sec. 860K).

Tax Preference Items

1425. TPIs Added Back to AMTI. Among the tax items that have been singled out as potential sources of extraordinary tax savings are tax preference items (TPIs) (Code Sec. 57).[11] Because these items are instrumental in generating tax savings by reducing a taxpayer's taxable income, they must be added back to the taxable income of either corporate or noncorporate taxpayers in computing AMTI so that unreasonably high tax breaks may be recaptured. The following is a complete list of TPIs:

(1) The amount by which the depletion deduction claimed by a taxpayer (other than an independent oil and gas producer) for an interest in a property exceeds the adjusted basis of the interest at the end of a tax year;

(2) The amount by which an integrated oil company's excess intangible drilling costs (i.e., the excess of the IDC deduction over the deduction that would have been allowed if the costs had been capitalized and ratably amortized over a 120-month period) is greater than 65 percent of the taxpayer's net income from oil, gas, and geothermal properties. Independent producers are not subject to this preference in tax years beginning after 1992. Their AMTI, however, may not be reduced by more than 40 percent (in tax years beginning

---

Footnote references are to paragraphs of the 2002 Standard Federal Tax Reports.

after 1993) of the AMTI that would otherwise be determined if the taxpayer were subject to this intangible drilling cost preference and did not compute an alternative tax net operating loss deduction;

(3) The excess of a financial institution's deduction for reasonable bad debt reserves over the deduction that would have been allowed had the institution maintained a reserve for all tax years on the basis of actual experience;

(4) Tax-exempt interest (less any related expenses) on specified private activity bonds, which generally are issued after August 7, 1986;

(5) For most property placed in service prior to 1987, the excess of accelerated depreciation on nonrecovery real property over straight-line depreciation;

(6) For most property placed in service by noncorporate taxpayers and personal holding companies prior to 1987, the excess of accelerated depreciation on leased personal property over straight-line depreciation;

(7) For most property placed in service prior to 1987, the excess of rapid amortization of pollution control facilities under Code Sec. 169 over the depreciation that would be allowed under Code Sec. 167;

(8) For most property placed in service by noncorporate taxpayers and personal holding companies prior to 1987, the excess of the ACRS deduction for leased recovery property (other than 19-year real property and low-income housing) over the straight-line depreciation deduction that would have been allowed if a half-year convention had been used, salvage value had been disregarded, and the following recovery periods had been used:

In the case of:	The recovery period is:
3-year property	5 years
5-year property	8 years
10-year property	15 years
15-year public utility property	22 years

(9) For most property placed in service by taxpayers prior to 1987, the excess of the ACRS deduction for 19-year real property or low-income housing over the deduction that would have been allowed if straight-line depreciation, with a 19-year recovery period for real property and a 15-year recovery period for low-income housing, had been used and computed without considering salvage value; and

(10) 42 percent of the amount of gain excluded from the sale or disposition of qualified small business stock (28 percent is substituted for 42 percent, in the case of stock, the holding period of which begins after December 31, 2000) (¶ 2396).

Adjustments to Selected Tax Items

1430. Adjustments Affecting Corporate and Noncorporate Taxpayers. In addition to TPIs, the AMT is aimed at recovering some of the tax savings generated by a variety of other deductions and methods for computing tax liability. This is achieved by requiring taxpayers to recompute certain regular tax deductions in a different, less preferential manner. Adjustments are usually required in order to eliminate "time value" tax savings that result from tax laws allowing the acceleration of deductions (e.g., the MACRS depreciation) or the deferral of income (e.g., the completed-contract method of determining income from long-term contracts). Thus, the recomputation of the items for AMT purposes usually results in an initial increase to AMTI.

Some adjustments have to be made solely by noncorporate taxpayers (see ¶ 1435), while others have to be made solely by corporate taxpayers (see ¶ 1440). All

taxpayers, whether corporate or noncorporate, must make the following adjustments when determining AMTI:

Depreciation. For property placed in service after 1998, if the 200-percent declining balance method is used for regular tax purposes for 3-, 5-, 7-, or 10-year property, then the 150-percent declining balance method and regular tax depreciation period must be used for AMT purposes (Code Sec. 56(a)(1)).[12] For all other property placed in service after 1998, no AMT adjustment is required, as AMT and regular tax depreciation are identical.

For property placed in service after 1986 and before 1999, if the 200-percent declining balance method is used for regular tax purposes for 3-, 5-, 7-, or 10-year property, then the 150-percent declining balance method and the ADS recovery period must be used for AMT purposes (Code Sec. 56(a)(1), prior to amendment by P.L. 105-34). If the 150-percent declining balance method is used for 15- or 20-year property, then the 150-percent declining balance method and the ADS recovery period is used for AMT purposes. If the 150-percent declining balance method election is in effect for regular tax purposes for 3-, 5-, 7-, 10-, 15-, or 20-year property, then no adjustment is required for AMT purposes, as the AMT and regular tax depreciation are computed the same way (i.e., using the 150-percent declining balance method over the ADS recovery period). In the case of 27.5-year residential real property, or in the case of 31.5- or 39-year real property, AMT depreciation is computed using the straight-line method and ADS recovery period (40 years). If the straight-line election is in effect for regular tax purposes for 3-, 5-, 7-, 10-, 15-, or 20-year property, then for AMT purposes the straight-line method and ADS recovery period must be used. If the MACRS ADS method (elective or nonelective) is used for regular tax purposes, then no adjustment is required for AMT purposes, as AMT and regular tax depreciation are computed the same way on real and personal property subject to such method.

Adjusting depreciation deductions, rather than treating them as TPIs, may provide taxpayers with some major benefits as they compute AMTI in the later years of a property's use. Although MACRS deductions will exceed AMT deductions in the early years of a property's use (assuming that AMT and MACRS deductions are not computed in the same manner), the reverse will be true in the later years. Thus, the higher deductions produced under the applicable AMT method in later years may be used to reduce AMTI and, therefore, reduce the potential for alternative minimum taxation. Another benefit from the adjustment approach to depreciation is that depreciation for all property is combined in calculating AMTI, allowing for the netting of excess MACRS deductions with excess alternative deductions. Consequently, a taxpayer who has excess MACRS deductions on a new piece of property may be able to avoid paying an AMT on the excess deductions by offsetting them with excess alternative deductions generated by an older piece of property.

No AMT adjustments have to be made to depreciation claimed for property which has been expensed under Code Sec. 179; motion pictures, video tapes, and public utility property for which the normalization method of accounting is not used; and property which is depreciated under the units of production method or under a depreciation method which is not based on a term of years (other than the retirement-replacement-betterment method or similar method).

When property that generated depreciation deductions is sold, its adjusted basis must be computed under the alternative minimum tax rules in order to determine the gain or loss from the sale for alternative minimum tax purposes (Code Sec. 56(a)(7)).[13] The difference between the regular tax gain or loss and the recomputed alternative minimum tax gain or loss is a tax preference adjustment in the year of sale.

Example 1. A taxpayer has purchased a piece of property for $100,000 and, over several tax years, has claimed a total of $25,000 of depreciation deductions in regular tax calculations. In AMTI calculations made during the same tax years, he has claimed adjusted depreciation deductions totaling $10,000. He sells the property in the current tax year for $150,000. The adjusted basis of the property in regular tax calculations is $75,000 ($100,000 − $25,000), leaving him with a regular tax gain of $75,000. However, the amount of gain that must be included in his AMTI calculations is only $60,000 ($150,000 − $90,000), since the adjusted basis of the property must reflect only adjusted depreciation deductions.

Mining Exploration and Development Costs. Taxpayers who have expensed mining exploration and development expenditures (or amortized these costs under Code Sec. 291) in computing their regular tax must, in calculating AMTI, capitalize and amortize these costs over a 10-year period, beginning with the tax year in which the expenditures were made (Code Sec. 56(a)(2)).[14] If a tax loss is incurred from a mine, all expenditures which have been capitalized but not yet amortized may be deducted from AMTI.

When property that generated mining exploration and development deductions is sold, its adjusted basis must be computed under the alternative minimum tax rules in order to determine the gain or loss from the sale for alternative minimum tax purposes (Code Sec. 56(a)(7)).[15] The difference between the regular tax gain or loss and the recomputed alternative minimum tax gain or loss is a tax preference adjustment in the year of sale.

Long-Term Contracts. The percentage-of-completion method of accounting for gain or loss from long-term contracts (other than home construction contracts) must be substituted for any other accounting method, such as the completed contract method or the cash basis method, to determine AMTI for long-term contracts (Code Sec. 56(a)(3)).[16] The percentage of completion is determined using simplified cost allocation procedures in the case of construction contracts of certain small contractors if the contract has an estimated duration of less than two years (Code Sec. 56(a)(3) and Code Sec. 460(e)(1)(B)).

Alternative Tax Net Operating Loss Deduction. Net operating loss deductions must be recomputed so that tax preferences (including TPIs and items that are subject to adjustment for AMTI) that make up an NOL are not a factor in reducing AMTI (Code Sec. 56(a)(4) and Code Sec. 56(d)).[17] A recomputed NOL, termed an alternative tax NOL, may not offset more than 90 percent of AMTI (computed without the alternative tax NOL deduction). An alternative tax NOL is computed in the same manner as an ordinary NOL, except that it is reduced by TPIs (items listed in Code Sec. 57), and tax items that must be adjusted for AMTI calculations (items listed in Code Sec. 56 and Code Sec. 58) must also be adjusted for NOL calculations. It does not have to be reduced by the TPIs listed in Code Sec. 57 if those items did not increase the amount of a regular tax NOL deduction.

Example 2. A taxpayer's income for a tax year is $75,000, while her losses total $100,000, of which $20,000 is from TPIs. Her NOL for regular taxation is $25,000. In computing AMTI, TPIs cannot be used. Consequently, only $80,000 of the losses may offset income, leaving the taxpayer with an alternative tax NOL of $5,000.

Pollution Control Facilities. For property placed in service after 1986 and before 1999, the five-year amortization method for depreciating pollution control facilities (Code Sec. 169) must be replaced by the alternative depreciation system (Code Sec. 168(g)). (See Code Sec. 56(a)(5).)[18] The pollution control facility adjust-

ment is computed under MACRS using the straight-line method for property placed in service after 1998.

When the pollution control facility is sold, its adjusted basis must be computed under the alternative minimum tax rules in order to determine the gain or loss from the sale for alternative minimum tax purposes (Code Sec. 56(a)(7)).[19] The difference between the regular tax gain or loss and the recomputed alternative minimum tax gain or loss is a tax preference adjustment in the year of sale.

1435. Adjustments Affecting Noncorporate Taxpayers. Noncorporate taxpayers must make the following adjustments when computing AMTI:

Alternative Tax Itemized Deductions. Some of the itemized deductions that a noncorporate taxpayer has claimed for regular tax purposes may not be claimed for AMTI purposes (Code Sec. 56(b)).[20] These deductions and the tax savings they generate have been targeted for recapture by the AMTI. They include miscellaneous itemized deductions that are subject to the 2% AGI floor under Code Sec. 67. This means that miscellaneous itemized deductions claimed in the computation of regular taxation must be added back to AMTI. State, local, or foreign tax payments are not deductible, and refunds of these taxes need not be included in AMTI. Deductions may be claimed for medical expenses, but the expenses must exceed AGI by 10 percent rather than 7.5 percent. Investment interest expenses are limited to the size of a taxpayer's net investment income. Tax-exempt interest on private activity bonds is included in investment income for this purpose, and interest expended to carry the bonds is included in investment interest expenses.

The limitation on itemized deductions of high-income taxpayers that applies for regular tax purposes (Code Sec. 68) does not apply for AMTI purposes (Code Sec. 56(b)(1)(F)).[21]

Among the itemized interest deductions that may be claimed against AMTI is qualified housing interest, which is similar to the qualified residence interest deduction that may be claimed against regular tax (Code Sec. 56(e)).[22] Qualified housing interest is interest paid on a loan used to purchase, build, or substantially improve (1) a taxpayer's principal residence and (2) another dwelling (i.e., a house, apartment, condominium, or mobile home that is not used on a transient basis) personally used by the taxpayer during a tax year for the greater of (a) 14 days or (b) 10 percent of the number of days during which the dwelling is leased (see Code Sec. 163(h)(4) and Code Sec. 280A(d)(1)). It is not subject to the limitation on investment interest deductions. Interest on a refinanced loan is also deductible if the loan does not exceed the balance remaining on the original loan.

Personal Exemptions and the Standard Deduction. No deduction for or in lieu of personal exemptions may be claimed against alternative minimum taxable income, and the standard deduction may not be claimed for AMTI purposes (Code Sec. 56(b)(1)(E)).[23]

Circulation and Research and Experimental Expenditures. Circulation expenditures (i.e., the costs (deductible under Code Sec. 173) of establishing, maintaining, or increasing a newspaper's, magazine's, or other periodical's circulation), which are expensed for regular tax calculations, must be capitalized for AMTI calculations and ratably amortized over a three-year period, which starts with the tax year in which the expenditures are made (Code Sec. 56(b)(2)); [24] research and experimental expenditures (Code Sec. 174) must be ratably amortized over a 10-year period. These adjustments, in effect, treat the excess of expense deductions over amortization deductions as a tax preference. Besides noncorporate taxpayers, personal holding companies must also recompute circulation costs for AMTI. No recomputation of research and experimental costs is required if a taxpayer has materially participated in the activity that generated the costs. If a loss is sustained on property that

---

Footnote references are to paragraphs of the 2002 Standard Federal Tax Reports.
[19] ¶ 5200   [21] ¶ 5200   [23] ¶ 5200
[20] ¶ 5200   [22] ¶ 5200   [24] ¶ 5200   **¶ 1435**

generated these research and experimental deductions or circulation expenditures, a deduction is allowed equal to the lesser of (1) the unamortized expenditures or (2) the amount that would be allowed as a loss had the expenditures remained capitalized. The adjusted basis of such property must be computed under the alternative minimum tax rules in order to determine the gain or loss from the sale for alternative minimum tax purposes (Code Sec. 56(a)(7)).[25] The difference between the regular tax gain or loss and the recomputed alternative minimum tax gain or loss is a tax preference adjustment in the year of sale.

Incentive Stock Options. AMTI must be increased by the amount by which the price actually paid by an individual for an incentive stock option is exceeded by the option's fair market value at the time his rights to the stock are freely transferable or are not subject to a substantial risk of forfeiture (Code Sec. 56(b)(3)).[26]

Passive Farm Tax Shelter Losses. Noncorporate taxpayers (including personal service corporations (see Code Sec. 469(j)(2))) who are not material participants in a farming business but use a farming tax shelter to avoid regular tax liability may not deduct passive farming losses in computing AMTI (Code Sec. 58(a)).[27] Farm tax shelters are farm syndicates (see Code Sec. 464(c)) or passive farm activities in which the taxpayer (or his spouse) is not a material participant (see Code Sec. 469(c)). The amount of denied losses must be reduced by the amount of a taxpayer's insolvency during a tax year. Insolvency is defined as the excess of a taxpayer's liabilities over the fair market value of his assets. Taxpayers may not net income and losses from various farming tax shelters to determine an overall loss or gain. Each tax shelter must be regarded separately. Thus, a taxpayer who suffers a $1,000 loss from one tax shelter, but has a $1,000 gain from another, must include a $1,000 gain in AMTI calculations. Also, tax preferences included in losses must be adjusted so that their preference is eliminated.

Farm losses that have been disallowed as deductions from AMTI in one tax year may be claimed as deductions from farm income from that activity in the succeeding tax year. Taxpayers who dispose of their interest in a farm tax shelter are allowed to claim their losses against AMTI.

Other Passive Business Activity Losses. With some modifications, the regular tax rules limiting the deductibility of losses from passive, nonfarm business activities must be followed in finding the minimum tax liability of individuals, trusts, estates, closely held C corporations, and personal service corporations. Thus, deductions for passive losses may be claimed only against passive income. One modification requires a taxpayer to reduce the amount of denied losses by the amount of his insolvency during a tax year. Furthermore, the passive activity loss is determined without regard to any qualified housing interest. Finally, passive losses must be adjusted, as they would be under other minimum tax rules, to eliminate tax preferences.

> **Example.** In calculating his regular tax, Doug Pratt has a passive loss deduction of $15,000 for net losses from real estate rentals. The losses are partially based on MACRS deductions, a tax preference (see ¶ 1430). His minimum tax liability must be determined by computing depreciation deductions under the alternative depreciation system. This leaves him with a passive loss deduction of only $5,000 against AMTI. Since he already has adjusted his depreciation deductions in determining whether there is a passive loss tax preference, he does not have to include them as part of any adjustment for depreciation tax preferences.

1440. Adjustments Affecting Corporate Taxpayers. Corporations must make the following adjustments to AMTI:

Adjusted Current Earnings. A portion of the difference between the AMTI and the adjusted current earnings (ACE) of corporations other than S corporations,

---

Footnote references are to paragraphs of the 2002 Standard Federal Tax Reports.

regulated investment companies, real estate investment trusts, or real estate mortgage investment conduits is treated as a tax preference for tax years beginning after 1989. This preference does not attempt to recapture the tax benefit derived by a corporation from the use of a particular tax deduction or exclusion, such as the depletion deduction described at ¶ 1425. Instead, it is aimed at recapturing some of the overall tax savings enjoyed by corporations that report large earnings to their shareholders and creditors but, due to a variety of tax benefits, pay little or no tax. To achieve recapture, a corporation's AMTI must be increased by 75 percent of the amount by which its ACE exceeds its AMTI, computed without the adjustments for either the ACE preference or alternative tax NOLs (Code Sec. 56(c)(1) and Code Sec. 56(g)).[28]

> **Example 1.** A corporation has AMTI of $100,000 before it makes adjustments for alternative tax NOLs or ACE. The current tax year's ACE amounts to $200,000, leaving the corporation with an ACE preference of $75,000 (.75 ($200,000 − $100,000)), which increases AMTI to $175,000 ($100,000 + $75,000).

In some years, AMTI may be decreased, rather than increased, by the ACE preference. If a corporation's ACE is less than its AMTI, ACE may reduce AMTI by 75 percent of the amount by which AMTI exceeds ACE (.75 (AMTI − ACE)). The overall amount by which the ACE preference may decrease AMTI over a period of years may not be greater than the overall amount by which the ACE preference has increased AMTI over that period. In a given tax year, this ceiling is determined by limiting the amount of AMTI available for reduction to the excess of prior year increases in AMTI caused by the ACE preference over prior year reductions caused by an ACE shortfall.

> **Example 2.** In a corporation's current tax year, it calculates ACE of $50,000 and AMTI of $70,000. Multiplying the difference between AMTI and ACE by .75 leaves the corporation with $15,000, an amount that may possibly be used to reduce AMTI and thereby reduce the amount of minimum tax to which AMTI may be subjected for other tax preferences. In its prior tax years, the corporation calculated an overall positive ACE preference of $10,000. This amount serves as a limit on the amount by which ACE may reduce AMTI in the current year, leaving the corporation with only a $10,000 reduction of AMTI rather than a $15,000 reduction. The possible reduction of $5,000 that remains may not be carried over to later tax years.

A quick look at the rather simple ACE preference formula makes it clear that the most important factor in establishing the size of the preference is determining what makes up a corporation's adjusted current earnings. In a broad view, ACE is made up of a corporation's earnings and profits—with a twist. The earnings and profits figure must be adjusted so that it takes on some of the principles used to calculate income for tax returns, including some of the principles for calculating the earnings and profits figure used to determine the taxation of dividend distributions to shareholders. Thus, the computation of ACE starts with AMTI as a base, which carries with it the built-in income, deductions, and exclusions used to determine regular as well as alternative taxable income.

For depreciable property placed into service before 1994, AMTI must be adjusted using the applicable ACE depreciation method, a method that may differ from that used for regular tax reporting, for corporate books, or even for the portion of AMTI that does not include the ACE preference. No ACE depreciation adjustment is made for property placed in service after 1993. The alternative (straight-line) MACRS method is used to determine allowable ACE depreciation for property placed in service after 1989 and before 1994 (Code Sec. 56(g)(4)(A)).

Footnote references are to paragraphs of the 2002 Standard Federal Tax Reports.

[28] ¶ 5200

Income, other than exempt discharge of indebtedness income, that is exempt from regular or minimum taxation but that is included in the computation of earnings and profits must be included in the computation of ACE. This includes items such as interest payments on state and local bonds that are excluded from regular taxation but typically are included in the earnings and profits corporations report in financial sheets disclosed to the public. Expenses incurred in earning this kind of income, while not deductible in determining regular or minimum taxation, are deductible in determining ACE.

Here is a sampling of other adjustments: (1) if a corporation does not claim a deduction against earnings and profits, it may not claim the deduction in the computation of ACE (except for certain dividends); (2) while they may be expensed or amortized in regular taxation, intangible drilling costs (other than the costs of a nonproductive well or costs incurred by independent producers related to oil or gas wells), the costs of organizing a corporation, and the costs of circulating periodicals must, in computing ACE, be capitalized; (3) ACE must be increased or decreased by an increase or decrease in a corporation's LIFO recapture amount, which is the amount by which the value of the corporation's inventory under the FIFO method of inventory valuation exceeds the value under the LIFO method; (4) the installment method of accounting, in most cases, may not be used in the computation of ACE to report income from installment sales; (5) income that has built up on a life insurance contract must be included in a corporation's ACE; (6) the cost depletion method must be used to determine depletion deductions of corporations other than independent oil and gas producers and royalty owners; (7) a corporation that has undergone an ownership change in which new shareholders have acquired more than half of the value of the corporation's stock must undertake a wholesale recomputation of the bases of its assets so that the basis of each asset takes on the value of the asset at the time of the corporation's acquisition by the new shareholders; (8) ACE may not include loss from the exchange of one pool of debt obligations for another pool that consists of obligations with the same effective interest rates and maturities as obligations in the first pool; (9) the adjusted basis of assets for purposes of making ACE preference adjustments is determined under these ACE preference rules; and (10) no adjustment related to the earnings and profits effect of charitable contributions is made to ACE.

Merchant Marine Capital Construction Funds. Contributions made by shipping companies to capital construction funds (established under Code Sec. 607 of the Merchant Marine Act of 1936, 46 U.S.C. 1177) may not be deducted from AMTI, and a fund's earnings (including gains or losses) may not be excluded from AMTI (Code Sec. 56(c)(2)).[29] No reduction in the basis of a vessel, barge, or container need be made to reflect amounts withdrawn from a fund if the amounts have been included in AMTI.

Blue Cross and Blue Shield Organizations. The special deduction from regular tax allowed to Blue Cross and Blue Shield organizations, under Code Sec. 833, for one-fourth of their annual claims and administrative expenses (less the prior tax year's adjusted surplus) may not be claimed against AMTI (Code Sec. 56(c)(3)).[30]

Property and Casualty Insurance Companies. A property and casualty insurance company that elects to be taxed only on taxable investment income for regular tax purposes determines its ACE without regard to underwriting income or underwriting expense in tax years beginning after 1997 (Code Sec. 56(g)(4)(B)(i)).

Cutbacks of Certain Corporate Tax Benefits

1445. Reductions in Tax Benefits v. Minimum Taxation. Under Code Sec. 291, several tax benefits that may be claimed by corporations must be reduced, in most cases, by 20 percent.[31] Like tax preferences that are subject to minimum

Footnote references are to paragraphs of the 2002 Standard Federal Tax Reports.

¶ **1445**   [29] ¶ 5200   [30] ¶ 5200   [31] ¶ 15,190

taxation, these tax items have been selected for reduction in order to prevent excessive tax benefits. However, the approach adopted under the preference cutback rules differs from the minimum tax principles. Rather than being subject to the minimum tax after they have been claimed against regular taxable income, these items are reduced in size before they may offset income. Some of these items are also tax preferences subject to minimum taxation, and, therefore, the AMT may be imposed if the tax benefit produced by these items after reduction remains too large (Code Sec. 59(f)).

The following reductions must first be made to these tax preferences:

(1) Corporations that have sold or otherwise disposed of Code Sec. 1250 property (depreciable real property) must provide ordinary income treatment to 20 percent of the portion of the gain on the disposition that has not been treated as ordinary income. The 20-percent treatment does not have to be applied if Code Sec. 1250 property was part of a certified pollution control facility (described in Code Sec. 169). Also, if a real estate investment trust (REIT) (Code Sec. 856) disposes of Code Sec. 1250 property, Code Sec. 1250 gain which is treated as not coming from ordinary income and is distributed to shareholders as a capital gain dividend is excluded from ordinary income treatment. Corporate shareholders of a REIT must treat capital gain dividends as subject to the 20-percent ordinary income treatment.

(2) The percentage depletion deduction (Code Sec. 613) for iron ore and coal (including lignite) must be reduced by 20 percent of the excess of (a) the percentage depletion deduction (determined before the 20-percent reduction is made) over (b) the adjusted basis (determined without including the depletion deduction claimed in a tax year) of the minerals at the close of the tax year.

(3) There must be a 20-percent reduction in the amount of deductions claimed by a financial institution (subject to Code Sec. 585 or Code Sec. 593) for certain interest expenses on debts incurred to purchase tax-exempt obligations acquired after December 31, 1982, and before August 8, 1986.

(4) The basis of certified pollution control facilities that is used under Code Sec. 169 for computing rapid amortization deductions must be reduced by 20 percent. ACRS depreciation must be used to depreciate the reduced basis.

(5) A corporation's (including an integrated oil company's) deductions for intangible drilling costs and mineral exploration and development costs (see Code Sec. 263, Code Sec. 616, and Code Sec. 617) must be reduced by 30 percent. Reduced deductions may be deducted ratably over a 60-month period that starts with the month in which costs are paid or incurred. Ratable deductions may be recaptured under Code Sec. 1254 if the related property is disposed of.

(6) The exemption from U.S. taxation allowed for 32 percent of the foreign sales corporation (FSC) foreign trade income that is determined without following FSC administrative pricing requirements (¶ 2470 and Code Sec. 923) must be reduced to 30 percent, while the exemption for 16/23 of the income that is determined under the pricing requirements is reduced to 15/23.

Rapid amortization deductions by pollution control facilities, bad debt reserve deductions claimed by financial institutions, percentage depletion deductions, and deductions for intangible drilling costs and mineral explorations and development costs are also subject to the minimum tax. They must be reduced before, rather than after, the minimum tax is imposed so that a double cutback of these items does not occur (Code Sec. 59(f)).[32]

Footnote references are to paragraphs of the 2002 Standard Federal Tax Reports.

Miscellaneous Rules

1450. Election to Avoid Tax Preference Status. Deductions for certain expenditures that are treated as tax preferences will not be treated as tax preferences, and therefore will not be subject to minimum taxation, if a taxpayer elects to claim these deductions ratably over a 3-year, 60-month, or 10-year period, beginning with the tax year (or month) in which the expenditures were made, rather than entirely in one tax year (Code Sec. 59(e)).[33] Taxpayers may limit their elections to only a portion of their deductions, leaving the remaining deductions subject to minimum taxation. The 3-year period may be claimed for circulation expenditures, the 60-month period may be claimed for intangible drilling and development expenditures, and the 10-year period may be claimed for research and experimental, mine development, and mining exploration expenditures. Partners and S corporation shareholders must make elections separately.

1455. S Corporations and Partnerships. S corporations and partnerships are not subject to the minimum tax (Code Sec. 701 and Code Sec. 1363(a)).[34] Shareholders and partners must compute their minimum tax liability separately. In determining the AMTI of a partner in an electing large partnership in post-1997 tax years, the partner must take into account his distributive share of the partnership's applicable net AMT adjustment, separately computed for passive loss limitation activities and other activities (Code Sec. 722), instead of making the separate adjustments provided in the alternative minimum tax rules with respect to the items of the partnership. The net AMT adjustment is determined by using the adjustments applicable to individuals (in the case of non-corporate partners) and the adjustments applicable to corporations (in the case of corporate partners). Except as provided in regulations, the applicable net AMT adjustment is treated as a deferral tax preference for purposes of computing the minimum tax credit (¶ 1370).

1460. Possessions Tax Credit. Corporate income for which the Puerto Rican economic activity credit of Code Sec. 30A or the possessions tax credit of Code Sec. 936 may be claimed is not includible in AMTI and therefore is not subject to the minimum tax (Code Sec. 59(b)).[35]

1465. REITs, RICs, and Common Trust Funds. Tax items which are treated differently for minimum taxation and regular taxation must be apportioned between REITs or RICs and their shareholders and holders of beneficial interests. Participants in common trust funds must apportion these items among themselves on a pro rata basis (Code Sec. 59(d)).[36]

1470. Corporate Preference Cutbacks. Minimum tax calculations may be performed only after specified corporate tax preferences have been reduced in accordance with Code Sec. 291 (see Code Sec. 59(f) and ¶ 1445).[37]

1475. Credit for Minimum Tax Payments. For details on the tax credit carryforward allowed against regular tax liability for minimum tax payments, see Code Sec. 53 and ¶ 1370.[38]

1480. Limitations on Certain Losses Recomputed for Minimum Taxation. The loss limitations on at-risk amounts (Code Sec. 465), on a partner's distributive share of partnership losses (Code Sec. 704(d)), and on an S corporation shareholder's losses (Code Sec. 1366(d)) are applied for purposes of computing AMTI (see Code Sec. 59(h)).[39]

Footnote references are to paragraphs of the 2002 Standard Federal Tax Reports.

[33] ¶ 5400
[34] ¶ 25,060, ¶ 32,060
[35] ¶ 5400
[36] ¶ 5400
[37] ¶ 5400
[38] ¶ 5002
[39] ¶ 5400

¶ 1450

Chapter 15

TAX ACCOUNTING

Accounting Period

1501. Tax Year. Taxable income is computed on the basis of a period called a tax year. A tax year is the annual accounting period on the basis of which the taxpayer regularly computes income in keeping its books and records. The annual period is usually a calendar year or a fiscal year. Special rules exist when (1) a taxpayer has no annual accounting period or keeps no books and records; (2) a 52-53-week fiscal-year period is elected (¶ 1503); (3) a foreign service corporation (FSC) (¶ 2470) or domestic international sales corporation (DISC) (¶ 2468) files a return for a period of at least 12 months; or (4) a taxpayer must file a return for a period that is less than 12 months (short-period return) (¶ 1505) (Code Sec. 441).[1]

Calendar v. Fiscal Year. A calendar year is a period of 12 months ending on December 31. A fiscal year is a period of 12 months ending on the last day of any month other than December or a 52-53-week tax year (see ¶ 1503). A *new* taxpayer may adopt either a calendar or a fiscal year on the first return (Temporary Reg. § 1.441-1T).[2] A fiscal year will be recognized only if it is established as the taxpayer's annual accounting period and only if the books are kept in accord with it. A taxpayer who has no annual accounting period, does not keep adequate records, or whose present tax year does not qualify as a fiscal year must compute taxable income on a calendar-year basis. Adoption of a tax year of exactly 12 months from the date business was begun is not permitted where the tax year does not begin on the first day of a calendar month (Rev. Rul. 85-22).[3] The IRS has issued procedures for changing from such an impermissible tax year to a calendar year Rev. Proc. 85-15.[4]

> **Example 1.** A corporation began doing business on August 15, 2001. The end of its first tax year cannot be later than July 31, 2002, since a tax year may not cover more than a 12-month period and it must end on the last day of a month, unless it is a 52-53-week tax year.

Footnote references are to paragraphs of the 2002 Standard Federal Tax Reports.

[1] ¶ 20,302 [3] ¶ 20,307.70 [4] ¶ 20,406.15
[2] ¶ 20,303

¶ 1501

Example 2. Assume that the new corporation in Example 1 can see no particular advantage in keeping its books on the basis of any year other than the calendar year. Therefore, it adopts the calendar-year basis. It should close its books as of December 31, 2001, and file its first return for the short period from August 15, 2001, through December 31, 2001. This is its first tax year. All its later tax years will be full calendar years until its dissolution or until it changes to a fiscal year.

A partnership generally must conform its tax year to the tax years of its owners, unless the partnership can establish a business purpose for having a different tax year (Code Sec. 706(b)).[5] An S corporation or a personal service corporation (¶ 219) must generally use the calendar year, unless the entities can establish a business purpose for having a different tax year (Code Sec. 441(i) and Code Sec. 1378(b)).[6] For this purpose, a corporation is not considered a personal service corporation (PSC) unless more than 10 percent of its stock (by value) is held by employee-owners. An employee-owner for this purpose is any employee that owns any stock of the PSC. If a corporation is a member of an affiliated group filing a consolidated return, all members of such group must be considered in determining whether such corporation is a PSC (Code Sec. 441(i)).[7]

A partnership must use the same tax year as the majority interest tax year (the tax year of one or more partners that own in total more than a 50-percent interest in partnership profits and capital) (Code Sec. 706(b)). If there is no majority interest tax year, the partnership must adopt the same tax year as that of its principal partners each of whom has at least a 5 percent interest in partnership profits or capital. Where neither condition is met, a partnership must use the calendar year.

Certain partnerships, S corporations, and personal service corporations may elect on Form 8716, "Election to Have a Tax Year Other than a Required Tax Year," to use a tax year other than a required tax year (Code Sec. 444).[8] To neutralize tax benefits resulting from such a tax year, electing partnerships and S corporations must compute and make any required payments (i.e., the amount of tax that would otherwise be due from partners and stockholders had such entities used the required tax year) exceeding $500 (Code Sec. 7519).[9] The required payment is due on or before May 15 of the calendar year following the calendar year in which the election year begins (Temporary Reg. § 1.7519-2T(a)(4)).[10] Electing personal service corporations must make minimum distributions to their employee-owners by the end of a calendar year falling within a tax year to avoid certain deduction deferrals for amounts paid to employee-owners (Code Sec. 280H).

Generally, such an election must be made by the earlier of: (1) the 15th day of the fifth month following the month that includes the first day of the tax year for which the election is first effective or (2) the due date (without extensions) of the return that results from the election (Temporary Reg. § 1.444-3T(b)(1)).[11] The election remains in effect until an entity changes its tax year or otherwise terminates such an election (Code Sec. 444(d)(2)).[12]

Such an election may not be made by an entity that is a member of a tiered structure unless the tiered structure consists only of partnerships or S corporations (or both), all of which have the same tax year (Code Sec. 444(d)(3)).[13]

Common trust funds (certain investment funds maintained by a bank) are required to adopt the calendar year as their tax year (Code Sec. 584(h)).[14]

Tax Year of FSC and DISC. The tax year of an FSC (¶ 2470) or a DISC (¶ 2468) must be the same as that of the shareholder or group of shareholders with the same tax year who have the highest percentage of voting power. Voting power is determined on the basis of total combined voting power of all classes of stock of the corporation entitled to vote. If two or more shareholders or groups are tied for the

---

Footnote references are to paragraphs of the 2002 Standard Federal Tax Reports.

[5] ¶ 25,160	[9] ¶ 42,770	[12] ¶ 20,600
[6] ¶ 20,302, ¶ 32,260	[10] ¶ 42,773	[13] ¶ 20,600
[7] ¶ 20,302	[11] ¶ 20,604	[14] ¶ 23,630
[8] ¶ 20,600		

highest percentage, the tax year used shall be that of any such shareholder or group (Code Sec. 441(h)).[15]

1503. 52- or 53-Week Accounting Period. A taxpayer may elect to use a fiscal tax year that varies from 52 to 53 weeks if such period always ends on the same day of the week (Monday, Tuesday, etc.), either the last such day in a calendar month or the closest such day to the last day of a calendar month (Code Sec. 441(f); Temporary Reg. § 1.441-2T).[16]

> **Example.** A new taxpayer wishes to have its accounting period end on the last Saturday in July. In 2001, its tax year ends on July 28, completing a 52-week year (July 29, 2000, through July 28, 2001). In 2002, its tax year ends on July 27, completing a 52-week year (July 28, 2001, through July 27, 2002). With this type of tax year, most of the taxpayer's tax years are 52 weeks long. As an alternative, the taxpayer could select a tax year that ends on the Saturday that is nearest to the end of July. In 2001, therefore, the tax year ends on July 28 (the Saturday nearest the end of July). In 2002, the tax year will end on July 27.

In determining when taxable income is included by a partner, S corporation shareholder, or personal service corporation shareholder, a 52- or 53-week tax year of such an entity is treated as ending on the last day of the calendar month ending nearest to the last day of such 52- or 53-week tax year (Temporary Reg. § 1.441-3T).[17]

Short-Period Return

1505. Tax for Portion of Year. Although no return ordinarily may be made for a period of more than 12 months except in the case of a 52-53-week tax year (Temporary Reg. § 1.441-1T),[18] a return for a period of less than 12 months may need to be filed (Code Sec. 443; Reg. § 1.443-1)[19] by a taxpayer who:

(1) changes the annual accounting period, e.g., from fiscal to calendar year (see ¶ 1513), or

(2) is in existence during only part of what would otherwise be the tax year.

Taxpayers who are not in existence for a full 12-month period include (a) a corporation that begins business or goes out of business at any time other than the beginning or end of its accounting period, (b) an individual taxpayer who dies prior to the end of the accounting period, and (c) a decedent's estate that comes into existence on the date of the decedent's death and adopts an accounting period ending less than 12 months from such date.

If the taxpayer is not in existence for a full tax year, the tax is computed as if the return had actually covered a full tax year. When a short period occurs as a result of a change in accounting period, the tax is computed on an annualized basis (see ¶ 1507). An alternative relief method is also available for taxpayers that change their accounting period (¶ 1509).

Special rules apply to taxpayers that change to or from a 52-53-week tax year (Code Sec. 441(f)(2)).[20] If such a change results in a short period of 359 days or more, the tax is computed as if the return had actually covered a full tax year. If the short period is less than seven days, the short period becomes a part of the following tax year. If the short period is more than six days but less than 359 days, the tax is computed under the annualized method discussed at ¶ 1507.

1507. Tax Recomputed on Annual Basis. When there has been a change in an accounting period that necessitates the filing of a short-period return, income for the period must be converted to an annual basis. This conversion is accomplished by: (1) multiplying the modified taxable income for the short period by 12, and (2) dividing the result by the number of months in the short period. Then the tax is

computed on the resulting taxable income by using the tax rate schedules and not the tax tables for individuals. The tax so computed is divided by 12 and multiplied by the number of months in the short period.

The modified taxable income for the short period is the gross income for the period less any allowable deductions (other than the standard deduction amount) and an adjusted personal exemption amount. Actual itemized deductions for the short period are allowed in lieu of the standard deduction amount. The adjusted personal exemption amount mentioned above is the total of an individual taxpayer's personal exemptions times the ratio of the number of months in the short period to 12 (Code Sec. 443).[21]

> **Example.** Tom has been making his returns on the basis of a fiscal year ending April 30. He changes to a year ending June 30 in 2001. He must file his return for the year ending April 30, 2001, on or before August 15, 2001. On or before October 16, 2001, he must file his return for the short period of two months beginning May 1, 2001, and ending June 30, 2001. His gross income for the short period is $9,566, and his itemized deductions total $600. He is married, age 60, and has no dependents. His wife has no income or deductions. The tax before credits on their joint return is computed as follows:

Gross income	$ 9,566
Itemized deductions *	600
Net income	$ 8,966
Less 2/12 of $5,800 (2 × $2,900) exemptions	966
Modified taxable income for short period	$ 8,000
Annualized taxable income—$8,000 × 12/2	$48,000
Tax on $48,000	$ 7,550
Tax for short period, 2/12 of $7,550	$ 1,258

> * Assume that the itemized deductions are not miscellaneous itemized deductions under Code Sec. 67 and that amounts are rounded up to the nearest dollar. An individual making a return under Code Sec. 443(a)(1) for a period of less than 12 months because of a change in annual accounting period is not eligible for the standard deduction (Code Sec. 63(c)(6)(C)).

When a short-period return is filed, the self-employment tax (¶ 2664) should be computed on the actual self-employment income for the short-period and not prorated for a portion of a 12-month period.[22] A net operating loss deduction should be applied against actual income for the short period before annualizing.[23]

A taxpayer that is changing to or from a 52-53-week fiscal tax year and that must annualize income will apply the same rules as other taxpayers in determining the income of the short period, but will calculate income on an annual basis by multiplying the income of the short period by 365 and dividing the result by the number of days in the short period (Code Sec. 441(f)(2)(B)(iii)). Tax is computed on such annualized income and, as computed, is multiplied by the ratio of the number of days in the short period to 365; the resulting figure is the tax for the short year.

1509. Relief from Annual Basis. Code Sec. 443(b)(2)[24] provides an alternative method for computing the short-period tax. Under this method, the tax for the short period is the greater of:

(1) a tax on the actual taxable income for the 12-month period beginning with the start of the short period (using the law in effect for that 12-month period) multiplied by the modified taxable income (¶ 1507) for the short period and divided by the modified taxable income for the 12-month period, or

(2) a tax on the modified taxable income for the short period.

Footnote references are to paragraphs of the 2002 Standard Federal Tax Reports.

¶ **1509**   [21] ¶ 20,500   [23] ¶ 20,406.27   [24] ¶ 20,500
                [22] ¶ 35,203.30

If a taxpayer does not exist at the end of the 12-month period described in (1), above, or if a corporate taxpayer has distributed substantially all its assets before the end of that period, the tax is computed by using a 12-month period ending with the last day of the short period (Code Sec. 443(b)(2)(B)(ii)).[25] In such cases, in order to claim the benefits of the alternative method, the taxpayer must attach a return covering the 12-month period ending on the last day of the short year to the return initially computed for the short period.

If there was a change in accounting period, with a resultant short period, the taxpayer must first compute the tax by use of the annualization method (¶ 1507) and file the return. If the alternate method would result in lower taxes, a claim for credit or refund must be filed not later than the due date by which a return would have been required to be filed if the 12-month period beginning with the short period were considered a tax year (Reg. § 1.443-1(b)(2)(v)(a)).[26] The application of the taxpayer for use of the alternate method is considered as a claim for credit or refund (Code Sec. 443(b)(2)(C)).[27]

1511. Returns of Decedents, New Corporations or Dissolving Corporations. Short-period returns of decedents and dissolving corporations and the first return of a new corporation are not required to be annualized (Reg. § 1.443-1).[28]

Change of Accounting Period

1513. IRS's Consent Generally Required. The change from one accounting period to another generally requires prior permission of the IRS and requires the filing of a return for the short period under the rules discussed at ¶ 1505-¶ 1509. To effect the change in cases where prior approval is required, Form 1128 "Application to Adopt, Change, or Retain a Tax Year" generally must be filed by the 15th day of the second month following the close of the short period for which a return is required. A change in the accounting period will be approved where it is established that a substantial business purpose exists for making the change (Reg. § 1.442-1(b)(1)) [29] but generally will not be approved where the sole purpose of the change is to maintain or obtain a preferential tax status.[30] Consideration will be given to all the facts and circumstances relating to the change, including the tax consequences. Among the nontax factors is the effect of the change on the taxpayer's annual cycle of business activity. The agreement between the taxpayer and the IRS under which the change is carried out will, in appropriate cases, provide terms, conditions, and adjustments necessary to prevent a substantial distortion of income that otherwise would result from the change. The following are examples of effects that would constitute substantial distortions of income: (1) deferring a substantial portion of the taxpayer's income or shifting a substantial portion of deductions from one year to another so as to reduce substantially the taxpayer's tax liability; (2) causing a similar deferral or shift in the case of any other person, such as a partner, a beneficiary, or an S corporation shareholder; or (3) creating a short period in which there is either (a) a substantial net operating loss or (b) in the case of an S corporation, a substantial portion of amounts treated as long-term capital gain (Reg. § 1.442-1(b)(1)).[31]

Corporations. In certain situations, a corporation need not obtain IRS consent for a change in accounting period. Under Reg. § 1.442-1(d),[32] a subsidiary corporation that is required to change its accounting period under the rules for affiliated groups filing consolidated returns need not file Form 1128 (see below) to effect the change, and under Reg. § 1.442-1(c),[33] a corporation (except for an S corporation or a DISC (¶ 2468)) may change its accounting period (including a change from a 52-53-week year)[34] without prior IRS approval if:

Footnote references are to paragraphs of the 2002 Standard Federal Tax Reports.

[25] ¶ 20,500	[29] ¶ 20,401	[32] ¶ 20,401
[26] ¶ 20,501	[30] ¶ 20,406.41	[33] ¶ 20,401
[27] ¶ 20,500	[31] ¶ 20,401	[34] ¶ 20,406.034
[28] ¶ 20,501		

(1) the corporation has not changed its accounting period at any time within the 10 calendar years ending with the calendar year that includes the beginning of the short period required to effect the proposed change;

(2) the short period required to effect the change is not one in which the corporation has a net operating loss (see below);

(3) the *taxable income* for the short period is, when annualized, at least 80 percent of the taxable income for the preceding tax year;

(4) a corporation which is a personal holding company, a foreign personal holding company, an exempt organization, or a nonresident foreign corporation has had the same status for both the short period and the preceding tax year; and

(5) the corporation does not try to make an S corporation election for the tax year which immediately follows the short period required to effect the change.

A statement indicating the change and the fulfillment of the five conditions must be filed with the local district director on or before the due date (including extensions) for the short-period return. In addition, the IRS has provided procedures under which certain corporations that are unable to meet the above tests because they experienced net operating losses in a short tax year may expeditiously obtain approval of changes in their annual accounting periods (Rev. Proc. 85-16 and Rev. Proc. 2000-11).[35]

Generally, a corporation other than an S corporation, a DISC (¶ 2468), an FSC (¶ 2470), a personal service corporation, a controlled foreign corporation, a PFIC (with certain exceptions), a tax-exempt organization or a cooperative association may change its accounting period without prior IRS approval if:

(1) the five conditions stated above are met, except that the 10-year waiting period of condition (1) is reduced to a six-year period;

(2) a Form 1128 is filed before the due date (including extensions) of the short period return; and

(3) a return is filed for the short period (Rev. Proc. 2000-11).[36]

Other Entities. Partnerships, S corporations, corporations that elect to become S corporations, and personal service corporations that want to adopt a tax year ending other than on December 31 must comply with the terms and conditions set forth in Rev. Proc. 87-32 [37] (see also Rev. Rul. 87-57).[38] Approval is granted (but see ¶ 1501) where such entities (1) retain a fiscal tax year that coincides with a natural business year or (2) change to a fiscal tax year that coincides with a natural business year and such year results in less deferral of income to the owners than the present tax year. Similarly, S corporations or corporations that elect to become S corporations may adopt, retain, or change to a fiscal tax year used by stockholders who own more than 50 percent of the outstanding stock of such entities.

An existing partnership may change its accounting period without prior IRS consent where all the principal partners have the same tax year to which the partnership changes or if all those who do not have such a tax year concurrently change to that year (but see ¶ 1501). However, the individual partners must always obtain permission to change (Reg. § 1.442-1(b)(2)).[39]

Individual. The only individual who may change his or her tax year without IRS consent is a newly married individual who is adopting the annual accounting period of his or her spouse in order to be able to file a joint return (Reg. § 1.442-1(e)).[40]

Footnote references are to paragraphs of the 2002 Standard Federal Tax Reports.

¶ 1513

[35] ¶ 20,406.17, ¶ 20,406.27
[36] ¶ 20,406.17
[37] ¶ 20,406.048
[38] ¶ 20,406.29
[39] ¶ 20,401
[40] ¶ 20,401

Accounting Method

1515. Cash v. Accrual Basis. Taxable income must be computed not only on the basis of a fixed accounting *period* but also in accordance with a *method* of accounting regularly employed in keeping the taxpayer's books. A "method of accounting" includes the overall method of accounting for income and expenses and the method of accounting for special items such as depreciation (Reg. § 1.446-1(a)).[41] There are two common overall methods of accounting for income: (1) the cash basis and (2) the accrual basis.

The cash basis (cash receipts and disbursements) is the method of accounting used by most individuals. Income is generally reported in the year that it is actually or constructively received in the form of cash or its equivalent or other property. The constructive receipt of income is income not actually received but within the taxpayer's control. However, there is no constructive receipt if there are substantial limits or restrictions on the right to receive it. Deductions or credits are generally taken for the year in which the related expenditures were actually paid, unless they should be taken in a different period to more clearly reflect income (examples would include depreciation allowances and prepaid expenses).

Under the accrual method, income is accounted for when the right to receive it comes into being—i.e., when all the events that determine the right have occurred. It is not the actual receipt but the *right to receive* that governs. Expenses are deductible on the accrual basis in the year incurred—i.e., when all the events have occurred that fix the amount of the item and determine the liability of the taxpayer to pay it. See ¶ 1539 for a discussion of this "all-events test" as it relates to economic performance.

When no books are kept, an individual not engaged in business must report income on the cash basis.[42] In other cases, the accounting method used must clearly reflect income. An approved standard method of accounting (such as the cash basis or the accrual basis) ordinarily is regarded as clearly reflecting income. A taxpayer may use one accounting method to keep his personal books and another for the books of his trade or business, or use different accounting methods if the taxpayer has two or more separate businesses as long as separate and distinct sets of records are maintained. Further, the use of multiple accounting methods is not permitted if there is a creation or shifting of profits or losses between the taxpayer's various trades or businesses (Reg. § 1.446-1(d)(3)).

Taxpayers that are required to use inventories must use the accrual method to account for purchases and sales (Reg. § 1.446-1(c)(2)).[43] Furthermore, the following taxpayers must generally use the accrual method of accounting as their overall method of accounting for tax purposes: (1) C corporations, (2) partnerships that have a C corporation as a partner, (3) trusts that are subject to the tax on unrelated trade or business income (charitable trusts), but only for such income, and (4) tax shelters (Code Sec. 448(a) and Code Sec. 448(d)(6)).[44] Qualified personal service corporations (¶ 219) are treated as individuals rather than as corporations for purposes of category (2), above. Notwithstanding the general requirement that these taxpayers use the accrual method, the cash method of accounting may be used instead if the entity is not a tax shelter and (1) is engaged in a farming or tree-raising business, (2) is a qualified personal service corporation, or (3) is an entity that has met the $5 million or less gross receipts test for all prior tax years beginning after 1985. An entity meets the $5 million gross receipts test if the average annual gross receipts for the three tax years ending with the prior tax year does not exceed $5 million. Furthermore, the cash method may also be used by most other taxpayers whose average annual gross receipts do not exceed $1,000,000 (Rev. Proc. 2000-22).

Certain farming corporations must use the accrual method (Code Sec. 447)[45] (see ¶ 2028).

Footnote references are to paragraphs of the 2002 Standard Federal Tax Reports.

[41] ¶ 20,607	[43] ¶ 20,607	[45] ¶ 20,700
[42] ¶ 20,620.0254	[44] ¶ 20,800	

An accrual-method publisher of magazines, paperbacks, or records may elect to exclude from gross income the income attributable to the qualified sale of magazines, paperbacks, or records that are returned before the close of the merchandise return period (Code Sec. 458).[46]

1517. Accruing Income Doubtful of Collection. On the accrual basis, income, such as interest, is taxable as it accrues even though it is received at a later date. However, if there is a real doubt that the interest is collectible when it becomes due, it need not be accrued.[47] But where the uncollectible item arises from a sale of property, the proper procedure is to report the sale and then take a bad debt deduction as appropriate.[48]

Generally, an accrual-basis taxpayer is not required to accrue as income any amount to be received for the performance of services that, based on experience, will not be collected (Code Sec. 448(d)(5); Temporary Reg. § 1.448-2T(e)).[49] This treatment with respect to such amounts is a method of accounting that must be elected by the taxpayer.

1519. Liability Uncertain or Unascertained. There can be no accrual of an expense until any contingency disappears and liability becomes fixed and certain (Reg. § 1.461-1(a)(2)(ii)).[50] See, also, ¶ 1539 on the economic performance rule. But where the taxpayer, while denying liability, has paid a claim, the entire amount may be deductible when paid. See ¶ 1521. For treatment of estimated expenses, see ¶ 1547.

1521. Accruing Contested Liability. A deduction is allowed for the year in which a transfer of money or other property takes place in satisfaction of an asserted liability if: (1) the taxpayer contests the asserted liability, (2) the contest exists after the transfer, and (3) the liability would otherwise be allowed as a deduction in the year of transfer (or an earlier tax year). This means that it must meet the economic performance requirement of the all-events test, discussed at ¶ 1539 (Code Sec. 461(f)).[51]

1523. Hybrid Accounting Methods. Under Code Sec. 446(c),[52] one or more hybrid methods of accounting may be authorized by regulation. The regulations allow use of a combination of methods if the combination clearly reflects income and is consistently used (Reg. § 1.446-1(c)(1)(iv)).[53] A taxpayer engaged in more than one business is permitted to use a different method for each trade or business.

1525. Method Prescribed by IRS. The IRS can prescribe a method of accounting that will clearly reflect income if, in the IRS's opinion, the method used by the taxpayer fails to do so (Code Sec. 446(b)).[54] If the IRS requires a change in accounting methods, the taxpayer must compute an income adjustment due to the change (Code Sec. 481(a)).[55] See ¶ 1531.

1527. Interest and Expenses Owed to Related Taxpayers. Where different methods of accounting are used by related taxpayers, accrued interest and expenses owed to each of the related taxpayers may not be deducted until the time that the interest or expense payment is includible in the gross income of the cash-basis payee (Code Sec. 267(a)(2)).[56] Thus, an accrual-basis payor is placed on the cash basis for the purpose of deducting business expenses and interest owed to a related cash-basis taxpayer. The deduction is deferred until the cash-basis payee takes the item into income.

The related taxpayers covered by this rule are those described in Code Sec. 267(b) and Code Sec. 267(e) and include such taxpayers as certain family members, members of a controlled group of corporations, controlling shareholders and controlled corporations, and "pass-through entities," such as a partnership and its partners and an S corporation and its shareholders.

Footnote references are to paragraphs of the 2002 Standard Federal Tax Reports.

[46] ¶ 21,540	[50] ¶ 21,805	[54] ¶ 20,606
[47] ¶ 5704.32	[51] ¶ 21,802	[55] ¶ 22,277
[48] ¶ 21,005.20	[52] ¶ 20,606	[56] ¶ 14,150
[49] ¶ 20,800, ¶ 20,802	[53] ¶ 20,607	

¶ **1517**

A personal service corporation may not deduct payments made to owner-employees before the tax year in which such persons must include the payment in gross income. For this purpose, a personal service corporation and any employee-owner are considered related taxpayers (Code Sec. 267(a)(2)).[57]

Change of Accounting Method

1529. IRS Permission Needed. As a general rule, a taxpayer may not change his method of accounting without obtaining advance permission from the IRS (Code Sec. 446(e); Reg. § 1.446-1(e)).[58]

A change of accounting method includes a change in the overall plan of accounting as well as a change in the treatment of any material item. In most cases, a method of accounting is not established for an item unless there is a pattern of consistent treatment. A change in the treatment of a material item is one involving the timing of its inclusion in income or deduction (not the traditional accounting meaning dealing with the relationship of amounts). Consent is required whether the change is made from an acceptable or an unacceptable method, and, if the taxpayer fails to file a request to change his method of accounting, the absence of IRS consent to the change will not be taken into account in order to prevent the imposition of penalties (or additions to tax) or to diminish such penalties (or additions to tax) (Code Sec. 446(f)).[59] Changes in accounting method include, but are not limited to—

(1) a change from the cash to the accrual basis (see Rev. Proc. 99-49) or vice versa,

(2) any change in the method of valuing inventories (¶ 1571),

(3) a change from the cash or accrual basis to one of the long-term contract methods (percentage-of-completion capitalized-cost and percentage-of-completion), or vice versa, or from one long-term contract method to the other (¶ 1551),

(4) a change involving the adoption, use or discontinuance of any other specialized basis, such as the crop method (¶ 1569), and

(5) a change where the Code and regulations specifically require that IRS consent be obtained.

Application for permission to change the method of accounting must generally be filed on Form 3115 during the tax year in which the taxpayer desires to make the proposed change (Reg. § 1.446-1(e)(3)(i)).[60]

1531. Adjustments Required by Changes in Method of Accounting. Taxpayers who voluntarily change their method of accounting with the IRS's permission, or who are compelled by the IRS to make a change because the method used does not clearly reflect income, must make certain adjustments to income in the year of the change (Code Sec. 481(a); Reg. § 1.481-1).[61] The adjustments are those determined to be necessary to prevent duplication or omission of items.

Since the adjustments for the year of change might result in the bunching of income, two statutory methods of limiting the tax in the changeover year may be applied if the adjustments for the changeover year increase taxable income by more than $3,000 (Reg. § 1.481-2).[62] If both limitations apply, the one resulting in the lower tax should be used. In order for the first of these methods to be used, the old method of accounting must have been used in the two preceding years; if so, the tax increase in the changeover year is limited to the tax increases that would result if the adjustments were spread ratably over that year and the two preceding years.

Under the second method, the taxpayer must be able to reconstruct his income under the new method of accounting for one or more consecutive years immediately preceding the changeover year. The increase in the changeover year's tax because of the adjustments may not be more than the net tax increases that would result if the adjustments were allocated back to those preceding years under the new method.

Footnote references are to paragraphs of the 2002 Standard Federal Tax Reports.

[57] ¶ 14,150	[59] ¶ 20,606	[61] ¶ 22,270, ¶ 22,271
[58] ¶ 20,606, ¶ 20,607	[60] ¶ 20,608	[62] ¶ 22,272

Any amounts that cannot be allocated back must be included in the changeover year's income for purposes of computing the limitation.

In addition to the statutorily prescribed methods of allocation limiting the tax in the changeover year described above, the IRS has prescribed conditions under which accounting change adjustments must be made as well as favorable "spread of adjustment" provisions for taxpayers that agree to the IRS conditions (Rev. Proc. 97-27 or Rev. Proc. 99-49).[63] Moreover, a taxpayer may request approval of an alternative method of allocating the amount of the adjustments (Reg. § 1.481-4).

A change in accounting method resulting from limitations placed on the use of the cash method of accounting under Code Sec. 448 (¶ 1501) is treated as a change initiated by the taxpayer with the consent of the IRS. The related Code Sec. 481 adjustment is includible in income over a period not generally exceeding four years (Code Sec. 448(d)(7)).[64]

Constructive Receipt and Payment

1533. Cash Basis and Constructive Receipt. It is not always necessary that money or property representing income actually be in the taxpayer's possession before it is considered received. Income that is constructively received is taxed to the cash-basis taxpayer as though it had been actually received.

There is constructive receipt when income is credited without restriction and made available to the taxpayer. There must be no substantial limitation or condition on the taxpayer's right to bring the funds within his control. An insubstantial forfeiture provision, a notice requirement, or the loss of bonus interest for deposits or accounts in certain financial institutions is not a substantial limitation (Reg. § 1.451-2(a)).[65]

Common examples of constructive receipt include matured and payable interest coupons, interest credited on savings bank deposits, and dividends unqualifiedly made subject to a stockholder's demand. However, if a dividend is declared payable on December 31 and the corporation follows a practice of paying the dividend by checks mailed so that the shareholders will not receive them until January of the following year, the dividend is not considered to be constructively received by the stockholders in December.[66] For the time of receipt by shareholders of certain mutual fund dividends, see ¶ 2303. Accrued interest on an unwithdrawn insurance policy dividend is gross income to the taxpayer for the first tax year during which the interest may be withdrawn.[67]

Salaries credited on corporate books are taxable to an officer in the year when the officer may withdraw the compensation at will if the corporation has funds available to pay the salaries without causing financial difficulties. Bonuses that are based on yearly sales and that are otherwise not available to an officer are taxable in the year of receipt.[68]

Accrued interest on a deposit that may not be withdrawn at the close of an individual's tax year because of an institution's actual or threatened bankruptcy or insolvency is not includible in the depositor's income until the year in which such interest is withdrawable (Code Sec. 451(g)).[69]

Any option to accelerate the receipt of any payment under a production flexibility contract (between certain eligible owners and producers and the Secretary of Agriculture) which is payable under the Federal Agriculture Improvement and Reform Act of 1996 (the FAIR Act) is to be disregarded in determining the taxable year in which such payment is properly included in gross income (Tax Relief Extension Act of 1999, P.L. 106-170, Act Sec. 525).

Footnote references are to paragraphs of the 2002 Standard Federal Tax Reports.

63 ¶ 20,620.075,   66 ¶ 21,007,   68 ¶ 21,007, ¶ 21,009.17,
   ¶ 20,620.285   ¶ 21,009.1235   ¶ 21,009.14
64 ¶ 20,800   67 ¶ 21,007   69 ¶ 21,002
65 ¶ 21,007

¶ 1533

1535. Notes as Income and Payment. The fact that the negotiable note of a responsible and solvent maker, received in payment of salary, interest, rent, etc., must be reported by a recipient on the cash basis as income to the extent of its fair market value when received does not mean that the maker (on a cash basis) may also deduct the same amount at that time.

The Supreme Court has held that delivery of a note is not a payment on the cash basis, and the deduction may be taken only in the year when the note is paid. Giving collateral to secure the note does not change the promise to pay into an actual payment.[70]

Deferred and Accrued Income and Expense

1537. Deferred and Accrued Income. *Deferred Income.* Payments received in advance are usually income to an accrual-basis taxpayer as well as to a cash-basis taxpayer in the year of receipt, provided that there is no restriction on the use of such payments. This is true even though the payments are returnable upon the happening of some specified event. A distinction must be made, however, between prepayments that may be refunded for services or goods and deposits over which the taxpayer does not have complete dominion and control upon receipt.[71] A utility company was not required to include deposits from uncreditworthy customers in income upon receipt since the utility was required to return the deposit upon request by a customer who established creditworthiness.

Inclusion in the year of receipt is required for amounts that are paid for future services.[72] However, the IRS has set up a special procedure to permit the deferral of prepayments for future services by accrual-basis taxpayers until the time of performance.[73] Deferral will not be allowed if any part of the services is to be performed at an unspecified future date that may fall beyond the end of the tax year after the tax year of receipt. The amount of the deferral is to be proportionate to the portion of services remaining unperformed at the end of the tax year of receipt. The amount deferred must be included in income in the tax year following the tax year of receipt regardless of whether the remaining services are all performed in that tax year.

> **Example.** Advance payment for 48 dancing lessons under a one-year contract is received on November 1, 2001, by a calendar-year taxpayer. Eight lessons are given in 2001. The remaining lessons are provided in 2002. If the dance studio, an accrual-basis taxpayer, elects the above deferral method, 1/6 of the payment is includible in 2001 income and 5/6 of it is taxable as 2002 income, even if not all of the remaining 40 lessons are given in 2002.

Certain accrual-basis membership organizations and publishers can defer prepaid dues and subscription income (Code Sec. 455 and Code Sec. 456).[74]

Inclusion in the year of receipt is also required for advance payments received on the sale of merchandise. However, under certain circumstances the IRS permits accrual-basis sellers to include certain advance payments in income in the tax year in which such payments are properly accruable under the method of accounting used for tax purposes if they are reported at that time or later for financial reporting purposes (Reg. § 1.451-5).[75] If the method used for financial reporting results in an earlier accrual, then the advance payments are taxed according to the financial reporting method. Where a long-term contract method of accounting (¶ 1551) is used, advances are included in income under that method without regard to how the income from these payments is accounted for in the seller's financial reports.

An advance payment for the above purposes is any amount received by an accrual-basis taxpayer under an agreement (1) for the sale or other disposition in a future tax year of goods held by the taxpayer primarily for sale to customers in the ordinary course of his trade or business or (2) for the building, installation, construc-

---

tion or manufacture of items by the taxpayer where the agreement is not completed within such tax year. An exception exists where substantial advance payments for inventoriable goods have been received and goods are on hand or available to satisfy the agreement in the year of receipt. Payments for gift certificates are substantial when received, but in other cases, advance payments are not substantial until they exceed the cost of goods to be sold. In such cases, all advance payments received by the last day of the second tax year following the year in which the substantial advance payments are received and not previously included in income under the taxpayer's method of accounting must be included in income in such second tax year (Reg. § 1.451-5(c)).[76]

Certain manufacturers, wholesalers and retailers that receive advance payments for multi-year service warranty contracts may elect to recognize income from such advance payments as a series of equal payments over the life of the contracts. This election is permitted only if an eligible taxpayer purchases insurance to cover its obligations under a service warranty contract within 60 days after the sale of the contract (Rev. Proc. 97-38).[77]

Tax Benefit Rule. An amount that has been deducted from gross income in a prior year must be included in income in the year of recovery, but only to the extent that the deduction had reduced taxable income in the year of the deduction (Code Sec. 111(a)).[78]

Accrued Income. A number of Code provisions may require cash-basis taxpayers to report income that has not yet been received. The computation of such income often uses present value concepts. In addition, such Code provisions may require accrual-basis taxpayers to compute income for tax purposes in a manner that differs from generally accepted accounting methods. For a discussion of accruals of rental payments (Code Sec. 467), see ¶ 1541. For a discussion of original issue discount (Code Sec. 1272), see ¶ 1952. For a discussion of certain debt instruments issued for property (Code Sec. 1274), see ¶ 1954.

1539. Deferred and Accrued Expense. *Prepaid Expenses for Cash-Basis Taxpayers.* Cash-basis taxpayers may deduct certain prepaid *expenses* in the year paid under certain conditions. A distinction is made between expenditures that are more in the nature of expenses and those that are capital in nature. If the payment creates an asset having a useful life extending substantially beyond the end of the tax year in which paid, the expenditure may not be deductible, or may be deductible only in part, in that year. If payment is made for a capital asset or is capital in nature, a deferment and charge-off for depreciation, amortization or other comparable allowance are proper.[79] See ¶ 1201.

Thus, if a calendar-year taxpayer signs a three-year business property lease on December 1 of the tax year and agrees to pay an "additional rental" of $18,000 plus a monthly rental of $1,000 for 36 months, he can deduct only $1,500 for the tax year ($1,000 rent plus 1/36 of $18,000). The $18,000 is an amount paid for securing the lease and must be amortized over the lease term.[80]

Cash-basis farmers and ranchers can deduct prepaid feed costs in the year of payment if: (1) the advance feed expenditure is a payment and not a deposit; (2) the payment is for a business purpose; and (3) the deduction does not cause a material distortion of income.[81] However, generally, no deduction is allowed to a cash-basis taxpayer (other than farming syndicates) in the year of prepayment for advance payments for feed, seed, fertilizer, or other supplies to the extent such prepayments exceed 50% of total deductible farming expenses (excluding prepaid supplies) (Code Sec. 464(f)).[82] (For rules applicable to farming syndicates, see ¶ 2032.) The limitation does not apply to a "farm-related taxpayer" if (1) the aggregate prepaid farm supplies for the preceding three tax years are less than 50% of the aggregate deductible farming expenses (other than prepaid farm supplies) for that period or

---

Footnote references are to paragraphs of the 2002 Standard Federal Tax Reports.

¶ **1539**

[76] ¶ 21,016	[79] ¶ 21,817.038	[81] ¶ 21,817.205
[77] ¶ 20,620.20	[80] ¶ 21,817.05,	[82] ¶ 21,840
[78] ¶ 7062	¶ 21,817.635	

(2) the taxpayer has excess prepaid farm supplies for the tax year by reason of any change in business operation directly attributable to extraordinary circumstances. A "farm-related taxpayer" is one whose principal residence is on a farm and who has a principal occupation of farming. Family members of such a taxpayer (as defined by Code Sec. 464(c)(2)(E)) also qualify for the exception.

In the *Keller* case,[83] the Eighth Circuit indicated that the three-pronged test for prepaid feed, described above, was appropriate in determining the deductibility of certain oil-drilling prepayments.

Estimated state income taxes paid in advance are deductible by a cash-basis taxpayer in the year paid (Rev. Rul. 56-124).[84]

See ¶ 1055 for a discussion of the allowance of deductions for prepaid interest payments. See, also, ¶ 2042 for a discussion of prepaid expenses of tax shelters.

Accrued Expenses for Accrual-Basis Taxpayers. Under the "all-events" test, an accrual-basis taxpayer is generally entitled to deduct the face amount of an accrued expense in the tax year in which (1) all of the events have occurred that determine the fact of liability and (2) the amount of the liability can be determined with reasonable accuracy. All of the events that establish liability for an amount, for the purpose of determining whether such amount has been incurred regarding any item, are treated as not occurring any earlier than the time that economic performance occurs (Code Sec. 461(h)).[85]

For a liability of a taxpayer that requires a payment for property or services, economic performance is deemed to occur as the property or services are provided to the taxpayer. If the liability arises out of the taxpayer's use of property, economic performance occurs as the taxpayer uses the property.

> **Example 1.** A partnership on the accrual basis contractually obligates itself in October 2001 to pay Techno Inc. $10,000 for research and development to be performed in 2002. No amount is deductible before performance is rendered in 2002.

However, taxpayers are permitted to accrue payments before services are rendered or property is received if the taxpayer can reasonably expect the services or property to be provided within 3½ months after payment (Reg. § 1.461-4(d)(6)(ii)).[86]

> **Example 2.** An accrual-method, calendar-year taxpayer makes payment on December 1, 2001, for goods it expects to receive by March 12, 2002. It may deduct the payment or otherwise take it into account for its 2001 tax year.

If the liability of the taxpayer requires him to provide services or property, then economic performance occurs as the taxpayer provides the services or property (Reg. § 1.461-4(d)).[87]

> **Example 3.** Zop Corp., a calendar-year, accrual-method taxpayer, sells lawn mowers under a three-year warranty that obligates Zop to make reasonable repairs to each mower it sells. In 2002, Zop repairs, at a cost of $2,500, 12 mowers sold in 2000. Economic performance with respect to Zop's liability to perform services under the warranty occurs as Zop incurs costs in connection with the liability. Consequently, the $2,500 expense incurred by Zop is a deduction for the 2002 tax year.

However, certain manufacturers, wholesalers and retailers that make advance payments to purchase insurance policies that cover their obligations under multi-year service warranty contracts must capitalize the cost of the policies and deduct such cost ratably over the life of the policies. This rule applies regardless of whether the taxpayer uses the cash or accrual method (Rev. Proc. 97-38).[88]

Footnote references are to paragraphs of the 2002 Standard Federal Tax Reports.

[83] ¶ 21,817.209
[84] ¶ 21,817.1875
[85] ¶ 21,802
[86] ¶ 21,810

[87] ¶ 21,810
[88] ¶ 20,620.20,
¶ 21,817.027,
¶ 22,277.40

¶ 1539

Under an exception to the above general rules for economic performance, payment is considered to be economic performance for the following: (1) liabilities to another person arising out of any workers' compensation, tort, or breach of contract claims against the taxpayer or any violation of law by the taxpayer; (2) rebates and refunds; (3) awards, prizes, and jackpots; (4) insurance, warranty and service contracts; and (5) taxes other than creditable foreign taxes. The IRS may specify additional "payment liabilities" in the future (Reg. § 1.461-4(g)).[89]

Under certain limited circumstances, an irrevocable payment to a court-ordered settlement fund that completely extinguishes specified tort liabilities will constitute economic performance (Code Sec. 468B).[90]

Certain recurring items are treated as incurred in advance of economic performance by taxpayers other than tax shelters. Under this exception, an item is treated as incurred during a tax year if (1) the all-events test, without regard to economic performance, is satisfied during such year, (2) the economic performance test is met within the shorter of 8½ months or a reasonable time after the close of such year, (3) the item is recurring in nature and the taxpayer consistently treats similar items as incurred in the tax year in which the all-events test is met, and (4) either the item is not material or accrual of the item in the year that the all-events test is met results in a better matching against the income to which it relates than accrual of the item in the tax year of economic performance. In determining whether an item is material or whether a more proper matching against income results from deduction of an expense prior to economic performance, the treatment of the expense on financial statements is to be taken into account but will not necessarily govern the tax treatment of the expense (Code Sec. 461(h)(3)).[91]

A taxpayer may adopt the recurring item exception as part of its method of accounting for any type of expense for the first tax year in which that type of expense is incurred. Generally, the rules of Code Sec. 446(e) and Reg. § 1.446-1(e) apply to changes to or from the recurring item exception as a method of accounting (Reg. § 1.461-5(d)).[92]

An item is recurring if it can generally be expected to be incurred from one tax year to the next (Reg. § 1.461-5(b)(3)).[93] However, a taxpayer may treat a liability as recurring even if it is not incurred in each tax year. Also, a liability that has never previously been incurred may be treated as recurring if it is reasonable to expect that it will be incurred on a recurring basis in the future.

1541. Deferred Payments Under Rental Agreements. Lessors and lessees of certain leaseback and long-term rental agreements under Code Sec. 467 and Reg. § 1.467-1 that involve the use of property must report income and expenses arising out of such agreements by applying statutory accrual-basis and present-value principles (Code Sec. 467).[94] Such treatment, in effect, is an extension of the principles embodied in the rules on taxation of original issue discount. Although the rules under Code Sec. 467 apply to the use of property, the IRS is given authority to extend similar rules to agreements for services.

"Section 467 rental agreements" cover tangible property with respect to which either (1) at least one amount, allocable to the use of property in the calendar year, is to be paid after the close of the following calendar year (deferred payments) or (2) there are increases in the amount to be paid as rent under the agreement (stepped rents). A "Section 467 rental agreement" does not encompass a rental agreement in which the sum of the amounts to be paid is $250,000 or less.

The lessor or lessee of any Section 467 agreement must report for any tax year (regardless of the accounting method used) the sum of (1) the accrued rental payments and (2) any interest for the year (calculated at the rate of 110% of the applicable federal rate compounded semiannually) on unpaid rents (amounts that were attributed to a prior tax year but are still unpaid as of the current tax year).

Footnote references are to paragraphs of the 2002 Standard Federal Tax Reports.

¶ 1541

89 ¶ 21,810   91 ¶ 21,802   93 ¶ 21,811
90 ¶ 21,950   92 ¶ 21,811   94 ¶ 21,910

The accrued rental payments—except in tax-avoidance transactions and agreements that do not allocate rents—are calculated by (1) allocating rents in accordance with the agreement and (2) including the present value of rents allocable to the period but paid after the close of the period. In tax-avoidance transactions and agreements that do not allocate rents, the rent that accrues during the tax year is equal to the allocable portion of the "constant rental amount." The "constant rental amount" is equal to the amount which, if paid as of the close of each lease period, would result in an aggregate present value equal to the present value of the aggregate payments required under the lease.

Claim-of-Right Repayments

1543. Claim-of-Right Doctrine. Under an established principle of tax law, payments must be included in gross income if the taxpayer receives them without restriction under a claim of right. This is true even though the taxpayer may discover in a later year that he had no right to the payments in the earlier year and is required to repay the same amount. Under this claim-of-right doctrine, the taxpayer may deduct the repayments in the year in which they are made.

When the repayments exceed income for the year of repayment or when the income (after subtraction of such repayments) is taxed at a rate lower than that at which the income in the year of inclusion was taxed, the deduction does not compensate the taxpayer adequately for the tax paid in the earlier year. The law eliminates this inequity if the amount repaid exceeds $3,000. In such case, the taxpayer is to reduce his tax for the year of repayment by the amount of tax for the previous year which was attributable to inclusion of this amount; any excess is to be claimed as a refund. However, if a smaller tax liability results from simply deducting the repaid amount in the year of repayment, the taxpayer is to claim the deduction instead (Code Sec. 1341; Reg. § 1.1341-1).[95]

In either case, the adjustment is made for the year of repayment. The return for the prior year, i.e., the year in which the item was received, is not reopened; in no case will there be an allowance for interest on the tax paid for the earlier year.

> **Example.** In 2000, a single taxpayer reported taxable income of $56,000 (adjusted gross income of $63,200 minus $2,800 personal exemption minus $4,400 standard deduction), consisting entirely of sales commissions, on which he paid a tax of $12,267.50. In 2001, it is determined that the commissions were erroneously computed for 2000. Accordingly, the taxpayer pays back $6,000 of the commissions. His taxable income for 2001, without regard to the $6,000 repayment, is $13,200.
>
> The tax for 2000 and 2001 will be computed using the tax tables as follows:

(a) Tax on $7,200 ($13,200 less $6,000)		$1,080
(b) Tax on $13,200		$1,980
Less: Difference between—		
Tax paid for 2000 on $56,000	$12,267.50	
Tax payable in 2000 on $50,000		
($56,000 − $6,000)	$10,587.50	1,680
		$ 300

> The tax for 2001 is the lesser of the amount computed under (a) or (b). In this case, the amount computed under (b) is less than the amount computed under (a). Thus, the tax for 2001 is $300, the amount computed under (b).

When the tax for the year of restoration under a claim of right is reduced by the amount of the tax already paid on the item in a previous year, the amount restored is not considered for any purpose. For example, taxpayers cannot use such amount in

---

Footnote references are to paragraphs of the 2002 Standard Federal Tax Reports.
[95] ¶ 31,880, ¶ 31,881

computing a net operating loss for the year of restoration (Reg. § 1.1341-1(b)(2)).[96]
The reduction of tax in the year of repayment does not apply where the taxpayer
did, in fact, have an unrestricted right to receive the amount in the prior year and
the obligation to repay arose as the result of subsequent events.

Reserves of Income and Expense

1545. Dealer's Reserve. Dealers who discount customers' installment paper with
financial institutions that withhold a small percentage of the price and credit
it to a "Dealer's Reserve Account" as security for the dealer's guaranty of payment
of the installment paper must accrue such credits as income in the year when the
installment paper is transferred to the financial institution.[97]

This has been applied to accrual-basis home sellers who guarantee buyers' loans
by requiring them to accrue as income in the year of sale the proceeds pledged as
loan security to the lender.[98] As to a cash-basis taxpayer, however, the pledged
amounts are taxable to him only as they become available for withdrawal (the
pledged amount was in a restricted savings account and could be withdrawn in
specified amounts only as the buyer reduced the loan principal by certain
amounts).[99]

1547. Reserve for Estimated Expense. Although reserves for contingent liabilities are often set up in business practice, amounts credited to them are
generally not deductible for income tax purposes because the fact of liability is not
fixed.[100] For example, advance deductions have been denied for additions to a
reserve for expected cash discounts on outstanding receivables,[101] amounts credited
by a manufacturer to a reserve for possible future warranty service,[102] and additions
to a reserve covering estimated liability of a carrier for tort claims.[103] However, to
the extent that the Code specifically provides for a deduction for a reserve for
estimated expenses, the economic performance rules of Code Sec. 461(h) do not
apply (Code Sec. 461(h)(5)).[104]

1549. Accrual of Vacation and Sick Leave Pay. A vacation or sick leave pay
deduction is generally limited to the amount of pay earned during the year to
the extent (1) the amount is paid to employees during the year or (2) the amount is
vested as of the last day of the tax year and is paid to employees within 2.5 months
after the end of the year. If such vacation or sick leave pay is not paid until after the
expiration of such period, the employer may deduct vacation pay when paid and
sick leave pay in its tax year that includes the last day of the employee's tax year for
which the payment is reported as income by the employee (Code Sec. 404(a)(5);
Temporary Reg. § 1.404(b)-1T, Q & A-1 and Q & A-2(b)).[105] However, vacation and
sick leave pay incurred with respect to the production of real and tangible personal
property or with respect to property acquired for resale is considered a direct labor
cost that must be capitalized by taxpayers subject to the uniform capitalization
rules (Reg. § 1.263A-1(e)(2)(B)).[106] See ¶ 991.

An employer may deduct FICA and FUTA taxes attributable to accrued
vacation pay only in the tax year that payments are actually made to employees.[107]

Long-Term Contract

1551. Special Treatment. A long-term contract is a building, installation, construction or manufacturing contract that is not completed within the tax year
in which it is entered into. However, a manufacturing contract will not be considered long term unless the contract involves the manufacture of (1) unique items not
normally carried in the finished goods inventory or (2) items normally requiring

Footnote references are to paragraphs of the 2002 Standard Federal Tax Reports.

[96] ¶ 31,881	[101] ¶ 21,817.034	[105] ¶ 18,330, ¶ 18,354,
[97] ¶ 21,005.032	[102] ¶ 21,817.034	¶ 21,817.033
[98] ¶ 21,005.032	[103] ¶ 21,817.65	[106] ¶ 13,811
[99] ¶ 21,005.032	[104] ¶ 21,802	[107] ¶ 21,817.033
[100] ¶ 21,817.688		

more than 12 calendar months to complete (regardless of the duration of the actual contract). The income from long-term contracts may be reported in either of the following ways:

(1) *Percentage-of-completion method.* Gross income may be reported annually according to the percentage of the contract completed in that year. The completion percentage, in the case of long-term contracts entered into after February 28, 1986, must be determined by comparing costs allocated and incurred before the end of the tax year with the estimated total contract costs (cost-to-cost method). In the case of contracts entered into before March 1, 1986, the completion percentage can be determined under the cost-to-cost method or by comparing the work completed to date with the total estimate of work to be completed. All expenditures made during the tax year must be deducted, taking into account unused material and supplies on hand at the beginning and end of the taxable period (Code Sec. 460(b)(1)(A) and Reg. § 1.460-4(b)).[108]

(2) *Completed-contract method.* In limited circumstances, net profit on the entire job may be reported in the year in which the contract is completed and accepted (Reg. § 1.460-4(a)).[109]

Under the completed-contract method, expenses allocable to the contract (i.e., contract costs) are deductible in the year in which the contract is completed. Expenses that are not allocated to the contract (i.e., period costs) are deductible in the year in which they are paid or incurred, depending on the method of accounting employed.[110] Regulations direct the proper allocation of expenses between contract costs and period costs (Reg. § 1.460-4(d)(5)) [111] and clarify when (1) a contract is to be considered completed, (2) separate contracts are to be considered as one contract, and (3) one contract is to be considered as several.

A taxpayer may change his method of accounting to conform with either of these special methods only after he secures permission from the IRS (Reg. § 1.460-4(a)).[112] (See ¶ 1529.) Permission is also required for a change from percentage-of-completion to completed-contract basis, or vice versa.

Long-Term Contracts After February 28, 1986. Most long-term contracts entered into after July 10, 1989, must be fully accounted for under the percentage-of-completion method. For long-term contracts entered into after February 28, 1986, and before July 11, 1989, for which the percentage-of-completion method is not used, taxpayers are required to use the percentage-of-completion capitalized-cost method. Under this method, a percentage of the contract items are taken into account under the percentage-of-completion method and a percentage of the contract items are taken into account under the taxpayer's normal method of accounting (e.g., the completed contract method, an accrual shipment method, etc.). For long-term contracts entered into after June 20, 1988, and before July 11, 1989 (other than certain qualified ship contracts), 90% of the contract items are taken into account under the percentage-of-completion method and 10% of the contract items are taken into account under the taxpayer's normal method of accounting. (For contracts entered into after October 13, 1987, and before June 21, 1988, 70% of the contract items are accounted for under the percentage-of-completion method and 30% are accounted for under the taxpayer's normal method of accounting, and for contracts entered into after February 28, 1986, and before October 14, 1987, the respective percentages are 40% and 60%.)

For example, if there is a long-term contract executed on July 10, 1989, a taxpayer who normally uses the completed-contract method can defer recognition of only 10% of the gross contract income, along with a deduction of 10% of the contract costs, until completion of the contract. The remaining 90% of such income and costs is, respectively, recognized and deducted to the same extent that it would be under the percentage-of-completion method (Code Sec. 460(a)).[113]

Footnote references are to paragraphs of the 2002 Standard Federal Tax Reports.
[108] ¶ 21,550, ¶ 21,560.44   [110] ¶ 21,560.044   [112] ¶ 21,560.50
[109] ¶ 21,560.029   [111] ¶ 21,560.044   [113] ¶ 21,550, ¶ 21,560.01

Home and Residential Construction Contracts. Neither the percentage-of-completion method nor the percentage-of-completion capitalized-cost method of accounting applies to home construction contracts (in which at least 80% of the estimated total costs to be incurred under the contract is attributable to dwelling units in a building with four or fewer dwelling units) and certain other construction contracts of small contractors (see below) (Code Sec. 460(e)).[114] The uniform capitalization rules apply to home construction contracts other than contracts of small contractors (Code Sec. 460(e)(1)).[115]

The percentage-of-completion capitalized-cost method applies to residential construction contracts that do not qualify as home construction contracts, but it is applied according to the 70%-30% rule rather than the 90%-10% rule discussed above (Code Sec. 460(e)(5)).[116]

Look-Back Rule. To the extent that the percentage-of-completion method applies to a long-term contract, a taxpayer who errs in his estimate of the contract price or costs must recompute his tax liability on the basis of the actual contract price and costs for the years that such method was used. Thus, if 40%, 70%, 90% or 100% (whichever applies) of the contract income was reported using the percentage-of-completion method, under the rule described above, the look-back rule is applied to that portion upon completion of the contract. The taxpayer may elect not to apply or reapply the look-back method if, for each prior contract year, the cumulative taxable income or loss under the contract, as determined using estimated contract price or costs, is within 10 percent of the cumulative taxable income or loss as determined using actual contract price and costs. A taxpayer will either pay or receive interest (at the rate for overpayment of tax provided by Code Sec. 6621, compounded daily) on the amount by which the recomputed tax liability for a year exceeds or is less than the previously reported tax liability (Code Sec. 460(b)(2)).[117] Only one rate of interest will apply for each "accrual period," the period which begins on the date after the original return due date for the tax year and which ends on the original return due date for the following tax year. The applicable "adjusted overpayment rate" of interest is the overpayment rate in effect for the calendar quarter in which the accrual period begins.

The look-back method does not apply to certain long-term contracts that are completed within two years of the contract commencement date and have a small gross contract price (Code Sec. 460(b) and Code Sec. 460(e)(1)(B)).[118]

Pass-through entities (partnerships, S corporations, and trusts) that are not closely held must use a simplified look-back method if substantially all of the income under a long-term contract is from sources in the United States (Code Sec. 460(b)(4)).[119] A closely held entity is an entity where 50% or more of the value of the beneficial interests are owned by five or fewer persons. The amount of taxes deemed overpaid or underpaid under a contract in any year is determined at the entity level and is the product of the amount of contract income overreported or underreported for the year times the top marginal tax rate applicable for the year (the top corporate tax rate, or the top individual tax rate if more than 50% of the beneficial interests in the entity are held by individuals).

Allocation and Capitalization of Costs. In general, all costs (including research and experimental costs) that directly benefit or are incurred because of a long-term contract are to be allocated to the contract under Code Sec. 451 and the regulations thereunder that apply to extended period long-term contracts. However, independent research and development costs, expenses incurred in making unsuccessful bids and proposals, and marketing, selling and advertising costs may be expensed. For a cost-plus or federal long-term contract, costs that are not allocated to the contract under the extended period long-term contract rules must be capitalized if identified by the taxpayer (or a related person) as attributable or allocable to the contract. Such an attribution or allocation can be created by the terms of the contract or by

---

Footnote references are to paragraphs of the 2002 Standard Federal Tax Reports.

¶ 1551   [114] ¶ 21,550   [116] ¶ 21,550   [118] ¶ 21,550
                [115] ¶ 21,550   [117] ¶ 21,550   [119] ¶ 21,550

federal, state, or local laws and regulations. Allocation of production period interest is governed by rules (Code Sec. 263A(f)) (see ¶ 1561) that apply to property not produced under a long-term contract (Code Sec. 460(c)).

Pension expense (including previously deducted pension expense that represents past service costs) is subject to the uniform capitalization rules (Code Sec. 263A) and the long-term contract cost allocation rules (Code Sec. 460). Thus, an allocable portion of all otherwise deductible pension costs, whether they relate to current or past services, is included in the basis of property that is produced or held for resale or is allocated to long-term contracts that are subject to the cost allocation rules.

Small Construction Contracts Exception. Small construction contracts are generally not subject to the 40%, 70%, 90% or 100% (whichever is applicable) current recognition requirement, the look-back rules or the cost allocation rules (except for the production period interest rules). A small construction contract is one that is (1) expected to be completed within the two-year period beginning on the commencement date of the contract and (2) performed by a taxpayer whose average annual gross receipts for the three tax years preceding the tax year in which the contract is entered into do not exceed $10 million (Code Sec. 460(e)).

Inventories

1553. Need for Inventories. The use of inventories at the beginning and end of each year is required in most every case where the production, purchase or sale of merchandise is an income-producing factor. Inventories must also be used wherever necessary to clearly reflect income, in the opinion of the IRS (Code Sec. 471(a); Reg. § 1.471-1).[120] A taxpayer whose average annual gross receipts do not exceed $1,000,000 is generally not required to use inventories or the accrual method of accounting (Rev. Proc. 2000-22). However, such taxpayer who does not otherwise use inventories must treat merchandise inventory in the same manner as a material or supply that is not incidental (see Reg. § 1.162-3); the uniform capitalization rules (Code Sec. 263A) will not apply to such merchandise inventory.

A farmer may use the cash method of accounting for purchases and sales if he desires. (But see the accrual method requirement for certain farming corporations at ¶ 2028.) However, any taxpayer, including a farmer, who uses inventories must use the accrual method of accounting for purchases and sales.

1555. Inventories Explained. Gross profit from business operations is calculated by subtracting from receipts the cost of goods sold. See ¶ 759. The cost of goods sold is calculated by adding the inventory at the beginning of the year to the cost of goods purchased or produced during the year and subtracting from this total the inventory at the end of the year. Use of the accrual basis and inventories more clearly reflects the income of a single accounting period through recognition of unsold goods on hand at the beginning and end of each tax year.

1557. Items Included in Inventory. An inventory is an itemized list, with valuations, of goods held for sale or consumption in a manufacturing or merchandising business. Taxpayers must usually verify the amount of items in inventory by a physical count of the items as of the last day of the tax year. Taxpayers may use estimates of inventory shrinkage that are confirmed by a physical count after year-end if the taxpayer normally does a physical inventory count at each location on a regular and consistent basis and the taxpayer makes proper adjustments to such inventories and to its estimating methods to the extent such estimates are greater than or less than the actual shrinkage.

Inventory should include all finished or partly finished goods, and only those raw materials and supplies which have been acquired for sale or which will physically become a part of merchandise intended for sale. Merchandise should be included in inventory only if title to it is vested in the taxpayer. A seller should

---

Footnote references are to paragraphs of the 2002 Standard Federal Tax Reports.
[120] ¶ 22,202, ¶ 22,203

include in inventory goods under contract for sale but not yet segregated and applied to the contract and goods out on consignment. The seller should not include goods sold (including containers) where title has passed to the buyer. A buyer should include in inventory merchandise purchased (including containers) where title has passed to him, even where the merchandise is in transit or has not been physically received (Reg. § 1.471-1).[121]

Permission to include real estate held for sale by a real estate dealer in inventory has been denied.[122] Likewise, capital assets, equipment, accounts, notes, investments, cash, or similar assets may not be included in inventories.

For inventories of farmers and dealers in securities, see ¶ 1569 and ¶ 1903.

1559. Valuation of Inventory. An inventory must conform to the best accounting practice in the particular trade or business and it must clearly reflect income. An inventory that, under the best accounting practice, can be used in a balance sheet showing the financial position of the taxpayer will generally be regarded as clearly reflecting income. In determining whether income is clearly reflected, great weight is given to consistency in inventory practice (Reg. § 1.471-2),[123] but a legitimate accounting system will be disallowed where it distorts income.[124]

It is necessary to identify the particular goods in inventory so that proper costs can be applied to the quantities. Identification of inventories is ordinarily accomplished by the first-in, first-out (FIFO) rule, unless the items are specifically identified. This rule is discussed at ¶ 1564. A taxpayer can also elect to identify inventory items by use of the last-in, first-out (LIFO) rule discussed at ¶ 1565.

Either of two common bases for valuing inventories may be adopted: (1) cost or (2) lower of cost or market (Reg. § 1.471-2).[125] Opening and closing inventories must be valued by the same method.[126] The second method must be consistently applied to each item in the inventory. Cost and market value are determined as to each item, and the lower amount is included in the inventory valuation. A taxpayer is not permitted to inventory the entire stock at cost and also at market and use the lower of the two results (Reg. § 1.471-4).[127] Deviations are permitted, however, as to goods inventoried under the LIFO method (¶ 1565) and as to animals inventoried under the "unit-livestock-price" method (¶ 1569).

Special rules apply to a dealer in securities. See ¶ 1903.

Whether the "cost" or the "lower of cost or market" method is used, inventoried goods that are unsalable, or unusable in normal transactions because of wear and tear, obsolescence or broken lots, should be valued at bona fide selling price, less cost of selling; that is, at the actual offering of goods during a period ending not later than 30 days after inventory date. Adjustment of the valuation on a reasonable basis, not less than scrap value, is permitted in the case of unsalable or unusable raw material or partly finished goods (Reg. § 1.471-2(c)).[128]

1561. Inventory at Cost: Uniform Capitalization Rules. Uniform capitalization rules govern the inclusion in inventory or capital accounts of all allocable costs that are incurred with respect to real and tangible personal property that is produced by the taxpayer or acquired for resale and would otherwise be considered in computing taxable income (Code Sec. 263A(a) and Code Sec. 263A(b)).[129] For this purpose, tangible personal property includes a film, sound recording, videotape, book, or similar property. Except for the interest capitalization rules, the uniform capitalization rules also apply to costs incurred with respect to real or personal (whether tangible or intangible) property that is acquired for resale. Certain small businesses with average annual gross receipts not exceeding $10 million for the three previous years that acquire personal property for resale are exempt from these rules (Code Sec. 263A(b)(2)(B)).[130]

Footnote references are to paragraphs of the 2002 Standard Federal Tax Reports.

[121] ¶ 22,203	[125] ¶ 22,205	[128] ¶ 22,205
[122] ¶ 22,204.36	[126] ¶ 22,206.12	[129] ¶ 13,800
[123] ¶ 22,205	[127] ¶ 22,209	[130] ¶ 13,800
[124] ¶ 22,206.01		

¶ 1559

Costs attributable to inventory must be added to costs of producing or acquiring the inventory, and costs attributable to producing other property must be capitalized. Direct costs (direct material costs and direct labor costs) and the portion of indirect costs (described in Reg. § 1.263A-1(e)(3)(ii)) allocable to such property are subject to these rules.

The uniform capitalization rules replace the inventory cost rules of Code Sec. 471 in the case of property to which they apply. The rules do not apply to inventories valued at market under either the market method or the lower of cost or market method if the market valuation used by the taxpayer generally equals the property's fair market value (i.e., price of sale to customers less direct disposition costs). However, the uniform capitalization rules do apply in determining the market value of any inventory for which market is determined with reference to replacement cost or reproduction cost (Reg. § 1.263A-1(a)(3)(iv)).[131]

Costs incurred with respect to property produced for personal use, timber (including certain ornamental trees), or property produced under long-term contracts, or costs deductible as Code Sec. 174 research and experimental expenditures or as certain oil, gas, and other mineral property, foreign drilling, amortizable or developmental expenditures, and costs (other than circulation expenditures) subject to the ten-year amortization rule for tax preferences are excluded from such rules (Code Sec. 263A(c)).[132]

Certain costs incurred by an individual (or personal service corporation, ¶ 219) engaged in the business of being a writer, photographer, or artist (¶ 990A) that are otherwise deductible are also exempt from such rules (Code Sec. 263A(h)).[133]

In addition, the following costs may be currently deducted under Reg. § 1.263A-1(e)(4)(iv): marketing and selling expenses and general and administration expenses that do not directly benefit production or the acquisition of inventory.[134]

Interest Capitalization Rules. Interest costs paid or incurred during the production period to finance the construction, building, installation, manufacture, development, or improvement of real or tangible personal property that is produced by the taxpayer must be capitalized (Code Sec. 263A(f); Reg. § 1.263A-8).[135] Property subject to the interest capitalization requirement includes property that is produced by the taxpayer for use in its trade or business or in an activity for profit and that has (1) a long useful life (real property or any other property with a class life of 20 years or more), (2) an estimated production period exceeding two years, or (3) an estimated production period exceeding one year and a cost exceeding $1 million. The production period begins on the date on which production of the property starts and ends on the date on which the property is ready to be placed in service or is ready to be held for sale.

The interest capitalization rules also apply to property that is produced for a taxpayer under a contract (Code Sec. 263A(g)(2)).[136] Thus, the portion of the taxpayer-customer's interest expense allocable to costs required to be capitalized (including progress payments, advances to the contractor, and an allocable portion of the general and administrative expenses of the taxpayer) must be capitalized.

Capitalization of interest is not required for property acquired for resale (inventory held by a dealer) (Code Sec. 263A(f)(1)(B)).[137] Interest that constitutes qualified residence interest under Code Sec. 163(h) is also excluded from the capitalization rules (Code Sec. 263A(f)(2)(B)).[138]

The determination of whether interest expense is allocable to the production of property is made under the following rules. Interest on a debt that financed production or construction costs of a particular asset is first allocated and capitalized as part of the cost of the item. If the production or construction costs for an asset exceed the amount of this direct debt, interest on other loans is also subject to capitalization under an avoided-cost rule to the extent of the excess. An assumed

---

Footnote references are to paragraphs of the 2002 Standard Federal Tax Reports.

[131] ¶ 13,811	[134] ¶ 13,811	[137] ¶ 13,800
[132] ¶ 13,800	[135] ¶ 13,800, ¶ 13,852	[138] ¶ 13,800
[133] ¶ 13,800	[136] ¶ 13,800	

¶ 1561

interest rate based on the average interest rates on the taxpayer's outstanding debt, excluding debt specifically traceable to production or construction, may be used for this purpose. For purposes of the interest allocation rule, production or construction expenditures include cumulative production costs (including previously capitalized interest) required to be capitalized (Reg. § 1.263A-9 and Reg. § 1.263A-11).[139]

Interest relating to property used to produce property subject to the interest capitalization rules is also subject to capitalization to the extent such interest is allocable to the produced property as determined under the above rules (Code Sec. 263A(f)(3)).[140]

For flow-through entities (partnerships, S corporations, estates and trusts), the interest capitalization rules are applied first at the entity level and then at the beneficiary level (Code Sec. 263A(f)(2)(C)).[141]

Farming Businesses. For the uniform capitalization rules pertaining to farm businesses, see ¶ 999.

Inventory at Cost: Code Sec. 471 Rules. The rules below are to be used to value inventory at cost where the uniform capitalization rules do not apply. For merchandise on hand at the beginning of the year, "cost" is the amount at which it was included in the closing inventory of the preceding period. For merchandise *bought* after the beginning of the year, "cost" means the invoice price less trade or other discounts, except cash discounts approximating a fair interest rate, which may be deducted from cost, or reported as income, at the option of the taxpayer. Cost also includes transportation or other acquisition charges. For merchandise *produced* by the taxpayer, the costs attributed to inventoried goods must be determined under the uniform capitalization rules (see above).

1563. Inventory at "Cost or Market." If a "cost or market" inventory is used, the market value of each item is compared with the cost of the item, and the lower of the two values must be used for that item (¶ 1559).

> **Example.** A lumber dealer has three grades of lumber at the end of his tax year. They are valued as follows:

Grade	Cost	Market	Lower of Two
A	$45,000	$60,000	$45,000
B	20,000	15,000	15,000
C	5,000	5,000	5,000
	$70,000	$80,000	$65,000

If the lumber dealer is using the cost method, his ending inventory is valued at $70,000. If he is using the lower of cost or market method, his ending inventory is valued at $65,000.

Under normal conditions, market value is the prevailing current bid price at the inventory date in the volume in which the items are usually purchased by the taxpayer. If a current bid price is unobtainable, the best available evidence of fair market value must be used. Specific purchases or sales by the taxpayer or others, or compensation paid for cancellation of contracts for purchase commitments, may be used (Reg. § 1.471-4).[142]

The market value of goods in process and finished goods, for a manufacturer or processor, is reproduction cost. This is the total that materials, labor and factory burden or overhead would cost at current prices to bring the article to a comparable state of completion (Reg. § 1.471-4).[143]

The market price basis does not apply to goods on hand or in the process of manufacture for delivery under firm sale contracts at fixed prices entered into before the inventory date, where the taxpayer is protected against actual loss. Such goods must be inventoried at cost (Reg. § 1.471-4).[144]

Footnote references are to paragraphs of the 2002 Standard Federal Tax Reports.

¶ 1563

[139] ¶ 13,856, ¶ 13,864	[141] ¶ 13,800	[143] ¶ 22,209
[140] ¶ 13,800	[142] ¶ 22,209	[144] ¶ 22,209

A merchant may also use the "retail method" to approximate the lower of cost or market (Reg. § 1.471-8).[145]

If inventories are valued at cost under the lower of cost or market method, such valuation is subject to the uniform capitalization rules at ¶ 1561.

1564. "First-In, First-Out" (FIFO) Rule. The "first-in, first-out" (FIFO) method assumes that items purchased or produced first are the first items sold, consumed or otherwise disposed of. Accordingly, items in inventory at the end of the year are matched with the costs of similar items that were most recently purchased or produced. The FIFO method of valuation is utilized for items taken in inventory that have been so comingled that they cannot be identified with specific invoices; thus, they are considered to be the items most recently purchased or produced. The cost is the actual cost of the items purchased and produced during the period in which the quantity of items in inventory was acquired.

In the absence of an election to use the "last-in, first-out" method, inventory is identified under the FIFO method (Code Sec. 471).[146]

1565. "Last-In, First-Out" (LIFO) Rule. The "last-in, first-out" (LIFO) method is a means of identifying items in inventory and is based on cost values (Code Sec. 472).[147] Under the LIFO method, inventory is taken at cost, but the items contained in the inventory are treated as being, first, those contained in opening inventory, to the extent of the opening inventory (whether or not they are physically on hand), and, second, those acquired during the tax year. The items treated as still in the opening inventory are taken in order of acquisition, except for the first year in which the method is used. For that year, the items in the opening inventory are taken at the average cost of those items. The closing inventory of the preceding year must also be adjusted and an amended return filed to reflect the changes. In the case of a retailer or certain manufacturers, items deemed to have been purchased during the year, that is, inventory increases, may be taken, at the taxpayer's election, on the basis of the most recent purchases, or at average cost for the year, or in order of acquisition.

A taxpayer need not obtain advance permission from the IRS to elect to use the LIFO method but must adopt it on the return for the year in which the method is first used. In addition, the taxpayer must file a Form 970, "Application to Use LIFO Inventory Method," with the return and accept any modifications or adjustments required by the IRS. The election applies only to the class or classes of goods specified in the application. Although the election to adopt LIFO must generally cover the entire inventory of a business, manufacturers or processors may elect to have the method apply to raw materials only, including those in finished goods and work-in-process (Reg. § 1.472-1(h)).[148] Furthermore, if LIFO is used for tax purposes, it generally must also be used in preparing annual financial statements for credit purposes or for the purpose of reports to stockholders, partners, or proprietors. For purposes of this "report rule," all members of the same group of financially related corporations are treated as one taxpayer.

Taxpayers using the LIFO method of accounting who acquire inventory items in a bulk bargain purchase at a substantial discount cannot use the cost of the inventory items as the base-year cost for substantially similar inventory items that are subsequently produced or acquired.[149] Taxpayers that voluntarily choose to change their method of accounting to conform to this rule must file Form 3115, "Application for Change in Accounting Method."

1567. Dollar-Value LIFO Method. Instead of determining quantity increases of each item in the inventory and then pricing them, as is required under regular LIFO, the "dollar-value" LIFO method may be used (Reg. § 1.472-8).[150] The increase in LIFO value is determined by comparing the total dollar value of the beginning and ending inventories at base year (first LIFO year) prices and then

Footnote references are to paragraphs of the 2002 Standard Federal Tax Reports.
[145] ¶ 22,217 [147] ¶ 22,230 [149] ¶ 22,277
[146] ¶ 22,204 [148] ¶ 22,231 [150] ¶ 22,239

¶ 1567

converting any dollar-value increase to current prices by means of an index. Taxpayers are allowed, under the dollar-value LIFO method, to determine base year dollars through the use of government indexes (Code Sec. 472(f)).[151]

Simplified Dollar-Value LIFO Method. Small businesses (those with average gross receipts for the three preceding years of $5 million or less) may elect to use a simplified dollar-value LIFO method to account for their inventories (Code Sec. 474(a)).[152] The election applies to all succeeding years unless the taxpayer obtains IRS permission to change to another method or becomes ineligible to use such method. If elected, it must be used to value all LIFO inventories.

The simplified dollar-value LIFO method replaces the single LIFO inventory pool method used by taxpayers with average annual gross receipts of $2 million or less. The single LIFO pool election may be revoked without the consent of the IRS or it may still be used by any taxpayer who continues to meet its requirements. However, the simplified dollar-value LIFO method may not be used for any year in which the single LIFO inventory pool method is used.

1569. Special Accounting Methods for Farmers. In addition to the standard cost and the lower of cost or market methods, a farmer on the accrual basis has a choice of two other systems. The "farm-price" method provides for the valuation of inventories at market price less the direct cost of disposition. If this method is used, it must be applied to the entire inventory except livestock which the taxpayer has elected to inventory under the "unit-livestock-price" method (Reg. § 1.471-6(d)).[153]

The "unit-livestock-price" method—adoptable when the farmer raises his own livestock or purchases young animals and raises them to maturity—provides for the valuation *of different classes* of animals at a standard unit price for each animal within a class. This method, once elected, must be applied to all livestock raised to maturity or purchased before maturity and raised to maturity, whether held for sale or for breeding, draft or dairy purposes.[154] This includes unweaned calves, according to the Tax Court.[155] Unit prices assigned to classes must account for normal cost of production. For purchased livestock, the cost should be increased in accordance with unit prices only for animals acquired in the first six months of the tax year (Reg. § 1.471-6(g)).[156]

The "crop" basis of accounting may be used with IRS consent for crops which have not been gathered and disposed of during the tax year in which they are planted (Reg. § 1.61-4(c)).[157] The entire cost of producing the crop must be deducted no earlier than in the year in which the crop income is realized.

1571. Change in Basis of Inventory. A change of inventory basis can be made only when authorized by the IRS. A change from a cash method to an inventory method is, in effect, a change to the accrual method of accounting for purchases and sales (Reg. § 1.446-1(c)(2) and Rev. Proc. 97-37). Permission to make such a change must generally be requested within the tax year that the change is to be effective (¶ 1529), with the exception of an election to change to the LIFO method. An election to use this method may be made by a statement on Form 970 attached to the first tax return in which it is used; however, adjustments will be required to prevent duplications and omissions of income and expenses (Reg. § 1.472-3 and Reg. § 1.472-4).[158]

Allocation and Reconstruction of Income

1573. Allocation by IRS. Where two or more organizations, trades, or businesses are owned or controlled by the same interests, the IRS may allocate gross income, deductions or credits between them if it determines such action is necessary to prevent evasion of taxes or to clearly reflect income (Code Sec. 482).[159] Moreover,

Footnote references are to paragraphs of the 2002 Standard Federal Tax Reports.

[151] ¶ 22,230	[154] ¶ 22,214	[157] ¶ 5601
[152] ¶ 22,260	[155] ¶ 22,214	[158] ¶ 22,234, ¶ 22,235
[153] ¶ 22,213	[156] ¶ 22,213	[159] ¶ 22,280

¶ **1569**

the IRS is specifically authorized by statute to allocate any income, deduction, credit, exclusion or other allowance between certain personal service corporations and their employee-owners where the principal purpose of forming or using such a corporation is to avoid or evade income tax. See ¶ 1575.

1575. Acquisitions to Avoid Tax. If a taxpayer acquires control of a corporation, directly or indirectly, to evade or avoid income tax by securing the benefit of a deduction, credit, or other allowance that would not otherwise be enjoyed, then such deduction, credit or other allowance will not be permitted. The same rules of disallowance apply to a corporation that acquires property of another corporation that was not controlled by the acquiring corporation or its stockholders and that acquires a basis determined by reference to the basis in the hands of the transferor corporation (Code Sec. 269(a)).[160] Code Sec. 269(b)[161] explicitly authorizes the IRS to deny an acquiring corporation the carryover and other tax benefits of a subsidiary corporation, acquired in a qualified stock purchase for which an election of asset acquisition treatment is not made, if the subsidiary corporation is liquidated under a plan adopted within two years of the acquisition date and the principal purpose of the liquidation is tax avoidance or evasion.

If (1) substantially all of the services of a personal service corporation are performed for, or on behalf of, one other corporation, partnership, or other entity and (2) the principal purpose for forming or using such personal service corporation is the avoidance or evasion of income tax by reducing the income of or securing the benefit of any expense, deduction, credit, exclusion or other allowance for any employee-owner that would not otherwise be available, then the IRS can allocate all income, credits, exclusions, or other allowances between such personal service corporation and its employee-owners in order to prevent tax evasion or avoidance or to clearly reflect the income of both (Code Sec. 269A).[162] A "personal service corporation" means a corporation the principal activity of which is the performance of personal services that are substantially performed by the employee-owners. The term "employee-owner" is defined as any employee who owns, on any day during the tax year, more than 10% of the personal service corporation's outstanding stock.

1577. Income Reconstruction. Where a taxpayer has kept either inadequate or no books or records, the IRS has authority to compute income in order to clearly reflect the taxpayer's income (Code Sec. 446(b)).[163] The methods for reconstructing income vary depending on the facts and circumstances, and the records that are available. The IRS has developed several methods for reconstructing a taxpayer's income. The methods used most often are:

(1) *Bank deposits and expenditures method.* All bank deposits are assumed to represent income unless the taxpayer can establish otherwise.[164]

(2) *Net worth method.* An opening net worth or total value of assets at the beginning of a given year is established. The IRS then shows increases in the taxpayer's net worth for each subsequent year and calculates the difference between the adjusted net values of the assets at the beginning and end of each year under examination. Nondeductible expenses are added to the increases. If the resulting amount is greater than reported taxable income for that year, then the excess is treated as unreported taxable income.[165]

(3) *Percentage or unit mark-up method.* Net income is determined by applying certain percentages, such as gross profits to sales, net income to gross income, or net income to sales, derived from other taxpayers in similar types of businesses.[166]

Footnote references are to paragraphs of the 2002 Standard Federal Tax Reports.
[160] ¶ 14,250 [163] ¶ 20,606 [165] ¶ 20,620.0462
[161] ¶ 14,250 [164] ¶ 20,620.046 [166] ¶ 20,620.047
[162] ¶ 14,300

¶ **1577**

Chapter 16

BASIS FOR GAIN OR LOSS

Computing Gain or Loss

1601. Basis. The basis for computing gain or loss or depreciation on property acquired in most common transactions is outlined below, with references to the paragraphs where additional details appear. This basis, after adjustments described at ¶ 1611—¶ 1617, is subtracted from the amount realized to determine the amount of gain or loss from a sale or exchange (Code Sec. 1001).[1] Except where other rules are prescribed, the basis for gain or loss is determined under the law in effect when the property is sold.

Type of acquisition	Basis for gain or loss
Bargain purchases	
arm's-length	Cost (¶ 789)
corporation's, from nonstockholder	Cost (¶ 789)
corporation's, from stockholder	Cost, unless saving is paid-in surplus (¶ 1660)
employee's	Cost plus amount taxable as compensation for services (¶ 789)
relative or friend	Cost, unless saving is a gift (¶ 1630)
stockholder's	Cost plus amount taxable as a dividend (¶ 789)
Bequests	For property acquired from a decedent, basis generally is fair market value at the date of the decedent's death (¶ 1633—¶ 1642)
property acquired in lieu of specific amount bequest	Value assigned in settlement (¶ 1633)
Cash purchases	Cost (¶ 1604)
mortgage also assumed, or property taken subject to the mortgage	Full price, including mortgage amount (¶ 1725)
purchase money mortgage also given	Full purchase price (¶ 1725)
purchase notes also given	Full purchase price (¶ 1725)
redeemable ground rent assumed, or property taken subject to ground rent	Full purchase price (¶ 1725)
Community property	
survivor (death of spouse)	See "Bequests," above

Footnote references are to paragraphs of the 2002 Standard Federal Tax Reports.

¶ **1601**   [1] ¶ 29,220

Corporate property	
acquired for stock by controlled corporation	Transferor's basis of property (¶ 1663)
acquired for stock in taxable exchange	Fair market value of stock at time of exchange (¶ 1648)
contributions by nonstockholders	Zero (¶ 1660)
paid-in surplus	Transferor's basis (¶ 1660)
Dividend property	
corporate, stockholder of domestic corporation	Fair market value (¶ 735)
corporate, stockholder of foreign corporation	Fair market value (¶ 735)
noncorporate, stockholder	Fair market value (¶ 735)
Divorce or separation agreement	See ¶ 1734
Gift property	Donor's basis, increased by gift tax in some cases; basis for loss *limited* to lesser of donor's basis or fair market value at time of gift (¶ 1630)
Inventory goods	Last inventory value (¶ 1561)
Joint tenancy	
after death of one tenant after 1953	For property acquired from a decedent, basis generally is fair market value at the date of the decedent's death (¶ 1633, ¶ 1636)
Lessor's acquisitions of lessee's improvements	Zero, if excluded from income (¶ 764)
Life estate	Zero, if disposed of after October 9, 1969 (¶ 1633)
Livestock	
inventoried	Last inventory value (¶ 767)
purchased	Cost (¶ 767)
raised by accrual-basis farmer	Cost of raising (¶ 767)
raised by cash-basis farmer	Zero, if costs were charged to expense (¶ 767)
Mortgaged property (or property subject to redeemable ground rent)	Basis includes mortgage (or ground rent) (¶ 1725)
Partners' property	
partnership interest in exchange for contribution	Partners' adjusted basis of property contributed (¶ 443)
partnership interest purchased	Cost (¶ 434)
received in distribution other than liquidation	Partnership's adjusted basis at time of distribution (limited to partner's basis of his interest) (¶ 456)
received in partnership liquidation	Adjusted basis of partnership interest less cash received (¶ 456)
Partnership property	
after transfer of partnership interest or distributions to partners	Unaffected, unless election is made to adjust values (¶ 459, ¶ 467)
capital contribution	Partner's adjusted basis (¶ 443)
Purchase for more than value	Cost (¶ 1604), but excess may be a gift (¶ 1657)
Rehabilitated buildings, other than certified historic structures, for which investment credit on qualified expenditures available	Basis is reduced by allowable investment credit (¶ 1360); recaptured credit is added to basis (¶ 1364)

¶ 1601

Repossessed property after installment sale	
personal property	Fair market value (¶ 1838)
real property reacquired in satisfaction of purchaser's indebtedness secured by property	Adjusted basis of indebtedness plus gain resulting from reacquisition and reacquisition costs (¶ 1843)
Residence after sale of old residence without recognition of gain	Cost minus gain not recognized (¶ 1706)
Spousal transfers	See ¶ 1734
Stock	
acquired in wash sale	Basis of stock sold, adjusted for difference between selling price of sold stock and purchase price of acquired stock (¶ 1939)
bonus stock	Allocable portion of basis of old stock (¶ 1620)
nontaxable stock dividend	Allocable share of basis of stock on which declared (¶ 1620)
qualified small business stock rollover	See ¶ 2397
purchased	See ¶ 1975, ¶ 1977
received for services	Amount reported as income, plus cash paid (¶ 1681)
S corporation	See ¶ 317
specialized small business investment company stock rollover	See ¶ 2397
taxable stock dividend	Fair market value when issued (¶ 738)
Stock rights	
nontaxable	Allocable share of basis of stock unless rights value is less than 15% of stock value (¶ 738)
taxable	Fair market value when issued (¶ 738)
Transfer in trust after Dec. 31, 1920	Grantor's basis, plus gain or minus loss, upon transfer (¶ 1678)

1604. Adjusted Basis of Property. To determine the gain or loss from a sale or other disposition of property, the amount realized must be compared with the basis of the property to the taxpayer—generally measured by the original capital investment, adjusted (¶ 1611—¶ 1617) to the date of sale (Code Sec. 1011; Reg. § 1.1011-1).[2]

In most situations, the basis of property is its cost to the taxpayer.[3] When property is acquired in a fully taxable exchange, the cost of the property acquired is the fair market value (¶ 1695) of the property given up.[4] Since, in an arm's-length transaction, both are presumed to be equal in value, the basis for the acquired property can be expressed as its fair market value.

1607. "Substituted" Basis. A "substituted" basis is one that is continued or carried through from one taxpayer to another, or from one piece of property to another, as for gifts (¶ 1630), some transfers in trust (¶ 1678), tax-free exchanges (¶ 1651—¶ 1666), and replaced residential property (¶ 1706).[5]

Property Acquired by Purchase

1611. Additions to Basis of Property. In computing gain or loss on the sale of business or investment property or gain on the sale of personal property, the cost or other basis must be *adjusted* for any expenditure, receipt, loss, or other item

Footnote references are to paragraphs of the 2002 Standard Federal Tax Reports.

           2 ¶ 29,310, ¶ 29,311   4 ¶ 29,335.01   5 ¶ 29,426.01

¶ 1604   3 ¶ 29,330

properly chargeable to the capital account (Code Sec. 1016(a)(1); Reg. § 1.1016-1— Reg. § 1.1016-9).[6] This necessitates an addition for improvements made to the property since its acquisition.[7] For example, the cost of capital improvements such as an addition or new roof on a home, installing central air conditioning, or rewiring a home is added to its basis. Other capital charges such as brokers' commissions, lawyers' fees, etc. incurred in buying real estate are added to its basis. Generally, expenditures incurred in defending or perfecting title to property are also a part of the cost of the property.[8] The basis of property is also increased by zoning costs[9] and the capitalized value of a redeemable ground rent (Code Sec. 1055).

Cost basis also includes sales tax, freight, installation and testing cost, excise taxes, and revenue stamps.[10]

Settlement Fees and Other Costs. The basis of real property includes settlement fees and closing costs such as abstract fees, charges for installing utility services, legal fees (including title search and preparation of the sales contract and deed), recording fees, surveys, transfer taxes, owner's title insurance, and amounts owed by the seller but paid by the buyer, such as back taxes or interest, recording or mortgage fees, charges for improvements or repairs, and sales commissions (Code Sec. 1012; Reg. § 1.1012-1(b); Rev. Rul. 68-528). A buyer may claim a current deduction for reimbursing the seller for real estate taxes paid by the seller for the buyer (Reg. § 1.1012-1(b)). Amounts placed in escrow for future payments of items such as insurance and taxes do not increase basis. A buyer increases basis by the amount of an existing mortgage that the buyer assumes and becomes liable for (*B.B. Crane*, SCt, 47-1 USTC ¶ 9217).[11] Fees and costs related to getting a loan to purchase the property are not included in the basis of the property.

Assessments. An assessment for improvements or other items that increase the value of a property are added to the basis of the property and not deducted as a tax. Such improvements may include streets, sidewalks, water mains, sewers, and public parking facilities. The amount of such an assessment may be a depreciable asset. For example, the cost of a mall enclosure paid for by a business taxpayer through an assessment is depreciable. Assessments for maintenance or repair or meeting interest charges on the improvements are currently deductible as a real property tax (Code Sec. 164(c)(1); Reg. § 1.164-4).

Legal fees for obtaining a decrease in an assessment levied against property to pay for local improvements are added to the basis of the property (Rev. Rul. 70-62).

Taxes. Any tax paid in connection with the acquisition of a property is included in the basis of the property. A tax paid in connection with the disposition of a property reduces the amount realized on the disposition (Code Sec. 164(a)).

Checklist. See the checklist at ¶ 57 to determine whether an expense is deductible or must be capitalized and added to basis.

1614. Additions to Basis for Carrying Charges. A taxpayer may elect to treat taxes or other carrying charges (such as interest) on some property as capital charges rather than as an expense of the tax year (Code Sec. 266). The items chargeable to capital account are:[12]

(1) in the case of unimproved and unproductive real property: annual taxes, interest on a mortgage, and other carrying charges;

(2) in the case of real property, whether improved or unimproved and whether productive or unproductive: interest on a loan, taxes of the owner of such property measured by compensation paid to the owner's employees, taxes of the owner on the purchase of materials or on the storage, use or other consumption of materials, and other necessary expenditures, all of which are

---

Footnote references are to paragraphs of the 2002 Standard Federal Tax Reports.
6 ¶ 29,410—¶ 29,426   9 ¶ 13,709.659   11 ¶ 29,313.03
7 ¶ 29,412.021   10 ¶ 29,335.021;   12 ¶ 14,102.01
8 ¶ 8526.038

¶ 1614

paid or incurred for the development or improvement of the property up to the time the development or construction work has been completed;

(3) in the case of personal property: taxes of an employer measured by compensation for services rendered in transporting machinery or other fixed assets to the plant or installing them, interest on a loan to buy such property or to pay for transporting or installing it, and taxes imposed on the purchase of such property or on the storage, use or other consumption, paid or incurred up to the date of installation or the date when the property is first put to use by the taxpayer, whichever is later; and

(4) any other taxes and carrying charges, otherwise deductible, which are chargeable to capital account under sound accounting principles.

The election in (1) above must be renewed each year if the taxpayer wishes to continue capitalizing. The election in (2) is effective until the development or construction work has been completed. The election in (3) is effective until the property is installed or first put to use, whichever date is later. The IRS determines whether the election in (4) is effective (Code Sec. 266; Reg. § 1.266-1).[13]

1617. Reductions in Basis. In order to determine the amount of gain or loss on the sale or other disposition of property, or the basis of property acquired in an exchange, and the basis for depreciation or depletion, the unadjusted basis (usually its cost, but in some cases the transferor's basis) of the property must be decreased by any items that represent a return of capital for the period during which the property has been held. These include the Code Sec. 179 expense deduction for certain depreciable business assets (¶ 1208), the investment credit (50% of the credit for energy and reforestation credits) (¶ 1360), tax-free dividends (¶ 738), recognized losses on involuntary exchanges (¶ 1687), casualty losses (¶ 1139), deductions previously allowed or allowable for amortization, depreciation, obsolescence or depletion (chapter 12), and unrecognized gains on tax-free exchanges (¶ 1719).[14]

Depreciation. The basis of property is reduced by the amount of depreciation claimed, or if greater, the depreciation which should have been claimed under the method chosen (Code Sec. 1016(a)(2); Reg. § 1.1016-3). If no depreciation was claimed, the basis is reduced by the full amount of depreciation which should have been claimed.

If excess depreciation was claimed on an asset, the basis of the asset is reduced by the amount of depreciation which should have been claimed plus the part of the excess depreciation deducted that actually reduced the taxpayer's tax liability.[15]

Automobiles. The basis of an automobile must be reduced by the amount of any gas guzzler tax imposed by Code Sec. 4064 when use of vehicle begins not more than one year after first retail sale (Code Sec. 1016(a)).[16] The basis of a diesel vehicle purchased before August 21, 1996 must be reduced by the amount of any credit or refund allowed under former Code Sec. 6727(g) for diesel-powered highway vehicles.[17] The basis of a vehicle for which the deduction for clean-fuel vehicles is claimed is reduced by the amount of the deduction (Code Sec. 179A(e)(6)). See ¶ 1286. A qualified electric vehicle for which a tax credit is allowable is reduced by the lesser of $4,000 or 10 percent of the vehicle's cost (Code Sec. 30(d)). See ¶ 1321.

Percentage Depletion. Even though a percentage depletion allowance is in excess of cost or other basis, it is not necessary to use a negative basis (less than zero) in computing gain on the sale of mineral property.[18] See ¶ 1294-¶ 1298.

Easements. Generally, the amount received for granting an easement for a limited use or for a limited period reduces the basis of the affected part of the property (Rev. Rul. 68-291). Gain is recognized to the extent that the amount received exceeds the basis of the affected part. The granting of a perpetual easement

Footnote references are to paragraphs of the 2002 Standard Federal Tax Reports.

¶ **1617**   13 ¶ 14,100, ¶ 14,101   15 ¶ 29,412.035   17 ¶ 4151.03
              14 ¶ 29,410   16 ¶ 29,410   18 ¶ 29,412.037

that denies the grantor any beneficial use of the property may be considered a sale of property even though the grantor retains legal title.[19]

Energy Subsidy. The basis of a dwelling unit for which an excludable energy conservation subsidy was provided by a public utility (¶ 884) must be reduced by the amount of the subsidy (Code Sec. 136).

Homes Sales—Pre-May 7, 1997 Gain. Gain postponed from the sale of a principal residence before May 7, 1997 reduces the basis of the new home by the amount of postponed gain. See ¶ 1706.

Adoption Credit. The basis of a residence must be reduced by the amount of the adoption tax credit that was claimed with respect to improvements that increased that basis of the home (Code Sec. 23(g)).[20]

Canceled Debt. See ¶ 791.

Substituted Basis. Where the basis of the property is a substituted basis, the same adjustments must be made for the period the property was held by the transferor, donor, or grantor, or during the period the property was held by the person for whom the basis is to be determined (Code Sec. 1016(b)).[21]

1620. Apportionment of Cost or Other Basis. When a sale is made of parts of property purchased as a unit, as in a subdivision of real estate, allocation of the total basis is required.[22] Other instances where allocation of the cost or other basis is necessary include stock of different classes received as a dividend or pursuant to a reorganization, a split-up, split-off, or spin-off; stock received as a bonus with the purchase of stock of a different character; stock purchase warrants attached to debenture bonds; and depreciable and nondepreciable property purchased for a lump sum.

Trade or Business Purchased. The applicable asset acquisition rules of Code Sec. 1060 require the allocation of the purchase price of a trade or business acquired after March 15, 2001 among the assets in proportion to their fair market values in the following order (Reg. § 1.1060-1, Reg. § 1.338-6):[23]

(1) Certificates of deposit, U.S. government securities, foreign currency, and actively traded personal property, including stock and securities.

(2) Assets marked to market at least annually and debt instruments, including accounts receivable.

(3) Stock in trade, inventory, and property held primarily for sale to customers.

(4) All other assets except section 197 intangibles, goodwill, and going concern value.

(5) Section 197 intangibles except goodwill and going concern value.

(6) Goodwill and going concern value whether or not they qualify as section 197 intangibles.

Before making the above allocation, the purchase price is first reduced by any cash which the acquired business holds as an asset. The allocation order for businesses acquired before March 16, 2001 are substantially similar.[24]

The buyer and seller of the assets of a trade or business are bound by any written agreements allocating consideration to the transferred assets. However, any allocation which is not found to be fair market value will be disregarded (Code Sec. 1060).[25]

The buyer and seller must attach Form 8594 (Asset Allocation Statement) to their income tax returns for the year of sale to report the allocation.

Footnote references are to paragraphs of the 2002 Standard Federal Tax Reports.

[19] ¶ 30,422.055   [22] ¶ 5605, ¶ 29,313.024   [24] ¶ 30,063.024
[20] ¶ 29,412.0253   [23] ¶ 30,063   [25] ¶ 30,060
[21] ¶ 29,410, ¶ 29,426.01

Land and Buildings. When a building and land are purchased for a lump sum, the purchase price must be allocated between the land and building on the basis of their fair market values. If the fair market values are uncertain, the allocation may be based on their assessed values for real estate tax purposes (Reg. § 1.61-6(a); Reg. § 1.167(a)-5).

Subdivided Lots. The basis of each lot of a subdivided property is equal to the purchase price of the entire property multiplied by a fraction, the numerator of which is the fair market value of the lot and the denominator of which is the fair market value of the entire property. The cost of common improvements is also allocated among the individual lots. A developer who sells subdivided lots before development work is completed may include, with IRS consent, an allocation of the estimated future cost for common improvements in the basis of the lots sold (Rev. Proc. 92-29).[26]

See ¶ 1762 for a special rule relating to the recognition of capital gain on the sale of subdivided lots.

1623. Allocation of Basis—Bargain Sale to Charity. If a charitable deduction is available, the basis of property sold to charity for less than its fair market value must be allocated between the portion of the property "sold" and the portion "given" to charity, based on the fair market value of each portion. Thus, the seller-donor realizes some taxable gain even if the selling price did not exceed the seller-donor's cost or other basis for the entire property.[27] The adjusted basis of the portion of property sold to a charity is computed as:

$$\frac{\text{Amount realized on sale to charity}}{\text{Fair market value of entire property}} \times \begin{array}{c}\text{Adjusted basis}\\\text{of}\\\text{entire property}\end{array}$$

1626. Basis of Residential or Converted Property. Where property has been occupied by the taxpayer as a residence continually since its acquisition, no adjustment of the basis is made for depreciation since none is allowable. The cost of permanent improvements to the property is added to the basis, as are special assessments paid for local benefits that improve the property.[28] Recoveries against a builder for defective construction reduce the basis.[29]

If residential property is converted to rental property, an adjustment for depreciation should be made but only from the date of the change. Thus, the basis for gain in the case of rented residential property is the taxpayer's cost or other statutory basis, less depreciation allowable while the property was rented or held for rental.

The basis for loss may not exceed the value at the time the residence was converted to rental use, taking into account subsequent basis adjustments, including reduction for allowable depreciation. This is only a limitation; if a smaller loss results from the use of the adjusted cost basis, it must be used (Reg. § 1.165-9(b)).[30] The value of the property upon conversion to rental use has no effect on the basis for gain. If converted property is sold for a price that is greater than the basis for loss but less than the basis for gain, there is no gain or loss.

If rental property is converted to a personal residence, adjustments to basis for depreciation end on the date of the conversion. Any gain on the sale of the property will be recognized (subject to the exclusion rules at ¶ 1705) and may be subject to depreciation recapture (¶ 1779). Loss will not be recognized.

Footnote references are to paragraphs of the 2002 Standard Federal Tax Reports.

¶ **1623**

[26] ¶ 29,313.028, ¶ 29,313.576
[27] ¶ 29,310, ¶ 29,313.021
[28] ¶ 9508, ¶ 29,410, ¶ 29,412.021
[29] ¶ 29,412.9968
[30] ¶ 10,102

Property Acquired by Gift, Bequest

1630. Property Acquired by Gift. If property was acquired by gift after 1920, the basis to the donee is the same as it would be in the hands of the donor or the last preceding owner by whom it was not acquired by gift (Code Sec. 1015(a); Reg. § 1.1015-1).[31] The basis for loss is the basis so determined (adjusted for the period prior to the date of the gift as provided in ¶ 1611—¶ 1617) or the fair market value of the property at the time of the gift, whichever is lower.

In some cases, there is neither gain nor loss on the sale of property received by gift because the selling price is less than the basis for gain and more than the basis for loss.

If a gift tax was payable on a gift made after September 1, 1958, and before 1977, the basis of the property is increased by the amount of the gift tax, but not above the fair market value of the property at the time of the gift. As to gifts made before September 2, 1958, and held by the donee on that date, the basis is also increased by the amount of the gift tax, but not by more than any excess of the fair market value of the property at the time of the gift over the basis of the property in the hands of the donor at the time of the gift (Code Sec. 1015(d); Reg. § 1.1015-1).[32]

In the case of a gift made after 1976 on which the gift tax is paid, the basis of the property is increased by the amount of gift tax attributable to the net appreciation in value of the gift. The net appreciation for this purpose is the amount by which the fair market value of the gift exceeds the donor's adjusted basis immediately before the gift (Code Sec. 1015(d)(6)).[33]

For the basis of a life estate acquired by gift, see ¶ 1633.

1633. Property Acquired from a Decedent. Except as indicated at ¶ 1636 and ¶ 1639, the basis of any property, real or personal, acquired from a decedent is its fair market value on the date of the decedent's death or on the alternate valuation date described at ¶ 1642. Principally, this "stepped-up" basis rule applies to property acquired by bequest, devise or inheritance. It also applies to property required to be included in the decedent's gross estate for federal estate tax purposes even though it was the subject of a lifetime transfer, unless the transferee sold or otherwise disposed of the property before the decedent died. Property acquired by the decedent's estate, as well as property acquired directly from the decedent without passing through the estate, qualifies for a "stepped-up" basis (Code Sec. 1014; Reg. § 1.1014-1—§ 1.1014-8).[34]

Since, in community property states, each spouse has an undivided half interest in community property, an heir, devisee or legatee acquires the decedent's half interest from the deceased spouse and is entitled to a stepped-up basis under the foregoing general rule. Under Code Sec. 1014(b)(6), the surviving spouse is also entitled to a stepped-up basis for his or her half interest if at least half of the community property in question is includible in the decedent's gross estate for estate tax purposes. This special provision applies only in the case of decedents dying after 1947.[35]

In most instances, a zero basis is assigned to a life estate that was acquired by gift or bequest and sold or disposed of after October 9, 1969. Interests covered by this exception to the usual rules are: (1) life interests in property, (2) interests for a term of years in property, and (3) income interests in trusts. The zero basis requirement does not apply where the life tenant and remainderman sell their interests simultaneously so that the entire ownership of the property is transferred to another person or group of persons.[36]

Effective for property acquired from a decedent dying after December 31, 2009, the stepped-up basis at death rules will be repealed (Code Sec. 1014, as

---

Footnote references are to paragraphs of the 2002 Standard Federal Tax Reports.

[31] ¶ 29,390, ¶ 29,391   [33] ¶ 29,390   [35] ¶ 29,370
[32] ¶ 29,390, ¶ 29,391   [34] ¶ 29,370—¶ 29,378   [36] ¶ 29,225.047   **¶ 1633**

amended by the Economic Growth and Tax Relief Reconciliation Act of 2001 (P.L.
107-16)) and replaced with modified carryover basis at death rules. More specifically, the recipient of the property will receive a basis equal to the lesser of the
adjusted basis of the property in the hands of the decedent or the fair market value
of the property on the date of the decedent's death. As a partial replacement for the
repealed basis step-up, executors will be able partially to increase the basis of estate
property by up to $1,300,000 or $3,000,000 in the case of property passing to a
surviving spouse (Code Sec. 1022(b), as added by P.L. 107-16).

1634. Joint Tenancy. When property is held in joint tenancy with right of survivorship (other than with a spouse), the basis of the property in the hands of
the survivor will depend upon the amount contributed by each joint tenant toward
the original purchase price and, in the case of depreciable property, the manner in
which income is divided under local (state) law (Reg. § 20.2040-1(a)).

> **Example 1.** Tom Smith and Susan Jones (unmarried) purchased a
> townhouse for $100,000 in 1990 which they held as joint tenants with right
> of survivorship. Tom contributed $30,000 and Susan $70,000. Susan died
> in 2001, when the property was worth $200,000. 70% of the fair market
> value or $140,000 is included in Susan's estate. Tom's basis in the property
> is $170,000 ($30,000 + $140,000).

> **Example 2.** Assume that Tom and Susan held the townhouse as a
> rental property and that $25,000 of depreciation was allowed prior to
> Susan's death. If Tom and Susan are entitled to one-half of the income
> from the property under local law, Tom's basis would be reduced by
> $12,500 to $157,500 ($170,000 − $12,500).

Qualified Joint Interests. A qualified joint interest is an interest in property
held by a husband and wife as tenants by the entirety or as joint tenants with the
right of survivorship if the husband and wife are the only joint tenants. One-half of
the fair market value of a qualified joint interest acquired after 1976 is included in
the deceased spouse's estate regardless of the amount contributed by the surviving
spouse (Code Sec. 2040(b)). The surviving spouse's basis in the remaining portion of
the qualified joint interest is one-half of the original cost (regardless of the amount
that the survivor actually contributed) reduced by any depreciation deductions that
are allocable to the surviving spouse (IRS Publication 559, Basis of Inherited
Property).[37]

> **Example 3.** Assume the same facts as in *Example 1,* except that Tom
> and Susan are married. Tom's basis in the property is $150,000 ($50,000
> (one-half of original cost) + $100,000 (one-half of fair market value
> included in Susan's estate).

1636. Carryover Basis Elections. Executors and administrators of estates of
decedents dying after 1976 and before November 7, 1978, could elect to
determine the basis under the otherwise repealed carryover basis rules.[38] The time
for elections expired July 31, 1980, but valid elections will continue to affect
computation of gain on dispositions of property to which such elections apply.

1639. Property Reacquired by Donor from Decedent. If a decedent who died
after December 31, 1981, acquired appreciated property as a gift within one
year of death and such property passed to, or was acquired by, the original donor or
the original donor's spouse, then the basis of such property to the donor or the
donor's spouse is the adjusted basis of such property to the decedent immediately
prior to the decedent's death (Code Sec. 1014(e)).[39]

1642. Estate Tax Value. In determining the basis of property acquired from a
decedent, the fair market value of the property at the time of the death of the
decedent is usually the property's value as appraised for estate tax purposes. If

there is no estate tax liability, the value is its appraised value as of the date of the decedent's death for the purpose of state inheritance or transmission taxes.[40] The Tax Court, however, has accepted a proven higher value.[41]

If the executor elects to value the decedent's estate for federal estate tax purposes by using the alternative valuation method prescribed by Code Sec. 2032, the value used to determine the basis of the property is not the value at the date of the decedent's death but, rather, the value at the date six months after death if the property is not sold, distributed, or otherwise disposed of within six months after the decedent's death. If the property is sold, distributed, or disposed of within six months of death, the value that is used in determining basis is the value of the property at the date of sale, distribution, or disposition.[42]

Property Acquired by Exchange

1648. Property Transferred to a Corporation in a Taxable Exchange for Its Stock. Where a corporation acquires property for its stock in an exchange taxable to the transferor, its basis for the property is the fair market value of the stock on the date of the exchange. If the stock has no established market value at that time, it may be considered to be the equivalent of the fair market value of the property received.[43]

1651. Tax-Free Exchange Generally. If property is acquired in an exchange on which no gain or loss is recognized, the basis of the property is the same as that for the property exchanged (Code Sec. 1031(d); Reg. § 1.1031(d)-1).[44] This basis is known as a "substituted basis." See ¶ 1607. It applies to: (1) exchanges of property held for productive use or investment solely for property of like kind (¶ 1721); (2) some exchanges of stock for stock of the same corporation (¶ 1728); (3) exchanges of property solely for stock or securities of a "controlled" corporation (¶ 1731); and (4) exchanges of stock or securities solely for stock or securities in a reorganization (¶ 2229).

1654. Equipment Partly Paid for by a Trade-In. No gain or loss is recognized when old business equipment is traded in as part payment on new equipment (¶ 1721). Since this is a "like-kind" exchange, the basis of the new equipment, for gain or loss or depreciation, is ordinarily the total of the adjusted basis of the trade-in plus whatever additional cash is needed.[45] In effect, the basis of the new property is its purchase price, increased or decreased according to whether the trade-in value of the old equipment is greater or less than its depreciated cost.

1657. Exchange Tax Free in Part. In an exchange, money or other property, which is not permitted to be received without the recognition of gain or loss (see ¶ 1723), may be received together with securities or property that is permitted to be received without the recognition of gain or loss. In such exchanges, the cost or other applicable basis of the property acquired is the same as that of the property exchanged, decreased by the amount of any money received by the taxpayer in the transaction and increased by the amount of gain or decreased by the amount of loss recognized in the exchange. If such "other property" is received in an exchange that is tax free in part, the cost or other basis of the property disposed of must be allocated between the property received tax free and such "other property," assigning to the "other property" an amount equivalent to its fair market value (Code Sec. 1031(d)).[46]

1660. Transfer to Corporation. If property was acquired by a corporation from a shareholder as paid-in surplus or as a contribution to capital, the basis of the

---

Footnote references are to paragraphs of the 2002 Standard Federal Tax Reports.

[40] ¶ 29,373, ¶ 29,380.01, ¶ 29,380.38
[41] ¶ 29,380.38
[42] ¶ 29,373, ¶ 29,380.01

[43] ¶ 29,225.272
[44] ¶ 29,602, ¶ 29,612

[45] ¶ 29,612
[46] ¶ 29,602

¶ 1660

property to the corporation is the same as it was in the hands of the transferor, increased by the amount of gain recognized by the transferor on the transfer (Code Sec. 362(a)(2)).[47]

As to property acquired for stock, the basis of the property is the fair market value of the stock at the time the property is acquired (¶ 1648), unless the transferors of the property "control" the property after the transfer (whether or not there is a reorganization). In such cases, the rules described at ¶ 1663 and ¶ 1666 govern.

As to property acquired upon liquidation of a subsidiary, see ¶ 2261.

Property contributed to a corporation by nonstockholders on or after June 22, 1954, has a zero basis. Money contributed by an outsider on or after that date reduces the basis of corporate property acquired with it within 12 months after the contribution is received. To the extent that the contribution is not used to acquire property within this 12-month period, it reduces, as of the last day of the period, the basis of any other property held by the company (Code Sec. 362(c)).[48]

1663. Property Acquired in Exchange by "Controlled" Corporation. The basis of property acquired by a corporation in an exchange described in ¶ 1731 is the same as it would be in the hands of the transferor, increased by any gain that is recognized by the transferor on the exchange (Code Sec. 362(a)(1); Reg. § 1.362-1).[49]

1666. Reorganization Transfer to Corporation. If property is acquired in a reorganization, the basis of the transferor (increased by any recognized gain) follows through to the transferee corporation (Code Sec. 362(b); Reg. § 1.362-1).[50]

1669. Assumption of Liabilities. Under certain facts in connection with a reorganization or transfer to a controlled corporation, the assumption of liabilities is not treated as the equivalent of cash. See ¶ 2233. In a determination of basis after such transfers, the corporation whose liabilities were assumed (or whose property was taken subject to the liabilities) will treat the assumption or acquisition as money received, to the extent of the liabilities (Code Sec. 358(d) and Code Sec. 1031(d)).[51]

This rule applies only to the corporation whose liabilities are assumed. It has no effect on the corporation that assumes the debts.

1672. Discharge of Debt. Under some conditions, a taxpayer realizes no income from a discharge of debt (¶ 791 and ¶ 885). Any amount so excluded from gross income reduces the basis of the property securing the debt (Code Sec. 1017).[52] Regulations prescribe the sequence of allocation where the debt is, or must be treated as, a general liability (Reg. § 1.108-4 and Reg. § 1.1017-1).[53]

Other Acquired Property

1678. Transfer in Trust. If property is acquired by a transfer in trust, other than by a transfer in trust by gift, bequest or devise (for example, sale to the trust by the grantor), after December 31, 1920, its basis is the same as it would be in the hands of the trust's grantor, increased by the gain, or decreased by the loss, recognized to the grantor under the law in effect as of the date of such transfer (Code Sec. 1015(b)).[54]

1681. Stock or Other Property Received for Services. If stock or other property is given as compensation for services instead of cash, the fair market value of the property is income unless the property is subject to a substantial risk of forfeiture.[55] The fair market value of the property included in income becomes its basis to the employee (Code Sec. 83). If the property is sold to the employee for less than its market value, the difference between the amount paid and the value of the

Footnote references are to paragraphs of the 2002 Standard Federal Tax Reports.

[47] ¶ 16,610	[50] ¶ 16,610, ¶ 16,611	[53] ¶ 7003E, ¶ 29,431
[48] ¶ 16,610	[51] ¶ 16,550, ¶ 29,602	[54] ¶ 29,390
[49] ¶ 16,610, ¶ 16,611	[52] ¶ 29,430	[55] ¶ 6390

¶ 1663

property is also income; in this case, the employee's basis for the property is the cash cost plus the amount reported as income (Reg. § 1.83-4(b)).[56]

If the stock or other property is subject to a substantial risk of forfeiture, no amount is included in income until the year that the property becomes substantially vested as the result of the removal of the risk of forfeiture (Code Sec. 83(a)). However, any income (such as a dividend) from the property, or right to use the property, that is subject to a substantial risk of forfeiture is included in income as compensation when received (Rev. Proc. 80-11; Rev. Proc. 83-22; Rev. Proc. 83-38). The fair market value of the property (less any amount paid for it) is included in income when the property becomes substantially vested (Code Sec. 83(a)); Reg. Sec. 1.83-1(a)(1); Reg. § 1.61-1(a)).[57] Property is considered substantially vested when (1) it is either transferable to another person who is not required to give up the property or its value if the substantial risk of forfeiture occurs or (2) it is no longer subject to a substantial risk of forfeiture (Reg. § 1.83-3(b); Reg. § 1.83-3(d)). A substantial risk of forfeiture exists if the right to the property depends on the future performance (or refraining from performance) of substantial services by any person, or the occurrence of a condition related to the transfer (Code Sec. 83(c)(1); Reg. § 1.83-3(c)(1)).[58]

If property that is not substantially vested is sold or disposed of in an arm's-length transaction, the amount realized less any amount paid by the taxpayer for the property is included in the taxpayer's income in the year of disposition (Code Sec. 83(a); Reg. § 1.83-1(b)(1)).[59]

A taxpayer who receives property subject to a substantial risk of forfeiture may make an election to include the fair market value of the property in income (less any amount paid for the property) in the year that the property is received (Code Sec. 83(b)).[60] If the election is made, no amount is included in income in the year that the property is no longer subject to a substantial risk of forfeiture. The basis for determining gain or loss when the property is sold is the amount included in income in the election year plus any amount paid for the property. If the property is forfeited after the election is made, there is a loss equal to the amount paid for the property plus the amount included in income during the election year (Reg. § 1.83-2(a)). The Code Sec. 83(b) election is made by filing a written statement with the IRS center where the tax return is filed no later than 30 days after the date the property was transferred. This statement must also be attached to the taxpayer's return for the election year and provided to the employer (Reg. § 1.83-2(b); Reg. § 1.83-2(c); Reg. § 1.83-2(d)). The election is revocable only with IRS consent (Reg. § 1.83-2(f)).[61]

> **Example.** ABC corporation transfers 100 shares of its stock to an employee for $50 a share in 2001 when the property has a fair market value of $150 per share. The employee must resell the stock to the corporation for $50 a share (regardless of its value) if the employee quits his job at any time within two years after receiving the stock. In this case, the right to the stock is subject to a substantial risk of forfeiture and no amount is included in income in 2001 unless an election is made under Code Sec. 83(b). If the election is made, $10,000 (100 shares × $100) is included in income in 2001 as compensation. The taxpayer's basis is $150 per share (amount paid per share ($50) + gain recognized per share ($100)).

For stock acquired under stock options, see ¶ 1922-¶ 1933.

1684. Equipment for Which Medical Deduction Claimed. The basis of equipment whose cost qualifies as a medical expense (see ¶ 1016) does not include that portion of its cost that has been claimed as an itemized deduction since such

---

[56] ¶ 6384
[57] ¶ 6390.03
[58] ¶ 6390.029
[59] ¶ 6390.032
[60] ¶ 6390.0735
[61] ¶ 6390.073

amounts are not properly chargeable to the capital account. However, the equipment's basis includes that portion of the cost that is nondeductible because of the 7.5-percent floor discussed at ¶ 1015. To determine this portion, the total amount of the limitation (7.5% of the taxpayer's adjusted gross income) is multiplied by a fraction whose numerator is the cost of the equipment and whose denominator is the total amount of the taxpayer's medical expenses. Similarly, if a taxpayer's total allowable itemized deductions exceed the taxpayer's adjusted gross income, or are limited by the overall limitation on itemized deductions of high-income taxpayers (see ¶ 1014), that portion of the equipment's cost attributable to the nondeductible expenses may also be included in the equipment's basis.[62]

1687. Involuntary Conversion. The basis of property purchased as the result of an involuntary conversion (see ¶ 1713) on which gain is not recognized is the cost of the replacement property, less the amount of gain not recognized on the conversion. If qualifying replacement property is received as the result of an involuntary conversion, the replacement property's basis is the same as the basis of the involuntarily converted property decreased by any loss recognized on the conversion and any money received and not spent on qualifying replacement property. The basis is increased by any gain recognized on the conversion and any cost of acquiring the replacement property (Code Sec. 1033(b)).[63]

1693. Property Transferred Between Spouses or Incident to Divorce. No gain or loss is recognized on a transfer of property from an individual to, or in trust for the benefit of, a spouse or a former spouse if the transfer is incident to the divorce of the parties (Code Sec. 1041). See ¶ 1734. In such case, the basis of the transferred property in the hands of the transferee is the transferor's adjusted basis in the property. This nontaxable carryover basis provision does not apply to a spouse (or former spouse) who is a nonresident alien (Code Sec. 1041(d)).

Nonrecognition of gain is not permitted with respect to the transfer of property in trust to the extent that the sum of the amount of any liabilities assumed, plus the amount of any liabilities to which the property is subject, exceeds the total of the adjusted basis of the property transferred (Code Sec. 1041(e)).[64] The transferee's basis is adjusted to take into account any gain recognized.

Valuation Rules

1695. Fair Market Value. Fair market value is the standard for valuing property acquired by a corporation for its stock and for valuing a decedent's property at date of death. It is also used in determining whether and to what extent property received in an exchange is the equivalent of cash. The IRS has recognized a judicial definition of fair market value as being the price which property will bring when offered for sale by a willing seller to a willing buyer, neither being obliged to buy or sell.[65] Only in rare and extraordinary cases does property have no determinable fair market value (Reg. § 1.1001-1).[66]

If the fair market value of an asset received in an exchange (such as a contract to receive royalties) cannot be determined with fair certainty, gain is not realized on the exchange until after the total payments received under the contract exceed the cost (or other basis) of the property surrendered in exchange.[67] The Tax Court has applied the *Cohan* rule (estimated or approximate value) to estimate the value of patents, patent applications, and stock rights, where the taxpayer could not prove their exact value.[68]

Footnote references are to paragraphs of the 2002 Standard Federal Tax Reports.

[62] ¶ 29,412.9963, ¶ 29,413   [65] ¶ 29,225.1071   [67] ¶ 29,225.153
[63] ¶ 29,640, ¶ 29,644   [66] ¶ 29,221   [68] ¶ 16,612.022
[64] ¶ 29,800

¶ 1687

Nonrecourse Indebtedness. In determining the amount of gain or loss (or deemed gain or loss) with respect to any property, the fair market value of such property is deemed not less than the amount of any nonrecourse indebtedness to which the property is subject (Code Sec. 7701(g)).[69]

1697. Valuation of Securities and Real Estate. The fair market value of securities traded on the open market, or on a recognized exchange, is ordinarily the average of the high and low quoted prices on the valuation date.[70] If only a minimal number of shares are traded on the valuation date, or if other abnormal market conditions exist, an alternative valuation method may be necessary.[71]

When corporate stock is not sold on the open market, its fair market value depends upon many factors, including the nature and history of the business, economic outlook and condition of the industry, book value of stock and financial condition of the business, earning capacity of the company, dividend-paying capacity, goodwill, prior sales, size of the block to be valued, and market price of similar but listed stock.[72] Isolated sales of small portions of the stock or forced sales are not considered evidence of fair market value.[73]

Restrictive sales agreements must be considered in the valuation of stock. If the stock is subject to a repurchase option, its value may not exceed the amount for which it may be repurchased. If there are restrictions making sale of stock impossible, and its value is highly speculative, it does not have a fair market value.[74]

Accepted evidence of the fair market value of real estate includes sales of like property in the same locality,[75] testimony of real estate experts,[76] and offers to purchase.[77] Appraisal affidavits of a retrospective nature, standing alone, are generally not accorded great weight.[78]

Footnote references are to paragraphs of the 2002 Standard Federal Tax Reports.

[69] ¶ 43,080
[70] ¶ 29,225.022
[71] ¶ 29,225.0505
[72] ¶ 29,225.228

[73] ¶ 29,225.234
[74] ¶ 29,225.256
[75] ¶ 29,225.518
[76] ¶ 29,225.481

[77] ¶ 29,225.511
[78] ¶ 29,225.0362,
¶ 29,225.1054,
¶ 29,225.1055

¶ **1697**

Chapter 17

SALES ☐ EXCHANGES
CAPITAL GAINS

SALES AND EXCHANGES

Recognition of Gain or Loss

1701. Gain from Sale or Exchange of Property. Gains from sales or exchanges of property are generally recognized for income tax purposes (Code Sec. 1001(c)).[1] The gain from a sale or exchange of property is the excess of the amount realized from the sale or exchange (¶ 1703) over the property's adjusted basis (Code Sec. 1001(a)).[2] The adjusted basis of an asset is generally the taxpayer's original cost plus the cost of any capital improvements and less any depreciation or depletion (Code Secs. 1011, 1012 and 1016)[3] (¶ 1604 et seq.). Some types of exchanges of property may be partially or totally tax free (see ¶ 1719 et seq.).

See ¶ 1601 for a chart prepared by CCH editors that may be used to determine a taxpayer's basis in property.

In order to determine the tax consequences of a sale or exchange, the following questions must be answered: (1) What is the *amount realized* on the sale? See ¶ 1703. (2) Is the gain or loss on the transaction *recognized*? See ¶ 1719. (3) What is the *amount* of gain or loss? See ¶ 1604. (4) Will the *capital gain and loss* provisions apply? See ¶ 1735. (5) Is any part of the gain attributable to depreciation recapture that must be treated as ordinary income? See ¶ 1779. Any *recognized gain* on a sale

---

Footnote references are to paragraphs of the 2002 Standard Federal Tax Reports.

¶ 1701
[1] ¶ 29,220
[2] ¶ 29,220
[3] ¶ 29,310, ¶ 29,330, ¶ 29,410

or exchange must be included in gross income. However, a *realized loss* on the sale or exchange of the same property is not always recognized.

Installment Payments. When real or personal property is sold by a nondealer and part or all of the selling price is to be paid after the year of sale, the *recognized gain* from the sale must be reported on the installment method unless the taxpayer elects *not* to apply the installment method (Code Sec. 453(d)). See ¶ 1801 et seq.

Rollover Into Specialized Small Business Investment Company Stock. Individuals and C corporations may elect to defer the recognition of capital gain from the sale of publicly traded securities if the sale proceeds are invested in the stock or a partnership interest of a "specialized small business investment company" (Code Sec. 1044).[4] See ¶ 2394.

Exclusion for Small Business Stock. A noncorporate taxpayer may exclude up to 50% of the gain from the sale of qualified small business stock issued after August 10, 1993 and held for more than five years (Code Sec. 1202(a)).[5] See ¶ 2396. In addition, a noncorporate taxpayer may elect to roll over the realized gain from the sale of qualified small business stock held for more than six months if other small business stock is purchased during the 60-day period beginning on the date of sale (Code Sec. 1045). See ¶ 2397.

1703. Amount Realized. The amount realized on a sale or exchange is the total of all money received plus the fair market value of all other property or services received (Code Sec. 1001(b)).[6] If the property received in an exchange has no readily determinable fair market value, it is generally treated as being equal in value to the property it was exchanged for (*Philadelphia Park Amusement Co.*).[7] Generally, the amount realized includes any liabilities from which the seller is relieved as a result of the sale or exchange (Reg. § 1.1001-2).[8]

A taxpayer who makes a gift of property on condition that the donee pay the resulting gift taxes realizes, and must recognize, a gain to the extent that the gift taxes paid by the donee exceed the donor's basis in the property (*V.P. Diedrich*).[9]

Gain or Loss from Sale of Residence

1705. Exclusion of Gain—Post-May 6, 1997. An individual may exclude from income up to $250,000 of gain ($500,000 on a joint return in most situations) realized on the sale or exchange of a principal residence (Code Sec. 121(b)). Ownership and use tests must be met (see "Ownership and Use," below). The exclusion may not be used more frequently than once every two years. For purposes of the two-year rule, sales prior to May 7, 1997, are not taken into account (Code Sec. 121(b)(3)).[10]

Ownership and Use. Gain may only be excluded if, during the five-year period that ends on the date of the sale or exchange, the individual owned and used the property as a principal residence for periods aggregating two years or more (i.e., a total of 730 days (365 × 2)). Short temporary absences for vacations or seasonal absences are counted as periods of use, even if the individual rents out the property during these periods of absence. However, an absence of an entire year is not considered a short temporary absence. The ownership and use tests may be met during nonconcurrent periods, provided that both tests are met during the five-year period that ends on the date of sale (Prop. Reg. § 1.121-1(c)).[11]

Married Individuals. The amount of excludable gain is $500,000 for married individuals filing jointly if:

(1) either spouse meets the ownership test;

(2) both spouses meet the use test; and

(3) neither spouse is ineligible for exclusion by virtue of a sale or exchange of a residence within the prior two years (Code Sec. 121(b)(2)).[12]

Footnote references are to paragraphs of the 2002 Standard Federal Tax Reports.

[4] ¶ 29,845	[7] ¶ 29,225.1523	[10] ¶ 7260
[5] ¶ 30,372	[8] ¶ 29,223	[11] ¶ 7261B
[6] ¶ 29,220	[9] ¶ 29,226.3062	[12] ¶ 7260

The exclusion is determined on an individual basis. Thus, if a single individual who is otherwise eligible for an exclusion marries someone who has used the exclusion within the two years prior to the sale, the newly married individual is entitled to a maximum exclusion of $250,000. Once both spouses satisfy the eligibility rules and two years have passed since the exclusion was allowed to either of them, they may exclude up to $500,000 of gain on their joint return (Prop. Reg. § 1.121-2).

Divorced Taxpayers. If a residence is transferred to an individual incident to a divorce, the time during which the individual's spouse or former spouse owned the residence is added to the individual's period of ownership. An individual who owns a residence is deemed to use it as a principal residence while the individual's spouse or former spouse is given use of the residence under the terms of a divorce or separation (Code Sec. 121(d)(3)).[13]

Hardship Relief. An individual who fails to meet the ownership and use requirements, or the minimum two-year time period for claiming the exclusion, may be granted relief in some situations. Relief may be granted when the sale of the home is due to a change in place of employment, health, or unforeseen circumstances (Code Sec. 121(c)(2)).[14] The IRS states that "unforeseen circumstances" may be defined in future regulations, letter rulings, forms, instructions or other appropriate guidance (Prop. Reg. § 1.121-3(a)).

Computing the Reduced Exclusion. If hardship relief is granted, the individual may be entitled to a reduced exclusion. The reduced exclusion is computed by multiplying the maximum allowable exclusion (i.e., $250,000 or $500,000) by a fraction.

The numerator of the fraction is the shortest of (a) the period of time that the individual owned the property as a principal residence during the five-year period ending on the date of sale or exchange; (b) the period of time that the individual used the property as a principal residence during the five-year period ending on the date of sale or exchange; or (c) the period between the date of the most recent prior sale or exchange to which the exclusion applied and the date of the current sale or exchange. The numerator may be expressed in days or months.

The denominator of the fraction is either 730 days or 24 months (depending on the measure of time used in the numerator) (Prop. Reg. § 1.121-3(a)).

> **Example 1.** Al Jackson is an unmarried taxpayer who owned and used a principal residence for 12 months and then sold it in 2001 because of a change in his place of employment. Jackson had not excluded gain from the sale of a residence within the prior two years. He may exclude up to $125,000 of his realized gain ($250,000 × 12/24 = $125,000).

> **Example 2.** On September 1, 2000, Bill and Ruth Green purchase a townhouse in Boston for $450,000. Ruth receives an offer of employment in Atlanta, and on July 1, 2001, the Greens sell their townhouse and move to Atlanta. Because they owned and resided in the townhouse for 10 months, they may exclude up to $208,333 of their realized gain ($500,000 × 10/24 = $208,333).

Incapacity. If an individual becomes physically or mentally incapable of self-care, the individual is deemed to use a residence as a principal residence during the time in which the individual owns the residence and resides in a licensed care facility (e.g., a nursing home). In order for this rule to apply, the taxpayer must have owned and used the residence as a principal residence for an aggregate period of at least one year during the five years preceding the sale or exchange (Code Sec. 121(d)(7)(B)).[15]

Widowed Individual. A widow or widower's period of ownership of a residence includes the period during which the taxpayer's deceased spouse owned the residence (Code Sec. 121(d)(2)).[16]

Footnote references are to paragraphs of the 2002 Standard Federal Tax Reports.

¶ 1705

[13] ¶ 7260
[14] ¶ 7260
[15] ¶ 7260
[16] ¶ 7260

Reporting Requirements. An individual who is qualified to exclude all of the realized gain from the sale of a home is not required to report the sale on the tax return for the year of sale. However, if there is a portion of the realized gain that must be recognized, the taxpayer reports the entire gain in Part I (Short-Term) or Part II (Long-Term) of Schedule D, Form 1040. Then, directly below the line where realized gain is reported, the amount of the prorated exclusion is entered and identified as "Section 121 exclusion." The exclusion is shown as a loss in Column (f).

Maintenance of Records. The $250,000 or $500,000 exclusion from income eliminates the need for many homeowners to keep records of capital improvements that increase the basis of their residences. However, records of capital improvements should be kept if there is any possibility that gain might be required to be recognized upon the sale of the principal residence. That situation might arise in the following circumstances:

(1) the individuals intend to live in the residence for a long period of time;

(2) the residence is rapidly appreciating in value;

(3) there is a possibility that the owners may claim a depreciation deduction for a home office or rental use of the residence; or

(4) there is a possibility that the owners may not use or own the residence long enough to qualify for the full amount of the exclusion.

Gain Recognized to Extent of Depreciation. The exclusion does not apply, and gain is recognized, to the extent of any depreciation adjustments with respect to the rental or business use of a principal residence after May 6, 1997 (Code Sec. 121(d)(6)).[17]

Ownership and Use of Prior Residences. In determining the period of ownership and use of a current residence, taxpayers may include periods of ownership and use of all prior residences with respect to which gain was rolled over to the current residence under former Code Sec. 1034 (Code Sec. 121(g)).[18]

Remainder Interests. The exclusion applies to gain on the sale or exchange of a remainder interest in a principal residence, provided the person acquiring the residence is not a member of the taxpayer's family or other related person as defined by Code Sec. 267(b) or 707(b) (Code Sec. 121(d)(8)).[19]

Expatriates. The exclusion is not available to nonresident alien individuals who are subject to Code Sec. 877(a)(1) because they gave up their U.S. citizenship for the principal purpose of tax avoidance (Code Sec. 121(e)).[20]

Involuntary Conversions. For purposes of determining the allowable exclusion, the destruction, theft, seizure, requisition, or condemnation of property is treated as a sale or exchange of the residence. In addition, the ownership and use of property acquired in an involuntary conversion generally includes the ownership and use of the property treated as sold or exchanged. For purposes of the rules governing involuntary conversions (i.e., Code Sec. 1033), the amount realized from the sale or exchange of property is equal to the amount of realized gain, reduced by the amount of gain that is permitted to be excluded from income under the $250,000/$500,000 exclusion (Code Sec. 121(d)(5)).[21]

Co-ops. The ownership of stock in a cooperative housing corporation is the equivalent of ownership of a residence, if the seller, during the five-year period ending on the date of sale, owned the stock for at least two years and lived in the house or apartment as a principal residence for at least two years (Code Sec. 121(d)(4)).[22]

Important Terms. In order to determine the gain or loss on the sale of a home, the individual must be able to determine "selling price," "amount realized," and "adjusted basis." The "selling price" of a home is the total amount received. This includes cash, notes, debts assumed by the buyer, and the fair market value of services or property received. The "amount realized" is selling price less selling

Footnote references are to paragraphs of the 2002 Standard Federal Tax Reports.
[17] ¶ 7260 [19] ¶ 7260 [21] ¶ 7260
[18] ¶ 7260 [20] ¶ 7260 [22] ¶ 7260

¶1705

expenses (e.g., commissions, legal fees, and advertising). "Adjusted basis" refers to the individual's original basis in the home, usually cost, plus such costs as capital improvements, and less such items as depreciation claimed. The "amount realized" minus "adjusted basis" results in the individual's realized gain or loss. A loss on the individual's principal residence cannot be deducted.

Prior Law. Although the $250,000/$500,000 exclusion applies to sales and exchanges after May 6, 1997, individuals may elect to apply prior law if they (1) sold a home in 1997 before August 6th, (2) had a binding sales contract in effect on August 5, 1997, that resulted in a sale after August 5, 1997, or (3) bought a rollover replacement home before August 6, 1997, or pursuant to a binding contract in effect on August 5, 1997 (Act Sec. 312(d) of P.L. 105-34).

1706. Postponement of Gain for All Taxpayers—Pre-May 7, 1997. The taxation of some or all of the gain from a principal residence sold before May 7, 1997, could be postponed (or "rolled over") if a new principal residence was bought or built within the period beginning two years before and ending two years after the sale of the old residence (Code Sec. 1034, repealed by P.L. 105-34).[23] This rollover provision has been replaced by the gain exclusion provisions effective for sales and exchanges of principal residences after May 6, 1997 (see ¶ 1705). Taxpayers could have elected to apply this rollover provision to sales or exchanges (1) made before August 5, 1997, (2) made after August 5, 1997, pursuant to a binding contract in effect on August 5, 1997, or (3) if the replacement residence was acquired on or before August 5, 1997, and the rollover provision would apply.

Under the rollover provisions, the new residence must have been used by the taxpayer as a principal residence within the two-year period. The gain on the sale was recognized only to the extent that the "adjusted sales price" of the old residence exceeded the cost of the new residence . If the cost of the new residence was as much as or more than the adjusted sales price of the old residence, none of the gain was recognized.

Military Personnel. A member of the Armed Forces who went on extended active duty after selling a principal residence was entitled to suspend the running of the two-year period for replacing the old residence during the period spent on active duty. The total extended period (two-year replacement period plus time on active duty) cannot exceed four years after the date of sale of the old residence (Code Sec. 1034(h)(1), repealed by P.L. 105-34).[24] Armed Forces members stationed overseas or who return from overseas duty and were forced to reside in on-base government housing due to the lack of adequate off-base housing at a remote base site may extend the replacement period until one year after the last day that the taxpayer was stationed overseas or resided in the on-base housing. However, this extended period cannot exceed eight years after the date of the sale (Code Sec. 1034(h)(2), repealed by P.L. 105-34).[25]

The rollover rules and their application to sales of a principal residence before May 7, 1997 are covered in the CCH STANDARD FEDERAL TAX REPORTER.[26]

1708. Once-in-a-Lifetime Exclusion—Pre-May 7, 1997. Effective for principal residences sold before May 7, 1997, taxpayers who attained age 55 prior to the date of the sale of a principal residence could have elected to exclude up to $125,000 of the gain realized on the sale. For married taxpayers filing separate returns, the maximum exclusion was $62,500 on each separate return (Code Sec. 121(b), prior to amendment by P.L. 105-34).[27] As with the rollover provisions (see ¶ 1706), the once-in-a-lifetime exclusion has been replaced by the exclusion of gain provisions (see ¶ 1705). Taxpayers could have elected to apply the $125,000 once-in-a-lifetime exclusion to sales or exchanges (1) made before August 5, 1997, or (2) made after August 5, 1997, pursuant to a binding contract in effect on August 5, 1997.

Footnote references are to paragraphs of the 2002 Standard Federal Tax Reports.

¶ 1706
[23] ¶ 29,660
[24] ¶ 29,660
[25] ¶ 29,660
[26] ¶ 29,662.01
[27] ¶ 7260

Under these former rules, in order to qualify for the exclusion, the taxpayer must have owned and used the property as a residence for a total of at least three years during the five-year period ending on the date of the sale (Code Sec. 121(a), prior to amendment by P.L. 105-34; Reg. § 1.121-1).[28]

Involuntary Conversion

1713. Gain or Loss from Involuntary Conversion. An involuntary conversion occurs when property is destroyed, stolen, condemned, or disposed of under the threat of condemnation and the taxpayer receives other property or money in payment (e.g., insurance proceeds or a condemnation award).

There are two specific sets of circumstances under which gain from compulsory or involuntary conversion of property is not recognized for tax purposes (Code Sec. 1033; Reg. § 1.1033(a)-1):[29]

(1) When property is converted involuntarily or by compulsion into other property that is similar or related in service or use, no gain is recognized. The basis of the old property is simply transferred to the new property. This rule applies regardless of the owner's intent (i.e., the owner does not have the right to recognize gain).

(2) When property is involuntarily converted into money (e.g., property is destroyed by fire and an insurance award is recovered), or into unlike property, then the owner may elect to postpone gain by buying qualified property within a specified replacement period. (See ¶ 1715 for information concerning replacement property.) If the involuntary conversion results in a gain, and if suitable replacement property or stock in a corporation owning suitable replacement property is purchased, an election may be made to recognize gain only to the extent that the amount realized from the converted property exceeds the cost of the replacement property. The election to defer all or part of the gain realized in the involuntary conversion is made by excluding the gain from gross income on the tax return for the year in which it is realized (Code Sec. 1033(a)(2)(A)). A taxpayer who has realized gain from an involuntary conversion must provide details of the involuntary conversion on the tax return for the tax year in which the gain is realized (see "Required Statement," below).

Loss from an involuntary conversion is deductible only if the converted property is used in a trade or business or for the production of income. However, casualty or theft losses on personal property may be deductible (¶ 1124 and ¶ 1748).

When an individual's principal residence has been involuntarily converted, the individual may exclude any realized gain, up to the $250,000/$500,000 maximum, (see ¶ 1705) as if the home had been sold (Code Sec. 121(d)(5)).[30] If the total realized gain is more than the maximum allowable exclusion, the individual may postpone recognizing the gain if replacement property is purchased. The sale of land within a reasonable period of time following the destruction of a principal residence qualified as part of the involuntary conversion of the residence on the date it was destroyed (Rev. Rul. 96-32).[31]

The destruction of livestock by disease, or the sale or exchange of livestock because of disease, is treated as an involuntary conversion (Code Sec. 1033(d); Reg. § 1.1033(d)-1).[32] Sales or exchanges of livestock (except poultry) solely on account of drought, flood, or other weather-related conditions that exceed the number normally sold may also be entitled to involuntary conversion treatment (Code Sec. 1033(e); Reg. § 1.1033(e)-1).[33] If, because of soil or other environmental contamination, it is not feasible for a farmer to reinvest the proceeds from involuntarily converted livestock in property similar or related in service or use, the proceeds may be invested in other property, including real property, used for farming. The replace-

---

Footnote references are to paragraphs of the 2002 Standard Federal Tax Reports.

[28] ¶ 7260, ¶ 7261	[30] ¶ 7260	[32] ¶ 29,640, ¶ 29,646
[29] ¶ 29,640, ¶ 29,641	[31] ¶ 29,643	[33] ¶ 29,640, ¶ 29,647

¶ 1713

ment property will then be treated as property similar or related in service or use to the converted livestock (Code Sec. 1033(f)).[34]

Reporting Requirements. Form 4797 (Sales of Business Property) is used to report the gain or loss from an involuntary conversion (other than from casualty or theft) of (a) business property, (b) capital assets used in a business, or (c) property held for rent or royalty income. Form 4684 (Casualties and Thefts) is used to report involuntary conversions from casualties and thefts. Schedule D (Capital Gains and Losses) is used to report gains from involuntary conversions (other than from casualty of theft) of capital assets not held for business or profit.

Required Statement. A taxpayer is required to attach a statement to the tax return for the year in which gain is realized (e.g., the year in which insurance proceeds are received) (Reg. § 1.1033(a)-2(c)(2)). The statement should include such information as the date and details of the involuntary conversion and the insurance or other reimbursement received. If replacement property was acquired before the tax return is filed, the statement is to include information concerning a description of the replacement property, the date of acquisition and the cost of the replacement property. If replacement is to be made after the year in which the gain is realized, the statement should also state that the taxpayer intends to replace the property within the required replacement period.

1715. Replacement of Converted Property. No gain is recognized if property, as a result of its destruction, theft, seizure, requisition, condemnation, or the threat or imminence thereof, was involuntarily converted into property similar to or related in service or use to the property converted. Further, a taxpayer may elect to not recognize gain, when property is involuntarily converted into money or other property, and an amount that equals or exceeds the net proceeds from the conversion (including severance damages if the property to which they relate is unusable) is spent for replacement property. To the extent that the net proceeds from an involuntary conversion are not invested in replacement property, gain is recognized (Code Sec. 1033(a)(2)(A)).[35]

Generally, "replacement property" refers to (a) the acquisition of other property *similar or related in service or use* to the property converted or (b) the acquisition of 80% control of a corporation owning such other property. An actual purchase must take place (e.g., title must have passed); an enforceable contract to purchase is not sufficient.[36] However, in a situation involving *real property* used in the taxpayer's trade or business (other than inventory or property held primarily for sale) or held for investment, the replacement property does not need to be *similar or related in service or use* to the converted property. Instead, the replacement property only needs to be of a "like-kind" to the converted property (¶ 1721) if held either for productive use in trade or business or for investment (Code Sec. 1033(g)).[37] However, this "like kind" test, which is more liberal than the "similar use" standard that is generally applied, is not applicable to acquisitions of 80% control of a corporation owning such property or to involuntary conversions by fire, storm, or other casualty (Code Sec. 1033(g)(2)).[38]

A taxpayer may elect to treat an outdoor advertising display as real property except when the election to expense the property under Code Sec. 179 (¶ 1208) has been made (Code Sec. 1033(g)(3)).[39]

As to the basis of property acquired as a replacement, see ¶ 1687.

Presidentially Declared Disasters. Another exception to the requirement that converted property be replaced with similar or related property is made for business or investment property that is compulsorily or involuntarily converted as a result of a presidentially declared disaster. The property will be treated as similar or related in service or use to *any* tangible property of a type held for productive use in a trade or business. Under this rule, a taxpayer may elect not to recognize gain with respect

---

Footnote references are to paragraphs of the 2002 Standard Federal Tax Reports.

¶ 1715

[34] ¶ 29,640	[36] ¶ 29,650.204	[38] ¶ 29,640
[35] ¶ 29,640	[37] ¶ 29,640	[39] ¶ 29,640

to the property if the tangible business or investment property is acquired within a specified time period (see "Replacement Period," below) (Code Sec. 1033(h)(2)).[40]

Acquisitions from Related Persons. Stock or other assets acquired from a related person by a C corporation or a partnership in which a C corporation has more than a 50% interest does not qualify as replacement property. An exception applies if the related person from whom the replacement property is acquired obtained the property from an unrelated person during the statutorily prescribed time period (see "Replacement Period," below) (Code Sec. 1033(i)).[41]

The ban on the acquisition of involuntary conversion replacement property from related parties also applies to all other taxpayers (including individuals) who do not meet a $100,000 *de minimis* exception (Code Sec. 1033(i)(2)).[42] Under the *de minimis* exception, gain realized from an involuntary conversion when the replacement property is acquired from a related person can nonetheless be deferred by taxpayers (other than C corporations and certain partnerships with majority corporate partners) if the aggregate realized gain is $100,000 or less. In the case of a partnership or S corporation, the $100,000 limitation applies to both the partnership and each partner and to both the S corporation and each shareholder.

Two-Year Replacement Period. Purchase of the replacement property, or of 80% control of a corporation that owns such property, must be within a period of time that begins on the actual date of the destruction, condemnation, etc., or the date on which the threat or imminence of condemnation or requisition begins, whichever is earlier. Generally, the replacement period ends two years (three years for certain real estate, as explained below) after the close of the first tax year in which any part of the gain on the conversion is realized. The IRS may extend the replacement period on application of the taxpayer (see "Application for Extension," below) (Code Sec. 1033(a)(2)(B)).[43]

> **Example.** Laura has a basis in a commercial building, excluding the underlying land, of $100,000. The building is destroyed by fire, and Laura receives a $120,000 settlement from her insurance company, thus realizing a gain of $20,000. If she acquires a new building for the same use for $120,000 (or more) within the prescribed replacement period, she may elect not to recognize any gain on the involuntary conversion. If the replacement building costs only $110,000, Laura must recognize $10,000 of gain, if she elects nonrecognition treatment. Without her election, she must recognize the entire $20,000 gain.

Real Property. For situations involving the condemnation of business or investment *real* property (other than inventory), the replacement period ends *three years*, rather than two years, after the close of the first tax year in which only part of the gain is realized (Code Sec. 1033(g)(4)).[44] The three-year period does not apply to property involuntarily converted through destruction (e.g., casualty) or theft.

For treatment of some gains and losses from involuntary conversions as capital gains and losses, see ¶ 1748.

Application for Extension. The replacement period may be extended by the IRS (Code Sec. 1033(a)(2)(B)).[45] The taxpayer applies for an extension with the IRS district office where the return was filed. The application should explain in detail the reasons for the extension request. An extension will not be granted based on an unfavorable financing climate and market conditions (Rev. Rul. 60-69).[46] The application should be filed before the statutory replacement period expires. However, a late request is considered if it is made within a reasonable period of time after the replacement period expires and there is reasonable cause for the untimely filing (Reg. § 1.1033(a)-2(c)(3)).[47]

Residence Damaged in Presidentially Declared Disaster. Special rules apply to a principal residence or the contents of a principal residence that are involuntarily

---

Footnote references are to paragraphs of the 2002 Standard Federal Tax Reports.

[40] ¶ 29,640
[41] ¶ 29,640
[42] ¶ 29,640
[43] ¶ 29,640
[44] ¶ 29,640
[45] ¶ 29,640
[46] ¶ 29,650.135
[47] ¶ 29,642

converted as the result of a disaster for which a presidential declaration is made (Code Sec. 1033(h)(4)).[48] No gain is recognized by reason of the receipt of insurance proceeds for *unscheduled* personal property that was part of the contents of the residence. This is true regardless of the use to which the taxpayer puts the insurance money.[49] All other insurance proceeds (i.e., insurance reimbursement for *scheduled* items) for the residence or its contents are treated as a common pool of funds received for the conversion of a single item of property. Funds received for scheduled property must be used to purchase property that is similar or related in service or use to the converted residence (or its contents) in order for the taxpayer to avoid recognition of gain. Gain is recognized only to the extent that the amount of the pool of funds exceeds the cost of any property similar or related in service or use to the converted residence or its contents. The replacement period is *four years* after the close of the first tax year in which any part of the gain upon the conversion is realized (Code Sec. 1033(h)(1)(B)). These rules also apply to the conversion of property in a rented residence if the rented residence served as the taxpayer's principal residence (Code Sec. 1033(h)(4)).[50]

1716. Condemnation Award. If only a portion of a tract of land is appropriated by a condemning authority, the condemnation award may have two components: (1) compensation for the converted portion and (2) severance damages for the retained portion. In this situation, the entire award is considered compensation for the condemned property unless it is established that a specific portion was for damage to retained property (Rev. Rul. 59-173).[51]

For purposes of determining gain or loss, compensation for the converted property and severance damages are treated separately. Thus, the owner's legal and other expenses and the basis of the property must be apportioned between the compensation for the part of the property taken and the severance damages for the part retained. If severance damages are for damage to only a portion of the retained property, only that part of the basis of the retained property properly allocable to the damaged portion can be taken into account (Rev. Rul. 68-37).[52] Severance damages reduce the basis of the retained property. Any excess of severance damages over such basis (plus allocated expenses) is gain.

Transactions Between Related Persons

1717. Losses Not Allowed. In most situations, a loss from the sale or exchange of property is not allowed when the sale or exchange is between (Code Sec. 267(b); Reg. § 1.267(b)-1):[53]

(1) Members of a family (brother, sister, spouse, ancestor, or lineal descendant);

(2) An individual and a corporation if the individual owns (directly or indirectly) more than 50% in value of the outstanding stock;

(3) Two corporations that are members of a controlled group (at least 50% owned) of corporations;

(4) A grantor and a fiduciary of any trust;

(5) A fiduciary of one trust and a fiduciary of another trust, if the same person is grantor of both trusts;

(6) A fiduciary of a trust and any beneficiary of such trust;

(7) A fiduciary of a trust and a beneficiary of another trust, if the same person is a grantor of both trusts;

(8) A fiduciary of a trust and a corporation more than 50% in value of the outstanding stock of which is directly or indirectly owned by or for the trust or a grantor of the trust;

Footnote references are to paragraphs of the 2002 Standard Federal Tax Reports.

¶ **1716**

[48] ¶ 29,640	[50] ¶ 29,640	[52] ¶ 29,650.504
[49] ¶ 29,650.059	[51] ¶ 29,650.504	[53] ¶ 14,150, ¶ 14,153

(9) A person and an exempt charitable or educational organization controlled by the person or, if the "person" is an individual, by the individual or his family;

(10) A corporation and a partnership if the same persons own (a) more than 50% in value of the outstanding stock of the corporation and (b) more than 50% of the capital interest or profits interest in the partnership;

(11) An S corporation and another S corporation if the same persons own more than 50% in value of the outstanding stock of each corporation; or

(12) An S corporation and a C corporation if the same persons own more than 50% in value of the outstanding stock of each corporation.

In determining stock ownership: (a) stock held by a corporation, partnership, estate, or trust is considered owned proportionately by its shareholders, partners, or beneficiaries; (b) individuals are considered to own stock owned by their families, as defined above; and (c) stock owned by an individual's partner is considered owned by the individual if the individual also owns stock in the corporation (Code Sec. 267(c)).[54]

When the rule results in a denial of a loss deduction to the transferor of property, gain is taxable to the original transferee upon disposition of the property to an outsider *only* to the extent that it exceeds the transferor's loss allocable to the property. This rule benefits only the original transferee (Reg. § 1.267(d)-1).[55]

> **Example.** A father sells business property with a $15,000 basis to his son for $5,000. The father's $10,000 realized loss is not deductible. Later, the son sells the property for $18,000 to an unrelated person. His realized gain is $18,000 minus $5,000, or $13,000, but only $3,000 ($13,000 minus the father's $10,000 disallowed loss) is recognized.

Tax-Free Exchanges

1719. Exchange of Property. Gains from exchanges of property are generally recognized for tax purposes (Code Sec. 1001(c)).[56] See ¶ 1701 for the recognition rules. However, some types of exchanges do not give rise to taxable gain or deductible loss. These types of tax-free exchanges are described in ¶ 1721-¶ 1734.

1721. Like-Kind Exchanges. No gain or loss is recognized upon the exchange of property held for productive use in a trade or business or for investment if the property received is of a like kind and is held either for productive use in a business or for investment. This nonrecognition rule does *not* apply to stock in trade or other property held primarily for sale, stocks, bonds, notes, certificates of trust, beneficial interests, partnership interests, securities or evidences of indebtedness or interest (Code Sec. 1031(a)(2); Reg. § 1.1031(a)-1).[57] It does cover "trade-in" allowances (see ¶ 1654).

Related Persons. If property received in a like-kind exchange between related persons (as defined at ¶ 1717) is disposed of within two years after the date of the last transfer that was part of the like-kind exchange, the original exchange will not qualify for nonrecognition treatment (Code Sec. 1031(f)).[58] Any gain or loss that was not recognized by the taxpayer on the original exchange must be recognized as of the date that the like-kind property is disposed of by either the taxpayer or the related party. The running of the two-year period may be suspended when the holder of the exchanged property has substantially diminished the risk of loss by the use of a put, short sale, holding by another person of a right to acquire such property, or any other transaction (Code Sec. 1031(g)).[59] A disposition that would otherwise require recognition of the original exchange is excepted from the related-person rule if (1) neither the original exchange nor the disposition had as one of its principal purposes the avoidance of federal income tax, (2) the disposition was due to the death of

---

[54] ¶ 14,150	[56] ¶ 29,220	[58] ¶ 29,602, ¶ 29,608.04
[55] ¶ 14,155	[57] ¶ 29,602, ¶ 29,603	[59] ¶ 29,602

482

U.S. Master Tax Guide

either related party, or (3) the disposition was due to the compulsory or involuntary conversion of the property (see ¶ 1713).

Basis. For the basis of property received in a like-kind exchange, see ¶ 1651.

Reporting. Form 8824 (Like-Kind Exchanges) is used to report the like-kind exchange.

Like-Kind Property Defined. Property is of like kind if it is of the same nature or character. Most exchanges of real properties qualify as like-kind exchanges (Reg. § 1.1031(a)-1(b) and (c)).[60] However, real property located in the U.S. and real property located outside the U.S. are not like-kind property (Code Sec. 1031(h)(1)).[61]

Personal properties are like kind if they are of a like kind or class. Depreciable tangible personal properties are of a like class if they fall within the same general asset class or the same product class. For depreciable tangible personal property, asset classes follow those used for depreciation purposes (see Rev. Proc. 87-56, which appears at ¶ 163.01 of the 2002 STANDARD FEDERAL TAX REPORTER and at ¶ 74 of the 2002 U.S. MASTER TAX GUIDE—Loose-Leaf Edition). Product classes are determined by reference to the four-digit product classes in Division D of the Standard Industrial Classification (SIC) codes, as set forth in the SIC Manual (Reg. § 1.1031(a)-2(b)).[62]

Personal property predominantly used in the U.S. and personal property predominantly used outside of the U.S. are not "like-kind" property (Code Sec. 1031(h)(2)).[63]

Exchanges involving intangible personal property or nondepreciable tangible personal property may qualify for like-kind exchange treatment only if the properties are like kind. For example, an exchange of a copyright on a novel for a copyright on another novel would generally be a like-kind exchange. However, an exchange of a copyright on a novel for a copyright on a song would not be a like-kind exchange. An exchange of goodwill or going concern value of one business for the goodwill or going concern value of another business is *not* a like-kind exchange (Reg. § 1.1031(a)-2(c)).[64]

1722. Deferred Like-Kind Exchanges. An exchange may qualify for like-kind treatment even if the replacement property is received after the relinquished property has been transferred by the taxpayer, provided that specific identification and receipt requirements are satisfied. This type of transaction has become known as a Starker exchange (*B. Starker*).[65] After transferring the relinquished property, the taxpayer must identify replacement property within 45 days and must receive the replacement property within 180 days (or, if earlier, by the due date (including extensions) of the transferor's return for the tax year in which the relinquished property was transferred) (Code Sec. 1031(a)(3); Reg. § 1.1031(k)-1).[66] Real property still under construction may qualify as like-kind exchange property (Reg. § 1.1031(k)-1(e)).[67] A taxpayer may identify up to three replacement properties or may identify any number of replacement properties if their aggregate value does not exceed 200% of the aggregate value of all relinquished properties (Reg. § 1.1031(k)-1(c)(4)).[68]

Identifying Property. Replacement property must be identified before the end of the "identification period" that begins on the date that the relinquished property is transferred and ends at midnight on the 45th day thereafter (Reg. § 1.1031(k)-1(b)(2)).[69] Replacement property is treated as identified only if it is designated as replacement property in either: (1) a written agreement covering the exchange that is signed by all parties before the end of the identification period or (2) a written document signed by the taxpayer and hand delivered, mailed, telecopied, or otherwise sent before the end of the identification period to a person involved in the exchange (such as an intermediary, escrow agent or title company)

Footnote references are to paragraphs of the 2002 Standard Federal Tax Reports.

[60] ¶ 29,603	[64] ¶ 29,602, ¶ 29,619	[67] ¶ 29,619
[61] ¶ 29,602	[65] ¶ 29,621.30	[68] ¶ 29,619
[62] ¶ 29,606	[66] ¶ 29,619	[69] ¶ 29,619
[63] ¶ 29,602		

¶ 1722

other than the taxpayer or a related party (Reg. § 1.1031(k)-1(c)).[70] In either case, the replacement property must be unambiguously described. For example, for transactions involving real property, a street address or legal description would generally be considered as adequate identification of the property.

Safe Harbors. The taxpayer may not actually or constructively receive cash and then use the proceeds to buy the replacement property. The following four safe harbors protect nonrecognition treatment in a deferred like-kind exchange in which a property or security interest is received by the transferor. The transferor is not considered in receipt of money or other property if the transaction involves (1) qualifying security or guarantee arrangements, (2) qualified escrow accounts or trusts, (3) a qualified intermediary, or (4) payment of interest or a growth factor (Reg. § 1.1031(k)-1(g)).[71]

An additional safe harbor is provided in situations involving what is termed a "reverse-Starker exchange" (i.e., an exchange in which replacement property is acquired before the relinquished property is transferred) (Rev. Proc. 2000-37).[72] If the provisions of this safe harbor are complied with, the IRS will not challenge the qualification of property as either "replacement property" or "relinquished property" or the treatment of the exchange accommodation titleholder as the beneficial owner of the property. In order for this safe harbor to come into play, the property must be held in a "qualified exchange accommodation arrangement" (QEAA). A QEAA must meet a number of requirements, including the following: (1) title of the property must be held by a person other than the taxpayer or a disqualified person, and (2) the combined time period that the properties are held in a QEAA must not exceed 180 days.

Direct Deeding of Property. In an exchange of real property involving three parties—the taxpayer, the transferee (a qualified intermediary), and a third party that supplies replacement property—the exchange may qualify as like kind even if the third party deeds the replacement property directly to the taxpayer. Therefore, it is not necessary for the transferee to take title to the replacement property and then transfer title to the taxpayer (Rev. Rul. 90-34).[73]

1723. Exchange for Property of Like Kind Plus Cash or Other Property. If, in an exchange of property for property of like kind, unlike property or money is received in addition to the like-kind property, gain is recognized, but only up to the sum of the money and the fair market value of the other property received (Code Sec. 1031(b); Reg. § 1.1031(b)-1).[74] Under no circumstances may a *loss* from a similar exchange be deducted (Code Sec. 1031(c); Reg. § 1.1031(c)-1).[75]

> **Example.** Bill exchanged unimproved real estate, with a basis of $10,000, for $4,000 cash and real estate with a fair market value of $12,000. His $6,000 gain is *recognized* only to the extent of the cash received. Bill must, therefore, recognize $4,000 as income from the exchange. His basis for the new property is $10,000 (the cost of the old property ($10,000), minus the cash received ($4,000), plus *recognized* gain ($4,000)).

See ¶ 1728 and ¶ 1731 for situations involving stock exchanged for stock in the same corporation and the tax-free transfer of property to a controlled corporation.

1724. Exchange of Contracts. No gain or loss results from an exchange of: (1) life insurance contracts; (2) a life insurance contract for an endowment or an annuity contract; (3) two annuity contracts; (4) an endowment insurance contract for an annuity contract; or (5) two endowment insurance contracts if the new contract provides for regular payments beginning on a date not later than the date payments would have begun under the contract that was exchanged (Code Sec. 1035(a); Reg. § 1.1035-1).[76]

Footnote references are to paragraphs of the 2002 Standard Federal Tax Reports.

[70] ¶ 29,619
[71] ¶ 29,621.30
[72] ¶ 29,620.01
[73] ¶ 29,621.30
[74] ¶ 29,602, ¶ 29,611
[75] ¶ 29,602, ¶ 29,612
[76] ¶ 29,680, ¶ 29,681

Policyholders who surrender life insurance or annuity contracts of a financially troubled insurance company may qualify for nonrecognition of gain if, within 60 days, all cash received is reinvested in another policy or contract issued by another insurance company or in a single custodial account (Rev. Proc. 92-44).[77]

1725. Exchange of Mortgaged Real Estate. When taxpayers exchange mortgaged real estate for other real estate in an otherwise tax-free "like kind" exchange, the amount of the mortgage from which they are relieved is treated as other property or money. If mortgaged property is exchanged for mortgaged property, the net reduction of the mortgage indebtedness is treated as other property or money (Reg. § 1.1031(d)-2).[78]

> **Example.** Kathy owned real property, which had a fair market value of $100,000 and an adjusted basis of $75,000 and was subject to a $70,000 mortgage. She exchanged the property for like-kind property, which had a fair market value of $60,000 and was subject to a $30,000 mortgage. Her entire realized gain must be recognized:

Fair market value of property received	$ 60,000
Less mortgage on that property	30,000
	$ 30,000
Mortgage on property transferred by Kathy	70,000
Total consideration received	$100,000
Less basis of property transferred	75,000
Gain realized	$ 25,000

The total realized gain is recognized because it is less than the $40,000 net mortgage reduction.

It is immaterial whether a mortgage is assumed by the purchaser or whether the property is acquired subject to a mortgage (Reg. § 1.1031(d)-2).[79]

1726. Exchange of Government Obligations. Obligations issued by the United States under chapter 31 of title 31, U.S.C., may be exchanged tax free for other such obligations (except to the extent that money is received in the exchange) (Code Sec. 1037; Reg. § 1.1037-1).[80] Municipal or state bonds may be exchanged pursuant to a refunding agreement without recognition of gain or loss, provided that there are no material differences in the terms of the exchanged bonds (Rev. Rul. 81-169).[81]

1728. Stock Exchanged for Stock of the Same Corporation. An exchange of common stock for common stock of the same corporation, or of preferred stock for preferred stock of the same corporation, does not result in a taxable gain or deductible loss (Code Sec. 1036(a); Reg. § 1.1036-1).[82] However, if money or other property is received in addition to the stock, gain (but not loss) may be recognized, but only to the extent of the money or fair market value of the other property received (¶ 1723) (Code Sec. 1031(b) and (c)).[83] Nonqualified preferred stock is not treated as stock for these purposes (Code Sec. 1036(b)).[84]

1729. Stock Exchanged for Property. No gain or loss is recognized to a corporation upon the receipt of money or other property in exchange for its stock (including treasury stock). Also, no gain or loss is recognized by a corporation upon the lapse or acquisition of an option to buy or sell its stock (or treasury stock) (Code Sec. 1032(a)).[85]

1731. Tax-Free Transfer of Property to Controlled Corporation. No gain or loss is recognized if one or more persons (individuals, trusts or estates, partnerships or corporations) transfer property to a corporation solely in exchange for its stock and, immediately after the transfer, are in "control" of the transferee

---

Footnote references are to paragraphs of the 2002 Standard Federal Tax Reports.

¶ 1725

[77] ¶ 29,682.10	[80] ¶ 29,720, ¶ 29,721	[83] ¶ 29,602
[78] ¶ 29,613, ¶ 29,615.035	[81] ¶ 29,226.1117	[84] ¶ 29,700
[79] ¶ 29,614	[82] ¶ 29,700, ¶ 29,701	[85] ¶ 29,622

corporation. "Control" means the ownership of at least 80% of the voting stock and at least 80% of all other stock of the corporation. Stock rights or warrants are not considered to be stock (Code Sec. 351(a); Reg. § 1.351-1).[86] Nonqualified preferred stock is not treated as stock (Code Sec. 351(g)). Stock is not considered issued in exchange for property if it is issued for services or unsecured debts of the transferee or for interest accrued to the transferor on debts owed by the transferee.[87]

If the transferor-stockholder receives other property (including securities) or cash in addition to the stock, any gain from the transfer (but not any loss) is recognized, but only up to the cash or the fair market value of the other property received (¶ 1723) (Code Sec. 351(b); Reg. § 1.351-2).[88] For the basis of the property to the controlled corporation, see ¶ 1663.

1732. Property Exchanged to Avoid Conflicts of Interest. If an officer or employee of the executive branch of the federal government sells, pursuant to a certificate of divestiture issued by the President or the Director of the Office of Government Ethics, any property in order to comply with conflict-of-interest requirements, the individual may elect to recognize only a portion of the gain from the sale (Code Sec. 1043).[89] The portion of the gain that must be recognized is the excess of (a) the amount realized on the sale over (b) the cost (reduced by any basis adjustment attributable to a prior sale) of any U.S. obligation or any diversified investment fund approved by the Office of Government Ethics and purchased by the individual during the 60-day period beginning on the date of the sale. Any nonrecognized gain is applied to reduce (in the order acquired) the basis of any qualified property that is purchased by the individual during the 60-day period.

These rules also apply to any spouse, minor or dependent child whose ownership of any property is attributable to a federal officer or employer under any applicable conflict-of-interest law. Also subject to these rules are sales made by a trustee if any person subject to the rules has a beneficial interest in the principal or income of the trust. Part IV of Form 8824 (Like-Kind Exchanges) is used to report conflict-of-interest sales.

1733. Tax-Free Sale of Stock to ESOP. Taxpayers (other than C corporations) may sell qualified securities to an ESOP or worker-owned cooperative and replace the securities with other securities without recognition of gain (Code Sec. 1042).[90]

1734. Transfers of Property Between Spouses or Former Spouses. No gain or loss is recognized for transfers of property from an individual to a spouse or to a former spouse incident to a divorce. The transferor's basis for the transferred property is carried over to the transferee. In the case of a transfer to a former spouse, the transfer must occur within one year after the date on which the marriage ceased or must be related to the cessation of the marriage. This nonrecognition treatment is not available for transfers to spouses or former spouses who are nonresident aliens (Code Sec. 1041).[91]

CAPITAL GAINS

Treatment of Capital Gain or Loss

1735. Characterization of Gain or Loss. The characterization of income as capital or ordinary and the differentiation between long-term and short-term capital gains and losses is necessary for income tax reporting purposes.

Gain or loss from the sale or exchange of a capital asset is characterized as either short-term or long-term depending on how long the asset was held by the taxpayer (¶ 1777). If a taxpayer has both long-term and short-term transactions during the year, each type is reported separately and gains and losses from each

---

Footnote references are to paragraphs of the 2002 Standard Federal Tax Reports.

[86] ¶ 16,402, ¶ 16,403	[88] ¶ 16,402, ¶ 16,404B	[90] ¶ 29,820
[87] ¶ 16,405.046	[89] ¶ 29,840	[91] ¶ 29,800

type are netted separately. The net long-term capital gain or loss for the year is then combined with the net short-term capital gain or loss for the year to arrive at an overall (net) capital gain or loss. When capital gains exceed capital losses, the overall gain is included with the taxpayer's other income but is generally subject to a maximum tax rate of 20% for sales of long-term capital assets and 35% for corporations (see ¶ 1736). When capital losses exceed capital gains, the deductible loss may be limited (see ¶ 1752 and ¶ 1757).

Losses from the sale of stock in a small business investment company (¶ 2392) or in a small business corporation (i.e., Code Sec. 1244 stock) (¶ 2395) may be considered ordinary rather than capital if certain requirements are satisfied.

Reporting. In most situations, individuals use Schedule D (Capital Gains and Losses) of Form 1040 to report the sale or exchange of a capital asset. However, some individuals may be able to report their capital gains on Form 1040A (e.g., the individual's only capital gains are from mutual fund distributions).

1736. Tax on Capital Gains—Individual, Estate, Trust—2001. Generally, for 2001, gain from the sale of long-term capital assets is subject to a maximum capital gains tax rate of 20% (10% for individuals in the 10% or 15% tax bracket). A special lower rate of 18% (8% for individuals in the 10% or 15% tax bracket) may apply to transactions after December 31, 2000, when the asset was held more than five years (Code Sec. 1(h)).[92] These rules are discussed in detail at "Tax Years Beginning After December 31, 2000," below.

These capital gains rates apply to individuals, estates and trusts. In addition, the rates apply when a taxpayer is computing the income tax under the alternative minimum tax.

Even though the lower capital gain rates apply to net capital gain for sales and exchanges after May 6, 1997, the legislative history of this provision states that the lower rate applies to *installment payments* received on or after May 7, 1997.[93] In addition, if a taxpayer elects to treat any amount of net capital gain as investment interest under Code Sec. 163(d)(4)(B)(iii), then that amount is subtracted from the total net capital gain in order to determine the amount subject to the maximum capital gains rate (¶ 1094).

Holding Period. A capital asset must be held "more than 12 months" in order for realized gain to be classified as long-term capital gain.

> **Example 1.** On November 2, 2000, John Aubrey purchased 100 shares of Gizmo Inc. for $5,000. On May 8, 2001, Aubrey sold the 100 shares for $20,000. Aubrey will compute his tax on his $15,000 capital gain by using his ordinary income tax rate (e.g., 10%, 15%, 27.5%, 30.5%, 35.5%, 39.1%). The ordinary income rates apply because he did not hold the stock more than 12 months.

> **Example 2.** Assume the same facts as in Example 1, except that Aubrey sold the shares on December 1, 2001. In this situation, he is entitled to use the long-term rate of 20% (or 10% if he is in the 10% or 15% tax bracket) because he held the stock more than 12 months.

Determining Holding Period. In determining how long an asset was held, the taxpayer begins counting on the date after the day the property was acquired. The same date of each following month is the beginning of a new month regardless of the number of days in the preceding month. For example, if property was acquired on February 1, 2001, the taxpayer's holding period began on February 2, 2001. The date the asset is disposed of is part of the holding period. See ¶ 1777 for additional information concerning the determination of a taxpayer's holding period.

Tax Years Beginning After December 31, 2000. In general, the capital gains rates of 20% or 10% will apply after December 31, 2000, provided the regular long-term holding period has been met (i.e., more than 12 months). However, a lower

---

Footnote references are to paragraphs of the 2002 Standard Federal Tax Reports.

capital gains rate of 18% (8% for individuals in the 10% or 15% tax bracket) may be applied if the individual held the asset more than five years (Code Sec. 1(h)(2)(B)).[94]

The date that the five-year holding period starts is different for individuals in a 10% or 15% tax bracket than for individuals in higher brackets. The following rules will be applied in order to determine when the five-year holding period begins:

(1) If the individual is in a tax bracket that is higher than 15%, the five-year holding period only applies to assets acquired after December 31, 2000. (Note: A special election allows these individuals to treat prior acquired assets as acquired on January 1, 2001. See "Special Election for Capital Assets Acquired in Tax Years Beginning Before January 1, 2001," below.)

(2) If the individual is in the 10% or 15% tax bracket, the asset does *not* have to be acquired after December 31, 2000 in order to have the five-year period begin.

> **Example 3.** On January 2, 2001, Bob Bailey purchased 10 shares of stock in Azor Inc. Assume he holds the stock more than five years and sells it at a gain. If his tax bracket in the year of sale is more than 15%, his net long-term capital gain will be taxed at a maximum rate of 18%. Conversely, if he holds the stock for more than 12 months but not more than five years, his gain will be subject to a maximum capital gains rate of 10% or 20% depending on his tax bracket in the year of sale.

> **Example 4.** In 1999, Jane Smith purchased 100 shares of stock. Assume she holds the stock more than five years and sells it at a gain. If her maximum tax bracket in the year of sale is 15% or less, she may compute her capital gains tax by using the special 8% rate. Because of her 15% or lower tax bracket, she did not have to acquire the stock after December 31, 2000, in order to have the five-year holding period apply. Conversely, if she holds the stock more than 12 months but not more than five years, her maximum capital gains rate will be 10% if her tax bracket is 15% or less in the year of sale.

Applying the 8% Capital Gains Rate on 2001 Tax Returns. For 2001, individuals will use a worksheet on page 8 of the Schedule D Instructions to compute their gains from eligible capital assets held more than five years. These gains will then be entered on Line 29 of Part IV of Schedule D where they will be part of the computations that are required to determine the individual's capital gains tax.

Property Acquired Under an Option. When property was acquired under an option or other right to acquire property, the five-year period includes the period that the option was held (Code Sec. 1(h)(2)(B)(ii)).[95]

Special Election for Capital Assets Acquired in Tax Years Beginning Before January 1, 2001. As a general rule, an individual in a marginal tax bracket higher than 15% must acquire an asset after December 31, 2000, in order to have the special lower capital gains rate for five-year property apply to the gain from the asset. However, these individuals may make a special election to treat pre-January 1, 2001, assets held on January 1, 2001 as being sold and then reacquired on the same date. As a result of their election, the property will be eligible for the five-year holding period rule. Any income tax due on the gain from this deemed sale of the asset must be paid. The deemed sale election will not apply to an asset that is disposed of in a recognition transaction before the close of the one-year period beginning on the date the asset would have been treated as sold under the election (Act Sec. 311(e)(3) of the Taxpayer Relief Act of 1997 (P.L. 105-34), as amended by Act Sec. 314(c) of the Community Renewal Tax Relief Act of 2000 (P.L. 106-554)). If the individual would realize a loss from this deemed sale, the loss is not recognized (Act Sec 311(e), P.L. 105-34).

Individuals who want to take advantage of this election may have it apply to readily tradable stock, open-end mutual fund, any other capital asset, and certain

---

property used in the taxpayer's trade or business (i.e., business property defined in Code Sec. 1231(b)).

> **Example 5.** Max Brand is in the highest marginal tax bracket. He purchases 10 shares of Binnacle Inc. in 1999 for $1,000. He still owns the shares on January 1, 2001. He plans on holding the stock for a few more years and wants to be able to take advantage of the 18% special long-term rate when he sells the stock. He may elect to treat the stock as if he sold it at its closing market price on January 2, 2001 and pay the applicable tax. Assume that the stock had a closing price of $1,500 on January 2, 2001. Max would pay the tax on his deemed $500 gain when he filed his tax return for 2001. His five-year holding period would begin and his basis in the stock would now be $1,500.

Making the Election on 2001 Tax Returns. To make the election, the deemed sale is reported on the 2001 tax return as if it was an actual sale. In addition, the taxpayer must attach a statement to the tax return indicating that an election is being made under Section 311 of the Taxpayer Relief Act of 1997. The statement must also included a list of the assets for which the election is being made. As a general rule, the tax return, with the election statement attached, must be filed no later than the due date of the return (including extensions). However, if the election was not made on a timely filed return for one or more eligible assets, the taxpayer is permitted to make the election on an amended return that is filed within six months of the due date of the tax return (including extensions). The following should appear at the top of the amended return, "Election Under Section 311 of the Taxpayer Relief Act of 1997." Once made, an election for any asset is irrevocable.

Depreciable Real Estate. A maximum 25% rate is imposed on long-term capital gain attributable to certain prior depreciation that had been claimed on real property. This depreciation is referred to as "unrecaptured Section 1250 gain." Unrecaptured Section 1250 gain is defined as the excess of (Code Sec. 1(h)(7)(A)):[96]

(1) the amount of long-term capital gain (not otherwise treated as ordinary income) that would be treated as ordinary income if Code Sec. 1250(b)(1) included all depreciation and the applicable percentage that applied under Code Sec. 1250(a) were 100% over

(2) the excess of 28%-rate loss over 28%-rate gain.

Even under these capital gains rules, Code Sec. 1250 will continue to treat some prior claimed depreciation (i.e., usually the amount claimed in excess of the amount allowable under the straight-line method) as ordinary income.

> **Example 6.** On December 1, 2001, William Drake sold a building for $1,000,000. The building had originally cost $700,000 and, over the years, Drake had claimed $300,000 in depreciation. Upon the sale of the building, Drake recognizes a total gain of $600,000. Of the $300,000 in claimed depreciation, $100,000 was in excess of that allowed under the straight-line method. Under the capital gains rules (Code Sec. 1(h)(7)(A)), $200,000 of the total claimed depreciation is classified as unrecaptured Section 1250 gain. This is because if Section 1250 had applied to all depreciation, and not only additional depreciation, $300,000 of Drake's long-term capital gain would have been treated as ordinary income. Based on these facts, the $100,000 in excess depreciation would be taxed as ordinary income, the $200,000 in unrecaptured Section 1250 gain would be subject to a maximum capital gains rate of 25%, and the remaining $300,000 of gain would be subject to a maximum capital gains rate of 20%.

Under MACRS, all depreciation on real property must be computed under the straight-line method. As a result, any gain on the sale of MACRS real property that was held more than 12 months and that is due to claimed deprecation will be classified as "unrecaptured Section 1250 gain" and subject to a maximum capital gains rate of 25%.

Footnote references are to paragraphs of the 2002 Standard Federal Tax Reports.

¶ 1736   [96] ¶ 3260

Pass-Through Entities. A pass-through entity (e.g., mutual funds, S corporations, partnerships, estates and trusts) may pass through capital gains to their shareholders or beneficiaries (Code Sec. 1(h)(11)).[97]

Collectibles. Generally, collectibles (e.g., stamps, antiques, gems, and most coins) are taxed at the maximum capital gain rate of 28% even if held more than 12 months (Code Sec. 1(h)(6)).[98]

Small Business Stock. When a taxpayer sells or exchanges certain small business stock (i.e., Sec. 1202 stock) that the taxpayer has held for more than five years, 50% of the gain may be excluded from the taxpayer's gross income. If the small business stock qualifies for this 50% exclusion, any recognized gain from the sale or exchange of the stock is subject to a maximum capital gains rate of 28% (Code Sec. 1(h)(5)(A)(ii)).[99] See ¶ 2396 for more information. The exclusion of gain from the sale or exchange of qualified small business stock is increased to 60% in the case of the sale or exchange of certain empowerment zone stock that was acquired after December 21, 2000 (Code Sec. 1202(a)(2)).

1737. Tax on Capital Gains—Individual, Estate, Trust—Pre-May 7, 1997. For sales of long-term capital assets before May 7, 1997, the maximum tax rate on the net capital gain of individuals, estates and trusts was 28%.

1738. Corporate Capital Gains. A corporation is taxed on net capital gain at the regular tax rates, including the additional phase-out rates for high-income corporations (¶ 219). Although the corporate alternative minimum tax on *net capital gain* is limited to 35%, this limitation applies only in tax years in which the regular corporate tax exceeds 35%, excluding the additional phase-out rates (Code Sec. 1201).[100] Effective for corporate tax years ending after December 31, 1997, the alternative minimum tax rate of 35% is applied to the *lesser of the corporation's net capital gain or its taxable income* (Code Sec. 1201).[101] However, because the alternative minimum tax rate only applies when a corporation's ordinary income tax rate *exceeds* 35%, and the top corporate tax rate is currently 35%, this change has no immediate impact on corporations.

See ¶ 1752 and ¶ 1756 for treatment of corporate capital losses.

1739. Netting of Gains and Losses. In order to calculate their recognized capital gain or loss for the tax year, noncorporate taxpayers have to follow specific netting procedures (Code Sec. 1(h)(1)).[102]

The basic netting procedure provides that within each tax rate group (e.g., 20% group), gains and losses are netted in order to arrive at a net gain or loss for the group. After this basic process has been completed, the following netting and ordering rules must be applied (Notice 97-59):[103]

(1) *Short-term capital gains and losses.* Short-term capital losses (including short-term loss carryovers from a prior year) are applied first to reduce short-term capital gains, if any, that would otherwise be taxable at ordinary income tax rates. A net short-term loss is used first to reduce any net long-term capital gain from the 28% group (Code Sec. 1(h)(5)).[104] Any remaining short-term loss is then used to reduce gain from the 25% group and then the 20% group (Notice 97-59).[105]

(2) *Long-term capital gains and losses.* A net loss from the 28% group (including long-term capital loss carryovers) is used first to reduce gain from the 25% group, then to reduce net gain from the 20% group. A net loss from the 20% group is used first to reduce net gain from the 28% group, and then to reduce gain from the 25% group.

Any resulting net capital gain that is attributable to a particular rate group is taxed at that group's marginal tax rate.

> **Example.** At the end of 2001, Ralph Helm had a short-term capital loss of $35,000. He also had long-term capital gains in the following amounts and tax rate groups: $28,000 (25% group-unrecaptured Section

---

Footnote references are to paragraphs of the 2002 Standard Federal Tax Reports.

97 ¶ 3260
98 ¶ 3260
99 ¶ 3260
100 ¶ 30,352
101 ¶ 30,352
102 ¶ 3260
103 ¶ 3285.55
104 ¶ 3260
105 ¶ 3285.55

¶ 1739

1250 gain), $5,000 (28% group-collectibles gain), and $10,000 (20% group). Helm would first apply $5,000 of his short-term loss against his 28% collectibles gain. Next he would apply $28,000 of his short-term loss against the 25% unrecaptured Section 1250 gain. His remaining $2,000 of short-term loss would then be applied against his $10,000 gain in the 20% group. The result of this netting and ordering procedure is that he has $8,000 of long-term gain subject to a maximum capital gains tax rate of 20%.

1740. Conversion Transactions. Capital gain from the disposition or termination of a position that is part of a "conversion transaction" is subject to recharacterization as ordinary income (Code Sec. 1258).[106] In general, the amount of capital gain treated as ordinary income is equal to the interest that would have accrued on the taxpayer's net investment at a yield equal to 120% of the applicable federal rate (¶ 83) compounded semiannually, or, if the term of the conversion transaction is indefinite, 120% of the federal short-term rates (¶ 83) in effect under Code Sec. 6621(b) compounded daily. The recharacterized gain is not considered interest income.

A transaction is a conversion transaction only if substantially all of the taxpayer's expected return is attributable to the time value of the taxpayer's net investment in the transaction (i.e., the taxpayer is in the economic position of a lender) (Code Sec. 1258(c)). In addition, the transaction must be: (1) a transaction in which the taxpayer acquires property and on a substantially contemporaneous basis enters into a contract to sell the property (or substantially identical property) at a predetermined price; (2) a straddle; (3) marketed or sold as producing capital gains from a transaction in which the taxpayer's return is substantially from the time value of the net investment; or (4) specified by the IRS in regulations.

> **Example.** Sam Jones purchases stock on January 2, 1999, for $100 and agrees on the same day to sell it to Wendell Johnson on January 2, 2001, for $115. A portion of the $15 gain from the sale of the stock on January 2, 2001, equal to 120% of the applicable federal rate compounded semiannually for two years and applied to the $100 investment is recharacterized as ordinary income.

Transactions of options dealers and commodities traders in the normal course of their trade or business of dealing in options or trading section 1256 contracts are *not* conversion transactions (Code Sec. 1258(d)(5)(A)).[107] However, this exception does not apply to certain gains allocated to limited partners and limited entrepreneurs.

Constructive Ownership Transactions. The amount of long-term capital gains that a taxpayer may recognize from certain constructive ownership transactions that arise from specified financial assets may be limited (Code Sec. 1260).[108] These "financial assets" include any equity interest in a pass-through entity (e.g., a partnership or REIT). The long-term gain is limited to the amount of gain that the taxpayer would have recognized if the financial asset had been held directly by the taxpayer during the term of the derivative contract. Any additional gain is recognized as ordinary income. Interest is imposed on the amount of ordinary income. These rules apply to transactions entered into on or after July 12, 1999.

1741. Capital Asset. A capital gain or loss arises from the sale or exchange of a *capital asset,* or an asset given this effect under the Code (see ¶ 1747). The term "capital asset" means property (whether or not connected with a trade or business) *except the following*:

(1) an inventoriable asset;

(2) property held primarily for sale to customers in the ordinary course of the taxpayer's trade or business (according to the Supreme Court, "primarily" means "of first importance" or "principally," and not merely "substantially");[109]

Footnote references are to paragraphs of the 2002 Standard Federal Tax Reports.

106 ¶ 31,125
107 ¶ 31,125
108 ¶ 31,140

109 ¶ 30,422.022,
¶ 30,575.021

¶ 1740

(3) a note or account receivable acquired in the ordinary course of trade or business for services rendered or from the sale of stock in trade or property held for sale in the ordinary course of business;

(4) depreciable business property;

(5) real property used in taxpayer's trade or business;

(6) a copyright, a literary, musical or artistic composition, a letter or memorandum, or similar property (but not a patent or invention) held by the taxpayer who created it, or by one whose basis in the property is determined by reference to the basis of the one who created it, or in the case of a letter, memorandum or similar property, a taxpayer for whom such property was prepared or produced; and

(7) a U.S. government publication (including the *Congressional Record*) held by a taxpayer who received it (or by another taxpayer in whose hands the publication would have a basis determined in whole or in part by reference to the taxpayer's basis) other than by purchase at the price at which the publication is offered to the public (Code Sec. 1221; Reg. § 1.1221-1).[110]

Additional Noncapital Assets. Recent legislation has added three new categories to the list of "noncapital" assets. These additions are: (1) commodities derivative financial instruments held by commodities derivatives dealers (Code Sec. 1221(a)(6));[111] (2) hedging transactions entered into in the normal course of the taxpayer's business (Code Sec. 1221(a)(7));[112] and (3) supplies of a type regularly used or consumed by the taxpayer in the ordinary course of business (Code Sec. 1221(a)(8)).[113] These additions are effective for any instrument held, acquired or entered into, any transaction entered into, and supplies held or acquired on or after December 17, 1999.

A taxpayer's household furnishings, personal residence and automobile are "capital assets" to which the capital gain provisions apply. Gain on the sale of this kind of property is treated as capital gain. However, loss from the sale is not recognized for income tax purposes unless the property was held for the production of income. For example, if an individual sells a residence that had been partially used as rental property, the individual would have to make a proper allocation of the cost of the building, the selling price, depreciation (applicable to the rental portion only), and the selling expenses between the personal and rental portions of the building as if there were two separate transactions.[114] Although gain on either portion would generally be recognized for income tax purposes, loss would be recognized only on the rental portion. (For additional information concerning the sale of a personal residence, see ¶ 1107, ¶ 1626, and ¶ 1705.) Stock and securities generally are considered to be held for production of income so that loss on their sale is a capital loss.

The disposition of property normally results in ordinary income or loss treatment only if it falls within one of the exceptions to capital asset treatment listed above. However, the Supreme Court has ruled that the definition of a capital asset must be broadly interpreted and that an asset must come within one of the statutory categories of "noncapital" assets in order for it to be excluded from capital asset treatment (*Arkansas Best Corp.*).[115] In its decision, the Court rejected the contention that ordinary income and loss treatment should apply to an asset that is otherwise capital simply because it is acquired for business purposes. Therefore, bank stock that was acquired by a holding company in order to prevent damage to the holding company's business reputation was held to be a capital asset even though it was acquired for a business purpose. In an earlier decision, the Supreme Court ruled that

---

Footnote references are to paragraphs of the 2002 Standard Federal Tax Reports.

[110] ¶ 30,420, ¶ 30,421	[112] ¶ 30,420	[114] ¶ 10,103.35
[111] ¶ 30,420	[113] ¶ 30,420	[115] ¶ 30,422.6865

¶ 1741

hedging transactions that were an integral part of a business's inventory-purchase system were a noncapital asset because they were inventory (*Corn Products Refining*).[116] Gains and losses from most business hedges entered into in order to reduce risk of price changes or currency fluctuations are treated as ordinary gains and losses. The hedge must relate to ordinary income property held or to be held by the taxpayer who enters into the hedge. A taxpayer must make a same-day identification in its books and records of the hedges entered into (Reg. § 1.1221-2(e)(1)).[117] After December 21, 2000, gain or loss on a securities futures contract may be eligible for capital gain treatment (Code Sec. 1234B).

In some situations, capital gain can result even when the property sold is held primarily for sale in the ordinary course of business. An example is the sale of a patent by an inventor under Code Sec. 1235. See ¶ 1767. For special rules on depreciable property, see ¶ 1779. For special rules on the disposition of certain farm property, see ¶ 1797. A partnership interest is generally treated as a single capital asset. See ¶ 434.

1742. Sale or Exchange Required. The capital gain and loss provisions apply only to a *sale or exchange* of a capital asset (Code Sec. 1222; Reg. § 1.1222-1).[118] In the case of real estate, a sale or exchange occurs on the earlier of the date of conveyance or the date when the burden and benefits of ownership pass to the purchaser.[119] Other transactions considered to be sales or exchanges include a liquidation distribution or other transaction described at ¶ 2253, loss on worthless securities (¶ 1764), and failure to exercise a privilege or option on property that would have been a capital asset if acquired (¶ 1919).

When bonds with past-due interest are purchased "flat," aggregate interest payments that are for the prepurchase period and that are in excess of the purchase price but less than the face value of the bonds are properly characterized as capital gains because they are considered to be amounts received on retirement of the bonds (Rev. Rul. 60-284).[120]

The sale of an endowment insurance policy before its maturity or of a paid-up annuity contract before the annuity starting date results in ordinary income (*E.J. Arnfeld*).[121]

1743. Sale of a Trade or Business. When a business is sold, generally each asset of the business is treated as being sold separately in determining the seller's income, gain or loss and the buyer's basis in each of the assets acquired (Rev. Rul. 55-79).[122] See ¶ 1620. The seller must make the allocation to determine the amount and character of any recognized gain or loss. The buyer must allocate the purchase price among the business assets to determine any allowable depreciation or amortization (Code Sec. 1060; Reg. § 1.1060-1(a)).[123]

Residual Method. Under the residual method the purchase price is first allocated to Class I assets (cash and cash equivalents). The remaining amount is then allocated in the following order: Class II assets (certificates of deposit, U.S. government securities, readily marketable stock or securities, and foreign currency); Class III assets (all assets other than Class I, II, IV, or V assets); Class IV assets (Section 197 intangibles, except those in the nature of goodwill or going concern value (e.g., workforce in place, copyrights, and covenants not to compete)); and Class V (goodwill and going concern value) (Reg. § 1.1060-1(c)).[124]

The buyer and seller may agree in writing to allocations of part or all of the consideration involved in the transaction and of the fair market value of any assets transferred. This allocation generally is binding on both parties, unless the IRS determines that the allocation is inappropriate (Code Sec. 1060(a)).[125]

Reporting. The purchaser and the seller must both file Form 8594 (Asset Acquisition Statement) to report the sale of assets used in a trade or business when

---

Footnote references are to paragraphs of the 2002 Standard Federal Tax Reports.

[116] ¶ 30,426.15	[120] ¶ 5704.3075	[123] ¶ 30,060, ¶ 30,061
[117] ¶ 30,424	[121] ¶ 30,422.58	[124] ¶ 30,061
[118] ¶ 30,440, ¶ 30,441	[122] ¶ 30,422.125	[125] ¶ 30,060
[119] ¶ 21,005.04		

goodwill or going concern value could be part of the sale. Form 8594 is attached to the tax return filed for the year in which the sale occurred.

Goodwill, Covenants Not to Compete, and Other Acquired Intangibles. See ¶ 1288 for information concerning the amortization of the cost of goodwill and other intangibles.

1744. Sale of Depreciable Assets Between Related Taxpayers. Capital gain treatment is denied when depreciable property (including patent applications) is sold or exchanged between related taxpayers. This covers sales or exchanges between a person and all entities that are controlled by such person and between a taxpayer and any trust in which the taxpayer or spouse is a beneficiary unless such beneficiary interest is a remote contingent interest (Code Sec. 1239).[126]

For purposes of this rule, entities that are controlled by a taxpayer include: (1) a corporation if the taxpayer owns (directly or indirectly) more than 50% of the value of its stock; (2) a partnership if the taxpayer owns (directly or indirectly) more than 50% of the capital or profits interest; and (3) certain entities that are related persons with respect to the taxpayer, including two corporations that are members of the same controlled group, a corporation and a partnership if the same persons own more than 50% of each, and two S corporations, or an S corporation and a C corporation, if the same persons own more than 50% of the stock of each (Code Sec. 1239(c); Reg. § 1.1239-1).[127]

Section 1231

1747. Property Used in Trade or Business. Business real estate or any depreciable business property is excluded from the definition of "capital assets" (¶ 1741). However, if the business property qualifies as Code Sec. 1231 property and gains from dealings in such property exceed any losses, then each gain or loss is treated as though it were derived from the sale of a long-term capital asset (Code Sec. 1231(a)).[128] If the losses exceed the gains, all gains and losses are treated as though they were ordinary gains and losses.

Taxpayers use Form 4797 (Sales of Business Property) to report Code Sec. 1231 transactions.

Code Sec. 1231 property includes (Code Sec. 1231(b); Reg. §§ 1.1231-1 and 1.1231-2): [129]

(1) Property used in the trade or business, subject to depreciation and held for the long-term holding period (¶ 1777) (but excluding property includible in inventory; property held primarily for sale to customers; a copyright; a literary, musical or artistic composition; a letter, memorandum or similar property (see item (6), ¶ 1741); and government publications (see item (7), ¶ 1741)).

(2) Real property used in the trade or business and held for the long-term holding period (¶ 1777) (but excluding property includible in inventory or held primarily for sale to customers).

(3) Trade or business property (items (1) and (2), above) held for the long-term holding period (¶ 1777) and involuntarily converted.

(4) Capital assets held for the long-term holding period (¶ 1777) and involuntarily converted (for rules, see ¶ 1748).

(5) A crop sold with the land where the land has been held for the long-term holding period (¶ 1777).

(6) Livestock, as explained at ¶ 1750.

(7) Timber, domestic iron ore, or coal under conditions described at ¶ 1772.

When Code Sec. 1231 property is also property subject to depreciation recapture under Code Sec. 1245 or 1250 or mining property with unrecaptured mining

---

exploration expenditures under Code Sec. 617, the amount of the Code Sec. 1231 gain on sales or exchanges is the amount by which the total gain exceeds amounts recaptured at ordinary income rates under Code Sec. 1245, 1250 or 617(d)(1) (see ¶ 1779 and following). The farmland expenditure recapture rules may also cause reductions in Code Sec. 1231 gain (see ¶ 1797).

A loss that is disallowed by other provisions of the law (e.g., a sale between family members) is not taken into account in comparing Code Sec. 1231 gains and losses.

Recapture of Net Section 1231 Losses. A taxpayer who has a net section 1231 gain (i.e., excess of section 1231 gains over section 1231 losses) for the tax year must review the five preceding tax years for possible recapture of net section 1231 losses for the prior years. If there were any net section 1231 losses during such period, the taxpayer must treat the current year's net section 1231 gain as ordinary income to the extent of the amount of unrecaptured net section 1231 losses for that past period (Code Sec. 1231(c)).[130] The losses are to be recaptured on a first-in, first-out (FIFO) basis.

> **Example.** A business taxpayer incurred a net section 1231 gain of $23,000 for 2001. The taxpayer had a net section 1231 loss of $12,000 in 1999 and a net section 1231 loss of $15,000 in 2000. The taxpayer must include the total 2001 $23,000 net section 1231 gain as ordinary income (i.e., recapture the $12,000 net section 1231 loss for 1999 and $11,000 of the $15,000 net section 1231 loss for 2000). The $4,000 balance of the net section 1231 loss for 2000 remains outstanding, to be recaptured should the taxpayer realize any net section 1231 gain during 2002-2005.

1748. Involuntary Conversions. Gains and losses from the involuntary conversion of depreciable business property, or capital assets held for more than one year that were either used in a trade or business or in a transaction entered into for profit, are covered by the general rules of Code Sec. 1231 unless the nonrecognition rules of Code Sec. 1033 apply (see ¶ 1713) (Reg. § 1.1231-1(e)).[131] Recognized gains and losses resulting from theft or seizure or an exercise of power of requisition or condemnation are treated as Sec. 1231 gains or losses.

Gains and losses from other casualties (i.e. fire, storm, shipwreck, theft) are separately grouped. This grouping must be made whether the casualty property was insured, partially insured or uninsured.

If casualty gains equal or exceed casualty losses, then the gains and losses are grouped with other Code Sec. 1231 transactions to determine whether there is an overall Code Sec. 1231 gain or loss. But if the separate grouping of the casualty or theft gains and losses results in a *net loss,* the transactions are not further grouped with other Code Sec. 1231 transactions. Instead, they are excluded from Code Sec. 1231, and the net loss is treated as an ordinary loss (Reg. § 1.1231-1(e)(3)).[132]

Personal Assets—Casualty and Theft Losses. Casualty and theft losses of personal assets (i.e., those not held in a trade or business or for investment) are excluded from the operation of Code Sec. 1231. Instead, gains and losses (in excess of the $100 floor per loss) from personal casualties and thefts are grouped separately. Any resulting net loss from casualties and thefts for the year is deductible as an ordinary loss to the extent it exceeds 10% of the taxpayer's adjusted gross income (AGI) (Code Sec. 165(h)).[133] See ¶ 1124. If there is a net gain, the gains and losses are treated as capital gains and losses—either long-term or short-term depending upon the holding period—and the losses are not subject to the 10% AGI floor.

1750. Sale of Livestock. Capital gain treatment under Code Sec. 1231 applies to a sale or involuntary conversion of livestock (not including poultry) held for draft, breeding, dairy or sporting purposes. To qualify for this treatment, horses and cattle must be held for at least 24 months and all other livestock must be held for at

Footnote references are to paragraphs of the 2002 Standard Federal Tax Reports.

130 ¶ 30,572	132 ¶ 30,573	133 ¶ 9802
131 ¶ 30,573,		
¶ 30,575.027		

¶ **1748**

least 12 months.[134] The holding period begins on the date of acquisition rather than on the date the animal is actually placed in one of the above uses (Code Sec. 1231(b)(3); Reg. § 1.1231-2).[135] Livestock includes fur-bearing animals such as chinchillas, mink and foxes.[136] For treatment of involuntary conversions of livestock due to disease, see ¶ 1713. For treatment of forced sales due to weather conditions (e.g., flood or drought), see ¶ 767.

1751. Lease or Distributor's Agreement Canceled. An amount received by a lessee for cancellation of a lease is treated as received in exchange for the lease. This rule applies also to amounts received by a distributor of goods for the cancellation of a distributor's agreement if the taxpayer has a substantial capital investment in the distributorship (Code Sec. 1241; Reg. § 1.1241-1).[137] Thus, if the lease or agreement is a Code Sec. 1231 asset, there will be a Code Sec. 1231 gain or loss.

Capital Loss Limitation, Carryover, Carryback

1752. Limitation on Capital Loss. To determine the deductibility of capital losses, all capital gains and losses (without distinction between long-term and short-term) incurred during the year must be totaled. Any capital losses are deductible only to the extent of any capital gains plus, in the case of noncorporate taxpayers, ordinary income of up to $3,000 (Code Sec. 1211).[138] Thus, both net long-term capital losses and net short-term capital losses may be used to offset up to $3,000 of an individual's ordinary income. Special rules for married persons, whether filing joint or separate returns, are at ¶ 1757.

Example. For 2001, Janet Green had $30,000 of ordinary income, a net short-term capital loss of $500 and a net long-term capital loss of $300. Green's total capital loss deduction is $800.

Corporations. A corporation can use capital losses for a tax year only to offset capital gains in that year (Code Sec. 1211(a)).[139] See ¶ 1756 for the carryback and/or carryforward of corporate capital losses.

1754. Individual's Net Capital Loss Carryover. Individuals and other noncorporate taxpayers may carry over a net capital loss for an unlimited time until the loss is exhausted. The capital loss carryover may be computed on a worksheet in the Schedule D, Form 1040 instructions.

A capital loss that is carried over to a later tax year retains its long-term or short-term character for the year to which it is carried. In determining the amount of the capital loss that can be carried over, short-term capital gain is increased by the lesser of (1) the ordinary income offset (whether $3,000 or the amount of the overall net loss) or (2) taxable income increased by that offset and the deduction for personal exemptions (any excess of allowable deductions over gross income for the loss year is treated as negative taxable income for this purpose) (Code Sec. 1212).[140]

A short-term capital loss carryover first offsets short-term gain in the carryover year. If a net short-term capital loss results, this loss first offsets net long-term capital gain, and then up to $3,000 of ordinary income (¶ 1752). A long-term capital loss carryover first reduces long-term capital gain in the carryover year, then net short-term capital gain, and finally up to $3,000 of ordinary income.

Example. Marvin Blue had taxable income of $30,000 in 2001 and filed a joint return. In computing taxable income, he reported a net short-term capital loss of $1,000 and a net long-term capital loss of $5,000. Blue would use his $1,000 net short-term loss to offset $1,000 of ordinary income; he would then use $2,000 of his net long-term capital loss to offset $2,000 of ordinary income. The remaining $3,000 of his net long-term capital loss would be carried over to 2002 ($3,000 is carried over because it

Footnote references are to paragraphs of the 2002 Standard Federal Tax Reports.
[134] ¶ 30,575.037 [137] ¶ 30,750, ¶ 30,751 [139] ¶ 30,390
[135] ¶ 30,572, ¶ 30,574 [138] ¶ 30,390 [140] ¶ 30,400
[136] ¶ 30,575.154

¶ **1754**

is less than Blue's taxable income of $30,000 increased by the ordinary income offset of $3,000 and the deduction for personal exemptions).

Code Sec. 1256 Contract Loss. An individual (but not an estate, trust, or corporation) who has a net Code Sec. 1256 contracts loss (net loss from futures contracts, foreign currency contracts, nonequity options, or dealer options) in a given tax year may elect to carry back the loss to the three prior tax years (Code Sec. 1212(c)).[141]

1756. Corporate Capital Loss Carryover and Carryback. A corporation may carry back a capital loss to each of the three tax years preceding the loss year. Any excess may be carried forward for five years following the loss year. However, the amount that can be carried back is limited to an amount that does not cause or increase a net operating loss in the carryback year (Code Sec. 1212(a)(1)).[142]

Any carryback or carryover is treated as short-term capital loss for the year to which it is carried. As such, it is grouped with any other capital losses for the year to which carried and is used to offset any capital gains. Any undeducted loss remaining after the three-year carryback and the five-year carryover is not deductible.

Foreign expropriation losses that can be carried over for 10 years are ineligible for three-year carryback. A foreign expropriation capital loss is the sum of the capital losses sustained (either directly or on securities that become worthless) by reason of the expropriation, intervention, seizure, or similar taking of property by the government of any foreign country, any political subdivision, or any agency or instrumentality of such a governmental unit (Code Sec. 1212(a); Reg. § 1.1212-1).[143]

A regulated investment company's capital loss can be carried over for eight years (Code Sec. 1212(a)(1)(C)(i)).[144]

A quick refund procedure is available for corporate net operating loss carrybacks for capital loss carrybacks (see ¶ 2773).

1757. Capital Gain or Loss of Husband and Wife. All the capital gains and losses of a husband and wife are computed on a joint return as if they were the gains and losses of one person (*W.C. Janney*).[145] If a husband and wife file separate returns, the capital loss deduction is limited to $1,500 (one-half of the limit for a joint return). If separate returns are filed the year after a net capital loss was reported on a joint return, any carryover is allocated on the basis of the individual net capital loss of the spouses for the prior joint return year (Reg. § 1.1211-1(b)(7)).[146]

1758. Partnership or S Corporation Capital Gain or Loss. The capital gains and losses of a partnership or S corporation are generally segregated from its ordinary net income and carried into the income of the individual partners or shareholders. Partners or shareholders treat their distributive share of the capital gain or loss as if it were their own capital gain or loss (see ¶ 431). The same rule applies for Code Sec. 1231 transactions (¶ 1747) (Code Secs. 702(a) and 1366(a)).[147] S corporations may be taxed on capital gains in very limited situations (see ¶ 337).

1760. Investors, Dealers and Traders. In order to determine whether a taxpayer's gains or losses are ordinary or capital in nature, it must be determined if the taxpayer entered into the transaction as an investor, dealer or trader. The following is an overview of how these terms are defined.

Investors. An investor is a taxpayer whose activities are limited to occasional transactions for his own account. The level of activity is less than that associated with a trade or business. Gains and losses of an investor are subject to the capital gains and loss rules.

Dealers. Capital gain and loss treatment does not apply to securities owned by a dealer, except for those securities held primarily for personal investment (Code Sec. 1236). Securities that are held by a dealer for investment purposes must be

---

Footnote references are to paragraphs of the 2002 Standard Federal Tax Reports.

[141] ¶ 30,400	[144] ¶ 30,400	[146] ¶ 30,391
[142] ¶ 30,400	[145] ¶ 30,392.125	[147] ¶ 25,080, ¶ 32,080
[143] ¶ 30,400, ¶ 30,401		

¶ 1756

clearly identified in the dealer's records before the close of the day on which they were acquired and must never be held primarily for sale to the dealer's customers (Code Sec. 1236(a)). A dealer regularly purchases securities from, and sells securities to, customers in the ordinary course of a trade or business. Because they are in the business of buying and selling, the gains and losses of dealers are classified as ordinary gain or loss. Capital gain and loss treatment does not apply to real estate sales by a dealer in realty, except for property held as an investment (*J.M. Welch*).[148]

Traders. A securities trader (including a "day trader") buys and sells securities for the trader's own account. A trader's expectation of making a profit depends upon such circumstances as a rise in value or an advantageous purchase to enable him to sell at a price in excess of cost. Because the securities that traders buy and sell are not held primarily for sale to customers, the gains and losses are generally treated as capital in nature and are reported on Schedule D (Code Sec. 1221(a)(1)).[149] (Traders may make a "mark-to-market" election that allows them to treat gains and losses as ordinary (see ¶ 1901).) Because traders are in the business of trading, they may claim their business expenses on Schedule C (Profit or Loss From Business). However, for the rules concerning the commissions they pay for buying and selling securities, see ¶ 1983.

Subdivision of Real Estate

1762. Subdivision and Sale of Real Estate. Noncorporate taxpayers and S corporations are not treated as real estate dealers solely because they have subdivided a tract of land for sale (Code Sec. 1237(a)).[150] At least part of the gain on the sale of a lot is treated as capital gain when (1) the taxpayer has not previously held the tract or any lot or parcel thereof for sale in the ordinary course of business, and, in the same tax year as the sale occurs, does not hold any other real estate for sale in the ordinary course of business (this automatically disqualifies a real estate dealer); (2) no "substantial" improvements are made while the tract is held by the taxpayer or pursuant to a contract of sale between the taxpayer and the buyer; and (3) the taxpayer has held the particular lot sold for at least five years, unless it was acquired by inheritance or devise, in which case there is no minimum holding period requirement (except the required time for long-term capital gain treatment) (Code Sec. 1237(a)(3)).[151]

There is an exception to the substantial-improvement rule noted at (2), above. Certain improvements, such as water, sewage, drainage, or road installation, are not considered substantial improvements if the property (including inherited property) is held for at least 10 years and would not have been marketable at the prevailing local price for similar building sites without such improvements and if the taxpayer elects not to adjust the basis of the property (or other property) or deduct the costs as expenses (Code Sec. 1237(b)(3)).

Making the Election. There are a number of special requirements that have to be met in order to make a successful election (e.g., the taxpayer has to submit a plat of the subdivision and a list of all improvements) (Code Sec. 1237(b)(3); Reg. § 1.1237-1(c)(5)).[152] The election and the required information are to be submitted with the tax return for the year in which the lots covered by the election were sold.

The profits realized on the sales of the first five lots or parcels from the same tract are capital gains. However, in the year in which the sixth sale or exchange is made, and thereafter, gain on each sale is taxed as ordinary income to the extent of 5% of the selling price. Selling expenses are deducted first from the 5% that would otherwise be considered ordinary income and then are used to reduce the capital gain on the sale or exchange. The selling expenses cannot be deducted from other income as ordinary business expenses (Code Sec. 1237(b)(2); Reg. § 1.1237-1).[153]

Footnote references are to paragraphs of the 2002 Standard Federal Tax Reports.
[148] ¶ 30,575.244 [150] ¶ 30,690 [152] ¶ 30,690, ¶ 30,691
[149] ¶ 30,420 [151] ¶ 30,690 [153] ¶ 30,690, ¶ 30,691

¶ 1762

> **Example 1.** Mark bought a tract of land in 1990. He subdivides it in 2001, and during the year sells three lots for $50,000 each. The adjusted basis for each lot is $30,000. Mark has a long-term capital gain of $20,000 from the sale of each lot.
>
> **Example 2.** Assume the same facts as in Example 1. Assume further that in 2001, Mark sells three additional lots, each having a $30,000 basis for gain or loss. The selling price of each lot is $50,000. Because he sold more than five lots, 5% of $50,000, or $2,500, of the gain on the sale of each of the six lots is ordinary income. The balance of the gain on each lot (i.e., $17,500) is treated as long-term capital gain.

If a taxpayer sells or exchanges any lots or parcels from a tract, and then does not sell or exchange any others for a period of five years from the last sale or exchange, the taxpayer can sell another five lots without having a portion of the gain taxed as ordinary income (Reg. § 1.1237-1(g)(2)).[154]

If a tract of land is bought with the purpose that it is to be subdivided and sold as separate lots or parcels, the seller must measure gain or loss on every lot or parcel sold on the basis of an equitable (not ratable) apportionment (such as their relative assessed valuations for real estate tax purposes) of the cost of the subdivision to each separate part (Reg. § 1.61-6(a)).[155]

Worthless Security

1764. Worthless Security. Loss from a security that becomes worthless is treated as a capital loss if the security is a capital asset. Generally, the loss is treated as occurring on the last day of the tax year in which the security becomes worthless (Code Sec. 165(g)).[156] This rule affects whether the capital loss is recognized as short-term or long-term. Deduction for *partial* worthlessness is not allowed.[157]

> **Example.** On December 10, 2000, Judy Green purchased shares of Xetco Corporation for $5,000. On May 1, 2001, she received formal notification that the shares of Xetco were worthless. In claiming a capital loss for the worthless shares on her 2001 tax return, Judy must treat the shares as becoming worthless on December 31, 2001. As a result, her $5,000 capital loss is recognized as long-term even though she did not own the shares for more than 12 months before they became worthless.

Special rules apply to stock issued, or some securities held, by a small business investment company (¶ 2392). A bank may claim a bad debt deduction on the worthlessness (in whole or in part) of certain securities (Code Sec. 582(a)).[158] A bank's net loss from a sale or exchange of a bond is deductible in full as an ordinary loss (Code Sec. 582(c)).[159]

Patents and Royalties

1767. Patents. An individual inventor, whether amateur or professional, and any other *individual* acquiring an interest in a patent from the original inventor for money or money's worth paid prior to actual reduction of the invention to practice treats profits and royalties from the sale or exchange of the patent as long-term capital gains, regardless of how long the patent is held. However, the individual may not be the inventor's employer or a related individual described in Code Sec. 267(b), except a brother or sister of the inventor or a controlled partnership described in Code Sec. 707(b). Also, a "25%-or-more" test is substituted for the more than 50% stock ownership test in items (2), (8) and (10)-(12) of the list at ¶ 1717 and for control of a partnership (Code Sec. 1235).[160]

1772. Timber, Coal or Iron Ore. A taxpayer may elect to treat the cutting of timber (for sale or for use in a trade or business) *as a sale or exchange* of

---

Footnote references are to paragraphs of the 2002 Standard Federal Tax Reports.

[154] ¶ 30,691	[157] ¶ 9905, ¶ 10,000	[159] ¶ 23,608
[155] ¶ 5605	[158] ¶ 23,608	[160] ¶ 30,650
[156] ¶ 9802		

timber cut during the year if the taxpayer owned the timber or held the contract right to cut the timber for more than one year (for property acquired after 1987) (Code Sec. 631; Reg. § § 1.631-1—1.631-2).[161] Under Code Sec. 1231, such timber is considered to be "property used in the trade or business" so that gain may be treated as long-term capital gain under certain conditions. See ¶ 1747.

Making the Election. In order to make the election, a taxpayer must file Form T (Timber) (Forest Activities Schedules) with the tax return for the year in which the election is to be effective.

Timber, coal or domestic iron ore royalties are also subject to Code Sec. 1231 (¶ 1747) treatment (except for any recapture of exploration expenditures under Code Sec. 617) when the owner of timber, coal, or iron ore or an economic interest therein (including a lessee) disposes of it under a contract (which may include a lease or sublease) with a retained economic interest. This treatment generally is not available in the case of coal or iron ore mined outside the United States or when the coal or iron ore property is owned and operated by the same parties (Code Secs. 272 and 631(b) and (c)).[162]

Franchise Grant and Sale

1774. Ordinary Income from Franchise Grant. Amounts received from the transfer of a franchise, trademark, or tradename are generally treated as ordinary income by the transferor if the transferor retains any significant power, right, or continuing interest over the franchise, trademark, or tradename (Code Sec. 1253(a)).[163] Ordinary income treatment also applies to amounts received from the transfer, sale, or other disposition of a franchise, trademark, or tradename which are contingent on the transferred asset's productivity, use, or disposition (Code Sec. 1253(c)).[164]

1775. Rules for Payments by Transferee. Amounts paid or incurred on account of the transfer of a franchise, trademark, or tradename are amortized over 15 years under Code Sec. 197 (see ¶ 1288). Amortization is claimed on Form 4562 (Depreciation and Amortization).

Contingent Serial Payments. A current business deduction may be claimed for certain contingent serial payments paid or incurred on account of a transfer, sale, or other disposition of a trademark, tradename, or franchise. The deduction is allowed for payments that are contingent on the asset's productivity, use, or disposition if (1) the contingent amounts are paid as part of a series of payments that are payable at least annually throughout the term of the transfer agreement and (2) the payments are substantially equal in amount or payable under a fixed formula (Code Sec. 1253(d)(1)).[165]

Holding Period of Capital Asset

1777. Rules on Determination of Holding Period. The holding period for a capital asset is the length of time that the taxpayer owned the property before disposing of it through sale or exchange. Determining whether the holding period was "short-term" or "long-term" will determine the tax treatment of any recognized gain or loss (Code Secs. 1222 and 1223).[166] The lowest long-term capital gain tax rate is generally available when a capital asset has been held more than 12 months. However, lower capital gains rates for assets held more than five years went into effect for tax years beginning after December 31, 2000 (Code Sec. 1(h)).[167] See ¶ 1736 for a discussion concerning the taxation of capital gains.

Calculating the Holding Period. In most situations when determining how long an asset was held, the taxpayer begins counting on the date after the day the

---

Footnote references are to paragraphs of the 2002 Standard Federal Tax Reports.

[161] ¶ 24,150, ¶ 24,151, ¶ 24,153
[162] ¶ 14,309, ¶ 24,150, ¶ 24,110
[163] ¶ 31,040
[164] ¶ 31,040
[165] ¶ 31,040
[166] ¶ 30,440, ¶ 30,460
[167] ¶ 3260

¶ 1777

property was acquired. The same date of each following month is the beginning of a new month regardless of the number of days in the preceding month (Rev. Rul. 66-7).[168] For example, if property was acquired on February 1, 2001, the taxpayer's holding period began on February 2, 2001. The date the asset is disposed is part of the holding period. However, there are special rules that must be applied when determining the holding period of assets acquired by gift, inheritance, exchange, etc. See "Special Holding Periods," below.

> **Example 1.** If an asset is acquired on March 23, 2000, the first day on which it may be considered to have been held for more than one year is March 24, 2001.

If an asset is acquired on the last day of a month, the first day on which it may be considered to have been held for more than one year is *the first day of the thirteenth calendar month following the calendar month of acquisition.*[169]

> **Example 2.** An asset acquired on March 31, 2000, must be held until April 1, 2001, in order to be considered held for more than one year.

Special Holding Periods. The general rule is that a taxpayer's holding period begins the day after the asset was acquired. However, in some situations a taxpayer's holding period is considered to have begun before that day. For example, the current owner is allowed to "tack on" a prior holding period when a tax-free exchange of property is involved. The following material presents an overview of the holding period rules.

Exchange. When property is received in an exchange without recognition of gain or loss (¶ 1706, ¶ 1721-¶ 1734, ¶ 2201 and¶ 2205-¶ 2265), the holding period of the property received in the exchange begins with the date of the taxpayer's acquisition of the property that he surrendered in the exchange (Code Sec. 1223).[170] This applies to property received in a tax-free exchange only if the property given in exchange was also a capital asset or Code Sec. 1231 property used in the trade or business at the time of the exchange.

Gift. The holding period of property acquired by gift or transfer in trust (see ¶ 1630 and ¶ 1678) includes the time the property was held by both the donor and the donee, if the donee is required to use as his basis the basis of the donor (Code Sec. 1223(2)).[171] When the fair market value at the time of the gift is used to determine the loss and such fair market value is greater than the donor's basis in the property, the holding period of the donor is not used (IRS Pub. 544).

Inherited. For property acquired from a decedent, the long-term holding period requirement is generally considered to be met (Code Sec. 1223(11)).[172]

Converted. The holding period of property acquired in an involuntary conversion includes the holding period of the property converted if the basis of the new property is determined by reference to the basis of the old (Code Sec. 1223(1)(A)).[173]

Stock. The holding period for stock purchased on an exchange begins on the day following the day of purchase (i.e., the trade date), and ends on, and includes, the date of sale (rather than the day when payment is received and delivery is made (i.e., the settlement date)) (Rev. Rul. 93-84).[174] The holding period for stock received in a nontaxable stock distribution or in a "spin-off" includes the holding period of the related stock on which the distribution is made (Code Sec. 1223(1) and (5)).[175]

Options. When assets are acquired by the exercise of a purchase option, the holding period starts the day after the option is exercised.[176]

Partnership Property. The holding period for property distributed to a partner includes the period for which the partnership held the property (Code Sec. 735(b)).[177]

Footnote references are to paragraphs of the 2002 Standard Federal Tax Reports.

[168] ¶ 30,463.3997	[172] ¶ 30,460	[175] ¶ 30,460
[169] ¶ 30,463.023,	[173] ¶ 30,460	[176] ¶ 30,463.4013
¶ 30,463.4099	[174] ¶ 30,463.4383	[177] ¶ 25,400
[170] ¶ 30,460		
[171] ¶ 30,460		

¶ 1777

Treasury Obligations. In determining the holding period of U.S. Treasury Notes and Bonds sold at auction on the basis of yield, the acquisition date is the date the Secretary of Treasury, through news releases, gives notification of the successful bidders. The acquisition date of U.S. Treasury Notes sold through an offering on a subscription basis at a specified yield is the date the subscription is submitted (Rev. Rul. 78-5).[178]

Disposition of Depreciable Property

1779. Depreciation Recapture Rules. *Code Sec. 1245 Property.* A gain on the sale or other disposition of Code Sec. 1245 property (¶ 1785) is taxed as ordinary income to the extent of all depreciation or amortization deductions previously claimed on the property. Amounts expensed under Code Sec. 179 (¶ 1208), Code Sec. 190, for the removal of architectural and transportation barriers (¶ 1287), and Code Sec. 193, for tertiary injectant costs, are considered amortization deductions (Code Sec. 1245(a)).[179]

The amount treated as ordinary income is the excess of the lower of (1) the property's recomputed basis or (2) the amount realized or fair market value over the adjusted basis of the Code Sec. 1245 property. The recomputed basis is the property's adjusted basis plus previously allowed or allowable depreciation or amortization reflected in the adjusted basis.

A disposition of Code Sec. 1245 property includes a sale in a sale-and-leaseback transaction and a transfer upon the foreclosure of a security interest but does not include a mere transfer of title to a creditor upon creation of a security interest or to a debtor upon termination of a security interest (Reg. § 1.1245-1).[180]

Code Sec. 1250 Property. Depreciable real property, other than that included within the definition of Code Sec. 1245 property, is subject to depreciation recapture under Code Sec. 1250. (Code Sec. 1250 property is defined at ¶ 1786.) Gain on the sale or other disposition of Code Sec. 1250 property is treated as ordinary income, rather than capital gain, to the extent of the excess of post-1969 depreciation allowances over the depreciation that would have been available under the straight-line method. See ¶ 1780. However, if Code Sec. 1250 property is held for one year or less, all depreciation (and not just the excess over straight-line depreciation) is recaptured (Code Sec. 1250(b)(1)).[181] See ¶ 1736 for capital gains treatment of "unrecaptured Section 1250 gain."

Special recapture rules phase out the recapture by reducing it by 1% for each full month the Code Sec. 1250 property is held over a specified period in the case of (1) residential rental property, (2) certain types of subsidized housing, and (3) Code Sec. 1250 property for which rapid depreciation of rehabilitation expenditures was claimed (Code Sec. 1250(a)(1)(B) and (2)(B)).[182]

The recapture rules apply notwithstanding any other provision of the Code. In the case of a sale to a related party (see ¶ 1717), gain that is not recaptured may still be treated as ordinary income under Code Sec. 1239.[183]

Code Sec. 1250 property may be made up of two or more "elements" with separate holding periods. Where this occurs, the recapture must be determined separately for each element (Code Sec. 1250(f)(3)).[184]

Installment Sale. In the case of disposal of recapture property in an installment sale, any recapture income (i.e., ordinary income under Code Sec. 1245 or 1250) is to be recognized in the year of the disposition, and any gain in excess of the recapture income is to be reported under the installment method (Code Sec. 453(i)).[185]

Additional Recapture from Corporations. For corporations, the amount treated as ordinary income on the sale or other disposition of Code Sec. 1250 property is increased by 20% of the additional amount that would be treated as ordinary income

---

Footnote references are to paragraphs of the 2002 Standard Federal Tax Reports.

[178] ¶ 30,463.67 [181] ¶ 31,000 [184] ¶ 31,000
[179] ¶ 30,902 [182] ¶ 31,000 [185] ¶ 21,402
[180] ¶ 30,903 [183] ¶ 30,730

¶ 1779

if the property were subject to recapture under the rules for Code Sec. 1245 property (Code Sec. 291(a)(1)).[186]

Reporting Recapture. Form 4797 (Sales of Business Property) is used to calculate and report the amount of recaptured depreciation.

1780. Depreciation Subject to Recapture. In general, depreciation on tangible property placed in service after 1986 is determined under the Modified Accelerated Cost Recovery System (MACRS). Property placed in service after 1980 and before 1987 is covered under the Accelerated Cost Recovery System (ACRS). See ¶ 1216 and following.

MACRS. Gain on the disposition of tangible personal property is treated as ordinary income to the extent of previously allowed MACRS deductions. If property from a general asset account is disposed of, the full amount of proceeds realized on the disposition is treated as ordinary income to the extent the unadjusted depreciable basis of the account (increased by amounts allowed as deductions under Code Secs. 179 and 190 for assets in the account) exceeds previously recognized ordinary income from prior dispositions (Reg. § 1.168(i)-1(e)).[187]

Residential rental property and nonresidential real property that is placed in service after 1986 and is subject to the MACRS rules must be depreciated under the straight-line MACRS method. Therefore, recapture of depreciation on such property is not required because no depreciation in excess of straight-line depreciation could have been taken.

ACRS. Gain on the disposition of personal recovery property and nonresidential real recovery property is treated as ordinary income to the extent of previously allowed ACRS deductions.[188] Gain on the disposition of residential rental real recovery property is treated as ordinary income to the extent that ACRS deductions exceed straight-line ACRS depreciation over the recovery period applicable to such property. Consequently, there would be no recapture if the straight-line ACRS method was elected for real property.

On the disposition of assets from mass asset accounts, taxpayers recognize the amount of the proceeds realized as ordinary income to the extent of the unadjusted basis in the account less any amounts previously included in income. Any excess proceeds realized are treated as capital gain, unless a nonrecognition provision applies. As far as the recovery of depreciation is concerned, the mass asset account is treated as though there was no disposition of the asset, and the unadjusted basis of the property is left in the capital account until fully recovered in future years (Code Sec. 168(d)(2), prior to amendment by P.L. 97-34).

Amounts Excluded from Depreciation Adjustments. In determining the amount of additional depreciation taken before the disposition of Code Sec. 1250 property, a taxpayer's depreciation adjustments do *not* include amortization of emergency facilities, pollution control facilities, railroad grading and tunnel bores, child care facilities, expenditures to remove architectural and transportation barriers to the handicapped and elderly, or tertiary injections (Code Sec. 1250(b)(3)).[189]

1783. Recapture of Investment Credit Basis Reductions. In determining the amount of gain that is recaptured as ordinary income on a sale or disposition of depreciable personal property (Code Sec. 1245) or depreciable realty (Code Sec. 1250), the amount of an investment credit downward basis adjustment is subject to recapture (see ¶ 1360).

1785. Code Sec. 1245 Property. Code Sec. 1245 property is property that is or has been depreciable (or subject to amortization under Code Sec. 197) and that is either (1) personal property (tangible and intangible) or (2) other tangible property (not including a building or its structural components) used as an integral part of (a) manufacturing, (b) production, (c) extraction, or (d) the furnishing of transportation, communications, electrical energy, gas, water, or sewage disposal services (Reg.

Footnote references are to paragraphs of the 2002 Standard Federal Tax Reports.

§ 1.1245-3).[190] The term "other tangible property" includes research facilities or facilities for the bulk storage of fungible commodities used in connection with the activities in (a)-(d). A leasehold of Code Sec. 1245 property is also treated as Code Sec. 1245 property (Reg. § 1.1245-3).[191]

Livestock is considered Code Sec. 1245 property, and depreciation on purchased draft, breeding, dairy and sporting livestock is recaptured as ordinary income when sold. Raised livestock generally has no basis for depreciation, but to the extent that it does have a basis and is depreciated, it would be subject to recapture.[192]

Code Sec. 1245 property also includes so much of any real property (except "other property" described at (2) above) that has an adjusted basis reflecting adjustments for amortization of pollution control facilities, child care facilities, or railroad grading and tunnel bores; expenditures for removal of architectural and transportation barriers to the handicapped and elderly, reforestation, or tertiary injectants; and amounts expensed under Code Sec. 179. Code Sec. 1245 property also includes single purpose agricultural and horticultural structures and storage facilities used in connection with the distribution of petroleum products (Code Sec. 1245(a)(3)).[193]

1786. Code Sec. 1250 Property. Code Sec. 1250 property is any real property that is or has been depreciable under Code Sec. 167 but is not subject to recapture under Code Sec. 1245. This includes all intangible real property (such as leases of land or Code Sec. 1250 property), buildings and their structural components, and all tangible real property except Code Sec. 1245 property (Code Sec. 1250(c)).[194] For real property covered by Code Sec. 1245 rather than Code Sec. 1250, see ¶ 1785.

1788. Gift of Code Sec. 1245 or 1250 Property. The recapture rules at ¶ 1779 do not apply in the case of disposition by gift or to transfers at death (except a taxable transfer of Code Sec. 1245 or 1250 property in satisfaction of a specific bequest of money) (Reg. § 1.1245-4).[195] Upon a later sale, however, the donee will realize the same amount of ordinary income that the donor would have realized if the donor had retained the property and sold it (except in the case of a tax-exempt donee). Also, if the taxpayer contributes Code Sec. 1245 or 1250 property to a charitable organization, the allowable charitable contribution deduction is reduced by the amount that would have been treated as ordinary income if the taxpayer had sold the asset at its fair market value (Code Sec. 170(e)).[196] See ¶ 1062 concerning charitable gifts of appreciated property.

1789. Disposal in Tax-Free Transaction. When Code Sec. 1245 or 1250 property is disposed of in certain tax-free transactions (i.e., Code Sec. 332, 351, 361, 721, or 731), the transferor takes into account Code Sec. 1245 or 1250 gain only to the extent that gain is recognized under those sections (Code Secs. 1245(b)(3) and 1250(d)(3)).[197] However, when there is an otherwise tax-free transfer under one of those sections to a tax-exempt organization (other than a cooperative described in Code Sec. 521), Code Sec. 1245 or 1250 gain is recognized in full to the transferor. On a later sale of Code Sec. 1245 or 1250 property received in one of the above tax-free transactions, the transferee realizes Code Sec. 1245 or 1250 gain to the extent of the transferor's unrecognized Code Sec. 1245 or 1250 gain plus depreciation deducted by the transferee (not to exceed the actual gain).

1790. Exchange or Conversion. If Code Sec. 1245 or 1250 property is exchanged for like-kind property (¶ 1721) or is involuntarily converted (¶ 1713), Code Sec. 1245 or 1250 gain is recognized to the extent of any gain recognized on the exchange (if money or other property is received) or on the conversion (when the conversion proceeds are not all spent on replacement property) plus the fair market value of any property received in the exchange or acquired as replacement property

---

Footnote references are to paragraphs of the 2002 Standard Federal Tax Reports.

[190] ¶ 30,905	[193] ¶ 30,902	[196] ¶ 11,600
[191] ¶ 30,905	[194] ¶ 31,000	[197] ¶ 30,902, ¶ 31,000
[192] ¶ 30,909.021	[195] ¶ 30,906	

¶ 1790

that is not Code Sec. 1245 or 1250 property (Reg. § § 1.1245-4(d) and 1.1250-3(d)).[198]

1792. Partnership Distribution. No Code Sec. 1245 or 1250 gain is recognized on a distribution by a partnership to a partner when no gain is recognized under Code Sec. 731. However, under Code Sec. 751(c) and for the purposes of Code Secs. 731 and 741, the term "unrealized receivables" includes Code Sec. 1245 and 1250 gains (computed as if the partnership sold the property at its fair market value when distributed) (Code Sec. 751(c)).[199] Thus, ordinary income is realized to the extent of potential Code Sec. 1245 and 1250 gains in the sale of a partnership interest and in distributions to a partner (Reg. § § 1.1245-4(f) and 1.1250-3(f)).[200]

1793. Corporate Disposition. When a corporation distributes Code Sec. 1245 or 1250 property as a dividend or in partial or complete liquidation and no gain is otherwise recognized to the corporation under Code Sec. 311 or 336, Code Sec. 1245 or 1250 gain has to be recognized by the corporation to the same degree that it would have been had the corporation sold the property at its fair market value on the date of distribution (Reg. § § 1.1245-1(c) and 1.1250-1(c)).[201]

1795. Adjustments to Basis. When Code Sec. 1245 or 1250 gain is recognized in an exchange of like-kind property under Code Sec. 1031 or an involuntary conversion under Code Sec. 1033 (¶ 1790), the basis of the acquired property is to be determined under those Code sections (Reg. § 1.1245-5).[202]

> **Example.** Greg exchanges Code Sec. 1245 property with an adjusted basis of $10,000 for like-kind Code Sec. 1245 property with a fair market value of $9,000 and unlike property with a fair market value of $3,500. Gain of $2,500 is recognized because unlike property was received. The basis of the property acquired by Greg is $12,500 ($10,000 adjusted basis of the transferred property plus $2,500 recognized gain), of which $3,500 (fair market value) is allocated to the unlike property and the remaining $9,000 is allocated to the acquired like-kind property.

Farmers' Recaptures

1797. Recapture on Land Sale. If farm land held for nine years or less is disposed of, a percentage of the total post-1969 deductions for soil and water conservation expenditures and land clearance expenditures will be recaptured as ordinary income on Form 4797 (Sales of Business Property) (Code Sec. 1252).[203] If the land is held for five years or less, the recapture percentage is 100%. The recapture percentage is 80% if disposal is within the sixth year after acquisition. For the seventh, eighth and ninth years, the recapture percentages are 60%, 40%, and 20%, respectively. There is no recapture after the ninth year (Code Sec. 1252(a)(3)).[204]

The recapture covers only *deductible* soil and water conservation expenditures. In the case of a transaction between related parties, gain that is not recaptured may be treated as ordinary income under Code Sec. 1239.[205] See ¶ 1779.

Exempt Transfers. Exceptions to the farm land expenditure recapture rule exist (similar to those in Code Sec. 1245(b), as explained at ¶ 1788 and ¶ 1789) for transfers by gift, transfers at death, and transfers in certain tax-free transactions (Reg. § 1.1252-2).[206]

Footnote references are to paragraphs of the 2002 Standard Federal Tax Reports.

[198] ¶ 30,906, ¶ 31,003	[201] ¶ 30,903, ¶ 31,001	[204] ¶ 31,020
[199] ¶ 25,500	[202] ¶ 30,907	[205] ¶ 30,730
[200] ¶ 30,906, ¶ 31,003	[203] ¶ 31,020	[206] ¶ 31,022

¶ 1792

Chapter 18

INSTALLMENT SALES
DEFERRED PAYMENT SALES

INSTALLMENT SALES

Reporting of Gain

1801. Use of Installment Method. The installment method is a special method of reporting gains (not losses) from sales of property when at least one payment is received in a tax year after the year of sale. Under the installment method, gain from an installment sale is prorated and recognized over the years in which payments are received.

Prohibition for Dealer Dispositions. The installment method may only be used for reporting gain from nondealer sales of property other than inventory. Dealer dispositions of property (see ¶ 1808) may not be reported under the installment method (Code Sec. 453(b)(2)(A)).[1] Thus, even though a dealer expects to receive payments from such dispositions in future years, all payments are treated as if they were received in the year of disposition.

Repeal of Prohibition for Accrual Taxpayers. The Installment Tax Correction Act of 2000 (P.L. 106-573) retroactively repealed the provision in the Ticket to Work and Work Incentives Improvement Act of 1999 (P.L. 106-170) which prohibited accrual basis taxpayers from using the installment method of accounting. The repeal applies to dispositions occurring on or after December 17, 1999 (the date of enactment of P.L. 106-170). The retroactive repeal allows businesses sold in 2000 under an installment sale to file for refunds on estimated tax payments and to ignore the repealed law entirely when filing 2000 tax year returns (Notice 2001-22).

Footnote references are to paragraphs of the 2002 Standard Federal Tax Reports.
[1] ¶ 21,402

¶ 1801

Gain Calculation. The amount of gain from an installment sale that is taxable in a given year is calculated by multiplying the payments received in that year by the gross profit ratio for the sale (Code Sec. 453(c)).[2] The gross profit ratio is equal to the anticipated gross profit divided by the total contract price (see ¶ 1813). However, gain from installment sales of depreciable property subject to recapture under Code Sec. 1245 or 1250 is determined under a special rule (see ¶ 1823).

> **Example.** On December 1, 2001, a calendar year taxpayer sells his *personal* automobile for a total contract price of $2,500. He receives a $1,000 down payment, with the balance due in monthly installments of $100 each, plus interest at the applicable federal rate, beginning on January 1, 2002. His anticipated gross profit from the sale is $500. Under the installment method, the taxpayer must report $200 ($1,000 × ($500 ÷ $2,500)) as income in 2001, $240 ($1,200 × ($500 ÷ $2,500)) in 2002, and $60 ($300 × ($500 ÷ $2,500)) in 2003.

Income from an installment sale is reported on Form 6252, "Installment Sale Income," which must be filed with the tax return in the year of sale and in each year payments are received.

1802. Character of Gain on Installment Sale. Although use of the installment method affects when gain from an installment sale is reported, it does not affect the characterization of the gain as capital gain or ordinary income. Such characterization depends on the nature of the asset sold (see ¶ 1735 and ¶ 1741).

1803. Election Out. A qualifying sale must be reported on the installment method unless the taxpayer elects not to use the installment method (Code Sec. 453(d)).[3] Such an election may be made by reporting the entire gain on a timely filed tax return for the year of sale. Untimely elections will generally not be permitted. Valid elections can be revoked only with IRS consent (Temporary Reg. § 15A.453-1(d)).[4]

1805. Publicly Traded Property and Revolving Credit Plans. The installment method may not be used for sales of personal property under a revolving credit plan, sales of stock or securities that are traded on an established securities market and, to the extent provided by regulations, sales of other property of a kind that is regularly traded on an established market. All payments to be received from such sales are treated as received in the year of disposition (Code Sec. 453(k)).[5]

Dealer Sales

1808. Dealers May Not Use Installment Method. Dealers in real and personal property may not use the installment method to report the gain from "dealer dispositions." A "dealer disposition" includes (1) any disposition of personal property by a person who regularly sells or otherwise disposes of such property on the installment plan and (2) any disposition of real property that is held by the taxpayer for sale to customers in the ordinary course of the taxpayer's trade or business (Code Sec. 453(l)(1)).[6] However, some exceptions to these general rules are provided for dispositions of farm property, residential lots and timeshares (Code Sec. 453(l)(2))[7] (¶ 1811).

1811. Exceptions to "Dealer Disposition" Rule. Gains from the following transactions may be reported using the installment method since these transactions have been excluded from the term "dealer disposition": (1) the disposition of any property used or produced in the trade or business of farming, (2) the disposition of any residential lot, provided that the dealer or any related person is not obligated to make any improvements to the lot, and (3) the disposition of timeshare rights to use or own residential real property for not more than six weeks per year or

---

Footnote references are to paragraphs of the 2002 Standard Federal Tax Reports.

¶ 1802   [2] ¶ 21,402   [4] ¶ 21,404   [6] ¶ 21,402
               [3] ¶ 21,402   [5] ¶ 21,402   [7] ¶ 21,402

a right to use specified campgrounds for recreational purposes. In order to use the installment method for the disposition of residential lots and timeshares, the taxpayer must elect to pay interest (at the applicable federal rate in effect at the time of sale, compounded semiannually (see ¶ 1875)) on the amount of tax that is attributable to the installment payments received during the year for the period beginning on the date of sale and ending on the date the payment is received (Code Sec. 453(l)(3)).[8]

Nondealer Sales

1813. Nondealer Dispositions of Property. For nondealer dispositions that are not subject to the Code Sec. 1245 or 1250 recapture provisions, the amount of income reported from an installment sale in any tax year (including the year of sale) is equal to the payments received during that year multiplied by the gross profit ratio for the sale. (For a discussion of the various forms of payment, see ¶ 1819.)

The gross profit ratio is equal to the gross profit on the sale divided by the total contract price. The gross profit is equal to the selling price of the property minus its adjusted basis. The selling price of the property is not reduced by any existing mortgage or encumbrance, or by any selling expenses, but is reduced by interest that is imputed under Code Sec. 483 (¶ 1868).

The total contract price (denominator of gross profit ratio) is equal to the selling price minus that portion of qualifying indebtedness (¶ 1815) assumed by, or taken subject to, the buyer that does not exceed the seller's basis in the property (adjusted to reflect commissions and other selling expenses) (Temporary Reg. § 15A.453-1(b)(2)).[9] In the case of an installment sale that is a partially nontaxable like-kind exchange (see ¶ 1723), the gross profit is reduced by that portion of the gain that is not recognized, and the total contract price is reduced by the value of the like-kind property received (Code Sec. 453(f)(6)).[10]

For certain nondealer sales of property for over $150,000, a special interest charge may apply (¶ 1825).

1815. Qualifying Indebtedness. Qualifying indebtedness, for the purpose of determining the total contract price, includes (1) any mortgage or other indebtedness encumbering the property and (2) any indebtedness not secured by the property but incurred or assumed by the purchaser incident to his acquisition, holding or operation of the property in the ordinary course of business or investment (Temporary Reg. § 15A.453-1(b)(2)).[11]

Qualifying indebtedness does not include an obligation of the seller incurred incident to *disposition* of the property nor does it include an obligation functionally unrelated to the acquisition, holding or operation of the property. Any obligation incurred or assumed in contemplation of disposition of the property is not qualifying indebtedness if recovery of the seller's basis is accelerated.

1817. Wrap-Around Mortgage. When property encumbered by an outstanding mortgage is sold in exchange for an installment obligation equal to the mortgage, the installment obligation is said to "wrap around" the mortgage. The seller generally uses the payments received from the installment obligation to pay the "wrapped" mortgage. In such a situation, the IRS will follow the Tax Court's position [12] and will not treat the buyer as having taken the property subject to, or as having assumed, the seller's mortgage. Thus, the seller will not have to reduce the total contract price by the amount of the wrapped mortgage.

1819. Installment Payments. When determining the amount of reportable income under the installment method, cash and the following debt instruments are treated as payments received: (1) evidence of indebtedness of a person other

---

[8] ¶ 21,402   [10] ¶ 21,402   [12] ¶ 21,412.036
[9] ¶ 21,404   [11] ¶ 21,404

than the buyer; (2) evidence of indebtedness of the buyer that is payable on demand, readily tradable, or issued with coupons or in registered form; (3) a bank certificate or treasury note; (4) qualifying indebtedness assumed by, or taken subject to, the buyer to the extent it exceeds the seller's basis for the sold property, as adjusted for selling expenses; (5) seller's indebtedness to the buyer that is canceled; and (6) indebtedness on the sold property (for which the seller is not personally liable), where the buyer is the obligee of the indebtedness (Temporary Reg. § 15A.453-1(b)(3)).[13]

Debt instruments in registered form that the seller can establish are not readily tradable are not considered payments. In addition, like-kind property received in a partially tax-free exchange (¶ 1723) that is part of an installment sales transaction is not treated as a payment for purposes of determining the amount of income to be reported under the installment method (Code Sec. 453(f)(6)).[14]

1821. Contingent Payment Sales. A contingent payment sale (i.e., one in which the total selling price is not determinable by the close of the tax year in which the sale occurs) must be reported on the installment method unless the seller elects out of the installment method treatment (Temporary Reg. § 15A.453-1(c)(1)).[15]

In a contingent payment sale, the basis of the property sold (including selling expenses) is allocated to payments received in each tax year and recovered as follows: (1) for sales with a stated maximum selling price, basis is recovered according to a profit ratio based on the stated maximum selling price; (2) for sales with a fixed payment period, basis is recovered ratably over the fixed period; and (3) for sales with neither a maximum selling price nor a fixed payment period, basis is recovered ratably over a 15-year period (Temporary Reg. § 15A.453-1(c)(2)–(4)).[16] However, alternate methods of basis recovery may be required where the normal method would substantially accelerate or defer the recovery of basis (Temporary Reg. § 15A.453-1(c)(7)).[17]

1823. Dispositions of Property Subject to Recapture Provisions. In the case of installment dispositions of real or personal property to which Code Sec. 1245 or 1250 applies, any recapture income must be reported in the year of disposition, whether or not an installment payment is received in that year (Code Sec. 453(i)).[18] The ordinary income amount reported in the year of sale is added to the property's basis, and this adjusted basis is used in determining the remaining profit on the disposition.[19] The remaining profit amount is used to compute the gross profit percentage to be applied to each installment payment.

> **Example.** On December 1, 2001, a calendar year taxpayer sells his rental building for a total contract price of $100,000, plus interest at the applicable federal rate. He receives a note due in yearly installments of $20,000, plus interest, beginning January 1, 2002. His basis in the building is $20,000. Assuming that $10,000 of the $80,000 gain is real property recapture income (the amount of depreciation recapturable under Code Sec. 1250), the entire $10,000 is included in ordinary income in 2001 (the year of sale). The $10,000 is added to his $20,000 basis for purposes of determining the gross profit on the remaining gain. Gross profit is, therefore, $70,000 ($100,000 − $30,000). Of each $20,000 payment received in the following years, $14,000 is includible in income ($20,000 × ($70,000 ÷ $100,000)).

1825. Special Interest Rule for Nondealers of Property. A special interest charge may apply to nondealer dispositions of real or personal property having a sales price of over $150,000 (Code Sec. 453A).[20] The interest charge does not apply to nondealer dispositions of (1) property used in the trade or business of

---

Footnote references are to paragraphs of the 2002 Standard Federal Tax Reports.

¶ 1821

[13] ¶ 21,404	[16] ¶ 21,404	[19] ¶ 21,402.049
[14] ¶ 21,402	[17] ¶ 21,404	[20] ¶ 21,450
[15] ¶ 21,404	[18] ¶ 21,402	

farming or (2) personal use property, which is property that is not substantially used in connection with the taxpayer's trade or business or in an investment activity. Also, the interest charge does not apply to dispositions of timeshares and residential lots (but the interest rule described in ¶ 1811 will apply).

The interest charge is imposed on the tax deferred under the installment method with respect to outstanding installment obligations, but the charge will not apply unless the face amount of all obligations of the taxpayer that arose during and remain outstanding at the close of the tax year exceeds $5,000,000 (Code Sec. 453A(b)(2)(B)).[21]

If any indebtedness is secured by a nondealer installment obligation that arises from the disposition of any real or personal property having a sales price of over $150,000, the net proceeds of the secured indebtedness will be treated as a payment received on the installment obligation on the later of the date that the indebtedness is secured or the date that the net proceeds are received.

Related-Party Sales

1833. Property Sales to Related Persons. When a person makes an installment sale of property to a related person (first disposition) who, in turn, sells the property before the installment payments are made in full (second disposition), the amount realized by the related party from the second disposition is treated as received by the initial seller at the time of the second disposition (Code Sec. 453(e)(1)).[22] A related person for this purpose includes the seller's spouse, child, grandchild, parent, grandparent, brother, sister, controlled corporation, partnership, trust, or estate (Code Sec. 453(f)(1)).[23] In most cases, however, the related-party rule will not apply if the second disposition took place more than two years after the first disposition (Code Sec. 453(e)(2)).[24]

In applying the resale rule, the amount treated as received by the initial seller is limited to the lesser of (1) the total amount realized from the second disposition before the close of the tax year of disposition or (2) the total contract price for the first disposition, reduced by the sum of the total amount received from the first disposition before the close of the year of the second disposition and the total amount treated as received for prior years under the resale rule (Code Sec. 453(e)(3)).[25]

Dispositions excluded from application of the resale rule are (1) first dispositions which are nonliquidating installment sales of stock to the issuing corporation, (2) second dispositions resulting from involuntary conversions of the property if the initial installment sale occurred before the threat or imminence of conversion, and (3) second dispositions occurring after the death of the installment seller or the related purchaser.

1835. Depreciable Property Sales. In most cases, the installment method cannot be used for installment sales of depreciable property between related persons. Therefore, all payments are deemed received in the year of disposition unless the disposition did not have as one of its principal purposes the avoidance of federal tax (Code Sec. 453(g)).[26] For this purpose, the term "related person" is defined in Code Sec. 1239(b) (¶ 1744) and includes corporations and partnerships that are more than 50 percent owned, either directly or indirectly, by the same person.

Repossessions of Property

1838. Repossession of Personal Property. When personal property that was sold in an installment sale is repossessed, the repossession is treated as a disposition of the installment obligation. Gain or loss is measured by the difference between

Footnote references are to paragraphs of the 2002 Standard Federal Tax Reports.

| [21] ¶ 21,450 | [23] ¶ 21,402 | [25] ¶ 21,402 |
| [22] ¶ 21,402 | [24] ¶ 21,402 | [26] ¶ 21,402 |

¶ 1838

the basis of the obligation in the hands of the seller and the fair market value of the property at the date of repossession. The basis of the obligation in the hands of the seller is equal to the face value of the obligation minus the deferred gross profit on the sale at the time of repossession (IRS Pub. 537, Installment Sales).[27] The character of the gain or loss, if any, on the repossession is the same as on the original sale.

If the installment obligation is not completely satisfied by repossession of the property, and the seller is unable to collect the balance of the debt, he may be able to claim a bad debt deduction for the portion of the obligation that is not satisfied through repossession (¶ 1145 and ¶ 1169).

1841. Repossession of Real Estate. When real property is sold on the installment plan and the seller accepts an installment debt secured by the property, the seller will recognize only a limited amount of gain and no loss upon repossession of the property. Gain on the repossession is limited to the lesser of:

(1) the sum of the money and fair market value of other property (other than buyer obligations) received before repossession minus the amount of the gain from the original sale that is reported as income for pre-repossession periods; or

(2) the gain on the original sale (selling price less adjusted basis) reduced by income reported for pre-repossession periods and by repossession costs (money and fair market value of property, other than buyer's obligations, paid or transferred by the seller in connection with reacquisition) (Code Sec. 1038; Reg. § 1.1038-1).[28]

The same rules apply where an estate or beneficiary repossesses real property sold by the decedent on the installment method (Code Sec. 1038(g)).[29]

Repossession of Principal Residence. Special repossession rules apply if a seller repossesses a principal residence that he sold under the installment method but deferred the tax due because he acquired a replacement residence or excluded gain under Code Sec. 121 (¶ 1705 (post-May 6, 1997 sales); ¶ 1706 (pre-May 7, 1997 sales by sellers age 55 or older)). Basically, if the seller resells the residence within one year of repossession, the original sale and the resale are treated as one transaction and his gain is determined on the combined sale and resale (Code Sec. 1038(e)).[30] If the resale does not take place within one year, the general rules for repossessions of real property apply.

1843. Basis After Repossession of Real Estate. Generally, the basis of repossessed real property is the adjusted basis to the seller of the debt secured by the property (determined at the time of the repossession), increased by any gain recognized at the time of the repossession and by the seller's repossession costs (Code Sec. 1038(c)).[31] If the debt to the seller is not discharged as a result of the repossession, the basis of the debt is zero. If the seller, before repossession, has treated the secured debt as having become worthless or partially worthless, he is considered as having received, upon repossession, an amount equal to that which he treated as worthless. However, his adjusted basis in the debt is increased by the same amount (Code Sec. 1038(d)).[32]

Dispositions of Installment Obligations

1846. Recognition of Gain or Loss. Gain or loss is generally recognized when installment obligations are sold, disposed of, or satisfied at other than their face value (Code Sec. 453B(a)).[33] The amount of gain or loss is the difference between the basis of the obligation and either (1) the amount realized, if the obligation is satisfied at other than face value or is sold or exchanged, or (2) the fair market value of the obligation, if the obligation is distributed or disposed of other

---

[27] ¶ 21,406.048	[30] ¶ 29,740	[32] ¶ 29,740
[28] ¶ 29,740, ¶ 29,741	[31] ¶ 29,740	[33] ¶ 21,470
[29] ¶ 29,740		

than by sale or exchange. For this purpose, the basis of the obligation to the transferor is the excess of the face value of the obligation over an amount equal to the income that would have been returnable had the obligation been satisfied in full (Code Sec. 453B(b)).[34]

Installment obligations that are canceled, or that lapse, are treated as dispositions other than sales or exchanges (Code Sec. 453B(f)).[35] This includes a self-canceling installment note that is extinguished at the death of the holder.[36] Therefore, gain or loss is computed based on the fair market value of the obligation.

The character of any resulting gain or loss on the disposition of an installment obligation is determined by reference to the character of the original asset that was sold, whether it be a capital or noncapital asset (Code Sec. 453B(a)).[37] For a discussion of capital assets, see ¶ 1741.

1849. Transfers Between Spouses. The transfer of an installment obligation between spouses or incident to divorce (other than a transfer in trust) will not trigger recognition of gain. Thus, the same tax treatment applies to the transferee spouse as would have applied to the transferor spouse (Code Sec. 453B(g)).[38]

1854. Effect of Death on Installment Obligations. Installment obligations acquired from a decedent are considered income in respect of a decedent (¶ 182) (Reg. § 1.453-9(e)).[39] The taxpayer who receives the installment payments (estate, beneficiary, etc.) must report as income the same portion of the payments that would have been taxable income to the decedent. The amount considered to be an item of gross income in respect of the decedent is the excess of the face value of the obligation over its basis in the hands of the decedent (Reg. § 1.691(a)-5).[40]

A decedent seller's estate is deemed to have made a taxable disposition of an installment obligation if the obligation is transferred by bequest, devise, or inheritance to the obligor or if the estate allows the obligation to become unenforceable. If the decedent and obligor-recipient of the obligation were related persons, the fair market value of the obligation may not be determined at less than its face amount (Code Secs. 453(f)(1) and 691(a)(5)).[41]

Sales of Accrual Corporations or Partnerships

1855. Sales of Accrual Corporations. A cash-basis shareholder of an accrual-basis C or S corporation can report the gain from the sale of nonpublicly traded stock in exchange for cash and an installment obligation on the installment method. Further, if such a C or S corporation engages in a direct sale of its *assets* in exchange for cash and an installment obligation, the corporation can report the gain on the installment method (Code Sec. 453(a)).

If a buyer of an accrual basis corporation's stock makes an election under Code Sec. 338(g) to treat the stock purchase as a purchase of the corporation's assets, the selling cash basis shareholder is not affected and can report the gain from the sale of the stock on the installment method. However, the corporation cannot report the gain from the deemed sale of assets on the installment method (Code Sec. 453(h)).

1855A. Sales of Accrual Partnerships. If a sale of a partnership interest otherwise qualifies for installment method reporting, a cash basis partner is not precluded from reporting on the installment method the gain arising from the sale of an interest in an accrual basis partnership in exchange for cash and an installment obligation. Also, an accrual basis partnership can report the gain from the sale of its assets on the installment method (Code Sec. 453(a)).

Footnote references are to paragraphs of the 2002 Standard Federal Tax Reports.

[34] ¶ 21,470 [37] ¶ 21,470 [40] ¶ 24,905
[35] ¶ 21,470 [38] ¶ 21,470 [41] ¶ 21,402, ¶ 24,900
[36] ¶ 21,471.15 [39] ¶ 21,416

¶ 1855A

Corporate Liquidations

1856. Reporting Gain. Liquidating corporations (other than certain liquidating S
corporations, see below) that distribute installment obligations to shareholders in exchange for their stock must currently recognize gain or loss from the
distribution. However, even if the liquidating corporation was accrual-based, the
shareholder that receives the installment obligation may use the installment method
to report the gain from the exchange under certain circumstances. An installment
obligation from a liquidating corporation whose stock is traded on an established
securities market is *not* a qualifying installment obligation. However, a shareholder
may use the installment method if the stock of the liquidating corporation is not
traded in established markets, even if the obligation arose from the sale by the
liquidating corporation of securities that are traded on the open market, provided
the liquidating corporation was not formed or used to get around the prohibition on
using the installment method for publicly traded stock.

Gain on the transfer of an installment obligation to a shareholder during a
liquidation (¶ 2253) is not immediately taxed to the shareholder. Instead, the
payments received under the installment obligation are treated as payments for the
stock, and any gain is included in the shareholder's income as payments are
received. This rule applies if: (1) stockholders exchange their stock in the corporation
in a Code Sec. 331 liquidation, (2) the corporation, during the 12-month period
beginning with the adoption of the plan of liquidation, had sold some or all of its
assets under the installment method, (3) the corporation, within that 12-month
period, distributes the installment notes acquired in connection with those sales to
the shareholders in exchange for their stock, and (4) the liquidation is completed
within that 12-month period. This rule does not apply to obligations arising from a
sale of inventory, stock in trade, or assets held for sale to customers in the ordinary
course of business unless those assets are sold in a bulk sale (Code Sec. 453(h)).[42]

S Corporation Liquidations. If an installment obligation is distributed by an S
corporation in a complete liquidation, and the receipt of the obligation is not treated
as payment for stock under the 12-month rule stated at ¶ 1856, then the corporation
generally recognizes no gain or loss on the distribution. This is true even for accrual
basis S corporations (Code Sec. 453B(h)).[43]

Subsidiary Liquidations. In a complete liquidation of a subsidiary in which gain
or loss on distributions of property generally is not recognized by the parent or the
subsidiary (¶ 2261), the distribution of installment obligations also will not cause
recognition of gain or loss (Code Sec. 453B(d)).[44]

DEFERRED PAYMENT SALES

Unstated Interest on Deferred Payment Sale

1859. Inadequate or Unpaid Interest on Nonpublic Debt Instruments. Generally, whenever a sale or exchange of property for more than $3,000 involves
the issuance of a debt instrument, adequate interest should be paid on the instrument. When adequate interest is not paid on a debt instrument, interest income
must be imputed to the seller or holder of the debt under the original issue discount
(OID) rules of Code Sec. 1274 or the unstated interest rules of Code Sec. 483. Code
Sec. 483 applies only if the transaction does not come within the scope of Code Sec.
1274 (Code Sec. 483(d)(1)).[45]

In some cases, however, neither Code Sec. 483 nor Code Sec. 1274 will operate
to impute interest to a transaction in which adequate interest is not charged or

Footnote references are to paragraphs of the 2002 Standard Federal Tax Reports.

¶ 1856 [42] ¶ 21,402   [44] ¶ 21,470   [45] ¶ 22,290
            [43] ¶ 21,470, ¶ 21,471.041

currently paid on a debt obligation given in exchange for property (Reg. § 1.483-1(a) and (c); Reg. § 1.1274-1(b)). In most of those cases, interest is imputed but is governed by other Code sections. For example, interest is imputed to certain obligations given in exchange for services or for the use of property under Code Secs. 404 and 467 (¶ 1541), respectively (Reg. § 1.1274-1(a)). Further, the interest imputation rules of Code Sec. 7872 will apply to certain below market demand loans (Reg. § 1.1274-1(b)(3)). Also, the Code Sec. 483 and 1274 rules do not apply to transfers of property between spouses, or incident to divorce, under Code Sec. 1041, to cash method debt instruments of Code Sec. 1274A(c), and to certain loans for personal use property of Code Sec. 1275(b).

The following steps should be applied with respect to deferred contracts: (1) determine whether the transaction is covered by either Code Sec. 483 or Code Sec. 1274; (2) test for unstated interest or OID; (3) compute the total unstated interest or OID under the contract; and (4) apportion the unstated interest or OID over the payments.

The unstated interest is income to the seller and, generally, a deduction to the buyer (Code Sec. 163(e)). Similarly, a portion of the OID must be included in income each year by the holder of the debt instrument, and an interest deduction is allowed to the issuer. However, there are exceptions as explained at ¶ 1887.

Unstated Interest or OID

1863. Scope of Code Sec. 1274. The OID rules apply to a debt instrument provided as consideration for the sale or exchange of property if (1) the stated redemption price at maturity for such debt instrument exceeds the stated principal amount (when there is adequate stated interest) or the imputed principal amount (in any other case) *and* (2) some or all of the payments under the instrument are due more than six months after the date of such sale or exchange. The term "stated redemption price at maturity" means the sum of all payments due under the debt instrument other than certain qualified interest payments (Code Sec. 1273(a)(2); Reg. § 1.1273-1(b)).[46] The "imputed principal amount" is equal to the sum of the present value of all payments due under the instrument, as determined by discounting the payments at 100% of the applicable federal rate in effect as of the date of the sale, compounded semiannually (Code Sec. 1274(b))[47] (¶ 1875).

Debt instruments that are given in consideration for the sale or exchange of property are covered by the unstated interest rules at ¶ 1868, rather than the OID rules, if the sale or exchange relates to (1) the sale of a farm for $1,000,000 or less by an individual, an estate, a testamentary trust, a small business corporation, or a partnership that meets requirements similar to those of a small business corporation; (2) the sale of a taxpayer's principal residence; (3) sales of property for $250,000 or less; (4) sales of publicly traded debt instruments or debt instruments issued for publicly traded property; (5) sales of patents to the extent that the amounts are contingent on the productivity, use, or disposition of the property transferred; and (6) land transfers of $500,000 or less between family members (Code Sec. 1274(c)(3); Reg. § 1.1274-1(b)).[48]

1868. Scope of Code Sec. 483. The unstated interest rules under Code Sec. 483 apply to any payments on the sale or exchange of property that are due more than six months after the sale or exchange if some payments are due more than one year after the sale or exchange.[49] Excepted from these rules are (1) debt instruments for which an issue price is determined under Code Sec. 1273(b)(1), (2) or (3) or Code Sec. 1274; (2) sales for $3,000 or less; (3) with respect to the buyer, any purchase of personal property or educational services (under Code Sec. 163(b)) on an installment basis if the interest charge cannot be ascertained and is treated as 6 percent; and (4)

Footnote references are to paragraphs of the 2002 Standard Federal Tax Reports.
[46] ¶ 31,280, ¶ 31,281   [48] ¶ 31,300, ¶ 31,301   [49] ¶ 22,290
[47] ¶ 31,300

¶ **1868**

sales or exchanges of patents to the extent of any payments that are contingent on the productivity, use or disposition of the property transferred (Code Sec. 483(d); Reg. § 1.483-1(c)).

1872. Testing for and Imputing OID or Unstated Interest. For purposes of the OID rules, there is adequate interest if the stated principal amount is less than or equal to the imputed principal amount (see ¶ 1863) (Code Sec. 1274(c)(2)).[50] Code Sec. 483 applies when there is "unstated interest." For this purpose, unstated interest is equal to the excess of the total payments (excluding any interest payments) due more than six months after the date of sale over the total of their present values (including the present values of any interest payments). The present value is generally determined by using a discount rate equal to the applicable federal rate (Code Sec. 483(b); Reg. § 1.483-3).[51] Different discount rates apply to certain transactions (see ¶ 1879).

1875. Applicable Federal Rates. For every calendar month, federal short-term, mid-term and long-term rates are determined by the IRS based on average market yields of specified maturities. For a sale or exchange, the applicable federal rate (AFR) is the lowest rate in effect for any month in the three-calendar-month period ending with the first calendar month in which there is a binding written contract (Reg. § 1.483-3(a); Reg. § 1.1274-4(a)). The AFR is determined by reference to the term of the debt instrument, including renewal and extension options, as shown in the following table (Code Sec. 1274(d)).[52]

Term of Debt Instrument:	Applicable Federal Rate:
Not over 3 years	Federal short-term rate.
Over 3 years but not over 9 years	Federal mid-term rate.
Over 9 years	Federal long-term rate.

For the applicable federal rates, see ¶ 83.

1879. Special Rates in Certain Situations. In computing the imputed principal amount for the OID rules or the present value of the total payments for the unstated interest rules, the 100-percent AFR discount rate does not apply in the following situations:

Sales and Leasebacks. A discount rate of 110 percent of the federal rate, compounded semiannually, applies to sale and leaseback transactions (Code Sec. 1274(e); Reg. § 1.1274-4(a)(2)).[53]

Qualified Debt Instruments. A discount rate not in excess of nine percent (if less than the AFR), compounded semiannually, applies to most debt instruments given in consideration for the sale or exchange of property if the stated principal amount does not exceed $2,800,000, adjusted for inflation in 1990 and thereafter (Code Sec. 1274A(a), (b) and (d); Reg. § 1.1274A-1(a)).[54] The 2001 inflation-adjusted amount is $4,085,900 for qualified debt instruments and $2,918,500 for cash-method debt instruments (Rev. Rul. 2000-55).[55]

Transfers of Land Between Family Members. The discount rate will not exceed six percent, compounded semiannually, in the case of transfers of land between family members. This rule only applies if the aggregate sales price of all prior land sales between the family members during the calendar year does not exceed $500,000. However, this limit on the discount rate does not apply if any party to the sale is a nonresident alien (Code Sec. 483(e); Reg. § 1.483-3(b)).[56]

1881. Assumptions of Debt. If any person in connection with the sale or exchange of property assumes any debt instrument or acquires any property subject to any debt instrument, in determining whether the unstated interest or OID rules apply, such assumption or acquisition is not taken into account unless the instru-

---

Footnote references are to paragraphs of the 2002 Standard Federal Tax Reports.

[50] ¶ 31,300	[53] ¶ 31,300, ¶ 31,304	[55] ¶ 22,299.03
[51] ¶ 22,290, ¶ 22,294	[54] ¶ 31,320, ¶ 31,321	[56] ¶ 22,290, ¶ 22,294
[52] ¶ 31,300		

¶ 1872

ment's terms and conditions are modified in a manner that would constitute an exchange (Code Sec. 1274(c)(4); Reg. § § 1.483-1(d) and 1.1274-5(b)).[57]

1883. Including the Imputed Interest. The amount of OID to be included in the income of the holder of the instrument is the sum of the daily portions of OID for each day of the tax year that the instrument is held. The daily portion is determined by allocating to each day in the accrual period the ratable portion of the increase in the adjusted issue price of the debt instrument. The increase in the issue price is computed by multiplying the adjusted issue price at the beginning of the accrual period by the yield to maturity (determined by compounding at the close of each accrual period) and subtracting from the result the sum of the interest payable under the instrument during such accrual period (Code Sec. 1272(a)(3); Reg. § 1.1272-1(b)).[58]

A special rule for determining OID applies to any regular interest in a REMIC (real estate mortgage investment conduit (¶ 2358)) or qualified mortgage held by a REMIC and to debt instruments that have a maturity that is initially fixed but is accelerated based on prepayments (or other events) made on other debt obligations securing the debt instrument (Code Sec. 1272(a)(6)).[59] Effective for tax years beginning after August 5, 1997, the special rules for determining OID also apply to pooled debt instruments.

The reporting of OID and unstated interest depends upon whether the seller is on the cash or accrual basis. Cash basis sellers include OID in income as accrued and unstated interest as interest income in the year payments are received. Sellers on the accrual basis include both OID and unstated interest in income in the year payments are due (Reg. § § 1.446-2(a) and 1.1272-1(a)).[60]

Treatment of Interest by Obligors

1887. Special Rules. In the case of the issuer of any debt instrument given in consideration for the sale or exchange of personal use property, the OID and unstated interest rules do not apply. Thus, OID or unstated interest is not deductible by the issuer but must be accrued by the holder. Personal use property means any property substantially all the use of which by the taxpayer is not in connection with the taxpayer's trade or business or the for-profit and other activities described in Code Sec. 212 (Code Sec. 1275(b)(1)).[61]

If a debt instrument is incurred in connection with the acquisition or carrying of personal use property by a cash-basis taxpayer, any OID or unstated interest is deductible only when paid (Code Sec. 1275(b)(2)).[62]

If a debt instrument issued after July 1, 1982 is held by a related foreign person, any OID is not deductible by the issuer until paid. However, this rule does not apply if the OID is effectively connected with the related foreign person's conduct of a trade or business in the United States (Code Sec. 163(e)).[63]

Footnote references are to paragraphs of the 2002 Standard Federal Tax Reports.

[57] ¶ 22,291, ¶ 31,300, ¶ 31,305
[58] ¶ 31,260, ¶ 31,261
[59] ¶ 31,260
[60] ¶ 20,610, ¶ 31,261
[61] ¶ 31,340
[62] ¶ 31,340
[63] ¶ 9102

Chapter 19

SECURITIES TRANSACTIONS

Treatment of Securities Transactions

1901. Securities Transactions. Gains and losses from a disposition of securities are generally calculated and taxed like gains and losses from dispositions of other property (see ¶ 1701). There are, however, exceptions and special rules. This chapter explains rules that are of special significance when securities are issued, sold, exchanged, or otherwise transferred.

1903. Dealer in Securities. Unlike securities held by investors, securities held for sale by dealers to their customers in the ordinary course of business are not capital assets. See ¶ 1760 for information concerning the proper classification of investors, dealers, and traders.

Mark-to-Market Requirements. The following mark-to-market rules apply to certain securities held by a dealer (Code Sec. 475(a)):[1] (1) any security that is inventory in the hands of the dealer must be included in inventory at its fair market value; and (2) any security that is not inventory in the hands of the dealer and that is held at the close of the tax year is treated as if sold by the dealer for its fair market value on the last business day of the year, and any gain or loss must be recognized in determining the dealer's gross income for the year.

If any gain or loss is taken into account under the second mark-to-market rule, then the amount of gain or loss realized on the eventual sale, exchange, or other disposition of the security is adjusted to reflect the gain or loss (Code Sec. 475(a)(2)).

The mark-to-market requirements do not apply to certain securities held by a dealer (e.g., those held for investment, notes and bonds acquired for the business but not held for sale and securities held for hedging purposes) (Code Sec. 475(b)(1)). However, in order for a security to be excluded from the mark-to-market requirements, it must be clearly identified in the dealer's records before the close of the day on which it was acquired, originated or entered into (Code Sec. 475(b)(2)).

The IRS has provided guidance on the mark-to-market requirement that addresses the definition of a dealer, exempt securities, and transitional issues (Rev. Rul. 97-39). Commodity dealers may elect to have the mark-to-market requirements apply to them in the same manner that the requirements apply to securities dealers (Code Sec. 475(b)(2)).

Footnote references are to paragraphs of the 2002 Standard Federal Tax Reports.

¶1901   [1] ¶ 22,265

Taxpayers can be dealers in securities and still trade other securities for their own investment purposes. As a result, if the business of being a dealer is simply a branch of the trading activities carried on by the taxpayer, the securities inventoried may include only those held for purposes of resale and not for investment (Reg. § 1.471-5).[2]

Traders In Securities or Commodities. Traders are defined as taxpayers who are in the business of buying and selling securities and/or commodities for their own accounts. Traders differ from investors in that traders seek to profit from daily market movements, their buying and selling activity is substantial, and they carry on the activity with continuity and regularity. Traders differ from dealers in that traders do not deal with customers. (See ¶ 1760 for more information concerning the difference in tax treatment between investors, traders and dealers.) Although traders are allowed to deduct expenses that are related to their trading activities as business expenses, gains and losses from their trading are generally treated as capital in nature. This is because noncapital asset treatment only covers securities that are held primarily for sale to customers (Code Sec. 1221(a)(1)). However, traders may make a mark-to-market election that allows them to treat their gains and losses as ordinary and not capital (Code Sec. 475(f)). The election is made by attaching a statement to the tax return for the year prior to the year in which the election is to take effect (e.g., the tax return for 2001 for the election to be effective for 2002). The statement should contain such information as: (1) the election is being made under Code Sec. 475(f), (2) the tax year for which the election is to be effective, and (3) the activity for which the election is being made (i.e., security trading). When a trader makes a mark-to-market election, as a general rule, the same mark-to-market requirements that apply to dealers also apply to the trader (Code Sec. 475(f)(1)(D)).

Income Items

1905. Taxation of Rights to Subscribe to Stock. Normally, a shareholder does not include in gross income the value of a stock dividend or a stock right declared by a corporation on its own shares (Code Sec. 305).[3] However, the distribution is taxed if it is: (1) in lieu of money, (2) a disproportionate distribution, (3) a distribution of convertible preferred stock, (4) a distribution of common and preferred stock, (5) a dividend on preferred stock, or (6) a transaction that increases the shareholder's proportionate interest. Under certain circumstances, a corporation may give "stock rights" (a right to purchase a certain amount of stock at a specified price) to some or all of its shareholders. Usually, the distribution of these rights is not a taxable event at the time of distribution (see ¶ 738). If "nontaxable" rights are granted, tax consequences occur when they are exercised or transferred (see ¶ 1907). In contrast, when "taxable" rights are received, their fair market value is includible in income at the time of receipt.

1907. Nontaxable Stock Distributions. The basis of stock on which a nontaxable distribution of stock or stock rights with a fair market value of 15% or more of the value of the stock is made is allocated between the stock and the rights (Code Sec. 307(b)). The allocation between the old stock and the new stock or the rights is made in proportion to their fair market values on the date of distribution. The date of distribution of the rights is the date on which the rights are distributed to the stockholder and *not* the record date (Reg. § 1.307-1).[4]

The taxpayer may *elect* to allocate basis in this way if nontaxable new stock or stock rights have a market value that is less than 15% of the value of the old stock on which the distribution was made. If the election is not made, the basis of the rights is zero and the basis of the stock on which the rights are issued remains unchanged (Reg. § 1.307-2).[5] (This is also the rule if the rights are allowed to lapse, regardless of their value.) The election to allocate basis to rights must be made in a

---

Footnote references are to paragraphs of the 2002 Standard Federal Tax Reports.

[2] ¶ 22,211   [4] ¶ 15,401   [5] ¶ 15,502.0215
[3] ¶ 15,303

¶ 1907

statement attached to the shareholder's return for the year in which the rights are received. The election is irrevocable with respect to the rights for which it is made. Also, the election must be made for all the rights received in a particular distribution by the shareholder on stock of the same class received by the shareholder at the time of the distribution.

> **Example.** Bob bought 100 shares of Yeta Company common stock at $125 per share and later received 100 rights entitling him to purchase 20 shares of new common stock in Yeta Company at $100 per share. When the rights were distributed, the old shares had a fair market value of $120 per share, and the rights had a fair market value of $3 each. Three weeks later, Bob sold his rights for $4 each. He elects to apportion basis.

Cost of old stock on which rights were distributed	$12,500.00
Market value of old stock at date of distribution of rights....	12,000.00
Market value of rights at date of distribution	300.00
Cost apportioned to old stock after distribution of rights (12,000/12,300 of $12,500)	12,195.12
Cost apportioned to rights (300/12,300 of $12,500).........	304.88
Selling price of rights	400.00
Gain ($400 − $304.88)	$ 95.12

> In determining gain or loss from any later sale of the stock on which the rights were distributed, the adjusted cost of the old stock is $12,195.12, or $121.95 a share.

The holding period of nontaxable stock rights includes the holding period of the stock on which the rights are distributed. The holding period of the stock acquired by the exercise of the rights begins on the date that the rights are exercised (Reg. § 1.1223-1(e)).[6]

1909. Basis After Exercise of Nontaxable Rights. The basis for gain or loss on a sale of stock acquired by exercise of nontaxable rights is found by adding the portion of the cost or other basis of the old stock allocated to the rights (determined as explained at ¶ 1907) to the subscription price of the new shares and dividing the sum by the number of shares obtained (Reg. § 1.307-1).[7]

1911. Corporation Dealing in Its Stock or Bonds. No gain or loss is recognized by a corporation when it receives money or other property in exchange for its own stock, including treasury stock, regardless of the nature of the transaction (Reg. § 1.1032-1(a)).[8] It is immaterial whether the stock is sold at a premium or a discount.

The nonrecognition rule also applies to the acquisition by a corporation of shares of its own stock in exchange for shares of its own stock (including treasury stock). Ordinarily, a corporation does not recognize gain or loss on the nonliquidation distribution of its stock (or rights) or on the distribution of property (e.g., a dividend) to shareholders. See ¶ 736. However, a corporation generally must recognize gain (but not loss) on the distribution to its shareholders of appreciated property. Gain is recognized to the extent that the property's fair market value exceeds its adjusted basis (Code Sec. 311(b)(1)).[9]

A corporation does not recognize gain or loss on bonds it issues at face value. If, however, it buys its bonds for less than their issue price or face value, the corporation will realize income (Reg. § 1.61-12(c)).[10] When bonds are issued on or after March 2, 1998, at a premium, the premium is income amortized as an offset to the corporation's allowable interest deduction (Reg. § 1.163-13(a)).[11] Any amount allocable to a conversion feature is not part of the premium (Code Sec. 171(b)(1)).[12] See also ¶ 1967.

Footnote references are to paragraphs of the 2002 Standard Federal Tax Reports.

[6] ¶ 30,461	[9] ¶ 15,450	[11] ¶ 9302D
[7] ¶ 15,401, ¶ 15,402.022	[10] ¶ 5801, ¶ 5804.47	[12] ¶ 11,850
[8] ¶ 29,623		

¶ 1909

Loss Items

1913. Surrender of Stock. Ordinarily, a stockholder's surrender of part of his stock to a corporation for resale, or to corporate creditors, will not result in a deductible loss even if other stockholders do not make a ratable contribution. The basis of the stock surrendered is reallocated to the basis of the remaining shares.[13]

1915. Loss from Worthless Stock. The cost or other basis of corporate stock is deducted in the year that it becomes completely worthless (Code Sec. 165(g); Reg. § 1.165-5).[14] No deduction is allowed for partially worthless stock. A loss from worthless stock that is a capital asset is ordinarily subject to the limitation on capital losses. See ¶ 1752 and ¶ 1764. However, in the case of loss on stock in a small business investment company, see ¶ 2392. The deduction for worthless securities is not available to dealers in securities that reflect the worthlessness of any security in inventories (Reg. § 1.165-5(g)).[15]

1917. Bond as Bad Debt. A bank, a financial institution described in Code Sec. 591, and a small business investment company operating under the Small Business Investment Act of 1958 are the only taxpayers that may treat wholly or partially worthless corporate bonds as ordinary losses (Code Sec. 582)[16] (see, also, ¶ 1764), except that a dealer in securities may take such losses by adjustments to inventory. For other taxpayers, a loss from any worthless security (bonds, debentures, notes, certificates, or other evidences of indebtedness, issued with interest coupons or in registered form) is deductible only when it is completely worthless (Code Sec. 165(g); Reg. § 1.165-4 and Reg. § 1.165-5),[17] and then it may be subject to the capital loss limitations (Code Sec. 1211).[18]

Options

1919. Option to Buy or Sell. An option is a right to buy or sell property at a stipulated price on or before a specified date. There is a capital gain or loss from sale or exchange of an option or a loss on failure to exercise it only if the property covered by the option is a capital asset in the hands of the taxpayer or would be a capital asset if acquired by him. For purposes of a loss from the failure of the holder to exercise an option, the option is deemed sold or exchanged on the day it expires (Code Sec. 1234(a)).[19]

In the case of an option on stock, securities, commodities or commodity futures, any gain of a nondealer grantor on the lapse of options is short-term capital gain. Also, any gain or loss of a nondealer grantor from a closing transaction is short-term capital gain or loss. The capital gain and loss provisions do not apply to options or privileges that are stock-in-trade of a taxpayer, such as a dealer in securities (Code Sec. 1234(b)).[20]

Gain or loss is recognized on the exercise of an option on Code Sec. 1256 contracts (regulated futures contracts, foreign currency contracts, nonequity options and dealer equity options) (Code Sec. 1234(c)).[21]

1921. "Puts" and "Calls." A "put" is an option purchased to have the right to sell a specified number of shares of stock to the optionee at a specific price within a certain time. A "call" is an option purchased to obtain the right to purchase a certain number of shares of stock at a stated price within a certain time. The purchaser of an option is usually called the holder. The seller is called a writer.[22]

The cost or premium of purchasing a put or call is a nondeductible capital expenditure (Rev. Rul. 71-521).[23] If a call is exercised, its cost is added to the seller's amount realized and to the buyer's basis of the purchased stock. If a put is exercised, its cost reduces the amount realized upon the sale of the underlying stock. Also, the

---

Footnote references are to paragraphs of the 2002 Standard Federal Tax Reports.

[13] ¶ 29,412.992	[17] ¶ 9802, ¶ 9905,	[21] ¶ 30,610
[14] ¶ 9802, ¶ 10,000	¶ 10,000	[22] ¶ 30,614.14
[15] ¶ 10,000	[18] ¶ 30,390	[23] ¶ 30,592.70
[16] ¶ 23,608	[19] ¶ 30,610	
	[20] ¶ 30,610	

¶ 1921

seller's cost basis in the stock he has sold is reduced by the amount received for the put. Gain or loss is short-term or long-term, depending upon the holding period of the stock involved.

If an option on stock or securities is allowed to expire without having been exercised, any gain to the grantor or loss to the purchaser is treated as a short-term capital gain or loss (Code Sec. 1234(b)(1)).[24] However, this rule does not apply when the taxpayer's trade or business is the granting of options.

1922. Qualified vs. Nonqualified Employee Stock Options. Employer corporations often grant their employees the right to purchase stock in the employers. These options are a form of compensation. Generally, stock options are *given* without cost to key employees both as a reward for past services and as an incentive for future activities on the employer's behalf. However, the options may also be *sold* to employees.

Stock Option Defined. There are two classifications of options: (1) statutory or qualified options (i.e., the tax treatment of the options is governed by specific Code sections) and (2) nonstatutory or nonqualified options (i.e., the tax treatment of the options is governed under the more general Code principles of compensation and the recognition of income). Either type of option is an agreement under which the holder of the option has the right, but not the obligation, to purchase corporate shares at a fixed price on a fixed date or within a range of dates (Reg. § 1.421-7(a)(1)).[25]

1923. Nonqualified Stock Options. A nonqualified stock option is one that does not meet the requirements of, and is not governed by, the rules of Code Secs. 421 through 424 (Reg. § 1.83-7(a)).[26]

Taxation upon Grant. A nonqualified stock option is taxed when it is granted if the option has a "readily ascertainable fair market value" at that time (Reg. § 1.83-1(a) and Reg. § 1.83-7(a)).[27]

An option that is not actively traded on an established market has a readily ascertainable fair market value only if *all* of the following requirements are met (Reg. § 1.83-7(b)(2)): [28] (1) the option must be transferable, (2) the option must be exercisable immediately and in full when it is granted, (3) there can be no condition or restriction on the option that would have a significant effect on its fair market value, and (4) the fair market value of the *option privilege* (under Reg. § 1.83-7(b)(3)) [29] must be readily ascertainable.

Because these requirements are seldom satisfied, most nonqualified options that are not traded on an established market do not have a readily ascertainable fair market value.

1924. Options Without Readily Ascertainable Fair Market Value. If the nonqualified option does not have a readily ascertainable fair market value, the grant of the option is not a taxable event; the purchase of the optioned stock triggers taxation (Reg. § 1.83-7(a)).[30] An employee recognizes ordinary income in the amount of the value of the stock purchased minus any amounts paid for the stock or the option. The gain or loss recognized when the employee sells the stock is capital in nature.

1925. Options With Readily Ascertainable Fair Market Value. If a nonqualified option is actively traded or has a readily ascertainable fair market value, the employee must recognize ordinary income in the amount of the fair market value in the year the option is granted (Reg. § 1.83-1(a)).[31] If the employee paid for the option, he recognizes the value of the option minus its cost. The employee is not taxed again when he exercises the option and buys the corporate stock; he is taxed when the stock is sold. The employee's basis in the stock is the fair market value of the option on which he paid taxes, plus the amount he paid for the stock. Any gain or loss recognized on the subsequent sale of the stock is capital in nature.

Footnote references are to paragraphs of the 2002 Standard Federal Tax Reports.

[24] ¶ 30,610, ¶ 30,614	[27] ¶ 6381, ¶ 6388	[30] ¶ 6388
[25] ¶ 19,607	[28] ¶ 6388	[31] ¶ 6381
[26] ¶ 6388	[29] ¶ 6388	

1926. Lapse of Options. If an option with a readily ascertainable fair market value is allowed to lapse, the capital loss is measured by the taxpayer's basis in the option (the value of the option that was taxed) (Code Sec. 1234(a)(2)).[32] Thus, if the stock value declines and the option holder never exercises the option, he has a capital loss of whatever he paid for the option. The option is treated as if it were sold or exchanged on the date that it lapsed (Reg. § 1.1234-1(b)).

1927. Determining the Holding Period. In determining whether a capital gain on stock is long-term or short-term, the holding period begins on the date after the option is exercised, not the date the option is granted. See ¶ 1777 for rules used to determine holding period of various types of capital assets.

1928. Taxation of Employer. An employer is allowed to deduct the value of a nonqualified stock option as a business expense for the tax year in which the option is included in the gross income of the employee. Thus, if the option has a readily ascertainable value and is included in the employee's income when the option is granted, the employer is allowed the deduction in the year of the grant. If the option does not have a readily ascertainable value and is not included in the employee's income until the year the option is exercised, the employer is allowed the deduction in the year of exercise. The amount of the employer's deduction is the same as the amount included by the employee in gross income (Code Sec. 83(h)).[33]

If the employer and the employee have different tax years, the employer claims the deduction in the tax year in which or with which the employee's tax year ends.

1929. Qualified Options. There are two kinds of statutory ("qualified") options (Reg. § 1.421-7(b)): [34] incentive stock options (Code Sec. 422) [35] and options granted under employee stock purchase plans (Code Sec. 423).[36]

In order to be recognized as a statutory option, the option may be exercisable only by the individual to whom it is granted unless the right to exercise passes by will or law at the grantee's death. The determination of whether an option qualified as a statutory option is made when the option is granted, not when it is exercised or the stock is sold (Reg. § 1.421-7(b)).[37]

1930. Incentive Stock Options. The rules governing incentive stock options (ISOs) prevent the taxation of the option as income to the employee at the time the option is granted *or at the time the employee exercises the option and buys the stock* (Code Sec. 421(a)). [38] The shares that were acquired by the ISO are taxed at capital gains rates when the employee *sells* the stock (Temporary Reg. § 14a.422A-1, Q&A-1).[39] There are requirements imposed on the terms of an ISO and how long the stock acquired by the ISO must be held.

1931. Requirements for Incentive Stock Options. The employee must have the option to receive shares of the employer corporation, its parent or its subsidiary corporation. The right to obtain the stock of a sister corporation (one that has a joint parent with the employer corporation) cannot qualify as an ISO. ISOs must be granted under a plan adopted by the corporation and approved by the shareholders that sets out the total number of shares that may be issued as options and the employees who may receive the options (Code Sec. 422(a)).

The options must be granted within 10 years from the date the plan is adopted or approved, whichever is earlier. Further, the option granted must be exercisable within 10 years from the date it is granted. The option price may not be less than the fair market value of the stock at the time the option is granted, and the option may not be transferred other than by death. The option may be exercised only by the employee. Finally, the employee, *at the time the option is granted,* may not own stock with more than 10% of the total combined voting power of all classes of stock of the employer corporation or its parent or any subsidiary (Code Sec. 422(b)).[40]

Footnote references are to paragraphs of the 2002 Standard Federal Tax Reports.

[32] ¶ 30,610	[35] ¶ 19,800	[38] ¶ 19,602
[33] ¶ 6380	[36] ¶ 19,900	[39] ¶ 19,801
[34] ¶ 19,607	[37] ¶ 19,607	[40] ¶ 19,800

The employee must remain an employee of the corporation from the time the option is granted until three months before the option is exercised. Once stock has been purchased under an incentive stock option, it cannot be sold within two years from the date the option was granted or within one year from the date the option was exercised and the stock was purchased, whichever is later (Code Sec. 422(a)).[41]

If the employee sells the shares before the required period, gain on the sale is treated as ordinary income (compensation). Gain, for this purpose, is an amount equal to the lesser of (1) the fair market value of the stock on the date of exercise minus the option price or (2) the amount realized on disposition minus the option price (Reg. § 14a.422A-1, Q&A-2). The gain is recognized for the tax year in which the sale occurs (Code Sec. 421(b)).[42] In determining whether stock has been held for the required period, each share of stock sold is treated separately (Reg. § 1.421-8(a)(2)).[43]

Alternative Minimum Tax. The exercise of an ISO does not give rise to taxable income to the employee. However, the difference between the option price and the fair market value of the stock at the time the employee's rights in the acquired stock became transferable or were no longer subject to a substantial risk of forfeiture must be recognized for alternative minimum tax purposes for the tax year in which the ISO is exercised (Code Sec. 56(b)(3)).[44] See ¶ 1435.

1932. Death of Option Holder. In the event the holder of an ISO dies, the deceased's representative may exercise the option (Code Sec. 422(b)(5)). The executor, administrator, or representative need not exercise the option within three months after the death of the employee (as would be the case if the employee left the service of the employer) (Reg. § 1.421-8(c)(1)).[45]

1933. Basis of Option. An employee's basis in an ISO is what he paid for it. If he paid nothing for it there is no loss to the employee if the option lapses without being exercised.

An employee's basis in *stock* purchased though an ISO is the amount he paid for the stock when the option was exercised (plus any amount he paid for the option). If the stock has been held for the required period, the employee recognizes a capital gain (or loss) in the amount of the difference between what he paid for the shares and what he sold them for (Code Sec. 1001(a)).[46]

1934. Employee Stock Purchase Plans. Employee stock purchase plans are written plans approved by the shareholders (Code Secs. 423(b)(1) and (2))[47] that give corporate employees the option to purchase shares of their employer's stock or the stock of a parent or subsidiary corporation.

If an option price is no less than 85% of the fair market value of the stock at the time the option was granted, the shareholder recognizes ordinary income in the amount of the *lesser* of: (1) the difference between the fair market value of the shares when sold (or the fair market value of the shares at the employee's death while owning the shares) and the option price for the shares or (2) the difference between the option price and the fair market value of the shares when the option was granted. The balance of any gain is treated as capital gain (Code Sec. 423(c)).[48]

1934A. Employee Stock Purchase Plan Special Rules. An employee stock purchase plan may grant employees the option to purchase stock in their employer or the employer's parent or subsidiary. To qualify for statutory treatment, the stock purchased under the option may not be sold within two years from the grant of the option and one year after the shares are transferred (Code Sec. 423(a)).[49]

Further requirements are that the employee remain an employee of the corporation during the option period; if the employee leaves employment with the corporation, he has three months from the time he leaves to exercise the option

Footnote references are to paragraphs of the 2002 Standard Federal Tax Reports.

¶ **1932**

[41] ¶ 19,800	[44] ¶ 5200	[47] ¶ 19,900
[42] ¶ 19,602	[45] ¶ 19,609	[48] ¶ 19,900
[43] ¶ 19,609	[46] ¶ 29,220	[49] ¶ 19,900

(Code Sec. 423(a)(2)).[50] No employee who has more than 5% of the voting power or value of the employer's stock, or that of any parent or subsidiary of the employer, can be granted a stock purchase plan option (Code Sec. 423(b)(3)).[51]

All full-time employees must be included in the plan, except those with less than two years of employment, highly compensated employees as defined in Code Sec. 414(q), part-time employees and seasonal workers (Code Sec. 423(b)(4)).[52] The plan may limit the amount of stock any employee can buy, and purchase of the stock may be tied to compensation (Code Sec. 423(b)(5)).

The option price may not be less than the lesser of 85% of the fair market value of the stock at the time the option is granted or the fair market value of the stock at the time the option is exercised (Code Sec. 423(b)(6)).[53] The option cannot be exercised later than 27 months from the date the option is granted or five years from the date the option is granted if the option price is not less than 85% of the fair market value of the stock at the time the option is exercised (Code Sec. 423(b)(7)).[54]

No employee can acquire the right to buy more than $25,000 of stock per year (valued at the time the option is granted) (Code Sec. 423(b)(8)).[55]

Wash Sales

1935. Wash Sale Losses Denied. A loss sustained upon a sale or other disposition of stock or securities is not allowed if, within a period beginning 30 days before the date of the sale or disposition and ending 30 days after that date, the taxpayer has acquired, or has entered into a contract or option to acquire, substantially identical stock or securities (Code Sec. 1091(a); Reg. § 1.1091-1).[56] Similarly, a loss realized on the closing of a short sale of stock or securities is disallowed if within 30 days before or after the closing substantially identical stock or securities are sold or another short sale of substantially identical stock or securities is entered into (Code Sec. 1091(e)).[57] The term "stock or securities" includes contracts or options to acquire or sell stock or securities (except as provided in regulations).

An acquisition by gift, bequest, inheritance, or tax-free exchange that is made within the 61-day period does not bring the wash sale rule into play. The proscribed period is not cut off by the end of a tax year. Also, nonrecognition of loss cannot be avoided by arranging for delivery outside the 61-day period since the contract date fixes the date of loss if the obligation to deliver becomes fixed on that date.[58] See, also, the discussion on short sales at ¶ 1944.

The wash sale rule applies to all classes of taxpayers, including corporations. However, the rule does not apply to stock or securities dealers for losses sustained in a transaction in the course of their business.

When shares of the same corporation are purchased in separate lots, sold at the same time, and then reacquired within the prohibited time period, a loss on one lot may not be claimed to reduce the gain from the other shares.[59] The U.S. Supreme Court has disallowed deduction of a loss incurred when identical securities were purchased by a taxpayer's spouse.[60]

For application of the wash sale rules to commodity futures contracts involving tax straddle positions, see ¶ 1948.

1937. "Substantially Identical" Securities. For purposes of the wash sale rules, securities are "substantially identical" if they are not substantially different in any material feature or in several material features considered together.

1939. Basis After Wash Sale. A substituted basis applies to the new stock or securities acquired in a wash sale. Assuming that the amount of new securities is exactly equal to the amount of the securities on which the wash sale rules disallowed a loss, the basis for the new securities is the same as for the old securities,

---

Footnote references are to paragraphs of the 2002 Standard Federal Tax Reports.

[50] ¶ 19,900	[54] ¶ 19,900	[58] ¶ 30,183.104
[51] ¶ 19,900	[55] ¶ 19,900	[59] ¶ 30,183.11
[52] ¶ 19,900	[56] ¶ 30,180, ¶ 30,181	[60] ¶ 30,183.109
[53] ¶ 19,900	[57] ¶ 30,180	

increased or decreased by the difference between the selling price of the old securities and the acquisition price of the new (identical) securities (Code Sec. 1091(d); Reg. § 1.1091-2).[61]

1941. Holding Period. When there has been a wash sale of securities, the holding period of the securities acquired includes the period for which the taxpayer held those securities on which the loss was not deductible (Code Sec. 1223(4); Reg. § 1.1223-1).[62] Rules for computation of the holding period when fractional parts of a month are involved are at ¶ 1777.

Short Sales

1944. Short Sales. A short sale is one in which the seller borrows the stock certificates or other property delivered to the buyer. At a later date, the seller either purchases similar stock or property necessary to "cover" the sale, and delivers it to the lender, or delivers stock or property that he already held but did not wish to transfer at an earlier date.[63]

A short sale results in a capital gain or loss only if the property used to close the sale, including a commodity future, is a capital asset. This rule does not apply to a hedging transaction, from which ordinary income or loss results (see ¶ 1949). A short sale includes a "put," or option to sell at a fixed price, except where the "put" is acquired on the same day as the property identified as intended to be used in exercising the "put" and the "put" is exercised through the sale of the property so identified (Code Sec. 1233; Reg. § 1.1233-1).[64] If the option is not exercised, its cost is added to the basis of the stock.

A short sale that is considered to be a sale of a capital asset normally results in a short-term gain or loss because the "covering" purchase is usually made at about the time delivery is made to the lender, at which time the transaction is closed. In this situation, the holding period for the covering stock is not more than the required holding period for long-term capital gain or loss treatment (¶ 1777). However, when the seller is in both a long and short position on substantially identical securities and when the substantially identical securities have been held for not more than the required holding period for long-term capital gain or loss treatment on the date of the short sale (not the date of closing) or are acquired after the short sale and on or before the date the sale is closed, (1) any gain on closing of the short sale is considered to be a short-term capital gain no matter when the property used in closing the "short" sale is acquired and (2) the holding period of the substantially identical property (that is not in excess of the property sold short) is considered to begin on the date that the short sale is closed, or on the date of a sale, gift, or other disposition of the property, whichever occurs earlier (Code Sec. 1233(b)).[65] Rule (1) does not apply to the portion of property sold short that exceeds the quantity of substantially identical property.

When there is a loss on the closing of the "short" sale, the loss is considered as a long-term capital loss if property substantially identical to that sold "short" has been held for more than the long-term holding period on the date of the "short" sale regardless of when the property used to close the short sale was acquired. This loss rule does not apply to the part of the property sold short that exceeds in quantity the substantially identical property held for more than the long-term holding period. Special holding period rules apply to brokers' arbitrage transactions (Code Sec. 1233(f); Reg. § 1.1233-1).[66]

Constructive Sale Treatment. "Constructive sale" provisions, enacted by the Taxpayer Relief Act of 1997, generally eliminated the tax deferral benefits of short sales. Prior to the Act, certain hedging strategies such as short sales against the box, forward contracts, and notional principal contracts could be used to lock in gains on appreciated financial positions without immediate recognition of income. Code Sec.

¶ 1941

[61] ¶ 30,180, ¶ 30,182
[62] ¶ 30,460, ¶ 30,461
[63] ¶ 30,592.355

[64] ¶ 30,590, ¶ 30,591, ¶ 30,614.14
[65] ¶ 30,590

[66] ¶ 30,590, ¶ 30,591

1259, generally effective for constructive sales entered into after June 8, 1997, limits an investor's ability to do this by treating certain hedging transactions as constructive sales (Code Sec. 1259).[67]

If there is a constructive sale of an appreciated financial position, the taxpayer must recognize gain as if the position were sold, assigned, or otherwise terminated at its fair market value *as of the date of the constructive sale* and immediately repurchased. Adjustments are made in the amount of any gain or loss subsequently realized on the position to reflect gain recognized on the constructive sale. The taxpayer's holding period begins as if the taxpayer had first acquired the position on the date of the constructive sale.

"Appreciated financial position" generally means any position with respect to any stock, debt instrument, or partnership interest where there would be gain if such position is sold, assigned, or otherwise terminated at its fair market value. However, there are two exceptions. One exception is made for any position that is marked to market. A second exception is made for any position with respect to debt instruments if three conditions are satisfied:

(1) the debt unconditionally entitles the holder to receive a specified principal amount;

(2) interest payments are payable based on a fixed rate or, to the extent provided in regulations, at a variable rate; and

(3) the debt is not convertible into stock of the issuer or any related person.

A taxpayer is treated as making a constructive sale of an appreciated position if the taxpayer enters into certain types of transactions or attempts to avoid Code Sec. 1259 by having a related person enter into one of these transactions. A constructive sale is deemed to occur when a taxpayer does any of the following:

(1) enters into a short sale of the same or substantially identical property;

(2) enters into an offsetting notional principal contract with respect to the same or substantially identical property;

(3) enters into a futures or forward contract to deliver the same or substantially identical property;

(4) has entered into a short sale, an offsetting notional principal contract, or a forward or futures contract and acquires a long position in the same property; or

(5) to the extent prescribed in regulations, enters into other transactions having substantially the same effect as the four types of transactions listed above.

Exclusions. Excluded from the definition of a constructive sale are contracts for the sale of appreciated financial assets that are not marketable securities (Code Sec. 1259(c)(2)). However, this exclusion only applies if the contract settles within one year after the date it was entered into. Also, excluded are certain securities that are marked-to-market (Code Sec. 475(f)(1)(C)) (see ¶ 1903).

Safe Harbor for Short-Term Hedges. Code Sec. 1259 provides a safe harbor for certain short-term hedges that would otherwise be treated as constructive sales (Code Sec. 1259(c)(3)).[68] Under this exception, a transaction that would otherwise be treated as a constructive sale is disregarded if three conditions are satisfied:

(1) the transaction is closed before the end of the 30th day after the end of the tax year in which the transaction was entered into;

(2) the taxpayer holds the appreciated financial position throughout the 60-day period beginning on the date the transaction is closed; and

(3) at no time during such 60-day period is the taxpayer's risk of loss with respect to the position reduced by a circumstance that would be described in Code Sec. 246(c)(4) if references to stock included references to such position.

The circumstances referred to in Code Sec. 246(c)(4) are as follows:

(1) the taxpayer has an option to sell, is under a contractual obligation to sell, or has made (but not closed) a short sale of substantially identical stock or securities;

---

(2) the taxpayer is the grantor of an option to buy substantially identical stock or securities; or

(3) under IRS regulations, the taxpayer has diminished his or her risk of loss by holding one or more other positions with respect to substantially similar or related property.

If a transaction that is closed is reestablished in a substantially similar position, the exception still applies, provided that the reestablished position is closed prior to the end of the 30th day after the close of the taxable year in which the original transaction occurred and that the taxpayer satisfies the two 60-day rules described above.

1946. Dividends and Payments in Lieu of Dividends. An amount equal to the dividend paid by an investor to one who lends him stock to sell short may be deductible as investment interest expense (as an itemized deduction). See ¶ 1094 for information on investment interest. The borrower may not deduct the payments unless the short sale is held open for at least 45 days. The 45-day period is extended to one year if extraordinary dividends are involved. If the short sale is closed by the 45th day after the date of the short sale (one year or less in the case of an extraordinary dividend), the taxpayer may not deduct the payment in lieu of dividend that was made to the lender. Instead, the taxpayer must increase the basis of the stock used to close the short sale by the amount of the payment (Code Sec. 263(h)(1)).[69]

These 45-day and one-year periods are suspended for any period in which the borrower holds options to buy substantially identical property or holds one or more positions in such property (Code Sec. 263(h)(4)).[70]

Tax Straddles

1948. Straddle Transactions. Taxpayers are prevented from using various tax-motivated straddle transactions (positions in a transaction that balance or offset each other) to defer income or to convert short-term capital gain into long-term capital gain. Losses incurred from actively traded personal property are deferred to the extent that the taxpayer had gains in offsetting positions that were not closed out by year-end. In the case of stock, this rule applies to straddles involving stock options traded on an exchange and to any other straddle in which at least one position is an option in actively traded stock (Code Sec. 1092).[71]

Generally, positions in regulated futures contracts, foreign currency contracts, nonequity options, and dealer equity options in an exchange using the mark-to-market system are treated as if they were sold on the last day of the year (Code Sec. 1256(b)). Any capital gains or losses arising under this rule are treated as if they were 60% long-term and 40% short-term without regard to the holding period (Code Sec. 1256(a)).[72]

Hedging transactions generally are exempt from the above rules. However, special rules apply to restrict limited partners' and limited entrepreneurs' deductions for hedging losses (Code Sec. 1092(e)[73] and Code Sec. 1256(e)-(f)).[74] Special rules also apply to grantors of qualified covered call options (Code Sec. 1092(c)(4)) and options market-makers and commodities traders (Code Sec. 1256(f)).

Taxpayers are prohibited from converting ordinary income into capital gains through the use of straddle transactions if substantially all the taxpayer's expected return is attributable to the time value of his net investment. These rules generally do not apply to the normal trade of options dealers (Code Sec. 1258(d)(5)).[75]

1949. Hedging Transactions. A hedging transaction is one a taxpayer enters into in the normal course of business primarily to reduce the risk of interest rate or price changes or currency fluctuations (Code Sec. 1221(a)(7); Reg. § 1.1221-2).[76] The property that is the subject of a hedging transaction is not considered capital

---

Footnote references are to paragraphs of the 2002 Standard Federal Tax Reports.

[69] ¶ 13,700	[72] ¶ 31,100	[75] ¶ 31,128.03
[70] ¶ 13,700	[73] ¶ 30,200	[76] ¶ 30,420, ¶ 30,424
[71] ¶ 30,200	[74] ¶ 31,100	

property, and gain or loss on most hedging transactions is ordinary in nature rather than capital. This treatment also applies if a short sale or option is part of a hedging transaction. In this case, it is the type of transaction that controls the tax treatment rather than the type of underlying property involved (Reg. § 1.1221-2(a)(2)).[77]

For a transaction to be a hedging transaction, the transaction must have a risk-reducing purpose (Reg. § 1.1221-2(c)(1)).[78] This is normally determined by looking at the taxpayer's entire operations. The acquisition of certain assets, such as investments, that are not acquired primarily to reduce risk is not a hedging transaction. Even though these assets may reduce risk, they typically are not acquired primarily to reduce risk (Reg. § 1.1221-2(c)(3)).[79] In the case of a hedge of property or of an obligation, the sale or exchange of the property could not produce capital gain or loss.

To qualify as a hedge, a transaction must be identified substantially contemporaneously with entering into the hedging transaction (Reg. § 1.1221-2(e)(1)).[80] The identification of the items that comprise the hedge must be made no more than 35 days after entering into the hedging transaction (Reg. § 1.1221-2(e)(3)). This time period should make it possible for taxpayers to identify the hedged item, items, or aggregate risk at the time they prepare monthly reports for nontax purposes. The identification must be clear and unambiguous for financial accounting purposes, such as by reflecting the transaction in a separate account used only for hedges of a specified item.

Corporate Bonds and Other Debt Instruments

1950. Discounts, Premiums, and Issue Expenses. A bond is issued at a discount when the issue price is less than the face value of the bond (see ¶ 1952). A bond is issued at a premium when the issue price is more than the amount payable at maturity, or at an earlier call date if the bond is callable. The premium amount is income to the corporation and is amortized over the life of the bond (Reg. § 1.61-12(c)).[81] Any expenses related to issuing the bond (that is, printing, advertising, legal fees) must be amortized over the life of the bond and deducted as a business expense.[82]

1952. Original Issue Discount. "Original issue discount" (OID) is the difference between the issue price (as defined in Code Sec. 1273(b))[83] and the stated redemption price at maturity. If the difference is less than 1/4 of 1% per year on the redemption price from the date of issue to the date of maturity, the OID is "zero" (Code Sec. 1273(a)(3)).[84]

Holders of bonds and debt instruments having a more-than-one-year maturity and originally issued after July 1, 1982, must include in income the sum of the daily portion of original issue discount determined for each day during the tax year the instrument is held (Code Sec. 1272(a)(1)). This does not apply to obligations issued by a natural person before March 2, 1984, certain loans between natural persons, debt instruments having a fixed maturity date of not more than one year from the date of issue, tax-exempt obligations, or U.S. Savings Bonds (Code Sec. 1272(a)(2)).[85]

The basis of any bond or other evidence of indebtedness in the hands of the holder is increased by the amount of OID that was included in gross income (Code Sec. 1272(d)(2)).[86]

Pre-July 2, 1982, and Post-May 27, 1969, Corporate Bonds. The holder of a corporate bond or other evidence of indebtedness issued after May 27, 1969, and before July 2, 1982, must include in income the ratable monthly portion of OID multiplied by the number of complete months and fractions thereof that the individual held the bond or other evidence of indebtedness during the tax year (Code Sec. 1272(b)).[87]

Footnote references are to paragraphs of the 2002 Standard Federal Tax Reports.

[77] ¶ 30,424	[81] ¶ 5801, ¶ 5804.47	[85] ¶ 31,260, ¶ 31,262
[78] ¶ 30,424	[82] ¶ 5804.01, ¶ 5804.22	[86] ¶ 31,260
[79] ¶ 30,424	[83] ¶ 31,280	[87] ¶ 31,260, ¶ 31,262.035
[80] ¶ 30,424	[84] ¶ 31,280	**¶ 1952**

Interest Deduction. In the case of any debt instrument issued after July 1, 1982, the portion of OID allowable as a deduction to the issuer for any tax year is equal to the aggregate daily portions of the OID for days during that tax year (Code Sec. 163(e)). The daily portions of OID for any day are to be determined under the formula contained in Code Sec. 1272(a)(3).[88]

Information Statement for Recipients. Any issuer with any bond outstanding or any other evidence of indebtedness in registered form issued at a discount must furnish the holder and the IRS with an information statement (Form 1099-OID) for the calendar year if there is OID of at least $10 for the calendar year and the term of the obligation is more than one year (Code Sec. 6049(c)).[89]

Stripped Bonds and Stripped Coupons. Special rules govern stripped bonds and stripped coupons purchased or sold after July 1, 1982 (Code Sec. 1286).[90] Prior to the adoption of these rules, a bond holder could sell bonds stripped of their interest coupons for less than he paid for the bond with the coupons and recognize a capital loss. He could also sell the coupons and retain the bonds, thus realizing immediate income. Now, the basis of the bond must be allocated between the bond without the coupons and the coupons, and the bond and coupons are treated as being issued with an original issue discount. The allocation is based on the fair market value of the bond and the coupons as of the date one is sold without the other. Further, the bond holder must also report any accrued and unreported interest income and include in income any accrued acquisition discount or market discount for the current year. The basis of the bond and/or coupons is adjusted accordingly.

Purchasers of stripped bonds or coupons must amortize the difference between the amount due at maturity of the bond or coupons and the allocated cost over the remaining life of the bond or coupons (Code Sec. 1286).[91] This is designed to prevent the conversion of ordinary income into capital gain by selling coupons before the maturity date and thus realizing a gain on the coupons rather than realizing interest income.

Stripped Stock. Preferred stock purchased after April 30, 1993, that has been stripped of some or all of its dividend rights is treated in the same manner as stripped bonds. There is an imputed original issue discount equal to the stated redemption price minus the amount paid for the stock (Code Sec. 305(e)).[92]

Tax-Exempt Bonds. Original issue discount on a tax-exempt bond is generally treated as tax-exempt interest (¶ 1956). However, where a tax-exempt bond is stripped, only a portion of the OID is treated as OID on a tax-exempt obligation. The balance is treated as OID on a taxable obligation. A process is set out in the Code for determining the tax-exempt portion of the deemed original issue discount (Code Sec. 1286(d)).[93] See also ¶ 1956.

1954. Certain Debt Instruments Issued for Property. The OID rules apply to debt instruments that are not publicly traded and that are given as consideration for the sale or exchange of property that is not publicly traded (Code Sec. 1274).[94] Code Sec. 1274 applies to such transactions if (1) some or all of the payments under the instrument are due more than six months after the sale and (2) the stated redemption price at maturity of the instrument exceeds (a) the instrument's stated principal amount if there is adequately stated interest or (b) its imputed principal amount if there is inadequately stated interest.

Exemptions. Specific statutory exemptions from Code Sec. 1274 coverage are provided for debt instruments arising from: (1) sales for $250,000 or less; (2) sales of principal residences; (3) sales of farms by individuals, estates, testamentary trusts, or small business corporations or partnerships for $1 million or less; (4) land transfers between related parties that are covered by Code Sec. 483; (5) in the case of the borrower, sales or exchanges of personal use property (Code Sec. 1275(b));[95] (6) sales or exchanges of certain annuity contracts governed by Code Sec. 72 (Code

---

Footnote references are to paragraphs of the 2002 Standard Federal Tax Reports.

¶ 1954

88 ¶ 31,260, ¶ 31,262.04	91 ¶ 31,480	94 ¶ 31,300
89 ¶ 36,020	92 ¶ 15,303	95 ¶ 31,340
90 ¶ 31,480, ¶ 31,481	93 ¶ 31,480.23	

Sec. 1275(a)(1)(B));[96] and (7) sales of patents for amounts that are contingent on the productivity, use, or disposition of the property transferred. If a debt-for-property transaction is not covered by the OID rules, it may be subject to the imputed interest rules of Code Sec. 483 (Code Sec. 1274).

Adequate Interest. Interest is adequate if its stated principal amount is less than or equal to the imputed principal amount. The imputed principal amount is determined by totaling the present values of all payments due on the instrument discounted at the applicable federal rate (AFR). For transactions in which a debt instrument is given in consideration for the sale or exchange of property (other than new Code Sec. 38 property) and the stated principal amount of the instrument does not exceed an inflation-adjusted amount ($3,960,100 for 2000 and $4,085,900 for 2001), a 9% rate may be substituted for the AFR (Code Sec. 1274A); [97] for a sale-leaseback transaction, a rate equal to 110% of that AFR applies.

Election Out of OID Rules. For sales or exchanges of property (other than new Code Sec. 38 property), the lender and borrower may jointly elect out of the OID rules and take the interest on the debt instrument into account under the cash receipts and disbursements method of accounting. The election can be made only if (1) the stated principal amount of the instrument does not exceed an inflation-adjusted amount ($2,828,700 for 2000 and $2,918,500 for 2001), (2) the lender is on the cash-basis method of accounting and is not a dealer with respect to the property sold or exchanged, and (3) the OID rules would otherwise have applied to the transaction (Code Sec. 1274A(c)).[98]

Applicable Federal Rate. The applicable federal rate, which is determined monthly, will depend upon the maturity of the debt instrument. See ¶ 83.

1956. OID on Tax-Exempt Bonds. Although OID on tax-exempt obligations is exempt from tax, OID must be accrued for purposes of increasing the holder's tax basis in determining gain or loss if the bond is sold prior to maturity. The holder is to accrue OID for various "accrual periods" using the constant-interest method, under which OID is allocated over the life of a bond by making adjustments to the issue price of the bond for each accrual period. The amount of OID allocated over an accrual period is determined by (1) multiplying the adjusted issue price of the bond by its yield to maturity and then (2) subtracting the interest payable as "qualified periodic interest" from the product. In determining OID on tax-exempt obligations, tax-exempt interest must be excluded. The tables at ¶ 84 present applicable federal interest rates that have been adjusted to account for tax-exempt interest (Code Sec. 1272(a)).[99] These rules apply to obligations issued after September 3, 1982, and acquired after March 1, 1984 (Code Sec. 1288).[100] A portion of OID on a stripped tax-exempt obligation may be subject to tax. See ¶ 1952.

1958. Market Discount Bonds. Gain from the sale of a market discount bond purchased after April 30, 1993, is treated as ordinary income to the extent of accrued market discount on the bond. Gain from the sale of a market discount bond purchased before May 1, 1993, is subject to these market discount rules only if the bond was originally issued after July 18, 1984, and produces taxable interest income.

A market discount bond is a bond that was purchased at a discount from face value. If the bond was originally issued at a discount, then the bond's revised issue price, or original issue price plus accrued OID, is substituted for the purchase price to determine if the bond is a market discount bond. Market discount bonds do not include obligations that mature within one year of issuance, U.S. savings bonds, installment bonds, and tax-exempt bonds purchased before May 1, 1993. The accrued market discount on a bond may be figured under either the ratable accrual method (Code Sec. 1276(b)(1)) or, upon the irrevocable election of the taxpayer with respect to a particular bond, the constant interest method (Code Sec. 1276(b)(2)).[101] Instead of recognizing interest income upon the disposition of a market discount bond, a taxpayer may elect to include market discount in income currently using

---

Footnote references are to paragraphs of the 2002 Standard Federal Tax Reports.

[96] ¶ 31,340   [98] ¶ 31,320   [100] ¶ 31,520, ¶ 31,521
[97] ¶ 31,320   [99] ¶ 31,260   [101] ¶ 31,360

¶ 1958

either the ratable accrual method or the constant interest method (Code Sec. 1278(b)).[102] This election, which is revocable only with the consent of the IRS, applies to all market discount bonds acquired during and after the tax year of the election. The election is made by filing a statement with the taxpayer's timely filed tax return that states that the market discount has been included in income under the provisions of Code Sec. 1276(b). The statement should also indicate how the amount included in income was calculated (Rev. Proc. 92-67).

Any partial payment of principal on a market discount bond is ordinary income to the extent of accrued market discount on the bond for obligations acquired after October 22, 1986 (Code Sec. 1276(a)(3)).[103] Any such payment that is included in gross income will reduce the amount of accrued market discount.

Net direct interest expenses on debt incurred to purchase or continue a market discount bond acquired after July 18, 1984, may be deducted currently only to the extent that the expenses exceed the market discount allocable to the number of days the bond is held by the taxpayer (Code Sec. 1277).[104] The taxpayer may elect to take any deferred interest deduction in a subsequent year to the extent of net interest income from the market discount bond. Any deferred interest expense that remains (whether or not the election is made) is deducted in the year of disposition.

1961. Discount on Short-Term Obligations. Short-term obligations (obligations with a one-year maturity or less) are generally exempt from the OID rules and from the acquisition discount rules. However, certain holders are required to include acquisition discount on short-term obligations in income on a level straight-line basis and, for obligations acquired after September 27, 1985, any interest (other than interest taken into account in determining the amount of the acquisition discount) payable on such obligations as it accrues. The holders in question are accrual-basis taxpayers, dealers, banks, regulated investment companies, common trust funds, and certain pass-through entities. This rule also applies to obligations identified under Code Sec. 1256(e)(2) [105] as hedging transactions and short-term stripped bonds or coupons held by the person who stripped the bond or coupon (Code Sec. 1281).[106] In the case of short-term obligations other than government obligations, current inclusion under the OID rules applies unless the holder elects to use the acquisition discount rules (Code Sec. 1283(c)).[107]

When mandatory accrual is not required, interest is deductible only to the extent that it exceeds the sum of the acquisition discount (excess of stated redemption price over basis) for each day during the year that the bond is held by the taxpayer and the amount of any interest payable on the obligation that accrues during the year but is not included in gross income for that year because of the taxpayer's accounting method. The daily portion of the acquisition discount is equal to the sum of the discount divided by the number of days from the acquisition date to the maturity date (Code Sec. 1282 and Code Sec. 1283).[108]

1963. Unregistered Obligations. Most corporate and government obligations are required to be in registered form (Code Sec. 163(f)(1)) if the payor is to deduct interest.[109] An excise tax is imposed on issues of registration-required obligations that are not in registered form (Code Sec. 4701).[110] In addition, certain bonds issued after August 15, 1986, must be in registered form in order to be tax exempt (Code Sec. 149),[111] although no excise tax is imposed (Code Sec. 4701(b)). The excise tax is equal to one percent of the principal amount of the obligation multiplied by the number of calendar years (or portions thereof) during the term of the obligation (Code Sec. 4701). This is the period beginning on the date of issuance of the obligation and ending on the date of maturity.

If any registration-required obligation is not in registered form, any gain realized on its sale or other disposition is taxed as ordinary income (Code Sec. 1287) [112] and loss deductions will be denied (Code Sec. 165(j)) [113] unless the issuance

---

Footnote references are to paragraphs of the 2002 Standard Federal Tax Reports.

102 ¶ 31,400	106 ¶ 31,420, ¶ 31,421	110 ¶ 33,941
103 ¶ 31,360	107 ¶ 31,460	111 ¶ 7900
104 ¶ 31,380	108 ¶ 31,440, ¶ 31,460	112 ¶ 31,500
105 ¶ 31,100	109 ¶ 9102	113 ¶ 9802

¶ 1961

of the obligation was subject to the excise tax under Code Sec. 4701 or certain other specified exceptions (Code Sec. 165(j)(3)) apply. Issuers of registration-required obligations face the loss of deductions for interest (including OID) on the bonds (Code Sec. 163(f)) [114] and cannot reduce earnings and profits by the amount of any interest on the obligation (Code Sec. 312(m)).[115]

1965. Discounted U.S. Bonds Received in Tax-Free Exchange. Certain U.S. savings bonds may be exchanged tax free for other such bonds, but only if the exchange is authorized by the IRS (Code Sec. 1037).[116] When the original bond was issued at a discount, an amount equal to what would have been ordinary income from OID if the exchange had been taxable is ordinary income when the bond received in exchange is disposed of or redeemed at a gain.

1967. Bond Premium Amortization by Bondholder. If a bond owner has paid a premium over the face amount of the bond, he has the option (1) of amortizing the premium until bond maturity and reducing his basis in the bond by the amortized amount or (2) not amortizing and treating the premium as part of his bond basis (Code Sec. 171).[117] Amortization is allowed only if it is properly elected (Reg. § 1.171-3).[118] The election is made by reporting the amortization on the tax return for the first year the election is to apply. In addition, the taxpayer must attach a statement that the amortization election is being made under Code Sec. 171. For a dealer in municipal bonds, see ¶ 1970.

No amortization is allowed for tax-exempt bonds. Reduction of the basis of the bond by the amount of the bond premium is nevertheless required (Code Sec. 1016(a)(5)).[119]

Effective generally for taxable bonds issued after September 27, 1985, the amount of bond premium that can be amortized for a tax year (and deducted currently) is calculated under a constant yield method. When taxpayers have a pre-September 28, 1985, election in effect to amortize and deduct bond premium, they are given the opportunity to choose whether the election will apply to obligations issued after September 27, 1985 (Code Sec. 171(b)).[120]

For a bond received in a post-May 6, 1986, exchange, in which the basis of the bond is determined at least in part from the basis of the property received, the basis of the bond cannot exceed its fair market value immediately after the exchange for purposes of determining bond premium. This rule generally does not apply to an exchange of securities in a reorganization (Code Sec. 171(b)(4)).[121]

Premium on Convertible Bond. Amortization is not allowed for any part of a premium that is paid for the conversion feature in a convertible bond (Code Sec. 171(b)(1); Reg. § 1.171-2).[122] A corporation's deduction for the premium it is called upon to pay to repurchase its own convertible indebtedness is generally limited to the amount of the normal call premium (Code Sec. 249).[123]

1970. Dealer in Municipal Bonds. A dealer in municipal bonds (tax-exempt securities) must amortize any premiums just as if the interest on the bonds had been taxable. A dealer who does not inventory his securities or who inventories them at cost must reduce the adjusted basis of any municipal bonds he sells during the year by the total amortization for the period they were held. A dealer who values his inventories at other than cost (for example, market value) must annually reduce the "cost of securities sold" by amortization on municipal bonds held during the year (Code Sec. 75(a)).

If a municipal bond is purchased and it (1) is sold or disposed of within 30 days after acquisition or (2) matures or is callable more than five years after it is acquired, an amortization adjustment must be made unless the bond is sold or disposed of at a gain. Thus, a dealer who inventories at other than cost and holds at the end of the year a bond maturing or callable more than five years after

---

Footnote references are to paragraphs of the 2002 Standard Federal Tax Reports.

[114] ¶ 9102
[115] ¶ 15,600
[116] ¶ 29,720, ¶ 29,723
[117] ¶ 11,850

[118] ¶ 11,853
[119] ¶ 29,410
[120] ¶ 11,850

[121] ¶ 11,850
[122] ¶ 11,850, ¶ 11,852
[123] ¶ 13,400

acquisition does not have to reflect amortization on it in his "cost of securities sold." If it is sold at a gain, no amortization adjustment is to be made. If it is not sold at a gain, his "cost of securities sold" is then reduced by the amortization for the entire period it was held (Code Sec. 75; Reg. § 1.75-1).[124]

Accounting Issues

1973. Time of Sale. Whether on the cash or accrual method of accounting, taxpayers who sell stock or securities traded on an established securities market must recognize gains and losses on the trade date and not on the settlement date. The installment rules do not apply to these sales (Code Sec. 453(k)).[125] For information concerning the rules used for calculating whether the holding period of a capital asset is short-term or long-term, see ¶ 1777.

1975. Identification of Stock. If a taxpayer can identify the shares of stock or bonds sold, his basis is the cost or other basis of the particular shares of stock or bonds. However, if a taxpayer buys and sells securities at various times in varying quantities and cannot adequately identify the shares that are sold, the basis of the securities sold is the basis of the securities acquired first (Reg. § 1.1012(c)).[126] See the " 'First-In, First-Out' Rule," below. Except for mutual fund shares, a taxpayer may *not* use the average price per share to figure gain or loss on the sale of the shares.

Mutual Fund Shares. A holder of mutual fund shares may choose to use the average basis of shares owned in a regulated investment company (mutual fund) if the shares were acquired at various times and prices and if they were left on deposit in an account kept by a custodian or agent for receiving or redeeming the shares (Reg. § 1.1012(e)).[127] The average basis is determined by using either the double-category method or the single-category method. Under the double-category method, all shares in an account at the time of each sale of shares are divided into two categories: those held for the long-term capital gain holding period and those held for the short-term capital gain holding period. The cost or other basis of each share in a category is the cost or other basis of all shares in that category at the time of the sale divided by the total number of shares in the category. Under the single-category method, all shares in an account are combined.[128]

"First-In, First-Out" Rule. If stock is sold from lots purchased on different dates and at different prices and the identity of the lots cannot be determined, the stock sold must ordinarily be charged first against the earliest purchases (Reg. § 1.1012-1(c)).[129] Most courts hold, however, that after a nontaxable reorganization in which the taxpayer receives shares of stock in another corporation in exchange for the original shares, the "first-in, first-out" rule is not applicable.[130]

1977. Allocation of Cost of Shares. When securities of different classes are purchased as a unit, as where one share of preferred and two of common stock are bought for a lump sum, their cost should be apportioned between the different classes according to their respective fair market values when acquired. If this is impracticable, no gain or loss is realized from any sale until after the proceeds exceed the aggregate cost of the entire unit.[131]

1980. Margin Trading Account. A margin trading account is not a unitary investment, and a taxpayer cannot merely report net gains or losses.[132] The records and tax return must account for each transaction.

1983. Commissions. A commission paid by a trader in purchasing securities is *part* of the cost of the security and may not be deducted as a business expense.[133] A commission paid by a trader in selling securities is an offset against the selling price and may not be deducted as a business expense, except by a dealer in securities, and then only as to securities held for sale to customers.[134]

Footnote references are to paragraphs of the 2002 Standard Federal Tax Reports.

[124] ¶ 6250, ¶ 6251	[128] ¶ 29,335.03	[132] ¶ 9805.912
[125] ¶ 21,402	[129] ¶ 29,331, ¶ 29,336	[133] ¶ 8521.1484
[126] ¶ 29,331	[130] ¶ 29,336.451	[134] ¶ 8521.1484
[127] ¶ 29,331	[131] ¶ 29,313.005	

Chapter 20

TAX SHELTERS □ AT-RISK RULES PASSIVE LOSSES

TAX SHELTERS

Administrative Provisions

2001. Tax Shelter Defined. A tax shelter that must be registered with the IRS is defined as any investment (1) with respect to which any person could reasonably infer, from the representations made or to be made in connection with any offer for sale of interests in the investment, that the tax shelter ratio (i.e., ratio of deductions and 350% of credits to investment) for any investor may be greater than 2 to 1 as of the close of any of the first five years ending after the date on which the investment is offered for sale and (2) that is (i) required to be registered under a federal or state law regulating securities, (ii) sold pursuant to an exemption from registration requiring the filing of a notice with a federal or state agency regulating the offering or sale of securities, or (iii) a substantial investment. An investment that meets these requirements will be considered a tax shelter regardless of whether it is marketed or customarily designated as a tax shelter (Code Sec. 6111(c)(1)).[1]

2004. Registration of Tax Shelters. An organizer of a tax shelter is required to register the shelter with the IRS on Form 8264 (Code Sec. 6111(a)).[2] If the principal organizer does not do so, the duty may fall upon any other participant in the organization of the shelter or any person participating in its sale or management. The shelter's identification number must be furnished to each investor who purchases or acquires an interest in the shelter. Failure to furnish this number to the tax shelter investors will subject the organizer to a $100 penalty for each such failure (Code Sec. 6707(b)(1)).[3]

Footnote references are to paragraphs of the 2002 Standard Federal Tax Reports.

[1] ¶ 37,000, ¶ 37,002   [2] ¶ 37,000, ¶ 37,002   [3] ¶ 40,085   **¶ 2004**

A penalty may be imposed against an organizer who fails without reasonable cause to timely register the shelter or who provides false or incomplete information with respect to it. The penalty is the greater of 1% of the aggregate amount invested in the shelter or $500 (Code Sec. 6707(a)(2)).

Any person claiming any tax benefit with respect to a shelter must report its registration number on his return by attaching Form 8271. Failure to do so without reasonable cause will subject that person to a $250 penalty (Code Sec. 6707(b)(2)).[4]

Confidential Corporate Tax Shelters. Promoters of confidential corporate tax shelters will be required to register such shelters after the IRS issues guidance that explains the registration requirements. A confidential corporate tax shelter is any investment, plan, arrangement or transaction (1) that has tax avoidance or evasion by a corporate participant as a significant purpose, (2) that is offered to any potential participant under conditions of confidentiality, and (3) for which the tax shelter promoters may receive total fees in excess of $100,000 (Code Sec. 6111(d)(1)).[5]

A transaction is offered under conditions of confidentiality if: (1) an offeree has an understanding or agreement with or for the benefit of any promoter to restrict or limit the offeree's disclosure of the tax shelter or any significant tax features of the tax shelter, or (2) the promoter claims, knows, or has reason to know that the transaction is proprietary to the promoter or any person other than the offeree, or is otherwise protected from disclosure or use (Code Sec. 6111(d)(2)).

The penalty for failing to timely register a confidential corporate tax shelter is the greater of $10,000 or 50 percent of the fees paid to all promoters with respect to offerings prior to the date of late registration (Code Sec. 6707(a)(3)). The penalty is applicable to promoters and to actual participants in any corporate tax shelter who were required to register the tax shelter but did not. With respect to participants, however, the 50-percent penalty requirement to register by either a promoter or a participant increases the 50-percent penalty to 75 percent of the applicable fees. For purposes of the substantial understatement penalty, the amount of the understatement is reduced by any portion attributable to an item if the item on the return is or was supported by substantial authority or if facts relevant to the tax treatment of the item were adequately disclosed on the return.

2008. Investor Lists. A person who organizes or sells an interest in a tax shelter subject to the registration rule (see ¶ 2004) or in any other potentially abusive plan or arrangement must maintain a list of the investors (Code Sec. 6112(a)).[6] A $50 penalty may be assessed for each name omitted from the list. The maximum penalty per year is $100,000 (Code Sec. 6708(a)).[7]

2011. Abusive Tax Shelters Penalty. A penalty is imposed against persons who promote abusive tax shelters (Code Sec. 6700(a)).[8] These persons may be enjoined from further promotion activity (Code Sec. 7408(a)).[9] The penalty is an amount equal to the lesser of $1,000 or 100% of the gross income derived or to be derived by the promoter from the activity. In applying the penalty maximum, promotion of each entity or activity is a separate activity and each sale of an interest in the shelter is a separate activity. According to the U.S. Court of Appeals for the Fifth Circuit, assessment of the penalty is not barred by any statute of limitations.[10]

2014. Accounting Method. Tax shelters are generally required to use the accrual method of accounting (see ¶ 1515).

Footnote references are to paragraphs of the 2002 Standard Federal Tax Reports.

[4] ¶ 40,085	[7] ¶ 40,095, ¶ 40,100.01	[9] ¶ 41,670, ¶ 41,673.01
[5] ¶ 37,000, ¶ 37,002.027	[8] ¶ 40,025, ¶ 40,030	[10] ¶ 38,963.42
[6] ¶ 37,020		

Oil, Gas, and Geothermal Wells

2025. Recapture of Intangible Drilling Costs. For property placed in service after 1986, when oil, gas, geothermal, or other mineral properties are disposed of, certain expensed costs are recaptured as ordinary income. Exploration and intangible drilling and development costs are recaptured to the extent that they would have been included in the adjusted basis of the property if they had not been deducted. Depletion is subject to recapture to the extent that it reduced the adjusted basis of such property. These recapture rules do not apply to property originally acquired under a binding written contract entered into before September 26, 1985.

For property placed into service before 1987, the amount recaptured is the lower of (a) the amounts deducted for intangible drilling expenses on a productive well that exceed the amounts which would have been allowed had the intangible drilling expenses been charged to a capital account instead of being deducted or (b) the excess of the gain realized from a sale, exchange, or involuntary conversion over the adjusted basis of the property or, in the case of any other disposition, the excess of fair market value over the adjusted basis of the property (Code Sec. 1254).[11]

Recapture is computed on Form 4797.

Farming Operations

2028. Accrual Accounting for Farm Corporations. Certain corporations and partnerships having a corporation as a partner that are engaged in the business of farming must use the accrual method of accounting (Code Sec. 447(a)).[12] In addition, these taxpayers are required to capitalize their preproductive period expenses (see ¶ 999) (Code Sec. 263A).[13]

All farming corporations are subject to the accrual accounting rule except (1) S corporations, (2) corporations or partnerships engaged in the trade or business of operating a nursery or soil farm, or raising or harvesting trees (other than fruit and nut trees), and (3) corporations having annual gross receipts of $1 million or less for each prior tax year beginning after 1975 (including the receipts of predecessor corporations and members of a controlled group). A family corporation meets the gross-receipts test if its gross receipts do not exceed $25 million for each prior tax year beginning after 1985. A family corporation is defined as (1) any corporation in which at least 50% of the total combined voting power of all classes of voting stock and at least 50% of all other classes of the corporation's stock are owned by members of the same family and (2) any of the closely held corporations described in Code Sec. 447(h) (Code Sec. 447(d)(2)(c)).[14]

If a corporation or qualified partnership (each of the partners of which is a corporation) has, for a 10-year period ending with its 1976 tax year and for all subsequent years, used an annual accrual method of accounting under which it either deducted preproductive period expenses currently or charged them to the current year's crops, it may continue to use this method (Code Sec. 447(g)).[15]

2032. Expenses of Farming Syndicates. A farming syndicate is a tax shelter (Code Sec. 461(i)(4))[16] and must use the accrual method of accounting (see ¶ 1515).

A farming syndicate is any farming partnership or enterprise (other than a corporation that is not an S corporation) if at any time (a) interests in the enterprise or partnership have been offered for sale in an offering required to be registered with any federal or state agency having authority to regulate such offering or (b) more than 35% of the losses during any period are allocable to limited partners or limited entrepreneurs (Code Sec. 464(c)(1)(B)). A limited entrepreneur is one who has an interest (other than a limited partnership interest) in an enterprise and who does not actively participate in the enterprise's management (Code Sec. 464(e)(2)(A)). An

---

Footnote references are to paragraphs of the 2002 Standard Federal Tax Reports.

[11] ¶ 31,066
[12] ¶ 20,700, ¶ 20,701
[13] ¶ 13,800, ¶ 13,833.01
[14] ¶ 20,700, ¶ 20,701.025
[15] ¶ 20,700
[16] ¶ 21,802

individual will not be treated as a limited partner or limited entrepreneur in a farming enterprise (other than one with respect to which securities have been registered) if the individual:

(1) has his principal residence on the farm on which the farming enterprise is being carried on;

(2) has an interest attributable to active participation in management of the farming enterprise for a period of not less than five years;

(3) as his principal business activity, actively participates in the management of a farming enterprise, regardless of whether he actively participates in the management of the enterprise in question; or

(4) actively participates in the management of another farming enterprise involving the raising of livestock (or is so treated under either (1) or (2)) and owns an interest in an enterprise involving the further processing of the livestock raised in the enterprise.

If an individual meets any of these conditions, any member of his family who owns an interest in a farming enterprise which is attributable to the individual's active participation will not be treated as a limited partner or limited entrepreneur (Code Sec. 464(c)(2)).[17]

Cash-method farmers who purchase feed, seed and similar supplies for use in a later tax year are limited in their ability to claim current deductions for these prepaid expenses. To the extent that prepaid farm expenses (including prepaid poultry expenses) exceed 50% of total deductible farming expenses, these expenses may be deducted only when used or consumed.

If the farmer qualifies for one of two possible exceptions, he may deduct the cost of the prepaid expenses (Code Sec. 464(f)).[18] The first exception applies if a farm-related taxpayer satisfies the 50% test on the basis of the three preceding years. The second exception applies if a farm-related taxpayer fails to satisfy the 50% test due to a change in business operations directly attributable to extraordinary circumstances.

Economic Performance

2042. Prepaid Expenses. Under Code Sec. 461(i),[19] a tax shelter is prohibited from using the recurring-item exception to the economic performance rule (see ¶ 1539). However, economic performance with respect to the drilling of an oil or gas well will be considered to have occurred within a tax year if drilling commences within 90 days of the close of the tax year. For purposes of these rules, a tax shelter is (a) any enterprise (other than a C corporation) that is required to register its offering with a state or federal agency, (b) any partnership, entity, plan, or arrangement, the principal purpose of which is tax evasion or avoidance, and (c) any partnership or entity (other than a C corporation) if more than 35% of its losses are allocable to limited partners or limited entrepreneurs. For transactions entered into after August 5, 1997, a tax shelter is defined as an entity that has the avoidance or evasion of federal income tax as a *significant* purpose (rather than a *principal* purpose).

AT-RISK RULES

Limitations on Loss Deductions

2045. Limit of Losses to Amount at Risk. Code Sec. 465 generally limits a taxpayer's deductible loss to the amount that the taxpayer has at risk with respect to an activity.[20] The rules, which apply to individuals and certain closely held corporations, are designed to prevent taxpayers from offsetting trade, business,

or professional income by losses from investments in activities that are largely financed by nonrecourse loans for which they are not personally liable. Even if it has been determined that the loss is deductible under the at-risk rules, the loss may still be limited by the passive activity loss rules (see ¶ 2053).

Under the at-risk rules, loss deductions are limited to the amount of the taxpayer's cash contribution and the adjusted basis of other property which he contributes to the activity, plus any amounts borrowed for use in the activity if the taxpayer has personal liability for the borrowed amounts or has pledged assets not used in the activity as security for the borrowed amounts. The taxpayer will not be considered at risk with respect to amounts protected against loss through nonrecourse financing, guarantees, stop-loss agreements, or similar arrangements (Code Sec. 465(b)).[21] Also, amounts are not at risk if they are borrowed from (1) a creditor who has an interest other than as a creditor (which has been defined as a capital or net profits interest) or (2) a person related to a person with such an interest (Code Sec. 465(b)(3)).[22]

Personal liability of the taxpayer for borrowed amounts generally hinges on whether the taxpayer is the ultimate obligor of the liability with no recourse against any other party.[23]

Generally, the at-risk rules apply to all activities engaged in as a trade or business or for the production of income. Code Sec. 465(c)[24] specifically includes: (1) holding, producing, or distributing motion pictures or video tapes, (2) farming, (3) leasing of Sec. 1245 property (see ¶ 1785), (4) exploring for, or exploiting, oil and gas resources, and (5) exploring for, or exploiting, geothermal deposits.

For investment tax credit at-risk rules, see ¶ 1356.

The two activities not subject to the at-risk rules are: (1) the holding of real estate (other than mineral property) placed in service before January 1, 1987, and (2) the leasing of equipment by closely held corporations (i.e., those with five or fewer individuals owning more than 50% of the stock) (Code Sec. 465(c)(4)).

In the case of the five specifically identified activities above, each film or tape, each piece of Sec. 1245 property, each farm and each oil, gas, or geothermal property is treated as a separate activity. However, for a partnership or an S corporation, all leased Sec. 1245 properties that are placed in service in the same tax year are treated as a single activity (Code Sec. 465(c)).[25] Trade or business activities subject to the at-risk rules are to be aggregated and treated as a single activity if the taxpayer actively participates in the management of the trade or business or, where the trade or business is carried on by a partnership or S corporation, if 65% or more of the losses for the tax year are allocable to persons who actively participate in the management (Code Sec. 465(c)(3)(B)).

Form 6198 is used to compute the deductible loss, if any, under the at-risk rules.

PASSIVE ACTIVITY LOSSES

Limitations on Losses and Credits

2053. General Rules. Generally, losses from passive activities may not be deducted from nonpassive income (for example, wages, interest, or dividends) (Code Sec. 469).[26] Similarly, tax credits from passive activities are generally limited to the tax allocable to those activities. In determining a taxpayer's allowable loss, the at-risk rules discussed at ¶ 2045 are applied before the passive activity loss rules.

Generally, to the extent that the total deductions from passive activities exceed the total income from these activities for the tax year, the excess (the passive activity loss) is not allowed as a deduction for that year. A disallowed loss is suspended and carried forward as a deduction from the passive activity in the next

---

Footnote references are to paragraphs of the 2002 Standard Federal Tax Reports.
21 ¶ 21,850, ¶ 21,893.05   23 ¶ 21,893.35   25 ¶ 21,850, ¶ 21,893.027
22 ¶ 21,850, ¶ 21,893.05   24 ¶ 21,850, ¶ 21,893.025   26 ¶ 21,960, ¶ 21,966   **¶ 2053**

succeeding tax year (Reg. § 1.469-1(f)(4)).[27] Any unused suspended losses are allowed in full when the taxpayer disposes of his entire interest in the activity in a fully taxable transaction (Code Sec. 469(g)) (see ¶ 2076).[28]

Special rules apply to rental real estate activities in which a taxpayer actively participates (see ¶ 2063). Losses and credits that are attributable to limited partnership interests are generally treated as arising from a passive activity (Code Sec. 469(h)(2)).[29] See ¶ 2059. Losses from a working interest in oil and gas property are not subject to the passive activity limitations if the working interest is held directly or through an entity that does not limit liability, such as an interest as a general partner (Code Sec. 469(c)(3)), Temp. Reg. § 1.469-1T(e)(4)(ii)).[30]

Forms. Most taxpayers use Forms 8582 and 8582-CR to calculate their allowable passive losses and credits. Form 8810 is used by personal service corporations and closely held C corporations. Form 8825 is used by partnerships and S corporations to report income and deductible expenses from rented real estate activities.

2054. Publicly Traded Partnerships. Special rules apply to losses from publicly traded partnerships (PTPs). A PTP is a partnership whose interests are traded on an established securities market or are readily tradable on a secondary market (or its substantial equivalent) (Code Sec. 469(k)(2)).[31] A taxpayer's net income from a PTP may not be used to offset net losses from other PTPs or net losses from other passive activities.[32] A disallowed loss from a PTP is carried forward and allowed as a deduction in a tax year when the PTP has net income or when the taxpayer disposes of his entire interest in the PTP (Code Sec. 469(k)).[33]

2056. Taxpayers Covered. The passive activity rules apply to individuals, estates, trusts (other than grantor trusts), and personal service corporations (Code Sec. 469(a)(2)).[34] Although the passive activity rules do not apply to grantor trusts, partnerships, and S corporations directly, the owners of these entities are subject to the rules.

Closely Held C Corporations. A rule preventing the offset of passive activity losses against portfolio income, but not against net active income, applies to closely held C corporations (other than personal service corporations). A closely held C corporation's net active income is equal to its taxable income figured without any income or loss from a passive activity or any portfolio income or loss (Code Sec. 469(e)(2)(A)).[35]

2058. Activity Defined. In order to correctly apply the passive loss rules, taxpayers must determine which of their operations constitute an "activity." For tax years ending after May 10, 1992, an activity is defined under Reg. § 1.469-4.[36]

One or more trade or business activities are treated as a single activity if they constitute an appropriate economic unit for the measurement of gain or loss for PAL purposes (Reg. § 1.469-4(c)).[37] Five factors listed in the regulations are given the greatest weight in determining whether an activity or group of activities constitutes an appropriate economic unit: (1) similarities or differences in types of business; (2) extent of common control; (3) extent of common ownership; (4) geographical location; and (5) business interdependencies among the activities.[38]

Once activities are grouped together or kept separate, they may not be regrouped by the taxpayer in future years unless the original grouping was clearly inappropriate or became inappropriate due to a material change in facts and circumstances (Reg. § 1.469-4(e)).[39] The IRS may disallow and regroup a taxpayer's grouping of activities that does not reflect an appropriate economic unit and has

---

Footnote references are to paragraphs of the 2002 Standard Federal Tax Reports.

[27] ¶ 21,961B
[28] ¶ 21,960
[29] ¶ 21,960
[30] ¶ 21,960
[31] ¶ 21,960
[32] ¶ 21,966.059
[33] ¶ 21,960

[34] ¶ 21,960, ¶ 21,966.02
[35] ¶ 21,960,
¶ 21,966.0205,
¶ 21,966.0545,
¶ 21,966.0285
[36] ¶ 21,964B,
¶ 21,966.021

[37] ¶ 21,964B
[38] ¶ 21,966.031
[39] ¶ 21,964B,
¶ 21,966.031

¶ 2054

circumvention of the passive activity loss rules as a primary purpose (Reg. § 1.469-4(f)(1)).[40]

Activities Held Through Partnerships or S Corporations. Activities are first grouped by partnerships or S corporations at the entity level (Reg. § 1.469-4(d)(5)).[41] If appropriate, a partner or shareholder should further combine these activities with other activities outside the entity.

Rental Activities. Rental activities are grouped according to the "appropriate economic unit" standard stated above (Reg. § 1.469-4(c)). However, a rental real estate activity may not be combined with an activity involving the rental of personal property (Reg. § 1.469-4(d)(2)). [42]

Combining Trade or Business and Rental Activities. A rental activity may not be grouped with a trade or business activity unless either the rental activity is insubstantial in relation to the trade or business activity or the trade or business activity is insubstantial in relation to the rental activity (Reg. § 1.469-4(d)(1)(i)).[43] The regulations add a third alternative—that each owner of the trade or business have the same proportionate ownership interest in the rental activity, in which case the portion of the rental activity that involves the rental of items of property to a trade or business activity may be grouped with the trade or business activity (Reg. § 1.469-4(d)(1)(i)(C)).

> *Example:* The Getaway Partnership owns a 10-story building in which it operates a travel agency on three floors and rents seven floors to tenants. The partnership is divided into two activities: a travel agency activity and a rental real estate activity. Deductions and credits attributable to the building are allocable to the travel agency activity only to the extent that they relate to the space occupied by the travel agency during the tax year.

Partial Disposition of Activity. If the taxpayer disposes of *substantially all* of an activity, he may treat the interest disposed of as a separate activity, provided that he can establish the amount of gross income, deductions and credits allocable to that part of the activity for the tax year (Reg. § 1.469-4(g)).[44] This provision is designed to allow taxpayers to claim suspended passive losses even though they have not disposed of their entire interest in an activity (see ¶ 2076).

2059. Passive Activity Defined. A passive activity is one that involves the conduct of any trade or business in which the taxpayer does not materially participate (Code Sec. 469(c)).[45] Any rental activity is a passive activity whether or not the taxpayer materially participates. However, there are special rules for real estate rental activities (see ¶ 2063) and real estate professionals (see ¶ 2064). The rental of a dwelling unit used for personal purposes during the year for more than the greater of 14 days or 10 percent of the number of days that the unit was rented is not a passive activity (Temp. Reg. § 1.469-1T(e)(5))[46]

Trading personal property that is actively traded, such as stocks and bonds, for the account of owners of interests in the activity is not a passive activity. For example, the activity of a partnership that trades stock using money contributed by the partners is not a passive activity (Temp. Reg. § 1.469-1T(e)(6)).

Generally, to be considered as materially participating in an activity during a tax year an individual must satisfy any one of the following tests: (1) he participates more than 500 hours; (2) his participation constitutes substantially all of the participation in the activity; (3) he participates for more than 100 hours and this participation is not less than the participation of any other individual; (4) the activity is a "significant participation activity" (see below) and his participation in all significant participation activities exceeds 500 hours; (5) he materially partici-

---

Footnote references are to paragraphs of the 2002 Standard Federal Tax Reports.

[40] ¶ 21,964B
[41] ¶ 21,964B,
¶ 21,966.0315
[42] ¶ 21,964B,
¶ 21,966.032

[43] ¶ 21,964B,
¶ 21,966.0325
[44] ¶ 21,964B,
¶ 21,966.033

[45] ¶ 21,960
[46] ¶ 21,962B,
¶ 21,966.021

pated in the activity for any five years of the 10 years that preceded the year in question; (6) the activity is a "personal service activity" (see below) and he materially participated in the activity for any three years preceding the tax year in question; or (7) he satisfies a facts and circumstances test that requires him to show that he participated on a regular, continuous, and substantial basis for more than 100 hours during the tax year. With respect to test (7), an individual's participation in managing the activity does not count toward the 100-hour requirement if any other person received compensation for managing the activity or any other person spent more time managing the activity (Temporary Reg. § 1.469-5T(a)).[47]

Limited Partners. Losses and credits attributable to limited partnership interests are treated as arising from a passive activity unless the limited partner participated for more than 500 hours (test (1)), materially participated in five of the 10 preceding tax years (test (5)), or the activity is a personal service activity in which the limited partner materially participated for any three preceding tax years (test (6)). A general partner who also holds a limited partnership interest is not treated as a limited partner (Code Sec. 469(h)(2), Temp. Reg. § 1.469-5T(e)).

Special rules are also provided for determining the material participation of limited partners (Temporary Reg. § 1.469-5T(e)(2)),[48] certain retired or disabled farmers (Temporary Reg. § 1.469-5T(h)(2)),[49] and personal service and closely held corporations (Temporary Reg. § 1.469-1T(g)(2) and Temporary Reg. § 1.469-1T(g)(3)(i)).[50]

Significant Participation Activity. A significant participation activity is one in which the taxpayer participates more than 100 hours during the tax year but does not materially participate under any of the other six tests set forth above (Temporary Reg. § 1.469-5T(c)).[51]

Personal Service Activity. A personal service activity involves the performance of personal service in (1) the fields of health (including veterinary services), law, engineering, architecture, accounting, actuarial services, the performing arts, or consulting or (2) any other trade or business in which capital is not a material income-producing factor (Temporary Reg. § 1.469-5T(d)).[52]

Definition of Participation. Generally, any work done by an individual with respect to an activity that the individual owns an interest in is treated as participation (Reg. § 1.469-5(f)(1)). However, participation does not include work that is not customarily done by an owner if one of the principal purposes for performing the work is to avoid the passive activity limitations (Temp. Reg. § 1.469-5T(f)(2)(i)).

Spouse's Participation. In applying the material participation tests, an individual's participation includes his spouse's participation even if the spouse does not own an interest in the activity and separate returns are filed (Temp. Reg. § 1.469-5T(f)(3)).

Participation as an Investor. Work done in an individual's capacity as an investor in an activity, such as studying and reviewing the activity's financial statements and operational reports, preparing summaries or analyses of the activity's finances or operations for personal use, and monitoring the finances or operations of the activity in a nonmanagerial capacity, is not counted as participation (Temp. Reg. § 1.469-5T(f)(2)(ii)).

Proving Participation. Participation may be established by any reasonable means. It is not necessary to maintain contemporaneous daily records of participation. An approximate number of hours of participation may be based on appointment books, calendars, or narrative summaries (Temp. Reg. § 1.469-5T(f)(4)).

Footnote references are to paragraphs of the 2002 Standard Federal Tax Reports.

¶ 2059
[47] ¶ 21,965, ¶ 21,966.026   [49] ¶ 21,965   [51] ¶ 21,965, ¶ 21,966.026
[48] ¶ 21,965   [50] ¶ 21,962   [52] ¶ 21,965, ¶ 21,966.026

Rental Activities

2062. Special Rules for Rental Activities. In general, a rental activity is treated as a passive activity (Code Sec. 469(c)(2)).[53] An activity is a "rental activity" if (1) during the tax year, tangible property held in connection with the activity is used by customers or is held for use by customers, and (2) the gross income of the activity represents amounts paid mainly for the use of the tangible property (Temporary Reg. § 1.469-1T(e)(3)(i)).[54] However, if any one of the following tests is met, the activity is not considered to be a rental activity for purposes of the passive loss rules: (1) the average period of customer use of the property is seven days or less; (2) the average period of customer use is 30 days or less and significant personal services are provided by or on behalf of the owner; (3) without regard to the period of customer use, extraordinary personal services are provided by or on behalf of the owner; (4) the rental of the property is incidental to a nonrental activity; (5) the property is customarily made available during defined business hours for the nonexclusive use of customers; or (6) the taxpayer provides property for use in an activity that is conducted by a partnership, S corporation, or joint venture in which the taxpayer owns an interest and the activity is not a rental activity (Temporary Reg. § 1.469-1T(e)(3)(ii)).[55]

2063. Active Participation in Rental Real Estate Activity. There is a limited exception to the passive loss rules in the case of losses from rental real estate in which the taxpayer or the taxpayer's spouse actively participates (Code Sec. 469(i)).[56] The exception is available only to individual taxpayers or their estates for tax years ending less than two years after the date of death. The estate qualifies during this period if the decedent actively participated before his death (Code Sec. 469(i)(4)(A)).

The active participation standard is less stringent than the material participation standard. An individual may meet the active participation requirement if he participates in the making of management decisions (for example, approving new tenants, deciding on rental terms, approving expenditures) or arranges for others to provide services (for example, repairs) in a significant and bona fide sense.[57] The requirement for active participation applies in the year in which the loss arose as well as the year in which the loss is allowed under the $25,000 allowance rule. (However, real estate professionals may be able to treat rental property activities as nonpassive activities (¶ 2064).)

Under this exception, up to $25,000 of passive losses and the deduction equivalent of tax credits that are attributable to rental real estate may be used as an offset against income from nonpassive sources (for example, dividends and wages) each year. To be eligible for this exception, the individual must own at least a 10% interest of all interests in the activity throughout the year. The interest of an individual's spouse is taken into account in determining 10% ownership (Code Sec. 469(i)(6)).[58] This $25,000 maximum amount is reduced, but not below zero, by 50% of the amount by which adjusted gross income exceeds $100,000.

"Adjusted gross income" is computed for purposes of this exception by disregarding: taxable social security and railroad retirement benefits, the exclusion for qualified U.S. savings bonds used to pay higher education expenses, the exclusion for employer adoption assistance payments, passive activity income or loss included on Form 8582, any overall loss from a publicly traded partnership, rental real estate losses allowed to real estate professionals, deductions for contributions to IRAs and pension plans, and the deductions for one-half of self-employment tax, interest on student loans, and higher education expenses (Code Sec. 469(i)(3)(E)).[59] The $25,000 is completely phased out when modified adjusted gross income reaches $150,000 (Code Sec. 469(i)(3)).[60]

Footnote references are to paragraphs of the 2002 Standard Federal Tax Reports.
[53] ¶ 21,960
[54] ¶ 21,962
[55] ¶ 21,962, ¶ 21,966.022
[56] ¶ 21,960, ¶ 21,966.035
[57] ¶ 21,966.0353
[58] ¶ 21,960
[59] ¶ 21,960
[60] ¶ 21,960

Separate Returns. For married taxpayers who file separate returns and live apart, up to $12,500 of passive losses may be used to offset income. This amount is reduced by 50% of the amount by which the taxpayer's modified adjusted gross income exceeds $50,000. The special allowance is completely phased out when modified adjusted gross income reaches $75,000. Married taxpayers who file separately and live together at any time during the tax year are not eligible for the special allowance (Code Sec. 469(i)(5)).[61]

Rehabilitation and Low-Income Housing Tax Credits. For the rehabilitation tax credit (see ¶ 1347) and low-income housing credits on property placed in service before 1990, the phaseout range for offsetting tax on up to $25,000 of nonpassive income is between $200,000 and $250,000 of adjusted gross income ($100,000 and $125,000 for a married taxpayer filing separately and living apart). No AGI limitation applies to the low-income housing credits for property placed in service after 1989 (¶ 1334) (Code Sec. 469(i)(3)(B) and (C)).[62] The individual need not actively participate in the activity to which the credits relate (Code Sec. 469(i)(6)(B)).[63]

2064. Real Estate Professionals. Certain real estate professionals may be able to treat rental real estate activities as nonpassive (Code Sec. 469(c)(7)).[64] To qualify, (1) more than one-half of the personal services performed in trades or businesses by the taxpayer during the tax year must involve real property trades or businesses in which the taxpayer (or the taxpayer's spouse) materially participates, and (2) the taxpayer must perform more than 750 hours of service during the tax year in real property trades or businesses in which the taxpayer (or the taxpayer's spouse) materially participates. These two requirements must be satisfied by one spouse if a joint return is filed. Assuming that the requirements for the exception are satisfied, the passive activity loss rules are not applied.

Personal services performed as an employee are not taken into account for purposes of (1) and (2) unless the employee owns more than a 5-percent interest in the employer.

A real property trade or business is a business with respect to which real property is developed or redeveloped, constructed or reconstructed, acquired, converted, rented or leased, operated or managed, or brokered (Code Sec. 469(c)(7)(C)).

The exception for real estate professionals is applied as if each interest of the taxpayer in rental real estate is a separate activity. However, a taxpayer may elect to treat all interests in rental real estate as a single activity for purposes of satisfying the material participation requirements.

A closely held corporation qualifies as a real estate professional if more than 50 percent of its annual gross receipts for the tax year are from real property trades or businesses in which it materially participates.

Portfolio Income

2066. Separate Accounting Required. Portfolio income is not treated as income from a passive activity; it must be accounted for separately, and passive losses and credits generally may not be applied against it. The term "portfolio income" includes interest, dividends, annuities and royalties, as well as gain or loss from the disposition of income-producing or investment property that is not derived in the ordinary course of a trade or business (Code Sec. 469(e)(1)).[65] No exception is provided for the treatment of portfolio income arising from working capital (amounts set aside for the reasonable needs of the business) (Code Sec. 469(e)(1)(B)).[66]

Footnote references are to paragraphs of the 2002 Standard Federal Tax Reports.

¶ 2064

[61] ¶ 21,960
[62] ¶ 21,960
[63] ¶ 21,960
[64] ¶ 21,960, ¶ 21,966.024
[65] ¶ 21,960, ¶ 21,966.042
[66] ¶ 21,960

Tax Treatment of Current Losses and Credits

2070. Current Losses. Generally, a loss arising from a passive activity is deductible against the net income of another passive activity. Losses that are not deductible for a particular tax year because there is insufficient passive activity income to offset them (suspended losses) are carried forward indefinitely and are allowed as deductions against passive income in subsequent years (Code Sec. 469(b)).[67] Unused suspended losses are allowed in full upon a fully taxable disposition of the taxpayer's entire interest in the activity (see ¶ 2076).

2073. Current Credits. Credits arising with respect to passive activities are generally treated in the same manner as losses, except that suspended credits are not allowed upon disposition of the activity.[68] Thus, credits may be used to offset the tax attributable to net passive income (the difference between the tax that the taxpayer would have to pay (1) on all income and (2) on taxable income other than net passive income). In both cases, the effect of credits is disregarded.

In general, unused credits can be carried forward indefinitely. However, the character of a credit relating to a passive activity changes, in effect, when the credit becomes allowable under the passive loss rules (either there is sufficient passive income to allow its use, or it is within the scope of the $25,000 benefit for real estate activities). At this time, the credit is aggregated with credits relating to nonpassive activities of the taxpayer to determine whether all such credits are allowable considering the other limitations that apply to the use of credits (see ¶ 1323).[69]

Tax Treatment of Suspended Losses and Credits

2076. Carryforward of Suspended Losses and Credits. When a taxpayer disposes of his entire interest in a passive activity in a taxable transaction, his suspended passive losses (see ¶ 2070) may be applied against his active income (Code Sec. 469(g)).[70] However, these losses must first be applied against the taxpayer's net income or gain from passive activities (Code Sec. 469(g)(1)(A)).[71] Suspended credits are not allowed upon the disposition of a passive activity.

Entire Interest. A disposition of a taxpayer's entire interest involves a disposition of the interest in all entities that are engaged in the activity and, to the extent the activity is held in the form of a sole proprietorship, of all of the assets used or created in the activity. If a partnership or S corporation conducts two or more separate activities and the entity disposes of all the assets used or created in one activity, the disposition constitutes a disposition of the entire interest. The same rule applies to grantor trusts.[72]

In some instances, a taxpayer may claim a deduction for suspended losses even though he disposes of less than his entire interest (see ¶ 2058).

Taxable Transactions. To qualify as a fully taxable disposition, the disposition generally must be a sale of the interest to a third party in an arm's-length transaction and must not be a sham, a wash sale, or a transfer of repurchase rights.[73]

If a taxpayer disposes of an interest in a passive activity in a taxable transaction with a related party as defined by Code Sec. 267(b)[74] or with a controlled partnership as defined by Code Sec. 707(b)(1),[75] the suspended losses will not be triggered (Code Sec. 469(g)(1)(B)).[76] In these circumstances the taxpayer will be able to claim the loss only when the related person or controlled partnership disposes of the activity in a taxable transaction with an unrelated person. Abandonment is a fully taxable disposition.

Footnote references are to paragraphs of the 2002 Standard Federal Tax Reports.

[67] ¶ 21,960, ¶ 21,966.0552
[68] ¶ 21,966.057
[69] ¶ 21,966.0575
[70] ¶ 21,960, ¶ 21,966.0552

[71] ¶ 21,960
[72] ¶ 21,966.0552
[73] ¶ 21,966.0552

[74] ¶ 14,150
[75] ¶ 25,480
[76] ¶ 21,960

¶ 2076

Installment Sales. An installment sale of a taxpayer's interest triggers the allowance of suspended losses. Losses are allowed in the ratio that the gain recognized in each year bears to the total gain. Gain from a pre-1987 installment sale that is recognized in post-1986 tax years may be treated as passive activity income if the activity would have been treated as a passive activity.[77]

Death. A transfer by reason of the taxpayer's death causes suspended losses to be allowed in the year of death to the extent that they exceed the amount by which the basis of the interest is increased under Code Sec. 1014.[78]

Gifts. Disposition of a passive activity by gift does *not* trigger the suspended losses. Instead, the basis of the transferred interest is increased by the amount of such losses (Code Sec. 469(j)(6)).[79]

Exchanges. An exchange of a taxpayer's interest in a passive activity in a nonrecognition transaction (e.g., a Code Sec. 1031 like-kind exchange—see ¶1721) does not trigger suspended losses. However, to the extent that the taxpayer recognizes gain on the transaction (for example, to the extent of boot received), the gain is treated as passive activity income against which passive losses may be deducted.[80]

Casualty or Theft. A casualty or theft loss involving property used in a passive activity does not constitute a complete disposition of the taxpayer's interest in the activity unless loss of all property used or created in the activity results.[81]

Activity No Longer Passive. In the tax year that an activity ceases to be a passive activity, previously suspended losses from that activity are permitted to be claimed as deductions against the activity's net income. Similarly, prior year unallowed passive activity credits may offset the current year's tax liability that is allocable to the current year's net income from the former passive activity. Tax liability for this purpose is figured on the net income as reduced by the prior year unallowed losses (Code Sec. 469(f)(1)).[82]

Cessation of Closely Held C Corporation or PSC Status. If a closely held C corporation or a personal service corporation (PSC) changes its status, suspended losses from prior years will continue to be subject to the limitations that were imposed before the status changed (see ¶2056). Losses arising in years after the year in which the corporation's status changes are not subject to the passive loss rules (Code Sec. 469(f)(2)).

Treatment of Loss on Disposition. When a taxpayer disposes of a passive activity in a taxable transaction, any net passive loss from the activity must first be applied against income or gain from the taxpayer's other passive activities. Any remaining loss from the activity is then classified as nonpassive and may be used to offset income from nonpassive activities (for example, wages and interest income) (Code Sec. 469(g)(1)(A)).[83]

Footnote references are to paragraphs of the 2002 Standard Federal Tax Reports.

¶2076

[77] ¶21,966.0541
[78] ¶21,960
[79] ¶21,960
[80] ¶21,966.0553
[81] ¶21,966.0553
[82] ¶21,960
[83] ¶21,960

Chapter 21

RETIREMENT PLANS

Types of Plans

2101. Introduction. An employer who wants to provide retirement benefits for employees will customarily establish a pension, profit-sharing or stock bonus plan that qualifies for certain tax benefits (Code Sec. 401).[1] Tax benefits of a qualified retirement plan include a tax exemption for the fund that is established to provide benefits (Code Sec. 501(a); Reg. § 1.401(f)-1(c)(1)),[2] deductions by the employer for contributions made to the fund (Code Sec. 404),[3] tax deferral for the employee for the employer's contributions and earnings thereon (Code Secs. 402(a) and 403(a)(1)),[4] and, in some instances, favorable tax treatment when benefits are paid (Code Sec. 402(c) and (d)).[5]

New Tax Incentive for Employers. Small employers (e.g., 100 employees or less) that establish qualified retirements plans in a tax year beginning after December 31, 2001, may be eligible to claim a tax credit based on 50% of the cost of establishing and/or maintaining the plan (Code Sec. 45E, as added by the Economic Growth and Tax Relief Reconciliation Act of 2001 (P.L. 107-16)). The maximum credit for any tax year is $500. Generally, the credit may be claimed for each of the first three years of the plan (Code Sec. 45E(b)(1), as added by P.L. 107-16). See ¶ 1344B.

New Tax Incentive for Individuals. For tax years beginning after December 31, 2001, individuals that meet specific requirements will be able to claim a nonrefundable tax credit based upon their qualified retirement savings contributions (Code Sec. 25B, as added by P.L. 107-16). See ¶ 1307 and ¶ 2175.

2103. Qualified Retirement Plans. There are two basic types of qualified retirement plans: defined benefit plans and defined contribution plans. *Defined benefit plans* include pension and annuity plans that promise specified retirement benefits (Code Sec. 414(j)).[6] These promised benefits usually are in the form of a monthly retirement pension based on levels of compensation and years of service. Contributions to the plan are actuarially calculated to provide the promised benefits

---

Footnote references are to paragraphs of the 2002 Standard Federal Tax Reports.

[1] ¶ 17,502
[2] ¶ 18,100, ¶ 22,602
[3] ¶ 18,330
[4] ¶ 18,202, ¶ 18,270
[5] ¶ 18,202
[6] ¶ 19,150

¶ 2103

(Reg. § 1.401-1(b)(1)(i)) [7] and are not allocated to individual accounts of participants. *Defined contribution plans* include profit-sharing, stock bonus, and money purchase plans. A separate account must be provided for each person covered by the plan (Code Sec. 414(i)).[8] Under a defined contribution plan, the employer promises a specific contribution on behalf of each participant (usually expressed as a percentage of compensation). The contributions are fixed and are not determined with reference to the employer's profits (Reg. § 1.401-1(b)(1)(i)).[9] The contributions must be allocated among individual accounts maintained for participants, and the plan must have a definite, written formula for the allocation. Future benefits are dependent upon such factors as contributions to participants' accounts and accumulations of income.

2105. Profit-Sharing Plans. Employer contributions to a profit-sharing plan are ordinarily based on profits. The employer is not required to contribute any particular percentage of profits, but contributions must be substantial and recurring. A profit-sharing plan must have a definite written formula for allocating profits among individual accounts maintained for the participants (Reg. § 1.401-1(b)(1)(ii)) [10] and is classified as a defined contribution plan (Code Sec. 414(i)).[11] The term "profit-sharing plan" is a misnomer because a plan may qualify as such even if contributions exceed current and accumulated profits and even if the plan is maintained by a not-for-profit organization (Code Sec. 401(a)(27)).[12] A more accurate name would be "discretionary contribution plan"—a name that distinguishes this type of plan from a money purchase plan (which must have a contribution formula).

2107. Annuity Plans. An annuity plan is a defined benefit plan funded through the direct purchase by the employer of an annuity contract or contracts (Code Secs. 403(a)(1) [13] and 404(a)(2)).[14]

2109. Stock Bonus Plans and ESOPs. A stock bonus plan is a defined contribution plan that provides benefits similar to those of a profit-sharing plan (Reg. § 1.401-1(b)(1)(iii)) [15] and is generally subject to the same rules as those governing such a plan. Generally, the benefits under the plan are distributed in stock of the employer.

ESOPs. Certain stock bonus plans (or combination stock bonus and money purchase pension plans)—so-called "employee stock ownership plans" (ESOPs) (Code Secs. 409 and 4975(e)(7)) [16]—may enable an employer corporation and others to qualify for additional tax advantages if special requirements are met. These advantages include the following:

(1) The ESOP will qualify for an exemption from certain of the prohibited transaction rules that apply in the case of loans made by disqualified persons to qualified plans (Code Sec. 4975(d)(3) and (e)(7)).[17]

(2) Under some circumstances a shareholder, other than a C corporation, may elect not to recognize gain on the sale of qualified securities to an ESOP (Code Sec. 1042(a)).[18] Nonrecognition depends upon the shareholder purchasing qualified replacement property within a specific period of time (Code Sec. 1042(c)(3)).[19]

(3) The employer corporation is entitled to a deduction for dividends on its stock held by an ESOP that are (a) paid in cash directly to participants in the ESOP, (b) paid to the ESOP and subsequently distributed to the participants in cash no later than 90 days after the end of the plan year in which the dividends are paid to the ESOP, or (c) used to repay an ESOP loan (Code Sec. 404(k)).[20] For tax years beginning after December 31, 2001, C corporations may deduct, at the

---

Footnote references are to paragraphs of the 2002 Standard Federal Tax Reports.

[7] ¶ 17,504	[12] ¶ 17,502	[17] ¶ 34,400
[8] ¶ 19,150	[13] ¶ 18,270	[18] ¶ 29,820
[9] ¶ 17,504	[14] ¶ 18,330	[19] ¶ 29,820
[10] ¶ 17,504	[15] ¶ 17,504	[20] ¶ 18,330
¶ **2105** [11] ¶ 19,150	[16] ¶ 18,950, ¶ 34,400	

election of plan participants or their beneficiaries, dividends paid to an ESOP and reinvested in qualified employer securities (Code Sec. 404(k)(2)(A)(iii)).[21]

(4) Contributions to an ESOP that are used to pay the principal on loans that were incurred to purchase employer securities may be deducted to the extent that they do not exceed 25% of the compensation paid to participants (Code Sec. 404(a)(9)(A)).[22] This contribution rule does not apply to S corporations (Code Sec. 404(a)(9)(C)).[23]

Participants in an ESOP maintained by an S corporation need not be given the ability to demand their distributions in the form of employer securities, provided that they have the right to receive the distributions in cash. This nondistribution rule also extends to stock that is substantially restricted to employee ownership (Code Sec. 409(h)(2)(B)).[24]

2110. SIMPLE Retirement Plans. A SIMPLE plan may be maintained in any year by an employer who has 100 or fewer employees who received at least $5,000 of compensation from the employer for the preceding year (Code Secs. 401(k)(11) and 408(p)(2)(C)(i)(I)).[25] Generally, the employer must not maintain any other employer-sponsored retirement plan, except for collectively bargained employees (Code Sec. 401(k)(11)(C) and (D)(i); Code Sec. 408(p)(2)(C)(i) and (D)).[26] An eligible employer who establishes and maintains a SIMPLE plan for at least one year, but subsequently fails to qualify as an eligible employer, will continue to be treated as an eligible employer for the two years following the last year in which it did qualify (Code Sec. 401(k)(11)(A) and (D)(i); Code Sec. 408(p)(2)(C)(i)(II)).[27]

A SIMPLE plan may take the form of an IRA established for each participant and it is tax exempt like any other IRA. However, it is not subject to the nondiscrimination and other qualification rules generally applicable to qualified plans (see ¶ 2185). As an alternative, the SIMPLE plan may take the form of a 401(k) arrangement (see ¶ 2112). SIMPLE is the acronym for "savings incentive match plans for employees."

2111. 401(k) Plans. Under a "401(k) plan," employer contributions to the plan will not be included in the income of a participant because the employee has the option of taking the contribution in cash or having it paid to the plan (an "elective contribution") or because the contribution coincides with a salary reduction arrangement (Code Secs. 401(k) and 402(e)(3); Reg. § § 1.401(k)-1 and 1.402(a)-1(d)).[28] These types of plans are sometimes referred to as "cash or deferred arrangements" (CODAs).

A 401(k) plan must generally be part of a profit-sharing or stock bonus plan that, in addition to meeting the general requirements of a qualified plan, must meet the special requirements summarized below.

Limit on Elective Deferrals. The total elective deferrals under the plans in which an individual participates (e.g., 401(k), 403(b) and/or 457 plans) are subject to an maximum annual limit (Code Sec. 402(g)(3)).[29] Generally, there is not a separate limit for each plan to which the employee makes elective deferrals. (After 2001, 457 plans are an exception to this rule; see ¶ 2197A.) For 2001, the limit is $10,500 ($11,000 for 2002) (Code Sec. 402(g)(1)).[30]

> **Example.** For 2001, Tony defers $8,000 under the 401(k) plan of Employer A and $5,000 under the 401(k) plan of Employer B. Tony has made an excess deferral in 2001 of $2,500 ($13,000 in deferrals − $10,500 deferral allowable).

Catch-Up Contributions. For tax years beginning after December 31, 2001, individuals age 50 or over may make an additional "catch-up" contribution to their

---

Footnote references are to paragraphs of the 2002 Standard Federal Tax Reports.

[21] ¶ 18,330	[26] ¶ 17,502, ¶ 18,902	[29] ¶ 18,202
[22] ¶ 18,330	[27] ¶ 17,502, ¶ 18,902	[30] ¶ 18,202
[23] ¶ 18,330	[28] ¶ 17,502, ¶ 18,110,	
[24] ¶ 18,950	¶ 18,202, ¶ 18,203	
[25] ¶ 17,502, ¶ 18,902		

401(k) plans and other types of elective deferral plans (e.g., 403(b) plans). For 2002, the additional "catch-up" contribution is $1,000 (Code Sec. 414(v)).[31] Catch-up contributions may only be made if the plan permits this type of contribution.

Amounts in excess of the limit are included in the participant's income. If the excess remains in the plan or plans, it is not treated as a part of the participant's investment in the plan and, therefore, is taxed again when distributed. However, the participant is entitled—before April 15 of the tax year following the year in which the excess is included in income—to withdraw the excess without tax consequences. The income attributable to the excess must also be withdrawn and is includible in the gross income of the participant for the tax year in which it is distributed. If the employee has made elective deferrals to more than one plan, then the employee can designate the amount of the excess that is to be withdrawn from each plan (Code Sec. 402(g)(2)(A)(i)).[32]

Matching Contributions from Employers. As a general rule, matching contributions made to a 401(k) plan by the employer are not treated as elective contributions and are, therefore, not subject to the annual limit (e.g., $10,500 for 2001, $11,000 for 2002). Matching contributions made to 401(k) plans for self-employed persons are not treated as part of the individual's elective contributions (Code Sec. 402(g)(9)).[33]

Special Qualification Requirements. A 401(k) plan must satisfy the following special requirements (Code Sec. 401(k)(2) and (4)): [34]

(1) It must give the participant the option of having the employer contribute amounts to the plan or receiving those amounts in cash.

(2) It must prohibit distributions of amounts attributable to elective contributions *earlier* than one of the following events: (a) separation from service ("severance from employment," for distributions made after December 31, 2001), death or disability; (b) termination of the plan without establishment of a successor plan; (c) attainment of age 59½; (d) before 2002, a corporate employer's disposition of substantially all of its assets or its interest in a subsidiary; or (e) hardship. Distributions at age 59½ or for hardship are not permitted in the case of a money purchase pension plan (Code Sec. 401(k)(2)(B)(i)).[35]

(3) It must provide that the participant's right to the value of the account that is attributable to elective contributions be fully vested at all times.

(4) It must not require as a condition of participation that an employee complete more than one year of service with the employer.

(5) It must not condition benefits under the 401(k) plan or any other benefit upon an employee's election to make contributions to the 401(k) plan. However, this prohibition does not apply to an employer's matching contributions.

Hardship Distribution. A hardship distribution is one that (1) is made because of the distributee's immediate and heavy financial need and (2) does not exceed the amount necessary to satisfy that need (Reg. § 1.401(k)-1(d)(2)(i)).[36] Types of expenses that satisfy the requirement of immediate and heavy financial need are: (a) medical expenses of the employee, spouse and dependents; (b) expenditures (excluding mortgage payments) to purchase a principal residence for the employee; (c) post-secondary tuition for the employee, spouse, children or dependents; and (d) expenditures to stave off eviction or foreclosure with respect to the employee's principal residence (Reg. § 1.401(k)-1(d)(2)(iii)(A) and (iv)(A)).

To satisfy the requirement that the funds are needed to satisfy an immediate and heavy financial need, the participant must first have exhausted all distributions and nontaxable loans available under all plans of the employer. A distribution will not qualify as a hardship distribution unless its receipt triggers the suspension of elective contributions and other employee contributions on behalf of the employee for at least 12 months (six months after December 31, 2001). Nor will a distribution qualify unless, by the terms of the plan, the applicable dollar limit on the employee's

Footnote references are to paragraphs of the 2002 Standard Federal Tax Reports.

¶2111
[31] ¶ 19,150
[32] ¶ 18,202
[33] ¶ 18,202
[34] ¶ 17,502
[35] ¶ 17,502
[36] ¶ 18,110

elective contributions for the tax year following the tax year of the distribution is reduced by the elective contributions made by the employee for the tax year of the hardship distribution (Reg. § 1.401(k)-1(d)(2)(iv)(B)(4)). A hardship distribution may *not* be rolled over into an IRA or other type of retirement plan (Code Sec. 402(c)(4)(C)).

An immediate and heavy financial need also includes any amounts necessary to pay any income taxes or penalties reasonably anticipated to result from the distribution (Reg. § 1.401(k)-1(d)(2)(iii)(B) and (iv)(B)). [37]

Special Nondiscrimination Rules. Unless the employer establishes a SIMPLE 401(k) (see ¶ 2112) or satisfies one of the alternative tests mentioned below, a qualified 401(k) must meet a special annual nondiscrimination test. The first step in the test is to determine the actual deferral ratio (ADR) (expressed as a percentage) of each highly compensated employee's elective contribution for the year being tested to his or her compensation for the same year. The next step is to determine the average of those individual ratios (expressed as a percentage). The average ADR for highly compensated individuals is then compared against the *preceding plan year* average ADR for rank and file employees. The average ratio (referred to as the actual deferral percentage (ADP)) of the highly compensated group may not exceed:

(a) 125% of the ADP of the rank and file group if the ADP of that group is 8% or more;

(b) 200% of the ADP of the rank and file group if the ADP of that group is 2% or less; or

(c) the ADP of the rank and file group plus two percentage points if the ADP of that group is between 2% and 8% (Code Sec. 401(k)(3)(A)(ii)). [38]

Election to Use Current Year ADP. The employer may elect to calculate the ADP for rank and file employees with reference to data for the current year. If made, this election may not be revoked without permission of the IRS. If the test year is the first year of the plan, and if the employer does not make this election, the ADP of rank and file employees for the preceding plan year is deemed to be 3% or, if the employer so elects, the ADP calculated on the basis of rank and file employees for the first plan year (Code Sec. 401(k)(3)(A)(ii) and (k)(3)(E)). [39]

For purposes of applying the nondiscrimination rule, the employer may elect to treat matching contributions and nonelective contributions as elective contributions if they satisfy the distribution and vesting rules (items (2) and (3) of the special qualification requirements discussed above) (Code Sec. 401(k)(3)(D)(ii)). [40]

The ADP test will be deemed satisfied if the employer establishes a SIMPLE 401(k). In addition, the ADP test will be deemed satisfied if the plan satisfies *either* one of the following alternatives:

(1) The employer must make matching contributions on behalf of each rank and file employee in an amount equal to (a) 100% of the employee's elective contributions not exceeding 3% of the employee's compensation and (b) 50% of the employee's elective contributions in excess of 3% but not in excess of 5% of the employee's compensation (Code Sec. 401(k)(12)(B)(i)). [41] Also, at any rate of elective contribution, the matching rate for any highly compensated employee must nct be greater than the matching rate for any rank and file employee (Code Sec. 401(k)(12)(b)(ii)). [42] Even though the rate of matching contribution with respect to any rate of elective contribution is not equal to the *percentage* required by the 100/50 match rule, the plan will be treated as having satisfied that rule if the design of the plan is such that (a) the rate of an employer's matching contribution does not increase as an employee's rate of elective contributions increases and (b) the aggregate *amount* of matching contributions at the rate of elective contribution is at least equal to the aggregate amount of matching contributions that would have been

---

Footnote references are to paragraphs of the 2002 Standard Federal Tax Reports.

[37] ¶ 18,110	[39] ¶ 17,502	[41] ¶ 17,502
[38] ¶ 17,502	[40] ¶ 17,502	[42] ¶ 17,502

made if matching contributions satisfied the 100/50 match rule (Code Sec. 401(k)(12)(B)(iii)).[43]

(2) The employer must contribute to a defined contribution plan at least 3% of compensation on behalf of each rank and file employee eligible to participate in the plan. The contribution must be made whether or not the employee makes an elective contribution or an after-tax contribution (Code Sec. 401(k)(12)(C)).[44]

Satisfaction of either alternative test by the same plan that includes the CODA being tested is not necessarily required. If the test is satisfied for each employee eligible to participate in the 401(k) plan by any plan maintained by the employer, the 401(k) qualifies (Code Sec. 401(k)(12)(F)).[45]

Correction of Excess Contributions. A plan is not disqualified because elective contributions on behalf of highly compensated employees exceed those permitted under the special nondiscrimination rule, provided that the excess is (1) recharacterized as an employee contribution or (2) distributed to the highly compensated employees. A distribution must include any income allocable to the excess contribution (Code Sec. 401(k)(8); Reg. § 1.401(k)-1(f)(1)).[46]

Penalty on Excess Contributions. There is a 10% penalty on excess contributions. The penalty will not apply if the excess is recharacterized or distributed within 2½-months following the plan year in which the excess contribution arose (Code Sec. 4979(f); Reg. § 1.401(k)-1(f)(6)(i); Reg. § 54.4979-1(c)).[47]

Highly Compensated Employees. A highly compensated employee is any employee who was:

(1) a 5% or more owner of the employer during the plan year or the preceding year or

(2) an employee who had compensation for the preceding year in excess of $85,000 for 2001 and, if the employer elects, was among the top 20% of employees by compensation for the preceding year (Code Sec. 414(q)(1)).[48]

2112. SIMPLE 401(k) Plans. Certain employers may maintain SIMPLE retirement plans (see ¶ 2110). One variety of a SIMPLE plan takes the form of an IRA established for each participating employee (see ¶ 2185). The other variety—a SIMPLE 401(k) plan—is discussed in the following material. Except as explained below, a SIMPLE 401(k) must generally satisfy the requirements that apply to other 401(k) plans.

In lieu of satisfying the ADP test (¶ 2111), a SIMPLE 401(k) plan established by an employer may qualify by satisfying the following requirements.

Elective Contributions. Each employee eligible to participate in the SIMPLE 401(k) plan must have the right to make annual elective contributions, expressed as a percentage of compensation and not exceeding $6,500 (for 2001) (Code Sec. 401(k)(11)(B)(i)).[49] A $7,000 limit is in effect for 2002 (Code Sec. 401(k)(11)(B)(i)(I)).[50] Matching contributions made for an employee, or a self-employed individual, are not treated as elective contributions and are, therefore, not included in the annual limit on elective contributions (Code Sec. 408(p)(9)).[51]

Matching Contributions. Unless the employer exercises the "nonelective contribution" option explained below, it must match the annual elective contribution of the employee in an amount not exceeding 3% of the employee's compensation (Code Sec. 401(k)(11)(B)(ii)).[52]

Vesting. All contributions must be fully vested when made, and the plan cannot impose any restrictions on withdrawals (Code Sec. 401(k)(11)(A)(iii)).[53]

Footnote references are to paragraphs of the 2002 Standard Federal Tax Reports.

43 ¶ 17,502	47 ¶ 18,110, ¶ 34,520,	51 ¶ 18,902
44 ¶ 17,502	¶ 34,522	52 ¶ 17,502
45 ¶ 17,502	48 ¶ 19,150	53 ¶ 17,502
46 ¶ 17,502, ¶ 18,110	49 ¶ 17,502	
	50 ¶ 17,502	

Employee Contributions and Rollovers. No contributions may be made to a SIMPLE 401(k) other than elective and matching contributions (Code Sec. 401(k)(11)(B)(I)(iii)).[54] As a result, nondeductible employee contributions and rollover contributions may not be made to the plan.

Employer May Maintain No Other Plan. No contributions (other than elective contributions, matching contributions, and nonelective contributions (see discussion below)) may be made, or benefits accrued, under any qualified plan of the employer on account of services performed by any employee eligible to participate in the SIMPLE 401(k) (Code Sec. 401(k)(11)(C)).[55] In this context, the term "qualified plan" also includes a SEP (see ¶ 2184), a tax-sheltered annuity (see ¶ 2167), and, in the case of a governmental unit, a nonqualified retirement plan (Code Sec. 401(k)(11)(C) and (D)(i); Code Sec. 408(p)(2)(D)(ii)).[56]

Matching Contribution Requirement Satisfied by Nonelective Contributions. An employer's matching contribution requirement is satisfied if the employer elects to make nonelective contributions of 2% of compensation for each employee who is eligible to participate in the arrangement and who has at least $5,000 of compensation from the employer for the calendar year. If the employer makes this election, employees must be notified within a reasonable period of time before the 60th day before the beginning of the calendar year (Code Sec. 401(k)(11)(B)(ii)). The compensation that may be taken into account in determining the 2% nonelective contributions may not exceed $170,000 for 2001 ($200,000 for 2002) (see ¶ 2128 for information on compensation limits) (Code Sec. 401(a)(17)).[57]

Top Heavy Rules. The strict rules that apply to "top-heavy plans" (see ¶ 2139) do not apply to SIMPLE 401(k) plans (Code Sec. 401(k)(11)(D)(ii)).[58]

Contribution and Distribution Rules. A SIMPLE 401(k) is a qualified plan (Code Secs. 401(k)(1), (2), and (11)).[59] Therefore, the rules governing the employer's deduction of contributions and the tax treatment of distributions are generally the same rules that apply to any other qualified plans (see ¶ 2147 et seq. and ¶ 2153 et seq.). However, an employer's deduction is limited to the *greater* of: (1) 15% (25% after 2001) of the compensation paid or accrued during the tax year to beneficiaries under a stock bonus or profit-sharing plan or (2) the amount that the employer is required to contribute to a SIMPLE 401(k) plan for the year (Code Sec. 404(a)(3)(A)(i)(I) and (II)).[60] Thus, an employer may deduct contributions to a SIMPLE 401(k) that are in excess of the general 15% of compensation limit (25% limit after 2001).

2113. Plans Covering Self-Employed Persons. No distinction is generally made between pension, profit-sharing and other retirement plans (including SEPs and SIMPLE accounts) established by corporations and those established by individual proprietors and partnerships (generally referred to as Keogh plans). Under the Code, the term "employee," unless otherwise indicated, includes a participant in a plan of an unincorporated enterprise who is a partner or a sole proprietor (Code Sec. 401(c)(1)).[61] References to "compensation," in the case of a proprietor or partner, are to the "earned income" of that person from the business or businesses for which the plan is established. Basically, "earned income" is the individual's net earnings from self-employment for purposes of the tax on self-employment income (see ¶ 2670) less: (1) the allowable deductions for contributions to the retirement plan on behalf of that individual and (2) the individual's income tax deduction for 50% of self-employment tax (see ¶ 923) (Code Sec. 401(c)(2)(A)).[62] (For details on the adjustment for the contribution and self-employment tax deductions, see ¶ 2152.) When references are made to the "employer," a sole proprietor is treated as his or her own employer, while a partnership is considered to be the employer of each partner (Code Sec. 401(c)(4)).[63] As a result, a sole proprietor may establish a Keogh

---

Footnote references are to paragraphs of the 2002 Standard Federal Tax Reports.

[54] ¶ 17,502	[58] ¶ 17,502	[61] ¶ 17,502
[55] ¶ 17,502	[59] ¶ 17,502	[62] ¶ 17,502
[56] ¶ 17,502	[60] ¶ 18,330	[63] ¶ 17,502
[57] ¶ 17,502		

¶2113

plan while a partner may not. The Keogh plan must be established by the partnership (see also ¶ 2152).

2115. Plans of S Corporations. Retirement plans established by S corporations are governed by the same rules that apply to plans established by other corporations.

Qualification and Other Plan Requirements

2117. Introduction. A retirement plan, its sponsoring employer and its participants are not eligible for the tax benefits mentioned at ¶ 2101 unless the plan becomes "qualified" by satisfying the requirements of Code Sec. 401.[64]

The fundamental requirement is that the plan not discriminate in coverage (see ¶ 2119) or in the amount or availability of contributions or benefits in favor of highly compensated employees as defined at ¶ 2111 (Code Sec. 401(a)(4) and (5); Reg. § § 1.401(a)(4)-1—1.401(a)(4)-13).[65] Certain plans that primarily benefit an employer's key employees ("top-heavy plans") are subject to additional qualification requirements (see ¶ 2139).[66]

The qualification requirements are numerous and complex. Highlights of the most important of these requirements are set forth below.

2119. Participation and Coverage. Two of the basic rules of most qualified plans are that they meet minimum participation standards and coverage requirements.

Participation. Generally, a qualified plan may not condition participation on the completion of more than one year of service or the attainment of more than 21 years of age, whichever occurs later. Once these conditions are met an individual must be eligible to participate within six months or, if earlier, by the first day of the plan's next accounting year. However, participation may be conditioned on completion of two years of service if, after no more than two years of service, each participant has a vested right to their accrued benefit under the plan (Code Sec. 410(a)).[67]

Minimum Coverage Requirement. Generally, a plan may meet the minimum coverage requirement in one of two ways:

(1) By satisfying a "ratio percentage test." Under this test, the percentage of rank and file employees who benefit from the plan is divided by the percentage of highly compensated employees who benefit. The test is satisfied if the ratio is at least 70% (Code Sec. 410(b)(1)(A), (B); Reg. § 1.410(b)-2(b)(2)).[68]

(2) By satisfying an "average benefit test." This test is satisfied if (a) the plan benefits such employees as qualify under a classification set up by the employer and found by the IRS not to discriminate in favor of highly compensated employees and (b) the average benefit percentage for nonhighly compensated employees is at least 70% of the average benefit percentage for highly compensated employees. An employee's "benefit percentage" comprises the employer-provided contributions (including forfeitures) or benefits under all qualified plans of the employer, expressed as a percentage of the employee's compensation (see ¶ 2128) (Code Sec. 410(b)(2); Reg. § § 1.410(b)-2, 1.410(b)-4 and 1.410(b)-5).[69]

For the definition of a highly compensated employee, see ¶ 2111.

50-40 Rule. Even if a defined benefit plan satisfies the coverage requirement, it must benefit at least the lesser of (1) 50 employees or (2) the greater of (a) 40% of all employees or (b) two employees (one employee if there is only one employee) (Code Sec. 401(a)(26)).[70]

Footnote references are to paragraphs of the 2002 Standard Federal Tax Reports.

[64] ¶ 17,507	[67] ¶ 18,970	[70] ¶ 17,502
[65] ¶ 17,502, ¶ 17,703,	[68] ¶ 18,970, ¶ 18,988	
¶ 17,715	[69] ¶ 18,970, ¶ 18,988,	
¶ 2115 [66] ¶ 19,250	¶ 18,990, ¶ 18,991	

2121. Vesting. A plan must satisfy a minimum vesting requirement (Code Sec. 411).[71] In the case of benefits attributable to employer contributions, most plans can do this in one of two ways:

Graded Vesting. Under this method, 20% of an employee's accrued benefit from employer contributions must vest after three years of service and an additional 20% must vest after each additional year of service (Code Sec. 411(a)(2)(B)).[72] After seven years of service, the employee will be 100% vested.

Cliff Vesting. Under this method, an employee has no vested interest in the accrued benefit from employer contributions until the employee has completed five years of service but then must be 100% vested (Code Sec. 411(a)(2)(A)).[73]

Vesting of Employer's Matching Contributions. For plan years beginning after December 31, 2001, a qualified plan must provide for faster vesting of an employer's matching contributions. The plan must either provide for "cliff vesting" of such contributions after three years of service or a "graded vesting" schedule that provides for 20% vesting after two years of service and an additional 20% each year until 100% vesting is achieved after six years of service (Code Sec. 411(a)(12)).

Benefits attributable to an employee's own contributions must be 100% vested at all times (Code Sec. 411(a)(1)).[74]

Cash-Out of Benefit. A qualified plan may pay the balance of a participant's account without the participant's consent if the present value of the benefit does not exceed $5,000 (Code Sec. 411(a)(11)(A)).[75]

2125. Contributions by Participants. Many defined contribution plans contemplate contributions by participants in addition to those made by the employer. These contributions may be mandatory, voluntary, or a condition to the employer making contributions. There is a special nondiscrimination test that applies to contributions by plan participants and matching contributions by employers (Code Sec. 401(m)(1)).[76] Matching contributions are those made by the employer on account of an after-tax contribution by a participant or on account of an elective contribution by a participant under a 401(k) plan (Code Sec. 401(m)(4)). The actual contribution percentage (ACP) test is essentially the same as the one imposed with respect to elective contributions under 401(k) plans, except that it is applied to employee contributions and matching contributions rather than the elective contributions.

If the employer establishes a qualifying SIMPLE 401(k) (see ¶ 2112), the plan is not required to satisfy the ACP test (Code Sec. 401(m)(10)).[77] In addition, the ACP test need not be satisfied if one of two alternative tests are satisfied (Code Sec. 401(m)(11)).[78] These tests call for satisfaction of one of the two alternative tests used in satisfying the ADP test (see ¶ 2111) and impose other requirements.

Failure to satisfy the ACP test will not result in disqualification of the plan if the excess participant and matching contributions (and the income allocable to them) are distributed within 12 months following the plan year in which they arose (Code Sec. 401(m)(6)(A)).[79] However, the excess contributions are subject to a 10% tax unless they (and the income allocable to them) are distributed to the highly compensated participants within 2½ months after the plan year in which they arose (Code Sec. 4979(f)(1)).[80] The amount of a corrective distribution (other than the portion representing the contributions of the distributee) is included in the distributee's gross income, but the 10% penalty on early distributions (see ¶ 2157) does not apply (Code Sec. 401(m)(7)).[81]

2127. Limits on Contributions and Benefits. A qualified plan must limit the benefits or contributions that may be provided for an individual participant (Code Sec. 415).[82] See ¶ 2148 for the limits imposed on annual *deductions.*

Footnote references are to paragraphs of the 2002 Standard Federal Tax Reports.

[71] ¶ 19,050, ¶ 19,076	[75] ¶ 19,050	[79] ¶ 17,502, ¶ 18,123.044
[72] ¶ 19,050, ¶ 19,076	[76] ¶ 17,502	[80] ¶ 34,520, ¶ 34,523
[73] ¶ 19,050, ¶ 19,076	[77] ¶ 17,502	[81] ¶ 17,502, ¶ 18,123.044
[74] ¶ 19,050, ¶ 19,076	[78] ¶ 17,502	[82] ¶ 19,200

Limits for Defined Benefit Plans. For 2001, the maximum annual retirement benefit for any participant may not exceed the *lesser* of $140,000 or 100% of the participant's average compensation (not exceeding $170,000) for the participant's three consecutive years of highest compensation (Code Sec. 415(b)(1)).[83] For 2002, the maximum annual retirement benefit is increased to $160,000 and the average compensation limit is increased to $200,000 (Code Sec. 415(b)(1)(A); Code Sec. 401(a)(17)).

The maximum annual benefit is actuarially reduced in the case of retirement before social security retirement age (after 2001, a reduction will be made if benefits are paid "before age 62") (Code Sec. 415(b)(2)(C)). It is actuarially increased in the case of retirement after social security retirement age (after 2001, an increase will be made if benefits are paid "after age 65") (Code Sec. 415(b)(2)(D)). However, if certain requirements are met, a minimum annual benefit of $10,000 may be provided by the plan. The benefit limit and the compensation limit are reduced in the case of individuals with less than 10 years of service with the employer (Code Sec. 415(b)(5)).[84]

Defined Contribution Plan Limits. For 2001, the annual contribution to a participant's account may not exceed the *lesser* of (1) 25% of the participant's compensation (not exceeding $170,000—see ¶ 2128) or (2) $35,000 (Code Sec. 401(a)(17); Reg. § 1.401(a)(17)-1; Code Sec. 415(c)(1)(A)). For 2002, the maximum contribution may not exceed the *lesser* of (1) 100% of a participant's compensation (not exceeding $200,000) or (2) $40,000 (Code Sec. 415(c)(1)(A)).

Catch-Up Contributions. After 2001, individuals who are at least 50 years of age will be permitted to make "catch-up" contributions to a variety of employer sponsored plans defined contribution plans (e.g., 401(k), SEP, SIMPLE, 403(b) and 457 plans). Catch-up contributions to IRAs (traditional or Roth) will also be permitted. The maximum amount of the catch-up contribution depends upon the type of plan involved. For example, for 2002, the maximum catch-up contribution to a 401(k), 403(b), or 457 plan will be $1,000. However, the maximum amount for a SIMPLE 401(k) or SIMPLE IRA will be $500. The annual allowable catch-up contributions will gradually increase until they reach a maximum in 2006. After 2006, they may be increased for inflation (Code Sec. 414(v), as added by P.L. 107-16).

2128. Compensation Taken into Account. A plan will not qualify unless the annual compensation of each employee taken into account under the plan for any year does not exceed an inflation indexed dollar amount (Code Sec. 401(a)(17)).[85] For 2001, the maximum amount of compensation that may be considered is $170,000 ($200,000 for 2002).

The compensation limit applies in the two following ways: (1) a plan may not base contributions or benefits on compensation in excess of the annual compensation limit and (2) the amount of a participant's annual compensation taken into account in applying the nondiscrimination rules is subject to the annual compensation limit (Reg. § 1.401(a)(17)-1(a)). [86]

Salary reduction amounts are generally taken into account when determining compensation for purposes of the qualified plan rules. For example, amounts contributed to a cafeteria plan or received as qualified transportation benefits are considered part of an employee's gross compensation when determining allowable contributions to a qualified plan (Code Sec. 415(c)(3)(D)).

2131. Requirement of Joint and Survivor and Pre-retirement Survivor Annuities. A plan that pays benefits in the form of an annuity must generally provide for their payment in the form of a joint and survivor annuity for the participant and the surviving spouse (Code Secs. 401(a)(11)(A)(i) and 417).[87] The annuity must be the actuarial equivalent of an annuity for the single life of the

---

Footnote references are to paragraphs of the 2002 Standard Federal Tax Reports.

¶ 2128
[83] ¶ 19,200	[85] ¶ 17,502	[87] ¶ 17,502, ¶ 19,260
[84] ¶ 19,200	[86] ¶ 17,902	

employee, and the survivor portion may not be less than 50% of the annuity paid during the joint lives of the employee and spouse (Code Sec. 417(b)).[88]

Also, a pre-retirement survivor annuity must be provided for the surviving spouse of a vested participant who dies prior to retirement. When a participant dies before reaching early retirement age, the annuity commences when the participant would have reached early retirement age (Code Sec. 417(c)).[89]

An employee may "elect out" of either the joint and survivor or pre-retirement survivor annuity but generally only with the written consent of the spouse in an instrument acknowledged by the spouse and witnessed by a notary public or plan representative (Code Sec. 417(a)(2)).[90] Consent cannot be given in an antenuptial agreement (Reg. § 1.401(a)-20, Q&A-28).[91]

2133. Commencement of Benefits. A plan will not qualify unless it provides that the payment of benefits must begin (unless the participant elects otherwise) not later than the 60th day after the *latest* of (1) the close of the plan year in which the participant attains the earlier of age 65 or normal retirement age, (2) the close of the plan year in which the participant marks the 10th anniversary of enrollment in the plan, or (3) the close of the plan year in which the participant terminates service with the employer (Code Sec. 401(a)(14)).[92] Except in the case of a 5% owner, distribution must begin not later than April 1 of the calendar year following *the later of*:

(1) the calendar year in which the participant attains age 70½, or

(2) the calendar year in which the employee retires (Code Sec. 401(a)(9)(C)(i)).[93]

For a 5% owner, distributions must generally begin not later than April 1 of the year following the year in which the individual reached age 70½.

2135. Period for Payment of Benefits—Required Minimum Distributions (RMDs). At a minimum, the Code requires that benefits from qualified plans must generally be paid out over a period that does not exceed the life or life expectancy of the participant or the combined lives or life expectancies of the participant and a designated beneficiary (Code Sec. 401(a)(9)(A)).[94] In January 2001, the IRS issued proposed regulations that provide guidance on the required minimum distributions (RMDs) from IRAs, as well as other types of retirement plans (e.g, qualified plans, 403(b) plans and 457 plans) (Proposed Reg. § 1.401(a)(9)-1, issued January 17, 2001).[95] These proposed regulations are to be used for determining RMDs for calendar years beginning on or after January 1, 2002. The IRS has stated that if future regulations are more restrictive than the 2001 proposals, the restrictions will not impact the calculations made for 2001. For 2001, taxpayers may either use the 2001 proposed regulations or proposed regulations that were issued in 1987. As a general rule, for 2001, taxpayers will find it to their advantage to use the 2001 proposed regulations because they allow for more flexibility in the naming of beneficiaries and the calculations used to determine RMDs will result in smaller distributions. See "Proposed Regulations Concerning RMD," below.

Distributions Started Before Death. When distributions are made to the participant before his or her death, any undistributed portion payable to a beneficiary of the participant is to be distributed at least as rapidly as under the method of distribution in effect before death (Code Sec. 401(a)(9)(B)(i)).[96]

Distributions Not Started Before Death. Generally, when distributions have not been made to the participant before his or her death, the entire interest is to be distributed to the beneficiary within five years after the employee's death (Code

Footnote references are to paragraphs of the 2002 Standard Federal Tax Reports.

[88] ¶ 19,260	[92] ¶ 17,502	[95] ¶ 17,723D, ¶ 17,724D,
[89] ¶ 17,729, ¶ 19,260	[93] ¶ 17,502	¶ 17,725D-¶ 17,725N,
[90] ¶ 17,729, ¶ 19,260	[94] ¶ 17,502	¶ 17,726.002
[91] ¶ 17,729,		[96] ¶ 17,502
¶ 17,730.0435		

Sec.401(a)(9)(B)(ii)).[97] However, the two following exceptions to this five-year distribution rule must be considered.

Under the *first exception*, the five-year rule does not apply if (1) any portion of the participant's interest is payable to (or for the benefit of) a designated beneficiary, (2) the portion of the participant's interest to which the beneficiary is entitled will be distributed over the life of the beneficiary (or over a period not extending beyond the life expectancy of the beneficiary), and (3) the distributions commence no later than one year after the date of the participant's death (Code Sec. 401(a)(9)(B)(iii)).[98]

The *second exception* applies if the designated beneficiary is the surviving spouse of the participant (Code Sec. 401(a)(9)(B)(iv)).[99] Here, the five-year rule does not apply if (1) the portion of the participant's interest to which the surviving spouse is entitled will be distributed over the life of that spouse (or over a period not exceeding his or her life expectancy) and (2) the distributions commence no later than the date on which the participant would have attained age 70½. If the surviving spouse dies before payments are required to begin, the five-year rule is to be applied as if the surviving spouse were the participant. Payments to a surviving spouse under a qualified joint and survivor annuity will satisfy this second exception. Life expectancies may be redetermined annually.

Proposed Regulations Concerning RMD. Benefits must satisfy required minimum distribution (RMD) rules in each calendar year. The rules are set forth in lengthy and complex proposed regulations that were issued in 1987 (Proposed Reg. § § 1.401(a)(9)-1 and 1.401(a)(9)-2).[100] In January 2001, the IRS issued new proposed regulations that contain simplified rules for determining RMDs from qualified plans, traditional IRAs, Sec. 457 plans and 403(b) plans (Proposed Reg. § § 1.401(a)(9)-0 through 1.401(a)(9)-8). In calculating RMDs for 2001, taxpayers have the option of using the rules contained in the 2001 regulations or those contained in the 1987 proposed regulations. As a practical matter, most taxpayers will find it to their advantage to use the calculations provided by the 2001 regulations. This is primarily because the new rules permit RMDs to be made over a longer period of time. Therefore, the tax deferred advantage of retirement plans is enhanced.

The 2001 proposed regulations provide a uniform table that all employees can use to determine the minimum distributions required during their lifetime (Proposed Reg. § 1.401(a)(9)-5, Q&A-4). This facilitates calculation of RMD because employees will no longer need to determine their beneficiary by their required beginning date, will no longer need to decide whether to recalculate their life expectancy each year in determining required minimum distributions, and will no longer need to satisfy a separate incidental death benefit rule. The 2001 proposed regulations allow calculation of the required minimum distribution during the employee's lifetime without regard to the beneficiary's age, with one exception (Proposed Reg. § 1.401(a)(9)-5, Q&A-1(b)). If a spouse is more than 10 years younger than the employee, required distributions can be reduced by taking the spouse's age into account using the joint life and last survivor life expectancy of the employee and spouse. Furthermore, under these proposed regulations, a beneficiary can be determined up to the end of the year following the year of the employee's death (Proposed Reg. § 1.401(a)(9)-4). This allows the employee to change designated beneficiaries after the required beginning date without increasing the required minimum distribution and it also allows the beneficiary to be changed after the employee's death (i.e., by one or more beneficiaries disclaiming or being cashed out). In some situations, the proposed rules also permit the calculation of post-death minimum distributions to take into account an employee's remaining life expectancy at the time of death (Proposed Reg. § 1.401(a)(9)-5, Q&A-5(a)). This allows distributions in all cases to be spread over a number of years after death.

Footnote references are to paragraphs of the 2002 Standard Federal Tax Reports.

¶2135

[97] ¶ 17,502
[98] ¶ 17,502
[99] ¶ 17,502
[100] ¶ 17,724, ¶ 17,725

Penalty. Failure of the plan to make minimum distributions will result in disqualification unless the failure is an isolated instance (Proposed Reg. § 1.401(a)(9)-1, A-5).[101] In addition to disqualification, an excise tax may be imposed on the distributee. The rate of this excise tax is 50% of the amount by which the required minimum distribution exceeds the distribution actually made (Code Sec. 4974(a)).[102] The excise tax may be waived if the shortfall is due to reasonable error and if steps are taken to correct it. The penalty is reported on Form 5329.

2137. Anti-Assignment Provision. A qualified plan must provide that benefits under the plan may not be assigned or otherwise transferred (Code Sec. 401(a)(13)(A)).[103] An exception is made for assignments ordered by a "qualified domestic relations order" (QDRO) issued under a state's domestic relations law (Code Secs. 401(a)(13)(B) and 414(p)).[104] (See ¶ 2166 concerning QDROs.)

Breach of Fiduciary Duty. A participant's benefits may be reduced when the individual has committed a breach of fiduciary duty or committed a criminal act against the plan (Code Sec. 401(a)(13)(C)).[105]

2139. Top-Heavy Plans. More stringent qualification requirements must be met for qualified plans or tax-sheltered annuity arrangements that primarily benefit an employer's key employees (see "Key Employees," below). Such plans are referred to as "top-heavy plans" (Code Sec. 416(a)).[106] The requirements need not be met by a SIMPLE 401(k) (¶ 2112) or a SIMPLE IRA (¶ 2185) (Code Secs. 401(k)(11)(D)(ii) and 416(g)(4)(G)).[107] The top-heavy rules have been eased for years beginning after 2001.

Accelerated Vesting. For any plan year in which a plan is top heavy, the benefits of each employee for that year must *either* be (1) 100% vested if the employee has at least three years of service or (2) 20% vested after two years of service with a 20% increase for each later year of service (Code Sec. 416(b)).[108] See ¶ 2121 for the vesting requirements that apply to most types of qualified plans.

Minimum Benefits and Contributions for Non-key Employees. In any plan year in which a *defined benefit plan* is top heavy, each participating non-key employee must be provided with a retirement benefit that is not less than 2% of average annual compensation for the employee's five consecutive years of highest compensation multiplied by years of service. However, if 2% multiplied by years of service exceeds 20% of such average annual compensation, the benefit need not exceed 20% (Code Sec. 416(c)(1)).[109]

In any plan year in which a *defined contribution plan* is top heavy, each participating non-key employee must be provided with a contribution that is not less than 3% of such employee's compensation for that year. After 2001, employer matching contributions are taken into account when determining if this contribution requirement has been met. If the contribution rate for the key employee receiving the largest contribution is less than 3%, the contribution rate for such key employee shall be used to determine the minimum contribution for non-key employees (Code Sec. 416(c)(2)).[110]

For the limitation on compensation taken into account for purposes of the maximum benefit and contribution rules, see ¶ 2128.

Key Employee Defined. For 2001, a key employee is any employee or former employee who, at any time during the plan year or any of the four preceding plan years, is: (1) an officer of the employer with annual compensation greater than 50% of the defined benefit plan contribution limit (i.e., 50% of $140,000), (2) one of the 10 employees owning the largest interests in the employer and who received annual compensation from the employer greater than the defined contribution plan dollar

---

Footnote references are to paragraphs of the 2002 Standard Federal Tax Reports.

[101] ¶ 17,724	[105] ¶ 17,502	[108] ¶ 19,250
[102] ¶ 34,380	[106] ¶ 19,250, ¶ 19,253	[109] ¶ 19,250
[103] ¶ 17,502, ¶ 17,733	[107] ¶ 17,502, ¶ 19,250	[110] ¶ 17,250
[104] ¶ 17,502, ¶ 17,733,		
¶ 19,150		

limit (i.e., $35,000), (3) a more-than-5% owner of the employer, or (4) a more-than-1% owner of the employer having an annual compensation of more than $150,000 (Code Sec. 416(i)(1)(A)).[111]

For years beginning after December 31, 2001, the definition of a key employee has been modified in several ways. An individual will now be considered as a key employee if the employee is: (1) an officer with compensation in excess of $130,000 (after 2002, subject to an inflation adjustment), (2) a more-than-5% owner, or (3) a more-than-1% owner who received more than $150,000 in compensation (Code Sec. 416(i)(1)(A), as amended by the Economic Growth and Tax Relief Reconciliation Act of 2001 (P.L. 107-16)). The new law has eliminated the four-year look-back period. Thus, individuals are key employees only if they meet the definition during the plan year.

2141. Minimum Funding Standards. In order to ensure that defined benefit pension plans are adequately funded, minimum and full-funding limits are imposed. Annual contributions to a defined benefit pension plan by the employer must meet a minimum funding standard which includes amortization of past service liability (liability arising from a participant's service before the plan was established) as well as current plan costs (Code Sec. 412(b)(1)).[112] In order to prevent employers from claiming tax deductions for contributions to a plan in excess of the amount necessary to fund plan benefits, plans are subject to a "full-funding limitation" (Code Sec. 404(a)(1)(a)). The formula for determining the full-funding limit will change for plan years beginning after December 31, 2001 and will be repealed for plan years beginning in 2004 (Code Sec. 412(c)(7)(A)(i)(I), as amended by the Economic Growth and Tax Relief Reconciliation Act of 2001 (P.L. 107-16)). As applied to a money purchase pension plan, the funding requirements are satisfied if the promised contributions are made in each year. The funding requirements do not apply to profit-sharing, stock bonus plans, and certain other types of qualified plans (Code Sec. 412(h)). The IRS may temporarily waive the requirement for a particular year in the event of business hardship. The funding requirements are not qualification requirements under Code Sec. 401. However, failure to meet and correct minimum funding requirements will subject the employer to special excise taxes (Code Sec. 4971).[113]

2143. Prohibited Transactions. Certain transactions between a qualified employees' trust and a plan fiduciary or other "disqualified person" are prohibited (Code Sec. 4975(c)).[114] The "disqualified person" who engages in the prohibited transaction is liable for excise taxes based upon the amount of the prohibited transaction. The basic excise tax rate is 15%. If the prohibited transaction is not corrected within the tax period, an additional tax of 100% is imposed (Code Sec. 4975(b)).[115] For years beginning after 2001, plan loans made to owner-employees are generally not considered to be prohibited transactions. As a result of this change, a plan loan will only be a prohibited transaction if made to a participant or beneficiary of an IRA, or an employer or association of employees that has established an IRA (Code Sec. 4975(f)(6)(B)(iii), as amended by the Economic Growth and Tax Relief Reconciliation Act of 2001 (P.L. 107-16)).

2145. Returns. Generally, annual returns for each funded plan of deferred compensation must be filed with the IRS (Code Sec. 6058).[116] Unless an extension is requested on Form 5558, the returns must be filed no later than the last day of the seventh month after the plan year ends (e.g., July 31 for calendar year plans). In most situations, Form 5500 is filed. However, a plan may file Form 5500-EZ if its only participants are an individual and spouse who together own the business (whether or not incorporated) for which the plan is established. Form 5500-EZ may also be used by the plan of a partnership if the only participants are partners and their spouses.

Footnote references are to paragraphs of the 2002 Standard Federal Tax Reports.

¶ 2141
[111] ¶ 17,250
[112] ¶ 19,100
[113] ¶ 34,320
[114] ¶ 34,400
[115] ¶ 34,400
[116] ¶ 36,500

Penalties may be imposed for failure to file the required annual information return or, in the case of defined benefit plans, the actuarial report (Schedule B of Form 5500) (Code Sec. 6652).[117]

Contributions Deduction

2147. Contributions by Employer and Participants. Contributions may be made to a qualified retirement plan both by the employer and by participants (see ¶ 2125). Contributions by participants are not deductible. However, elective deferrals under a 401(k) plan (see ¶ 2111) are equivalent to deductible contributions by the participant because they are made with pre-tax dollars.

2148. Limits on Contributions and Deductions. The *limits on contributions* are discussed at ¶ 2127. The *limits on the deduction of contributions* are discussed at ¶ 2151. The limits on deductions and limits on contributions are related. In the case of a defined contribution plan (¶ 2103 and ¶ 2105), the Code prohibits the deduction of contributions that are in excess of the maximum amount determined by the calculations set forth at ¶ 2127 (Code Sec. 404(j)(1)(B)).[118] In the case of a defined benefit plan (¶ 2103), the Code prohibits the deduction of contributions that are in excess of the amount that is actuarially necessary to provide the maximum benefit described at ¶ 2127 (Code Sec. 404(j)(1)(A)).[119] As a result of these rules, the maximum deduction for a particular year (see ¶ 2151) may be less than the maximum allowable contribution.

A 10% excise tax is generally imposed on contributions in excess of the deductible amount (Code Sec. 4972).[120] Some exceptions to the penalty are provided (Code Sec. 4972(c)(6)).[121]

2149. General Rules for Deduction for Contributions. A deduction is allowed for contributions to a qualified plan whether or not the rights of the participants to the contributions are forfeitable. With the exception of contributions that may be carried over to a later year (see ¶ 2151), contributions are deductible only for the tax year when paid regardless of whether the taxpayer uses the cash or accrual method of accounting. A deductible contribution is deemed made on the last day of the tax year if it is paid no later than the due date (including extensions) of the taxpayer's return (Code Sec. 404(a)(6)).[122] It should be noted that in the case of most defined benefit plans, the deadline for making the required contribution to the funding standard account is 8½ months after the close of the plan year (Code Sec. 412(c)(10)). As a result, the required funding date may actually come before the last day for making deductible contributions. Interest may be charged if the contribution to the standard account is not made by the due date (Code Sec. 412(m)).

Elective and matching contributions under a 401(k) plan (see ¶ 2111) are not deductible by the employer for a tax year if they are attributable to compensation earned by participants after the end of that year (Rev. Rul. 90-105).[123]

2151. Limits on Deductions for Contributions. Limitations are imposed on deductions for contributions to a qualified plan. In applying these limitations, the amount of compensation of an employee that may be taken into account under the plan may not exceed a specific dollar limit (e.g., $170,000 for 2001 and $200,000 for 2002) (see ¶ 2128) (Code Sec. 404(l), as amended by the Economic Growth and Tax Relief Reconciliation Act of 2001 (P.L. 107-16)).[124]

Defined Benefit Pension Plans. Generally, there are two annual dollar limits imposed on defined benefit plans: limits on benefits (Code Sec. 415(b)(l)) and limits on deductible contributions (Code Sec. 404(a)).

Footnote references are to paragraphs of the 2002 Standard Federal Tax Reports.

[117] ¶ 39,480, ¶ 39,490.025	[120] ¶ 34,340	[123] ¶ 18,347.27
[118] ¶ 18,330	[121] ¶ 34,340	[124] ¶ 18,330
[119] ¶ 18,330	[122] ¶ 18,330	

The law permits an employer to use either one of the following two methods for determining the annual limit on the deduction that may be claimed for contributions to a defined benefit plan (Code Sec. 404(a)(1)(A)).[125]

Level Funding Method. An amount necessary to provide, for all participants under the plan, the remaining unfunded cost of their past and current service credits distributed as a level amount or level percentage of compensation over the remaining service of each participant. Under this method, the past service liability for each participant is deducted ratably over the employee's projected years of service until retirement.

Normal Cost Method. An amount equal to the normal ("current") cost of the plan plus, if past service or other supplementary credits are provided, an amount not in excess of that necessary to amortize these credits in equal payments over 10 years.

Prior to 2002, there is a special rule that permits deductible contributions to certain defined benefit plans to be equal to the plan's unfunded current liability. For plan years beginning after December 31, 2001, this special rule has been expanded to include all defined benefit plans (Code Sec. 404(a)(1)(D), as amended by P.L. 107-16).[126]

Profit-Sharing and Stock Bonus Plans. Generally, in the case of a profit-sharing or stock bonus plan, the maximum deduction that may be claimed for contributions is 15% (25% after 2001) of the compensation of all participants in the plan (Code Sec. 404(a)(3)(A)(i)(I), as amended by P.L. 107-16).[127]

> **Example.** In 2002, Titanic Corporation paid $1,250,000 in compensation to its employees covered by its profit-sharing plan. As a result of the new percentage limit that went into effect after 2001, the corporation will be able to contribute and deduct a maximum of $312,500 ($1,250,000 × 25%) to the profit-sharing plan. This is an increase of $125,000 over the amount that would have been permissible under the rule that was in effect for 2001 ($1,250,000 × 15% = $187,500).

Money Purchase Pension Plans. For 2001, the maximum deduction for a money purchase plan is the *lesser* of 25% of the participant's compensation or $35,000 ($40,000 for 2002) (Code Sec. 415(c)).[128] For years beginning after December 31, 2001, except as provided by IRS regulations, money purchase plans will be treated the same as stock bonus or profit-sharing plans (Code Sec. 404(a)(3)(A)(v), as amended by P.L. 107-16).[129]

Employer Maintaining More Than One Type of Plan. If an employer makes contributions to a defined contribution plan and also to a defined benefit plan, there is an overall limit on the deduction of these contributions. The deduction is limited to the *greater* of (1) 25% of the compensation paid or accrued for that year to the participants in all such plans or (2) the amount necessary to satisfy the minimum funding standards of Code Sec. 412. The overall limitation does not apply in cases in which no individual is a participant in more than one plan maintained by the employer (Code Sec. 404(a)(7)(A) and (C)).[130]

Elective Deferrals. For years beginning after December 31, 2001, elective deferrals made by employees are not taken into account when determining deduction limits for stock bonus and profit sharing plans, combination defined benefit and defined contribution plans, and ESOPs (Code Sec. 404(n), as added by P.L. 107-16).

Compensation. For years beginning after December 31, 2001, the definition of "compensation" for purposes of deduction limits for stock bonus and profit sharing plans, combination defined benefit and defined contribution plans, self-employed plans and ESOPs, includes amounts that are generally excluded from gross income (e.g., certain disability benefits and elective deferrals) (Code Sec. 404(a)(12), as added by P.L. 107-16).

Footnote references are to paragraphs of the 2002 Standard Federal Tax Reports.

¶ 2151

[125] ¶ 18,330		[127] ¶ 18,330		[129] ¶ 18,330	
[126] ¶ 18,330		[128] ¶ 19,200		[130] ¶ 18,330	

Carryovers. If an employer's contribution exceeds the maximum deductible amount, the excess amount may be carried over and deducted in later tax years. However, the total of the carryovers and the regular contributions in the carryover year may not exceed the deductible limit for that year (Code Sec. 404(a)(1)(E) and (3)(A)(ii)). [131]

Similarly, if the 25% overall limit for contributions to different types of plans is exceeded, the excess may be carried over. However, the combination of carryovers and regular deductions for any succeeding year may not exceed 25% of the compensation paid to participants in that year (Code Sec. 404(a)(7)(B)). [132]

2152. Plan Covering Self-Employed Participants. Contributions and deductions for a self-employed participant covered by a qualified plan are subject to essentially the same rules and limitations as those that apply in the case of a participant who is a common law employee. However, a few special rules must be considered.

Earned Income. The "compensation" of a self-employed participant is that participant's "earned income" (Code Sec. 401(c)(2)(A)). [133] See ¶ 2113 for information concerning the determination of "earned income." In calculating earned income, net earnings from self-employment must be reduced by the following two adjustments.

(1) A reduction must be made for the deduction allowed for contributions made on behalf of the self-employed participant (Code Sec. 401(c)(2)(A)(v)). [134] In situations when the entire contribution is deductible, the equivalent of this reduction is achieved by limiting the contribution to a percentage of earned income (calculated without regard to the deduction) determined by dividing the nominal rate by the integer 1 plus that rate.

> **Example.** If the plan calls for a contribution equal to 10% of each participant's compensation, the contribution on behalf of a self-employed participant would be 10% divided by 1.10, or 9.0909%.

(2) A reduction must also be made for the self-employment tax deduction claimed by the self-employed participant (Code Sec. 401(c)(2)(A)(vi)). [135] As explained at ¶ 923, this is 50% of the self-employment tax owed by the participant.

Limits on Contributions and Benefits. The qualified plan must provide that contributions or benefits cannot exceed certain limits. The limits depend upon whether the plan is a defined contribution plan or a defined benefit plan.

Defined Benefit Plan. For 2001, the annual pension benefit for a participant is generally the *lesser* of $140,000 ($160,000 for 2002) or 100% of the participant's average compensation for the highest three consecutive years (not exceeding $170,000 ($200,000 for 2002)) (see ¶ 2127) (Code Sec. 415(b)(1)(A), as amended by the Economic Growth and Tax Relief Reconciliation Act of 2001 (P.L. 107-16)). The deduction for contributions to a defined benefit plan must be based upon the computations of an actuary.

Defined Contribution Plan. For 2001, a defined contribution plan's annual contributions to the account of a participant cannot be more than the *lesser* of $35,000 or 25% of the participant's compensation (compensation is limited to a maximum of $170,000) (see ¶ 2127). After 2001, the maximum contribution is the *lesser* of $40,000 or 100% of compensation (compensation is limited to a maximum of $200,000) (Code Sec. 415(c)(1)(A), as amended by P.L. 107-16). The limit on deductible contributions depends upon whether the plan is a profit-sharing plan or a money purchase plan (see ¶ 2151 for the applicable limits).

Calculating the Deduction. For 2001, in Publication 560 (Retirement Plans for the Self-Employed), the IRS provides the procedure for calculating deductible

Footnote references are to paragraphs of the 2002 Standard Federal Tax Reports.
131 ¶ 18,330   133 ¶ 17,502   135 ¶ 17,502
132 ¶ 18,330   134 ¶ 17,502

¶ 2152

contributions to a plan that defines contributions as a percentage of compensation (e.g., a money purchase pension plan). The procedure is as follows:

(1) The self-employed participant's net earnings from self-employment are reduced by 50% of the self-employment tax.

(2) The net earnings as reduced in (1) are multiplied by the reduced contribution rate applicable to self-employed participants (see the previous example). Except as stated below, the product is the deductible contribution of the participant.

Percentage Equivalents. For 2001, in Publication 560 (Retirement Plans for the Self-Employed), the IRS provides a rate table that may be used to determine the reduced contribution rate for a self-employed individual. For example, under the rate table, the maximum deduction percentage for contributions to the self-employed individual's own profit-sharing plan is 13.0435%, while it is 15% for the employees. The maximum deduction percentage to a money purchase plan for the self-employed individual is 20%, while it is 25% for the employees. The rate table is also reproduced in CCH's STANDARD FEDERAL TAX REPORTS.[136]

Contribution for Partner. A partnership's deduction for contributions on behalf of a partner must be allocated solely to that partner (Reg. § 1.404(e)-1A(f)).[137] See ¶ 428 and ¶ 431. It cannot be allocated among all of the partners pursuant to the partnership agreement. This rule applies to elective contributions under a 401(k) plan (see ¶ 2111), as well as to other employer contributions, including those made by the partnership to match elective contributions of a partner or to match contributions made by the partner as an employee.[138]

Contribution Is Not a Business Expense. A contribution to a qualified plan for the benefit of a self-employed individual is not a business expense of that individual.[139] Thus, it is not deductible on Schedule C of Form 1040 or page 1 of Form 1065 and, therefore, is not deductible in calculating self-employment tax. For a sole proprietorship, the contribution may only be claimed as an adjustment to gross income on page 1 of Form 1040. For a partnership, it is shown on Schedule K-1 of Form 1065 and carried to page 1 of Form 1040 as a deduction from gross income.

Taxation of Benefits

2153. Treatment of Lump-Sum Distribution. For many years, lump-sum distributions have been subject to special, favorable tax treatment. As a general rule, this treatment is no longer available for lump-sum distributions made in tax years beginning after 1999 (Sec. 1401(a) of P.L. 104-188).[140] However, in the case of a lump-sum distribution made to an employee who had attained age 50 before January 1, 1986 (i.e., the employee was born before 1936), the individual may be able to use a 10-year averaging method or a flat 20% tax (see below for details) (Secs. 1401(a) and (c) of P. L. 104-188).[141]

Lump-Sum Distribution Defined. A lump-sum distribution is a distribution of a participant's entire interest in a qualified plan. The amount distributed (or, in the case of multiple distributees, a distributee's portion of it) must be received within a single tax year of the distributee. In the case of a participant other than a self-employed person, the distribution must be made (1) because of the participant's death, (2) due to separation from the service of the employer, or (3) after the individual has attained age 59½. In the case of a self-employed person, the distribution must be made because of the individual's death or it must be made after age 59½, unless the individual was previously disabled (Code Sec. 402(d)(4)(A), before amendment by P.L. 104-188).[142]

Separation From Service. Prior to 2002, under what is commonly known as the "same desk rule," an employee is generally treated as having separated from service

---

¶ **2153**

only when the individual retires, resigns, or is discharged and not when the individual continues on in the same job (Rev. Rul. 79-336).[143] It has been held that a change in the employing entity, coupled with a substantial change in the ownership of the business, will cause employees associated with that business to be separated from service (*P.R. Smith*).[144] If at least 85% of an employer's assets have been sold, an employee will be treated as having been separated from service even if the individual continues performing the same tasks for the new employer (Reg. § 1.401(k)-1(d)(4)).[145] In 2000, the IRS ruled that employees had been separated from service even though less than 85% of a business had been sold. The ruling was based on the finding that, even though the employees continued performing the same activities after the sale, they did not continue on in the same business. As a result, distributions from their former employer's 401(k) plan were made after the employees had separated from service (Rev. Rul. 2000-27).[146] For distributions made after December 31, 2001, the term "separation from service" will be replaced by "severance from employment"(Code Sec. 401(k)(2)(B)(i)(I), as amended by the Economic Growth and Tax Relief Reconciliation Act of 2001 (P.L. 107-16)).[147] This change, which will improve the portability of retirement benefits, also applies 403(b) plans (see ¶ 2167) and 457 plans (see ¶ 2197A).

Determining Taxable Amount. The entire amount of the lump-sum distribution is not always subject to taxation. To determine the taxable portion of the lump-sum distribution, subtract from the total amount of the distribution the following: (1) nondeductible amounts contributed to the plan by the participant (less any previous distributions the participant received that were not includible in gross income); (2) any premiums paid by the plan to furnish a participant with life insurance protection that were included in gross income (see ¶ 2156); (3) any repayments of loans from the plan that were included in gross income (¶ 2164); (4) the current actuarial value of any annuity contract that was included in the lump-sum distribution; and (5) net unrealized appreciation in any employer securities that were distributed as part of the lump-sum distribution (unless the taxpayer elects to be taxed on this appreciation). If the net unrealized appreciation is excluded from gross income upon distribution of the securities, tax is deferred until the securities are sold or exchanged. The cost or other basis of the employer securities is included in the taxable portion of the distribution (Code Sec. 402(e)(4)(B)). [148]

Special Tax Treatment. For 2001, a lump-sum distribution may be eligible for special treatment under the rules discussed immediately below. However, this calculation for a lump-sum distribution is available only if the employee with respect to whom the distribution is made was born before 1936 and only if the recipient elects special tax treatment for all such amounts received during the tax year (Code Sec. 402(d)(4)(B), before amendment by P.L. 104-188). In addition, special treatment is not available if any portion of the lump-sum distribution is rolled over under the rules discussed at ¶ 2188 (Code Sec. 402(d)(4)(K), before amendment by P.L. 104-188).[149]

Age 50 Attained Before January 1, 1986. If a participant was age 50 or older before January 1, 1986 (i.e, born before 1936), the distributee may choose among the options listed below for taxation of a lump-sum distribution. However, choices (2) and (3) may be selected only if the participant was a participant during at least five tax years preceding the year of distribution (Code Sec. 402(d)(4)(F), before amendment by P.L. 104-188).[150]

(1) A distributee may include the entire taxable amount in gross income. If this is done, it will be combined with all other gross income and, after deductions, taxed at the normal rates applying to income received in the tax year.

Footnote references are to paragraphs of the 2002 Standard Federal Tax Reports.

[143] ¶ 18,217A.57	[146] ¶ 18,112.10	[149] ¶ 18,202
[144] ¶ 18,217A.62	[147] ¶ 17,502	[150] ¶ 18,202
[145] ¶ 18,110	[148] ¶ 18,202	

(2) A distributee may calculate a separate tax on the entire taxable amount by employing a 10-year averaging method (Sec. 1122(h)(5) of the Tax Reform Act of 1986).[151]

(3) A distributee may (a) pay a separate 20% tax on the pre-1974 portion of the taxable amount and (b) calculate a separate tax under the 10-year averaging method for the post-1973 portion of the taxable amount (Sec. 1122(h)(3) of the Tax Reform Act of 1986).[152] Note that if the 20% flat tax is elected, the 20% rate is applied to the entire pre-1974 amount and not to that amount after it has been reduced by capital losses.

Five-Year Averaging. The use of the five-year averaging method was repealed for tax years after 1999.

Making the Election. The distributee must make an election to use the averaging method (Code Sec. 402(d)(4)(B)(ii), before amendment by P.L. 104-188).[153] An election must also be made in order to use the flat 20% tax for the pre-1974 portion of a lump-sum distribution (Sec. 1122(h)(3) and (4) of the Tax Reform Act of 1986).[154] There are no special procedures for making an election. All that is necessary is to fill out the applicable return in such a way as to take advantage of the option selected. The tax form used for choosing the various options with respect to lump-sum distributions is Form 4972.

An election to use 10-year averaging may be made only once with respect to a particular participant (Code Sec. 402(d)(4)(B), before amendment by P.L. 104-188; Sec. 1122(h)(5) of the Tax Reform Act of 1986).[155] Therefore, a person is permitted to make an averaging election for amounts received as a participant in a plan and may make another election for amounts received as a beneficiary of another participant in a plan.

An election to apply a flat 20% tax to the pre-1974 portion of such a distribution can be made only once with respect to the same participant. The election is treated as an election to use averaging, thus precluding any averaging for a subsequent lump-sum distribution with respect to the same participant (Sec. 1122(h) of the Tax Reform Act of 1986).[156]

10-Year Averaging Computation. Under 10-year averaging, a tax is computed (using the tax rates in the table below) on 1/10 of the excess of (1) the portion of the distribution subject to averaging over (2) the minimum distribution allowance. The tax so computed is then multiplied by 10.

The minimum distribution allowance is (1) the lesser of (a) $10,000 or (b) one-half of the portion subject to averaging, reduced, but not below zero, by (2) 20% of the amount by which the portion subject to averaging exceeds $20,000. If the amount subject to averaging is $70,000 or more, the minimum distribution is zero.

Ten-Year Averaging Rate Table

Over—	But Not Over—	The Tax Is	of the Amount Over—
$ –0–	$ 1,190	. . . . . 11%	$ –0–
1,190	2,270	$ 130.90 + 12%	1,190
2,270	4,530	260.50 + 14%	2,270
4,530	6,690	576.90 + 15%	4,530
6,690	9,170	900.90 + 16%	6,690
9,170	11,440	1,297.70 + 18%	9,170
11,440	13,710	1,706.30 + 20%	11,440
13,710	17,160	2,160.30 + 23%	13,710
17,160	22,880	2,953.80 + 26%	17,160
22,880	28,600	4,441.00 + 30%	22,880
28,600	34,320	6,157.00 + 34%	28,600
34,320	42,300	8,101.80 + 38%	34,320
42,300	57,190	11,134.20 + 42%	42,300
57,190	85,790	17,388.00 + 48%	57,190
85,790	. . . . . .	31,116.00 + 50%	85,790

Footnote references are to paragraphs of the 2002 Standard Federal Tax Reports.

[151] ¶ 18,217A.021   [154] ¶ 18,217A.021   [156] ¶ 18,217A.021
[152] ¶ 18,217A.021   [155] ¶ 18,202,
[153] ¶ 18,202   ¶ 18,202.002

¶ 2153

565

securities. Distributions of an employer's securities under circumstanceving a lump-sum distribution (e.g., distributions spread over more r) are subject to the above rules except for unrealized appreciation hares that were purchased with the employee's own contributions (4)(A)).[164] The appreciation is taxed when the securities are sold.

2156. Cost of Life Insurance Protection. Some retirement plans provide incidental life insurance protection for participants. Indeed, many pension plans are funded with retirement income or similar endowment contracts under which the cash surrender value is the source of retirement benefits, while the excess of the face value over the cash value represents current protection against death. Even though a plan is qualified, the cost of current life insurance protection provided by it is included in the participant's gross income. The amount of current life insurance protection for a year is equal to the excess of the amount payable upon death over the cash value of the policy at the end of the year. The cost of this protection is a reasonable net premium cost, as determined under the second table reproduced at ¶ 721 (Code Sec. 72(m)(3)(B); Reg. § 1.72-16).[165]

2157. Early Distributions. Generally, distributions from a qualified retirement plan are subject to an additional 10% tax if they are made before the participant reaches age 59½ (Code Sec. 72(t)(1)). It is important to note that this 10% tax will only apply to the amount of the early distribution that is included in gross income. Therefore, distributions which are rolled over will not be subject to this tax.

Exceptions to 10% Tax. The 10% tax does *not* apply to (1) distributions upon death or disability of the participant; (2) distributions after separation from service that are part of a series of substantially equal periodic payments over the life of the participant or the joint lives of the participant and the beneficiary; (3) distributions after separation from service, if the separation occurred during or after the calendar year in which the participant reached age 55 (Notice 87-13, Q&A-20);[166] (4) distributions to a nonparticipant under a qualified domestic relations order (see ¶ 2166); (5) distributions not exceeding deductible medical expenses (determined without regard to whether deductions are itemized) (Code Sec. 72(t)(2)(B));[167] and (6) certain distributions by ESOPs of dividends on employer securities (Code Sec. 72(t)(2)(A)).[168] The 10% tax is reported on Part I of Form 5329. The fact that a lump-sum distribution qualifies for special tax averaging treatment (see ¶ 2153) does not mean that it is not subject to the 10% tax. To be exempt, it must fall within one of the foregoing exceptions.[169]

Separation From Service. The rules governing 401(k), 403(b) and 457 plans provide that amounts in the plans may not be distributed prior to certain specified events. One of these events is the employee's "separation from service" (Code Sec. 401(k)(2)(B)(i)(I)). The interpretation of this term and its change to "severance from employment" for distributions after December 31, 2001 is discussed at ¶ 2153.

2160. Community Property Laws. The special rules applicable to lump-sum distributions are applied without regard to community property laws (Code Sec. 402(e)(4)(D)(iii)).[170] As a result, a lump-sum distribution is considered to belong entirely to the participant, rather than half to the participant and half to his or her spouse (*R.L. Karem*).[171] However, a spouse may acquire an interest in retirement plan assets by means of a qualified domestic relations order (see ¶ 2166).

2164. Loans from Qualified Plans. As a general rule, a loan to a participant by a qualified plan or tax-sheltered annuity arrangement (including a pledge or assignment of a participant's interest) is treated as an in-service distribution, taxable under the rules discussed at ¶ 2155. The same is true of a pledge or

---

Footnote references are to paragraphs of the 2002 Standard Federal Tax Reports.

[164] ¶ 18,202	[168] ¶ 6102	[170] ¶ 18,202
[165] ¶ 6126, ¶ 6140.0255	[169] ¶ 6140.068,	[171] ¶ 18,207.11
[166] ¶ 6140.775	¶ 6140.0688	
[167] ¶ 6102		

assignment of any part of a participant's interest in the plan (Code Sec. 72(p)(1)(B); Reg. § 1.72(p)-1).[172] A loan to a participant is not treated as an actual distribution for purposes of the qualification for qualified retirement plans or TSAs. For example, it is not considered to violate the restrictions on distributions by 401(k) plans (see ¶ 2111) (Reg. § 1.72(p)-1, Q&A-12).[173]

Exceptions. Within limits, a loan will not be treated as a distribution if: (1) the loan must be repaid within five years or (2) the loan proceeds must be used (within a reasonable time after the date of the loan) to acquire a dwelling unit that is the principal residence of the participant. Under these exceptions, the loan will be treated as a distribution only to the extent that, when added to the balances of all other loans to the participant (whenever made), the proceeds exceed the *lesser* of:

(1) $50,000 (reduced as explained below) or

(2) half the present value (but not less than $10,000) of the participant's vested benefits under the plan.

The $50,000 amount must be reduced by the excess (if any) of (1) the highest outstanding balance of loans from the plan during the one-year period ending on the day preceding the date of the loan over (2) the outstanding balance of those loans on the date of the loan (Code Sec. 72(p)(2)).[174]

Example. Jane Smith is a participant in her employer's qualified profit-sharing plan. She wishes to borrow the maximum amount subject to the five-year repayment rule on July 1, 2001. On that date, the value of her vested interest in the plan is $100,000. Her highest loan balance during the period July 1, 2000, through June 30, 2001, was $40,000, and her balance on July 1, 2001 (ignoring the contemplated further loan) is $35,000. The maximum amount that Jane may borrow on July 1, 2001, is $10,000. This is the amount that, when added to her $35,000 loan balance, does not exceed $45,000. The figure $45,000 is the amount determined under (1) ($50,000 reduced by the excess of $40,000 over $35,000) because that amount is less than the amount determined under (2) (half the value of her vested interest in the plan).

In applying the exceptions, all plans of the employer are treated as a single plan (Code Sec 72 (p)(2)(D)(ii)).[175] The exceptions do not apply unless substantially level amortization of the loan is required, with payments not less frequent than quarterly (Code Sec. 72(p)(2)(C); Reg. § 1.72(p)-1, Q&A-4, -9, and -10).[176]

2166. Distribution to a Nonparticipant Incident to Divorce or Separation. A distribution made by a qualified plan to a spouse or ex-spouse of the participant pursuant to orders of state divorce courts incident to annulment, divorce or separation is taxable to the spouse or ex-spouse and not to the participant (Code Sec. 402(e)(1)(A)).[177]

The court orders are those by which a state court directs an assignment of all or a portion of a participant's benefits to satisfy his or her alimony or child support obligations or to secure to a participant's spouse or former spouse a property interest in those benefits. The order must meet specified requirements as to content and generally may not require the plan to pay benefits that are not otherwise payable under the terms of the plan. An order meeting these requirements is called a "qualified domestic relations order" (QDRO) (Code Sec. 414(p)).[178]

Payment of the entire amount due the spouse or ex-spouse under a QDRO is eligible for special tax averaging treatment (see ¶ 2153) if it would be so eligible if paid to the participant (ignoring the portion, if any, paid to the participant) and if paid within one tax year to the spouse or former spouse. See ¶ 2191 for rollover options of distributions made under a QDRO.

Footnote references are to paragraphs of the 2002 Standard Federal Tax Reports.

[172] ¶ 18,207.11	[175] ¶ 6102	[177] ¶ 18,202
[173] ¶ 6140.0362	[176] ¶ 6140.0374	[178] ¶ 19,150
[174] ¶ 6102		

The participant's "investment in the contract" (see ¶ 2155) is allocated between the participant and the spouse or ex-spouse, pro rata, on the basis of the present value of all benefits awarded to the spouse or ex-spouse and the present value of all benefits reserved to the participant (Code Sec. 72(m)(10)).[179]

403(b) and 457 plans. The rules regarding taxability of a nonparticipant spouse or former spouse also apply to distributions under tax-sheltered annuity arrangements described at ¶ 2167 (i.e., 403(b) plans) (Code Sec. 414(p)(9)).[180] For distributions made after December 31, 2001, QDROs apply to 457 plans (see ¶ 2167) (Code Sec. 414(p)(12), as amended by the Economic Growth and Tax Relief Reconciliation Act of 2001 (P.L. 107-16)).

Tax-Sheltered Annuity Arrangements

2167. Deferred Compensation Plans of Exempt Organizations and Public Schools. A public school system, an exempt educational charitable, or religious organization, or, with respect to its civilian faculty and staff, the Uniformed Services University of the Health Sciences may provide retirement benefits for its employees through the purchase of annuities or by contributing to a custodial account invested in mutual funds (Code Sec. 403(b)(1)(A)).[181] These plans are commonly referred to as "403(b) plans" or "tax-sheltered annuity plans" (TSAs). Whichever funding medium is used, the employee's rights must be nonforfeitable except, in the case of an annuity contract, for nonpayment of future premiums (Code Sec. 403(b)(1) and (7)).[182]

Limit on Contributions. Subject to limitations, employer contributions for a covered employee may be excluded from the employee's gross income. For purposes of this exclusion, employer contributions include elective contributions made by an employee.

For tax years beginning before December 31, 2001, the amount excludable is the *lesser* of: (1) the employer's contributions; (2) the exclusion allowance; (3) the annual employer contribution limit; or (4) the limit on elective deferrals for the employee's tax year (Code Sec. 403(b)(1)).[183] Generally, for 2001, an employer's contributions could not be more than the lesser of: (1) $35,000 or (2) 25% of the employee's compensation (the maximum compensation that can be taken into account is $170,000). In Publication 571 (Tax-Sheltered Annuity Programs for Employees of Public Schools and Certain Tax Exempt Organizations), the IRS provides worksheets that may be used to calculate the exclusion allowance, the annual employer contribution limit, and the annual limit on elective deferrals.

For tax years beginning after December 31, 2001, the amount excludable is the *lesser* of: (1) the employer's contributions; (2) the annual employer contribution limit; or (3) the limit on elective deferrals for the employee's tax year (Code Sec. 403(b)(1), as amended by the Economic Growth and Tax Relief Reconciliation Act of 2001 (P.L. 107-16)).[184] Generally, for 2002, an employer's contributions can not be more than the lesser of: (1) $40,000 or (2) 100% of the employee's compensation (the maximum compensation that can be taken into account is $200,000). The exclusion allowance provision has been repealed for years beginning after 2001.

Maximum Elective Deferrals. There are limits on the amount of elective deferrals that an employee may make to a 403(b) plan. For 2001, the limit is $10,500. Over the next few years the limit will be increased (e.g., $11,000 for 2002, $12,000 for 2003 and $13,000 2004) (Code Sec 402(g)(1), as amended by P.L 107-16).

Catch-Up Contributions. For tax years beginning after December 31, 2001, individuals who are age 50 or older may make "catch-up contributions" to most types of retirement plans. For 2002, the maximum catch-up contribution to a 403(b) plan is $1,000 (Code Sec. 414(v), as added by P.L. 107-16).

Footnote references are to paragraphs of the 2002 Standard Federal Tax Reports.

¶ 2167

[179] ¶ 6102	[181] ¶ 18,270	[183] ¶ 18,270
[180] ¶ 19,150	[182] ¶ 18,270	[184] ¶ 18,270

Employees of Certain Organizations. Qualified employees of certain organizations (e.g., schools, hospitals, churches, and home health service organizations) who are covered by an annuity contract under a 403(b) plan may defer additional amounts of their compensation (Code Sec. 402(g)(7)(A)). A "qualified employee" is one who has completed 15 years of service with the organization (Code Sec. 402(g)(7)(C)).

Distributions. Payments to an employee under the annuity contract or from the custodial account are taxable to the employee when made, under the annuity rules as explained at ¶ 817 and following, but any contributions by the employer which were excludable from the employee's income under the above rules are not treated as part of the employee's investment in the contract. Distributions from a custodial account may generally be made because of the employee's death, disability, separation from the employer's service (after 2001, "severance from employment"), attainment of age 59½, or financial hardship (Code Sec. 403(b)(7)(A)(ii)). The required distribution rules applicable to qualified plans apply (see ¶ 2133, ¶ 2135).

Rollovers. Prior to 2002, eligible distributions may only be rolled over into an IRA or another 403(b) annuity. However, distributions made after December 31, 2001 may also be rolled over into a qualified plan (e.g., a 401(k) plan) or 457 plan (Code Sec. 403(b)(8)(A), as amended by P.L. 107-16). Although the participant has the right to make the rollover, the other plans (i.e., 403(b), 457, or qualified plans) do not have the obligation to accept the rollover.

Early Distributions. Payments to an employee under an annuity contract or custodial account are subject to the 10% tax on early distributions discussed at ¶ 2157 (Code Sec. 72(t)(1)).[185]

Ministers. Contributions to a church plan on behalf of a self-employed minister are excludable from the minister's income to the extent that the contribution would be excludable if the minister was an employee of the church and the contribution was made to the plan (Code Sec. 414(e)(5)(E)).[186] In addition, if a minister is employed by an organization other than a church and the organization is not otherwise participating in a church plan, then the minister does not have to be included as an employee under the retirement plan of the organization for purposes of the nondiscrimination rules (Code Sec. 414(e)(5)(C)).[187]

Indian Tribal Government Plans. Employees participating in 403(b) annuities offered by Indian tribal governments may roll over amounts received from a 403(b) plan annuity contract purchased before 1995 by an Indian tribal government to a 401(k) plan sponsored by the Indian tribal government (Act Sec. 1601(d)(4) of the Taxpayer Relief Act of 1997).

Individual Retirement Accounts

2168. Introduction. Individuals who receive compensation ("earned income" in the case of a self-employed individual) that is includible in gross income and who are not age 70½ or older during the tax year may make contributions to traditional individual retirement accounts (IRAs) (Code Sec. 219 and Code Sec. 408).[188] Individuals may also have access to Roth IRAs (see ¶ 2180). Amounts earned in a traditional IRA are not taxed until distributions are made (Code Sec. 408(e)(1)).[189] In addition, contributions to a traditional IRA may be deducted, subject to limitations in the case of persons who are active participants in employer-maintained retirement plans (Code Sec. 219(g)).[190] Subject to limitations, contributions in excess of the amount deductible may be made to a traditional IRA and/or a Roth IRA (Code Sec. 408(o)).[191] The primary focus of the following material is on traditional IRAs. Roth IRAs are discussed at ¶ 2180.

Footnote references are to paragraphs of the 2002 Standard Federal Tax Reports.

[185] ¶ 6102	[188] ¶ 18,902	[190] ¶ 12,650
[186] ¶ 19,150	[189] ¶ 18,902	[191] ¶ 18,902
[187] ¶ 19,150		

¶2168

Maximum Contribution. For 2001, the maximum combined contribution to a traditional IRA and Roth IRA is $2,000. For tax years 2002 through 2004, the maximum combined contribution will be $3,000. For 2005 through 2007, it will be $4,000 and in 2008 it will be $5,000. Starting in 2009, the maximum contribution is subject to an annual inflation adjustment (Code Sec. 219(b)(5)(A)).

"Catch-Up" Contributions. For tax years 2002 through 2005, individuals who are at least age 50 will be able to make an additional contribution to their traditional or Roth IRA. For 2002 through 2005, the maximum annual amount of the catch-up contribution will be $500. After 2005, the maximum amount will be $1,000 (Code Sec. 219(b)(5)(B)).

Compensation. The term "compensation" includes earned income as well as alimony. The term does *not* include pensions, annuities or other forms of deferred compensation. The IRS will accept as compensation the amount properly shown on the Form W-2 box 1 for wages, tips, and other compensation less any amount properly shown for nonqualified plans (e.g., box 11 of the 2001 Form W-2) (Rev. Proc. 91-18).[192] The compensation of a self-employed person is the individual's "earned income," as defined at ¶ 2113 (Code Sec. 219(f)(1)).[193]

Allowable Investments. An IRA is generally prohibited from investing in "collectibles" (e.g., antiques and stamps). However, certain U.S. gold and silver bullion coins minted since October 1986 may be held by an IRA. An IRA may also hold certain platinum and state issued coins, as well as gold, silver, platinum, and palladium bullion (Code Sec. 408(m)(3)).[194]

Deemed IRAs. For plan years beginning after December 31, 2002, qualified plans may allow employees to make voluntary contributions to an account that will be deemed to be an IRA if the account meets all the requirements of an IRA (Code Sec. 408(q), as added by the Economic Growth and Tax Relief Reconciliation Act of 2001 (P.L. 107-16)). An employee's contribution to this account will count towards the maximum annual contribution that may be made to an IRA (e.g., $2,500 for 2003).

2168A. Time When Contribution Considered Made. Individuals have until the due date of their tax returns to make contributions to their IRAs (e.g., April 15). Filing extensions are *not* taken into account. If the contribution is made by the due date, it will be treated as having been made on the last day of the tax year for which the return is filed (Code Sec. 219(f)(3)).[195]

A deduction may be claimed for a contribution even though the contribution had not yet been made when the return is filed, provided that it is in fact made before the due date for filing the return (Rev. Rul. 84-18).[196]

2169. Carryovers. If a contribution to a traditional IRA is less than the amount deductible for the tax year, the difference may not be contributed and deducted in a succeeding year without regard to the limitation for that succeeding year. If a contribution exceeds the amount deductible, the excess contribution may be carried over and deducted in succeeding years to the extent that the contributions in succeeding years are less then the amounts deductible in those years (Code Sec. 219(f)(6)).[197] However, the excess contribution is subject to a 6% penalty tax each year until it is corrected (Code Sec. 4973(a)).[198] See ¶ 2174.

2170. Deduction and Contribution Limits in General. There are limits on the amount of contributions that may be made annually to IRAs maintained by an individual (Code Sec. 219(b)).[199] Also, deductible contributions may be limited when the individual (or spouse) is an active participant in a retirement plan maintained by an employer (including qualified plans, simplified employee pensions (SEPs), SIMPLE accounts, and governmental retirement plans) (Code Sec.

Footnote references are to paragraphs of the 2002 Standard Federal Tax Reports.

¶ **2168A**

[192] ¶ 18,922.0232	[195] ¶ 18,922.0227	[198] ¶ 34,360
[193] ¶ 12,650	[196] ¶ 18,922.87	[199] ¶ 12,650
[194] ¶ 18,902	[197] ¶ 18,922.0228	

219(g)).[200] The application of the contribution and deduction limitations are different for spouses filing joint returns than for other individuals.

Active Participation Rules for Spouses. An individual is *not* considered an active participant in an employer-sponsored plan merely because the individual's spouse is treated as an active participant (Code Sec. 219(g)(7)).[201] However, the maximum deductible IRA contribution for an individual who is not an active participant, but whose spouse is an active participant, is phased out at adjusted gross income between $150,000 and $160,000 (jointly computed).

>**Example 1.** Barney is covered by a 401(k) plan sponsored by his employer. His wife, Betty, is not employed. The couple files a joint income tax return for 2001, reporting adjusted gross income of $120,000. Betty may make a deductible contribution to a traditional IRA for the year because she is not an active participant in an employer-sponsored retirement plan and the combined AGI of the couple is below $150,000. However, Barney may not make a deductible IRA contribution because the combined AGI of the couple is above the phaseout range for active participants who are married and filing jointly ($53,000 to $63,000 for 2001) (see ¶ 2172 for the threshold range).

>**Example 2.** Assume the same facts as in Example 1, except that the couple's AGI was $200,000 for 2001. Neither Barney nor Betty would be able to make a deductible contribution to traditional IRAs.

Active Participant Defined. In the case of a defined benefit pension plan, an individual is considered to be an active participant if eligible to participate for any part of the plan year ending with or within the tax year, even though the individual may elect not to do so. In the case of a money-purchase pension plan, an individual is an active participant if any employer contribution or any forfeiture is required to be allocated to his account for the plan year ending with or within the tax year. In the case of a profit-sharing or stock bonus plan, an individual is an active participant if any employer contribution (including an elective contribution under a 401(k) plan) or any forfeiture is allocated to the individual's account during the tax year. Finally, an individual is an active participant for any tax year in which the individual makes a voluntary or mandatory employee contribution (Notice 87-16).[202] Neither social security nor Railroad Retirement (Tier I or Tier II) is considered to be retirement arrangements for purposes of determining active participation.

Social Security Recipients. An employed individual (either the taxpayer or spouse) who (1) is covered by a retirement plan, (2) is currently receiving social security benefits, and (3) wants to determine the allowable deduction for IRA contributions must compute taxable social security benefits twice. The first computation is for the purpose of determining the tentative amount of social security benefits that must be included in gross income if the taxpayer did not make any IRA contribution. This first computation determines the amount of hypothetical adjusted gross income for purposes of the IRA phase-out provision. The second computation determines the actual amount of taxable social security benefits by taking into account the deductible IRA contribution that was determined under the first computation. The necessary worksheets for these computations are contained in Publication 590 (Individual Retirement Arrangements (IRAs)). See ¶ 716 concerning the taxation of social security benefits.

2171. Deduction Limit for Single Persons and Married Persons Filing Separate Returns. For a single individual, head of household, or a married individual who files a separate return, contributions to traditional IRAs are deductible to the extent that they do not exceed the lesser of (1) the "deductible amount" (e.g., $2,000 for 2001) or (2) the individual's compensation for that year that is

Footnote references are to paragraphs of the 2002 Standard Federal Tax Reports.
[200] ¶ 18,922.023, ¶ 18,922.0231   [201] ¶ 12,650   [202] ¶ 18,922.865

¶2171

includible in gross income ("includible compensation") (Code Sec. 219(b)(1)).[203] For 2002, the "deductible amount" is generally $3,000. However, under the catch-up provision that applies to individuals who are at least 50 years of age (see ¶ 2168), the maximum deduction will increase to $3,500.

The maximum deduction (e.g., $2,000 for 2001) is reduced if the individual is an active participant in an employer maintained retirement plan (Code Sec. 219(g)).[204] For 2001, the reduction is in an amount that bears the same ratio to $2,000 as the individual's adjusted gross income in excess of the "applicable dollar amount" bears to $10,000. For 2001, the applicable dollar amount for a single individual or head of household is $33,000. For such a taxpayer, the deduction limit becomes zero when adjusted gross income is $43,000 or more. The applicable dollar amount for a married person filing separately is $0. Thus, for such a taxpayer, the deduction limit becomes zero when adjusted gross income is $10,000 or more. See ¶ 2172 for the deduction limits imposed on married persons filing joint returns.

A short-cut method of calculating the reduced dollar limit is to subtract the adjusted gross income from the dollar amount at which the limit becomes zero and multiply the difference by .20.

If the calculation of the reduced dollar limit produces a result that is not a multiple of $10, it is rounded to the next highest multiple of $10 (for example, $611.40 is rounded to $620). However, if the result is less then $200, but more than zero, the reduced limit is $200.

In applying the above rules, spouses who file separate returns and live apart at all times during a tax year are *not* considered to be married during that tax year (Code Sec. 219(g)(4)).[205]

Modified Adjusted Gross Income. For purposes of the reduction in the dollar limitation, the taxpayer's AGI is modified by taking into account Code Sec. 86 (the inclusion in income of social security and railroad retirement benefits) and Code Sec. 469 (the disallowance of passive activity losses) and by not taking into account Code Sec. 135 (exclusion of interest on educational U.S. Savings Bonds), Code Sec. 137 (exclusion of employer paid adoption assistance), Code Sec. 221 (deduction for student loan interest), Code Sec. 911 (foreign earned income and housing exclusion), and the deduction for contributions to IRAs (Code Sec. 219(g)(3)(A)).[206] After 2001, modified AGI is computed without taking into account Code Sec. 222 (deduction for qualified tuition and related expenses).

Future AGI Limits for Single Individuals. The AGI limits for single individuals and heads of households is being gradually increased over the next few years. For example, for 2002, the AGI phaseout range will be from $34,000 to $44,000. For 2005 and thereafter, the maximum range will be from $50,000 to $60,000 (Code Sec. 219(g)(2)(A)(ii)).

2172. Deduction Limit for Married Persons Filing Joint Returns. If a married couple files a joint return, each spouse may, in the great majority of cases, make deductible contributions to his or her IRA up to the dollar limitation (e.g., for 2001, $2,000 reduced by AGI limits). The compensation limitation will come into play only in a situation when the combined includible compensation of the spouses for the tax year is less than the sum of their dollar limitations. In effect, a spouse with little or no compensation may "borrow" his or her spouse's compensation for purposes of obtaining the maximum limitation (Code Sec. 219(c)).[207]

For 2001, the IRAs of the spouse with the greater amount of includible compensation ("higher-paid spouse") may receive deductible contributions of up to the lesser of (a) $2,000 (as reduced for active participation) or (b) his or her includible compensation. The IRAs of the spouse with the lesser amount of includible compensation ("lower-paid spouse") may receive deductible contributions equal to the lesser of:

Footnote references are to paragraphs of the 2002 Standard Federal Tax Reports.

¶ 2172

[203] ¶ 18,922.023	[205] ¶ 18,922.023	[207] ¶ 18,922.0231
[204] ¶ 18,922.023	[206] ¶ 12,650	

(a) $2,000 (as reduced for active participation) or

(b) the sum of—

(1) the includible compensation of the lower paid spouse and

(2) the includible compensation of the higher paid spouse reduced by: (i) the deduction allowed to the higher paid spouse for IRA contributions, (ii) the amount of any designated nondeductible IRA contribution on behalf of the higher paid spouse, and (iii) the amount of any contribution on behalf of the higher paid spouse to a Roth IRA (Code Sec. 219(c)(1)(B)).

Deductible Limits After 2001. After 2001, the maximum IRA contribution will be increased. For 2002 through 2004, the maximum annual contribution will be $3,000. For 2005 through 2007, it will be $4,000 and in 2008 it will be $5,000. In addition, individuals who are age 50 or over may make additional catch-up contributions (e.g., $500 for tax years 2002 through 2005) (Code Sec. 219(b)(5)(B)).

AGI Limits for Married Individuals. If both individuals are covered by an employer's retirement plan, their ability to claim a deduction for contributions made to traditional IRAs depends upon the amount of their modified AGI (see ¶ 2171 for rules used when calculating modified AGI.) For 2001, the deduction will be reduced when modified AGI is between $53,000 and $63,000. For 2002, the phaseout range will be $54,000 to $64,000. For 2007 and thereafter, the maximum range will be from $80,000 to $100,000 (Code Sec. 219(g)(2)(A)(ii)).[208]

> **Example.** Ralph and Alice file a joint return for 2001. They are both employed and both are covered by their employers' qualified plans. Their AGI for 2001 is $80,000. Because they are both active participants in qualified plans sponsored by their employers and their AGI exceeds the maximum phaseout range for 2001 (i.e., $63,000), they are not able to make deductible IRA contributions for 2001. They may make nondeductible contributions to traditional IRAs. As an alternative, they should consider the tax advantages of making their contributions to Roth IRAs (see ¶ 2180).

Special Active Participation Rules for Spouses. An individual will not be considered an active participant in an employer sponsored plan merely because the individual's spouse is treated as an active participant (Code Sec. 219(g)(7)).[209] However, the maximum deductible IRA contribution for an individual who is not an active participant, but whose spouse is, will be phased out at an AGI between $150,000 and $160,000 (jointly computed). See Examples 1 and 2 at ¶ 2170 for illustrations of this rule.

2173. Nondeductible Contributions to Traditional IRAs. An individual may make nondeductible contributions to a traditional IRA. These contributions may not exceed the excess of (1) the amount allowable as a deduction under the rules at ¶ 2170—¶ 2172, without regard to any required reduction in the dollar limitations, over (2) the amount actually allowable as a deduction under those rules (Code Sec. 408(o)).[210] In applying this rule, an individual may elect to treat otherwise deductible contributions as nondeductible contributions. This might be done if the individual had no taxable income for the year after taking into account other deductions, thereby preventing taxation (upon ultimate distribution) of amounts that had been contributed without tax benefit.

> **Example.** In 2001, Bill Webb is single, has compensation in excess of $2,000, and has an AGI of $45,000. He is an active participant in an employer-maintained retirement plan. Because his AGI exceeds $43,000, his contribution to a traditional IRA would not be deductible. As an alternative to making a contribution to a traditional IRA, he should consider the long-range tax advantages of making a contribution to a Roth IRA for 2001 (see ¶ 2180).

Footnote references are to paragraphs of the 2002 Standard Federal Tax Reports.

[208] ¶ 12,650
[209] ¶ 12,650

[210] ¶ 18,902,
¶ 18,922.0238

Designation of Nondeductible Contributions. Nondeductible contributions must be designated on Form 8606, which is attached to Form 1040 or Form 1040A. Like deductible contributions, nondeductible contributions may be made up to and including the due date of the return for the tax year (a filing extension does *not* extend the due date of the contribution) (see ¶ 2168A).

2174. Excess Contributions. Contributions to a traditional IRA or Roth IRA in excess of the permissible deductible and nondeductible amounts (¶ 2170—¶ 2173) are subject to a cumulative 6% excise tax, which is reported on Form 5329 (Code Sec. 4973).[211] However, this tax can be avoided through one of the nontaxable distributions described at ¶ 2178.

2175. Tax Credit for Contributions. For tax years beginning after December 31, 2001 and ending before January 1, 2007, individuals with a low to moderate income may be able to claim a nonrefundable credit based upon their contributions to IRAs (traditional and/or Roth) as well as most other types of qualified retirement plans (Code Sec. 25B, as added by the Economic Growth and Tax Relief Reconciliation Act of 2001 (P.L. 107-16)). The credit is equal to the applicable percentage multiplied by the amount of the qualified retirement savings contributions (not to exceed $2,000). The "applicable percentage" is determined by the taxpayer's filing status and modified adjusted gross income (MAGI) (Code Sec. 25B(b), as added by P.L. 107-16). The credit may be used against the taxpayer's regular and alternative minimum tax liability (Code Sec. 25B(g), as added by P.L. 107-16).

Applicable Percentage. The applicable percentage, which may be 10%, 20% or 50%, depends upon the taxpayer's modified adjusted gross income (MAGI) and filing status. For *joint returns,* with MAGI that does not exceed $30,000, the applicable percentage rate is 50%. The rate drops to 20% for a MAGI over $30,000 but not over $32,500. It drops to 10% for MAGI over $32,500 but not over $50,000. Over $50,000 the credit may not be claimed. For a *head of household,* the 50% credit applies when MAGI does not exceed $22,500, the 20% rate applies when MAGI is over $22,500 but not over $24,375, the 10% rate applies when MAGI is over $24,375 but not over $37,500, and no credit may be claimed when MAGI exceeds $37,500. For *all other* returns, the 50% credit rate applies when MAGI does not exceed $15,000, the 20% rate applies when MAGI is over $15,000 but not over $16,250, the 10% rate applies when MAGI is over $16,250 but not over $25,000, and no credit may be claimed when MAGI exceeds $25,000 (Code Sec. 25B(b), as added by P.L. 107-16).

Eligible Individuals. To be eligible for the credit, the individual making the contribution to a qualified retirement savings plan must be at least 18 years of age as of the close of the tax year, must *not* be claimed as a dependent on someone else's tax return, and must *not* be a student as defined at Code Sec. 151(c)(4) (Code Sec. 25B(c), as added by P.L. 107-16).

2177. Distribution Requirements. Distributions to the owner of a traditional IRA must begin no later than April 1 following the calendar year in which the owner reaches age 70½. The period over which distributions must be made to an owner (or to a beneficiary following the death of an owner) and the required minimum distributions (RMDs) are governed by rules similar to those that apply to qualified employer-sponsored plans and are imposed by Code Sec. 401(a)(9) (Code Sec. 408(a)(6) and (b)(3)).[212] See ¶ 2135 for discussion of the RMD rules.

Proposed Regulations. In calculating RMDs for 2001, taxpayers have the option of using the rules contained in the proposed regulations that were issued in January 2001 (Proposed Reg. § 1.408-8, issued January 17, 2001) or those contained in the 1987 proposed regulations. In most situations, taxpayers will benefit by using the proposed regulations issued in 2001 because calculating the RMDs is made much simpler and the amount of the annual RMDs will be smaller (Proposed Reg. § 1.401(a)(9)-5, Q&A-4, issued January 17, 2001). The IRS has stated that if final

---

Footnote references are to paragraphs of the 2002 Standard Federal Tax Reports.

[211] ¶ 34,360   [212] ¶ 18,902

regulations are more restrictive than the proposed regulations issued in 2001, the restrictions will not impact the RMD calculations made for 2001 (Preamble to Proposed Regulations). See ¶ 2135 for discussion of the RMD rules.

Inherited IRA. A surviving spouse may elect to treat the inherited traditional IRA as his or her own. The surviving spouse will be treated as having made this election if: (1) any amounts in the IRA are not distributed within the time period that applied to the decedent or (2) the individual makes contributions (including rollover contributions) to the inherited IRA (Proposed Reg. § 1.408-8, Q&A-5, issued January 17, 2001).[213] If the election is not made, the distribution requirements that applied to the deceased will now apply to the surviving spouse. If the election is made, the funds must be distributed under the requirements that apply to the surviving spouse. When an individual, other than the decedent's spouse, inherits a lump sum distribution from an IRA, the individual may not rollover that distribution into another IRA and the distribution, minus the aggregate amount of the owner's nondeductible IRA contributions, will be taxed as ordinary income in the year the distribution is received (Rev. Rul. 92-47).[214] If the individual does not receive a lump sum distribution from the inherited IRA, then the distribution requirements depend upon whether the deceased had begun to receive the required minimum distributions before death. For more information concerning RMDs from traditional IRAs, as well as other types of retirement plans, see ¶ 2135.

More Than One IRA. If an individual is required to receive a minimum distribution from more than one traditional IRA in a calendar year, the amount of the minimum distribution from each must be calculated separately and the separate amounts totalled. However, the total may be withdrawn from either or both IRAs in whatever amounts the individual chooses (Notice 88-38).[215]

2178. Taxation of Distributions. The taxation of distributions from traditional IRAs (whether to the owner or to a beneficiary of the owner) is generally determined under the same rules that apply to nonannuity payments (see ¶ 2155) under Code Sec. 72 (Code Sec. 408(d)(1)). Applying the computational rules of Code Sec. 72 was made necessary because taxpayers may make nondeductible contributions to traditional IRAs. These nondeductible IRA contributions create a basis, or "investment in the contract" with respect to the traditional IRA, that must be recovered tax free when distributions are made. When applying these rules: (1) all traditional IRAs of an individual (including SEPs described at ¶ 2184 and SIMPLE accounts described at ¶ 2185) are treated as a single contract; (2) all distributions during the individual's tax year are treated as one distribution; (3) the value of the contract, the income on the contract, and the investment in the contract are calculated (after adding back distributions made during the year) as of the close of the calendar year in which the tax year of the distribution begins; and (4) total withdrawals excludable from income in all tax years cannot exceed the taxpayer's investment in the contract in all tax years. The individual's investment in the contract is made up of the aggregate nondeductible contributions to the IRA (Code Sec. 408(d)(1), (2)).[216]

> **Example.** Jane Albright owns two traditional IRAs. During the past few years, Jane made a deductible contribution of $1,000 to IRA 1 and a nondeductible contribution of $500 to IRA 2. During 2001, Jane withdrew $1,500 from IRA 1 and made a $2,000 nondeductible contribution to IRA 2. At the end of 2001, Jane's investment (i.e., basis) in the IRAs was $2,500 (the total of her nondeductible contributions to both IRAs). At that time, the account balance of IRA 1 was $8,500, and the value of the account balance of IRA 2 was $6,000. The excludable portion of the $1,500 distribution was $2,500/$16,000 × $1,500, or $234.38. The balance of the distribution ($1,265.62) was includible in Jane's gross income for 2001. The numerator of the above fraction is the aggregate of nondeductible

---

Footnote references are to paragraphs of the 2002 Standard Federal Tax Reports.
213 ¶ 18,917B   215 ¶ 18,922.272   216 ¶ 18,902
214 ¶ 18,922.26

¶2178

contributions to both IRAs at the end of 2001, while the denominator is the aggregate value of both IRAs at the end of 2001 plus the $1,500 distribution from IRA 1 during 2001.

If the distributee is the beneficiary of the IRA owner and the value of the IRA is included in the owner's estate for federal estate tax purposes, the distributee is entitled to deduct the estate tax allocable to the IRA (Rev. Rul. 92-47).[217] See ¶ 191.

A distribution is not included in income under the annuity rules if it represents the return of a contribution made for any tax year to an IRA and if (1) the distribution is made before the due date (including extensions) of the individual's tax return for that year, (2) no deduction is allowed with respect to the contribution, and (3) the distribution includes any net income earned by the contribution. The net income earned by the contribution is included in income for the tax year in which the contribution was made even if it is received in the following year (Code Sec. 408(d)(4)).[218]

2179. Early Distributions. Distributions from a traditional IRA to a participant before the individual has reached age 59½ are generally subject to the same 10% penalty that applies to early distributions from qualified plans. Many of the exceptions to the early distribution penalty also apply to early distributions from a traditional IRA. See ¶ 2157 concerning the penalty and its exceptions. However, the early retirement exception to the penalty does *not* apply in the case of an IRA (Code Sec. 72(t)(3)(A)).[219] The following exceptions to the 10% penalty also apply when early distributions are made from an IRA.

Medical Insurance Premiums. To the extent that they do not exceed qualifying medical insurance premiums, distributions by an IRA (including a SEP or SIMPLE account) to certain unemployed individuals are not subject to the 10% penalty (Code Sec. 72(t)(2)(D)).[220] Eligible unemployed individuals are those who have received federal or state unemployment compensation for 12 consecutive weeks. A self-employed individual will be treated as having received unemployment compensation if, under Federal or State law, the individual would have received unemployment compensation but for being self-employed. Qualifying premiums are deductible premiums for the medical care of the unemployed individual, spouse and dependents. To be excludable, the distributions must be received in the tax year during which unemployment compensation is received or in the following year. In determining whether the premiums are deductible, the 7.5% medical expense floor (¶ 1015) is ignored. This exception to the 10% penalty imposed on certain early distributions ceases to apply after the individual has been reemployed for 60 days (not necessarily consecutive) after initial unemployment.

Education Expenses. The 10% penalty will not be charged if the individual uses the IRA money to pay for "qualified higher education expenses" for the individual, the individual's spouse, child, or grandchild of the individual or the individual's spouse. Qualified expenses included tuition at a post secondary educational institution, books, fees, supplies and equipment (Code Sec. 72(t)(2)(E)).[221]

First-Time Homebuyer Expenses. The 10% penalty will not be charged if the individual uses the IRA money for certain expenses associated with buying a principal residence. Only $10,000 during the individual's lifetime may be withdrawn without a penalty for this purpose. Qualified expenses include acquisition costs, settlement charges and closing costs. The principal residence may be for the individual or the individual's spouse, child, grandchild or ancestor of the individual or the individual's spouse. In order to be considered a "first-time homebuyer," the individual (and spouse, if married) must not have had an ownership interest in a principal residence during the two-year period ending on the date that the new home is acquired (Code Sec. 72(t)(2)(F)).[222]

Footnote references are to paragraphs of the 2002 Standard Federal Tax Reports.

¶ 2179

[217] ¶ 18,922.26	[219] ¶ 6102	[221] ¶ 6102
[218] ¶ 18,902	[220] ¶ 6102	[222] ¶ 6102

Reporting Exceptions to 10% Penalty. The 10% early distribution penalty is generally reported on Part I of Form 5329. If an exception to the penalty exists (e.g., early distribution due to total and permanent disability), the individual provides this information to the IRS on Line 2 of Part I of Form 5329.

2180. Roth IRA. Contributions to a Roth IRA are not deductible (Code Sec. 408A(c)(1)).[223] The advantage of the Roth IRA is that the buildup within the IRA (e.g., interest, dividends and/or price appreciation) may be free from federal income tax when the individual withdraws money from the account. To be treated as a Roth IRA, the account must be designated as such when it is established. A Roth IRA is treated like a traditional IRA (see ¶ 2168) except for the special rules described below.

Contribution Limits. For 2001, the maximum total yearly contribution that can be made by an individual to all IRAs (traditional and Roth) is $2,000, not counting rollover contributions (Reg. § 1.408A-3, Q&A-3(c)).[224] The maximum amount that may be contributed to a Roth IRA will increase to $3,000 for tax years beginning in 2002 through 2004, $4,000 for tax years beginning in 2005 through 2007, and $5,000 for tax years beginning in 2008 and thereafter. In addition, catch-up contributions (e.g., $500 for 2002) will be allowed for individuals who are at least 50 years of age (see ¶ 2168). Unlike traditional IRAs, individuals are allowed to make contributions to a Roth IRA even after age 70½ (Code Sec. 408(c)(4)).[225]

Income Limits. The ability of an individual to make a contribution to a Roth IRA depends upon the amount of the individual's modified AGI. The maximum yearly contribution that can be made to a Roth IRA is phased out for a single individual with a modified AGI between $95,000 and $110,000, for joint filers with modified AGI between $150,000 and $160,000, and for married filing separately with modified AGI between $0 and $10,000 (Reg. § 1.408A-3, Q&A-3(b)).[226] These AGI limits are *not* adjusted for inflation (Code Sec. 408A(c)(3)(C)(ii)). Modified AGI is generally calculated under the same procedure as that used for traditional IRAs (see ¶ 2171). However, for Roth IRA purposes, modified AGI does not include the income reported from the conversion of a traditional IRA into a Roth IRA (Code Sec. 408A(c)(3)(C)(i)).

Taxation of Distributions. Qualified distributions from a Roth IRA are not included in the individual's gross income and are not subject to the additional 10% penalty for early withdrawals. To be treated as a "qualified distribution," the distribution must satisfy a five-year holding period and must meet one of four requirements (see below).

To satisfy the five-year holding period, the Roth IRA distribution (including distributions allocable to rollover contributions) may not be made before the end of the five-tax-year period beginning with the first tax year for which the individual made a contribution to the Roth IRA (Reg. § 1.408A-6, Q&A-2).[227] Generally, each Roth IRA owner has only one five-year period for all of the Roth IRAs that the individual owns. (However, see "Distributions of Conversion Contributions," below, for determination of the five-year period.) Due to this five-year requirement, no qualified Roth IRA distributions may occur before tax years beginning in 2003.

> **Example.** Jack Matrin made his first contribution to a Roth IRA on September 15, 1998. The contribution was for the 1998 tax year. The five-year holding period for all of Jack's Roth IRAs began on January 1, 1998.

In addition to satisfying the five-year holding period, a qualified distribution must be: (1) made on or after the date on which individual attains age 59½; (2) made to a beneficiary (or the individual's estate) on or after the individual's death; (3) attributable to the individual's being disabled; or (4) a distribution to pay for "qualified first-time homebuyer expenses" (¶ 2179) (Code Sec. 408A(d)(2)).[228] Even if the distribution from a Roth IRA is not "qualified," it may escape the usual 10%

Footnote references are to paragraphs of the 2002 Standard Federal Tax Reports.

[223] ¶ 18,925
[224] ¶ 18,927
[225] ¶ 18,925
[226] ¶ 18,927
[227] ¶ 18,928
[228] ¶ 18,925

¶ 2180

early withdrawal penalty if it satisfies one of the exceptions for traditional IRAs (see the list of exceptions at ¶ 2179) (Reg. § 1.408A-6, Q&A-5(a)).[229]

Distribution Ordering Rules. Ordering rules determine what amounts are withdrawn from the Roth IRA. Under these rules, regular Roth contributions are deemed to be withdrawn first, then amounts transferred from traditional IRAs (starting with amounts first transferred). Withdrawals of transferred amounts are treated as coming first from amounts that were included in income. Earnings are treated as withdrawn after contributions (Reg. § 1.408A-6, Q&A-8).[230]

Pre-death Distribution Rules. The pre-death required beginning distribution rules of Code Sec. 401(a)(9)(A) that apply to qualified plans and traditional IRAs do not apply to Roth IRAs. Thus, the holders of a Roth IRA need not take a distribution by April 1 of the calendar year in which they attain age 70½. Also, the incidental death benefit rules of Code Sec. 401(a)(9)(G) do not apply to Roth IRAs (Reg. § 1.408A-1, Q&A-2).[231]

Rollovers and Conversions. Distributions from one Roth IRA can be rolled over or converted tax free to another Roth IRA. Amounts in a traditional IRA can be rolled over or converted into a Roth IRA but only if: (1) the taxpayer's adjusted gross income for the tax year does not exceed $100,000 and (2) the taxpayer is not married filing separately (Code Sec. 408A(c)(3)(B)).[232] Generally, amounts transferred or converted from a traditional IRA into a Roth IRA must be included in gross income but are not considered when determining the $100,000 AGI limit (Code Sec. 408A(c)(3)(C)(i)).[233]

Distributions of Conversion Contributions. If, within the five-year period starting with the year in which the individual made a conversion contribution of an amount from a traditional IRA to a Roth IRA, the individual takes a distribution from a Roth IRA of an amount that is attributable to the portion of the conversion contribution that was included in income, then, as general rule, the individual will be liable for the 10% penalty that applies to early distributions (Reg. § 1.408A-6, Q&A-5). However, there are a number of exceptions to the penalty (e.g., disability) (see ¶ 2179). The five-year period is separately determined for each conversion contribution made to a Roth IRA. See ¶ 2179 for information concerning the reporting of the 10% penalty and exceptions to the penalty.

Pre-1999 Rollover. If a rollover from a traditional IRA to a Roth IRA was made before January 1, 1999, the amount that would have been included in gross income if the individual had taken a distribution is included in gross income "ratably" over a four-tax-year period beginning with the tax year in which the payment or distribution is made (Reg. § 1.408A-4, Q&A-10).[234] The tax return for 2001 will include the last ratable distribution.

If the individual dies during the four-year period, usually the remaining portion of the taxable amount of the converted amount must be included on the individual's final return. However, if the surviving spouse is the sole beneficiary of the Roth IRA, the spouse may elect to continue the deferral of the taxable amount over the remaining portion of the four-year period (Code Sec. 408A(d)(3)(E)).[235]

Deemed Roth IRA. For plan years beginning after December 31, 2002, qualified plans may allow employees to make voluntary contributions to an account that will be deemed to be a Roth IRA if the account meets all the requirements of a Roth IRA (Code Sec. 408(q), as added by the Economic Growth and Tax Relief Reconciliation Act of 2001 (P.L. 107-16)). An employee's contribution to this account will count towards the maximum annual contribution that may be made to a Roth IRA (e.g., $2,500 for 2003).

Roth Contributions to 401(k) or 403(b) Plans. For tax years beginning after December 31, 2005, 401(k) and 403(b) plans may contain a provision that would

---

Footnote references are to paragraphs of the 2002 Standard Federal Tax Reports.

¶ 2180

[229] ¶ 18,928	[232] ¶ 18,925	[234] ¶ 18,927B
[230] ¶ 18,928	[233] ¶ 18,925	[235] ¶ 18,925
[231] ¶ 18,926B		

allow employees to designate all or part of their elective deferrals to the plan to be treated as after-tax Roth contributions (Code Sec. 402A, as added by P.L. 107-16). As with regular Roth IRAs, earnings generated by these elective contributions will not be currently taxed and, if certain qualifications are met, distributions will not be taxed.

2182. Coverdell Education Savings Accounts (f/k/a "Education IRAs"). During 2001, Congress changed the name of "Education IRAs" to "Coverdell Education Savings Accounts." The tax ramifications of these accounts are discussed at ¶ 898.

Simplified Employee Pensions

2184. Simplified Employee Pensions (SEPs). A simplified employee pension, or SEP, is a program under which the employer makes contributions to IRAs of employees (Code Sec. 408(k)).[236] The IRA of each participating employee typically takes the form of a separate account in a group IRA established under Code Sec. 408(c).[237] In the case of a SEP established by an unincorporated employer, the "compensation" of a self-employed participant (partner or proprietor) is "earned income" (see ¶ 2113 and ¶ 2151) (Code Sec. 408(k)(7)(A), (B)).[238]

Employer Contributions. Annual contributions by an employer to a SEP are excluded from the participant's gross income to the extent that they do not exceed the lesser of 15% of the participant's compensation ($170,000 maximum for 2001, $200,000 for 2002) or $35,000 (maximum for 2001) ($40,000 for 2002) (Code Sec. 402(h)).[239] If the employer exceeds this limit, the employee is generally taxed on the amount of the excess (see ¶ 2174) (Code Sec. 4973(a)).[240]

A SEP may be maintained on either a calendar year or a tax year basis. If a calendar year is employed, contributions for the calendar year are deductible for the tax year with or within which the calendar year ends, and the contributions are treated as made on the last day of the calendar year if they are made by the due date (including extensions) of the employer's tax return for the tax year. If a tax year is employed, contributions are deductible for the tax year and are treated as made on the last day of the tax year if they are made by the due date (including extensions) of the employer's tax return for the tax year (Code Sec. 404(h)).[241]

Although the employer's deduction cannot exceed 15% of the employee's compensation (not in excess of $170,000 for 2001, $200,000 for 2002) paid to employees for the calendar year, any excess can be carried over and deducted (subject to the 15% limitation for the carryover year) in later years. In addition, the deduction for contributions to a SEP reduces the limitation on contributions to qualified profit-sharing and stock bonus plans and the 25% limitation on deductible contributions to a combination of plans (see ¶ 2151) (Code Sec. 404(h)(2)).[242]

Nondiscriminatory employer contributions under a SEP must be made for each employee who (1) has reached age 21, (2) has performed services for the employer during at least three of the immediately preceding five years, and (3) received at least the indexed dollar amount of compensation from the employer for the year ($450 for 2001) (Code Sec. 408(k)(2)).[243]

Salary Reduction SEPs (SARSEPs). In plan years beginning before 1997, an employer could establish a salary reduction (cash or deferred) arrangement as part of a SEP.[244] Such an arrangement—commonly known as a SARSEP—may not be established in plan years beginning after 1996. However, SARSEPs established before 1997 may continue to operate after 1996, subject to the same conditions and requirements that have always applied (Sec. 1421(c) of P. L. 104-188).[245] That is, if eligible to do so under the rules discussed below, participating employees (including

---

Footnote references are to paragraphs of the 2002 Standard Federal Tax Reports.

[236] ¶ 18,902	[240] ¶ 34,360	[243] ¶ 18,902
[237] ¶ 18,902	[241] ¶ 18,330	[244] ¶ 18,902
[238] ¶ 18,902	[242] ¶ 18,330	[245] ¶ 18,902
[239] ¶ 18,202		

those hired after 1996) may continue to make cash or deferred elections in plan years beginning after 1996.

Employee's Contributions. An employee for whom an employer contributes under a SEP may also make contributions to the SEP-IRA, subject to the usual rules regarding contributions by an individual to an IRA (see ¶ 2170-¶ 2173).

Distributions. Distributions from a SEP are subject to tax based on the rules that apply to distributions from an IRA (Code Sec. 402(h)(3)).[246] See ¶ 2178.

Top-Heavy SEP. If a SEP is top heavy (see ¶ 2139), each participant who is not a key employee must be provided with a contribution that is not less than 3% of his compensation. If the rate for the key employee receiving the largest contribution is less than 3%, the contribution rate for that employee is used to determine the minimum contribution for non-key employees (Code Sec. 408(k)(1)(B)).[247]

SIMPLE Retirement Accounts

2185. Generally. Certain small employers (see ¶ 2110) may maintain SIMPLE retirement plans. One variety of a SIMPLE plan takes the form of a SIMPLE 401(k) plan (see ¶ 2112). The other variety is a SIMPLE IRA which is discussed below.

No Other Plan Allowed. Generally, if an employer maintains a SIMPLE IRA, it may not, in the same plan year, maintain another tax-favored plan to which contributions are made or under which benefits are accrued. Tax-favored plans include qualified plans, tax-sheltered annuity arrangements (TSAs), simplified employee pensions (SEPs or SARSEPs), and nonqualified governmental plans (Code Sec. 408(p)(2)(D)).[248] However, employers may adopt a SIMPLE IRA for noncollectively bargained employees, even if the employer also maintains a qualified plan for collectively bargained employees (Code Sec. 408(p)(2)(D)).[249]

2185A. Eligible Employees. If the employer has established a SIMPLE account, an employee must be eligible to participate in any calendar year if he or she received at least $5,000 of compensation from the employer during each of the two preceding calendar years and is reasonably expected to receive at least $5,000 in compensation during the current calendar year (Code Sec. 408(p)(4)(A)).[250] Nonresident alien employees and employees covered by a collective bargaining agreement may be excluded from participation (Code Sec. 408(p)(4)(B)).[251] A self-employed individual is treated as an employee and may participate in a SIMPLE plan if the compensation threshold is exceeded (Code Sec. 408(p)(6)(B)).[252] For this purpose, compensation means earned income (see ¶ 2113) (Code Sec. 408(p)(6)(A)(ii)).[253]

Members of Certain Religious Faiths. For tax years beginning after December 31, 2001, self-employed persons who have elected out of the self-employment tax (SECA) on religious grounds (Code Sec. 1402(g)) may base their retirement plan contributions, including SIMPLE IRAs, on their self-employment income that is exempt from SECA.

2185B. Elective Contributions Must Be Permitted. A SIMPLE IRA must permit each eligible employee to elect to have the employer make payments either (1) directly to the employee in cash or (2) as a contribution (expressed as a percentage of compensation) to the SIMPLE account (Code Sec. 408(p)(2)(A)(ii)).[254]

No Other Contributions. Prior to January 1, 2002, no contributions other than elective contributions, employer matching contributions (see ¶ 2185C), and nonelective employer contributions (see ¶ 2185C) may be made to a SIMPLE account by the employer or the employee (Code Sec. 408(p)(2)(A)(iv)).[255] However, a rollover from another SIMPLE account may be received (Code Sec. 408(d)(3)(G)).[256] For

---

Footnote references are to paragraphs of the 2002 Standard Federal Tax Reports.

[246] ¶ 18,202	[250] ¶ 18,902	[254] ¶ 18,902
[247] ¶ 18,902	[251] ¶ 18,902	[255] ¶ 18,902
[248] ¶ 18,902	[252] ¶ 18,902	[256] ¶ 18,902
[249] ¶ 18,902	[253] ¶ 18,902	

¶ 2185

distributions after December 31, 2001, if the employee has participated in the SIMPLE IRA for at least two years the distribution may be rolled over into other types of retirement plans (e.g., employer qualified plans, 403(b) plans and 457 plans) (Code Sec. 408(d)(3)(A)).

Dollar Limitation. Elective contributions for 2001 are limited to $6,500 ($7,000 for 2002 and increasing in $1,000 annual increments until the limit reaches $10,000 in 2005) (Code Sec. 408(p)(2)(A)(ii) and (E)).[257] The maximum employee deferral (e.g., $6,500 for 2001) may be matched by the employer, resulting in a maximum deferral to the SIMPLE IRA of $13,000 for 2001 (Code Sec. 408(p)(8)). Matching contributions to SIMPLE IRAs that are made on behalf of self-employed individuals are not treated as elective contributions made by the individuals (Code Sec. 408(p)(9)).[258] After 2001, individuals who are at least 50 years old may make additional "catch-up" contributions to IRAs ($500 for 2002, $1,000 for 2003, $1,500 for 2004, $2,000 for 2005, and $2,500 for 2006 and later) (Code Sec. 414(v)(2)(B)(ii), as added by the Economic Growth and Tax Relief Reconciliation Act of 2001 (P.L. 107-16)).

Election to Participate or Modify Elective Contributions. Under the arrangement, each eligible employee must have the right to elect, during the 60-day period preceding the beginning of any calendar year (and the 60-day period preceding the first day of eligibility), to participate in the arrangement for that calendar year or to modify the amount of his or her elective contributions under the arrangement for that calendar year (Code Sec. 408(p)(5)(C)).[259]

Termination of Participation. An employee may terminate participation in the arrangement at any time during a calendar year. However, the arrangement may prohibit reentry until the beginning of the following calendar year (Code Sec. 408(p)(5)(B)).[260]

2185C. Matching Contributions Required. Ordinarily, the employer must match the elective contribution of an employee in an amount not exceeding 3% of the employee's compensation (Code Sec. 408(p)(2)(A)(iii)).[261] However, an employer may elect to limit its match, for all eligible employees, to a smaller percentage of compensation (not less than 1%). The election may not be made by an employer in more than two out of every five years. If the SIMPLE account did not exist during the full five-year period, the election may still be made in up to two of the years in which it did exist (Code Sec. 408(p)(2)(C)(ii)).[262]

Nonelective Contributions as Alternative to Matching Contributions. The matching contribution requirement is considered to be satisfied if the employer elects to make nonelective contributions of 2% of compensation for each employee who is eligible to participate in the arrangement and who has at least $5,000 of compensation from the employer for the calendar year. The compensation that may be taken into account in determining the 2% nonelective contributions may not exceed the limitation explained at ¶ 2128 (i.e., $170,000 for 2001 and $200,000 for 2002) (Code Sec. 408(p)(2)(B)(ii)).[263]

2185D. Vesting. The employee's right to both elective contributions and matching contributions (and the earnings on these contributions) must be fully vested at all times. In addition, the plan may not contain any employer-imposed prohibition on withdrawals from the account (Code Sec. 408(p)(3)).[264]

2185E. Tax Treatment of Contributions to SIMPLE IRAs. Even though a SIMPLE IRA is treated as a traditional IRA for most purposes, SIMPLE IRAs must comply with their own set of rules (Code Secs. 219(b)(4) and 408(p)(2)(A)(iv)).[265] Elective contributions of employees are not includible in gross income when made (Code Secs 402(h) and 408(k)).[266] They are taxable only under

---

Footnote references are to paragraphs of the 2002 Standard Federal Tax Reports.

[257] ¶ 18,902 [261] ¶ 18,902 [264] ¶ 18,902
[258] ¶ 18,902 [262] ¶ 18,902 [265] ¶ 12,650, ¶ 18,902
[259] ¶ 18,902 [263] ¶ 18,902 [266] ¶ 18,202, ¶ 18,902
[260] ¶ 18,902

the distribution rules discussed at ¶ 2185F. The employer is entitled to a deduction for its contributions to a SIMPLE, including elective contributions made under a SIMPLE 401(k) plan (Code Sec. 404(m)).[267] Elective and nonelective contributions made in lieu of matching contributions made during any calendar year are deductible for the employer's tax year in which or with which the calendar year ends. These contributions are treated as made for a tax year if they are made on account of that tax year and are made not later than the time prescribed by law for filing the return for that tax year (including extensions of time).

For deduction purposes, employer contributions to a SIMPLE account are treated as if they were made to a plan subject to the requirements of Code Sec. 404, which governs the deduction of contributions by an employer to qualified plans, nonqualified plans of the funded variety, and SEPs (Code Sec. 404(m)).[268]

2185F. Distributions (Withdrawals) from SIMPLE Accounts. Distributions by a SIMPLE account are taxable to the employee (or the beneficiary or estate of the employee) under the rules that govern distributions from traditional IRAs (see ¶ 2178) (Code Sec. 408(p)(1)(A)).[269]

Rollovers. A distribution from a SIMPLE account may be rolled over free of tax to another SIMPLE account, but, prior to 2002, it may not be rolled over to a qualified plan or TSA. It may be rolled over to a traditional or Roth IRA, but only after two years have elapsed since the employee's inception of participation in the salary reduction arrangement. For distributions after December 31, 2001, after two years of participation, an employee's funds in a SIMPLE plan may be generally rolled over into a other types of qualified plans (e.g., 401(k), 403(b) or 457 plans) (Code Sec. 408(d)(3)(G), as amended by the Economic Growth and Tax Relief Reconciliation Act of 2001 (P.L. 107-16)).[270]

Early Distributions. A 25% tax on early distributions (¶ 2157) applies to distributions from SIMPLE accounts in the case of nonexempt distributions made within two years following the date of the employee's first participation in a SIMPLE arrangement (Code Sec. 72(t)(6)).[271]

2185G. Top Heavy Rules Do Not Apply. The special rules for top heavy plans (see ¶ 2139) do not apply to SIMPLE plans (Code Sec. 416(g)(4)(G)).[272]

Rollovers

2186. Tax-Free Rollovers Between Traditional IRAs and Employer Plans. An individual may withdraw all or part of the assets of one traditional IRA and exclude the withdrawal from income if the individual transfers it to another traditional IRA or returns it to the same IRA. However, the transfer or return must be accomplished within 60 days after the withdrawal. It is not necessary that the entire amount withdrawn be transferred, but only the amount that is in fact transferred during the 60-day period will be free from tax. Any portion of the withdrawal that is not rolled over within the 60-day period will be taxed as ordinary income and may be subject to a 10% penalty on premature distributions if the distributee is less than 59½ years old (see ¶ 2157). For distributions made after December 31, 2001, the IRS has the authority to grant a waiver of the 60-day rule in situations involving equity, good conscience, or situations beyond the control of the individual. Once an individual has made a tax-free rollover, the individual must wait at least one year from the date of receipt of the amount withdrawn before becoming eligible to engage in another (Code Sec. 408(d)(3)(B)).[273] The IRS takes the position that the one-year limitation applies to each separate IRA owned by the taxpayer (IRS Publication 590). Thus, a distribution received from one IRA of the taxpayer may be rolled over even though a distribution from another IRA of the taxpayer was received less than a year before and was also rolled over. A mere

---

Footnote references are to paragraphs of the 2002 Standard Federal Tax Reports.

267 ¶ 18,922.0272	270 ¶ 18,902	272 ¶ 19,250
268 ¶ 18,922.0272	271 ¶ 6102	273 ¶ 18,902
269 ¶ 18,902		

¶ 2185F

change of trustee or custodian for an IRA is not considered a rollover (although it too is tax free), and, therefore, the one-year limitation does not apply.[274]

Rollover from one traditional IRA to another is not available for a mandatory distribution (see ¶ 2177) (Code Sec. 408(d)(3)(E)).[275] See ¶ 2180 regarding a rollover from a traditional IRA into a Roth IRA.

Although a SIMPLE account is a type of IRA and is treated as an IRA for most purposes, its assets may *not* be rolled over to a traditional or Roth IRA until two years after the inception of the employee's participation (Code Sec. 408(d)(3)(G)).[276] In addition, prior to 2002, a distribution from a traditional IRA may not be rolled over to a SIMPLE account. This is because a SIMPLE account may receive only elective contributions of participants, matching contributions of the employer, and, in some instances, nonelective contributions of the employer (Code Sec. 408(p)(2)(A)(iv)).[277] However, for distributions after December 31, 2001, after two years of participation, an employee's funds in a SIMPLE plan may be generally rolled over into a other types of qualified plans (e.g., 401(k), 403(b) or 457 plans) (Code Sec. 408(d)(3)(G), as amended by the Economic Growth and Tax Relief Reconciliation Act of 2001 (P.L. 107-16)).

Rollovers From IRAs to Employer Plans. Prior to 2002, in most situations, an IRA may not be rolled over into a qualified employer retirement plan, including 403(b) and 457 plans. The only exception to the ban on rollovers from IRAs to employer plans is that amounts from a qualified plan which are rolled into an IRA may be rolled back into another qualified plan if the amounts in the IRA are attributable solely to rollovers from qualified plans (Code Sec. 402(c)(5). The IRA used to achieve this result is commonly known as a "conduit IRA." No additional contributions can be made to a conduit IRA in order for the funds to remain eligible for transfer to a qualified plan. A similar exception exists for amounts that are rolled over from a Code Sec. 403(b) annuity to an IRA and subsequently rolled back into a Code Sec. 403(b) annuity.

For distributions made after December 31, 2001, the rollover options have been greatly expanded. Generally, an eligible rollover distribution from an IRA may be rolled over into a qualified plan, 403(b) plan or 457 plan (Code Sec. 408(d)(3)(A), as amended by P.L. 107-16). This is true whether or not the distributing IRA qualifies as a "conduit IRA." A rollover of after-tax contributions may be made from one IRA to another but may not be made into an employer plan (Code Sec. 408(d)(3)(A)(ii), as amended by P.L. 107-16).

2188. Tax-Free Rollover from Qualified Plan to a Traditional IRA or to Another Qualified Plan. In many situations, a distribution from a qualified plan may be rolled over and thus excluded from income (Code Sec. 402(c)).[278] Any part of the taxable portion of a distribution from a qualified plan may, within 60 days, be rolled over to a traditional IRA or to another qualified plan, unless the distribution is one of a series of substantially equal payments made (1) over the life (or life expectancy) of the participant or the joint lives (or joint life expectancies) of the participant and his or her beneficiary or (2) over a specified period of 10 years or more (Code Sec. 402(c)(4)).[279] In addition, a distribution may not be rolled over if it is required to be made under the minimum distribution rules discussed at ¶ 2135 (Code Sec. 402(c)(4)(B)).[280]

Ten-year averaging and the special 20% tax (see ¶ 2177) are not available if any part of a lump-sum distribution is rolled over (Code Sec. 402(d)(4)(K), before amendment by P.L. 104-188).[281] Also, if a distribution that is not a lump-sum distribution is rolled over, averaging is not available as to a subsequent lump-sum distribution (Code Sec. 402(c)(10), before amendment by P.L. 104-188).[282]

Direct Transfers. All qualified plans must permit a participant (or a spouse or ex-spouse of a participant who is an alternate payee under a QDRO) to elect to have any distribution that is eligible for rollover treatment transferred directly to an eligible transferee plan specified by the participant (Code Sec. 401(a)(31)(A)).[283] A transferee plan is eligible if it is a traditional IRA or a qualified plan. In the case of a qualified plan funded by a trust (instead of an annuity contract or contracts), the plan must be a defined contribution plan the terms of which permit the acceptance of rollover distributions. Prior to 2002, a direct transfer is not permitted for that portion of a distribution that would not be included in the gross income of the distributee even if no rollover was involved (i.e., the employee's after-tax contributions).

Rollovers After December 31, 2001. The rollover options between employer plans has been greatly expanded for distributions made after December 31, 2001. The term "eligible retirement plan" for purposes of rollover distributions will include IRAs, qualified plans, 403(b) plans and 457 plans (Code Sec. 402(c)(8)(B), as amended by the Economic Growth and Tax Relief Reconciliation Act of 2001 (P.L. 107-16)). Rollovers of after-tax amounts may be rolled over into an employers plan if the new plan agrees to separately account for these amounts (Code Sec. 401(a)(31)(B), as amended by P.L. 107-16).

Mandatory Rollovers. A direct rollover from a qualified plan into an IRA will become mandatory for distributions made after the IRS issues regulations on the subject. This will be applied when an involuntary distribution from a qualified plan exceeds $1,000 and the plan specifies that nonforfeitable benefits that do not exceed $5,000 must be distributed immediately. However, the employee will have the right to elect to receive the distribution or have it rolled over into another IRA or qualified plan (Code Sec. 401(a)(31), as amended by P.L. 107-16).

Withholding. If a distributee does not elect a direct transfer—instead receiving the distribution and transferring it to an eligible plan within 60 days—the payor of the distribution must withhold 20% of the distribution (Code Sec. 3405(c)).[284] If the distributee does elect a direct transfer, there is no withholding. It is important to be aware that the amount withheld from a distribution will not be excluded from the distributee's gross income unless an equivalent amount is contributed to the transferee plan or IRA within the 60-day rollover period.

Written Explanation. The plan administrator must provide a written explanation to a recipient of the distribution options (including the direct trustee-to-trustee transfer option) within a reasonable period of time before making an eligible rollover distribution (Code Sec. 402(f)).[285] Additional information concerning the tax implications of the rollover must be provided to the employee for distributions made after December 31, 2001 (Code Sec. 402(f)(1)(E), as added by P.L. 107-16).

Tax-Sheltered Annuities. Rules similar to the foregoing rules also apply in the case of tax-sheltered annuity arrangements (Code Sec. 403(a)(4)(B)).[286]

2190. Rollover by Successor After Death of Participant. If any part of a distribution from a qualified plan that would be eligible for rollover treatment if made to the employee is received by the participant's surviving spouse, the spouse may roll over that distribution to a traditional IRA under the same terms and conditions that would have applied to the employee (Code Sec. 402(c)(9)).[287] For distributions made after December 31, 2001, the expanded rollover options (see ¶ 2188) are available to the surviving spouse. Other successors who receive a distribution from a qualified plan are not entitled to roll over that distribution to an IRA or to another qualified plan (Code Sec. 402(c)(4)).[288]

The surviving spouse of the owner of an IRA is also eligible to roll over any amount received from that IRA to another IRA (Code Sec. 408(d)(3)(C)(ii)(II)).[289]

Footnote references are to paragraphs of the 2002 Standard Federal Tax Reports.

¶ 2190

[283] ¶ 17,502	[286] ¶ 18,270	[288] ¶ 18,202
[284] ¶ 33,620	[287] ¶ 18,202	[289] ¶ 18,902
[285] ¶ 18,202		

See ¶ 2186 for allowable rollovers. This cannot be done by any other successor (Code Sec. 408(d)(3)(C)).[290]

2191. Rollovers Incident to Divorce. When a participant's spouse or former spouse is awarded all or part of the participant's interest in a qualified plan or 403(b) plan by a qualified domestic relations order (QDRO) (see ¶ 2166), the distribution of any part of that interest to the spouse or former spouse may be rolled over on the same terms that would apply if the distribution were made to the participant (Code Sec. 414(p)(10)).[291] For transfers, distributions and payments made after December 31, 2001, the QDRO provisions also apply to 457 plans (i.e., eligible deferred compensation plans of state and local governments and tax-exempt organizations) (see ¶ 2197A).

The transfer of all or a portion of an IRA to a spouse or former spouse under a divorce or separation instrument that meets the definition established by Code Sec. 71(b)(2) is a nontaxable transaction as to both parties, and the IRA is thereafter treated as that of the spouse or former spouse (Code Sec. 408(d)(6)).[292] Accordingly, the spouse or former spouse may roll over to another IRA or IRAs all or any part of the interest transferred to him or her (see ¶ 2186).

2192. IRA as Conduit for Transfers Between Qualified Plans. For distributions made prior to January 1, 2002, an amount rolled over to a traditional IRA from a qualified plan may later be rolled over to another qualified plan if the IRA at no time holds assets other than those rolled over from the qualified plan, assets attributable to reinvestment of those assets, and earnings of those assets. In this situation, the IRA is used strictly as a "holding account," or conduit, and no contributions may be made to the account. For distributions made after December 31, 2001, the rollover options available to individuals have been greatly expanded (Code Sec. 408(d)(3)(A)(ii), as amended by the Economic Growth and Tax Relief Reconciliation Act of 2001 (P.L. 107-16)).[293] See ¶ 2186 for rollovers between IRAs. See ¶ 2188 for rollovers between qualified plans and IRAs.

2193. Rollovers of 403(b) and 457 Plan Assets. See ¶ 2167 for the rollover of assets from a 403(b) plan. See ¶ 2197A for the rollover of 457 plan assets. Rollovers between various types of qualified plans is discussed at ¶ 2188.

Nonqualified Plans

2194. Nonqualified Plans. An employer may maintain a retirement or other deferred compensation plan that is not a qualified plan. If such a plan is *funded* (i.e., the employer makes contributions to a trust or purchases an annuity contract or contracts), the participants realize income and the employer is entitled to deductions under the rules set forth below. As to *unfunded* deferred compensation plans, see ¶ 723 and ¶ 906.

2195. Income of the Plan. In the case of a plan funded through a trust, the trust is not exempt (i.e., the plan's earnings are generally taxable to the trust) (Code Sec. 641).[294] The grantor trust rules (see ¶ 573 and following) ordinarily do not apply to a nonqualified plan. Therefore, the participant is not usually treated as the owner of his share of the trust's assets and is not subject to tax on the trust's income. However, if a participant's contributions as of any date exceed the employer's contributions on behalf of the participant, the participant is treated as the owner of the portion of the trust attributable to his contributions and is subject to tax on the income from that portion (Reg. § 1.402(b)-1(b)(6)).[295]

2196. Income of a Participant. Contributions of (or premiums paid by) the employer in the case of a nonqualified plan are taxable to a participant when

---

made if they are substantially vested at that time. If contributions are made to a nonqualified plan at a time when the participant's interest in the plan is not substantially vested and the interest subsequently becomes substantially vested, the value of the participant's interest that is attributable to the employer's contributions after August 1, 1969, is includible in the employee's income at the time of vesting. If only a portion of a participant's interest becomes substantially vested, the amount included in income is the amount that would have been included if the entire interest had vested multiplied by the percentage that did become substantially vested.

Rank-and-file employees are not taxable on amounts contributed to, or earned by, a trust that is not exempt solely because of the plan's failure to satisfy the nondiscriminatory coverage requirements described at ¶ 2119. However, each highly compensated employee (as defined at ¶ 2111) is subject to tax on the value of the vested accrued benefit attributable to employer contributions as of the close of the employer's tax year that ends with or within the tax year in which the trust loses its exemption. If the trust continues to be nonexempt for failure to satisfy the coverage requirements, a highly compensated employee is subject to tax on the excess of the current value of his or her vested accrued benefit attributable to employer contributions over the value of the previously taxed portion of that benefit (Code Sec. 402(b)(4)).[296]

The participant's investment (basis) in a nonqualified plan is increased by any amounts included in his or her income under the above rules.

Actual distributions from a nonqualified plan are taxed under the rules described at ¶ 817 et seq. if they take the form of an annuity. Otherwise, they are considered to be derived first from plan earnings and asset appreciation (taxable gain) rather than from the employee's investment (basis) in the plan (Code Secs. 402(b) and 403(c)).[297]

2197. Employer's Deduction. The employer is entitled to a deduction for contributions to, or premiums paid under, a nonqualified plan on behalf of an employee in the tax year of the employer in which an amount attributable to the contribution is includible in the gross income of the employee under the rules discussed at ¶ 2196 (Code Sec. 404(a)(5)).[298] If more than one employee participates, this rule applies only if separate accounts are maintained for each employee.

2197A. Deferred Compensation Plans of Exempt Employers ("Sec. 457 Plans"). Special rules apply to certain deferred compensation plans sponsored by state and local governments and private tax-exempt organizations (commonly referred to as Sec. 457 plans). Prior to 2002, compensation deferred under these plans and any increase attributable to that compensation are included in gross income only for the tax year in which they are paid or otherwise made available to the participant or beneficiary. After December 31, 2001, under a state or local government plan, compensation deferred under the plan is only included in income when it is paid to the employee. For plans of tax-exempt organizations, the rule remains unchanged that deferred compensation is includible when paid or made available (Code Sec. 457(a)(1), as amended by the Economic Growth and Tax Relief Reconciliation Act of 2001 (P.L. 107-16)). As with other types of retirement plans, special requirements have to be met by Sec. 457 plans.

Availability of Benefits. Compensation is deferred for any calendar month under a Sec. 457 plan only if an agreement providing for deferral is entered into before the beginning of that month (Code Sec. 457(b)(4)). Benefits are not considered to be made available under the plan if the participant or beneficiary may elect, before any benefits become payable, to defer payment of some or all of them to a fixed or determinable future time. In addition, amounts deferred under an eligible

---

Footnote references are to paragraphs of the 2002 Standard Federal Tax Reports.

¶ 2197　　　[296] ¶ 18,202　　　　　[297] ¶ 18,202, ¶ 18,270　　　[298] ¶ 18,330

plan are not considered to be made available to the participant solely because the individual may choose among various investment options under the plan, whether before or after benefit payments have commenced (Reg. § 1.457-1(b)(1)).[299] After benefits have become payable but before they have commenced, the participant or beneficiary may elect to defer them to a date later than that originally elected. Only one such election may be made (Code Sec. 457(e)(9)(B)).[300]

Limitation on Deferral. For 2001, the maximum amount that may be deferred for the tax year may not exceed the *lesser* of (1) one-third of the participant's compensation attributable to services performed for the employer and includible in gross income or (2) $8,500. Prior to 2002, when applying the dollar limit, elective deferrals under qualified plans, SEPs, and tax-sheltered annuity arrangements are combined with deferrals under the Sec. 457 plan (see ¶ 2111). For years beginning after December 31, 2001, the maximum amount that can be deferred is the *lesser* of: (1) 100% of the participant's includible compensation or (2) a specific dollar amount (Code Sec. 457(b)(2), as amended P.L. 107-16).[301] The "specific dollar amount" will increase over the next few years (e.g., $11,000 for 2002, $12,000 for 2003 and $13,000 for 2004) (Code Sec. 457(e)(15), as amended by P.L. 107-16).[302] In addition, after 2001, it is no longer necessary to coordinate the maximum deferral to a Sec. 457 plan with contributions made to other types of retirement plans (Code Sec. 457(c), as amended by P.L. 107-16).[303] Participants in a Sec. 457 plan are permitted to make additional deferrals of income for one or more of the last three tax years that end before normal retirement age (Code Sec. 457(b)(3)). This additional deferral may be as high as twice the applicable dollar amount for the tax year (e.g., $22,000 for 2002).

Catch-Up Contributions. After 2001, participants in a Code Sec. 457 state or governmental plan who are at least 50 years of age will be able to make special catch-up contributions to the plan (Code Sec. 414(v), as added by P.L. 107-16). The maximum catch-up contribution will increase over the next few years ($1,000 for 2002, $2,000 for 2003, $3,000 for 2004, $4,000 for 2005, and $5,000 for tax years beginning in 2006 and thereafter).

Other Requirements. For distributions made prior to 2002, special minimum distribution rules have to be met (Code Sec. 457(d)). For distributions made after December 31, 2001, a Sec. 457 plan must satisfy the minimum distribution rules that are generally imposed on qualified plans (see ¶ 2135) (Code Sec. 457(d)(2), as amended by P.L. 107-16). Deferred amounts must not be made available before the calendar year in which the participant attains age 70½, is separated from the service of the employer ("severance from employment" after 2001), or is faced with an unforeseen emergency (Code Sec. 457(d)(1)).[304]

Rollovers. Generally, prior to 2002, rollovers may only be made between Sec. 457 plans (Code Sec. 457(e)(10)). However, the rollover options have been greatly expanded for distributions made after December 31, 2001 (Code Sec. 457(e)(16), as added by P.L. 107-16). Under these new provisions, an employee participating in a governmental Sec 457 plan may rollover plan assets into a variety of retirement plans (e.g., IRAs, 401(k) plans and 403(b) plans). Similarly, in some circumstances, assets from these plans may be rolled over into a Sec. 457 plan. See ¶ 2186 and ¶ 2188 for more information on rollovers.

Ineligible Plans. Compensation deferred under a nonqualified plan of a state or local government or other tax-exempt organization that is not an eligible Sec. 457 plan is includible in the income of a participant or beneficiary for the first tax year in which there is no substantial risk of forfeiture (Code Sec. 457(f)(1)(A); Code Sec. 457(f)(2)(E)).[305]

Footnote references are to paragraphs of the 2002 Standard Federal Tax Reports.

[299] ¶ 21,532	[302] ¶ 21,531	[304] ¶ 21,531
[300] ¶ 21,531	[303] ¶ 21,531	[305] ¶ 21,531
[301] ¶ 21,531		

¶ 2197A

Welfare Benefits

2198. Unfunded Welfare Benefits. Welfare benefits provided directly by an employer to an employee are deductible by the employer only in its tax year that includes the end of the tax year in which the employee includes the benefits in gross income (or would include such benefits in gross income if they were taxable to the employee) (Code Sec. 404(b)(2)(A)).[306] An employer may not accrue and deduct unpaid welfare benefits. This rule applies to any benefit which—if it were classified as compensation—would be deferred compensation. See ¶ 906.

2199. Funded Welfare Benefits. Special rules govern deductions for employer contributions to funded welfare benefit plans (Code Sec. 419).[307] The rules also govern contributions to welfare benefit plans on behalf of independent contractors.

Essentially, the rules for welfare benefit funds prevent an employer from deducting contributions to a welfare benefit plan in excess of the benefits actually paid by the plan during the tax year. However, under some circumstances, for plans providing disability, medical, supplemental unemployment and severance pay, and life insurance benefits, deductions may also be taken for additions to a reserve (referred to as a "qualified asset account") (Code Sec. 419A(a)).[308] Specifically, the employer may deduct contributions paid or accrued to a welfare benefit fund to the extent that the contributions do not exceed the "qualified cost" of the fund for its tax year ending with or within the tax year of the employer, reduced by the "after-tax income" of the fund for that tax year.

Qualified Cost. The qualified cost of the fund consists of two elements: (1) the qualified direct cost and (2) the allowable addition, if any, to a qualified asset account (Code Sec. 419(c)(1)).[309]

A qualified asset account is one maintained by a welfare benefit fund for the payment of such costs as medical, SUB, severance pay and life insurance benefits (including associated administrative costs) (Code Sec. 419A(a)).[310] Generally, the allowable addition for a tax year is the amount that will bring the account to a level (the "account limit") that is reasonably and actuarially necessary to fund the payment of incurred but unpaid benefits and, in the case of post-retirement medical and life insurance benefits, to fund the payment of such benefits on a level basis over the working lives of the covered employees (based on current medical costs). For employers who do not support higher additions to a qualified asset account by actuarial certifications, there are safe harbor additions for the various benefits. Limits are placed on the level of disability and SUB or severance pay benefits that may be considered in establishing the account limit for such benefits.

After-Tax Income. The after-tax income of a welfare benefit plan is its gross income reduced by the sum of (a) the deductions allowed by the Code that are directly connected with the production of that income and (b) the federal income tax imposed on the fund (Code Secs. 419 and 419A; Temporary Reg. § § 1.419-1T, 1.419A-1T and 1.419A-2T).[311]

Footnote references are to paragraphs of the 2002 Standard Federal Tax Reports.

[306] ¶ 18,330	[310] ¶ 19,298
[307] ¶ 19,295	[311] ¶ 19,295, ¶ 19,296,
[308] ¶ 19,298	¶ 19,298, ¶ 19,299,
[309] ¶ 19,295	¶ 19,300

¶ 2198

Chapter 22

CORPORATE ACQUISITIONS REORGANIZATIONS LIQUIDATIONS

Corporate Division

2201. "Spin-Off," "Split-Off," and "Split-Up" Exchanges. Nonrecognition-of-gain benefits apply to receipt of stock in connection with corporate exchanges in distributions known as "spin-offs," "split-offs," or "split-ups."

Spin-Off. A "spin-off" occurs when a corporation distributes stock or securities in another corporation controlled by it (through at least 80 percent stock ownership) without requiring shareholders to surrender any shares. The distribution is pro rata. The recipients do not surrender any of their stock in the controlling corporation (Code Sec. 355; Reg. § 1.355-1).[1] A new or existing corporation may be used for the spin-off (Reg. § 1.355-1(b)).[2]

Split-Off. A "split-off" is a type of corporate separation in which a parent corporation distributes to some or all of its shareholders stock in a newly formed or pre-existing controlled corporation, under the same conditions as in a "spin-off," except that the shareholders surrender a part of their stock in the parent corporation for the stock in the controlled corporation. The distribution may be pro rata but usually is not.

Split-Up. In a "split-up," the distributing corporation's shareholders surrender all shares held in the distributing corporation and in return receive new shares in two or more controlled subsidiaries it controlled immediately before the distribution. The subsidiaries may be pre-existing or newly formed.

To attain nonrecognition treatment, the transaction must have a valid corporate business purpose and it cannot be principally a tax-avoidance device (Reg. § 1.355-2).[3] Also, after the transaction, both the distributing and controlled corporations must actively conduct the businesses previously owned and operated (directly or indirectly) by the distributing corporation for at least five years (Code Sec. 355(a)(3)(B); Reg. § 1.355-3).[4] Other limitations relate to continuity of interest on the part of the owners (Reg. § 1.355-2(c)),[5] the amount of securities distributed, taxable acquisitions within five years, and receipt of other property or "boot" (Code Sec. 355(a)(3)). [6]

Footnote references are to paragraphs of the 2002 Standard Federal Tax Reports.

[1] ¶ 16,460, ¶ 16,462   [3] ¶ 16,463   [5] ¶ 16,463
[2] ¶ 16,460   [4] ¶ 16,460, ¶ 16,464   [6] ¶ 16,460

Basis Rules. With an exchange of stock and/or securities, the basis of the old becomes the basis of the new ("substituted basis"). If the exchange is partially taxable, the basis of the old stock or securities is decreased by the sum of the money and fair market value of "other property" received and increased by the amount of gain recognized and the amount treated as a dividend. If any loss is recognized, the basis of the property received is decreased by that amount. If some old stock is retained, allocation is made as though the stock were first surrendered and then received in exchange (Code Sec. 358).[7]

Morris Trust Rules. Restrictions have been imposed on certain spin-offs that follow the structure of *Morris Trust* (66-2 USTC ¶ 9718) (Code Sec. 355(e)).[8] If either the controlled or distributing corporation is acquired pursuant to a plan or arrangement in existence on the date of distribution, gain is generally recognized by the other corporation as of the date of the distribution. Recognition can be avoided if more than 50 percent of the historical shareholders retain ownership in the distributing and acquiring corporations. Acquisitions occurring within the four-year period beginning two years before the date of distribution are presumed to have occurred pursuant to a plan or arrangement.

Corporate Reorganization

2205. Tax-Free Exchange in "Reorganization." A corporation recognizes no gain or loss on the exchange of property solely for stock or securities of another corporation when the exchange is made pursuant to a plan of reorganization (Code Sec. 351 and Code Sec. 368).[9] Both sides of the transaction are eligible for nonrecognition. However, to achieve such a favorable tax outcome, transactions must satisfy strict statutory and nonstatutory requirements.

Although no gain or loss is generally recognized by a transferor on the transfer of property pursuant to a plan of reorganization, gain is recognized on any "boot" (property that does not qualify for nonrecognition treatment) as if it were sold to the distributee at its fair market value. In addition, no gain or loss is recognized by a corporation on the disposition, pursuant to a plan of reorganization, of stock or securities that were received under the plan and are in another corporation that is a party to the reorganization (Code Sec. 361).[10] There cannot be a tax-free "reorganization" unless there is an "exchange" of properties as distinguished from a "sale" (Code Sec. 368; Reg. § 1.368-2).[11]

For exchanges of depreciable property, see ¶ 1779.

Basis Rules. Generally, the basis of stock and securities received by a corporation in a reorganization is the same as the basis of the property transferred to the acquiring corporation, adjusted for any gain or loss recognized on the exchange and the value of any money or other property ("boot") received (Code Sec. 358(a)).[12] Boot received from the acquiring corporation generally takes a basis equal to its fair market value at the time of the transaction (Code Sec. 362(b)).[13]

2209. "Reorganization" Defined. A qualified "reorganization" must fall within one of seven categories (each referred to by letter corresponding to the statutory provisions of Code Sec. 368): [14]

(A) a statutory merger or consolidation (that is, a merger or consolidation under the corporation laws of the United States, or a state, or the District of Columbia);

(B) the acquisition by one corporation of stock of another corporation, in exchange solely for all or a part of its own or its parent's voting stock, if the acquiring corporation has control (see below) of the other immediately after the acquisition, whether or not it had control before the acquisition;

Footnote references are to paragraphs of the 2002 Standard Federal Tax Reports.

[7] ¶ 16,550	[10] ¶ 16,580	[13] ¶ 16,610
[8] ¶ 16,460	[11] ¶ 16,750, ¶ 16,752	[14] ¶ 16,750
[9] ¶ 16,402, ¶ 16,750	[12] ¶ 16,550	

(C) the acquisition by one corporation of substantially all the properties of another corporation, in exchange solely for all or a part of its own or its controlling parent's voting stock, followed (unless waived by the IRS) by the acquired corporation's distribution of all its property pursuant to the plan of reorganization;

(D) a transfer by a corporation of all or a part of its assets to another corporation if, immediately after the transfer, the transferor or one or more of its shareholders is in control of the corporation to which the assets are transferred. The term "shareholders" includes those who were shareholders immediately before the transfer, but only if the stock or securities of the corporation to which the assets are transferred are distributed under the plan of reorganization in a transaction described at ¶ 2201 or ¶ 2205;

(E) a recapitalization (¶ 2225);

(F) a mere change in the identity, form, or place of organization of one corporation; or

(G) a transfer by a corporation in bankruptcy of all or part of its assets to another corporation, but only if stocks or securities of the transferee corporation are distributed to the shareholders tax free or partially tax free.

"Control" Defined. The term "control" means the ownership of stock possessing at least 80 percent of the combined voting power of all classes of stock entitled to vote and at least 80 percent of the total number of shares of all other classes of stock of the corporation (Code Sec. 368(c)).[15] The 80-percent figures are changed to 50 percent in the case of nondivisive (D) reorganizations (Code Sec. 368(a)(2)(H)(i) and Code Sec. 304(c)).[16]

2211. "Solely for Voting Stock." Under a (B) reorganization, "solely for voting stock" means that the acquiring corporation cannot use cash or nonvoting stock in the exchange or the reorganization becomes taxable (Reg. § 1.368-2(c)).[17] The "solely" requirement is relaxed for a (C) reorganization in that "substantially all the assets" must be acquired solely for voting stock (¶ 2217).[18]

2213. "Securities" Defined. Ordinarily, the term "securities" would include corporate bonds and debentures and any other corporate obligations in the nature of registered certificates, numbered serially, maturing after a relatively long period, bearing interest coupons, and secured by property of the corporation. The U.S. Supreme Court (*Pinellas Ice and Cold Storage Co.*) has held that ordinary promissory notes are not "securities." [19]

2217. "Substantially All." What constitutes "substantially all" of the properties of a corporation for purposes of a C reorganization (Code Sec. 368(a)(1)(C))[20] is not spelled out in the Code. It has been held that a transfer of about two-thirds in value of the assets, or 68 percent or even 75 percent of all the corporate property, is not "substantially all." One court held, however, that 85.2 percent, which included all property except cash, was "substantially all" (*Western Industries Co.*).[21] Other cases held substantially all the voting stock was transferred when over 90 percent of the stock changed hands (*B.R. Britt* and *Cortland Specialty Co.*).[22]

The IRS interprets the "substantially all" requirement, for the purpose of issuing ruling letters, as requiring a transfer of assets representing at least 90 percent of the fair market value of the net assets and at least 70 percent of the fair market value of the corporation's gross assets held immediately before the transfer (Rev. Proc. 77-37).[23]

2221. "Party to a Reorganization"—"Plan of Reorganization." Code Sec. 368(b) [24] contains a limited definition of "a party to a reorganization" (see

Footnote references are to paragraphs of the 2002 Standard Federal Tax Reports.

[15] ¶ 16,750	[19] ¶ 16,433.61	[22] ¶ 16,753.709
[16] ¶ 16,750, ¶ 15,375	[20] ¶ 16,750	[23] ¶ 16,753.53
[17] ¶ 16,752	[21] ¶ 16,753.709	[24] ¶ 16,750
[18] ¶ 16,750,		
¶ 16,753.0231		

¶ 2205), including a corporation resulting from a reorganization and both corporations in a reorganization resulting from the acquisition by one corporation of stock or properties of another. In an (A), (B), (C) or (G) reorganization (¶ 2209), a party to a reorganization includes a controlling corporation if its stock is exchanged and likewise includes a controlled subsidiary that receives any of the assets or stock exchanged.

A plan of reorganization is required in connection with a tax-free exchange (Reg. § 1.368-2).[25] The plan does not need to be a formal written document; however, the safest practice would be to incorporate the plan into the corporate records. The plan may be amended as circumstances change so long as the reorganization remains in compliance with Code Sec. 368(a) (¶ 2209).

2225. Recapitalization. The Code does not define the term "recapitalization," but the U.S. Supreme Court (*Southwest Consolidated Corporation*)[26] has stated that the term contemplates "reshuffling of a capital structure within the framework of an existing corporation." Thus, an (E) reorganization (¶ 2209) takes place, for example, when a corporation discharges outstanding bond indebtedness by issuing preferred stock to the shareholders in exchange for the bonds instead of paying them off in cash; when 25 percent of a corporation's preferred stock is surrendered for cancellation and no-par-value common stock is issued; or when previously authorized but unissued preferred stock is issued in exchange for outstanding common stock (Reg. § 1.368-2(e)).[27]

2229. Exchange of Securities or Property for Securities. An exchange of securities in a reorganization is tax free only to the extent that the principal amount received does not exceed the principal amount surrendered (Code Sec. 354(a)(2))[28] (¶ 2201 and ¶ 2205). No gain or loss is recognized if a party to a reorganization (¶ 2221) exchanges property pursuant to the plan of reorganization (¶ 2221) solely for stock or securities (¶ 2213) in another corporation that is a party to the reorganization (Code Sec. 361).[29] Unlike the exchange of securities, the party exchanging property must be a corporation and the principal amount is not subject to a percentage test. However, securities received in a Code Sec. 351 exchange are treated as boot (¶ 1731). Nonqualified preferred stock is treated as boot (Code Sec. 351(g)).[30]

2233. Assumption of Liabilities. A release from liabilities assumed by a transferee or a disposition of property subject to liabilities in (1) an exchange in reorganization under Code Sec. 361 (¶ 2229), (2) a transfer to a controlled corporation under Code Sec. 351 (¶ 1731), or (3) certain bankruptcy reorganizations or foreclosures (¶ 2247) is not "other property or money" received by the taxpayer and does not prevent the transaction from being tax free (Code Sec. 357).[31] But if it appears that the principal purpose of the assumption of liabilities is to avoid income tax, or the purpose is not a bona fide business purpose, the liability assumed is treated as other property or money (unless the taxpayer can prove to the contrary) (Code Sec. 357(b)(1)).[32]

In a Code Sec. 351 exchange in which liabilities are assumed, if a cash-basis transferor's payment of such liabilities would have given rise to a deduction, the amount of liability assumed for purposes of Code Sec. 357(c)[33] does not include such liability. This rule does not apply to the extent incurring the liability results in the creation of, or an increase in, the basis of any property (Code Sec. 357(c)(3)).[34]

If the liabilities assumed, or to which the property is subject, exceed the total basis of all the properties transferred in a Code Sec. 351 exchange or a (D) reorganization (¶ 2209), the excess is treated as gain from a sale or exchange of a

---

Footnote references are to paragraphs of the 2002 Standard Federal Tax Reports.

[25] ¶ 16,752	[29] ¶ 16,580	[32] ¶ 16,520
[26] ¶ 16,753.476	[30] ¶ 16,402	[33] ¶ 16,520
[27] ¶ 16,752	[31] ¶ 16,520	[34] ¶ 16,520
[28] ¶ 16,431		

capital asset or a noncapital asset, depending on the nature of the encumbered asset transferred (Code Sec. 357(c)(1) and Code Sec. 357(c)(2)).[35] As to the basis of property after an assumption of liabilities, see ¶ 1669.

2237. Dividend Distribution in Reorganization. A distribution of money or other property to a stockholder as part of a plan of reorganization may be taxed as a dividend if it has the effect of a taxable dividend, even if the money or other property is received in an exchange which is in part tax free (Code Sec. 356; Reg. § 1.356-1).[36] The constructive ownership rules discussed at ¶ 743 are applied in determining dividend equivalency. A distribution within this provision is taxable as a dividend, not to exceed the recognized gain, to the extent the distributing company has on hand earnings or profits sufficient to cover the distribution.

2241. Liquidation as Part of Reorganization. Under a plan of reorganization, a corporation often acquires, for all or part of its stock, all the stock in another corporation from the stockholders of the latter. As the final step in the reorganization, the acquiring corporation may liquidate the latter company, acquiring those assets by surrendering its own stock. This last step in the reorganization may be accomplished tax free under Code Sec. 332, relating to property received by a corporation on complete liquidation of another (¶ 2261).

Enforced Reorganization

2247. Federal Order or Bankruptcy Act. In general, no gain is recognized to a corporation transferring property to another corporation which is a member of the same "system group" if the transfer is ordered by the Securities and Exchange Commission (Code Sec. 1081).[37]

Special provisions cover the nonrecognition of gain or loss with respect to certain bankruptcy, foreclosure and similar proceedings (Code Sec. 368(a)(1)(G)).[38]

Corporate Liquidation

2253. Gain or Loss to Shareholders. Amounts distributed in complete liquidation of a corporation are usually treated as full payment in exchange for the stock (Code Sec. 331; Reg. § 1.331-1).[39] The shareholder's gain or loss from a distribution is determined by comparing the amount distributed (including the fair market value of any property received) with the cost or other basis of the stock. The gain cr loss is capital.

If property received in a complete liquidation is subject to a liability, the distributee's recognition of gain or loss is adjusted to reflect this assumption. Thus, if a shareholder receives property on which he otherwise would recognize a gain of $8,000 but which is subject to a liability of $3,000, the gain recognized would the $5,000 (*B.B. Crane*, 47-1 USTC ¶ 9217).[40]

A distribution that is one of a series of distributions in redemption of all a corporation's stock pursuant to a plan is treated as a complete liquidation (Code Sec. 346(a)).[41] If a liquidation distribution is made as one of a series of distributions intended eventually to result in complete liquidation of the corporation, no gain is realized by the shareholder until the entire cost of the stock is recovered. If complete liquidation covers two or more consecutive tax years, the distribution first offsets the shareholder's basis for the stock and the excess is gain in the year received. The gain is not allocable to all of the years in which distributions were received (Rev. Rul. 85-48).[42]

Partial Liquidation. A distribution of corporate assets to a *noncorporate* shareholder is treated as being in exchange for stock (whether or not stock is actually

---

Footnote references are to paragraphs of the 2002 Standard Federal Tax Reports.

[35] ¶ 16,520
[36] ¶ 16,490, ¶ 16,491
[37] ¶ 30,120
[38] ¶ 16,750
[39] ¶ 16,002, ¶ 16,003
[40] ¶ 29,225.042
[41] ¶ 16,351
[42] ¶ 16,004.163

surrendered) if the distribution is in partial liquidation of the corporation. Such a distribution must not be essentially equivalent to a dividend (determined by reference to the effect on the corporation rather than the effect on the shareholders) but rather must be made pursuant to a plan and must occur within the tax year in which the plan is adopted or within the succeeding tax year. The Code does not provide a definition of "partial liquidation"—it is generally understood that the phrase refers to a contraction of the business of the corporation—but does provide a "safe harbor," under which a distribution will qualify as a partial liquidation if it is attributable to the corporation's ceasing to conduct a trade or business that it actively conducted for at least five years ending with the date of the distribution and if the corporation continues to conduct at least one other trade or business immediately after the distribution (Code Sec. 302(b)(4) and (e)(3)).[43]

2257. Recognition of Gain or Loss. Generally, property distributed in a complete liquidation of a corporation is deemed to have been sold by the corporation at its fair market value and any gain or loss will be recognized by the liquidating corporation (Code Sec. 336).[44] If the distributed property is subject to a liability or if the distributee assumes a liability upon the distribution, the fair market value of the property is deemed to be no less, for purposes of determining gain or loss, than the amount of the liability. The following exceptions to this general recognition rule apply:

(1) No gain or loss is recognized upon any exchange or distribution that is tax free under the corporate organization and reorganization provisions (Code Secs. 351–368; [45] see ¶ 1731 and ¶ 2201-¶ 2241).

(2) No gain or loss is generally recognized in connection with the complete liquidation of a controlled subsidiary into its parent corporation (see ¶ 2261).

(3) No loss is recognized with respect to a distribution of property to a related person within the meaning of Code Sec. 267[46] (see ¶ 905), unless the property (a) is distributed to all shareholders on a pro rata basis and (b) was not acquired by the liquidating corporation in a Code Sec. 351[47] transaction or as a contribution to capital during the five years preceding the distribution (Code Sec. 336(d)(1)).[48]

(4) Recognition of loss may be limited if the distributed property was initially acquired by the liquidating corporation, either by tax-free transfer to a controlled corporation or as a contribution to capital, as part of a plan a principal purpose of which is the recognition of loss on the property in connection with the liquidation. In these circumstances, the basis of the property for purposes of determining loss is reduced, but not below zero, by the excess of the adjusted basis of the property on the date of contribution over its fair market value. There is a presumption of tax-avoidance purpose with respect to any such transfer within the two-year period prior to the adoption of the plan of liquidation (Code Sec. 336(d)(2)).[49]

(5) No gain or loss is recognized if a corporation owning 80 percent of the voting power and value of another corporation elects to treat any disposition (sale, exchange or distribution) of the subsidiary's stock as a disposition of all of the subsidiary's assets (Code Sec. 336(e)).[50]

2261. Liquidation of Subsidiary. If distributions in complete liquidation are made by a subsidiary to a parent corporation (owning at least 80 percent by value and voting power of the subsidiary), then no gain or loss on the distributions is recognized by either (1) the parent corporation (Code Sec. 332) [51] or (2) the liquidating subsidiary (Code Sec. 337).[52] Property distributed to a controlling parent

---

Footnote references are to paragraphs of the 2002 Standard Federal Tax Reports.

[43] ¶ 15,325	[47] ¶ 16,402	[50] ¶ 16,200
[44] ¶ 16,200	[48] ¶ 16,200	[51] ¶ 16,050
[45] ¶ 16,402—¶ 16,750	[49] ¶ 16,200	[52] ¶ 16,225
[46] ¶ 14,150		

¶ 2257

corporation (but not a foreign corporation) in satisfaction of a debt owed by the liquidating subsidiary is treated as a distribution in liquidation and, accordingly, no gain or loss is recognized to the liquidating subsidiary (Code Sec. 337(b)(1)).[53]

If a minority shareholder receives property in such a liquidation, the distribution is treated as a nonliquidating redemption. Thus, gain (but not loss) is recognized by the liquidating corporation (Code Sec. 336).[54] Gain or loss also is recognized on distributions to 80-percent distributees that are foreign corporations (Code Sec. 367(e))[55] and tax-exempt organizations, unless the property is used by that organization in a trade or business unrelated to its tax-exempt purpose (Code Sec. 337(b)(2)).[56]

The 80-percent control test must be met by direct ownership and not by reason of the aggregation rules (Reg. § 1.1502-34)[57] for affiliated groups filing consolidated returns (Code Sec. 337(c)).[58]

Basis. The parent corporation's basis in the assets acquired from the liquidation of a subsidiary is the same as it would be in the hands of the subsidiary (Code Sec. 334(b)).[59]

2265. Acquisition of Stock Treated as Acquisition of Assets. If a parent corporation acquires by purchase 80-percent control of a second corporation (the subsidiary) within a 12-month period, the parent may irrevocably elect to have the subsidiary treated as if it had sold and purchased its own assets (Code Sec. 338; Temporary Reg. § 1.338-3T(b)(4); Code Sec. 1504(a)(2)).[60] If the election is made, the subsidiary is treated as a new corporation after the date of acquisition of 80-percent control. The hypothetical sale is deemed to have occurred on the date of acquisition of control. The subsidiary's tax year as the "selling corporation" ends on that date, its carryovers and other tax attributes disappear, and, as the "purchasing corporation," it becomes a member of the affiliated group including the parent on the day following that date. Gain or loss will be recognized by the subsidiary as though it had sold all of its assets at fair market value in a single transaction on the acquisition date. Recapture items will typically be taken into account on the final return of the "selling corporation." The election is to be made no later than the 15th day of the 9th month, beginning after the month in which 80-percent control is acquired.

The parent is not required to liquidate the subsidiary, but, if it does, it will succeed to the basis of the subsidiary as increased by the hypothetical purchase.

There are detailed rules to ensure consistency of treatment for acquisitions of stock or assets by and from members of an affiliated group of corporations (Temporary Reg. § 1.338-4T).[61] A corporate seller may treat a sale of its 80-percent-controlled subsidiary as a sale of the subsidiary's underlying assets. The assets receive a stepped-up basis to fair market value, and the selling consolidated group recognizes gain or loss attributable to the assets, but there is no separate tax on the seller's gain attributable to the stock. This treatment also applies in situations when the selling corporation owns 80 percent of the subsidiary's stock by value and voting power but does not file a consolidated return (Code Sec. 338(h)(10)(B)).[62]

Collapsible Corporation

2273. "Collapsible" Corporation. Despite the general rule relating to complete liquidation outlined at ¶ 2253, a shareholder owning more than five percent of the stock in a "collapsible" corporation is denied capital gain treatment on a distribution of the corporation's assets or a sale of the stock. This rule applies regardless of the holding period of the stock.

Footnote references are to paragraphs of the 2002 Standard Federal Tax Reports.

[53] ¶ 16,225	[57] ¶ 33,185	[60] ¶ 33,260
[54] ¶ 16,200	[58] ¶ 16,225	[61] ¶ 16,279
[55] ¶ 16,640	[59] ¶ 16,150	[62] ¶ 16,275
[56] ¶ 16,225		

A "collapsible" corporation is formed principally to manufacture, construct, produce or purchase certain property—or to hold stock in another corporation formed for the same purpose—with a view to distributing the property or selling or exchanging the corporation's stock before the corporation realizes two-thirds of the taxable income to be derived from the property. In this way, the shareholders could realize capital gains for the bulk of the assets rather than ordinary income (Code Sec. 341).[63] Property held in a collapsible corporation is called "Code Sec. 341 property."

The presumption that a corporation is collapsible arises if the fair market value of its Sec. 341 assets is (1) 50 percent or more of the fair market value of its total assets (not including cash, stock in other corporations, or bonds, debentures, investment notes, etc., that are capital assets, or any U.S., state or local bonds) and (2) 120 percent or more of the adjusted basis of its Sec. 341 assets (Reg. § 1.341-3).[64] This presumption may be overcome by evidence.

The collapsible corporation provisions do not apply if, at the time of the sale or exchange or distribution, the net unrealized appreciation in "subsection (e)" assets of the corporation does not exceed 15 percent of its net worth (Reg. § 1.341-6).[65] "Subsection (e)" assets are, in general, property of the corporation which would result in ordinary income if they were sold for a gain. (Code Sec. 341(e)).[66]

The collapsible corporation provisions do not apply to a sale of stock in a corporation which consents to a recognize gain on the disposition of corporate assets (Code Sec. 341(f)).[67]

Carryforwards

2277. Carryforwards Permitted for Many Types of Transactions. The law allows a successor corporation to use carryovers of a predecessor to a limited extent. This privilege is available to the following corporations:

(1) a parent after complete liquidation of a subsidiary (¶ 2261); and

(2) the transferee in a nontaxable corporate acquisition of property in a type (A), (C), (D), (F) or (G) reorganization (¶ 2209). In a (D) or (G) reorganization, however, substantially all the assets must be acquired and the transferor must distribute all its assets (Code Sec. 381; Reg. § 1.381(a)-1).[68]

These carryover provisions are mandatory, even though in some cases they will work to the disadvantage of the successor. They do not apply after a split-up, split-off, or spin-off type of reorganization (¶ 2201), or other divisive reorganization.

The carryforward items are listed in Code Sec. 381(c).[69]

Note that in the complete liquidation of a subsidiary, if the election described in ¶ 2265 is made, there is no carryforward of attributes of the subsidiary for the periods prior to the parent's acquisition.

Carrybacks. Carrybacks of net operating losses (¶ 1176) and net capital losses are permitted from one corporate entity to another only in the case of an (F) reorganization—i.e., a mere change in identity, form, or place of organization.

2281. Limitations on Use of Carryforwards. After a reorganization or other change in corporate ownership, the use of certain carryforwards may be limited or prohibited. The carryforwards involved concern: (1) net operating losses, (2) unused general business credit, (3) corporate minimum tax credit, (4) foreign tax credit, and (5) capital loss carryovers (Code Sec. 382 and Code Sec. 383).[70]

After an ownership change (see below), the amount of *income* that a corporation may offset each year by preacquisition net operating loss carryforwards is generally limited to an amount determined by multiplying the value of the equity of

---

Footnote references are to paragraphs of the 2002 Standard Federal Tax Reports.

[63] ¶ 16,300	[66] ¶ 16,300	[69] ¶ 17,002, ¶ 17,031.01
[64] ¶ 16,305	[67] ¶ 16,300	[70] ¶ 17,101, ¶ 17,200
¶ 2277 [65] ¶ 16,310	[68] ¶ 17,002, ¶ 17,003	

the corporation just prior to the ownership change by the federal long-term tax-exempt rate (see ¶ 85) in effect on the date of the change (Code Sec. 382(b)(1)).[71] Any unused limitation may be carried forward and added to the next year's limitation. In addition, NOL carryforwards are eliminated completely unless the business continuity requirements for reorganizations (Reg. § 1.368-1(d)) [72] are satisfied for the two-year period following the ownership change. The annual income limitation is reduced by the recognition of any built-in losses (the amount by which a corporation's adjusted basis in its assets exceeds their fair market value on the date of the ownership change) and increased by the recognition of built-in gains. An exception to the limitations on NOL carryforwards is provided in bankruptcy situations, with certain restrictions (Code Sec. 382(l)(5); Reg. § 1.382-9).[73]

Two kinds of ownership changes can trigger the income limitation: (1) a change involving a five percent shareholder and (2) any tax-free reorganization (other than divisive and (F) reorganizations). In either case, one or more of the 5 percent shareholders must have increased their percentage of ownership in the corporation by more than 50 percent over their lowest pre-change ownership percentage (generally within three years of the ownership change) (Code Sec. 382; Temporary Reg. § 1.382-2T).[74]

Similar rules apply to the other carryforwards, including those for net capital losses, unused general business credit and foreign taxes (Code Sec. 383; Reg. § 1.383-1).[75]

Pre- and Post-change Allocation. A loss corporation must allocate net operating loss or taxable income and net capital loss or gain for the change year between the pre-change period and the post-change period either by (1) ratably allocating an equal portion to each day in the change year or (2) electing to treat its books as closed on the date of the change (Reg. § 1.382-6).[76] If a "closing of the books" election is made, the amounts allocated to either period may not exceed the NOL or taxable income and net capital loss or gain for the change year.

Worthless Stock. In order to prevent a double tax benefit, the NOLs of a corporation may not be carried forward after an ownership change if a shareholder with 50 percent or more control (prior to the ownership change) claims, within three years, a worthless stock deduction with respect to the stock (Code Sec. 382(g)(4)(D)).[77]

Tax Avoidance Purpose. NOLs and other carryforwards may be disallowed if an acquisition is made with a tax avoidance purpose (see ¶ 1575).

2285. Limitation on Preacquisition Losses. A corporation (or any member of its affiliated group) may not use its preacquisition losses (NOLs, net built-in losses, net capital losses, and credit carryforwards) against the built-in gains of a company (1) whose assets are acquired in an (A), (C) or (D) reorganization (¶ 2209) or (2) that becomes directly or indirectly controlled (80 percent ownership of its stock by vote and value) by the acquiring corporation. The restriction generally applies to built-in gains recognized within five years of the acquisition date, unless 50 percent or more of the gain company has been owned by the loss corporation (or a member of its group) for five years prior to the acquisition (Code Sec. 384).[78]

The unrealized built-in gains of either the acquired or acquiring corporation are subject to the restriction. It applies to any successor corporation to the same extent as to its predecessor, and all members of the same affiliated group before the acquisition are treated as one corporation.

Footnote references are to paragraphs of the 2002 Standard Federal Tax Reports.

[71] ¶ 17,101
[72] ¶ 16,751
[73] ¶ 17,101, ¶ 17,111F
[74] ¶ 17,101, ¶ 17,107D
[75] ¶ 17,200, ¶ 17,204
[76] ¶ 17,111
[77] ¶ 17,101
[78] ¶ 17,300

Chapter 23

SPECIAL CORPORATE STATUS

Regulated Investment Company

2301. Elective Treatment. Regulated investment companies, commonly known as mutual funds, are corporations that act as investment agents for their shareholders, typically investing in government and corporate securities and distributing dividend and interest income earned from the investments as dividends. They may escape corporate taxation if certain distribution requirements are met.

A regulated investment company (RIC) is any domestic corporation that derives at least 90 percent of its gross income from dividends, interest, payments with respect to certain securities loans, and gains on the sale or other disposition of stock and securities, and meets other specified Code requirements.

Principally, this classification includes corporations registered under the Investment Company Act of 1940 and some venture capital companies. In order to be classified as a regulated investment company, an election, which is binding for later years, is required (Code Sec. 851; Reg. § 1.851-1–Reg. § 1.851-7).[1]

If the company distributes currently at least 90 percent of its dividend and interest income (exclusive of capital gain dividend distributions) and meets certain other conditions, it is not taxed on amounts distributed to shareholders. Two of the requirements for RIC classification are that at least 50 percent of the company's assets must be invested in cash and cash items and in securities and that not more that 25 percent in value of the company's assets may be invested in the securities of any one issuer (or in two or more issuers if they are engaged in the same or similar trades or businesses or related trades or businesses and are controlled by the company) (Code Sec. 851(b)(3)). To meet the 50-percent requirement, the securities of any one issuer held by the RIC may not exceed five percent of the value of the RIC's total assets or 10 percent of the issuer's outstanding voting securities.

A nondeductible excise tax equal to four percent of the excess, if any, of the "required distribution" for the calendar year ending within the tax year of the RIC over the "distributed amount" for the calendar year is imposed on any RIC (Code Sec. 4982).[2] For purposes of the excise tax, the "required distribution" for a taxable year is the sum of 98 percent of the company's ordinary income plus 98 percent of

---

Footnote references are to paragraphs of the 2002 Standard Federal Tax Reports.

its capital gain net income. Special rules apply to gain or loss attributable to a Code Sec. 988 foreign currency transaction.[3] A RIC may reduce its capital gain net income by the amount of any "net ordinary loss" but not below its "net capital gain" in determining the amount it must distribute in order to avoid the excise tax.

2303. Distributions to Shareholders. Within 60 days after the close of its tax year, a RIC must notify its shareholders as to what portion of the distributions made represents capital gain dividends, what portion represents ordinary income dividends, and what portion represents other income. The shareholder is then taxed on the distributions (¶ 237) (Code Sec. 854(b)).[4]

The IRS has ruled that the percentage of dividends distributed by a RIC to a class of shareholders out of a class of dividends cannot exceed the overall percentage of dividends that has been earmarked for the shareholders under the terms of the company's investment arrangement with its shareholders.[5]

Dividends declared in October, November or December and made payable to shareholders of record in any of these months are deemed to have been paid by the RIC and received by its shareholder on December 31 of such year, as long as the dividends are actually paid during January of the following year (Code Sec. 852(b)(7)). Regulations prescribe the manner in which a RIC must treat a post-October capital or currency loss for purposes of determining its taxable income, its earnings and profits, and the amount that it may designate as capital gain dividends for the tax year in which the loss is incurred and in the succeeding year (Reg. § 1.852-11).[6]

2304. Taxation of Shareholders. A capital gain dividend is treated by a share-holder as a gain from the sale or exchange of a capital asset held for more than 12 months (Code Sec. 852(b)(3)). Dividends (other than extraordinary dividends) received from a RIC by a corporate shareholder qualify for the dividends-received deduction (¶ 237) to the extent that they are designated as dividends. The aggregate amount designated cannot exceed the aggregate amount of dividends received by the RIC for the tax year (¶ 2311) (Code Sec. 854(b)(1)). Capital gains dividends do not qualify for the corporate dividends-received deduction (Code Sec. 854; Reg. § 1.854-1–Reg. § 1.854-3).[7]

A RIC may pass through to its shareholders tax-exempt interest from state and municipal bonds, qualified scholarship funding bonds, and other exempt obligations, if at least one half of the value of the RIC's assets consists of such obligations at the close of each quarter of its tax year (Code Sec. 852(b)(5)).[8]

2305. Sale of RIC Stock. Where RIC stock is sold at a loss and the stock was held for less than six months, the loss is, nevertheless, treated as a long-term (not short-term) capital loss to the extent of the capital gains dividend on the stock. However, any loss from the sale of stock in a RIC will be disallowed to a seller who has held such stock for six months or less to the extent that tax-exempt interest dividends were paid on the stock (Code Sec. 852(b)(4)(B)).

Dividends on stock owned by a RIC must be included in the company's income no later than the date on which the share became ex-dividend with respect to the dividends or the date on which the mutual investment company acquired the share (Code Sec. 852(b)(9)).

2309. Retention of Capital Gains. A RIC may elect to retain and pay income tax on net long-term capital gains received during the tax year. Shareholders must include their proportionate share of these undistributed long-term capital gains in their income as long-term capital gains. The RIC is deemed to have paid the

---

Footnote references are to paragraphs of the 2002 Standard Federal Tax Reports.

[3] ¶ 28,900	[6] ¶ 26,432	[8] ¶ 26,420
[4] ¶ 26,460	[7] ¶ 26,460, ¶ 26,461—	
[5] ¶ 26,433.032,	¶ 26,464	
¶ 26,433.28		

shareholder's share of the tax, which can be credited or refunded to the shareholder. The basis of the shareholder's shares is increased by the amount of the undistributed long-term capital gains (less the amount of capital gains tax paid by the RIC) included in the shareholder's total long-term capital gains (Code Sec. 852(b)(3)(D); Reg. § 1.852-4).[9] The undistributed capital gains are assigned to the shareholders for purposes of the minimum tax on tax preferences (¶ 1465) (Code Sec. 59(d)).[10]

If the company elects to retain capital gains, it files Form 2438, "Undistributed Capital Gains Tax Return," and pays the tax on such gains (Code Sec. 1201(a)).[11] The company must advise each shareholder who is a shareholder at the close of the company's tax year of his or her share of the undistributed capital gains and report the tax on Form 2439, "Notice to Shareholder of Undistributed Long-Term Capital Gains." Copy A of Form 2439 and Form 2438 should be filed with Form 1120–RIC, "U.S. Income Tax Return for Regulated Investment Companies" (Reg. § 1.852-9).[12]

2311. Method of Taxation. The tax rates for qualifying RICs are the same as those for corporations generally. The tax is computed on "investment company taxable income," which is determined by excluding from taxable income any net capital gain and without allowing the deduction for net operating loss and the special deductions for corporations (dividends received, deficiency dividends, and dividends paid by public utilities on certain preferred stock) (Code Sec. 852(b)).[13]

Dividends on stock owned by a RIC must be included in the company's income no later than the date on which the share became ex-dividend with respect to the dividends or the date on which the mutual investment company acquired the share (Code Sec. 852(b)(9)).

2317. Deficiency Dividend Procedures. A company may become eligible for RIC status for any tax year for which it had been determined that it did not qualify if, within 90 days after a determination of ineligibility is made, it distributes property in an amount equal to the accumulated earnings and profits attributable to the non-RIC year, less any interest charge. The distribution must be designated as being taken into account for the disqualified year (Code Sec. 852(e)). A RIC is allowed a deduction for deficiency dividends paid in the year for which the deficiency is determined. A RIC will only be allowed this deduction if the deficiency dividend is paid within 90 days of the determination and a claim for deduction is filed within 120 days of the determination.

2318. Mutual Fund Load Charges. Under certain circumstances, a load charge on a mutual fund will not be taken into account as part of the purchaser's basis for purposes of computing profit or loss on a sale of the mutual fund shares (Code Sec. 852(f)). This rule applies only if the mutual fund shares are disposed of before the 91st day following their acquisition and where the purchaser subsequently acquires mutual fund shares pursuant to a reinvestment right received when the original shares were purchased. The omission of the load charge from basis applies to the extent the charge does not exceed the reduction in the load charge for the new investment. To the extent that a load charge is not taken into account in determining the purchaser's gain or loss, it is treated as incurred in connection with the acquisition of the second-acquired shares. A purchaser who acquires stock in a RIC from another person in a transaction in which no gain or loss is recognized shall succeed to the treatment of the other person under these rules.

2320. Foreign Tax Credit Allowed to Shareholders. A regulated investment company may elect to have its foreign tax credit taken by its shareholders on their individual returns if more than 50 percent of the value of its total assets at the close of the tax year consists of stock or securities in foreign corporations and it has

Footnote references are to paragraphs of the 2002 Standard Federal Tax Reports.

¶ **2311**

[9] ¶ 26,420, ¶ 26,425   [11] ¶ 30,352   [13] ¶ 26,420
[10] ¶ 5400   [12] ¶ 26,430

distributed at least 90 percent of its (1) investment company taxable income and (2) net tax-exempt interest (Code Sec. 853; Reg. § 1.853-1–Reg. § 1.853-4).[14]

2323. Distribution After Tax Year Ends. A RIC may throw back to the prior tax year all or part of a dividend (including a capital gain dividend) that is declared after the year is closed but before the due date for the filing of its return, including any extension, *if* the entire declared dividend is paid (1) within the 12-month period following the close of the tax year and (2) not later than the date of the first regular dividend payment after the declaration (Code Sec. 855).[15]

Real Estate Investment Trust

2326. Definition. A corporation (other than a bank or insurance company), trust, or association that specializes in investments in real estate and real estate mortgages, meets certain status requirements as to ownership and purpose, and satisfies gross income and diversification requirements may elect to be taxed as a real estate investment trust (REIT). A foreign corporation cannot be a REIT (Rev. Rul. 89-130).[16]

A trust or an association may elect REIT status in its first year even though it fails to satisfy the ownership test or the personal holding company stock ownership test (50 percent in value of the stock owned directly or indirectly by five or fewer individuals). However, it must meet these requirements for its second year. To determine indirect ownership, attribution to an individual of stock owned by or for the individual's partner is ignored (Code Sec. 856(a) and (h)).[17]

A REIT is not disqualified to hold any property primarily for sale to customers in the ordinary course of business, but it is subject to a 100-percent tax on the net income from sales of such property (called "prohibited transactions"), excluding foreclosures (Code Secs. 856(c) and 857(b)(6)). A REIT is not liable for the 100-percent penalty if certain conditions are met (Code Sec. 857(b)(6)).

There are two income tests that a trust or association must meet to qualify as a REIT for any tax year (Code Sec. 856(c)):

(1) at least 95 percent of gross income must be from dividends, interest, rents from real property, gains from sales of stock, securities and real property (other than from inventory or property held for sale to customers in the ordinary course of business), abatements and refunds of taxes on real property, and income from foreclosure property; and

(2) at least 75 percent of gross income must come from rents, interest on mortgages, gain from sales of real property and mortgage interests, income from other qualified REITs, abatements and refunds of real property taxes, income from foreclosure property, amounts received or accrued as consideration for entering into agreements to make loans secured by mortgages on real property or interests in real property or to purchase or lease real property, gain from the sale or disposition of a real estate asset that is not a prohibited transaction (a sale or other disposition of property described in Code Sec. 1221(1) that is not foreclosure property) and qualified temporary investment income. For purposes of qualified temporary investment income, "debt instrument" has the same meaning as under Code Sec. 1275(a)(1) and "new capital" includes amounts received in exchange for certificates of beneficial ownership in the trust other than those received pursuant to a dividend reinvestment plan. If a REIT receives new equity capital and temporarily invests the proceeds in stock or debt instruments, then, for a one-year period beginning on the date the capital is received from these investments (interest, dividends, or

---

Footnote references are to paragraphs of the 2002 Standard Federal Tax Reports.
[14] ¶ 26,440—¶ 26,444   [16] ¶ 26,512.313   [17] ¶ 26,500
[15] ¶ 26,480—¶ 26,481

¶ 2326

gains from the sale of the instruments), the capital is treated as qualifying income for purposes of the 75-percent income test (Code Sec. 856(c)).[18]

Foreclosure property is any real property interest acquired as a result of bidding on the interest at foreclosure or having reduced such property to ownership by arrangement or process of law after a default. A REIT must elect to treat property as foreclosure property on or before the due date of its return for the year in which the property was acquired. Property does not cease to be foreclosure property until the close of the third tax year following the tax year in which the REIT acquired the property. A REIT is limited to one extension of the grace period, which cannot extend the period beyond the close of the third tax year following the last tax year of the initial grace period.[19]

For purposes of the 95- and 75-percent gross income tests, the general rule is that impermissible tenant services income is not treated as allowable rent from real property. This includes (1) services provided to the property's tenants or (2) fees for managing or operating the property. However, charges for services *customarily* furnished or rendered in connection with the rental or real property, such as water, heat, light, general maintenance, trash collection, etc., still qualify as rent from real property (Code Sec. 856(d)).[20] In addition, a REIT may receive a small amount (one percent of amounts received or accrued with respect to the property) of income from furnishing impermissible tenant services without causing all of the amount received with respect to a property to fail to qualify as rent (Code Sec. 856(d)(7)).

Failure to meet the 75-percent and 95-percent tests will not result in disqualification if (a) the REIT sets forth the source and nature of its gross income on its tax return; (b) incorrect information is not fraudulently included on the return with the intent to evade tax; and (c) the failure to meet the tests is due to reasonable cause and not willful neglect. However, a tax is imposed on the net income attributable to the greater of the amount by which the trust fails to meet the 75-percent test or the amount by which 90-percent of the trust gross income exceeds the amount of gross income derived from sources referred to in the 95-percent test. (Code Sec. 856(c)(6) and Code Sec. 857(b)(5)).

In addition, at the close of each quarter, at least 75 percent of the value of a REIT's total assets must consist of real estate (including mortgage interest), cash and cash items (including receivables), and government securities. Also, not more than 25 percent of the value of its total assets must be represented by securities, other than government securities, and the trust may not own securities of any one issuer greater in value than 5 percent of the trust's total assets or own more than 10 percent of any one issuer's outstanding voting securities (Code Sec. 856(c)(4); Reg. § 1.856-2(d)).[21]

A REIT may own a "qualified REIT subsidiary" and treat all of the subsidiary's assets, liabilities and items of income, deduction and credit as its own; thus, a REIT and its wholly owned subsidiaries are treated as a single taxpayer (Code Sec. 856(i)).

Special rules apply when a REIT receives or accrues amounts with respect to real or personal property from a tenant that derives substantially all of its income from such property pursuant to a sublease (Code Sec. 856(d)(6)).

REITs may increase their operational flexibility through the use of a "taxable REIT subsidiary." To qualify as a taxable REIT subsidiary, a corporation must be owned, in whole or in part, by the REIT and both entities must join in an election. In addition, any corporation in which a taxable REIT subsidiary owns securities representing 35 percent of the corporation's vote or value will itself be treated as a taxable REIT subsidiary (Code Sec. 856(l)(2)).[22]

Footnote references are to paragraphs of the 2002 Standard Federal Tax Reports.

¶ 2326

[18] ¶ 26,500	[20] ¶ 26,500	[22] ¶ 26,500
[19] ¶ 26,512.0732	[21] ¶ 26,500, ¶ 26,503	

2327. Pension Fund Investment in REITs. A pension trust generally will not be treated as a single individual for purposes of the five-or-fewer rule (Code Sec. 542(a)(2) and Code Sec. 856(h)).[23] Instead, beneficiaries of the pension trust are treated as if they held stock in the REIT in proportion to their actuarial interests in the trust (Code Sec. 856(h)(3)). However, this lookthrough rule does not apply if disqualified persons (Code Sec. 4975(e)(2))[24] together own five percent or more of the value of the REIT stock and the REIT has earnings and profits attributable to a period during which it did not qualify as a REIT.

2329. Taxation of Real Estate Investment Trust. A REIT that distributes at least 90 percent (95 percent for tax years beginning before January 1, 2001) of its taxable income for the tax year and complies with the recordkeeping requirements of Reg. § 1.857-8 is taxable at the regular corporate rates on retained earnings other than capital gains (Reg. § 1.857-1).[25] Distributed earnings are taxed to the beneficiaries and the trust is allowed a dividends-paid deduction.

A net operating loss for a REIT's tax year cannot be carried back to a preceding year but can be carried over to each of the following 20 years (NOLs for tax years beginning before August 6, 1997, may only be carried forward 15 years). An NOL for a year that is not a REIT year cannot be carried back to a REIT year (Code Sec. 172(b)(1)(B) and Code Sec. 857(b)(2)).[26] For purposes of determining the maximum amount of capital gain dividends that a REIT may pay for a tax year, the REIT may not offset its net capital gain with the amount of any NOL, whether current or carried over from a previous tax year, thus increasing the amount available for capital gain treatment. To the extent that a REIT elects to pay capital gain dividends in excess of its net income, the REIT must increase the amount of its NOL carryover by such amount (Code Sec. 857(b)(3)).

Dividends declared in October, November or December and paid to shareholders of record in such a month are deemed to have been paid by the REIT and received by its shareholders on December 31 of that year, so long as the dividends are actually paid during January of the following year (Code Sec. 857(b)(9)).

2331. Beneficiaries. REIT taxable income that is distributed is taxable to the beneficiaries as ordinary income. Capital gains of the trust, to the extent they are distributed, are taxed to beneficiaries as long-term capital gains rather than as ordinary income; distributed capital gains belong to the shareholder for purposes of the minimum tax on tax preferences (Code Sec. 59(d) and Code Sec. 291(d)).[27] (See ¶ 1445 and ¶ 1465.)

A REIT may elect to retain its net long-term capital gains and pay the tax on such gains, while its shareholders include their proportionate share of the undistributed long-term capital gains in income and receive a credit for their share of the tax paid by the REIT.[28]

2334. Sale of Real Estate Investment Trust Stock. Any loss on the sale or exchange of stock or a beneficial interest in a REIT held by the shareholder for six months or less is long-term capital loss to the extent that the shareholder received a long-term capital gain dividend distribution with respect to the stock or beneficial interest (Code Sec. 857(b)(8)). However, the holding period requirement does not apply to losses incurred on the disposition of stock or beneficial interest pursuant to a plan that provides for the periodic liquidation of the shares. For purposes of determining whether a taxpayer has held REIT stock or beneficial interest for six months, rules similar to those in Code Sec. 246(c)(3) and Code Sec. 246(c)(4) regarding the holding period requirements for the dividends-received deduction, are to be applied (Code Sec. 857(b)(8)(B)).

Footnote references are to paragraphs of the 2002 Standard Federal Tax Reports.

[23] ¶ 23,190, ¶ 26,500   [25] ¶ 26,521   [27] ¶ 5400, ¶ 15,190
[24] ¶ 34,400   [26] ¶ 12,002, ¶ 26,520   [28] ¶ 26,520

¶ 2334

2337. Deficiency Dividends. If the amount that a REIT is required to distribute for a tax year in order to meet the 90-percent test (95 percent before January 1, 2001) (¶ 2326) is increased, or if the amount of dividends previously distributed for that year is decreased, because of a determination (such as a final court decision or closing agreement), a deficiency dividend may be distributed within 90 days of the determination to avoid disqualification (Code Sec. 860).[29] A claim for the deficiency dividend deduction must be filed within 120 days after the date of the determination. This deficiency dividend procedure is available only if the failure to meet the distribution test was not the result of fraud with intent to evade tax or of willful failure to file a return. Interest is to be assessed on the deficiency at the same rate as that for other tax deficiencies. A nondeductible excise tax will be imposed on any REIT for each calendar year equal to 4 percent of the excess, if any, of the "required distribution" for the calendar year over the "distributed amount" for that calendar year. The tax is due on or before March 15 of the year following the calendar year for which it is calculated (Code Sec. 4981).[30] For purposes of the excise tax, a REIT may reduce its capital gain net income by the amount of any "net ordinary loss."

2339. Distribution After Tax Year Ends. A REIT may elect to throw back to the prior tax year all or part of a dividend (including a capital gain dividend) that is declared after the year is closed but before the due date for filing its return, including any extension, if the entire declared dividend is paid (1) within the 12-month period following the close of the tax year and (2) not later than the date of the first regular dividend payment after the declaration (Code Sec. 858).[31]

2340. Accounting Period. A REIT may not change to or adopt any annual accounting period other than the calendar year (Code Sec. 859),[32] but a taxpayer who has not engaged in an active trade or business may change its accounting period to a calendar year, without consent, in connection with its initial election of REIT status. REITs must annually file Form 1120-REIT by the 15th day of the third month following the end of the tax year.

REMIC

2343. Qualification of a Real Estate Mortgage Investment Conduit. In general, a real estate mortgage investment conduit (REMIC) is a fixed pool of mortgages with multiple classes of interests held by investors. It is treated like a partnership, with its interests allocated to, and taken into account by, the holders of the interests in the REMIC (Code Sec. 860D). However, a REMIC is subject to tax on prohibited transactions, on income from foreclosure property, and on certain contributions received after startup day. It also may be required to withhold on amounts paid to foreign holders of regular or residual interests. Substantially all of the REMIC's assets at the close of the third month ending after the startup day and at all times thereafter must consist of "qualified mortgages" and "permitted investments."[33]

A qualified mortgage is any obligation principally secured by an interest in real property that is (Code Sec. 860G(a)(3)): (1) transferred to the REMIC on the startup day in exchange for regular or residual interests in the REMIC or is purchased by the REMIC within the three-month period beginning on the startup day if (unless otherwise provided in the regulations) the purchase is made pursuant to a fixed price contract in effect on the startup day; (2) any qualified replacement mortgage; and (3) any regular interest in another REMIC transferred to the REMIC on the startup day in exchange for regular or residual interests in the REMIC. The startup day is the day on which the REMIC issues all of its regular

Footnote references are to paragraphs of the 2002 Standard Federal Tax Reports.

¶ **2337**　[29] ¶ 26,580　[30] ¶ 34,620　[31] ¶ 26,540　[32] ¶ 26,560　[33] ¶ 26,660

and residual interests. A qualified mortgage also includes a regular FASIT (¶ 2369), provided certain conditions are met (Code Sec. 860G(a)(3)(D)).

Permitted investments are of three types: (1) cash flow investments, (2) qualified reserve assets, and (3) foreclosure property (Code Secs. 860A, 860D, 860F and 860G).[34] An entity that elects to be treated as a REMIC, as well as an issuer of a collateralized debt obligation, must file Form 8811, "Information Return for Real Estate Mortgage Investment Conduits (REMICs) and Issuers of Collateralized Debt Obligations," 30 days after the startup day of the REMIC (or 30 days after the issue date of the collateralized debt obligation) (Reg. § 1.6049-7).[35]

A REMIC must use a reasonable arrangement designed to ensure that residual interests are not held by disqualified organizations (Code Sec. 860E(e)).[36] Information for the tax on certain transfers of residual interests must be made available on Schedule Q, "Quarterly Notice to Residual Interest Holder of REMIC Taxable Income or Net Loss Allocation," of Form 1066, "U.S. Real Estate Mortgage Investment Conduit Income Tax Return" (Reg. § 1.860F-4).[37]

2346. Investors' Interests. All of the interests in a REMIC must be either regular interests or a single class of residual interests. A regular interest is any interest in a REMIC that is issued on the startup day with fixed terms and that is designated as a regular interest if (1) the interest unconditionally entitles the holder to receive a specified principal amount or other similar amount and (2) interest payments or other similar amounts are payable based on a fixed rate (or at a variable rate if provided in regulations (Reg. § 1.860G-1(a)(3)) or consist of a specified portion of the interest payments on qualified mortgages and the portion does not vary during the period the interest is outstanding. A residual interest is an interest in a REMIC that is issued on the startup day, that is not a regular interest, and that is designated as a residual interest. There may not be more than one class of residual interests, and all distributions (if any) with respect to such interests must be pro rata (Code Sec. 860D(a); Code Sec. 860G(a)(1) and (2)).

2349. Transfer of Property to REMIC. No gain or loss is recognized to a transferor on the transfer of property to a REMIC in exchange for a regular or residual interest. The aggregate adjusted bases of the interests received in exchange for property equal the aggregate adjusted bases of the property transferred to the REMIC plus organizational expenses (Reg. § 1.860F-2(b)(3)). If the transferor receives more than one interest in the REMIC (that is, both a regular and residual interest), the transferor's basis must be allocated among the interests in the REMIC in accordance with their respective fair market values (Code Sec. 860F(b)).

When the issue price of a regular interest exceeds its adjusted basis, the excess is included in gross income as if it were market discount on a bond and a Code Sec. 1278(b) election had been made to include the market discount currently in gross income. In the case of a residual interest, the excess is included in gross income ratably over the anticipated weighted average life of the REMIC (Code Sec. 860F(b)(1)(C); Reg. § 1.860F-2(b)(4)).[38]

If the adjusted basis of any regular interest received in a transfer exceeds its issue price, the excess is allowable as a deduction under rules similar to those governing amortizable bond premiums (Code Sec. 171) and, for a residual interest, the excess is allowable as a deduction ratably over the anticipated weighted average life of the REMIC (Code Sec. 860F(b)(1)(D)).

Generally, the issue price of either a regular or residual interest in a REMIC is determined under the rules governing the determination of issue price for original discount purposes (Code Sec. 1273(b)) in the same manner as if the interest were a debt instrument (Code Sec. 860G(a)(10)).

Footnote references are to paragraphs of the 2002 Standard Federal Tax Reports.

[34] ¶ 26,600, ¶ 26,660,   [36] ¶ 26,680   [38] ¶ 26,700, ¶ 26,700B
¶ 26,700, ¶ 26,720   [37] ¶ 26,701
[35] ¶ 36,036

2352. Taxation of the REMIC. In general, a REMIC is not taxed on its income. Instead, the income of a REMIC is taxable to the holders of the interests in the REMIC (Code Sec. 860A).[39] A holder of a regular interest is taxed on the portion of the REMIC's income that would be taken into account by an accrual-method holder of a debt instrument with terms equivalent to those of the holder's regular interest (Code Sec. 860B).[40] A holder of a residual interest is taxed on the holder's daily portion of the REMIC's taxable income or net loss for each day during the year that the interest is held (Code Sec. 860C).[41]

In determining a REMIC's taxable income or net loss, it must use the accrual method of accounting. A deduction is allowed for those amounts that would be deductible as interest if the regular interests were treated as debt. However, a REMIC is not permitted to claim deductions that are not allowed to a partnership under Code Sec. 703(a)(2). The market discount on any market discount bond is included in gross income for the tax year to which it is attributable under the rules governing accrued market discount (Code Sec. 1276(b)(2), without regard to Code Sec. 1276(a) or Code Sec. 1277). No item of income, gain, loss or deduction allocable to a prohibited transaction is taken into account. The amount of net income from foreclosure property must be reduced by the amount of tax on income from foreclosure property imposed by Code Sec. 860G(c). A REMIC's net loss is the excess of the deductions allowable in computing its taxable income over its gross income (Code Sec. 860C(b)).[42]

2355. Prohibited Transactions. A REMIC is required to pay a 100-percent tax on its net income from prohibited transactions, which is computed without taking into account any items from such transactions that result in a loss. Prohibited transactions include the disposition of any qualified mortgage unless the disposition is pursuant to: (1) the substitution of a qualified replacement mortgage for a qualified mortgage (or the repurchase in lieu of substitution of a defective obligation); (2) the bankruptcy or insolvency of the REMIC; (3) a disposition incident to the foreclosure, default, or imminent default of the mortgage; or (4) a qualified liquidation. A disposition required to prevent default on a regular interest where the threatened default results from a default on one or more qualified mortgages is not deemed a prohibited transaction (Code Sec. 860F(a)(1), (2)(A) and (5)).[43]

Other prohibited transactions include the receipt of any income from assets other than assets permitted to be held by the REMIC, the receipt of any compensation for services, and the disposition of any cash flow investment other than a disposition made pursuant to a qualified liquidation (Code Sec. 860F(a)(2)(B)-(D)).

2356. Foreclosure Property. REMICs must pay a tax, based on the highest corporate income tax rate, on their net income from foreclosure property (Code Sec. 860G(c)).[44] However, REMIC taxable income is reduced by the amount of tax paid. Net income from foreclosure property is the same as it would be if the REMIC were a real estate investment trust. A REIT's net income from foreclosure property is defined as the excess of gain from the sale or other disposition of foreclosure property described in Code Sec. 1221(1) (stock in trade or property held for sale to customers in the ordinary course of trade or business) plus the gross income derived from foreclosure property described in Code Sec. 856(e) over deductions that are derived from the production of the foregoing gain and gross income (Code Sec. 857(b)(4)(B)).[45] Property ceases to be foreclosure property two years after it is acquired by a REMIC, unless extensions are granted.

2357. Contributions Made After Startup Day. REMICs that receive contributions of property after their startup day must pay the full value of the contribution as a tax. No tax, however, is imposed against the following cash

---

Footnote references are to paragraphs of the 2002 Standard Federal Tax Reports.

[39] ¶ 26,600	[42] ¶ 26,640	[44] ¶ 26,720
[40] ¶ 26,620	[43] ¶ 26,700	[45] ¶ 26,520
[41] ¶ 26,640		

¶ 2352

contributions: (1) contributions to facilitate a clean-up call or a qualified liquidation, (2) guarantee payments, (3) contributions during the three-month period that begins on the startup day, (4) contributions by holders of residual interests in REMICs to qualified reserve funds, or (5) contributions cited in regulations (Code Sec. 860G(d)). A clean-up call is the redemption of a class of regular interests at a time when administrative costs associated with servicing the class outweigh the benefits of maintaining it (Reg. § 1.860G-2(j)).[46]

2358. Taxation of Regular Interests. Holders of regular interests generally are taxed as if their regular interests were debt instruments and they must account for income relating to an interest in a REMIC using the accrual method of accounting, regardless of the method of accounting otherwise used. Gain on the disposition of a regular interest is treated as ordinary income to the extent of unaccrued original issue discount computed at 110 percent of the applicable federal rate effective at the time the interest was acquired (Code Sec. 860B).[47]

2361. Taxation of Residual Interests. Income or loss of a REMIC is passed through to holders of residual interests who are required to take into account their daily portion of the taxable income or net loss of the REMIC for each day during the tax year on which they held their interest. The daily portion is determined on the basis of quarterly computations of the REMIC's taxable income or net loss and is allocated among all residual interests in proportion to their respective holdings on that day. All such income is treated as ordinary income and losses are treated as ordinary losses (Code Sec. 860C(a)-(e)).[48]

Losses for a quarter that are passed through in this manner to a residual interest holder may not be taken into account by the holder to the extent they exceed the holder's adjusted basis (determined without regard to the required basis decreases). Any loss disallowed by this rule may be carried to succeeding calendar quarters indefinitely (Code Sec. 860C(e)(2)).

Distributions to holders of residual interests are received tax free to the extent that they do not exceed the holder's adjusted basis in the interest. Any excess is treated as gain from the sale or exchange of the interest. A holder's basis is increased by the amount of REMIC taxable income that the holder takes into account. Basis is decreased, but not below zero, by the amount of any distribution received and the amount of the REMIC's net loss taken into account (Code Sec. 860C(c)).

A holder of a residual interest may not reduce taxable income for the tax year below the holder's "excess inclusion" for the year, which is equal to the excess (if any) of the net income passed through to the holder over a deemed interest component that is referred to as the "daily accrual" (Code Sec. 860E(a) and Code Sec. 860E(c)).[49] The effect of this rule is to prevent a holder from offsetting the excess inclusion with any NOLs. Excess inclusions are also treated as unrelated business income for tax-exempt holders. Where a residual interest is held by a REIT, a portion of the dividends paid by the REIT is treated as excess inclusions for REIT shareholders. Moreover, excess inclusions attributable to residual interests held by regulated investments companies, common trust funds, and subchapter T cooperatives are allocated to shareholders of such entities using rules similar to those applied to a REIT and its shareholders (Code Sec. 860E(c) and (d)).

Where a residual interest is received in exchange for property, any excess of the issue price of the interest over the basis of the interest immediately after the exchange is amortized and included in the holder's income ratably over the expected life of the REMIC (Code Sec. 860F(b)(1)(c)).[50] Any excess of the holder's basis in the interest over its issue price is deductible ratably over the anticipated weighted average life of the REMIC (Reg. § 1.860F-2(b)(4)).

Footnote references are to paragraphs of the 2002 Standard Federal Tax Reports.

[46] ¶ 26,720B   [48] ¶ 26,640   [50] ¶ 26,700

[47] ¶ 26,620   [49] ¶ 26,680   **¶ 2361**

The wash sale rules (Code Sec. 1091) apply to dispositions of residual interests where a seller of the interest acquires any residual interest in any REMIC (or any interest in a taxable mortgage pool that is comparable to a residual interest) within a period beginning six months before the date of sale or disposition and ending six months after that date (Code Sec. 860F(d)).

If a tax-exempt organization holds a residual interest in a REMIC, the REMIC must pay a quarterly tax on the amount of the organization's nontaxable excess inclusions at the highest corporate tax rate (Code Sec. 860E(e)). An organization is treated as holding a residual interest in a REMIC even if it holds its interest indirectly through one or more partnerships, trusts, or other pass-through entities.

2364. REMIC Interests Owned by Financial Institutions and REITs. Regular and residual interests are treated as qualifying real property loans for purposes of Code Sec. 593(d)(1), which deals with reserves for losses on loans, and Code Sec. 7701(a)(19), which deals with domestic building and loan associations. In the case of a residual interest, the amount treated as a qualifying real property loan should not exceed the basis of that interest.[51]

Both regular and residual interests are treated as real estate assets in the same proportion that the assets of the REMIC would be treated as real estate assets for purposes of determining eligibility for REIT status. Also, an interest in a REMIC is treated as a real estate asset and income from the interest is treated as an obligation secured by a mortgage on real property. In the case of a residual interest, the fair market value of the residual interest and not the fair market value of all the REMIC's assets is used in applying the REIT asset test under Code Sec. 856(c)(5).[52]

When one REMIC owns interests in a second REMIC, the character of the second REMIC's assets flow through for purposes of determining whether interests in the first REMIC constitute qualifying assets to a building and loan association under Code Sec. 7701(a)(19). Further, the 95-percent test under Code Sec. 593(d)(4), Code Sec. 856(c)(5)(E) and Code Sec. 7701(a)(19)(C)(xi) is applied only once with respect to a REMIC that is part of a tiered structure.

2367. Foreign Taxpayers. If the holder of a residual interest in a REMIC is a nonresident alien (Code Sec. 871(a) and Code Sec. 1441)[53] or a foreign corporation (Code Sec. 881 and Code Sec. 1442),[54] then (1) amounts includible in the holder's gross income are taken into account when paid or distributed, or when the interest is disposed of, and (2) no exemption from the 30 percent tax imposed on income not connected to a U.S. business applies to any excess inclusion (Code Sec. 860G(b)) (see ¶ 2431).[55]

2368. Taxable Mortgage Pools. A taxable mortgage pool (TMP) is taxed as a corporation but may not be part of a group filing a consolidated return (Code Sec. 7701(i)).[56] An entity (other than a REMIC (see ¶ 2343) or a FASIT (see ¶ 2369)) is a TMP if (1) substantially all its assets consist of debt obligations (or interests therein) and more than 50 percent of the obligations (or interests) consist of real estate mortgages, (2) the entity is the obligor under debt obligations with two or more maturities, and (3) the terms for payment under the entity's obligations are tied to payments being made on the obligations held by the entity. An entity that would otherwise be taxed as a TMP may, if applicable requirements are met, elect to be treated as a REIT.

Footnote references are to paragraphs of the 2002 Standard Federal Tax Reports.

¶ 2364   [51] ¶ 26,600, ¶ 26,600B   [53] ¶ 27,320, ¶ 32,702   [55] ¶ 26,720
               [52] ¶ 26,500   [54] ¶ 27,480, ¶ 32,720   [56] ¶ 43,080

Financial Asset Securitization Investment Trust

2369. Definition. A qualified entity can elect to be treated as a financial asset securitization investment trust (FASIT) (Code Sec. 860L).[57] A FASIT is a pass-through entity used to secure debt obligations such as credit card receivables, home equity loans and auto loans. A FASIT must be entirely owned by a taxable C corporation. The advantage offered by a FASIT is the certainty that instruments issued by a FASIT will be treated as debt for federal tax purposes, thereby ensuring that interest paid to investors is deductible and not subject to tax at the entity level.

Insurance Companies

2370. Taxation of Life Insurance Companies. A corporation is taxable as a life insurance company if its life insurance reserves plus unearned premiums and unpaid losses on noncancellable life, health, or accident policies not included in life insurance reserves comprise more than 50 percent of the total reserves (Code Sec. 816(a)).[58] An annual income tax is imposed at corporate tax rates on a life insurance company's taxable income. "Life insurance company taxable income" means life insurance gross income minus life insurance deductions (Code Sec. 801(b)).[59] The deduction for an increase in reserves takes into account increases due to both premiums and interest credited to the reserves. The net increase or net decrease in reserves is computed by comparing the closing balance for reserves, reduced by the policyholders' share of tax-exempt interest, to the opening balance of the reserves where the closing balance of the reserves for one tax year becomes the opening balance for the following year (Code Sec. 807).[60]

2373. Policyholder Dividends. The amount of the deduction for dividends or similar distributions to policyholders is the amount of policyholder dividends paid or accrued during the tax year rather than the amount of the increase in the reserves for policyholder dividends. Thus, no income or loss is recognized with respect to amounts in existing policyholder dividend reserves (Code Sec. 808(c)).[61]

2375. Reduced Deduction for Mutual Life Insurance Companies. The general rules and definitions pertaining to policyholder dividends apply to both stock and mutual life insurance companies except that, in the case of mutual companies, the deduction for policyholder dividends must be reduced by the "differential earnings amount." This amount is computed by multiplying the company's "average equity base" for the tax year by the "differential earnings rate" for that year (Code Sec. 809(a)(3)).[62] The "differential earnings rate" is the excess of the "imputed earnings rate" over the "average mutual earnings rate" (Code Sec. 809(c), (d) and (e)).[63] If the differential earnings amount exceeds the otherwise allowable deduction, then the excess reduces the closing balance of the company's reserves.

2377. Operations Loss Deduction. A life insurance company may claim an "operations loss deduction," which is the excess of life insurance deductions over life insurance gross income. The loss from operations may be carried back three years and carried forward 15 years. If the company qualifies as a new life insurance company, the loss may be carried forward 18 years (Code Sec. 810(b)(1) and (e)).[64]

2378. Taxation of Insurance Companies Other than Life Insurance Companies. Tax at corporate tax rates is imposed on the gross income less allowable deductions (Code Sec. 832)[65] of insurance companies other than life insurance companies (Code Sec. 831(a)).[66]

Mutual and stock property and casualty companies are eligible for exemption from income tax if the greater amount of their net or direct written premiums does not exceed $350,000 (Code Sec. 501(c)(15)).[67] A small insurance company, with net

---

Footnote references are to paragraphs of the 2002 Standard Federal Tax Reports.

[57] ¶ 26,738	[61] ¶ 25,830	[65] ¶ 26,150
[58] ¶ 25,990	[62] ¶ 25,850	[66] ¶ 26,130
[59] ¶ 25,710	[63] ¶ 25,850	[67] ¶ 22,602
[60] ¶ 25,810	[64] ¶ 25,870	

¶ 2378

written premiums of more than $350,000 but not more than $1,200,000 for the tax year, may elect to be taxed on its taxable investment income, such as gross investment income less deductions for tax-free interest, investment expenses, real estate expenses, depreciation, paid or accrued interest, capital losses, trade or business deductions and certain corporate deductions (Code Sec. 831(b) and Code Sec. 834).[68]

2379. Deduction for Loss Reserves. Property and casualty companies, as well as life insurance companies that are not subject to the life insurance company reserve rules (Code Sec. 807),[69] are required to discount reserves to account for the time value of money. The deduction for unpaid losses is limited to the amount of discounted unpaid losses. Any net decrease in loss reserves results in income inclusion, but the inclusion is computed on a discounted basis (Code Sec. 846).[70] Insurance companies that are required to discount unpaid losses may claim an additional deduction up to the excess of (1) undiscounted unpaid losses over (2) related discounted unpaid losses (Code Sec. 847).[71]

2380. Foreign Companies. A foreign company carrying on an insurance business within the United States that would qualify as an insurance company if it were a domestic company is taxable on its income effectively connected with the conduct of any U.S. trade or business (Code Sec. 842).[72]

Bank or Mutual Institution

2383. Bank as Taxpayer. A bank is taxed at the same rates and in the same manner as any ordinary corporation (Reg. § 1.581-1).[73] A bank is permitted to add to its bad debt reserves and, except for large banks, may claim a deduction for only the amount called for on the basis of its experience as indicated by losses for the current year and the preceding five years (Code Sec. 585(b) and Code Sec. 585(c)).[74] A large bank, i.e., one with gross assets in excess of $500 million, may not use the reserve method of computing deductions for bad debts but must use the specific charge-off method.

2386. Mutual Institution. A mutual savings bank, building and loan association, or cooperative bank is treated as a bank and, like other corporations, pays income tax at corporate levels. It may deduct amounts paid or credited to the accounts of depositors (Code Sec. 591; Reg. § 1.591-1).[75] Also, it may make a deductible addition to a reserve for bad debts. The reserve method of accounting for bad debts utilized by thrift institutions is repealed. Thrift institutions that qualify as small banks can use the experience method of accounting for bad debts. Thrift institutions that are treated as large banks are required to use the charge-off method (Code Secs. 585 and 593)[76] (see ¶ 2383). Reserves for nonqualifying loans are computed on the basis of the six-year moving average of the institution's own experience (Code Sec. 593(b)).

2389. Sale or Exchange of Securities. In the case of financial institutions (commercial banks, mutual savings banks, building and loan associations, cooperative banks, business development corporations and small business investment companies), the sale or exchange of a bond, debenture, note, certificate, or any regular or residual interest in a REMIC (¶ 2346), any regular interest in a FASIT (¶ 2369), or other evidence of indebtedness is not considered a sale or exchange of a capital asset. Financial institutions treat net gains from these transactions as ordinary income instead of capital gains. Net losses from these sales or exchanges are treated as ordinary losses (Code Sec. 582).[77]

Footnote references are to paragraphs of the 2002 Standard Federal Tax Reports.

¶ **2379**

[68] ¶ 26,130, ¶ 26,190	[72] ¶ 26,250	[75] ¶ 23,690, ¶ 23,691
[69] ¶ 25,810	[73] ¶ 23,603	[76] ¶ 23,650, ¶ 23,710
[70] ¶ 26,330	[74] ¶ 23,650	[77] ¶ 23,608
[71] ¶ 26,350		

Small Business Investment Company

2392. Loss on Stock. An investor in a small business investment company is allowed an ordinary, rather than a capital, loss deduction on a loss from the worthlessness, or from the sale or exchange, of stock in such a company. A small business investment company operating under the Small Business Investment Act of 1958 may also treat as an ordinary loss any loss on stock received under the conversion privilege of convertible debentures acquired under Sec. 304 of the Small Business Investment Act of 1958 (Code Sec. 1242 and Code Sec. 1243).[78] Gain or loss on convertible debentures held by a small business investment company (or a business development corporation) is ordinary gain or loss (Code Sec. 582(c)).[79]

2393. Dividends Received. Amounts received as dividends from a domestic corporation by a small business investment companies are fully deductible (Code Sec. 243(a)(2)).[80]

2394. Rollover Election. A taxpayer (other than an estate, trust, partnership or S corporation) may elect to roll over the gain realized on the sale of publicly traded securities into a specialized small business investment company (SSBIC) (Code Sec. 1044).[81] An SSBIC is a partnership or corporation licensed under section 301(d) of the Small Business Investment Act of 1958 and includes investment companies that finance small business concerns owned by disadvantaged persons.

A taxpayer who makes the rollover election and buys a common stock or partnership interest in a specialized small business investment company within 60 days of selling publicly traded securities will only recognize gain from the securities sale to the extent that the sale amount exceeds the cost of the SSBIC interest. The election must be made by the due date (including extensions) for the income tax return for the year in which the publicly traded securities are sold. The election is made by reporting the entire gain from the sale on Schedule D of the taxpayer's return and by attaching a statement to Schedule D that shows how the nonrecognized gain was calculated and includes other information about the SSBIC stock (Reg. § 1.1044(a)-1(b)).[82]

The amount of gain that an individual can roll over in one tax year is limited to the lesser of (a) $50,000 or (b) $500,000, reduced by the amount of gain from prior tax years that has already been deferred under the rollover provision ($25,000 or $250,000 for a married person filing separately). For a C corporation, the maximum deferral is $250,000 or $1,000,000, reduced by previously deferred gain. All corporations that are members of the same controlled group are treated as one taxpayer, and any gain excluded by the predecessor of a C corporation is treated as gain excluded by the successor corporation (Code Sec. 1044(b)).

The deferred gain is reflected as a basis reduction. However, basis is not reduced when calculating gain eligible for the 50-percent exclusion for qualified small business stock[83] (see ¶ 2396).

Small Business Corporation

2395. Code Sec. 1244 Stock. An individual may deduct, as an ordinary loss, a loss from sale or exchange, or from worthlessness, of "small business stock" (more commonly called "Code Sec. 1244 stock") issued by a qualifying small business corporation. The maximum amount deductible as an ordinary loss in any one year is $50,000 ($100,000 on a joint return) (Code Sec. 1244(b)). The ordinary loss allowed on this stock is a business loss for the purpose of determining a net operating loss

---

Footnote references are to paragraphs of the 2002 Standard Federal Tax Reports.

[78] ¶ 30,753, ¶ 30,770	[80] ¶ 13,051	[82] ¶ 29,845B
[79] ¶ 23,608	[81] ¶ 29,845	[83] ¶ 30,372

¶2395

deduction (Code Sec. 1244(d)(3)).[84] The stock must have been issued to the taxpayer or to the taxpayer's partnership directly from the corporation.

A corporation qualifies as a "qualifying small business corporation" if the amount of money and other property it receives as a contribution to capital, and as paid-in surplus, does not exceed $1 million (Code Sec. 1244(c)(3)). This determination is to be made at the time the stock is issued and must take into account amounts received for such stock and for all stock previously issued. Property (other than money) is taken into account at its adjusted basis to the corporation for figuring gain, less any liabilities to which the property was subject or that were assumed by the corporation. In addition to satisfying many statutory requirements, including one stipulating a percentage of gross receipts from nonpassive sources, the corporation must be "largely an operating company."[85]

Small Business Stock

2396. Excludable Gain. A noncorporate taxpayer can exclude 50 percent of any gain from the sale or exchange of qualified small business stock held for more than five years (Code Sec. 1202(a)).[86] Gain eligible for the 50-percent exclusion may not exceed the greater of $10,000,000 or 10 times the taxpayer's basis in the stock. The remaining gain is capital gain, taxed at a maximum rate of 28 percent (Code Sec. 1(h)).[87] However, 28 percent of the amount excluded from gross income claimed is an AMT preference item for stock where the holding period begins after December 31, 2000 (Code Sec. 57(a)(7)).[88] The preference is 42 percent for stock where the holding period begins before January 1, 2001.

The stock must be issued after August 10, 1993, and acquired by the taxpayer at its original issue (directly or through an underwriter) in exchange for money or property or as compensation for services provided to the corporation. A qualified small business is a domestic C corporation with aggregate gross assets that do not exceed $50,000,000 as of the date of issuance. All corporations that are members of the same parent-subsidiary controlled group are treated as one corporation in determining whether the qualified small business requirements have been met.

At least 80 percent, by value, of the corporation's assets must be used in the active conduct of one or more qualified trades or businesses. The performance of services in the fields of health, law, engineering, architecture, etc., is not a qualified trade or business, nor are the hospitality, farming, insurance, financing or mineral extraction industries. However, a specialized small business investment company, licensed under section 301(d) of the Small Business Investment Act of 1958, will meet the active business test (see ¶ 2394).

An eligible corporation may be any domestic corporation except a DISC or former DISC, a corporation that has elected the Code Sec. 936 tax credit for corporations in Puerto Rico or U.S. possessions, a RIC, a REIT, a REMIC, a FASIT, or a cooperative (Code Sec. 1202(e)(4)).

2397. Rollover of Gain. A noncorporate taxpayer may elect to roll over capital gain from the sale of qualified small business stock held for more than six months if other small business stock is purchased during the 60-day period beginning on the date of sale. The replacement stock must meet the active business requirement for the six-month period following its purchase. Except for purposes of determining whether the active business test six-month holding period is met, the holding period of the stock purchased includes the holding period of the stock sold. The basis of the newly purchased stock must be reduced by the amount of gain rolled over (Code Sec. 1045).[89]

Footnote references are to paragraphs of the 2002 Standard Federal Tax Reports.

¶ 2396

[84] ¶ 30,790
[85] ¶ 30,800
[86] ¶ 30,372
[87] ¶ 3260
[88] ¶ 5300
[89] ¶ 29,850

Chapter 24

U.S. TAXATION OF FOREIGN ACTIVITIES AND FOREIGN TAXPAYERS

Overview

2401. Taxation of Worldwide Income. The United States taxes the worldwide income of U.S. citizens, resident aliens and domestic corporations, without regard to whether the income arose from a transaction or activity originating outside its geographic borders. Foreign corporations and nonresident alien individuals, however, are only taxed on income that is either "effectively connected" with a trade or business conducted within the United States or "fixed and determinable, annual, or periodic income" from sources within the United States. Thus, "international taxation" generally covers the rules for the following categories of persons:

(1) U.S. persons with foreign activities or income, such as the exclusion for foreign earned income (¶ 2402) and the foreign tax credit (¶ 2475);

(2) foreign persons with U.S. activities or income, such as income from U.S. sources (¶ 2431), income effectively connected with a U.S. trade or business (¶ 2429), the taxation of U.S. branch profits of foreign corporations (¶ 2433) and the disposition of U.S. real property interests by foreign persons (¶ 2442);

(3) U.S. persons with foreign activities or income and foreign persons with U.S. activities or income, such as the rules for sourcing of income and deductions (¶ 2431) and the translation of foreign currency items (¶ 2497); and

(4) special status entities, such as possession corporations (¶ 2463), DISCs (¶ 2468), FSCs (¶ 2470) and FPHCs (¶ 2472).

¶ 2401

U.S. Citizen—Foreign Earned Income

2402. U.S. Citizen Working in Foreign Country. A qualifying individual (see below) who works abroad and receives earned income from foreign sources may elect to exclude up to $78,000 for calendar year 2001 of foreign earned income attributable to the period of residence in a foreign country as well as certain employer-provided housing costs (Code Sec. 911(a)(1) and (b)(2); Reg. § 1.911-1).[1] The amount of foreign earned income that may be excluded is the lesser of: (1) the qualified individual's foreign earned income for the tax year in excess of foreign housing costs (see ¶ 2403) excluded under Code Sec. 911(a)(2) or (2) the product of $78,000 (for calendar year 2001) multiplied by a fraction the numerator of which is the number of qualifying days of residence or physical presence in the tax year and the denominator of which is the number of days in the tax year (Reg. § 1.911-3(d)).[2]

In applying the exclusion amount, foreign earned income is considered received in the tax year in which the services to which the income is attributable are performed. For the definition of "earned income," see ¶ 2405.

The exclusion is scheduled to increase to $80,000 for 2002 and thereafter (Code Sec. 911(b)).

Qualifying Individual. In order to qualify for either the exclusion for foreign housing costs or the foreign earned income exclusion, a U.S. citizen working abroad must make a tax home in a foreign country and meet either the bona fide residence test or the physical presence test. A U.S. resident alien working abroad can qualify for either exclusion provided he or she meets the physical presence test. A U.S. resident alien may also qualify under the bona fide resident test, provided that the resident alien is a citizen of a foreign country with which the United States has a treaty containing a nondiscrimination clause.[3]

Tax Home. The individual's tax home is his regular or principal place of business. If he has no regular or principal place of business, then his tax home is his regular place of abode. The taxpayer cannot have a tax home in a foreign country when his abode or principal residence is in the United States. However, maintenance of a dwelling in the United States, whether or not that dwelling is used by the taxpayer's spouse and dependents, does not necessarily mean that the individual's abode is in the United States.

Bona Fide Residence Test. A taxpayer must be a bona fide resident of a foreign country or countries for an uninterrupted period that includes a full tax year (Code Sec. 911(d)(1)(A); Reg. § 1.911-2).[4] During a period of bona fide residence, a taxpayer may leave the foreign country for brief or temporary trips elsewhere for vacations or business. Once the bona fide residence test is met, the excess housing costs exclusion (¶ 2403) or the foreign earned income exclusion is available for any partial tax year in which the period of residence began or ended.

> **Example 1.** An individual became a bona fide resident of a foreign country on January 1, 2000, and continued such residence through the first 90 days of 2001. Since the taxpayer had established a full tax year (2000) of bona fide foreign residence, he may exclude, if he so elects, up to $19,233 (90/365 × $78,000) of his 2001 foreign earned income.

An individual will not be considered to be a bona fide resident of a foreign country if he or she files a statement of nonresidency with the foreign authorities and is held exempt from such country's income tax (Code Sec. 911(d)(5); Reg. § 1.911-2(c)).[5]

Physical Presence Test. An individual meets the physical presence test if 330 full days out of any 12-consecutive-month period are spent in a foreign country (or countries) (Code Sec. 911(d)(1)(B); Reg. § 1.911-2).[6]

Waiver of Time Requirements. Relief from the residence requirements is provided for taxpayers who would otherwise satisfy the bona fide residence or the physical presence tests except for the fact that they were forced to flee foreign

---

Footnote references are to paragraphs of the 2002 Standard Federal Tax Reports.

¶ **2402**

[1] ¶ 28,040	[3] ¶ 28,049.101	[5] ¶ 28,040, ¶ 28,042
[2] ¶ 28,043	[4] ¶ 28,040, ¶ 28,042	[6] ¶ 28,040, ¶ 28,042

countries because of civil unrest, war, or other adverse conditions (Code Sec. 911(d)(4)).

To qualify, the taxpayer must:

(1) be a bona fide resident of, or present in, a foreign country for any period;

(2) establish that he or she left the foreign country during the period when adverse conditions existed; and

(3) establish that he or she could reasonably have expected to have satisfied the bona fide residence or physical presence test had the adverse condition not arisen.

The IRS publishes the names of foreign countries where such conditions exist and the dates between which such conditions were deemed to exist.[7]

Physical presence in 2000 can be counted in determining whether a taxpayer meets the 330-day physical presence test during a consecutive 12-month period for purposes of the 2001 exclusion.

> **Example 2.** An individual was physically present in a foreign country on a construction job that began July 1, 2000, and ended June 15, 2001. Since the taxpayer met the physical presence test, he may elect to exclude up to $42,953 ($201/365 \times \$78,000$) of his 2001 foreign earned income. The number of qualifying days is determined by counting back 330 days from the last full day he was in the foreign country (June 15, 2001) to July 20, 2000, and then counting the total days during 2001 (201) that fall within the 12-month period that begins July 20, 2000, and ends July 19, 2001.

Foreign Country. A foreign country usually is any territory (including the air space, territorial waters, sea bed, and subsoil) under a government other than that of the United States. The term "foreign country" includes Continental Shelf areas over which the foreign country has exclusive rights under international law to explore and exploit the natural resources (Reg. § 1.911-2(h)).[8]

The foreign earned income exclusion and the housing expense exclusion (or deduction) are denied to a taxpayer who is present in a foreign country in which travel for U.S. citizens and residents is generally restricted by regulations issued under the Trading with the Enemy Act or the International Emergency Economic Powers Act (Code Sec. 911(d)(8)).

2403. Exclusion for Excess Housing Expenses. In addition to the election to exclude foreign earned income, taxpayers who meet the bona fide residence test or physical presence test may also exclude an amount based upon employer-provided foreign housing costs (Code Sec. 911(a)(2) and (c); Reg. § 1.911-1).[9] This exclusion is equal in amount to the excess of the reasonable cost of providing housing for the taxpayer and his family (including a second residence for family members who do not reside with the taxpayer because of adverse conditions) over an amount equal to 16% of the salary of a federal employee at grade level GS-14, step 1 ($65,983 for 2001 and $67,765 for 2002), multiplied by a fraction, the numerator of which is the number of qualifying days of residence or physical presence and the denominator of which is the number of days in the tax year (Code Sec. 911(c)(1); Reg. § 1.911-4).[10] The housing cost amount is excludable only to the extent of the lesser of the individual's housing cost amount attributable to employer-provided amounts or the individual's foreign earned income for the tax year (Reg. § 1.911-4(d)).[11] Housing costs include amounts attributable to utilities, insurance and similar operating expenses but exclude expenses that are separately deductible under the Code (interest and taxes) and expenses for lavish housing.

However, this exclusion (or deduction) will be denied to a taxpayer who is present in a foreign country in which travel for U.S. citizens and residents is generally restricted by regulations issued under the Trading with the Enemy Act or the International Emergency Economic Powers Act (Code Sec. 911(d)(8)).[12]

Footnote references are to paragraphs of the 2002 Standard Federal Tax Reports.

[7] ¶ 46,434
[8] ¶ 28,042
[9] ¶ 28,040, ¶ 28,041
[10] ¶ 28,040, ¶ 28,044
[11] ¶ 28,044
[12] ¶ 28,040

¶ 2403

A taxpayer electing the housing exclusion must compute such exclusion before computing his foreign earned income exclusion and may not claim less than the full amount of foreign housing exclusion to which he is entitled. A housing exclusion election limits a taxpayer's foreign earned income exclusion to the lesser of: (1) total foreign earned income minus the amount of the foreign housing exclusion or (2) $78,000 (for 2001) multiplied by a fraction (number of qualifying days over the number of days in the tax year). Thus, a taxpayer's combined foreign earned income exclusion and foreign housing exclusion can never exceed his total foreign earned income.

The housing expense exclusion applies to those costs attributable to employer-provided amounts (this amount would include salary and any reimbursement for housing expenses). If an individual's housing amount is not provided by an employer (i.e., when he is self-employed), it is deductible in computing adjusted gross income.

Taxpayers who have foreign earned income consisting entirely of non-employer-provided amounts (self-employed persons) are required to limit their housing deduction to the amount of foreign earned income that exceeds the foreign earned income exclusion. For example, a self-employed individual with $100,000 of foreign earned income in 2001 who exercises the election to exclude $78,000 from gross income may further deduct up to $22,000 of his housing expenses from gross income. A taxpayer who is unable to deduct the full amount of his excess housing expense under this limitation may carry over any remaining amount to the following year only and to the extent that he receives foreign earned income in such succeeding year.

Taxpayers who have foreign earned income consisting of both employer-provided amounts and self-employment amounts may elect to exclude that part of their housing cost attributable to employer-provided amounts and also claim a deduction for the remainder of their housing cost attributable to self-employment income. To determine the housing exclusion in this case, multiply the housing amount by the amount provided by the employer and then divide the result by the amount of foreign earned income. The balance of the housing amount may be deducted, but this deduction is limited to the amount of foreign earned income that exceeds the foreign earned income exclusion and any housing exclusion for that year. For a discussion on how to make the election, see ¶ 2408.

2405. Earned Income. The term "earned income" means wages, salaries, or professional fees, and other amounts received as compensation for personal services actually rendered during the period in which the bona fide residence test or physical presence test is met. If a taxpayer is engaged in a trade or business in which both personal services and capital are material income-producing factors, a reasonable allowance as compensation for the personal services, not in excess of 30% of his share of the net profits of such trade or business, is considered as earned income (Code Sec. 911(d)(2)(B); Reg. § 1.911-3).[13] Foreign earned income does not include a number of items, such as amounts (1) paid by the United States or its agencies to its employees, (2) received after the close of the tax year following the tax year in which the services were performed, (3) received as pensions, annuities and social security payments, (4) included in income from a nonexempt trust or nonqualified annuity, (5) amounts included in income as recaptured unallowable moving expenses, and (6) allowances for meals or lodging furnished by an employer and excluded from the employee's gross income (Code Sec. 911(b)(1)(B) and Reg. § 1.911-3(c)).[14]

2406. Camps Located in a Foreign Country. In addition to the two elective exclusions discussed above, an individual may also be able to exclude the value of meals and lodging provided by an employer in a camp located in a foreign country if three requirements are met. First, the lodging must be provided for the convenience of the employer because the place where services are rendered is in a remote area where satisfactory housing is unavailable. Second, the location of the

---

Footnote references are to paragraphs of the 2002 Standard Federal Tax Reports.

[13] ¶ 28,040, ¶ 28,043
[14] ¶ 28,040, ¶ 28,043, ¶ 28,049.025

¶ 2405

camp is as near as practicable to the place where the employee's services are performed. Third, the lodging must be provided in a common area, not open to the public, that normally accommodates 10 or more employees (Code Sec. 119(c)).[15]

2408. Electing the Exclusion. The foreign earned income exclusion (¶ 2402), the housing expense exclusion (¶ 2403) and the housing expense deduction (¶ 2403) are computed on Form 2555 (Foreign Earned Income), which is to be attached to Form 1040 (Reg. § 1.911-7). Form 2555-EZ may be used by certain taxpayers to compute the foreign earned income exclusion.

Form 673 (Statement for Claiming Benefits Provided by Section 911 of the Internal Revenue Code) should be submitted to the employer to exclude wages from income tax withholding.

A qualified individual must make a separate election with respect to each exclusion. The election is made by filing a Form 2555 (Foreign Earned Income). If both a husband and wife qualify for the foreign earned income exclusion or the foreign housing exclusion or deduction, each must file a separate Form 2555—even if filing a joint return. Each election must be filed with the taxpayer's timely income tax return (including extensions), amended return or a late-filed return if filed within one year after the due date for the first year for which the election is to be effective. Later dates may be applicable if, after taking into account the exclusicn, no tax is owed and the taxpayer makes the election prior to the issue being raised by the IRS (Reg. § 1.911-7(a)(2)(i)(D)). No separate election is required for the housing cost deduction.

An individual that claims the foreign earned income or housing exclusion may not claim the foreign tax credit for the income excluded. Claiming the foreign tax credit may result in the revocation of the foreign earned income or housing exclusion.[16] Also, the earned income credit may not be claimed if income is excluded by either the foreign earned income or housing exclusion.

Once made, the election remains in effect for all subsequent tax years until revoked. If revoked with IRS consent, the election may be made subsequently with IRS approval. If revoked without IRS consent, a new election may not be made until the sixth tax year following the year of revocation (Reg. § 1.911-7(b)).[17]

2410. Resident of U.S. Possession. U.S. citizens who are bona fide residents of American Samoa during an entire tax year are subject to U.S. tax in the same manner as a U.S. resident. However, gross income for U.S. tax purposes does not include income derived from sources within American Samoa, Guam or the Commonwealth of the Northern Mariana Islands or income that is effectively connected with the conduct of a trade or business by such resident within those possessions. Deductions (other than personal exemptions) and credits that are properly allocated and apportioned to such excluded income are not allowed for U.S. tax purposes. Bona fide residents of American Samoa are required to file Form 1040 and pay taxes on a net basis if they receive income from sources outside American Samoa (either U.S. or foreign source income) (Code Sec. 931).[18] In order to exclude income from sources inside American Samoa, bona fide residents must complete Form 4563 and attach it to their tax return.

2415. Resident of Puerto Rico. A U.S. citizen who is a bona fide resident of Puerto Rico during an entire tax year is taxed by the United States on all his income except income derived from Puerto Rican sources (unless earned as an employee of the United States). Any deduction that can be tied to income that is excluded is not allowed on the United States return. Such individual is also subject to Puerto Rican income tax on income from any source but is entitled to a credit against the Puerto Rican tax for income taxes paid to the United States.

If a United States citizen has been a bona fide resident of Puerto Rico for at least two years before he changes his residence from Puerto Rico, he can exclude income derived from Puerto Rican sources (unless earned as an employee of the

---

Footnote references are to paragraphs of the 2002 Standard Federal Tax Reports.

[15] ¶ 7220   [17] ¶ 28,040, ¶ 28,047   [18] ¶ 28,240
[16] ¶ 46,428

United States) for that period preceding the change (Code Sec. 933; Reg. § 1.933-1).[19] For withholding of tax, see ¶ 2492.

2416. Resident of Virgin Islands. A bona fide resident of the Virgin Islands on the last day of the tax year is not required to file a U.S. federal income tax return for any tax year, provided that he or she reports and pays taxes on income from all sources to the Virgin Islands and identifies the sources of the income on the return (Code Sec. 932(c)).[20] Citizens or residents of the United States who have income from sources in the Virgin Islands or income effectively connected with the conduct of business in the Virgin Islands and who are not bona fide residents of the Virgin Islands at the close of their tax years must file identical tax returns with the United States and the Virgin Islands. The tax owed to the Virgin Islands is figured by multiplying the total tax owed on the U.S. return (after certain adjustments) by a decimal. This decimal is found by dividing the adjusted gross income from the Virgin Islands by worldwide adjusted gross income (Code Sec. 932(b)).[21] Form 8689 (Allocation of Individual Income Tax to the Virgin Islands) is used for this computation.

2417. Foreign Spouse—Community Property. In the case of a married couple, one or both of whom are nonresident alien individuals and who have community income for the tax year, the community income is to be treated as follows: (1) the earned income (other than trade or business or partnership income) is treated as the income of the spouse who earned it; (2) trade or business income is treated as the husband's income unless the wife substantially controls and manages the business, while a distributive share of partnership income is included in computing the net earnings from self-employment of such partner with no part of such share taken into account in computing the net earnings from self-employment of the spouse of such partner; (3) income not described in (1) or (2), above, that is derived from separate property of one spouse is considered the income of the spouse who owns the property; and (4) other income is accorded the same treatment it is given under the applicable community property law (Code Sec. 879).[22] Thus, where both spouses are nonresident aliens, one spouse's income that is effectively connected with a U.S. trade or business is treated as income of that spouse, regardless of foreign community property law.

The above rules do not apply if the spouses make the election described at ¶ 2427 to be taxed on worldwide income.

Resident Alien

2421. Taxed as U.S. Citizen. A resident alien is taxed in the same manner as a U.S. citizen (Reg. § 1.1-1).[23] See ¶ 2423, below, for definitions of resident and nonresident aliens.

To be eligible to file a joint return, a husband and wife who are citizens of a foreign country must be U.S. residents on the last day of the tax year and make a special election.[24] See ¶ 2427 for special elections that are available to a nonresident alien who is married to a U.S. citizen or resident.

Midyear change to resident status does not qualify an individual alien to file a final return for a fractional part of a tax year (unless the election described at ¶ 2427 is made). However, he is not liable for tax on any income from a source outside the United States received before he became a resident.[25] Such dual-status aliens cannot take advantage of the standard deduction and must itemize allowable deductions.[26] A departing alien who files Form 1040C (Departing Alien's Income Tax Return) must later file a final return for the year (either Form 1040 or 1040NR).

2423. Definitions of Resident and Nonresident Alien. An alien is considered to be a U.S. resident for income tax purposes if he (1) is a lawful permanent

---

Footnote references are to paragraphs of the 2002 Standard Federal Tax Reports.

[19] ¶ 28,300, ¶ 28,301	[22] ¶ 27,460	[25] ¶ 3290.102
[20] ¶ 28,280	[23] ¶ 3265	[26] ¶ 27,343.30
[21] ¶ 28,280	[24] ¶ 35,167, ¶ 35,169	

resident of the U.S. at any time during the calendar year (Code Sec. 7701(b)(1)(A)(i); Reg. § 301.7701(b)-1(b)),[27] (2) meets the requirements of the "substantial presence" test (Code Sec. 7701(b)(1)(A)(ii) and (b)(3); Reg. § 301.7701(b)-1(c)),[28] or (3) makes the first-year election under Code Sec. 7701(b)(4) and Reg. § 301.7701(b)-4(c)(3).[29] An alien who does not qualify under either of these tests will be treated as a nonresident alien for purposes of the income tax (Code Sec. 7701(b)(1)(B)).[30]

An alien individual is a lawful permanent resident of the United States if the alien has the status of having been lawfully given the privilege of residing permanently in the United States as an immigrant and such status has not been revoked or administratively or judicially determined to have been abandoned.

An alien individual meets the substantial presence test if: (1) the alien is present in the United States for at least 31 days during the calendar year and (2) the sum of the number of days on which such individual was present in the United States during the current year and the two preceding calendar years (when multiplied by the applicable multiplier—1 for the current year, 1/3 for the first preceding year, and 1/6 for the second preceding year) equals or exceeds 183 days.

Even though an alien individual otherwise meets the requirements of the substantial presence test, there are circumstances when an alien will not be considered a resident of the United States (see Code Sec. 7701(b)(3)(B)).[31]

Special rules are provided for determining when U.S. residency begins and ends (Code Sec. 7701(b)(2); Reg. § 301.7701(b)-4)[32] and determining nonresident alien status under income tax treaties (Reg. § 301.7701(b)-7).[33]

Nonresident Alien and Foreign Corporation

2425. Method of Taxation. A nonresident alien individual and a foreign corporation are taxed in the same manner as U.S. citizens and domestic corporations on all income which is effectively connected with their conduct of a trade or business in the U.S. They are also taxed at a flat 30% rate on U.S. source fixed or determinable periodical income (¶ 2431) that is not effectively connected with the conduct of a U.S. trade or business (Code Secs. 871 and 881).[34] For treatment of capital gains, see ¶ 2435. For payment of estimated taxes by a nonresident alien, see ¶ 2685. Moreover, excluded from the 30% withholding tax for nonresident aliens are winnings from blackjack, roulette, baccarat, craps, and big six wheel.

A nonresident alien individual who is married to a citizen or resident and has effectively connected income must use the rate schedule for married individuals filing separate returns since the alien is not entitled to file a joint return unless one of the elections at ¶ 2427 is made. If the alien is unmarried, the rate schedule for unmarried individuals (other than surviving spouses and heads of households) must be used. A nonresident alien may not use the head of household rate schedule (Reg. § 1.2-2(b)(6)).[35]

2427. Election To Be Treated as Resident. An alien individual may elect to be treated as a U.S. resident even though he moves to the United States too late in a calendar year to qualify as a resident for that year under the substantial presence test and does not otherwise qualify. To qualify for the election, the alien must not have qualified as a resident for the calendar year immediately preceding the election year, must meet the substantial presence test in the year following the election year, must be present in the U.S. for at least 31 consecutive days in the election year, and must be present in the U.S. for at least 75% of the number of days in the period beginning with the first day of the 31-day presence and ending with the last day of the election year. The electing alien individual is to be treated as a resident for that portion of the election year that begins on the first day of the earliest presence period that satisfies both the 31-day and 75% tests. The election may not be made, however, before the individual has met the substantial presence

---

Footnote references are to paragraphs of the 2002 Standard Federal Tax Reports.

[27] ¶ 43,080, ¶ 43,117   [30] ¶ 43,080   [33] ¶ 43,123
[28] ¶ 43,080, ¶ 43,117   [31] ¶ 43,080   [34] ¶ 27,320, ¶ 27,480
[29] ¶ 43,080, ¶ 43,120   [32] ¶ 43,080, ¶ 43,120   [35] ¶ 3325

test for the calendar year following the election year (Code Sec. 7701(b)(4); Reg. § 301.7701(b)-1).[36]

A U.S. citizen or resident who is married to a nonresident alien may elect to have the nonresident alien spouse treated as a resident alien for income tax purposes. Thus, the couple may file joint returns but will be taxed on their worldwide income. As part of this election, both spouses must agree to supply all necessary information pertinent to the determination of tax liability (Code Sec. 6013(g)).[37] If the election is made, the nonresident alien will be treated as a U.S. resident for purposes of normal income tax rules and for purposes of withholding of tax on wages.

The privilege of filing a joint return is also available in the year in which a nonresident alien who is married to a U.S. citizen or resident becomes a U.S. resident. Both spouses must join in making the election (Code Sec. 6013(h)).

2429. Effectively Connected Rules. In determining whether periodical income is effectively connected with a U.S. business, two factors are considered: (1) whether the income is derived from assets used in, or held for use in, the conduct of a U.S. business and (2) whether the activities of the U.S. business were a material factor in the realization of the income. In applying these factors, due regard is given to whether or not the asset or income involved was separately accounted for on the books of account kept for the U.S. business, but this, by itself, is not a controlling factor (Code Sec. 864(c)(2)).[38]

In order to reach foreign businesses that try to use the U.S. as a tax haven, the effectively connected rules apply to three limited categories of foreign source income in certain situations where definite U.S. economic connections are present. This applies only when the nonresident alien individual or foreign corporation has a fixed place of business in the U.S. and the income is attributable to that place of business. These three types of income are:

(1) Rents and royalties derived from the active conduct of a licensing business.

(2) Dividends, interest, or gain from securities or debt obligations derived in the active conduct of a banking, financing, or similar business.

(3) The sale or exchange (through the U.S. office) of inventory property, stock in trade, or property held primarily for sale to customers in the ordinary course of trade or business outside the U.S. (Code Sec. 864(c)(4)).[39]

2431. Fixed or Determinable Periodic Income. U.S. source fixed or determinable periodic income of a nonresident alien individual or foreign corporation is taxed at a flat 30% (or lower treaty) rate if such income is not effectively connected with the conduct of a U.S. trade or business. If periodic income falls within the effectively connected rules (¶ 2429), it is subject to regular U.S. tax rates. Fixed or determinable periodical income includes interest (but see ¶ 2440), dividends, rents, salaries, wages, premiums, annuities, and other fixed or determinable annual or periodical gains, profits, and income (Code Secs. 871(a) and 881).[40]

Social Security Benefits. 85% of Social Security benefits (as defined in Code Sec. 86(d)) received by nonresident aliens is subject to the 30% tax under Code Sec. 871(a)(3).[41]

Tax on Original Issue Discount Obligations. The 30% tax on nonresident aliens and foreign corporations with respect to income that is not effectively connected with a U.S. business applies to original issue discount obligations held by such individuals and corporations (Code Secs. 871(a) and 881(a)).[42] The tax is imposed on the sale or exchange of such an obligation or when interest with respect to such an obligation is paid. When a nonresident alien or foreign corporation receives an interest or principal payment on an OID obligation, the amount taxable is equal to the OID accrued on the obligation that has not before been subject to tax, whether or not the OID accrued since the last payment of interest. However, such OID will be taken into account for this purpose only to the extent that the tax on the OID does

Footnote references are to paragraphs of the 2002 Standard Federal Tax Reports.

¶ 2429
[36] ¶ 43,080, ¶ 43,117
[37] ¶ 35,160
[38] ¶ 27,180
[39] ¶ 27,180
[40] ¶ 27,320, ¶ 27,480
[41] ¶ 27,320
[42] ¶ 27,320, ¶ 27,480

not exceed the payment less the 30% tax imposed. On the sale or exchange of an OID obligation, the amount of the OID accruing while the foreign investor held the obligation is subject to tax to the extent that such discount was not taken into account previously. The term "original issue discount obligation" means any bond or other evidence of indebtedness having original issue discount. OID is the difference between the issue price and the stated redemption price at maturity (Code Sec. 1273).[43] For purposes of the 30% rate, an original issue discount obligation does not include (1) any obligation payable 183 days or less from its date of original issue or (2) any tax-exempt obligation.

Portfolio Investment Interest. The 30% tax on U.S. source income not effectively connected with the conduct of a U.S. trade or business is generally inapplicable to interest received by nonresident aliens on two categories of portfolio investments (Code Sec. 871(h)).[44] The first is any obligation that is not in registered form but meets the following three requirements: (1) arrangements exist that are reasonably designed to ensure that such obligations will be sold or resold only to non-U.S. persons, (2) the interest is payable only outside of the U.S., and (3) on the face of the obligation, there is a statement that any U.S. person who holds it will be subject to limitations under the U.S. tax law. The second type of obligation is any registered obligation with respect to which the U.S. person who would otherwise be required to withhold tax from interest paid on the obligation has received a statement stating that the beneficial owner is not a U.S. person (a valid Form W-8BEN will satisfy this requirement).

The 30% tax remains applicable to portfolio interest paid to a 10% shareholder; in the case of an obligation issued by a corporation, a 10% shareholder is any person who owns 10% or more of the total combined voting power of all classes of voting stock. In the case of an obligation issued by a partnership, a 10% shareholder is any person who owns 10% of the capital or profits interest in the partnership.

Portfolio interest received by a foreign corporation generally is treated in the same manner as that received by nonresident aliens (Code Sec. 881(c)(1) and (4)).[45] In the case of a foreign corporation, however, the term "portfolio interest" does not include interest: (1) received by a 10% shareholder, (2) except in the case of interest paid on an obligation of the U.S., received by a bank on an extension of credit made pursuant to a loan agreement entered into in the ordinary course of its trade or business, or (3) received by a controlled foreign corporation from a related person under Code Sec. 864(d)(5). Special rules apply for controlled foreign corporations.

Generally, the portfolio interest exemption does not apply to contingent interest (Code Secs. 871(h)(4) and 881(c)(4)). The IRS will determine the appropriate portion of the value of a debt instrument that provides for both contingent and noncontingent interest that is attributable to U.S. property (Code Sec. 2105(b)).

Certain Interest and Dividend Income. Nonresident aliens and foreign corporations are not subject to U.S. tax on interest from bank deposits that are not effectively connected with a U.S. trade or business. The exemption also applies to income from a foreign central bank of issue from bankers' acceptances and a percentage of any dividend paid by a domestic corporation that meets the 80-percent foreign business requirements (Code Secs. 871(i) and 881(d)).

Guam and Virgin Islands Corporations. A corporation created or organized in, or under the laws of, Guam, American Samoa, the Northern Mariana Islands, or the U.S. Virgin Islands is not considered a "foreign" corporation and thus is not subject to the 30% withholding tax imposed by Code Sec. 881(a) if certain requirements are met (Code Sec. 881(b)).[46]

2433. Branch Profits Tax. Foreign corporations that operate businesses in the U.S. must pay a branch profits tax equal to 30% of the foreign corporation's dividend equivalent amount (Code Sec. 884(a)).[47] This tax is in addition to U.S. corporate income taxes on its effectively connected income (see ¶ 2429).

Footnote references are to paragraphs of the 2002 Standard Federal Tax Reports.

[43] ¶ 31,280	[45] ¶ 27,480	[47] ¶ 27,540
[44] ¶ 27,320	[46] ¶ 27,480	

The dividend equivalent amount is approximately the amount that would have been distributed as a dividend if the branch were a U.S. subsidiary. The dividend equivalent comprises the after-tax earnings of the foreign corporation's U.S. trade or business that are not reinvested in the business by the close of the tax year or that are disinvested in a later tax year. Changes in the equity in the business are used to measure whether earnings have been reinvested or disinvested (Code Sec. 884(a)-(c); Reg. § 1.884-1).[48] In addition to the branch profits tax, interest paid by a U.S. trade or business of a foreign corporation is treated as if it had been paid by a domestic corporation. Thus, the interest may be subject to U.S. tax (see ¶ 2429) and withholding (see ¶ 2492) (Code Sec. 884(f); Reg. § 1.884-4).[49]

With a few exceptions, no foreign corporation can be exempt from the tax (or subject to a reduced amount) because of an income tax treaty between the U.S. and a foreign country (Code Sec. 884(e)).

Generally, a foreign government that is treated as a corporate resident of its country of residence under Code Sec. 892(a)(3) is treated as a corporation and, therefore, is subject to the branch-profits tax (Code Sec. 884; Reg. § 1.884-0(a)).[50]

2435. Capital Gain. The U.S.-source capital gain net income of a nonresident alien individual is subject to U.S. tax if effectively connected with the conduct of a U.S. business. Other capital gain (except that considered as periodical income (¶ 2431)) escapes tax unless the individual is present in the U.S. for at least 183 days during the tax year. If the 183-day period is met, capital gain not effectively connected with a U.S. business is taxed at a flat 30% (or lower treaty) rate (Code Sec. 871(a)(2)).[51]

In the case of a foreign corporation, capital gain net income effectively connected with the conduct of a U.S. business is taxed at U.S. tax rates. Otherwise, the gain (unless it is fixed or determinable periodical income (¶ 2431)) is not taxed (Code Secs. 881 and 882).[52]

2436. Trade or Business. Generally, a nonresident alien who performs personal services within the United States during the tax year is engaged in a U.S. trade or business. However, this does not extend to personal services performed by a nonresident alien individual who is temporarily present in the United States for 90 days or less during the tax year and whose compensation does not exceed $3,000 when services are performed (1) for a nonresident alien individual, foreign partnership, or foreign corporation not engaged in a U.S. business or (2) for a branch office or place of business maintained in a foreign country or U.S. possession by a U.S. citizen or resident or by a domestic partnership or corporation (Code Sec. 864(b)(1)).[53]

A nonresident alien individual (or foreign corporation) who is not engaged in a U.S. trade or business but realizes income from investment real estate located in the United States may elect to treat the income from the property as income effectively connected with a U.S. business. In this way, income from the property may be offset by the allowable income tax deductions attributable to such income (Code Secs. 871(d) and 882(d)).[54] See ¶ 2442 for treatment of dispositions of U.S. real property interests.

2438. Trading in Securities. Trading in stocks, securities, or commodities in the United States for one's own account, whether done personally or through a resident broker or agent (irrespective of whether the agent has discretionary authority to act), does not constitute the conduct of a U.S. trade or business by a nonresident alien individual or foreign corporation. This rule, however, does not apply to a dealer in stocks or securities. Further, in the tax years beginning before 1998, the rule does not apply to a foreign investment corporation if it has its principal office in the U.S. (Code Sec. 864(b)(2)).[55]

2440. Income from U.S. Sources. What "income from sources within the United States" comprises is determined by a set of technical rules (Code Sec. 861).[56]

Footnote references are to paragraphs of the 2002 Standard Federal Tax Reports.

¶ **2435**

[48] ¶ 27,540, ¶ 27,542	[51] ¶ 27,320	[54] ¶ 27,320, ¶ 27,500
[49] ¶ 27,540, ¶ 27,545	[52] ¶ 27,480, ¶ 27,500	[55] ¶ 27,180
[50] ¶ 27,540, ¶ 27,541	[53] ¶ 27,180	[56] ¶ 27,120

For example, the source of an interest payment is generally the residence of the obligor. Similar rules exist for determining foreign-source income (Code Sec. 862).

Source rules for personal property sales provide generally that income from sales by U.S. residents are from U.S. sources and sales by nonresidents are from sources outside the U.S., with some exceptions and special provisions (Code Sec. 865).[57]

Rules for mixed source income provide that all income from transportation that both begins and ends in the United States is treated as U.S.-source income. Special rules apply to transportation between the United States and any of its possessions. The term "transportation income" means any income derived from or in connection with (1) the use (or hiring or leasing for use) of a vessel or aircraft or (2) the performance of services directly related to the use of a vessel or aircraft. The term "vessel or aircraft" includes any container used in connection with either of those modes of transportation (Code Sec. 863(c)).[58]

2442. Disposition of U.S. Real Property Interest. A gain or loss from the disposition by a nonresident alien or foreign corporation of a U.S. real property interest (including an interest in a mine, well, or other natural deposit) is treated as a gain or loss that is effectively connected with a U.S. trade or business (Code Sec. 897).[59] A gain or loss from the disposition of an interest in a domestic corporation by a nonresident alien or foreign corporation is considered a gain or loss from a disposition of a U.S. real property interest unless the taxpayer establishes that such corporation was not a U.S. real property holding corporation (RPHC) at any time during the shorter of (1) the period the interest was held by the taxpayer after June 18, 1980, or (2) the five-year period ending on the date of disposition of such interest.

Gain will not be recognized if, at the time of the receipt of the distributed property, the transferee would be subject to a realized gain on a subsequent disposition of the distributed property and the basis of the distributed property in the hands of the transferee is no greater than the adjusted basis of such property before the distribution, increased by the amount of gain recognized by the transferor corporation (Code Sec. 897(d)(2)).[60]

A disposition of an interest in a foreign corporation is not considered a disposition of any U.S. real property that such corporation owns. Instead, the foreign corporation is taxed on any distribution (whether or not in liquidation) of any appreciated U.S. real property interest (a direct interest in U.S. real property or an interest in RPHC stock) to the extent of the excess of the fair market value of the interest over its adjusted basis. The tax is likewise imposed if such appreciated interest is sold in connection with a liquidation of the foreign corporation. The foreign corporation is taxed on any gains it realizes on the disposition of any U.S. real property interest.

When a nonresident alien or foreign corporation disposes of an interest in a partnership, trust or estate, the amount of any money and the fair market value of other property received for such interest, to the extent attributable to U.S. real property interests, are considered amounts received from the sale or exchange in the United States of such property. In effect, the gain on the disposition of such interest is taxed to the extent that the gain represents the taxpayer's pro rata share of appreciation in the value of the U.S. real property interests of the entity.

A distribution by a real estate investment trust is treated as gain on the disposition of a U.S. real property interest to the extent of the nonresident alien's or the foreign corporation's pro rata share of the net capital gain of the REIT. In the case of a REIT that is controlled by U.S. persons, a sale of a REIT interest is not subject to tax (except in the case of distribution by the REIT) (Code Sec. 897(h)).

A corporation is an RPHC if the fair market value of its U.S. real property interests equals or exceeds 50% of the sum of its (1) U.S. real property interests, (2) interests in foreign real property, and (3) other assets used or held for use in its trade

---

Footnote references are to paragraphs of the 2002 Standard Federal Tax Reports.

[57] ¶ 27,200   [59] ¶ 27,700   [60] ¶ 27,700
[58] ¶ 27,160

or business. If any class of stock of an RPHC is regularly traded on an established securities market, stock of such class shall be treated as a U.S. real property interest only in the case of a person who owns more than 5% of such class of stock.

In order to insure that foreign investors in U.S. real property interests will pay taxes on gain realized on the disposition of such interests, a withholding tax is imposed on dispositions of U.S. real property interests (Code Sec. 1445).[61] Generally, the transferee of any U.S. real property interest is required to withhold and deduct a tax equal to 10% of the amount realized by the foreign person-transferor.

The reporting requirements pertaining to real property interests in the United States are set forth in Code Sec. 6039C.

2444. Deductions. A nonresident alien individual or foreign corporation engaged in a U.S. trade or business is allowed to take income tax deductions to the extent that they relate to income effectively connected with the U.S. trade or business, plus the deduction for charitable contributions (without regard to its relation to effectively connected income). In addition, a nonresident alien individual may take a casualty or theft loss deduction on property located within the United States and the deduction for personal exemptions (except for residents of Mexico, Canada, nationals of the United States and, under certain circumstances, residents of Japan or the Republic of Korea, a nonresident alien engaged in a trade or business in the United States is allowed only one personal exemption) (Code Secs. 873 and 882).[62]

2445. Foreign Tax Credit. A nonresident alien individual or a foreign corporation engaged in a U.S. business is allowed a foreign tax credit for any foreign income, war profits, or excess profits tax paid or accrued on foreign income which is subject to U.S. tax. This applies to the three types of foreign-source income that are treated and taxed as income effectively connected with a U.S. business under the rules discussed at ¶ 2429. Certain limitations (see ¶ 2477) apply to this credit (Code Sec. 906).[63] No credit will be allowed for income, war profits, and excess profits taxes paid or accrued with respect to the foreign trade income of a foreign sales corporation (¶ 2470) (Code Sec. 906(b)(5)).[64]

2449. Conditions for Allowance of Deductions and Credits. A nonresident alien individual is entitled to deductions and credits, to the extent qualified, only if a timely return is filed, or caused to be filed, by the nonresident alien. If a return should have been filed and was not, the IRS will have one prepared but will allow no deductions or credits (other than the credit for taxes withheld or the credit for federal excise taxes on gasoline and special fuels) (Code Sec. 874; Reg. § 1.874-1).[65]

2451. Change of Residence During Tax Year. An alien who establishes or abandons U.S. residence during the tax year is taxable for that year as if it were comprised of two separate periods—one of residence and one of nonresidence. For the period of nonresidence, the alien need not include any income from sources outside the United States unless that income is effectively connected with a U.S. trade or business. Income for the period of nonresidence from sources within the United States, which is not effectively connected with a U.S. trade or business, is subject to the usual 30% rate or lower treaty rate. All income for the period of residence, from whatever source, is subject to tax under the same rules that apply to citizens (Reg. § 1.871-13).[66]

An alien whose residence status changes during the tax year is entitled to one personal exemption (or, in the case of an individual mentioned at ¶ 2444, any additional exemptions to which he may be entitled). In addition, he is entitled to the same exemptions as a citizen, provided that these may not exceed his taxable income (without deduction for exemptions) for the period in the tax year during which he is a resident of the United States.

Definitions of the terms "nonresident alien" and "resident alien" have been codified (Code Sec. 7701(b)); [67] rules are provided for determining when an alien is

---

Footnote references are to paragraphs of the 2002 Standard Federal Tax Reports.

[61] ¶ 32,780	[64] ¶ 27,920	[66] ¶ 27,341
[62] ¶ 27,360, ¶ 27,500	[65] ¶ 27,363, ¶ 27,364	[67] ¶ 43,080
[63] ¶ 27,920		

¶ 2444

considered to have established a U.S. residence, and rules are provided regarding an alien's first and last years of U.S. residency. See ¶ 2423.

2453. Foreign Student or Exchange Visitor. A nonresident alien individual who is not otherwise engaged in a U.S. trade or business and who is temporarily present in the U.S. as a nonimmigrant under Sec. 101(a)(15)(F), (J) or (M) of the Immigration and Nationality Act (relating to visiting students, teachers, trainees, etc.) is considered to be engaged in a U.S. business. This means that any taxable portion of a scholarship or fellowship grant and expenses incidental thereto (see ¶ 879), to the extent derived from U.S. sources, are taxable at the same rates (but subject only to a 14% withholding rate) applicable to a U.S. citizen. Payments received by these individuals from a foreign employer are fully exempt from tax. Also, a scholarship or a fellowship received by a foreign student or exchange visitor from a foreign government or from certain binational, multinational, and international organizations is exempt from tax, subject to the limitations described at ¶ 879 (Code Secs. 117, 871(c), 872(b) and 1441(b)).[68]

2455. Foreign Ship or Aircraft. U.S.-source earnings of a foreign ship or aircraft are exempt from U.S. taxation if such exemption is available to foreign persons who reside in a country that grants a U.S. citizen or corporation a tax exemption for the transportation income (Code Sec. 883).[69]

2457. Expatriation to Avoid Income Tax. Generally, every nonresident alien individual who, within the 10-year period immediately preceding the close of the tax year, lost U.S. citizenship is taxed at regular U.S. rates (including minimum tax and lump-sum distribution tax) on income that is effectively connected and other U.S. source income specified under Code Sec. 871(b), unless such citizenship loss did not have for one of its principal purposes the avoidance of tax. With some exceptions, a tax-avoidance motive will be presumed for these expatriates if either: (1) the individual's average annual net income tax for the five years preceding the termination exceeds $112,000 in 2001 (Rev. Proc. 2001-13) or (2) the individual's net worth equals at least $562,000 in 2000 (Rev. Proc. 2001-13) (Code Sec. 877).[70] Individuals may rebut the presumption of tax avoidance if they submit a complete ruling request in good faith (Notice 98-34).[71]

For calendar year 2002, CCH unofficially projects the thresholds used to determine whether an individual's loss of United States citizenship had the avoidance of United States taxes as one of its principal purposes to be $120,000 for "average annual net income tax" and $599,000 or more for "net worth."

The amount included in an expatriate's gross estate (see ¶ 2912) by reason of ownership in a CFC may be subject to foreign estate tax and a credit for foreign death taxes. This credit is computed by a formula specified in Code Sec. 2107(c)(2).

2458. Alien Departing from the United States. Generally, no alien (whether resident or nonresident) is permitted to depart from the country without first obtaining from the District Director a certificate of compliance (popularly known as the sailing permit or departure permit) as proof that he has discharged his income tax liability. This document is part of the income tax form an alien must file before leaving the country. An alien will receive a sailing or departure permit as a result of filing a Form 1040C or Form 2063. Advance payment of the tax is not required if the Treasury determines that tax collection will not be jeopardized by the alien's departure (Code Sec. 6851(d)).[72]

2460. Returns. A nonresident alien individual (other than one whose wages are subject to withholding) and a foreign corporation (other than one having an office or place of business in the U.S. or an FSC or former FSC) must file income tax returns on or before the 15th day of the 6th month following the close of the tax year (Code Sec. 6072(c)).[73] In other cases, returns are due at the same time as those that are applicable to a U.S. citizen or domestic corporation. A nonresident alien individual uses Form 1040NR. A foreign corporation uses Form 1120F.

Footnote references are to paragraphs of the 2002 Standard Federal Tax Reports.

[68] ¶ 7170, ¶ 27,320, ¶ 27,344, ¶ 32,702
[69] ¶ 27,520
[70] ¶ 27,420
[71] ¶ 27,425.17
[72] ¶ 40,402
[73] ¶ 36,720

Tax Treaties

2462. Tax Treaties. A nonresident alien individual or a foreign corporation is taxed on fixed or determinable, annual or periodic income received from U.S. sources at a flat rate of 30% unless a lower rate is set under an income tax treaty ratified by the United States. See ¶ 2431. The United States has negotiated a network of treaties with other countries to avoid international double taxation and to prevent tax evasion. Provisions are included to prevent fraudulent evasion and also to restrict legal avoidance.

When a taxpayer claims that a U.S. treaty overrules (or otherwise modifies) an internal revenue law, the taxpayer must disclose such fact on his tax return, under Code Sec. 6114, or in a manner prescribed by the Secretary. A penalty may be imposed pursuant to Code Sec. 6712 for failure to comply with the disclosure requirement, but the Secretary may waive it. Also, provisions of the Internal Revenue Code are to be applied to any taxpayer's exclusion of certain items from gross income with due regard to any treaty obligation of the United States that is applicable to such taxpayer (Reg. § 301.6114-1).[74]

A foreign person is not entitled to a reduced rate of withholding tax under a tax treaty on an item of income derived through a partnership (or other fiscally transparent entity) if all of the following apply: (1) the income item is not treated by the treaty partner as an item of income to such foreign person; (2) the foreign country does not impose tax on a distribution of the item by the U.S. entity to the foreign person; and (3) the treaty does not contain a provision addressing the applicability of the treaty in the case of an item of income derived through a partnership (Code Sec. 894(c)).[75]

U.S. Possession Corporations

2463. U.S. Possession Corporations. The Puerto Rico and possession tax credit is terminated for tax years beginning after December 31, 1995 (Code Sec. 931(j)).[76] Special phaseout rules apply in the case of existing credit claimants with respect to the portion of the credit attributable to active business income. "Qualified possession source investment income" (QPSII) is not included in the phaseout; rather, such income is excluded in determining if it is received or accrued on or after July 1, 1996. An existing credit claimant is a corporation that was actively conducting a trade or business in a possession on October 13, 1995, and that has a Code Sec. 936 election in effect for the corporation's tax year which includes October 13, 1995. A corporation can also qualify as an existing credit claimant if it acquires all of the trade or business of an existing credit claimant. An existing credit claimant that adds a substantial new line of business after October 13, 1995, will cease to be eligible for the credit in the tax year in which the new line of business is added and thereafter. When an existing credit claimant with respect to a possession other than Puerto Rico uses the economic activity limitation, the current possession tax credit is allowed for tax years beginning after December 31, 1995, and before January 1, 2002. An existing credit claimant with respect to Puerto Rico that uses the economic activity limitation calculates its tax credit under Code Sec. 30A for tax years beginning after December 31, 1995, and before January 1, 2006. Code Sec. 30A contains the same rules found in Code Sec. 936(a)(1)(A) and (4) for calculating the economic activity credit, and applies a cap on possession business income, for tax years beginning after December 31, 2001. When an existing credit claimant elects a reduced credit using the applicable percentage limitation in lieu of using the economic activity limitation, the possession tax credit is allowed for tax years beginning after December 31, 1995, and before January 1, 1998. The election to claim a reduced credit becomes irrevocable unless revoked for the taxpayer's first tax year beginning in 1997 and all subsequent tax years. Following the initial period, existing credit claimants that use either the economic activity limitation or the applicable percentage limit may continue to claim the credit throughout the last tax year beginning before January 1, 2006, subject to a cap on possession business

Footnote references are to paragraphs of the 2002 Standard Federal Tax Reports.

¶ **2462**   [74] ¶ 37,061   [75] ¶ 27,640   [76] ¶ 4058

income. For tax years beginning in 2006 and thereafter, the credit is scheduled to expire. In the case of an existing credit claimant, the possession tax credit continues to apply without change to Guam, American Samoa, and the Commonwealth of the Northern Mariana Islands for tax years beginning after December 31, 1995, and before January 1, 2006, when the credit is scheduled to expire.

"Controlled" Foreign Corporation

2465. U.S. Shareholder Taxed on Undistributed Earnings. Where a foreign corporation (see ¶ 2472 for foreign personal holding companies) is controlled for an uninterrupted period of 30 or more days by U.S. shareholders, such shareholders are taxed on some of the corporation's undistributed earnings as well as on its distributed earnings.

A U.S. shareholder is a U.S. person who actually or constructively owns 10% or more of a foreign corporation's voting interest. A "U.S. person" includes a U.S. citizen or resident, a domestic partnership, a domestic corporation, and an estate or trust (other than a foreign estate or trust whose income from sources without the U.S. is not includible in the beneficiaries' gross income). A controlled foreign corporation generally is one in which more than 50% of the voting interest or total value is owned by U.S. shareholders on any day in the corporate tax year (Code Secs. 951, 957 and 958; Reg.§ § 1.951-1, 1.957-1—1.957-4 and 1.958-1—1.958-2).[77]

A U.S. shareholder must include in his gross income his share of the corporation's (1) "subpart F income," including previously excluded "subpart F income" withdrawn from investment in foreign base company shipping operations and from investment in less developed countries (Code Sec. 951(a)(1)(A)), (2) earnings invested in U.S. property determined under Code Sec. 956 (Code Sec. 951(a)(1)(B)), and (3) earnings invested in excess passive assets determined under Code Sec. 956A, for tax years of controlled foreign corporations beginning after September 30, 1993 and for tax years of U.S. shareholders in which or with which such tax years of controlled foreign corporations end (Code Sec. 951(a)(1)(C)).[78] Item (3) above is repealed for tax years of foreign corporations beginning after December 31, 1996, and to tax years of U.S. shareholders within which or with which such tax years of foreign corporations end. The term "U.S. property" for purposes of (2), above, does not include property held by a foreign sales corporation that is related to its export activities. Consequently, an FSC's foreign trade income and any deductions allocated to such income are not taken into account in determining amounts included in the gross income of shareholders under Subpart F (Code Sec. 956(b)(2)(I)).[79]

A controlled foreign corporation's subpart F income includes the sum of (1) insurance income (as defined under Code Sec. 953), (2) foreign base company income (as determined under Code Sec. 954), (3) an amount equal to the product of (a) income of the controlled foreign corporation other than income that is attributable to earnings and profits of the foreign corporation included in the gross income of a U.S. person under Code Sec. 951 or described under Code Sec. 952(b) multiplied by (b) the international boycott factor (as determined under Code Sec. 999), (4) the sum of the amounts of any illegal bribes, etc., paid by or on behalf of the corporation to a government official (payments which would be unlawful under the Foreign Corrupt Practices Act of 1977 if the payor were a U.S. person), and (5) the income of the controlled foreign corporation derived from any foreign country during any period during which Code Sec. 901(j) applies to such country (Code Sec. 952). (See ¶ 2496 and ¶ 2497 regarding international boycotts and illegal payments.)

The gross income items, above, are included only for the period during the year that the corporation was "controlled" by U.S. shareholders. Amounts which would, except for Code Sec. 951(d), be included in the gross income of a U.S. shareholder for any tax year both under the Subpart F rules and the foreign personal holding

---

Footnote references are to paragraphs of the 2002 Standard Federal Tax Reports.

[77] ¶ 28,470, ¶ 28,471,
¶ 28,590, ¶ 28,591—
¶ 28,595, ¶ 28,610,
¶ 28,611—¶ 28,612

[78] ¶ 28,470, ¶ 28,570,
¶ 28,580

[79] ¶ 28,570

company provisions are included in the gross income of such shareholder only under the Subpart F rules (Code Sec. 951(d)).[80]

An individual U.S. shareholder may elect to be taxed as a domestic corporation upon undistributed earnings of a controlled foreign corporation and thereby become eligible for the foreign tax credit (Code Sec. 962; Reg. § § 1.962-1—1.962-4).[81]

2466. Returns. An annual information return on Form 5471 must be made by certain U.S. persons (see ¶ 2465) who have an interest in a foreign corporation. The threshold for stock ownership of a foreign corporation that triggers the information reporting requirements under Code Sec. 6046 on Form 5471 is 10 percent of either total value of corporate stock or the total combined voting power of all classes of stock with voting rights (Code Sec. 6046(a)).[82] Failure to file such return will result in penalties (Code Sec. 6038; Reg. § 1.6038-2).[83]

DISC

2468. Interest Charge Domestic International Sales Corporations. The pre-1985 system of tax deferral for export income of domestic international sales corporations (DISCs) generally has been replaced by a system of foreign sales corporations (FSCs) (¶ 2470). DISCs, however, have not been entirely abolished. A DISC can elect to be an interest charge DISC, whose benefits are geared toward small businesses. Individual shareholders of an interest charge DISC generally may defer income attributable to $10 million or less of qualified export receipts and corporate shareholders may defer 16/17 of DISC income attributable to $10 million or less of qualified export receipts.[84] A shareholder of a DISC must, however, pay interest on the amount of the DISC-related deferred tax liability (Code Sec. 995(f)).[85] This interest is due at the same time as the shareholder's regular tax and is subject to a penalty for late payment (Code Sec. 6601).[86] The election is made on Form 4876A and is due on or before the 15th day of the 9th month following the end of its tax year (Code Secs. 6011(c) and 6072(b)).[87]

FSC

2470. Foreign Sales Corporations. As pointed out at ¶ 2468, above, DISCs were generally replaced by the foreign sales corporation (FSC) system (Code Secs. 921-927).[88] Under this system, a portion of the foreign trade income of an FSC is exempt from tax at the corporate level, provided it is derived from the foreign presence and economic activity of the FSC. In contrast, under the DISC system, there is no corporate income tax imposed on DISC income, and there is a partial deferral of taxes at the shareholder level.

FSC Repeal. On November 15, 2000, the FSC Repeal and Extraterritorial Income Exclusion Act of 2000 (P.L. 106-519) was signed into law. The Act repealed the rules regarding foreign sales corporations (Code Secs. 921-927) in an effort to comply with a World Trade Organization (WTO) decision that ruled that the FSC provisions were an illegal export subsidy. The FSC rules have been replaced with rules providing for the exclusion from gross income of extraterritorial income (Code Sec. 114 and Code Secs. 941-943). The rules regarding extraterritorial income are expected to result in tax benefits that are comparable to those available under the FSC rules. The repeal was effective for transactions after September 30, 2000. No corporation may elect FSC status after that date, while FSCs that were in existence on September 30, 2000 will not be subject to the new rules before January 1, 2002.

2471. Extraterritorial Income Exclusion. Effective September 30, 2000, gross income does not include extraterritorial income to the extent that such income is qualifying foreign trade income (Code Sec. 114).[89] Qualifying foreign trade income is the amount of gross income which, if excluded, would result in a reduction of

Footnote references are to paragraphs of the 2002 Standard Federal Tax Reports.

[80] ¶ 28,470	[84] ¶ 29,020, ¶ 29,033.01	[88] ¶ 28,080, ¶ 28,100—
[81] ¶ 28,690—¶ 28,694	[85] ¶ 29,020	¶ 28,200
[82] ¶ 35,940	[86] ¶ 39,410	[89] ¶ 7105
[83] ¶ 35,540, ¶ 35,543	[87] ¶ 35,120, ¶ 36,720	

¶ **2466**

taxable income by the greatest of: (1) 15% of foreign trade income, (2) 1.2% of foreign trading gross receipts, or (3) 30% of foreign sale and lease income.

Foreign Trading Gross Receipts. Foreign trading gross receipts are receipts derived from certain activities in connection with qualifying foreign trade property. However, foreign trading gross receipts may not include receipts of a taxpayer arising from a transaction if the qualifying foreign trade property or services are for ultimate use in the United States or by the United States or any instrumentality if such use is required by law. Foreign trading gross receipts also do not include receipts arising from any transaction accomplished through the use of a subsidy of the country in which the property is manufactured, grown, produced, or extracted (Code Sec. 942).[90]

Property is qualifying foreign trade property if it meets three requirements. First, the property must be manufactured, produced, grown or extracted within the United States or outside the United States if certain other conditions are met. Second, the property must be held for sale, lease, or rental in the ordinary course of trade or business for direct use, consumption, or disposition outside the United States. Finally, no more than 50 percent of the fair market value of the property may be attributable to (1) articles manufactured, produced, grown, or extracted outside the United States and (2) direct costs for labor performed outside the United States. The following types of property cannot be qualifying foreign trade property: property leased or rented for use by any related person; patents, inventions, certain copyrights, goodwill, trademarks, trade brands, franchises, or other like property; oil or gas; any unprocessed timber which is a softwood; and any property that has been designated as in short supply by executive order as long as such order remains in effect.

Property which is otherwise qualifying foreign trade property and is manufactured outside the United States shall be treated as qualifying foreign trade property only if it is manufactured by: (1) a domestic corporation, (2) an individual who is a citizen or resident of the United States, (3) a foreign corporation that has elected under Code Sec. 943(e) to be treated as a domestic corporation for tax purposes, or (4) a partnership or pass through entity all the members of which are listed in (1) - (3) above.

Foreign Trade Income. Foreign trade income is taxable income attributable to foreign trade gross receipts (Code Sec. 941(b)).

Foreign Sale and Lease Income. "Foreign sale and lease income" is foreign trade income that is properly allocable to activities described in Code Sec. 942(b)(2)(A)(i) or Code Sec. 942(b)(3). Activities that are described in Code Sec. 942(b)(2)(A)(i) are transactions in which a taxpayer (or person acting under contract with a taxpayer) has participated outside the United States in the solicitation, negotiation, or making of the contract relating to the transaction. Activities that are described in Code Sec. 942(b)(3) are any of the following with respect to qualifying foreign trade property: (1) advertising and sales promotions, (2) the processing of customer orders or arranging for delivery, (3) transportation outside the United States in connection with delivery to a customer, (4) the determination or final transmittal of a final invoice or statement of account or the receipt of payment, and (5) the assumption of credit risk (Code Sec. 941(c)).[91]

Returns. All taxpayers that claim the extraterritorial income exclusion must use Form 8873, "Extraterritorial Income Exclusion," to determine the amount to be excluded from gross income. The form must be attached to the taxpayer's income tax return.

WTO Decision. On August 20, 2001, the WTO found that the rules regarding extraterritorial income violated the WTO rules by illegally subsidizing the foreign sales of domestic businesses. The United States has appealed this decision.

Footnote references are to paragraphs of the 2002 Standard Federal Tax Reports.

[90] ¶ 28,410   [91] ¶ 28,400   **¶ 2471**

Foreign Personal Holding Company

2472. Foreign Personal Holding Company. A U.S. shareholder is subject to tax on undistributed income, as well as on distributed income, of a foreign personal holding company (Code Sec. 551; Reg. § 1.551-1).[92] The tax on undistributed income is imposed only on a shareholder who is a U.S. citizen or resident, a domestic corporation, a domestic partnership, or a domestic estate or trust as though the income had been actually distributed as dividends.

A foreign corporation is usually classified as a foreign personal holding company if:

(a) at least 60% (50% after the first tax year) of its gross income (not gross receipts) consists of dividends, interest (whether or not treated as rent), royalties (except for active business computer software royalties), annuities, rents (unless amounting to 50% or more of gross income), gains in stock and commodity transactions, income from personal service contracts and other specified types of income; and

(b) more than 50% of either the total combined voting power of all classes of voting stock or the total value of its outstanding stock is owned directly or indirectly by five or fewer U.S. citizens or residents (Code Secs. 552 and 553; Reg. § § 1.552-2, 1.552-3 and 1.553-1).[93]

For purposes of (b), above, stock owned by a nonresident alien individual (other than a foreign trust or estate) will not be treated as owned by a U.S. citizen or by a resident alien who is not the spouse of the nonresident individual and who does not otherwise own stock in the corporation. The attribution rules will not apply to a foreign person's partners who are citizens or U.S. residents unless they own stock, as determined by application of the attribution rules (other than attribution through partners) (Code Sec. 554(c)).[94]

Stock of a foreign personal holding company owned, directly or indirectly, by a foreign partnership, estate, or trust, or a foreign corporation that is not a foreign personal holding company will be considered as owned proportionately by its partners, beneficiaries, or shareholders (Code Sec. 551(f)).[95]

For purposes of the foreign personal holding company rules, dividends and interest received from certain related foreign corporations will be excluded—either as foreign personal holding company income or as non-foreign personal holding company income—in determining whether a foreign corporation is a foreign personal holding company (Code Sec. 552(c)).[96] To qualify under this rule, the dividends and interest must be received from a corporation that (1) is related to the recipient or (2) is created or organized under the laws of the recipient's country and (3) has a substantial part of its assets used in its trade or business located in that same foreign country.

2473. Returns. A U.S. citizen or resident who is an officer or director of a foreign personal holding company or who is a stockholder owning 10% or more in value of the outstanding stock of such company must file an annual return on Form 5471 (Code Sec. 6035; Reg. § 1.6035-1).[97]

Foreign Tax Deduction and Credit

2475. Deductions and Credits. A taxpayer may deduct foreign income tax paid or accrued, or may apply it as a credit against U.S. income tax (Code Secs. 901-908).[98] Form 1116 is used to report the credit.

The credit for foreign tax may be taken for income or profits taxes imposed by a foreign country or a U.S. possession upon a domestic corporation or a U.S. citizen,

---

Footnote references are to paragraphs of the 2002 Standard Federal Tax Reports.

[92] ¶ 23,310, ¶ 23,311	[96] ¶ 23,350	¶ 27,902, ¶ 27,920,
[93] ¶ 23,330, ¶ 23,332,	[97] ¶ 31,480, ¶ 31,481	¶ 27,940, ¶ 27,964
¶ 23,334, ¶ 23,350,	[98] ¶ 27,820, ¶ 27,840,	
¶ 23,351	¶ 27,860, ¶ 27,880,	
[94] ¶ 23,370		
[95] ¶ 23,310		

¶ 2472

whether resident or nonresident (or imposed by a U.S. possession upon a U.S. resident), and paid or accrued during the tax year (Code Sec. 901).[99] Generally, the amount of the credit allowed for citizens and domestic corporations, residents of the United States or Puerto Rico, nonresident alien individuals and foreign corporations, and partnerships and estates is subject to certain limitations imposed under Code Sec. 904 (see ¶ 2477) (Code Sec. 901(b)).[100]

An alien resident of the U.S. or a resident of Puerto Rico for the entire tax year may credit taxes paid or accrued to any U.S. possession. A resident alien or a bona fide resident of Puerto Rico during the entire tax year is allowed a credit for such a tax assessed by any foreign country only (within the discretion of the President of the United States) if the country of which he is a citizen or subject in imposing such taxes allows a like credit to citizens of the United States residing in such country (Code Sec. 901(b)(3) and (c)).[101]

Except in the case of a reduction of credit because of participation in a foreign boycott (see ¶ 2496), a taxpayer who chooses the credit against the tax for any tax year is prohibited from deducting foreign tax from U.S. income for that year (Code Sec. 275(a)(4)(A); Reg. § 1.164-2).[102] In addition, no deduction is allowed for income, war profits, and excess profits taxes imposed by any foreign country or possession of the U.S. if such taxes are paid or accrued with respect to foreign trade income of a foreign sales corporation (¶ 2470) (Code Sec. 275(a)(4)(B)).[103] Also, a taxpayer cannot take a credit for some foreign taxes and a deduction for others in one tax year except where credit has been reduced for taxes paid on foreign-boycott-produced income. A taxpayer can, however, change from deduction to credit (or vice versa) in different tax years. An individual may claim the foreign tax credit even though he elects not to itemize his deductions.[104]

While the credit is intended to cover foreign income taxes, it is also permitted to cover taxes imposed in lieu of income taxes otherwise generally imposed by the particular country (Code Sec. 903).[105] However, where the tax of a particular foreign country is not determined to be the substantial equivalent of an income tax, it will not qualify for the credit. Regulations limit the types of foreign taxes that qualify for the credit and provide comprehensive guidance in determining what types of foreign taxes are creditable against U.S. tax liability (Reg. § § 1.901-2 and 1.903-1).[106]

A holding period is imposed for purposes of crediting foreign taxes associated with foreign-source dividends. In general, no credit is allowed for foreign withholding taxes paid for dividends if a 16-day holding period for the dividend-paying stock (or a 46-day holding period for certain dividends on preferred stock) is not satisfied. The 16-day holding period must be met within the 30-day period beginning 15 days before the ex-dividend date. If the stock is held for 15 days or less during the 30-day period, the foreign tax credit for the withholding tax on the dividend is disallowed. Securities dealers holding securities in the active conduct of their securities businesses in a foreign country are excepted from the holding-period rule (Code Sec. 901(k)).

2477. Limitations. In computing the amount of the "credit against tax" on account of foreign taxes, taxpayers are subject to a limitation that prevents using foreign tax credits to reduce U.S. tax liability on income from sources within the U.S. The method by which this limitation is computed is called the overall limitation method (Code Sec. 904(a)).[107] An individual with $300 ($600 for joint filers) or less of creditable foreign taxes may be exempt from the foreign tax credit limitation, provided he has no foreign source income other than qualified passive income. The exemption is not automatic; it must be elected each year (Code Sec. 904(j)).

Under the overall limitation method, a taxpayer totals the taxes paid to all foreign countries and possessions (but see ¶ 2463 for the special treatment accorded

---

Footnote references are to paragraphs of the 2002 Standard Federal Tax Reports.
99 ¶ 27,820   102 ¶ 9503, ¶ 14,500   105 ¶ 27,860
100 ¶ 27,820   103 ¶ 14,500   106 ¶ 27,822, ¶ 27,861
101 ¶ 27,820   104 ¶ 27,826.021   107 ¶ 27,880

¶ 2477

to corporations electing the possessions tax credit). This total is then subjected to a limitation computed by multiplying the U.S. tax liability by a fraction in which the numerator consists of taxable income from foreign sources and the denominator consists of the worldwide taxable income.

The foreign tax credit limitation is computed separately for several types of income (¶ 2480) (Code Sec. 904(d); Reg. § 1.904-4).[108] The numerator of the foreign tax credit limitation formula—foreign-source taxable income—is determined by reducing foreign source income for deductions directly related to foreign source income and the allocation of deductions unrelated to the production of foreign source income. The allocation rules are found in Reg. § 1.861-8 and often result in reduction of the taxpayer's available foreign tax credits. Individuals, estates and trusts must compute taxable income without taking any deductions for personal exemptions under Code Sec. 151 (individuals) or Code Sec. 642(b) (estates and trusts) (Code Sec. 904(b)(1)).

In computing the foreign tax credit limitation, losses involving income from foreign countries reduce income from other foreign countries and reduce the amount of foreign taxes that can be used from those countries as a credit against U.S. tax. Foreign losses reduce U.S. tax on U.S. income only in cases where foreign losses exceed foreign income from all foreign countries for the tax year. However, in such cases the benefits are subject to recapture (see ¶ 2479, below).

The extent to which foreign source capital gain can be used in computing the limitation on the foreign tax credit is restricted. The general effect of the limitation is to require domestic source net capital loss to be taken into account in determining foreign source capital gain.[109] After doing so, a corporation must make further reductions under special rules (Code Sec. 904(b)(2)).[110]

The following amounts derived from U.S.-owned foreign corporations may be treated as U.S. source income for purposes of the limitations on foreign tax credits: (1) interest, (2) dividends, (3) subpart F inclusions, and (4) foreign personal holding company income (Code Sec. 904(g) and Reg. § 1.904-5(c)). Generally, subpart F inclusions, foreign personal holding company income and interest are treated as U.S. source income to the extent such amounts are attributable to the U.S. source income of the U.S.-owned foreign corporation. Dividends are generally treated as U.S. source in proportion to the U.S. source earnings and profits of the U.S.-owned foreign corporation. A *de minimis* exception applies to interest and dividends. The term "United States-owned foreign corporation" means any foreign corporation if 50% or more of the total combined voting power of all classes of stock in the corporation entitled to vote, or the total value of the stock of the corporation, is held by U.S. persons (Code Sec. 904(g); Reg. § 1.904-5(m)).[111] The IRS has been authorized to issue regulations that would require taxpayers to resource the income of any member of an affiliated group of corporations, or to modify the consolidated return regulations, to the extent necessary to prevent avoidance of the foreign tax credit limitation rules (Code Sec. 904(i)).[112]

There are special limitations on the amount of foreign taxes on foreign oil and gas extraction income that can qualify for the foreign tax credit (Code Sec. 907; Reg. § § 1.907-0—1.907(f)-1A).[113]

2479. Recapture of Foreign Losses. Overall foreign loss sustained in a tax year is subject to recapture in later years (Code Sec. 904(f)).[114] The general effect of the recapture rule is to limit foreign tax credits in a year subsequent to an overall loss year by recharacterizing some foreign source income as domestic source income. The recapture rule also applies to the credit under Code Sec. 936 for tax attributable to possession source income. (See ¶ 2463.)

An overall foreign loss is the amount by which gross income from foreign sources is exceeded by the sum of expenses, losses and other deductions properly

---

Footnote references are to paragraphs of the 2002 Standard Federal Tax Reports.

[108] ¶ 27,880, ¶ 27,885	[112] ¶ 27,880	[114] ¶ 27,880
[109] ¶ 27,901.0212	[113] ¶ 27,940, ¶ 27,941—	
[110] ¶ 27,880	¶ 27,950	
[111] ¶ 27,880, ¶ 27,886		

¶ 2479

allocable to such foreign source income. Any net operating loss deduction, foreign expropriation losses and uncompensated casualty or theft losses are not taken into account.

Generally, the amount of foreign source income that will be recharacterized is limited to the lesser of the overall foreign loss for the earlier year or 50% of the foreign source taxable income for the current year. However, a taxpayer may choose to have more than 50% of his foreign source taxable income recharacterized as domestic source income.

Gain on the disposition of business property predominantly used outside the U.S. during the preceding three-year period also is subject to the recapture rule unless the property was not a material factor in the realization of income by the taxpayer. The amount recharacterized is 100% of the gain or, if less, the overall foreign loss. Generally, nonrecognized gain as well as recognized gain is subject to recapture. Foreign source gain that otherwise would not be recognized is recognized and recharacterized. Therefore, a disposition of foreign business property may result in both a reduction of the limitation on foreign tax credit and an increase in the taxpayer's income.

Foreign losses may not be used to offset U.S. income before all foreign income has been offset. Thus, a taxpayer may not offset a category of separate limitation losses solely against the corresponding category of separate limitation income and then apply excess losses against U.S. income without first using the excess to offset overall limitation income or another category of separate limitation income. Moreover, foreign losses must be allocated proportionately among the different categories of separate or overall limitation income, and the percentage of foreign losses that may offset a category of income must equal the category's percentage share of total foreign income.

Also, for qualified stock purchases under Code Sec. 338(d)(3), any income that might be foreign source because of a Code Sec. 338(h)(10) election will be recharacterized as U.S. source and therefore will allow the United States to recoup the tax that was previously lost because of foreign losses.

2480. Special Computation for Certain Categories of Income. The foreign tax credit must be computed separately for several categories of income. These categories include: (1) passive income, (2) high withholding tax interest, (3) financial services income (which includes high withholding tax interest), (4) shipping income, (5) dividends received by corporations from each noncontrolled Code Sec. 902 corporation (all non-PFIC noncontrolled Code Sec. 902 corporations are treated as one for this purpose, for tax years beginning after December 31, 2002) (Code Sec. 904(d)(2)(E)(iv)), (6) certain dividends from an IC-DISC or former DISC, (7) foreign trade income, (8) certain distributions from an FSC or former FSC out of earnings and profits attributable to foreign trade income, interest or carrying charges (¶ 2470), and (9) all other income not included in the above categories (general limitation income) (Code Sec. 904(d); Reg. § 1.904-4).[115]

Look-Through Rules. Interest, subpart F inclusions (Code Sec. 951(a)(1)(A)), rents, or royalties and dividends received or accrued by a U.S. shareholder from a controlled foreign corporation must be treated as separate limitation income if these items were a separate limitation income of the corporation before they were passed on to the U.S. shareholder. A *de minimis* exception provides that these rules will not be applied against foreign-base company income and gross insurance income received from a controlled corporation if the sum of the income is less than the lesser of 5% of gross income or $1,000,000, provided none of the income is financial services income. (Code Secs. 904(d)(3), 904(d)(3)(E) and 954(b)(3)(A); Reg. § 1.904-5).[116]

Look-through treatment of interest subject to a 5% or greater gross basis tax that is paid to a U.S. shareholder by a controlled foreign corporation would apply only to that portion of the interest payments that exceeds the payor's interest

---

Footnote references are to paragraphs of the 2002 Standard Federal Tax Reports.

[115] ¶ 27,880, ¶ 27,885
[116] ¶ 27,880, ¶ 27,886,
¶ 28,530

income (or its equivalent) that would be treated as financial services income under the look-through rule.

2482. Carryback and Carryover of Credit. Where the tax paid or accrued to any foreign country (or U.S. possession) is more than the amount allowable as a credit under the limitation discussed at ¶ 2477, the excess may be carried back to the two preceding tax years and then forward to the five succeeding tax years (Code Sec. 904(c)).[117] The amount of carryback or carryover that can be utilized is limited to the amount by which the applicable limitation for the year exceeded the amount of tax paid (or accrued) to foreign countries or possessions for that year.

The 10-year limitations period for filing a claim for credit or refund of a carryforward is determined by reference to the date for filing the return for the year in which the foreign taxes were paid or accrued, rather than the year to which the foreign tax credits are carried (Code Sec. 6511(d)(3)(A), reversing *Ampex Corp*, 80-1 USTC ¶ 9358). In addition, the restricted interest rule, which formerly applied only in the case of an overpayment of tax created by a foreign tax credit carryback, is extended to an underpayment of tax (Code Sec. 6601(d)(2)).

2483. Refunded Tax. If foreign tax is refunded and the taxpayer must pay a tax on the refund, in redetermining the U.S. tax for the year in which a credit was originally taken, the foreign tax refunded is reduced by the tax imposed on the refund. No separate credit or deduction is allowed for the foreign tax imposed on the refund (Code Sec. 905(c)).[118]

A taxpayer whose foreign tax payments are returned to the taxpayer in the form of a subsidy (such as a refund or a credit) from a foreign country is prohibited from claiming foreign tax credits for the payments. Credits are also denied if the subsidies are given to persons related to the taxpayer or persons who participated in a transaction or a related transaction with the taxpayer (Code Sec. 901(i)).[119]

2485. Credit for Taxes of a Foreign Subsidiary. A domestic corporation that receives a dividend payment in a post-1986 tax year from a foreign subsidiary in which it owns 10% or more of the voting stock must compute its foreign tax credit (deemed-paid credit), for foreign taxes paid by the subsidiary on the dividend, by multiplying the subsidiary's total post-1986 foreign tax payments by the ratio of the dividend payment (determined without regard to Code Sec. 78) to the subsidiary's post-1986 undistributed earnings (accumulated in tax years beginning after 1986). The subsidiary's post-1986 foreign tax payments include the subsidiary's foreign tax payments in the year of the dividend, as well as tax payments made between the start of the 1987 tax year and the start of the dividend year, to the extent that such taxes were not attributable to dividends distributed by the foreign corporation in prior tax years (Code Sec. 902(b)).[120]

A U.S. corporation is deemed to have paid taxes paid by a second- or third-tier foreign corporation under certain circumstances. This indirect foreign tax credit is extended to fourth-, fifth-, and sixth-tier corporations under certain circumstances (Code Sec. 902(b)).[121]

For purposes of qualifying to claim the deemed paid credit, a domestic corporation and its affiliated group may not aggregate their share holdings in a foreign corporation in order to meet the 10% voting stock requirement of Code Sec. 902(a).[122]

Foreign tax credit may also be taken where a domestic corporation (or individual U.S. shareholder electing to be taxed as a domestic corporation) is required to include undistributed earnings of a controlled foreign corporation in gross income (see ¶ 2465) (Code Sec. 960).[123] For purposes of determining the credit, the inclusion is treated as if it were a dividend, and the method for determining the deemed-paid credit for dividend distributions applies.

Footnote references are to paragraphs of the 2002 Standard Federal Tax Reports.

¶ 2482

[117] ¶ 27,880
[118] ¶ 27,902
[119] ¶ 27,820
[120] ¶ 27,820
[121] ¶ 27,820
[122] ¶ 27,840
[123] ¶ 28,650

Transfer Involving Foreign Entity

2487. Foreign Investment Company Stock. Special provisions govern the gain from the sale or exchange of foreign investment company stock by U.S. shareholders. Where a foreign investment company is registered as such with the Securities and Exchange Commission or 50% or more of its voting stock or total value of stock is held by U.S. persons (see ¶ 2465), gain from the sale or exchange of company stock held for more than one year will be treated as ordinary income to the extent of the shareholder's ratable share of the company earnings and profits accumulated in years beginning after 1962 (Code Sec. 1246).[124]

2488. Sale, Exchange or Redemption of Stock in Controlled Foreign Corporation. Special provisions govern the sale or exchange of stock in certain foreign corporations or the surrender of stock to certain foreign corporations for redemption in a transaction that would be treated as a sale or exchange under Code Sec. 302 or a complete or partial liquidation under Code Sec. 331. These provisions affect U.S. shareholders owning 10% or more of the total combined voting power of all classes of voting stock of a foreign corporation at any time during the five-year period ending on the date of sale or exchange, provided the corporation was a controlled foreign corporation at any time the stock was owned by the shareholder. In such case, gain on the transaction will be included in the gross income of the shareholder-seller as a dividend to the extent of that portion of the gain that is attributable to the earnings and profits of the foreign corporation allocable to the stock, accumulated in corporate tax years beginning after 1962, but only while the stock was held and while the corporation was "controlled." Certain distributions, however, are excepted from this tax treatment (Code Sec. 1248; Reg. § § 1.1248-1—1.1248-7).[125]

Any taxpayer that is not eligible to receive deemed paid credits on dividends from a foreign corporation is not subject to the separate limitations for dividends from noncontrolled Code Sec. 902 corporations. Also, dividends from a controlled foreign corporation received by a related person with respect to that controlled foreign corporation, out of earnings for periods during which the dividend recipient was not a related person with respect to that corporation, will be treated as dividends from a noncontrolled Code Sec. 902 corporation.

CFC Gain on Stock Sales. Gain recognized on the sale or exchange of stock in a foreign corporation by a controlled foreign corporation (CFC) is included in the CFC's gross income as a dividend to the same extent that it would have been included under Code Sec. 1248(a) if the CFC were a U.S. person. This provision does not affect the determination of whether the corporation whose stock is sold or exchanged is a CFC (Code Sec. 964(e)).[126]

2489. Sale to, or Exchange of Patent, Etc., with, Foreign Corporation. Recognized gain from the taxable sale to, or exchange by a U.S. person with, a foreign corporation controlled by the transferor of a patent, an invention, model, or design (whether or not patented), a copyright, a secret formula or process, or any other similar property right is treated as ordinary income rather than capital gain (Code Secs. 958, 1249 and 7701(a); Reg. § 1.1249-1).[127]

2489A. Transfer of Intangibles. The treatment of deemed royalty income on transfers of intangibles to a foreign corporation in exchange for stock or as part of a corporate reorganization as U.S.-source income is no longer subject to a special source rule. Instead, the income will be considered as foreign source to the extent that an actual payment made by the foreign corporation under a license or sale agreement with the transferor would be treated as foreign-source income. Regulatory authority is granted to apply the Code Sec. 367(d) deemed royalty payment in the case of a transfer of intangible property to a partnership (Code Secs. 367(d) and 721(d)).[128]

Footnote references are to paragraphs of the 2002 Standard Federal Tax Reports.
[124] ¶ 30,920   [126] ¶ 28,710   [128] ¶ 25,240
[125] ¶ 30,960—¶ 30,967   [127] ¶ 28,610

¶ 2489A

2490. Transfers to Foreign Trusts. A U.S. person who transfers property to a foreign trust that has U.S. beneficiaries generally is treated as the owner of the portion of the trust attributable to such property. However, this rule does not apply to transfers in exchange for fair market value consideration. For purposes of determining whether the transfers of property after February 6, 1995, by a U.S. person to a foreign trust with U.S. beneficiaries is made in exchange for fair market value consideration, the obligations of the trust owner and certain persons related to the trust owner are not taken into account. Thus, trust owners (and related persons) join trust grantors and beneficiaries as "persons described" in Code Sec. 679(a)(3)(C). The obligations of described persons are disregarded in applying the fair market value exception to the rule that treats a U.S. transferor of property to a foreign trust with U.S. beneficiaries as the trust owner (Code Sec. 679(a)(3)(C)).[129]

A foreign trust is any trust that does not meet the two-part test of Code Sec. 7701(a)(30)(E). A trust is a U.S. person if both (1) a U.S. Court can exercise primary supervision over the administration of the trust and (2) one or more U.S. persons have the authority to control all substantial decisions of the trust.

2491. Passive Foreign Investment Companies. A passive foreign investment company (PFIC) is a foreign corporation that meets either passive income or passive assets thresholds. The passive income threshold is met if 75 percent or more of the corporation's gross income for the tax year is passive. The assets test is met if 50 percent or more of the average fair market value of the corporation's assets consists of assets that either produce or are held for the production of passive income (Code Sec. 1298).[130] A publicly traded foreign corporation is a PFIC if the fair market value of its passive income-producing assets equals or exceeds 50 percent of the sum of the market value of its outstanding stock plus its liabilities (Code Sec. 1297(e)).[131]

If the PFIC is a qualified electing fund under Code Sec. 1295, U.S. shareholders are taxed currently on their respective shares of the PFIC's earnings, but may elect to defer payment of tax on income not currently received, subject to an interest charge under Code Sec. 1291. If a PFIC is a nonqualified fund, U.S. shareholders are taxed on realized PFIC income and charged interest on deferred, unrealized income.

A U.S. shareholder of a PFIC may make a mark-to-market election with the PFIC stock if such stock is marketable (Code Sec. 1296). Under the election, any excess of the full market value of the PFIC stock at the close of the tax year over the shareholder's adjusted basis in the stock is included in the shareholder's income. The rules of Code Sec. 1291 applicable to nonqualified funds generally do not apply to a shareholder for tax years for which the mark-to-market election is in effect.

PFICs That Are CFCs. A corporation that otherwise would be a PFIC will not be treated as such with respect to 10-percent U.S. shareholders if the corporation is also a CFC (see ¶ 2465). That means shareholders who are taxed currently on their pro rata shares of subpart F income of a CFC will not be subject to the PFIC income inclusion provisions with respect to the same stock. There are special rules for PFICs that are not qualified electing funds and for shareholders who cease to be 10-percent U.S. shareholders (Code Sec. 1296(e)).[132]

2491A. Information Reporting on Foreign Partnerships. A number of reporting requirements apply with respect to foreign partnerships. A foreign partnership must by statute file a return if it has gross income that is either U.S. source or effectively connected with a U.S. trade or business (Code Sec. 6031(e)).[133] Also, a U.S. partner that controls a foreign partnership is required to file an annual information return, similar in scope to Form 5471 (Code Sec. 6038).[134] Furthermore, the requirement that a U.S. person report the acquisition or disposition of an interest in a foreign partnership or a change in his proportional interest in the partnership applies only to a 10-percent partner (Code Sec. 6046A(d)).[135] Moreover, a civil penalty of $10,000 applies for failure to file a return for changes in ownership

---

Footnote references are to paragraphs of the 2002 Standard Federal Tax Reports.

[129] ¶ 24,820	[132] ¶ 31,610	[134] ¶ 35,540
[130] ¶ 31,640	[133] ¶ 35,381	[135] ¶ 35,960
[131] ¶ 31,620		

of a foreign partnership (Code Sec. 6046A).[136] Finally, U.S. persons must report the contribution of property to a foreign partnership (Code Sec. 6038B).[137]

Withholding on Payment to Nonresident

2492. Withholding on Income Other Than Wages. The IRS has issued regulations to govern the withholding of tax on certain U.S.-source income paid to foreign persons. Due to the tremendous increase in cross-border payments that have occurred since the 1980s, the IRS has issued these regulations to standardize and coordinate the conditions under which withholding is required and the documentation that the withholding agent may rely upon to determine the status of a payee or beneficial owner as a U.S. person or a foreign person. The regulations went into effect on January 1, 2001 (Notice 99-25).

Under the regulations, the duty to withhold rests on the withholding agent. However, a withholding agent need not withhold where the foreign person assumes responsibility for withholding as a qualified intermediary or as a U.S. branch of a foreign person or as an authorized withholding agent.

The treatment of a payee as a U.S. person or a foreign person has an impact on whether information returns are required. Payees that are foreign persons are generally not required to file information returns. Thus, the withholding rules have consequences outside the context of the general withholding area (Reg. § 1.1441-1(b)(1)).

Withholding Rules. To ensure collection of the tax, withholding and payment are required by the person paying the income, rather than the one receiving it, in the case of a payment to a nonresident alien individual, a foreign partnership or a foreign corporation (¶ 2425) of fixed or determinable annual or periodical U.S. source income that is not effectively connected with a U.S. trade or business (see ¶ 2431) (Code Secs. 1441 and 1442; Reg. § § 1.1441-1—1.1441-5),[138] including royalties and patronage dividends.[139] Withholding is also required on OID where a nonresident alien or a foreign corporation is required to include a ratable portion of such discount in income (Code Sec. 1441(c)(8)).[140]

Income effectively connected with a nonresident alien individual's or a foreign corporation's U.S. business is not subject to withholding (Code Sec. 1441(c); Reg. § 1.1441-4).[141] Compensation for personal services of a nonresident alien individual is subject to withholding in the same manner as compensation to a U.S. citizen or resident (Reg. § 1.1441-4).[142]

Also, withholding by a U.S. or foreign partnership in 2001 is required on the partnership's "effectively connected taxable income" allocable to foreign partners at a rate of 39.1% for individuals and non-corporate partners and 35% for foreign partners that are corporations. Effectively connected taxable income is the partnership's taxable income computed with certain adjustments (Code Sec. 1446).[143]

There is a 30% U.S. withholding tax on payments of U.S. source interest, dividends, and other passive income to corporations created in or organized under the laws of Guam, American Samoa, the Northern Mariana Islands or the Virgin Islands (however, such income may be exempt from withholding if certain requirements are met) (Code Sec. 1442(c)).[144]

When a foreign taxing authority uses withholding simply as a collection mechanism, it will not necessarily follow that the mechanism results in interest being treated as high withholding tax interest.

2493. Rate of Withholding. The withholding rate for a nonresident alien is 30% (14% for certain scholarship income of nonresident aliens who have nonimmigrant status), except for compensation, as noted at ¶ 2492, and except where modified by treaty (Code Secs. 1441 and 1442; Reg. § § 1.1441-1—1.1441-4).[145]

Footnote references are to paragraphs of the 2002 Standard Federal Tax Reports.

[136] ¶ 35,960	[140] ¶ 32,702	[144] ¶ 32,720
[137] ¶ 35,580	[141] ¶ 32,702, ¶ 32,708	[145] ¶ 32,702—¶ 32,708,
[138] ¶ 32,702—¶ 32,710,	[142] ¶ 32,708	¶ 32,720
¶ 32,720	[143] ¶ 32,800	
[139] ¶ 32,716.23		

2494. Returns on Withholding. Every person required to withhold and pay a tax on income paid to a nonresident alien individual, a foreign partnership or a foreign corporation must make an annual return on Form 1042 and file it with the Internal Revenue Service Center in Philadelphia, Pa., on or before March 15 of the following year (Code Sec. 1461; Reg. § 1.1461-2).[146] See, also, ¶ 2650. Annual information returns on payments (except those shown on a W-2 Form) to nonresident alien individuals, foreign corporations and foreign partnerships are required on Form 1042S (Reg. § 1.1461-2(c)).[147]

Filing Requirements. The IRS has issued documentation requirements for the foreign withholding regulations (see ¶ 2492). The withholding certificates that are valid under the regulations are listed below.

Form W-8BEN (Certificate of Foreign Status of Beneficial Owner for United States Tax Withholding) should be provided to a withholding agent or payer by a beneficial owner to claim foreign status, claim beneficial ownership of income and, if applicable, claim a reduced rate of or exemption from withholding.

Form W-8ECI (Certificate of Foreign Person's Claim for Exemption From Withholding on Income Effectively Connected With the Conduct of a Trade or Business in the United States) should be used to establish foreign status, claim beneficial ownership and claim that income is effectively connected with the conduct of a trade or business in the United States.

Form W-8EXP (Certification of Foreign Government and Other Foreign Organizations for United States Tax Withholding) should be provided to a withholding agent or payor by a foreign government, international organization, foreign central bank of issue or foreign tax-exempt organization to establish foreign status, claim beneficial ownership and, if applicable, claim a reduced rate of or exemption from withholding.

Form W-9 (Request for Taxpayer Identification Number and Certification) may be used to determine whether to treat a payee or beneficial owner as a U.S. person.

These forms replace Form W-8 (Certificate of Foreign Status); Form 1001 (Ownership, Exemption, or Reduced Rate Certificate); Form 1078 (Certificate of Alien Claiming Residence in the United States); Form 4224 (Exemption From Withholding of Tax on Income Effectively Connected With the Conduct of a Trade or Business in the United States); Form 8709 (Exemption from Withholding on Investment Income of Foreign Governments and International Organizations); and the statement under Reg. 1.1441-5, relating to an individual's claim to be a U.S. citizen or resident, or a partnership or corporation's claim that it is a domestic entity. These forms were available for use in 1999 and 2000.

International Boycotts, Illegal Payments, Records

2496. International Boycotts. Participation in or cooperation with an international boycott may result in the reduction of available foreign tax credit, the denial of certain benefits otherwise allowable to U.S. shareholders of foreign controlled corporations, DISCs, and FSCs, and the denial of deferral of tax. The amount of the benefits to be denied is determined from the ratio of the value of the sales or purchases of goods and services (or other transactions) arising from the boycott activity to the total value of the foreign sales or purchases of goods and services (or other transactions) of the corporation.

Participation in, or cooperation with, an international boycott occurs when a person, in order to do business in a certain country, agrees not to do business with a specified second country or with other countries doing business in specified countries. An agreement not to hire employees of or to do business with other companies whose employees are of a specified nationality, race or religion is also boycott activity (Code Sec. 999(b)(3)).[148]

The following countries may require participation in, or cooperation with, an international boycott within the meaning of the Code: Bahrain, Iraq, Kuwait, Lebanon, Libya, Oman, Qatar, Saudi Arabia, Syria, United Arab Emirates and Republic of Yemen.[149] The reduction of foreign tax credit (¶ 2475) extends to the credit that the taxpayer is entitled to as a shareholder as well as to the credit for foreign taxes he paid himself (Code Sec. 908).[150] Taxpayers who participate in or cooperate with a boycott and derive income from such activities must report such information to the IRS by filing Form 5713 when their income tax is due (including extensions).

2496A. Illegal Payments. If an illegal bribe, kickback, or other payment is made by, or on behalf of, a controlled foreign corporation or a DISC, either directly or indirectly, to an official, employee, or agent-in-fact of a government, the amount of the bribe, kickback or other payment will affect shareholders. In the case of a controlled foreign corporation, the amount is included as Subpart F income for the year and thus is included in the shareholder's income (Code Sec. 952(a)(4)).[151] In the case of a DISC, the amount is considered a constructive dividend and must be included in the shareholders' income (Code Sec. 995(b)(1)(F)(iii)).[152] However, see ¶ 972 for rules permitting the deduction of certain payments that may be deducted, despite their possible illegality.

2496B. Information from Foreign Sources. Procedures have been established for formal document requests to obtain from a taxpayer foreign-based information regarding the taxpayer's tax affairs (Code Sec. 982).[153]

Foreign Currency Transactions

2497. Functional Currency. All federal income tax determinations must be made in the taxpayer's functional currency (Code Sec. 985(a)). Code Sec. 985—Code Sec. 989 provide rules for determining the functional currency of a reporting unit or taxpayer. Most often, the functional currency of a U.S. taxpayer will be the U.S. dollar. However, a qualified business unit (QBU), such as a foreign corporation or a foreign subsidiary of a U.S. corporation, may be required to adopt the functional currency of the economic environment in which it conducts a significant part of its activities and which is used in keeping its books and records (Code Sec. 985(b)(1)(B)). The taxable income or loss of a foreign branch and the foreign taxes, earnings and profits and other items of a foreign corporation must be translated into U.S. dollars (Code Secs. 986 and 987).[154]

Taxpayers who, for foreign tax credit purposes, account for foreign taxes on an accrual basis generally may translate foreign income taxes accrued into U.S. dollars at the average exchange rate for the tax year to which the taxes relate. All foreign taxes not eligible for translation at the yearly average exchange rate must be translated using the exchange rate for date of payment. However, the IRS has authority to specify periodic average exchange rates that may be used instead of actual daily exchange rates (Code Sec. 986(a) and Code Sec. 905(c)).[155]

2498. Nonfunctional Currency Transactions. Foreign currency gain or loss attributable to a nonfunctional currency transaction is treated separately from the underlying transaction and generally results in ordinary gain or loss (Code Sec. 988).[156] However, exchange gain of an individual from the disposition of foreign currency in a personal transaction is not taxable, provided that the gain realized does not exceed $200. A "personal transaction" is any transaction other than one with respect to which properly allocable expenses are deductible as trade or business expenses under Code Sec. 162 or expenses incurred in the production of income under Code Sec. 212(1) and Code Sec. 212(2). It also refers to an individual's currency exchange transactions that are entered into in connection with business travel, but does not affect tax treatment of capital losses (Code Sec. 988(e)).[157]

Footnote references are to paragraphs of the 2002 Standard Federal Tax Reports.

[149] ¶ 29,083.15	[153] ¶ 28,820	[156] ¶ 28,900
[150] ¶ 28,204	[154] ¶ 28,840, ¶ 28,860,	[157] ¶ 28,900
[151] ¶ 28,490	¶ 28,880, ¶ 28,920	
[152] ¶ 29,020	[155] ¶ 28,860	

Chapter 25

RETURNS □ PAYMENT OF TAX

	Par.

Filing

2501. Income Tax Returns—Types of Returns. Individuals who must file an income tax return use Form 1040EZ, 1040A, or 1040, along with any appropriate schedules; fiduciaries of estates and trusts who must file an income tax return use Form 1041; corporations must file an income tax return on Form 1120 or 1120-A; and partnerships must file an information return on Form 1065.

The following specialized income tax return forms for individuals also exist: Form 1040-C for a departing alien; Form 1040NR for a nonresident alien; Form 1040-SS (self-employment) for a resident of the Virgin Islands, Guam, American Samoa or the Northern Mariana Islands; and Form 1040-PR or 1040SS (self-employment) for a resident of Puerto Rico.

Specialized forms for certain types of corporations also exist: Schedule PH, attached to Form 1120, for a U.S. personal holding company; Form 1120-IC-DISC for an interest charge domestic international sales corporation; Form 1120F for a foreign corporation; Form 1120-FSC for a foreign sales corporation; Form 1120L for a life insurance company; Form 1120-PC for a property and casualty insurance company; Form 1120-POL for a political organization; Form 1120-REIT for a real estate investment trust; Form 1120-RIC for a regulated investment company; and Form 1120S for an S corporation.

Rules for determining which individuals must file an income tax return are set out at ¶ 109; rules for determining who must pay estimated tax are covered at ¶ 2682. Rules for corporation returns appear at ¶ 211. For rules applicable to partners and partnerships, see ¶ 406.

Employers who withhold income tax, social security tax, or both from their employees' wages are required to file quarterly returns on Form 941 to report the amount of tax withheld and their share of social security tax.[1] Schedule H (Form 1040) is to be filed by individuals who pay annual cash wages of $1,300 or more in 2001 for domestic service in their private homes ($1,300 for 2002). It is used to report and pay employer and employee social security taxes and any income tax withheld at the employee's request. Form 943 is to be filed annually by employers who pay wages for agricultural labor (including household employees in a private home on a farm operated for profit). It is used to report and pay social security taxes and voluntary income tax withholding. Form 940 is an annual form filed by employers and is used to report and pay federal unemployment taxes.

Footnote references are to paragraphs of the 2002 Standard Federal Tax Reports.

¶ 2501   [1] ¶ 33,662.01

2503. Electronic Filing. Electronic filing is a method by which qualified filers transmit tax return information directly to an IRS Service Center over telephone lines in the format of the official IRS forms. The IRS e-file program allows taxpayers to file their tax returns through an electronic return originator or by using a personal computer, modem, and commercial tax preparation software (the Form 1040 On-Line Filing Program). Taxpayers who e-file their returns can authorize direct debit payment from their checking or savings account on a specified date. Taxpayers may also charge their taxes by credit card (Internal Revenue News Release 2001-33).

At one time, electronic filers were required to submit their signatures on paper documents, i.e., Form 8453. However, taxpayers now have the option of filing electronically without submitting any paperwork. This version of paperless filing can be used by taxpayers who use a self-select personal identification number (Internal Revenue News Release 2001-01).

2505. Income Tax Returns—When to File. Subject to an exception for deadlines falling on a Saturday, Sunday or holiday (see ¶ 2549), the due dates for income tax returns are as follows:

Individual, trust, and estate income tax returns and the partnership information return are due on or before the 15th day of the 4th month following the close of the tax year (April 15 in the case of a calendar-year taxpayer) (Code Sec. 6072; Reg. § 1.6072-1(a)).[2] The final income tax return of a decedent for a fractional part of a year is due on the 15th day of the 4th month following the close of the 12-month period that began on the first day of that fractional year (Reg. § 1.6072-1(b)).[3]

The corporate income tax return of a domestic corporation or foreign corporation having a U.S. office is due on or before the 15th day of the 3rd month after the close of the tax year (March 15 for a calendar-year corporation). The U.S. income tax return of a foreign sales corporation is due by the 15th day of the 3rd month after the end of its tax year (Instructions for Form 1120-FSC). The return of an IC-DISC, an exempt farmers' cooperative, or other cooperative organization is due on or before the 15th day of the 9th month following the close of the tax year (September 15 for a calendar-year taxpayer) (Reg. § 1.6072-2).[4]

The due date for income tax returns of an organization exempt from tax under Code Sec. 501(a) (other than employees' trusts under Code Sec. 401(a)) is the 15th day of the 5th month following the close of the tax year (Reg. § 1.6072-2(c)).[5]

A taxpayer filing as a nonresident alien who is not subject to the wage withholding described at ¶ 2601 and a foreign corporation not having an office or place of business in the U.S. may file a return as late as the 15th day of the 6th month after the close of the tax year (Reg. § 1.6072-1(c) and Reg. § 1.6072-2(b)).[6] However, a nonresident alien who has wages subject to withholding is required to file a return on or before the 15th day of the 4th month following the close of the tax year.

A taxpayer may correct an error in a return, without incurring interest or penalties, by filing an amended return (Form 1040X) and paying any additional tax due on or before the last day prescribed for filing the original return.[7]

2509. Extension of Time. An individual is granted an automatic extension of four months for filing a return (but *not* for payment of tax), provided that Form 4868 is properly filed before the normal due date of the return (Reg. § 1.6081-4).[8] Filing extensions can be obtained without making tax payments if taxpayers properly estimate their tax liability on the form. If tax is not properly estimated, the extension request will be disallowed and the late-filing penalty will be assessed. If the amount of tax included with the extension request is less than sufficient to cover the taxpayer's liability, the taxpayer will be charged interest on the overdue

---

Footnote references are to paragraphs of the 2002 Standard Federal Tax Reports.
[2] ¶ 36,720, ¶ 36,721   [5] ¶ 36,724   [7] ¶ 35,141
[3] ¶ 36,721   [6] ¶ 36,721, ¶ 36,724   [8] ¶ 36,793
[4] ¶ 36,724

¶ 2509

amount. No late-payment penalty will be imposed if the tax paid through withholding, estimated tax payments, or any payment accompanying Form 4868 is at least 90% of the total tax due with Form 1040 and if the remaining unpaid balance is paid with the return within the extension period (Reg. § 1.6081-4 and Reg. § 301.6651-1).[9] An automatic extension should not be requested if the taxpayer has asked the IRS to compute the tax or if the taxpayer is under a court order to file the return by the original due date.

Except in cases of undue hardship, no additional extension of time for filing an individual income tax return will be granted unless an individual first takes advantage of the automatic extension. The total extension of time may not exceed six months, including the four months allowed under the automatic extension (except for U.S. taxpayers abroad, discussed below). Any further extension of time beyond the four-month automatic extension must be applied for in writing to the Internal Revenue Service Center where the individual will file the return (see ¶ 3) and must be specifically granted. The application for an extension beyond the automatic four-month extension period may be in the form of a letter, or Form 2688 may be used by individuals who file Form 1040 or 1040A. If an application for an extension beyond the automatic four-month extension period is denied, a taxpayer may be granted a 10-day grace period from the date of the denial or the due date of the return, whichever is later. However, the Tax Court denied the grace period where a taxpayer sought and was denied an extension which would have extended the due date beyond the six-month limit.[10]

Individual Residing Outside the United States. U.S. citizens or residents living outside the U.S. and Puerto Rico (including military personnel) are granted an automatic extension up to and including the 15th day of the sixth month following the close of their tax year for filing a return if they attach a statement to their return showing that they are entitled to such an extension (Reg. § 1.6081-5(a) and Reg. § 1.6081-5(b)).[11] In addition, the time for payment of tax is also extended for two months unless the IRS specifies otherwise. However, interest will be assessed on any unpaid tax from the due date of the return (without regard to the automatic extension) until the tax is paid (IRS Publication 54). The automatic filing extension runs concurrently with the automatic four-month extension allowed to all individuals. Thus, the maximum automatic extension is only four months from the regular due date. However, the application for the automatic four-month extension is timely if it is filed by the due date established by the two-month extension. If an individual outside the United States needs more than the automatic extension in order to meet either the bona fide residence or the physical presence test for the foreign earned income or housing exclusion, Form 2350 should be filed. Such filing will entitle the individual to additional time for filing the return but not for paying the tax. Any further extensions must be applied for under the rules discussed above (Reg. § 1.6081-4).[12]

Corporations. A corporation or an S corporation is entitled to an automatic extension of six months for filing its return, provided that it timely and properly files Form 7004 and deposits the full amount of the tax due with Form 8109. This extension, however, can be terminated by the IRS at any time by mailing to the taxpayer, or to the person requesting the extension, notice of such termination at least 10 days prior to the termination date fixed in the notice (Reg. § 1.6081-3(d)).[13]

Other Entities. An automatic extension of time (through the 15th day of the 6th month following the close of the tax year) is also granted to a partnership that keeps its books and records outside the United States and Puerto Rico, a domestic corporation that transacts its business and keeps its books and records outside the United States and Puerto Rico, a foreign corporation that maintains an office or place of business within the United States, and a domestic corporation whose principal income is from sources within U.S. possessions (Reg. § 1.6081-5(a)).[14] Form

---

Footnote references are to paragraphs of the 2002 Standard Federal Tax Reports.

¶ 2509

  [9] ¶ 36,794.01   [11] ¶ 36,795   [13] ¶ 36,790
  [10] ¶ 36,789.1195   [12] ¶ 36,793   [14] ¶ 36,795

2758 is to be used by the following entities to apply for extensions of time for filing returns: estates filing Form 1041; various trusts filing Forms 1041-A, 3520-A, 5227, and 6069; and certain exempt organizations filing Forms 990, 990-PF, 990-BL, and 4720. Partnerships filing Form 1065, real estate mortgage investment conduits filing Form 1066, and trusts filing Form 1041 should use Form 8736 to apply for a filing extension.

Sufficient Cause. Clear reasons must be given for a nonautomatic extension. "Illness" or "Practitioner too busy" are too vague without further explanation. However, the IRS will generally grant extensions where the taxpayer's tax preparer was unable to complete the tax return for reasons beyond the preparer's control or where, in spite of reasonable efforts, the taxpayer was unable to get professional help in time.[15]

2513. Place for Filing Returns. The return of an individual, estate, or trust is filed with the Service Center indicated at ¶ 3, except for certain charitable and split-interest trusts and pooled-income funds (see Instructions for Form 1041).

The return of a corporation, S corporation or partnership is filed with the Service Center indicated in the instructions to the entity's return (Form 1120, Form 1120S or Form 1065).

2517. Return Preparers. In addition to the prohibition against disclosure of return information (see ¶ 2894), a person who prepares income tax returns (or refund claims) for compensation is subject to the following rules:

(1) The preparer must include his identifying number (either social security number or alternative preparer identification number) on the taxpayer's return (Temporary Reg. § 1.6109-2T). Such a preparer must manually sign the return after the return is completed but before it is given to the taxpayer for signature. A signature stamp or label is generally unacceptable. However, if the preparer is employed to prepare returns for compensation, the employer is responsible for furnishing the identifying numbers of both the employer and the preparer (Code Sec. 6109(a) and Code Sec. 7701(a)(36); Reg. § 1.6695-1(b)).[16]

(2) The preparer must furnish the taxpayer with a completed copy of the prepared return no later than the time the original return is presented for signing. The preparer must also keep for three years (following the close of the return period) a copy of the return or a list of the names, identification numbers, and tax years of taxpayers for whom returns were prepared (Code Sec. 6107; Reg. § 1.6107-1).[17] The preparer need not sign the taxpayer's copy of the return.

(3) The preparer must keep a record, for three years following the close of the return period (the 12-month period beginning on July 1 of each year) to which the record relates, of the name, taxpayer identification number (TIN), and principal place of work of each income tax return preparer employed or engaged by the preparer at any time during the return period (Reg. § 1.6060-1).[18]

2518. Return Preparer Penalties. Several potential penalties may be assessed against tax return preparers.

Failure to Follow Procedures. Penalties assessable for failure to meet the requirements in (1)-(3) as described in ¶ 2517, unless such failure is due to reasonable cause and not to willful neglect, are (1) $50 for each failure to sign a return, to furnish an identifying number, or to furnish the taxpayer with a copy of the prepared return; (2) $50 for each failure to retain a copy of prepared returns or a list of taxpayers for whom returns were prepared; and (3) $50 for each failure to retain and make available a record of preparers employed, plus $50 for each failure to include an item required in such record. The penalty for failure to sign a return will not be imposed against preparers of Forms 1041 who use a facsimile signature and meet certain other requirements. A $500 penalty is assessable against a preparer

---

Footnote references are to paragraphs of the 2002 Standard Federal Tax Reports.
[15] ¶ 36,789.25   [17] ¶ 36,920, ¶ 36,921   [18] ¶ 36,561
[16] ¶ 36,962, ¶ 39,966, ¶ 43,113

who endorses or negotiates another's refund check (other than a bank preparer who negotiates customers' refund checks for bank account deposits) (Code Sec. 6695; Reg. § 1.6695-1).[19]

Understatement of Taxpayer's Liability Due to Unrealistic Position. A $250 penalty may be imposed against a return preparer for each tax return or claim for refund that understates the taxpayer's liability due to an unrealistic position (Code Sec. 6694(a)).[20] The penalty is increased to $1,000 per return or refund claim if the understatement is willful or reckless (Code Sec. 6694(b)).[21]

To avoid the penalty, positions taken on a return or refund claim must have a realistic possibility of being sustained on the merits or must be disclosed and have a reasonable basis. A realistic possibility of success means at least a one-in-three chance (Reg. § 1.6694-2(b)(1)).[22] Disclosures generally must be made on Form 8275 or 8275-R, as appropriate, except that the disclosure may be made on a return pursuant to an annual revenue procedure (Reg. § 1.6662-4(f) and Reg. § 1.6694-2(c)(3)).[23] The penalty may be excused if there is a reasonable cause for the understatement and the return preparer acted in good faith.

Failure To Be Diligent in Claiming Earned Income Credit. Income tax preparers must comply with due diligence requirements (to be imposed by the IRS through regulations) for claims for refunds or returns they prepare claiming the earned income credit (Code Sec. 6695(g)).[24] Each failure to observe the requirements regarding the amount of, or eligibility for, the credit will result in a penalty of $100, in addition to any other penalty imposed.

Aiding or Abetting in Tax Liability Understatement. Return preparers also may be penalized $1,000 for aiding or abetting in an understatement of tax liability on a return, claim or other document ($10,000 in the case of a corporation) (Code Sec. 6701).[25] Only one penalty may be imposed per taxpayer per period. The time period is not necessarily a year; for instance, understatements on quarterly employment tax returns may give rise to four separate penalties for a calendar year (Code Sec. 6701(b)(3)).[26] According to the Sixth Circuit, no statute of limitations applies to bar the penalty.[27] If this understatement penalty applies, the penalties for promoting abusive tax shelters (see ¶ 2011) and for a taxpayer's unrealistic position on a return of refund claim do not apply with respect to the same documents or conduct (Code Sec. 6701(f)).[28]

2521. Protest Returns. A civil penalty of $500 will be imposed upon an individual who files a purported income tax return if (1) the purported return fails to contain sufficient information from which the substantial correctness of the amount of tax liability can be judged or contains information that on its face indicates that the amount of tax shown is substantially incorrect and (2) such conduct arises from a frivolous position or from a desire to delay or impede administration of the tax laws. This penalty is imposed in addition to any other penalties imposed on the taxpayer (Code Sec. 6702).[29] Also, up to $25,000 may be assessed by the Tax Court against a taxpayer who institutes or maintains proceedings primarily for delay or on frivolous grounds or who unreasonably fails to pursue available administrative remedies. Other courts may require a taxpayer to pay a penalty of up to $10,000 if the taxpayer's action against the IRS for unauthorized collection activities appears to be a frivolous or groundless proceeding (Code Sec. 6673).[30] The Tax Court has held that a penalty for instituting proceedings primarily for delay is properly assessed against the tax matters person of an S corporation, rather than against the entity or its other shareholders.[31]

Footnote references are to paragraphs of the 2002 Standard Federal Tax Reports.

[19] ¶ 39,965, ¶ 39,966	[24] ¶ 39,965	[28] ¶ 40,033
[20] ¶ 39,955, ¶ 39,956A.01	[25] ¶ 40,033	[29] ¶ 40,040
[21] ¶ 39,955	[26] ¶ 40,033, ¶ 40,035.10	[30] ¶ 39,785
[22] ¶ 39,957	[27] ¶ 40,035.10	[31] ¶ 39,790.47
[23] ¶ 39,651H, ¶ 39,957		

¶ **2521**

Payment of Tax

2525. Place of Payment. The tax shown on the tax return is to be paid to the internal revenue officer with whom the return is filed unless, as in the case of corporations, the tax is required to be deposited with an authorized depository. See ¶ 2513.

The IRS requests that individuals use a payment voucher, Form 1040-V, for any balance due on any Forms 1040.

2529. Time of Payment. In general, the tax shown on an income tax return is to be paid, without assessment or notice and demand, at the time fixed for filing the return, determined without regard to any extension of time for filing the return. See ¶ 2505. However, exceptions apply when (1) a taxpayer shows that payment on the return due date will result in undue hardship (see ¶ 2537, below); (2) a taxpayer is residing outside the United States on the return due date (see ¶ 2509); or (3) a taxpayer elects to have the IRS compute the tax (¶ 124), in which case payment is due within 30 days after the IRS mails a notice and demand (Code Sec. 6151(b)(1)).[32]

The IRS also has the authority to enter into a written agreement with the taxpayer, allowing for the payment of any tax in installments, if such an agreement will facilitate the collection of a tax liability (Code Sec. 6159).[33] The fee for entering into an installment agreement is $43.[34]

2533. Taxes of Member of Armed Forces upon Death. When a member of the Armed Forces dies while serving in a combat zone or as a result of wounds, disease, or injury incurred while so serving, the income tax for the year of death and any prior year ending on or after the first day served in a combat zone is canceled, and any unpaid taxes of such individual that relate to tax years prior to service in a combat zone may also be abated. A similar tax forgiveness rule applies to U.S. military and civilian employees who die as the result of wounds or injury occurring outside the United States in a terroristic or military action against the United States or any of its allies (Code Sec. 692).[35] (Note that, as this publication goes to press, both the House and the Senate have proposals that would extend similar relief to victims of the September 11, 2001 terrorist attacks in New York City and Washington, DC.)

2537. Extension of Time for Payment of Tax. As noted at ¶ 2509, an extension of time for filing the return ordinarily does not postpone the time for payment. The IRS, however, may extend the time of payment of the tax shown on the return for up to six months (or longer if the taxpayer is abroad) upon a showing of undue hardship. A taxpayer applying for an extension of the time to pay tax must file Form 1127 on or before the original due date for payment of the tax. The application must be accompanied by evidence showing the undue hardship that would result if the extension were refused, a statement of the assets and liabilities of the taxpayer, and a statement of the receipts and disbursements of the taxpayer for the three months preceding the original due date for payment of tax (Code Sec. 6161(a); Reg. § 1.6161-1).[36]

As a condition to the granting of an extension, the taxpayer may be required to furnish a bond (Code Sec. 6165; Reg. § 1.6165-1).[37] If an extension of time for payment of tax is granted, interest is payable on any unpaid balance (see ¶ 2838) from the original due date to the date on which payment is received (Reg. § 1.6161-1(d)).[38]

Military and Government Personnel. Armed Forces members and civilians serving in support of the Armed Forces who serve in a designated combat zone (see ¶ 895) or are hospitalized outside the United States as a result of an injury received

---

Footnote references are to paragraphs of the 2002 Standard Federal Tax Reports.

[32] ¶ 37,080	[35] ¶ 24,920	[37] ¶ 37,260, ¶ 37,261
[33] ¶ 37,180	[36] ¶ 37,200, ¶ 37,201	[38] ¶ 37,201
[34] ¶ 37,180B		

while serving in a combat zone qualify for an extension for filing returns and paying tax for the period of combat service or hospitalization plus 180 days (Code Sec. 7508(a)).[39] This extension is also available to such a taxpayer's spouse who wishes to file a joint return (Code Sec. 7508(c)).[40]

Disaster Areas. The IRS is authorized to postpone deadlines for filing returns and paying taxes for up to 120 days (90 days prior to June 7, 2001) for taxpayers affected by a presidentially declared disaster (Code Sec. 7508A).[41]

Taxpayers (other than individuals) that were affected by the September 11, 2001 terrorist attacks in New York City and Washington, DC, and had an original filing deadline on or after September 11, 2001 through November 30, 2001, were given a 120-day postponement plus a six-month extension—to run consecutively—to file any return, declaration, statement or other document required by the Code or regulations for which the IRS has the authority under Code Sec. 6081, Code Sec. 6161 or Code Sec. 7508A to extend and to pay the taxes owed (Notice 2001-61).

2541. Extension of Time for Payment of Deficiency in Tax. An extension of time for payment of a deficiency of tax may be granted for a period of not more than 18 months where timely payment of the deficiency would result in undue hardship. Such an extension may be applied for according to the procedure for an extension of time for payment of tax outlined in ¶ 2537. An additional period of not more than 12 months may be granted in an exceptional case. A request for an extension will be refused if the deficiency was due to negligence, intentional disregard of income tax rules and regulations, or fraud (Code Sec. 6161(b); Reg. § 1.6161-1(a)(2) and Reg. § 1.6161-1(c)).[42]

2545. Forms of Payment. Payment of income tax must be made in cash or by bank check or money order or by any commercially acceptable means deemed appropriate by the IRS (Code Sec. 6311).[43] This includes, for example, electronic funds transfers, including those arising from credit cards, debit cards and charge cards (Temporary Reg. § 301.6311-2T). The IRS has also launched an on-line option, EFTPS-OnLine (EFTPS is short for the Electronic Federal Tax Payment System), for paying federal taxes for businesses and individuals (Internal Revenue News Release 2001-77).

Weekend and Holiday Deadlines

2549. "Deadlines" Falling on a Weekend or Holiday. If the last day for performing any act (such as filing a return, paying tax, or filing a claim for credit or refund) falls on Saturday, Sunday, or a legal holiday, the act is timely if it is performed on the next day that is not a Saturday, Sunday, or a legal holiday (Reg. § 301.7503-1).[44] The term "legal holiday" means a legal holiday in the District of Columbia. In the case of a return, statement, or other document required to be filed with an IRS office, the term "legal holiday" also includes a statewide legal holiday in the state in which the office is located (such as Patriots' Day in Massachusetts) (Code Sec. 7503).[45]

2553. Timely Mailing as Timely Filing and Paying. Any return, claim, statement, or document that must be filed with the IRS or the Tax Court, or any payment required to be made on or before a particular date, is regarded as having been timely filed or paid if it is actually delivered by mail or the date of the U.S. postmark falls on or before the due date (Code Sec. 7502(a)).[46] A taxpayer's testimony that she saw a clerk postmark her return has been held sufficient to prove a postmark date.[47] Federal tax returns (not claims, statements, or other documents) mailed from outside the U.S. are timely if they bear the official timely dated postmark of the foreign country.[48] However, unlike returns mailed from within the

---

Footnote references are to paragraphs of the 2002 Standard Federal Tax Reports.

[39] ¶ 42,686	[43] ¶ 38,085	[46] ¶ 42,620
[40] ¶ 42,686	[44] ¶ 42,631	[47] ¶ 42,625.428
[41] ¶ 42,687A	[45] ¶ 42,630	[48] ¶ 42,625.25
[42] ¶ 37,200, ¶ 37,201		

¶ **2541**

United States, returns bearing foreign postmarks must be *received* by the due date (*E.M. Sarrell*, 117 TC —, No. 11, CCH Dec. 54,494).

Returns, claims, statements or other documents properly sent by registered mail are considered to have been filed on time if the date of registration falls on or before the due date of the document. Such documents properly sent by certified mail are timely filed if the certified mail sender's receipt is postmarked on or before the due date of the document. Delivery by properly registered or certified mail is presumed to have occurred if the envelope or package was correctly addressed to the office for filing (Reg. § 301.7502-1(c)(2) and Reg. § 301.7502-1(d)).[49] The IRS is authorized to issue regulations that extend to electronically filed returns rules similar to those that apply to paper returns sent by registered mail (Code Sec. 7502(c)).[50]

The IRS has expanded the timely-mailed-is-timely-filed rule to designated private delivery services (Code Sec. 7502(f)).[51] See ¶ 3 for a listing of the available delivery services.

The timely-mailed-is-timely-filed rule has also been expanded to cover returns filed electronically (Temp. Reg. § 301.7502-1T). The date of an electronic postmark given by an authorized electronic return transmitter will be deemed to be the filing date if the date of the electronic postmark is on or before the filing due date.

A tax deposit received by an authorized depository (no longer including Federal Reserve Banks) after the due date for the deposit is timely if it has been properly mailed at least two days before the prescribed due date. However, if any person is required to deposit tax more than once a month and the deposit amounts to $20,000 or more, the deposit must be received on or before the prescribed due date in order to be timely (Code Sec. 7502(e)).[52]

Signature

2557. Signatures on Returns. Forms 1040, 1040A, and 1040EZ must be signed by the individual taxpayer (Reg. § 1.6061-1).[53] The return contains a declaration that it is made under the penalties of perjury (Code Sec. 6065).[54] In the case of a joint return, both the husband and the wife must sign. If the taxpayer did not prepare the return, the return must be signed by the taxpayer and the tax return preparer (see ¶ 2517). If a decedent's return is filed by a representative, the representative should sign the return on the line indicated for the taxpayer and attach a written power of attorney.

Fiscal-Year Taxpayers

2561. Proration. When the effective date of a tax rate change occurs within a tax year, a taxpayer must compute the tax for the entire tax year by using both the old and the new rates (Code Sec. 15).[55] The final tax is the sum of (1) the tax calculated at the old rates that is proportionate to the portion of the tax year before the effective date of the new tax and (2) the tax calculated at the new rates that is proportionate to the portion of the tax year beginning with the effective date.

When the tax rate change involves the highest rate of income tax, the taxpayer must compute the tax for the year by using a weighted average of the highest rates before and after the change determined on the basis of the respective portions of the tax year before the date of change and on or after the date of change.

Information Returns and Payment at Source

2565. Payments Made in Course of Trade or Business. Every person engaged in a trade or business, including a partnership and a nonprofit organization,

---

[49] ¶ 42,621 [52] ¶ 42,620 [54] ¶ 36,680
[50] ¶ 42,620 [53] ¶ 36,603 [55] ¶ 3385
[51] ¶ 42,620

must file information returns for each calendar year for certain payments made during such year in the course of the payer's trade or business (Code Sec. 6041— Code Sec. 6050S).[56] In many cases the information contained on such returns must be reported to the IRS by means of magnetic media (tapes, tape cartridges and diskettes) or electronic filing. Recipients must be furnished a copy of the information return or a comparable statement. While payee statements are generally required to be in written form, persons required to furnish recipients copies of Form W-2, Form 1098-E or Form 1098-T (see below) may furnish electronic payee statements to recipients with the permission of the recipient (Temp. Reg. § 1.6041-2T, Temp. Reg. § 1.6050S-2T, and Temp. Reg. § 31.6051-1T). The following information returns are currently being filed:

Form 1098. Persons file this form if they receive $600 or more in mortgage interest from an individual in the course of a trade or business. Points paid directly by a borrower (including seller-paid points) for the purchase of a principal residence must be reported on Form 1098.[57] Refunds and reimbursements of overpaid mortgage interest must also be reported on Form 1098 (Reg. § 1.6050H-2).[58]

Form 1098-E. This form is filed by financial institutions, governmental units or educational institutions that, in the course of a trade or business, receive interest of $600 or more in a calendar year on a student loan that is used solely to pay for qualified higher education expenses.

Form 1098-T. This form is filed by an educational institution that receives qualified tuition and related expenses on behalf of a student.

Form 1099-A. Persons who lend money in connection with their trade or business and, in full or partial satisfaction of the debt, acquire an interest in property that is security for the debt must file this form. The form must also be filed if the person has reason to know that the property securing the debt has been abandoned.

Form 1099-B. Brokers are to use this form to report sales (including short sales) of stock, bonds, commodities, regulated futures contracts, foreign currency contracts, forward contracts, and debt instruments. Barter exchanges are to use the form to report exchanges of property or services through the exchange (Code Sec. 6045).[59] Filing is not required for transactions involving property or services with a fair market value of less than $1 (Notice 2000-6.)

Form 1099-C. Financial institutions, credit unions and federal agencies must file this form for each debtor for which a debt of $600 or more was cancelled. Multiple discharges of debt of less than $600 during a year need not be aggregated unless the separate discharges occurred with the purpose of evading the reporting requirements. The returns must be filed regardless of whether the debtor is subject to tax on the discharged debt. For example, debts discharged in bankruptcy must be reported (Code Sec. 6050P).[60]

Form 1099-DIV. Corporate payers file this form for each person (1) to whom payments of $10 or more in distributions, such as dividends, capital gains, or nontaxable distributions, were made on stock; (2) for whom any foreign tax was withheld and paid on dividends and on other distributions on stock if the recipient can claim a credit for the tax; (3) for whom any federal income tax was withheld under the backup withholding rules; or (4) to whom payments of $600 or more were made as part of a liquidation. S corporations use this form only to report distributions made during the calendar year out of accumulated earnings and profits.

Form 1099-G. Government units use this form to report payments of $10 or more for unemployment benefits and state and local tax refunds, credits, or offsets, and payments of $600 or more in taxable grants.

Form 1099-INT. Payers file this form for each person to whom payments of $10 or more in interest were paid, including interest on bearer certificates of deposit and

Footnote references are to paragraphs of the 2002 Standard Federal Tax Reports.

¶ 2565   [56] ¶ 35,820 et seq.   [58] ¶ 36,184   [60] ¶ 36,310
             [57] ¶ 36,186.035   [59] ¶ 35,920

interest on U.S. Savings Bonds, Treasury bills, Treasury notes, and Treasury bonds. Interest paid in the course of a trade or business is reportable when the amount totals $600 or more for any person. Form 1099-INT must also be filed to report interest of $10 or more (other than original issue discount) accrued to a REMIC regular interest holder during the year or paid to the holder of a collateralized debt obligation.

Form 1099-MISC. This form is filed by payers for each person to whom at least $10 in gross royalty payments, or $600 for rents or services in the course of a trade or business, was paid. Some of the items reported on this form are: (1) payments for real estate, machine and pasture rentals; (2) royalties paid to authors; (3) prizes and awards that were not paid for services rendered; (4) amounts withheld as backup withholding; (5) payments by medical and health care insurers to each physician or health care provider under health, accident and sickness insurance programs; (6) compensation, such as fees, commissions and awards, and golden parachute payments, paid to a nonemployee for services (including payments to attorneys for legal services (Code Sec. 6045(f))); (7) notification of the occurrence of sales of $5,000 or more of consumer products to a person on a buy-sell or commission basis for resale anywhere other than in a permanent retail establishment; (8) fishing boat proceeds; and (9) crop insurance proceeds of $600 or more.

Form 1099-OID. Issuers of bonds or certificates of deposit use this form to report original issue discount of $10 or more.

Form 1099-PATR. Cooperatives use this form to report distributions of $10 or more to patrons.

Form 1099-R. Payers file this form to report any distributions of $10 or more from retirement or profit-sharing plans, individual retirement arrangements (IRAs), simplified employee pensions (SEPs), annuities or insurance contracts.

Form 1099-S. This form is used to report the sale or exchange of real estate and the real property taxes imposed on the purchaser as a result of the sale or exchange. Included are sales or exchanges of residences, land, commercial buildings, condominium units, and stock in cooperative housing corporations.[61] The form must be filed by the person responsible for closing the real estate transaction or, if no such person exists, by the mortgage lender, the transferor's broker, the transferee's broker or the transferee, in that order. Payments of timber royalties under a "pay-as-cut" contract are also reported on the form.

Form 5498. This form is filed for each person for whom an IRA or a SEP was maintained. It is used to report the contributions made during the year to the IRA (including rollover contributions and contributions under a SEP plan) and the fair market value of the IRA or SEP account on December 31. Form 5498 is due by May 31 of the year following the year of contribution.

Form 8027. Each employer that runs a "large food or beverage establishment" (see ¶ 2601) must file an annual return of the receipts from food or beverage operations and tips reported by employees. In addition, in certain circumstances, the employer is required to allocate amounts as tips to employees.

Form 8300. Each person engaged in a trade or business who, in the course of such trade or business, receives more than $10,000 in cash in one transaction (or two or more related transactions) must file this form. The form is to be filed with the IRS by the 15th day after the transaction, and a similar statement is to be provided to the payer on or before January 31 of the calendar year following the year of receipt.

Form W-2. This form is to be furnished to both the Social Security Administration and the recipient. Employers use the form to report wages, tips, other compensation, withheld income and FICA taxes, and advance earned income credit (EIC) payments. Bonuses, vacation allowances, severance pay, moving expense payments, some kinds of travel allowances and third-party payments of sick pay are included.

Due Dates. Unless otherwise specified, the above information returns for 2001 are to be provided to the IRS by February 28, 2002, and to recipients by January 31, 2002. Form W-2 is to be provided to the Social Security Administration by February 28, 2002, and to recipients by January 31, 2002. The due date for filing information returns with the IRS is extended from February 28 to April 1, 2002, for returns filed electronically (Code Sec. 6071(b); Reg. § 31.6071(a)-1(a)(3)(i)). Form 8809 is used to request a 30-day extension of time to file Forms 1098, 1099 and 5498 with the IRS or Form W-2 with the Social Security Administration. This form cannot be used to request an extension of time to furnish required statements to recipients.

Other Information Returns. Other information returns are required with respect to: a U.S. person's acquisition of, or change of interest in, a foreign partnership (Code Sec. 6046A); cases of liquidation or dissolution of a corporation, including an exempt organization (Code Sec. 6043); corporate acquisitions and recapitalizations (Code Sec. 6043); organizations or reorganizations of foreign corporations (Code Sec. 6046); creation of, or transfers to, foreign trusts or the death of a U.S. citizen or resident who had been treated as the owner of, or whose estate included any portion of, a foreign trust (Code Sec. 6048); U.S. persons who own interests in foreign partnerships or corporations (Code Sec. 6038); U.S. persons who transfer property to foreign partnerships or corporations (Code Sec. 6038B); payors of long-term care benefits (Code Sec. 6050Q); U.S. persons (other than tax-exempt organizations) that receive foreign gifts during the tax year totaling more than $10,000 ($11,273 in 2001 and $11,642 projected for 2002) (Code Sec. 6039F); individuals who lose citizenship, and long-term residents who terminate residency in the United States (Code Sec. 6039G); the purchase of fish for resale (Code Sec. 6050R); and applicable to tax years beginning after June 7, 2001, Alaska Native Settlement Trusts (Code Sec. 6039H, as added by the Economic Growth and Tax Relief Reconciliation Act of 2001).

In addition, the head of each federal executive agency generally must file Forms 8596 and 8596-A on a quarterly basis stating the name, address, and taxpayer identification number (TIN) of each person to whom the agency makes payments of remuneration of $600 or more (Code Sec. 6041A).[62]

2570. Interest in Foreign Bank. A U.S. person who has a financial interest in or signature authority over any bank, securities, or other financial account in a foreign country that exceeded $10,000 in aggregate value at any time during the calendar year must report that relationship by filing Form TD F 90-22.1 with the Treasury Department before July 1 of the following year.[63]

2579. Taxpayer Identification Number. Persons filing returns and other documents must record on such items a taxpayer identification number (TIN). Individuals use their social security number on Forms 1040, 1040A, and 1040EZ. Executors of individuals' estates who must file Form 706 are to use both their social security number and the decedent's social security number. For corporations, partnerships, estates and trusts, and similar nonindividual taxpayers, the identifying number is the employer identification number.

A prospective adoptive parent can apply for an adoptive taxpayer identification number (ATIN) for a child who is in the process of being adopted (Reg. § 301.6109-3). Application for an ATIN must be made on Form W-7A.

Persons who file information returns (see ¶ 2565) may request the recipient of any payments to furnish his TIN on Form W-9.

A penalty of $50 per failure applies to a taxpayer who omits his own TIN from a required return, statement, or document. Failure to furnish one's TIN to another person when so required or to include another person's TIN in any document for information reporting purposes will also give rise to a $50 penalty. The maximum penalty per calendar year for failure to include TINs is $100,000 (Code Sec. 6723 and Code Sec. 6724(d)(3)).[64]

Footnote references are to paragraphs of the 2002 Standard Federal Tax Reports.

¶ 2570   [62] ¶ 35,840   [63] ¶ 35,141   [64] ¶ 40,250, ¶ 40,275

Chapter 26

WITHHOLDING □ ESTIMATED TAX

WITHHOLDING

Withholding on Wages

2601. Withholding of Income Tax on Wages. Withholding of income tax by an employer is required on each of an employee's wage payments. Generally, the term "wages" includes all remuneration (other than fees paid to a public official) for services performed by an employee for an employer, including the cash value of all remuneration (including benefits) paid in any medium other than cash (Code Sec. 3401(a)).[1] Salaries, fees, bonuses, commissions on sales or on insurance premiums, taxable fringe benefits, pensions and retirement pay (unless taxed as an annuity) are, if paid as compensation for services, subject to withholding (Reg. § 31.3401(a)-1(a)(2)).[2]

    The term "employer" includes not only individuals and organizations engaged in trade or business, but also organizations exempt from income, social security and unemployment taxes (Reg. § 31.3401(d)-1).[3] Withholding also applies to wages and salaries of employees, corporate officers, or elected officials of federal, state, and local government units (Code Sec. 3401(c)).[4]

    The term "employee" must be distinguished from an "independent contractor" for purposes of employment tax obligations. An employer does not generally have to withhold taxes on payments to independent contractors. In addition to the common law definition that focuses on the control that is exercised over what work is done and how it is done, the IRS will use a 20-factor test to assist in making this determination. The factors are (1) employee compliance with instructions required; (2) training; (3) integration of worker's services into the business; (4) services are

---

Footnote references are to paragraphs of the 2002 Standard Federal Tax Reports.
[1] ¶ 33,502   [3] ¶ 33,537   [4] ¶ 33,502
[2] ¶ 33,503   **¶ 2601**

rendered personally; (5) ability to hire, supervise and pay assistants; (6) a continuing relationship; (7) set hours of work are established; (8) full time is required; (9) work performed on business's premises; (10) services performed in a set order or sequence; (11) oral or written reports required; (12) payment by hour, week or month; (13) payment of business and/or travel expenses; (14) tools and materials furnished; (15) worker invests in facilities; (16) worker can realize a profit or loss; (17) worker performs services for more than one business at a time; (18) worker makes services available to the general public; (19) business has the right to discharge worker; and (20) worker has the right to terminate the relationship (Rev. Rul. 87-41).[5]

Tips. Cash tips paid directly to an employee by a customer and tips paid over to the employee for charge customers must be accounted for by the employee in a written statement furnished to the employer on or before the 10th day of the month following the month when they are received. The employee reports the tips on Form 4070, "Employee's Report of Tips to Employer," or on a similar statement. An exception exists if the tips received by the employee in the course of his employment by a single employer amount to less than $20 in a calendar month (Code Sec. 3401(a)(16) and Code Sec. 6053(a)).[6] These tips are subject to withholding (Code Sec. 3401(a)(16)(B)).[7] However, the only tips that an employer must report on Form W-2 are those that are actually reported to him by the employee (Code Sec. 6051(a)).[8]

A large food and beverage establishment (one which normally has more than 10 employees on a typical business day and in which tipping is customary) must file annual information returns (Form 8027; see ¶ 2565). These returns must report gross food and beverage sales receipts, employee-reported tip income, total charge receipts, and total charge tips (Code Sec. 6053(c); Reg. § 31.6053-3).[9] Such employers must allocate among their employees who customarily receive tip income an amount equal to the excess of 8 percent of gross receipts over reported tips. This allocation is not required if the employees voluntarily report total tips equal to at least 8 percent of gross sales. If it can be shown that average tips are not 8 percent of gross sales, the employer or a majority of its employees may apply to the IRS to have the allocation reduced from 8 percent, but not to below 2 percent (Code Sec. 6053(c)).[10]

Compensation. Retroactive wages and overtime payments under the Fair Labor Standards Act are subject to withholding, but payments under the Act for liquidated damages are not.[11] Back pay awards by the NLRB are also subject to withholding.[12]

The basis used in determining compensation, whether piecework, percentage of profits, hourly rate, or fixed salary, is immaterial. Overtime, vacation allowances[13] and dismissal payments[14] are wages subject to withholding, as are Christmas gift merchandise certificates given to employees (although the value of turkeys, hams or other merchandise of nominal value distributed at Christmas or on other holidays to promote goodwill is *not* subject to withholding) [15] and payments by employers made directly to employees for medical insurance.[16]

Withholding is based on *gross* wage payments before deductions such as those under the federal or state unemployment insurance laws, those for pension funds (except deductible contributions to IRAs, (see ¶ 2609)), insurance, etc., or those for liabilities of the employee paid by the employer.[17]

Employers required to withhold tax with respect to non-cash fringe benefits may deem those benefits paid at any time on or after the date on which they are provided but no later than the last day of the calendar quarter in which they are

---

Footnote references are to paragraphs of the 2002 Standard Federal Tax Reports.

[5] ¶ 33,538.66	[10] ¶ 36,460	[14] ¶ 33,506.1853
[6] ¶ 33,502, ¶ 36,460	[11] ¶ 33,506.1866	[15] ¶ 33,506.1825
[7] ¶ 33,502	[12] ¶ 33,506.1813	[16] ¶ 33,506.1871
[8] ¶ 36,420	[13] ¶ 33,506.397,	[17] ¶ 33,506.023
[9] ¶ 36,460, ¶ 36,463	¶ 33,562.01	

¶ 2601

provided (Reg. § 31.3501(a)-1T).[18] Withholding on payments, other than wages, to nonresident aliens is governed by special rules covered at ¶ 2492-¶ 2494.

2604. Included and Excluded Wages. If an employee works on two jobs for the same employer, and only a part of the remuneration is "wages" (e.g., a construction worker who also works on his employer's farm (exempt employment)), all of the remuneration is treated alike—either (1) all is subject to withholding if more than half of the time is spent performing services for which wages are received or (2) all is excluded if more than half of the time spent is in exempt services— provided the payroll period is not longer than 31 consecutive days (Reg. § 31.3402(e)-1).[19]

An employer is required to withhold income tax from "wages" paid for "employment" regardless of the circumstances under which the employee is employed or the frequency or size of amounts of the individual wage payments.[20] Tax must be withheld from the wages paid for *each* payroll period.[21] However, see ¶ 2634 as to an employee's possible exemption from withholding.

When a retail commission salesperson is occasionally paid other than in cash, the employer is not required to withhold income tax for the noncash pay (Reg. § 31.3402(j)-1).[22] However, the fair market value of the noncash pay, such as prizes, must be included on the Form W-2 furnished to the employee as part of the total pay earned by the employee during the calendar year.[23]

Withholding is also available, if the payee so requests, for wage continuation payments (i.e., sick pay) received from a third party pursuant to a health or accident plan in which the employer participates (Code Sec. 3402(o); Reg. § 31.3402(o)-3).[24] Payments of sick pay made directly by employers to their employees are automatically subject to withholding.[25] Employers who are third-party payors of sick pay are not required to withhold income taxes from payments unless the employee has requested withholding on Form W-4S.[26]

2607. Certain Gambling Winnings. Certain gambling winnings are subject to withholding. For winnings paid after August 6, 2001, an amount equal to the product of the third lowest rate of tax applicable to single filers is required to be withheld. For 2001, the applicable tax rate is 30.5 percent. However, winnings paid on or before August 6, 2001 are subject to a 28-percent withholding (Act Sec. 101(c)(8) of the Economic Growth and Tax Relief Reconciliation Act of 2001)[27] (see IRS Publication 15-T). This withholding requirement is imposed on winnings of more than $5,000 from sweepstakes, wagering pools, and lotteries. Withholding is generally imposed on other types of gambling winnings (including pari-mutual pools with respect to horse races, dog races and jai alai) only if the winnings exceed $5,000 and at least 300 times the wager. In addition, the payor of gambling winnings from these activities must report winnings of more than $600 by filing Form W-2G "Certain Gambling Winnings." Backup withholding (see¶ 2645) is required if the winner of reportable amounts does not furnish his TIN to the payor. No withholding is required on winnings from bingo, keno, or slot machines. However, for winnings of $1,200 or more from a bingo game or slot machine and for winnings of $1,500 or more from a keno game, the payor must file Form W-2G (Code Sec. 3402(q) and Code Sec. 6041; Reg. § 7.6041-1).[28] Withholding is imposed on proceeds from wagering transactions other than bingo, keno or slot machines at the rate stated above if such proceeds exceed $5,000, regardless of the odds of the wager.

Footnote references are to paragraphs of the 2002 Standard Federal Tax Reports.

[18] ¶ 33,661, ¶ 33,662.058
[19] ¶ 33,551
[20] ¶ 33,593.165
[21] ¶ 33,544.20
[22] ¶ 33,574
[23] ¶ 33,575.01, ¶ 33,575.20
[24] ¶ 33,542, ¶ 33,584
[25] ¶ 33,542, ¶ 33,585.021
[26] ¶ 33,584, ¶ 33,585.021, ¶ 36,424
[27] ¶ 33,589.25
[28] ¶ 33,542, ¶ 35,820, ¶ 35,835

2609. Exempt Remuneration of Employees. Some types of salaries or wages are *specifically* excluded by law from the definition of "wages" for income tax *withholding* purposes. Specifically excluded are amounts paid for the services of:

newspaper carriers under age 18 delivering to customers;

newspaper and magazine vendors buying at fixed prices and retaining excess from sales to customers;

domestic workers;

agricultural workers who are not subject to FICA withholding;

cash or noncash tips of less than $20 per month;

moving expenses;

certain employer contributions to IRAs and deferred compensation plans;

individuals not working in the course of the employer's business (less than $50 paid and less than 24 days worked during the current or preceding quarter);

employees of foreign governments and international organizations;

armed forces personnel serving in a combat zone;

foreign earned income if excludable from gross income; and

members of a religious order performing services for the order or associated institution.

The employer's cost of group-term life insurance, including any amount in excess of $50,000 coverage, which is taxable to the employee as compensation, is exempt from withholding (Code Sec. 79(a)(1) and Code Sec. 3401(a)(14); Reg. § 31.3401(a)(14)-1).[29] However, the employer must report the cost of the insurance coverage includible in the employee's gross income on Form W-2 (Reg. § 1.6052-1).[30] An employer's reimbursement of an employee's moving expenses is also exempt if it is reasonable to believe a moving expense deduction will be allowable to the employee under Code Sec. 217 (Code Sec. 3401(a)(15)).[31] In addition, the value of any meals or lodging excludable by the employee from gross income under Code Sec. 119 (see ¶ 873) is exempt from withholding (Reg. § 31.3401(a)-1(b)(9)).[32]

Benefits provided by an employer to an employee in the form of certain educational assistance (see ¶ 871),[33] dependent care assistance, fellowship or scholarship grants, or nontaxable fringe benefits (such as working condition fringe benefits (see ¶ 863)) are not subject to withholding if it is reasonable to believe that the employee is entitled to exclude the payment from income. Benefits provided by the employer in the form of medical care reimbursement made to or for the benefit of an employee under a self-insured medical reimbursement plan are excluded from wages for withholding purposes (Code Sec. 3401(a)(20)).[34] Amounts paid to, or on behalf of, an employee or his beneficiary to an individual retirement plan pursuant to a simplified employee pension are not wages subject to withholding if it is reasonable to believe that the employee will be entitled to an exclusion for such payments (Code Sec. 3401(a)(12)).[35]

In many cases, however, employee and employer may enter into a mutual agreement to withhold from the employee's remuneration (Code Sec. 3402(p)).[36] To effectuate this agreement, the employee must submit Form W-4 to the employer, and the employer must begin withholding.

Certain Federal Payments. Taxpayers may request voluntary withholding from certain federal payments. The payments include social security benefits, crop disaster payments, Commodity Credit Corporation loans, and any other payment to be specified in regulations by the IRS (Code Sec. 3402(p)(1)).[37]

Unemployment Benefits. Similarly, states are required to permit voluntary withholding on unemployment compensation at a rate of 10 percent (Code Sec.

Footnote references are to paragraphs of the 2002 Standard Federal Tax Reports.

[29] ¶ 6360, ¶ 33,502, ¶ 33,527
[30] ¶ 36,441
[31] ¶ 33,502, ¶ 33,506.207

[32] ¶ 33,503, ¶ 33,506.1880, ¶ 33,506.189
[33] ¶ 7353.01
[34] ¶ 33,502
[35] ¶ 33,502

[36] ¶ 33,542
[37] ¶ 33,542

¶ 2609

3402(p)(2) and Act Sec. 101(c)(7) of the Economic Growth and Tax Relief Reconciliation Act of 2001).[38]

2611. Other Payments *Not* Subject to Withholding. Generally, withholding does not apply to payments made to physicians, lawyers, dentists, veterinarians, contractors, and others pursuing an independent trade, business or profession, because they are not considered employees (Reg. § 31.3401(c)-1(c)).[39]

Payments of supplemental unemployment compensation are treated as wages, but withholding applies only to the extent that such benefits are includable in the employee's gross income (Code Sec. 3402(o)).[40] Guaranteed annual wage payments made during periods of unemployment pursuant to a collective bargaining agreement are "wages" subject to withholding.[41] However, strike benefits (other than hourly wages received for strike-related duties) paid by a union to its members are not subject to withholding.[42]

Death benefit payments to beneficiaries or to the estates of deceased employees and payments to such persons of compensation due but unpaid at the time of the decedent's death are not subject to withholding.[43]

Benefits paid under workers' compensation laws (other than nonoccupational disability benefits) are not taxable compensation for services performed and are not subject to withholding[44] nor are amounts received by employees as reimbursements for medical care or as payments for permanent injury or for loss of bodily function (Code Sec. 3401(a)(20)).[45] Also, employer-provided health insurance coverage paid for by salary reduction does not constitute wages for withholding purposes.[46]

For more information concerning amounts paid to employees as advances or reimbursements for traveling, meals, etc., see ¶ 2662 and ¶ 2663.

Methods of Withholding

2614. Major Methods of Withholding. The law provides two methods of computing the tax to be withheld: (1) the "percentage" method (see ¶ 2616) and (2) the "wage bracket" method (see ¶ 2619) (Code Sec. 3402(b), Code Sec. 3402(c) and Code Sec. 3402(h)).[47] For other permissible methods of withholding, see ¶ 2627.

Regardless of which method is used, the amount of withholding will depend upon the amount of wages paid, the number of exemptions claimed by the employee on the withholding exemption certificate (see ¶ 2634), the employee's marital status, and the payroll period of the employee (see ¶ 2621) (Code Sec. 3402(a), Code Sec. 3402(f) and Code Sec. 3402(g)).[48]

See "Employer's Tax Guide (Circular E)," IRS Publication 15, for additional information.

2616. Percentage Method. If the employer selects the percentage method of withholding, he must: (1) multiply the amount of one withholding exemption for the payroll period by the number of exemptions claimed on the employee's Form W-4; (2) subtract the amount determined in (1) from the employee's wages; and (3) apply the appropriate percentage rate table to the resulting figure to determine the amount of withholding (Code Sec. 3402(a)).[49]

Percentage method withholding tables for both single (including heads of household) and married employees for each of the payroll periods are provided for use in determining the amount of tax to be withheld (Code Sec. 3402(a)).[50] The IRS has approved and issued alternative formula tables for percentage method withholding that were devised for computing withheld tax under different payroll systems and equipment.[51]

Footnote references are to paragraphs of the 2002 Standard Federal Tax Reports.

[38] ¶ 33,542	[43] ¶ 33,506.1856	[48] ¶ 33,542
[39] ¶ 33,536	[44] ¶ 33,506.43	[49] ¶ 33,542
[40] ¶ 33,542	[45] ¶ 33,502	[50] ¶ 151—¶ 152, ¶ 33,542
[41] ¶ 33,506.3683	[46] ¶ 33,506.1871	[51] ¶ 153
[42] ¶ 33,506.3678	[47] ¶ 33,542	

2619. Wage Bracket Method. The wage bracket tables provided by the IRS for graduated withholding cover weekly, biweekly, semimonthly and monthly payroll periods.[52] Separate tables for each period are provided for single persons (including heads of household) and married persons. The proper columns to be used by the employer are determined by the total number of exemptions claimed on the employee's withholding exemption certificate. These tables produce about the same result as the percentage method tables and are designed to accommodate different payroll systems and equipment. See IRS Publication 15.

If the wage bracket method is used, wages in excess of the highest wage bracket in the tables may, at the election of the employer, be rounded off to the nearest dollar (Reg. § 31.3402(c)-1(e)).[53]

2621. Payroll Period. The employee's correct "payroll period" (the period of service for which a payment of wages is ordinarily made to an employee) will determine the exemption amount (see ¶ 2616 and ¶ 2619) to be used if the employer uses the percentage method or the correct table to be used if the employer uses the wage bracket method. Daily, weekly, biweekly, semimonthly, monthly, quarterly, semiannual and annual payroll periods have separate tables for the percentage computation. Any other payroll period is a miscellaneous payroll period. Wages may also be paid for periods that are not payroll periods (see ¶ 2624).

2624. Computation of Withholding Allowance. If an employee has an established payroll period, the amount of the withholding allowance (for the percentage method) is determined by the payroll period, without regard to the time the employee is actually engaged in performing services during such period.

If the payment is for a period that is not a payroll period, such as when wages are paid upon completion of a particular project, the exemption (or the amount withheld, if the wage bracket method is used) is computed based on a miscellaneous payroll period containing a number of days (including Sundays and holidays) equal to those in the period covered by the payment (Code Sec. 3402(b); Reg. § 31.3402(c)-1(c)(2)).[54]

If the wages are paid without regard to any period, the tax to be withheld is the same as for a miscellaneous payroll period containing the number of days equal to the days (including Sundays and holidays) which have elapsed since (1) the date of the last payment of wages by the employer during the calendar year, (2) the date of commencement of employment with the employer during such year, or (3) January 1 of such year, whichever is later (Code Sec. 3402(b); Reg. § 31.3402(c)-1(c)(3)).[55]

2627. Alternative Methods of Withholding. An employer may withhold on the basis of average wages by using estimated quarterly wages, annualized wages, cumulative wages, or any method which produces substantially the same amount of withholding as the percentage or wage bracket method (Code Sec. 3402(h); Reg. § 31.3402(h)(1)-1—Reg. § 31.3402(h)(4)-1).[56]

2629. Employee Requests to Increase Withholding. An employee may request on Form W-4 that the employer withhold additional amounts. However, the IRS has not yet prescribed rules for decreases in the amount of withholding (Code Sec. 3402(i); Reg. § 31.3402(i)-1 and Reg. § 31.3402(i)-2).[57]

In addition, amounts may be voluntarily withheld from certain types of income that are not subject to mandatory withholding (see¶ 2609). Thus, for example, magazine vendors, domestic workers, etc., may enter into an agreement with their employer to have income tax withheld (Code Sec. 3402(p); Reg. § 31.3401(a)-3).[58]

Footnote references are to paragraphs of the 2002 Standard Federal Tax Reports.

¶ 2619

[52] ¶ 154	[55] ¶ 33,542, ¶ 33,547	[57] ¶ 33,542, ¶ 33,571,
[53] ¶ 33,547	[56] ¶ 33,542, ¶ 33,566—	¶ 33,572
[54] ¶ 33,542, ¶ 33,547	¶ 33,569	[58] ¶ 33,508, ¶ 33,542

Withholding Exemptions

2632. Claiming Withholding Exemptions. Every employee is entitled to his or her own withholding exemption and one for each dependent. A married employee may claim a withholding exemption for his or her spouse if the latter does not claim one. A student or a child under age 19 may claim a withholding exemption even though a dependency exemption is claimed by his parent (Code Sec. 3402(f)(1)).[59] No withholding exemption is allowed for unborn children even though the birth is expected to occur within the tax year. Employees with more than one job may not claim an exemption that is currently in effect with another employer (Code Sec. 3402(f)(7)).[60]

In order to avoid excess withholding, a standard deduction allowance may be claimed by an employee, provided that the employee does not have a spouse who is receiving wages subject to withholding and does not have withholding certificates in effect with more than one employer. The standard deduction allowance is equivalent to one withholding exemption (or more than one if regulations so prescribe) (Code Sec. 3402(f)(1)(E)).[61]

Additional withholding allowances are available to an employee who can show that he or she will have large itemized deductions, deductible alimony payments, moving expenses, employee business expenses, retirement contributions, net losses from Schedules C, D, E, and F of Form 1040, or tax credits. An eligible employee should file Form W-4 with the employer (Code Sec. 3402(m); Reg. § 31.3402(m)-1).[62]

2634. Withholding Exemption Certificate. Before an employee is allowed any withholding exemptions, he must file a withholding exemption certificate (Form W-4) with his employer showing the number of exemptions to which he is entitled (Code Sec. 3402(f)(2); Reg. § 31.3402(f)(2)-1).[63] Otherwise, withholding must be computed as if the employee were single and claiming no other exemptions. A widow or widower may claim "married" status for purposes of withholding if she or he qualifies as a surviving spouse (Code Sec. 3402(l)(3)).[64] See ¶ 175.

An employee who certifies to his employer that he had no income tax liability for his preceding tax year and anticipates none for the current tax year may be exempt from the withholding provisions (Code Sec. 3402(n); Reg. § 31.3402(n)-1).[65] Form W-4 should be used, and should be renewed annually, by any employee claiming this exemption.

If an employee claims an excessive number of exemptions, the IRS may determine the number to which he is actually entitled. Generally, the employer is bound by this determination until otherwise advised by the IRS.[66] A $500 civil penalty may be assessed against any individual who decreases his rate of withholding by claiming excess withholding allowances on Form W-4 (Code Sec. 6682).[67] In addition, a criminal penalty may be imposed against any individual who willfully supplies false withholding information or fails to supply withholding information (Code Sec. 7205).[68]

2637. Change in Status. An employee must file an amended withholding exemption certificate reducing the number of his exemptions within 10 days after the occurrence of any of the following events (Code Sec. 3402(f)(2)(B); Reg. § 31.3402(f)(2)-1(b)):[69]

1. The spouse for whom the employee has been claiming an exemption is divorced or legally separated from the employee, or claims his or her own exemption on a separate certificate.

2. The support of a claimed dependent is taken over by someone else, and the employee no longer expects to claim that person as a dependent.

Footnote references are to paragraphs of the 2002 Standard Federal Tax Reports.

[59] ¶ 33,542	[63] ¶ 33,542, ¶ 33,554	[67] ¶ 39,845
[60] ¶ 33,542	[64] ¶ 33,542	[68] ¶ 41,325
[61] ¶ 33,542	[65] ¶ 33,542, ¶ 33,580	[69] ¶ 33,542, ¶ 33,554
[62] ¶ 33,542, ¶ 33,579	[66] ¶ 33,560.19	

¶ 2637

3. The employee discovers that a dependent (other than a child under age 19 or a student) for whom an exemption was claimed will receive sufficient income of his own for the calendar year to disqualify him as a dependent (see ¶ 137).

4. Circumstances have changed so that the employee is no longer entitled to claim an exemption based on one of the deduction or credit items listed at ¶ 2632.

An employee who claimed "no liability" (see ¶ 2634) must file a new Form W-4 within 10 days from the time he anticipates that he will incur liability for the year, or before December 1 if he anticipates liability for the next year (Reg. § 31.3402(f)(2)-1(c)).[70]

The death of a spouse or dependent does not affect the withholding exemption for that year (Reg. § 31.3402(f)(2)-1(b)(1)(ii)) unless the employee's tax year is not a calendar year and the death occurs in that part of the calendar year preceding the employee's tax year.[71]

An employee may file an amended withholding exemption certificate, increasing the number of exemptions, at any time that he becomes eligible for an additional dependency or an extra exemption based on one of the deduction or credit items listed at ¶ 2632.

A withholding exemption certificate furnished to the employer that replaces an existing certificate can be effective for the first payment after the certificate is received if so elected by the employer. However, the replacing certificate must be effective for the first payroll period that ends on or after the 30th day after the day on which the new certificate is furnished (Code Sec. 3402(f)(3)(B)).[72]

Supplemental Wages

2639. Supplemental Payments and Tips. Special rules apply when the employee is paid supplemental wages (bonus, overtime pay, commissions, etc.).

If supplemental wages are paid at the same time as regular wages, the two are added together and the withholding tax is computed on the total as a single wage payment. If the supplemental wages are not paid at the same time as the regular wages, the supplemental wages may be added either to the regular wages for the preceding payroll period or for the current payroll period within the same calendar year. Under an alternative method, the employer may treat the supplemental wages as wholly separate from regular wages and withhold at a flat rate on the supplemental wage payment without any allowance for exemptions and without reference to any regular payment of wages. For amounts paid on or before August 6, 2001, the flat rate cannot be less than 28 percent. For amounts paid after August 6, 2001, the flat rate cannot be less than the third lowest rate of tax applicable to single filers. This rate is 30.5 percent for tax years beginning in 2001 (Reg. § 31.3402(g)-1, Act Sec. 13273 of the Revenue Reconciliation Act of 1993 and Act Sec. 101(c)(11) of the Economic Growth and Tax Relief Reconciliation Act of 2001)[73] (see IRS Publication 15-T).

A vacation allowance is subject to withholding as if it were a regular wage payment for the vacation period. If the vacation allowance is paid in addition to the regular wage, it is a "supplemental payment" (Reg. § 31.3402(g)-1(c)).[74]

An employer must collect both income tax and employee social security or railroad retirement tax on tips reported by an employee from wages due the employee or other funds that the employee makes available. Tips may be treated as if they were supplemental wages subject to the flat 28 percent withholding rate without allowance for exemptions, provided that income tax has been withheld on the employee's regular wages. Otherwise, the tips must be treated as part of the

---

Footnote references are to paragraphs of the 2002 Standard Federal Tax Reports.

¶ 2639

[70] ¶ 33,554	[72] ¶ 33,542	[74] ¶ 33,561
[71] ¶ 33,554	[73] ¶ 33,561	

current or preceding wage payment of the same calendar year and are subject to the regular graduated withholding rates.[75]

Withholding on Pensions, Interest and Dividends

2643. Pensions, Annuities and Certain Deferred Income. In the case of taxable payments from an employer-sponsored pension, annuity, profit-sharing, stock bonus or other deferred compensation plan, withholding is required unless the recipient elects not to have tax withheld (Code Sec. 3405).[76] The same rule applies to an IRA or an annuity, endowment, or life insurance contract issued by a life insurance company. The recipient's election not to have withholding apply remains in effect until revoked. The payor must notify the recipient that an election may be made and of the right to revoke such election. The election is generally not available with respect to foreign-delivered payments to persons subject to U.S. tax on their world-wide income. "Foreign-delivered," for this purpose, means outside the U.S. or its possessions.[77]

Amount Withheld. The amount withheld depends on whether the distributions are periodic payments or nonperiodic payments.

For periodic payments (annuity and similar periodic payments), withholding is made as though the payment was a payment of wages for the appropriate payroll period and, if the recipient does not have a withholding exemption certificate (Form W-4P) in effect, he is treated as a married individual claiming three exemptions. However, these exemptions are not available to a payee failing to file a certificate if the payee fails to furnish a taxpayer identification number (TIN) to a payor or if the IRS notifies the payor that the payee's TIN is incorrect (Code Sec. 3405(a)). Under the general rule, the withholding rate on nonperiodic distributions is 10 percent (Code Sec. 3405(b)).[78] Special withholding rules apply to distributions that were eligible for rollover but not directly transferred from the distributing plan to an eligible transferee plan. The withholding rate on such distributions is 20 percent instead of 10 percent. The withholding requirement is mandatory and distributees cannot elect to forego withholding on rollover eligible distributions (Code Sec. 3405(c)).[79]

2645. Backup Withholding. A backup withholding system requires a payor to deduct and withhold income tax from reportable payments, such as interest or dividends, if (1) the payee fails to furnish his TIN to the payor in the manner required;[80] (2) the IRS notifies the payor that the TIN furnished by the payee is incorrect;[81] (3) there has been a notified payee underreporting, described in Code Sec. 3406(c),[82] of interest, dividend, patronage dividend income, or other reportable payments; or (4) there has been a payee certification failure described in Code Sec. 3406(d) with respect to interest, dividend, patronage dividend payments, or other reportable payments.[83] For amounts paid on or before August 6, 2001, the payor is required to withhold at the rate of 31 percent. For amounts paid after August 6, 2001, the payor is required to withhold an amount equal to the product of the fourth lowest rate of tax applicable to single filers. This rate is 27.5 percent for tax years beginning in 2001 (Act Sec. 101(c)(10) of the Economic Growth and Tax Relief Reconciliation Act of 2001).

FICA Tax

2648. FICA Tax Rates. Under the Federal Insurance Contributions Act, an employer is required to withhold social security taxes (including hospital insurance tax) from wages paid to an employee during the year and must also match the tax withheld from the employee's wages. For 2001 (and 2002), the combined tax

---

Footnote references are to paragraphs of the 2002 Standard Federal Tax Reports.

[75] ¶ 33,506.056	[78] ¶ 33,620	[81] ¶ 33,654.30
[76] ¶ 33,620	[79] ¶ 33,620	[82] ¶ 33,640, ¶ 33,654.026
[77] ¶ 33,620.75	[80] ¶ 33,654.034	[83] ¶ 33,640, ¶ 33,654.032

rate is 7.65 percent, which consists of a 6.2 percent component for old-age, survivors, and disability insurance (OASDI) and a 1.45 percent component for hospital insurance (Medicare). The OASDI rate applies only to wages paid within an OASDI wage base ($80,400 in 2001 and $84,900 in 2002). There is no cap on wages subject to the Medicare tax (Code Sec. 3101, Code Sec. 3111 and Code Sec. 3121(a)).[84]

If an employee works for more than one employer, each employer must withhold and pay FICA taxes on the wages paid. In such instance, the employee's FICA tax withheld for the year might exceed the maximum employee tax for the year. If this happens, the employee must take the excess as a credit against his income tax (see ¶ 1372 as to limitation) (Reg. § 1.31-2)[85] or, if he is not required to file an income tax return, he may file a special refund claim (Reg. § 31.6413(c)-1).[86] The same rule applies to taxes withheld under the Railroad Retirement Tax Act.

If an individual is concurrently employed by two or more related corporations and all remuneration is disbursed to the individual through a common paymaster for the group, the common paymaster is responsible for the reporting and payment of FICA and FUTA taxes. However, the other related corporations remain jointly and severally liable for their appropriate share of the taxes (Reg. § 31.3121(s)-1).

In the case of persons performing domestic services in a private home of the employer and persons performing agricultural labor, if the employer pays the employee's liability for FICA taxes or state unemployment taxes without deduction from the employee's wages, those payments are not wages for FICA purposes (Code Sec. 3121(a)(6)).

Return and Payment by Employer

2650. Employer Return and Deposit of Taxes. An employer subject to either income tax withholding or social security taxes, or both, must file a quarterly return. Form 941 is the quarterly return form, which combines the reporting of income and FICA taxes withheld from wages, tips, supplemental unemployment compensation benefits, and third-party payments of sick pay (see ¶ 2604). Taxes on wages for agricultural employees, including domestic services on a farm operated for profit, are reported annually on Form 943. Nonpayroll items are separately deposited and annually reported on Form 945.

Form 941 is due on or before the last day of the month following the quarter involved. However, an extension of time for filing is automatically granted to the 10th day of the second month following the close of the calendar quarter if the return is accompanied by depositary receipts showing timely deposits in full payment of taxes due for the period (Reg. § 31.6071(a)-1).[87]

Forms W-2, 1099-R, and Transmittal Form W-3 must be filed with the Social Security Administration by the last day of February of the year following the year included in the return. The SSA transmits the income tax information on the return to the IRS.

Domestic Workers/Nanny Tax. Employers must withhold and pay FICA taxes on the wages of their household workers if cash wages paid in calendar year 2001 total $1,300 or more ($1,300 in 2002) (Code Sec. 3121(a)(7)(B) and Code Sec. 3121(x)).

Employers must report and pay required employment taxes for domestic employees on Schedule H of their own Forms 1040 or 1040A. While withheld amounts no longer have to be deposited on a monthly basis, employers do need an employer identification number (EIN) to include on Form W-2 (see ¶ 2655) and Schedule H. To obtain an EIN, employers should complete Form SS-4, "Application for Employer Identification Number."

Footnote references are to paragraphs of the 2002 Standard Federal Tax Reports.

[84] ¶ 114
[85] ¶ 4063
[86] ¶ 38,754
[87] ¶ 36,702

Employers must increase either their quarterly estimated tax payments or the income tax withholding on their own wages in order to satisfy employment tax obligations with respect to domestic workers. Failure to withhold for domestic workers results in liability for the penalty for underpayment of estimated tax (see ¶ 2682).

Deposit Rules. Generally, an employer must deposit the income tax withheld and the FICA taxes with an authorized commercial bank depositary.

Depositors are classified as either monthly or semiweekly depositors. An employer's status for a given calendar year is determined annually, based on the employer's employment tax reporting history during a 12-month lookback period ending on June 30 of the preceding year. The IRS will inform employers by November of each year which schedule they are to follow for the upcoming year.

An employer generally must deposit employment taxes on a monthly basis during 2002 if, during the lookback period from July 1, 2000, through June 30, 2001, the amount of the aggregate employment taxes reported was $50,000 or less. Monthly depositors are required to deposit each month's taxes on or before the 15th day of the following month.

An employer that reported more than $50,000 in aggregate employment taxes during the 2000-2001 lookback period will be a semiweekly depositor in 2001. Semiweekly depositors generally are required to deposit their taxes by the Wednesday after payday, if payday falls on a Wednesday, Thursday or Friday. For all other paydays, the deposit is due by the Friday following payday. Both monthly and semiweekly depositors will always have at least three banking days after the payday to make the deposit.

Notwithstanding these general rules, employers with $100,000 or more of accumulated liability during a monthly or semiweekly period are required to deposit the funds by the first banking day after the $100,000 threshold is reached. Also, employers accumulating deposits of less than $2,500 in 2001 during the quarter may skip the deposits entirely and send full payment with their quarterly employment tax returns. As a result, employers with employment tax liabilities of less than $2,500 per return period in 2001 are no longer required to make monthly deposits but may instead send a payment with the return filed for that period (see IRS Publication 15).

The deposit rules apply to employment taxes that are reported on a quarterly or annual basis, such as Form 941, "Employer's Quarterly Federal Tax Return," and Form 943, "Employer's Annual Tax Return for Agricultural Workers."

As a safe harbor, employers that fail to deposit the full amount of taxes will not be penalized if the shortfall does not exceed the greater of $100 or 2 percent of the amount of employment taxes required to be deposited, provided that the shortfall is deposited on or before a prescribed makeup date.

Penalties will also be abated if an employer shows that a failure to deposit the full amount of the employment taxes was due to reasonable cause, as provided in Code Sec. 6656 (Reg. § 31.6302-1).[88]

Amounts withheld under the Code Sec. 3406 backup withholding requirements are treated as employment taxes subject to these deposit rules. However, employers are permitted to treat the backup withholding amounts separately from other employment taxes for purposes of the deposit rules (Reg. § 31.6302-3).[89]

Different monthly and semimonthly deposit requirements apply to taxes withheld from nonresident aliens and foreign corporations (Reg. § 1.6302-2).[90]

Only an original Form 8109, "Federal Tax Deposit Coupons," may be used to make a deposit. Under the IRS's AUTOGEN program, taxpayers automatically receive new FTD coupon books as they are needed.[91]

Footnote references are to paragraphs of the 2002 Standard Federal Tax Reports.
[88] ¶ 38,055B
[89] ¶ 38,055D
[90] ¶ 38,062
[91] ¶ 38,070.075, ¶ 38,070.107

Electronic Fund Transfer. The IRS has issued final regulations that change which taxpayers must make deposits using Electronic Fund Transfer (EFT) (Reg. § 31.6302-1(h)).[92] Taxpayers that exceed threshold aggregate amounts of employment and other taxes during a determination period (12-month period) must deposit by EFT (Reg. § 31.6302-1(h)(2)).[93] A taxpayer is required to make deposits using EFT in 2001 if (1) the total deposits of all depositary taxes (such as employment tax, excise tax and corporate income tax) in 1999 was more than $200,000 or (2) the taxpayer was required to use EFT in 2000.The date on which taxpayers must begin using EFT depends on when the threshold level of $200,00 is met. A chart showing new and old threshold amounts, including the determination period for these amounts, and the date when deposits by EFT must begin, follows:

Threshold Amount	Determination Period	Effective Date
$ 50,000	1/1/1995—12/31/1995	July 1, 1997
50,000	1/1/1996—12/31/1996	January 1, 1998
50,000	1/1/1997—12/31/1997	January 1, 1999
200,000	1/1/1998—12/31/1998	January 1, 2000
200,000	1/1/1999—12/31/1999	January 1, 2001
200,000	1/1/2000—12/31/2000	January 1, 2002
200,000	1/1/2001—12/31/2001	January 1, 2003

Once a taxpayer is required to make EFT deposits applying the new threshold, all future deposits must be made by EFT, regardless of whether the amount is reached in each calendar year thereafter. If a taxpayer is required to use EFT and fails to do so, a 10-percent penalty may be imposed. Also, taxpayers that are not required to use EFT may participate in the payment system voluntarily (Reg. § 31.6302-1(h)(2)).[94]

Timeliness of Deposits. The timeliness of deposits is determined by the date they are received by an authorized depositary. However, a deposit received by the depositary after the due date is considered timely if the employer establishes that it was mailed on or before the second day before the prescribed due date (Code Sec. 7502(e)). In determining banking days for deposit purposes, Saturdays, Sundays and legal holidays are excluded, but the mailing date (on or before the second day before the prescribed due date) is not extended under such circumstances. However, the above timely mailing exception does not apply to a large depositor (i.e., with respect to any deposit of $20,000 or more by any person who is required to deposit the tax more than once a month). This type of deposit must be made by the due date, regardless of the method of delivery (Code Sec. 7502(e)(3)).[95]

2653. Advance Payment of Earned Income Credit. Although advance payments of the earned income credit (see ¶ 1375) are not compensation for withholding purposes, the payments must be separately reported on Form W-2. Failure to make advance payments when required is considered a failure to deduct and withhold taxes (Code Sec. 3507).[96]

An employer may reduce its deposit of employment taxes due with respect to each payroll period for all employees by the sum of any credits advanced during the same period.[97]

2655. Statements to Employees. On or before January 31, every employer is required to furnish every employee with copies of Form W-2 for taxes withheld during the preceding calendar year. When employment terminates before the end of the calendar year, there is no reasonable expectation of reemployment, and the employee submits a written request for the information, Form W-2 must be furnished within 30 days of the written request, if the 30-day period ends before January 31 (Code Sec. 6051(a)).[98]

Form W-2 is a multiple-part wage statement with several copies; Copy A is sent to the SSA, Copy 1 is sent to the state, Copy B is kept by the employee and attached

---

Footnote references are to paragraphs of the 2002 Standard Federal Tax Reports.

[92] ¶ 38,055B	[95] ¶ 42,620	[97] ¶ 33,781, ¶ 33,783
[93] ¶ 38,055B	[96] ¶ 33,780	[98] ¶ 36,420
[94] ¶ 38,055B		

to his or her federal tax return, Copy C is retained for the employee's records, Copy 2 is attached to the employee's state, city, or local tax return, and Copy D is kept in the employer's records. Employers must use magnetic media rather than paper returns if 250 or more Forms W-2 or W-2p are to be filed with the SSA. Hardship waivers may be requested.[99]

If the social security tax imposed on tips reported by the employee exceeds the tax that has been collected by the employer, the employer is required to furnish the employee with a statement showing the amount of the excess (Code Sec. 6053(b)).[100]

2658. Employer Penalties. Every employer required to withhold tax on wages is liable for payment of the tax whether or not it is collected. The employer's liability is relieved, however, after showing that the employee's related income tax liability has been paid (Reg. § 31.3402(d)-1).[101]

Any responsible person—typically a corporate officer or employee—who willfully fails to withhold, account for, or pay over withholding tax to the government is subject to a penalty equal to 100 percent of such tax (Code Sec. 6672).[102] The penalty is a collection device, usually assessed only when the tax cannot be collected from the employer, and results in a personal liability not dischargeable by bankruptcy.[103]

Civil and criminal penalties can be imposed under Code Sec. 6674 and Code Sec. 7204 if an employer willfully fails to furnish or furnishes a false or fraudulent Form W-2 statement (see ¶ 2655) to an employee.[104]

Failure to Make Timely Deposits. A four-tier graduated penalty applies to failures to make timely deposits of tax, unless the failure is due to reasonable cause and not willful neglect. The penalty amount varies with the length of time within which the taxpayer corrects the failure to make the required deposit. The penalty is assessed as follows: (1) 2 percent of the amount of the underpayment if the failure is for no more than five days; (2) 5 percent of the amount of the underpayment if the failure is for more than five days but for no more than 15 days; and (3) 10 percent of the amount of the underpayment if the failure is for more than 15 days. However, the penalty will be imposed at the rate of 15 percent of the amount of the underpayment if a required tax deposit is not made on or before the day that is 10 days after the date of the first delinquency notice to the taxpayer, or, if earlier, on or before the day on which notice and demand for immediate payment of tax is given in cases of jeopardy (Code Sec. 6656(a) and Code Sec. 6656(b)).[105]

Deposits are applied in order against deposit liabilities arising in due-date order for purposes of computing the failure to timely deposit penalty. Thus, a deposit is first applied to satisfy any past due underdeposits for the same return period, with the oldest underdeposit being satisfied first. Amounts delivered to an IRS office, rather than being deposited in an authorized depository, are not treated as deposits for purposes of computing the penalty (Rev. Proc. 91-52 and Rev. Proc. 99-10).[106]

FUTA Tax

2661. FUTA Tax Rate. The Federal Unemployment Tax Act imposes a tax on employers who employed one or more persons in covered employment on at least one day in each of 20 weeks during the current or preceding calendar year, or who paid wages (in covered employment) of at least $1,500 ($20,000 for agricultural labor or $1,000 for domestic labor) in a calendar quarter in the current or preceding calendar year. The tax is based on the first $7,000 of certain wages paid during the calendar year to each employee. The full rate of tax is 6.2 percent, but the employer is allowed a partial credit against this tax based on its state unemployment insurance tax liability (Code Sec. 3301).

Footnote references are to paragraphs of the 2002 Standard Federal Tax Reports.

[99] ¶ 33,594.03	[102] ¶ 39,775	[105] ¶ 39,580
[100] ¶ 36,460	[103] ¶ 39,780.53	[106] ¶ 39,585.01, ¶ 46,258,
[101] ¶ 33,549	[104] ¶ 39,795, ¶ 41,320	¶ 46,416

In the case of persons performing domestic services in a private home of the employer and persons performing agricultural labor, if the employer pays the employee's liability for FICA taxes or state unemployment taxes without deducting those taxes from the employee's wages, the amounts paid by the employer are not wages for FUTA purposes (Code Sec. 3306(b)(6)), but they are wages for income tax withholding purposes (see ¶ 2601).[107] The temporary surtax rate of 0.2 percent is extended through December 31, 2007 (Code Sec. 3301).

Withholding on Expense Allowances

2662. Accountable Plans v. Nonaccountable Plans. An employer's withholding obligations with respect to amounts paid to employees under an expense allowance or reimbursement arrangement depend upon whether the amounts are paid under an accountable or a nonaccountable plan (see ¶ 943). Amounts paid under an accountable plan, to the extent of an employee's substantiated expenses, may be excluded from an employee's gross income, are not required to be reported on the employee's Form W-2, and are exempt from withholding of income and employment taxes (FICA, FUTA, railroad retirement, and railroad unemployment taxes) (Reg. § 1.62-2(c)(4), Reg. § 1.62-2(h)(1) and Reg. § 31.3401(a)-4(a)).[108] Amounts paid under a nonaccountable plan are included in the employee's gross income, reported on Form W-2 and subject to withholding (Reg. § 1.62-2(c)(5)).[109] If expenses are reimbursed under an accountable plan, but either the expenses are not substantiated within a reasonable period of time or amounts in excess of substantiated expenses are not returned within a reasonable period of time, the excess or unsubstantiated amounts paid are treated as paid under a nonaccountable plan and are subject to withholding no later than the first payroll period following the end of the reasonable period of time (Reg. § 1.62-2(h)(2)(i)(A) and Reg. § 31.3401(a)-4(b)(1)).[110]

Withholding Rate. Expense reimbursements that are subject to withholding may be added to the employee's regular wages for the appropriate payroll period, and withheld taxes may be computed on the total. Alternatively, the employer may withhold at the flat rate applicable to supplemental wages (see ¶ 2639) if the expense reimbursement or allowance is paid separately or is separately identified (Reg. § 31.3401(a)-4(c), Act Sec. 13273 of the Revenue Reconciliation Act of 1993 and Act Sec. 101(c)(11) of the Economic Growth and Tax Relief Reconciliation Act of 2001).[111]

2663. Per Diem Allowances for Automobile, Meal, and Lodging Expenses. If the amount of an employee's expenses is substantiated through the use of an IRS-approved per diem allowance, any amounts paid to the employee exceeding the amounts deemed substantiated are subject to income and employment tax withholding (Reg. § 1.62-2(h)(2)(i)(B) and Reg. § 31.3401(a)-4(b)(1)(ii)).[112] (See ¶ 947 for standard mileage rate and FAVR allowances for automobile expenses; see ¶ 954 et seq. for per diem methods relating to meal and lodging expenses.)

For per diem or mileage allowances paid in advance, withholding on any excess must occur no later than the first payroll period following the payroll period in which the expenses for which the advance was paid (i.e., the days or miles of travel) are substantiated by the employee. For a per diem or mileage allowance paid as a reimbursement, the excess amounts reimbursed are subject to withholding when paid.

Footnote references are to paragraphs of the 2002 Standard Federal Tax Reports.

¶ 2662

[107] ¶ 114, ¶ 33,506.021	[109] ¶ 6004	[111] ¶ 33,508A
[108] ¶ 6004, ¶ 33,508A	[110] ¶ 6004, ¶ 33,508A	[112] ¶ 6004, ¶ 33,508A

Self-Employment Tax

2664. Rate and Payment. The combined rate of tax on self-employment income (see ¶2670) is 15.3 percent.[113] The rate consists of a 12.4 percent component for old-age, survivors, and disability insurance (OASDI) and a 2.9 percent component for hospital insurance (Medicare). See IRS Publication 533.

The self-employment tax, which is computed on Schedule SE of Form 1040, is treated as part of the income tax and must also be taken into account for purposes of the estimated tax (Code Sec. 6654(f)).[114] A married couple filing a joint return must file separate Schedules SE where each spouse is self-employed.

2667. Persons Subject to Tax. An individual who is self-employed is subject to the self-employment tax, the purpose of which is to provide social security and Medicare benefits to such individuals. This tax is assessed on the individual's self-employment income (see ¶2670). However, members of religious orders who have taken vows of poverty are not subject to the tax when they perform duties connected with their religious order (Code Sec. 1402(c)).[115]

A duly ordained, commissioned, or licensed minister of a church, a member of a religious order (who has not taken a vow of poverty), or a Christian Science practitioner may elect not to be covered by social security by filing an exemption certificate, Form 4361, which contains a statement indicating that he is opposed by conscience or religious principle to the acceptance of any public insurance. The statement must include a declaration that he has informed the ordaining, commissioning, or licensing body of the church of his opposition to such insurance (Code Sec. 1402(e)(1)).[116]

An individual who has conscientious objections to insurance by reason of an adherence to established tenets or teachings of a religious sect of which he is a member may also be exempt (Code Sec. 1402(g)).[117] A qualified individual must apply for an exemption on or before the due date of the income tax return for the second tax year for which he had earnings from self-employment of $400 or more from his religious activities (Reg. § 1.1402(e)-3A).[118]

Services performed by employees for a church or church-controlled organization may be excluded from social security coverage if the church or organization makes a valid election under Code Sec. 3121(w). However, such employees will be liable for self-employment tax on remuneration paid for such services unless the remuneration is less than $100 per year (Code Sec. 1402(a)(14) and Code Sec. 1402(j)).[119]

A U.S. citizen who works for an employer that is exempt from the social security tax because it is either a foreign government or instrumentality or an international organization is treated as self-employed and wages are subject to the self-employment tax (Code Sec. 1402(c)(2)).[120] Also, a resident of Puerto Rico, the Virgin Islands, Guam or American Samoa who is not a citizen of the United States is subject to the self-employment tax (Code Sec. 1402(b)).[121]

2670. Self-Employment Income. The self-employment tax is 15.3 percent and consists of two taxes—an OASDI (i.e., social security) tax of 12.4 percent and a Medicare tax of 2.9 percent. The tax is based on "self-employment income," which is defined as "net earnings from self-employment." For 2001, the OASDI base is $80,400 ($84,900 in 2002). There is no cap for the Medicare component. However, if wages subject to social security or railroad retirement tax are received during the tax year, the maximum is reduced by the amount of wages on which these taxes were paid (Code Sec. 1402(b)).[122] If net earnings from self-employment are less than $400, no self-employment tax is payable.

Footnote references are to paragraphs of the 2002 Standard Federal Tax Reports.
[113] ¶32,541, ¶32,543.07   [117] ¶32,560   [120] ¶32,560
[114] ¶39,550   [118] ¶32,593   [121] ¶32,560
[115] ¶32,560   [119] ¶32,560   [122] ¶32,560
[116] ¶32,560

"Net earnings from self-employment" consist of: (1) the gross income derived from any trade or business, less allowable deductions attributable to the trade or business, and (2) the taxpayer's distributive share of the ordinary income or loss of a partnership engaged in a trade or business (Reg. § 1.1402(a)-1).[123] The term "trade or business" does not include services performed as an employee other than services relating to certain: (1) newspaper and magazine sales, (2) sharing of crops, (3) foreign organizations, and (4) sharing of fishing catches (Code Sec. 1402(c)(2)).[124]

There are special rules for computing net earnings from self-employment (including a special optional method of computing net earnings from nonfarm self-employment) (Code Sec. 1402(a)).[125] Rents from real estate and from personal property leased with the real estate, and the attributable deductions, are excluded unless received by the individual in the course of his business as a real estate dealer.

Dividends and interest from any bond, debenture, note, certificate or other evidence of indebtedness issued with interest coupons or in registered form by any corporation are excluded from net earnings from self-employment income unless received by a dealer in stocks and securities in the course of his business. Other interest received in the course of any trade or business is not excluded. Gain or loss from the sale or exchange of property that is not stock in trade or held primarily for sale is excluded, as is gain or loss from the sale or exchange of a capital asset.

Termination payments received by former insurance salespersons are excludable from self-employment tax under certain circumstances specified under Code Sec. 1402(k).[126]

Even though the rental value of a parsonage (or a parsonage rental allowance) and the value of meals and lodging furnished for the convenience of the employer are not included in a minister's gross income for income tax purposes (see ¶ 873 and ¶ 875), they are taken into account in calculating net earnings from self-employment (Code Sec. 1402(a)(8)).[127] The same is true of amounts excluded from gross income as foreign earned income (see ¶ 2401). However, self-employment income does not include a minister's retirement benefits received from a church plan or the rental value of a parsonage allowance as long as each was furnished after the date of retirement.[128]

One business deduction that cannot be taken in calculating net earnings from self-employment for the tax year is the deduction allowed for 50 percent of the self-employment tax for the same tax year (see ¶ 923). However, the law provides a substitute for that deduction. This is an amount determined by multiplying net earnings from self-employment (calculated without regard to the substitute deduction) by one-half of the self-employment tax rate for the year (Code Sec. 1402(a)(12)).[129] For 2001, this is 7.65 percent of the net earnings from self-employment.

> **Example.** Aileen Smith, a self-employed individual, has $40,000 of net earnings from self-employment in 2001 (determined without regard to the substitute deduction). Her self-employment tax for 2001 would be computed as follows:

Self-employment net earnings	$40,000
Less: $40,000 × 7.65%	3,060
Reduced self-employment net earnings	$36,940
Tax rate on self-employment income	× 15.3%
Self-employment tax for 2001	$ 5,652

Footnote references are to paragraphs of the 2002 Standard Federal Tax Reports.

¶ 2670

[123] ¶ 32,561	[126] ¶ 32,560	[128] ¶ 32,599.58
[124] ¶ 32,560	[127] ¶ 32,560	[129] ¶ 32,560, ¶ 32,543.07
[125] ¶ 32,560		

2673. Optional Method for Nonfarm Self-Employment. A taxpayer may be able to use an optional method to compute net earnings from self-employment if the net earnings from nonfarm self-employment are: (a) less than $1,600 and (b) less than two-thirds of gross nonfarm income. In addition, this optional method may only be used if the taxpayer had net earnings from self-employment of $400 or more in at least two of the three years immediately preceding the year in which the nonfarm optional method is elected.

If the taxpayer is eligible to use this optional method, he may elect to report two-thirds of his gross nonfarm income, up to $1,600, as his net earnings from self-employment. The purpose of this optional method is to permit taxpayers to pay into the social security system and thus obtain or increase their benefits, even though they are not otherwise eligible because their net self-employment income is under $400. This optional method may not be used more than five times by any individual.[130] Note that the $1,600 amount refers to net earnings after reduction by the 7.65 percent deduction amount.

2676. Farmer's Self-Employment Income. A special method for determining self-employment net earnings is provided for farm operators whether they own the land they farm, rent on a fixed rental basis, or rent under a share-farming arrangement. Rentals received by the owner or tenant of the land under a share-farming arrangement—the farm is operated by a third party (share-farmer who may be a subtenant)—are treated as self-employment income if the owner or tenant participates materially with the share-farmer working the land in the production or management of the production of an agricultural or horticultural commodity. (There is no material participation if the owner or tenant does not participate in operations and has turned over management of the land to an agent, such as a professional farm management company.) The share-farmer is also considered a self-employed person (Code Sec. 1402(a)(1)).[131]

A self-employed farmer has to pay the self-employment tax if his net earnings from self-employment are $400 or more (Code Sec. 1402(b)).[132] However, an optional method for reporting income from farming, providing for greater credit toward benefits under old-age and survivors insurance, is available to a farmer. If his gross income for the tax year is not more than $2,400, he can report two-thirds of his gross income as net earnings from self-employment (Code Sec. 1402(a)).[133]

> **Example.** In 2001, Breanna Jones had $2,200 of gross income from her farm operations. Although her actual net earnings amounted to $1,300, she reported $1,466.67 (2/3 of $2,200) as net earnings from self-employment subject to self-employment tax. In electing to pay the tax on the larger amount, she receives a greater credit toward social security benefits.

If a farmer has more than $2,400 of gross income from farm operations, he may report either his actual net earnings or, if his net earnings are less than $1,600, $1,600 as net earnings (Code Sec. 1402(a)).[134] As in the case of the nonfarm optional method, the $1,600 amount refers to net earnings after reduction by the 7.65 percent deduction. There is no limit on the number of times a taxpayer may use this optional method.

Footnote references are to paragraphs of the 2002 Standard Federal Tax Reports.
[130] ¶ 32,578.034   [132] ¶ 32,560   [134] ¶ 32,560
[131] ¶ 32,560   [133] ¶ 32,560

ESTIMATED TAX

Payment of Estimated Taxes

2679. Purpose. To provide for current payment of income taxes not collected through withholding, the law requires individuals in some instances to pay a portion of their tax currently. The general rule is that at least 90 percent of an individual's final income tax is to be paid through either withholding or estimated tax payments.

For the payment of estimated taxes, an individual is to use the appropriate payment voucher attached to Form 1040-ES. Estimated tax installments required of an individual are based on the penalty exception provisions of Code Sec. 6654.[135]

In general, the estimated tax is the amount of income and self-employment tax (as well as other taxes reported on Form 1040) that an individual estimates will have to be paid for the tax year after subtracting any estimated credits against tax. For rules on payment of corporate estimated tax, see ¶ 225-¶ 231. For a discussion of the estimated tax rules for trusts and estates, see ¶ 518.

2682. Who Should Estimate for 2002? No penalty for failure to pay estimated tax will apply to an individual whose tax liability for the year, after credit for withheld taxes, is less than $1,000. Also, a U.S. citizen or resident need not pay estimated tax if he or she had no tax liability for the preceding tax year, provided such year was a 12-month period. Under circumstances of hardship or following an individual's retirement or disability, the penalty may be waived (Code Sec. 6654(e)).[136]

Individuals who do not qualify for any of these exceptions may generally avoid the penalty for failure to pay estimated tax by (1) paying at least 90 percent of the tax shown on the current year's return, (2) paying 100 percent of the tax shown on the prior year's return, or (3) paying installments on a current basis under an annualized income installment method. However, an individual may not use the 100-percent-of-prior-year's-tax safe harbor if the prior year was not a 12-month period.

The required payments may be made either through withholding or payment of annual installments. The annualization method is suitable for taxpayers whose income is received or accrued more heavily in one part of the year (Code Sec. 6654(d)).

A special rule applies to individuals with adjusted gross income for the previous tax year in excess of $150,000 ($75,000 for married individuals filing separately). In order to qualify for the prior year safe harbor for any estimated tax installment payment due for tax years beginning after December 31, 1999, five rules apply: (1) if the preceding tax year begins in 1998, the prior year safe harbor percentage is 105 percent; (2) if the preceding tax year begins in 1999, the prior year safe harbor percentage is 108.6 percent; (3) if the preceding tax year begins in 2000, the prior year safe harbor percentage is 110 percent; (4) if the preceding tax year begins in 2001, the prior year safe harbor percentage is 112 percent; or (5) if the preceding tax year begins in 2002 or thereafter, the prior year safe harbor percentage is 110 percent (Code Sec. 6654(d)(1)(C), as amended by P.L. 106-170).[137]

Employers of domestic workers who fail to satisfy their obligations for FICA and FUTA withholding, through regular estimated tax payments or increased tax withholding from their own wages, may be liable for estimated tax penalties (see ¶ 2650).

Footnote references are to paragraphs of the 2002 Standard Federal Tax Reports.

¶ 2679   [135] ¶ 39,550   [136] ¶ 39,550   [137] ¶ 39,550

Payment Requirements

2685. Estimated Tax Payment Due Dates. For estimated tax purposes, the year is broken down into four payment periods,[138] and a 2002 calendar-year individual is required to pay his estimated tax in four installments as follows:

Installment	Due date
First	April 15, 2002
Second	June 17, 2002
Third	September 16, 2002
Fourth	January 15, 2003

For fiscal-year individuals, the due dates for the four estimated tax payments are: (1) the 15th day of the fourth month of the fiscal year, (2) the 15th day of the sixth month of the fiscal year, (3) the 15th day of the ninth month of the fiscal year, and (4) the 15th day of the first month after the end of the fiscal year.

If the due date for making an estimated tax payment falls on a Saturday, Sunday or legal holiday, the payment will be timely if made on the next day that is not a Saturday, Sunday or legal holiday.[139]

If an individual is not liable for estimated tax on March 31, 2002, but his tax situation changes so that he becomes liable for estimated tax at some point after March 31, then he must make estimated tax payments as follows: (1) if he becomes required to pay estimated tax after March 31 and before June 1, then he should pay 50 percent of his estimated tax on or before June 17, 2002, 25 percent on September 16, 2002, and 25 percent on January 15, 2003; (2) if he becomes required to pay estimated tax after May 31 and before September 1, then he should pay 75 percent of his estimated tax on or before September 16, 2002, and 25 percent on January 15, 2003; or (3) if he becomes required to pay estimated tax after August 31, then he should pay 100 percent of his estimated tax by January 15, 2003 (Form 1040-ES).

Nonresident Alien Individuals. Nonresident alien individuals (except those whose wages are subject to withholding) must pay estimated taxes in three installments (June 17 and September 16 in 2002 and January 15 in 2003). Fifty percent of the annual payment must be made on the first installment due date and 25 percent on each of the remaining two installment due dates (Code Sec. 6654(j)).[140]

2688. Return as Substitute for Last Installment of 2001 Estimated Tax. The fourth (last) tax installment for a tax year need not be made if the taxpayer files a Form 1040 tax return and pays the balance of the tax on or before January 31, 2002, or, for a fiscal year, on or before the last day of the month following the close of the fiscal year. Filing a final 2001 return by January 31, 2002, with payment of any tax due will not avoid an addition to tax for underpayment of any of the first three installments that were due for the year, but it will terminate the period of underpayment (and therefore the accrual of further additions) as of January 15, 2002 (Code Sec. 6654(h)).[141]

2691. Farmer or Fisherman. A farmer or fisherman who expects to receive at least two-thirds of his gross income for the tax year from farming or fishing, or who received at least two-thirds of his gross income for the previous tax year from farming or fishing, may pay estimated tax for the year in one installment. Thus, a qualifying farmer or fisherman may wait until January 15, 2002, to make his 2001 estimated tax payment. The entire amount of 2001 estimated tax must be paid at that time. However, this January 15 payment date may be ignored if the farmer or fisherman files his income tax return for 2001 and pays the entire tax due by March 1, 2002. The penalty for underpayment of estimated tax (see ¶ 2875) does not apply unless a farmer or fisherman underpays his tax by more than one-third (Code Sec. 6654(i)).[142] If a joint return is filed, a farmer or fisherman must consider his or her spouse's gross income in determining whether at least two-thirds of gross income is from farming or fishing.

Footnote references are to paragraphs of the 2002 Standard Federal Tax Reports.
[138] ¶ 39,560.0215   [140] ¶ 39,550   [142] ¶ 39,550
[139] ¶ 42,635.01   [141] ¶ 39,550

¶ 2691

Chapter 27

EXAMINATION OF RETURNS COLLECTION OF TAX

Organization of IRS

2701. Organization and Functions. The Internal Revenue Service is the Treasury Department unit that has responsibility for determining, assessing, and collecting internal revenue taxes and enforcing the internal revenue laws. The Internal Revenue Service consists of a National Office in Washington, D.C., and a field organization. The National Office is the Office of the Commissioner of Internal Revenue, who heads the Internal Revenue Service. Among the principal offices of the IRS are: the Office of the Deputy Commissioner (Operations); the Office of the Associate Commissioner (Policy and Management); the Office of the Associate Commissioner (Computer Services); the Office of the Assistant Commissioner (Taxpayer Service and Returns Processing); and the Office of the Chief Counsel. The Office of Inspector General of the Treasury Department has oversight responsibility for the internal investigations performed by the Office of Assistant Commissioner (Inspection) of the IRS.

Until recently, IRS field offices were divided into four geographic regions, each headed by a Regional Commissioner. The Regional Offices were situated in the following cities: Atlanta, Georgia; Dallas, Texas; New York, New York; and San Francisco, California. There also were IRS district offices in the principal cities of the United States, each headed by a District Director.

However, pursuant to the IRS Restructuring and Reform Act of 1998, the IRS has reorganized itself by doing away with the four regional divisions and organizing itself into four units serving groups of taxpayers with similar needs. As of October 1, 2000, the IRS has put into operation the following operating divisions: (1) Wage and Investment, serving individual taxpayers with wage and investment income; (2) Small Business/Self-Employed, serving self-employed individuals and small businesses (C corporations, S corporations and partnerships) with assets of less than $5 million; (3) Large and Mid-Size Business, serving corporations with assets of at least $5 million; and (4) Tax-Exempt and Government Entities, serving employee plans, exempt organizations, and government entities. The IRS has informally indicated

¶ 2701

that it is planning to raise the $5 million threshold for determining status as a small or mid/large-size business to $10 million.

IRS field offices also include 10 IRS service centers, with mailing addresses in the following cities: Austin, Texas; Kansas City, Missouri; Andover, Massachusetts; Ogden, Utah; Atlanta, Georgia; Philadelphia, Pennsylvania; Memphis, Tennessee; Holtsville, New York; Cincinnati, Ohio; and Fresno, California. The service centers currently receive and process tax and information returns, manage accounts, and conduct simple audits through correspondence based on a taxpayer's geographic location. However, these activities are in the process of being assigned to service centers based on whether a taxpayer's return relates to an individual or a business, the taxpayer's geographical location, and the operating division to which the center, as part of the IRS reorganization, will eventually report.

The IRS also maintains a national computer center located near Martinsburg, West Virginia.

In addition, a nine-member IRS Oversight Board has been created to ensure that the IRS is organized and operated to carry out its new mission to place a greater emphasis on serving the public and meeting taxpayers' needs (Code Sec. 7802).[1]

2703. Office of Chief Counsel. The legal work of the Internal Revenue Service is performed by the Office of the Chief Counsel.[2] The Chief Counsel is a member of the Commissioner's executive staff and acts as counsel and legal adviser to the Commissioner in all matters pertaining to the administration and enforcement of the Internal Revenue laws. There also used to be Regional Counsels, subject to the general supervision of the Chief Counsel, in each of the former four geographical regions. As part of the IRS reorganization (see ¶ 2701), however, the Regional Counsels have been replaced by Division Counsels aligned with the new operating divisions.

2705. Appeals Procedure. If a tax return is examined by the IRS and the taxpayer does not agree with the results of the examination, further appeal within the IRS is permitted.[3] Once the IRS has issued a preliminary 30-day letter, the taxpayer has the right to appeal to a local Appeals Office by filing a written request for appellate consideration. This is the only level of appeal within the IRS (disregarding the functions of the National Taxpayer Advocate (¶ 2707)). Appeals conferences are conducted in an informal manner. A taxpayer who requests a conference may also need to file a formal written protest. However, if the protested amount is not more than $25,000, a small case request may be made instead of a formal written protest (IRS Publication 556 (Rev. Nov. 2000)). Taxpayers who wish to forego the right to submit a protest to the Appeals Office after receiving a 30-day letter can file a petition in the Tax Court within 90 days after the receipt of a statutory notice of deficiency.

The IRS is required to develop certain appeals dispute resolution procedures (Code Sec. 7123).[4] Accordingly, the IRS has established procedures under which any taxpayer may request early referral of issues from the examination or collection division to the Office of Appeals (Rev. Proc. 99-28). Additionally, procedures have been developed under which either a taxpayer or the Office of Appeals may request nonbinding mediation of any unresolved issue involving examination adjustments of at least $1 million at the conclusion of the appeals procedure or an unsuccessful attempt to enter into a closing agreement or an offer in compromise (Ann. 98-99). Mediation procedures for issues involving less than $1 million are in the process of being developed. Finally, a pilot program under which the Office of Appeals and the taxpayer may jointly request binding arbitration is also being developed.

2707. Taxpayer Assistance Orders. The National Taxpayer Advocate assists taxpayers in resolving problems with the IRS and has the authority to issue a taxpayer assistance order where the taxpayer is suffering, or is about to suffer,

Footnote references are to paragraphs of the 2002 Standard Federal Tax Reports.
[1] ¶ 43,254   [3] ¶ 43,336, ¶ 43,352.033   [4] ¶ 41,132
[2] ¶ 43,258

significant hardship as a result of the IRS's actions (Code Sec. 7803(c); Code Sec. 7811).[5] "Significant hardship" means any serious privation caused to the taxpayer as the result of the IRS's administration of revenue laws. Mere economic or personal inconvenience to the taxpayer does not constitute significant hardship (Reg. § 301.7811-1(a)(4)).[6] The following four specific factors, among other things, must be considered by the Advocate when determining whether there is a significant hardship: (1) whether there is an immediate threat of adverse action; (2) whether there has been a delay of more than 30 days in resolving the taxpayer's account problems; (3) whether the taxpayer will have to pay significant costs (including fees for professional representation) if relief is not granted; or (4) whether the taxpayer will suffer irreparable injury, or a long-term adverse impact, if relief is not granted (Code Sec. 7811(a)).[7]

An application for a taxpayer assistance order may be filed by the taxpayer or a duly authorized representative who may request remedial action, such as the release of the taxpayer's property from IRS levy or the immediate reissuance of a lost refund check. Form 911 is to be used for this purpose. Any relevant limitations period is suspended from the date on which the application is filed until the Advocate makes a decision on the application, unless the order provides for the continuation of the suspension beyond the date of the order. Such orders are binding on the IRS unless modified or rescinded by the Advocate, IRS Commissioner or Deputy Commissioner. The Advocate can take independent action and issue an assistance order without an application by the taxpayer. The statute of limitations, however, is not suspended when the Advocate issues an order independently.[8]

Examination

2708. Examination of Return. The IRS examines a taxpayer's books and records either at the place of business where the books and records are maintained (a field examination) or at an IRS office.[9] The type of examination affects the internal appeals procedure (see ¶ 2705).

The Taxpayer Bill of Rights requires the IRS to provide a written statement detailing the taxpayer's rights and the IRS's obligations during the audit, appeals, refund and collection process. The IRS must also explain the audit and collection (Code Sec. 7521(b)).[10]

The taxpayer has the right to make an audio recording of any in-person interview conducted by the IRS, upon ten days' advance notice (Code Sec. 7521(a)).[11] Moreover, a taxpayer is guaranteed the right to be represented by any individual currently permitted to practice before the IRS, unless the IRS notifies the taxpayer that the representative is responsible for unreasonable delay or hindrance (Code Sec. 7521(c)).[12] Any interview must be suspended when the taxpayer clearly requests the right to consult with a representative.[13] Further, unless it issues an administrative summons, the IRS cannot require the taxpayer to accompany the representative to the interview.[14]

The IRS has granted administrative relief to taxpayers in hostage situations or in a combat zone, or who are continuously hospitalized as a result of injuries received in a combat zone, or who are affected by a presidentially declared disaster area, by suspending tax examination and collection actions during their detention. Examination and collection actions that can be precluded or suspended include tax return audits, mailings of notices and other actions involving the collection of overdue taxes.[15]

2709. Third-Party Summonses. The IRS may issue summonses to third-party recordkeepers (attorneys, enrolled agents, banks, brokers, accountants, etc.)

Footnote references are to paragraphs of the 2002 Standard Federal Tax Reports.

[5] ¶ 43,304, ¶ 43,312
[6] ¶ 43,308
[7] ¶ 43,304
[8] ¶ 43,304, ¶ 43,308, ¶ 43,312.01
[9] ¶ 43,332, ¶ 43,352.021
[10] ¶ 42,790, ¶ 42,791.01
[11] ¶ 42,790, ¶ 42,791.021
[12] ¶ 42,790, ¶ 42,791.035
[13] ¶ 42,790, ¶ 42,791.03
[14] ¶ 42,760, ¶ 42,791.035
[15] ¶ 42,686

and other third parties for the production of records concerning the business transactions or affairs of a taxpayer. The taxpayer is to be notified of the summons within three days of service of the summons (but in no case later than the 23rd day before the day fixed in the summons for production of records). However, notice is not required with respect to any summons: (1) served on the person with respect to whose liability the summons is issued, or any officer or employee of the person; (2) issued to determine whether or not records of the business transactions or affairs of an identified person have been made or kept; and (3) issued in certain criminal investigations. Any taxpayer who is entitled to notice may intervene in any proceeding for the enforcement of the summons in question. The taxpayer also has the right to begin a proceeding to quash the summons if, within 20 days after the day the notice of summons was served on or mailed to him, he files a petition to quash the summons in a district court having jurisdiction and notifies the IRS and the third party by mailing a copy of the petition by certified or registered mail to each one. Although notice is not required for a "John Doe" summons (i.e., issued to determine the identity of a person having a numbered bank account or similar arrangement), such a summons may be issued only after the IRS has shown adequate grounds for serving the summons, and an ex parte court proceeding is held to determine its validity (Code Sec. 7609).[16]

If a taxpayer intervenes in a dispute between the IRS and a third party and the dispute is not resolved within six months, the statute of limitations period will be suspended beginning on the date that is six months after the summons is served and continuing until the dispute is resolved. This provision also applies with respect to "John Doe" summonses (Code Sec. 7609(e)).[17]

The IRS is required to provide reasonable notice in advance to a taxpayer before contacting third parties with respect to examination or collection activities regarding the taxpayer (Code Sec. 7602(c)).[18] However, notice is not required: (1) with respect to any contact authorized by the taxpayer; (2) if the IRS determines that the notice would jeopardize collection of any tax; or (3) with respect to any pending criminal investigation.

Assessment and Collection of Tax

2711. Assessment of Deficiency. A "deficiency" is the excess of the correct tax liability over the tax shown on the return (if any), plus amounts previously assessed (or collected without assessment) as a deficiency, and minus any rebates made to the taxpayer (Code Sec. 6211).[19] For this purpose, the tax shown on the return is the amount of tax before credits for estimated tax paid, withheld tax, or amounts collected under a termination assessment (Code Sec. 6211(b)).[20]

The IRS is authorized to assess taxes (Reg. § 301.6201-1).[21] The collection process begins when a notice of deficiency is sent to the taxpayer's last known address by registered or certified mail (Code Sec. 6212).[22] In each deficiency notice, the IRS must provide a description of the basis for the assessment, an identification of the amount of tax, interest and penalties assessed (Code Sec. 7522)[23] and the date determined to be the last day on which the taxpayer may file a petition with the Tax Court (Code Sec. 6213(a)).[24] However, the failure by the IRS to specify the last day on which to file a petition will not invalidate an otherwise valid deficiency notice if the taxpayer was not prejudiced by the omission.[25]

Within 90 days after notice of the deficiency is mailed (or within 150 days after mailing if the notice is addressed to a person outside the U.S.), the taxpayer may file a petition with the Tax Court for a redetermination of the deficiency (Code Sec. 6213).[26] Payment of the assessed amount after the deficiency notice is mailed does not deprive the Tax Court of jurisdiction over the deficiency (Reg. § 301.6213-1(b)(3)).[27]

Footnote references are to paragraphs of the 2002 Standard Federal Tax Reports.

[16] ¶ 42,890	[20] ¶ 37,535	[24] ¶ 37,545
[17] ¶ 42,890, ¶ 42,897.021	[21] ¶ 37,503	[25] ¶ 37,544.25
[18] ¶ 42,820, ¶ 42,897.021	[22] ¶ 37,540	[26] ¶ 37,545
[19] ¶ 37,535	[23] ¶ 42,800	[27] ¶ 37,546

¶ 2711

If the taxpayer does not file a Tax Court petition within the 90-day time period, the tax may be collected (see ¶ 2735). A taxpayer's property may be seized to enforce collection if there is a failure to pay an assessed tax within 30 days after notice of levy (Code Sec. 6331(d)(2)).[28] However, the notice and waiting period does not apply if the IRS finds that the collection of tax is in jeopardy (see ¶ 2713). Notices of levy must provide a description of the levy process in simple and nontechnical terms (Code Sec. 6331).[29]

Mathematical or Clerical Errors. A notice of tax due because of mathematical or clerical errors is not a deficiency notice, and the taxpayer has no right to file a petition with the Tax Court for redetermining the deficiency. A taxpayer who receives notice of additional tax due to mathematical or clerical error has 60 days after the notice is sent in which to file a request for abatement of any part of the assessment. Any reassessment must be made under the regular notice-of-deficiency procedures. During the 60-day period, the IRS cannot proceed to collect upon the summary assessment (Code Sec. 6213(b)(1) and (f)).

2712. Waiver of Deficiency Restrictions. The taxpayer has the right to waive the restrictions on assessment and collection of all or part of a deficiency at any time, whether or not a notice of deficiency has been issued (Code Sec. 6213(d)).[30] This is done by executing Form 870. Execution of a waiver of the restrictions on assessment and collection of the entire deficiency in advance of the statutory ("90-day") notice relieves the IRS of sending such a notice and precludes appeal to the Tax Court.[31] However, an appeal to the Tax Court is not precluded if the waiver covers only part of the deficiency or is executed after receipt of the 90-day deficiency notice. Payment of an amount as tax before issuance of the statutory notice has the effect of a waiver,[32] and, if the amount paid equals or exceeds the amount of a subsequently determined deficiency, it deprives the Tax Court of jurisdiction (Reg. § 301.6213-1(b)(3)).[33]

2713. Jeopardy and Termination Assessments. The IRS can immediately assess a deficiency if the assessment and collection of tax would be jeopardized by delay or if the collection of tax would be otherwise jeopardized, as, for example, when a taxpayer is leaving the country or seeking to hide assets (Code Sec. 6851;[34] Code Sec. 6861[35]). If a jeopardy assessment is made prior to the mailing of the notice of deficiency, the notice must be mailed to the taxpayer within 60 days after the assessment (Code Sec. 6861(b)).[36] If a termination assessment is made, the assessment ends the taxpayer's tax year only for purposes of computing the amount of tax that becomes immediately due and payable. It does not end the tax year for any other purpose. In the case of a termination assessment, the IRS must issue the taxpayer a notice of deficiency within 60 days of the later of (1) the due date (including extensions) of the taxpayer's return for the full tax year or (2) the day on which the taxpayer files the return (Code Sec. 6851(b)).[37]

The IRS may presume that the collection of tax is in jeopardy if an individual in physical possession of more than $10,000 in cash or its equivalent does not claim either ownership of the cash or that it belongs to another person whose identity the IRS can readily ascertain and who acknowledges ownership of the cash. In this case, the IRS may treat the entire amount as gross income taxable at the highest rate specified in Code Sec. 1. The possessor of the cash is entitled to notice of, and the right to challenge, the assessment. However, should the true owner appear, he will be substituted for the possessor and all rights will vest in him (Code Sec. 6867).[38]

2719. Injunction to Restrain Collection. The Code prohibits a suit to restrain the assessment or collection of any tax (Code Sec. 7421(a)) [39] or to restrain the enforcement of liability against a transferee or fiduciary (Code Sec. 7421(b)).[40] Nevertheless, injunctive relief may be available in rare cases if irreparable harm[41]

---

[28] ¶ 38,185	[33] ¶ 37,546	[38] ¶ 40,580
[29] ¶ 38,185	[34] ¶ 40,402	[39] ¶ 41,680
[30] ¶ 37,545	[35] ¶ 40,460	[40] ¶ 41,680
[31] ¶ 37,549.9612	[36] ¶ 40,460	[41] ¶ 41,683.70
[32] ¶ 37,549.032	[37] ¶ 40,402	

will be done to the taxpayer and the taxpayer shows, at the outset of the suit, that the government could not collect the tax under any circumstances.[42] However, injunctive relief may be obtained for assessment or collection actions (other than jeopardy or termination assessments) if a notice of deficiency has not been mailed to the taxpayer, the period for filing a Tax Court petition has not expired, or a Tax Court proceeding with respect to the tax is pending (Code Sec. 6213(a)).[43]

2721. Closing Agreement. The IRS is authorized to enter into a written agreement with a taxpayer in order to determine conclusively the tax liability for a tax period that ended prior to the date of the agreement (Form 866) or to determine one or more separate items affecting the tax liability for any tax period (Form 906). A closing agreement may also be entered for tax periods that end subsequent to the date of the agreement. Closing agreements may be entered into in order to finally resolve questions of tax liability (Code Sec. 7121; Reg. § 301.7121-1).[44] For example, a fiduciary may desire a final determination before an estate is closed or trust assets distributed. Closing agreements are final, conclusive, and binding upon both parties. They cannot be reopened or modified except upon a showing of fraud or malfeasance or the misrepresentation of a material fact.[45] Generally, the IRS is not precluded from later determining additions to tax absent terms in the agreement that specifically address the issue of additions to tax.[46]

2723. Compromise of Tax and Penalty. The IRS may compromise the tax liability in most civil or criminal cases before referral to the Department of Justice for prosecution or defense. The Attorney General or a delegate may compromise any case after the referral. However, the IRS may not compromise certain criminal liabilities arising under internal revenue laws relating to narcotics, opium, or marijuana. Interest and penalties, as well as tax, may be compromised (Code Sec. 7122; Temp. Reg. § 301.7122-1T).[47] Offers in compromise are submitted on Form 656 accompanied by a financial statement on Form 433-A for an individual or Form 433-B for businesses (if based on inability to pay) (Reg. § 601.203(b)).[48] A taxpayer who faces severe or unusual economic hardship may also apply for an offer in compromise by submitting Form 656. If the IRS accepts an offer in compromise, the payment is allocated among tax, penalties, and interest as stated in the collateral agreement with the IRS. If no allocation is specified in the agreement and the amounts paid exceed the total tax and penalties owed, the payments will be applied to tax, penalties, and interest in that order, beginning with the earliest year. If the IRS agrees to an amount that does not exceed the combined tax and penalties, and there is no agreement regarding allocation of the payment, no amount will be allocated to interest.[49]

2724. Partial Payments. Allocations for partial payments of assessed federal income taxes, penalties and interest made by a cash-basis taxpayer will be respected.[50] A partial payment on deficiencies received without instructions for its application will be applied to tax, penalties, and interest in that order, starting with the earliest period.

Limitation Period for Assessment and Collection of Tax

2726. General Three-Year Period. Generally, all income taxes must be assessed within three years after the original return is filed (the last day prescribed by law for filing if the return was filed before the last day).[51] In the case of pass-through entities, the three-year rule begins to run at the time the pass-through entity's shareholder or other beneficial owner files an individual income tax return. A return filed prior to its due date is deemed to have been filed on the due date. A proceeding in court without assessment for collection of the tax must commence

---

Footnote references are to paragraphs of the 2002 Standard Federal Tax Reports.

[42] ¶ 41,683.69	[46] ¶ 41,090.279	[49] ¶ 9104.63
[43] ¶ 37,545	[47] ¶ 41,110, ¶ 41,111	[50] ¶ 9104.664
[44] ¶ 41,080, ¶ 41,081,	[48] ¶ 43,372	[51] ¶ 38,960, ¶ 38,963
¶ 41,090, ¶ 43,364		
[45] ¶ 41,080, ¶ 41,081,		
¶ 41,090.279, ¶ 43,364		

within the same period (Code Sec. 6501; Reg. § 301.6501(a)-1).[52] The period can be extended by a written agreement between the taxpayer and the IRS (Code Sec. 6501(c)(4); Reg. § 301.6501(c)-1(d)).[53] Interest on any tax may be assessed and collected at any time during the period within which the tax itself may be collected (but only up to the date on which payment of the tax is received) (Reg. § 301.6601-1(f)).[54]

If, within the 60-day period ending on the last day of the assessment period, the IRS receives an amended return or written document from the taxpayer showing that additional tax is due for the year in question, the period in which to assess such additional tax is extended for 60 days after the day on which the IRS receives the amended return or written document (Code Sec. 6501(c)(7)).[55]

If unused foreign tax credits have been carried back, the statute of limitations on assessment and collection for the year to which the carryback is made will not close until one year after the expiration of the period within which a deficiency may be assessed for the year from which the carryback was made (Code Sec. 6501(i); Reg. § 301.6501(i)-1).[56]

Deficiencies attributable to carryback of a net operating loss, a capital loss or the general business credit and research credit may be assessed within the period that applies to the loss or credit year. Deficiencies attributable to the carrying back of one of those credits as a result of the carryback of a net operating loss, capital loss or other credit may be assessed within the period that applies to the loss or other credit year (Code Sec. 6501(h) and (j)).[57]

2728. Request for Prompt Assessment. A corporation that is contemplating dissolution, is in the process of dissolving, or has actually dissolved, or a decedent or an estate of a decedent (for taxes other than the estate tax imposed by chapter 11), may request a prompt assessment (Code Sec. 6501(d)).[58] If such a request is made, an assessment or a proceeding in court without assessment for the collection of any tax must then be begun within 18 months after the receipt of a written request for a prompt assessment. In the case of a corporation, however, the 18-month period will not apply unless the corporation has completed or will eventually complete its dissolution at or before the end of the 18-month period. This provision does not apply in the cases described at ¶ 2732 and ¶ 2734. It also does not apply for personal holding company taxes in certain instances or where a waiver filed by the taxpayer extends the assessment period beyond the 18-month period (Reg. § 301.6501(d)-1).[59]

2730. Return Executed by IRS Official. A return executed by an IRS official or employee in which the taxpayer has not filed a return will not start the running of the statute of limitations on assessment and collection (Code Sec. 6020 and Code Sec. 6501(b)(3); Reg. § 301.6501(b)-1(c)).[60]

2732. False Return or No Return. Tax may be assessed or a court proceeding to collect tax may be commenced at any time if (1) the return is false or fraudulent; (2) there is a willful attempt to evade tax; or (3) no return is filed (Reg. § 301.6501(c)-1).[61]

In addition, in the case of a fraudulent return, the government may impose additional taxes at any time, without regard to statutes of limitations, although the burden of proof falls on the government to prove fraud by the taxpayer.[62]

2734. Omission of Over 25% of Income. If the taxpayer omits from gross income (total receipts, without reduction for cost) an amount in excess of 25% of the amount of gross income stated in the return, a six-year limitation period on

---

Footnote references are to paragraphs of the 2002 Standard Federal Tax Reports.

[52] ¶ 38,960, ¶ 38,961	[58] ¶ 38,960	[61] ¶ 38,960, ¶ 38,966,
[53] ¶ 38,960, ¶ 38,966,	[59] ¶ 38,960, ¶ 38,968,	¶ 38,967.021
¶ 38,967.025	¶ 38,969.01	[62] ¶ 38,967.04
[54] ¶ 39,412	[60] ¶ 35,240, ¶ 35,241,	
[55] ¶ 38,960	¶ 38,960, ¶ 38,963.65,	
[56] ¶ 38,960, ¶ 38,977	¶ 38,964	
[57] ¶ 38,960, ¶ 39,080.034		

assessment applies. An item will not be considered as omitted from gross income if information sufficient to apprise the IRS of the nature and amount of such item is disclosed in the return or in any schedule or statement attached to the return (Code Sec. 6501(e); Reg. § 301.6501(e)-1(a)).[63]

2735. Collection After Assessment. After assessment of tax made within the statutory period of limitation (¶ 2726), the tax may be collected by levy or a proceeding in court commenced within 10 years after the assessment or within any period for collection agreed upon in writing between the IRS and the taxpayer before the expiration of the 10-year period. The period agreed upon by the parties may be extended by later written agreements so long as they are made prior to the expiration of the period previously agreed upon. The IRS has to notify taxpayers of their right to refuse an extension each time one is requested (Code Sec. 6501(c)(4)). If a timely court proceeding has commenced for the collection of the tax, then the period during which the tax may be collected is extended until the liability for tax (or a judgment against the taxpayer) is satisfied or becomes unenforceable.

Generally effective after 1999, the 10-year limitations period on collections may not be extended if there has been no levy on any of the taxpayer's property. If the taxpayer entered into an installment agreement with the IRS, however, the 10-year limitations period may be extended for the period that the limitations period was extended under the original terms of the installment agreement plus 90 days. If, in any request made on or before December 31, 1999, a taxpayer agreed to extend the 10-year period of limitations on collections, the extension will expire on the latest of (1) the last day of the original 10-year limitations period, (2) December 31, 2002, or (3) in the case of an extension in connection with an installment agreement, the 90th day after the extension.

The 10-year limitation period referred to above applies in the case of (1) taxes assessed after November 5, 1990, and (2) taxes assessed on or before that date if six years had not expired following assessment as of that date. In the case of taxes assessed before that date, the limitation period was six years (Code Sec. 6502(a)).[64]

Interest accrues on a deficiency from the date the tax was due (determined without regard to extensions) until the date payment is received at the rate specified at ¶ 2838 (Reg. § 301.6601-1(a)(1)).[65] Interest may be assessed and collected during the period in which the related tax may be collected (Code Sec. 6601(g)).[66]

2736. Suspension of Assessment Period. When an income, estate or gift tax deficiency notice is mailed, the running of the period of limitations on assessment and collection of any deficiency is suspended for 90 days (150 days for a deficiency notice mailed to persons outside the United States) (not counting Saturday, Sunday, or a legal holiday in the District of Columbia as the 90th or 150th day), plus an additional 60 days thereafter in either case (Code Sec. 6503(a)(1)).[67] If a petition is filed with the Tax Court, the running of the period of limitations is suspended until the Tax Court's decision becomes final, and for an additional 60 days thereafter (Code Sec. 6503(a)(1); Reg. § 301.6503(a)-1).[68]

The 10-year statute of limitations for collection after assessment is also suspended from the date the IRS wrongfully seizes or receives a third party's property to 30 days after the earlier of (1) the date the IRS returns the property or (2) the date on which a judgment secured in a wrongful levy action becomes final. Similarly, with respect to wrongful liens, the 10-year limitations period is suspended from the time the third-party owner is entitled to a certificate of discharge of lien until 30 days after the earlier of (1) the date that the IRS no longer holds any amount as a deposit or bond that was used to satisfy the unpaid liability, or that was refunded or released or (2) the date that the judgment in a civil action becomes final (see ¶ 2755) (Code Sec. 6503(f)).[69]

Footnote references are to paragraphs of the 2002 Standard Federal Tax Reports.

[63] ¶ 38,960, ¶ 38,970, ¶ 38,971.021
[64] ¶ 39,010, ¶ 39,020.021
[65] ¶ 39,412
[66] ¶ 39,410
[67] ¶ 39,030
[68] ¶ 39,030, ¶ 39,031
[69] ¶ 39,030

¶ 2736

For Chapter 11 bankruptcy cases, the running of the period of limitations is suspended during the period of the automatic stay on collection of taxes and for an additional period ending 60 days after the day the stay is lifted for assessments and for six months thereafter for collection (Code Sec. 6503(h)).[70] In receivership and other bankruptcy cases (such as Chapter 13) where a fiduciary is required to give written notice to the IRS of an appointment or authorization to act, the assessment period is suspended from the date the proceedings are instituted and ending 30 days after the day of notice to the IRS of such appointment. The extension period cannot exceed two years (Code Sec. 6872).[71]

If the taxpayer and the IRS agree to the rescission of a deficiency notice, the statute of limitations again begins to run as of the date of the rescission and continues to run for the period of time that remains on the date the notice was issued (Code Sec. 6212(d)).[72]

2738. Suit for Recovery of Erroneous Refund. The government may sue to recover an erroneous refund (including, but not limited to, one made after the applicable refund period described in ¶ 2763) within two years after such refund was paid (Code Sec. 6532(b)).[73] However, a suit may be commenced within five years if any part of the refund was induced by fraud or misrepresentation of a material fact (Code Sec. 6532(b); Reg. § 301.6532-2).[74]

2740. Criminal Prosecution. A criminal prosecution must generally be started within three years after the offense is committed (Code Sec. 6531).[75] However, a six-year period applies in a case where there is (1) fraud or an attempt to defraud the United States or an agency thereof, by conspiracy or otherwise; (2) a willful attempt to evade or defeat any tax or payment; (3) willful aiding or assisting in the preparation of a false return or other document; (4) willful failure to pay any tax or make any return (except certain information returns) at the time required by law; (5) a false statement verified under penalties of perjury or a false or fraudulent return, statement or other document; (6) intimidation of a U.S. officer or employee; (7) an offense committed by a U.S. officer or employee in connection with a revenue law; and (8) a conspiracy to defeat tax or payment (Code Sec. 6531).[76]

Claim Against Transferee or Fiduciary

2743. Collection from Transferee of Property. The liability of a transferee of property is generally assessed and collected in the same manner as is any other deficiency imposed by the IRS (Reg. § 301.6901-1(a)).[77] The term "transferee" includes an heir, legatee, devisee, distributee of an estate of a deceased person, the shareholder of a dissolved corporation, the assignee or donee of an insolvent person, the successor of a corporation, a party to a Code Sec. 368(a) reorganization, and all other classes of distributees. Such term also includes, with respect to the gift tax, a donee (without regard to the solvency of the donor) and, with respect to the estate tax, any person who, under Code Sec. 6324(a)(2), is personally liable for any part of such tax (Reg. § 301.6901-1(b)).[78]

2745. Transferee Assessment and Collection Period. Unless a taxpayer has filed a false return with intent to evade tax (¶ 2732), an assessment against a transferee or fiduciary must be made within the following periods: (1) in the case of an initial transferee, within one year after the expiration of the period of limitation for assessment against the taxpayer; (2) in the case of a transferee of a transferee, within one year after the expiration of the period of limitation for assessment against the preceding transferee or three years after the expiration of the period of limitation for assessment against the taxpayer, whichever of these two periods expires first; (3) if a timely court proceeding has been brought against the taxpayer

---

Footnote references are to paragraphs of the 2002 Standard Federal Tax Reports.

[70] ¶ 39,030	[74] ¶ 39,270, ¶ 39,280.01	[77] ¶ 40,701, ¶ 40,720.01
[71] ¶ 40,640	[75] ¶ 39,240	[78] ¶ 40,701
[72] ¶ 37,540	[76] ¶ 39,240	
[73] ¶ 39,270, ¶ 39,272, ¶ 39,280.01		

¶ **2738**

or last preceding transferee, within one year after the return of execution in such proceeding; or (4) in the case of a fiduciary, within one year after the liability arises or within the limitations period for collection of the tax (¶ 2726), whichever is the later (Code Sec. 6901; Reg. § 301.6901-1(c)).[79]

2747. Collection from Fiduciary. In order to receive advance notice from the IRS with respect to assessments, every fiduciary must give written notice to the IRS of his fiduciary capacity. If this notice (Form 56) is not filed, the IRS may proceed against the property in the hands of the fiduciary after mailing notice of the deficiency or other liability to the taxpayer's last known address, even if the taxpayer is then deceased or is under legal disability. The fiduciary may be relieved of any further liability by filing with the IRS written notice and evidence of the termination (Reg. § 301.6903-1).[80]

Bankruptcy or Receivership of Taxpayer

2750. Tax Collection Procedure. When a taxpayer's assets are taken over by a receiver appointed by the court, the IRS may immediately assess the tax if it has not already been lawfully assessed. The IRS may also assess the tax on (1) the debtor's estate under U.S. Code title 11 bankruptcy proceedings or (2) the debtor, if the tax liability has become *res judicata* pursuant to a title 11 bankruptcy determination (Code Sec. 6871(a) and (b)).[81] Tax claims may be presented to the court before which the receivership (or a title 11 bankruptcy) is pending, despite the pendency of proceedings in the Tax Court. However, in the case of a receivership proceeding, no petition shall be filed with the Tax Court after the appointment of the receiver (Code Sec. 6871(c)).[82] The trustee of the debtor's estate in a title 11 bankruptcy proceeding may intervene on behalf of the debtor's estate in any Tax Court proceeding to which the debtor is a party (Code Sec. 7464).[83]

Liens and Levies

2751. Property Subject to Liens. If a taxpayer fails to pay an assessed tax for which payment has been demanded, the amount due (including interest and penalties) constitutes a lien in favor of the United States upon all the taxpayer's property (real, personal, tangible, and intangible), including after-acquired property and rights to property (Reg. § 301.6321-1).[84] Whether the taxpayer owns or has an interest in property is determined under the appropriate state law.[85] Once the taxpayer's rights in the property are established, federal law determines priorities among competing creditors (Code Sec. 6323) [86] and controls whether specific property is exempt from levy (see ¶ 2753). Once a tax lien arises, it continues until the tax liability is paid or the lien becomes unenforceable due to a lapse of time (Code Sec. 6322).[87] Time has lapsed if 10 years have passed from the date of assessment (or longer, if the taxpayer waives restrictions on collection) during which the IRS has not attempted to collect the tax either by suit or distraint (Code Sec. 6502(a)).[88]

2753. Property Subject to Levy. Although a tax lien attaches to all the debtor's property, some property is exempt from levy. The following are among the items that are exempt from levy to some extent: (1) wearing apparel and school books; (2) fuel, provisions, furniture, and personal effects; (3) unemployment benefits; (4) books and tools of a trade, business, or profession; (5) undelivered mail; (6) certain annuity and pension payments; (7) workers' compensation; (8) judgments for support of minor children; (9) certain AFDC, social security, state and local welfare payments and Job Training Partnership Act payments; (10) certain amounts of wages, salary, and other income; and (11) certain service-connected disability payments (Code Sec. 6334(a)).[89]

Footnote references are to paragraphs of the 2002 Standard Federal Tax Reports.

[79] ¶ 40,700	[83] ¶ 42,120	[87] ¶ 38,140
[80] ¶ 40,730, ¶ 40,811	[84] ¶ 38,135A, ¶ 38,136	[88] ¶ 39,020.021
[81] ¶ 40,610	[85] ¶ 38,136.01	[89] ¶ 38,210, ¶ 38,225.01
[82] ¶ 40,610, ¶ 40,630.01	[86] ¶ 38,145	

Certain specified payments are not exempt from levy if the Secretary of the Treasury approves the levy. Among the items so covered are certain wage replacement payments as specified at Code Sec. 6334(f).[90]

The IRS may not seize any real property used as a residence by the taxpayer or any real property of the taxpayer (other than rental property) that is used as a residence by another person in order to satisfy a liability of $5,000 or less (including tax, penalties and interest). In the case of the taxpayer's principal residence, the IRS may not seize the residence without written approval of a federal district court judge or magistrate (Code Sec. 6334(a)(13); Code Sec. 6334(e)).[91] Unless collection of tax is in jeopardy, tangible personal property or real property (other than rented real property) used in the taxpayer's trade or business may not be seized without written approval of an IRS district or assistant director. Such approval may not be given unless it is determined that the taxpayer's other assets subject to collection are not sufficient to pay the amount due and the expenses of the proceedings. Where a levy is made on tangible personal property essential to the taxpayer's trade or business, the IRS must provide an accelerated appeals process to determine whether the property should be released from levy (Code Sec. 6343(a)(2)).[92] See ¶ 2755.

Levies are prohibited if the estimated expenses of the levy and sale exceed the fair market value of the property (Code Sec. 6331(f)).[93] Also, unless the collection of tax is in jeopardy, a levy cannot be made on any day on which the taxpayer is required to respond to an IRS summons (Code Sec. 6331(g)).[94] Further, financial institutions are required to hold amounts garnished by the IRS for 21 days after receiving notice of the levy to provide the taxpayer time to notify the IRS of any errors (Code Sec. 6332(c)).[95]

2754. Recording and Priority of Tax Liens. Until notice of a tax lien has been properly recorded, it is not valid against any bona fide purchaser for value, mechanic's lienor, judgment lien creditor or holder of a security interest (such as a mortgagee or pledgee, for example) (Code Sec. 6323(a)).[96] Also, even a properly recorded tax lien may not be valid against so-called superpriorities, which include purchases of securities and automobiles, retail purchases, casual sales of less than $1,100 in 2001 ($1,130 projected for 2002), certain possessory liens securing payment for repairs to personal property, real property taxes and special assessment liens, mechanic's liens for repairs and improvements to certain residential property, attorneys' liens, certain insurance contracts and deposit secured loans (previously referred to as passbook loans) (Code Sec. 6323(b)).[97] In addition, security interests arising from commercial financing agreements may be accorded superpriority status (Code Sec. 6323(c)).[98]

Notice of a federal tax lien must be filed in the one office designated by the state in which the property is situated (Code Sec. 6323(f)).[99] Generally, personal property is situated in the state where the taxpayer resides (rather than where domiciled); for real property, the situs is its physical location. If, in the case of either real or personal property, the state designates more than one office or does not designate an office where notice must be filed, notice of the lien must be filed with the Clerk of the U.S. District Court for the district in which the property is situated. If state law provides that a notice of lien affecting personal property must be filed in the county clerk's office located in the taxpayer's county of residence and also adopts a federal law that requires a notice of lien to be filed in another location in order to attach to a specific type of property, the state is deemed to have designated only one office for the filing of the notice. Thus, to protect its lien, the IRS need only file its notice in the county clerk's office located in the taxpayer's home county. Notice regarding property located in the District of Columbia is filed with the

---

Footnote references are to paragraphs of the 2002 Standard Federal Tax Reports.

[90] ¶ 38,210	[95] ¶ 38,185	[98] ¶ 38,145,
[91] ¶ 38,210, ¶ 38,225.01	[96] ¶ 38,145,	¶ 38,160.03—
[92] ¶ 38,270, ¶ 38,274.01	¶ 38,160.021—	38,160.0155
[93] ¶ 38,185	38,160.0119	[99] ¶ 38,145
[94] ¶ 38,185	[97] ¶ 38,145	

¶ 2754

Recorder of Deeds of the District of Columbia. Special rules apply in a state that requires public indexing for priority liens against realty.

A forfeiture under local law of property seized by any law enforcement agency or other local governmental branch relates back to the time the property was first seized, unless, under local law, a claim holder would have priority over the interest of the government in the property (Code Sec. 6323(i)(3)).[100]

The IRS may not levy against property while a taxpayer has a pending offer in compromise or installment agreement (Code Sec. 6331(k)).[101] If the offer in compromise or installment agreement is ultimately rejected, the levy prohibition remains in effect for 30 days after the rejection and during the pendency of any appeal of the rejection, providing the appeal is filed within 30 days of the rejection. No levy may be made while the installment agreement is in effect. If the installment agreement is terminated by the IRS, no levy may be made for 30 days after the termination and during the pendency of any appeal.

2754A. Notice and Opportunity for Hearing. The IRS must notify any person subject to a lien of the existence of the lien within five days of the lien being filed (Code Sec. 6320; Temp. Reg. § 301.6320-1T). Among other requirements, the notice must address the person's right to request a hearing during the 30-day period beginning on the sixth day after the lien is filed. Similarly, at least 30 days prior to the IRS filing a notice of levy on any person's property or right to property, the IRS must provide notice of the right to a hearing (Code Sec. 6330; Temp. Reg. § 301.6320-1T). Whether in connection with the notice of lien or notice of intent to levy, the hearing is to be held by the IRS Office of Appeals. At the hearing, the taxpayer may raise any issue relevant to the appropriateness of the proposed collection activity if such issue was not raised at a previous hearing. The taxpayer has 30 days after the hearing determination to appeal the determination to the Tax Court or, if the Tax Court lacks jurisdiction over the underlying tax liability, to a federal district court.

2755. Release of Tax Liens and Levies. Taxpayers may appeal the filing of a notice of lien in the public record and petition for release. If filed in error, the IRS must release the lien and state that the lien was erroneous (Code Sec. 6326(b)). The request for relief must be based on one of the following grounds: (1) the tax liability had been satisfied before the lien was filed; (2) the assessing of the tax liability violated either the notice of deficiency procedures or the Bankruptcy Code; or (3) the limitations period for collecting the liability had expired prior to the filing of the lien (Code Sec. 6326; Reg. § 301.6326-1).[102]

Further, the IRS may withdraw a public notice of tax lien before payment in full if: (1) the filing of the notice was premature or not in accord with administrative procedures; (2) the taxpayer has entered into an installment agreement to satisfy the tax liability; (3) withdrawal of the notice would facilitate the collection of the tax liability; or (4) the withdrawal of the notice would be in the best interest of the taxpayer and the government, as determined by the National Taxpayer Advocate (Code Sec. 6323(j)).[103] The withdrawal of a notice of tax lien does not affect the underlying tax lien; rather, the withdrawal simply relinquishes any lien priority the IRS had obtained when the notice was filed.

The IRS is required to release a levy if: (1) the underlying liability is satisfied or becomes unenforceable due to lapse of time; (2) the IRS determines that the release of the levy will facilitate the collection of tax; (3) an installment payment agreement has been executed by the taxpayer with respect to the liability; (4) the IRS determines that the levy is creating a financial hardship; or (5) the fair market value of the property exceeds the liability, and the partial release of the levy would not hinder the collection of tax (Code Sec. 6343(a)).[104] In addition, a taxpayer may

Footnote references are to paragraphs of the 2002 Standard Federal Tax Reports.
100 ¶ 38,145   102 ¶ 38,175, ¶ 38,176   104 ¶ 38,270, ¶ 38,274.01
101 ¶ 38,185   103 ¶ 38,160.0756

request that the IRS sell the levied property (Code Sec. 6335(f); Reg. § 301.6335-1(d)).[105]

The IRS has been given authority to return property that has been levied upon if: (1) the levy was premature or not in accordance with administrative procedure; (2) the taxpayer has entered into an installment agreement to satisfy the tax liability, unless the agreement provides otherwise; (3) the return of the property will facilitate collection of the tax liability; or (4) with the consent of the taxpayer or the Taxpayer Advocate, the return of the property would be in the best interests of the taxpayer and the government (Code Sec. 6343(d)).[106] Property is returned in the same manner as if the property had been wrongfully levied upon, except that the taxpayer is not entitled to interest.

A taxpayer may bring a suit in federal district court if an IRS employee knowingly or negligently fails to release a tax lien on the taxpayer's property after receiving written notice from the taxpayer of the IRS's failure to release the lien (Code Sec. 7432).[107] The taxpayer may recover actual economic damages plus the costs of the action. Injuries such as inconvenience, emotional distress, and loss of reputation are not compensable damages unless they result in actual economic harm. Costs of the action that may be recovered are limited generally to certain court costs and do not include administrative costs or attorney's fees, although attorney's fees may be recoverable under Code Sec. 7430 (see ¶ 2796) (Reg. § 301.7432-1(c)).[108] A two-year statute of limitations, measured from the date on which the cause of action accrued, applies (Code Sec. 7432(d)(3)).[109]

Third-Party Owners. A third-party owner of property against which a federal tax lien has been filed may obtain a certificate of discharge with respect to the lien on such property (Code Sec. 6325(b)(4)).[110] The certificate is issued if (1) the third-party owner deposits with the IRS an amount of money equal to the value of the government's interest in the property as determined by the IRS or (2) the third-party owner posts a bond covering the government's interest in the property in a form acceptable by the IRS.

If the IRS determines that (1) the liability to which the lien relates can be satisfied from other sources or (2) the value of the government's interest in the property is less than the IRS's prior determination of the government's interest in the property, then the IRS will refund (with interest) the amount deposited and release the bond applicable to such property. Within 120 days after a certificate of discharge is issued, the third-party owner may file a civil action against the United States in a federal district court for a determination of whether the government's interest in the property (if any) has less value than that determined by the IRS (Code Sec. 7426(a)(4); Code Sec. 7426(b)(5)).[111]

Mitigation of Effect of Statute of Limitations

2756. Correction of Errors in Certain Cases. The Code provides rules in Secs. 1311-1314 (Reg. § 1.1311(a)-1—Reg. § 1.1314(c)-1) [112] for relief from some of the inequities caused by the statute of limitations and other provisions that would otherwise prevent equitable adjustment of various income tax hardships. Adjustments are permitted even though the limitation period forassessment or refund for the year at issue may have otherwise expired, when a determination under the income tax laws: (1) requires the inclusion in gross income of an item that was erroneously included in the income of the taxpayer for another tax year or in the gross income of a "related taxpayer"; (2) allows a deduction or credit that was erroneously allowed to the taxpayer for another tax year or to a "related taxpayer"; (3) requires the exclusion from gross income of an item included in a return filed by the taxpayer or with respect to which tax was paid and which was erroneously excluded or omitted from the gross income of the taxpayer for another tax year or

---

Footnote references are to paragraphs of the 2002 Standard Federal Tax Reports.

¶ 2756

[105] ¶ 38,230, ¶ 38,231,	[108] ¶ 41,761	[111] ¶ 41,710
¶ 38,234.025	[109] ¶ 41,760	[112] ¶ 31,800—¶ 31,865
[106] ¶ 38,274.023	[110] ¶ 38,165	
[107] ¶ 41,760, ¶ 41,768.01		

from the gross income of a "related taxpayer" for the same or another tax year; (4) requires the correction of income or deduction items of estates or trusts or beneficiaries of either as between such "related taxpayers"; (5) establishes the basis of property by making adjustments to such basis for items that should have been added to, or deducted from income of preceding years; (6) requires the allowance or disallowance of a deduction or credit to a corporation where a correlative deduction or credit should have been allowed (or disallowed) to a related taxpayer that is a member of an affiliated group of corporations (where there is an 80% common ownership); (7) requires the exclusion from gross income of an item not included in a return filed by the taxpayer and with respect to which the tax was not paid but which is includible in the gross income of the taxpayer for another tax year or in the gross income of a related taxpayer; or (8) disallows a deduction or credit that should have been allowed, but was not allowed, to the taxpayer for another tax year or to a related taxpayer for the same or another tax year.[113]

Refunds and Credits

2759. Claim for Refund or Credit. A claim for refund for an overpayment of income taxes is generally made on the appropriate income tax return. However, once the return has been filed and the taxpayer believes the tax is incorrect, the claim for refund by an individual who filed Form 1040, 1040A, or 1040EZ is made on Form 1040X. The refund claim is made on Form 1120X by a corporation that filed Form 1120.[114] A claim for refund or credit for an overpayment of income taxes for which a form other than Form 1040, 1040A, 1040EZ, 1120, or 990T was filed is made on the appropriate amended tax return (Reg. § 301.6402-3).[115]

2760. Amendment of Refund Claim. A timely claim for refund based upon one or more specific grounds may not be amended to include other and different grounds after the statute of limitations has expired (Reg. § 301.6402-2(b)).

2761. Refund or Credit After Appeal to Tax Court. Where the taxpayer has been mailed a notice of deficiency and has filed a petition with the Tax Court (see ¶ 2778), no credit or refund is allowable, and the taxpayer may not sue in any other court for any part of the tax for the tax year in question (Code Sec. 6512).[116] A credit or refund may be allowed or a suit may be instituted, however, to recover (1) an overpayment determined by a decision of the Tax Court that has become final; (2) any amount collected in excess of an amount computed in accordance with a final decision of the Tax Court; (3) any amount collected after the expiration of the period of limitation upon the beginning of levy or a proceeding in court for collection; (4) overpayments attributable to partnership items; (5) any amount that was collected within the period following the mailing of a notice of deficiency during which the IRS is prohibited from collecting by levy or through a court proceeding; and (6) any amount that is not contested on an appeal from a Tax Court decision.

The Tax Court can order the refund of a tax overpayment plus interest if the IRS has not made a refund to the taxpayer within 120 days after the decision fixing the amount of the refund has become final (Code Sec. 6512(b)).[117]

The Tax Court is empowered to resolve disputes regarding the amount of interest to be charged on a tax deficiency redetermined pursuant to a Tax Court order. The action must be brought within one year from the date on which the decision ordering the redetermination of taxes became final. Further, the taxpayer must pay the entire redetermined deficiency, plus the entire amount of interest, before the Tax Court can hear the case (Code Sec. 7481(c)).[118]

2763. Limitations on Credit or Refund. Generally, a taxpayer may file a claim for refund within three years from the time the return was filed or within two years from the time the tax was paid, whichever is later. If no return was filed by

---

Footnote references are to paragraphs of the 2002 Standard Federal Tax Reports.

[113] ¶ 31,820, ¶ 31,829.021
[114] ¶ 38,518, ¶ 38,519.01, ¶ 38,519.075
[115] ¶ 38,518, ¶ 38,519.12, ¶ 38,519.26
[116] ¶ 39,090, ¶ 39,100.01
[117] ¶ 39,090, ¶ 39,100.021
[118] ¶ 42,420

¶ 2763

the taxpayer, the claim must be filed within two years from the time the tax was paid (Code Sec. 6511(a)).[119] For this purpose, a return filed before the due date is treated as filed on the due date (Code Sec. 6513(a)).[120] Taxpayers who fail to file a return as of the date the IRS mails a deficiency notice may recover in the Tax Court taxes paid during the three years preceding the IRS mailing date (Code Sec. 6512(b)(3)).[121]

If the claim relates to the deductibility of bad debts or worthless securities, the period is seven years; if it relates to the credit for foreign taxes, the period is 10 years. If the refund claim relates to a net operating loss or a capital loss carryback, the period is that period which ends three years after the time prescribed by law for filing the return (including extensions thereof) for the tax year of the NOL or capital loss carryback. To the extent that an overpayment is due to unused credit carrybacks that arise as the result of the carryback of an NOL or capital loss, the claim may be filed during the period that ends three years after the time prescribed by law for filing the return (including extensions thereof) for the tax year of the unused credit that results in such carryback (Code Sec. 6511(d); Reg. § 301.6511(d)-2).[122]

The statute of limitations on refund claims is suspended during any period that an individual is "financially disabled," i.e., under a medically determinable mental or physical impairment that: (1) can be expected to result in death or that has lasted or can be expected to last for a continuous period of not less than one year and (2) renders the person unable to manage his or her financial affairs (Code Sec. 6511(h)).[123] The suspension of the limitations period does not apply for any period during which the taxpayer's spouse or another person is authorized to act on behalf of the individual in financial matters.

2764. Refund Reduction for Past-Due, Legally Enforceable Debts. The Treasury Department's Financial Management Service (FMS) (no longer the IRS since 1998) will reduce the amount of any tax refund payable to a taxpayer by the amount of any past-due, legally enforceable nontax debt that is owed to any federal agency. Debts that are less than $25 and those that have been delinquent for more than 10 years are exempt. In most cases, the creditor federal agencies must have first attempted to collect the debt by using salary offset and administrative procedures. The federal agency is also required to notify the taxpayer that a debt will be referred to the FMS for refund offset if the debt remains unpaid after 60 days or if there is insufficient evidence that the debt is either not past due or not legally enforceable (31 CFR § 285.2).

The FMS has also promulgated rules governing the offset of tax refunds against past-due child and spousal support (31 CFR § 285.3) and against state income tax debts reduced to judgment (31 CFR § 285.8).

2765. Interest on Refund Claim. When a return has been properly filed in processible form, interest is allowed on a refund from the date of overpayment to a date preceding the date of the refund check by not more than 30 days (Code Sec. 6611(b)(2)).[124] If a return is filed late, no interest is allowed for any day before the date on which it is filed (Code Sec. 6611(b)(3)).[125] No interest is payable on a refund arising from an original tax return if the refund is issued by the 45th day after the later of the due date for the return (determined without regard to any extensions) or the date the return is filed (Code Sec. 6611(e)).[126]

The interest rate the IRS must pay for overpayment of taxes by corporate taxpayers is the short-term federal rate plus two percentage points (Code Sec. 6621(a)(1)).[127] The rate of interest on overpayments for noncorporate taxpayers is equal to the federal short-term rate plus three percentage points (which is equal to the interest rate on underpayments of tax). For large corporate overpayments (any portion that exceeds $10,000), the rate is reduced to the sum of the short-term federal rate plus one-half of one percentage point. These rates are adjusted quar-

---

Footnote references are to paragraphs of the 2002 Standard Federal Tax Reports.

¶ **2764**

[119] ¶ 39,060	[122] ¶ 39,060, ¶ 39,067	[125] ¶ 39,430
[120] ¶ 39,120	[123] ¶ 39,060	[126] ¶ 39,430
[121] ¶ 39,090	[124] ¶ 39,430	[127] ¶ 39,450

terly, with each successive rate becoming effective two months after the date of each quarterly adjustment. The rate for the first quarter of 2001 was 9% for noncorporate taxpayers and 8% for corporate taxpayers (6.5% for large corporate overpayments); the rate for the second quarter of 2001 was 8% for noncorporate taxpayers and 7% for corporate taxpayers (5.5% for large corporate overpayments); the rate for the third and fourth quarters of 2001 was 7% for noncorporate taxpayers and 6% for corporate taxpayers (4.5% for large corporate overpayments).[128]

Overlapping Overpayments and Underpayments. The interest rates for overpayments and underpayments have been equalized (sometimes referred to as "global interest netting") for any period of mutual indebtedness between taxpayers and the IRS (Code Sec. 6621(d)). No interest is imposed to the extent that underpayment and overpayment interest run simultaneously on equal amounts. The net zero interest rate applies regardless of whether an underpayment otherwise would be subject to the increased interest rate imposed on large corporate underpayments or an overpayment otherwise would be subject to a reduced interest rate because it was a corporate overpayment in excess of $10,000. Although global interest netting is available to both corporate and noncorporate taxpayers, its effect on noncorporate taxpayers is mitigated due to the equalization of the underpayment and overpayment interest rates for such taxpayers.

2773. Quick Carryback Refund and Postponement of Tax Payment. A corporation (other than an S corporation) that has an overpayment of tax as a result of a net operating loss, capital loss, business and research credits, or a claim-of-right adjustment can file an application on Form 1139 for a tentative adjustment or refund of taxes for a year affected by the carryback of such loss or credits or by such adjustment. A noncorporate taxpayer can apply for similar adjustments on Form 1045.[129] For provisions on the quick refund of a capital loss carryback, see ¶ 1188.

The application itself is not a formal refund claim and its rejection in whole or in part cannot be made the basis of a refund suit. However, the taxpayer can file a regular claim for refund within the limitation period (see ¶ 2763), and this claim can be made the basis for a suit. For losses and credits, the IRS must allow or disallow the refund or credit within 90 days from the later of (1) the date the application is filed or (2) the last day of the month in which the return for the loss or unused credit year is due (giving effect to extensions of time). For claim-of-right adjustments, the IRS must allow or disallow the refund or credit within 90 days from the later of (1) the date the application is filed or (2) the date of the overpayment (Code Sec. 6411(b) and Code Sec. 6411(d)).[130]

If a corporation (but no other taxpayer) expects a net operating loss carryback from the current (unfinished) tax year, it can, subject to certain limitations, extend the time for payment of all or a part of the tax still payable for the immediately preceding year by filing a statement on Form 1138 (Reg. § 1.6164-1).[131]

The Courts

2776. Organization of Tax Court. The primary function of the U.S. Tax Court is to review deficiencies asserted by the IRS for additional income, estate, gift, or self-employment taxes (Code Sec. 7442)[132] or special excise taxes imposed on taxpayers under Chapters 41-44 of the Code (Code Sec. 6512).[133] The Tax Court is the only judicial body from which relief may be obtained without the payment of tax. The Tax Court also may issue declaratory judgments on the initial or continuing qualification of a retirement plan under Code Secs. 401-415, a tax-exempt organization under Code Sec. 501(c)(3) or Code Sec. 170(c)(2), a private foundation under Code Sec. 509(a) or a private operating foundation under Code Sec. 4942(j)(3). It also may rule on the tax-exempt interest status of a government bond issue (Code

---

Footnote references are to paragraphs of the 2002 Standard Federal Tax Reports.

[128] ¶ 39,455.01	[130] ¶ 38,720	[132] ¶ 42,058.01
[129] ¶ 38,726	[131] ¶ 37,241	[133] ¶ 39,090

Secs. 7428, 7476 and 7478; Tax Court Rule 210).[134] Declaratory judgment powers are also provided for (1) estate tax installments, (2) gift tax revaluations, and (3) employment status determinations.

The Tax Court's offices and trial rooms are located in Washington, D.C., but trials are also conducted in principal cities throughout the country. At the time of filing a petition, the taxpayer should file a request indicating where he prefers the trial to be held. The court imposes a filing fee of $60 (Code Sec. 7451).[135]

In any Tax Court case, other than small tax cases (see ¶ 2784), the findings of fact and opinion must generally be reported in writing. However, in appropriate cases, a Tax Court judge may state orally, and record in the transcript of the proceedings, the findings of fact or opinion in the case (Code Sec. 7459).[136] In such cases, the court must provide to all parties in the case either a copy of the transcript pages, which record the findings or opinion, or a written summary of such findings or opinion (Tax Court Rule 152).[137]

2778. Appeal to the Tax Court. Before the IRS can assess a deficiency, it generally must mail a deficiency notice to the taxpayer. The taxpayer then has an opportunity to appeal, within 90 days after the notice is mailed, to the Tax Court, if it has jurisdiction. (See ¶ 2711.) A notice based solely upon a mathematical or clerical error is not considered a notice of deficiency (Code Sec. 6213).[138] If the notice is mailed to a person outside the United States, the period is 150 days instead of 90 days (Code Sec. 6213).[139] The period is counted from midnight of the day on which the notice is mailed.[140] Saturday, Sunday, or a legal holiday in the District of Columbia is not counted as the 90th or 150th day (Reg. § 301.6213-1(a)).[141]

When a petition to the Tax Court is properly addressed and mailed within the prescribed time for filing, with the postage prepaid, the date of the U.S. postmark stamped on the cover in which the petition is mailed is the date of filing. (For a petition that is mailed from a foreign country, the petition must be *received* by the due date to be timely (*E.M. Sarrell*, 117 TC —, No. 11, CCH Dec. 54,494).) If a petition is sent by registered or certified mail, the date of registration or certification is the date of mailing and is prima facie evidence that the petition was delivered to the Tax Court (Reg. § 301.7502-1).[142]

If a taxpayer has filed a Tax Court petition before a jeopardy assessment or levy is made, the Tax Court is given concurrent jurisdiction with the federal district courts with respect to the taxpayer's challenge of the jeopardy assessment or levy (Code Sec. 7429(b)(2)).[143] Similarly, if there is a premature assessment of tax made while a proceeding with respect to that tax is pending in the Tax Court, the Tax Court has concurrent jurisdiction with the federal district court to restrain the assessment and collection of tax (Code Sec. 6213).[144]

2782. Burden of Proof. The IRS has the burden of proof in the Tax Court with respect to a factual issue that is relevant to determining a taxpayer's tax liability if the taxpayer presents credible evidence with respect to that issue *and* satisfies three applicable conditions discussed below (Code Sec. 7491):

(1) The taxpayer must comply with the substantiation and recordkeeping requirements of the Internal Revenue Code and regulations.

(2) The taxpayer must cooperate with reasonable requests by the IRS for witnesses, information, documents, meetings and interviews.

(3) Taxpayers *other than individuals* must meet the net worth limitations that apply for awarding attorneys' fees under Code Sec. 7430. Thus, corporations, trusts, and partnerships whose tax worth exceeds $7 million cannot benefit from this provision.

Footnote references are to paragraphs of the 2002 Standard Federal Tax Reports.

[134] ¶ 41,720, ¶ 42,134, ¶ 42,154, ¶ 42,370	[138] ¶ 37,545	[142] ¶ 42,621
[135] ¶ 42,072	[139] ¶ 37,545	[143] ¶ 41,725, ¶ 41,736.025
[136] ¶ 42,110	[140] ¶ 37,549.34	[144] ¶ 37,545
[137] ¶ 42,312	[141] ¶ 37,546	

¶ **2778**

Further, in any court proceeding where the IRS solely uses statistical information from unrelated taxpayers to reconstruct an item of an *individual* taxpayer's income, such as the average income for taxpayers in the area in which the taxpayer lives, the burden of proof is on the IRS with respect to that item of income. Also with respect to individuals only, the IRS must initially come forward with evidence that it is appropriate to apply a penalty, addition to tax, or additional amount before the court can impose the penalty.

In cases in which the burden of proof does not shift to the IRS, in general, the taxpayer has the burden of proof in the Tax Court. However, a taxpayer must only establish that the IRS is in error and not whether any tax is owed (Tax Court Rule 142).[145] The IRS bears the burden of proof with respect to any new matter, increase in deficiency, or affirmative defenses raised in its answer. Further, the burden of proving fraud and liability as a transferee is upon the IRS (Code Sec. 6902 and Code Sec. 7454).[146] The IRS also has the burden of proof in certain proceedings involving foundation managers, e.g., where a manager knowingly participated in self-dealing.[147]

2784. Small Tax Cases. The Tax Court maintains relatively informal procedures for the filing and handling of cases where neither the tax deficiency in dispute (including additions to tax and penalties) nor the amount of claimed overpayment exceeds $50,000. Usually taxpayers represent themselves, although they may be represented by anyone admitted to practice before the Tax Court. Each decision is final and cannot be appealed by either the taxpayer or the government (Code Sec. 7463).[148] The filing fee is $60.[149]

2786. Appeal from Tax Court Decision. A taxpayer who loses in the Tax Court may appeal the case (unless the case was tried as a small tax case, ¶ 2784) to the proper U.S. Court of Appeals[150] by filing a notice of appeal with the clerk of the Tax Court. The notice must be filed within 90 days after the Tax Court decision is entered. However, if one party to the proceeding files a timely notice of appeal, any other party to the proceeding may take an appeal by filing a notice of appeal within 120 days after the decision of the Tax Court is entered (Code Sec. 7483).[151]

A taxpayer who wants the assessment postponed pending the outcome of the appeal must file an appeal bond with the Tax Court guaranteeing payment of the deficiency as finally determined (Code Sec. 7485).[152]

2788. Acquiescence and Nonacquiescence by Commissioner. The IRS announces in the Internal Revenue Bulletin if it has decided to acquiesce or not acquiesce in a regular decision of the Tax Court. Any acquiescence or nonacquiescence may be withdrawn, modified or reversed at any time and any such action may be given retrospective, as well as prospective, effect.[153]

An acquiescence or nonacquiescence relates only to the issue or issues decided adversely to the government. Acquiescence means the IRS accepts the conclusion reached and does not necessarily mean acceptance and approval of any or all of the reasons assigned by the court for its conclusions. Acquiescences are to be relied on by IRS officers and others concerned as conclusions of the IRS only with respect to the application of the law to the facts in the particular case.

2790. Suits for Refund of Tax Overpayments. After the IRS rejects a refund claim for an alleged tax overpayment, suit can be maintained in the Court of Federal Claims or a District Court. A suit may be brought in the Court of Federal Claims against the United States to recover any overpayment of tax, regardless of amount (Judicial Code Sec. 1491).[154] Final decisions of the Court of Federal Claims are appealable to the Court of Appeals for the Federal Circuit.[155] All civil actions against the United States for the recovery of any internal revenue tax (regardless of

---

Footnote references are to paragraphs of the 2002 Standard Federal Tax Reports.

[145] ¶ 42,302,	[148] ¶ 42,118	[152] ¶ 42,500
¶ 42,302.615	[149] ¶ 42,072, ¶ 42,180	[153] ¶ 43,282.01
[146] ¶ 40,780, ¶ 42,081,	[150] ¶ 42,440	[154] ¶ 41,571, ¶ 41,605.01
¶ 42,302	[151] ¶ 42,477	[155] ¶ 41,605.045
[147] ¶ 42,081, ¶ 42,302		

¶ 2790

amount) alleged to have been erroneously or illegally assessed or collected may be brought against the United States as defendant in a U.S. District Court with right of trial by jury in any action, if either party makes a specific request for a jury trial.[156] Filing a proper claim for refund or credit (see ¶ 2759) is a condition precedent to a suit for recovery of overpaid taxes (Code Sec. 7422(a)).[157]

If, prior to the hearing on a taxpayer's refund suit in a District Court or the Court of Federal Claims, a notice of deficiency is issued on the subject matter of the taxpayer's suit, then the District Court or Court of Federal Claims proceedings are stayed during the period of time in which the taxpayer can file a petition with the Tax Court and for 60 days thereafter. If the taxpayer files a petition with the Tax Court, then the District Court or the Court of Federal Claims loses jurisdiction as to any issues over which the Tax Court acquires jurisdiction. If the taxpayer does not appeal to the Tax Court, the United States may then counterclaim in the taxpayer's suit within the period of the stay of proceedings even though the time for such pleading may otherwise have expired (Code Sec. 7422(e)).[158]

2792. Time to Bring Suit. A suit or proceeding based upon a refund claim must be brought within two years from the date the IRS mails, by registered or certified mail, notice of disallowance of the part of the claim to which such suit or proceeding relates or within two years from the date the taxpayer waives notification of disallowance of his claim. The two-year period of limitation for filing suit may be extended by written agreement between the taxpayer and the IRS (Code Sec. 6532(a)).[159]

Unless a bankruptcy proceeding has begun, no action can be brought before the expiration of six months from the date of filing the refund claim unless the IRS renders a decision on the claim before the six months are up. In bankruptcy proceedings, the six-month period is reduced to 120 days (Code Sec. 6532(a)).[160]

2794. Supreme Court. Either party may seek a review of a Court of Appeals decision by the Supreme Court (Code Sec. 7482(a)) [161] through a petition for a writ of certiorari.

2796. Attorneys' Fees and Court Costs. A "prevailing party"—any party (other than the United States or a creditor of the taxpayer) who has substantially prevailed with respect to the amount in controversy or the most significant issue or issues—may be awarded litigation costs in most civil tax litigation, including declaratory judgment proceedings (Code Sec. 7430).[162] In addition, a prevailing party can recover reasonable administrative costs incurred after the earlier of (1) the date the taxpayer received the decision notice from the IRS Office of Appeals, (2) the date of the deficiency notice, or (3) the date on which the first letter of proposed deficiency is sent that allows the taxpayer an opportunity for administrative review in the IRS Office of Appeals. Such awards may be made if the taxpayer meets certain net worth limitations and the IRS fails to prove that its position was substantially justified. When litigation costs are involved, the IRS's position is the government's position taken in the litigation proceeding or administratively by the IRS District Counsel. In the case of administrative costs, the IRS's position is the position taken as of the earlier of (1) the date the taxpayer received a decision notice from the IRS Office of Appeals or (2) the date of the deficiency notice. Litigation costs include (1) expenses of expert witnesses, (2) costs of any study, analysis, engineering report, test, or project, which was found by the court to be necessary for the preparation of its case, (3) fees of an individual authorized to practice before the court or the IRS, whether or not an attorney (generally not in excess of $140 per hour for 2001 (projected to increase to $150 for proceedings commenced during 2002), unless an affidavit is presented that establishes a special factor for a higher rate, such as the unavailability of qualified representatives at the customary rate), and (4) court costs. Reasonable attorneys' fees may also be awarded to specified

---

Footnote references are to paragraphs of the 2002 Standard Federal Tax Reports.

¶ **2792**

[156] ¶ 41,605.01	[159] ¶ 39,270	[161] ¶ 41,583, ¶ 42,440
[157] ¶ 41,685	[160] ¶ 39,270	[162] ¶ 41,740
[158] ¶ 41,685		

persons who represent, on a pro bono basis or for a nominal fee, taxpayers who are prevailing parties (Code Sec. 7430).[163]

A taxpayer is considered to have substantially prevailed if the liability determined by the court is equal to or less than the amount for which the taxpayer would have been prepared to settle the case (Code Sec. 7430(c)(4)(E) and Code Sec. 7430(g)).[164] The written qualified settlement offer must be made at any time during the time from the issuance of the 30-day letter to a date 30 days before the date the case is first set for trial.

However, no costs will be awarded where the prevailing party failed to exhaust all of the administrative remedies within the IRS (Code Sec. 7430(b); Reg. § 301.7430-1).[165] The tender of a qualified settlement offer (see preceding paragraph) does not satisfy the requirement to exhaust all administrative remedies (*Haas & Associates Accounting Corporation*, 117 TC —, No. 5, CCH Dec. 54,447). Further, costs will be denied for any portion of the proceeding where the prevailing party caused unreasonable delay (Code Sec. 7430(b)(4)).[166] A taxpayer who prevails in an IRS proceeding must apply to the IRS for administrative costs before the 91st day after the date the final IRS determination of tax, interest or penalty was mailed to the taxpayer. If the IRS denies the application for costs, the taxpayer must petition the Tax Court within 90 days of the IRS mailing of the denial.

An order granting or denying an award for litigation costs becomes part of the decision or judgment in the case and is subject to appeal in the same manner as the decision or judgment (Code Sec. 7430).[167]

2798. Suit for Damages in Connection with Collection of Tax. A taxpayer may bring a suit in federal district court for damages sustained in connection with the collection of any federal tax because an IRS employee recklessly or intentionally disregarded any provision of the Internal Revenue Code, any IRS regulations or certain provisions of the Bankruptcy Code (Code Sec. 7433).[168] A suit may also be brought for negligent disregard of the Internal Revenue Code or any IRS regulations. Except as provided in Code Sec. 7432 relating to damage awards for failure to release liens (see ¶ 2755), this action is the taxpayer's exclusive remedy for recovering damages caused by reckless, intentional or negligent disregard of such provisions and regulations by IRS employees. The suit must be brought within two years after the right of action accrues. The award is limited to the costs of the action plus any actual direct economic damages sustained by the taxpayer, up to a maximum award of $1 million for reckless or intentional actions and $100,000 for acts of negligence (Reg. § 301.7433-1(b)).[169] The IRS must comply with certain provisions of the Fair Debt Collection Practices Act so that the treatment of tax debtors by the IRS is at least equal to that required of private sector debt collectors (Code Sec. 6304). Taxpayers may bring a damages action under Code Sec. 7433 against the IRS for violations of these provisions.

Footnote references are to paragraphs of the 2002 Standard Federal Tax Reports.

[163] ¶ 41,740	[166] ¶ 41,740	[168] ¶ 41,770, ¶ 41,778
[164] ¶ 41,740	[167] ¶ 41,740	[169] ¶ 41,771
[165] ¶ 41,740, ¶ 41,742		

¶ 2798

Chapter 28

PENALTIES □ INTEREST

Failure to File Returns or Pay Tax

2801. Failure to File Returns. A failure to file any tax return within the time prescribed by the Code may result in an addition to tax. This penalty is 5% for each month (or fraction thereof) during which there is a failure to file any return, up to 25%. If the tax return is not filed within 60 days of the prescribed due date (including extensions), the penalty will not be less than the lesser of $100 or 100% of the tax due on the return (Code Sec. 6651(a)).[1] The late filing addition runs for the period up to the date the IRS actually receives the late return (Rev. Rul. 73-133).[2] The penalty is computed only on the net amount of tax due, if any, on the return after credit has been given for amounts paid through withholding, estimated tax and any other credits claimed on the return (Code Sec. 6651(b); Reg. § 301.6651-1(a), (b) and (d)).[3]

The fraud and accuracy-related penalties will not apply in the case of a fraudulent failure to file a return. Instead, the failure-to-file penalty is increased to 15% for each month, up to 75% (Code Sec. 6651(f)).[4]

The failure-to-file penalty is not imposed where the taxpayer can show that the failure to file was due to reasonable cause and not to willful neglect. Mere absence of willful neglect is not "reasonable cause." [5] "Reasonable cause" did not exist where: (1) the taxpayer relied upon the advice of an agent; (2) the taxpayer relied on the accountant to perform the purely ministerial function of filing;[6] or (3) an officer of the corporate taxpayer misjudged the extension date.[7] However, failure to file a return upon a lawyer's or certified public accountant's advice that there was no income to report, or that the taxpayer was not liable for tax, has been held to be reasonable cause where the taxpayer supplied complete information to the tax professional.[8]

2805. Failure to Pay Tax. A penalty is imposed for failure to pay, when due, those taxes (other than estimated taxes) shown by a taxpayer on his return, unless the failure is due to reasonable cause (Code Sec. 6651(a)(2)).[9] The same

---

Footnote references are to paragraphs of the 2002 Standard Federal Tax Reports.

[1] ¶ 39,470	[5] ¶ 39,475.028,	[8] ¶ 39,475.41,
[2] ¶ 39,475.021,	¶ 39,475.34	¶ 39,475.68
¶ 39,475.33	[6] ¶ 39,475.42,	[9] ¶ 39,470
[3] ¶ 39,470, ¶ 39,472	¶ 39,475.72	
[4] ¶ 39,470, ¶ 39,475.022	[7] ¶ 39,475.705	

penalty is imposed on additional taxes determined to be due on audit for which the IRS has made a demand for payment, but this penalty runs only for the period of nonpayment beginning after the 21st *calendar* day (10th *business* day if the amount demanded is at least $100,000) following the demand (Code Sec. 6651(a)(3)).[10] The addition to tax is one-half of 1% of the tax not paid, for each month (or part of a month) it remains unpaid, up to a maximum of 25%. The penalty increases to 1% per month beginning with either the 10th day after notice of levy is given or the day on which notice and demand is made in the case of a jeopardy assessment. For taxpayers who enter into installment agreements with the IRS, the penalty for failure to timely pay taxes is reduced to one-quarter of 1% of the tax not paid (Code Sec. 6651(h); Reg. § 301.6651-1(a)(4)). If a taxpayer files a late return that is subject to both the failure-to-file and failure-to-pay penalties, the former may be reduced by the latter. However, if no return is filed or if a late-filed return understates the amount required to be shown on the return, the failure-to-pay penalty attributable to additional tax demanded by the IRS may not be used to offset any portion of the failure-to-file penalty. If the penalty for failure to file beyond 60 days applies, the penalty may not be reduced by a failure-to-pay penalty that is also imposed below the lesser of $100 or 100% of the tax due (Code Sec. 6651(a), Code Sec. 6651(c) and Code Sec. 6651(d)).[11]

2809. Automatic Extension of Time for Filing. An automatic extension of time to file a tax return (¶ 2509) is not an extension of time to pay the tax due under the return (Reg. §§ 1.6081-3(c) and 1.6081-4(b)).[12] However, an individual taxpayer can avoid a failure-to-pay penalty by making an estimate of the tax due and paying that estimate (reduced by any amounts already paid in through withholding or estimated tax payments over the course of the tax year) with the request for extension of time to file. If the balance of tax due is remitted when the income tax return is filed, no penalty for failure to pay will apply, unless the unpaid amount is more than 10% of the total tax liability. Similar rules apply for corporations (Reg. § 301.6651-1(c)(3) and Reg. § 301.6651-1(c)(4)).[13]

2811. Frivolous Return Penalty. In addition to other penalties that may be imposed, there is a $500 penalty for filing a frivolous return. A frivolous return is one that omits information necessary to determine the taxpayer's tax liability, shows a substantially incorrect tax, is based upon a frivolous position (e.g., that wages are not income) or is based upon the taxpayer's desire to impede the collection of tax. A return based on the taxpayer's altering or striking out the "penalty of perjury" language above the signature line also constitutes a frivolous return (Code Sec. 6702).[14]

2813. Abatement of Penalties and/or Interest. The IRS must abate certain penalties that result from reliance on incorrect IRS advice if (1) the advice was furnished in writing in response to a specific written request from the taxpayer and (2) the taxpayer reasonably relied upon the advice (Code Sec. 6404(f)).[15] However, penalties will be abated only if the taxpayer furnished adequate and accurate information in making the request. Taxpayers entitled to abatement should file Form 843 (Claim for Refund and Request for Abatement) with copies of the relevant written documents attached (Reg. § 301.6404-3(d)).[16]

If the IRS extends the due date for filing income tax returns and for paying income for any taxpayer located in a presidentially declared disaster area, the IRS will abate the interest that would otherwise accrue for the extension period (Code Sec. 6404(h)).[17]

Footnote references are to paragraphs of the 2002 Standard Federal Tax Reports.

[10] ¶ 39,470, ¶ 39,475.022 [14] ¶ 40,040, ¶ 40,043.01, [16] ¶ 38,576
[11] ¶ 39,470   ¶ 40,043.60, ¶ 40,043.70 [17] ¶ 38,570
[12] ¶ 36,790, ¶ 36,793 [15] ¶ 38,570
[13] ¶ 39,472

The accrual of interest and penalties will be suspended after 18 months (12 months after 2003) unless the IRS sends the taxpayer a notice within 18 months following the later of: (1) the original due date of the return (without regard to extensions) or (2) the date on which a timely return is filed (Code Sec. 6404(g)).[18] The suspension of interest and penalties is available only for individuals and only for income taxes. Further, the suspension pertains only to tax related to timely filed returns (i.e., returns filed by the original due date or by the extended due date). The suspension begins on the day after the end of the 18-month period and ends on the day that is 21 days after the date on which the notice is made. The suspension does not stop the accrual of:

(1) the failure to pay and failure to file penalties;

(2) any interest, penalty or other addition to tax in a case involving fraud;

(3) any interest, penalty, addition to tax, or additional amount with respect to any tax liability shown on the return; or

(4) any criminal penalty.

Document and Information Return Penalties

2814. Information Reporting Penalties. Three distinct categories of penalties apply to failures to file required information returns and payee statements: (1) failure to file an information return or to include correct information on an information return (Code Sec. 6721);[19] (2) failure to file a payee statement or to include correct information on a payee statement (Code Sec. 6722);[20] and (3) failure to comply with other information reporting requirements, which includes all reporting failures not covered by the other two categories (Code Sec. 6723).[21]

2816. Failure to File Correct Information Returns. A time-sensitive three-tier penalty structure is imposed for (1) any failure (other than a failure due to reasonable cause and not to willful neglect) to file correct information returns (see ¶ 2565) with the IRS on or before the required filing date, (2) any failure to include all the information required to be shown on a return, or (3) the inclusion of incorrect information (Code Sec. 6721(a)).[22] The penalty applies also to any failure to file, when required, by means of magnetic media, but is imposed only on the number of returns exceeding 250 (Code Sec. 6724(c)).[23] The penalty amounts for each of the prescribed time periods are as follows:

(1) For any reporting failure corrected within 30 days after the return's filing date, the amount of the penalty is $15 per return, up to a maximum of $75,000 for a calendar year (Code Sec. 6721(b)(1)).[24] The calendar-year maximum is $25,000 for small businesses (i.e., firms having average annual gross receipts of less than $5 million for the three most recent tax years (fiscal or calendar) ending before the calendar year for which the return was filed) (Code Sec. 6721(d)(1)(B)).[25]

(2) For any reporting failure corrected within the period beginning 31 days after the return's filing date up to August 1 of the calendar year in which the return had to be filed, the penalty is $30 per return, up to a maximum of $150,000 ($50,000 for small businesses) for a calendar year (Code Sec. 6721(b)(2) and Code Sec. 6721(d)(1)(C)).[26]

(3) For any reporting failure corrected after August 1, the penalty is $50 per return, up to a maximum of $250,000 ($100,000 for small businesses) for a calendar year (Code Sec. 6721(a)(1) and Code Sec. 6721(d)(1)(A)).[27]

Footnote references are to paragraphs of the 2002 Standard Federal Tax Reports.

[18] ¶ 38,570	[22] ¶ 40,210, ¶ 40,220.023	[25] ¶ 40,210, ¶ 40,220.027
[19] ¶ 40,210	[23] ¶ 40,275, ¶ 40,285.021	[26] ¶ 40,210, ¶ 40,220.027
[20] ¶ 40,230	[24] ¶ 40,210	[27] ¶ 40,210, ¶ 40,220.027
[21] ¶ 40,250		

¶ 2814

A certain *de minimis* number of returns timely filed with incorrect or omitted information that are corrected on or before August 1 of the calendar year in which the returns are due will be treated as having been filed correctly, and no penalty will be imposed on them. This exception is limited to the greater of (1) 10 returns or (2) one-half of 1% of the total number of information returns required to be filed during the calendar year. The *de minimis* exception does not apply to a failure to file an information return (Code Sec. 6721(c)).[28]

If the failure to file an information return or to include all the required correct information is due to intentional disregard of the filing requirements, neither the three-tier penalty nor the *de minimis* exception will apply. Instead, the penalty for each failure is the greater of (1) $100 or (2) 10% of the aggregate amount of the items required to be reported correctly in the case of a return other than a return required under Code Sec. 6045(a) (brokers' transactions with customers), Code Sec. 6041A(b) (payments of remuneration for direct sales), Code Sec. 6050H (information on mortgage interest received in a trade or business from individuals), Code Sec. 6050I (information on cash receipts from a trade or business), Code Sec. 6050J (information on foreclosures and abandonments of security), Code Sec. 6050K (information on exchanges of certain partnership interests), or Code Sec. 6050L (information on certain dispositions of donated property). The penalty equals the greater of $100 or 5% for returns required under Code Sec. 6045(a), Code Sec. 6050K, or Code Sec. 6050L. In the case of a return required under Code Sec. 6050I(a) (cash receipts of more than $10,000 in a trade or business), the greater of (1) $25,000 or (2) the amount of cash received in the transaction, up to a maximum of $100,000. In addition, the intentional disregard penalties are not considered in figuring the yearly maximum penalty of $250,000 for failures not attributable to intentional disregard (Code Sec. 6721(e)).[29]

No penalty is imposed for inconsequential omissions and inaccuracies that do not prevent or hinder the IRS from adequately processing the return. Errors and omissions that relate to a taxpayer identification number, to the surname of a person required to receive a copy of the information provided, or to any monetary amounts are never considered inconsequential (Reg. § 301.6721-1(c)).[30]

2823. Failure to Furnish Correct Payee Statement. A penalty of $50 per statement (up to a maximum of $100,000 per payor per calendar year) may be imposed for (1) any failure (other than a failure due to reasonable cause and not to willful neglect) to furnish a payee statement on or before the required filing date, (2) any failure to include all the information required to be shown on a payee statement, or (3) the inclusion of incorrect information with respect to a payee statement. Payee statements include the following: (1) information-at-source payments under Code Sec. 6041(d); (2) payments in connection with services and direct sales under Code Sec. 6041A(e); (3) brokers under Code Sec. 6045(b) or (d); (4) certain stock options under Code Sec. 6039(a); (5) group-term life insurance under Code Sec. 6052(b); (6) catch shares of certain fishing boat crews under Code Sec. 6050A(b); (7) income tax withheld from employees' wages under Code Sec. 6051; (8) tip income reportable by employers under Code Sec. 6053(b) or (c); (9) mortgage interest payments under Code Sec. 6050H(d); (10) cash payments in excess of $10,000 under Code Sec. 6050I(e), (g)(4) or (g)(5); (11) foreclosures and abandonments under Code Sec. 6050J(e); (12) exchanges of certain partnership interests under Code Sec. 6050K(b); (13) certain dispositions of donated property under Code Sec. 6050L(c); (14) pass-through income, deductions, etc., to partners under Code Sec. 6031(b) or (c) to beneficiaries of estates and trusts under Code Sec. 6034A, and to S corporation shareholders under Code Sec. 6037(b); (15) payments of royalties under Code Sec. 6050N(b); (16) statements relating to returns regarding payments of dividends and corporate earnings and profits under Code Sec. 6042(c); (17)

---

statements regarding payments of patronage dividends under Code Sec. 6044(e); (18) statements regarding interest payments under Code Sec. 6049(c); (19) statements relating to certain purchasers of diesel and aviation fuels under Code Sec. 4093(c)(4)(B); (20) statements relating to the cancellation of indebtedness by certain financial entities under Code Sec. 6050P(d); (21) payments for certain purchases of fish for resale under Code Sec. 6050R; (22) distributions from individual retirement accounts under Code Sec. 408(i) and from employee benefit plans under Code Sec. 6047(d); (23) payments relating to qualified tuition and related expenses under Code Sec. 6050S; and (24) returns relating to certain company-owned life insurance held by a natural person where a trade or business is directly or indirectly the beneficiary under the policy under Code Sec. 264(f)(5)(A)(iv).[31]

In the case of intentional disregard of the requirements with respect to payee statements, the penalty imposed is identical to that for failures to file an information return or to include correct information. See ¶ 2816. Similarly, the intentional disregard penalty is not considered in applying the yearly maximum penalty of $100,000 for failures not attributable to intentional disregard (Code Sec. 6722(c)).[32] In addition, the regulatory exception from penalty (Reg. § 301.6721-1(c)) [33] in the case of inconsequential omissions and inaccuracies on a payee statement continues to apply. See ¶ 2816.

2833. Failure to Comply with Other Information Reporting Requirements. A penalty of $50, up to a maximum of $100,000 for a calendar year, is imposed for each failure to comply with any specified information reporting requirement on or before the prescribed time (Code Sec. 6723).[34] The penalty will not be imposed if it can be shown that the failure was due to reasonable cause and not to willful neglect.

The specified information reporting requirements that are subject to the penalty include: (1) the requirement that a transferor of an interest in a partnership promptly give notice to the partnership concerning the transfer; (2) the requirement that a person include his taxpayer identification number (TIN) on any return, statement, or other document (other than an information return or payee statement), furnish his TIN to another person, or include the TIN of another person on any return, statement or other document made with respect to that person; (3) the requirement on returns reporting alimony payments that the TIN of the payee be furnished to the payor or that the payee's TIN be included on the payor's return; (4) the requirement that a person include the TIN of any dependent on his return; and (5) the requirement that a person who deducts qualified residence interest under Code Sec. 163 on any seller-provided financing include the name, address and TIN of the person to whom such interest is paid or accrued (Code Sec. 6724(d)(3)).[35]

Underpayments of Tax—Interest

2838. Interest on Underpayment of Tax. Interest on underpayments of tax is imposed at the federal short-term rate plus three percentage points (Code Sec. 6621(a)(2)). The interest rates, which are adjusted quarterly, are determined during the first month of a calendar quarter and become effective for the following quarter.

Interest accrues from the date the payment was due (determined without regard to any extensions of time) until it is received by the IRS. Interest is to be compounded daily, except for additions to tax for underpayment of estimated tax by individuals and corporations (Code Sec. 6601).[36] The interest rate on underpayments for the first quarter of 2001 was 9%; the interest rate on underpayments for the

---

Footnote references are to paragraphs of the 2002 Standard Federal Tax Reports.

[31] ¶ 40,230, ¶ 40,275	[35] ¶ 40,275	¶ 39,455.01, ¶ 39,460,
[32] ¶ 40,230, ¶ 40,240.023	[36] ¶ 39,410, ¶ 39,412,	¶ 39,560.01
[33] ¶ 40,213	¶ 39,415.01, ¶ 39,450,	
[34] ¶ 40,250, ¶ 40,265.01		

¶ 2833

second quarter of 2001 was 8%; and the interest rate for the third and fourth quarters of 2001 was 7%.[37]

If a carryback of a net operating loss, investment credit, work incentive program credit, jobs credit, or a net capital loss eliminates or reduces a deficiency otherwise due for such earlier year, the taxpayer remains liable for interest on unpaid income taxes (including deficiencies later assessed by the IRS) for the carryback year. The entire amount of the deficiency will be subject to interest from the last date prescribed for payment of the income tax of the carryback year up to the due date (excluding extensions) for filing the return for the tax year in which the loss or credit occurred (Code Sec. 6601(d); Reg. § 301.6601-1(e)).[38]

Large Corporate Tax Underpayments. Interest on large underpayments of tax by corporations is imposed at the federal short-term rate plus five percentage points (Code Sec. 6621(c)(1); Reg. § 301.6621-3).[39] A large corporate underpayment is any tax underpayment by a C corporation that exceeds $100,000 for any tax period. For purposes of determining the $100,000 threshold, underpayments of different types of taxes (for example, income and employment taxes) as well as underpayments relating to different tax periods are not added together. The tax period is the tax year in the case of income tax or, in the case of any other tax, the period to which the underpayment relates (Code Sec. 6621(c)(3)).[40]

The interest rate applies to time periods after the 30th day after the earlier of (1) the date the IRS sends the first letter of proposed deficiency that allows the taxpayer an opportunity for administrative review in the IRS Office of Appeals (a 30-day letter) or (2) the date the IRS sends a deficiency notice under Code Sec. 6212 (a 90-day letter) (see ¶ 2778). The 30-day period does not begin unless the underpayment shown in the letter or notice exceeds $100,000 (Code Sec. 6621(c)(2)(B)(iii)). An IRS notice that is later withdrawn because it was issued in error will not trigger the higher rate of interest on large corporate underpayments (Code Sec. 6621(c)(2)(A)).[41] If the underpayment is not subject to deficiency payments, the 30-day period begins to run following the sending of any letter or notice by the IRS that notifies the taxpayer of the assessment or proposed assessment of the tax. A letter or notice is disregarded if the full amount shown as due is paid during the 30-day period (Code Sec. 6621(c)(2)(B)).[42] The interest rate on large corporate underpayments for the first quarter of 2001 was 11%; the interest rate for the second quarter of 2001 was 10%; and the interest rate for the third and fourth quarters of 2001 was 9%.[43]

Overlapping Overpayments and Underpayments. The interest rates for overpayments and underpayments have been equalized (sometimes referred to as "global interest netting") for any period of mutual indebtedness between taxpayers and the IRS. See ¶ 2765.

Abatement of Interest. The IRS has the authority to abate interest in cases where the additional interest was caused by IRS errors or delays (Code Sec. 6404(e)). However, the IRS may act only if there was an error or delay in performing either a ministerial act or a managerial act (including loss of records by the IRS, transfers of IRS personnel, extended illness, extended personnel training or extended leave) and only if the abatement relates to a tax of the type for which a notice of deficiency is required. Such taxes would be those relating to income, generation-skipping transfers, estate, gift and certain excise taxes, but not abatement of interest for employment taxes or other excise taxes.

Taxpayers requesting an abatement of interest generally must file a separate Form 843 for each tax period for each type of tax with the IRS Service Center where

---

Footnote references are to paragraphs of the 2002 Standard Federal Tax Reports.

[37] ¶ 39,455.021
[38] ¶ 39,410, ¶ 39,415.026
[39] ¶ 39,450, ¶ 39,453, ¶ 39,455.03
[40] ¶ 39,450
[41] ¶ 39,450, ¶ 39,455.03
[42] ¶ 39,450, ¶ 39,455.03
[43] ¶ 39,455.021

¶ 2838

their tax return was filed or, if unknown, with the Service Center where their most recent tax return was filed. The claim must clearly state across the top, "Request for Abatement of Interest Under Rev. Proc. 87-42."

2845. Interest on Additions and Penalties. Interest on penalties and additions to tax for failure to file, for failure to pay the stamp tax, and for the accuracy-related and fraud penalties (see ¶ 2854 and ¶ 2866) will be imposed for the period beginning on the due date of the return (including extensions) and ending on the date of payment. However, if payment is made within 21 calendar days after notice and demand is made (10 *business* days if the amount demanded is at least $100,000), then interest will stop running after the date of notice and demand (Code Sec. 6601(e)(3)). For all other penalties, interest will be imposed only if the addition to tax or penalty is not paid within the 21- or 10-day period after notice and demand is made and then only for the period from the date of notice and demand to the date of payment (Code Sec. 6601(e)(2)).[44] For rules governing the allocation of interest on tax liabilities paid pursuant to a compromise or partial payment, see ¶ 2723 and ¶ 2724, respectively.

Underpayments of Tax—Penalties

2854. Accuracy-Related Penalty. The two penalties primarily applicable to underpayments of tax are the accuracy-related penalty (Code Sec. 6662)[45] and the fraud penalty (Code Sec. 6663).[46] See ¶ 2866.

The accuracy-related penalty consolidates all of the penalties relating to the accuracy of tax returns. It is equal to 20% of the portion of the underpayment that is attributable to one or more of the following: (1) negligence or disregard of rules or regulations (¶ 2856), (2) substantial understatement of income tax (¶ 2858), (3) substantial valuation misstatement (¶ 2860), and (4) substantial overstatements of pension liabilities (¶ 2862) (Code Sec. 6662(a) and (b)).[47]

The accuracy-related penalty is entirely separate from the failure to file penalty (¶ 2801) and will not be imposed if no return, other than a return prepared by the IRS when a person fails to make a required return, is filed (Code Sec. 6664(b)).[48] In addition, the accuracy-related penalty will not apply to any portion of a tax underpayment on which the fraud penalty is imposed. Also, no penalty is imposed with respect to any portion of any underpayment if the taxpayer shows that there was reasonable cause for the underpayment and that the taxpayer acted in good faith (Code Sec. 6664(c)).[49]

2856. Negligence or Disregard of Rules and Regulations. If any part of an underpayment of tax is due to negligence or careless, reckless or intentional disregard of rules and regulations, the 20% accuracy-related penalty will be imposed on that portion of the underpayment attributable to the negligence or intentional disregard of rules and regulations (Code Sec. 6662(a) and (c)).[50] Negligence includes the failure to reasonably comply with tax laws, to exercise reasonable care in preparing a tax return, to keep adequate books and records, or to substantiate items properly (Reg. § 1.6662-3(b)(1)).[51] Taxpayers may not avoid the negligence penalty merely by adequately disclosing a return position which is "not frivolous" on Form 8275, "Disclosure Statement," or Form 8275-R, "Regulation Disclosure Statement" (Conference Committee Report to P.L. 103-66).[52]

2858. Substantial Understatement of Income Tax. The IRS may impose the 20% accuracy-related penalty where there is a substantial understatement of

Footnote references are to paragraphs of the 2002 Standard Federal Tax Reports.

44 ¶ 39,410	48 ¶ 39,660, ¶ 39,661.03	51 ¶ 39,651D,
45 ¶ 39,651	49 ¶ 39,660, ¶ 39,661.022	¶ 39,651G.01
46 ¶ 39,656	50 ¶ 39,651,	52 ¶ 39,651.45
47 ¶ 39,651	¶ 39,651G.01	

¶ 2845

tax. A substantial understatement exists when the understatement for the year exceeds the greater of (1) 10% of the tax required to be shown on the return (including self-employment tax) or (2) $5,000 ($10,000 for corporations other than S corporations or personal holding companies) (Code Sec. 6662(d)).[53] Taxpayers generally may avoid all or part of the penalty by showing (a) that they acted in good faith and there was reasonable cause for the understatement, (b) that the understatement was based on substantial authority, or (c) if there was a reasonable basis for the tax treatment of an item, the relevant facts affecting the item's tax treatment were adequately disclosed on Form 8275 (Form 8275-R for return positions contrary to regulations) (Code Sec. 6662(d)(2) and Code Sec. 6664(c); Reg. § 1.6662-4(d)—Reg. § 1.6662-4(f)).[54] Substantial authority generally means that the likelihood that a taxpayer's position is correct is somewhere between 50% and the more lenient reasonable basis standard used in applying the negligence penalty. The disclosure exception does not apply to tax shelter items. Further, a corporation does not have a reasonable basis for its tax treatment of an item attributable to a multi-party financing transaction if the treatment does not clearly reflect the income of the corporation. Some items may be disclosed on the taxpayer's return, instead of on Form 8275, pursuant to an IRS Revenue Procedure relating to the tax year.

Only the following are authority for purposes of determining whether a position is supported by substantial authority:

(1) the Internal Revenue Code and other statutory provisions,

(2) proposed, temporary and final regulations construing the statutes,

(3) revenue rulings and procedures,

(4) tax treaties and the regulations thereunder, and Treasury Department and other official explanations of such treaties,

(5) court cases,

(6) congressional intent as reflected in committee reports, joint explanatory statements of managers included in conference committee reports, and floor statements made prior to enactment by one of a bill's managers,

(7) General Explanations of tax legislation prepared by the Joint Committee on Taxation (the Blue Book),

(8) private letter rulings and technical advice memoranda issued after October 31, 1976,

(9) actions on decisions and general counsel memoranda issued after March 12, 1981 (as well as general counsel memoranda published in pre-1955 volumes of the Cumulative Bulletin),

(10) Internal Revenue Service information and press releases, and

(11) notices, announcements and other administrative pronouncements published by the IRS in the Internal Revenue Bulletin (Reg. § 1.6662-4(d)(3)(iii)).[55]

2860. Substantial Valuation Misstatement. The 20% accuracy-related penalty is imposed on any portion of an underpayment resulting from any substantial income tax valuation misstatement. There is a substantial valuation misstatement if (1) the value of any property, or adjusted basis of any property, claimed on a tax return is 200% or more of the amount determined to be the correct amount of the valuation or the adjusted basis, (2) the price for any property, or use of property, or services in connection with any transaction between persons described in Code Sec. 482 is 200% or more, or 50% or less, of the correct Code Sec. 482 valuation, or (3) the net Code Sec. 482 transfer price adjustment exceeds the lesser of $5 million or 10 percent of the taxpayer's gross receipts.

Footnote references are to paragraphs of the 2002 Standard Federal Tax Reports.

[53] ¶ 39,651   [54] ¶ 39,651, ¶ 39,660, ¶ 39,651H, ¶ 39,652.022   [55] ¶ 39,651H

¶ 2860

The penalty is doubled to 40% in cases of "gross valuation misstatements" where claimed value or adjusted basis exceeds the correct value or adjusted basis by 400% or more. A gross valuation misstatement occurs if the price claimed exceeds 400% or more, or 25% or less, of the amount determined to be the correct price or the net Code Sec. 482 transfer price adjustment for the year exceeds the lesser of $20 million or 20% of the taxpayer's gross receipts.

No penalty is imposed unless the portion of the underpayment attributable to the substantial valuation misstatement exceeds $5,000, or $10,000 in the case of corporations other than S corporations or personal holding companies (Code Sec. 6662(a), (e), and (h)).[56] The penalty will not be imposed if it is shown that there was reasonable cause for an underpayment and the taxpayer acted in good faith (Code Sec. 6664(c)).[57]

2862. Substantial Overstatement of Pension Liabilities. The 20% accuracy-related penalty is imposed on any portion of any underpayment resulting from a substantial overstatement of pension liabilities. A substantial overstatement occurs if the actuarial determination of pension liabilities is 200% or more of the amount determined to be correct. The penalty is doubled to 40% of the underpayment if a portion of the substantial overstatement to which the penalty applies is attributable to a gross valuation misstatement of 400% or more. The penalty applies only if the portion of the underpayment attributable to the overstatement exceeds $1,000 (Code Sec. 6662(a), (f), and (h)).[58] The penalty will not be imposed if it is shown that there was a reasonable cause for an underpayment and the taxpayer acted in good faith (Code Sec. 6664(c)).[59]

2866. Fraud. The fraud penalty is imposed at the rate of 75% on the portion of any underpayment that is attributable to fraud (Code Sec. 6663).[60] The fraud penalty will not apply, however, if no return is filed, other than a return prepared by the IRS when a person fails to make a required return (Code Sec. 6664(b)).[61] Although the failure to file penalty is entirely separate from the fraud penalty, in cases of a fraudulent failure to file, the failure to file penalty will be imposed at a higher rate. See ¶ 2801. If any portion is attributable to fraud, it is presumed that the entire underpayment is attributable to fraud, unless the taxpayer establishes otherwise by a preponderance of the evidence with respect to any item. The accuracy-related penalty will not apply to any portion of an underpayment on which the fraud penalty is imposed. The IRS must meet its burden of proof in establishing fraud by clear and convincing evidence (Code Sec. 6663(b)).[62]

Underpayments of Estimated Tax

2875. Addition to Tax for Underpayment of Estimated Tax by Individuals.
An underpayment of estimated tax by an individual and most trusts and estates will result in imposition of an addition to tax equal to the interest that would accrue on the underpayment for the period of the underpayment (Code Sec. 6654(a)).[63] For the applicable rate of interest, see ¶ 2838. In determining the addition to tax for an underpayment of individual estimated tax, the federal short-term rate that applies during the third month following the tax year of the underpayment will also apply during the first 15 days of the fourth month following such tax year (Code Sec. 6621(b)(2)(B)).[64] Changes in the interest rate apply to amounts of underpayments outstanding on the date of change or arising thereafter.[65] An individual can avoid any penalty for underpayment of estimated tax by

---

Footnote references are to paragraphs of the 2002 Standard Federal Tax Reports.

¶**2862**

56 ¶ 39,651, ¶ 39,654.02, ¶ 39,654.03, ¶ 39,654.04
57 ¶ 39,660, ¶ 39,661.022
58 ¶ 39,651, ¶ 39,654A.01
59 ¶ 39,660, ¶ 39,661.022
60 ¶ 39,656, ¶ 39,658.01
61 ¶ 39,660, ¶ 39,661.03
62 ¶ 39,656, ¶ 39,658.022
63 ¶ 39,550
64 ¶ 39,450
65 ¶ 39,451

making payments as set forth in ¶2679 et seq. See ¶518 for the rules regarding trusts and estates.

2881. Waiver of Underpayment Penalty. The IRS is authorized to waive the penalty for underpayment of estimated tax if the underpayment is either due to casualty, disaster, or other unusual circumstances and the imposition of the penalty would be against equity and good conscience. The penalty may also be waived for an individual who retired after having attained age 62, or who became disabled, in the tax year for which the estimated payment was due or in the preceding tax year and the underpayment was due to reasonable cause and not to willful neglect (Code Sec. 6654(e)(3)).[66] Otherwise, the addition to tax is mandatory where there is an underpayment.[67]

2889. "Underpayment" Form 2210. When insufficient estimated tax was paid during the year, the taxpayer should complete and attach Form 2210 (Form 2210F for farmers and fishermen) to explain which test (¶2682) was met to avoid the addition to tax or, if no tests were met, how the amount of the addition to tax due was computed.

2890. Underpayment of Estimated Tax by Corporations. If estimated taxes are underpaid by a corporation (including an S corporation), a penalty is imposed in the amount of the interest that accrues on the underpayment for the period of the underpayment (Code Sec. 6655). The rate of interest is the rate charged on underpayment of taxes determined under Code Sec. 6621 (¶2838). The additions are calculated for quarterly periods ending with the installment due dates. Generally, additions to tax apply to the difference between payments made by the due date of the installment and the lesser of an installment based on (1) 100% of the tax shown on the current year's tax return or (2) 100% of the tax shown on the preceding year's return (for a 12-month tax year). No additions to tax will be assessed if the corporation's tax liability is less than $500 for the tax year.[68]

Unauthorized Disclosures

2892. Confidentiality of Returns. Returns and tax return information are confidential and may not be disclosed to federal or state agencies or employees except as provided in Code Sec. 6103.[69] A return is defined as any tax return, information return, declaration of estimated tax, or claim for refund filed under the Internal Revenue Code. Return information includes the taxpayer's identity, the nature, source or amount of income, payments, receipts, deductions, net worth, tax liability, deficiencies, closing (and similar) agreements, and information regarding the actual or possible investigation of a return. The prohibition on disclosure applies to all officers and employees of the United States, of any state, and of any local child support enforcement agency. It also applies to most other persons who have had access to returns or return information by virtue of permitted disclosures of such returns or information under Code Sec. 6103.[70]

Agreements and information received under a tax convention with a foreign government (including a U.S. possession) are confidential and generally cannot be disclosed (Code Sec. 6105).

2893. Remedies for Unauthorized Disclosures. Taxpayers whose privacy has been invaded by an unlawful disclosure of returns or return information may bring a civil suit for damages. Upon a finding of liability, the taxpayer may recover the greater of $1,000 for each unauthorized disclosure or the amount of the actual damages sustained as a result of the disclosure. Punitive damages, as well as

---

Footnote references are to paragraphs of the 2002 Standard Federal Tax Reports.

[66] ¶39,550, ¶39,560.01, ¶39,560.03
[67] ¶39,560.21
[68] ¶39,565, ¶39,575.023
[69] ¶36,880, ¶36,894
[70] ¶36,894.026

¶2893

litigation costs, may be recovered if the disclosure was willful or grossly negligent.[71] Felony charges can also be brought against individuals who have made unauthorized and willful disclosures of any return information (Code Sec. 7213).[72]

2894. Disclosure of Return Information. A return preparer who uses return information for any purpose other than to prepare a return, or who makes an unauthorized disclosure of return information, is subject to a $250 penalty for each disclosure, up to a maximum of $10,000. If the action is undertaken knowingly or recklessly, the preparer may be subject to criminal penalties or a fine of up to $1,000, or up to a year in jail, or both, together with the cost of prosecution (Code Sec. 6713 and Code Sec. 7216).[73] A taxpayer may bring a civil action for damages against the U.S. government if an IRS employee offers the taxpayer's representative favorable tax treatment in exchange for information about the taxpayer (Code Sec. 7435).[74]

Unauthorized Return Inspections

2896. Penalties for Unauthorized Inspections. A taxpayer may bring a civil action against the United States if a government employee knowingly or negligently inspects, without authorization, any return or return information pertaining to that taxpayer. The same action may also be taken against any other person who browses through returns or return information without proper authorization (Code Sec. 7431).[75] Criminal penalties for willful unauthorized return inspection can also be imposed against any federal employee or IRS contractor. In addition, penalties may be imposed against any state employee or other person who acquires the return or return information under Code Sec. 6103, which permits the use of federal return information for other government purposes, such as state tax and child support collection, law enforcement, social welfare program administration, and statistical use (Code Sec. 7213A).[76]

Criminal Penalties

2898. Crimes. Criminal penalties may be incurred when the taxpayer (a) willfully fails to make a return, keep records, supply required information, or pay any tax or estimated tax, (b) willfully attempts in any manner to evade or defeat the tax, or (c) willfully fails to collect and pay over the tax. In addition to the felony charges listed in the preceding sentence, misdemeanor charges can be brought for (1) making fraudulent statements to employees, (2) filing a fraudulent withholding certificate, or (3) failing to obey a summons. The criminal penalties are in addition to the civil penalties (Code Sec. 7201-Code Sec. 7212). A good faith misunderstanding of the law or a good faith belief that one is not violating the law negates the willfulness element of a tax evasion charge.[77]

Footnote references are to paragraphs of the 2002 Standard Federal Tax Reports.

[71] ¶41,750, ¶41,758.055	[74] ¶41,785	[76] ¶41,354
[72] ¶41,350, ¶41,353.01	[75] ¶41,750	[77] ¶41,318.034
[73] ¶40,155, ¶41,365, ¶41,370		

¶2894

Chapter 29

ESTATE, GIFT AND GENERATION-SKIPPING TRANSFER TAX

Unified Transfer Tax System

2901. Estate, Gift and Generation-Skipping Transfer Taxes. The estate, gift and generation-skipping transfer (GST) taxes form a unified transfer tax system. The estate tax is based on all property transferred at death, and the gift tax is based on all property transferred during life. The generation-skipping transfer tax is designed to ensure that property does not skip a generation without a transfer tax being assessed. However, pursuant to tax legislation enacted in 2001, the estate and GST taxes will not apply to the estates of decedents dying after December 31, 2009 (Code Sec. 2210(a), as added by the Economic Growth and Tax Relief Reconciliation Act of 2001 (P.L. 107-16)). The gift tax will be retained following the repeal of the estate and GST taxes, although in a modified form. Beginning in 2002, the highest estate and gift tax rates will gradually decrease (from 55 percent in 2001 to 45 percent in 2009, and in 2010 the gift tax top rate will be 35 percent), and the exemption for estate and GST taxes will gradually increase. All changes made by P.L. 107-16, however, are subject to a "sunset provision," which states that the provisions shall not apply to estates of decedents dying, gifts made, or generation-skipping transfers, after December 31, 2010. Thus, unless Congress intervenes, the original Code provisions governing the estate, GST and gift taxes will be administered as if P.L. 107-16 had not been enacted. For a detailed discussion of these rules, see the CCH FEDERAL ESTATE AND GIFT TAX REPORTS and the 2002 U.S. MASTER ESTATE AND GIFT TAX GUIDE.

Applicable Credit Amount. The estate and gift tax currently share a unified progressive rate schedule (see ¶ 42) and an applicable credit that shelters a total of $675,000 (applicable exclusion amount) from the gift and estate tax for decedents dying, and gifts made, in 2001 ($1 million in 2002 and 2003). The applicable exclusion amount for estate (but not gift) tax purposes will be gradually increased to $3.5 million by 2009, the year prior to repeal of the estate and GST taxes. The applicable exclusion amount in effect for the years leading up to repeal is: $1.5 million in 2004 and 2005; $2 million in 2006, 2007, and 2008; and $3.5 million in 2009 (Code Sec. 2010(c), as amended by P.L. 107-16). Beginning with gifts made in 2002, the applicable exclusion amount for gift tax purposes will be increased to $1 million (Code Sec. 2505(a)(1), as amended by P.L. 107-16). However, unlike the gradual increase in the estate tax applicable exclusion amount in the years leading up to repeal, the gift tax applicable exclusion amount will remain at $1 million and is not indexed for inflation.

2902. Computing the Gift Tax Liability. The gift tax is calculated by adding the current year's taxable gifts to all prior years' taxable gifts and then calculating the tentative tax by applying the applicable tax rate from the unified rate schedule to the total amount of taxable gifts. Taxable gifts are the total of all gifts made by a donor during the calendar year, less the amount of marital and charitable deductions. Taxable gifts do not include those gifts protected by the annual $10,000 (indexed for inflation after 1998 but unchanged for 2001, and projected by CCH to increase to $11,000 in 2002) per donee exclusion allowed for gifts of a present interest and the unlimited exclusion for educational and medical expenses paid on behalf of another person.[1] The gift tax presently payable is determined by applying the applicable tax rate to the sum of all prior years' taxable gifts and then subtracting that sum from the tentative tax (Code Sec. 2502(a)). The tentative tax is then reduced by the amount of the unified credit (Code Sec. 2505). The value of a gift is its fair market value on the date of the gift.[2] If a gift is adequately disclosed on the gift tax return and the gift tax statute of limitations has expired, the IRS may not revalue the donor's lifetime gifts when computing the estate tax liability upon the donor's death (Code Sec. 2001(f)). There is a three-year statute of limitations for gift tax returns (Code Sec. 2504(c)).

For years 2002 through 2009, the applicable credit amount is determined as if the applicable exclusion amount was $1 million (Code Sec. 2505(a)(1), as amended by P.L. 107-16). For years 2010 and thereafter, the amount of the credit allowed against the gift tax is: (1) the amount of the tentative tax that would be determined under a new gift tax-only rate schedule if the amount with respect to which such tentative tax is to be computed was $1 million, reduced by (2) the sum of the amounts allowable as a credit for all preceding calendar periods.

2903. Computing the Estate Tax Liability. The estate tax computation begins with a calculation of the gross estate. The gross estate is valued at the fair market value on the decedent's date of death or, if elected, on the alternate valuation date, which is six months after the date of death (Code Sec. 2031). The charitable and marital deductions and estate administration expenses as well as other allowable deductions are subtracted to find the taxable estate (Code Sec. 2051). The amount of taxable gifts made after 1976 is added to the taxable estate. A tentative tax is computed by applying the applicable tax rates from the unified tax rate schedule to the sum of the amount of the taxable estate and the taxable gifts. The tentative tax is then reduced by the amount of gift tax payable on the post-1976 gifts and the unified credit. Credits for state and foreign death taxes paid (Code Sec. 2011), tax on transfers from a person who died within ten years before or two years after the decedent (Code Sec. 2013), and gift tax paid on pre-1977 gifts included in the gross estate (Code Sec. 2012) are available.[3]

2904. Qualified Disclaimers. The beneficiary of a bequest or donee of a gift may disclaim the entire interest or a portion of it without making a taxable gift. A

Footnote references are to paragraphs of the Federal Estate and Gift Tax Reports.

¶ **2902**   [1] ¶ 9649   [3] ¶ 1201, ¶ 1551, ¶ 3011,
                [2] ¶ 10,622   ¶ 4801, ¶ 6010

qualified disclaimer must be made in writing and within nine months of the date of the gift or bequest. The beneficiary may not accept any of the benefits of the gift (Code Sec. 2518).[4]

2905. Excess Accumulations in Qualified Plans. The additional 15-percent estate tax levied on excess accumulations in qualified retirement plans and IRAs has been repealed for decedents dying after December 31, 1996 (Code Sec. 4980A(d)(1)).[5]

Gift Tax

2906. What Is a Gift. The gift tax applies to the transfer of property by gift, whether the gift is direct or indirect, and whether the transfer is in trust or otherwise. The property transferred may be real, personal, tangible or intangible, but does not include donated services (Code Sec. 2511; Reg. § 25.2511-1(a)). The donor makes a gift to the extent that the value of the property transferred exceeds the consideration received for the transfer (Code Sec. 2512(b)). The transferred property or evidence of it must be delivered to the donee and the donor must relinquish all control over the property for the gift to be subject to tax. A promise to make a gift is taxable when it is enforceable under state law. Once made, gifts cannot be rescinded.[6]

Indirect gifts, such as the cancellation of indebtedness, are gifts subject to the gift tax (Code Sec. 2511). Other indirect gifts include the conversion of an annuity for an individual to one with a survivorship provision, and the payment by an employer of a death benefit on behalf of an employee's beneficiary (Reg. § 25.2511-1(c), Reg. § 25.2511-1(h)). A spouse's waiver of the right to a joint and survivor annuity in a qualified plan is not a gift.[7]

2907. Transfers Subject to Gift Tax. A transfer to or from a corporation may be a gift to or from shareholders of the corporation (Reg. § 25.2511-1(h)). The creation of a family partnership also often involves a gift. Gratuitous transfers made by guardians or conservators under court orders are gifts. A transfer under a will contest settlement is not a gift unless the possibility of litigation is remote. A transfer of life insurance is a gift if the proceeds are payable to someone other than the donor. Transfer of stock and securities is a gift even if the securities are exempt from tax. The transfer of an option is a gift. However, transfers to political organizations are not gifts (Code Sec. 2501(a)(5)).[8] The making of a loan bearing no interest or a below-market interest rate is a gift of the interest forgone by the lender (Code Sec. 7872(e)(2)).[9]

Interests retained by the transferor are disregarded for gift tax valuation purposes when the transferor transfers an interest in a corporation, partnership, or trust to family members as part of an estate valuation freeze. Under this rule the value of the transferred interest is not discounted when the gift tax is applied at the time of the transfer (Code Secs. 2701, 2702).[10]

Gift Tax Exclusions

2908. Per Donee Annual Exclusion. The first $10,000 of gifts made by a donor during the 2001 calendar year to any donee are not included in the total amount of the donor's taxable gifts during that year (Code Sec. 2503(b)). The annual exclusion amount is indexed for inflation and is projected by CCH to increase to $11,000 in 2002. If the donor's spouse is not a U.S. citizen, an annual exclusion of $106,000 for 2001 (Rev. Proc. 2001-13) (projected to be $110,000 in 2002) is allowed for present interest gifts to the spouse that would qualify for the marital deduction if the spouse were a U.S. citizen (Code Sec. 2523(i)(2)).[11] The annual exclusion is

---

Footnote references are to paragraphs of the Federal Estate and Gift Tax Reports.

[4] ¶ 11,339
[5] ¶ 15,025, ¶ 16,079, ¶ 18,375
[6] ¶ 10,514
[7] ¶ 10,181.05, ¶ 10,514
[8] ¶ 9245, ¶ 10,514
[9] ¶ 18,525,¶ 18,575, ¶ 18,601, ¶ 18,625, ¶ 18,650
[10] ¶ 13,551, ¶ 14,001, ¶ 14,651
[11] ¶ 9649, ¶ 11,662, ¶ 11,850

available to all donors, including nonresident citizens. Also, spouses who consent to split their gifts may transfer a total of $20,000 per donee in 2001 (projected to be $22,000 in 2002) free of gift and generation-skipping transfer tax (Code Sec. 2513(a)).[12]

The annual exclusion is not allowed for gifts of future interests in property. Future interests include any interest, whether vested or contingent, that is not available to the donee's use, possession or enjoyment until some future date or time (Reg. § 25.2503-3(b)). The annual exclusion is allowed for an outright gift to a minor whether made to the minor's legal guardian or to a custodian under a state statute such as the Uniform Gifts to Minors Act (Code Sec. 2503(c)).[13]

2909. Annual Exclusion for Transfers in Trust. A transfer to a trust that allows a beneficiary the unrestricted right to the immediate use, possession or enjoyment of the transferred property or the income from the property, such as a life estate or term certain, is a present interest gift that qualifies for the annual exclusion (Reg. § 25.2503-3(b)). The number of annual exclusions available for a gift in trust is determined by the number of trust beneficiaries who have a present interest in the gifted property. Discretionary powers in the trustee or grantor to distribute, accumulate and sprinkle income or principal of a trust disqualify gifts in trust as present interest gifts. A beneficiary's power to withdraw trust income or principal (*Crummey* power) is a present interest that qualifies for the annual exclusion.[14]

A gift in trust for a minor beneficiary qualifies for the annual exclusion if the beneficiary holds a *Crummey* power.[15] Gifts, in trust or otherwise, that do not qualify for the annual exclusion because they are gifts of future interests nevertheless qualify for the exclusion if the property and income from it may be expended by or for the benefit of the minor, and any income and principal not expended must be paid to the minor at age 21, or to his estate if the minor dies before age 21 (Code Sec. 2503(c); Reg. § 25.2503-4(a)).[16] However, if a transfer of property is made under a parent's legal obligation to support a minor, the transfer is not a gift.[17]

2910. Exclusion for Educational or Medical Payment. In addition to the annual exclusion, an unlimited gift tax exclusion is allowed for amounts paid on behalf of a donee *directly* to an educational organization, provided such amounts constitute tuition payments. Amounts paid for books, dormitory fees, or board on behalf of the donee are not eligible for the exclusion. Amounts paid *directly* to health care providers for medical services on behalf of a donee also qualify for the unlimited gift tax exclusion. Medical expense payments are excludable without regard to the percentage limitations imposed for income tax purposes. Both the medical and tuition exclusions are available without regard to the relationship between the donor and donee (Code Sec. 2503(e)).[18]

Filing Gift Tax Return and Paying the Gift Tax

2911. Donor Is Primarily Liable to File Return and Pay Gift Tax. Gift tax returns must be filed by individual donors for gifts of more than $10,000 in 2001 (projected by CCH to be $11,000 in 2002) that do not qualify for an exemption (Code Sec. 6019). Gift tax returns must be filed on Form 709, U.S. Gift (and Generation-Skipping Transfer) Tax Return. However, if a donor elects gift-splitting for all of his gifts and no gift tax is due, Form 709-A, U.S. Short Form Gift Tax Return, may be used (Reg. § 25.6019-1(a)). The donor is primarily liable for the payment of the gift tax (Code Sec. 6019).[19]

Footnote references are to paragraphs of the Federal Estate and Gift Tax Reports.

12 ¶ 10,960	16 ¶ 9996	¶ 15,412, ¶ 15,450,
13 ¶ 9649, ¶ 10,041	17 ¶ 9649, ¶ 11,284	¶ 15,825, ¶ 15,995
14 ¶ 9649, ¶ 9891,	18 ¶ 9649, ¶ 10,095	
¶ 9950.07	19 ¶ 9245, ¶ 11,339,	
15 ¶ 9649, ¶ 9891,	¶ 15,045, ¶ 15,108,	
¶ 9950.07		

¶ 2909

Estate Tax—Determining the Gross Estate

2912. Property in Which Decedent Held an Interest. The gross estate of a U.S. citizen or resident decedent includes the value of all property in which the decedent had an interest at the time of his death (Code Sec. 2033; Reg. § 20.2033-1(a)). Effectively executed disclaimers prevent the property subject to the disclaimer from being included in the gross estate (Code Secs. 2046 and 2518).[20]

Qualified terminable interest property (QTIP) for which an election was made to qualify it for the marital deduction in the estate of the first spouse to die, or on the gift tax return of the donor spouse, is included in the gross estate of the surviving or donee spouse (Code Sec. 2044(a)).[21]

2913. Transferred Property in Which Decedent Retained an Interest. When a decedent retains some control over gifts of property made during his life, the property may be added back to his gross estate. The transfers subject to this rule include:

(1) gifts in which the decedent retains a life estate[22] or the right to the income,[23] possession, or enjoyment of the property[24] or the right to designate who will enjoy the property (Code Sec. 2036),[25] including gifts of stock in which voting rights are retained,[26] and gifts related to estate valuation freezes;[27]

(2) gifts in which the decedent retains a right to a reversionary interest that exceeds five percent of the value of the transferred property (Code Sec. 2037(a));[28] and

(3) gifts in which the decedent holds a power to alter, amend, revoke, or terminate the gift (Code Sec. 2038(a)(1); Reg. § 20.2038-1(a)).[29]

An estate valuation freeze is a technique used to limit the value of closely held business interests owned by an individual by transferring the future appreciation in value of the business to the next generation of the owner's family while retaining certain interests in the business. This technique has been severely limited by the special valuation rules (Code Secs. 2701-2704) which treat transfers of family business interests unfavorably for gift tax purposes by valuing certain types of interests retained by the donor in such exchanges at zero.[30]

If income from transferred property is used to discharge a legal obligation of the decedent, such as the decedent's obligation to support his dependents, the decedent is considered to have a right to income from the property and the property is includible in his gross estate (Reg. § 20.2036-1(b)(2)).[31]

2914. Gifts Made Within Three Years of Death. Gifts made within three years of the donor's death ordinarily are not includible in the donor's gross estate. However, gifts made within three years of death are included in his gross estate if the gift consists of interests in property that would otherwise be included in the gross estate because of the donor's retained powers, such as the power to alter, amend, revoke or terminate the gift (Code Sec. 2035(a)). Similarly, a gift of life insurance that would otherwise be includible in the decedent's gross estate because of his retention of incidents of ownership in the policy is also includible if the policy is transferred within three years of the decedent's date of death (Code Sec. 2035(a)). The gross estate of a decedent dying after August 5, 1997, however, does not include transfers from a revocable trust made within three years of the decedent's death (Code Sec. 2035(e)). Such transfers are treated as if made directly by the decedent (Code Sec. 2035 and Code Sec. 2038). Gift tax paid on all transfers made within three years of death is included in the gross estate (Code Sec. 2035(b)).[32]

If a lifetime transfer is a sale for adequate and full consideration, the property that is transferred is not included in the transferor's gross estate (Code Sec.

Footnote references are to paragraphs of the Federal Estate and Gift Tax Reports.

[20] ¶ 5980, ¶ 11,339	[25] ¶ 4901	[30] ¶ 13,551,¶ 14,001,
[21] ¶ 5901	[26] ¶ 4901	¶ 14,501, ¶ 14,651
[22] ¶ 4901	[27] ¶ 3195	[31] ¶ 4925
[23] ¶ 4901	[28] ¶ 5001	[32] ¶ 4801, ¶ 5101, ¶ 5651
[24] ¶ 4901	[29] ¶ 5101	

2036(a)). The amount included in the decedent's estate is the full value of the property subject to the decedent's retained interest. However, if the interest or right is reserved over only part of the property transferred, only the reserved portion is included in the gross estate (Reg. § 20.2036-1(a)).[33]

Life Insurance

2915. When Included in Gross Estate. Proceeds of insurance on decedent's life payable to or for benefit of estate, and insurance payable to other beneficiaries when decedent retained incident of ownership in policy, are included in the decedent's gross estate (Code Sec. 2042(1), (2); Reg. § 20.2042-1(b)(1)). Insurance that is paid to a named beneficiary but must be used to meet estate expenses such as debts and taxes is included in the insured's gross estate.[34]

2916. Incidents of Ownership in the Policy. If proceeds of insurance on the life of a decedent are payable to a beneficiary other than the decedent's estate, they are included in the decedent's gross estate when the decedent has retained an incident of ownership in the life insurance policy on the date of his death (Code Sec. 2042(2); Reg. § 20.2042-1(c)). Some incidents of ownership include a reversionary interest exceeding five percent of the value of the policy, the power to change the beneficiary, or the ability to pledge the policy as security for a loan or borrow against the policy. If the decedent transfers a life insurance policy or an incident of ownership within three years of his death, the proceeds are included in his gross estate (Code Sec. 2035(a)).[35] However, only one half of the proceeds of life insurance purchased with community property are included in the estate of the insured spouse, even if he possesses an incident of ownership (Reg. § 20.2042-1(b)(2)).[36]

Key-employee insurance on an executive's life is included in the executive's gross estate if he retains an incident of ownership in the policy.[37]

Annuities and Retirement Benefits

2917. Portion Included in Gross Estate. The value of an annuity or other payment is included in a decedent's gross estate to the extent the payment is attributable to amounts paid by the decedent if:

(1) the payments are receivable by a beneficiary by reason of surviving the decedent;

(2) the payments arise under a contract or agreement;

(3) the decedent possessed the right to receive the payments during his lifetime; and

(4) payments under the contract are determined based on the decedent's life or life expectancy (Code Sec. 2039(a)).[38]

The value of an annuity or other payment included in a decedent's gross estate is the portion of its value attributable to the portion of the purchase price contributed by the decedent. Any contribution made by a decedent's employer or former employer by reason of his employment is considered to be made by the decedent (Code Sec. 2039(b)).[39]

Powers of Appointment

2918. General Powers Includible in Gross Estate. Property subject to a general power of appointment is included in the gross estate of the holder if the power exists at death (Code Sec. 2041(a)(2)). The exercise or release of a general power during the life of the holder is a transfer subject to gift tax (Code Sec. 2514(b)).[40] A power of appointment is a right given to someone other than the donor of property to dispose of the property. The holder of the power of appointment has a general power if he may exercise it in favor of himself, his creditors, his estate or the creditors of his

---

Footnote references are to paragraphs of the Federal Estate and Gift Tax Reports.

[33] ¶ 4901	[36] ¶ 5670	[39] ¶ 5201
[34] ¶ 5651, ¶ 5670	[37] ¶ 5670, ¶ 5760	[40] ¶ 5501, ¶ 11,054
[35] ¶ 4801, ¶ 5651	[38] ¶ 5201	

¶ **2915**

estate (Code Sec. 2041(b), Code Sec. 2514(c)). Powers that cannot be exercised in favor of any of these are special or limited powers (Reg. § 20.2041-1(c)(1)). A power is not general if its exercise is limited by an ascertainable standard (Code Sec. 2041(b)(1)(A), Code Sec. 2514(c)(1)). A power is not general if the creator of the power must join in its exercise or if a co-holder of the power has a substantial adverse interest (Code Sec. 2041(b)(1)(C), Code Sec. 2514(c)(3)(A)). The incompetence of the holder of the power to exercise the power does not affect whether the power is taxable to the power holder.[41]

Jointly Held Property

2919. Portion Includible in Gross Estate. The entire value of jointly held property with the right of survivorship, including joint bank accounts and U.S. savings bonds registered in two names, is included in a decedent's gross estate except for the portion of the property for which the surviving joint tenant furnished consideration. If the joint property is received by the decedent and the other joint tenants as a gift or bequest, the decedent's fractional share of the property is included in his gross estate (Code Sec. 2040(a)).[42] If the joint tenants are spouses, it generally does not matter who furnished the consideration for the property; one half of the property is included in the gross estate of the first spouse to die (Code Sec. 2040(b)).[43]

2920. Gift Tax Consequences on Creation. The creation of a joint interest in property results in a taxable gift to the person supplying the consideration if the noncontributing joint tenant has a right to sever the joint interest under local law. Creation of a joint bank account or joint brokerage account is not a taxable gift until a joint owner withdraws funds (Reg. § 25.2511-1(h)). The severance of joint tenancy is a gift from one joint owner to the other if the joint owner gets less than the value of his share. A transfer of joint property to a third party is a gift of the value of each joint owner's share.[44]

Taxation of Community Property

2921. Amount Included in Gross Estate. Community property is all property acquired by means other than gift, devise, bequest, and inheritance by spouses domiciled in community property jurisdictions. Separate property is property other than community property.[45]

One half of the value of all community property owned by a married couple is includible in the gross estate of the first of the spouses to die (Code Sec. 2033). This rule of inclusion applies even though the surviving spouse elects to allow his share of the community property to pass in accordance with the will of the decedent spouse.[46]

Value of Property Included in the Gross Estate

2922. Date of Death Fair Market Value. The value of property that is included in the gross estate is its fair market value on the date of the decedent's death, considering the facts as known at the time of valuation (Code Sec. 2031; Reg. § 20.2031-1(b)).[47]

2923. Alternate Valuation Date. If both the value of the gross estate and the amount of estate tax due will decrease as a result, the executor may elect to value the gross estate at the fair market value of the property on the alternate valuation date, which is the date six months after the date of the decedent's death. The alternate valuation election is irrevocable (Code Sec. 2032). The election is made on Form 706 (U.S. Estate (and Generation-Skipping Transfer) Tax Return).

Footnote references are to paragraphs of the Federal Estate and Gift Tax Reports.

[41] ¶ 5001, ¶ 5101, ¶ 5501, ¶ 11,054
[42] ¶ 5401, ¶ 6501
[43] ¶ 5401, ¶ 6501
[44] ¶ 10,528, ¶ 11,662
[45] ¶ 4675, ¶ 5401
[46] ¶ 4601, ¶ 4675
[47] ¶ 3001, ¶ 3801, ¶ 4001

The amount of any marital or charitable deduction is based on the alternate value of assets passing to charity or a surviving spouse when the election is made (Code Sec. 2032(b); Reg. § 20.2032-1(g)).[48] If property is sold, exchanged, distributed or otherwise disposed of during the six-month period, it is valued on the date of disposition rather than the alternate valuation date (Code Sec. 2032(a)(1)).[49] When the alternate valuation election is made, all property included in the gross estate is valued at the alternate valuation date (Reg. § 20.2032-1(d)).[50]

2924. Special Use Valuation. If a farm or real property used in a closely held business is included in the gross estate, the executor may elect to value the property at its special use value rather than at its fair market value. Special use valuation is the irrevocable election by an executor to value real property used in a farm, trade or business at its business use value rather than its fair market value at its highest and best use. The reduction in value was limited to $750,000 for estates of decedents dying in 1983 through 1998 and is indexed for inflation thereafter (Code Sec. 2032A).[51] For 2001, the limitation on the reduction in value resulting from special use valuation is $800,000 (projected by CCH to be $820,000 in 2002). Special use value is also elected on the estate tax return by completing the notice of election and submitting a recapture agreement. If the executor makes the election and submits the agreement but some of the required information or signatures are omitted, the executor has 90 days to supply it (Code Sec. 2032A(d)).[52] If the qualified heir ceases to use the farm property for farming or if he sells the property within ten years of the decedent's date of death, an additional estate tax, the recapture tax, is due (Code Sec. 2032A(c)).[53]

Taxable Estate—Deductions

2925. Administration Expenses Must Be Allowable Under Local Law. A deduction from the gross estate is allowed for funeral expenses, administration expenses, claims against the estate, certain taxes and unpaid mortgages or other indebtedness. Expenses, claims or other indebtedness must be allowable under the local law governing the administration of the decedent's estate (Code Sec. 2053(a)). For expenses that are not paid before filing the estate tax return, an estimated amount may be deducted if it is ascertainable with reasonable certainty (Reg. § 20.2053-1(b)(3)). Estate administration expenses may generally be deducted on either the decedent's estate tax return or the estate's income tax return but not on both (Code Sec. 642(g); Reg. § 1.642(g)-1).[54]

Expenses incurred in connection with the decedent's funeral, including reasonable expenses for a tombstone, mausoleum or burial lot, are deductible (Code Sec. 2053(a)(1)).[55] Administration expenses are deductible if actually and necessarily incurred in the administration of the estate. Administration expenses include fees paid to surrogates, appraisers and accountants. Paid attorney's fees or fees reasonably expected to be paid are also deductible (Code Sec. 2053(a)(2); Reg. § 20.2053-3(a)).[56] Claims that are a personal obligation of the decedent, existing and enforceable against him at the time of his death, and allowable under local law, are deductible. Liabilities imposed by law or arising out of torts committed by the decedent are also deductible (Reg. § 20.2053-4).[57] The full value of any unpaid mortgage or other indebtedness charged against property for which the decedent is personally liable, plus interest accrued on the debt to the date of death, is deductible if the property's entire value undiminished by the mortgage or indebtedness is included in the gross estate (Code Sec. 2053(a)(4)).[58] Estate, succession, legacy or inheritance taxes are not deductible, but unpaid gift taxes on gifts made before death are deductible. Unpaid income taxes are deductible if they are on income properly includible in an income tax return of a decedent for a period before his death (Reg. § 20.2053-6).[59] A deduction is allowed for losses arising from fires,

Footnote references are to paragraphs of the Federal Estate and Gift Tax Reports.

¶ 2924

48 ¶ 3801, ¶ 3830
49 ¶ 3801
50 ¶ 3830
51 ¶ 4001

52 ¶ 4001
53 ¶ 4001
54 ¶ 6040, ¶ 16,675
55 ¶ 6040

56 ¶ 6040, ¶ 16,675
57 ¶ 6040
58 ¶ 6040
59 ¶ 6210

storms, shipwrecks or other casualties, or thefts that are incurred during estate administration and not compensated for by insurance (Code Sec. 2054).[60]

Estate and Gift Tax Marital Deduction

2926. Unlimited Estate and Gift Tax Marital Deduction. The unlimited gift tax marital deduction allows spouses to transfer property between themselves free of the gift tax. The gift tax marital deduction is a deduction from gifts made during the calendar year. The gift tax marital deduction is not available if the spouse of the donor is not a U.S. citizen at the time of the gift (Code Sec. 2523).[61] The unlimited estate tax marital deduction is available if the husband and wife have a valid marriage under applicable state law at the time of the decedent spouse's death (Code Sec. 2056(a)). The transferee spouse must survive the decedent spouse; a presumption of survivorship in the decedent's will or under local law is recognized for this purpose (Reg. § 20.2056(c)-2(e)). If the surviving spouse is a noncitizen, the property transferred must pass from the decedent to a qualified domestic trust (QDOT) (Code Sec. 2056(d)(2); Reg. § 20.2056A-1(a)).[62]

2927. Passing Requirement. Property must pass from the decedent to a surviving spouse for a transfer to be deductible (Code Sec. 2056(a)). Bequests and inheritances, dower and curtesy interests, joint property, property received under antenuptial agreements, and annuities and life insurance may pass from the decedent to the surviving spouse. Property received by a spouse under her state law right of election against the will satisfies the passing requirement (Code Sec. 2056(c); Reg. § 20.2056(e)-1(a)). Property passing to the spouse as a result of another person's qualified disclaimer is considered to pass from the decedent (Reg. § 20.2056(d)-2(b)).[63]

2928. Terminable Interest Rule. The terminable interest rule bars deduction for any nondeductible terminable interest. A terminable interest in property is an interest that terminates or fails because of the lapse of time or the occurrence of an event (Code Sec. 2056(b)(1)). A nondeductible terminable interest is an interest in which a person, other than the surviving spouse, receives an interest in property from the decedent and, upon the termination of the spouse's interest in the same property, the other person may possess or enjoy the property. Property interests passing to a spouse that are conditioned on the spouse's survival of a period of six months or less, or on the spouse's survival in a common disaster, are not subject to the terminable interest rule (Code Sec. 2056(b)(3)).[64]

2929. Qualified Terminable Interest Property. Qualified terminable interest property (QTIP) is excluded from the terminable interest rule. To qualify as QTIP, the surviving spouse must have the right to all the income from the property for life, payable no less frequently than annually (Code Sec. 2056(b)(7); Reg. § 20.2056(b)-7(a)). A surviving spouse's income interest may be contingent upon the executor's QTIP election and still be considered a "qualifying income interest for life" (Temp. Reg. § 20.2056(b)-7T).[65] In addition, no person may have a power to appoint any of the property to any person other than the surviving spouse for her life. An election on the Form 706 (U.S. Estate (and Generation-Skipping Transfer) Tax Return) is necessary to designate property as QTIP (Code Sec. 2056(b)(7)(B)(v)). Once the QTIP election is made, the surviving spouse must include the property remaining at her death in her gross estate even though she has no control over its disposition (Code Sec. 2044). However, the estate tax that is attributable to the QTIP included in the spouse's estate may be recovered from the QTIP (Code Sec. 2207A).[66]

2930. Life Estate with Power of Appointment. A life estate with a power of appointment qualifies for the marital deduction if:

Footnote references are to paragraphs of the Federal Estate and Gift Tax Reports.

[60] ¶ 6320	[63] ¶ 6501, ¶ 6975	[66] ¶ 5901, ¶ 6501, ¶ 8800,
[61] ¶ 16,662	[64] ¶ 6501	¶ 11,432
[62] ¶ 6501, ¶ 7030, ¶ 7045	[65] ¶ 6850.07	

(1) the surviving spouse is entitled to all the income from the entire interest or a specific portion for her life;

(2) the income is payable at least annually;

(3) the spouse has the power to appoint the property or a specific portion to herself or her estate;

(4) the power is exercisable by the spouse alone and in all events; and

(5) no other person has the power to appoint property to anyone but the surviving spouse (Code Sec. 2056(b)(5)).

There is a similar exception to the terminable interest rule for life insurance proceeds held by an insurer in which the spouse has a right to all payments and a power of appointment (Code Sec. 2056(b)(6); Reg. § 20.2056(b)-6(c)).[67]

2931. Amount of Marital Deduction. The marital deduction is limited to the net value of property passing to the spouse. Death taxes, debts and administration expenses payable from the marital bequest, mortgages on property passing to the spouse and insufficient estate assets to fund the marital bequest all reduce the amount of the deduction (Code Sec. 2056(b)(4); Reg. § 20.2056(b)-4(a)).[68] However, administration expenses allocable to an estate's income do not necessarily reduce the amount of the marital deduction (*Hubert Est.*, SCt, 97-1 USTC ¶ 60,261).[69]

Charitable Deduction

2932. Unlimited Estate and Gift Tax Charitable Deduction. An unlimited estate and gift tax charitable deduction is available for transfers to federal, state and local governmental entities; charitable organizations; fraternal societies (if the property is used for charitable purposes); or veterans' organizations. The bequest or gift must have a public rather than a private purpose (Code Secs. 2055(a), 2522(a)).[70]

2933. Transfers of Partial Interests. If an interest in property passes from a transferor to a charity and an interest in the same property passes to a noncharitable recipient, the transfer must take one of the following forms:

(1) charitable remainder annuity trust, which provides for a fixed-dollar amount to be paid to a noncharity annually, or charitable remainder unitrust, which provides for a fixed percentage of trust assets, valued annually, to be paid to a noncharity annually (Code Secs. 2055(e)(2), 2522(c)(2));[71]

(2) charitable lead trust with guaranteed annuity or unitrust amount paid to charity (Code Secs. 170(f)(2), 2055(e)(2), 2522(c)(2));[72]

(3) remainder interest in a farm or personal residence (Code Secs. 2055(e)(2), 2522(c)(2));[73]

(4) copyrightable work of art separate from its copyright (Code Secs. 2055(e)(4), 2522(c)(3));[74] or

(5) qualified conservation contribution (Code Secs. 170(f)(3), 2055(e)(2), 2522(c)(2)).[75]

The amount of the estate tax deduction must be reduced by the administration expenses and death taxes paid from the property transferred to charity (Code Sec. 2055(c); Reg. § 20.2055-3(a)).[76] However, administration expenses allocable to an estate's income do not necessarily reduce the amount of the charitable deduction (*Hubert Est.*, SCt, 97-1 USTC ¶ 60,261).[77]

Footnote references are to paragraphs of the Federal Estate and Gift Tax Reports.

[67] ¶ 6501, ¶ 6801	[71] ¶ 6360, ¶ 11,486,	[75] ¶ 6360, ¶ 11,486
[68] ¶ 6501, ¶ 6745	¶ 16,901	[76] ¶ 3011, ¶ 3801, ¶ 6360,
[69] ¶ 6755.674	[72] ¶ 6360, ¶ 11,486	¶ 6430
[70] ¶ 6360, ¶ 11,486,	[73] ¶ 6360, ¶ 16,079	[77] ¶ 6380.18
¶ 11,891	[74] ¶ 6360	

¶ 2931

Family-Owned Business Deduction

2933A. Amount of the Deduction. Certain estates of decedents dying after December 31, 1997 and before January 1, 2004, can elect to deduct up to $675,000 of a qualified family-owned business interest (QFOBI) from the decedent's gross estate (Code Sec. 2057).[78] The deduction is allowed in addition to other special provisions in effect for closely-held businesses, such as the special use valuation provisions (see ¶ 2924) and the installment payment of estate tax provisions (see ¶ 2939). The QFOBI deduction is not available for gift tax or generation-skipping transfer tax purposes and will be repealed for the estates of decedents dying after December 31, 2003 (Code Sec. 2057, as amended by the Economic Growth and Tax Relief Reconciliation Act of 2001 (P.L. 107-16)).

2933B. Qualifying Estates. In order for an estate to qualify for the QFOBI deduction, the decedent must have been a U.S. citizen or resident at the time of death, and the aggregate value of QFOBIs passed to heirs must exceed 50 percent of the decedent's adjusted gross estate. For this purpose, qualified heirs include members of the decedent's family as well as individuals actively employed by the business for at least 10 years prior to the decedent's death.

2933C. Ownership Requirement. To qualify as a QFOBI, the interest must be in a trade or business with a principal place of business in the U.S. and owned: (1) at least 50 percent by one family, (2) 70 percent by two families, or (3) 90 percent by three families. If the interest is held by more than one family, the decedent's family must own at least 30 percent of the trade or business. An interest does not qualify as a QFOBI if its stock was publicly-traded within three years of the decedent's death or if more than 35 percent of the adjusted gross income from the business for the year of the decedent's death was personal holding company income.

2933D. Participation Requirement. In order for the decedent's interest to qualify as a QFOBI, the decedent, or a member of the decedent's family, must have owned and materially participated in the business for at least five of the eight years preceding the decedent's death. Further, a qualified heir is subject to a recapture tax if the heir, or a member of the heir's family, does not materially participate in the business for at least five years of any eight-year period within 10 years following the decedent's death. The principal factors to be considered regarding "material participation" include physical work and participation in management. Note that the recapture tax provisions *may* continue to apply after the repeal of the estate tax (in 2010).

2933E. Coordination With Applicable Exclusion. The QFOBI deduction and the applicable exclusion amount in effect at the date of the decedent's death (see ¶ 2901) are coordinated so that a maximum of $1.3 million of the value of the QFOBI may be shielded from estate tax. If the maximum $675,000 QFOBI deduction is taken, the applicable exclusion amount is limited to $625,000, regardless of the date of decedent's death. If the QFOBI deduction is less than $675,000, the $625,000 applicable exclusion amount is increased by the excess of $675,000 over the amount of the QFOBI deduction taken. Note, however, that the applicable exclusion amount may not be increased above the amount that would apply to the estate if no QFOBI deduction had been elected.

    Example 1. Charlie dies in 2000 when the applicable exclusion amount is $675,000. His estate includes $1.4 million of QFOBIs and his executor elects to take the maximum $675,000 deduction. Since the estate is electing to take the maximum QFOBI deduction, the applicable exclusion amount is limited to $625,000.

    Example 2. Fred dies in 2002 when the applicable exclusion amount is $1 million. Fred's $1.4 million estate includes $600,000 of QFOBIs. The estate qualifies for and elects to take a $600,000 QFOBI deduction. Fred's estate will be entitled to an applicable exclusion amount of $700,000 ($625,000 + ($675,000 − $600,000)).

Credits Against the Estate Tax

2934. State Death Taxes. Other than the unified credit, there are four credits available to offset the federal estate tax liability. The estate tax may be offset by state death taxes actually paid to a state or the District of Columbia. This credit for state death taxes is limited by a graduated rate table that uses the adjusted taxable estate as a base. The adjusted taxable estate is the taxable estate reduced by $60,000 (Code Sec. 2011).[79] See ¶ 43. The state death tax credit will be reduced by 25 percent beginning in 2002 and will continue to decrease until it is repealed entirely in 2005 (Code Sec. 2011(b), as amended by the Economic Growth and Tax Relief Reconciliation Act of 2001 (P.L. 107-16)). The reduction in the credit will be 50 percent for the estates of decedents dying in 2003 and 75 percent for the estates of decedents dying in 2004. For estates of decedents dying after 2004, the credit will be repealed and replaced by a *deduction* until the phaseout of the federal estate tax is complete (in 2010). In addition, the new state tax deduction will be subject to a limitations period, which will generally require the deduction to be claimed within four years after the estate tax return is filed.

2935. Federal Estate Tax Paid on Prior Transfers. A credit is available for federal estate tax paid on prior transfers to the decedent from a person who died within 10 years before or two years after the decedent. The credit is limited to the lesser of the estate tax attributable to the transferred property in the transferor's estate or the estate tax attributable to the transferred property in the decedent's estate (Code Sec. 2013).[80]

2936. Foreign Death Taxes. A credit against estate tax is available for foreign death taxes paid on property located in a foreign country but included in the gross estate of a U.S. citizen or resident. The credit is limited to the lesser of the foreign or the U.S. tax attributable to the property. If a treaty exists with the foreign country, the credit provided for under the treaty may be used instead (Code Sec. 2014).[81]

2937. Gift Tax Paid on Gifts Included in Gross Estate. For gifts made before 1977, the gift tax paid on gifts included in the gross estate is a credit to the estate tax. The credit is limited to the lesser of the gift tax paid or the estate tax attributable to inclusion of the gift in the taxable estate (Code Sec. 2012).[82]

Filing the Estate Tax Return and Paying the Tax

2938. Filing Estate Tax Return and Liability for Payment. Form 706 (United States Estate (and Generation-Skipping Transfer) Tax Return) must be filed for every U.S. citizen or resident decedent whose gross estate exceeds $675,000 in 2001 (and $1 million in 2002 and 2003) (Code Sec. 6018(a)). The return must be filed by the executor, administrator or person in possession of the estate's assets (Code Secs. 2203; 6018(a)). The return is due within nine months of a decedent's date of death, but a six-month extension of time to file is available (Code Sec. 6075(a); Reg. § 20.6075-1).[83] The six-month extension applies automatically to estate tax returns due after July 25, 2001 upon application by the executor. The estate tax must be paid within nine months after the decedent's death (Code Secs. 6075(a); 6151(a)) by the executor or person in possession of the estate's property (Code Sec. 2002; Reg. § 20.2002-1)). The tax may be paid with a check or money order,[84] or with certain government bonds (flower bonds) (Code Sec. 6311(a); Reg. § 20.6151-1(c)).[85] The time for payment of the estate tax may be extended for a period of one year past the due date (Code Sec. 6161(a)(1)). For reasonable cause, the time for payment may be extended for up to ten years (Code Sec. 6161(a)(2)).[86]

2939. Election to Pay Estate Tax in Installments. If an estate includes a farm or closely held business whose value exceeds 35 percent of the adjusted gross

Footnote references are to paragraphs of the Federal Estate and Gift Tax Reports.

¶ **2934**

79 ¶ 1551	83 ¶ 15,108	86 ¶ 15,108, ¶ 15,180,
80 ¶ 2001	84 ¶ 15,108, ¶ 15,180	¶ 15,194, ¶ 15,209,
81 ¶ 2301	85 ¶ 15,181, ¶ 15,304	¶ 15,212
82 ¶ 1901		

estate, the executor may elect to pay the estate and generation-skipping transfer taxes in as many as ten annual installments following a deferral period of as many as five years (Code Sec. 6166(a)(1)). The amount of tax that may be deferred is limited to the tax attributable to the business interest (Code Sec. 6166(a)(2)). For decedents dying in 1998 and later years, a *two-percent* interest rate applies to that portion of the estate tax deferred on the first $1 million in *taxable* value of the closely held business, computed as follows: the tentative tax on the sum of $1 million plus the applicable exclusion amount, reduced by the applicable credit amount. The $1 million dollar amount is indexed for inflation after 1998 (Code Sec. 6601(j)). The inflation-adjusted figure for 2001 is $1,060,000 (projected by CCH to be $1,100,000 in 2002). In 2001, the two-percent portion is $441,000 (a tentative tax of $648,050 is computed on the sum of $1,060,000 plus the applicable exclusion amount of $675,000; the applicable credit amount of $220,550 is then subtracted from the tentative tax figure). A closely held corporation may redeem stock from the estate of a decedent or from the beneficiaries of the estate to pay estate taxes and administrative expenses if the stock comprises 35 percent of the gross estate. This redemption of stock is generally not treated as a disqualifying disposition for purposes of the installment payment of the estate tax (Code Sec. 6166(g)(1)(B)).[87]

Estate and Gift Taxation of Nonresident Aliens

2940. Transfers Subject to Estate and Gift Tax. A decedent who is neither a U.S. citizen nor a U.S. resident (a nonresident alien)[88] is subject to gift tax on transfers of real and tangible property situated in the United States (Code Secs. 2101(a), 2501(a)). Transfers of intangible property are not subject to gift tax (Code Sec. 2501(a)(2)). Taxable gifts are taxed at the same rates that apply to U.S. citizens (Code Sec 2501(a)(1)).[89] The gross estate of a nonresident alien that is subject to the estate tax includes real, tangible and intangible property situated in the United States (Code Sec. 2103). Intangible property situated in the United States includes stock in domestic corporations, bonds and debt obligations of U.S. obligors, U.S. partnership assets and U.S. property owned by a trust in which the nonresident alien has an interest.[90]

2941. Determining Estate Tax Liability. The estate of a nonresident alien is taxed at the same estate tax rates that apply to U.S. citizens' estates (Code Sec. 2101(b); Reg. § 20.2101-1). Except where provided by treaty, the unified credit is $13,000 (Code Sec. 2102(c)(1)). The estate may claim deductions for a pro rata share of expenses, debts and losses, a marital deduction if the surviving spouse is a U.S. citizen, and a charitable deduction (Code Sec. 2106(a)(1); Reg. § 20.2106-2(a)(2)). An estate tax return must be filed if a nonresident alien's gross estate situated in the United States exceeds $60,000 (Code Sec. 6018(a)(2)).[91] The estate of a nonresident alien or long-term resident alien who lost U.S. citizenship within 10 years of his death and who had a principal purpose of tax avoidance for the loss of citizenship (an expatriate) is taxed at the same rates applicable to U.S. citizens (Code Secs. 2107(a), 2501(a)(3)(B); Reg. §§ 20.2107-1(a), 25.2511-1(b)). The expatriate is also subject to gift tax on transfers of property situated in the United States (Code Sec. 2501(a)(3)).[92] An individual is considered to have lost his U.S. citizenship, or long-term residency status, for the principal purpose of tax avoidance if his average annual net income for the five years preceding his loss was greater than $100,000 or his net worth on the date of loss is $500,000 or more (Code Secs. 877(a)(2), 2107(a)(2)(A), 2501(a)(3)(B)).[93] The estate and gift tax Code provisions may be affected by provisions contained in foreign tax treaties (Code Sec. 7852(d)).[94]

Footnote references are to paragraphs of the Federal Estate and Gift Tax Reports.

[87] ¶ 15,212, ¶ 15,650	[91] ¶ 7525, ¶ 7550, ¶ 8055,	[93] ¶ 8125, ¶ 10,514
[88] ¶ 7550	¶ 8225, ¶ 15,025	[94] ¶ 16,215
[89] ¶ 9245	[92] ¶ 8150, ¶ 9245,	
[90] ¶ 7725, ¶ 7825	¶ 10,514, ¶ 10,528	**¶ 2941**

Generation-Skipping Transfer Tax

2942. Transfers Subject to Tax. Every generation-skipping transfer (GST) is subject to the GST tax (Code Sec. 2601). However, the GST tax will not apply to GSTs made after December 31, 2009 as the GST tax is scheduled to be repealed along with the estate tax in 2010 (Code Sec. 2664, as added by the Economic Growth and Tax Relief Reconciliation Act of 2001 (P.L. 107-16)). The GST tax rate is 55 percent in 2001 and 50 percent in 2002. A GST takes one of three forms. A direct skip is a transfer to a skip person that is also subject to estate or gift tax. A skip person is two generations or more younger than the transferor (Code Sec. 2612(c)(1); Reg. § 26.2612-1(a)(1)). However, if the parent of the grandchild is dead, a gift to the grandchild is not a direct skip (Code Sec. 2612(c)(2)). A taxable termination occurs when an interest in property held in trust terminates and trust property is held for or distributed to a skip person (Code Sec. 2652(c)). Finally, a taxable distribution is any distribution from a trust that is not a taxable termination or direct skip (Code Sec. 2612(b)). Transfers that are not subject to gift tax because of the gift tax annual exclusion and unlimited exclusion for direct payment of medical and tuition expenses are not subject to GST tax (Code Sec. 2642(c)(1)). [95]

2943. Lifetime $1 Million Exemption. Individual taxpayers are allocated a lifetime exemption that shields $1 million in GSTs from the tax (Code Sec. 2631). For 2001, the GST tax exemption increases for inflation to $1,060,000 (projected by CCH to be $1,100,000 in 2002) and will continue to be adjusted for inflation through 2003. Married couples may treat transfers as if made one-half by each spouse, which qualifies them for a total exemption of $2,120,000 (Code Sec. 2652(a)(2)). Prior to the repeal of the GST tax in 2010, the GST tax exemption is scheduled to increase as follows: $1.5 million in 2004 and 2005; $2 million in 2006, 2007, and 2008; and $3.5 million in 2009 (Code Sec. 2631(c), as amended by P.L. 107-16). The tax is computed by multiplying the taxable amount of the transfer by the applicable rate (Code Sec. 2602). The applicable rate is the product of the highest estate and gift tax rate multiplied by the inclusion ratio (Code Sec. 2641(a); Reg. § 26.2641-1). The inclusion ratio is found by allocating all or a portion of the transferor's $1,060,000 lifetime exemption to the transfer (Code Sec. 2642(a)(2); Reg. § 26.2642-2(b)). [96]

2944. Filing the Return and Paying the GST Tax. The executor must file the return and pay the tax for direct skips occurring at death. The transferor is responsible for filing the return and paying the tax on lifetime direct skips (Code Sec. 2603(a)(3); Reg. § 26.2662-1(c)(1)). The trustee is responsible for filing the return and paying the tax on taxable terminations (Code Sec. 2603(a)(2)). The transferee is responsible for paying the tax and filing the return for taxable distributions (Code Sec. 2603(a)(1); Reg. § 26.2662-1(c)(1)). [97]

Footnote references are to paragraphs of the Federal Estate and Gift Tax Reports.

¶ 2942

[95] ¶ 12,025, ¶ 12,225, ¶ 12,315   [96] ¶ 12,585, ¶ 12,625, ¶ 12,170, ¶ 12,790   [97] ¶ 13,160, ¶ 13,200, ¶ 13,225, ¶ 15,402, ¶ 15,415, ¶ 15,423

TOPICAL INDEX

References are to paragraph (¶) numbers

ACC

ASS

CAP

CAP

COS

DEF

DEF

DIV

EMP

2

FOS

JUR

MAR

MAR

PAR

REC

REC

SAL

STA

TAX